Europe on a
Shoestring

Scandinavia
p137

Russia &
the Baltic Coast
p777

Great Britain &
Ireland
p51

Germany &
Benelux
p209

Central &
Eastern Europe
p687

France, Switzerland
& Austria
p295

Balkans
p603

Spain &
Portugal
p389

Italy, Greece & Turkey
p489

THIS EDITION WRITTEN AND RESEARCHED BY
Mark Baker, Tom Masters, Korina Miller,
Simon Richmond, Andy Symington, Nicola Williams

PLAN YOUR TRIP

LA SAGRADA FAMÍLIA,
BARCELONA P417

ON THE ROAD

ASTRONOMICAL CLOCK,
PRAGUE P701

SZÉCHENYI BATHS,
BUDAPEST P739

Contents

GUINNESS STOREHOUSE,
DUBLIN P108

ON THE ROAD

ROYAL ALBERT HALL,
LONDON P72

THE MATTERHORN,
SWITZERLAND P355

CATHÉDRALE NOTRE DAME
DE PARIS P305

Contents

SURVIVAL GUIDE

SPECIAL FEATURES

Welcome to Europe

Even on a shoestring budget, a journey through the cultural storehouse that is Europe can be fun, exciting and wonderfully life enhancing.

Urban Adventures

Some of Europe's headline locations can suck up your cash like a herd of thirsty elephants. But for every London or Paris there's a more affordable Lviv or Porto. Scattered among the 40 countries covered in this guide, ranging from Iceland to Turkey, there are hundreds of fascinating cities, towns and villages to discover. Take a taxi tour of the mural art of Belfast; ride the ferry across the Bosphorus in İstanbul, enjoy an ice cream on Venice's Piazza San Marco – many of Europe's most memorable experiences needn't break the bank, and a surprising amount can be done for free. Be flexible and you'll soon find your funds stretching further than you ever imagined.

Scenic Wonders

Europe's lovely landscapes are the gift that keeps on giving. Stride across English meadows or the sand dunes of the Baltic States. Sail down Norwegian fjords or Germany's Rhine. Climb, ski or just marvel at the Swiss and French Alps. Relax on Croatian beaches or Greek islands. Explore the honeycombed hills of Cappadocia or cycle past Dutch tulip fields in full bloom. Picture-postcard views are around every corner, whichever route you take.

Cultural Kaleidoscope

With thousands of years of civilisation under its belt, Europe's cultural diversity is its trump card. Religions, philosophies and artistic movements that changed the world developed in Athens, Rome, Moscow, Leipzig, Vienna – we could go on and on. Europe has in the region of 450 Unesco World Heritage Sites, the most of any continent, with 51 in Italy alone! Be it climbing up Skellig Michael off Ireland's west coast, soaking up the architectural majesty of Granada's Alhambra, or witnessing whirling dervishes in action, Europe's range of cultural attractions is unsurpassed.

Join the Party

Europe has some of the best nightlife in the world. Globally famous DJs keep the party going in London, Berlin and Paris, all of which also offer top-class entertainment, especially theatre and live music. Other key locations for high-energy nightlife include Moscow, Belgrade, Budapest and Madrid, while those hankering for something more cosy can add Dublin's pubs or Vienna's cafes to their itinerary. Continue to party on the continent's streets at a multiplicity of festivals and celebrations, from city parades attended by hundreds of thousands to intimate concerts in an ancient amphitheatre.

Why I Love Europe

By Simon Richmond Writer

You're likely to feel a little overwhelmed, but once you dive into Europe, these fears will be replaced by wonder and fascination – plus something, perhaps, unexpected: a sense of connection. Very few places in the world, if any, remain untouched by European history, culture and influence. As continents go, Europe's broad variety and excellent transport infrastructure – be it air or roads, or the old standby of the Grand Tour, rail – is hard to beat and is sure to push you on to new experiences and unexpected discoveries.

For more about our writers, see page 896

Above: Manarola (p513), Cinque Terre, Italy

Europe

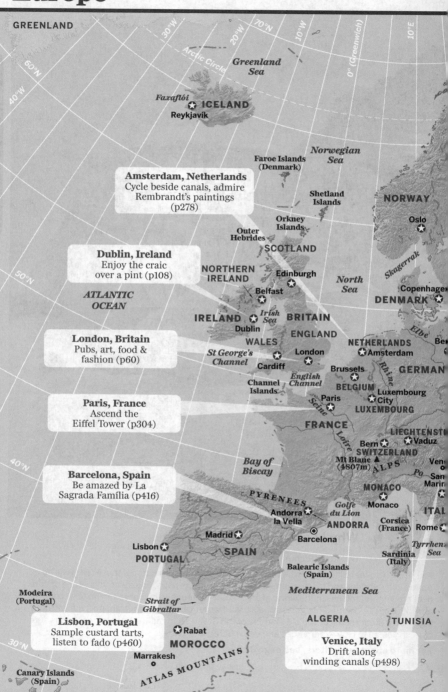

GREENLAND

Greenland Sea

Arctic Circle

Faxaflói ⭐ ICELAND
Reykjavík

Norwegian Sea

Faroe Islands
(Denmark)

Shetland
Islands

NORWAY

Orkney
Islands

Oslo ⭐

Outer
Hebrides

SCOTLAND

Skagerrak

Amsterdam, Netherlands
Cycle beside canals, admire
Rembrandt's paintings
(p278)

Dublin, Ireland
Enjoy the craic
over a pint (p108)

NORTHERN
IRELAND

Edinburgh ⭐

*North
Sea*

Copenhagen ⭐

Belfast ⭐

DENMARK ⭐

*ATLANTIC
OCEAN*

IRELAND ⭐ *Irish
Sea*

BRITAIN

Dublin

ENGLAND

Elbe

London, Britain
Pubs, art, food &
fashion (p60)

WALES

London ⭐

NETHERLANDS
⭐ Amsterdam

Ber

*St George's
Channel*

Cardiff ⭐

Brussels ⭐

Rhine

GERMAN

Channel
Islands

*English
Channel*

BELGIUM

Luxembourg
⭐ City

Paris ⭐

Paris, France
Ascend the
Eiffel Tower (p304)

Seine

LUXEMBOURG

FRANCE

LIECHTENST
⭐ Vaduz

Loire

Bern ⭐
SWITZERLAND

Barcelona, Spain
Be amazed by La
Sagrada Família (p416)

*Bay of
Biscay*

Mt Blanc ▲
(4807m)

ALPS

Ven
San
Mari

PYRENEES

*Golfe
du Lion*

MONACO

Po

Andorra ⭐
la Vella

ANDORRA

Monaco ⭐

ITAL

Madrid ⭐

Corsica
(France)

Rome ⭐

Lisbon ⭐

SPAIN

⊙
Barcelona

*Tyrrhen
Sea*

PORTUGAL

Sardinia
(Italy)

Balearic Islands
(Spain)

Mediterranean Sea

Modeira
(Portugal)

*Strait of
Gibraltar*

ALGERIA

TUNISIA

Lisbon, Portugal
Sample custard tarts,
listen to fado (p460)

⭐ Rabat

MOROCCO

Venice, Italy
Drift along
winding canals (p498)

Marrakesh

ATLAS MOUNTAINS

Canary Islands
(Spain)

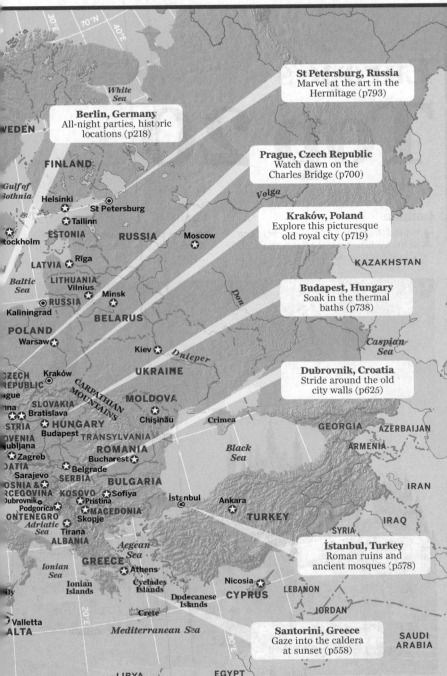

800 km
500 miles

St Petersburg, Russia
Marvel at the art in the
Hermitage (p793)

Berlin, Germany
All-night parties, historic
locations (p218)

Prague, Czech Republic
Watch dawn on the
Charles Bridge (p700)

Kraków, Poland
Explore this picturesque
old royal city (p719)

Budapest, Hungary
Soak in the thermal
baths (p738)

Dubrovnik, Croatia
Stride around the old
city walls (p625)

İstanbul, Turkey
Roman ruins and
ancient mosques (p578)

Santorini, Greece
Gaze into the caldera
at sunset (p558)

White
Sea

SWEDEN

FINLAND

Gulf of
Bothnia

Helsinki

St Petersburg

Tallinn

Stockholm

ESTONIA

RUSSIA

Moscow

Volga

LATVIA   Rīga

Baltic
Sea

LITHUANIA
Vilnius

Minsk

KAZAKHSTAN

RUSSIA

Kaliningrad

BELARUS

Don

Caspian
Sea

POLAND

Warsaw

Kiev   Dnieper

UKRAINE

CZECH
REPUBLIC

Kraków

Prague

CARPATHIAN
MOUNTAINS

MOLDOVA

Vienna

SLOVAKIA

Bratislava

AUSTRIA

HUNGARY

Chișinău

Crimea

GEORGIA

AZERBAIJAN

SLOVENIA
Ljubljana

Budapest

TRANSYLVANIA

ROMANIA

Black
Sea

ARMENIA

Zagreb

CROATIA

Sarajevo

Bucharest

Belgrade

SERBIA

BULGARIA

IRAN

BOSNIA &
HERCEGOVINA

KOSOVO

Sofiya

İstanbul

Ankara

Dubrovnik

Pristina

TURKEY

IRAQ

Podgorica

MACEDONIA

MONTENEGRO

Skopje

SYRIA

Adriatic
Sea

Tirana

ALBANIA

Aegean
Sea

Italy

Ionian
Sea

GREECE

Athens

Ionian
Islands

Cyclades
Islands

Nicosia

LEBANON

CYPRUS

Dodecanese
Islands

JORDAN

Valletta

Crete

MALTA

Mediterranean Sea

LIBYA

EGYPT

SAUDI
ARABIA

Europe's
Top 20

London

1 Hit the streets and free museums of one of the world's greatest capital cities. (p60)
Below: Houses of Parliament

Paris

2 Paris offers sophistication, great architecture and art, and delicious food. (p304) Right: Cathédrale Notre Dame de Paris (p305)

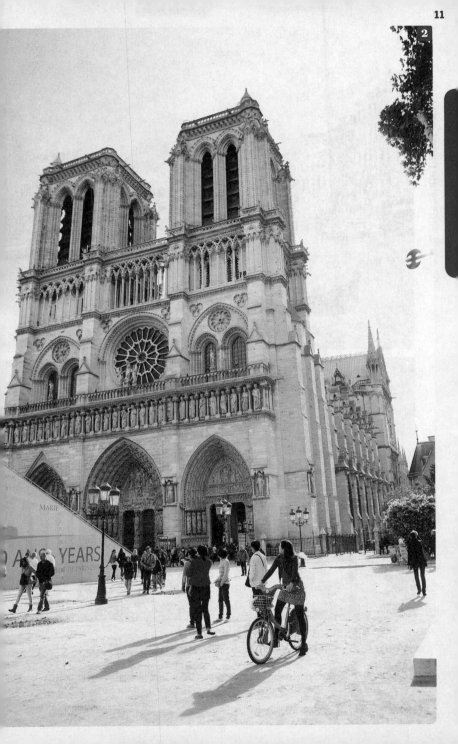

Venice

3 Glide down the canals past Gothic palaces, domed churches and crumbling piazzas. (p498) Top: Grand Canal (p514)

Berlin

4 Diverse, tolerant and packed with historical sights, Berlin is cool, edgy and ready to party. (p218) Above: Brandenburger Tor

St Petersburg

5 Russia's imperial capital offers grand palaces, stunning art collections and a hedonistic vibe. (p793) Top right: Church on the Spilled Blood

Santorini

6 A volcanic caldera submerged in the sparkling blue Aegean with whitewashed clifftop towns. (p558)

W. EBIKO / GETTY IMAGES ©

Dubrovnik

7 Marble streets, baroque buildings and ancient city walls overlooking the shimmering Adriatic. **(p625)** Below: Minčeta Tower and City Walls

Kraków

8 A former royal capital of Poland, Kraków's old town is one of Europe's most picturesque. **(p719)** Right: St Mary's Basilica (p721)

7

FRANCESCO IACOBELLI / GETTY IMAGES ©

Prague

9 Gothic, Renaissance, art nouveau and cubist styles jostle for attention in this Central European stunner. (p700) Top right: Old Town Square (p701)

Zermatt

10 Ride trains through spellbinding alpine scenery that includes superstar peak, the Matterhorn. (p355)

DANITA DELIMONT / GETTY IMAGES ©

Budapest

11 Soak away your hangover from the city's pumping nightlife in one of its soothing thermal baths. (p738) Top left: Gellért Baths (p739)

Dublin

12 Georgian architecture, great museums and fine pubs. (p108) Top right: Long Room, Trinity College

Amsterdam

13 Cycle alongside the World Heritage–listed canals, admiring gabled houses and enjoying the free-spirited atmosphere. (p278)

Rome

14 Ancient and modern life collide in this pulsating city studded with architectural and artistic masterpieces. p516) Below top: Roman Forum (p517)

Barcelona

15 View Guadí's still unfinished masterpiece of a cathedral and enjoy Catalan culture. (p416) Below bottom: Interior, La Sagrada Família (p417)

Tallinn

16 Look out over the onion-dome-studded skyline of Estonia's modern-meets-medieval capital. (p806)

Vienna

17 Waltz around a city of grand palaces, parks and coffee houses. (p367) Bottom: Schloss Schönbrunn (p371)

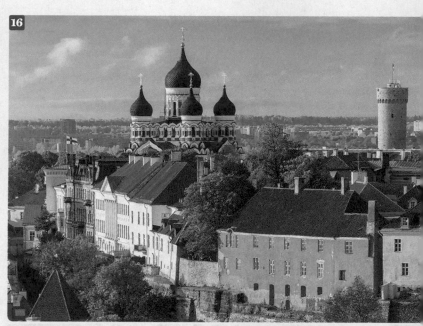

MICHELE FALZONE / GETTY IMAGES ©

İstanbul

18 Haggle in its Grand Bazaar, gawp at the monumental Aya Sofya and tour the glittering Topkapı Palace. (p578)

Lisbon

19 Navigate Lisbon's cobblestone streets to find Moorish ruins, white-domed cathedrals, grand plazas and sun-drenched cafes. (p460)

Athens

20 Experience the apex of ancient Greece at the iconic Acropolis, the Agora and Olympian temples. (p544) Above Monastiraki and the Acropolis

Need to Know

For more information, see Survival Guide (p849)

Currency

Euro (€), Pound (£), Swiss franc (Sfr), Rouble (R)

Language

English, French, German, Italian, Spanish, Russian, Hungarian, Greek, Turkish

Visas

EU citizens don't need visas for other EU countries. Australians, Canadians, New Zealanders and Americans don't need visas for visits of less than 90 days.

Money

ATMs are common; credit and debit cards are widely accepted.

Mobile Phones

Europe uses the GSM 900 network. If you're coming from outside Europe it's worth buying a prepaid local SIM.

Time

Britain, Ireland and Portugal (GMT), Central Europe (GMT plus one hour), Greece, Turkey and Eastern Europe (GMT plus two hours), Russia (GMT plus three hours).

When to Go

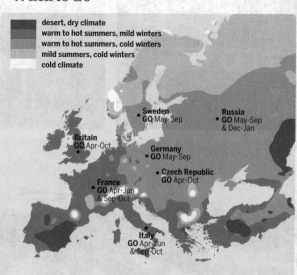

desert, dry climate
warm to hot summers, mild winters
warm to hot summers, cold winters
mild summers, cold winters
cold climate

Sweden
GO May-Sep

Russia
GO May-Sep
& Dec-Jan

Britain
GO Apr-Oct

Germany
GO May-Sep

Czech Republic
GO Apr-Oct

France
GO Apr-Jun
& Sep-Oct

Italy
GO Apr-Jun
& Sep-Oct

High Season
(Jun–Aug)

➡ Everybody comes to Europe and all of Europe hits the road.

➡ Hotel prices and temperatures are their highest.

➡ Expect all the major attractions to be nightmarishly busy.

Shoulder Season (Apr–May & Sep–Oct)

➡ Crowds and prices drop, except in Italy where it's still busy.

➡ Temperatures are comfortable but it can be hot in Southern Europe.

➡ Overall these are the best months to travel in Europe.

Low Season
(Nov–Mar)

➡ Outside ski resorts, hotels drop their prices or close down.

➡ The weather can be cold and days short, especially in Northern Europe.

➡ Some places, such as resort towns, are like ghost towns.

Useful Websites

Lonely Planet (www.lonely planet.com/thorntree) Ask other travellers questions.

Hidden Europe (www.hidden europe.co.uk) Fascinating magazine and online dispatches from all the continent's corners.

VisitEurope (www.visiteurope. com) With information about travel in 33 member countries.

Spotted by Locals (www.spot tedbylocals.com) Insider tips for cities across Europe.

In Your Pocket (www.inyour pocket.com) Up-to-date guides to more than 100 European cities.

Opening Hours

In most of Europe businesses are open 9am to 6pm Monday to Friday, and 9am to 1pm or 5pm on Saturday. In smaller towns there may be a one- to two-hour closure for lunch. Some shops close on Sunday. Businesses also close on national holidays and local feast days.

Banks have the shortest opening times, often closing between 3pm and 5pm, and occasionally even shutting for lunch. They only open on weekdays.

Restaurants typically open from noon until midnight and bars open around 6pm. Museums usually close on Monday or (less commonly) on Tuesday.

Exchange Rates

Australia A$1	£0.50	€0.64
Canada C$1	£0.53	€0.68
Japan ¥100	£0.63	€0.81
NZ NZ$1	£0.46	€0.61
US US$1	£0.69	€0.89

For current exchange rates see www.xe.com.

Daily Costs
Budget:
Less than €60

➡ Dorm beds: €10–€20

➡ Admission to museums: €5–€15

➡ Pizza or pasta: €8–12

Midrange:
€60–€200

➡ Double room in a small hotel: €50–€100

➡ Short taxi trip: €10–€20

➡ Meals in good restaurants: around €20 per person

Top end:
More than €200

➡ Stay at iconic hotels: from €150

➡ Car hire: from around €30 per day

➡ Theatre tickets: €15–€150

Emergency Number

The phone number ☑112 can be dialled free for emergencies in all EU states. See individual countries for country-specific emergency numbers.

Arriving in Europe

Schiphol Airport, Amsterdam (p284) Trains to the centre (20 minutes).

Heathrow Airport, London (p106) Trains (15 minutes) and Tube (one hour) to the centre.

Aéroport de Charles de Gaulle, Paris (p317) Many buses (one hour) and trains (30 minutes) to centre.

Frankfurt Airport, Frankfurt (p243) Trains (15 minutes) to the centre.

Leonardo da Vinci Airport, Rome (p530) Buses (one hour) and trains (30 minutes) to centre.

Barajas Airport, Madrid (p402) Buses (40 minutes) and Metro (15 minutes) to the centre.

Euro Reading List

➡ *A Time of Gifts* (1977), *Between the Woods and the Water* (1986) and *The Broken Road: Travels from Bulgaria to Mount Athos* (2013) Patrick Leigh Fermor's classic trilogy about his experiences at the age of 18 in 1934 when he walked from Hoek van Holland to İstanbul.

➡ *Neither Here nor There: Travels in Europe* (1992; Bill Bryson) Twenty years after his 1970s European tour Bryson retraces his steps with humour and acute observation.

➡ *Continental Drifter* (2000; Tim Moore) Musings on the origins of the 17th-century European Grand Tour and a modern day re-creation of it.

➡ *Rite of Passage: Tales of Backpacking 'round Europe* (2003; Edited by Lisa Johnson) Stories by young travellers about conquering the continent for the first time.

➡ *In Europe* (2008; Geert Mak) Fascinating account by a Dutch journalist of his Euro-wanderings in 1999.

First-Time Europe

For more information, see Survival Guide (p849)

Checklist

→ Check passport validity and visa requirements

→ Read travel advisory websites

→ Arrange travel insurance

→ Check airline baggage restrictions

→ Download country-related travel apps and music

What to Pack

→ Flip-flops (thongs) for beach and hostel bathrooms.

→ Hiking boots for Europe's fantastic walks.

→ Ear plugs – helpful anywhere, but especially in hostels.

→ Anti-mosquito plugs – useful in summer.

→ Travel plug (adaptor)

→ An unlocked mobile phone for use with a local SIM card for making cheap calls.

→ Raincoat, waterproof jacket or umbrella for the weather that keeps Europe green.

→ Smart clothes so you look the part when breaking the budget.

→ Pocket knife with corkscrew

Top Tips for Your Trip

→ Visit in spring, autumn and winter (except for ski resort areas) – crowds will be thinner and accommodation costs cheaper.

→ To ensure your plastic works wherever you go, tell banks and credit card providers your travel dates and the countries you plan to visit.

→ Check local happy hours for budget drinking at bars. Hostel bars are sometimes cheaper.

→ When first arriving in a new city search out the tourism bureau and enquire about local discounts, free maps, festivals, events and activities such as walking tours.

→ Consider investing in city tourist cards – they can save you money if you plan on doing a lot of sightseeing.

→ Book budget airline, bus and train tickets as far in advance as possible to get the best discount fares.

What to Wear

Cities To avoid standing out from the urban crowd, smart-casual is the way to go, particularly if dining out, attending the theatre or the like. A light sweater or waterproof jacket is useful in spring and autumn.

Countryside Casual is fine and the further south you go in Europe, the more relaxed fashion becomes. Sturdy shoes are a good idea when visiting archaeological sites or going hiking.

Beach resorts Bikini tops and bare male chests are fine on the sand but think about covering up when back on the street.

Sleeping

For major cities and resorts it's a good idea to book a night or two in advance (especially during the busy summer season). Elsewhere you can usually just turn up and find a room.

Hostels There's no shortage of these across Europe, including the fancier 'poshtels' and 'flashpacker' hostels.

B&Bs and homestays Great for character-filled accommodation and connecting with locals.

Camping Cheap but seldom are campsites in convenient locations for sightseeing.

Safe Travel

With terrorist attacks on the rise it's easy to become a little paranoid about how safe travel across Europe currently is. To ease your mind, consider the following:

➡ Statistically you are many times more likely to be killed in a car crash or by gun crime than you are of becoming a victim of terrorism in Europe.

➡ Register with your own country before you travel so that you can be more easily found or contacted in an emergency (see http://dfat.gov.au/travel in Australia and https://step.state.gov in the USA).

➡ Stay in touch with friends and family back home so they always know where you are.

WALTER BIBIKOW / GETTY IMAGES ©

Sozopol (p683), Bulgaria

Bargaining

Bargaining isn't common in much of Europe, but is known in and around the Mediterranean. In Turkey it's virtually a way of life.

Tipping

Tipping has become more complicated, with 'service charges' increasingly added to bills. In theory this means you're not obliged to tip. In practice that money often doesn't go to the server and they might make it clear they still expect a gratuity. Don't pay twice. If the service charge is optional, remove it from the bill and pay a tip. If the service charge is not optional, don't tip.

Etiquette

Greetings A handshake is fine with strangers. Across Continental Europe cheek-skimming kisses – at least two, but up to four – are the way to greet friends.

Language Learn a few simple phrases and useful words in the language of each of the countries you plan to visit – your efforts will be greatly appreciated by locals.

Religion At churches, mosques or other religious buildings be respectful and dress modestly (cover shoulders, torsos and thighs).

Eating

➡ Most hostels have kitchens and you learn a lot about a country by shopping in their supermarkets and convenience stores.

➡ Search out weekly morning markets – there's no finer opportunity for mingling with locals. Take your own shopping bag or basket.

➡ While it might be tempting to favour restaurants with a menu in English, the very best (and best-loved by locals) rarely offer a translation.

➡ Avoid 'tourist menus' but do look out for places that offer a bargain set lunch – this can be a great way of sampling food at fancy restaurants usually beyond your budget.

If You Like...

Castles & Palaces

Versailles, France The vast formal palace against which all others are measured includes the Hall of Mirrors and sumptuous gardens. (p320)

Schloss Neuschwanstein, Germany So what if it's not even 150 years old? Neuschwanstein, in the heart of the Bavarian Alps, is everybody's (including Disney's) castle fantasy. (p236)

Winter Palace, Russia Forever associated with the Russian Revolution, this golden-green baroque building is unmatched anywhere for sheer tsarist splendour. (p793)

Bran Castle, Romania Better known as Dracula's Castle, this Transylvanian beauty is straight out of a horror movie. (p758)

Alhambra, Spain This exquisite Islamic palace complex in Granada is a World Heritage–listed wonder. (p448)

Gravensteen, Belgium The turreted stone castle of the Counts of Flanders looms over the beautiful Belgian city of Ghent. (p266)

Windsor Castle, Britain The world's largest and oldest occupied fortress is one of the British monarch's principal residences. (p74)

Topkapı Palace, Turkey Tour the opulent pavilions and jewel-filled Treasury of the former court of the Ottoman empire in İstanbul. (p580)

Ancient Wonders

Stonehenge, Britain The UK's most iconic – and mysterious – archaeological site, dating back some 5000 years. (p74)

Pompeii, Italy Wander the streets and alleys of this great ancient city, buried by a volcanic eruption. (p531, 532-3)

Athens, Greece Ancient wonders include the Acropolis, Ancient Agora, Temple of Olympian Zeus and more. (p544)

Rome, Italy The gladiatorial arena of the Colosseum is the most thrilling of the city's archaeological sights which include the Palatino, Roman Forum and Pantheon. (p516)

Ephesus, Turkey Europe's most complete classical metropolis includes the Library of Celsus, Temple of Hadrian and Great Theatre large enough for 25,000 spectators. (p578)

Urban Architecture

Amsterdam's Canal Ring, Netherlands Stroll the Dutch capital's Golden Age canals lined with gabled buildings. (p278)

Moscow's Kremlin, Russia The seat of power to medieval tsars and modern tyrants alike, Moscow's vast Kremlin offers incredible sights. (p784)

Sarajevo, Bosnia & Hercegovina Enjoy the bustling old Turkish quarter of arguably the Balkans' most charming town – and a proud survivor. (p630)

Brussels' Grand Place, Belgium This cobblestone square surrounded by antique guildhalls is one of the world's most unforgettable urban ensembles. (p257)

Chemin de la Corniche, Luxembourg 'Europe's most beautiful balcony' is a pedestrian promenade that winds along the course of the 17th-century city ramparts. (p275)

Museo Guggenheim, Spain Frank Gehry's architectural masterpiece is the catalyst that transformed the industrial port of Bilbao into a vibrant cultural centre. (p407)

Beaches & Islands

Rhodes, Greece The largest of Greece's Dodecanese Islands. Lose yourself within the medieval walls of the city's Old Town and then head for sandy beaches. (p562)

The Balearic Islands, Spain Beach tourism destinations par excellence, Mallorca, Menorca, Ibiza and Formentera, each retain much of their individual character and beauty. (p428)

Top: Svartifoss, Skaftafell (p205), Iceland
Bottom: Bathhouse, Pompeii (p531), Italy

Drymades Beach, Albania The stuff of legend among backpackers, this white-sand beach on Albania's fast-disappearing undeveloped coastline remains the one to head for. (p652)

Sozopol, Bulgaria Avoid the big resort towns on Bulgaria's Black Sea coast and head instead to this charming old town of meandering cobbled streets and pretty wooden houses. (p683)

Hvar Island, Croatia Famed for its verdancy and lilac fields, this luxurious and sunny island is the jumping-off point for the wooded Pakleni Islands. (p623)

Isle of Skye, Scotland A 50-mile-long smorgasbord of velvet moors, jagged mountains, sparkling lochs and towering sea cliffs. (p104)

Spectacular Scenery

The Alps, Switzerland There's no competition for the most stunning landscape in Europe – even its neighbours wouldn't dare suggest that theirs could rival that of beautiful Switzerland. (p355)

Fjords, Norway From the precipitous coastline to the impossibly steep gashes that cut into the interior, Norway's fjords are simply unmissable. (p188)

Cappadocia, Turkey In the centre of Turkey, Anatolia's mountain-fringed plains give way to a land of other-worldly rock formations and underground cities – definitely one of the region's strangest landscapes. (p594)

High Tatras, Slovakia Offering pristine snowfields, ultramarine mountain lakes, thundering waterfalls, undulating pine forests and shimmering alpine meadows. (p714)

Vatnajökull National Park, Iceland Skaftafell is the jewel in the crown of this breathtaking collection of peaks and glaciers. (p205)

Zugspitze, Germany On good days, views from Germany's rooftop near Garmisch-Partenkirchen extend into four countries. (p236)

Nightlife

Berlin, Germany Kreuzberg and Friedrichshain are currently the edgiest bar-hopping grounds. The liberal city is also one of the world's biggest and most diverse LGBT playgrounds. (p223)

London, Britain Whether it's a quiet session down at the local pub or a full-blown night on the tiles of East London, you can be sure to have a good time in the hedonistic bars and clubs of London town. (p70)

Madrid, Spain Has more bars per capita than anywhere else on earth and no one goes to bed here before killing the night. (p400)

Reykjavík, Iceland Join in the *djammið*, a raucous weekend pub crawl around the Icelandic capital's vibrant cafe-bar scene. (p201)

Belgrade, Serbia The Serbian capital is one of the most vibrant places to party the night away – in summer, the Danube and Sava rivers are clogged with *splavovi* (floating clubs). (p664)

Art Collections

Louvre, France The exhaustive quantity of treasures from Europe and all over the planet here will simply dazzle you – better yet, it's free the first Sunday of

each month and for some age groups. (p308)

Florence, Italy It starts with the Duomo, continues through the Uffizi Gallery and crosses the Ponte Vecchio – the entire Renaissance embodied in one city. (p508)

Hermitage, Russia Housed in the Winter Palace, this is quite simply one of the world's greatest art collections – everything from Egyptian mummies to a hoard of Picassos and Matisses; free to students and on the first Thursday of the month. (p793)

Amsterdam, The Netherlands The Rijksmuseum is packed with Rembrandts and Vermeers while the Van Gogh Museum offers the world's largest collection by Van Gogh. (p278)

Madrid, Spain With the Prado, Thyssen and Reina Sofia within a single golden mile of art, Madrid is one of Europe's premier destinations for art lovers. (p396)

London, England Come face to face with kings, queens, and a cast of celebrities in the National Portrait Gallery, then nip around the corner for the old masters in the National Gallery. Both are free. (p60)

Music

Berlin, Germany Everything from the world's most acclaimed techno venue to the celebrated Berliner Philharmoniker can be seen in Germany's music-obsessed capital. (p224)

Galway, Ireland The Irish love their music and it takes little – sometimes just a pint of beer – to get them singing; this West Coast city's music pubs, are a great place to start. (p124)

Fado, Portugal Portuguese love the melancholic and nostalgic

songs of *fado*; hear it in Lisbon's Alfama district. (p465)

Trubači, Serbia While this wild brass music is celebrated en masse at Guča each August, ragtag *trubači* bands wander the streets of many Serbian towns year-round: if you hear a trumpet, follow that sound. (p668)

Seville, Spain Few musical forms capture the spirit of a nation quite like passionate flamenco, with this Andalucian city the heartland for Spain's best-loved musical tradition. (p443)

Cafes & Bars

Vienna's coffee houses, Austria Unchanged in decades and redolent with the air of refinement; pause for a cup served just so. (p372)

Irish pubs, Ireland Come and join the warm and gregarious crowds of locals in any pub in Ireland for a true cultural experience. (p113)

Paris cafe society, France What's more clichéd: the practised curtness of the Parisian waiter or the studied boredom of the customer? Both are, probably, and we wouldn't miss the show for anything. (p309)

Amsterdam's tiny havens, Netherlands The Dutch call them 'brown cafes' for the former tobacco stains on the walls from legions of smokers, but they should just call them cosy, for the warm and friendly atmosphere. (p283)

Budapest's ruin pubs, Hungary So-called 'ruin pubs' – essentially pop-up bars in abandoned buildings – are popular (and uniquely Budapest) seasonal outdoor venues in summer. (p744)

Month by Month

January

It's cold but most towns are relatively tourist free and hotel prices are rock bottom.

✿ Orthodox Christmas, Eastern Europe

Christmas is celebrated in different ways in Eastern Europe: many countries celebrate on Christmas Eve (24 December), with an evening meal and midnight Mass. In Russia, Ukraine, Belarus, Moldova, Serbia, Montenegro and Macedonia, Christmas falls in January, as per the Gregorian calendar.

✿ Kiruna Snöfestivalen, Sweden

In the last weekend of January this Lapland snow festival (www.snofestival en.com), based around a snow-sculpting competition, draws artists from all over Europe. There's also a husky-dog competition and a handicrafts fair.

February

Carnival in all its manic glory sweeps the Catholic regions. Cold temperatures are forgotten amid masquerades, street festivals and general bacchanalia. Expect to be kissed by a stranger.

✿ Carnaval, Netherlands

Pre-Lent is celebrated with greater vigour in Maastricht than anywhere else in Northern Europe. While the rest of the Netherlands hopes the canals will freeze for ice skating, this Dutch corner cuts loose with a celebration that would have done its former Roman residents proud.

✿ Carnevale, Italy

In the period before Ash Wednesday, Venice goes mad for masks (www.venice-carnival-italy.com). Costume balls, many with traditions centuries old, enliven the social calendar in this storied old city. Even those without a coveted invite are swept up in the pageantry.

✿ Fasching, Germany

Germany doesn't leave the pre-Lent season solely to its neighbours. Karneval is celebrated with abandon in the traditional Catholic regions including Bavaria, along the Rhine and particularly vibrantly in Cologne (www.koelner karneval.de/en/cologne -carnival).

March

Spring arrives in Southern Europe. Further north the rest of the continent continues to freeze, though days are often bright.

✿ St Patrick's Day, Ireland

Parades and celebrations are held on 17 March in Irish towns big and small to honour the beloved patron saint of Ireland. While elsewhere the day is a commercialised romp of green beer, in his home country it's time for a parade and celebrations with friends and family.

☆ Budapest Spring Festival, Hungary

This two-week festival in late March is one of Europe's top classical music events (www.springfestival. hu). Concerts are held in a number of beautiful venues, including stunning churches, the opera house and the national theatre.

April

The bulb fields of Holland and the orchards of Spain burst into flower. On the most southern beaches it's time to shake the sand out of the umbrellas.

🎉 Semana Santa, Spain

There are parades of penitents and holy icons in Spain, notably in Seville, during Easter week (www.semana-santa.org). Thousands of members of religious brotherhoods parade in traditional garb before thousands of spectators. Look for the pointed *capirotes* (hoods).

🎉 Settimana Santa, Italy

Italy celebrates Holy Week with processions and passion plays. By Holy Thursday Rome is packed with the faithful and even nonbelievers are swept up in the emotion and piety of hundreds of thousands thronging the Vatican and St Peter's Basilica.

🎉 Orthodox Easter, Greece

The most important festival in the Greek Orthodox calendar has an emphasis on the Resurrection, so it's a celebratory event. The most significant part is midnight on Easter Saturday, when candles are lit and fireworks and a procession hit the streets.

🎉 Feria de Abril, Spain

Hoods off! A week-long party in Seville in late April counterbalances the religious peak of Easter (http://feriadesevilla. andalunet.com). The beautiful old squares of this gorgeous city come alive during the long, warm nights for which the nation is known.

🎉 Koninginnedag (Queen's Day), Netherlands

The nationwide celebration on 27 April is especially fervent in Amsterdam, awash with orange costumes and fake Afros, beer, dope, leather boys, temporary roller coasters, clogs and general craziness.

May

This is an excellent time to visit. It's not too hot or too crowded, though you can still expect the big destinations to feel busy.

🍺 Beer Festival, Czech Republic

An event dear to many travellers' hearts, this Prague beer festival (www. ceskypivnifestival.cz) offers lots of food, music and –

most importantly – around 70 beers from around the country from mid to late May.

☆ Brussels Jazz Marathon, Belgium

Around-the-clock jazz performances hit Brussels during the second-last weekend in May (www. brusselsjazzmarathon.be). The saxophone is the instrument of choice for this international-flavoured city's most joyous celebration.

🎉 Queima das Fitas, Portugal

Coimbra's annual highlight is this boozy week of *fado* music and revelry that begins on the first Thursday in May, when students celebrate the end of the academic year.

🎉 Karneval der Kulturen, Germany

This joyous street carnival (www.karneval-berlin.de) celebrates Berlin's multicultural tapestry with parties, global nosh and a fun parade of flamboyantly costumed dancers, DJs, artists and musicians.

June

The huge summer travel season hasn't started yet, but the sun has broken through the clouds and the weather is generally gorgeous across the continent.

🎉 Festa de São João, Portugal

Elaborate processions, live music on Porto's plazas and

merrymaking all across Portugal's second city. Squeaky plastic hammers (for sale everywhere) come out for the unusual custom of whacking one another. Everyone is fair game – expect no mercy.

✻✻ White Nights in Northern Europe

By mid-June the Baltic sun only just sinks behind the horizon at night, leaving the sky a grey-white colour and encouraging locals to forget their routines and party hard. The best place to join the fun is St Petersburg, Russia, where balls, classical-music concerts and other summer events keep spirits high.

☆ Glastonbury Festival, Britain

The town's youthful summer vibe peaks for this long weekend of music, theatre and New Age shenanigans (www.glastonburyfestivals. co.uk). It's one of England's favourite outdoor events and more than 100,000 turn up to writhe around in the grassy fields (or deep mud) at Pilton's Worthy Farm.

☆ Roskilde Festival, Denmark

Northern Europe's largest music festival (www. roskilde-festival.dk) rocks Roskilde each summer. It takes place in late June but advance ticket sales are on offer in December and the festival usually sells out.

op: Carnevale (p27), Venice, Italy
ottom: Eggs painted for Orthodox Easter (p28), Greece

July

One of the busiest months for travel across the continent with outdoor cafes, beer gardens and beach clubs all hopping. Expect beautiful – even steamy – weather anywhere you go.

🏃 Sanfermines (Running of the Bulls), Spain

The Fiesta de San Fermín (Sanfermines) is the week-long nonstop festival and party in Pamplona with the daily *encierro* (running of the bulls) as its centrepiece (www.bullrunpamplona.com). Anything can happen, but it rarely ends well for the bull. The antibull-fighting event, the Running of the Nudes (www.runningofthenudes.com), takes place two days earlier.

🎆 Bastille Day, France

Fireworks, balls, processions, and – of course – good food and wine, for France's national day on 14 July, celebrated in every French town and city. Go to the heart of town and get caught up in this patriotic festival.

🎆 EXIT Festival, Serbia

Eastern Europe's most talked-about music festival (www.exitfest.org) takes place within the walls of the Petrovaradin Fortress in Serbia's second city, Novi Sad. Book early as it attracts music lovers from all over the continent with big international acts headlining.

☆ Gentse Feesten, Belgium

Ghent is transformed into a 10-day party of music and theatre, a highlight of which is a vast techno celebration called 10 Days Off (www.gentsefeesten.be).

🎆 Medieval Festival of the Arts, Romania

The beautiful Romanian city of Sighişoara hosts open-air concerts, parades and ceremonies, all glorifying medieval Transylvania and taking the town back to its fascinating 12th-century origins.

☆ Bažant Pohoda, Slovakia

Slovakia's largest music festival (www.pohodafestival.sk) represents all genres of music from folk and rock to orchestral over eight different stages. It's firmly established as one of Europe's biggest and best summer music festivals.

🎆 Amsterdam Gay Pride, Netherlands

Held at the end of July and first week of August this is one of Europe's best LGBT events (www.amsterdamgaypride.nl).

August

Half of Europe shuts down to enjoy the traditional month of holidaying with the other half. If it's near the beach, from Germany's Baltic to Spain's Balearics, it's mobbed and the temperatures are hot, hot, hot!

🎆 Zürich Street Parade, Switzerland

Zürich lets its hair down with an enormous techno parade (www.street-parade.ch). All thoughts of numbered accounts are forgotten as bankers, and everybody else in this otherwise staid burg, party to orgasmic, deep-base thump, thump, thump.

🎆 Notting Hill Carnival, England

This is Europe's largest – and London's most vibrant – outdoor carnival, where London's Caribbean community shows the city how to party (www.thenottinghillcarnival.com). Food, frolic and fun are just a part of this vast multicultural two-day celebration.

☆ Edinburgh International Festival, Scotland

Three weeks of innovative drama, comedy, dance, music and more (www.eif.co.uk). Two weeks overlap with the celebrated Fringe Festival (www.edfringe.com), which draws innovative acts from around the globe. Expect cutting-edge productions that often defy description.

☆ Sziget Music Festival, Hungary

A week-long, great-value world-music festival (www.sziget.hu) held all over Budapest. Sziget features bands from around the world playing at more than 60 venues.

September

It's cooling off in every sense, from the northern countries to the romance started on a dance floor in Ibiza. Maybe the best time to visit: the weather's still good and the crowds have thinned.

Oktoberfest, Germany

Despite its name, Germany's legendary beer-swilling party (www.oktoberfest. de) starts mid-September in Munich and finishes a week into October. Millions descend for litres of beer and carousing that has no equal. If you didn't plan ahead, you'll have to sleep in Austria.

Festes de la Mercè, Spain

Barcelona knows how to party until dawn and it outdoes itself for the Festes de la Mercè (around 24 September). The city's biggest celebration has four days of concerts, dancing, *castellers* (human-castle builders), fireworks and *correfocs* – a parade of fireworks-spitting dragons and devils.

October

Another good month to visit – almost everything is still open, while prices and visitor numbers are way down. Weather can be unpredictable, though and even cold in Northern Europe.

☆ Festival at Queen's, Northern Ireland

Belfast hosts the second-largest arts festival (www. belfastfestival.com) in the UK for three weeks in late October/early November in and around Queen's University. It's a time for the city to shed its gritty legacy, and celebrate the intellectual and the creative without excessive hype.

Wine Festival, Moldova

Wine-enriched folkloric performances in Moldova draw oenophiles and anyone wanting to profit from the 10-day visa-free regime Moldova introduces during the festival.

November

Snow may have started falling in Northern Europe and even in the temperate zones around the Med it can get chilly, rainy and blustery. Most seasonal attractions have closed for the year.

Guy Fawkes Night, Britain

Bonfires and fireworks erupt across Britain on 5 November, recalling the foiling of a plot to blow up the Houses of Parliament in the 1600s. Go to high ground in London to see glowing explosions erupt everywhere.

☆ Iceland Airwaves, Iceland

Roll on up to Reykjavík for this great music festival featuring both Icelandic and international acts (www. icelandairwaves.is).

December

Despite freezing temperatures this is a magical time to visit Europe, with Christmas decorations brightening the dark streets. Prices remain low provided you avoid Christmas and New Year's Eve.

Natale, Italy

Italian churches set up an intricate crib or a *presepe* (nativity scene) in the lead-up to Christmas. Some are quite famous, most are works of art, and many date back hundreds of years and are venerated for their spiritual ties.

Christmas Markets

In December Christmas Markets are held across Europe, with particularly good ones in Germany, Austria, Slovakia and Czech Republic. The most famous are in Nuremberg (the Christkindlmarkt) and Vienna. Warm your hands through your mittens holding a hot mug of mulled wine and find that special (or kitsch) present.

Plan Your Trip
Itineraries

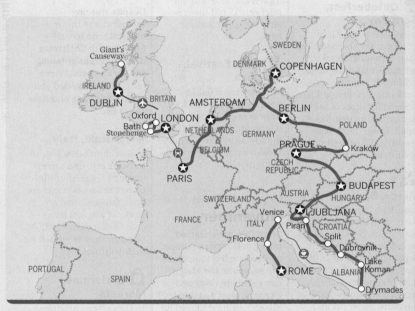

8 WEEKS First-Time Europe

This combo of major league countries, such as France and Germany, and left-field destinations like Slovenia and Albania, provides an irresistible mix of world-famous sights and unforgettable experiences for the European novice.

Ease into the first two weeks by concentrating on Ireland and Great Britain. The atmosphere of a **Dublin** bar provides the perfect introduction, followed by a few days exploring the city's museums and literary haunts. It costs nothing to walk across the Unesco-listed **Giant's**

Causeway in Northern Ireland, which leaves more money to enjoy your next stop: **London**. The city is pricey, but focus on the free museums and royal parks and you're sure to stay on budget. Travel west to marvel at **Stonehenge** and wander the historic streets of **Oxford** and **Bath**.

Return to London to board the Eurostar for the next couple of weeks hopping between some of the continent's iconic northern metropolises. In **Paris** you will be dazzled by the Louvre, Eiffel Tower and Versailles. Check out more classic art, plus *those* cafes, in enchanting **Amsterdam**.

Giant's Causeway (p131), Northern Ireland

Get a taste of Scandinavia in **Copenhagen**, the coolest kid of the Nordic bloc. And unleash your inner party animal in **Berlin** where you can also see the remains of the wall.

Go through the former Iron Curtain to the gorgeous old Polish royal capital of **Kraków**, which was miraculously spared destruction in WWII. If you thought that was stunning wait till you see the architectural glories of **Prague**. Continue on to **Budapest**, where you can freshen up at the thermal baths and enjoy numerous cafes and bars, followed by Slovenia's eco-friendly capital **Ljubljana**.

The Venetian-style seaside resort of **Piran** is a good starting point for a journey down the scenic Dalmatian Coast via **Split** and **Dubrovnik** both of which have ancient ruins to explore. End up way off the beaten track in Albania where you can sail on a ferry across beguiling **Lake Koman** and relax at a campsite by the beach in **Drymades** on the Albanian Riviera.

Cruise across the Adriatic on one of the ferry services to Italy, where your final week's pit stops include hauntingly beautiful **Venice**, the exquisite Renaissance time capsule of **Florence**, and the eternal city of **Rome**.

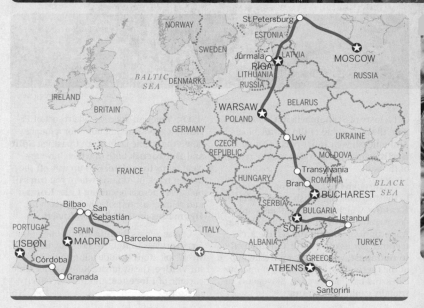

East to West

8 WEEKS

This trans-European journey kicks off in the east, a dynamic part of Europe yet where you'll also encounter under-the-radar attractions. Then enjoy a more leisurely pace of life along the balmy Mediterranean coast as you continue west towards to the resorts of Spain and Portugal.

Begin in Russia's capital **Moscow**, where the imposing Kremlin and adjacent Red Square are guaranteed to strike you with awe. Take an overnight train to **St Petersburg**, home to the magnificent art collection of the Hermitage and gorgeously restored imperial palaces. Another overnight train will whisk you to Latvia's lovely art-nouveau captial **Rīga** where you can get a taste of the Baltic. If the weather's fine consider a day trip to the chic beach resort of **Jūrmala**.

Poland's capital **Warsaw** is a vibrant city that's survived all that history could throw at it. Continue into Ukraine and spend a few days in Unesco World Heritage–listed **Lviv** which oozes Central European charm. Move on to **Transylvania** and sharpen your fangs at 'Dracula's' castle in **Bran**. Romania's dynamic capital **Bucharest** is next, with its good museums, parks and trendy cafes.

Sofia, Bulgaria's relaxed capital is another recommended pitstop en route to beautiful, chaotic **İstanbul**: when you've had your fill of sightseeing you can relax in a hamam (Turkish bath).

Time to explore the ancient world staring with the Acropolis in **Athens**. You could easily spend a couple of weeks island hopping around Greece but with limited time focus on volcanic **Santorini**, then pick up the pace by flying to Spain for the final leg of your trip.

Admire the genius of Gaudí and wallow in cultural riches and glorious food in supercool **Barcelona**. Zip north to Basque seaside resort **San Sebastián**, with its delicious food scene, and then to the shimmering Museo Guggenheim in happening **Bilbao**. Turn south, making a beeline for energetic **Madrid**, for some of Europe's best galleries and bars.

Head south to see the beautiful Moorish architecture of the Alhambra in **Granada** and the stunning Mezquita of **Córdoba**. Cross over to Portugal, where the fascinating capital **Lisbon** offers clattering bright-yellow trams, a lamplit old quarter and superb *pastéis de nata* (custard tarts) in the waterside Belém district.

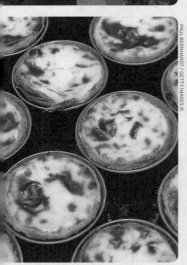

Top: Oia (p561), Santorini, Greece
Bottom: *Pastéis de nata* (custard tarts), Portugal

Off the Beaten Track – Europe

N ↑

0 — 1,000 km
0 — 500 miles

THE WESTFJORDS (ICELAND)

Surround yourself in Iceland's most dramatic landscapes, including jagged bird cliffs, broad multihued beaches, jaw-dropping coastal fjords, immense central mountains and tiny fishing villages embracing traditional ways of life. (p202)

ABISKO (SWEDEN)

A prime viewing spot for the Aurora Borealis, Abisko lies near the national park of the same name and is the start or endpoint for the spectacular 425km Kungsleden hiking trail. (p170)

INARI (FINLAND)

This tiny village is home to the wonderful Siida museum devoted to Sámi culture and environment, and a great base for hiking in the nearby Lemmenjoki National Park and Kevo Strict Nature Reserve. (p184)

DAUGAVPLIS (LATVIA)

With a fairly well-preserved historical centre and a mighty fortress, Daugavpils has more recently been put on the tourist map by the new Rothko Centre devoted to contemporary art. (p832)

BREST (BELARUS)

This relatively prosperous and cosmopolitan border town has plenty of charm as well as the impressive 19th century Brest Fortress. Reconstruction has been rampant as Brest gears up for its millennial

REYKJAVÍK ✪ ICELAND

The Westfjords

SCOTLAND
EDINBURGH ✪
NORTHERN
IRELAND
BELFAST ✪ BRITAIN
DUBLIN ✪

NORWAY
OSLO ✪

Abisko

SWEDEN
STOCKHOLM ✪

Inari

FINLAND
HELSINKI ✪

St Petersburg ◉

TALLINN ✪

MOSCOW ✪

COPENHAGEN ✪

Kaliningrad ◉

RĪGA ✪ Daugavpils ◉

VILNIUS ✪

BELARUS ✪

MINSK

RUSSIA

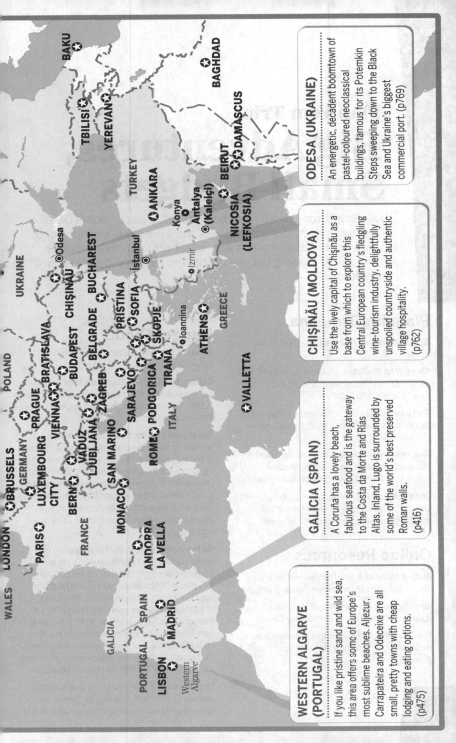

WALES · LONDON · BRUSSELS · GERMANY · POLAND · UKRAINE · TBILISI ★ BAKU ★ YEREVAN ★ BAGHDAD ★

WESTERN ALGARVE (PORTUGAL)

If you like pristine sand and wild sea, this area offers some of Europe's most sublime beaches. Aljezur, Carrapateira and Odeceixe are all small, pretty towns with cheap lodging and eating options. (p475)

GALICIA (SPAIN)

A Coruña has a lovely beach, fabulous seafood and is the gateway to the Costa da Morte and Rías Altas. Inland, Lugo is surrounded by some of the world's best preserved Roman walls. (p416)

CHIŞINĂU (MOLDOVA)

Use the lively capital of Chişinău as a base from which to explore this Central European country's fledgling wine-tourism industry, delightfully unspoiled countryside and authentic village hospitality. (p762)

ODESA (UKRAINE)

An energetic, decadent boomtown of pastel-coloured neoclassical buildings, famous for its Potemkin Steps sweeping down to the Black Sea and Ukraine's biggest commercial port. (p769)

Plan Your Trip

Big Adventures, Small Budgets

Travelling Europe on a limited budget? Yes, it can be done! Despite the fearsome costs of some places, there are many locations and experiences that are light on your wallet or simply free. Advance planning and thinking outside the box are the keys to a great Euro adventure.

Planning Timeline

12 months before Calculate a trip budget and start saving.

Six months Pick which countries to visit and book a flight. Take out travel insurance and make sure your passport is up to date.

Six to four weeks Get any necessary visas and vaccinations. Book tickets for any special events and festivals.

Four to two weeks Reserve high-season transport and accommodation in popular destinations, as well as specialist activities such as cooking courses.

One week Download travel apps and music playlist. Test out full backpack and repack leaving half out – you can get by with much less than you think.

Online Resources

Budget Traveller (http://budgettraveller.org) Tons of tips from an award-winning travel blogger.

Eurocheapo (www.eurocheapo.com) More budget-stretching advice on travelling Europe.

The Savvy Backpacker (http://thesavvyback packer.com) Trip planning and useful city price guides.

Budget Guide

Some of the many different elements to take into account:

Getting there This could cost anything from nothing, if you already live in Europe, to, say, NZ$1500 (€960) for a return air ticket from Auckland, New Zealand to London.

Travel gear & protection A good backpack is a worthwhile investment. An unlocked smart phone is also very handy, enabling you to combine staying in touch, surfing the internet and photography. Don't skimp on travel insurance and be sure your policy covers theft or damage to your equipment. The cost of the policy will also depend on how long you plan to travel, as well as the countries covered.

On the road Our breakdown of daily costs is a useful starting point. Some countries are going to be much more expensive than others. According to Eurostat (http://ec.europa.eu) in 2014 the top five most costly European nations for a bundle of goods and services were Switzerland, Norway, Denmark, Sweden and Finland, while the cheapest were Romania, Bosnia-Herzegovina, Serbia, Albania and Bulgaria. That said, if you stay away from the booze, then the Scandinavian countries, where alcohol is pricey, become much more affordable.

Time of year Avoid high season (June to August, and over Christmas & New Year and winter school holidays in ski resorts areas) and you will also find prices to be lower, particularly for accommodation and transport. Even for the busy times, booking transport well in advance or using some kind of travel pass can cut your costs considerably.

All this said, you could assume a rock-bottom budget of €50/37/30 a day for an expensive/mid-range/cheap country. This would entail a pretty spartan standard of accommodation and eating with little more than the occasional beer. Add at least €20 more to each of these daily amounts to account for more comfort and fun during your travels.

Accommodation

Hostels and camping are among the cheapest forms of accommodation. Also consider sites that link travellers with thousands of global residents who'll let you occupy their couch, spare room, even their garden in your own tent – and sometimes show you around town – for free. These include the following:

Couchsurfing (www.couchsurfing.com)

Camp in My Garden (http://campinmygarden.com)

Global Freeloaders (www.globalfreeloaders.com)

Hospitality Club (www.hospitalityclub.org)

5W (www.womenwelcomewomen.org.uk)

Check the rules of each organisation. And always let friends and family know where you're staying.

Discount Cards
Camping Cards

The Camping Card International (CCI; http://campingcardinternational.com) is an ID that can be used instead of a passport when checking into a camping ground. Many camping grounds offer a small discount if you sign in with one and it includes third-party insurance.

Transport Passes

If you plan to visit more than a few countries, or one or two countries in-depth, you might save money with a rail or bus pass.

Student Cards

The International Student Identity Card (www.isic.org), available for students, teachers and under-26s, offers thousands

of worldwide discounts on transport, museum entry, youth hostels and even some restaurants. Apply for the cards online or via issuing offices, which include **STA Travel** (www.statravel.com).

For under-26s, there's also the **European Youth Carde** (www.eyca.org). Many countries have raised the age limit for this card to under 30.

City Passes

Enquire at tourist offices about passes that provide free and/or discounted entry to many key local attractions, experiences and services. These can work out to be good value but do your sums before you buy.

Best Budget Experiences

The following are our author picks for the best locations, sights and experiences across Europe for budget travellers:

Great Britain Entry to London's amazing selection of museums and galleries usually costs nothing, and it's free entry to Glasgow and Edinburgh's premier cultural storehouses, too. The inspiring landscapes of the Lake District or along Hadrian's Wall can be appreciated gratis.

Ireland Dublin's Trinity College and the National Gallery are a couple of the city's free attractions. In Northern Ireland, Derry's City Walls and the People's Gallery Murals are both no-charge highlights.

Denmark Copenhagen's National Museum and National Gallery are both free. So is a wander in the intriguing alternative 'republic' of Christiania or a peek at the underwhelming Little Mermaid. Plus, free walking tours can show you around town.

Sweden Some major state-run museums in Stockholm, such as the excellent Historiska Museet, are free. Major cathedrals at Uppsala and Lund will also cost you nothing to enter.

Finland It's a cheap ferry ride from Helsinki to the fortress islands of Suomenlinna, with a fascinating view of the harbour on the way. Once there, you can wander the fortifications to your heart's content.

Norway Not known as a budget destination, but Oslo's iconic opera house is free to wander around, while Bergen's classic Bryggen district is the city's major highlight.

DAILY COSTS

COUNTRY	BUDGET	MIDRANGE	TOP END
Albania	<€50	€50-120	>€120
Austria	<€100	€100-200	>€200
Belgium	<€100	€100-200	>€200
Bosnia & Hercegovina	<€60	€60-130	>€130
Britain	<€80	€80-160	>€160
Bulgaria	<€50	€50-120	>€120
Croatia	<€60	€60-130	>€130
Czech Republic	<€80	€80-200	>€200
Denmark	<€120	€120-220	>€220
Estonia	<€60	€60-120	>€120
Finland	<€120	€120-250	>€250
France	<€110	€110-220	>€220
Germany	<€100	€100-200	>€200
Greece	<€60	€60-120	>€120
Hungary	<€60	€60-130	>€130
Iceland	<€110	€110-220	>€220
Ireland	<€60	€60-120	>€120
Italy	<€100	€100-250	>€250
Kosovo	<€60	€60-130	>€130
Latvia	<€60	€60-120	>€120
Lithuania	<€60	€60-120	>€120
Luxembourg	<€100	€100-200	>€200
Macedonia	<€60	€60-120	>€120
The Netherlands	<€100	€100-200	>€200
Norway	<€140	€140-220	>€220
Poland	<€50	€50-90	>€90
Portugal	<€60	€60-130	>€130
Romania	<€50	€50-120	>€120
Russia	<€20	€20-50	>€50
Serbia	<€60	€60-130	>€130
Slovakia	<€50	€50-120	>€120
Slovenia	<€50	€80-100	>€100
Spain	<€80	€80-180	>€180
Sweden	<€110	€120-220	>€220
Switzerland	<€180	€180-270	>€270
Turkey	<€50	€50-100	>€100
Ukraine	<€20	€20-50	>€50

Vondelpark (p279), Amsterdam, Netherlands.

Iceland Grab a bike from Reykjavik and head out to explore the Golden Circle attractions, none of which charge admission. Many more of Iceland's natural wonders are free to visit.

Germany Two of the biggest Berlin attractions are free. The iconic Brandenburg Gate is a symbol of the city, while the nearby Reichstag offers marvellous city views from its glass dome. In Hamburg, see the harbour for a pittance by jumping on one of the regular ferry services.

Belgium Brussels' magnificent Grand Place is one of the world's most unforgettable city squares. Nearby, the cheeky Manneken Pis statue, a tiny statue of a boy urinating is a major drawcard.

Luxembourg City It's not a cheap town, but it's a beautiful one, and wandering its ramparts is its most spectacular attraction. Plus, for just €2, you can head out to explore anywhere in this small country by train or bus.

The Netherlands It costs nothing to spend a glorious afternoon in Amsterdam's Vondelpark, a slice of idyllic Dutch life on a sunny day.

France It doesn't cost a cent to scamper up, cartwheel across or simply laze on the golden sands and gorge on extraordinary sea views of Dune du Pilat, Europe's largest sand dune.

Switzerland Let your hair down and boogie with the best of them at Europe's largest street party, aka Zurich's wild and wacky, larger-than-life Street Parade in August.

Austria There is no cheaper thrill in Austria than a hair-raising motor along the 36 hairpins of Grossglockner Road, with staggering views of snow-capped mountain peaks and plunging waterfalls guaranteed. Rub shoulders with 28 dwarfs, scale a staircase encrusted with angels and relive scenes from *The Sound of Music* - all for free at Salzburg's Schloss Mirabell.

Spain Madrid's Museo del Prado is free in the late afternoon. The nearby Reina Sofía and Museo Thyssen-Bornemisza are also free at certain times. Order a drink in Granada, León or some other cities and you'll get a free tapas portion to accompany it. Santiago de Compostela, one of Europe's most memorable cathedrals, is free to enter, as is Barcelona's Mercat de la Boqueria covered market.

Portugal Accommodation in Portugal offers the best value in Western Europe, and eating out certainly doesn't break the budget either. The extraordinary cathedrals in Braga and Coimbra, among other places, don't charge admission.

Italy Explore the Cinque Terre, an endless network of hiking trails linking five coastal medieval villages packed with pastel buildings, castles and burgeoning gardens.

Greece The Meteora Monasteries, perched atop towering rock pinnacles, make for an otherworldly setting. See the world from the viewpoint of 11th century hermit monks. With world famous climbing, once-secret hiking trails, stunning chapels and truly dramatic views, you'll understand why they stayed so long.

Turkey Is there a more Turkish experience than visiting a grand, historic hamam? Head to İstanbul for a cultural soak.

Albania For just a handful of lek, ride the ferry down enormous Lake Koman on a three-hour voyage through a chain of spectacular mountain gorges stopping off at various tiny hamlets on the way. Some travellers enjoy the scenery so much they do the journey in both directions in one day: others continue to the Accursed Mountains for more stunning scenery.

Kosovo The Pristina Bear Sanctuary, a superb NGO-run project in the countryside around the Kosovan capital can be visited for free (though donations are accepted), and the journey here is part of the fun. The resident bears have all been rescued from restaurants where they were once kept as caged 'mascots', and it's wonderful to see them finally enjoying good living conditions.

Belarus The centre of Minsk is surprisingly attractive: a uniform conurbation that features colourful 1950s architectural flourishes that are far grander than you might expect from Soviet-era style.

Czech Republic Kutná Hora's Sedlec Ossuary (aka the 'Bone Church') is at the top of the list of every backpacker's must-do list. It's cheap to enter and relatively easy to get to from Prague by bus or train.

Slovakia The High Tatras feature true Alpine peaks, arising seemingly in the middle of nowhere. There are miles of excellent hiking trails, and entry to the mountains is free.

Poland It's free to enter the grounds of the Auschwitz-Birkenau Memorial & Museum to bear witness to one of history's greatest crimes: the murder of more than a million Jews and many others by Nazi German occupiers in WWII.

Georgia The best way to experience Georgia on a budget is simply to stroll through old Tbilisi, with its winding lanes, balconied houses, leafy squares and handsome churches.

Slovenia Lake Bled is lovely to behold from almost any vantage point, and makes a stunning backdrop for the 6km walk along the perimeter, which doesn't cost a penny and is beautiful any time of year.

Clifftop monasteries, Meteora (p559), Greec

Hungary No trip to Budapest is complete without a dip in the pool and hot tub, and the Széchenyi Baths are the most popular and accessible.

Romania Bucharest's enormous Palace of Parliament is the world's second-largest building and a testament to the egos of dictators. Students pay half price for the guided tour.

Moldova Try to make it over to the country's separatist, Russian-speaking region of Transdniestr. It's a time-warp kind of place, where the Soviet Union reigns supreme and busts of Lenin line the main boulevards.

Ukraine Lviv's Ploshcha Rynok, the city's amazing market square, lies at the heart of the Unesco-protected heritage zone. It's free to enjoy.

Russia Moscow's Red Square, Lenin's Tomb and Gorky Park are among its not-to-be-missed free attractions. Time your visit to St Petersburg's magnificent Hermitage Museum for the first Thursday of the month when it's free entry to all.

The Baltic States There's no charge for enjoying the beaches at Pärnu in Estonia, Jūrmala in Latvia and in the Curonian Spit National Park in Lithuania.

Plan Your Trip
Getting Around
Europe

For many, trains or buses will be the preferred mode of Euro transport. Flights are useful for covering distances quickly and are affordable, if booked in advance. If time isn't an issue, then cycling can get you from one end of the continent to the other, and keep you fit.

Air

In the face of competition from low-cost airlines, many national carriers have dropped their prices and/or offer special deals. For a comprehensive overview of which low-cost carriers fly to or from which European cities, check out the excellent www.flycheapo.com.

Air Passes

Depending on which airline you fly into Europe, you may be able to purchase one of the following air passes. Check the details carefully and compare prices with budget airlines, taking into account taxes and any luggage surcharges.

Visit Europe Pass (www.oneworld.com/flights/single-continent-fares/visit-europe)

Europe Airpass (http://www.staralliance.com/en/airpass-details)

Charter Flights

Charter flights are organised by tour operators for travellers who have purchased a holiday package that includes transportation and accommodation. Depending on when you fly they can be a very good deal. Certain charter airlines such as Condor (www.condor.com) and Monarch Airlines (www.monarch.co.uk) also sell flights directly without the accommodation packages.

Transport Types

Train Europe's network covering 240,000km is fast and efficient but rarely a bargain unless you book well in advance or use a rail pass wisely.

Bus Usually taken for short trips in more remote areas, though long-distance intercity buses can be very cheap.

Car You can hire a car or drive your own through Europe. Roads are excellent but petrol is expensive.

Ferry Boats connect Britain and Ireland with mainland Europe, Scandinavia to the Baltic countries and Germany, and Italy to the Balkans and Greece.

Plane Speed things up by flying from one end of the continent to the other. Book well ahead for cheapest fares.

Bicycle Slow things down on a two-wheeler, a great way to get around just about anywhere.

Train

Comfortable, frequent and reliable, trains are *the* way to get around Europe.

➡ Many state railways have interactive websites publishing their timetables and fares, including www.bahn.de (Germany) and www.sbb.ch (Switzerland), which both have pages in English. Eurail (www.eurail.com) links to 28 European train companies.

➡ The very comprehensive, The Man in Seat 61 (www.seat61.com) is a gem, while the US-based Budget Europe Travel Service (www.budgeteuropetravel.com) can also help with tips.

➡ European trains sometimes split en route to service two destinations, so even if you're on the right train, make sure you're also in the correct carriage.

➡ A train journey to almost every station in Europe can be booked via Voyages-sncf.com (http://uk.voyages-sncf.com/en), which also sells InterRail and other passes.

International Rail Passes

If you're covering lots of ground, a rail pass (which usually needs to be purchased in your home country) is the way to go.

➡ You can buy online from sites such as www.raileurope.com, www.railpass.com and www.interrail.eu. If you're already in Europe arrange for the pass to be sent to parents or friends from where it can be forwarded on.

➡ Do some price comparisons of point-to-point ticket charges and rail passes beforehand to make absolutely sure you'll break even.

SLEEPING IN AIRPORTS

Sometimes the cheapest flights are for very early morning departures or late arrivals after public transport has stopped for the night. In such cases, it may be worth checking out whether it's possible to snooze at the airport. Start your research at The Guide to Sleeping at Airports (www.sleepinginairports.net): in Europe it lists Munich, Helsinki and Zurich within the top 10 airports to sleep in, and Paris Beauvais-Tille as one of the 10 worst.

➡ Shop around for rail-pass prices as prices do vary between outlets. When weighing up options, look into cheap deals that include advance-purchase reductions, one-off promotions or special circular-route tickets, particularly over the internet.

➡ Normal point-to-point tickets are valid for two months, and you can make as many stops as you like en route; make your intentions known when purchasing and inform train conductors how far you're going before they punch your ticket.

➡ Supplementary charges (eg for some express and overnight trains) and seat reservation fees (mandatory on some trains, a good idea on others) are not covered by rail passes. Always ask. Note that European rail passes also give reductions on Eurostar, the Channel Tunnel and on certain ferries.

➡ Pass-holders must always carry their passport with them for identification purposes. The railways' policy is that passes cannot be replaced or refunded if lost or stolen.

National Rail Passes

National rail operators might also offer their own passes, or at least a discount card, offering substantial reductions on tickets purchased (eg the Bahn Card in Germany or the Half-Fare Card in Switzerland).

Look at individual train operator sites via http://uk.voyages-sncf.com/en/ to check. Such discount cards are usually only worth it if you're staying in the country a while and doing a lot of travelling.

Bus

If you really want to make your budget go further then buses are always going to be a cheaper (but slower) form of transport around Europe.

One recent entrant into the market is **Megabus** (http://uk.megabus.com) which offers discount bus tickets throughout the UK and to cities in Belgium, France, Germany, Italy, The Netherlands, Ireland and Spain.

Bus Passes

Eurolines Pass (www.eurolines.com/en/eurolines-pass) Allows passengers to visit a choice of 53 cities across Europe over 15 or 30 days. In 2016/17 the high season (mid-June to mid-September)

Above: The train journey to Jungfraujoch (p358), Switzerland

Right: Women cycling in Barcelona (p416), Spain

WESTEND61 / GETTY IMAGES ©

passes for 15/30 days cost €270/350 for those aged under 26, or €320/425 for those 26 and over. It's cheaper in other periods.

Busabout (www.busabout.com) Offers a 'hop-on, hop-off' service around Europe, stopping at major cities every two days from May to the end of October. Buses are often oversubscribed, so book each sector to avoid being stranded.

Car

While driving a car will give you the greatest flexibility in the places you can see across Europe, it will also be the most expensive way to travel unless you happen to be travelling in a group that can share the cost.

If that's not the case then hitching is another option – it's never entirely safe, though, and we cannot recommend it.

A variation on hitching is car pooling, where you arrange a lift in advance. Scan student noticeboards in colleges, or check out services such as Bla Bla Car (www.blablacar.co.uk) or Drive2Day (www.drive2day.de).

Bicycle

Much of Europe is ideally suited to cycling. Popular cycling areas include the whole of the Netherlands, the Belgian Ardennes, the west of Ireland, the upper reaches of the Danube in southern Germany and anywhere in northern Switzerland, Denmark or the south of France. Exploring the small villages of Turkey and Eastern Europe also provides up-close access to remote areas.

A primary consideration on a cycling trip is to travel light, but you should take a few tools and spare parts, including a puncture-repair kit and an extra inner tube. Panniers are essential to balance your possessions on either side of the bike frame. Wearing a helmet is not compulsory in most countries, but is certainly sensible.

Seasoned cyclists can average 80km a day, but it depends on what you're carrying and your level of fitness.

Cyclists' Touring Club (CTC; www.ctc.org.uk) The national cycling association of the UK runs organised trips to Continental Europe.

European Cyclists' Federation (www.ecf.com) Has details of 'EuroVelo', the European cycle network of 12 pan-European cycle routes, plus tips for other tours.

SwitzerlandMobility (www.veloland.ch/en/cycling-in-switzerland.html) Details of Swiss national routes and more.

Transporting a Bicycle

For major cycling trips, it's best to have a bike you're familiar with, so consider bringing your own rather than buying on arrival. If coming from outside Europe, ask about the airline's policy on transporting bikes before buying your ticket.

From the UK to the continent, Eurostar (the train service through the Channel Tunnel) charges £25 to £30 to send a bike as registered luggage on its routes.

For only £20 extra you can transport your bicycle and yourself on Eurotunnel through the Channel Tunnel; see www.eurotunnel.com/uk/traveller-info/vehicles/bicycles.

With a bit of tinkering and dismantling (eg removing wheels), you might be able to get your bike into a bag or sack and take it on a train as hand luggage.

Alternatively, the European Bike Express (www.bike-express.co.uk) is a UK-based coach service where cyclists can travel with their bicycles to various cycling destinations on the continent.

Once on the continent, you can put your feet up on the train if you get tired of pedalling or simply want to skip a boring section. On slower trains, bikes can usually be transported as luggage, subject to a small supplementary fee. Some cyclists have reported that Italian and French train attendants have refused bikes on slow trains, so be prepared for regulations to be interpreted differently by officious staff.

Fast trains can rarely accommodate bikes; they might need to be sent as registered luggage and may end up on a different train from the one you take. This is often the case in France and Spain.

Regions at a Glance

Europe is like a bumper pack of sweets – so many tempting options! To stop your head from spinning we've divided this guide's On the Road chapters into clusters of neighbouring countries that share not only borders but often overlapping histories and cultures. Rather than spreading your travels thinly across broad swathes of Europe, consider the benefits of concentrating on a smaller region. The key elements of each region are spelled out so you'll know where to go if you're looking for beaches and nightlife rather than history and culture.

Great Britain & Ireland

History
Landscape
Nightlife

The Romans came 2000 years ago and so should you. Capitals London and Dublin simply rock but also make time to see some of the region's other highlights, from the rugged Scottish highlands to Ireland's convivial pubs.

p51

Scandinavia

Cities
Forests
Outdoor Activities

Design savvy cities that know how to party and pristine swathes of nature perfect for outdoor pursuits are among the prime draws of this region that includes Denmark, Finland, Iceland, Norway and Sweden.

p137

Germany & Benelux

Landscapes
Cities
Drinking

Edgy architecture, art and culture are enlivened by beer halls and convivial cafes in Germany, Belgium, Luxembourg and the Netherlands. History is writ large across a region that includes incredible castles and memorials to WWII.

p209

GARY YEOWELL / GETTY IMAGES ©

Above: Acropolis of Lindos (p567) and harbour, Rhodes, Greece

Left: Shop selling gourmet produce, Tuscany, Italy

France, Switzerland & Austria

Food & Drink
Art
Mountains

Gastronomic delights, classic works of art and awe-inspiring landscapes are the major highlights on this trio of nations spanning the Alps and stretching from the English Channel to the shores of the Med.

p295

Spain & Portugal

Beaches
Scenery
Food & Drink

When much of the rest of Europe is shivering you can be sure of some sunshine on the Iberian Peninsula. And even if the weather isn't playing ball, there are plenty of cultural attractions including amazing museums and fabulously tasty food.

p389

Italy, Greece & Turkey

History
Beaches
Food & Drink

The attractions of these crucibles of the ancient world encompass incredible ruins, idyllic beaches and a budget-friendly spread of gastronomic goodies. The southeastern Med's warmth is also reflected in the friendliness of the locals.

p489

Balkans

Beaches
Festivals
Scenery

Travel here may not be as smooth as other parts of Europe, but it's still possible to discover some delightful off-the-radar treasures, such as Albania's amazing beaches. There are also ancient towns, cool cities and plenty of fab festivals.

p603

Central & Eastern Europe

Food & Drink
Scenery
Outdoor Adventures

The combination of mountain rusticity with old-world style captivates here. Come for Teutonic villages and graffiti-decorated Renaissance squares as well as alpine activities and an abundance of outdoor cafes and beer halls.

p687

Russia & the Baltic Coast

Architecture
History
Scenery

Moscow and St Petersburg are packed with architectural and artistic must-sees. but it's not all about Russia. It's easy and fun to travel between the Baltic States each with their own distinct cultures and gorgeous scenery.

p777

On the Road

Great Britain & Ireland

Why Go?

Britain, which includes England, Wales and Scotland, can be traversed from tip to toe in around half a day. However, you could spend a lifetime exploring this historic and beautiful island – from ancient Stonehenge and the great medieval cathedrals of Westminster, Canterbury and York, to the colleges of Oxford and Cambridge and the castles and magnificent scenery of Wales and Scotland.

West across the Irish Sea, lies Ireland, made up of the Republic and the British province of Northern Ireland. The Ireland of postcards very much exists. You'll find it along the peninsulas of the southwest, in the brooding loneliness of Connemara and the dramatic wildness of the Causeway Coast. This is also a very modern country, but some things endure. Linger in the yard of a thatched-cottage pub on a warm evening and you'll experience a country that has changed little in generations.

Best Places to Eat

➜ Kerbisher & Malt (p69)

➜ Coffee Barker (p88)

➜ Mums (p97)

➜ Maggie May's (p129)

➜ Fumbally (p113)

Best Places to Sleep

➜ Clink78 (p68)

➜ River House (p88)

➜ Malone's Old Town Hostel (p97)

➜ Vagabonds (p129)

➜ Isaacs Hostel (p112)

Fast Facts

Capitals London (England), Cardiff (Wales), Edinburgh (Scotland), Belfast (Northern Ireland), Dublin (Republic of Ireland)

Emergency ☎999 (Great Britain and Northern Ireland); ☎999 or ☎112 (Republic of Ireland)

Currency Pound £ (Great Britain and Northern Ireland); Euro € (Republic of Ireland)

Languages English, Scottish Gaelic, Welsh (Great Britain); English, Irish (Ireland)

Visas Not required for most EU citizens, Australia, New Zealand, USA and Canada

Mobile Phones Most foreign phones work in Great Britain and Ireland (beware roaming charges). Local SIMs and basic handsets available.

Great Britain & Ireland Highlights

1 London
Experience the many delights of one of the world's greatest capital cities. (p60)

2 Oxford Get lost among the dreaming spires of this ancient university town. (p77)

3 Bath Visit Roman baths and admire grand Georgian architecture. (p75)

4 Snowdonia National Park Climb or ride the train up the 1085m mountain. (p88)

5 Manchester Dive into the northern powerhouse's wealth of cultural institutions and cracking nightlife scene. (p85)

0 — 100 km
0 — 50 miles

WORTH A TRIP: ISLE OF SKYE

Head north through the Scottish Highlands to experience the epic scenery of this island. (p104)

Shetland Islands
● Lerwick

NORTH SEA

Orkney Islands
Stromness ● ● Kirkwall
South Ronaldsay

Thurso ● ● Wick

● Helmsdale

Fraserburgh

● Stornoway
Isle of Lewis
Isle of Harris
The Minch

Tarbert ●
North Uist
Lochmaddy ●
Dunvegan ●
South Uist
Lochboisdale ●
Barra

ATLANTIC OCEAN

St Kilda

Uig ●
Isle of Skye **7**

Kyle of Lochalsh ●

Mallaig ●

Sea of the Hebrides

Isle of Mull
Isle of Iona

Isle of Jura

Isle of Islay

Campbeltown ●

Mull of Kintyre

Buncrana ●
Coleraine ●

Ullapool ●

Inverness
Loch Ness

Fort Augustus ●

Fort William ●
Ben Nevis (1344m) ▲

Glencoe ●
● Kinlochleven

Loch Lomond & Trossachs National Park

Oban ●

Brodick ●
Isle of Arran

Ayr ●

● Stromness

● Helmsdale

Nairn ●
Moray Firth Elgin

Cairngorms National Park
Kingussie ●

● Aberdeen

● Stonehaven

Montrose ●

Perth ● ● Dundee
● St Andrews

Stirling ●
Loch Lomond

Dumbarton ●
Glasgow ● ● Hamilton
Kilmarnock ●

SCOTLAND

6 Edinburgh ●
Peebles ●
Lanark ●

Melrose ●
Jedburgh ●

● Berwick-upon-Tweed

Kelso ●

Northumberland National Park

Galloway Forest Park
Dumfries ●

Hadrian's

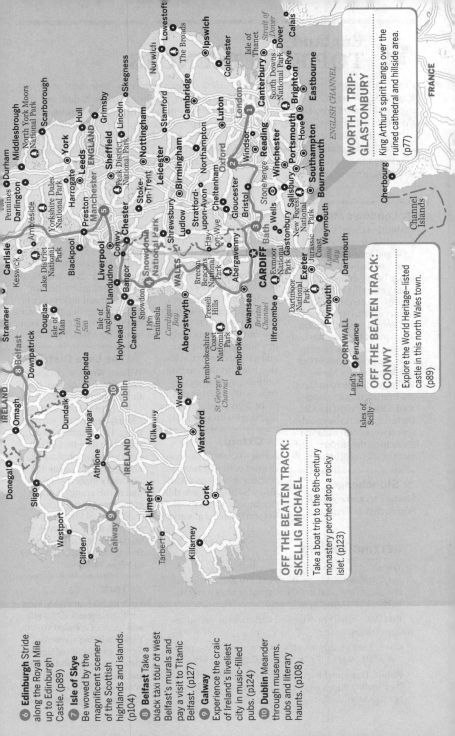

6 Edinburgh Stride along the Royal Mile up to Edinburgh Castle. (p89)

7 Isle of Skye Be wowed by the magnificent scenery of the Scottish highlands and islands. (p104)

8 Belfast Take a black taxi tour of West Belfast's murals and pay a visit to Titanic Belfast. (p127)

9 Galway Experience the craic in one of Ireland's liveliest city in music-filled pubs. (p124)

10 Dublin Meander through museums, pubs and literary haunts. (p108)

OFF THE BEATEN TRACK:
SKELLIG MICHAEL

Take a boat trip to the 6th-century monastery perched atop a rocky islet. (p123)

OFF THE BEATEN TRACK:
CONWY

Explore the World Heritage–listed castle in this north Wales town. (p89)

WORTH A TRIP: **GLASTONBURY**

King Arthur's spirit hangs over the ruined cathedral and hillside area. (p77)

England's
TOP EXPERIENCES

From the Roman remains of Hadrian's Wall to London's incomparable theatre scene, England (p60) is full of astounding variety. In the cities, the streets buzz day and night, filled with tempting shops and restaurants, and some of the finest museums in the world. After dark, cutting-edge clubs, top-class performing arts and formidable live music provide a string of nights to remember. Next day, you're deep in the English countryside or enjoying a classic seaside resort. There really is something for everyone, whether you're eight or 80, going solo or travelling with your friends, your kids or your grandma.

⭐ London's Museums

Institutions bright and beautiful, great and small, wise and wonderful – London's got them all. The range of museums is vast: from generalist exhibitions (British Museum, V&A) to specific themes (Imperial War Museum, London Transport Museum, Natural History Museum), from intriguing private collections (Sir John Soane's Museum, Wallace Collection) to those celebrating people associated with the city (Handel, Dickens, Freud).You could spend weeks without even scratching the surface. And most of it's free! (p60)

⭐ Stonehenge

Mysterious and compelling, Stonehenge is England's most iconic ancient site. People have been drawn to this myth-rich ring of boulders for more than 5000 years, and we still don't know quite why it was built. Most visitors gaze at the 50-tonne stones from behind the perimeter fence, but with enough planning you can arrange an early morning or evening tour and gain access to the inner ring itself. In the slanting sunlight, away from the crowds, it's an ethereal place. This is an experience that stays with you. (p74)

⭐ Oxford

A visit to Oxford is as close as most of us will get to the brilliant minds and august institutions that made this city famous across the globe. But you'll catch a glimpse of this rarefied world in the cobbled lanes and ancient quads where student cyclists and dusty academics roam. The beautiful college buildings, archaic traditions and stunning architecture have changed little over the centuries, leaving the centre much as Einstein or Tolkien would have found it. (p77)

⭐ The Lake District

William Wordsworth and his Romantic friends were the first to champion the charms of the Lake District and it's easy to see what stirred them. The dramatic landscape of whale-backed hills, deep valleys, mountain lakes and high peaks (including England's highest summit) makes this craggy corner of the country the spiritual home of English hiking. Strap on the boots, stock up on mint cake and drink in the views: inspiration is sure to follow. (p86)

⭐ York

With its Roman and Viking heritage, ancient city walls and maze of cobbled streets, York is a living showcase for the highlights of English history. Join a walking tour and plunge into the network of narrow alleys, each one the focus of a ghost story or

---

GETTING AROUND

Train Britain's comprehensive rail network connects major cities and towns. Book well in advance for the cheapest fares and avoid travelling at peak times (ie before 10am Monday to Friday).

Bus Bus routes are extensive and cover places where trains don't reach.

Car Britain's roads are extensive and of a high standard. Motorways link major cities. Car hire is pricey.

Public Transport Excellent (but expensive) in London; mainly buses and light rail in other big cities such as Manchester.

historical character. Explore the intricacies of York Minster, the biggest medieval cathedral in all of northern Europe, or admire the exhibits from more recent times at the National Railway Museum, the world's largest collection of historical locomotives. (p82)

★ Bath

In a nation packed with pretty cities, Bath stands out as the belle of the ball. Founded by the Romans, who established the spa resort of Aquae Sulis to take advantage of the area's hot springs, Bath hit its stride in the 18th century when the rich industrialist Ralph Allen and architects John Wood the Elder and John Wood the Younger oversaw the city's reinvention as a model of Georgian architecture. Awash with amber town houses, sweeping crescents and Palladian mansions, Bath demands your undivided attention. (p75)

★ Cambridge

Abounding with exquisite architecture and steeped in tradition, Cambridge is a university town extraordinaire. The tightly packed core of ancient colleges, the picturesque riverside 'Backs' (college gardens and parks) and the surrounding green meadows give Cambridge a more tranquil appeal than its historic rival Oxford. Highlights include the intricate vaulting of King's College Chapel, while no visit is complete without an attempt to steer a punt (flat-bottomed boat) along the river and under the quirky Mathematical Bridge. You'll soon wonder how you could have studied anywhere else. (p81)

★ Stratford-upon-Avon

The pretty English Midlands town of Stratford-upon-Avon is famed around the world as the birthplace of the nation's best-known dramatist, William Shakespeare. Today, the town's tight knot of Tudor streets form a living map of Shakespeare's life and times, while crowds of fans and would-be thespians come to enjoy a play at the theatre or visit the five historic houses owned by Shakespeare and his relatives, with a respectful detour to the old stone church where the Bard was laid to rest. (p80)

★ Hadrian's Wall

Hadrian's Wall is one of Britain's most revealing and dramatic Roman ruins, its sturdy line of battlements, forts, garrisons, towers and castles disclosing much about the everyday life of the battalions posted along its length almost 2000 years ago. Hadrian's edge-of-empire barrier symbolised the boundary of civilised order. To the south was the orderly Roman world of tax-paying, bathhouses and underfloor heating, while to the north was the unruly land of the marauding Celts. (p87)

if England were 100 people

85 would be British
4 would be South Asian
2 would be African & Afro Caribbean
9 would be other

belief systems
(% of population)

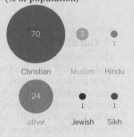

70 Christian 3 Muslim 1 Hindu
24 other 1 Jewish 1 Sikh

population per sq km

ENGLAND SCOTLAND USA

↟ ≈ 35 people

When to Go

London

°C/°F **Temp**   Rainfall Inches/mm

30/86 —   — 4.9/125
              — 3.9/100
20/68 —   — 2.9/75
              — 2/50
10/50 —   — 1/25
0/32 —   — 0

J F M A M J J A S O N D

Wales' & Scotland's
TOP EXPERIENCES

Lying to the west of England, Wales (p87) is a nation with Celtic roots, its own language and a rich historic legacy. The country also offers myriad opportunities for escaping into nature. Humans have been shaping this land for millennia but there are plenty of lonely corners to explore, lurking behind mountains, within river valleys and along surf-battered cliffs. An extensive network of paths makes Wales a hiker's paradise – and thousands of people duck across the border from England each year for that reason alone.

Scotland (p89) also has many treasures crammed into its compact territory – big skies, lonely landscapes, spectacular wildlife, superb seafood and hospitable, down-to-earth people. This is a land with a rich, multilayered history, which also harbours some of the largest areas of wilderness left in Western Europe. At museums such as Glasgow's Kelvingrove, you can also learn about the Scottish artists, engineers, explorers, writers and inventors who have shaped the modern world.

⭐ Cardiff

The transformation of stinky Cardiff Bay into the shiny architectural showcase of today is a textbook example of urban renewal at its best. Yes, it's cut off from the city centre and there are still abandoned buildings on its fringes, but Cardiff Bay is a worthy testament to the rebirth of an ancient nation as a modern democratic country, increasingly in control of its own destiny. And the transformation is ongoing, with the recent opening of the Doctor Who Experience, right next to BBC Wales' flash new studio complex. (p87)

⭐ Snowdonia

The rugged northwest corner of Wales has rocky mountain peaks, glacier-hewn valleys and lakes, sinuous ridges, sparkling rivers and charm-infused villages. The busiest part is around Snowdon itself, where hordes hike to the summit and many more take the less strenuous cog railway from Llanberis. Elsewhere in Snowdonia's rugged mountains are rarely trodden areas perfect for off-the-beaten-track exploration. Glorious under the summer sun and even better under a blanket of snow, Snowdonia is one of Wales' absolute treasures. (p88)

⭐ Conwy Castle

The golden age of castle building coincided with the golden age of 'let's show the Welsh what's what'. There's barely a town in Wales of any note that doesn't have a castle towering over it. None has a more symbiotic relationship with its settlement than Conwy. The castle still stretches out its enfolding arms to enclose the historic town in a stony embrace, originally designed to keep a tiny English colony safe from the populace they displaced. Even today it's an awe-inspiring sight. (p89)

⭐ Edinburgh

Scotland's capital may be famous for its festivals, but there's much more to

---

GETTING AROUND

Bus Extensive networks and the cheapest way to get around, but also the slowest.

Train Invest in a discount pass to get the best value out of riding the rails. Many routes pass through beautiful scenery, particularly in Scotland's Highlands.

Car Wales' and Scotland's roads are generally good and far less busy than those in England.

Bicycle Travelling around by bicycle in these compact countries is certainly feasible, and particularly suited to Scotland's islands.

it than that. Edinburgh is a city of many moods: visit out of season to see the Old Town silhouetted against a blue spring sky and a yellow haze of daffodils; or on a chill December morning with the fog snagging the spires of the Royal Mile, rain on the cobblestones and a warm glow beckoning from the window of a pub. (p89)

★ Glasgow

Scotland's biggest city lacks Edinburgh's classical beauty, but more than makes up for it with a barrelful of things to do and a warmth and energy that leave every visitor impressed. Edgy and contemporary, it's a great spot to browse art galleries and museums, and to discover the works of local hero Charles Rennie Mackintosh. Add what is perhaps Britain's best pub culture and one of the world's best live-music scenes, and the only thing to do is live it. (p99)

★ Isle of Skye

In a country famous for stunning scenery, the Isle of Skye takes top prize. From the craggy peaks of the Cuillins and the bizarre pinnacles of the Old Man of Storr and Quiraing to the spectacular sea cliffs of Neist Point, there's a photo opportunity at almost every turn. Walkers can share the landscape with red deer and golden eagles, and refuel at the end of the day in convivial pubs and top seafood restaurants. (p104)

★ Loch Lomond

Despite being less than an hour's drive from the bustle and sprawl of Glasgow, the 'bonnie banks' and 'bonnie braes' of Loch Lomond – immortalised in the words of one of Scotland's best-known songs – comprise one of the most scenic parts of the country. At the heart of Scotland's first national park, the loch begins as a broad, island-peppered lake in the south, its shores clothed in bluebell woods, narrowing in the north to a fjord-like trench ringed by 900m-high mountains. (p103)

★ Whisky

After tea, Britain's best-known drink is whisky. And while this amber spirit is also made in England and Wales, it is always most associated with Scotland. With more than 2000 whisky brands available, there are distilleries dotted across Scotland, many open to visitors, with Speyside one of the main concentrations and a favourite spot for connoisseurs. Before enjoying your tipple, heed these warnings: never spell whisky with an 'e' (that's the Irish variety); and when ordering at the bar, never ask for 'Scotch'. What else would you drink in Scotland?

if Scotland were 100 people

98 would be white
1 would be South Asian
1 would be other

Welsh speaking
(% of population)

74
don't understand
Welsh at all

19
speak
Welsh

5
understand but
can't speak Welsh

2
read but don't
speak Welsh

population per sq km

WALES   UK   USA

= 3 people

When to Go

Edinburgh

°C/°F Temp

40/104 —
30/86 —
20/68 —
10/50 —
0/32 —
-10/14 —

Rainfall Inches/mm

— 10/250
— 8/200
— 6/150
— 4/100
— 2/50
— 0

J F M A M J J A S O N D

Ireland's
TOP EXPERIENCES

From shamrocks and shillelaghs (Irish fighting sticks) to leprechauns and loveable rogues, there's a plethora of platitudes to wade through before you reach the real Ireland (p108). But it's well worth looking beyond the tourist tat, for the Emerald Isle is one of Europe's gems, a scenic extravaganza of lakes, mountains, sea and sky. From picture-postcard County Kerry to the rugged coastline of Northern Ireland (part of the UK, distinct from the Republic of Ireland; p127), there are countless opportunities to get outdoors and explore, whether cycling the Causeway Coast or hiking the hills of Connemara.

There are cultural pleasures too in the land of Joyce and Yeats, U2 and the Undertones. Dublin, Cork and Belfast all have world-class art galleries and museums, while you can enjoy foot-stomping traditional music in the bars of Galway and Killarney. So push aside the shamrocks and experience the real Ireland.

★ Dublin

Ireland's capital and largest city by some stretch is the main gateway into the country, and it has enough distractions to keep visitors engaged for at least a few days. From world-class museums and entertainment, superb dining and top-grade hotels, Dublin has all the baubles of a major international metropolis. But the real clinchers are Dubliners themselves, who are friendlier, more easy-going and welcoming than the burghers of virtually any other European capital. And it's the home of Guinness. (p108)

★ Galway

One word to describe Galway City? Craic! Ireland's liveliest city literally hums through the night at music-filled pubs where you can hear three old guys playing spoons and fiddles or listen to a hot, young band. Join the locals as they bounce from place to place, never knowing what fun lies ahead but certain of the possibility. Add in local bounty such as the famous oysters and nearby adventure in the Connemara Peninsula and the Aran Islands and the fun never ends. (p124)

★ Kilkenny

From its regal castle to its soaring medieval cathedral, Kilkenny exudes a permanence and culture that have made it an unmissable stop on journeys to the south and west. Its namesake county boasts scores of artisans and craftspeople and you can browse their wares at Kilkenny's classy shops and boutiques. Chefs eschew Dublin in order to be close to the source of Kilkenny's wonderful produce and you can enjoy the local brewery's brews at scores of delightful pubs. (p116)

GETTING AROUND

Bus The bus network is extensive and generally quite competitive – although journey times can be slow and lots of the points of interest outside towns are not served.

Train Given Ireland's relatively small size, train travel can be quick and advance-purchase fares are competitive with buses.

Car Compared with many countries, hire rates are cheap in Ireland so it's worth considering as a way to see more in a short space of time.

Bicycle Ireland's compact size and scenic landscapes make it a good cycling destination but be prepared for inclement weather.

⭐ Rock of Cashel

Soaring up from the green Tipperary pastures, this ancient fortress takes your breath away at first sight. The seat of kings and churchmen who ruled over the region for more than a thousand years, it rivalled Tara as a centre of power in Ireland for 400 years. Entered through the 15th-century Hall of the Vicars Choral, its impervious walls guard an awesome enclosure with a complete round tower, a 13th-century Gothic cathedral and the most magnificent 12th-century Romanesque chapel in Ireland. (p119)

⭐ Cliffs of Moher

Bathed in the golden glow of the late afternoon sun, the iconic Cliffs of Moher are but one of the splendours of County Clare. From a boat bobbing below, the towering stone faces have a jaw-dropping dramatic beauty that's enlivened by scores of sea birds, including cute little puffins. Down south in Loop Head, pillars of rock towering above the sea have abandoned stone cottages whose very existence is inexplicable. All along the coast are cute little villages like trad-session-filled Ennistymon and the surfer mecca of Lahinch. (p126)

⭐ Giant's Causeway

County Antrim's Causeway Coast is an especially dramatic backdrop for *Game of Thrones* filming locations. Put on your walking boots by the swaying Carrick-a-Rede rope bridge, then follow the rugged coastline for 16.5 spectacular kilometres, passing Ballintoy Harbour (aka the Iron Islands' Lordsports Harbour) and the geological wonder of the Giant's Causeway's outsized basalt columns, as well as cliffs and islands, sandy beaches and ruined castles, before finishing with a dram at the Old Bushmills Distillery. (p131)

⭐ Titanic Belfast

The construction of the world's most famous ocean liner is celebrated in high-tech, multimedia glory at this wonderful museum. Not only can you explore virtually every detail of the *Titanic*'s construction – including a simulated 'fly-through' of the ship from keel to bridge – but you can place yourself in the middle of the industrial bustle that was Belfast's shipyards at the turn of the 20th century. The experience is heightened by the use of photography, audio and – perhaps most poignantly – the only footage of the actual *Titanic* still in existence. (p127)

if Ireland were 100 people

85 would be Irish
10 would be other white
2 would be Asian
1 would be black
2 would be mixed and other

belief systems
(% of population)

| 85 | 3 | 1 |
| Roman Catholic | Church of Ireland | Muslim |

| 3 | 8 |
| other Christian | other or none |

population per sq km

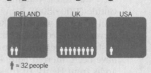

| IRELAND | UK | USA |

👤 ≈ 32 people

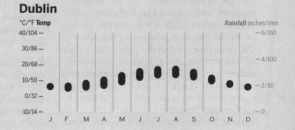

When to Go

Dublin

°C/°F Temp   Rainfall inches/mm
40/104 —   — 6/150
30/86 —
20/68 —   — 4/100
10/50 —
0/32 —   — 2/50
-10/14 —   — 0
          J F M A M J J A S O N D

ENGLAND

London

📙 020 / POP 8.5 MILLION

Everyone comes to London with preconceptions. Whatever yours are, prepare to have them exploded by this endlessly intriguing city. Its streets are steeped in fascinating history, magnificent art, imposing architecture and popular culture. When you add a bottomless reserve of cool to this mix, it's hard not to conclude that London is one of the world's great cities, if not the greatest.

It's certainly not a cheap city, but with some careful planning and a bit of common sense, you can find excellent bargains and freebies among the popular attractions. And many of London's best assets – its wonderful parks, bridges, squares and boulevards, not to mention many of its landmark museums – come completely free.

◎ Sights

◎ Westminster & St James's

★ **Westminster Abbey**   CHURCH
(Map p65; 📙 020-7222 5152; www.westminster -abbey.org; 20 Dean's Yard, SW1; adult/child £20/9, verger tours £5, cloister & gardens free; ⊙ 9.30am-4.30pm Mon, Tue, Thu & Fri, to 7pm Wed, to 2.30pm Sat; ⊜Westminster) Westminster Abbey is a mixture of architectural styles, but considered the finest example of Early English Gothic (1190–1300). It's not merely a beautiful place of worship, though. The Abbey serves up the country's history cold on slabs of stone. For centuries the country's greatest have been interred here, including 17 monarchs from Henry III (died 1272) to George II (1760). Westminster Abbey has never been a cathedral (the seat of a bishop). It's what is called a 'royal peculiar', administered directly by the Crown.

Houses of Parliament   HISTORIC BUILDING
(Map p65; www.parliament.uk; Parliament Sq, SW1; ⊜Westminster) FREE A visit to the Houses of Parliament is a journey to the heart of UK democracy. Officially called the Palace of Westminster, the Houses of Parliament's oldest part is 11th-century **Westminster Hall**, which is one of only a few sections that survived a catastrophic fire in 1834. Its roof, added between 1394 and 1401, is the earliest known example of a hammerbeam

roof. Most of the rest of the building is a neo-Gothic confection built by Charles Barry and Augustus Pugin (1840–58).

The palace's most famous feature is its clock tower, called Elizabeth Tower, aka **Big Ben**. Ben is actually the 13.5-ton bell, named after Benjamin Hall, who was Commissioner of Works when the tower was completed in 1858.

Tate Britain   GALLERY
(www.tate.org.uk; Millbank, SW1; ⊙10am-6pm, to 10pm 1st Fri of month; ⊜Pimlico) FREE Splendidly refurbished with a stunning new art-deco-inspired staircase and a rehung collection, the more elderly and venerable of the two Tate siblings celebrates paintings from 1500 to the present, with works from Blake, Hogarth, Gainsborough, Hepworth, Whistler, Constable and Turner, as well as vibrant modern and contemporary pieces from Lucian Freud, Francis Bacon, Henry Moore and Tracey Emin. Join free 45-minute **thematic tours** (⊙11am, noon, 2pm & 3pm) and 15-minute **Art in Focus talks** (⊙1.15pm Tue, Thu & Sat).

◎ West End

★ **British Museum**   MUSEUM
(Map p70; 📙 020-7323 8000; www.britishmuseum. org; Great Russell St, WC1; ⊙10am-5.30pm Sat-Thu, to 8.30pm Fri; ⊜Russell Sq, Tottenham Court Rd) FREE The country's largest museum and one of the oldest and finest in the world, this famous museum boasts vast Egyptian, Etruscan, Greek, Roman, European and Middle Eastern galleries, among many others. It is frequently London's most visited attraction, drawing over six million visitors each year.

Among the must-sees are the **Rosetta Stone**, the key to deciphering Egyptian hieroglyphics, discovered in 1799; the controversial **Parthenon Sculptures**, taken from the Parthenon in Athens by Lord Elgin (the British ambassador to the Ottoman Empire); the large collection of **Egyptian mummies**; the Anglo-Saxon **Sutton Hoo burial relics**; and the **Winged Bulls from Khorsabad**.

★ **National Gallery**   GALLERY
(Map p65; www.nationalgallery.org.uk; Trafalgar Sq, WC2; ⊙10am-6pm Sat-Thu, to 9pm Fri; ⊜Charing Cross) FREE With some 2300 European paintings on display, this is one of the world's richest art collections, with seminal

paintings from every important epoch in the history of art – from the mid-13th to the early 20th century, including works by Da Vinci, Michelangelo, Titian, Van Gogh and Renoir.

Many visitors flock to the East Wing (1700–1900), where works by 18th-century British artists such as Gainsborough, Constable and Turner, and seminal Impressionist and post-Impressionist masterpieces by Van Gogh, Renoir and Monet await.

Trafalgar Square   SQUARE
(Map p65; ⊖ Charing Cross) In many ways Trafalgar Sq is the centre of London, where rallies and marches take place, tens of thousands of revellers usher in the New Year and locals congregate for anything from communal open-air cinema and Christmas celebrations to various political protests. It is dominated by the 52m-high **Nelson's Column** and ringed by many splendid buildings, including the National Gallery and St Martin-in-the-Fields.

National Portrait Gallery   GALLERY
(Map p65; www.npg.org.uk; St Martin's Pl, WC2; ⊘10am-6pm Sat-Wed, to 9pm Thu & Fri; ⊖ Charing Cross, Leicester Sq) **FREE** What makes the National Portrait Gallery so compelling is its familiarity; in many cases you'll have heard of the subject (royals, scientists, politicians, celebrities) or the artist (Andy Warhol, Annie Leibovitz, Sam Taylor-Wood). Highlights include the famous 'Chandos portrait' of William Shakespeare, the first artwork the gallery acquired (in 1856) and believed to be the only likeness made during the playwright's lifetime, and a touching sketch of novelist Jane Austen by her sister.

Piccadilly Circus   SQUARE
(Map p65; ⊖ Piccadilly Circus) John Nash had originally designed Regent St and Piccadilly in the 1820s to be the two most elegant streets in town but, curbed by city planners, couldn't realise his dream to the full. He may be disappointed, but suitably astonished, with Piccadilly Circus today: a traffic maelstrom, deluged with visitors and flanked by flashing advertisement panels. A seething hubbub, 'it's like Piccadilly Circus', as the expression goes, but it's certainly fun.

◉ **The City**

★**St Paul's Cathedral**   CATHEDRAL
(Map p62; 020-7246 8350; www.stpauls.co.uk; St Paul's Churchyard, EC4; adult/child £18/8; ⊘8.30am-4.30pm Mon-Sat; ⊖ St Paul's) Tower-

CHANGING OF THE GUARD

London's most famous open-air freebie, the Changing of the Guard in the forecourt of **Buckingham Palace** (Map p65; 020-7766 7300; www.royalcollection.org.uk; Buckingham Palace Rd, SW1; adult/child £20.50/11.80; ⊘9.30am-7.30pm late Jul–Aug, to 6.30pm Sep; ⊖St James's Park, Victoria, Green Park) takes place at 11.30am from April to July (and alternate days, weather permitting, August to March). Alternatively, catch the changing of the mounted guard at **Horse Guards Parade** (Map p65; www.changing-the-guard.com/london-programme.html; Horse Guards Parade, off Whitehall, W1; ⊘11am Mon-Sat, 10am Sun; ⊖Westminster, St James's Park) at 11am (10am on Sundays).

ing over Ludgate Hill, in a superb position that's been a place of Christian worship for over 1400 years, St Paul's Cathedral is one of London's most majestic and iconic buildings. For Londoners, the vast dome, which still manages to dominate the skyline, is a symbol of resilience and pride, standing tall for over 300 years. Viewing Sir Christopher Wren's masterpiece from the inside and climbing to the top for sweeping views of the capital is an exhilarating experience.

★**Tower of London**   CASTLE
(Map p62; 0844 482 7777; www.hrp.org.uk/toweroflondon; Tower Hill, EC3; adult/child £22/10, audioguide £4/3; ⊘9am-5.30pm Tue-Sat, 10am-5.30pm Sun & Mon Mar-Oct, 9am-4.30pm Tue-Sat, 10am-4.30pm Sun & Mon Nov-Feb; ⊖Tower Hill) The unmissable Tower of London (actually a castle of 22 towers) offers a window into a gruesome and compelling history. This was where two kings and three queens met their death and countless others were imprisoned. Come here to see the colourful Yeoman Warders (or Beefeaters), the spectacular Crown Jewels, the soothsaying ravens and armour fit for a *very* large king.

Tower Bridge   BRIDGE
(Map p62; ⊖Tower Hill) London was a thriving port in 1894 when elegant Tower Bridge was built. Designed to be raised to allow ships to pass, electricity has now taken over from the original steam and hydraulic engines. A lift leads up from the northern tower to the **Tower Bridge Exhibition** (Map p62;

Central London

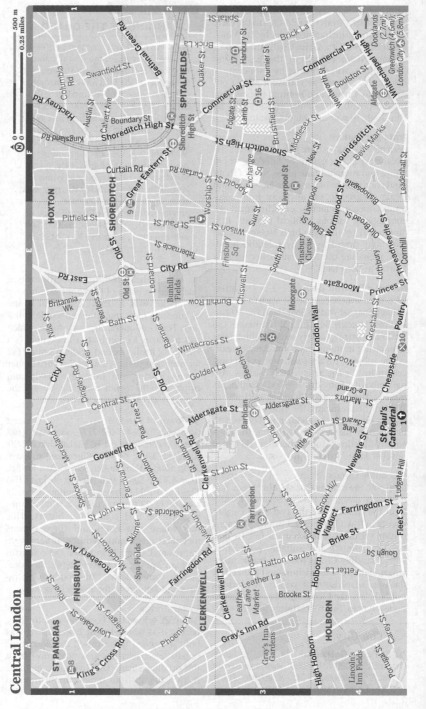

500 m
0.25 miles

ST PANCRAS

FINSBURY

HOXTON

SHOREDITCH

SPITALFIELDS

CLERKENWELL

HOLBORN

St Paul's Cathedral

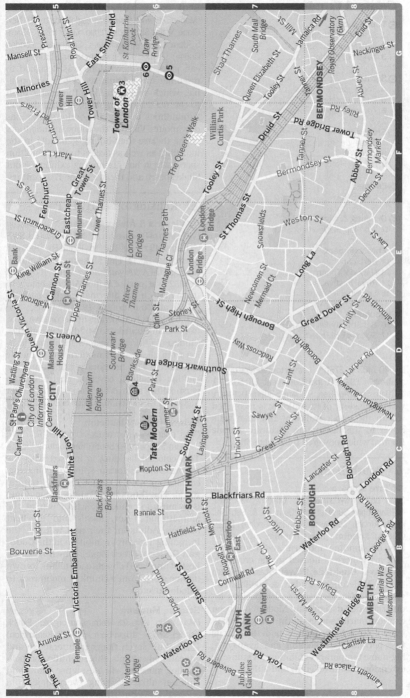

Central London

📞 020-7403 3761; www.towerbridge.org.uk; adult/child £9/3.90, incl Monument £10.50/4.70; ⏰ 10am-6pm Apr-Sep, 9.30am-5.30pm Oct-Mar), where the story of its building is recounted within the upper walkway. You then walk down to the fascinating Victorian Engine Rooms, which powered the bridge lifts.

◎ South Bank

★ Tate Modern   MUSEUM
(Map p62; www.tate.org.uk; Queen's Walk, SE1; ⏰ 10am-6pm Sun-Thu, to 10pm Fri & Sat; 👪; 🚇 Blackfriars, Southwark, London Bridge) FREE One of London's most popular attractions, this outstanding modern and contemporary art gallery is housed in the creatively revamped **Bankside Power Station** south of the Millennium Bridge. A spellbinding synthesis of modern art and capacious industrial brick design, Tate Modern has been extraordinarily successful in bringing challenging work to the masses, both through its free permanent collection and fee-paying, big-name temporary exhibitions. A stunning extension was unveiled in mid-2016.

Shakespeare's Globe   HISTORIC BUILDING
(Map p62; www.shakespearesglobe.com; 21 New Globe Walk, SE1; adult/child £13.50/8; ⏰ 9am-5.30pm; 👪; 🚇 Blackfriars, Southwark, London Bridge) Unlike other venues for Shakespearean plays, the new Globe was designed to resemble the original as closely as possible, which means having the arena open to the fickle London skies, leaving the 700 'groundlings' to stand in London's notorious downpours. Visits to the Globe include tours of the theatre (half-hourly, generally in the morning) as well as access to the exhibition space, which has fascinating exhibits about Shakespeare and theatre in the 17th century.

◎ Kensington & Hyde Park

★ Victoria & Albert Museum   MUSEUM
(V&A; Map p68; www.vam.ac.uk; Cromwell Rd, SW7; ⏰ 10am-5.45pm Sat-Thu, to 10pm Fri; 🚇 South Kensington) FREE The Museum of Manufactures, as the V&A was known when it opened in 1852, was part of Prince Albert's legacy to the nation in the aftermath of the successful Great Exhibition of 1851. It houses the world's largest collection of decorative arts, from Asian ceramics to Middle Eastern rugs, Chinese paintings, Western furniture, fashion from all ages and modern-day domestic appliances. The temporary exhibitions are another highlight, covering anything from personalities such as late designer Alexander McQueen to special materials and trends.

Natural History Museum   MUSEUM
(Map p68; www.nhm.ac.uk; Cromwell Rd, SW7; ⏰ 10am-5.50pm; 🚇 South Kensington) FREE This colossal building is infused with the irrepressible Victorian spirit of collecting, cataloguing and interpreting the natural world. The **Dinosaurs Gallery** (Blue Zone) is a must for children, who gawp at the animatronic T-Rex, fossils and excellent displays. Adults for their part will love the intriguing Treasures exhibition in the **Cadogan Gallery** (Green Zone), which houses a host of unrelated objects each telling its own unique story, from a chunk of moon rock to a dodo skeleton.

Science Museum   MUSEUM
(Map p68; www.sciencemuseum.org.uk; Exhibition Rd, SW7; ⏰ 10am-6pm; 🚇 South Kensington) FREE With seven floors of interactive and educational exhibits, this scientifically spellbinding museum will mesmerise adults and children alike, covering everything from

West End & Westminster

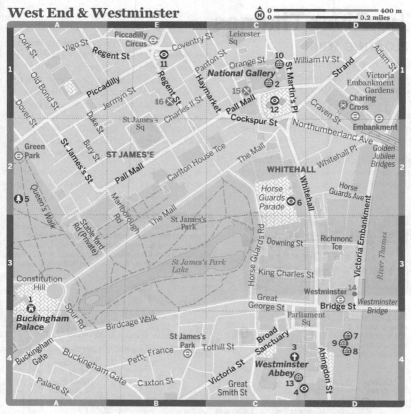

early technology to space travel. A perennial favourite is **Exploring Space**, a gallery featuring genuine rockets and satellites and a full-size replica of 'Eagle', the lander that took Neil Armstrong and Buzz Aldrin to the Moon in 1969. The **Making the Modern World Gallery** next door is a visual feast of locomotives, planes, cars and other revolutionary inventions.

🛏 Sleeping

During university holidays (generally mid-March to late April, late June to September, and mid-December to mid-January), student dorms and halls of residence are open to paying visitors. Choices include **LSE Vacations** (☎020-7955 7676; www.lsevacations.co.uk; s/tw/tr from £45/66/89), whose eight halls include **Bankside House** (Map p62; ☎020-7107 5750; 24 Sumner St, SE1; ⊖Southwark) and **High Holborn Residence** (Map p70; ☎020-7107 5737; 178 High Holborn, WC1; ⊖Holborn).

West End & Westminster

The River Thames

A FLOATING TOUR

London's history has always been determined by the Thames. The city was founded as a Roman port nearly 2000 years ago and over the centuries since then many of the capital's landmarks have lined the river's banks. A boat trip is a great way to experience the attractions.

There are piers dotted along both banks at regular intervals where you can hop on and hop off the regular services to visit

places of interest. The best place to board is Westminster Pier, from where boats head downstream, taking you from the City of Westminster, the seat of government, to the original City of London, now the financial district and dominated by a growing band of skyscrapers. Across the river, the once shabby and neglected South Bank now bristles with as many top attractions as its northern counterpart, including the slender Shard.

In our illustration we've concentrated on the top highlights you'll enjoy from a waterborne

MARK DAFFEY / GETTY IMAGES ©

St Paul's Cathedral
Though there's been a church here since AD 604, the current building rose from the ashes of the 1666 Great Fire and is architect Christopher Wren's masterpiece. Famous for surviving the Blitz intact and for the wedding of Charles and Diana, it's looking as good as new after a major clean-up for its 300th anniversary.

Blackfriars

Somerset House
This grand neoclassical palace was once one of many aristocratic houses lining the Thames. The huge arches at river level gave direct access to the Thames until the Embankment was built in the 1860s.

3 · Temple

Blackfriars Pier
Blackfriars Bridge

Charing Cross

Savoy Pier

Victoria Embankment Gardens

Waterloo Bridge

National Theatre

OXO Tower

Embankment

Queen Elizabeth Hall
Southbank Centre

London Eye
Built in 2000 and originally temporary, the Eye instantly became a much-loved landmark. The 30-minute spin takes you 135m above the city from where the views are unsurprisingly amazing.

2

Westminster Pier

Waterloo Millennium Pier

Houses of Parliament
Rebuilt in neo-Gothic style after the old palace burned down in 1834, the most famous part of the British parliament is the clocktower. Generally known as Big Ben, it's named after Benjamin Hall who oversaw its construction.

Westminster

Westminster Bridge

1

RICHARD I'ANSON / GETTY IMAGES ©

vessel. These are, from west to east, the **Houses of Parliament ❶**, the **London Eye ❷**, **Somerset House ❸**, **St Paul's Cathedral ❹**, **Tate Modern ❺**, **Shakespeare's Globe ❻**, the **Tower of London ❼** and **Tower Bridge ❽**.

Apart from covering this central section of the river, boats can also be taken upstream as far as Kew Gardens and Hampton Court Palace, and downstream to Greenwich and the Thames Barrier.

BOAT HOPPING

Thames Clippers hop-on/hop-off services are aimed at commuters but are equally useful for visitors, operating every 15 minutes on a loop from piers at Embankment, Waterloo, Blackfriars, Bankside, London Bridge and the Tower. Other services also go from Westminster. Oyster cardholders get a discount off the boat ticket price.

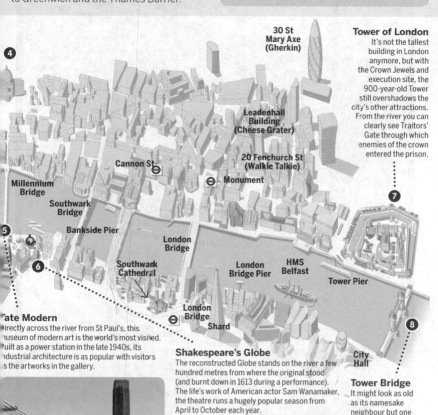

30 St Mary Axe (Gherkin)

Tower of London
It's not the tallest building in London anymore, but with the Crown Jewels and execution site, the 900-year-old Tower still overshadows the city's other attractions. From the river you can clearly see Traitors' Gate through which enemies of the crown entered the prison.

Leadenhall Building (Cheese Grater)

20 Fenchurch St (Walkie Talkie)

Cannon St ⊖

Monument ⊖

Millennium Bridge

Southwark Bridge

Bankside Pier

London Bridge

Southwark Cathedral

London Bridge Pier

HMS Belfast

Tower Pier

London Bridge ⊖

Shard

City Hall

Tate Modern
Directly across the river from St Paul's, this museum of modern art is the world's most visited. Built as a power station in the late 1940s, its industrial architecture is as popular with visitors as the artworks in the gallery.

Shakespeare's Globe
The reconstructed Globe stands on the river a few hundred metres from where the original stood (and burnt down in 1613 during a performance). The life's work of American actor Sam Wanamaker, the theatre runs a hugely popular season from April to October each year.

Tower Bridge
It might look as old as its namesake neighbour but one of the world's most iconic bridges was only completed in 1894. Not to be confused with London Bridge upstream, this one's famous raising bascules allowed tall ships to dock at the old wharves to the west and are still lifted up to 1000 times a year.

Hyde Park

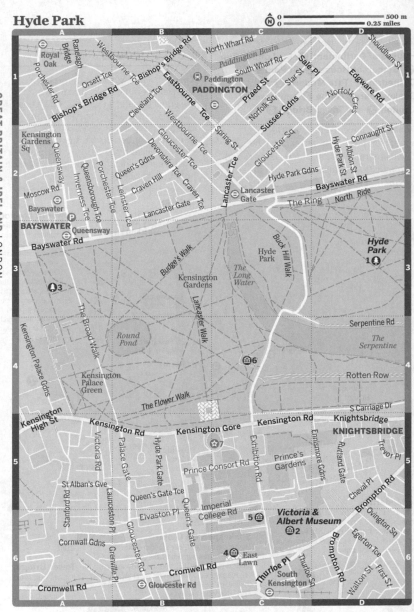

★ **Clink78**   HOSTEL £
(Map p62; ☎020-7183 9400; www.clinkhostels.
com/london/clink78; 78 King's Cross Rd, WC1; dm/r
from £13/50; @☎; ⊖King's Cross/St Pancras)
This fantastic 630-bed hostel is housed in a
19th-century magistrates courthouse where
Dickens once worked as a scribe and members of the Clash made an appearance in
1978. Rooms feature pod beds (including
overhead storage space) in four- to 16-bed
dormitories. There's a top kitchen with a
huge dining area and the busy Clash bar in
the basement.

Hyde Park

◎ Top Sights
1 Hyde Park D3
2 Victoria & Albert Museum C6

◎ Sights
3 Kensington Gardens................. ....A3
4 Natural History Museum C6
5 Science Museum C6
6 Serpentine Galleries................. .... C4

◎ Entertainment
7 Royal Albert Hall C5

★ **Hoxton Hotel**　　　　　　　HOTEL £
(Map p62; ☎020-7550 1000; www.hoxtonhotels.com; 81 Great Eastern St, EC2; r from £49; ❋@☎; ◉Old St) In the heart of hip Shoreditch, this sleek hotel takes the easyJet approach to selling its rooms – book long enough ahead and you might pay just £49. The 209 recently renovated rooms are small but stylish; there are flat-screen TVs, a desk, fridge with complimentary bottled water and milk, and breakfast in a bag delivered to your door.

Generator　　　　　　　　HOSTEL £
(Map p70; ☎020-7388 7666; www.generatorhostels.com/london; 37 Tavistock Pl, WC1; dm/r from £18/55; @☎; ◉Russell Sq) With its industrial lines and funky decor, the huge Generator (over 870 beds) is one of central London's grooviest budget spots. The bar, complete with pool tables, stays open until 2am and there are frequent themed parties. Dorm rooms have between six and 12 beds; backing it all up are twin, triple and quad rooms.

✗ Eating

Eating in London can be pricey. If your budget is limited, zone on homegrown chains such as Pret a Manger (www.pret.com), Real Greek (www.therealgreek.com), Tas (www.tasrestaurants.co.uk) and Wagamama (www.wagamama.com). They're all good value and made even cheaper by regular voucher offers: check out www.vouchercodes.co.uk and www.myvouchercodes.co.uk.

★ **Kerbisher & Malt**　　　FISH & CHIPS £
(www.kerbisher.co.uk; 164 Shepherd's Bush Rd, W6; mains £6-7; ◷noon-2.30pm & 4.30-10pm Tue-Thu, noon-10pm Fri & Sat, to 9pm Sun; ☎; ◉Hammersmith) 🍴 Every day save Monday is Fry Day at popular, peacock-blue-fronted Kerbisher & Malt, where the sustainably sourced, delectable, battered or grilled coley, haddock, pollock, cod and plaice has made waves. Served in a box to go, the chip butties (£2) and tasty double-fried chips (£2) are all good news, while white-tile walls and chunky wooden tables casts Kerbisher & Malt as a no-nonsense, but handsome, chippie.

★ **Shoryu**　　　　　　　　NOODLES £
(Map p65; www.shoryuramen.com; 9 Regent St, SW1; mains £9-15; ◷11.15am-midnight Mon-Sat, to 10.30pm Sun; ◉Piccadilly Circus) Compact, well-mannered noodle parlour Shoryu draws in reams of noodle diners to feast at its wooden counters and small tables. It's busy, friendly and efficient, with informative staff. Fantastic tonkotsu ramen is the name of the game here, sprinkled with *nori* (dried, pressed seaweed), spring onion, *nitamago* (soft-boiled eggs) and sesame seeds. No bookings.

DON'T MISS

LONDON PARKS

London's central parks (find details of them all at www.royalparks.org.uk) are among its prime assets and they're all free to explore.

Start with **Hyde Park** (Map p58; ◷5am-midnight; ◉Marble Arch, Hyde Park Corner, Queensway). At 145 hectares, this is central London's largest open space with an astonishing variety of landscapes and trees. The Serpentine lake separates it from **Kensington Gardens** (Map p68; ◷6am-dusk; ◉Queensway, Lancaster Gate), where you'll find the **Serpentine Galleries** (Map p68; www.serpentinegalleries.org; ◷10am-6pm Tue-Sun) **FREE** showing great contemporary art for free.

Across Hyde Park Corner is the aptly named **Green Park** (Map p65; ◷24hr; ◉Green Park), followed by lovely **St James Park** (Strawberry Pl) south of the Mall. Should you hunger for more greenery, head north to the elaborate and formal **Regent's Park** (◷5am-9.30pm; ◉Regent's Park).

Bloomsbury

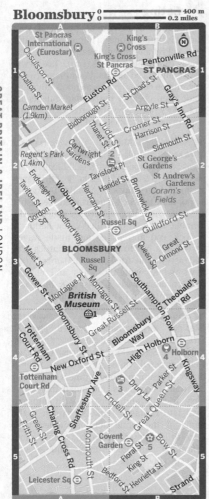

Bloomsbury

◎ Top Sights
1 British Museum.................................A4

🛏 Sleeping
2 Generator...B2
3 High Holborn Residence....................B4

🍷 Drinking & Nightlife
4 Princess Louise..................................B4

★ Entertainment
5 Royal Opera House.............................B5

Pimlico Fresh   CAFE £
(86 Wilton Rd, SW1; mains from £4.50; ⊙7.30am-
7.30pm Mon-Fri, 9am-6pm Sat & Sun; ⊜Victoria)
This friendly two-room cafe will see you
right whether you need breakfast (French
toast, bowls of porridge laced with honey
or maple syrup), lunch (homemade quiches
and soups, 'things' on toast) or just a good
old latte and cake.

🍷 Drinking & Nightlife

For up-to-the-minute listings see *Time Out*
or the *Evening Standard*.

Princess Louise   PUB
(Map p70; http://princesslouisepub.co.uk; 208
High Holborn, WC1; ⊙11am-11pm Mon-Fri, noon-
11pm Sat, noon-6.45pm Sun; ⊜Holborn) This
late-19th-century Victorian pub is spectacularly decorated with a riot of fine tiles,
etched mirrors, plasterwork and a stunning
central horseshoe bar. The old Victorian
wood partitions give drinkers plenty of
nooks and alcoves to hide in. Beers are Sam
Smith's only but cost just under £3 a pint,
so it's no wonder many elect to spend the
whole evening here.

Worship St Whistling Shop   COCKTAIL BAR
(Map p62; ☐020-7247 0015; www.whistlingshop.
com; 63 Worship St, EC2A; ⊙5pm-midnight Mon-
Thu, to 2am Fri & Sat; ⊜Old St) While the name
is Victorian slang for a place selling illicit
booze, this subterranean drinking den's master mixologists explore the futuristic outer
limits of cocktail chemistry and aromatic
science. Many ingredients are made with the
rotary evaporators in the on-site lab.

Cat & Mutton   PUB
(www.catandmutton.com; 76 Broadway Market,
E8; ⊙noon-midnight; ☐394) At this fabulous
Georgian pub, Hackney hipsters sup pints
under the watchful eyes of hunting trophies,

Café Below   CAFE £
(Map p62; ☐020-7329 0789; www.cafebelow.
co.uk; St Mary-le-Bow, Cheapside, EC2; mains £9-
11, 3-course set dinner £20; ⊙7.30am-2.30pm
Mon & Tue, to 9.15pm Wed-Fri; ☐; ⊜Mansion
House, St Paul's) This atmospheric cafe-
restaurant, in the crypt of one of London's
most famous churches, offers excellent
value and such tasty dishes as pan-fried
sea bream with chermoula (spicy North
African sauce) and aubergine Parmigiana.
There are as many vegetarian choices as
meat ones. Summer sees tables outside in
the shady courtyard.

DON'T MISS

LONDON MARKETS

Visitors are rightly drawn to London's famed markets. A treasure trove of small designers, unique jewellery pieces, original framed photographs and posters, colourful vintage pieces and bric-a-brac, they are the antidote to impersonal, carbon-copy shopping centres.

The most popular markets are **Camden** (www.camdenmarket.com; Camden High St, NW1; ⊙10am-6pm; ◉Camden Town), **Old Spitalfields** (Map p62; www.oldspitalfieldsmarket. com; Commercial St, E1; ⊙10am-5pm; ◉Shoreditch High St) and **Portobello Road** (www. portobellomarket.org; Portobello Rd, W10; ⊙8am-6.30pm Mon-Wed, Fri & Sat, to 1pm Thu; ◉Notting Hill Gate, Ladbroke Grove), which operate most days, but there are dozens of others, such as Brick Lane's excellent **Sunday Upmarket** (Map p62; www.sundayupmarket. co.uk; Old Truman Brewery, 91 Brick Lane, E1; ⊙10am-5pm Sun; ◉Shoreditch High St), which only pop up on the weekend. Camden and Old Spitalfields are both mainly covered, but even the outdoor markets are busy, rain or shine.

black-and-white photos of old-time boxers and a large portrait of Karl Marx. If it's crammed downstairs, as it often is, head up the spiral staircase to the comfy couches. DJs spin funk, disco and soul on the weekends.

Trafalgar Tavern PUB
(☑020-8858 2909; www.trafalgartavern.co.uk; 6 Park Row, SE10; ⊙noon-11pm Mon-Sat, to 10.30pm Sun; ⊠DLR Cutty Sark) This elegant tavern with big windows overlooking the Thames is steeped in history. Dickens apparently knocked back a few here – and used it as the setting for the wedding breakfast scene in *Our Mutual Friend* – and prime ministers Gladstone and Disraeli used to dine on the pub's celebrated whitebait.

☆ Entertainment

Some of the world's best theatre can be seen in London. Enquire at the theatre's own box office about cut-price standby tickets or limited late releases for otherwise sold-out shows. Student standby tickets are sometimes available one hour or so before performances start. On the day of performance, you can buy discounted tickets, sometimes up to 50% off, for West End productions from **Tkts Leicester Sq** (www.tkts.co.uk/leicester-square; ⊙10am-7pm Mon-Sat, 11am-4.30pm Sun; ◉Leicester Sq).

National Theatre THEATRE
(Map p62; ☑020-7452 3000; www.nationaltheatre. org.uk; South Bank, SE1; ◉Waterloo) England's flagship theatre showcases a mix of classic and contemporary plays performed by excellent casts in three theatres (Olivier, Lyttelton and Dorfman). Outstanding artistic director Nicholas Hytner oversaw a golden decade at the theatre, with landmark productions

such as *War Horse*. His replacement, Rufus Norris, started in April 2015.

Travelex tickets costing just £15 are available to certain performances during the peak period; same-day tickets also cost £15. Under-18s pay half-price.

Southbank Centre CONCERT VENUE
(Map p62; ☑0844 875 0073; www.southbankcentre. co.uk; Belvedere Rd, SE1; ◉Waterloo) The Southbank Centre's Royal Festival Hall seats 3000 in its amphitheatre and is one of the best places for catching world and classical music artists. The sound is fantastic, the programming impeccable and there are frequent free gigs in the wonderfully expansive foyer.

Barbican PERFORMING ARTS
(Map p62; ☑0845 121 6823, box office 10am-8pm Mon-Sat, from 11am Sun 020-7638 8891; www.barbican.org.uk; Silk St, EC2; ◉Barbican) Home to the wonderful London Symphony Orchestra and its associate orchestra, the less-known BBC Symphony Orchestra, the arts centre also hosts scores of other leading musicians, focusing in particular on jazz, folk, world and soul artists. Dance is another strong point here.

Royal Opera House OPERA
(Map p70; ☑020-7304 4000; www.rch.org.uk; Bow St, WC2; tickets £7-250; ◉Covent Garden) The £210 million redevelopment for the millennium gave classic opera a fantastic setting in London, and coming here for a night is a sumptuous – if pricey – affair. Although the program has been fluffed up by modern influences, the main attractions are still the opera and classical ballet – all are wonderful productions and feature world-class performers.

Midweek matinees are usually cheaper than evening performances and restricted-view seats cost as little as £7. There are same-day tickets (one per customer available to the first 67 people in the queue) from 10am for £8 to £44 and student standby tickets for £10. Half-price standby tickets four hours before the performance are only occasionally available. Free lunchtime recitals are held on Mondays, when possible, in the Crush Room or Paul Hamlyn Hall, depending on the program.

Royal Albert Hall CONCERT VENUE
(Map p68; ☎0845 401 5034; www.royalalberthall.com; Kensington Gore, SW7; ☺South Kensington) This splendid Victorian concert hall hosts classical music, rock and other performances, but is most famously the venue for the BBC-sponsored Proms. Booking is possible, but from mid-July to mid-September Proms punters also queue for £5 standing (or 'promenading') tickets that go on sale one hour before curtain-up. Otherwise, the box office and prepaid ticket collection counter are both through door 12 (south side of the hall).

ℹ Information

City of London Information Centre (Map p62; www.visitthecity.co.uk; St Paul's Churchyard, EC4; ☺9.30am-5.30pm Mon-Sat, 10am-4pm Sun; ☎; ☺St Paul's) Tourist information, fast-track tickets to City attractions and guided walks (adult/child £7/6).

Visit London (☎0870 156 6366; www.visitlondon.com) Visit London can fill you in on everything from tourist attractions and events (such as the Changing of the Guard and Chinese New Year parade) to river trips and tours, accommodation, eating, theatre, shopping, children's London, and LGBT venues. There are helpful kiosks at Heathrow Airport (Terminal 1, 2 & 3 Underground station; ☺7.30am-7.30pm), King's Cross St Pancras Station (☺8.15am-6.15pm), Liverpool Street Station (☺7.15am-7pm Sun-Thu, to 9pm Fri & Sat), Piccadilly Circus Underground Station (☺8am-7pm Mon-Fri, 9.15-6pm Sat & Sun) and Victoria Station (☺7.15am-8pm Mon-Sat, 8.15am-7pm Sun).

ℹ Getting There & Away

BUS & COACH
The London terminus for long-distance buses (called 'coaches' in Britain) is **Victoria Coach Station** (164 Buckingham Palace Rd, SW1; ☺Victoria).

TRAIN
Most of London's main-line rail terminals are linked by the Circle line on the tube.
Euston Manchester, Liverpool, Glasgow
King's Cross Cambridge, York, Edinburgh
Liverpool Street Stansted Airport (Express), Cambridge
London Bridge Gatwick Airport
Paddington Heathrow Airport (Express), Oxford, Bath, Cardiff
St Pancras Gatwick and Luton Airports, Canterbury, Paris Eurostar
Victoria Gatwick Airport (Express)
Waterloo Salisbury

ℹ Getting Around

TO/FROM THE AIRPORTS
Heathrow Airport Trains, London Underground (tube) and buses to central London from just after 5am to before midnight (night buses run later) £5.70 to £21.50; taxi £45 to £85.
Gatwick Airport Trains to central London from 4.30am to 1.35am £10 to £20; hourly buses to central London around the clock from £5; taxi £100.
London City Airport DLR trains to central London from 5.30am to 12.30am Monday to Saturday, 7am to 11.15pm Sunday from £2.80; taxi around £30.
Luton Airport Trains to central London from 7am to 10pm from £14; round-the-clock buses to central London £10; taxi £110.
Stansted Airport Trains to central London from 5.30am to 1.30am £23.40; round-the-clock buses to central London from £12; taxi from £130.

BICYCLE
Tens of thousands of Londoners cycle to work every day, and it is generally a good way to get around the city, although traffic can be intimidating for less confident cyclists. The city has tried hard to improve the cycling infrastructure, however, opening new 'cycling superhighways' for commuters and launching **Santander Cycles** (☎0343 222 6666; www.tfl.gov.uk), which is particularly useful for visitors.

Transport for London (www.tfl.gov.uk) publishes 14 free maps of London's cycle routes. You can order them via the website or by ringing ☎0843-222 1234.

PUBLIC TRANSPORT
Boat
Thames Clippers (www.thamesclippers.com; adult/child £6.50/3.25) offers commuter services; they're fast, pleasant and you're almost always guaranteed a seat and a view.

Boats run every 20 minutes from 6am to between 10pm and 11pm. Discounts apply for pay-as-you-go Oyster Card holders (£6.44) and Travelcard holders (paper ticket or on an Oyster Card; £4.75).

Bus

London's ubiquitous red double-decker buses afford great views of the city but be aware that the going can be slow, thanks to traffic jams and dozens of commuters getting on and off at every stop. Bus services normally operate from 5am to 11.30pm.

Underground, DLR & Overground

The London Underground ('the tube'; 11 colour-coded lines) is part of an integrated transport system that also includes the Docklands Light Railway (DLR; a driverless overhead train operating in the eastern part of the city) and Overground network (mostly outside of Zone 1 and sometimes underground).

The first trains operate from around 5.30am Monday to Saturday and 6.45am Sunday. The last trains leave around 12.30am Monday to Saturday and 11.30pm Sunday.

Additionally, the Victoria and Jubilee lines, plus most of the Piccadilly, Central and Northern lines run all night on Fridays and Saturdays, with trains every 10 minutes or so.

Taxi

Black cabs are available for hire when the yellow sign above the windscreen is lit; just stick your arm out to signal one.

Fares are metered, with the flagfall charge of £2.40 (covering the first 310m during a weekday) rising by increments of 20p for each subsequent 168m.

Minicabs are a cheaper alternative to black cabs and will quote trip fares in advance. Only use drivers from proper agencies; licensed minicabs aren't allowed to tout for business or pick you up off the street without a booking.

TICKETS & PASSES

➡ The cheapest and most convenient way to pay for public transport is to buy an Oyster Card, a smart card on which you can store credit. The card works on the entire transport network and can be purchased from all tube and train stations and some shops.

➡ Oyster Cards will work out whether to charge you per journey, for a return or for a day travelcard.

➡ You need to pay a £5 deposit per Oyster Card, which you will get back when you return the card, along with any remaining credit.

➡ If you're staying for more than just a few days, consider getting a weekly or monthly pass (which can be loaded on the Oyster card).

➡ Paper tickets are still available but are more expensive than Oyster fares.

CANTERBURY

Canterbury tops the charts for English cathedral cities. Many consider the World Heritage–listed **cathedral** (www.canterbury-cathedral.org; adult/concession £12/10.50, tours £5/4, audio tours £4/3; ⊙9am-5.30pm Mon-Sat, 12.30-2.30pm Sun) that dominates its centre to be one of Europe's finest, and the town's narrow medieval alleyways, riverside gardens and ancient city walls are a joy to explore.

Staff at the **tourist office** (☏01227-862162; www.canterbury.co.uk; 18 High St; ⊙9am-5pm Mon-Wed, Fri & Sat, to 7pm Thu, 10am-5pm Sun) located in the Beaney House of Art & Knowledge, can help book accommodation, excursions and theatre tickets.

The city's **bus station** (St George's Lane) is just within the city walls. There are two train stations: Canterbury East for London Victoria, and Canterbury West for London's Charing Cross and St Pancras stations.

➡ Contactless cards can be used instead of Oyster Cards (they benefit from the same 'smart fare' system); just check for international fees with your card issuer.

Windsor & Eton

☏01753 / POP 33,400

Dominated by the massive bulk of Windsor Castle, these twin towns have a rather surreal atmosphere, with the morning pomp and ceremony of the changing of the guards in Windsor, and the sight of schoolboys dressed in formal tailcoats wandering the streets of tiny Eton, home to Eton College, the largest and most famous public (meaning private and fee-paying) school in England.

◎ Sights

★ **Windsor Great Park**   PARK
(☏01753-860222; www.windsorgreatpark.co.uk; Windsor; ⊙dawn-dusk) **FREE** Stretching behind Windsor Castle almost all the way to Ascot, Windsor Great Park covers just under 8 sq miles and features a lake, walking tracks, a bridleway and gardens. The Long Walk is a jaunt of just under 3 miles from King George IV Gate south of the castle to the Copper Horse statue of George III on Snow Hill, the highest point of the park.

Windsor Castle   CASTLE, PALACE

(🖵 0303 123 7304; www.royalcollection.org.uk; Castle Hill; adult/child £20/11.70; ⏰ 9.30am-5.15pm Mar-Oct, 9.45am-4.15pm Nov-Feb; 🚻; 🚌 702 from London Victoria, 🚆 London Waterloo to Windsor & Eton Riverside, 🚆 London Paddington to Windsor & Eton Central via Slough) The world's largest and oldest continuously occupied fortress, Windsor Castle is a majestic vision of battlements and towers. It's used for state occasions and is one of the Queen's principal residences; if she's at home, the Royal Standard flies from the Round Tower. Join a free guided tour (every half-hour) of the wards or take a handheld multimedia tour of the lavish State Apartments and beautiful chapels. Some sections may be off-limits on any given day if they're in use.

🛈 Information

Tourist Office (🖵 01753-743900; www.windsor.gov.uk; Old Booking Hall, Windsor Royal Shopping Arcade, Thames St; ⏰ 10am-5pm Apr-Sep, 10am-4pm Oct-Mar) Pick up a heritage walk brochure (50p).

🛈 Getting There & Away

➡ Green Line (www.greenline.co.uk) coaches head to London (£5, 1½ hours).

➡ Trains from Windsor Riverside station go directly to London Waterloo (£9.80, one hour), although trains from Windsor Central, changing at Slough for London Paddington, are considerably quicker (between 26 and 44 minutes).

Salisbury & Stonehenge

🖵 01722 / POP 45,000

Centred on a majestic cathedral that's topped by the tallest spire in England, Salisbury makes an appealing Wiltshire base. It's been an important provincial city for more than a thousand years, and its streets form an architectural timeline ranging from medieval walls and half-timbered Tudor townhouses to Georgian mansions and Victorian villas. Salisbury is also the access point for tours to nearby Stonehenge, Britain's most iconic archaeological site.

⊙ Sights

★ **Stonehenge**   ARCHAEOLOGICAL SITE

(EH; 🖵 0370 333 1181; www.english-heritage.org.uk; adult/child on-the-day ticket £18/11, advance booking £15.50/9.30; ⏰ 9am-8pm Jun-Aug, 9.30am-7pm Apr, May & Sep, 9.30am-5pm Oct-Mar; 🅿) An ultra-modern makeover at ancient Stonehenge has brought an impressive visitor centre and the closure of an intrusive road (now restored to grassland). The result is a far stronger sense of historical context; dignity and mystery returned to an archaeological gem.

A pathway frames the ring of massive stones. Although you can't walk in the circle, unless on a recommended **Stone Circle Access Visit** (🖵 0370 333 0605; www.english-heritage.org.uk; adult/child £32/19), you can get close-up views. Admission is through timed tickets; secure a place well in advance.

★ **Salisbury Cathedral**   CATHEDRAL

(🖵 01722-555120;   www.salisburycathedral.org.uk; Cathedral Close; requested donation adult/child £7.50/none; ⏰ 9am-5pm Mon-Sat, noon-4pm Sun) England is endowed with countless stunning churches, but few can hold a candle to the grandeur and sheer spectacle of 13th-century Salisbury Cathedral. This Early English Gothic–style structure has an elaborate exterior decorated with pointed arches and flying buttresses, and a sombre, austere interior designed to keep its congregation suitably pious. Its statuary and tombs are outstanding; don't miss the daily **tower tours** (adult/child £12.50/8) and the Cathedral's original, 13th-century copy of the **Magna Carta**.

Salisbury Museum   MUSEUM

(🖵 01722-332151; www.salisburymuseum.org.uk; 65 Cathedral Close; adult/child £8/4; ⏰ 10am-5pm Mon-Sat, plus noon-5pm Sun Jun-Sep) The hugely important archaeological finds here include the Stonehenge Archer, the bones of a man found in the ditch surrounding the stone circle – one of the arrows found alongside probably killed him. With gold coins dating from 100 BC and a Bronze Age gold necklace, it's a powerful introduction to Wiltshire's prehistory.

✖ Eating

Fish Row   DELI, CAFE £

(www.fishrowdelicafe.co.uk; 3 Fish Row; snacks from £5; ⏰ 8.30am-5.30pm Mon-Sat, 9.30am-4.30pm Sun; 🖋) Local produce is piled high at this heavily beamed deli-cafe – the New Forest Blue, Old Sarum and Nanny Williams cheeses come from just a few miles away. Grab one of 10 types of hand-made scotch eggs to go, or duck upstairs to eat alongside weathered wood, stained glass and old church pews.

ℹ Information

Tourist Office (📞 01722-342860; www.visitsalisbury.co.uk; Fish Row; ⊙ 9am-5pm Mon-Fri, 10am-4pm Sat, 10am-2pm Sun)

ℹ Getting There & Away

BUS

Direct National Express services include Bath (£11, 1¼ hours, one daily) and London (£17, three hours, three daily) via Heathrow. **Stonehenge Tour** (📞 01202-338420; www.thestonehenge-tour.info; adult/child £27/17) buses leave regularly.

TRAIN

Half-hourly connections include **Bath** (£10, one hour) and **London Waterloo** (£25, 1½ hours)

Bath

📞 01225 / POP 88,900

Britain's littered with beautiful cities, but precious few compare to Bath. Home to some of the nation's grandest Georgian architecture – not to mention one of the world's best-preserved Roman bathhouses – this slinky, sophisticated, snooty city has been a tourist draw for nigh-on 2000 years.

Founded on top of natural hot springs, Bath's heyday really began during the 18th century, when local entrepreneur Ralph Allen and his team of father-and-son architects, John Wood the Elder and Younger, turned this sleepy backwater into the toast of Georgian society, and constructed fabulous landmarks such as the Circus and Royal Crescent.

⊙ Sights

★ Roman Baths   HISTORIC BUILDING

(📞 01225-477785; www.romanbaths.co.uk; Abbey Churchyard; adult/child £15/9.50; ⊙ 9am-9pm Jul-Aug, to 5pm Sep-Jun) In typically ostentatious style, the Romans constructed a complex of bathhouses above Bath's three natural hot springs, which emerge at a steady 46°C (115°F). Situated alongside a temple dedicated to the healing goddess Sulis Minerva, the baths now form one of the best-preserved ancient Roman spas in the world, and are encircled by 18th and 19th century buildings. Bath's premier attraction can get very busy. To dodge the worst crowds, avoid weekends and July and August.

★ Royal Crescent   ARCHITECTURE

(Royal Cres) Bath is famous for its glorious Georgian architecture, and it doesn't get any grander than this semicircular terrace of majestic townhouses overlooking the green sweep of Royal Victoria Park. Designed by John Wood the Younger (1728–82) and built between 1767 and 1775, the houses appear perfectly symmetrical from the outside, but the owners were allowed to tweak the interiors, so no two houses are quite the same. **No 1 Royal Crescent** (📞 01225-428126; www.no1royalcrescent.org.uk; 1 Royal Cres; adult/child/family £10/4/22; ⊙ 10.30am-5.30pm Tue-Sun noon-5.30pm Mon Feb-early Dec) offers you an intriguing insight to life inside.

Bath Abbey   CHURCH

(www.bathabbey.org; Abbey Churchyard; requested donation adult/student £2.50/1.50; ⊙ 9.30am-5.30pm Mon, 9am-5.30pm Tue-Fri, 9am-6pm Sat, 1-2.30pm & 4.30-5.30pm Sun) Looming above the city centre, Bath's huge abbey church was built between 1499 and 1616, making it the last great medieval church raised in England. Its most striking feature is the west facade, where angels climb up and down stone ladders, commemorating a dream of the founder, Bishop Oliver King.

Tower tours (adult/child £6/3; ⊙ 10am-5pm Apr-Aug, 11am-3pm Sep-Mar) leave on the hour from Monday to Friday, and every half-hour on Saturday (no tours Sunday).

Holburne Museum   GALLERY

(📞 01225-388569; www.holburne.org; Great Pulteney St; ⊙ 10am-5pm Mon-Sat, 11am-5pm Sun) **FREE** Sir William Holburne, 18th-century aristocrat and art fanatic, amassed a huge collection which now forms the core of the Holburne Museum, in a lavish mansion at the end of Great Pulteney St. The museum houses a roll-call of works by artists including Turner, Stubbs, Hoare and Gainsborough, as well as 18th-century majolica and porcelain.

Jane Austen Centre   MUSEUM

(📞 01225-443000; www.janeausten.co.uk; 40 Gay St; adult/child £11/5.50; ⊙ 9.45am-5.30pm Apr-Oct, 10am-4pm Nov-Mar) Bath is known to many as a location in Jane Austen's novels, including *Persuasion* and *Northanger Abbey*. Although Austen only lived in Bath for five years from 1801 to 1806, she remained a regular visitor, and a keen student of the city's social scene. Here, guides in Regency costumes regale you with Austen-esque tales as you tour memorabilia relating to the writer's life in Bath.

Bath

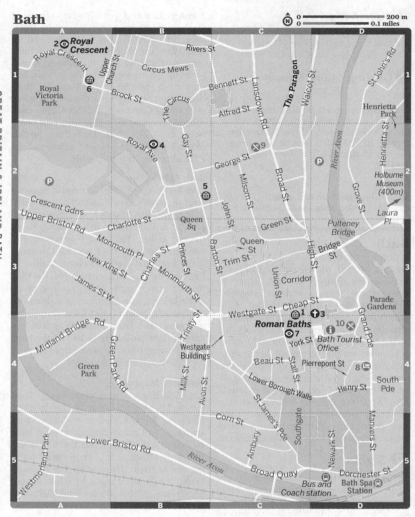

🛏 Sleeping & Eating

Bath YHA HOSTEL £
(☎0845 371 9303; www.yha.org.uk; Bathwick Hill; dm £13-22, d from £39; ⊙reception 7am-11pm; ℗@�) Split across an Italianate mansion and a modern annexe, this impressive hostel is a steep climb (or a short hop on bus U1 or U18) from the city. The listed building means the rooms are huge, and some have period features such as cornicing and bay windows.

Bath Backpackers HOSTEL £
(☎01225-446787; www.hostels.co.uk/bath; 13 Pierrepont St; dm £12-17) The showers are scarce and it's a bit grimy and battered, but it's beloved by budget travellers for bargain rates, prime location, a friendly vibe and a 24-hour 'dungeon' (in truth a soundproofed basement where you don't have to 'keep the noise down').

Adventure Cafe Bar CAFE £
(www.adventurecafebar.co.uk; 5 Princes Bldgs, George St; mains £5-10; ⊙8.30am-3am Mon-Fri, from 9am Sat & Sun) This cool cafe-bar, just a slipper's throw from the Assembly Rooms, offers something to everyone at most times of the day: morning cappuccino, lunchtime

Bath

◉ Top Sights
1 Roman Baths.............................. ....C3
2 Royal Crescent.......................... .... A1

◉ Sights
3 Bath Abbey..D3
4 Georgian Garden.................................B2
5 Jane Austen Centre.............................B2
6 No 1 Royal Crescent A1
7 Pump Room...C4

◎ Activities, Courses & Tours
Bath Abbey Tower Tours............ ... (see 3)

◉ Sleeping
8 Bath Backpackers D4

◉ Eating
9 Adventure Cafe Bar............... ....C2
10 Café Retro.. D4

ciabatta and late-night beer and cocktails. There's great outdoor seating in the back.

Café Retro   CAFE £
(☑ 01225-339347; www.caferetro.co.uk; 18 York St; mains £5-11; ⊙9am-5pm Mon-Sun) A poke in the eye for the corporate coffee chains. The paint job's scruffy, the crockery's ancient and none of the furniture matches, but that's all part of the charm: this is a cafe from the old school, and there are few places better for burgers, butties or cake. Takeaways (in biodegradable containers) are available from Retro-to-Go next door.

ⓘ Information

Bath Tourist Office (☑ 0844 847 5256; www.visitbath.co.uk; Abbey Chambers, Abbey Churchyard; ⊙9.30am-5.30pm Mon-Sat, 10am-4pm Sun) Calls are charged at the premium rate of 50p per minute.

ⓘ Getting There & Away

BUS

Bath's **bus and coach station** (Dorchester St) is near the train station.

National Express coaches run direct to London (£33, 3½ hours, eight to 10 daily). Two-hourly services also run to London Heathrow (£27, three hours).

TRAIN

Bath Spa station is at the end of Manvers St. Direct services include Cardiff Central (£20, one hour, hourly), London Paddington (£38, 1½ hours, half-hourly) and Salisbury (£18, one hour, hourly).

Oxford

☑ 01865 / POP 171,000

One of the world's most famous university cities, Oxford is a privileged place. It is steeped in history and studded with august buildings, yet it maintains the feel of a young town, thanks to its large student population. It's a wonderful place to ramble: the oldest colleges date back 750 years, and little has changed inside the hallowed walls since then (with the notable exception of female admissions, which only began in 1878).

WORTH A TRIP

GLASTONBURY

To many people, Glastonbury is synonymous with the **Glastonbury Festival of Contemporary Performing Arts** (www.glastonburyfestivals.co.uk; tickets from £228), a majestic (and frequently mud-soaked) extravaganza of music, theatre, dance, cabaret, carnival, spirituality and general all-round weirdness that's been held on and off on farmland in Pilton, just outside Glastonbury, for the last 40-plus years (bar the occasional off-year to let the farm recover).

Outside of the festival, the area is still worth visiting for the scattered ruins of **Glastonbury Abbey** (☑01458-832267; www.glastonburyabbey.com; Magdalene St; adult/child £7.60/4.70; ⊙9am-8pm Jun-Aug to 6pm Mar-May & Sep-Oct, to 4pm Nov-Feb) and **Glastonbury Tor** (NT; www.nationaltrust.org.uk) FREE, a grassy hump about a mile from town, topped by the ruins of St Michael's Church. According to local legend, the tor is said to be the mythical Isle of Avalon, King Arthur's last resting place. It's also allegedly one of the world's great spiritual nodes, marking the meeting point of many mystical lines of power known as leylines.

Bus 37/375/376 runs to Wells (£3.50, 15 minutes, several times an hour), which has a train station.

DON'T MISS

PUNTING IN OXFORD

A quintessential Oxford experience, punting is all about sitting back and quaffing Pimms (the typical English summer drink) as you watch the city's glorious architecture float by. Which, of course, requires someone else to do the hard work – punting is far more difficult than it appears. If you decide to go it alone, a deposit for the punt is usually charged. Most punts hold five people including the punter. The most central location to hire a punt is **Magdalen Bridge Boathouse** (☑01865-202643; www.oxfordpunting.co.uk; High St; chauffered 4-person punt per 30min £30, punt rental per hour £24; ☉9.30am-dusk Feb-Nov).

◉ Sights

★ Ashmolean Museum MUSEUM

(☑01865-278000; www.ashmolean.org; Beaumont St; ☉10am-5pm Tue-Sun) **FREE** Britain's oldest public museum, second in repute only to London's British Museum, was established in 1683 when Elias Ashmole presented the university with the collection of curiosities amassed by the well-travelled John Tradescant, gardener to Charles I. A 2009 makeover has left the museum with new interactive features, a giant atrium, glass walls revealing galleries on different levels and a beautiful rooftop restaurant.

★ Christ Church COLLEGE

(☑01865-276492; www.chch.ox.ac.uk; St Aldate's; adult/child £8/7; ☉10am-4.15pm Mon-Sat, 2-4.15pm Sun) The largest of all of Oxford's colleges and the one with the grandest quad, Christ Church is also its most popular. Its magnificent buildings, illustrious history and latter-day fame as a location for the *Harry Potter* films have tourists coming in droves. The college was founded in 1524 by Cardinal Thomas Wolsey, who suppressed the monastery existing on the site to acquire the funds for his lavish building project.

★ Pitt Rivers Museum MUSEUM

(☑01865-270927; www.prm.ox.ac.uk; South Parks Rd; ☉noon-4.30pm Mon, 10am-4.30pm Tue-Sun) **FREE** Hidden away through a door at the back of the main exhibition hall of the Oxford University Museum of Natural History, this wonderfully creepy anthropological museum houses a treasure trove of objects from around the world – more than enough to satisfy any armchair adventurer. One of the reasons this museum is so brilliant is because there are no computers here or shiny modern gimmicks. The dim light lends an air of mystery to the glass cases stuffed with the prized booty of Victorian explorers.

Magdalen College COLLEGE

(☑01865-276000; www.magd.ox.ac.uk; High St; adult/child £5/4; ☉1-6pm Oct-Jun, noon-7pm Jul-Sep) Set amid 40 hectares of lawns, woodlands, river walks and deer park, Magdalen (*mawd-*lin), founded in 1458, is one of the wealthiest and most beautiful of Oxford's colleges. It has a reputation as an artistic college, and some of its famous students have included writers Julian Barnes, Alan Hollinghurst, CS Lewis, John Betjeman, Seamus Heaney and Oscar Wilde, not to mention Edward VIII, TE Lawrence 'of Arabia' and Dudley Moore.

Radcliffe Camera LIBRARY

(www.bodleian.ox.ac.uk; Radcliffe Sq) The Radcliffe Camera is the quintessential Oxford landmark and one of the city's most photographed buildings. The spectacular circular library/reading room, filled with natural light, was built between 1737 and 1749 in grand Palladian style, and has Britain's third-largest dome. The only way to see the interior is to join one of the extended tours (£13, 90 minutes) of the **Bodleian Library** (☑01865-287400; www.bodleian.ox.ac.uk/bodley; Catte St; tours £6-14; ☉9am-5pm Mon-Sat, 11am-5pm Sun).

🛏 Sleeping & Eating

Oxford YHA HOSTEL £

(☑01865-727275; www.yha.org.uk; 2a Botley Rd; dm £18-25, r £55-59; 🛜) Particularly convenient for budget travellers arriving by train, this hostel has simple but comfortable four- and six-bed en suite dorms, private rooms and loads of facilities, including restaurant, library, garden, laundry and a choice of lounges.

Central Backpackers HOSTEL £

(☑01865-242288; www.centralbackpackers.co.uk; 13 Park End St; dm £20-25; 🛜) A friendly budget option located above a bar and right in the centre of town, this small hostel has basic, bright and simple rooms that sleep four to 12 people, a rooftop terrace and a small lounge with satellite TV.

Edamamé JAPANESE £

(☑01865-246916; www.edamame.co.uk; 15 Holywell St; mains £6-9.50; ☉11.30am-2.30pm Wed, 11.30am-2.30pm & 5-8.30pm Thu-Sat, noon-3.30pm Sun; 🍴) The queue out the door

Oxford

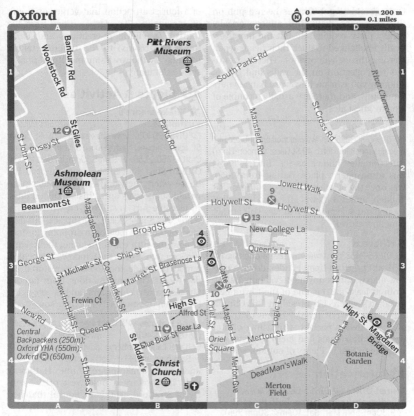

speaks volumes about the quality of food here. This tiny joint, all light wood and friendly bustle, is the best place in town for authentic Japanese cuisine. Arrive early and be prepared to wait.

Vaults & Garden　　　　　　　　CAFE £
(☎01865-279112; www.thevaultsandgarden.com; University Church of St Mary the Virgin, Radcliffe Sq; mains £7-10; ⊙8.30am-6pm; 🛜🍴) Set in the vaulted 14th-century Old Congregation House at the University Church, this place serves a wholesome line of soups, salads, pastas and paellas with plenty of choice for vegetarians. It's one of the most beautiful lunch venues in Oxford, with a lovely garden overlooking Radcliffe Sq. Come early for lunch as it's a local favourite.

🍷 Drinking & Nightlife

Bear Inn　　　　　　　　　　　PUB
(☎01865-728164; www.bearoxford.co.uk; 6 Alfred St; ⊙11am-11pm, to midnight Fri & Sat) Arguably

Oxford

⦿ Top Sights
1 Ashmolean Museum	A2
2 Christ Church	B4
3 Pitt Rivers Museum	B1

⦿ Sights
4 Bodleian Library	B3
5 Christ Church Cathedral	B4
6 Magdalen College	D4
7 Radcliffe Camera	C3

⊕ Activities, Courses & Tours
8 Magdalen Bridge Boathouse	D4

⊗ Eating
9 Edamame	C2
10 Vaults & Garden	C3

⊕ Drinking & Nightlife
11 Bear Inn	B4
12 Eagle & Child	A2
13 Turf Tavern	C3

Oxford's oldest pub (there's been a pub on this site since 1242), this atmospherically creaky place requires all but the most vertically challenged to duck their heads when passing through doorways. There's a curious tie collection on the walls and ceiling (though you can no longer exchange yours for a pint), and there are usually a couple of worthy guest ales.

Eagle & Child   PUB
(☑ 01865-302925; www.nicholsonspubs.co.uk/theeagleandchildoxford; 49 St Giles; ⊙ noon-11pm) Affectionately known as the 'Bird & Baby', this atmospheric place, dating from 1650, was once the favourite haunt of authors JRR Tolkien and CS Lewis. Its wood-panelled rooms and selection of real ales still attract a mellow crowd.

Turf Tavern   PUB
(☑ 01865-243235; www.turftavern-oxford.co.uk; 4-5 Bath Pl; ⊙ 11am-11pm) Hidden down a narrow alleyway, this tiny medieval pub (dating from at least 1381) is one of the town's best loved; it's where US president Bill Clinton famously 'did not inhale'. Home to 11 real ales, it's always packed with a mix of students, professionals and lucky tourists who manage to find it. Plenty of outdoor seating.

ⓘ Information

Tourist Office (☑ 01865-686430; www.experienceoxfordshire.com; 15-16 Broad St; ⊙ 9.30am-5pm Mon-Sat, 10am-3.30pm Sun)

ⓘ Getting There & Away

BUS
Oxford's main bus/coach station is at Gloucester Green, near the corner of Worcester and George Sts. Destinations include Cambridge (X5, £12.50, 3¾ hours) and London Victoria (Oxford Tube/X90, £14, 1¾ hours).

TRAIN
Oxford's train station is conveniently placed at the west of the city centre. Destinations include London Paddington (£25, 1¼ hours) and Manchester (£60, three hours).

Stratford-upon-Avon

☑ 01789 / POP 27,800

The author of some of the most quoted lines ever written in the English language, William Shakespeare was born in Stratford in 1564 and died here in 1616. The five houses linked to his life form the centrepiece

of a tourist attraction that verges on a cult of personality. Experiences range from the touristy (medieval re-creations and Bard-themed tearooms) to the sublime (taking in a play by the world-famous Royal Shakespeare Company).

⊙ Sights & Activities

★ Shakespeare's
Birthplace   HISTORIC BUILDING
(☑ 01789-204016; www.shakespeare.org.uk; Henley St; adult/child incl Nash's House & New Place & Halls Croft £17.50/11.50; ⊙ 9am-5.30pm Jul-Sep, to 5pm Oct-Jun) Start your Shakespeare quest at the house where the world's most popular playwright supposedly spent his childhood days. In fact, the jury is still out on whether this really was Shakespeare's birthplace, but devotees of the Bard have been dropping in since at least the 19th century, leaving their signatures scratched onto the windows. Set behind a modern facade, the house has restored Tudor rooms, live presentations from famous Shakespearean characters, and an engaging exhibition on Stratford's favourite son.

Anne Hathaway's Cottage   HISTORIC BUILDING
(☑ 01789-204016; www.shakespeare.org.uk; Cottage Lane, Shottery; adult/child £9.50/5.50; ⊙ 9am-5pm mid-Mar–Oct) Before tying the knot with Shakespeare, Anne Hathaway lived in Shottery, a mile west of the centre of Stratford, in this delightful thatched farmhouse. As well as period furniture, it has gorgeous gardens and an orchard and arboretum, with examples of all the trees mentioned in Shakespeare's plays. A footpath (no bikes allowed) leads to Shottery from Evesham Pl.

Holy Trinity Church   CHURCH
(☑ 01789-266316; www.stratford-upon-avon.org; Old Town; Shakespeare's grave adult/child £2/1; ⊙ 8.30am-6pm Mon-Sat, 12.30-5pm Sun Apr-Sep, reduced hours Oct-Mar) The final resting place of the Bard is said to be the most visited parish church in all of England. Inside are handsome 16th- and 17th-century tombs (particularly in the Clopton Chapel), some fabulous carvings on the choir stalls and, of course, the grave of William Shakespeare, with its ominous epitaph: 'cvrst be he yt moves my bones'.

🛏 Sleeping & Eating

Stratford-upon-Avon YHA   HOSTEL £
(☑ 0845 371 9661; www.yha.org.uk; Hemmingford House, Alveston; dm/d from £19/40; P@🖤) Set

in a large 200-year-old mansion, 1.5 miles east of the town centre along Tiddington Rd, this superior hostel attracts travellers of all ages. Of its 32 rooms and dorms, 16 are en suite. There's a canteen, bar and kitchen. Buses 18 and 18A run here from Bridge St. Wi-fi is available in common areas.

Fourteas TEAROOM £
(☑ 01789-293908; www.thefourteas.co.uk; 24 Sheep St; dishes £3-7. afternoon tea with/without Prosecco £17/12.50; ⏰ 9.30am-5pm Mon-Fri, 9am-5.30pm Sat, 11am-4pm Sun) Breaking with Stratford's Shakespearian theme, this tearoom takes the 1940s as its inspiration with beautiful old teapots, framed posters and staff in period costume. As well as premium loose-leaf teas and homemade cakes, there are hearty breakfasts, delicious sandwiches (fresh poached salmon, brie and grape), a hot dish of the day and indulgent afternoon teas.

☆ Entertainment

Royal Shakespeare Company THEATRE
(RSC; ☑ 0844 800 1110; www.rsc.org.uk; Waterside; tickets £10-62.50) Coming to Stratford without seeing a Shakespeare production would be like visiting Beijing and bypassing the Great Wall. The three theatre spaces run by the world-renowned Royal Shakespeare Company have witnessed performances by such legends as Lawrence Olivier, Richard Burton, Judi Dench, Helen Mirren, Ian McKellan and Patrick Stewart.

Stratford has two grand stages – the **Royal Shakespeare Theatre** and the **Swan Theatre** on Waterside – as well as the smaller **Courtyard Theatre** (☑ 0844 800 1110; www.rsc.org.uk), a short walk away, on Southern Lane. Contact the RSC for the latest news on performance times. There are often special deals for under 25-year-olds, students and seniors, and a few tickets are held back for sale on the day of the performance, but get snapped up fast. Book well ahead.

ⓘ Information

Tourist Office (☑ 01789-264293; www.shakespeare-country.co.uk; Bridge Foot; ⏰ 9am-5.30pm Mon-Sat, 10am-4pm Sun) Just west of Clopton Bridge on the corner with Bridgeway.

ⓘ Getting There & Away

National Express coaches and other bus companies run from Stratford's Riverside bus station (behind the Stratford Leisure Centre on Bridgeway). Services include London Victoria (£7, three hours, three daily) and Oxford (£10.70, one hour, twice daily).

Cambridge
☑ 01223 / POP 123,900

Abounding with exquisite architecture, oozing history and tradition, and renowned for its quirky rituals, Cambridge is a university town extraordinaire. The tightly packed core of ancient colleges, the picturesque 'Backs' (college gardens) leading on to the river and the leafy green meadows that surround the city give it a far more tranquil appeal than its historic rival Oxford.

◉ Sights

Cambridge University comprises 31 colleges, though not all are open to the public. Opening hours are only a rough guide, so contact the colleges or the tourist office for more information.

★ **King's College Chapel** CHURCH
(☑ 01223-331212; www.kings.cam.ac.uk/chapel; King's Pde; adult/child £9/6; ⏰ 9.30am-3.15pm Mon-Sat, 1.15-2.30pm Sun term time, 9.30am-4.30pm daily, to 3.30pm Dec & Jan, university holidays) In a city crammed with show-stopping buildings, this is the scene-stealer. Grandiose 16th-century King's College Chapel is one of England's most extraordinary examples of Gothic architecture. Its inspirational, intricate 80m-long, fan-vaulted ceiling is the world's largest and soars upwards before exploding into a series of stone fireworks. This hugely atmospheric space is a fitting stage for the chapel's world-famous choir; hear it in full voice during the magnificent, free, evensong (in term time only – 5.30pm Monday to Saturday, 10.30am and 3.30pm Sunday).

★ **Trinity College** COLLEGE
(www.trin.cam.ac.uk; Trinity St; adult/child £3/1; ⏰ 10am-4.30pm, closed early Apr–mid-Jun) The largest of Cambridge's colleges, Trinity offers an extraordinary Tudor gateway, an air of supreme elegance and a sweeping Great Court – the largest of its kind in the world. It also boasts the renowned and suitably musty **Wren Library** (www.trin.cam.ac.uk; Trinity College; ⏰ noon-2pm Mon-Fri, plus 10.30am-12.30pm Sat term time only) FREE, containing 55,000 books dated before 1820 and more than 2500 manuscripts. Works include those by Shakespeare, St Jerome, Newton and Swift – and AA Milne's original *Winnie the Pooh;* both Milne and his son, Christopher Robin, were graduates.

DON'T MISS

PUNTING ON THE CAMBRIDGE BACKS

Behind the Cambridge colleges' grandiose facades and stately courts, a series of gardens and parks line up beside the river. Collectively known as the Backs, the tranquil green spaces and shimmering waters offer unparalleled views of the colleges and are often the most enduring image of Cambridge for visitors.

Gliding a self-propelled punt along the Backs is a blissful experience – once you've got the hang of it; it can also be a manic challenge to begin. If you wimp out you can always opt for a relaxing chauffeured punt.

Punt hire costs around £19 per hour, one-hour chauffeured trips of the Backs cost about £15, and a return trip to Grantchester (2½ hours) will set you back around £27.

★ **Fitzwilliam Museum** MUSEUM
(www.fitzmuseum.cam.ac.uk; Trumpington St; donation requested; ⊙10am-5pm Tue-Sat, noon-5pm Sun) FREE Fondly dubbed 'the Fitz' by locals, this colossal neoclassical pile was one of the first public art museums in Britain, built to house the fabulous treasures that the seventh Viscount Fitzwilliam bequeathed to his old university. Expect Roman and Egyptian grave goods, artworks by many of the great masters and some more quirky collections: banknotes, literary autographs, watches and armour.

🛏 Sleeping & Eating

Cambridge YHA HOSTEL £
(☑0845-371 9728; www.yha.org.uk; 97 Tenison Rd; dm £18-26 d £39-59; @🛜) Busy, recently renovated, popular hostel with compact dorms and good facilities near the railway station.

Fitzbillies BAKERY, CAFE £
(www.fitzbillies.com; 52 Trumpington St; cafe mains £6-12; ⊙8am-6pm Mon-Fri, 9am-7pm Sat, 10am-6pm Sun) Cambridge's oldest bakery has a soft, doughy place in the hearts of generations of students, thanks to its ultrasticky Chelsea buns and other sweet treats. Pick up a bag-full to take away or munch in comfort in the quaint cafe next door.

Espresso Library CAFE £
(www.espressolibrary.co.uk; 210 East Rd; mains £5-9; ⊙7am-7pm Mon & Tue, 7am-9pm Wed & Thu, 7am-11pm Fri & Sat, 9am-6pm Sun; 🛜) This funky new cafe combines industrial-chic-meets-contemporary-art decor with a constantly changing, innovative menu, the chef's repertoire including imaginative salads and mostly vegetarian lunch mains. Come for breakfast, lunch or brunch or savour one of the signature coffees alongside the laptop-toting clientele.

ℹ Information

Tourist Office (☑01223-791500; www.visitcambridge.org; Peas Hill; ⊙10am-5pm Mon-Sat, 11am-3pm Sun Apr-Oct, 10am-5pm Mon-Sat Nov-Mar)

ℹ Getting There & Away

BUS
Buses leave from Parkside. Destinations include Gatwick (£20, 4½ hours, hourly), Heathrow (£17, four hours, hourly), Oxford (£15, 3½ hours, every 30 minutes) and Stansted (£10, 50 minutes, hourly).

TRAIN
The train station is 1.5 miles southeast of the centre. Destinations include London King's Cross (£18, one hour, two to four per hour) and Stansted (£15, 30 minutes to 1¼ hours, two per hour).

York

☑01904 / POP 198,000

Nowhere in northern England says 'medieval' quite like York, a city of extraordinary cultural and historical wealth that has lost little of its pre-industrial lustre. A magnificent circuit of 13th-century walls enclose a medieval spider's web of narrow streets with the awe-inspiring York Minster at its heart.

⊙ Sights

★ **York Minster** CATHEDRAL
(www.yorkminster.org; Deangate; adult/child £10/free, combined ticket incl tower £15/5; ⊙9am-5.30pm Mon-Sat, 12.45-5.30pm Sun, last admission 5pm) The remarkable York Minster is the largest medieval cathedral in all of northern Europe, and one of the world's most beautiful Gothic buildings. Seat of the archbishop of York, primate of England, it is second in importance only to Canterbury, seat of the primate of *all* England – the separate titles were created to settle a debate over the true centre of the English church. If this is the only cathedral you visit in England, you'll still walk away satisfied.

York

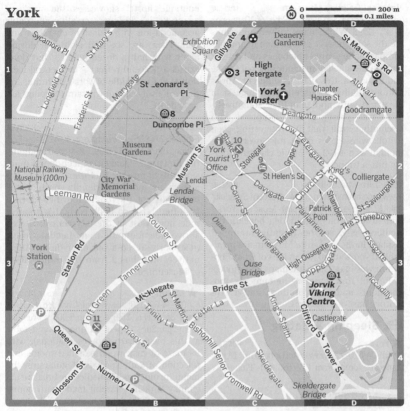

York

◎ Top Sights
1 Jorvik Viking Centre	D3
2 York Minster	C1

◎ Sights
3 Bootham Bar	C1
4 City Walls	C1
5 Micklegate Bar Museum	B4
6 Monk Bar	D1
7 Richard III Museum	D1
8 Yorkshire Museum	B1

⬤ Sleeping
9 Fort	C2

✖ Eating
10 Mannion's	C2
11 Your Bike Shed	A4

★ **Jorvik Viking Centre**   MUSEUM
(www.jorvik-viking-centre.co.uk; Coppergate;
adult/child £9.95/6.95; ⊙10am-5pm Apr-Oct, to
4pm Nov-Mar) Interactive multimedia exhibits aimed at bringing history to life often
achieve exactly the opposite, but the much-
hyped Jorvik manages to pull it off with
aplomb. It's a smells-and-all reconstruction
of the Viking settlement unearthed here
during excavations in the late 1970s, brought
to you courtesy of a 'time-car' monorail that
transports you through 9th-century Jorvik.
You can reduce time waiting in the queue
by booking your tickets online and choosing
the time you want to visit (£ extra).

City Walls   ARCHAEOLOGICAL SITE
(⊙8am-dusk) FREE If the weather's good,
don't miss the chance to walk the City Walls,
which follow the line of the original Roman
walls and give a whole new perspective on
the city. Allow 1½ to two hours for the full
circuit of 4.5 miles or, if you're pushed for
time, the short stretch from **Bootham Bar**
to **Monk Bar** is worth doing for the views
of the minster.

National Railway Museum
MUSEUM

(www.nrm.org.uk; Leeman Rd; ⊙10am-6pm; P🚻) FREE While many railway museums are the sole preserve of lone men in anoraks comparing dog-eared notebooks and getting high on the smell of machine oil, coal smoke and nostalgia, this place is different. York's National Railway Museum – the biggest in the world, with more than 100 locomotives – is so well presented and crammed with fascinating stuff that it's interesting even to folk whose eyes don't mist over at the thought of a 4-6-2 A1 Pacific class thundering into a tunnel.

Yorkshire Museum
MUSEUM

(www.yorkshiremuseum.org.uk; Museum St; adult/child £7.50/free; ⊙10am-5pm) Most of York's Roman archaeology is hidden beneath the medieval city, so the recently revamped displays in the Yorkshire Museum are invaluable if you want to get an idea of what Eboracum was like. There are maps and models of Roman York, funerary monuments, mosaic floors and wall paintings, and a 4th-century bust of Emperor Constantine.

🛏 Sleeping & Eating

★ Fort
HOSTEL £

(☎01904-620222; www.thefortyork.co.uk; 1 Little Stonegate; dm/d from £22/68; 🕾) This new

---

boutique hostel showcases the work of young British designers, creating affordable accomodation with a dash of character and flair. There are six- and eight-bed dorms, along with half a dozen doubles, but don't expect a peaceful retreat – the central location is in the middle of York's nightlife, and there's a lively club downstairs (earplugs are provided!).

York YHA
HOSTEL £

(☎0845 371 9051; www.yha.org.uk; 42 Water End, Clifton; dm/q from £21/99; P@🕾) Originally the Rowntree (Quaker confectioners) mansion, this handsome Victorian house makes a spacious and child-friendly youth hostel, with most of its rooms four-bed dorms. It's often busy, so book early. It's about a mile northwest of the city centre; there's a riverside footpath from Lendal Bridge (it's poorly lit, so avoid after dark). Alternatively, take bus 2 from the train station or Museum St.

★ Mannion's
CAFE, BISTRO £

(☎01904-631030; www.mannionandco.co.uk; 1 Blake St; mains £5-9; ⊙9am-5.30pm Mon-Sat, 10am-5pm Sun) Expect to queue for a table at this busy bistro (no reservations), with its maze of cosy, wood-panelled rooms and selection of daily specials. Regulars on the menu include eggs Benedict for breakfast, a chunky Yorkshire rarebit made with home-baked bread, and lunch platters of cheese and charcuterie from the attached deli. Oh, and pavlova for pudding.

Your Bike Shed
CAFE £

(☎01904-633777; www.yourbikeshed.co.uk; 148-150 Micklegate; mains £3-7; ⊙9am-5pm Mon-Sat, 10am-5pm Sun; 🕾🚲🚻) 🍴 Reinvigorated by the 2014 Tour de France, York's cycling scene has latched onto this cool new cafe and bike workshop. Fitted out with recycled furniture and colourful artwork, it serves reviving portions of halloumi burger, pie and peas, or carrot cake to hungry cyclists, washed down with excellent coffee.

ℹ Information

York Tourist Office (☎01904-550099; www.visityork.org; 1 Museum St; ⊙9am-6pm Mon-Sat, 10am-5pm Sun Apr-Sep, shorter hours Oct-Mar) Visitor and transport info for all of Yorkshire, plus accommodation bookings, ticket sales and internet access.

> WORTH A TRIP
>
> ## CASTLE HOWARD
>
> Stately homes may be two-a-penny in England, but you'll have to try pretty damn hard to find one as breathtakingly stately as Castle Howard (www.castle-howard.co.uk; adult/child house & grounds £14/7.50, grounds only £9.50/6; ⊙house 11am-4.30pm Apr-Oct, grounds 10am-5pm Mar-Oct & Dec, to 4pm Nov, Jan & Feb; P). A work of theatrical grandeur and audacity set in the rolling Howardian Hills, 15 miles northeast of York, this is one of the world's most beautiful buildings, instantly recognisable from its starring role in both the TV series and film of *Brideshead Revisited* based on Evelyn Waugh's 1945 novel of nostalgia for the English aristocracy. Stephenson's of Easingwold (www.stephensonsofeasingwold.co.uk) operates a bus service (£7.50 return, 40 minutes, three times daily Monday to Saturday) from York.

🛈 YORK PASS

Using a York Pass (www.yorkpass.com; 1/2/3 days adult £36/48/58, child £20/24/28) can save you money. It covers access to more than 30 pay-to-visit sights in and around York, including York Minster, Jorvik and Castle Howard. You can buy it at York tourist office or online.

🛈 Getting There & Away

BUS

For timetable information, call **Traveline Yorkshire** (☑ 0871-200 2233; www.yorkshiretravel.net) or check the computerised 24-hour information points at the train station and Rougier St. All local and regional buses stop on Rougier St, about 200m northeast of the train station. Connections include London (£31, 5½ hours, three daily).

TRAIN

From this major railway hub there are direct connections to Edinburgh (£80, 2½ hours, every 30 minutes), London King's Cross (£80, two hours, every 30 minutes) and Manchester (£17, 1½ hours, every 15 minutes).

Manchester

☑ 0161 / POP 503,100

The uncrowned capital of the north is well deserving of the title. It has a rich history and culture, easily explored in its myriad museums and galleries. You can also dine, drink and dance yourself into happy oblivion in the swirl of hedonism that is one of Manchester's most cherished characteristics.

⊙ Sights

★**Manchester Art Gallery** ART MUSEUM
(☑ 0161-235 8888; www.manchestergalleries.org; Mosley St; ⊙ 10am-5pm Mon-Wed & Fri-Sun, to 9pm Thu) FREE A superb collection of British art and a hefty number of European masters are on display at the city's top gallery. The older wing has an impressive selection that includes 37 Turner watercolours, as well as the country's best assemblage of Pre-Raphaelite art. The newer gallery is home to 20th-century British art starring Lucien Freud, Francis Bacon, Stanley Spencer, Henry Moore and David Hockney.

★**Museum of Science & Industry** MUSEUM
(MOSI; ☑ 0161-832 2244; www.mosi.org.uk; Liverpool Rd; charges vary for special exhibitions; ⊙ 10am-5pm) FREE If there's anything you want to know about the Industrial (and post-Industrial) Revolution and Manchester's key role in it, you'll find the answers here among this collection of steam engines and locomotives, factory machinery from the mills, and the excellent exhibition telling the story of Manchester from the sewers up.

★**People's History Museum** MUSEUM
(☑ 0161-838 9190; www.phm.org.uk; Left Bank, Bridge St; ⊙ 10am-5pm) FREE The story of Britain's 200-year march to democracy is told in all its pain and pathos at this superb museum, housed in a refurbished Edwardian pumping station. You clock in on the 1st floor (literally: punch your card in an old mill clock, which managers would infamously fiddle with so as to make employees work longer) and plunge into the heart of Britain's struggle for basic democratic rights, labour reform and fair pay.

Whitworth Art Gallery GALLERY
(☑ 0161-275 7450; www.whitworth.manchester.ac.uk; Oxford Rd, University of Manchester; ⊙ 10am-5pm, to 9pm Thu) FREE Manchester's second-most important art gallery is a wonderful space that reopened after an impressive renovation and extension in 2015. Light flows in from great windows that open up onto the surrounding park. Inside is a fine collection of British watercolours and the best selection of historic textiles outside London. Galleries are devoted to the work of artists from Dürer and Rembrandt to Lucien Freud and David Hockney. All this high art aside, you may find that the most interesting part of the gallery is the group of rooms dedicated to wallpaper – proof that bland pastels and horrible flowery patterns are not the final word in home decoration.

John Rylands Library LIBRARY
(☑ 0161-306 0555; www.library.manchester.ac.uk; 150 Deansgate; ⊙ noon-5pm Mon & Sun, 10am-5pm Tue-Sat) Less a library and more a cathedral to books, Basil Champneys' stunning building is a breathtaking example of Victorian Gothic, no more so than the Reading Room, complete with high-vaulted ceilings and stained-glass windows. The collection of early printed books and rare manuscripts is equally impressive, and includes a Gutenberg Bible, the earliest extant New Testament text and the country's second-largest assembly of works by Britain's first printer, William Caxton.

🛏 Sleeping & Eating

Hatters
HOSTEL **£**

(📞0161-236 9500; www.hattersgroup.com; 50 Newton St; dm/s/d/tr from £16/30/55/70; 🅿@🕏) The old-style lift and porcelain sinks are the only leftovers of this former milliner's factory, now one of the best hostels in town, with location to boot – smack in the heart of the Northern Quarter, you won't have to go far to get the best of alternative Manchester.

Richmond Tea Rooms
CAFE **£**

(📞0161-237 9667; www.richmondtearooms.com; Richmond St; mains £5-8) You've never seen Victorian tearooms like this. Or maybe you have – in Tim Burton's *Alice in Wonderland*. Bold, clashing colours, a potpourri of period furniture and a counter painted to resemble cake icing are just some of the features that make the Richmond one of the city's best new additions. Sandwiches and light meals (rarebit, quiche) are the menu's mainstay, but the real treat is the selection of afternoon teas, complete with four-fingered sandwiches, scones, cakes and, of course, your choice of teas.

🍸 Drinking & Nightlife

Bluu
BAR

(📞0161-839 7740; www.bluu.co.uk; Smithfield Market Bldgs, Thomas St; ⊘10am-midnight; 🕏) Our favourite of the Northern Quarter's collection of great bars. Bluu is cool, comfortable and comes with a great terrace on which to enjoy a pint and listen to music selected by folks with really good taste.

Britons Protection
PUB

(📞0161-236 5895; www.britons-protection.com; 50 Great Bridgewater St; ⊘noon-11pm) Whisky – over 300 different kinds of it – is the beverage of choice at this liver-threatening, proper English pub that also does home-style meals. An old-fashioned boozer with open fires in the back rooms and a cosy atmosphere...perfect on a cold evening.

❶ Information

Tourist Office (www.visitmanchester.com; Piccadilly Plaza, Portland St; adult/child guided tours daily £7/6; ⊘10am-5.15pm Mon-Sat, to 4.30pm Sun) This is mostly a self-service tourist office, with brochures and interactive maps to help guide visitors.

❶ Getting There & Around

The excellent public transport system can be used with a variety of Day Saver tickets. For enquiries about local transport, including night buses, contact **Travelshop** (📞0161-228 7811; www.tfgm.com; 9 Portland St, Piccadilly Gardens; ⊘8am-8pm).

AIR
Manchester Airport (📞0161-489 3000; www.manchesterairport.co.uk), 12 miles south of the city, is the largest UK airport outside London. A train to or from Victoria station costs £4.10/3.50 peak/off-peak, and a coach is £3.50. A taxi is nearly four times as much in light traffic.

BUS
National Express (📞08717 81 81 81; www.nationalexpress.com) serves most major cities almost hourly from the coach station (Chorlton St) in the city centre. Destinations include London (£26.20, 3¾ hours, hourly).

TRAIN
Manchester Piccadilly (east of the Gay Village) is the main station for trains to and from the rest of the country. Destinations include London Euston (£78.70, three hours, seven daily).

Lake District National Park

The Lake District (or Lakeland, as it's often known round these parts) is by far and away the UK's most popular national park. Every year, some 15 million people pitch up to explore the region's fells and countryside, and it's not hard to see why. Ever since the Romantic poets arrived in the 19th century, its postcard panorama of craggy hilltops, mountain tarns and glittering lakes has been stirring the imaginations of visitors.

◉ Sights

Stretching for 10.5 miles between Ambleside and Newby Bridge, **Windermere** isn't just the queen of Lake District lakes – it's also the largest body of water anywhere in England, closer in stature to a Scottish loch. It's been a centre for tourism since the first trains chugged into town in 1847, and it's still one of the national park's busiest spots.

Grasmere is a gorgeous little Lakeland village, all the more famous because of its links with Britain's leading Romantic poet, William Wordsworth. Literary pilgrims will want to see **Dove Cottage** (📞015394-35544; www.wordsworth.org.uk; adult/child £7.50/4.50; ⊘9.30am-5.30pm), his former home.

The main town of the north Lakes, **Keswick** sits beside lovely Derwent Water, a silvery curve studded by wooded islands and criss-crossed by puttering cruise boats, operated by the **Keswick Launch** (☑017687-72263; www.keswick-launch.co.uk; round-the-lake adult/child £9.25/4.50).

Sleeping

There are more than 20 YHA hostels, many of which can be linked by foot if you wish to hike.

In addition to the four excellent campsites run by the National Trust (near Ambleside, Great Langdale, Wasdale and Coniston), there are more great places to sleep under the stars.

Lake District Backpackers Lodge HOSTEL £ (☑015394-46374; www.lakedistrictbackpackers.co.uk; High St, Windermere Town; dm/r £16/36; @) Not the fanciest hostel in the Lake District, but these Windermere digs are about the only option in town for backpackers. There are two small four-bed dorms, plus two private rooms with a double bed and a single bed above.

Information

The national park's main visitor centre is at **Brockhole** (☑015394-46601; www.lake-district.gov.uk; ☺10am-5pm Easter-Oct, to 4pm Nov-Easter), just outside Windermere. Other tourist offices include the following:

Ambleside (☑015394-32582; tic@thehubof ambleside.com; Central Bldgs, Market Cross; ☺9am-5pm)

Bowness-on-Windermere (☑015394-442895; bownesstic@lake-district.gov.uk; Glebe Rd; ☺9am-5pm)

Carlisle (☑01228-625600; www.historic-carlisle.org.uk; Greenmarket; ☺9.30am-5pm Mon-Sat, 10.30am-4pm Sun)

Coniston (☑015394-41533; www.conistontic.org; Ruskin Ave; ☺9.30am-5.30pm Easter-Oct, to 4pm Nov-Easter)

Keswick (☑017687-72645; keswicktic@lake-district.gov.uk; Moot Hall, Market Pl; ☺9.30am-5.30pm Apr-Oct, to 4.30pm Nov-Mar)

Windermere (☑015394-46499; www.windermereinfo.co.uk; Victoria St; ☺8.30am-5pm)

All have information on local sights, activities, accommodation and public transport, and can help with accommodation bookings.

Getting There & Away

BUS

National Express coaches run direct from London Victoria and Glasgow to Windermere, Carlisle and Kendal.

WORTH A TRIP

HADRIAN'S WALL

Named in honour of the emperor who ordered it built, Hadrian's Wall was one of Rome's greatest engineering projects, a spectacular 73-mile testament to ambition and the practical Roman mind. It was constructed between AD 122 and 128 to separate Romans and Scottish Picts.

A variety of buses along the route of the wall are covered by the **Hadrian's Wall Rover Ticket** (adult/child one-day £9/4.50, three-day £18/9, seven-day £36/18), available from bus drivers and tourist offices, where you can also get timetables. The railway line between Newcastle and Carlisle (Tyne Valley Line; £12.20, one hour, hourly) has stations at Corbridge, Hexham, Haydon Bridge, Bardon Mill, Haltwhistle and Brampton for access to the wall. Not all services stop at all stations.

TRAIN

To get to the Lake District, you need to change train off the West Coast Main Line between London and Glasgow, at Oxenholme for Kendal and Windermere. The lines around the Cumbrian Coast and between Settle and Carlisle are particularly scenic.

WALES

Cardiff

☑029 / POP 346,000

Welsh capital since only 1955, Cardiff has embraced the role with vigour, emerging in the new millennium as one of Britain's leading urban centres. Caught between an ancient fort and an ultramodern waterfront, compact Cardiff seems to have surprised even itself with how interesting it has become.

Sights

★**Cardiff Castle** CASTLE (☑029-2087 8100; www.cardiffcastle.com; Castle St; adult/child £12/9, incl guided tour £15/11; ☺9am-5pm) There's a medieval keep at its heart, but it's the later additions to Cardiff Castle that capture the imagination of many visitors. During the Victorian era, extravagant mock-Gothic features were grafted onto this relic, including a clock tower and a lavish banqueting hall. Some but not all of this flamboyant fantasy world can be accessed with a regular castle entry; the rest can be visited as part of a guided tour.

Wales Millennium Centre ARTS CENTRE
(☑ 029-2063 6464; www.wmc.org.uk; Bute Pl, Cardiff Bay; tours adult/child £6/free; ☺ 9am-7pm)
The centrepiece and symbol of Cardiff Bay's regeneration is the superb Wales Millennium Centre, an architectural masterpiece of stacked Welsh slate in shades of purple, green and grey topped with an overarching bronzed steel shell. Designed by Welsh architect Jonathan Adams, it opened in 2004 as Wales' premier arts complex, housing major cultural organisations such as the Welsh National Opera, National Dance Company, BBC National Orchestra of Wales, Literature Wales, HiJinx Theatre and Tŷ Cerdd (Music Centre Wales).

National Museum Cardiff MUSEUM
(☑ 0300 111 2 333; www.museumwales.ac.uk; Gorsedd Gardens Rd; ☺ 10am-4pm Tue-Sun) FREE
Devoted mainly to natural history and art, this grand neoclassical building is the centrepiece of the seven institutions dotted around the country that together form the Welsh National Museum. It's one of Britain's best museums; you'll need at least three hours to do it justice, but it could easily consume the best part of a rainy day.

🛏 Sleeping & Eating

River House HOSTEL £
(☑ 029-2039 9810; www.riverhousebackpackers.com; 59 Fitzhamon Embankment, Riverside; dm/s/d incl breakfast from £17/40/42; @ 🛜)
Professionally run by a helpful young brother-and-sister team, the River House has a well-equipped kitchen, small garden and cosy TV lounge. The private rooms are basically small dorm rooms and share the same bathrooms. A breakfast of cereal, toast, pastries and fruit is provided.

Coffee Barker CAFE £
(Castle Arcade; mains £5.50-8.50; ☺ 8.30am-5.30pm Mon-Sat, 10.30am-4.30pm Sun; 🛜🚼)
Slink into an armchair, sip on a silky coffee and snack on salmon scrambled eggs or a sandwich in what is Cardiff's coolest cafe. There are plenty of magazines and toys to keep everyone amused.

🍷 Drinking & Nightlife

Gwdihŵ BAR
(☑ 029-2039 7933; www.gwdihw.co.uk; 6 Guildford Cres; ☺ 3pm-midnight Sun-Wed, noon-2am Thu-Sat) The last word in Cardiff hipsterdom, this cute little bar has an eclectic line-up of entertainment (comedy, DJs and lots of live music, including microfestivals that spill over into the car park) but it's a completely charming place to stop for a drink at any time. If you're wondering about the name, it's the Welsh take on an owl's call.

❶ Information

Tourist Office (☑ 029-2087 3573; www.visitcardiff.com; Wales Millennium Centre, Bute Pl, Cardiff Bay; ☺ 10am-6pm Mon-Sat, to 4pm Sun) Information, advice and souvenirs.

❶ Getting There & Away

AIR
Cardiff Airport (☑ 01446-711111; www.cardiff-airport.com) is 12 miles southwest of the city. Buses connect either directly with Central bus station or Rhoose Cardiff Airport train station.

BUS
➡ Cardiff's Central bus station has closed for a major redevelopment and is due to reopen near the train station in a revitalised Central Square in 2018. In the meantime there are temporary bus stops scattered all around the inner city. See www.traveline.cymru for details.

➡ National Express (www.nationalexpress.com) coaches depart from **Cardiff Coach Station** (Sophia Gardens), with destinations including Tenby (£18, 2¾ hours, daily), Swansea (£3.50, one hour, four daily), Chepstow (from £4.80, one hour, four daily), Bristol (£6.10, one hour, four daily) and London (from £5, 3½ hours, four daily).

TRAIN
Trains from major British cities arrive at Cardiff Central station. Direct services include London Paddington (£41, 2¼ hours).

Snowdonia National Park

Snowdonia National Park (Parc Cenedlaethol Eryri; www.eryri-npa.gov.uk) was founded in 1951, making it Wales' first national park. Around 350,000 people travel to the national park to climb, walk or take the train to the summit of Mt Snowdon (1085m), Wales' highest mountain.

On a clear day the views from the mountain stretch to Ireland and the Isle of Man. Even on a gloomy day you could find yourself above the clouds. At the top is the striking **Hafod Eryri** (☺ 10am to 20min before last train departure; 🛜) visitor centre. Clad in granite and curved to blend into the mountain, it's

CONWY

A visit to Britain's most complete walled town should be high on the itinerary for anyone with even a mild crush on things historic. The World Heritage–listed **castle** (Cadw; 🌐01492-592358; cadw.wales.gov.uk; Castle Sq; adult/child £7.95/5.60; ⊙9.30am-5pm Mar-Jun & Sep-Oct, to 6pm Jul & Aug, to 4pm Nov-Feb; P) continues to dominate the town, as it's done ever since Edward I first planted it here in the late 13th century.

For a small town, Conwy really packs in the historical interest. All within a short stroll of each other, Conwy's three key properties – **Plas Mawr** (Cadw; cadw.wales.gov.uk; High St; adult/child £6/4.20; ⊙9.30am 5pm Easter-Sep), **Aberconwy House** (NT; nationaltrust. org.uk; Castle St; adult/child £4/2; ⊙11am-5pm late-Feb-Oct) and **Royal Cambrian Academy** (🌐01492-593413; rcaconwy.org; Crown Lane; ⊙11am-5pm Tue-Sat) FREE – encapsulate the town's rich heritage and its continuing role in the Welsh art scene.

Conwy's train station is just inside the town walls, on Rosemary Lane. Most buses stop by the train station.

a wonderful building, housing a cafe, toilets and ambient interpretative elements built into the structure itself.

Six paths of varying length and difficulty lead to the summit, all taking around six hours return, or you can cheat and catch the **Snowdon Mountain Railway** (🌐0844 493 8120; www.snowdonrailway.co.uk; adult/child return diesel £27/18, steam £35/25; ⊙9am-5pm mid-Mar–Oct), opened in 1896 and still the UK's only public rack-and-pinion railway. However you get to the summit, take warm, waterproof clothing, wear sturdy footwear and check the weather forecast before setting out.

🛏 Sleeping

Bryn Gwynant YHA   HOSTEL £
(🌐0800 0195 465; www.yha.org.uk; Nantgwynant; dm/tw/f £19/50/73; ⊙Mar-Oct; P) Of all of the park's youth hostels, Bryn Gwynant has the most impressive building and the most idyllic setting, occupying a grand Victorian mansion facing over a lake to Snowdon – although it's certainly not flash inside. It's located 4 miles east of Beddgelert, near the start of the Watkin Path.

Snowdon Ranger YHA   HOSTEL £
(🌐0800 0191 700; www.yha.org.uk; dm/tr/q £19/57/73; P @) On the A4085, 5 miles north of Beddgelert at the trailhead for the Snowdon Ranger Path, this former inn has its own adjoining lakeside beach. Accommodation is basic.

ℹ Getting There & Away

The **Welsh Highland Railway** (🌐01766-516000; www.festrail.co.uk; adult/child return £38/34.20) and **Snowdon Sherpa** (🌐0870 608 2608) buses

link various places in Snowdonia with the town of Bangor, which can be reached by train from London Euston (£86, 3¼ hours, hourly).

SCOTLAND

Edinburgh

🌐0131 / POP 460,400

Edinburgh is a city that begs to be explored. Its Old Town is filled with quirky, come-hither nooks that tempt you to walk just a little bit further. And every corner turned reveals sudden views and unexpected vistas – green sunlit hills, a glimpse of rust-red crags, a blue flash of distant sea.

But there's more to Edinburgh than sightseeing. This is a city of pub crawls and impromptu music sessions, mad-for-it clubbing and all-night parties, overindulgence and wandering home through cobbled streets at dawn. All these superlatives come together at festival time in August, when it seems as if half the world descends on Edinburgh for one enormous party. If you can possibly manage it, join them.

◉ Sights

★**Edinburgh Castle**   CASTLE
(www.edinburghcastle.gov.uk; Castle Esplanade; adult/child £16.50/9.90, audioguide £3.50 extra; ⊙9.30am-6pm Apr-Sep, to 5pm Oct-Mar, last admission 1hr before closing; 🚌23, 27, 41, 42) Edinburgh Castle has played a pivotal role in Scottish history, both as a royal residence – King Malcolm Canmore (r 1058–93) and Queen Margaret first made their home here in the 11th century – and as a military stronghold.

Royal Mile

A GRAND DAY OUT

Planning your own procession along the Royal Mile involves some tough decisions – it would be impossible to see everything in a single day, so it's wise to decide in advance what you don't want to miss and shape your visit around that. Remember to leave time for lunch, for exploring some of the Mile's countless side alleys and, during festival time, for enjoying the street theatre that is bound to be happening in High St.

The most pleasant way to reach the Castle Esplanade at the start of the Royal Mile is to hike up the zigzag path from the footbridge behind the Ross Bandstand in Princes Street Gardens (in springtime you'll be knee-deep in daffodils). Starting at **Edinburgh Castle ❶** means that the rest of your walk is downhill. For a superb view up and down the length of the Mile, climb the **Camera Obscura's Outlook Tower ❷** before visiting **Gladstone's**

ROYAL VISITS TO THE ROYAL MILE

1561: Mary, Queen of Scots arrives from France and holds an audience with John Knox.
1745: Bonnie Prince Charlie fails to capture Edinburgh Castle, and instead sets up court in Holyroodhouse.
2004: Queen Elizabeth II officially opens the Scottish Parliament building.

Edinburgh Castle

If you're pushed for time, visit the Great Hall, the Honours of Scotland and the Prisons of War exhibit. Head for the Half Moon Battery for a photo looking down the length of the Royal Mile.

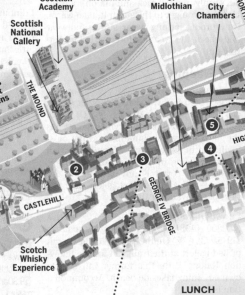

Royal Scottish Academy

Scott Monument

Heart of Midlothian

City Chambers

NORTH BRI

Scottish National Gallery

Princes Street Gardens

THE MOUND

❷

❸

❺

❹

HIGH

CASTLEHILL

GEORGE IV BRIDGE

❶

Scotch Whisky Experience

Gladstone's Land

The 1st floor houses a faithful recreation of how a wealthy Edinburgh merchant lived in the 17th century. Check out the beautiful Painted Bedchamber, with its ornately decorated walls and wooden ceilings.

LUNCH BREAK

Burger and a beer at **Holyrood 9A**; steak and chips at **Maxie's Bistro**; slap-up seafood at **Ondine**.

Land **3** and **St Giles Cathedral** **4**. If history's your thing, you'll want to add **Real Mary King's Close** **5**, **John Knox House** **6** and the **Museum of Edinburgh** **7** to your must-see list.

At the foot of the mile, choose between modern and ancient seats of power – the **Scottish Parliament** **8** or the **Palace of Holyroodhouse** **9**. Round off the day with an evening ascent of Arthur's Seat or, slightly less strenuously, Calton Hill. Both make great sunset viewpoints.

TAKING YOUR TIME

Minimum time needed for each attraction:

- » **Edinburgh Castle**: two hours
- » **Gladstone's Land**: 45 minutes
- » **St Giles Cathedral**: 30 minutes
- » **Real Mary King's Close**: one hour (tour)
- » **Scottish Parliament**: one hour (tour)
- » **Palace of Holyroodhouse**: one hour

Real Mary King's Close
The guided tour is heavy on ghost stories, but a highlight is standing in an original 17th-century room with tufts of horsehair poking from the crumbling plaster, and breathing in the ancient scent of stone, dust and history.

Canongate Kirk

CANONGATE

6

ST MARY'S ST

SOUTH BRIDGE

7

8

9

Our Dynamic Earth

Scottish Parliament
Don't have time for the guided tour? Pick up a 'Discover the Scottish Parliament Building' leaflet from reception and take a self-guided tour of the exterior, then hike up to Salisbury Crags for a great view of the complex.

RICK LEW/GETTY IMAGES © ARCHITECT: ENRIC MIRALLES

Palace of Holyroodhouse
Find the secret staircase joining Mary, Queen of Scots' bedchamber with that of her husband, Lord Darnley, who restrained the queen while his henchmen stabbed to death her secretary (and possible lover), David Rizzio.

St Giles Cathedral
Look out for the Burne-Jones stained-glass window (1873) at the west end, showing the crossing of the River Jordan, and the bronze memorial to Robert Louis Stevenson in the Moray Aisle.

RIEGER BERTRAND/GETTY IMAGES ©

Trinity College, Dublin

STEP INTO THE PAST

Ireland's most prestigious university, founded on the order of Queen Elizabeth I in 1592, is an architectural masterpiece, a cordial retreat from the bustle of modern life in the middle of the city. Step through its main entrance and you step back in time, the cobbled stones transporting you to another era, when the elite discussed philosophy and argued passionately in favour of empire.

Standing in Front Square, the 30m-high **Campanile ❶** is directly in front of you with the **Dining Hall ❷** to your left. On the far side of the square is the Old Library building, the centrepiece of which is the magnificent **Long Room ❸**, which was the inspiration for the computer-generated imagery of the Jedi Archive in *Star Wars Episode II: Attack of the Clones*. Here you'll find the university's greatest treasure, the **Book of Kells ❹**. You'll probably have to queue to see this masterpiece, and then only for a brief visit, but it's very much worth it.

Just beyond the Old Library is the very modern **Berkeley Library ❺**, which nevertheless fits perfectly into the campus' overall aesthetic: directly in front of it is the distinctive **Sphere Within a Sphere ❻**, the most elegant of the university's sculptures.

For more information on Trinity College and Dublin's other sights, see p108-16.

DON'T MISS

» Douglas Hyde Gallery, the campus' designated modern-art museum.

» cricket match on pitch, the most elegant of pastimes.

» pint in the Pavilion Bar, preferably while watching the cricket.

» visit to the Science Gallery, where science is made completely relevant.

RAQUEL PEDROSA PEREZ / GETTY IMAGES ©

Campanile
Trinity College's most iconic bit of masonry was designed in the mid-19th century by Sir Charles Lanyon; the attached sculptures were created by Thomas Kirk.

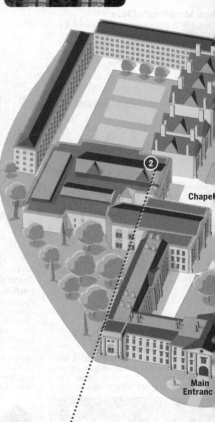

Chapel

Main Entrance

Dining Hall
Richard Cassels' original building was designed to mirror the Examination Hall directly opposite on Front Square: the hall collapsed twice and was rebuilt from scratch in 1761.

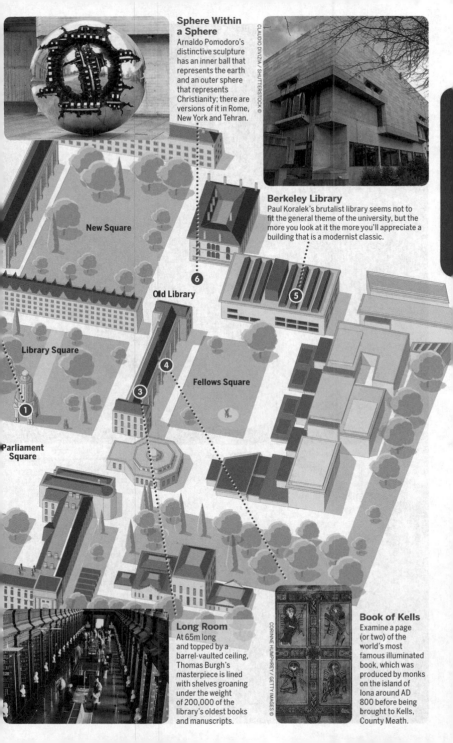

Sphere Within a Sphere
Arnaldo Pomodoro's distinctive sculpture has an inner ball that represents the earth and an outer sphere that represents Christianity; there are versions of it in Rome, New York and Tehran.

Berkeley Library
Paul Koralek's brutalist library seems not to fit the general theme of the university, but the more you look at it the more you'll appreciate a building that is a modernist classic.

New Square

Old Library

Library Square

Fellows Square

Parliament Square

Long Room
At 65m long and topped by a barrel-vaulted ceiling, Thomas Burgh's masterpiece is lined with shelves groaning under the weight of 200,000 of the library's oldest books and manuscripts.

Book of Kells
Examine a page (or two) of the world's most famous illuminated book, which was produced by monks on the island of Iona around AD 800 before being brought to Kells, County Meath.

1

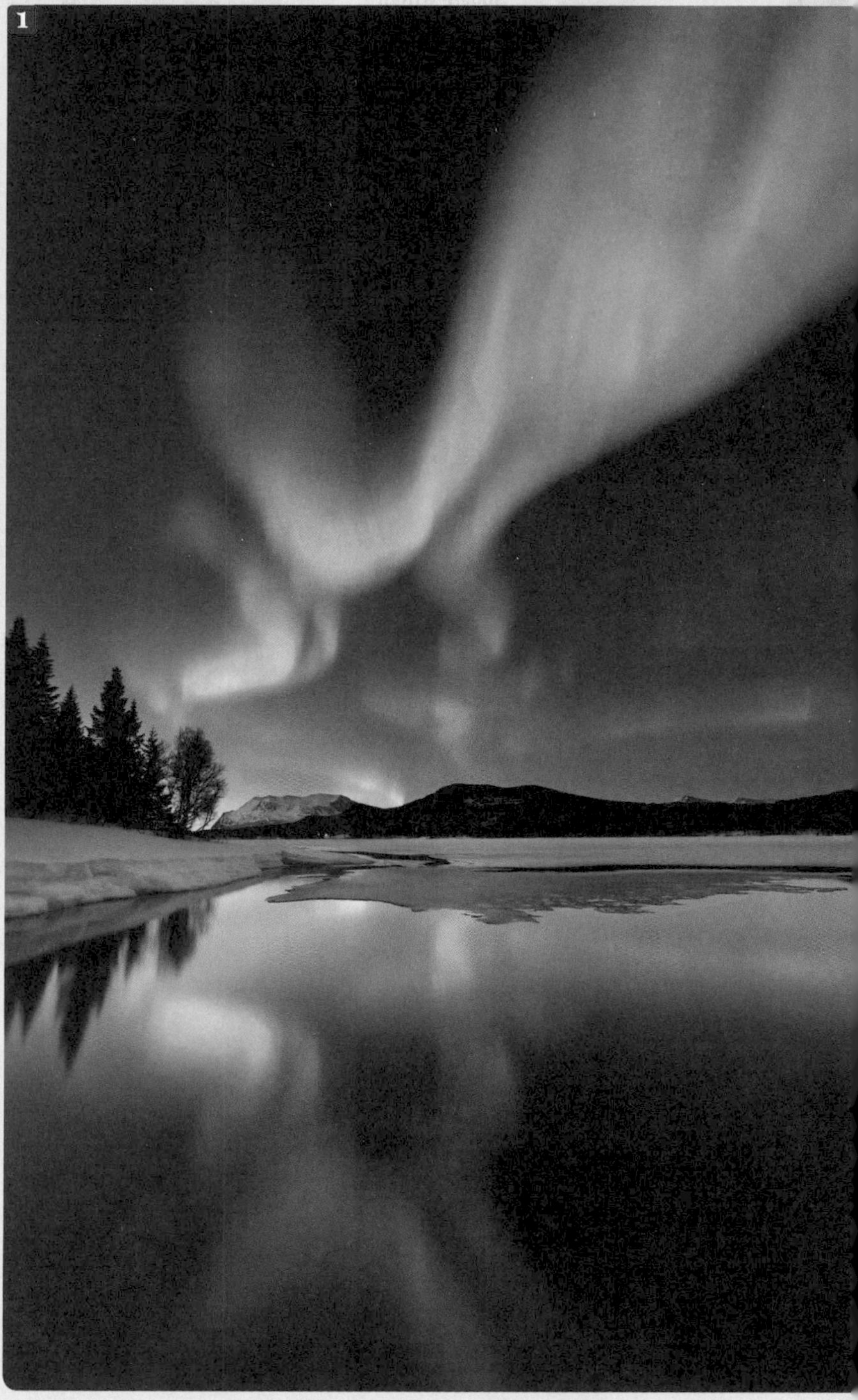

MEDIOIMAGES / PHOTODISC / GETTY IMAGES ©

T.STUDIO / SHUTTERSTOCK ©

1. Northern Lights, Norway
The aurora borealis (Northern Lights: p197) dances across the sky in northern Norway.

2. Edinburgh Castle, Britain
The imposing castle (p89) watches over the Scottish capital.

3. Stockholm, Sweden
Be enchanted by Stockholm's fairy-tale Old Town, Gamla Stan (p161).

4. Blue Lagoon, Iceland
Soak your troubles away in one of Iceland's most popular tourist attractions (p200).

TUUL AND BRUNO MORANDI / GETTY IMAGES ©

Central Edinburgh

Central Edinburgh

⊙ Top Sights

⊙ Sights

🛏 Sleeping

✕ Eating

🍷 Drinking & Nightlife

✪ Entertainment

The castle last saw military action in 1745; from then until the 1920s it served as the British army's main base in Scotland. Today it is one of Scotland's most atmospheric and most popular tourist attractions.

★ **Real Mary King's Close**   HISTORIC BUILDING
(☑0845 070 6244; www.realmarykingsclose.com; 2 Warriston's Close, High St; adult/child £14.50/8.75; ⊙10am-9pm daily Apr-Oct, 10am-5pm Sun-Thu & 10am-9pm Fri & Sat Nov-Mar; ▣23, 27, 41, 42) Edinburgh's 18th-century City Chambers were built over the sealed-off remains of Mary King's Close, and the lower levels of this medieval Old Town alley have survived almost unchanged amid the foundations for 250 years. Now open to the public, this spooky, subterranean labyrinth gives a fascinating insight into the everyday life of 17th-century Edinburgh. Costumed characters lead tours through a 16th-century town house and the plague-stricken home of a 17th-century gravedigger. Advance booking recommended.

National Museum of Scotland MUSEUM
(www.nms.ac.uk; Chambers St; fee for special
exhibitions; ⊙10am-5pm; ♿; ⏹2, 23, 27, 35, 41,
42, 45) FREE Broad, elegant Chambers St is
dominated by the long facade of the National Museum of Scotland. Its extensive collections are spread between two buildings, one
modern, one Victorian – the golden stone
and striking modern architecture of the new
building, opened in 1998, is one of the city's
most distinctive landmarks. The five floors
of the museum trace the history of Scotland
from geological beginnings to the 1990s,
with many imaginative and stimulating exhibits – audioguides are available in several
languages.

**Scottish
Parliament Building** NOTABLE BUILDING
(☎0131-348 5200; www.scottish.parliament.uk;
Horse Wynd; ⊙9am-6.30pm Tue-Thu & 10am-5pm
Mon, Fri & Sat in session, 10am-5pm Mon-Sat in re-
cess; ⏹35, 36) FREE The Scottish parliament
building, built on the site of a former brewery, was officially opened by HM the Queen
in October 2005. Designed by Catalan architect Enric Miralles (1955–2000), the ground
plan of the parliament complex represents
a 'flower of democracy rooted n Scottish
soil' (best seen looking down from Salisbury Crags). Free, one-hour guided tours
(advance booking recommended) include
a visit to the Debating Chamber, a commit-
tee room, the Garden Lobby and an MSP's
(Member of the Scottish Parliament) office.

Arthur's Seat LANDMARK
(Holyrood Park) The rocky peak of Arthur's
Seat (251m), carved by ice sheets from the
deeply eroded stump of a long-extinct volcano, is a distinctive feature of Edinburgh's
skyline. The view from the summit is well
worth the walk, extending from the Forth
Bridges in the west to the distant conical hill of North Berwick Law in the east,
with the Ochil Hills and the Highlands on
the northwestern horizon. You can hike
from Holyrood to the summit in around 45
minutes.

🛏 Sleeping

⭐**Malone's Old Town Hostel** HOSTEL £
(☎0131-226 7648; www.maloneshostel.com; 14
Forrest Rd; dm £12-20; @🤙; ⏹2, 23, 27, 41, 42, 45)
No fancy decor or style credentials here, but
they've got the basics right: it's clean, comfortable and friendly, and set upstairs from
an Irish pub where guests get discounts on

FESTIVAL CITY
....

Edinburgh hosts an amazing number
of festivals throughout the year, notably the **Edinburgh International
Festival** (☎0131-473 2000; www.eif.
co.uk), the **Edinburgh Festival Fringe**
(☎0131-226 0026; www.edfringe.com) and
the **Military Tattoo** (☎0131-225 1188;
www.edintattoo.co.uk), all in August. **Hog-
manay**, Scotland's New Year's celebrations, is also a peak party time.

food and drink. The cherry on the cake is its
superbly central location, an easy walk from
the Royal Mile, the castle, the Grassmarket
and Princes St.

Safestay Edinburgh HOSTEL £
(☎0131-524 1989; www.smartcityhostels.com; 50
Blackfriars St; dm £13-20; @🤙) A big, modern
hostel, with a convivial cafe where you can
buy breakfast, and mod cons such as key-
card access and charging stations for mobile
phones, MP3 players and laptops. Lockers in
every room, a huge bar and a central location
just off the Royal Mile make this a favourite among the young, party-mad crowd –
don't expect a quiet night!

Budget Backpackers HOSTEL £
(☎0131-226 6351; www.budgetbackpackers.com; 9
Cowgate; dm £13-18, tw £60; @🤙; ⏹2) This fun
spot piles on the extras, with bike storage,
pool tables, laundry and a colourful chill-out
lounge. You'll pay a little more for four-bunk
dorms, but larger dorms are great value.
The only downside is that prices increase at
weekends, but otherwise a brilliant spot to
doss.

🍴 Eating

⭐**Mums** CAFE £
(☎0131-260 9806; www.monstermashcafe.co.uk;
4a Forrest Rd; mains £8-11; ⊙9am-10pm Mon-Sat,
10am-10pm Sun; 🤙♿; ⏹23, 27, 41, 42) 🌱 This
nostalgia-fuelled cafe serves up classic British
comfort food that wouldn't look out of place
on a 1950s menu – bacon and eggs, bangers
and mash, shepherd's pie, fish and chips. But
there's a twist – the food is all top-quality
nosh freshly prepared from local produce, including Crombie's gourmet sausages. There's
even a wine list, though we prefer the real
ales and Scottish-brewed cider.

Elephant House
CAFE £

(www.elephanthouse.biz; 21 George IV Bridge; mains £5-10; ⊙8am-10pm Mon-Thu, to 11pm Fri, 9am-11pm Sat, 9am-10pm Sun; 🔲🚼; 🔲2, 23, 27, 41, 42, 45) Here you'll find counters at the front, tables and views of the castle at the back (where JK Rowling famously wrote in the days before Harry Potter was published), and little effigies and images of elephants everywhere. Excellent coffee and tasty, homemade food – pizzas, quiches, pies, sandwiches and cakes – at reasonable prices.

David Bann
VEGETARIAN ££

(🖉0131-556 5888; www.davidbann.com; 56-58 St Mary's St; mains £11-13; ⊙noon-10pm Mon-Fri, 11am-10pm Sat & Sun; 🔲; 🔲35) 🍴 If you want to convince a carnivorous friend that cuisine à la veg can be as tasty and inventive as a meat-muncher's menu, take them to David Bann's stylish restaurant – dishes such as parsnip and blue cheese pudding, and spiced aduki bean and cashew pie, are guaranteed to win converts.

🍷 Drinking & Nightlife

Café Royal Circle Bar
PUB

(www.caferoyaledinburgh.co.uk; 17 West Register St; ⊙11am-11pm Mon-Wed, to midnight Thu, to 1am Fri-Sat, 12.30-11pm Sun; 🛜; 🔲Princes St) Perhaps *the* classic Edinburgh pub, the Café Royal's main claims to fame are its magnificent oval bar and its Doulton tile portraits of famous Victorian inventors. Sit at the bar or claim one of the cosy leather booths beneath the stained-glass windows, and choose from the seven real ales on tap.

Cabaret Voltaire
CLUB

(www.thecabaretvoltaire.com; 36-38 Blair St; ⊙5pm-3am Mon-Thu, noon-3am Fri-Sun; 🛜; 🔲all South Bridge buses) An atmospheric warren of stone-lined vaults houses this self-consciously 'alternative' club, which eschews huge dance floors and egotistical DJ worship in favour of a 'creative crucible' hosting an eclectic mix of DJs, live acts, comedy, theatre, visual arts and the spoken word. Well worth a look.

Bow Bar
PUB

(www.thebowbar.co.uk; 80 West Bow; ⊙noon-midnight Mon-Sat, to 11.30pm Sun; 🍸; 🔲2, 23, 27, 41, 42) One of the city's best traditional-style pubs (it's not as old as it looks), serving a range of excellent real ales and a vast selection of malt whiskies, the Bow Bar often has standing-room only on Friday and Saturday evenings.

☆ Entertainment

The comprehensive source for what's on is The List (www.list.co.uk).

★ Sandy Bell's
TRADITIONAL MUSIC

(www.sandybellsedinburgh.co.uk; 25 Forrest Rd; ⊙noon-1am Mon-Sat, 12.30pm-midnight Sun; 🔲2, 23, 27, 41, 42, 45) This unassuming pub is a stalwart of the traditional music scene (the founder's wife sang with the Corries). There's music almost every evening at 9pm, and from 3pm Saturday and Sunday, plus lots of impromptu sessions.

Henry's Cellar Bar
ROCK, BLUES

(🖉0131-629 2992; 16 Morrison St; admission free-£6; ⊙5pm-1am Sun-Thu, to 3am Fri-Sat; 🔲all Lothian Rd buses) One of Edinburgh's most eclectic live-music venues, Henry's has something going on most nights of the week, from rock and indie to 'Balkan-inspired folk', funk to hip-hop to hardcore, staging both local bands and acts from around the world. Open till 3am at weekends.

ℹ Information

Edinburgh Information Centre (🖉0131-473 3868; www.edinburgh.org; Waverley Mall, 3 Princes St; ⊙9am-7pm Mon-Sat & 10am-7pm Sun Jul & Aug, to 6pm Jun, to 5pm Sep-May; 🛜; 🔲St Andrew Sq) Includes an accommodation booking service, currency exchange, gift and bookshop, internet access and counters selling tickets for Edinburgh city tours and Scottish Citylink bus services.

ℹ Getting There & Around

AIR

Edinburgh Airport (🖉0844 448 8833; www.edinburghairport.com) is 8 miles west of the city. **Airlink** (www.flybybus.com) bus service 100 runs from Waverley Bridge, outside the train station, to the airport (one way/return £4/7, 30 minutes, every 10 minutes, 4am to midnight) via the West End and Haymarket.

Edinburgh Trams (www.edinburghtrams.com) run from the airport to the city centre (one way/return £4.50/7.50, 33 minutes, every six to eight minutes, 6am to midnight).

BUS

Scottish Citylink (🖉0871 266 3333; www.citylink.co.uk) buses connect Edinburgh with all of Scotland's cities and major towns, including Glasgow (£7.30, 1¼ hours, every 15 minutes), Stirling (£8, one hour, hourly) and Inverness (£30, 3½ hours to 4½ hours, hourly).

National Express (www.nationalexpress.com) operates a direct coach service from London (£26, 10 hours, one daily). It's also worth checking with **Megabus** (☑ 0900 1600 900; www.megabus.com) for cheap interc ty bus fares from Edinburgh to London, Glasgow and Inverness.

TRAIN

Edinburgh's main terminus is Waverley train station. Trains arriving from, and departing for, the west also stop at Haymarket station, which is more convenient for the West End.

First ScotRail (☑ 0344 811 0141; www.scotrail. co.uk) operates a regular shuttle service between Edinburgh and Glasgow (£13.20, 50 minutes, every 15 minutes), and frequent daily services to all Scottish cities, includ ng Stirling (£8.30, one hour, twice hourly Monday to Saturday, hourly Sunday) and Inverness (£72, 3½ hours). There are also regular trains to London King's Cross (£85, 4½ hours, hourly via York.

Glasgow

☑ 0141 / POP 595,100

Disarmingly blending sophistication and earthiness, Scotland's biggest city has evolved over the last couple of decades to become one of Britain's most intriguing metropolises.

At first glance, the soberly handsome Victorian buildings, legacies of wealth generated from manufacturing and trade, suggest a staid sort of place. Very wrong. They are packed with stylish bars, top-notch restaurants, hedonistic clubs and one of Britain's best live-music scenes. The place's sheer vitality is gloriously infectious: the combination of edgy urbanity and the residents' legendary friendliness is captivating.

◎ Sights

Glasgow's main square in the city centre is grand **George Square**, built in the Victorian era to show off the city's wealth, and dignified by statues of notable Scots including Robert Burns, James Watt, John Moore and Sir Walter Scott.

★ Burrell Collection   GALLERY
(☑ 0141-287 2550; www.glasgowmuseums.com; Pollok Country Park; ⊙ 10am-5pm Mon-Thu & Sat, 11am-5pm Fri & Sun) **FREE** One of Glasgow's top attractions was amassed by wealthy industrialist Sir William Burrell then donated to the city and is housed in an outstanding museum, in a park 3 miles south of the city centre. Burrell collected all manner of art from his teens to his death at 97, and this idiosyncratic collection of treasure includes everything from Chinese porcelain and medieval furniture to paintings by Degas and Cézanne. It's not so big as to be overwhelming, and the stamp of the collector lends an intriguing coherence.

★ Kelvingrove
Art Gallery & Museum   GALLERY, MUSEUM
(www.glasgowmuseums.com; Argyle St; ⊙ 10am-5pm Mon-Thu & Sat, 11am-5pm Fri & Sun) **FREE** A magnificent stone building, this grand Victorian cathedral of culture is a fascinating and unusual museum, with a bewildering variety of exhibits. You'll find fine art alongside stuffed animals, and Micronesian shark-tooth swords alongside a Spitfire plane, but it's not mix 'n' match: rooms are carefully and thoughtfully themed, and the collection is a manageable size. There's an excellent room of Scottish art, a room of fine French Impressionist works, and quality Renaissance paintings from Italy and Flanders.

Riverside Museum   MUSEUM
(☑ 0141-287 2720; www.glasgowmuseums.com; 100 Pointhouse Pl; ⊙ 10am-5pm Mon-Thu & Sat, 11am-5pm Fri & Sun; ⊕) **FREE** This visually impressive modern museum at Glasgow Harbour (west of the centre – get bus 100 from the north side of George Sq, or the Clyde Cruises boat service) owes its striking curved forms to British-Iraqi architect Zaha Hadid. A transport museum forms the main part of the collection, featuring a fascinating series of cars made in Scotland, plus assorted railway locos, trams, bikes (including the world's first pedal-powered bicycle from 1847) and model Clyde-built ships.

Glasgow Cathedral   CATHEDRAL
(HES; ☑ 0141-552 8198; www.historicenvironment. scot; Cathedral Sq; ⊙ 9.30am-5.30pm Mon-Sat, 1-5pm Sun Apr-Sep, 10am-4pm Mon-Sat, 1-4pm Sun Oct-Mar) **FREE** Glasgow Cathedral has a rare timelessness. The dark, imposing interior conjures up medieval might and can send a shiver down the spine. It's a shining example of Gothic architecture, and, unlike nearly all Scotland's cathedrals, survived the turmoil of the Reformation mobs almost intact. Most of the current building dates from the 15th century.

⊨ Sleeping

Euro Hostel   HOSTEL £
(☑ 08455 399956; www.euro-hostels.co.uk; 318 Clyde St; dm £16-26, d £50-80; ⊛) With hundreds of beds, this mammoth hostel is

Glasgow

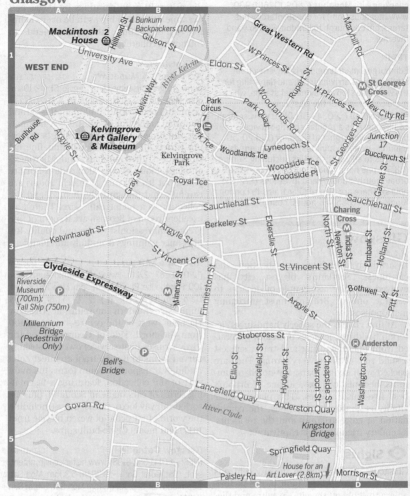

handily central. While it can feel over-businesslike, and is often booked out by rowdy groups, it has lots of facilities, including en-suite dorms (some recently modernized) with lockers, a compact kitchen, breakfast, bar, games room and laundry. Aimed at groups, the 'suites' section is attractively modern, with its own little garden and lounge area.

Glasgow Metro Youth Hostel
HOSTEL £

(☏ 0345 293 7373; www.syha.org.uk; 89 Buccleuch St; s without/with bathroom £27/34; ☺ late Jun-Aug; ☎) Student accommodation belonging to the nearby Glasgow School of Art

provides the venue for this summer hostel. All rooms are comfortable singles (many of them en suite), there are kitchen facilities, and it's a very good deal for solo travellers or groups. It's slightly cheaper midweek.

Glasgow SYHA
HOSTEL £

(☏ 0141-332 3004; www.syha.org.uk; 8 Park Tce; dm/tw £26/62; @ ☎) Perched on a hill overlooking Kelvingrove Park in a charming town house, this place is one of Scotland's best official hostels. Dorms are mostly four to six beds with padlock lockers and all have their own en suite. The common rooms are spacious, plush and good for lounging

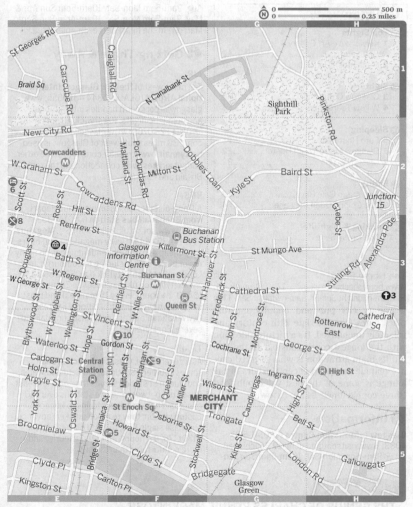

about. There's no curfew, a good kitchen, and meals are available. The prices listed reflect maximums and are usually cheaper.

🍴 Eating & Drinking

⭐ Saramago Café Bar
CAFE £

(📞 0141-352 4920; www.facebook.com/saramagocafebar; 350 Sauchiehall St; light meals £3-9; ⏱ food noon-10pm Sun-Wed, noon-11.30pm Thu-Sat; 📶🕎) In the airy atmosphere of the Centre for Contemporary Arts, this place does a great line in eclectic vegan fusion food, with a range of top flavour combinations from around the globe. The upstairs bar has a great deck on steep Scott St and packs out inside with a friendly hipstery crowd enjoying the eclectic DJ sets and quality tap beers.

The Chippy Doon the Lane
FISH & CHIPS £

(📞 0141-225 6650; www.thechippyglasgow.com; McCormick Lane, 84 Buchanan St; meals £6-12; ⏱ noon-9.30pm; 📶) 🍴 Don't be put off by its location in a down-at-heel alleyway off the shopping precinct: this is a cut above your average chip shop. Sustainable seafood is served in a chic space, all old-time brick, metal archways and jazz. Otherwise, chow down on your takeaway at the wooden tables in the lane or out on Buchanan St itself.

Glasgow

⊚ Top Sights
1 Kelvingrove Art Gallery &
  Museum A2
2 Mackintosh House...............................A1

⊚ Sights
3 Glasgow Cathedral H3
4 Willow Tearooms E3

🛏 Sleeping
5 Euro Hostel..F5
6 Glasgow Metro Youth Hostel E2
7 Glasgow SYHA B2

✖ Eating
8 Saramago Café Bar E3
9 The Chippy Doon the Lane.................F4

🍷 Drinking & Nightlife
10 The Horse Shoe F4

The Horse Shoe   PUB
(www.horseshoebar.co.uk; 17 Drury St;
⊙10am-midnight Sun-Fri, 9am-midnight Sat) This
legendary city pub and popular meeting
place dates from the late 19th century and
is largely unchanged. It's a picturesque spot,
with the longest continuous bar in the UK,
but its main attraction is what's served over
it – real ale and good cheer. Upstairs in the
lounge is some of the best value pub food
(three-course lunch £4.50) in town.

ℹ Information

Glasgow Information Centre (☎0141-566
4083; www.visitscotland.com; 10 Sauchiehall
St; ⊙9am-6pm Mon-Sat, 10am-5pm Sun Jun-
Aug, 9am-5pm Mon-Sat, 10am-5pm Sun Apr &
May, 9am-5pm Mon-Sat, 10am-4pm Sun Sep-
Mar; 🖥) In the heart of the shopping area.

ℹ Getting There & Away

AIR
Ten miles west of the city, **Glasgow International Airport** (GLA; ☎0844 481 5555; www.
glasgowairport.com) handles international
and domestic flights. **Prestwick Airport** (PIK;
☎0871 223 0700; www.glasgowprestwick.
com), 30 miles southwest of Glasgow, is used
by **Ryanair** (www.ryanair.com) and some other
budget airlines, with connections to the rest of
Britain and Europe.

BUS
All long-distance buses arrive at and depart
from **Buchanan bus station** (☎0141-333
3708; www.spt.co.uk; Killermont St). **Megabus**
(☎0141-352 4444; www.megabus.com) offers
very cheap demand-dependent prices on many
major bus routes, including to Edinburgh and
London. **Scottish Citylink** (☎0871 266 3333;
www.citylink.co.uk) has buses to Edinburgh
(£7.30, 1¼ hours, every 15 minutes) and most
major towns in Scotland. National Express
(www.nationalexpress.com) also runs daily to
several English cities.

TRAIN
As a general rule, Glasgow Central station
serves southern Scotland, England and Wales,
and Queen St station serves the north and east.
Buses run between the two stations every 10
minutes. There are direct trains to London's
Euston station; they're much quicker (advance
purchase single £56, full fare off-peak/peak
£130/176, 4½ hours, more than hourly) and
more comfortable than the bus.

DON'T MISS

THE GENIUS OF CHARLES RENNIE MACKINTOSH

Charles Rennie Mackintosh (1868–1928) is to Glasgow what Gaudí is to Barcelona. Ad
esigner, architect and master of the art-nouveau style, his quirky, linear and geometric
designs are seen all over Glasgow. Many of his buildings are open to the public, though
his masterpiece, the **Glasgow School of Art**, was closed after being badly damaged
by fire in 2014. If you're a fan, the **Mackintosh Trail ticket** (£10), available at the tourist office or any Mackintosh building, gives you a day's free admission to all his creations,
plus unlimited bus and subway travel. Highlights include the following:

Willow Tearooms (www.willowtearooms.co.uk; 217 Sauchiehall St; ⊙9am-5pm Mon-Sat,
10.30am-5pm Sun) FREE

Mackintosh House (www.hunterian.gla.ac.uk; 82 Hillhead St; adult/child £5/3; ⊙10am-5pm
Tue-Sat, 11am-4pm Sun)

House for an Art Lover (☎0141-353 4770; www.houseforanartlover.co.uk; Bellahouston
Park, Dumbreck Rd; adult/child £4.50/3; ⊙10am-4pm Mon-Wed, to 12.30pm Thu-Sun)

Scotrail (📞 0344 811 0141; www.scotrail.co.uk) runs Scottish trains. Destinations include Edinburgh (£12.50, 50 minutes, every 15 minutes) and Inverness (£84.70, 3½ hours, 10 daily, four on Sunday).

Inverness & Loch Ness

📞 01463 / POP 61,200

Inverness has a great location astride the River Ness at the northern end of the Great Glen. In summer it overflows with visitors intent on monster hunting at nearby Loch Ness, but it's worth a visit in its own right for a stroll along the picturesque River Ness, a cruise on Loch Ness, and a meal in one of the city's excellent restaurants.

◉ Sights

Loch Ness Centre & Exhibition
INTERPRETATION CENTRE

(📞 01456-450573; www.lochness.com; adult/child £7.95/4.95; ☉ 9.30am-6pm Jul & Aug, to 5pm Easter-Jun, Sep & Oct, 10am-3.30pm Nov-Easter; 🅿 🚻) This Nessie-themed attraction adopts a scientific approach that allows you to weigh the evidence for yourself. Exhibits include the original equipment – sonar survey vessels, miniature submarines, cameras and sediment coring tools – used in various monster hunts, as well as original photographs and film footage of sightings. You'll find out about hoaxes and optical illusions, as well as learning a lot about the ecology of Loch Ness – is there enough food in the loch to support even one 'monster', let alone a breeding population?

Urquhart Castle
CASTLE

(HS; 📞 01456-450551; adult/child £8.50/5.10; ☉ 9.30am-6pm Apr-Sep, to 5pm Oct, to 4.30pm Nov-Mar; 🅿) Commanding a brilliant location 1.5 miles east of Drumnadrochit, with outstanding views (on a clear day), Urquhart Castle is a popular Nessie-watching hot spot. A huge visitor centre (most of which is beneath ground level) includes a video theatre (with a dramatic 'unveiling' of the castle at the end of the film) and displays of medieval items discovered in the castle.

🛏 Sleeping & Eating

Bazpackers Backpackers Hotel
HOSTEL £

(📞 01463-717663; www.bazpackershostel.co.uk; 4 Culduthel Rd; dm/tw £18/50; @ 🛜) This may be Inverness' smallest hostel (34 beds), but it's hugely popular. It's a friendly, quiet place – the main building has a convivial

WORTH A TRIP

LOCH LOMOND

The 'bonnie banks' and 'bonnie braes' of Loch Lomond have long been Glasgow's rural retreat. The main tourist focus is on the loch's western shore, along the A82. The eastern shore, followed by the West Highland Way long-distance footpath, is quieter. The region's importance was recognised when it became the heart of **Loch Lomond & the Trossachs National Park** (www.lochlomond-trossachs.org) – Scotland's first national park, created in 2002.

The main centre for Loch Lomond boat trips is Balloch, where **Sweeney's Cruises** (📞 01389-752376; www.sweeneyscruises.com; Balloch Rd) offers a range of outings, including a one-hour cruise to Inchmurrin and back (adult/child £8.50/5, departs hourly). Balloch is connected to Glasgow by bus (£4.50, 1½ hours, at least two per hour) or train (£5.10, 45 minutes, every 30 minutes).

lounge centred on a wood-burning stove, and a small garden and great views (some rooms are in a separate building with no garden). The dorms and kitchen can be a bit cramped, but the showers are great.

Velocity Cafe
CAFE £

(📞 01463-419956; velocitylove.co.uk; 1 Crown Ave; mains £4-7; ☉ 9am-5pm Mon, Wed, Fri & Sat, 9am-9pm Thu, 11am-5pm Sun; 🛜 🚼 🚻) 🍴 This cyclists' cafe serves soups, sandwiches and salads prepared with organic, locally sourced produce, as well as yummy cake and coffee. There's also a workshop where you can repair your bike or book a session with a mechanic.

ⓘ Information

Inverness Tourist Office (📞 01463-252401; www.visithighlands.com; Castle Wynd; internet access per 20min £1; ☉ 9am-5pm Mon-Sat & 10am-3pm Sun, longer hours Mar-Oct) Bureau de change and accommodation booking service; also sells tickets for tours and cruises.

ⓘ Getting There & Around

BUS

Services depart from **Inverness bus station** (Margaret St) and include Edinburgh (£30, 3½ to 4½ hours, hourly), Glasgow (£30, 3½ to 4½ hours, hourly) and London (£45, 13 hours, one daily; more frequent services requiring a change at Glasgow).

If you book far enough in advance, **Megabus** (☎ 0141-352 4444; www.megabus.com) offers fares from as little as £1 for buses from Inverness to Glasgow and Edinburgh, and £10 to London.

Buses from Inverness to Fort William run along the shores of Loch Ness (six to eight daily, five on Sunday); those headed for Skye turn off at Invermoriston. There are bus stops at Drumnadrochit (£3.20, 30 minutes) and Urquhart Castle car park (£3.50, 35 minutes).

TRAIN
Edinburgh £41, 3½ hours, eight daily
Glasgow £41, 3½ hours, eight daily
London £100, eight to nine hours, one daily direct; others require a change at Edinburgh

Isle of Skye

POP 10,000

The second-largest of Scotland's islands is a 50-mile-long patchwork of velvet moors, jagged mountains, sparkling lochs and towering sea cliffs. Skye takes its name from the old Norse *sky-a*, meaning 'cloud island', a Viking reference to the often mist-enshrouded **Cuillin Hills**, Britain's most spectacular mountain range. The stunning scenery is the main attraction, including the cliffs and pinnacles of the **Old Man of Storr, Kilt Rock** and the **Quiraing**, but there are plenty of cosy pubs to retire to when the rain clouds close in. There are also dozens of art galleries and craft studios (ask at Portree tourist office for the free *Gallery & Studio Trails* booklet).

The tourist hordes tend to stick to Portree, Dunvegan and Trotternish – it's almost always possible to find peace and quiet in the island's further-flung corners. Come prepared for changeable weather: when it's fine it's very fine indeed, but all too often it isn't.

⊙ Sights & Activities

Skye offers some of the finest – and in places, the roughest and most difficult – **walking** in Scotland.

The Cuillin Hills is a playground for **rock climbers**, and the two-day traverse of the Cuillin Ridge is the finest mountaineering expedition in the British Isles.

The sheltered coves and sea lochs around Skye's coast also provide water lovers with magnificent sea-kayaking opportunities.

Dunvegan Castle   CASTLE
(☎ 01470-521206;   www.dunvegancastle.com; adult/child £10/7; ⊙ 10am-5.30pm Apr–mid-Oct;

P) Skye's most famous historic building, and one of its most popular tourist attractions, Dunvegan Castle is the seat of the chief of Clan MacLeod. It has played host to Samuel Johnson, Sir Walter Scott and, most famously, Flora MacDonald. The oldest parts are the 14th-century keep and dungeon but most of it dates from the 17th to 19th centuries.

Aros Centre   INTERPRETATION CENTRE
(☎ 01478-613750;   www.aros.co.uk;   Viewfield Rd, Portree; sea-eagle exhibition £4.75; ⊙ 9am-5.30pm; P ⛵) On the southern edge of Portree, the Aros Centre is a combined visitor centre, book and gift shop, restaurant, theatre and cinema. The visitor centre (Easter to October) offers a look at fascinating, live CCTV images from local sea-eagle nests, and a wide-screen video of Skye's impressive scenery (it's worth waiting for the aerial shots of the Cuillin).

🛏 Sleeping & Eating

Bayfield Backpackers   HOSTEL £
(☎ 01478-612231; www.skyehostel.co.uk; Bayfield; dm £18; P @ �🛜) Clean, central and modern, this hostel provides the best backpacker accommodation in town. The owner really makes you feel welcome, and is a fount of advice on what to do and where to go in Skye.

Café Arriba   CAFE £
(☎ 01478-611830;   www.cafearriba.co.uk;   Quay Brae; mains £5-10; ⊙ 7am-6pm daily May-Sep, 8am-5pm Thu-Sat Oct-Apr; ✍) 🌿 Arriba is a funky little cafe, brightly decked out in primary colours and offering delicious flatbread melts (bacon, leek and cheese is our favourite) as well as the best choice of vegetarian grub on the island, ranging from a vegie breakfast fry-up to felafel wraps with hummus and chilli sauce. Also serves excellent coffee.

❶ Getting There & Away

BOAT
Despite the bridge, there are still a couple of ferry links between Skye and the mainland. Ferries also operate from Uig on Skye to the Outer Hebrides.

Mallaig to Armadale (www.calmac.co.uk; per person/car £4.65/23.90) The Mallaig to Armadale ferry (30 minutes, eight daily Monday to Saturday, five to seven on Sunday) is very popular on weekends and in July and August, so book ahead if you're travelling by car.

OTHER BRITISH HIGHLIGHTS

Cornwall The southwestern tip of Britain is ringed with rugged granite seacliffs, sparkling bays, picturesque fishing villages and white sandy beaches.

Liverpool The city's waterfront is a World Heritage Site crammed with top museums including the International Slavery Museum and the Beatles Story.

Pembrokeshire Wales' western extremity is famous for its beaches and coastal walks, as well as being home to one of Britain's finest Norman castles.

Glen Coe Scotland's most famous glen combines those two essential qualities of Highlands landscape: dramatic scenery and deep history.

Climbing Ben Nevis Join the 100,000 people who reach the 1344m peak, the highest point in the British Isles.

Glenelg to Kylerhea (www.skyeferry.co.uk; car with up to four passengers £15; ☺ Easter-mid Oct) Runs a tiny vessel (six cars only) on the short Kylerhea to Glenelg crossing (five minutes, every 20 minutes). The ferry operates from 10am to 6pm daily (till 7pm June to August).

BUS
Glasgow to Portree £41, seven hours, three daily
Glasgow to Uig £41, 7½ hours, two daily; via Crianlarich, Fort William and Kyle of Lochalsh
Inverness to Portree £24, 3¼ hours, three daily

Great Britain Survival Guide

ℹ Directory A–Z

ACCOMMODATION
Accommodation can be difficult to find during holidays (especially around Easter and New Year) and major events (such as the Edinburgh Festival). In summer, popular spots (York, Canterbury, Bath etc) get very crowded, so booking ahead is essential. Local tourist offices often provide an accommodation booking service for a small fee.

Hostels The two main types are those run by the Youth Hostels Association (www.yha.org.uk) and Scottish Youth Hostels Association (www.syha.org.uk); and independent hostels, most of which are listed in the Independent Hostels Guide (www.independenthostelguide.co.uk). The simplest hostels cost around £15 per person per night. Larger hostels with more facilities are £18 to £25. London's YHA hostels cost from £30.

B&Bs Bed and breakfast (B&B) is a great British institution. At smaller places it's pretty much a room in somebody's house; larger

places may be called a 'guesthouse' (halfway between a B&B and a full hotel). Prices start from around £25 per person for a simple bedroom and shared bathroom; for around £30 to £35 per person you get a private bathroom – either down the hall or an en suite.

Camping Campsites range from farmers' fields with a tap and basic toilet, costing from £3 per person per night, to smarter affairs with hot showers and many other facilities, charging up to £13. You usually need all your own equipment.

INTERNET RESOURCES
Visit Britain (www.visitbritain.com) Comprehensive national tourism website.

LGBT TRAVELLERS
Resources include the following:
Diva (www.divamag.co.uk)
Gay Times (www.gaytimes.co.uk)
London Lesbian & Gay Switchboard (www.llgs.org.uk)

OPENING HOURS
Standard opening hours:
Banks 9.30am to 4pm or 5pm Monday to Friday; main branches 9.30am to 1pm Saturday
Post Offices 9am to 5pm (5.30pm or 6pm in cities) Monday to Friday, 9am to 12.30pm Saturday (main branches to 5pm)
Pubs 11am to 11pm Sunday to Thursday, 11am to midnight or 1am Friday and Saturday
Restaurants lunch noon to 3pm, dinner 6pm to 10pm; hours vary widely

PUBLIC HOLIDAYS
In many areas of Britain, bank holidays are just for the banks – many businesses and visitor attractions stay open.
New Year's Day 1 January
Easter March/April (Good Friday to Easter Monday inclusive)
May Day First Monday in May

ℹ PRICE RANGES

In accommodation reviews, a budget listing (indicated by the symbol **£**) refers to a double room with a private bathroom or a dorm bed in a hostel for less than £60 (£100 in London).

In restaurant/food reviews, the prices we quote are for a main course at dinner unless otherwise indicated. The symbol used in each review (**£**) indicates premises where a meal costs less than £9.

Spring Bank Holiday Last Monday in May
Summer Bank Holiday Last Monday in August
Christmas Day 25 December
Boxing Day 26 December

TELEPHONE

The UK uses the GSM 900/1800 network, which covers the rest of Europe, Australia and New Zealand, but isn't compatible with the North American GSM 1900. Most modern mobiles can function on both networks – but check before you leave home just in case.

Area codes in the UK do not have a standard format or length. In our reviews, area codes and phone numbers have been listed together, separated by a hyphen.

Other codes include ✆ 0500 or ✆ 0800 for free calls, ✆ 0845 for local rates, ✆ 087 for national rates and ✆ 089 or ✆ 09 for premium rates.

Mobile phones start with ✆ 07 and calling them is more expensive than calling a landline.

Dial ✆ 100 for an operator and ✆ 155 for an international operator as well as reverse-charge (collect) calls.

To call outside the UK, dial ✆ 00, then the country code, the area code (you usually drop the initial zero) and the number.

ℹ Getting There & Away

AIR

London is served by five airports; **Heathrow** (LHR; www.heathrowairport.com; ☎) and **Gatwick** (LGW; www.gatwickairport.com; ☎) are the busiest. Regional airports include **Cardiff** (p88), **Manchester** (p86), **Edinburgh** (p98) and **Glasgow** (GLA; ✆ 0844 481 5555; www.glasgowairport.com).

LAND
Bus & Coach

The international network **Eurolines** (www.eurolines.com) connects a huge number of European destinations via the Channel Tunnel or ferry crossings. Services to and from Britain are operated by **National Express** (www.nationalexpress.com).

Train

The quickest way to Europe from Britain is via the Channel Tunnel. High-speed **Eurostar** (www.eurostar.com) passenger services shuttle at least 10 times daily between London and Paris (2½ hours) or Brussels (two hours) via the Channel Tunnel. The normal one-way fare between London and Paris/Brussels costs £140 to £180; cheaper fares as low as £39 one way are possible via advance booking and by travelling off-peak.

Vehicles use the **Eurotunnel** (www.eurotunnel.com) at Folkestone in England or Calais in France. The trains run four times an hour from 6am to 10pm, then hourly. The journey takes 35 minutes. The one-way cost for a car and passengers is between £75 and £165 depending on time of day; promotional fares often bring it down to £55.

Travelling between Ireland and Britain, the main train–ferry–train route is Dublin to London, via Dun Laoghaire and Holyhead. Ferries also run between Rosslare and Fishguard or Pembroke (Wales), with train connections on either side.

SEA

Ferries sail from southern England to French ports in a couple of hours; other routes connect eastern England to the Netherlands, Germany and northern Spain, and Ireland from southwest Scotland and Wales.

The main ferry routes between Britain and mainland Europe include Dover to Calais or Boulogne (France), Harwich to Hook of Holland (Netherlands), Hull to Zeebrugge (Belgium) or Rotterdam (Netherlands), and Portsmouth to Santander or Bilbao (Spain). Routes to and from Ireland include Holyhead to Dun Laoghaire. Competition from the Eurotunnel and budget airlines means ferry operators discount heavily at certain times of year. The short cross-channel routes such as Dover to Calais or Boulogne can be as low as £20 for a car plus up to five passengers, although around £50 is more likely.

If you're a foot passenger, or cycling, crossings can start from as little as £10 each way. Broker sites covering all routes and options include www.ferrybooker.com and www.directferries.co.uk.

ℹ Getting Around

For travellers on a budget, public transport is the best way to go. Cheapest but slowest are long-distance buses (called coaches in Britain). Trains are faster but much more expensive.

AIR

Britain's domestic air companies include **British Airways** (www.britishairways.com), **Flybe/Loganair** (%0871 700 2000; www.loganair.co.uk), **EasyJet** (www.easyjet.com) and **Ryanair** (www.ryanair.com). On most shorter routes (eg London to Newcastle, or Manchester to Bristol), it's often faster to take the train once airport downtime is factored in.

BUS

Long-distance buses (coaches) nearly always offer the cheapest way to get around. Many towns have separate stations for local buses and intercity coaches; make sure you're in the right one.

National Express (www.nationalexpress.com) is England's main coach operator. North of the border, **Scottish Citylink** (www.citylink.co.uk) is the leading coach company. Tickets are cheaper if you book in advance and travel at quieter times. As a rough guide, a 200-mile trip (eg London to York) will cost around £15 to £30 if booked a few days in advance.

Also offering cheap fares (if you're lucky, from £1) is **Megabus** (www.megabus.com), which serves about 30 destinations around Britain.

Bus Passes

National Express offers discount passes to full-time students and under-26s, called Young Persons Coachcards. They cost £10 and give 30% off standard adult fares. Also available are coachcards for people over 60, families and travellers with a disability.

For touring the country, National Express offers Brit Xplorer passes, allowing unlimited travel for seven days (£79), 14 days (£139) and 28 days (£219).

CAR & MOTORCYCLE

Car rental is expensive in Britain; you'll pay from around £120 per week for the smallest model, or £250 per week for a medium-sized car (including insurance and unlimited mileage). All the major players including Avis, Hertz and Budget operate here.

Using a rental-broker site such as JK Car Hire (www.ukcarhire.net) or Kayak (www.kayak.com) can help find bargains. It's illegal to drive a car or motorbike in Britain without (at least) third-party insurance. This is included with all rental cars.

TRAIN

About 20 different companies operate train services in Britain, while Network Rail operates tracks and stations. For some passengers this system can be confusing at first, but information and ticket-buying services are mostly centralised. If you have to change trains, or use two or more train operators, you still buy one ticket – valid for the whole journey. The main railcards and passes are also accepted by all train operators.

National Rail Enquiries (08457 48 49 50; www.nationalrail.co.uk) provides booking and timetable information for Britain's entire rail network.

Classes, Cost & Reservations

Rail travel has two classes: 1st and standard. Travelling 1st class costs around 50% more than standard. At weekends some train operators offer 'upgrades' to first class for an extra £5 to £25 on top of your standard class fare, payable on the spot.

The earlier you book, the cheaper it gets. You can also save if you travel 'off-peak' (ie the days and times that aren't busy). If you buy online, you can have the ticket posted (UK addresses only), or collect it from station machines on the day of travel.

There are three main fare types:

Anytime Buy anytime, travel anytime – usually the most expensive option.

Off-peak Buy anytime, travel off-peak (what is off-peak depends on the journey).

Advance Buy in advance, travel only on specific trains (usually the cheapest option).

Train Passes

If you're staying in Britain for a while, passes known as railcards (www.railcard.co.uk) are available:

16–25 Railcard For those aged 16 to 25, or a full-time UK student.

Senior Railcard For anyone over 60.

Family & Friends Railcard Covers up to four adults and four children travelling together. Railcards cost £30 (valid for one year, available from major stations or online) and get 33% discount on most train fares, except those already heavily discounted. With the Family card, adults get 33% and children get 60% discounts, so the fee is easily repaid in a couple of journeys.

Various local train passes are also available covering specific areas and lines – ask at a local train station to get an idea of what's available.

National Passes

For country-wide travel, **BritRail** (www.britrail.net) passes are available for visitors from overseas. They must be bought in your country of origin (not in Britain) from a specialist travel agency. Available in seven different versions (eg England only; Scotland only; all Britain; UK and Ireland) for periods from four to 30 days.

IRELAND

Dublin

☑ 01 / POP 1.3 MILLION

Sultry rather than sexy, Dublin exudes personality as only those who've managed to turn careworn into carefree can. The halcyon days of the Celtic Tiger (the Irish economic boom of the late 1990s), when cash cascaded like a free-flowing waterfall, have long since disappeared, and the city has once again been forced to grind out a living. But Dubliners still know how to enjoy life. They do so through their music, art and literature – things that Dubs often take for granted but, once reminded, generate immense pride.

There are world-class museums, superb restaurants and the best range of entertainment available anywhere in Ireland – and that's not including the pub, the ubiquitous centre of the city's social life and an absolute must for any visitor. And should you wish to get away from it all, the city has a handful of seaside towns at its edges that make for wonderful day trips.

⊙ Sights

Dublin's finest Georgian architecture, including its famed doorways, is found around **St Stephen's Green** (⊙ dawn-dusk; 🚇 all city centre, 🚇 St Stephen's Green) and **Merrion Square** (⊙ dawn-dusk; 🚇 7 & 44 from city centre) just south of Trinity College; both are prime picnic spots when the sun shines.

O'Connell St, Dublin's grandest avenue, is dominated by the needle-like **Spire** (🚇 all city centre, 🚇 Abbey). It rises more than 120m from the spot once occupied by a statue of Admiral Nelson, which was blown up by the Irish Republican Army (IRA) in 1966. Nearby is the 1815 **General Post Office** (☎ 01-705 7000; www.anpost.ie; Lower O'Connell St; ⊙ 8am-8pm Mon-Sat; 🚇 all city centre, 🚇 Abbey), an important landmark of the 1916 Easter Rising, when the Irish Volunteers used it as a base for attacks against the British army.

★**Trinity College**　　　HISTORIC BUILDING
(☎ 01-896 1000; www.tcd.ie; College Green; ⊙ 8am-10pm; 🚇 all city centre) **FREE** Ireland's most prestigious university is a bucolic retreat in the heart of the city that puts one in mind of the great universities like Oxford, Cambridge or Harvard. Just ambling about its cobbled squares it's easy to imagine it in those far-off days when all good gentlemen (for they were only men) came equipped with a passion for philosophy and a love of empire. The student body is a lot more diverse these days, even if the look remains the same.

★**Long Room**　　　NOTABLE BUILDING
(www.tcd.ie/visitors/book-of-kells; East Pavilion, Library Colonnades, Trinity College; adult/student/child €10/9/free; ⊙ 9.30am-5pm Mon-Sat year-round, noon-4.30pm Sun Oct-Apr, 9.30am-4.30pm Sun May-Sep; 🚇 all city centre) Trinity's greatest treasures are kept in the Old Library's stunning 65m Long Room, which houses about 200,000 of the library's oldest volumes, including the **Book of Kells**, a breathtaking, illuminated manuscript of the four Gospels of the New Testament, created around AD 800 by monks on the Scottish island of Iona. Other displays include a rare copy of the **Proclamation of the Irish Republic**, which was read out by Pádraig Pearse at the beginning of the Easter Rising in 1916.

★**Guinness Storehouse**　　　BREWERY, MUSEUM
(www.guinness-storehouse.com; St James's Gate, South Market St; adult/student/child €18/16/6.50, connoisseur experience €48; ⊙ 9.30am-5pm Sep-Jun, to 7pm Jul & Aug; 🚇 21A, 51B, 78, 78A, 123 from Fleet St, 🚇 James's) The most popular visit in town is this multimedia homage to Guinness, one of Ireland's most enduring symbols. A converted grain storehouse is the only part of the 26-hectare brewery that is open to the public, but it's a suitable cathedral in which to worship the black gold. Across its seven floors you'll discover everything about Guinness before getting to taste it in the top-floor **Gravity Bar**, with its panoramic views. Pre-booking your tickets online will save you money.

★**Chester Beatty Library**　　　MUSEUM
(☎ 01-407 0750; www.cbl.ie; ⊙ 10am-5pm Mon-Fri, 11am-5pm Sat, 1-5pm Sun year-round, closed Mon Nov-Feb, free tours 1pm Wed, 3pm & 4pm Sun) **FREE** This world-famous library, in the grounds of **Dublin Castle** (☎ 01-677 7129; www.dublincastle.ie; Dame St; adult/child €8.50/6.50; ⊙ 9.45am-4.45pm Mon-Sat, noon-4.45pm Sun; 🚇 all city centre), houses the collection of mining engineer Sir Alfred Chester Beatty (1875–1968), bequeathed to the Irish State on his death. And we're immensely grateful for Chester's patronage: spread over two floors, the breathtaking collection includes more than 20,000 manuscripts, rare

books, miniature paintings, clay tablets, costumes and other objects of artist c, historical and aesthetic importance.

★ **Kilmainham Gaol**   MUSEUM
(www.heritageireland.com; Inchicore Rd; adult/child €7/3; ⊙9.30am-6pm daily Apr-Sep, 9.30am-5.30pm Mon-Sat, 10am-6pm Sun Oct-Mar; 🚌26, 51X, 68, 69, 79 from city centre) If you have *any* desire to understand Irish history – especially the juicy bits about resistance to British rule – then a visit to this former prison is an absolute must. This threatening grey building, built between 1792 and 1795, played a role in virtually every act of Ireland's painful path to independence, and even today, despite closing in 1924, it still has the power to chill.

★ **National Gallery**   MUSEUM
(www.nationalgallery.ie; West Merrion Sq; ⊙9.30am-5.30pm Mon-Wed, Fri & Sat, to 8.30pm Thu, noon-5.30pm Sun; 🚌7, 44 from city centre) **FREE** A magnificent Caravaggio and a breathtaking collection of works by Jack B Yeats – William Butler's younger brother – are the main reasons to visit the National Gallery, but not the only ones. Its excellent collection is strong in Irish art, and there are also high-quality collections of every major European school of painting.

★ **St Patrick's Cathedral**   CATHEDRAL
(www.stpatrickscathedral.ie; St Patrick's Close; adult/student/child €6/5/free; ⊙9.30am-5pm Mon-Fri, 9am-6pm Sat, 9-10.30am & 12.30-2.30pm Sun; 🚌50, 50A, 56A from Aston Quay, 54, 54A from Burgh Quay) Ireland's largest church is St Patrick's Cathedral, built between 1191 and 1270 on the site of an earlier church that had stood here since the 5th century. It was here that St Patrick himself reputedly baptised the local Celtic chieftains, making this bit of ground some fairly sacred turf: the well in question is in the adjacent St Patrick's Park, which was once a slum but is now a lovely spot to sit and take a load off.

★ **Museum of Natural History**   MUSEUM
(National Museum of Ireland – Natural History; www.museum.ie; Upper Merrion St; ⊙10am-5pm Tue-Sat, 2-5pm Sun; 🚌7, 44 from city centre) **FREE** Dusty, weird and utterly compelling, this window into Victorian times has barely changed since Scottish explorer Dr David Livingstone opened it in 1857 – before disappearing into the African jungle for a meeting with Henry Stanley. It is a fine example of

ℹ **DISCOUNT CARDS**

Dublin Pass (adult/child one day €49/29, three day €79/49) For heavy-duty sightseeing, the Dublin Pass will save you a packet. It provides free entry to over 25 attractions (including the Guinness Storehouse), discounts at 20 others and guaranteed fast-track entry to some of the busiest attractions. To avail of the free Aircoach transfer to and from the airport, order the card online so you have it when you land. Otherwise, it's available from any Discover Ireland Dublin Tourism Centre.

Heritage Card (adult/child & student €25/10) This card entitles you to free access to all sights in and around Dublin managed by the Office of Public Works (OPW). You can buy it at OPW sites or Dublin Tourism offices.

Victorian charm and scientific wonderment, and its enormous collection is a testament to the skill of taxidermy.

★ **National Museum of Ireland – Decorative Arts & History**   MUSEUM
(www.museum.ie; Benburb St; ⊙10am-5pm Tue-Sat, 2-5pm Sun; 🚌25, 66, 67, 90 from city centre, 🚇Museum) **FREE** Once the world's largest military barracks, this splendid early neoclassical grey-stone building on the Liffey's northern banks was completed in 1704 according to the design of Thomas Burgh, whose CV also includes the Old Library in Trinity College and St Michan's Church. It is now home to the Decorative Arts & History collection of the National Museum of Ireland.

National Museum of Ireland – Archaeology   MUSEUM
(www.museum.ie; Kildare St; ⊙10am-5pm Tue-Sat, 2-5pm Sun; 🚌all city centre) **FREE** Ireland's most important cultural institution was established in 1877 as the primary repository of the nation's archaeological treasures. These include the most famous of Ireland's crafted artefacts, the **Ardagh Chalice** and the **Tara Brooch**, dating from the 12th and 8th centuries respectively. They are part of the **Treasury**, itself part of Europe's finest collection of Bronze and Iron Age gold artefacts, and the most complete assemblage of medieval Celtic metalwork in the world.

Dublin

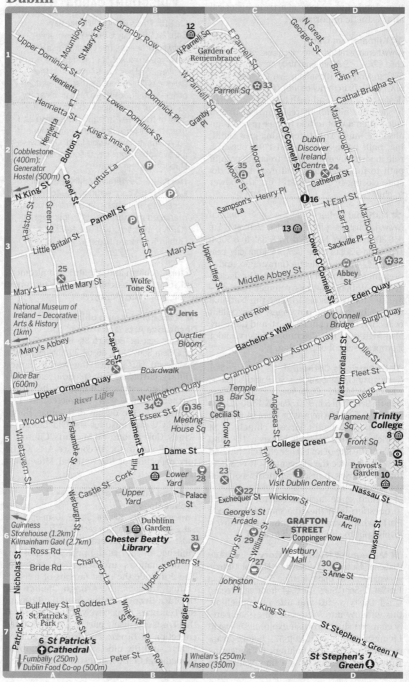

Map labels

N 0 — 200 m
0 — 0.1 miles

Gloucester Pl
Diamond Park
Lower Gloucester Pl
Lower Seán MacDermot St
Lower Buckingham St
Railway St
Lower Gardiner St
Corporation St
Foley St
Connolly
Talbot St
Moland Pl
Frenchman's La
20 Pl
Talbot St
19 Busáras
Lower Major St
Lower Abbey St
Memorial Rd
Epic Ireland (150m)
Beresford Pl
Custom House Quay
River Liffey
Talbot Memorial Bridge
George's Quay
City Quay
Tara St Station
Poolbeg St
Tara St
Moss St
Dowlings Ct
Townsend St
Bord Gáis Energy Theatre (600m)
Botany Bay
Pearse St
Artisan Parlour & Grocery (1.6km)
Library Sq
New Sq
21
Westland Row
Long Room
Fellows' Sq
9
College Park
Lincoln Pl
Frederick La
4 National Gallery
Clare St
Molesworth St
Clare La
National Museum of Ireland – Archaeology
5
W Merrion Sq
3 Museum of Natural History
14
S Merrion Sq
Kildare St
James Toner's (250m)

Dublin

◎ Top Sights

1 Chester Beatty Library B6
2 Long Room E5
3 Museum of Natural History E7
4 National Gallery F6
5 National Museum of Irelanc –
  Archaeology E7
6 St Patrick's Cathedral A7
7 St Stephen's Green D7
8 Trinity College D5

◎ Sights

9 Arts & Social Science Building E5
10 Douglas Hyde Gallery of
   Modern Art D5
11 Dublin Castle B5
12 Dublin City Gallery – Hugh
   Lane B1
13 General Post Office C3
14 Merrion Square F7
15 Old Library D5
16 Spire D3

⊕ Activities, Courses & Tours

Historical Walking Tour .... (see 17)
17 Trinity College Walking Tour D5

⊟ Sleeping

18 Barnacles C5
19 Isaacs Hostel E3
20 Jacob's Inn F2
21 Trinity College E5

✕ Eating

22 Fallon & Byrne C6
23 Honest to Goodness C5
24 M&L D2
25 Oxmantown A3
   Silk Road Café .... (see 1)
26 Soup Dragon B4

⊙ Drinking & Nightlife

27 Clement & Pekoe C6
28 George B5
29 Grogan's Castle Lounge C6
30 Kehoe's D6
31 Long Hall B6

✿ Entertainment

32 Abbey Theatre D3
33 Gate Theatre C1
34 Workman's Club B5

⊞ Shopping

35 Moore Street Market C2
36 Temple Bar Food Market B5

Dublin City Gallery – Hugh Lane   GALLERY

(☑01-222 5550; www.hughlane.ie; 22 N Parnell Sq; ⊙10am-6pm Tue-Thu, to 5pm Fri & Sat, 11am-5pm Sun; ☐3, 7, 10, 11, 13, 16, 19, 46A, 123) **FREE** Whatever reputation Dublin has as a repository of world-class art has a lot to do with the simply stunning collection at this exquisite gallery, housed in the equally impressive Charlemont House, designed by William Chambers in 1763. Within its walls you'll find the best of contemporary Irish art, a handful of impressionist classics and the relocated Francis Bacon's studio.

Epic Ireland   MUSEUM

(☑01-531 3688; epicirelandchq.com; CHQ Building, Custom House Quay; adult/child €16/€8; ⊙9am-7pm; ☐George's Dock) Dublin's newest museum is a high-tech, interactive exploration of emigration and its effect on Ireland and the 70 million or so people spread throughout the world that claim Irish ancestry. Start your visit with a 'passport' and proceed through 21 galleries examining why they left, where they went and how they maintained their relationship with their ancestral home.

☞ Tours

Download **iWalks** (www.visitdublin.com/iwalks) from the tourist-office website and explore the city with an expert's voice leading the way.

★Historical Walking Tour   WALKING TOUR

(☑01-878 0227; www.historicaltours.ie; Trinity College Gate; adult/child €12/free; ⊙11am & 3pm May-Sep, 11am Apr & Oct, 11am Fri-Sun Nov-Mar; ☐all city centre) Trinity College history graduates lead this 'seminar on the street' that explores the Potato Famine, Easter Rising, Civil War and Partition. Sights include Trinity, City Hall, Dublin Castle and Four Courts. In summer, themed tours on architecture, women in Irish history and the birth of the Irish state are also held. Tours depart from the College Green entrance.

Trinity College Walking Tour   WALKING TOUR

(Authenticity Tours; www.tcd.ie/Library/bookofkells/trinity-tours; Trinity College; tours €6, incl Book of Kells €13; ⊙10.15am-3.40pm Mon-Sat, to 3.15pm Sun May-Sep, fewer midweek tours Oct & Feb-Apr) A great way to see Trinity's grounds is on a student-led walking tour, which depart from the College Green entrance every 20 to 40 minutes.

🛌 Sleeping

★Isaacs Hostel   HOSTEL €

(☑01-855 6215; www.isaacs.ie; 2-5 Frenchman's Lane; dm/tw from €10/54; @ 🛜; ☐all city centre, 🚇Connolly) The north side's best hostel – hell, for atmosphere alone it's the best in town – is in a 200-year-old wine vault just around the corner from the main bus station. With summer barbecues, live music in the lounge, internet access and colourful dorms, this terrific place generates consistently good reviews from backpackers and other travellers.

★Generator Hostel   HOSTEL €

(☑01-901 0222; www.generatorhostels.com; Smithfield Sq; dm/tw from €16/70; @ 🛜) This European chain brings its own brand of funky, fun design to Dublin's hostel scene, with bright colours, comfortable dorms (including women-only) and a lively social scene. It even has a screening room for movies. Good location right on Smithfield Sq, next to the Old Jameson Distillery.

CAMPUS ACCOMMODATION

During the summer months, visitors can opt to stay in campus accommodation, which is both convenient and comfortable.

Trinity College (☑01-896 1177; www.tcd.ie; Accommodations Office, Trinity College; s/d from €76/124; ⊙May-Sep; 🅿 @ 🛜; ☐all cross-city) The closest thing to living like a student at this stunningly beautiful university is crashing in their rooms when they're on holidays. Rooms and two-bed apartments in the newer block have their own bathrooms; those in the older blocks share facilities, though there are private sinks. Breakfast is included.

Dublin City University (DCU; ☑01-700 5736; www.summeraccommodation.dcu.ie; Larkfield Apartments, Campus Residences, Dublin City University; s/d from €60/100; ⊙mid-Jun–mid-Sep; ☐11, 11A, 11B, 13, 13A, 19, 19A from city centre) This accommodation is proof that students slum it in relative luxury. The modern rooms have plenty of amenities at hand, including a kitchen, common room and fully equipped health centre. The Glasnevin campus is only 15 minutes by bus or car from the city centre.

Jacob's Inn   HOSTEL €

(✐ 01-855 5660; www.jacobsinn.com; 21-28 Talbot Pl; dm/d from €12/70; ⚡; 🖥 all city centre, 🚇 Connolly) Sister hostel to Isaacs (p112) around the corner, this clean and modern hostel offers spacious accommodation with private bathrooms and outstanding facilities, including some wheelchair-accessible rooms, a bureau de change, bike storage and a self-catering kitchen.

Barnacles   HOSTEL €

(✐ 01-671 6277; www.barnacles.ie; 19 Lower Temple Lane; dm/tw from €18/60; 🅿 ⚡; 🖥 all city centre) If you're here for a good time, not a long time, then this bustling Temple Bar hostel is the ideal spot to meet fellow revellers, and tap up the helpful and knowledgeable staff for the best places to cause mischief. Rooms are quieter at the back.

✗ Eating

★ Fumbally   CAFE €

(✐ 01-529 8732; www.thefumbally.ie; Fumbally Lane; mains €5-8; ⊘ 8am-5pm Tue-Fri, 10am-5pm Sat, also 7-9.30pm Wed; 🖥 49, 54A, 77X from city centre) A bright, airy warehouse cafe favoured by hipsters, who come for the healthy breakfasts, salads and sandwiches – and the guitarist strumming away in the corner. In 2016 it introduced Wednesday Dinner (mains €15), where a single organic, locally sourced dish (and its vegetarian variant) is served in a communal dining experience; advance bookings suggested

★ Oxmantown   CAFE €

(16 Mary's Abbey, City Markets; sandwiches €5.50-6.90; ⊘ 7.30am-4pm Mon-Fri; 🚇 Four Courts, Jervis) Delicious breakfasts and excellent sandwiches make this relatively new cafe one of the standout places for daytime eating on the north side of the Liffey. Locally baked bread, coffee supplied by Cloud Nine (Dublin's only micro-roastery) and meats sourced from Irish farms are the ingredients, but it's the way it's all put together that makes it so worthwhile.

★ M&L   CHINESE €

(13/14 Cathedral St; mains €9-13; ⊘ 11.30am-10pm Mon-Sat, noon-10pm Sun; 🖥 all city centre) Beyond the plain frontage and the cheap-looking decor is Dublin's best Chinese restaurant...by some distance. It's usually full of Chinese people, who come for the authentic Szechuan-style cuisine – spicier than Cantonese and with none of the concessions usually made to Western palates (no prawn crackers or curry chips).

Artisan Parlour & Grocery   MODERN IRISH €

(11 Fitzwilliam St, Ringsend; mains €6-9, 3-course supper club €26.50; ⊘ 8am-3.30pm Mon-Fri, 10am-3.30pm Sat, also 6-10pm Fri 🖥 1, 47, 56A, 77A, 84N from city centre.) A fine example of Dublin's recent focus on 'village identity' is this excellent deli and cafe, which serves artisan sandwiches (the slow-roasted Lynch's pork belly with lettuce, tomato and Dijonnaise is divine), salads and homemade desserts to an appreciative local clientele. The Friday Supper Club has well-made Irish classics such as fish pie and blade of beef

Honest to Goodness   PIZZA €

(www.honesttogoodness.ie; 12 Dame Ct; mains €6-15; ⊘ 8am-5pm Mon, to 10pm Tue & Wed, to 11pm Thu & Fri, 9am-11pm Sat, 10am-4pm Sun; 🖥 all city centre) By day, the downstairs cafe serves wholesome sandwiches, tasty soups and a near-legendary sloppy joe. By night, the upstairs restaurant serves what might be the best pizza in town – authentic enough to earn a Neapolitan's approval. Terrific staff, wonderful atmosphere.

Soup Dragon   FAST FOOD €

(✐ 01-872 3277; www.soupdragon.com; 168 Capel St; mains €5-8; ⊘ 8am-5pm Mon-Fri; ✐; 🖥 all city centre, 🚇 Jervis) Queues are a regular feature outside this fabulous spot which specialises in soups on the go – but it also does excellent stews, sandwiches, bagels and salads. The all-day breakfast options are excellent – we especially like the mini breakfast quiche of sausage, egg and bacon. Bowls come in two sizes, and prices include fresh bread and a piece of fruit.

♟ Drinking & Nightlife

The plethora of pubs in Temple Bar are a favourite place to start. We urge you to explore further afield: the pubs around Grafton St are a great mix of old-style pubs and stylish modern spots. Camden St, southwest of St Stephen's Green, is very popular, as is Dawson St and Merrion Row – the latter has a couple of long-established favourites.

North of the Liffey has a selection of fine old pubs and genuine locals (read: visitors will be given the once-over), but there are a handful of popular bars, including the **George** (www.thegeorge.ie; 89 S Great George's St; ⊘ 2-11.30pm Mon, 2pm-2.30am Tue-Fri, 12.30pm-2.30am Sat, 12.30pm-1.30am Sun; 🖥 all city centre), Dublin's best gay bar.

SELF-CATERING

If you're looking to self-cater, there are some excellent options, especially south of the river, including **Fallon & Byrne** (www.fallonandbyrne.com; Exchequer St; mains €5-10; ⊘8am-9pm Mon-Wed, 8am-10pm Thu & Fri, 9am-9pm Sat, 11am-7pm Sun; ⊡all city centre), the **Dublin Food Co-op** (www.dublinfoodcoop.com; 12 Newmarket; ⊘noon-8pm Wed-Fri, 9.30am-4.30pm Sat, 11am-5pm Sun; ⊡49, 54A, 77X from city centre) in Newmarket and the **Temple Bar Food Market** (www.templebar.ie; Meeting House Sq; ⊘10am-4.30pm Sat; ⊡all city centre) – not to mention a fine selection of cheesemongers and bakeries. North of the river, the traditional **Moore Street Market** (Moore St; ⊘8am-4pm Mon-Sat; ⊡all city centre) is the city's most famous, where the colour of the produce is matched by the language of the spruikers.

★ **Anseo**   BAR
(18 Lower Camden St; ⊘10.30am-11.30pm Mon-Thu, to 12.30am Fri & Sat, 11am-11pm Sun; ⊡all city centre) Unpretentious, unaffected and incredibly popular, this cosy alternative bar – which is pronounced 'an-*shuh*', the Irish for 'here' – is a favourite with those who live by the credo that to try too hard is far worse than not trying at all. The pub's soundtrack is an eclectic mix; you're as likely to hear Peggy Lee as Lee Perry.

★ **Grogan's Castle Lounge**   PUB
(www.groganspub.ie; 15 S William St; ⊘10.30am-11.30pm Mon-Thu, to 12.30am Fri & Sat, 12.30-11pm Sun) This place, known simply as Grogan's (after the original owner), is a city-centre institution. It has long been a favourite haunt of Dublin's writers and painters, as well as others from the alternative bohemian set, who enjoy a fine Guinness while they wait for that inevitable moment when they're discovered.

★ **James Toner's**   PUB
(139 Lower Baggot St; ⊘10.30am-11.30pm Mon-Thu, to 12.30am Fri & Sat, noon-11pm Sun; ⊡7, 44 from city centre) Toner's, with its stone floors and antique snugs, has changed little over the years and is the closest thing you'll get to a country pub in the heart of the city. The shelves and drawers are reminders that it once doubled as a grocery shop.

★ **Kehoe's**   PUB
(9 S Anne St; ⊘10.30am-11.30pm Mon-Thu, to 12.30am Fri & Sat, noon-11pm Sun; ⊡all city centre) This is one of the most atmospheric pubs in the city centre and a favourite with all kinds of Dubliners. It has a beautiful Victorian bar, a wonderful snug, and plenty of other little nooks and crannies. Upstairs, drinks are served in what was once the publican's living room – and looks it!

★ **Long Hall**   PUB
(51 S Great George's St; ⊘10.30am-11.30pm Mon-Thu, to 12.30am Fri & Sat, noon-11pm Sun; ⊡all city centre) Luxuriating in full Victorian splendour, this is one of the city's most beautiful and best-loved pubs. Check out the ornate carvings in the woodwork behind the bar and the elegant chandeliers. The bartenders are experts at their craft, an increasingly rare attribute in Dublin these days.

Clement & Pekoe   CAFE
(www.clementandpekoe.com; 50 S William St; ⊘8am-7pm Mon-Fri, 10am-6pm Sat, noon-6pm Sun; ⊡all city centre) Our favourite cafe in town is this hipster version of an Edwardian tearoom. Walnut floors, art-deco chandeliers and wall-to-wall displays of handsome tea jars are the perfect setting in which to enjoy the huge selection of loose leaf teas and carefully made coffees, along with a selection of cakes.

☆ Entertainment

For events, reviews and club listings, pick up a copy of the fortnightly music review *Hot Press* (www.hotpress.com), or go online to read Totally Dublin (www.totallydublin.ie). Friday's *Irish Times* (www.irishtimes.com) has a pullout section called 'The Ticket' that has reviews and listings of all things arty.

Whelan's   LIVE MUSIC
(☎01-478 0766; www.whelanslive.com; 25 Wexford St; ⊡16, 122 from city centre) Perhaps the city's most beloved live-music venue is this midsized room attached to a traditional bar. This is the singer-songwriter's spiritual home: when they're done pouring out the contents of their hearts on stage, you can find them filling up in the bar along with their fans.

Cobblestone
PUB

(N King St; ⊘10.30am-11.30pm Mon-Thu, to 12.30am Fri & Sat, noon-11pm Sun; 🔲Smithfield) This pub in the heart of Smithfield has a great atmosphere in its cosy upstairs bar, where there are superb nightly music sessions performed by traditional musicians (especially Thursday) and up-and-coming folk acts.

Workman's Club
LIVE MUSIC

(📞01-670 6692; www.theworkmansclub.com; 10 Wellington Quay; free-€20; ⊘5pm-3am; 🔲all city centre) A 300-capacity venue and bar in the former workingmen's club of Dublin, with an emphasis on keeping away from the mainstream, which means everything from singer-songwriters to electronic cabaret. When the live music at the Workman's Club (Twitter: @WorkmansClubs) is over, DJs take to the stage, playing everything from rockabilly to hip hop and indie to house.

Gate Theatre
THEATRE

(📞01-874 4045; www.gatetheatre.ie 1 Cavendish Row; ⊘performances 7.30pm Mon-Sat, matinees 2.30pm Wed; 🔲all city centre) The city's most elegant theatre, housed in a late-13th-century building, features a generally unflappable repertory of classic Irish, American and European plays. Orson Welles and James Mason played here early in their careers. Even today it is the only theatre in town where you might see established international movie stars work on their credibility with a theatre run.

Bord Gáis Energy Theatre
THEATRE

(📞01-677 7999; www.grandcanaltheatre.ie; Grand Canal Sq; 🚇Grand Canal Dock) Forget the uninviting sponsored name: Daniel Libeskind's masterful design is a three-tiered, 2100-capacity auditorium where you're as likely to be entertained by the Bolshoi or a touring state opera as you are to see Disney on Ice or Barbra Streisand. It's a magnificent venue – designed for classical, paid for by the classics.

Abbey Theatre
THEATRE

(📞01-878 7222; www.abbeytheatre.ie; Lower Abbey St; performances 8pm Mon-Sat, matinees 2.30pm Sat; 🔲all city centre, 🚇Abbey) Ireland's national theatre was founded by WB Yeats in 1904 and was a central player in the development of a consciously native cultural identity. Its relevance has waned dramatically in recent decades but it still provides a mix of Irish classics (Synge, O'Casey etc), established international names (Shepard, Mamet) and contemporary talent (O'Rowe, Carr et al).

ℹ️ Information

Visit Dublin Centre (www.visitdublin.com; 25 Suffolk St; ⊘9am-5.30pm Mon-Sat, 10.30am-3pm Sun; 🔲all city centre) The main tourist information centre, with free maps, guides and itinerary planning, plus booking services for accommodation, attractions and events.

Dublin Discover Ireland Centre (14 Upper O'Connell St; ⊘9am-5pm Mon-Sat; 🔲all city centre)

Grafton Medical Centre (📞01-671 2122; www.graftonmedical.ie; 34 Grafton St; ⊘8.30am-6pm Mon-Fri, 11am-2pm Sat; 🔲all city centre) One-stop shop with male and female doctors and physiotherapists.

St James's Hospital (📞01-410 3000; www.st-james.ie; James's St; 🚇James's) Dublin's main 24-hour accident and emergency department.

ℹ️ Getting There & Away

AIR

Dublin Airport (📞01-814 1111; www.dublinairport.com) Dublin Airport, 13km north of the centre, is Ireland's major international gateway airport. It has two terminals: most international flights (including most US flights) use the newer Terminal 2; Ryanair and select others use Terminal 1. Both terminals have the usual selection of pubs, restaurants, shops, ATMs and car-hire desks.

There is no train service to/from the airport, but there are bus and taxi options.

BOAT

There are direct ferries from Holyhead in Wales to **Dublin Port** (📞01-855 2222; Alexandra Rd), 3km northeast of the city centre, and to **Dun Laoghaire** (📞01-280 1905; 🚌7A or 8 from Burgh Quay, 46A from Trinity College, 🚇Dun Laoghaire), 13km southeast. Boats also sail direct to Dublin Port from Liverpool and from Douglas, on the Isle of Man.

BUS

The main bus terminal **Busáras** (📞01-836 6111; www.buseireann.ie; Store St; 🚇Connolly) is just north of the river behind Custom House.

It's possible to combine bus and ferry tickets from major UK centres to Dublin on the bus network. The journey between London and Dublin takes about 12 hours and costs around €34 return. For details, contact **Eurolines** (📞0870 514 3219; www.eurolines.com).

From here, Bus Eireann buses serve the whole national network, including buses to towns and cities in Northern Ireland.

ℹ LEAP CARD

The Leap Card (www.leapcard.ie) is a plastic smart card available in most newsagents. Once you register it online, you can top it up with whatever amount you need. When you board a bus, Luas or suburban train, just swipe your card and the fare – usually 20% less than a cash fare – is automatically deducted.

TRAIN

Dublin has two main train stations:

Heuston Station (☑ 01-836 5421; ⛉ Heuston Station) On the western side of town near the Liffey, for services to Cork, Galway, Killarney, Limerick and most other points south and west.
Connolly Station (☑ 01-836 3333; ⛉ Connolly Station, ⛉ Connolly Station) North of the Liffey, behind the Custom House, with services to Belfast.

Connolly Station is a stop on the DART line into town; the Luas Red Line serves both Connolly and Heuston stations.

ℹ Getting Around

BICYCLE

One of the most popular ways to get around the city is with the blue bikes of Dublinbikes (www.dublinbikes.ie), a pay-as-you-go service similar to the Parisian Vélib system: cyclists purchase a €10 Smart Card (as well as pay a credit-card deposit of €150) – either online or at any of the 40 stations throughout the city centre – before 'freeing' a bike for use, which is then free of charge for the first 30 minutes and €0.50 for each half-hour thereafter.

BUS

Dublin Bus (www.dublinbus.ie) Local buses cost from €2 to €3.30 for a single journey. You must pay the exact fare when boarding; drivers don't give change.
Freedom Ticket (adult/child €33/14) Three-day unlimited travel on all bus services, including Airlink and Dublin Bus Hop-On, Hop-Off tours.

TRAIN

The **Dublin Area Rapid Transport** (DART; ☑ 01-836 6222; www.irishrail.ie) provides quick train access to the coast as far north as Howth (about 30 minutes) and as far south as Greystones in County Wicklow. Pearse Station is convenient for central Dublin south of the Liffey, and Connolly Station for north of the Liffey. A one-way DART ticket from Dublin to Dun Laoghaire or Howth costs €3.25.

TRAM

The Luas (www.luas.ie) light-rail system has two lines: the green line (running every five to 15 minutes) connects St Stephen's Green with Sandyford in south Dublin via Ranelagh and Dundrum; the red line (every 20 minutes) runs from the Point Village to Tallaght via the north quays and Heuston Station.

There are ticket machines at every stop or you can use a tap-on, tap-off Leap Card. A typical short-hop fare (around four stops) is €2.30.

TAXI

All taxi fares begin with a flag-fall of €3.60 (€4 from 10pm to 8am), followed by €1.10 per kilometre thereafter (€1.40 from 10pm to 8am).

Taxis can be hailed on the street. Numerous taxi companies, such as **National Radio Cabs** (☑ 01-677 2222; www.nrc.ie), dispatch taxis by radio. You can also try Lynk (www.lynk.ie), a taxi app.

The Southeast

Kilkenny

☑ 056 / POP 24,400

Kilkenny (Cill Chainnigh) is the Ireland of many visitors' imaginations. Its majestic riverside castle, tangle of 17th-century passageways, rows of colourful, old-fashioned shopfronts and centuries-old pubs with traditional live music all have a timeless appeal, as does its splendid medieval cathedral. It's also one of Ireland's creative crucibles, a centre for arts and crafts, and home to a host of fine restaurants, cafes, pubs and shops.

⊙ Sights

★ **Kilkenny Castle**   CASTLE
(www.kilkennycastle.ie; Castle Rd; adult/child €7/3; ⊙ 9.30am-5pm Mar-Sep, to 4.30pm Oct-Feb) Rising above the River Nore, Kilkenny Castle is one of Ireland's most visited heritage sites. Stronghold of the powerful Butler family, it has a history dating back to the 12th century, though much of its present look dates from Victorian times.

During the winter months (November to January) there are 40-minute guided tours, which shift to self-guided February to October. Highlights include the Long Gallery with its painted roof and carved marble fireplace. There's an excellent tearoom in the former castle kitchens, all white marble and gleaming copper.

Kilkenny

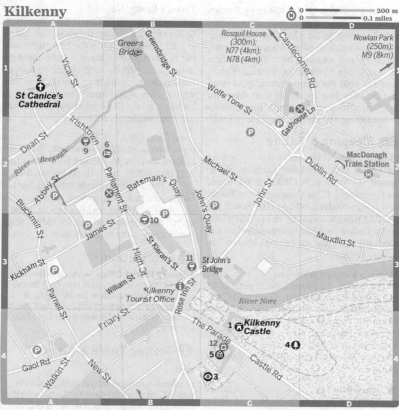

⭐ **St Canice's Cathedral** CATHEDRAL
(www.stcanicescathedral.ie; St Canice's Pl; cathedral €4, round tower €3, combined €6; ⊙9am-6pm Mon-Sat, 1-6pm Sun, shorter hours Sep-May) Ireland's second-largest medieval cathedral (after St Patrick's in Dublin) has a long and fascinating history. The first monastery was built here in the 6th century by St Canice, Kilkenny's patron saint. The present structure dates from the 13th to 16th centuries, with extensive 19th-century reconstruction, its interior housing ancient grave slabs and the tombs of Kilkenny Castle's Butler dynasty. Outside stands a 30m-high round tower, one of only two in Ireland that you can climb.

National Craft Gallery GALLERY
(www.nationalcraftgallery.ie; Castle Yard ⊙10am-5.30pm Tue-Sat, 11am-5.30pm Sun; ◉) FREE Contemporary Irish crafts are showcased at these imaginative galleries, set in former stables across the road from Kilkenny Castle,

Kilkenny

next to the shops of the **Kilkenny Design Centre** (☑ 056-772 2118; www.kilkennydesign. com; Castle Yard; ☉ 10am-7pm). Ceramics dominate, but exhibits often feature furniture, jewellery and weaving from the members of the Crafts Council of Ireland. Family days are held the second Saturday of every month, with free hands-on workshops for children at 10am and 12.30pm. For additional workshops and events, check the website.

🛏 Sleeping & Eating

Kilkenny Tourist Hostel HOSTEL €
(☑ 056-776 3541; www.kilkennyhostel.ie; 35 Parliament St; dm/tw from €17/42; @ 🛜) Inside an ivy-covered 1770s Georgian town house, this fairly standard, 60-bed IHH hostel has a sitting room warmed by an open fireplace, and a timber- and leadlight-panelled dining room adjoining the self-catering kitchen. Excellent location.

Mocha's Vintage Tearooms CAFE €
(4 The Arches, Gashouse Lane; mains €6-13; ☉ 8.30am-5.30pm Mon-Sat) Cute retro tearoom with picture-cluttered walls and rose-patterned china. As well as tea and cakes, there's a breakfast menu (until 11.30am) with a choice of bagels or a full Irish fry-up, and hot lunch specials including fish and chips.

★ Foodworks BISTRO, CAFE €€
(☑ 056-777 7696; www.foodworks.ie; 7 Parliament St; lunch mains €7-14, 3-course dinners €28; ☉ noon-9.30pm Wed-Fri, to 10pm Sat, 12.30-4.30pm Sun; 🛜 🍴) 🥢 The owners of this cool and casual bistro keep their own pigs and grow their own salad leaves, so it would be churlish not to try their pulled pork brioche or confit pig's trotter – and you'll be glad you did. Delicious food, excellent coffee and friendly service make this a justifiably popular venue; best to book a table.

🍷 Drinking & Nightlife

★ Kyteler's Inn PUB
(www.kytelersinn.com; 27 St Kieran's St; ☉ 11am-midnight Sun-Thu, to 2am Fri & Sat) Dame Alice Kyteler's old house was built back in 1224 and has seen its share of history: she was charged with witchcraft in 1323. Today the rambling bar includes the original building, complete with vaulted ceiling and arches. There is a beer garden, a courtyard and a large upstairs room for the live bands (6.30pm March to October), ranging from trad to blues.

Tynan's Bridge House PUB
(St John's Bridge; ☉ 10.30am-11.30pm Mon-Thu, to 12.30am Fri & Sat, 11.30am-11pm Sun) This historic 1703 Georgian pub is the best traditional bar in town. There's barely a right angle left in the place, with its sagging, granite-topped horseshoe bar, original wood panelling, wonky shelves and loyal clientele of crusty locals – and no TV! Trad music on Wednesdays and weekends at 9pm.

John Cleere's PUB
(www.cleeres.com; 22 Parliament St; ☉ 11.30am-11.30pm Mon-Thu, to 12.30am Fri & Sat, 1-11pm Sun) One of Kilkenny's finest venues for live music, theatre and comedy, this long bar has blues, jazz and rock, as well as trad music sessions on Monday and Wednesday. Food is served throughout the day, including soup, sandwiches, pizza and Irish stew.

ℹ Information

Kilkenny Tourist Office (www.visitkilkenny.ie; Rose Inn St; ☉ 9.15am-5pm Mon-Sat) Stocks guides and walking maps. Located in Shee Alms House, dating from 1582 and built in local stone by benefactor Sir Richard Shee to help the poor.

ℹ Getting There & Away

BUS
Bus Éireann services stop at the train station and on Ormonde Rd (nearer the town centre); JJ Kavanagh (www.jjkavanagh.ie) buses to Dublin airport stop on Ormonde Rd only. Services include Cork (€21.50, three hours, two daily), Dublin (€14, 2¼ hours, eight daily) and Dublin airport (€20, two to three hours, six daily).

TRAIN
Kilkenny's MacDonagh train station is a 10-minute walk northeast of the town centre. Services include Dublin Heuston (€26, 1½ hours, six daily).

The Southwest

Cork
☑ 021 / POP 120,000
Ireland's second city is first in every important respect – at least according to the locals, who cheerfully refer to it as the 'real capital of Ireland'. It's a liberal, youthful and cosmopolitan place with a developing hipster scene, but the best of the city is still happily traditional – snug pubs with live-music sessions, restaurants dishing up top-quality lo-

cal produce, and a genuinely proud welcome from the locals.

⊙ Sights

The best sight in Cork is the city itself – soak it up as you wander the streets. A new conference and events centre, complete with 6000-seat concert venue, tourist centre, restaurants, shops, galleries and apartments, is planned for the former **Beamish & Crawford brewery site**, fronted by the landmark mock-Tudor 'counting house', a block west of the English Market.

★ English Market
MARKET
(www.englishmarket.ie; main entrance Princes St; ⊙8am-6pm Mon-Sat) It could just as easily be called the Victorian Market for its ornate vaulted ceilings and columns, but the English Market is a true gem, no matter what you name it. Scores of vendors sell some of the regions's very best local produce, meats, cheeses and takeaway food. On a sunny day, take your lunch to nearby Bishop Lucey Park, a popular alfresco eating spot.

Crawford Municipal Art Gallery
GALLERY
(☑021-480 5042; www.crawfordartgallery.ie; Emmet Pl; ⊙10am-5pm Mon-Wed, Fri & Sat, to 8pm Thu) **FREE** Cork's public gallery houses a small but excellent permanent collection covering the 17th century through to the modern day. Highlights include works by Sir John Lavery, Jack B Yeats and Nathaniel Hone, and a room devoted to Irish women artists from 1886 to 1978 – don't miss the pieces by Mainie Jellet and Evie Hone.

Cork City Gaol
MUSEUM
(☑021-430 5022; http://corkcitygaol.com; Convent Ave; adult/child €8/5; ⊙9.30am-5pm Apr-Sep, 10am-4pm Oct-Mar) This imposing former prison is well worth a visit, if only to get a sense of how awful life was for prisoners a century ago. An audio tour guides you around the restored cells, which feature models of suffering prisoners and sadistic-looking guards. Take a bus to UCC – from there walk north along Mardyke Walk, cross the river and follow the signs uphill (10 minutes).

🛏 Sleeping

Sheila's Hostel
HOSTEL €
(☑021-450 5562; www.sheilashostel.ie; 4 Belgrave Pl, off Wellington Rd; dm €15-18, tw €44-5€; @ 🎧) Sheila's heaves with young travellers, and

WORTH A TRIP

ROCK OF CASHEL

The iconic and much-photographed **Rock of Cashel** (www.heritageireland.ie; adult/child €7/3; ⊙9am-7pm early Jun–mid-Sep, to 5.30pm mid-Mar–early Jun & mid-Sep–mid-Oct, to 4.30pm mid-Oct–mid-Mar) is one of Ireland's true highlights. The 'rock' is a fortified hill, the defences of which shelter a clutch of historical, religious monuments. The site has been a defensive one since the 4th century and its compelling features include the towering 13th-century Gothic cathedral, a 15th-century four-storey castle, an 11th-century round tower and a 12th-century Romanesque chapel.

The rock is a five-minute stroll along Bishop's Walk from appealing market town **Cashel**. There are eight buses daily between Cashel and Cork (€15.50, 1½ hours) via Cahir (€6, 20 minutes, six daily). The bus stop for Cork is outside the Bake House on Main St. The Dublin stop (€15.50, three hours, six daily) is opposite.

it's no wonder given its excellent central location. Facilities include a sauna, lockers, laundry service, a movie room and a barbecue. Cheaper twin rooms share bathrooms. Breakfast is €3 extra.

Brú Bar & Hostel
HOSTEL €
(☑021-455 9667; www.bruhostel.com; 57 MacCurtain St; dm/tw incl breakfast from €17/40; @ 🎧) This buzzing hostel has its own internet cafe, with free access for guests, and a fantastic bar, popular with backpackers and locals alike. The dorms (each with a bathroom) have four to six beds and are both clean and stylish – ask for one on the upper floors to avoid bar noise.

🍴 Eating

Quay Co-op
VEGETARIAN €
(☑021-431 7026; www.quaycoop.com; 24 Sullivan's Quay; mains €5-11; ⊙10am-9pm; 🖉🏠) 🍃 Flying the flag for alternative Cork, this cafeteria offers a range of self-service vegetarian dishes, all organic, including big breakfasts and rib-sticking soups and casseroles. It also caters for gluten-, dairy- and wheat-free needs, and is amazingly child-friendly.

GREAT BRITAIN & IRELAND THE SOUTHWEST

Cork

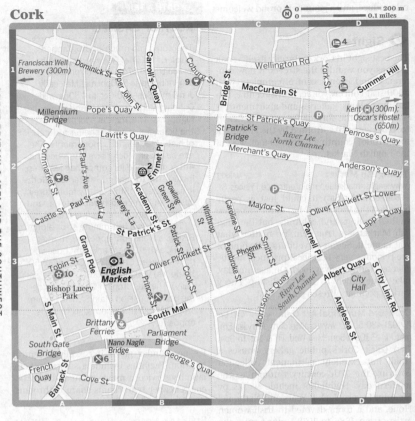

Cork

◉ Top Sights
1 English Market B3

◉ Sights
2 Crawford Municipal Art Gallery B2

🛏 Sleeping
3 Brú Bar & Hostel D1
4 Sheila's Hostel D1

🍽 Eating
5 Farmgate Cafe B3
6 Quay Co-op A4
7 Wildways B3

🍸 Drinking & Nightlife
8 Rising Sons A2
9 Sin É B1

🎭 Entertainment
10 Triskel Arts Centre A3

Wildways   SANDWICHES €
(www.wildways.net; 21 Princes St; mains €5-10;
⏱ 7.45am-5pm Mon-Fri, 8.30am-4pm Sat; 🍴)
🍃 Cork's first organic soup and sandwich
bar serves such a variety of delicious and
healthy food that even the pickiest of eaters
will find something scrumptious. If you're
around for breakfast, make sure to try the
excellent chocolate-chip pancakes.

★ **Farmgate Cafe**   CAFE, BISTRO €€
(📞 021-427 8134; www.farmgate.ie; Princes St,
English Market; mains €6.50-17.50; ⏱ 8.30am-5pm
Mon-Sat) 🍃 An unmissable experience at the
heart of the English Market, the Farmgate is
perched on a balcony overlooking the food
stalls below, the source of all that fresh local produce on your plate – everything from
crab and oysters to the lamb for an Irish
stew. Up the stairs and turn left for table
service, right for counter service.

Drinking & Nightlife

★ Sin É
PUB

(www.corkheritagepubs.com; 8 Coburg St; ⊙12.30-11.30pm Sun-Thu, to 12.30am Fri & Sat) You could easily while away an entire day at this great old place, which is everything a craic-filled pub should be – long on atmosphere and short on pretension (Sin É means 'that's it!'). There's music most nights (regular sessions Tuesday at 9.30pm, Friday and Sunday at 6.30pm), much of it traditional, but with the odd surprise.

Franciscan Well Brewery
PUB

(www.franciscanwellbrewery.com; 14 North Mall; ⊙3-11.30pm Mon-Thu, to 12.30am Fri & Sat, to 11pm Sun; ⊚) The copper vats gleaming behind the bar give the game away: the Franciscan Well brews its own beer. The best place to enjoy it is in the enormous beer garden at the back. The pub holds regular beer festivals together with other small independent Irish breweries.

Rising Sons
MICROBREWERY

(⊘021-241 1126; www.risingsonsbrewery.com; Cornmarket St; ⊙noon-late) This huge, warehouse-like, red-brick building houses Cork's newest microbrewery. The industrial decor of exposed brick, riveted iron and gleaming copper brewing vessels recalls American West Coast brewpubs. It turns out 50 kegs a week, some of them full of its lip-smacking trademark stout, Mi Daza, and has a food menu that extends as far as pizza, and no further.

☆ Entertainment

Cork's cultural life is generally of a high calibre. To see what's happening grab *Whaz On?*(www.whazon.com), a free monthly booklet available from the tourist office, newsagencies, shops, hostels and B&Bs.

Triskel Arts Centre
ARTS CENTRE

(⊘021-472 2022; www.triskelart.com; Tobin St; ⊙10am-5pm Mon-Sat; ⊚) A fantastic cultural centre housed partly in a renovated church building – expect a varied program of live music, installation art, photography and theatre at this intimate venue. There's also a cinema (from 6.30pm) and a great cafe.

ℹ Information

Cork City Tourist Office (⊘021-425 5100; www.discoverireland.ie/corkcity; Grand Pde; ⊙9am-6pm Mon-Sat year-round, plus 10am-5pm Sun Jul & Aug) Souvenir shop and information desk. Sells Ordnance Survey maps.

ℹ Getting There & Around

AIR
Cork Airport (⊘021-431 3131; www.cork-airport.com) is 8km south of the city. Bus Éireann service 226A shuttles between the train station, bus station and Cork Airport every half-hour between 6am and 10pm (€7.40, 30 minutes). A taxi to/from town costs €20 to €25.

BOAT
Brittany Ferries (⊘021-427 7801; www.brittanyferries.ie; 42 Grand Pde) sails to Roscoff (France) weekly from the end of March to October. The crossing takes 14 hours; fares vary widely. The ferry terminal is at Ringaskiddy, 15 minutes by car southeast of the city centre along the N28. Taxis cost €28 to €35. Bus Éireann runs a service from Cork's bus station to link up with departures (adult/child €7.90/5.60, 40 minutes); confirm times.

BUS
Bus Éireann (⊘021-450 8188; www.buseireann.ie) operates from the bus station, while **AirCoach** (⊘01-844 7118; www.aircoach.ie) and **Citylink** (⊘091-564 164; www.citylink.ie; ⊚) services depart from St Patrick's Quay, across the river. **GoBus** (⊘091-564 600; www.gobus.ie; ⊚) uses a stop around the corner on Parnell Pl. Services include Dublin (from €15, 3¾ hours, six to nine services daily), Kilkenny (€21, three hours, two daily) and Killarney (€27, two hours, hourly).

TRAIN
Kent Train Station (⊘021-450 4777) is north of the River Lee on Lower Glanmire Rd, a 10- to 15-minute walk from the city centre. Bus 205 runs into the city centre (€2, five minutes, every 15 minutes). Services include Dublin (€64, 2¼ hours, eight daily), Galway (€57, four to six hours, seven daily, two or three changes) and Killarney (€28, 1½ to two hours, nine daily).

Killarney
⊘064 / POP 14,200

This well-oiled tourism machine is set in the midst of sublime scenery. Its manufactured tweeness is renowned – the shops selling soft-toy *shillelaghs* (Irish fighting sticks) and shamrocks, the placards on street corners pointing to trad-music sessions. However, it has attractions beyond its proximity to lakes, waterfalls and woodland spreading beneath a skyline of 1000m-plus peaks. In a town that's been practising the tourism game for

Killarney

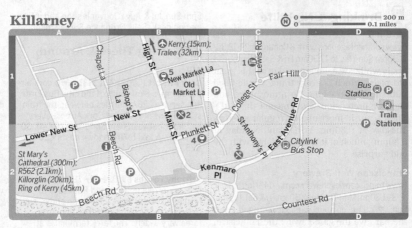

Killarney

⊕ Activities, Courses & Tours
O'Connors Tours...........................(see 5)

🛏 Sleeping
1 Súgán Hostel..............................C1

✗ Eating
2 Jam...B1
3 Lir Café....................................C2

🍷 Drinking & Nightlife
4 Courtney's................................B2
5 O'Connor's................................B1

more than 250 years, competition keeps standards high and visitors on all budgets can expect to find good restaurants, great pubs and comfortable accommodation.

👁 Sights & Activities

Killarney's biggest attraction, in every sense, is the nearby Killarney National Park. The town itself can easily be explored on foot in an hour or two.

The 214km **Kerry Way** (www.kerryway.com), the Republic's longest way-marked footpath, starts and ends in Killarney. It takes around 10 days to complete the whole route; with less time it's worth hiking the first three days as far as Glenbeigh, from where a bus or a lift could return you to Killarney.

Killarney National Park   PARK
(www.killarneynationalpark.ie) FREE Enclosed within Killarney's 102-sq-km national park are beautiful Lough Leane (the Lower Lake or 'Lake of Learning'), Muckross Lake and the Upper Lake, as well as the Mangerton,

Torc, Shehy and Purple Mountains. Areas of oak and yew woodland stretch for miles. This is wonderful walking and biking country.

O'Connors Tours   BUS, BOAT TOUR
(☏064-663 0200; www.gapofdunloetours.com; 7 High St; ⊙Mar-Oct) In summer the Gap of Dunloe, a gloriously scenic mountain pass squeezed between Purple Mountain and Carrauntouhill (at 1040m, Ireland's highest peak), is a tourist bottleneck. Rather than join the crowds taking pony-and-trap rides, O'Connors Tours can arrange a bike and boat circuit (€15; highly recommended) or bus and boat tour (€30) taking in the Gap.

🛏 Sleeping & Eating

★**Fleming's White Bridge**
Caravan & Camping Park   CAMPGROUND €
(☏086 363 0266; www.killarneycamping.com; White Bridge, Ballycasheen Rd; sites per vehicle plus 2 adults €25, hiker €10; ⊙mid-Mar–Oct; 🛜🐾) A lovely, sheltered, family-run campsite about 2km southeast of the town centre off the N22, Fleming's has a games room, bike hire, campers' kitchen, laundry and free trout fishing on the river that runs alongside. Your man Hillary at reception can arrange bus, bike and boat tours, if he doesn't talk the legs off you first!

Súgán Hostel   HOSTEL €
(☏064-663 3104; Lewis Rd; dm €15-18, tw €40-44; 🅿🛜) Behind its publike front, 250-year-old Súgán is an amiably eccentric hostel with an open fire in the cosy common room, low, crazy-cornered ceilings and hardwood floors. Check in at the next-door pub, a handy spot for a pint of Guinness once you're settled in.

Jam
CAFE €

(☑064-663 7716; www.jam.ie; 77 Old Market Lane; mains €4-11; ⊗8am-5pm Mon-Sat, 9am-5pm Sun; 🖪) 🖋 Duck down the alley to this local hideout for a changing menu of deli sandwiches, coffee and cake, and hot lunch dishes like shepherd's pie. It's all made with locally sourced produce and there are a few tables out front.

Lir Café
CAFE €

(☑064-663 3859; www.lircafe.com; Kenmare Pl; mains €3-7; ⊗8am-9pm Mon-Thu, to 9.30pm Fri & Sat, to 7pm Sun; 🖪) Great coffee and hip atmosphere in Killarney's coolest cafe; food is limited to cakes, biscuits and the real treat, handmade chocolates, including Bailey's truffles.

🍷 Drinking & Nightlife

★O'Connor's
PUB

(http://oconnorstraditionalpub.com; 7 High St; ⊗10.30am-11pm Mon-Thu, to 12.30am Fri & Sat, 12.30-11pm Sun) This tiny traditional pub with leaded-glass doors is one of Killarney's most popular haunts. Live music plays every night; good bar food is served daily in summer. In warmer weather, the crowds spill out onto the adjacent lane.

Courtney's
PUB

(www.courtneysbar.com; Plunkett St; ⊗2-11.30pm Sun-Thu, to 12.30am Fri & Sat, from 5pm winter) Inconspicuous on the outside, inside this timeless pub bursts at the seams with Irish music sessions many nights year-round. This is where locals come to see their old mates perform and to kick off a night on the town.

❶ Information

Tourist Office (☑064-663 1633; www.killarney.ie; Beech Rd; ⊗9am-5pm Mon-Sat; 🖪) Can handle most queries; especially good with transport intricacies.

❶ Getting There & Around

BICYCLE
Bicycles are ideal for exploring the scattered sights of the Killarney area, many of which are accessible only by bike or on foot.

BUS
Bus Éireann (☑064-663 0011; www.buseireann.ie) operates from the **bus station** on Park Rd. For Dublin (€40, six hours, six daily) you need to change at Cork (€27, two hours, hourly) – the train is much faster. **Citylink** (☑091 564164; www.citylink.ie) buses to Galway (€30, three hours, two daily) leave from the coach stop outside the Malton Hotel on East Avenue Rd.

TRAIN
Killarney's train station is behind the Malton Hotel, just east of the centre. Although close to the bus station, there is no direct connection – you have to walk down to East Avenue Rd and back through Killarney Outlet Centre mall.

There are one or two direct services per day to Cork (€27.80, 1½ hours) and Dublin (€69, 3¼ hours, every two hours); otherwise you'll have to change at Mallow.

Ring of Kerry

The Ring of Kerry is the longest and the most diverse of Ireland's big circle drives, combining jaw-dropping coastal scenery with emerald pastures and villages.

The 179km circuit usually begins in Killarney and winds past pristine beaches, the island-dotted Atlantic, medieval ruins,

---

OFF THE BEATEN TRACK

SKELLIG MICHAEL

The jagged, 217m-high rock of **Skellig Michael** (www.heritageireland.ie; ⊗mid-May-Sep) **FREE** is the larger of the two Skellig Islands and a Unesco World Heritage Site. If it looks familiar that's because the island was a location in the *Star Wars* saga *The Force Awakens*.

Early Christian monks survived at this forbidding site from the 6th until the 12th or 13th century. The 12km crossing can be rough but is well worth making. There are no toilets or shelter, so bring something to eat and drink, and wear stout shoes and weatherproof clothing. Trips usually run from Easter until September, depending on weather.

Boats leave Portmagee (1½ hours), Ballinskelligs (35 minutes to one hour) and Derrynane (1¾ hours) at around 10am and return at 3pm, and cost about €45 per person. Boat owners generally restrict you to two hours on the island, which is the bare minimum to see the monastery, look at the birds and have a picnic.

mountains and loughs (lakes). The coastline is at its most rugged between Waterville and Caherdaniel in the southwest of the peninsula. It can get crowded in summer, but even then, the remote Skellig Ring can be uncrowded and serene – and starkly beautiful.

The Ring of Kerry can easily be done as a day trip, but if you want to stretch it out, places to stay are scattered along the route. Killorglin and Kenmare have the best dining options, with some excellent restaurants; elsewhere, basic (sometimes very basic) pub fare is the norm.

ℹ Getting There & Around

Bus Éireann (☑ 064-663 0011; www.buseireann.ie) runs a once-daily Ring of Kerry bus service (No 280) from late June to late August. Buses leave Killarney at 11.30am and stop at Killorglin (€7.80, 30 minutes), Glenbeigh, Caherciveen (€17, 1¼ hours), Waterville (€19.20, 1¾ hours), Caherdaniel (€20.70, 2¼ hours) and Molls Gap, arriving back at Killarney (€22.50) at 4.45pm.

Travel agencies and hostels in Killarney offer daily coach tours of the Ring for about €20 to €25, year-round, lasting from 10.30am to 5pm.

The West Coast

Galway

☑ 091 / POP 75,600

Often referred to as the 'most Irish' of Ireland's cities, arty and bohemian Galway (Gaillimh) is renowned for its pleasures. Brightly painted pubs heave with live music, while cafes offer front-row seats for observing street performers, weekend parties run amok, lovers entwined and more. Steeped in history, for sure, but the city buzzes with a contemporary and cultured vibe as students make up a quarter of the population.

◉ Sights

★ **Galway City Museum**   MUSEUM
(www.galwaycitymuseum.ie; Spanish Pde; ⊙10am-5pm Tue-Sat year-round, noon-5pm Sun Easter-Sep) FREE This modern museum has exhibits on the city's history from 1800 to 1950, including an iconic Galway Hooker fishing boat, a collection of *currachs* (boats made from animal hides) and sections covering Galway and the Great War and the city's cinematic connections.

★ **Spanish Arch**   HISTORIC SITE
The Spanish Arch is thought to be an extension of Galway's medieval city walls, designed to protect ships moored at the nearby quay while they unloaded goods from Spain, although it was partially destroyed by the tsunami that followed the 1755 Lisbon earthquake. Today it reverberates to the beat of bongo drums, and the lawns and riverside form a gathering place for locals and visitors on sunny days, as kayakers negotiate the tidal rapids of the River Corrib.

Lynch's Castle   HISTORIC BUILDING
(cnr Shop & Upper Abbeygate Sts; ⊙10am-4pm Mon-Wed & Fri, 10am-5pm Thu) Considered the finest town castle in Ireland, this old stone town house – now part of AIB Bank – was built in the 14th century, though much of what you see today dates from around 1600. Stonework on the facade includes ghoulish gargoyles and the coats of arms of Henry VII, the Lynches (the most powerful of the 14 ruling Galway 'tribes') and the Fitzgeralds of Kildare. On the inside, it's worth a gander at the hefty and magnificent fireplace.

🛏 Sleeping

★ **Kinlay Hostel**   HOSTEL €
(☑091-565 244; www.kinlayhouse.ie; Merchants Rd; dm €17-29, d €54-70; @ ☎) Easy-going staff, a full range of facilities and a cream-in-the-doughnut location just off Eyre Sq make this a top choice, with four- to 10-bed dorms and doubles. Spanning two huge, brightly lit floors, amenities include two self-catering kitchens and two cosy TV lounges, with a pool table. Some rooms have bay views and newer beds have electric sockets and USB points.

Barnacles   HOSTEL €
(☑091-568 644; www.barnacles.ie; 10 Quay St; dm €14-35, d €50-75; @ ☎) This highly central and very well-run hostel is housed in a medieval building with a modern extension. Rooms are all clean and well kept, the kitchen is spacious, and there's a warm common room with a big gas fireplace and games consoles. There's a free pasta evening on Sunday and on Wednesday musicians can 'play to stay'. Breakfast includes scones and soda bread.

✗ Eating & Drinking

Most pubs in Galway have live music at least a couple of nights a week. **Róisín Dubh** (www.roisindubh.net; Upper Dominick St; ⊙5pm-2am Sun-Thu, till 2.30am Fri & Sat) is the

Galway City

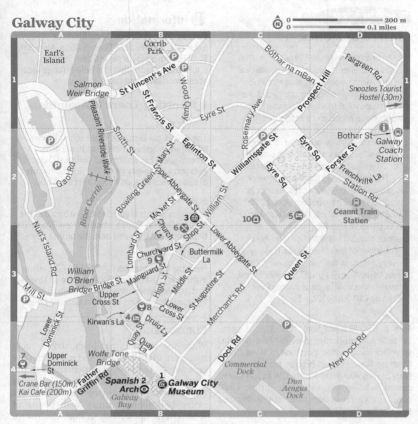

best place for bands; **Tig Cóilí** (Manguard St; ☺10.30am-midnight Mon-Thu, to 12.30am Fri & Sat, to 11pm Sun) excels at trad sessions.

★ **McCambridge's**　　　　CAFE, GROCERY €
(www.mccambridges.com; 38/39 Shop St; snacks from €3, mains €7-13; ☺cafe 9am-5.30pm Mon-Wed, 9am-9pm Thu-Sat, 10.30am-6pm Sun, grocery 8am-7pm Mon-Wed, 8am-9pm Thu-Sat, 10.30am-6pm Sun) The long-running food hall here has some superb prepared salads, hot foods and other more exotic treats. Create the perfect picnic or enjoy your pickings at the tables out front. All high ceilings, blond wood and busy staff, the upstairs cafe is lovely with an ever-changing menu of modern Irish fare plus gourmet sandwiches, salads, silky soups and tip-top coffee.

★ **Kai Cafe**　　　　　　CAFE €€
(☎091-526 003; www.kaicaferestaurant.com; 20 Sea Rd; lunch/dinner mains from €11.50/18.50; ☺9.30am-4pm Mon-Fri, 10.30am-4pm Sat, noon-

Galway City

WORTH A TRIP

CLIFFS OF MOHER

Star of a million tourist brochures, the Cliffs of Moher in County Clare are one of the most popular sights in Ireland. But like many an ageing star, you have to look beyond the famous facade to appreciate its inherent attributes. In summer the site is overrun with day trippers, but there are good rewards if you're willing to walk along the clifftops for 10 minutes to escape the crowds.

The landscaped **Cliffs of Moher Visitor Centre** (www.cliffsofmoher.ie; adult/child €6/free; ⊙9am-9pm Jul-Aug, to 7pm May-Jun & Sep, to 6pm Mar-Apr & Oct, to 5pm Nov-Feb) has exhibitions about the cliffs and their natural history. A number of bus tours leave Galway every morning for here, including **Burren Wild Tours** (⊡087 877 9565; www.burrenwalks.com; departs Galway Coach Station; €10-25; ⊙10am-5pm).

4pm & 6.30-10.30pm Sun; ☞) This fantastic cafe on happening Sea Rd is a delight, whether for a coffee, portions of West Coast Crab or Roscommon hogget and glasses of Galway Hooker Sixty Knots IPA in a relaxed, casual, wholesome and rustic dining environment. Great at any time of the day, but reserve for din-dins.

★**Crane Bar**   PUB
(www.thecranebar.com; 2 Sea Rd; ⊙10.30am-11.30pm Mon-Fri, 10.30am-12.30am Sat, 12.30-11pm Sun) This atmospheric old pub west of the Corrib is the best spot in Galway to catch an informal *céilidh* (session of traditional music and dancing) most nights. Talented bands play its rowdy, good-natured upstairs bar; downstairs at times it seems straight out of *The Far Side*.

★**Séhán Ua Neáchtain**   PUB
(www.tighneachtain.com; 17 Upper Cross St; ⊙10.30am-11.30pm Mon-Thu & Sun, 10.30am-12.30am Fri & Sat) Painted a bright cornflower blue, this 19th-century pub, known simply as Neáchtain's (*nock*-tans) or Naughtons, has a wraparound string of tables outside, many shaded by a large tree. It's a place where a polyglot mix of locals plop down and let the world pass them by – stop and join them for a pint. Good lunches.

❶ Information

Galway Tourist Office (www.discoverireland.ie; Forster St; ⊙9am-5.45pm Mon-Sat, 9am-1.15pm Sun) Large, efficient regional information centre that can help arrange local accommodation and tours.

❶ Getting There & Around

BICYCLE
The Coca-Cola Zero bike share scheme (www.bikeshare.ie/galway.html) has 16 stations around town. For visitors, €3 (with €150 deposit) gets you a three-day pass. The first 30 minutes of each hire is free; up to two hours is €1.50.

BUS
Several private bus companies are based at the modern **Galway Coach Station** (New Coach Station; Bothar St), located near the tourist office.

TRAIN
From the **train station** (⊡091-564 222; www.irishrail.ie), just off Eyre Sq, there are up to nine fast, comfortable trains daily to/from Dublin's Heuston Station (one way from €35, 2¼ hours).

Connemara

With its shimmering black lakes, pale mountains, lonely valleys and more than the occasional rainbow, Connemara in the northwestern corner of County Galway is one of Ireland's most gorgeous corners. It's prime hillwalking country with plenty of wild terrain, none more so than the Twelve Bens, a ridge of rugged mountains that form part of **Connemara National Park** (www.connemaranationalpark.ie; off N59; ⊙visitor centre 9am-5.30pm Mar-Oct, park 24hr) FREE .

Connemara's 'capital', Clifden (An Clochán), is an appealing Victorian-era country town with an oval of streets offering evocative strolls. The **Sky Road** is a spectacular 12km route looping out to the township of Kingston and back to Clifden, taking in some rugged, stunningly beautiful coastal scenery en route. It can be easily walked or cycled.

🛌 Sleeping & Eating

Clifden Town Hostel   HOSTEL €
(⊡095-21076; www.clifdentownhostel.com; Market St; dm €17-20, s/d from €25/40) Right in the centre of town, this cheery IHH hostel is set in a cream-coloured house framed by big picture windows, with sunlit rooms and 34 beds.

★ Connemara Hamper DELI €
(www.connemarahamper.com; Lower Market St; snacks from €3; ⊙10am-5pm Mon-Sat) The jolly ladies here will gladly package up a chicken and leek pie or other savoury treat for your picnic. There's a wide range of prepared foods and fresh breads.

❶ Information

Tourist Office (www.clifdenchamber.ie; Galway Rd/N59; ⊙10am-5pm Mon-Sat Easter-Jun & Sep, 10am-5pm daily Jul & Aug) In the Clifden Station House complex.

❶ Getting There & Away

Bus Éireann (www.buseireann.ie) and **Citylink** (www.citylink.ie) have several services daily to Galway along the N59. Fares start at €14.50 and the trip takes 90 minutes.

Northern Ireland

📋 028 / POP 1.8 MILLION

When you cross from the Republic into Northern Ireland you notice a couple of changes: the accent is different, the road signs are in miles, and the prices are in pounds sterling. However, as the two countries are in a customs union, there's no passport control and no customs declarations. All of a sudden, you're in the UK.

Dragged down for decades by the violence and uncertainty of the Troubles, Northern Ireland today is a nation rejuvenated. Since the 1998 Good Friday Agreement laid the groundwork for peace this UK province has seen a huge influx of investment and redevelopment. Belfast has become a happening place with a famously wild nightlife; Derry has come into its own as a cool, artistic city; and the stunning Causeway Coast gets more and more visitors each year.

Belfast

POP 280,900

Belfast is in many ways a brand-new city. In recent years it has pulled off a remarkable transformation from bombs-and-bullets pariah to a hip-hotels-and-hedonism party town. The old shipyards on the Lagan continue to give way to the luxury apartments of the Titanic Quarter, whose centrepiece, the stunning, star-shaped edifice housing the Titanic Belfast centre, covering the ill-fated liner's construction here, has become the city's number-one tourist draw. New venues keep popping up – WWI warship HMS *Caroline* is set to become a floating museum in 2016. They all add to a list of attractions that includes beautifully restored Victorian architecture, a glittering waterfront lined with modern art, a fantastic foodie scene and music-filled pubs.

◎ Sights

★ Titanic Belfast EXHIBITION
(www.titanicbelfast.com; Queen's Rd; adult/child £17.50/7.25; ⊙9am-7pm Jun-Aug, to 6pm Apr-May & Sep, 10am-5pm Oct-Mar) The head of the slipway where the *Titanic* was built is now occupied by the gleaming, angular edifice of Titanic Belfast, an unmissable multimedia extravaganza that charts the history of Belfast and the creation of the world's most famous ocean liner. Cleverly designed exhibits enlivened by historical images, animated projections and soundtracks chart Belfast's rise to turn-of-the-20th-century industrial superpower, followed by a high-tech ride through a noisy, smells-and-all re-creation of the city's shipyards.

★ SS Nomadic HISTORIC SITE
(www.nomadicbelfast.com; Hamilton Dock, Queen's Rd; adult/child £7/5; ⊙10am-5pm daily Apr-Sep, Tue-Sun Oct-Mar) Built in Belfast in 1911, the SS *Nomadic* is the last remaining vessel of the White Star Line. The little steamship ferried 1st- and 2nd-class passengers between Cherbourg Harbour and the ocean liners that were too big to dock at the French port. On 10 April 1912 it delivered 172 passengers to the ill-fated *Titanic*. First-come, first-served guided tours run every 30 minutes from 10am until an hour before closing. Alternatively, you're free to roam at will (don't miss the 1st-class toilets!).

★ Ulster Museum MUSEUM
(www.nmni.com; Botanic Gardens; ⊙10am-5pm Tue-Sun) FREE You could spend hours browsing this state-of-the-art museum, but if you're pressed for time don't miss the **Armada Room**, with artefacts retrieved from the 1588 wreck of the Spanish galleon *Girona*; the **Egyptian Room**, with Princess Takabuti, a 2500-year-old Egyptian mummy unwrapped in Belfast in 1835; and the **Early Peoples Gallery**, with the bronze Bann Disc, a superb example of Celtic design from the Iron Age.

Free tours (10 people maximum; first come, first served) run at 2.30pm Tuesday to Friday and 1.30pm Sunday.

Belfast

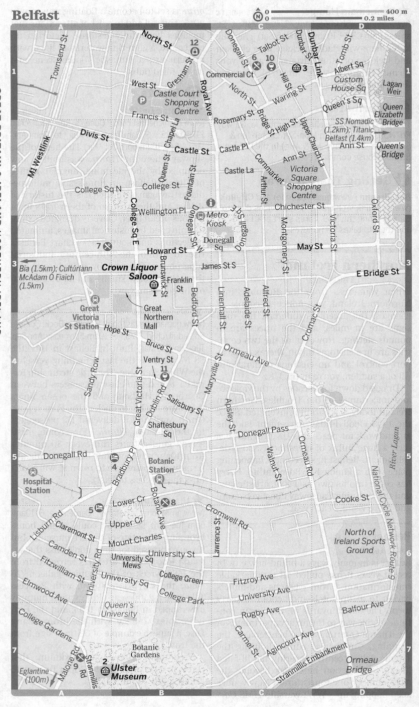

North St

Townsend St

M1 Westlink

Divis St

West St

Gresham St

Royal Ave

Francis St

Chapel La

Castle Court Shopping Centre

North St

Commercial Ct

Donegall St

Talbot St

Dunbar St

Dunbar Link

Tomb St

Albert Sq

Custom House Sq

Lagan Weir

Queen Elizabeth Bridge

Queen's Sq

SS Nomadic (1.2km); Titanic Belfast (1.4km)

Queen's Bridge

Rosemary St

Bridge St

Waring St

Hill St

High St

Upper Church La

Ann St

Ann St

Oxford St

Castle St

Castle Pl

Castle La

Commarket

Arthur St

Victoria Square Shopping Centre

Chichester St

Queen St

Fountain St

College St

Wellington Pl

College Sq N

College Sq E

Metro Kiosk

Donegall Sq

Donegall Sq W

Donegall Sq

Montgomery St

Victoria St

May St

E Bridge St

Howard St

Brunswick St

James St S

Bia (1.5km); Cultúrlann McAdam Ó Fiaich (1.5km)

Crown Liquor Saloon

Franklin St

Great Northern Mall

Great Victoria St Station

Hope St

Bedford St

Linenhall St

Adelaide St

Alfred St

Cromac St

Bruce St

Ventry St

Salisbury St

Ormeau Ave

Maryville St

Apsley St

Donegall Pass

Ormeau Rd

Walnut St

River Lagan

Shaftesbury Sq

Great Victoria St

Dublin Rd

Sandy Row

Donegall Rd

Bradbury Pl

Botanic Station

Hospital Station

Lower Cr

Upper Cr

Botanic Ave

Cromwell Rd

Cooke St

North of Ireland Sports Ground

National Cycle Network Route 9

Lisburn Rd

Claremont St

Camden St

Fitzwilliam St

Elmwood Ave

College Gardens

University Rd

University St

University Sq Mews

University Sq

Mount Charles

College Green

College Park

Lawrence St

Fitzroy Ave

University Ave

Rugby Ave

Balfour Ave

Queen's University

Carmel St

Agincourt Ave

Stranmillis Embankment

Ormeau Bridge

Eglantine (100m)

Malone Rd

Stranmillis Rd

Botanic Gardens

Ulster Museum

0 400 m
0 0.2 miles

Belfast

◉ Top Sights
1 Crown Liquor Saloon............................B3
2 Ulster Museum..................................A7

◉ Sights
3 Oh Yeah Music Centre.........................C1

🛏 Sleeping
4 Belfast Youth Hostel.............................B5
5 Vagabonds...A6

✕ Eating
6 John Hewitt Bar & Restaurant............C1
7 John Long's..A3
8 Maggie May's......................................B5
9 Maggie May's......................................A7

🍷 Drinking & Nightlife
10 Duke of York......................................C1
11 Filthy Quarter....................................B4
   John Hewitt Bar &
   Restaurant..................................(see 6)

🛍 Shopping
12 Good Vibrations................................B1

★ **Crown Liquor Saloon**   HISTORIC BUILDING
(www.nationaltrust.org.uk; 46 Great Victoria St; ☺11.30am-11pm Mon-Wed, to midnight Thu-Sat, 12.30-10pm Sun) FREE There are not too many historical monuments that you can enjoy while savouring a pint of beer, but the National Trust's Crown Liquor Saloon is one of them. Belfast's most famous bar was refurbished by Patrick Flanagan in the late 19th century and displays Victorian decorative flamboyance at its best (he was looking to pull in a posh clientele from the newfangled train station and Grand Opera House across the street).

Cave Hill   HILL
The best way to get a feel for Belfast's natural setting is to view it from above. In the absence of a private aircraft, head for Cave Hill (368m) which looms over the northern fringes of the city. The view from its summit takes in the whole sprawl of the city, the docks and the creeping fingers of urbanisation along the shores of Belfast Lough. On a clear day you can even spot Scotland lurking on the horizon.

Ulster Folk & Transport Museum   MUSEUM
(www.nmni.com; Cultra, Holywood; adult/child £9/5.50, combined ticket to both museums £11/6; ☺10am-5pm Tue-Sun Mar-Sep, 10am-4pm Tue-Fri & 11am-4pm Sat & Sun Oct-Feb) One of Northern Ireland's finest, the Ulster Folk & Transport Museum is really two museums in one: the **Ulster Folk Museum** and the **Ulster Transport Museum**, which lie on either side of the A2 road to Bangor, about 14km northeast of central Belfast, just north of Holywood.

Buses to Bangor stop nearby. Cultra station on the Belfast to Bangor train line is within a 10-minute walk.

☞ Tours

Belfast iTours (http://belfastitours.com) offers 10 self-guided video tours of the city that you can download to your mobile device.

Black taxi tours of West Belfast's murals are offered by a large number of taxi companies and local cabbies. These can vary in quality and content, but in general they're an intimate and entertaining way to see the sights. Drivers will pick you up from anywhere in the city centre.

Several companies also offer day-long bus tours around filming locations used for *Game of Thrones* – visit www.discover northernireland.com/gameofthrones.

🛏 Sleeping

★ **Vagabonds**   HOSTEL £
(☎028-9023 3017; www.vagabondsbelfast.com; 9 University Rd; dm £13-16, d & tw £40; @🛜) Comfy bunks, lockable luggage baskets, private shower cubicles and a relaxed atmosphere are what you get at one of Belfast's best hostels, run by a couple of experienced travellers. It's conveniently located close to both Queen's and the city centre.

Belfast Youth Hostel   HOSTEL £
(☎028-9031 5435; www.hini.org.uk; 22-32 Donegall Rd; dm £11.50-14.50, tw £30-42, d £38-42; @🛜) Handy amenities at this big, bright HI (Hostelling International) hostel include laundry facilities, secure on-site parking, 24-hour reception (with no lock-out or curfew), and a breakfast-specialist cafe.

✕ Eating

Maggie May's   CAFE £
(www.maggiemaysbelfastcafe.co.uk; 50 Botanic Ave; mains £4-14; ☺8am-11pm Mon-Sat, 9am-11pm Sun; 🍴👶) This is a classic little cafe with cosy wooden booths, murals of old Belfast and a host of hungover students wolfing down huge Ulster fry-ups. The all-day breakfast menu includes French toast and maple syrup, while lunch can be soup and a sandwich or beef lasagne. BYO.

① BELFAST VISITOR PASS

The **Belfast Visitor Pass** (per 1/2/3 days £6.50/11/14.50) allows unlimited travel on bus and train services in Belfast and around, and discounts on admission to Titanic Belfast and other attractions. You can buy it at airports, main train and bus stations, the Metro kiosk on Donegall Sq and the **Visit Belfast Welcome Centre** (p130).

John Hewitt Bar & Restaurant   PUB FOOD £
(www.thejohnhewitt.com; 51 Donegall St; mains £7-9; ☺kitchen noon-3pm Mon-Thu, to 5.30pm Fri & Sat; ✍) Named for the Belfast poet and socialist, this is a modern pub with a traditional atmosphere and a weekly changing menu that includes a soup of the day, beef and chicken dishes, and a couple of vegetarian options.

John Long's   FISH & CHIPS £
(www.johnlongs.com; 39 Athol St; fish & chips £4-8; ☺11.30am-6.30pm Mon-Sat) A wonderfully down-to-earth Belfast institution, this 1914-opened chippie is hidden in an inconspicuous red-brick building adjoining a car park, and is covered in mesh grills (a legacy of having its windows blown out when the nearby Europa Hotel was bombed). Inside, it fries up classic cod and chips in beef dripping, served at 1970s Formica booths. Cash only.

Bia   CAFE £
(www.biabelfast.com; 216 Falls Rd; mains £8-22; ☺9am-6pm Mon, 8am-8pm Tue-Sat, 10am-6pm Sun; ☏♿) Inside the Irish-language and arts centre **Cultúrlann McAdam Ó Fiaich** (www.culturlann.ie; ☺9am-5.30pm Mon-Sat, 10am-4.30pm Sun), Bia (meaning 'food') serves home-cooked stews, soups, roasts, steaks, burgers and lighter bites such as cakes, scones and pastries.

🍷 Drinking & Nightlife

★**Duke of York**   PUB
(www.dukeofyorkbelfast.com; 11 Commercial Ct; ☺11.30am-11.30pm Mon-Wed, to 1am Thu & Fri, to 2am Sat, 2-8pm Sun) Down an inconspicuous alley in the heart of the city's former newspaper district, the snug, traditional Duke has a hang-out for print workers and journalists. Sinn Féin leader, Gerry Adams, worked behind the bar here during his student days in 1971. The entire alley takes on a street-party atmosphere in warm weather.

★**Eglantine**   PUB
(www.eglantinebar.com; 32 Malone Rd; ☺11.30am-midnight Mon & Tue, to 1am Wed-Sun; ☏) The 'Eg' is a local institution, and widely reckoned to be the best of Belfast's many student pubs. It serves good beer and good food, and hosts numerous events: Monday is cinema club, Tuesday is vinyl night, other nights see DJs spin and bands perform. Bonus: Pac-Man machine.

★**Filthy Quarter**   BAR
(www.thefilthyquarter.com; 45 Dublin Rd; ☺1pm-1am Mon-Sat, to midnight Sun) Four individually and collectively fabulous bars make up the Filthy Quarter: retro-trad-style, bric-a-brac-filled **Filthy McNastys**, hosting local musicians from 10pm nightly; the fairy-lit **Secret Garden**, a two-storey beer garden with watering cans for drinks coolers; **Gypsy Lounge** (Tuesday, Thursday, Friday, Saturday and Sunday nights), with a gypsy caravan DJ booth; and a chandelier- and candelabra-adorned cocktail bar, **Filthy Chic**.

☆ Entertainment

Good places to get the low-down on live music and club nights include the **Good Vibrations** (89-93 North St; ☺8am-6pm) record shop, and the **Oh Yeah Music Centre** (www.ohyeahbelfast.com; 15-21 Gordon St; ☺museum 11am-3pm Mon-Fri, noon-5pm Sat) **FREE**.

Other resources include:

➡ Visit Belfast Welcome Centre (http://visit-belfast.com)

➡ Big List (www.thebiglist.co.uk)

➡ Culture Northern Ireland (www.culturenorthernireland.org)

➡ Belfast Music (www.belfastmusic.org)

① Information

Visit Belfast Welcome Centre (☏028-9024 6609; http://visit-belfast.com; 9 Donegall Sq N; ☺9am-7pm Mon-Sat, 11am-4pm Sun Jun-Sep, 9am-5.30pm Mon-Sat, 11am-4pm Sun Oct-May; ☏) Provides information about the whole of Northern Ireland and books accommodation. Services include left luggage (not overnight), currency exchange and free wi-fi.

① Getting There & Away

Contact **Translink** (☏028-9066 6630; www.translink.co.uk) for timetable and fares information for buses and trains.

AIR

Belfast International Airport (BFS; ☑ 028-9448 4848; www.belfastairport.com) is 30km northwest of the city; **George Best Belfast City Airport** (BHD; ☑ 028-9093 9093; www.belfastcityairport.com; Airport Rd) is 6km northeast of the city centre.

BOAT

Apart from Steam Packet Company and Stena Line services, other car ferries to and from Scotland and England dock at Larne, 37km north of Belfast. Trains to the terminal at Larne Harbour depart from Great Victoria St station.

BUS

There are **information desks** (☉ 7.45am-6.30pm Mon-Fri, 8am-6pm Sat) at both of Belfast's bus stations, where you can pick up regional bus timetables.

National Express (☑ 08717 818 178; www.nationalexpress.com) runs a daily coach service between Belfast and London (£37 one way, 15½ hours) via the Cairnryan ferry. The ticket office is in the Europa Bus Centre.

Scottish Citylink (☑ 0871 266 3333; www.citylink.co.uk) operates three buses a day from Glasgow to Belfast (£32, six hours) via the Cairnryan ferry.

TRAIN

Belfast has two main train stations: Great Victoria St, next to the Europa Bus Centre, and Belfast Central, east of the city centre. If you arrive by train at Central Station, your rail ticket entitles you to a free bus ride into the city centre. A local train also connects with Great Victoria St.

The **NIR Travel Shop** (☑ 028-9024 2420; Great Victoria St Station; ☉ 9am-5pm Mon-Fri, to 12.30pm Sat) books train tickets, ferries and holiday packages. Destinations include Dublin (£30, 2¼ hours, eight daily Monday to Saturday, five Sunday).

ℹ Getting Around

TO/FROM THE AIRPORT

Belfast International Airport Airport Express 300 bus runs to the Europa Bus Centre (one way/return £7.50/10.50, 30 minutes) every 10 or 15 minutes between 7am and 8pm, every 30 minutes from 8pm to 11pm, and hourly through the night; a return ticket is valid for one month. A taxi costs about £30.

George Best Belfast City Airport Airport Express 600 bus runs to the Europa Bus Centre (one way/return £2.50/3.80, 15 minutes) every 20 minutes between 6am and 9.30pm Monday to Saturday, and every 40 minutes on Sunday. A return ticket is valid for one month. The taxi fare to the city centre is about £10.

BICYCLE

Belfast Bike Tours (☑ 07812 114235; www.belfastbiketours.com; per person £15; ☉ 10.30am & 2pm Mon, Wed, Fri & Sat Apr-Aug, Sat only Sep-Mar) rents bikes.

BUS

Metro (☑ 028-9066 6630; www.translink.co.uk) operates the bus network in Belfast. Most city services depart from various stops on and around Donegall Sq, at City Hall and along Queen St. You can pick up a free bus map (and buy tickets) from the **Metro kiosk** (☉ 8am-5.30pm Mon-Fri) at the northwest corner of the square.

Buy your ticket from the driver (change given); fares range from £1.50 to £2.30 depending on distance. The driver can also sell you a **Metro Day Ticket** (£3.90), giving you unlimited bus travel within the City Zone all day Monday to Saturday. Cheaper versions allow travel any time after 10am Monday to Saturday or all day Sunday (£3.40).

The Causeway Coast

Ireland isn't short of scenic coastlines, but the Causeway Coast between Portstewart and Ballycastle – climaxing in the spectacular rock formations of the Giant's Causeway – and the **Antrim Coast** between Ballycastle and Belfast are as magnificent as they come.

◉ Sights

★ **Giant's Causeway**   LANDMARK
(www.nationaltrust.org.uk; ☉ dawn-dusk) FREE
This spectacular rock formation – Northern Ireland's only Unesco World Heritage Site – is one of Ireland's most impressive and atmospheric landscape features, a vast expanse of regular, closely packed, hexagonal stone columns looking for all the world like the handiwork of giants. The phenomenon is explained in the **Giant's Causeway Visitor Experience** (☑ 028-2073 1855; adult/child with parking £9/4.50, without parking £7/3.25; ☉ 9am-7pm Apr-Sep, to 6pm Feb, Mar & Oct, to 5pm Nov-Jan) 🍃, a spectacular new ecofriendly building half-hidden in a hillside above the sea.

Visiting the Giant's Causeway itself is free of charge but you pay to use the car park and the visitor centre. (The admission fee is reduced by £1.50 if you arrive by bus, bike or on foot.)

From the centre it's an easy 10- to 15-minute walk downhill to the Causeway itself, but a more interesting approach is to follow the clifftop path northeast for 2km to the

Chimney Tops headland, then descend the Shepherd's Steps to the Causeway. For the less mobile, a minibus shuttles from the visitor centre to the Causeway (£2 return).

★ **Carrick-a-Rede Rope Bridge** BRIDGE
(www.nationaltrust.org.uk; Ballintoy; adult/child £5.90/3; ⊙ 9.30am-7pm Apr-Aug, to 6pm Mar, Sep & Oct, to 3.30pm Nov-Feb) This 20m-long, 1m-wide bridge of wire rope spans the chasm between the sea cliffs and the little island of Carrick-a-Rede, swaying 30m above the rock-strewn water. Crossing the bridge is perfectly safe, but frightening if you don't have a head for heights, especially if it's breezy (in high winds the bridge is closed). From the island, views take in Rathlin Island and Fair Head to the east.

There's a small National Trust information centre and cafe at the car park.

🛏 Sleeping

There are several hostels along the coast, including the excellent **Sheep Island View Hostel** (☑ 028-2076 9391; www.sheepislandview.com; 42a Main St; dm/d/tr/f £18/40/60/80; P @ 🛜), **Ballycastle Backpackers** (☑ 028-2076 3612; www.ballycastlebackpackers.net; 4 North St; dm/tw from £15/35, cottage £80; P @ 🛜) and **Bushmills Hostel** (☑ 028-2073 1222; www.hini.org.uk; 49 Main St; dm/tw from £19.50/41; ⊙ closed 11.30am-2.30pm Jul & Aug, 11.30am-5pm Mar-Jun, Sep & Oct; @ 🛜).

ℹ Getting There & Away

As well as the **Antrim Coaster** (Bus 252; www.translink.co.uk; adult/child £9/4.50; ⊙ Easter, May bank holiday weekends & Jul-Aug; 🛜) and **Causeway Rambler** (Bus 402; www.translink.co.uk; adult/child £6.50/3.25; ⊙ Easter-Sep) services and **Giant's Causeway & Bushmills Railway** (☑ 028-2073 2844; www.freewebs.com/giantscausewayrailway; adult/child return £5/3), bus 172 from Ballycastle (£4.40, 30 minutes, eight daily Monday to Friday, three Saturday and Sunday) to Coleraine (£2.80, 25 minutes) and Bushmills (£2.30, five minutes) stop at the Giant's Causeway year-round. From Coleraine, trains run to Belfast or Derry.

Derry/Londonderry

POP 108,000

Northern Ireland's second-largest city continues to flourish as an artistic and cultural hub. Derry's city centre was given a striking makeover for its year as the UK City of Culture 2013, with the new Peace Bridge, Ebrington Square, and the redevelopment of the waterfront and Guildhall area making the most of the city's splendid riverside setting.

There's lots of history to absorb here, from the Siege of Derry to the Battle of the Bogside and Bloody Sunday – a stroll around the 17th-century city walls that encircle the city is a must, as is a tour of the Bogside murals – along with the burgeoning live-music scene in the city's lively pubs.

⊙ Sights

★ **Derry's City Walls** CITY WALLS
(www.derryswalls.com; ⊙ dawn-dusk) FREE The best way to get a feel for Derry's layout and history is to walk the 1.5km circumference of the city's walls. Completed in 1619, Derry's city walls are 8m high and 9m thick, and are the only city walls in Ireland to survive almost intact. The four original gates (Shipquay, Ferryquay, Bishop's and Butcher's) were rebuilt in the 18th and 19th centuries, when three new gates (New, Magazine and Castle) were added.

Guildhall NOTABLE BUILDING
(☑ 028-7137 6510; www.derrycity.gov.uk/Guildhall; Guildhall St; ⊙ 10am-5.30pm) FREE Standing just outside the city walls, the neo-Gothic Guildhall was originally built in 1890, then rebuilt after a fire in 1908. Its fine stained-glass windows were presented by the London Livery companies, and its clock tower was modelled on London's Big Ben. Inside, there's a historical exhibition on the Plantation of Ulster, and a tourist information point.

Tower Museum MUSEUM
(www.derrycity.gov.uk/museums; Union Hall Pl; adult/child £4/2; ⊙ 10am-5.30pm) Head straight to the 5th floor of this award-winning museum inside a replica 16th-century tower house for a view from the top. Then work your way down through the excellent **Armada Shipwreck** exhibition, and the **Story of Derry**, where well-thought-out exhibits and audiovisuals lead you through the city's history from the founding of the monastery of St Colmcille (Columba) in the 6th century to the Battle of the Bogside in the late 1960s. Allow at least two hours.

People's Gallery Murals MURALS
(Rossville St) The 12 murals that decorate the gable ends of houses along Rossville St, near Free Derry Corner, are popularly referred to as the People's Gallery. They are

Derry

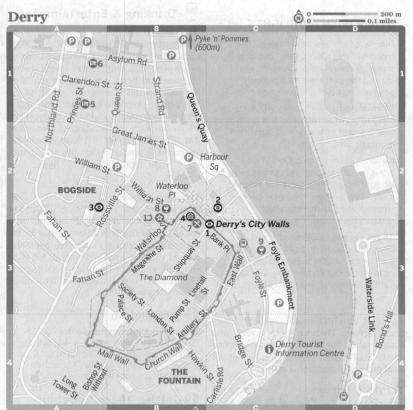

the work of Tom Kelly, Will Kelly and Kevin Hasson, known as 'the Bogside Artists'. The three men have spent most of their lives in the Bogside, and lived through the worst of the Troubles. The murals can be clearly seen from the northern part of the City Walls.

🛏 Sleeping & Eating

Derry City Independent Hostel HOSTEL **£**
(📞028-7128 0542; www.derry-hostel.co.uk; 12 Princes St; dm/d/tr £15/38/54; @🛜) Run by experienced backpackers and decorated with souvenirs from their travels around the world, this small, friendly hostel is set in a Georgian town house a short walk northwest of the bus station.

Derry Palace Hostel HOSTEL **£**
(📞028-7130 9051; www.paddyspalace.com; 1 Woodleigh Tce, Asylum Rd; dm/tw from £19/70; 🅿@🛜) Part of the Ireland-wide Paddy's Palace chain, this recently renovated hostel

---

Derry

◉ **Top Sights**
1 Derry's City Walls C3

◉ **Sights**
2 Guildhall C2
3 People's Gallery Murals A2
4 Tower Museum B2

🛏 **Sleeping**
5 Derry City Independent Hostel A1
6 Derry Palace Hostel A1

🍽 **Eating**
7 Green Man B3

🍷 **Drinking & Nightlife**
8 Peadar O'Donnell's B2
9 Sandino's Cafe-Bar C3

🎭 **Entertainment**
10 Gweedore Bar B2

OTHER IRISH HIGHLIGHTS

Dingle (65km west of Killarney) The charms of this special spot have long drawn runaways from across the world, making this port town a surprisingly cosmopolitan and creative place.

Glendalough (50km south of Dublin) Nestled between two lakes, this lovely spot is one of Ireland's most significant monastic sites.

Kinsale (28km south of Cork) This picturesque yachting harbour has been labelled the gourmet capital of Ireland; it certainly contains more than its fair share of international-standard restaurants.

Slieve League (120km southwest of Derry/Londonderry) Spend a day walking along the top of these awe-inspiring cliffs via the slightly terrifying One Man's Path to Malinbeg, near Glencolumbcille.

is central, comfortable and has a great party atmosphere. There's a sunny garden (and heated patio), free bikes and musical instruments. Staff regularly organise nights out at local pubs with traditional music.

★ **Pyke 'n' Pommes** BURGERS £
(behind Foyle Marina, off Baronet St; dishes £5-15; ☺ noon-3pm Tue-Thu, to 5pm Fri & Sat, hours vary; 🖼🚻) 🍴 Derry's best eatery is this quayside shipping container. Chef Kevin Pyke's amazing, mostly organic burgers span his signature Notorious Pig (pulled pork, crispy slaw, beetroot and crème fraîche), Cheeky Monkey (monkfish, warm potato and smoked-apple purée) and Veganderry (chickpeas, lemon and coriander) to his Legenderry Burger (Wagyu beef, pickled onions and honey-mustard mayo). Seasonal specials might include mackerel or oysters.

★ **Green Man** DELI £
(Craft Village, Shipquay St; ☺ 9.30am-6pm Mon-Sat) 🍴 The Green Man is the ultimate place to pick up artisan picnic fare from around the Emerald Isle: Haven Smokehouse turf-smoked salmon, Durrus farmhouse cheese, Filligans preserves and chutneys, Fermanagh black and white pudding, Knochnarea honey, and Guinness bread, as well as sweet treats like Glastry Farm ice cream and Melting Pot Irish fudge.

🍷 Drinking & Entertainment

★ **Peadar O'Donnell's** PUB
(www.peadars.com; 59-63 Waterloo St; ☺ 11.30am-1.30am Mon-Sat, 12.30pm-12.30am Sun) Done up as a typical Irish pub/grocery – with shelves of household items, shopkeepers scales on the counter and a museum's worth of old bric-a-brac – Peadar's has traditional music sessions every night and often on weekend afternoons as well. Its adjacent **Gweedore Bar** (59-61 Waterloo St; ☺ 11.30am-1.30am Mon-Sat, noon-12.30am Sun) hosts live rock bands every night, and a Saturday night disco upstairs.

Sandino's Cafe-Bar BAR
(www.sandinos.com; 1 Water St; ☺ 11.30am-1am Mon-Sat, noon-midnight Sun) From the posters of Che to the Free Palestine flag to the fair-trade coffee and gluten-free beer, this relaxed cafe-bar exudes a liberal, left-wing vibe. DJs spin from Thursday to Saturday in Club Havana; there's traditional Irish music on Sunday afternoons.

ℹ Information

Derry Tourist Information Centre (📞 028-7126 7284; www.visitderry.com; 44 Foyle St; ☺ 9am-5.30pm Mon-Fri, 10am-5pm Sat & Sun; 📶) Sells books and maps, has a bureau de change and can book accommodation.

ℹ Getting There & Around

BUS
The **bus station** (📞 028-7126 2261; Foyle St) is just northeast of the walled city. Services include Belfast Europa Bus Centre (£12, 1¾ hours, half-hourly Monday to Friday, hourly Saturday and Sunday) and Galway (£16.50, 5½ hours, five daily).

TRAIN
Derry's train station (traditionally referred to as Londonderry in Northern Ireland timetables) is on the eastern side of the River Foyle; a free Rail Link bus connects it with the bus station. Services include Belfast (£12, 2½ hours, nine daily Monday to Saturday, six on Sunday).

Ireland Survival Guide

ℹ Directory A–Z

ACCOMMODATION
Hostels in Ireland can be booked solid in summer. An Óige (www.anoige.ie) and Hostelling International Northern Ireland (HINI; www.

hini.org.uk) are branches of Hostelling International (HI); An Óige has 26 hostels in the Republic, while HINI has five in the North. Other hostel associations include Independent Holiday Hostels of Ireland (www.hostels-ireland.com) and the Independent Hostel Owners of Ireland (www.independenthostelsireland.com).

From June to September a dorm bed at most hostels costs €10 to €25 (£7 to £18). Many hostels now have family and double rooms.

Typical B&Bs cost around €35 to €40 (£25 to £30) per person a night (sharing a double room), though more luxurious B&Bs can cost upwards of €55 (£40) per person. Most B&Bs are small, so in summer they quickly fill up.

Commercial camping grounds typically charge €12 to €20 (£10 to £18) for a tent or campervan and two people. Unless otherwise indicated, prices quoted for 'campsites' are for a tent, car and two people.

INTERNET RESOURCES

Failte Ireland (www.discoverireland.ie) Official tourism site.

Northern Ireland Tourist Board (www.discovernorthernireland.com) Official tourism site.

Entertainment Ireland (www.entertainment.ie) Countrywide entertainment listings.

LGBT TRAVELLERS

Resources include the following:

Gaire (www.gaire.com) Message board and info for a host of gay-related issues.

Gay & Lesbian Youth Northern Ireland (www.cara-friend.org.uk/projects/glyni) Voluntary counselling, information, health and social space organisation for the gay community.

National Lesbian & Gay Federation (NLGF; ☏ 01-671 9076; http://nxf.ie) Publishes the monthly *Gay Community News* (http://theoutmost.com).

Northern Ireland Gay Rights Association (Nigra; ☏ 9066 5257; http://nigra.org.uk)

Outhouse (☏ 01-873 4932; www.outhouse.ie; 105 Capel St; ⬚ all city centre) Top gay, lesbian and bisexual resource centre in Dublin.

The Outmost (www.theoutmost.com) Excellent and resourceful for gay news, entertainment, lifestyle and opinion.

OPENING HOURS

Hours in both the Republic and Northern Ireland are roughly the same.

Banks 10am to 4pm Monday to Friday (to 5pm Thursday)

Post Offices Northern Ireland 9am to 5.30pm Monday to Friday, 9am to 12.30pm Saturday; Republic 9am to 6pm Monday to Friday, 9am to 1pm Saturday

Pubs In Northern Ireland: 11.30am to 11pm Monday to Saturday, 12.30pm to 10pm Sunday;

pubs with late licences open until 1am Monday to Saturday and midnight Sunday. In the Republic: 10.30am to 11.30pm Monday to Thursday, 10.30am to 12.30am Friday and Saturday, noon to 11pm Sunday (30 minutes of 'drinking up' time allowed); pubs with bar extensions open to 2.30am Thursday to Saturday.

Restaurants Noon to 10.30pm in Dublin, till 9pm outside (aim to be seated by 8pm at the latest); many close one day of the week

Shops 9am to 5.30pm or 6pm Monday to Saturday (until 8pm on Thursday and sometimes Friday), noon to 6pm Sunday (in bigger towns only)

PUBLIC HOLIDAYS

The following are public holidays in both the Republic and Northern Ireland:

New Year's Day 1 January

St Patrick's Day 17 March

Easter (Good Friday to Easter Monday inclusive) March/April

May Holiday 1st Monday in May

Christmas Day 25 December

St Stephen's Day (Boxing Day) 26 December

St Patrick's Day and St Stephen's Day holidays are taken on the following Monday when they fall on a weekend. In the Republic, nearly everywhere closes on Good Friday even though it isn't an official public holiday. In the North, most shops open on Good Friday, but close the following Tuesday.

TELEPHONE

Area codes in the Republic have three digits except for Dublin, which has a two-digit code (☏ 01). Always use the area code if calling from a mobile phone, but you don't need it if calling from a fixed-line number within the area code.

In Northern Ireland, the area code for all fixed-line numbers is ☏ 028, but you only need to use it if calling from a mobile phone or from outside

> ### ℹ️ EATING PRICE RANGES
>
> The following price indicators are used to indicate the cost of a main course at dinner:
>
> **Republic of Ireland**
>
> € less than €12
>
> €€ €12 to €25
>
> **Northern Ireland**
>
> £ less than £12
>
> ££ £21 to £20

Northern Ireland. To call Northern Ireland from the Republic, use ☑ 048 instead of ☑ 028, without the international dialling code.

ℹ️ Getting There & Away

AIR

Ireland's main airports:

Cork Airport (p121) Airlines servicing the airport include Aer Lingus and Ryanair.

Dublin Airport (p115) Ireland's major international gateway airport, with direct flights from the UK, Europe, North America and the Middle East.

Shannon Airport (SNN; ☑ 061-712 000; www.shannonairport.com; 🛜) In County Clare; has a few direct flights from the UK, Europe and North America.

Northern Ireland's airports:

Belfast International Airport (p131) Has direct flights from the UK, Europe and North America.

SEA

Competition from budget airlines has forced ferry operators to discount heavily and offer flexible fares.

A useful website is www.ferrybooker.com, which covers all sea-ferry routes and operators to Ireland. Main operators include the following:

Brittany Ferries (www.brittanyferries.com) Cork to Roscoff; April to October.

Irish Ferries (www.irishferries.com) Dublin to Holyhead ferries (up to four per day year-round); and France to Rosslare (three times per week).

P&O Ferries (www.poferries.com) Daily sailings year-round from Dublin to Liverpool, and Larne to Cairnryan. Larne to Troon runs March to October only.

Stena Line (www.stenaline.com) Daily sailings from Holyhead to Dublin Port, from Belfast to Liverpool and Cairnryan, and from Rosslare to Fishguard.

ℹ️ Getting Around

BICYCLE

Ireland is a great cycling destination. However, dodgy weather, many very narrow roads and some very fast drivers are major concerns. A good tip for cyclists in the west is that the prevailing winds make it easier to cycle from south to north.

Buses will carry bikes, but only if there's room. For trains, bear in mind:

➡ Intercity trains charge up to €10 per bike.

➡ Book in advance (www.irishrail.ie), as there's only room for two bikes per service.

BUS

Bus Éireann (☑ 01-836 6111; www.buseireann.ie) The Republic's main bus line.

Translink (☑ 028-9066 6630; www.translink.co.uk) Northern Ireland's main bus service; includes Ulsterbus and Goldline.

CAR & MOTORCYCLE

Advance rates can be as low as €10 to €20 per day for a small car (unlimited mileage). Shop around and use price comparison sites as well as company sites (which often have deals not available on booking sites).

Other tips:

➡ Most cars are manual; automatic cars are available, but they're much more expensive to hire.

➡ If you're travelling from the Republic into Northern Ireland, it's important to be sure that your insurance covers journeys to the North.

➡ The majority of hire companies won't rent you a car if you're under 23 and haven't had a valid driving licence for at least a year.

TRAIN

Irish Rail (Iarnród Éireann; ☑ 1850 366 222; www.irishrail.ie) Operates trains in the Republic.

Translink NI Railways (☑ 028-9066 6630; www.translink.co.uk) Operates trains in Northern Ireland.

Scandinavia

Best Places to Eat

→ Noma (p155)

→ Oli Nico (p159)

→ Hietalahden Kauppahalli (p174)

→ Baklandet Skydsstasjon (p193)

→ Þrír Frakkar (p201)

Best Places to Sleep

→ Icehotel (p171)

→ Dream Hostel (p179)

→ Svinøya Rorbuer (p195)

→ Generator Hostel (p151)

→ Odense City B&B (p157)

Why Go?

Effortlessly chic cities and remote forests; rocking festivals and the majestic aurora borealis; endless day and perpetual night: Scandinavia's menu is anything but bland.

Stolid Nordic stereotypes dissolve completely in the region's vibrant capitals. Crest-of-the-wave design can be seen across them all, backed up by outstanding modern architecture, excellent museums, acclaimed restaurants and a sizzling nightlife.

The great outdoors is rarely greater than in Europe's big north. Epic expanses of wilderness and intoxicatingly pure air mean that engaging with nature is an utter pleasure. It's rare to find such inspiring landscapes that are so easily accessible.

Despite the scary subzero winter temperatures, there's still a wealth of things to do: skiing, sledding behind huskies or reindeer, taking snowmobile safaris, spending romantic nights in snow hotels, visiting Santa Claus and gazing at the soul-piercing Northern Lights.

Explosive summer's long days are filled with festivals, beer terraces and wonderful boating, hiking and cycling.

Fast Facts

Capitals Copenhagen (Denmark), Stockholm (Sweden), Helsinki (Finland), Oslo (Norway), Reykjavík (Iceland)

Emergency ☑112

Currency krone (Dkr, Denmark), krona (Skr, Sweden), euro (€, Finland), krone (Nkr, Norway), króna (Ikr, Iceland)

Languages Danish, Swedish, Finnish, Norwegian, Icelandic, Sámi languages

Time Zone Central European (Denmark, Sweden, Norway; UTC/GMT plus one hour), Eastern European (Finland; UTC/GMT plus two hours), Western European (Iceland; UTC/GMT)

Country Codes ☑45 (Denmark), ☑46 (Sweden), ☑358 (Finland), ☑47 (Norway), ☑354 (Iceland)

Population 5.6 million (Denmark), 9.6 million (Sweden), 5.4 million (Finland), 5.1 million (Norway), 332,500 (Iceland)

Scandinavia Highlights

1 Copenhagen
Shop, nosh and chill in Scandinavia's capital of cool. (p150)

2 Stockholm Tour urban waterways, explore museums and wander the Old Town of Sweden's capital. (p161)

3 Helsinki
Immerse yourself in harbourside Helsinki, for the latest in Finnish design and nightlife. (p172)

4 Rovaniemi Cross the Arctic Circle, hit the Arktikum museum and visit Santa in his grotto in Finnish Lapland. (p183)

5 Kiruna Hike wild reindeer-filled landscapes, explore Sámi culture and sleep in the world-famous Icehotel in Jukkasjärvi. (p170)

6 Lofoten Head for the Arctic Ocean and arguably Europe's most beautiful archipelago. (p194)

7 Hurtigruten
Journey Norway's peerless coast on the characterful, spectacular Hurtigruten ferry. (p191)

8 Fjordland From Bergen, Norway's most attractive city, explore the south-western fjords. (p188)

9 Vatnajökull National Park
Discover Skaftafell glacier and the icebergs at nearby Jökulsárlón. (p205)

10 Reykjavík Party till dawn on the weekend pub crawl *djammið* in Iceland's lively capital, then hit museums, shops and cafes. (p197)

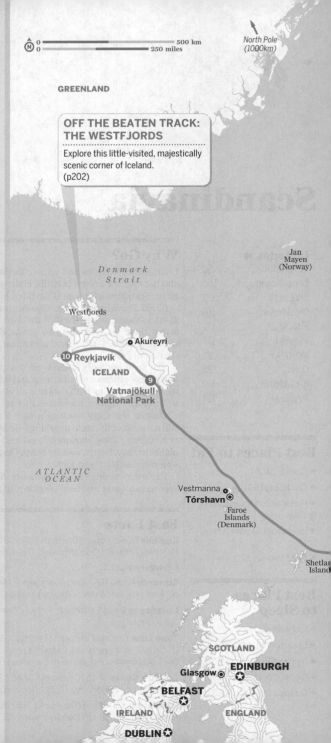

OFF THE BEATEN TRACK: THE WESTFJORDS

Explore this little-visited, majestically scenic corner of Iceland. (p202)

OFF THE BEATEN TRACK: INARI

Learn about Sámi culture in this fascinating Lapland village.
(p184)

GREENLAND SEA

Svalbard (Norway)

BARENTS SEA

NORWEGIAN SEA

Nordkapp ○ Vardø

○ Murmansk

Tromsø ○

Inarijärvi
Inari

Lofoten Islands   Narvik
Lofoten ○ **6**
Bodø ○   **5** Kiruna   Rovaniemi
4

RUSSIA

Oulu ◎
Oulujärvi

SWEDEN

FINLAND

Hurtigruten
7

Umeå ○   Vaasa   Kuopio ○   Saimaa

Trondheim ○   Östersund ○   Jyväskylä ○   Lappeenranta ○
Lake Ladoga
Vyborg ○

NORWAY
Ålesund ○
Galdhøpiggen (2469m) ▲   Gulf of Bothnia   Tampere ○   Helsinki   St Petersburg ◎

Lillehammer ○   Turku ○   **3**

8 Fjordland
○ Bergen   Åland   Gulf of Finland   RUSSIA

Uppsala ○   TALLINN ★   Lake Peipsi

OSLO ✪   Västerås ○   ESTONIA
Örebro ○   **2** Stockholm

Stavanger ○   Norrköping ○
Vänern   Linköping ○

Kristiansand   Vättern   Gotland

Skagen   **Göteborg**   Jönköping ○   BALTIC SEA   **RĪGA** ★   LATVIA

NORTH SEA   Skagerrak   Öland

Aalborg ○   **OFF THE BEATEN TRACK: ÅLAND**

Aarhus ○   Helsingør ○ Helsingborg
DENMARK   ○ **1**   Cycle this bucolic, flat archipelago
Esbjerg ○   **Copenhagen** ○ **Malmö**   between Sweden and Finland.
Odense ○   Funen   Bornholm   (p179)

Denmark's
TOP EXPERIENCES

Denmark (p150) is the bridge between Scandinavia and northern Europe. To the rest of Scandinavia, the Danes are chilled, frivolous party animals, with relatively liberal, progressive attitudes. Their culture, food, architecture and appetite for conspicuous consumption owe as much, if not more, to their German neighbours to the south than to their former colonies (Sweden, Norway and Iceland) to the north. Packed with intriguing museums, shops, bars, nightlife and award-winning restaurants, Denmark's capital, Copenhagen, is one of the hippest, most accessible cities in Europe. And while Danish cities such as Odense and Aarhus harbour their own urban drawcards, Denmark's other chief appeal lies in its photogenic countryside, sweeping coastline and historic sights.

Copenhagen

You may find it hard to suppress your envy for residents of Scandinavia's coolest capital. While this 850-year-old harbour town retains much of its historic good looks (think copper spires, cobbled squares and pastel-coloured gabled houses), the focus here is on the innovative. Denmark's high-achieving capital is home to a thriving design scene, a futuristic metro system, and clean, green developments. Its streets are awash with effortlessly hip shops, cafes and bars, world-class museums and art collections, brave new architecture, and no fewer than 15 Michelin-starred restaurants. (p150)

Danish Dining

Sure, some trendspotters predicted the end of New Nordic cuisine's time in the global spotlight – but then Noma popped up to reclaim the title of world's number one restaurant in 2014 (after temporarily losing the crown). New Nordic isn't going anywhere, and its effects are being warmly felt. Emboldened by the attention and praise lavished on Danish produce and innovative chefs, food producers are re-embracing old-school culinary delights. Expect new spins on beloved rye breads and pastries, smørrebrød (open sandwiches), smoked fish and even humble pork-and-potato dishes, and to eat damn well in unexpected corners of the country. (p155)

Cycling

Is Denmark the best nation for bike touring in the world? Probably, thanks to its extensive national network of cycle routes, terrain that is either flat or merely undulating, and a culture strongly committed to two-wheeled transport. But you needn't embark on lengthy tours to enjoy cycle touring. The cities are a breeze to pedal around, and many have public bike-sharing schemes with free (or cheap) bike usage. More than 50% of Copenhagen commuters travel by bicycle – it's easy to follow their lead, especially with fabulous new initiatives such as Cykelslangen,

---

GETTING AROUND

Transport in Denmark is reasonably priced, quick and efficient. Your best friend is the journey-planning website www.rejseplanen.dk (download the Rejseplanen app to your phone).

Train Reasonably priced, with comprehensive coverage of the country and frequent departures.

Bike Extensive bike paths link towns throughout the country. Bikes can be hired in every town.

Bus All large cities and towns have a local and regional bus system. Long-distance buses run a distant second to trains.

Boats Ferries link virtually all of Denmark's populated islands.

an elevated bike lane over the harbour.

⭐ Legoland

Legoland theme park celebrates the 'toy of the century' (as adjudged by *Fortune* magazine in 2000) in the country in which it was invented, also 'the world's happiest nation' (according to a Gallup World Poll). So you've got to believe Legoland will be something special – and it is. Billund, the Lego company's hometown, is positioning itself as the 'Capital of Children' – theme parks, waterparks and an inspired new cultural centre (designed to resemble gigantic Lego bricks) make this region Happy Families HQ in a country that's already overflowing with child-friendly attractions. (p158)

⭐ Summer Music Festivals

There's a fat calendar of festivals countrywide, from folk music in Tønder to riverboat jazz in the Lake District around Silkeborg. The capital lets loose the hepcats at its largest electric, Copenhagen Jazz Festival, over 10 days in early July, but also celebrates electronic beats at Strøm in August. Meanwhile in Aarhus, NorthSide is helping to augment the city's music-fest street cred. But it's the festivals outside the cities that draw the biggest crowds: Roskilde rocks with Scandinavia's largest music festival, and Skanderborg hosts Denmark's 'most beautiful' event, lakeside Smukfest. (p151)

⭐ Kronborg Slot

Something rotten in the state of Denmark? Not at this fabulous 16th-century castle in Helsingør, made famous as the Elsinore Castle of Shakespeare's *Hamlet*. Kronborg's primary function was as a grandiose toll house, wresting taxes for more than 400 years from ships passing through the narrow Øresund between Denmark and Sweden. The fact that Hamlet, Prince of Denmark, was a fictional character hasn't deterred legions of sightseers from visiting the site. It's the venue for glorious summer performances of Shakespeare's plays during the HamletScenen festival. (p156)

⭐ Skagen

Skagen is an enchanting place, both bracing and beautiful. It lies at Denmark's northern tip and acts as a magnet for much of the population each summer, when the town is full to capacity yet still manages to charm. In the late 19th century artists flocked here, infatuated with the radiant light's impact on the rugged landscape. Now tourists flock here to enjoy the output of the 'Skagen school' artists, soak up that luminous light, devour the plentiful seafood and laze on the fine sandy beaches. (p159)

if Denmark were 100 people

87 would live in urban areas
13 would live in rural areas

belief systems
(% of population)

95
Evangelical Lutheran

3
other Christian

2
Muslim

population per sq km

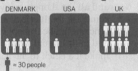

DENMARK USA UK

👤 ≈ 30 people

When to Go

Copenhagen

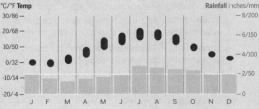

°C/°F Temp   Rainfall inches/mm

J F M A M J J A S O N D

Sweden's
TOP EXPERIENCES

As progressive and civilised as it may be, Sweden (p161) is a wild place. Its scenery ranges from barren moonscapes and impenetrable forests in the far north to sunny beaches and lush farmland further south.

Its short summers and long winters mean that people cling to every last speck of summer sunshine, while in winter locals rely on candlelight and glögg to warm their spirits. But lovers of the outdoors will thrive here in any season: winter sees skiing and dog-sledding, while the warmer months invite long hikes, swimming, sunbathing, canoeing and cycling...you name it.

For less rugged types, there's always restaurant- and nightclub-hopping and museum-perusing in cosmopolitan Stockholm, lively Göteborg and beyond.

 ## Stockholm

The nation's capital calls itself 'beauty on water', and it certainly doesn't disappoint in the looks department. Stockholm's many glittering waterways reflect slanted northern light onto spice-hued buildings, and the crooked cobblestone streets of Gamla Stan are magic to wander. Besides its aesthetic virtues, Stockholm also has top-notch museums, first-class dining and all the shopping anyone could ask for. Its clean and efficient public transport, and multilingual locals, make it a cinch to navigate, and at the end of the day you can collapse in a cushy designer hotel. (p161)

 ## Northern Delights

The twin phenomena that have made the north of Sweden so famous – one natural, one artificial – are both found beyond the Arctic Circle. No other natural spectacle compares to the aurora borealis – the shape-shifting lights that dance across the night sky during the Arctic winter (October to March). The Icehotel (p171), humble igloo turned ice palace, just outside Kiruna, takes its inspiration from the changeable nature of the northern lights, and is recreated in a slightly different form every winter.

 ## Medieval Visby

It's hard to overstate the beauty of the Hanseatic port town of Visby, in itself justification for making the ferry trip to Gotland. Inside its thick medieval walls are twisting cobblestone streets, fairy-tale cottages draped in flowers, and gorgeous ruins atop hills with stunning Baltic views. The walls themselves, with 40-plus towers and the spectacular church ruins within, are a travel photographer's dream, and the perimeter makes an ideal scenic stroll. The city is also a food-lover's heaven, packed with top-notch restaurants accustomed to impressing discriminating diners. (p169)

Göteborg

The edgy alter ego to Stockholm's confident polish, Göteborg is a city of contrasts, with slick museums, raw industrial landscapes, pleasant parks, can-do designers and cutting-edge

---

GETTING AROUND

Transport in Sweden is reliable and easy to navigate. Roads are generally in good repair, and buses and trains are comfortable, with plenty of services on-board and in stations. There's a good trip planner at http://reseplanerare.resrobot.se.

Train Affordable and extensive; speed depends on whether the route is local, regional or express.

Bus A more extensive network than for trains, and often equally quick and cheap (if not more so).

Car Expensive but ideal if you want to explore smaller roads and remote places, especially for camping and outdoor activities.

food. Try delectable shrimp and fish – straight off the boat or at one of the city's five Michelin-rated restaurants. There's the thrill-packed chaos of Sweden's largest theme park, the cultured quiet of the many museums, and you can't leave without window-shopping in Haga and Linné. For a unique way of getting there, jump on a boat and cruise the 190km of the Göta Canal. (p168)

★ Inlandsbanan

Take a journey through Norrland along this historic train line (summer only), which passes small mining towns, deep green forests, herds of reindeer and, if you're lucky, the occasional elk (moose). Built during the 1930s and rendered obsolete by 1992, the line has more than enough charm and historical appeal to make up for its lack of speed – you'll have plenty of time to contemplate the landscape, in other words. It's a beautiful, oddball means of transport, best suited to those for whom adventure trumps efficiency. (p172)

★ Winter Sports

Winter sports up north are a major draw. To go cross-country skiing, just grab a pair of skis and step outside; for downhill sports, be it heli-skiing or snowboarding, there are several spots. Few pastimes are as enjoyable as rushing across the Arctic wasteland pulled by a team of dogs, the sled crunching through crisp snow – but if you want something with a motor, you can test your driving (and racing) skills on the frozen lakes instead.

Norrland Hiking

Sweden has some absolutely gorgeous hiking trails, most of which are well maintained and supplied with conveniently located mountain huts along the way. The season is relatively short, but it's worth a bit of extra planning to get out into the wilderness: its natural landscape is one of Sweden's best assets. A good place to start your venture is the Norrland village of Abisko, at the top of the Kungsleden long-distance trail – it's a hiker headquarters and easily reached by train. (p170)

★ Vasamuseet

Stockholm's unique Vasamuseet is a purpose-built preservation and display case for an ancient sunken battleship. The ship was the pride of the Swedish Crown when it set out in August 1628, but pride quickly turned to embarrassment when the top-heavy ship tipped and sank to the bottom of Saltsjön, where it would await rescue for 300 years. The museum explains – in fascinating multimedia – how it was found, retrieved and restored, why it sank in the first place, and what it all means to the Swedish people.

if Sweden were 100 people

89 would be Swedish
3 would be Finn & Sami (Lapp)
1 would be Yugoslav
1 would be Iranian
6 would be other

belief systems

(% of population)

87 Lutheran

13 other

population per sq km

SWEDEN   NORWAY   UK

♦ ≈ 8 people

When to Go

Stockholm

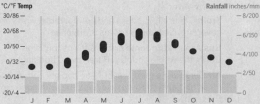

°C/°F Temp   Rainfall inches/mm

30/86 — 　　　　　　　　　　　　　 — 8/200
20/68 — 　　　　　　　　　　　　　 — 6/150
10/50 — 　　　　　　　　　　　　　 — 4/100
0/32 — 　　　　　　　　　　　　　 — 2/50
-10/14 —
-20/-4 —　　　　　　　　　　　　　 — 0

J F M A M J J A S O N D

Finland's
TOP EXPERIENCES

There's something pure, vital and exciting in the Finnish air; an invitation to get out and active. How about a post-sauna dip through the ice under the majestic aurora borealis (Northern Lights), after whooshing across the snow behind a team of huskies, for an inspiring winter's day? Hiking or canoeing under the midnight sun through pine forests populated by wolves and bears isn't your typical tanning-oil summer either. Although socially and economically in the vanguard of nations, large parts of Finland (p172) remain gloriously remote; trendsetting modern Helsinki is counterbalanced by forested wildernesses. Nordic peace in lakeside cottages, summer sunshine on convivial beer terraces, avant-garde design, dark melodies, and cafes with home-baking aromas are other facets of Suomi seduction, as are the independent, loyal and welcoming Finns, who do their own thing and are much the better for it.

 Design in Helsinki

Functional, elegant, outrageous or wacky: the choice is yours. The capital's decidedly nonmainstream chic is evident throughout and best explored by browsing the vast variety of design shops that spatter its centre. Whether examining iconic 20th-century Finnish forms in the flagship emporia of brands such as Iittala, Marimekko and Artek, or tracking down the cutting-edge and just plain weird in the bohemian Punavuori district, you're sure to find something you didn't know you needed but just can't do without. And yes, they all deliver... (p173)

 Food Markets

Counters selling local cheeses, rough rye breads, handmade chocolates, Finnish sausages and smoked fish fill each town's indoor kauppahalli (covered market). Tampere's is typical, filled with delicious aromas – try traditional *mustamakkara* (blood sausage). In summer the kauppatori (market square) in each town bursts with straight-from-the-garden vegetables: tiny new potatoes, nutty and sweet; mouthfuls of juicy red strawberries; or peas popped fresh from the pod. Autumn's approach is softened by piles of peppery

chanterelles and glowing Lapland cloudberries, appearing in August like a magician's trick. (p181)

Lakeland

The Lakeland, Finland's most beautiful corner, seems to have more water than land, so it would be a crime not to get out on it. There are numerous paddling opportunities around beautiful Savonlinna., and historic lake boats still ply what were once important transport arteries; head out from any town on short cruises, or make a day of it and head from Savonlinna right up to Kuopio or across Saimaa, Finland's largest lake. (p182)

Traditional Saunas

These days most Finns have saunas at home, but there are still a few of the old public ones left. They smell of old pine, tar shampoo and long tradition, with birch whisks and no-nonsense scrub-downs available as extras. Weathered Finnish faces cool down on the street outside, loins wrapped in a towel and hand wrapped around

---

GETTING AROUND

You can set your watch by Finnish transport. For bus timetables, head to www.matkahuolto.fi, for trains it's www.vr.fi.

Train Generally modern and comfortable, with good coverage. Book busy routes in advance.

Bus Around the same price as trains, but slower. Cover the whole country. Rarely need booking.

Air Generally expensive, but you can get some good deals on Lapland routes, saving time and money over the train.

a cold beer. Helsinki and Tampere are the best places for this, while further north you'll encounter rustic log sweat-boxes, smoke saunas and more. A jump in the lake or a roll in the snow is compulsory if available.

★ Lapland Activities

Fizzing across Lapland behind a team of huskies under the low winter sun is tough to beat. Short jaunts are great, but overnight safaris give you time to feed and bond with your dogs and try a wood-fired sauna in the middle of the winter wilderness. It's no fairy-tale ride though; expect to eat some snow before you learn to control your team. If you're more of a cat person, you can enjoy similar trips on a snowmobile or behind reindeer. In summer, the hiking in national parks is magnificent. (p183)

★ Sámi Culture

Finland's indigenous northerners have used technology to ease the arduous side of reindeer herding while maintaining an intimate knowledge of Lapland's natural world. Their capital, Inari, and the nearby Lemmenjoki National Park are the best places to begin to learn about Sámi culture and traditions, starting at the marvellous Siida museum. Arrange wilderness excursions with Sámi guides, meet reindeer, and browse high-quality handicrafts and music, the sale of which benefits local communities. (p184)

★ Music Festivals

Are you a chamber-music aficionado? Or do you like rock so raucous it makes your ears bleed? Whatever your pleasure, Finland has a music festival to suit. Savonlinna's castle is the dramatic setting for a month-long opera festival (p182); fiddlers gather at Kaustinen for full-scale folk; Pori, Espoo and Tampere attract thousands of jazz fans; workaday Seinäjoki flashes sequins and high heels during its five-day tango festival; Turku's Ruisrock is one of several kicking rock festivals; and the Sibelius Festival in Lahti ushers in autumn with classical grace.

★ Cycling in Åland

Charming Åland is best explored by bicycle: you'll appreciate its understated attractions all the more if you've used pedal power to reach them. Bridges and ferries link many of its 6000 islands, and well-signposted routes take you off 'main roads' down winding lanes and forestry tracks. Set aside your bicycle whenever the mood takes you, to pick wild strawberries, wander castle ruins, sunbathe on a slab of red granite, visit a medieval church, quench your thirst at a cider orchard, or climb a lookout tower to gaze at the glittering sea. (p179)

if Finland were 100 people

91 would speak Finnish
6 would speak Swedish
1 would speak Russian
3 would speak other languages

belief systems
(% of population)

78 Lutheran
1 Orthodox
1 other Christian
20 none

population per sq km

FINLAND SWEDEN USA

♦ ≈ 6 people

When to Go

Helsinki

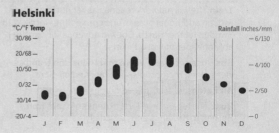

Norway's
TOP EXPERIENCES

Norway (p185) is a once-in-a-lifetime destination and the essence of its appeal is remarkably simple: this is one of the most beautiful countries on earth. Impossibly steep-sided fjords cut deep gashes into the interior, grand and glorious glaciers snake down from Europe's largest ice fields, and the appeal of the Arctic is primeval. The counterpoint to so much natural beauty is found in the country's vibrant cultural life. Norwegian cities are cosmopolitan and brimful of architecture that showcases the famous Scandinavian flair for design. Yes, Norway is one of the most expensive countries on the planet, but it'll pay you back with never-to-be-forgotten experiences many times over.

Geirangerfjord

The 20km chug along Geirangerfjord, a Unesco World Heritage Site, must rank as the world's loveliest ferry journey. Long-abandoned farmsteads still cling to the fjord's near-sheer cliffs, while ice-cold cascades tumble, twist and gush down to emerald-green waters. Take the ferry from Geiranger and enjoy the calm as you leave this small, heaving port or hop aboard at altogether quieter Hellesylt. Prime your camera, grab a top-deck open-air seat and enjoy what's literally the only way to travel Geirangerfjord's secluded reaches. (p192)

Lofoten

Few visitors forget their first sighting of the Lofoten Islands. The jagged ramparts of this astonishing island chain rise abruptly from the sea in summer greens and yellows or the stark blue and white of winter, their razor-sharp peaks stabbing at a clear, cobalt sky or shrouded mysteriously in swirling mists. Postcard-perfect villages with wooden *rorbuers* (cabins) cling to the shoreline, while the A-frame racks for drying fish tell of a land and a culture intimately entwined with the sea. (p194)

Hurtigruten Coastal Ferry

So much more than merely a means of getting around, the iconic Hurtigruten coastal ferry takes you on one of the most spectacular coastal journeys anywhere on earth. On its daily path between Bergen and Kirkenes, it dips into coastal fjords, docks at isolated villages barely accessible by road, draws near to dramatic headlands and crosses the Arctic Circle, only to return a few days later. In the process, it showcases the entire length of Norway's most glorious coast. (p191)

⭐ Bryggen, Bergen

Set amid a picturesque and very Norwegian coastal landscape of fjords and mountains, Bergen is one of Europe's most beautiful cities. A celebrated history of seafaring trade has bequeathed to the city the stunning (and Unesco World Heritage–listed) waterfront district of Bryggen, an archaic tangle of wooden buildings. A signpost to a history at once prosperous and tumultuous, the titled

GETTING AROUND

Train The rail network reaches as far north as Bodø, with an additional branch line connecting Narvik with Sweden further north. Book in advance for considerably cheaper *minipris* tickets.

Bus Buses go everywhere that trains don't, and services along major routes are fast and efficient.

Air Extensive, well-priced domestic network.

Boat The legendary Hurtigruten ferry sails from Bergen to Kirkenes and back daily.

and colourful structures now shelter the artisan boutiques and traditional restaurants for which the city is increasingly famous. (p189)

★ Oslo–Bergen Railway

Often cited as one of the world's most beautiful rail journeys, the Oslo–Bergen rail line is an opportunity to sample some of the best scenery in Norway. After passing through the forests of southern Norway, it climbs up to the horizonless beauty of the Hardangervidda Plateau and then continues down through the pretty country around Voss and on into Bergen. En route it passes within touching distance of the fjords and connects (at Myrdal) with the steep branch line down to the fjord country that fans out from Flåm. (p191)

★ Pulpit Rock

As lookouts go, Preikestolen (Pulpit Rock) has few peers. Perched atop an almost perfectly sheer cliff that hangs more than 600m above the waters of gorgeous Lysefjord, Pulpit Rock is one of Norway's signature images and most eye-catching sites. It's the sort of place where you'll barely be able to look as travellers dangle far more than seems advisable over the precipice, even as you find yourself drawn inexorably toward the edge. The hike to reach it takes two hours and involves a full-day trip from Stavanger. (p189)

★ Tromsø

Tromsø, a cool 400km north of the Arctic Circle, is northern Norway's most significant city with, among other superlatives, the world's northernmost cathedral, brewery and botanical garden. Its busy clubs and pubs – more per capita than in any other Norwegian town – owe much to the university (another northernmost) and its students. In summer, Tromsø is a base for round-the-clock, 24-hour daylight activity. Once the first snows fall, the locals slip on their skis or snowshoes, head out of town and gaze skywards for a glimpse of the northern lights. (p195)

★ Oslo

Oslo is reinventing itself. This is a city that is aiming to become nothing less than a world-renowned centre of art and culture. It's already bursting at the seams with top-notch museums, art galleries and a glacier-white opera house that could make even Sydney jealous, but in the past couple of years it's achieved a striking rebirth of its waterfront district, complete with daring architecture, a grade-A modern-art gallery, new restaurants and even a beach. (p185)

if Norway were 100 people

94 would be Norwegian
4 would be other European
2 would be other

belief systems
(% of population)

82 Church of Norway

4 other Christian

2 Roman Catholic

2 Muslim

10 other

population per sq km

NORWAY   SWEDEN   UK

👤 ≈ 8 people

When to Go

Oslo

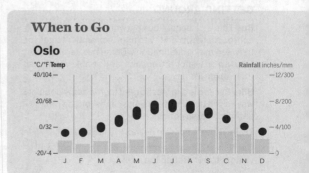

°C/°F Temp
40/104 —
20/68 —
0/32 —
-20/-4 —

Rainfall inches/mm
—12/300
—8/200
—4/100
—0

J F M A M J J A S C N D

Iceland's
TOP EXPERIENCES

The energy is palpable on this magical island (p197), where astonishing natural phenomena inspire the welcoming, creative locals and draw an increasing number of visitors in search of its untrammelled splendour. A vast volcanic laboratory, here the earth itself is restless and alive. Admire thundering waterfalls, glittering glaciers carving their way to black-sand beaches, explosive geysers, rumbling volcanoes and contorted lava fields. In summer, permanent daylight energises the already zippy inhabitants of Iceland's quaint capital, Reykjavík, with its wonderful cafe and bar scene. Fashion, design and music are woven into the city's fabric, and the museums are tops. In winter, with luck, you may see the Northern Lights shimmering across the sky. Year-round, though, adventure tours abound, getting you up close and personal with sights and sounds that will stay with you for life.

⭐ Hot Water

Iceland's unofficial pastime is splashing around in its surplus of geothermal water. There are 'hot-pots' everywhere – from downtown Reykjavík to the isolated peninsular tips of the Westfjords – and not only are they incredibly relaxing, they're the perfect antidote to a hangover, and a great way to meet locals (this is their social hub, the Icelanders' equivalent of the local pub or town square). Everyone knows that the Blue Lagoon (p200) is the big cheese: its steaming lagoon full of silica deposits sits conveniently close to Keflavík airport, making it the perfect send-off before flying home.

⭐ Jökulsárlón

A ghostly procession of luminous blue icebergs drifts serenely through the 25-sq-km Jökulsárlón lagoon before floating out to sea. This surreal scene (handily, right next to the Ring Road) is a natural film set: in fact, you might have seen it in *Batman Begins* and *Die Another Day*. The ice calves from Breiðamerkurjökull glacier, an offshoot of the mighty Vatnajökull ice cap. Boat trips are popular, or you can simply wander the lakeshore, scout for seals, and exhaust your camera's memory card. (p203)

⭐ Northern Lights

Everyone longs to glimpse the aurora borealis, the celestial kaleidoscope known for transforming long winter nights into natural lava lamps. The lights form when solar flares are drawn by the earth's magnetic field toward the North Pole. The results are ethereal veils of green, white, violet or red light, shimmering and dancing in a display like silent fireworks. Peak aurora sightings occur in winter, but look for the lights in clear, dark skies any time between October (maybe September) and April.

⭐ Vatnajökull National Park

Europe's largest national park covers nearly 14% of Iceland and safeguards mighty Vatnajökull, the largest ice cap outside the poles (three times the size of Luxembourg). Scores of outlet glaciers flow down from its frosty bulk, while underneath it are active volcanoes and mountain peaks.

GETTING AROUND

Bus There's a decent bus network operating from approximately mid-May to mid-September to get you between major destinations. Some bus services are focused on visitor attractions, and enable you to visit them on day trips.

Bike Cycling is a fantastic (and increasingly popular) way to see the country's landscapes, but be prepared for harsh conditions.

Train There is no train network in Iceland.

Car Rental cars are expensive, but a common way for visitors to get around the island.

Yes, this is ground zero for those 'fire and ice' clichés. You'll be spellbound by the diversity of landscapes, walking trails and activities inside this super-sized park. Given its dimensions, access points are numerous – start at Skaftafell in the south or Ásbyrgi in the north. (p205)

★ The Ring Road

There's no better way to explore Iceland than Route 1, affectionately known as the Ring Road. This 1330km tarmacked trail loops around the island, passing through verdant dales decked with waterfalls, past glacier tongues dripping from ice caps like frosting from a cake, desert-like plains of grey outwash sands, and velvety, moss-covered lava fields. It's supremely spectacular – but don't forget to take some of the detours. Use the Ring Road as your main artery and follow the veins as they splinter off into the wilderness.

★ Westfjords

Iceland's sweeping spectrum of superlative nature comes to a dramatic climax in the Westfjords – an off-the-beaten-path adventure par excellence. Broad beaches flank the southern coast, bird colonies abound, fjordheads tower above and then plunge into the deep, and a network of ruddy roads twists throughout, adding to the adventure. The region's uppermost peninsula, Hornstrandir, is the final frontier; the sea cliffs are perilous, the Arctic foxes are foxier, and hiking trails amble through pristine patches of wilderness that practically kiss the Arctic Circle. (p202)

★ Fimmvörðuháls

If you haven't the time to complete one of Iceland's multiday treks, the 23km, day-long Fimmvörðuháls trek will quench any wanderer's thirst. Start at the shimmering cascades of Skógafoss, hike up into the hinterland to discover a veritable parade of waterfalls, then tiptoe over the steaming remnants of the Eyjafjallajökull eruption before hiking along the stone terraces of a flower-filled kingdom that ends in silent Þórsmörk, a haven for campers, hemmed by a crown of glacial ridges. (p204)

★ Reykjavík's Cafe Culture & Beer Bars

The ratio of coffee houses to citizens in Iceland's capital is nothing short of staggering. The local social culture is built around these low-key hang-outs that crank up the intensity after hours, when tea is swapped for tipples and dancing breaks out. Handcrafted caffeine hits and designer microbrews are prepared with the utmost seriousness for accidental hipsters sporting well-worn *lopapeysur* (Icelandic woollen sweaters). (p201)

if Iceland were 100 people

89 would be Icelandic
3 would be Polish
1 would be German
2 would be Asian
2 would be other Nordic
3 would be other

belief systems
(% of population)

77 Evangelical Lutheran
5 Free Lutheran
3 Catholic
1 independent congregation
9 other
5 no religion

population per sq km

ICELAND   CANADA   USA

🧍 = 3 people

When to Go

Reykjavík

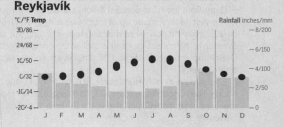

DENKMARK
DENMARK

Copenhagen

POP 1.26 MILLION

Copenhagen is the coolest kid on the Nordic block. Edgier than Stockholm and worldlier than Oslo, the Danish capital gives Scandinavia the X-factor. While this 850-year-old harbour town has managed to retain much of its historic good looks – think copper spires and cobbled squares – the focus here is on the innovative and cutting edge. Denmark's over-achieving capital is home to a thriving design scene, its streets awash with effortlessly hip shops, cafes and bars, world-class museums and art collections, intelligent new architecture, and a galaxy of Michelin-starred restaurants.

◉ Sights

★ Tivoli Gardens — AMUSEMENT PARK
(www.tivoli.dk; adult/child under 8yr Dkr110/free; ⊙11am-11pm Sun-Thu, to midnight Fri & Sat Apr-Sep, reduced hours rest of year; ⍭; ☐2A, 5A, 9A, 12, 26, 250S, 350S, ☐S-train København H) Dating from 1843, tasteful Tivoli wins fans with its dreamy whirl of amusement rides, twinkling pavilions, carnival games and open-air stage shows. Visitors can ride the renovated, century-old roller-coaster, take in the famous Saturday evening fireworks display or just soak up the storybook atmosphere.

★ Statens Museum for Kunst — MUSEUM
(www.smk.dk; Sølvgade 48-50; special exhibitions adult/youth under 27/child Dkr110/85/free; ⊙11am-5pm Tue & Thu-Sun, to 8pm Wed; ☐6A, 26, 42, 173E, 184, 185) FREE Denmark's National Gallery straddles two contrasting, interconnected buildings: a late-19th-century 'palazzo' and a sharply minimalist extension. The museum houses medieval and Renaissance works, and impressive collections of Dutch and Flemish artists including Rubens, Breughel and Rembrandt. It claims the world's finest collection of 19th-century Danish 'Golden Age' artists, foreign greats such as Matisse and Picasso, and modern Danish heavyweights.

★ Nationalmuseet — MUSEUM
(National Museum; www.natmus.dk; Ny Vestergade 10; ⊙10am-5pm Tue-Sun; ⍭; ☐1A, 2A, 11A, 33, 40, 66, ☐S-train København H) FREE For a crash course in Danish history and culture, spend an afternoon at Denmark's National Museum. It has first claims on virtually every antiquity uncovered on Danish soil, including Stone Age tools, Viking weaponry, rune stones and medieval jewellery. Among the many highlights is a finely crafted 3500-year-old Sun Chariot, as well as bronze *lurs* (horns), some of which date back 3000 years and are still capable of blowing a tune.

★ Christiania — AREA
(www.christiania.org; Prinsessegade; ☐9A, 2A, 40, 350S, ☐Christianshavn) Escape the capitalist crunch at Freetown Christiania, a dreadlocks-heavy commune straddling the eastern side of Christianshavn. Since its establishment by squatters in 1971, the area has drawn nonconformists from across the globe, attracted by the concept of collective business, workshops and communal living. Explore beyond the settlement's infamous 'Pusher St' – lined with shady hash and marijuana dealers – and you'll stumble upon a semi-bucolic wonderland of whimsical DIY homes, cosy gardens, and a handful of craft shops, eateries, beer gardens and music venues.

WORTH A TRIP

A MODERN ART DRAWCARD

Even if you don't have a consuming passion for modern art, Denmark's outstanding Louisiana (www.louisiana.dk; Gammel Strandvej 13, Humlebæk; adult/child Dkr115/free; ⊙11am-10pm Tue-Fri, to 6pm Sat & Sun) should be high on your to-do list. It's a striking modernist gallery, made up of four huge wings, which stretch across a sculpture-filled park, burrowing down into the hillside and nosing out again to wink at the sea (and Sweden). The collection itself is stellar, covering everything from constructivism, CoBrA movement artists and minimalist art, to abstract expressionism, pop art and photography.

Louisiana is in leafy Humlebæk, 30km north of Copenhagen. Trains run at least twice hourly from Copenhagen (Dkr108, 35 minutes) and Helsingør (Dkr36, 10 minutes). If day-tripping it from Copenhagen, the 24-hour ticket (adult/child Dkr130/65) is much better value.

★ Rosenborg Slot · CASTLE

(www.kongernessamling.dk/en/rosenborg; Øster Voldgade 4A; adult/child Dkr105/free incl Amalienborg Slot Dkr145/free; ⏱10am-5pm daily Jun-Aug, 10am-4pm daily May, Sep & Oct, reduced hours rest of year; 🚌6A, 11A, 42, 150S, 173E, 184, 185, 350S, Ⓜ Nørreport) A 'once-upon-a-time' combo of turrets, gables and moat, the early-17th-century Rosenborg Slot was built between 1606 and 1633 by King Christian IV in Dutch Renaissance style to serve as his summer home. Today, the castle's 24 upper rooms are chronologically arranged, housing the furnishings and portraits of each monarch from Christian IV to Frederik VII. The pièce de résistance, however, is the basement Treasury, home to the dazzling crown jewels, among them Christian IV's glorious crown and the jewel-studded sword of Christian III.

★ Designmuseum Danmark · MUSEUM

(www.designmuseum.dk; Bredgade 68; adult/child Dkr100/free; ⏱11am-5pm Tue & Thu-Sun, to 9pm Wed; 🚌1A) The 18th-century Frederiks Hospital is now the outstanding Denmark Design Museum. A must for fans of the applied arts and industrial design, its fairly extensive collection includes Danish silver and porcelain, textiles and the iconic design pieces of modern innovators such as Kaare Klint, Poul Henningsen and Arne Jacobsen. Also on display are ancient Chinese and Japanese ceramics, and 18th- and 19th-century European decorative arts.

Carlsberg Visitors Centre · BREWERY

(☎33 27 12 82; www.visitcarlsberg.dk; Gamle Carlsberg Vej 11, Vesterbro; adult/child Dkr85/60; ⏱10am-5pm Tue-Sun; 🚌18, 26) Adjacent to the architecturally whimsical Carlsberg brewery, the Carlsberg Visitors Centre explores the history of Danish beer. The self-guided tour ends at the bar, where you can knock back two free beers.

Little Mermaid · MONUMENT

(Den Lille Havfrue; 🚌1A, ⛴Nordre Toldbod) When the world thinks of Copenhagen, chances are they're thinking of the Little Mermaid. Love her or loathe her (watch Copenhageners cringe at the very mention of her), this small, underwhelming statue is arguably the most photographed sight in the city, as well as the cause of countless 'Is that it?' shrugs from tourists who have trudged the kilometre or so along an often windswept harbour front to see her.

ℹ COPENHAGEN CARD

The **Copenhagen Card** (www.copenhagencard.com; adult/child 10-15 24hr Dkr379/199, 48hr Dkr529/269, 72hr Dkr629/319, 120hr Dkr839/419), available at the Copenhagen Visitors Centre or online, gives you free access to 72 museums and attractions in the city and surrounding area, as well as free travel for all S-train, metro and bus journeys within the seven travel zones.

☞ Tours

Copenhagen Free Walking Tours · WALKING TOUR

(www.copenhagenfreewalkingtours.dk) FREE Departing daily at 11am and 3pm from outside Rådhus (City Hall), these free, three-hour walking tours take in famous landmarks and interesting anecdotes. Tours are in English and require a minimum of five people. Free 90-minute tours of Christianshavn depart at 4pm from the base of the Bishop Absalon statue on Højbro Plads.

☆ Festivals & Events

Copenhagen Jazz Festival · MUSIC

(www.jazz.dk) Copenhagen's single largest event, and the largest jazz festival in northern Europe, hits the city over 10 days in early July. The program covers jazz in all its forms, with an impressive line-up of local and international talent.

🛏 Sleeping

★ Generator Hostel · HOSTEL €

(☎78 77 54 00; www.generatorhostel.com; Adelgade 5-7; dm Dkr150-350, r Dkr800-1200; @🖨; 🚌11A, 350S, Ⓜ Kongens Nytorv) A solid choice for 'cheap chic', upbeat, design-literate Generator sits on the very edge of the city's medieval core. It's kitted out with designer furniture, slick communal areas (including a bar and outdoor terrace) and friendly, young staff. While the rooms can be a little small, all are bright and modern, with bathrooms in both private rooms and dorms.

Danhostel Copenhagen City · HOSTEL €

(☎33 11 85 85; www.danhostel.dk/copenhagencity; HC Andersens Blvd 50; dm/d Dkr240/675; @🖨; 🚌12, 33, 1A, 2A, 11A, 40, 66) With interiors by design company Gubi and a cafe-bar in the lobby, this friendly, ever-popular hostel is set in a tower block overlooking the harbour

Central Copenhagen (København)

Assistens
Kirkegård

NØRREBRO

Møllegade
Guldbergsgade
Sankt
Hans Torv
20

Elmegade
Nørrebrogade
Fælledvej

Skt Hans Gade

Ravnsborggade

Sortedam Dossering

Læssøesgade
Ryesgade

Fredensbro

Sølvgade

Sortedams
Sø

Øster Søgade

Stengade
Baggesensgade
Griffenfeldsgade
Kapelvej

Rantzausgade

Blågårds
Plads
Korsgade

Dronning
Louises
Bro

Frederiksborggade

Øster Farimagsgade

Åblvd

Peblinge Dossering

Peblinge
Sø

Vendersgade

Rømersgade
Gothersgade

H C Ørsteds Vej

Rosenørns Allé

M
Forum

VESTERBRO

Sankt Marcus Allé

Gyldenløvesgade

Nørre Søgade

Turesensgade

Nansensgade

Nørre Farimagsgade

16

Israels
Plads

Limesgade

Nørreport
S

Rosengården

Fiolstræde

Danasvej

Vester Søgade

Nyropsgade

Kampmannsgade

Vester Farimagsgade

H C Andersens Blvd

Nørre Voldgade

Ørsteds
Parken

Nørre Voldgade

Nørregade

Krystalgade

Kannikestræde

Larslejsstræde

Studiestræde

Vor Frue
Plads

Gammeltorv

Rådhusstræde

Niels Ebbesens Vej

Forhåbningsholms Allé

Vodroffsvej

Sankt
Jørgens Sø

Vesterport
S

Hammerichsgade

Jernbanegade

Axeltorv

Ved Vesterport

Vestergade

Frederiksberggade

STRØGET

Rådhuspladsen

8

Lavendelstræde

Regnbuepladsen

19

Bag Rådhuset

6
Tivoli
Gardens

i
Copenhagen
Visitors
Centre

TIVOLI

Stormgade

Vester

Dantes
Plads

Gammel Kongevej

Vesterbrogade

18

Viktoriagade

Istedgade

Banegårdspladsen

Central Station
(København
Hovedbanegården)
S

Tietgensgade

Eskildsgade
Gasværksvej

Halmtorvet

Eurolines

9

Hambrosgade

Dannebrogsgade

Absalonsgade

Skydebanegade

Sønder Blvd

VESTERBRO

Kødbyen
(Meatpacking
District)

Ingerslevsgade

12

Kalvebod Brygge

Pony (600m);
Carlsberg Visitors
Centre (1.6km)

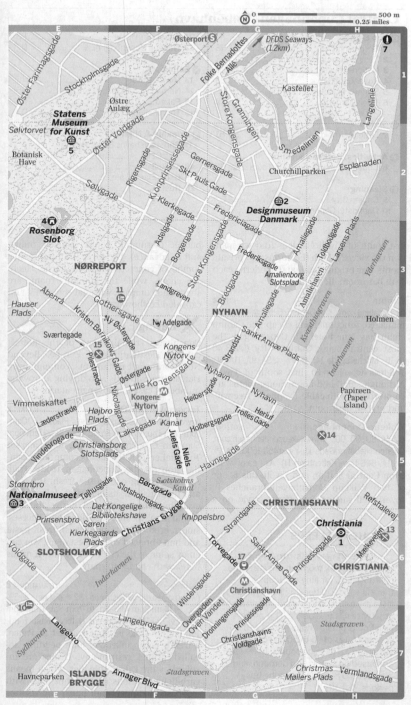

500 m
0.25 miles

Østerport

DFDS Seaways
(1.2km)

Kastellet

Langelinie

Øster Farimagsgade

Stockholmsgade

Østre
Anlæg

Folke Bernadottes Allé

Grønningen

Store Kongensgade

Statens
Museum
for Kunst
5

Sølvtorvet

Øster Voldgade

Smedelinien

Esplanaden

Botanisk
Have

Sølvgade

Rigensgade

Kronprinsessegade

Gernersgade

Skt Pauls Gade

Churchillparken

Designmuseum
Danmark 2

Amaliegade

Toldbodgade

Larsens Plads

Yderhavnen

4 Rosenborg
Slot

Kr Klerkegade

Adelgade

Borgergade

Fredericiagade

Frederiksgade

Store Kongensgade

Amalienborg
Slotsplad

Amaliegade

Amaliehaven

NØRREPORT

Landgreven

Bredgade

Holmen

Abenrå

Gothersgade 11

Ny Østergade

Ny Adelgade

NYHAVN

Sankt Annæ Plads

Kvæsthusgraven

Inderhavnen

Hauser
Plads

Kristen Berntows Gade

Sværtegade 15

Piiestræde

Østergade

Kongens
Nytorv

Strandstr

Nyhavn

Papirøen
(Paper
Island)

Vimmelskaftet

Læderstræde

Nikolajgade

Kongens
Nytorv

Heibergsgade

Nyhavn

Herluf

Højbro
Plads

Holmens
Kanal

Trolles Gade

Højbro

Laksegade

Holbergsgade

Vindebrogade

Christiansborg
Slotsplads

Niels
Juels Gade

Havnegade

14

Stormbro

Nationalmuseet
3

Tøjhusgade

Slotsholmsgade

Børsgade

Slotsholms
Kanal

CHRISTIANSHAVN

Refshalevej

Prinsensbro

Det Kongelige
Bibilotekshave
Søren
Kierkegaards
Plads

Christians Grygge

Knippelsbro

Strandgade

Christiania
1

13

SLOTSHOLMEN

Torvegade

Sankt Annæ Gade

Prinsessegade

Mælkevejen

CHRISTIANIA

Voldgade

10

Inderhavnen

Langebro

Wildersgade

17

Overgaden
Oven Vandet

Dronningensgade

Prinsessegade

Langebrogade

Christianshavn

Christianshavns
Voldgade

Sydhavnen

Havneparken

ISLANDS
BRYGGE

Amager Blvd

Stadsgraven

Stadsgraven

Christmas
Møllers Plads

Vermlandsgade

Central Copenhagen (København)

just south of Tivoli Gardens (did we mention the views?). Both the dorms and private rooms are bright, light and modern, each with bathroom. Book ahead.

Cabinn   HOTEL €
(www.cabinn.com; s/d Dkr495/625; @ 🛜) Well managed, functional and cheap, the Cabinn chain has four hotels in Copenhagen, the most central being **Cabinn City** (✆33 46 16 16; Mitchellsgade 14; @ 🛜; 🚌5A, 9A, 11A, 30, 🚉S-train København H), just south of Tivoli. Although small and anonymous, rooms are comfortable, with cable TV, phone, free wifi, and private bathroom.

Wakeup Copenhagen   HOTEL €€
(✆44 80 00 00; www.wakeupcopenhagen.com; Carsten Niebuhrs Gade 11; r Dkr450-1500; @ 🛜; 🚌11A, 🚉S-train København H) An easy walk from Central Station and Tivoli, this is one of two Wakeup Copenhagen branches in town, well known for offering style on a

budget (assuming you've booked online and in advance). The foyer is an impressive combo of concrete, glass and Arne Jacobsen chairs, while the 500-plus rooms are sharp and compact, with flat-screen TV and capsule-like showers.

✖ Eating

Copenhagen remains one of the hottest culinary destinations in Europe. Beyond New Nordic cult restaurants, contemporary Danish innovation is also driving a growing number of casual, midrange eateries.

Torvehallerne KBH   MARKET €
(www.torvehallernekbh.dk; Israels Plads; ⏰10am-7pm Mon-Thu, to 8pm Fri, to 6pm Sat, 11am-5pm Sun) Since opening in 2011, food market Torvehallerne KBH has become an essential stop on the Copenhagen foodie trail. A gut-rumbling ode to the fresh, the tasty and the artisanal, its beautiful stalls peddle everything from seasonal herbs and berries to smoked meats, seafood and cheeses, smørrebrød (open sandwiches), fresh pasta and hand-brewed coffee. Best of all, you can enjoy some of the city's best sit-down meals here...with change to spare.

Palæo   INTERNATIONAL €
(www.palaeo.dk; Pilestræde 32; dishes Dkr59-85; ⏰10am-8pm Mon-Fri, to 7pm Sat, 11am-5pm Sun; 🛜; 🚌11A, Ⓜ Kongens Nytorv) Fast food, Flintstones-style is what you get at Palæo, a trendy eat-in/takeaway joint peddling so-called 'primal gastronomy'. Dishes are inspired by the Palæolithic diet, which means carb-light creations such as hot dogs with egg-based wrappers (not buns) and risottos

---

❶ CHEAP SLEEPS

The **Copenhagen Visitors Centre** (p155) can book rooms in private homes (Dkr350/500 for singles/doubles); there is a Dkr100 booking fee if you do it via the tourist office when you arrive, otherwise it is free online. This office also books unfilled hotel rooms at discounted rates of up to 50% (sometimes even more). These discounts, however, are based on supply and demand, and are not always available during busy periods.

that give rice the flick for celeriac kernels. But if you're thinking mungbean mediocrity, think again: behind the menu is Michelin-starred chef Thomas Rode Andersen.

Morgenstedet
VEGETARIAN €

(www.morgenstedet.dk; Langgaden; mains Dkr90-110; ⊙ noon-9pm Tue-Sun; ⏸; ⏹ 9A, 2A, 40, 350S, Ⓜ Christianshavn) A homely, hippy bolthole in the heart of Christiania, Morgenstedet offers but two dishes of the day, one of which is usually a soup. Choices are always vegetarian and organic, and best devoured in the bucolic bliss of the cafe garden.

Pony
MODERN DANISH €€

(⏸ 33 22 10 00; www.ponykbh.dk; Vesterbrogade 135; 2/3/4-course menu Dkr295/375/450; ⊙ 5.30-10pm Tue-Sun; ⏹ 6A) If your accountant forbids dinner at famed Kadeau, opt for its bistro spin-off, Pony. While the New Nordic grub here is simpler, it's no less stunning, with palate-punching marvels such as tartar with black trumpet mushrooms, blackberries and mushroom broth or lemon sole with cauliflower, pickled apples, kale, almonds and capers. The vibe is convivial and intimate. Book ahead online, especially on Friday and Saturday.

🍸 Drinking & Nightlife

Copenhagen is packed with a diverse range of drinking options – slinky cocktail hideouts, rowdy and nicotine-stained *bodegas* (pubs), and everything in between.

Mikkeller Bar
BAR

(www.mikkeller.dk; Viktoriagade 8B-C; ⊙ 1pm-1am Sun-Wed, to 2am Thu & Fri, noon-2am Sat; ⏸; ⏹ 6A, 10, 14, 26, ⏹ S-train København H) Low-slung lights, moss-green floors and 20 brews on tap: cult-status Mikkeller flies the flag for craft beer, its rotating cast of suds including Mikkeller's own acclaimed creations and guest drops from microbreweries from around the globe. The bottled offerings are equally inspired, with cheese and snacks to soak up the foamy goodness.

Christianshavns Bådudlejning og Café
BAR

(⏸ 32 96 53 53; www.baadudlejningen.dk; Overgaden Neden Vandet 29; ⊙ 9am-midnight Jun-mid-Aug, reduced hours Apr, May & mid-Aug–Sep, closed Oct-Mar; ⏸; ⏹ 2A, 9A, 40, 350S, Ⓜ Christianshavn) Right on Christianshavn's main canal, this festive, wood-decked cafe-bar is a wonderful spot for drinks by the water. It's a cosy, affable hangout, with jovial crowds,

strung lights and little rowboats (available for hire) docked like bath-time toys. Grub is available for hungry punters, and there are gas heaters and tarpaulins to ward off any northern chill.

Oscar Bar & Cafe
GAY

(www.oscarbarcafe.dk; Regnbuepladsen 77; ⊙ 11am-11pm Sun-Thu, to 2am Fri & Sat; ⏸; ⏹ 12, 26, 33, 11A, ⏹ S-train København H) In the shadow of Rådhus, this corner cafe-bar remains the most popular gay in the village. There's food for the peckish and a healthy quota of eye-candy locals and out-of-towners. In the warmer months, its alfresco tables are packed with revellers, one eye on friends, the other on Grindr.

Rust
CLUB

(⏸ 35 24 52 00; www.rust.dk; Guldbergsgade 8, Nørrebro; ⊙ hours vary, club usually 11pm-5am Fri & Sat; ⏹ 3A, 5A, 350S) A smashing place attracting one of the largest, coolest crowds in Copenhagen. Live acts focus on alternative or upcoming indie rock, hiphop or electronica, while the club churns out hip hop, dancehall and electro on Wednesdays, and house, electro and rock on Fridays and Saturdays.

❶ Information

Copenhagen Visitors Centre (⏸ 70 22 24 42; www.visitcopenhagen.com; Vesterbrogade 4A; ⊙ 9am-8pm Jul-Sep, to 5pm Mon-Fri, to 2pm Sat Oct-Feb, to 5pm Mon-Fri, to 4pm Sat & Sun Mar-Jun; ⏸) Copenhagen's excellent information centre has multilingual staff, as well as a bakery and lounge with free wi-fi and power sockets. It's the best source of information in town, with free maps, masses of brochures and guides to take away, and booking services and hotel reservations available for a fee.

❶ Getting There & Away

➜ Copenhagen's user-friendly international airport is Scandinavia's busiest hub, with direct flights to cities in Europe, North America and Asia.

➜ DFDS Seaways (☑ 33 42 30 10; www.dfds-seaways.com; Dampfærgevej 30) runs one daily service to/from Oslo (one-way from Dkr750, 17¼ hours), which leaves from Søndre Frihavn, just north of Kastellet.

➜ Eurolines (☑ 33 88 70 00; www.eurolines. dk; Halmtorvet 5) operates buses to several European cities. The ticket office is behind Central Station.

➜ All long-distance trains arrive at and depart from Københavns Hovedbanegård (Central Station). Destinations include Hamburg (from Dkr635, 4½ hours, several daily), Odense (Dkr276, 1½ hours, at least twice hourly) and Aarhus (Dkr382, three to 3½ hours, twice hourly).

❶ Getting Around

➜ Copenhagen has an extensive public transit system consisting of a metro, rail, bus and ferry network. All tickets (billets) are valid for the whole network. Click onto the very handy www. rejseplanen.dk for routes and schedules.

➜ The cheapest ticket, costing Dkr24/12 per adult/child ages 12 to 15 years) covers two zones, offers unlimited transfers and is valid for one hour. Children under 12 travel free if accompanied by an adult.

➜ If you plan on exploring sights outside the city, you're better off buying a 24-hour ticket (all zones Dkr130/65 per adult/child) or a seven-day FlexCard (all zones Dkr590).

➜ Copenhagen vies with Amsterdam as the world's most bike-friendly city. Most streets have cycle lanes and there's a high-tech city-bike scheme.

Helsingør

POP 46,400

The main sight at the busy port town of Helsingør (Elsinore) is imposing Kronborg Slot, a brute of a castle that dominates the narrowest point of the Øresund. It was made famous as Elsinore Castle in Shakespeare's *Hamlet*.

◉ Sights

★ **Kronborg Slot**   CASTLE
(www.kronborg.dk; Kronborgvej; interior incl guided tour adult/child Dkr90/45; ⊙ 10am-5.30pm Jun-Sep, 11am-4pm Apr-May, 11am-4pm Tue-Sun Oct-Mar) The World Heritage–listed Kronborg Slot began life as Krogen, a formidable toll-house built by Danish king Erik of Pomerania in the 1420s. Expanded by Frederik II in 1585, the castle was ravaged by fire in 1629, leaving little but the outer walls. The tireless builder-king Christian IV rebuilt Kronborg, preserving the castle's earlier Renaissance style and adding his own baroque touches. The galleried chapel was the only part of the original castle buildings that escaped the flames in 1629 and gives a good impression of the castle's pre-restoration appearance.

⬛ Sleeping & Eating

Danhostel Helsingør   HOSTEL €
(☑ 49 28 49 49; danhostelhelsingor.dk; Nordre Strandvej 24; dm/s/d/tr Dkr225/495/550/595; ℙ 🛜) This 180-bed hostel is based in a coastal manor house 2km northwest of town, on a little beach looking directly across to Sweden. The run-of-the-mill dorms are in one of the smaller attached buildings. Facilities include a self-catering kitchen, small playground and outdoor ping-pong tables to keep kids amused. From Helsingør, bus 842 (Dkr24) will get you there.

Rådmand Davids Hus   DANISH €
(☑ 49 26 10 43; Strandgade 70; dishes Dkr38-98; ⊙ 10am-5pm Mon-Sat) What better place to gobble down Danish classics than a snug, lopsided 17th-century house, complete with cobbled courtyard? Refuel with honest, solid staples such as smørrebrød, herring, and the special 'shopping lunch', typically a generous plate of salad, salmon pâté, and slices of pork, cheese and homemade rye bread. Leave room for the Grand Marnier pancakes.

❶ Getting There & Away

Trains to Copenhagen (Dkr108, 45 minutes) run about three times hourly from early morning to around midnight.

Scandlines (☑ 33 15 15 15; www.scandlines. dk) sails between Helsingør and Helsingborg in Sweden (Dkr59/745 return per person/car plus nine passengers, 20 minutes).

Roskilde

POP 48,720

Most foreigners who have heard of Roskilde know it either as the home of one of Europe's best music festivals, or the site of several remarkable Viking ship finds, housed in an excellent, purpose-built museum. To the Danes, however, it is a city of great royal and religious significance, and was capital city long before Copenhagen.

⊙ Sights

★ Roskilde Domkirke
CATHEDRAL

(www.roskildedomkirke.dk; Domkirkepladsen; adult/child Dkr60/free; ⊙10am-6pm Mon-Sat, 1-6pm Sun Apr-Sep, to 4pm Oct-Mar) Not merely the crème de la crème of Danish cathedrals, this twin-towered giant is a designated Unesco World Heritage site. Started by Bishop Absalon in 1170, the building has been rebuilt and tweaked so many times that it's now a superb showcase of 800 years' worth of Danish architecture. As the royal mausoleum, it contains the crypts of 37 Danish kings and queens.

★ Viking Ship Museum
MUSEUM

(Vikingskibsmuseet; ☑46 30 02 00; www.viking eskibsmuseet.dk; Vindeboder 12; adult/child May-mid-Oct Dkr120/free, mid-Oct–Apr Dkr85/free, boat trip excl museum Dkr100; ⊙10am-5pm late Jun–mid-Aug, to 4pm mid-Aug–late Jun boat trips daily mid-May–Sep) Viking fans will be wowed by this superb museum, which displays five Viking ships discovered at the bottom of Roskilde Fjord. The museum is made up of two main sections – the Viking Ship Hall, where the boats themselves are kept, and Museumsø, where archaeological work takes place. In summer, if you've always had an urge to leap aboard a longboat for a spot of light pillaging, join one of the museum's hour-long boat trips.

✹ Festivals & Events

Roskilde Festival
MUSIC

(www.roskilde-festival.dk) Northern Europe's largest music festival. This four-day-long binge of bands and booze rocks Roskilde every summer on the last weekend in June.

⛤ Sleeping

Danhostel Roskilde
HOSTEL €

(☑46 35 21 84; www.danhostel.dk/roskilde Vindeboder 7; dm/s/d Dkr250/575/700; 🅿🛜) Roskilde's modern hostel sits right next door to the Viking Ship Museum, on the waterfront. Pimped with funky black-and-white murals, each of the 40 large rooms has its own shower and toilet. Staff are friendly, although the mattresses can be frustratingly lopsided. Cheekily, wi-fi is an extra Dkr20 per hour (Dkr100 per 24 hours).

❶ Getting There & Away

Trains run frequently between Copenhagen and Roskilde (Dkr96, 25 minutes).

Odense

POP 172,500

The millennium-old capital of the island of Funen is a cheerful, compact city ideal for feet or bicycles, with enough diversions to keep you hooked for a couple of days. The city makes much ado about being the birthplace of Hans Christian Andersen.

⊙ Sights

★ HC Andersens Hus
MUSEUM

(www.museum.odense.dk; Bangs Boder 29; adult/child Dkr95/free; ⊙10am-5pm Jul & Aug, 10am-4pm Tue-Sun Sep-Jun) Lying amid the miniaturised streets of the old poor quarter (now often referred to as the HCA Quarter), this birthplace museum delivers a thorough, lively telling of Andersen's extraordinary life and times. His achievements are put into an interesting historical context and leavened by some engaging audiovisual material and quirky exhibits (such as the display on his height – HCA was 25cm taller than the national average at the time).

★ Brandts
MUSEUM

(www.brandts.dk; Brandts Torv 1; combined ticket adult/child Dkr85/free; ⊙10am-5pm Tue, Wed & Fri-Sun, noon-9pm Thu) The former textile mill on Brandts Passage has been beautifully converted into a sprawling art centre, with thought-provoking, well-curated changing displays. Brandts Samling (the permanent collection) traces 250 years of Danish art, from classic to modern, and includes an impressive assemblage of international photography.

⛤ Sleeping

★ Odense City B&B
B&B €

(☑71 78 71 77; www.odensecitybb.dk; Vindegade 73B; s/d from Dkr250/350; 🛜) We're almost reluctant to share the secret of this ace B&B. In a prime central location (Brandts and eating options are just outside the door), a well-travelled couple have established this guesthouse above their home, with five fresh rooms sharing two bathrooms and a small kitchenette. The prices are wonderful value; breakfast costs Dkr50.

Danhostel Odense City
HOSTEL €

(☑63 11 04 25; www.odensedanhostel.dk; Østre Stationsvej 31; dm/d from Dkr250/570; @🛜) Perfectly placed for travellers, with the train and bus stations as neighbours and

DON'T MISS

LEGOLAND

Revisit your tender years at Denmark's most visited tourist attraction (beyond Copenhagen). Located 1km north of the Lego company town of Billund, the sprawling theme park **Legoland** (www.legoland.dk; Nordmarksvej; adult/child Dkr309/289; ⏰10am-8pm or 9pm Jul–mid-Aug, shorter hours Apr-Jun & mid-Aug–Oct, closed Nov-Mar; 🚻) is a gobsmacking ode to those little plastic building blocks, with everything from giant Lego models of famous cities, landmarks and wild beasts, to re-created scenes from the Star Wars film series. In 2017 the 'experience centre' Lego House is set to open in Billund town itself.

By train, the most common route is to disembark at Vejle and catch a bus from there (take bus 43 or 143). Buses run up to 10 times daily between Aarhus and Billund airport (Dkr160, one hour), close to the park.

Kongens Have (a large park) directly opposite. All rooms at this large, modern hostel have bathrooms, and there's a guest kitchen, laundry and a basement TV room.

✕ Eating & Drinking

Bazar Fyn   INTERNATIONAL €
(www.bazarfyn.dk; Thriges Plads 3; ⏰10am-9pm Tue-Sun) More than just a great place to buy groceries, Bazar Fyn offers an insight into the multicultural side of Odense. The roofed market is about five minutes' walk from the train station. There's fresh fruit and veg and deli items (stores close 6pm), plus a food court where you can eat cheaply: Lebanese shwarma, Greek souvlaki, Indian curries, Vietnamese pho.

★**Den Smagløse Café**   BAR
(http://densmagloesecafe.dk; Vindegade 57; ⏰noon-midnight or later; 🛜) This friendly, offbeat place describes itself as 'bringing to mind your grandmother's living room or your German uncle Udo's campervan'. It's *hyggelig* (cosy) in a slightly mad, wonderful way: old sofas and lamps, books and bric-a-brac. It serves all manner of drinks (coffee, cocktails, beer) and you can bring food if you like (there are pizzerias nearby).

ℹ Information

Tourist Office (📋63 75 75 20; www.visitodense.com; Vestergade 2; ⏰9.30am-6pm Mon-Fri, 10am-3pm Sat, 11am-2pm Sun Jul & Aug, 10am-4.30pm Mon-Fri, to 1pm Sat Sep-Jun) Helpful, well-stocked office in the town hall, about 700m from the train station.

ℹ Getting There & Away

Odense is accessible by the main railway line between Copenhagen (Dkr276, 1½ hours, at least hourly), Aarhus (Dkr240, 1¾ hours, at least hourly) and Esbjerg (Dkr218, 1½ hours, hourly)

Aarhus

POP 310,000

Sure, Aarhus (*oar*-hus) may be Denmark's second-largest city, but it feels more like a relaxed and friendly big town, a little bashful in the shadow of its glamorous big sister, Copenhagen. The museums and restaurants are first-rate, while the sizable student population (around 40,000) enlivens Aarhus' parks and cobblestone streets (and fill its bars). Expect its stature to grow in 2017, when it is one of the European Capitals of Culture.

◉ Sights

★**ARoS Aarhus Kunstmuseum**   ART MUSEUM
(www.aros.dk; Aros Allé 2; adult/youth 18-28/child Dkr110/90/free; ⏰10am-5pm Tue & Thu-Sun, to 10pm Wed; 🚻) Inside the cubist, red-brick walls of Aarhus' showpiece art museum are nine floors of sweeping curves, soaring spaces and white walls, showcasing a wonderful selection of Golden Age works, Danish modernism, and an abundance of arresting and vivid contemporary art. The museum's 'cherry on top' is the spectacular **Your Rainbow Panorama**, a 360-degree rooftop walkway offering technicolour views of the city through its glass panes in all shades of the rainbow.

★**Moesgård Museum**   MUSEUM
(www.moesgaardmuseum.dk; Moesgård Allé; adult/child Dkr110/free; ⏰10am-5pm Tue & Thu-Sun, to 9pm Wed) Don't miss the reinvented Moesgård Museum, 10km south of the city. It reopened in October 2014 in a spectacularly designed, award-winning modern space, next door to the manor house that once accommodated its excellent prehistory exhibits. The museum's star attraction is the 2000-year-old **Grauballe Man**, whose astonishingly well-preserved body was found in 1952. Bus 18 runs here frequently.

🛏 Sleeping & Eating

City Sleep-In HOSTEL €
(☑ 86 19 20 55; www.citysleep-in.dk; Havnegade 20; dm Dkr190, d without/with bathroom Dkr460/520; @ 🖥) The most central hostel option has small, basic rooms – you'll be more drawn to the communal areas, such as the pretty courtyard or 1st-floor TV room. There are helpful staff, a global feel and decent amenities (lockers, kitchen, pool table, laundry).

CabInn Aarhus Hotel HOTEL €
(☑ 86 75 70 00; www.cabinn.com; Kannikegade 14; s/d/tr from Dkr495/625/805; P @ 🖥) 'Best location, best price' is the CabInn chain's motto, and given that this branch recently doubled in size, it's clearly doing something right. The functional rooms are based on ships' cabins (hence the name) – the cheapest is *tiny*, but all come with bathroom, kettle and TV. The location is indeed top-notch. Breakfast costs Dkr75.

★ Oli Nico INTERNATIONAL €
(www.olinico.dk; Mejlgade 35; dishes Dkr55-125; ☻ 11.30am-2pm & 5.30-9pm Mon-Fri, noon-2pm & 5.30-9pm Sat, 5.30-9pm Sun) You may need to fight for one of the sought-after tables at Oli Nico, a small deli-restaurant with a menu of classic dishes at astoundingly good prices (*moules frites* for Dkr60, rib-eye steak for Dkr125 – both with homemade chips!). The daily-changing three-course dinner menu (for a bargain Dkr130) may be Aarhus' best-kept food secret. No reservations; takeaway available.

🍷 Drinking & Entertainment

Aarhus is the nation's music capital, with no shortage of quality music gigs in venues from dignified concert halls to beer-fuelled boltholes. For the lowdown click onto www.visitaarhus.com or www.aoa.dk.

★ Strandbaren BAR
(www.facebook.com/strandbarenaarhus; Havnebassin 7, pier 4; ☻ May-Sep) Plonk shipping containers and sand on a harbour-front spot and voila: beach bar. This chilled hang-out at Aarhus Ø (just beyond the ferry port) offers food, drink, flirting and weather-dependent activities and events. Check hours and location on the Facebook page (opening hours are 'when the sun is shining'). Bus 33 runs out th s way.

ℹ Information

VisitAarhus (☑ 87 31 50 10; www.visitaarhus.com) Information online, by phone, at the bus station and at several touchscreens and summer kiosks around the city.

ℹ Getting There & Away

Trains to Copenhagen (Dkr382, three to 3½ hours), via Odense (Dkr240, 1¾ hours), leave Aarhus roughly half-hourly.

Abildskou (☑ 70 21 08 88; www.abildskou.dk) bus 888 runs up to 10 times daily between Aarhus and Copenhagen's Valby station (Dkr310, three to 3½ hours), with connections to Copenhagen airport. Good online discounts available.

Skagen

POP 8200

The town of Skagen (pronounced 'skain') is a busy working harbour and Denmark's northernmost settlement, just a couple of kilometres from the dramatic sandy spit beloved of artists, where the country finally peters out at Grenen, a slender point of wave-washed sand, where seals bask and seagulls soar.

◉ Sights

★ Skagens Museum MUSEUM
(www.skagensmuseum.dk; Brøndumsvej 4; adult/child Dkr100/free; ☻ 10am-5pm, to 9pm Wed May-Aug, 10am-5pm Thu-Tue Sep-Apr) Artists discovered Skagen's luminous light and its wind-blasted heath-and-dune landscape in the mid-19th century; their work established a vivid figurative style of painting that became known internationally as the 'Skagen School'. This wonderful gallery showcases the outstanding art that was produced in Skagen between 1870 and 1930.

Grenen OUTDOORS
Appropriately enough for such a neat and ordered country, Denmark doesn't end untidily at its most northerly point, but on a neat finger of sand just a few metres wide. You can actually paddle at its tip, where the waters of the Kattegat and Skagerrak clash, and you can put one foot in each sea – but not too far. Bathing here is forbidden because of the ferocious tidal currents.

🛏 Sleeping & Eating

Danhostel Skagen HOSTEL €
(☑ 98 44 22 00; www.danhostelskagen.dk; Rolighedsvej 2; dm/s/d Dkr180/525/625; ☻ Mar-Nov; P 🖥) Always a hive of activity, this hostel is modern, functional and spick-and-span. It's decent value, particularly for families or groups. Low-season prices drop sharply. It's

1km toward Frederikshavn from the Skagen train station (if you're coming by train, get off at Frederikshavnsvej).

★ **Skagens Museum Cafe** CAFE **€**
(www.skagensmuseum.dk; Brøndumsvej 4; lunch mains Dkr85-100; ⏱ 10am-5pm) For lunch or a cuppa in a magical setting, head to the Garden House cafe at Skagens Museum, serving lunchtime dishes plus a super spread of home-baked cakes and tarts. Note: you don't need to pay the museum's admission if you're just visiting the cafe.

❶ Getting There & Away

Trains run hourly to Frederikshavn (Dkr60, 35 minutes), where you can change for destinations further south.

The summertime bus 99 connects Skagen with other northern towns and attractions.

Denmark Survival Guide

❶ Directory A–Z

ACCOMMODATION
➜ Campgrounds, hostels and B&B accommodation generally offer an excellent standard of accommodation and are good ways to secure comfort on a budget.

➜ During July and August it's advisable to book ahead.

LGBT TRAVELLERS
➜ Denmark is a tolerant, popular destination for gay and lesbian travellers. Copenhagen in particular has an active, open gay community with a healthy number of venues, but you'll find gay and lesbian venues in other cities as well.

➜ A useful website for travellers with visitor information and listings in English is www.copenhagen-gay-life.dk. Also see www.out-and-about.dk.

---

❶ PRICE RANGES

The following price ranges refer to a double room in high season:

€ less than Dkr700

€€ Dkr700–1500

€€€ more than Dkr1500

For eating choices, the following price ranges refer to a standard main course.

€ less than Dkr125

€€ Dkr125–250

€€€ more than Dkr250

➜ The main gay and lesbian festival of the year is Copenhagen Pride (www.copenhagenpride.dk), a five-day queer fest that takes place in August.

MONEY
➜ One krone is divided into 100 øre. There are 50 øre, Dkr1, Dkr2, Dkr5, Dkr10 and Dkr20 coins. Notes come in denominations of 50, 100, 200, 500 and 1000 kroner.

➜ ATMs are widely available. Credit cards are accepted in most hotels, restaurants and shops.

➜ Hotel and restaurant bills and taxi fares include service charges in the quoted prices. Further tipping is unnecessary, although rounding up the bill is not uncommon when service has been especially good.

OPENING HOURS
Banks 10am to 4pm Monday to Friday

Bars 4pm to midnight, to 2am or later Friday and Saturday

Cafes 8am to 5pm or midnight

Restaurants noon to 10pm

Shops 10am to 6pm Monday to Friday, to 4pm Saturday, some Sundays

Supermarkets 8am to 9pm

PUBLIC HOLIDAYS
Many Danes take their main work holiday during the first three weeks of July.

New Year's Day (Nytårsdag) 1 January

Maundy Thursday (Skærtorsdag) Thursday before Easter

Good Friday (Langfredag) Friday before Easter

Easter Day (Påskedag) Sunday in March or April

Easter Monday (2. påskedag) Day after Easter

Great Prayer Day (Stor Bededag) Fourth Friday after Easter

Ascension Day (Kristi Himmelfartsdag) Sixth Thursday after Easter

Whitsunday (Pinsedag) Seventh Sunday after Easter

Whitmonday (2. pinsedag) Seventh Monday after Easter

Constitution Day (Grundlovsdag) 5 June

Christmas Eve (Juleaften) 24 December (from noon)

Christmas Day (Juledag) 25 December

Boxing Day (2. juledag) 26 December

New Year's Eve (Nytårsaften) 31 December (from noon)

TELEPHONE
➜ All telephone numbers in Denmark have eight digits; there are no area codes.

➜ Country code: ☑ 45.

➜ International access code: ☑ 00.

➜ Local SIM cards with data packages are easily available and cheap.

ⓘ JUTLAND FERRY PORTS

Ferries to Sweden, Norway and Iceland run from two ports at the top tip of Jutland: Frederikshavn (Stena Line to Gothenburg and Oslo) and Hirtshals (Color Line & Fjord Line to Bergen, Kristiansand, Stavanger, Langesund and Larvik (Norway), Smyril Line to Seyðisfjörður (Iceland) via Tórshavn (Faroe Islands). See www.directferries.com for all routes.

Trains run from Copenhagen via Odense, Aarhus and Aalborg to Frederikshavn; change at Hjørring for Hirtshals.

ⓘ Getting There & Around

For getting around in Denmark, the essential website is www.rejseplanen.dk. Download the app for easy mobile access.

AIR

The majority of overseas flights into Denmark land at Copenhagen International Airport (www.cph.dk) in Kastrup, about 9km southeast of central Copenhagen.

BUS

Copenhagen is well connected to the rest of Europe by daily (or near daily) buses. Eurolines operates most international routes.

Within the country, all large cities and towns have a local and regional bus system. Long-distance buses run a distant second to trains.

FERRY

→ Ferry connections are possible between Denmark and Norway, Sweden, Germany, Poland (via Sweden), Iceland and the Faroe Islands. Check www.directferries.com for details.

→ Boats link virtually all of Denmark's populated islands.

TRAIN

→ Denmark has a very reliable train system with reasonable fares and frequent services. **Danske Statsbaner** (DSB; ☑70 13 14 15; www.dsb.dk) runs virtually all trains in Denmark.

→ There are regular international links from Copenhagen to Sweden (via the bridge) and Germany (via ferry).

SWEDEN

Stockholm

☑08 / POP 1.46 MILLION (URBAN AREA)

Beautiful capital cities are no rarity in Europe, but Stockholm is near the top of the list for sheer loveliness. Its 14 islands rise starkly out of the surrounding ice-blue water, each boasting saffron-and-cinnamon buildings that stand honeyed in sunlight and frostily elegant in cold weather. The city's charms are irresistible. From its movie-set Old Town (Gamla Stan) to its ever-modern fashion sense and impeccable taste in food and design, the city acts like an immersion school in aesthetics.

◉ Sights & Activities

Stockholm is strewn across 14 islands connected by more than 50 bridges. Gamla Stan, the old town, is Stockholm's historic and geographic heart.

Kungliga Slottet PALACE
(Royal Palace; ☑08-402 61 30; www.kungahuset.se; Slottsbacken; adult/child Skr150/75, valid for 7 days; ☉8.30am-5pm Jul & Aug, 10am-5pm mid-May–Jun & early Sep, 10am-4pm Tue-Sun mid-Sep–mid-May; ☑43, 46, 55, 59 Slottsbacken, Ⓜ Gamla Stan) With 608 rooms, this is the world's largest royal castle still used for its original purpose. Kungliga Slottet was built on the ruins of Tre Kronor castle, which burned down in 1697. Free 45-minute tours in English (check the website for times) are worthwhile. The Changing of the Guard takes place in the outer courtyard at 12.15pm Monday to Saturday and 1.15pm Sunday from May through August. The rest of the year it's Wednesdays, Saturdays and Sundays only.

★ Skansen MUSEUM
(www.skansen.se; Djurgårdsvägen; adult/child Skr180/60; ☉10am-4pm, 6pm or 8pm; 🚻; ☑44, 🚤Djurgårdsfärjan, 🚋7, Djurgården) The world's first open-air museum, Skansen was founded in 1891 to give visitors an insight into how Swedes lived once upon a time. You could easily spend a day here and still not see it all. Around 150 traditional houses and other exhibits from across the country dot the hilltop – it's meant to be 'Sweden in miniature', complete with villages, nature, commerce and industry. Prices and opening times vary greatly by date: check the website.

Storkyrkan CHURCH
(Great Church; www.stockholmsdomkyrkoforsamling.se; Trångsund 1; adult/child Skr40/free; ☉9am-4pm; Ⓜ Gamla Stan) The one-time venue for royal weddings and coronations, Storkyrkan is both Stockholm's oldest building (consecrated in 1306) and its cathedral. Behind a baroque facade, the Gothic-baroque interior includes extravagant royal-box pews.

Stockholm

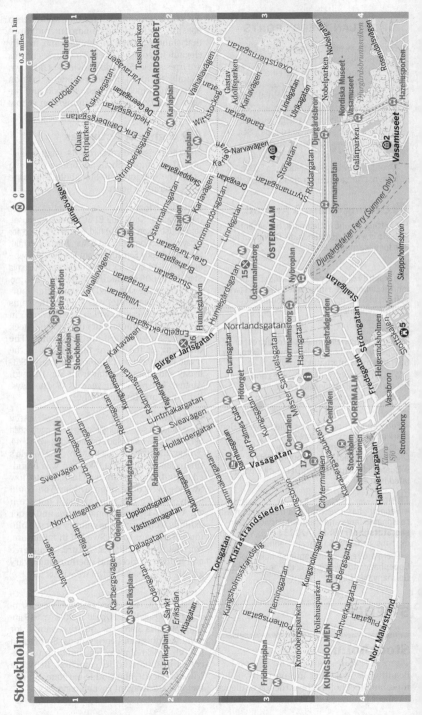

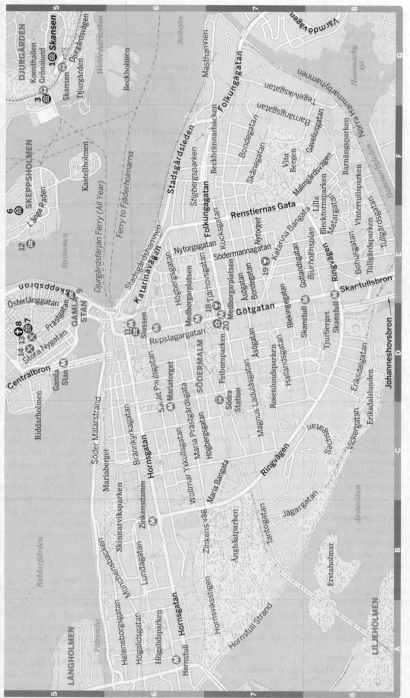

Stockholm

ABBA: The Museum MUSEUM
(📞 08-12 13 28 60; www.abbathemuseum.com; Djurgårdsvägen 68; adult/child Skr195/65; ⊙10am-8pm, shorter hours in winter; 🚌44, 🚢Djurgårdsfärjan, 🚊7) A sensory-overload experience that might appeal only to devoted Abba fans, this long-awaited and wildly hyped cathedral to the demigods of Swedish pop is almost aggressively entertaining. It's packed to the gills with memorabilia and interactivity.

Historiska Museet MUSEUM
(📞 08-51 95 56 00; www.historiska.se; Narvavägen 13-17; ⊙11am-6pm Jun-Sep, noon-6pm Tue-Fri, 11am-6pm Sat & Sun Oct-May, also to 8pm Wed Sep-May; 🚌44, 56, Ⓜ Karlaplan, Östermalmstorg) FREE The national historical collection awaits at this enthralling museum. From Iron Age skates and a Viking boat to medieval textiles and Renaissance triptychs, it spans over 10,000 years of Swedish history and culture. An undisputed highlight is the subterranean Gold Room.

Nobelmuseet MUSEUM
(www.nobelmuseet.se; Stortorget; adult/child Skr100/free; ⊙10am-8pm; Ⓜ Gamla Stan) Nobelmuseet presents the history of the Nobel Prizes and their recipients, with a focus on the intellectual and cultural aspects of invention. It's a slick space with fascinating displays, including short films on the theme of creativity, interviews with laureates such as Ernest Hemingway and Martin Luther King, and cafe chairs signed by the visiting prize recipients (flip them over to see!).

Moderna Museet MUSEUM
(📞 08-52 02 35 00; www.modernamuseet.se; Exercisplan 4; ⊙10am-8pm Tue, to 6pm Wed-Sun; 🚌65, 🚢Djurgårdsfärjan) FREE Moderna Mu-

seet is Stockholm's modern-art maverick, its permanent collection ranging from paintings and sculptures to photography, video art and installations.

Stockholm City Bikes BICYCLE RENTAL
(www.citybikes.se; 3-day/season card Skr165/300) City Bikes has around 90 self-service bicycle-hire stands across the city. Bikes can be borrowed for three-hour stretches and returned at any City Bikes stand. You'll need to purchase a bike card online or from the tourist office.

🛏 Sleeping

★**City Backpackers** HOSTEL €
(📞 08-20 69 20; www.citybackpackers.org; Upplandsgatan 2a; dm Skr200-300, s/d/tr Skr550/690/920; ☕@🛜; Ⓜ T-Centralen) The closest hostel to Centralstationen has clean rooms, friendly staff, free bike hire and excellent facilities, including sauna, laundry and kitchen (with a free stash of pasta). En suite private rooms are also available. Bonus for female guests: there are four- and eight-bed female-only dorms if you prefer, and you can borrow a hairdryer from reception.

★**Vandrarhem af Chapman
& Skeppsholmen** HOSTEL €
(📞 08-463 22 66; www.stfchapman.com; Flaggmansvägen 8; dm from Skr190, r from Skr590; ☕@🛜; 🚌65 Skeppsholmen) The *af Chapman* is a storied vessel that has done plenty of travelling of its own. It's anchored in a superb location, swaying gently off Skeppsholmen. Bunks are in dorms below deck. Apart from showers and toilets, all facilities are on dry land in the Skeppsholmen hostel, including a good kitchen, a laid-back common room and a TV lounge.

2kronor Hostel Old Town HOSTEL €

(📞 08-22 92 30; www.2kronor.se; Skeppsbron 40; dm Skr195, s/d Skr495/590; 🕓@🛜; Ⓜ Gamla Stan, Slussen) This small, quiet, family-run hostel has a fantastic location and a friendly vibe. Rooms are on the basement level, slightly cavelike but pretty and well kept (and there are windows). Shared bathrooms are down the hall. Breakfast isn't available, but there's a guest kitchen and dining area by the reception upstairs. Dorms (six- and eight-bed rooms with bunks) are mixed. Check-in is from 3pm to 6pm.

★ Hotel Anno 1647 HOTEL €€

(📞 08-442 16 80; www.anno1647.se; Mariagränd 3; s/d budget from Skr570/740, standard from Skr890/990; 🅿🕓@🛜; Ⓜ Slussen) Just off buzzing Götgatan, this historical hotel in two beautiful buildings has labyrinthine hallways, gorgeous wooden floors and spiral staircases, affable staff, and budget as well as standard rooms – both are recommended. The latter have antique rococo wallpaper, all modern amenities and the odd chandelier. The location and reduced high-season rates make this a fantastic deal.

✕ Eating

Stockholm is a city of foodies. Its epicurean highlights don't come cheap, but you can find great value in the abundant cafes, coffee shops and vegetarian buffets.

★ Vurma CAFE €

(www.vurma.se; Birger Jarlsgatan 36; sandwiches Skr60-80, salads Skr108; 🕓11am-10pm Mon & Tue, to 11pm Wed-Fri, noon-midnight Sat; 🛜🖊🚻; Ⓜ Rådhuset) Squeeze in among the locals at this friendly cafe-bakery, a reliably affordable place to get a healthy and substantial meal in an unfussy setting. They offer scrumptious sandwiches and the salads are inspired, with ingredients such as halloumi, falafel, cured salmon, avocado and greens over quinoa or pasta. The homemade bread that comes with your order is divine.

Östermalms Saluhall MARKET €

(www.ostermalmshallen.se; Östermalmstorg; 🕓9.30am-6pm Mon-Thu, to 7pm Fri, to 4pm Sat; Ⓜ Östermalmstorg) Stockholm's historic gourmet food market feeds all the senses with fresh fish, seafood and meat, fruit, vegetables and hard-to-find cheeses, as well as cafes for a quick lunch or snack. The 1885 building, a Stockholm landmark, is closed for renovations from 2015 to 2017, with a temporary market set up in the square.

Chokladkoppen CAFE €

(www.chokladkoppen.se; Stortorget 18; cakes Skr40-80; 🕓9am-11pm Jun-Aug, shorter hours rest of year; Ⓜ Gamla Stan) Arguably Stockholm's best-loved cafe, hole-in-the-wall Chokladkoppen sits slap bang on the old town's enchanting main square. It's a gay-friendly spot, with cute waiters, a look-at-me summer terrace and yummy grub such as broccoli-and-blue-cheese pie and scrumptious cakes.

★ Hermitage VEGETARIAN €€

(www.hermitage.gastrogate.com; Stora Nygatan 11; buffet lunch/dinner & weekends Skr120/130; 🕓11am-8pm Mon-Fri, noon-8pm Sat & Sun, to 9pm Jun-Aug; 🖊; Ⓜ Gamla Stan) Herbivores love Hermitage for its simple, tasty, vegetarian buffet, easily one of the best restaurant bargains in Gamla Stan. Salad, homemade bread, tea and coffee are included in the price. Pro tip: don't miss the drawers of hot food hiding under the main buffet tabletop.

🍷 Drinking & Entertainment

Pet Sounds Bar BAR

(www.psb.bar; Skånegatan 80; beer Skr72, cocktails Skr118; 🕓5pm-midnight Sun-Tue, to 1am Wed & Thu, 4pm-1am Fri & Sat; Ⓜ Medborgarplatsen) A SoFo favourite, this jamming bar pulls in music journos, indie culture vultures and the odd goth rocker. While the restaurant serves decent Italian-French grub, the real fun happens in the basement. Head down for a mixed bag of live bands, release parties and DJ sets. Hit happy hour (2pm to 6pm) for drink specials.

Kvarnen BAR

(📞 08-643 03 80; www.kvarnen.com; Tjärhovsgatan 4; 🕓11am-1am Mon & Tue, to 3am Wed-Fri, noon-3am Sat, noon-1am Sun; Ⓜ Medborgarplatsen) An old-school Hammarby football-fan hangout, Kvarnen is one of the best bars in Söder. The gorgeous beer hall dates from 1907 and seeps tradition; if you're not the clubbing type, get here early for a nice pint and a meal (mains Skr139 to Skr195). As the night progresses, the nightclub vibe takes over. Queues are fairly constant but justifiable

Icebar BAR

(📞 08-50 56 35 20; www.icebarstockholm.se; Vasaplan 4, Nordic 'C' Hotel; prebooked online/drop in Skr195/205; 🕓4.30-11.15pm Sun-Thu, 3.45pm-1am Fri & Sat) It's touristy. Downright gimmicky! And you're utterly intrigued, admit it: a bar built entirely out of ice, where you drink from glasses carved of ice at tables made of ice. The admission price gets you warm booties, mittens, a parka and one drink. Refill drinks cost Skr95.

Debaser   LIVE MUSIC
(✆ 08-694 79 00; www.debaser.se; Medborgarplatsen 8; ⊘ 7pm-1am Sun-Thu, 8pm-3am Fri & Sat; Ⓜ Medborgarplatsen) This mini-empire of entertainment has its flagship rock venue (Debaser Medis) on Medborgarplatsen. Emerging or bigger-name acts play most nights, while the killer club nights span anything from rock-steady to punk and electronica.

❶ Information

Stockholm Visitors Center (✆ 08-508 28 508; www.visitstockholm.com; Kulturhuset, Sergels Torg 3; ⊘ 9am-7pm Mon-Fri, to 6pm winter, 9am-4pm Sat, to 6pm Jul & Aug, 10am-4pm Sun; Ⓜ T-Centralen) The main visitors centre occupies a space inside Kulturhuset on Sergels Torg.

❶ Getting There & Away

➡ Stockholm's and Sweden's main airport, Arlanda, is 45km north of the city centre.

➡ Stockholm is connected by ferry to Turku and Helsinki in Finland via the Åland archipelago, and also to Tallinn (Estonia), Riga (Latvia) and St Petersburg (Russia).

➡ Most long-distance buses arrive at and depart from **Cityterminalen** (www.cityterminalen.com; ⊘ 7am-6pm), which is connected to Centralstationen.

➡ Stockholm is the hub for national and international train services run by **Sveriges Järnväg** (SJ; ✆ 0771-75 75 75; www.sj.se).

❶ Getting Around

The **Arlanda Express** (www.arlandaexpress.com; one-way Skr280) airport train service from Centralstationen takes 20 minutes to reach Arlanda. From Thursday to Sunday, two adults can travel together for Skr300.

A cheaper option is the **Flygbuss** (www.flygbussarna.se) service between Stockholm Arlanda and Cityterminalen. Buses (Skr119, 50 minutes, every 10 or 15 minutes) leave from stop 11 in Terminal 5. Tickets are cheapest online.

Storstockholms Lokaltrafik (SL; ✆ 08-600 10 00; www.sl.se; Centralstationen, Sergels Torg; single trip Skr25-50, unlimited 24hr/72hr/7-day pass Skr115/230/300, students & seniors half-price) runs all *tunnelbana* (metro) trains, local trains and buses within Stockholm county. Refillable SL travel cards (Skr20) can be loaded with single-trip or unlimited-travel credit.

Uppsala

☑ 018 / POP 156,000

Drenched in history but never stifled by the past, Uppsala has the party vibe of a university town to balance out its large number of important buildings and general atmosphere of weighty cultural significance. It's a terrific combination, and one that makes the town both fun and functional, not to mention very rewarding for the interested traveller.

◎ Sights

Domkyrka   CHURCH
(Cathedral; www.uppsaladomkyrka.se; Domkyrkoplan; ⊘ 8am-6pm) ᖴᖇᗴᗴ The Gothic Domkyrka dominates the city, just as some of those buried here, including St Erik, Gustav Vasa and the scientist Carl von Linné, dominated their country. Tours are available in English at 11am and 2pm Monday to Saturday, and 4pm Sunday, in July and August.

Gamla Uppsala   ARCHAEOLOGICAL SITE
(www.arkeologigamlauppsala.se; ⊘ 24hr; 🅿; 🚲2) ᖴᖇᗴᗴ One of Sweden's largest and most important burial sites, Gamla Uppsala (4km north of Uppsala) contains 300 mounds from the 6th to 12th centuries. Legend has it that the impressive earliest three contain the pre-Viking kings Aun, Egil and Adils, who appear in *Beowulf* and *Ynglingsaga*. More recent evidence suggests the occupant of Östhögen (East Mound) was a woman. The **museum** (www.raa.se; adult/child Skr80/free; ⊘ 10am-4pm Apr-late Jun & mid-Aug–Sep, 11am-5pm late Jun–mid-Aug, noon-4pm Mon, Wed, Sat & Sun Oct-Mar; 🅿) contains finds from the cremation mounds and various boat graves in and around the site.

🛏 Sleeping & Eating

Uppsala City Hostel   HOSTEL €
(✆ 018-10 00 08; www.uppsalacityhostel.se; Sankt Persgatan 16; dm/s/d from Skr220/440/560; ⊘ reception 8am-11pm; ⊜@☎) The no-nonsense Uppsala City Hostel is recommended for its sheer convenience – you really can't stay anywhere more central for these prices. Rooms, all named after famous Uppsala landmarks, are small but decent (although dorms suffer from traffic and level-crossing noise). There's wi-fi access in parts of the hostel. Breakfast costs Skr55, and a kitchen is available.

Saluhallen   MARKET €
(Sankt Eriks Torg; ⊘ 10am-6pm Mon-Thu, to 7pm Fri, to 4pm Sat, restaurants 11am-4pm Sun) Stock

up on meat, fish, cheese and fancy chocolate at this indoor market, or hit one of the restaurant corners for a bite; a couple stay open late for dinner, with pleasant terrace bars available in summer.

ℹ️ Information

Tourist Office (📞 018-727 48 00; www.destinationuppsala.se; Kungsgatan 59; ⊙10am-6pm Mon-Fri, to 3pm Sat, plus 11am-3pm Sun Jul & Aug) In a prime spot directly in front of the train station, the tourist office has helpful advice, maps and brochures for the whole county.

ℹ️ Getting There & Away

Swebus Express runs buses to Stockholm (Skr59, one hour, at least hourly). There are also direct buses to Arlanda airport.

Trains operate to/from Stockholm (Skr70 to Skr110, 35 to 55 minutes one way) via Arlanda airport.

Malmö

📞 040 / POP 300,000

Sweden's third-largest city has a multicultural, progressive contemporary feel. Home to Scandinavia's tallest building, beautiful parks, edgy contemporary museums and some seriously good cuisine, the opening of the Öresund bridge in 2000 has also been undeniably positive, connecting the city to bigger, cooler Copenhagen and creating a dynamic new urban conglomeration.

👁 Sights

⭐ **Malmö Museer**   MUSEUM
(www.malmo.se/museer; Malmöhusvägen; adult/child Skr40/free, audio guides Skr20; ⊙10am-5pm; 👪) Various museums in and around the imposing Malmöhus Slott (castle) make up the maze-like Malmö Museer. You can walk through royal apartments, learn about the castle's history, descend into the prison with displays on crime and punishment, check out vehicles through the ages, and see works by important Swedish artists. Don't miss the nocturnal hall at the Aquarium, wriggling with everything from bats to electric eels, plus local swimmers such as cod and pike.

🛏 Sleeping & Eating

STF Vandrarhem Malmö City   HOSTEL €
(📞 040-611 62 20; www.svenskaturistforeningen.se; Rönngatan 1; dm/d from Skr230/560; @ 🕲) Don't be put off by the exterior; this is a sparkling hostel right in the city centre with

WORTH A TRIP

LUND

The centrepiece of the appealing university town of Lund, just 15 minutes from Malmö on the train, is the splendid Romanesque **cathedral** (lundsdomkyrka.se; Kyrkogatan; ⊙8am-6pm Mon-Fri, 9.30am-5pm Sat, 9.30am-6pm Sun) FREE, with some fantastic gargoyles over the side entrances, a giant turned to stone in the eerie crypt and an astronomical clock that sends the wooden figures whirring into action (noon and 3pm Monday to Saturday and 1pm and 3pm Sunday).

a bright and airy communal kitchen and an outdoor patio. Staff are enthusiastic and helpful.

Falafel No. 1   FELAFEL €
(📞 040-84 41 22; www.falafel-n1.se; Österportsgatan 2; felafel from Skr35) Malmö residents are so fond of felafel that it even features in songs by local rapper Timbuktu. Falafel No. 1 (also known as the Orient House) is a long-standing favourite.

Salt & Brygga   SWEDISH €€
(📞 040-611 59 40; www.saltobrygga.se; Sundspromenaden 7; mains lunch Skr98-135, dinner Skr175-225; ⊙11am-2pm & 5-11pm Mon-Fri, 12.30-4pm & 5-11pm Sat; 🍴) 🌿 With an enviable view overlooking the Öresund bridge and the small harbour, this stylish slow-food restaurant presents updated Swedish cuisine with a clear conscience. Everything is organic (including the staff uniforms), waste is turned into biogas, and the interior is allergy free. Flavours are clean and strictly seasonal.

ℹ️ Information

Tourist Office (📞 040-34 12 00; www.malmotown.com; Skeppsbron 2; ⊙9am-7pm Mon-Fri, 10am-4pm Sat & Sun, shorter hours winter) Across from the Centralstationen.

ℹ️ Getting There & Away

➡ Train services include Copenhagen (Skr105, 35 minutes, three per hour), Göteborg (from Skr240, 2½ to 3¼ hours, several daily) and Stockholm (from SKR750, 4½ hours, hourly).

➡ From **Travelshop** (Malmö Buss & Resecenter; 📞 040-33 05 70; www.travelshop.se; Carlsgatan 4A), Swebus Express services run two to four times daily direct to Stockholm (from Skr539, 8½ hours) and up to 10 times daily to

Göteborg (from Skr139, three to four hours); five continue to Oslo (from Skr219, eight hours).

➡ Finnlines runs two to three daily ferries to Travemünde in Germany (8¾ hours).

Göteborg

☑ 031 / POP 549,800

Though often caught in Stockholm's shadow, gregarious, chilled-out Göteborg (*yurte-borry*, Gothenburg in English) actually has greater appeal for many visitors (and resident Swedes) than the fast-paced capital. Some of the country's finest talent hails from the streets of this cosmopolitan port, including music icons José González and Soundtrack of Our Lives. Neoclassical architecture lines its tram-rattled streets, grit-hip cafes hum with bonhomie, and there's always some cutting-edge art and architecture to grab your attention.

◉ Sights

The Haga district is Göteborg's oldest suburb, dating back to 1648. A hardcore hippie hangout in the 1960s and '70s, its cobbled streets and vintage buildings are now a gentrified blend of cafes, op shops and boutiques.

Konstmuseum GALLERY
(www.konstmuseum.goteborg.se; Götaplatsen; adult/youth under 25yr Skr40/free; ☉11am-6pm Tue & Thu, to 8pm Wed, 11am-5pm Fri-Sun; ♿; ☐4, 5, 7, 10 Berzeliigatan) Göteborg's premier art collection, this gallery hosts works by the French Impressionists, Rubens, Van Gogh, Rembrandt and Picasso. Scandinavian masters such as Bruno Liljefors, Edvard Munch, Anders Zorn and Carl Larsson have pride of place in the **Fürstenburg Galleries**.

Other highlights include a superb sculpture hall, the **Hasselblad Center** with its annual *New Nordic Photography* exhibition, and temporary displays of next-gen Nordic art.

Stadsmuseum MUSEUM
(City Museum; www.stadsmuseum.goteborg.se; Norra Hamngatan 12; adult/under 25yr Skr40/free; ☉10am-5pm Tue & Thu-Sun, to 8pm Wed; ♿; ☐1, 3, 4, 5, 6, 9 Brunnsparken) At Stadsmuseum, admire the remains of the *Äskekärrkeppet*, Sweden's only original Viking vessel, alongside silver treasure hoards, weaponry and jewellery from the same period in the atmospheric semigloom.

★**Röda Sten** GALLERY
(www.rodasten.com; Röda Sten 1; adult/free; ☉noon-5pm Tue & Thu-Sun, to 7pm Wed; ☐3, 9 Vagnhallen Majorna) Occupying a defunct, graffitied power station beside the giant Älvsborgsbron, Röda Sten's four floors are home to edgy temporary exhibitions. The indie-style cafe hosts weekly live music and club nights, and offbeat events. To get there, walk toward the Klippan precinct, continue under Älvsborgsbron and look for the brown-brick building.

★**Liseberg** AMUSEMENT PARK
(www.liseberg.se; Södra Vägen; 1-/2-day pass Skr415/595; ☉11am-11pm Jun–mid-Aug; ♿; ☐2, 4, 5, 6, 8, 10 Korsvägen) The attractions of Liseberg, Scandinavia's largest amusement park, are many and varied. Adrenalin blasts include the venerable wooden roller coaster Balder, its 'explosive' colleague Kanonen, where you're blasted from 0km/h to 75km/h in under two seconds, AtmosFear, Europe's tallest (116m) free-fall tower, and thrilling rollercoaster Helix.

🛏 Sleeping

STF Vandrarhem Slottsskogen HOSTEL €
(☑031-42 65 20; www.sov.nu; Vegagatan 21; hostel dm/s/d from Skr195/395/540, hotel s/d Skr550/790; ℗@🛜; ☐1, 2, 6 Olivedalsgatan) Like a good university dormitory, big, friendly Slottsskogen is a cracking place for meeting people. The facilities are top-notch, with comfortable beds, individual reading lights, lockable storage under the beds, a dressing table in the women's dorm and a good ratio of guests per bathroom. Proximity to the nightlife area is a bonus, and the buffet breakfast (Skr70) is brilliant.

Linné Vandrarhem HOSTEL €
(☑031-12 10 60; www.linnehostel.com; Vegagatan 22; dm/s/d Skr290/490/690; @🛜; ☐1, 6, 7, 10 Prinsgatan) The helpful staff really brighten up this central, homey hostel. Make sure you have your door code if arriving after office hours and avoid the windowless 'economy' rooms (read: ovens) in summer.

🍴 Eating & Drinking

Kungsportsavenyn brims with beer-downing tourists, but there are still some savvier options. The Linné district is home to several friendly student hang-outs serving extremely cheap beer.

Saluhall Briggen
MARKET €

(www.saluhallbriggen.se; Nordhemsgatan 28; ⊙9am-6pm Mon-Fri, to 3pm Sat; ☑; ☐1,6 ,7, 10 Prinsgatan) This covered market will have you drooling over its bounty of fresh bread, cheeses, quiches, seafood and ethnic treats. It's particularly handy for the hostel district.

Smaka
SWEDISH €€

(☑031-13 22 47; www.smaka.se; Vasaplatsen 3; mains Skr130-225; ⊙5pm-late; ☐1, 2, 3, 7, 10 Vasaplatsen) For top-notch Swedish husmanskost (home cooking), such as the speciality meatballs with mashed potato and lingonberries, it's hard to do better than this smart yet down-to-earth restaurant-bar. Mod-Swedish options might include hake with suckling pig cheek or salmon tartar with pickled pear.

ⓘ Information

Tourist Office (☑031-368 42 00; www.goteborg.com; Kungsportsplatsen 2; ⊙9.30am-8pm late Jun–mid-Aug, shorter hours rest of year) Central and busy; has a good selection of free brochures and maps.

ⓘ Getting There & Away

➧ **Stena Line** (www.stenaline.se; ☐3, 9, 11 Masthuggstorget) run ferries to Kiel n Germany (Skr599, daily, 14½ hours) and Fredrikshavn in Denmark (Skr99, 5 daily, 3¼ hours).

➧ Bus services include Stockholm (Skr389, 6½ to seven hours, four to five daily), Copenhagen (Skr239, 4¾ to five hours, four daily) Malmö (Skr159, 3½ to four hours, five to eight daily) and Oslo (Skr189, 3½ hours, five to 10 daily).

➧ Trains run to Copenhagen (Skr450, 3¾ hours, hourly), Malmö (Skr195, 2½ to 3¼ hours, hourly), Oslo (Skr299, four hours, three daily) and Stockholm (Skr419, three to five hours, one to two an hour)

Gotland

☑0498 / POP 57,300

Gorgeous Gotland, an island adrift in the Baltic, has much to brag about: a Unesco-lauded medieval capital, truffle-sprinkled woods, dining hot spots, talented artisans, and more hours of sunshine than anywhere else in Sweden. It's also one of the country's richest historical regions, with around 100 medieval churches and countless prehistoric sites.

ⓘ Getting There & Away

Year-round car ferries between Gotland and both Nynäshamn (just south of Stockholm) and Oskarshamn (between Stockholm and Malmö) are operated by **Destination Gotland** (☑0771-22 33 00; www.destinationgotland.se).

Visby

The Unesco-listed medieval port town of Visby alone warrants a trip to Gotland. Within its sturdy city walls await twisting cobbled streets, fairy-tale wooden cottages, evocative church ruins and steep hills with impromptu Baltic views. The wining and dining options are similarly superb. It gets very busy in summer.

⊙ Sights

★**Gotlands Museum**
MUSEUM

(www.gotlandsmuseum.se; Strandgatan 14; adult/child Skr120/free; ⊙11am-4pm Tue-Sun) The Fornsalen section of Gotlands Museum is one of the mightiest regional museums in Sweden. While highlights include amazing 8th-century pre-Viking picture stones, human skeletons from chambered tombs and medieval wooden sculptures, the star turn is the legendary Spillings horde. At 70kg it's the world's largest booty of preserved silver treasure.

🛏 Sleeping & Eating

Fängelse Vandrarhem
HOSTEL €

(☑0498-20 60 50; www.visbyfangelse.se; Skeppsbron 1; dm/s/d Skr290/450/700; 🛜) This hostel offers beds year-round in the small converted cells of an old prison. It's in a handy location, between the ferry dock and the harbour restaurants, and there's an inviting terrace bar in summer. Reception is open from 9am to 2pm, so call ahead if you are arriving outside these times.

Bakfickan
SEAFOOD €€

(www.bakfickanvisby.se; Stora Torget; lunch specials Skr100, mains Skr148-275; ⊙11am-10pm Mon-Fri, noon-10pm Sat & Sun) White-tiled walls, merrily strung lights and boisterous crowds define this foodie-loved bolt-hole, where enlightened seafood gems might include *toast skagen* (shrimps, dill and mayonnaise), pickled herrings on Gotland bread or Bakfickan's fish soup. Delicious!

ⓘ Information

Tourist Office (☑0498-20 17 00; www.gotland. info; Donners Plats 1; ⊙8am-7pm summer, 9am-5pm Mon-Fri, 10am-4pm Sat rest of year)

Around Gotland

Renting a bicycle and following the well-marked Gotlandsleden cycle path is one of the best ways to spend time on Gotland. It loops all around the island, sometimes joining the roadways but more often winding through quiet fields and forests. You can hire cycles at several locations in Visby.

Norrland

Norrland, the northern half of Sweden, is a paradise for nature lovers who enjoy hiking, skiing and other outdoor activities; in winter in particular, the landscape is transformed by snowmobiles, dog sleds and the eerie aurora borealis. The far north is home to the Sámi people and their reindeer.

Östersund

📞 063 / POP 44,330

This pleasant town by Storsjön lake, in the chilly waters of which is said to lurk Sweden's answer to the Loch Ness monster, is an excellent activity base and gateway town for further explorations of Norrland.

☉ Sights & Activities

Östersund is a major winter sports centre. You can also ask at the tourist office about monster-spotting lake cruises in summer.

★ Jamtli   MUSEUM
(www.jamtli.com; adult/child Skr70/free, entry late Aug-late Jun free; ⊙11am-5pm daily late Jun-late Aug, Tue-Sun rest of year; 🖘) Jamtli, 1km north of the centre, consists of two parts. One is an open-air museum comprising painstakingly reconstructed wooden buildings. The stars of the indoor museum are the Över-

---

OFF THE BEATEN TRACK

ABISKO

A stunning hiking destination and one of the best spots in Sweden for viewing the aurora borealis (p197). Abisko lies near the national park of the same name and is the start- or end-point for the 425km Kungsleden hiking trail. The hostel, trailhead and national park are at Abisko Turiststation, 4km west of the principal village. Abisko is easily reached from Kiruna or Narvik, Norway, by bus or train.

---

hogdal Tapestries, the oldest of their kind in Europe – Christian Viking relics from AD 1100 that feature animals, people, ships and dwellings.

🛏 Sleeping & Eating

STF Ledkrysset Hostel   HOSTEL €
(📞063-10 33 10; www.ostersundledkrysset.se; Biblioteksgatan 25; dm/s/d Skr170/300/460; 🖘) This well-run, central hostel is in a converted old fire station and is your best shoestring bet.

Törners Konditori   CAFE €
(www.tornerskonditori.se; Storgatan 24; sandwiches Skr60-70; ⊙7.30am-7pm Mon-Fri, 9am-5pm Sat, 11am-5pm Sun; 🖉) This large, cafeteria-style cafe seems perpetually filled with locals, who come for the cakes (Skr35), chunky sandwiches – from open-faced prawn to toasted pulled-pork baguettes – as well as salads and daily lunch specials ranging from goulash to chicken curry.

ⓘ Getting There & Away

SJ departures include two trains daily to Stockholm (Skr670; five hours) via Uppsala. There are onward connections to Trondheim, Norway. Bus and summer train options head further north.

Kiruna

📞 0980 / POP 22,945

Scarred by mine works, Kiruna may not be the most aesthetically appealing city, but its proximity to great stretches of hikeable wilderness, the iconic Icehotel and the proliferation of winter activities make it an excellent base.

Due to danger of collapse from mining, plans are to move the entire city a couple of miles northwest within the space of 20 years; the town centre move is already under way.

☞ Tours

Nutti Sámi Siida   CULTURAL TOUR, ADVENTURE TOUR
(📞0980-213 29; www.nutti.se) 🖉 This specialist in sustainable Sámi ecotourism arranges visits to the Ráidu Sámi camp to meet reindeer herders (Skr1880), reindeer-sledding excursions (from Skr2750), northern-lights tours (Skr2700), and four-day, multi-activity Lappland tours that take in dogsledding and more (Skr9450). In summer you can visit their reindeer yard in Jukkasjärvi.

DON'T MISS

ICEHOTEL

The winter wonderland that is the **Icehotel** (☑0980-668 00; www.icehotel.com; Marnadsvägen 63; s/d/ste from Skr2300/3200/5300, cabins from Skr1900; P) in Jukkasjärvi, 18km east of Kiruna, is an international phenomenon. The enormous hotel building is constructed using 30,000 tonnes of snow and 4,000 tonnes of ice with international artists and designers coming to contribute innovative ice sculptures every year. In the ice rooms, the beds are made of compacted snow and covered with reindeer skins and serious sleeping bags, guaranteed to keep you warm despite the -5°C temperature inside the rooms. Come morning, guests are revived with a hot drink and a sauna. The attached Ice Church is popular for weddings, while the ice bar and restaurants provide refreshment. Nonguests can visit the Icehotel in winter and take part in a range of activities and guided tours. Summer activities include ice-sculpting and a look at next season's building blocks in a chilled warehouse.

🛏 Sleeping & Eating

STF Vandrarhem & Hotell City   HOSTEL, HOTEL €€
(☑0980-17 000; www.kirunahostel.com; Bergmästaregatan 7; dm/s/d from Skr250/450/500, hotel s/d/tr Skr750/850/1100; P🛜) This catch-all hotel-and-hostel combo has a gleaming red-and-white colour scheme in its modern hotel rooms and cosy dorms. Sauna and breakfast cost extra for hostel guests, but there are handy guest kitchens.

★ Camp Ripan Restaurang   SWEDISH €€
(☑0980-63 000; www.ripan.se; Campingvägen 5; lunch buffet weekday/weekend Skr100/125, dinner mains Skr245-355; ⊙11am-2pm & 6-9.30pm Mon-Fri, noon-2pm & 6-9.30pm Sat & Sun 🖉) The unusually veggie-heavy lunch buffet is good value, but the real draw is the Sámi-inspired à la carte menu featuring local, seasonal produce. The restaurant's located at the local campground.

ℹ Information

Tourist Office (☑0980-188 80; www.kiruna lapland.se; Lars Janssonsgatan 17; ⊙8.30am-9pm Mon-Fri, to 6pm Sat & Sun) Inside the Folkets Hus visitor centre; can book various tours.

ℹ Getting There & Away

➤ Kiruna Airport, 7km east of the town, has flights with SAS and Norwegian to Stockholm.
➤ There's a daily bus to Narvik (Norway; Skr280, 2¾ hours). Other departures include Jukkasjärvi (Skr40, 30 minutes, two to six daily).
➤ There is a daily overnight train to Stockholm (Skr960, 17½ hours) via Uppsala (Skr960, 16¾ hours). Other destinations include Narvik (Norway; Skr227, 3½ to 3¾ hours, two daily).

Sweden Survival Guide

ℹ Directory A–Z

ACCOMMODATION

Sweden has hundreds of hostels (vandrarhem), usually with excellent facilities. There's a scarcity of dormitories; hostels are more likely to have singles and doubles. They keep very short reception opening times, so prebook by telephone. Before leaving, you must clean up after yourself; cleaning materials are provided.

DISCOUNT CARDS

Göteborg, Malmö, Stockholm and Uppsala have tourist cards that get you into their major attractions and offer parking, travel on public transport and discounts at participating hotels, restaurants and shops.

LGBT TRAVELLERS

Sweden is a famously liberal country that has been a leader in establishing LGBT rights.

A good source of local information is the free monthly magazine QX. You can pick it up at many clubs, shops and restaurants in Stockholm, Göteborg and Malmö.

MONEY

➤ Sweden uses the krona (plural kronor) as currency. One krona is divided into 100 öre.
➤ Credit and debit cards are extremely widely used, even for small purchases, and a few stores and museums are even cash-free.
➤ Tipping isn't expected, except at dinner (when around 10% for good service is customary).

OPENING HOURS

Banks 9.30am to 3pm Monday to Friday; some city branches 9am to 5pm or 6pm.
Bars & pubs 11am or noon to 1am or 2am.
Restaurants 11am to 2pm and 5pm to 10pm; often closed on Sunday and/or Monday.

ⓘ PRICE RANGES

Room price codes are for a double room in the summer season (mid-June through August):

€ less than Skr800

€€ Skr800–1600

€€€ more than Skr1600

Price categories for eating listings refer to the average price of a main dish:

€ less than Skr100

€€ Skr100–200

€€€ more than Skr200

Shops 9am to 6pm Monday to Friday, 9am to 1pm Saturday.

Supermarkets 8am or 9am to 7pm or 10pm.

Systembolaget (alcohol store) 10am to 6pm Monday to Friday, 10am to 2pm (often until 5pm) Saturday, sometimes with extended hours on Thursday and Friday evenings.

Tourist offices Usually open daily Midsummer to mid-August, Monday to Friday only the rest of the year.

PUBLIC HOLIDAYS

Midsummer brings life almost to a halt for three days.

New Year's Day (Nyårsdag) 1 January

Epiphany (Trettondedag Jul) 6 January

Good Friday, Easter Sunday and Monday (Långfredag, Påsk, Annandag Påsk) March/April

Labour Day (Första Maj) 1 May

Ascension Day (Kristi Himmelsfärdsdag) May/June

Whit Sunday and Monday (Pingst, Annandag Pingst) Late May/early June

Midsummer's Day (Midsommardag) Saturday between 19 and 25 June

All Saints Day (Alla Helgons dag) Saturday, late October/early November

Christmas Day (Juldag) 25 December

Boxing Day (Annandag Jul) 26 December

TELEPHONE

→ Country code: 📞46.

→ International access code: 📞00.

→ Local SIM cards are readily available (around Skr95); data packages are relatively cheap.

ⓘ Getting There & Around

AIR

Stockholm Arlanda links Sweden with major European and North American cities. Stockholm Skavsta (100km south of Stockholm, near Nyköping) and Göteborg City are both served by budget airline Ryanair.

BUS

Eurolines connect Sweden's major cities with many other European destinations. Swebus Express runs to Copenhagen. There are many cross-border buses to Norway.

Swebus Express (📞0771-21 82 18; www.swebus.se) has the largest network of express buses, but they only serve the southern half of the country. **Svenska Buss** (📞0771-67 67 67; www.svenskabuss.se) and **Nettbuss** (📞0771-15 15 15; www.nettbuss.se) also connect many southern towns and cities with Stockholm; prices are often slightly cheaper than Swebus Express prices, but services are less frequent.

In the north, connections with Stockholm are provided by several smaller operators. There are also services into Finland and Norway.

FERRY

Sweden has numerous international ferry connections to Denmark, Norway, Finland, Germany, Poland, Estonia and Latvia. Check www.directferries.com for all routes.

TRAIN

Sweden is linked by rail to Denmark and the rest of Europe via the Öresund bridge. Trains shuttle between Copenhagen and Malmö, where you can change to Swedish services. There are some through trains to Stockholm and Göteborg. There are regular train services between Sweden and Norway.

Sweden has an extensive and reliable railway network, and trains are almost always faster than buses.

Inlandsbanan (📞0771-53 53 53; www.inlandsbanan.se) One of the great rail journeys in Scandinavia is this slow and scenic 1300km route from Kristinehamn to Gällivare.

Sveriges Järnväg (SJ; 📞0771-75 75 75; www.sj.se) National network covering most main lines, especially in the southern part of the country.

Tågkompaniet (📞0771-44 41 11; www.tagkompaniet.se) Operates excellent overnight trains from Göteborg and Stockholm north to Kiruna and Narvik.

FINLAND

Helsinki

📞09 / POP 1.09 MILLION (URBAN AREA)

It's fitting that harbourside Helsinki, capital of a country with such watery geography, melds so graciously into the Baltic. Half the city seems liquid, and the complex, undulating coastlines include any number of bays, inlets and islands. The design scene here is legendary, whether you're browsing showroom brands or taking the backstreet hipster trail. The city's gourmet side is also flourishing, with new gastro eateries offering locally sourced tasting menus popping up at dizzying speed.

Sights & Activities

Kauppatori
SQUARE

The heart of central Helsinki is the harbourside kauppatori (market square), where cruises and ferries leave for archipelago islands. It's completely touristy these days, with reindeer souvenir stands having replaced most market stalls, but there are still some berries and flowers for sale, and adequate cheap food options. Alongside it, the Vanha Kauppahalli is a magnificent traditional covered market.

★ Kiasma
GALLERY

(www.kiasma.fi; Mannerheiminaukio 2; adult/child €12/free; ⊙10am-5pm Tue & Sun, to 8.30pm Wed-Fri, to 6pm Sat) Now just one of a series of elegant contemporary buildings in this part of town, curvaceous and quirky metallic Kiasma is still a symbol of the city's modernisation. It exhibits an eclectic collection of Finnish and international modern art and keeps people on their toes with its striking contemporary exhibitions. The interior, with its unexpected curves and perspectives, is as invigorating as the outside.

★ Ateneum
GALLERY

(www.ateneum.fi; Kaivokatu 2; adult/child €15/free; ⊙10am-6pm Tue & Fri, to 8pm Wed & Thu, to 5pm Sat & Sun) The top floor of Finland's premier art gallery is an ideal crash course in the nation's art. It houses Finnish paintings and sculptures from the 'golden age' of the late 19th century through to the 1950s. There's also a small but interesting collection of 19th- and early 20th-century foreign art.

★ Suomenlinna
FORTRESS

(Sveaborg; www.suomenlinna.fi) Just a 15-minute ferry ride from the Kauppatori, a visit to Suomenlinna, the 'fortress of Finland', is a Helsinki must-do. Set on a tight cluster of islands connected by bridges, the Unesco World Heritage site was originally built by the Swedes as Sveaborg in the mid-18th century.

From the main quay, a blue-signposted walking path connects the main attractions.

Design Museum
MUSEUM

(www.designmuseum.fi; Korkeavuorenkatu 23; adult/child €10/free; ⊙11am-6pm Jun-Aug, to 8pm

DESIGN SHOPPING

Helsinki is a design epicentre, from the latest fashion to furniture and homewares. Central but touristy Esplanadi has the chic boutiques of Finnish classics. The most intriguing area to browse is nearby Punavuori, with a great retro-hipster vibe and numerous boutiques, studios and galleries to explore. A couple of hundred of these are part of **Design District Helsinki** (www.designdistrict.fi), whose invaluable map you can find at the tourist office.

Tue, to 6pm Wed-Sun Sep-May) The Design Museum has a permanent collection that looks at the roots of Finnish design in the nation's traditions and nature. Changing exhibitions focus on contemporary design – everything from clothing to household furniture.

★ Kotiharjun Sauna
SAUNA

(www.kotiharjunsauna.fi; Harjutorinkatu 1; adult/child €12/6; ⊙2-8pm Tue-Sun, sauna to 9.30pm, closed Sundays Jun–mid-August) This traditional public wood-fired sauna in Kallio dates back to 1928. This type of place largely disappeared with the advent of shared saunas in apartment buildings, but it's a classic experience, where you can also get a scrub down and massage. There are separate saunas for men and women; bring your own towel or rent one (€3). It's a short stroll from Sörnäinen metro station.

Sleeping

Hostel Domus Academica
HOSTEL €

(☎09-1311-4334; www.hostelacademica.fi; Hietaniemenkatu 14; dm/s/d €29/60/73; ⊙Jun-Aug; P@♠≋) Finnish students live well, so in summer take advantage of this residence, a clean busy spot packed with features (pool and sauna) and cheery staff. The modern rooms are great, and all come with bar fridges and their own bathrooms. Dorms have only two or three berths, so there's no overcrowding. It's also environmentally sound. Breakfast available. HI discount.

Wi-fi doesn't reach all rooms, but you can get a cable for laptops.

Hostel Erottajanpuisto
HOSTEL €

(☎09-642169; www.erottajanpuisto.com; Uudenmaankatu 9; dm/s/d €31/62/77; @♠) Helsinki's most characterful and laid-back hostel occupies the top floor of a building in a

Helsinki

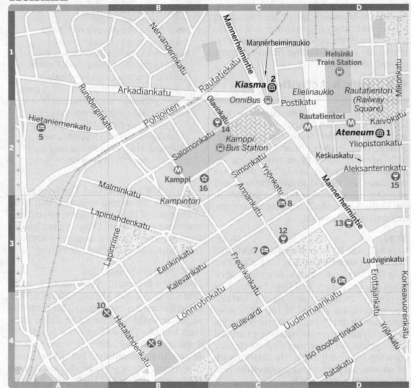

lively street of bars and restaurants. Forget curfews, lockouts, school kids and bringing your own sleeping sheet – this is more like a guesthouse with (crowded) dormitories. Shared bathrooms are new; private rooms offer more peace, and there's a great lounge and friendly folk. HI members get 10% off; breakfast is extra.

Eurohostel HOSTEL €
(☑ 09-622-0470; www.eurohostel.eu; Linnankatu 9; dm €29, s €55-62, d €61-72; @ 🖵) On Katajanokka island close to the Viking Line ferry and easily reached on tram 4, this hostel is busy and convenient, if a little impersonal. Two grades of room are similar and both come with share bathrooms; the 'Eurohostel' rooms are more modern with TV and parquet floors. Dorm rates mean sharing a twin – a good deal.

The cafe-bar serves breakfast and other meals, and there's a morning sauna included. HI and online-booking discount. Rates vary widely.

Omenahotelli HOTEL €€
(☑ 0600-18018; www.omenahotels.com; r €79-139; 🖵) This good-value staffless hotel chain has two handy Helsinki locations: **Lönnrotinkatu** (Lönnrotinkatu 13); **Yrjönkatu** (Yrjönkatu 30). As well as a double bed, rooms have fold-out chairs that can sleep two more, plus there's a microwave and minifridge. Book online or via a terminal in the lobby. Windows don't open, so rooms can be stuffy on hot days.

🍴 Eating

Good budget options are in short supply: cafes offer lunch choices and there are plenty of self-catering opportunities.

⭐ **Hietalahden Kauppahalli** MARKET
(www.hietalahdenkauppahalli.fi; Lönnrotinkatu 34; ⊙ 8am-6pm Mon & Tue, to 10pm Wed-Sat, also opens Sun Jun-Aug; 🖉) 🍽 This renovated market at Hietalahti has a fabulous range of food stalls and eateries, including enticing cafes with upstairs seating at each end. Take tram 6.

Helsinki

Konstan Möljä FINNISH €
(☎ 09-694-7504; www.konstanmolja.fi; Hietalah-
denkatu 14; buffet €19; ⊙ 5-10pm Tue-Fri, 4-11pm
Sat) The maritime interior of this old sailors'
eatery hosts an impressive husband-and-
wife team who turn out a great-value Finnish
buffet for dinner. Though these days it sees
plenty of tourists, it serves solid traditional
fare, with salmon, soup, reindeer and friendly explanations of what goes with what.
There's also limited à la carte available.

🍷 Drinking & Entertainment

Finns don't mind a drink and Helsinki has
some of Scandinavia's most diverse nightlife.
Some bars and club nights have a minimum
age of 20 or older, so check event details on
websites before you arrive.

Bar Loose BAR, CLUB
(www.barloose.com; Annankatu 21; ⊙ 5pm-2am
Tue, to 4am Wed-Sun; 🛜) The opulent blood-
red interior and comfortably cosy seating
seem too stylish for a rock bar, but this is
what this is, with portraits of guitar heroes
lining one wall and an eclectic mix of people filling the upstairs room, served by two
bars. Downstairs is a club area, with live music more nights than not and DJs spinning
everything from metal to mod/retro classics.

Zucchini VEGETARIAN €
(Fabianinkatu 4; lunch mains €8-12; ⊙ 11am-4pm
Mon-Fri; 🍴) One of the city's few vegetarian
cafes, this is a top-notch lunchtime spot;
queues out the door are not unusual. Piping-hot soups banish winter chills, and
fresh-baked quiche on the sunny terrace out
the back is a summer treat. For lunch, you
can choose soup or salad/hot dish or both.

Café Bar 9 CAFE €
(www.bar9.net; Uudenmaankatu 9; mains €10-16;
⊙ 11am-11pm Mon-Fri, noon-11pm Sat & Sun; 🛜)
It's tough to find low-priced food at dinnertime in Helsinki that's not shaved off a
spinning stick, so this place stands out. It
would anyway, with its retro red formica tables and unpretentious artsy air. Plates vary,
with some solid Finnish fare backed up by
big sandwiches, Thai-inspired stir-fries and
pastas.

★ **Teerenpeli**   PUB
(www.teerenpeli.com; Olavinkatu 2; ⊙noon-2am
Mon-Thu, to 3am Fri & Sat, to midnight Sun; 🛜) Get
away from the Finnish lager mainstream
with this excellent pub right by Kamppi bus
station. It serves very tasty ales, stouts and
berry ciders from its microbrewery in Lahti, in a long, split-level place with romantic
low lighting, intimate tables and an indoor
smokers' patio.

Wanha Kauppakuja   BAR
This covered laneway off Aleksanterinkatu
has a boisterous, meat-markety summer
scene once the restaurant terraces are done
with serving food for the night. There's usually a €5 admission charge.

DTM   GAY, CLUB
(www.dtm.fi; Mannerheimintie 6B; ⊙9pm-4am;
🛜) Finland's most famous gay venue (Don't
Tell Mama) now occupies smart premises in
a very out-of-the-closet location on the city's
main street. There are various club nights
with variable entry fees.

Tavastia   LIVE MUSIC
(www.tavastiaklubi.fi; Urho Kekkosenkatu 4;
⊙8pm-1am Sun-Thu, to 4am Fri & Sat) One of
Helsinki's legendary rock venues, Tavastia
attracts both up-and-coming local acts and
bigger international groups. There's a band
every night of the week. Also check out
what's on at Semifinal, the venue next door.

ℹ Information

Helsinki City Tourist Office (📞 09-3101-
3300; www.visithelsinki.fi; Pohjoisesplanadi 19;
⊙10am-8pm May-Sep, 10am-6pm Mon-Sat,
noon-6pm Sun Oct-Apr) Busy multilingual
office with a great quantity of information on
the city. An event and tour booking service
shares the office.

THE CALL OF KALLIO

For Helsinki's cheapest beer (around
€3 to €4 a pint), hit working-class Kallio
(near Sörnäinen metro station), north
of the city centre. Here, there's a string
of dive bars along Helsinginkatu, but
on this street as well as on the parallel
Vaasankatu and crossing Fleminginkatu
you'll find several more characterful
bohemian places: go for a wander and
you'll soon find a venue you like.

ℹ Getting There & Away

→ Helsinki-Vantaa airport (www.helsinki-
vantaa.fi), Finland's main air terminus, is
served from many European and intercontinental cities. It's 19km north of Helsinki.

→ International ferries travel to Stockholm,
Tallinn, St Petersburg and German destinations.
There is also regular fast-boat service to Tallinn.

→ Kamppi bus station (www.matkahuolto.fi)
has departures to all of Finland. OnniBus (www.
onnibus.com) runs budget routes to several
Finnish cities from a stop outside Kiasma: book
online in advance for the best prices.

→ Helsinki's train station (Rautatieasema; www.
vr.fi) is central, linked to the metro (Rautatien-
tori stop) and a short walk from Kamppi bus
station. There are services all over Finland and
also to Russia.

ℹ Getting Around

→ Trains run from the airport to central Helsinki
every ten minutes (€3.20, 30 minutes). Bus
services also run between the airport and the
train station.

→ With a flat inner city and well-marked cycling
paths, Helsinki is ideal for cycling. Get hold of a
copy of the Helsinki cycling map at the tourist
office.

→ The city's public-transport system **HSL**
(www.hsl.fi) operates buses, metro and local
trains, trams and a ferry to Suomenlinna. A
one-hour flat-fare ticket for any HSL transport
costs €3.20 when purchased on board or
€2.70 when purchased in advance. You can buy
rechargeable cards and multi-day tickets at the
tourist office, R-kioski shops and elsewhere.

Turku

📞 02 / POP 182,500
The historic castle and cathedral point to the
city's rich cultural history when it was capital, and contemporary Turku is a hotbed of
experimental art and vibrant festivals, thanks
in part to its spirited population from its university (the country's second largest), who
make Turku's nightlife young and fun. As the
first city many visitors encounter arriving by
ferry from Sweden and Åland, it's a splendid
introduction to the Finnish mainland.

⊙ Sights

★ **Turun Tuomiokirkko**   CATHEDRAL
(Turku Cathedral; 📞 040-341-7100; www.turun
seurakunnat.fi; Tuomiokirkonkatu 1; cathedral free,
museum adult/child €2/1; ⊙cathedral & museum
9am-6pm) The 'mother church' of Finland's
Lutheran faith, Turku Cathedral towers over

the town. Consecrated in 1300, the colossal brick Gothic building was rebuilt many times over the centuries after damaging fires. Upstairs, a small **museum** traces the stages of the cathedral's construction, and contains medieval sculptures and religious paraphernalia.

★**Aboa Vetus & Ars Nova**   MUSEUM, GALLERY
(📞020-718-1640; www.aboavetusarsnova.fi; Itäinen Rantakatu 4-6; adult/child €9/5.50; ⊙11am-7pm; 🚻) Art and archaeology unite here under one roof. Aboa Vetus (Old Turku) draws you underground to Turku's medieval streets, showcasing some of the 37,000 artefacts unearthed from the site (digs still continue). Back in the present, Ars Nova hosts contemporary art exhibitions. The themed Turku Biennaali (www.turku biennaali.fi) takes place here during summer in odd-numbered years.

★**Luostarinmäen**
Käsityöläismuseo   MUSEUM
(Luostarinmäki Handicrafts Museum; 📞02-262-0350; www.turku.fi/handicraftsmuseum; Vartiovuorenkatu 2; adult/child €6/4, guided tours €2.50; ⊙10am-6pm Jun-Aug, 10am-6pm Tue-Sun May & early Sep–mid-Sep, 10am-4pm Tue-Sun Dec–mid-Jan) When the savage Great Fire of 1827 swept through Turku, the lower-class quarter Luostarinmäki escaped the flames. Set along tiny lanes and around grassy yards, the 19th-century wooden workshops and houses now form the outdoor handicrafts museum, a national treasure since 1940.

Turun Linna   CASTLE
(Turku Castle; 📞02-262-0300; www.turunlinna. fi; Linnankatu 80; adult/child €9/5, guided tours €2; ⊙10am-6pm daily Jun-Aug, Tue-Sun Sep-May) Founded in 1280 at the mouth of the Aurajoki, mammoth Turku Castle is easily Finland's largest. Highlights include two dungeons and sumptuous banqueting halls, as well as a fascinating **historica museum** of medieval Turku in the castle's Old Bailey. Models depict the castle's growth from a simple island fortress to a Renaissance palace. Guided tours in English run several times daily from June to August.

🎊 **Festivals & Events**

★**Ruisrock**   MUSIC
(www.ruisrock.fi; 1-/3-day ticket €78/128) For three days in July, Finland's oldest and largest annual rock festival – held since 1969 and attracting 100,000-strong crowds – takes over Ruissalo island.

WORTH A TRIP

PORVOO

Finland's second-oldest town is an ever-popular day trip or weekender from Helsinki. Porvoo (Swedish: Borgå) officially became a town in 1380, but even before that it was an important trading post. The town's fabulous historic centre includes the famous brick-red former warehouses along the river that once stored goods bound for destinations across Europe. During the day, Old Town craft shops are bustling with visitors, but staying on a weeknight will mean you could have the place more or less to yourself. The old painted buildings are spectacular in the setting sun.

Buses depart for Porvoo from Helsinki's Kamppi bus station every 30 minutes or so (€11.80, one hour).

🛏 **Sleeping**

Laivahostel Borea   HOSTEL €
(📞040-843 6611; www.msborea.fi; Linnankatu 72; s/tr/q €50/110/134, d €80-106; 🛜) Built in Sweden in 1960, the enormous passenger ship S/S *Bore* is docked outside the Forum Marinum museum, just 500m northeast of the ferry terminal. It now contains an award-winning HI-affiliated hostel with vintage ensuite cabins. Most are squishy, but if you want room to spread out, higher-priced doubles have a lounge area. Rates include a morning sauna.

🍴 **Eating & Drinking**

CaféArt   CAFE €
(www.cafeart.fi; Läntinen Rantakatu 5; dishes €2.20-4.80; ⊙10am-7pm Mon-Fri, to 5pm Sat, 11am-5pm Sun) With freshly ground coffee, prize-winning baristas, a beautifully elegant interior and artistic sensibility, there's no better place to get your caffeine-and-cake fix. In summer, the terrace spills onto the riverbank, shaded by linden trees.

Tintå   GASTROPUB €€
(📞02-230-7023; www.tinta.fi; Läntinen Rantakatu 9; mains lunch €8.50-13.50, pizza €12-16, dinner €25-30; ⊙11am-midnight Mon, to 1am Tue-Thu, to 2am Fri, noon-2am Sat, noon-10pm Sun) With a cosy exposed-brick interior, this riverside wine bar also offers weekday lunches, gourmet pizzas such as asparagus and smoked feta or prosciutto and fig, and classy mains such as organic beef skewers with

SCANDINAVIA TURKU

Turku

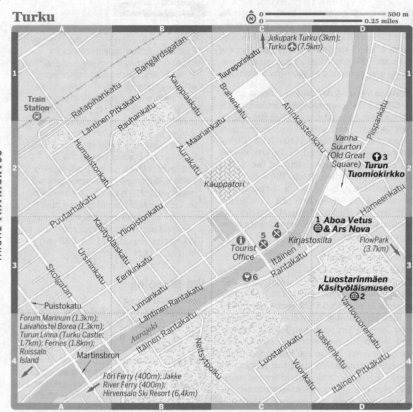

Turku

◎ Top Sights
1 Aboa Vetus & Ars Nova.......................D3
2 Luostarinmäen
  Käsityöläismuseo D3
3 Turun Tuomiokirkko...........................D2

⊗ Eating
4 CaféArt...C3
5 Tintå...C3

⊜ Drinking & Nightlife
6 Boat Bars..C3

horseradish aioli. Grab a glass of wine and
watch the world walking along the shore
from the summer terrace.

Boat Bars BAR
Summer drinking begins on the decks of
the boats lining the south bank of the river. Although most serve food, they are primarily floating beer terraces with music
and shipboard socialising. If the beer prices
make you wince, join locals gathering on the
grassy riverbank drinking takeaway alcohol.

ⓘ Information

Tourist Office (☑ 02-262-7444; www.visit
turku.fi; Aurakatu 4; ⊘ 8.30am-6pm Mon-Fri,
9am-4pm Sat & Sun Apr-Sep, 8.30am-6pm
Mon-Fri, 10am-3pm Sat & Sun Oct-Mar) Busy
but helpful office with information on the entire
region.

ⓘ Getting There & Away

➡ Turku is a major gateway to Sweden via
Åland. The harbour, about 3km southwest of
the city centre, has its own train station. Silja
Line and Viking Line sail to Stockholm (11
hours) via the Åland archipelago (six hours).
Bus 1 connects the centre with the harbour.

➡ Major intercity bus services include Helsinki
(€31.50, 2½ hours, hourly) and Tampere
(€25.60, 2½ hours).

→ Train destinations include Helsinki (€34, two hours, at least hourly), Rovaniemi (€91.40, 12 hours, four daily, usually with a change) and Tampere (€28.20, 1¾ hours, two hourly).

Tampere

🔊 03 / POP 217,400

Scenic Tampere, set between two vast lakes, has a down-to-earth vitality that makes it a favourite for many visitors. Through its centre churns the Tammerkoski rapids, the grassy banks of which contrast with the red brick of the imposing fabric mills that once drove the city's economy. Regenerated industrial buildings now house quirky museums, enticing shops, pubs, cinemas and cafes.

◎ Sights & Activities

There are plenty of summer cruise options on Tampere's two magnificent lakes.

★ Tuomiokirkko   CHURCH
(www.tampereenseurakunnat.fi; Tuomiokirkonkatu 3; ⊙10am-5pm May-Aug, 11am-3pm Sep-Apr) **FREE** An iconic example of National Romantic architecture, Tampere's cathedral dates from 1907. Hugo Simberg created the frescoes and stained glass; you'll appreciate that they were controversial. A procession of ghostly childlike apostles holds the 'garland of life', graves and plants are tended by skeletal figures, and a wounded angel is stretchered off by two children. There's a solemn, almost mournful feel; the altarpiece, by Magnus Enckell, is a dreamlike Resurrection in similar style.

★ Särkänniemi   AMUSEMENT PARK
(www.sarkanniemi.fi; day pass adult/child €36/30; ⊙rides roughly 10am-7pm mid-May–Aug) This promontory amusement park complex offers dozens of rides, an observation tower, art gallery, aquarium, farm zoo and planetarium. (The park has recently decided to close its dolphinarium and rehouse the animals, a move applauded by wildlife campaigners.) It's possible to buy all-inclusive entry or to pay per attraction (€10/5 per adult/child). Opening times are complex; check the website. Indoor attractions stay open year-round. Take bus 20 from the train station or central square.

★ Amurin Työläismuseokorttel   MUSEUM
(Amuri Museum of Workers' Housing; www.tampere.fi/amuri; Satakunnankatu 49; adult/child €7/3; ⊙10am-6pm Tue-Sun mid-May–mid-Sep) An

ÅLAND

The glorious Åland archipelago is a geopolitical anomaly: the islands belong to Finland, speak Swedish, but have their own parliament, flag and stamps. Åland is the sunniest spot in northern Europe and its sweeping white-sand beaches and flat, scenic cycling routes have great appeal. Outside the lively capital, Mariehamn, a sleepy haze hangs over the islands' tiny villages, and finding your own remote beach among the 6500 skerries and islets is surprisingly easy. A lattice of bridges and free cable ferries connect the central islands, while larger car ferries run to the archipelago's outer reaches. Several ferries head to Åland, including those that connect Turku and Helsinki with Stockholm. Bikes are the best way to explore and are easily rented.

entire block of 19th-century wooden houses, including 32 apartments, a bakery, a shoemaker, two general shops and a cafe, is preserved here. It's one of the most realistic house-museums in Finland and entertaining backstories (English translation available) give plenty of historical information.

🛏 Sleeping

★ Dream Hostel   HOSTEL €
(🔊045-236-0517; www.dreamhostel.fi; Åkerlundinkatu 2; dm €25-31, tw/q €81/112; P@🖥) Sparky, stylish and spacious, this is Finland's best hostel. Helpful staff, super-comfortable wide-berth dorms (unisex and female) in various sizes, a heap of facilities including bike hire, original decor and the right attitude about everything make it a real winner. It's a short walk from the train station in a quiet area.

Upstairs are compact en-suite rooms for those that want hostel atmosphere without sharing a shower.

Omenahotelli   HOTEL €€
(🔊0600-18018; www.omenahotels.com; Hämeenkatu 7; r €65-99; 🖥) On the main drag and very handy for the train station, this receptionless hotel offers the usual comfortable rooms with twin beds, a microwave, a kettle and a fold-out couch. Rooms are great value for a family of four, for example. Book online or via the terminal at the entrance.

Tampere

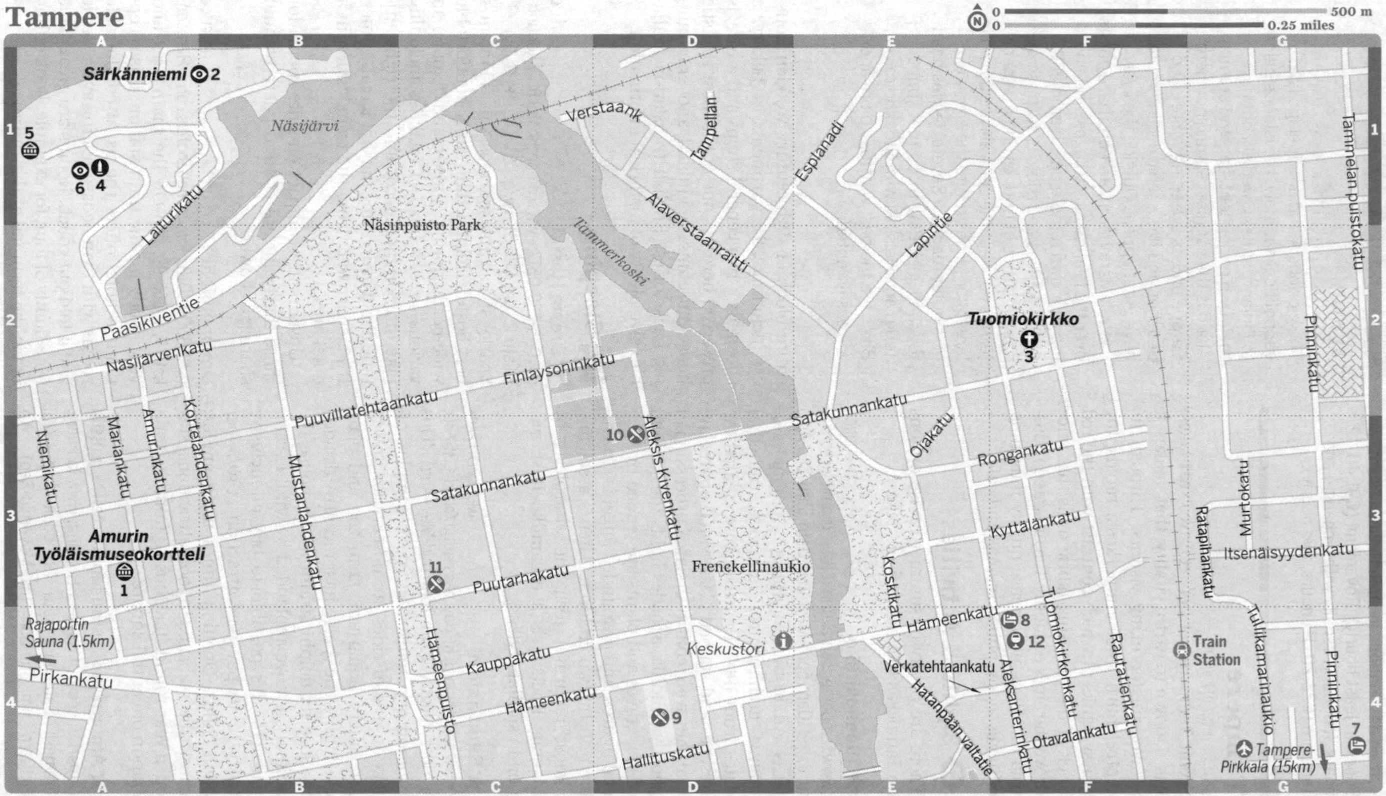

0 500 m
0 0.25 miles
N
A
B
C
D
E
F
G
1
2
3
4
Särkänniemi 2
Näsijärvi
5
6 4
Laiturikatu
Näsinpuisto Park
Paasikiventie
Näsijärvenkatu
Verstaank
Tampellan
Esplanadi
Alaverstaanraitti
Tammerkoski
Lapintie
Tammelan puistokatu
Tuomiokirkko
3
Pinninkatu
Finlaysoninkatu
Puuvillatehtaankatu
Satakunnankatu
10
Aleksis Kivenkatu
Ojakatu
Rongankatu
Niemikatu
Mariankatu
Amurinkatu
Kortelahdenkatu
Mustanlahdenkatu
Satakunnankatu
Kyttälänkatu
Murtokatu
Ratapihankatu
Itsenäisyydenkatu
Amurin Työläismuseokortteli
1
11
Puutarhakatu
Frenckellinaukio
Koskikatu
Hämeenkatu
8
12
Tuomiokirkonkatu
Rautatienkatu
Tullikamarinaukio
Train Station
Rajaportin Sauna (1.5km)
Pirkankatu
Hämeenpuisto
Kauppakatu
Keskustori
Verkatehtaankatu
Aleksanterinkatu
Hatanpään valtatie
Hämeenkatu
9
Hallituskatu
Otavalankatu
Pinninkatu
7
Tampere-Pirkkala (15km)

Tampere

✕ Eating & Drinking

Tampere's speciality, *mustamakkara*, is a mild, rather tasty sausage made with cow's blood, normally eaten with lingonberry jam. Try it at the kauppahalli (covered market) or Laukontori.

Kauppahalli   MARKET €
(Hämeenkatu 19; ◷ 8am-6pm Mon-Fri, to 3pm Sat; ⚡) ◐ This intriguing indoor market is one of Finland's best, with picturesque wooden stalls serving a dazzling array of wonderful meat, fruit, baked goodies and fish. There are good places to eat here, too; this is the best place to try cheap *mustamakkara* with berry jam.

Panimoravintola Plevna   BREWPUB €
(www.plevna.fi; Itäinenkatu 8; mains €11-23; ◷ 11am-10pm Mon-Sat, noon-10pm Sun; ⚡) Inside the Finlayson Centre, this barn of a place offers a wide range of delicious beer, cider and perry brewed here, including an excellent strong stout. Meals are large and designed to soak it all up: massive sausage platters and enormous slabs of pork in classic beer-hall style. Vegetables here mean potatoes and onions, preferably fried, but it's all tasty, and service is fast.

★ Tuulensuu   GASTROPUB €€
(www.gastropub.net/tuulensuu; Hämeenpuisto 23; mains €17-26; ◷ 11am-midnight Mon-Fri, noon-midnight Sat, 3pm-midnight Sun; ⚡) The best of several Tampere gastropubs, this has a superb range of Belgian beers, good wines and a lengthy port menu. Food is lovingly prepared and features staples such as liver or schnitzel, as well as more elaborate plates such as duck confit and other bistro fare inspired by Belgium and northeastern France. Even the bar snacks are gourmet: fresh-roasted almonds. Closed Sundays in summer.

★ Café Europa   BAR
(www.ravintola.fi/europa; Aleksanterinkatu 29; ◷ noon-midnight Mon & Tue, to 1am Wed & Thu, to 3am Fri & Sat, 1pm-midnight Sun; ⚡) Lavishly furnished with horsehair couches, armchairs, mirrors, chandeliers and paintings, this venue successfully fuses a re-creation of a 1930s-style old-Europe cafe, and is a popular meeting spot for students and anyone else.

🛈 Information

Visit Tampere (☎ 03-5656-6800; www.visittampere.fi; Hämeenkatu 14B; ◷ 10am-6pm Mon-Fri, to 3pm Sat & Sun Jun-Aug, 10am-5pm Mon-Fri, to 3pm Sat Sep-May; ⚡) On the main street in the centre of town. Can book activities and events.

🛈 Getting There & Away

→ Regular express buses run from Helsinki (€27, 2¾ hours) and Turku (€25.60, two to three hours), and most other major towns in Finland are served from here.

→ The train station is central. Express trains run hourly to/from Helsinki (€39, 1¾ hours), and there are direct trains to Turku (€33.30, 1¾ hours) and other cities.

SAUNAS

For centuries the sauna has been a place to bathe, meditate, warm up and even give birth, and most Finns still use it at least once a week. Bathing is done in the nude (public saunas are nearly always sex-segregated) and Finns are quite strict about its nonsexual – even sacred – nature. Shower first. Once inside (with a temperature of 80°C to 100°C), water is thrown onto the stove using a *kauhu* (ladle), producing *löyly* (steam). A *vihta* (whisk of birch twigs and leaves) is sometimes used to lightly strike the skin, improving circulation. Cool off with a cold shower or preferably by jumping into a lake. Repeat. The sauna beer afterwards is also traditional.

DON'T MISS

VISITING SANTA

The southernmost line at which the sun does not set on at least one day a year, the Arctic Circle (Napapiiri in Finnish) crosses the Sodankylä road 8km north of Rovaniemi. Surrounding the marker is **Santa Claus Village** (www.santaclausvillage.info; ⊗ 9am-6pm Jun-Aug, 10am-5pm Sep-Nov & mid-Jan–May, 9am-7pm Dec–mid-Jan) FREE, a touristy complex of shops, winter activities and cottage accommodation. Santa Claus Post Office (www.santa claus.posti.fi) here receives over half a million letters yearly from children (and adults) all over the world. But the top attraction for most is, of course, Santa himself, who sees visitors year-round in a rather impressive grotto (www.santaclauslive.com), where a huge clock mechanism (it slows the earth's rotation so that Santa can visit the whole world's children on Christmas night) eerily surrounds those queuing for an audience. The portly saint is quite a linguist, and an old hand at chatting with kids and adults alike. A private chat (around two minutes) is absolutely free, but you can't photograph the moment, and official photos of your visit start at an outrageous €25. Bus 8 heads here from Rovaniemi train station (adult/child €7.20/4 return), passing through the centre of town.

Lakeland

Most of southern Finland could be dubbed 'lakeland', but this spectacular area takes it to extremes. It often seems there's more water than land here, and what water it is: sublime, sparkling and clean, reflecting sky and forests like a mirror. It's a land that leaves an indelible impression on every visitor.

Savonlinna

📞 015 / POP 27,420

One of Finland's prettiest towns, Savonlinna shimmers on a sunny day as the water ripples around its centre. Set on islands between Haapavesi and Pihlajavesi lakes, it's a classic Lakeland settlement with a major attraction: perched on a rocky islet is one of Europe's most visually dramatic castles, Olavinlinna. The castle hosts July's world-famous opera festival in a spectacular setting.

⊙ Sights & Activities

From June to August, Savonlinna passenger harbour is buzzing with dozens of daily scenic cruises.

★ **Olavinlinna**　　　　　　　　　CASTLE
(www.olavinlinna.fi; adult/child €9/4.50; ⊗ 11am-6pm Jun–mid-Aug, 10am-4pm Mon-Fri, 11am-4pm Sat & Sun mid-Aug–mid-Dec & Jan-May) Standing immense and haughty, 15th-century Olavinlinna is one of the most spectacularly situated castles in northern Europe and, as well as being an imposing fortification, is also the stunning venue for the month-long Savonlinna Opera Festival. The castle's been heavily restored, but is still seriously impressive,

not least in the way it's built directly on a rock in the middle of the lake. To visit the upper part of the interior, including the towers and chapel, you must join a guided tour (around 45 minutes).

★ Festivals & Events

★ **Savonlinna Opera Festival**　　　OPERA
(📞 015-476-750; www.operafestival.fi; Olavinkatu 27) Savonlinna Opera Festival is Finland's most famous festival, with an enviably dramatic setting: the covered courtyard of Olavinlinna Castle. It offers four weeks of top-class opera performances from early July to early August. The atmosphere in town during the festival is reason enough to come; it's buzzing.

🛏 Sleeping & Eating

The lakeside kauppatori is the place for casual snacking. A traditional *lörtsy* (turnover) comes savoury with meat *(lihalörtsy)* or sweet.

Kesähotelli Vuorilinna　　　　　　HOTEL €
(📞 015-73950; www.spahotelcasino.fi; Kylpylaitoksentie; dm/hostel s €32/42, s/d €73/95; ⊗ Jun-Aug; 🅿) Set in several buildings used by students during term time, this is run by the Spahotel Casino and has an appealing location across a beautiful footbridge from the town centre. Rooms are clean and comfortable; the cheaper ones share bathroom and kitchen (no utensils) between two. Happily, dorm rates get you the same deal, and there's a HI discount.

Kalastajan Koju　　　　　　　　SEAFOOD €
(www.kalastajankoju.com; Kauppatori; muikku with potatoes and salad €15; ⊗ 10.30am-9pm Mon-Thu, to 10pm Fri & Sat, 11am-6pm Sun Jun-Aug) On the

water by the kauppatori, this is a summer hit for its traditionally fried *muikku* (vendace).

Information

Savonlinna Travel (0600-30007; www.savonlinna.travel; Puistokatu 1; 10am-6pm Mon-Sat, to 2pm Sun Jul, 9am-4pm Mon-Fri Aug-Jun) Tourist information including accommodation reservations, cottage booking, farmstays, opera festival tickets and tours.

Getting There & Away

- There are several express buses a day from Helsinki (€49.90, five to 5½ hours).
- Trains from Helsinki (€65.70, 4¼ hours) and Joensuu (€34, 2¼ hours) both require a change in Parikkala.
- In summer, boats connect Savonlinna with other Lakeland towns.

Lapland

Extending hundreds of kilometres above the Arctic Circle, Lapland is Finland's true wilderness and casts a powerful spell. The midnight sun, the Sámi peoples, the aurora borealis (Northern Lights) and the wandering reindeer are all components of Lapland's magic, as is good old ho-ho-ho himself, who 'officially' resides up here.

Rovaniemi

016 / POP 60,900

A tourism boomtown, the 'official' terrestrial residence of Santa Claus is the capital of Finnish Lapland and a more-or-less obligatory northern stop. Its wonderful Arktikum museum is the perfect introduction to the mysteries of these latitudes, and Rovaniemi is a good place from which to organise activities. It's also Lapland's transport hub.

Sights & Activities

Rovaniemi is great for winter (snowmobiling, skiing, husky-sledding) and summer activities, offering frequent departures with multilingual guides.

★Arktikum MUSEUM
(www.arktikum.fi; Pohjoisranta 4; adult/child/family €12/5/28; 9am-6pm Jun-Aug, 10am-6pm Dec–mid-Jan, 10am-6pm Tue-Sun mid-Jan–May & Sep-Nov) With its beautifully designed glass tunnel stretching out to the Ounasjoki, this is one of Finland's best museums and well worth the admission fee if you are interested in the north. One side deals with Lapland, with information on Sámi culture and the history of Rovaniemi. The other side offers a wide-ranging display on the Arctic, with superb static and interactive displays focusing on flora and fauna, as well as on the peoples of Arctic Europe, Asia and North America.

Sleeping

Guesthouse Borealis GUESTHOUSE €
(044-313-1771; www.guesthouseborealis.com; Asemieskatu 1; s/d/tr €58/68/99; P @) Cordial hospitality and proximity to trains make this family-run spot a winner. Rooms are simple, bright and clean; some have a balcony.

Hostel Rudolf HOSTEL €
(016-321-321; www.rudolf.fi; Koskikatu 41; dm/s/d mid-Jan–Mar €56/72/99, Apr-Nov €47/59/68, Christmas period €63/80/114; P) Run by Hotel Santa Claus, where you inconveniently have to go to check-in, this staffless hostel is Rovaniemi's only one and can fill up fast. Rooms are private and good for the price, with spotless bathrooms, solid desks and bedside lamps; dorm rates get you the same deal. HI discount.

Eating & Drinking

Mariza FINNISH €
(www.ruokahuonemariza.fi; Ruokasenkatu 2; lunch €7.50-9.50; 10am-1.30pm Mon-Fri;) A couple of blocks from the town centre in untouristed territory, this simple lunch place is a real find, and offers a buffet of home-cooked Finnish food, including daily

OFF THE BEATEN TRACK

HIKING IN LAPLAND

Northern Finland's great swaths of protected forests and fells make it one of Europe's prime hiking destinations. Head to the Karhunkierros near Kuusamo for a striking terrain of hills and sharp ravines, never prettier than in autumn. The Urho Kekkonen National Park in Lapland is one of Europe's great wildernesses; the spectacular gorge of the Kevo Strict Nature Reserve and the fell scenery of Pallas-Yllästunturi National Park are other great northern options. A network of camping huts makes itinerary planning easy and are good spots to meet Finns. The key resource for walking is the excellent national parks website www.outdoors.fi.

OFF THE BEATEN TRACK

INARI

The tiny village of Inari (Sámi: Anár) is Finland's most significant Sámi centre and it boasts the wonderful **Siida** (www.siida.fi; adult/child €10/5; ⊙9am-7pm Jun-Aug, 9am-6pm Sep, 10am-5pm Tue-Sun mid-Sep–May) museum, the place to begin to learn something of their culture and environment. Inari is also a great base for locations such as Lemmenjoki National Park and the Kevo Strict Nature Reserve, primo hiking spots. The village sits on Lapland's largest lake, Inarijärvi; a couple of campsites provide budget cabin accommodation. Two daily buses hit Inari from Rovaniemi (€60.10, five hours) and continue to Norway.

---

changing hot dishes, soup and salad. Authentic and excellent.

★**Kauppayhtiö**   BAR
(www.kauppayhtio.fi; Valtakatu 24; ⊙11am-9pm Tue-Thu, to 2.30am Fri, noon-2.30am Sat, 1-6pm Sun; 🛜) Rovaniemi's most personable cafe-bar, this is an oddball collection of retro curios with a coffee and gasoline theme and colourful plastic tables.

❶ Information

Tourist Information (📲016-346-270; www.visitrovaniemi.fi; Maakuntakatu 29; ⊙9am-5pm Mon-Fri, plus 10am-3pm Sat mid-Jun–mid-Aug & late Nov-early Jan; 🛜) On the square in the middle of town. Very helpful.

❶ Getting There & Away

➡ Rovaniemi's airport is a major winter destination for charter flights. Finnair and Norwegian fly daily from Helsinki.

➡ There are night buses to Helsinki (€130.20, 12¾ hours). Daily connections serve just about everywhere else in Lapland. Some buses head on north into Norway.

➡ The train between Helsinki and Rovaniemi (€84 to €102, 10 to 12 hours, three daily) is quicker and cheaper than the bus.

Finland Survival Guide

❶ Directory A–Z

ACCOMMODATION

➡ Many accommodation choices open only in summer, usually campsites or converted student residences.

➡ Almost all campgrounds have cabins or cottages for rent, which are usually excellent value; from €40 for a basic double cabin.

DISCOUNT CARDS

Finland's three main cities offer visitors a discount card that gives free public transport, admission to sights, and discounts on activities and restaurants. They can be worthwhile if you're planning a sightseeing-heavy itinerary.

LGBT TRAVELLERS

Finland's cities are open, tolerant places and Helsinki, though no Copenhagen nor Stockholm, has a small but welcoming gay scene.

MONEY

➡ Finland uses the euro (€). The one- and two-cent coins used in other Eurozone nations are not accepted in Finland.

➡ Credit cards are widely accepted and Finns are dedicated users of the plastic even to buy a beer or cup of coffee.

➡ Service is considered to be included in bills, so there's no need to tip at all unless you want to reward exceptional service. Doormen in bars and restaurants expect a cloakroom tip if there's no mandatory coat charge.

OPENING HOURS

Many attractions in Finland, particularly outdoor ones, only open for a short summer season.

Alko (state alcohol store) 9am to 8pm Monday to Friday, to 6pm Saturday

Banks 9am to 4.15pm Monday to Friday

Businesses & shops 9am to 6pm Monday to Friday, to 3pm Saturday

Nightclubs 10pm to 4am Wednesday to Saturday

Pubs 11am to 1am (often later on Friday and Saturday)

Restaurants 11am to 10pm, lunch 11am to 3pm. Last orders generally an hour before closing.

PUBLIC HOLIDAYS

National public holidays:

New Year's Day 1 January

Epiphany 6 January

Good Friday, Easter Sunday & Monday March/April

May Day 1 May

Ascension Day May

Whitsunday Late May or early June

Midsummer's Eve & Day Weekend in June closest to 24 June

All Saints Day First Saturday in November

Independence Day 6 December

Christmas Eve 24 December

Christmas Day 25 December

Boxing Day 26 December

TELEPHONE

→ Country code: ☑ 358.

→ International access code: ☑ 00.

→ Local SIM cards with data packages are easily available and cheap.

ℹ **Getting There & Away**

Finland is easily accessed from Europe and beyond. There are direct flights from numerous destinations, while Baltic ferries are another good option.

AIR

Finland is easily reached by air, with direct flights to Helsinki from many European, American and Asian destinations.

BOAT

→ The daily Stockholm–Helsinki and Stockholm–Turku ferries are popular ways to get here. There are several other Sweden–Finland services.

→ Helsinki is linked to nearby Tallinn, Estonia, by very regular ferries and fast ferries.

→ Other ferries connect Finland with Russia and Germany. See www.directferries.com for all routes.

BUS

There are bus connections with Russia and, in the far north, with Norway and Sweden.

TRAIN

Finland's only international trains are to/from Moscow and St Petersburg in Russia. There is no train between Finland and Sweden, but train passes give significant discounts on ferry and bus connections.

ℹ **Getting Around**

→ A useful combined journey planner for Finland's public transport network is online at www.journey.fi.

→ There are competitive fares on domestic flights from Helsinki to Rovaniemi in Lapland that can compare to the train price.

→ Bus is the main form of long-distance transport, with a far more comprehensive network than the train. Ticketing is handled by Matkahuolto (www.matkahuolto.fi), the excellent website of which has all timetables.

→ State-owned Valtion Rautatiet (VR; www.vr.fi) runs Finnish trains: a fast, efficient service, with prices roughly equivalent to buses on the same route. Discounted advance fares are available online.

NORWAY

Oslo

POP 616,700

Oslo is home to world-class museums and galleries to rival anywhere else on the European art trail and is fringed with forests, hills and lakes. Add to this mix a thriving cafe and bar culture and top-notch restaurants and the result is a thoroughly intoxicating place in which to forget about the fjords for a while.

◉ **Sights**

★ **Astrup Fearnley Museet** GALLERY

(Astrup Fearnley Museum; ☑ 22 93 60 60; www.afmuseet.no; Strandpromenaden 2; adult/student/child Nkr120/80/free, guided tours Nkr50; ⊙ noon-5pm Tue, Wed & Fri, to 7pm Thu, 11am-5pm Sat & Sun) A stunning architectural creation at the centre of Oslo's waterfront, this museum, which contains all manner of zany contemporary art, is Oslo's latest flagship project and the artistic highlight of the city. Designed by Renzo Piano and completed in 2012, the museum resides within a wonderful wooden building floating on jetties and rafts, with sail-like roofs that, appropriately, give the building the look of an old wooden boat.

★ **Oslo Opera House** ARCHITECTURE

(Den Norske Opera & Ballett; ☑ 21 42 21 21; www.operaen.no; Kirsten Flagstads plass 1; admission to foyer free; ⊙ foyer 10am-9pm Mon-Fri, 11am-9pm Sat, noon-9pm Sun) The centrepiece of a major waterfront modernisation is the magnificent Opera House, a creation that is fast becoming one of the iconic modern buildings of Scandinavia.

Vikingskipshuset MUSEUM

(Viking Ship Museum; ☑ 22 13 52 80; www.khm.uio.no; Huk Aveny 35; adult/child Nkr80/free; ⊙ 9am-6pm May-Sep, 10am-4pm Oct-Apr) Even in repose, there is something intimidating about the sleek, dark hulls of the Viking ships *Oseberg* and *Gokstad* – the best preserved such ships in the world. There is also a third boat at the Vikingskipshuet, the *Tune*, but only a few boards and fragments remain. This museum is a must for anyone who enjoyed childhood stories of Vikings (so that's everyone).

Nasjonalgalleriet GALLERY

(National Gallery; ☑ 21 98 20 00; www.nasjonalmuseet.no; Universitetsgata 13; adult/child Nkr100/free, Thu free; ☺ 10am-6pm Tue, Wed & Fri, to 7pm Thu, 11am-5pm Sat & Sun) One of Oslo's major highlights, the National Gallery houses the nation's largest collection of Norwegian art, including works from the Romantic era, as well as more-modern works from 1800 to WWII. Some of Edvard Munch's best-known creations are on display here, including his most renowned work, *The Scream*. There's also an impressive collection of European art.

Akershus Slott CASTLE

(Akershus Castle; ☑ 22 41 25 21; www.nasjonalefestningsverk.no; adult/child Nkr70/30, with Oslo pass free; ☺ 10am-4pm Mon-Sat, noon-4pm Sun May-Aug, noon-5pm Sat & Sun Sep-Apr, guided tours 11am, 1pm, 3pm mid-Jun–mid-Aug, shorter hours May–mid-Jun & mid-Aug–Sep) In the 17th century, Christian IV renovated Akershus Castle into a Renaissance palace, although the front remains decidedly medieval. In its dungeons you'll find dark cubby-holes where outcast nobles were kept under lock and key, while the upper floors contained sharply contrasting lavish banquet halls and staterooms.

Munchmuseet GALLERY

(Munch Museum; ☑ 23 49 35 00; www.munchmuseet.no; Tøyengata 53; adult/child Nkr100/free; ☺ 10am-4pm, to 5pm mid-Jun–late Sep) Fans of Edvard Munch (1863–1944) won't want to miss this museum, dedicated to his life's work and holding most of the pieces not

Oslo

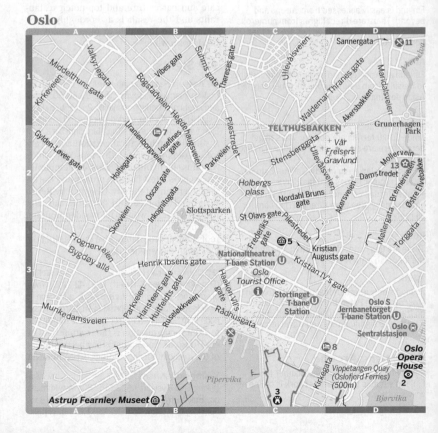

contained in the National Gallery. To get here, take bus 20 or the T-bane to Tøyen.

⌲ Tours

Norway in a Nutshell
TOUR

(☑81 56 82 22; www.norwaynutshell.com) This popular Norwegian highlights tour has lots of customisable options. The classic route from Oslo includes a rail trip across Hardangervidda to Myrdal, descent to along the dramatic Flåmbanen, a cruise along Nærøyfjorden to Gudvangen, a bus to Voss, a connecting train to Bergen for a short visit, then an overnight return rail trip to Oslo; you can also stay in Bergen.

🛌 Sleeping

★ Saga Poshtel Oslo
HOSTEL €

(☑23 10 08 00; www.sagahotelcentral.no; Kongens gate 7; dm Nkr395-485, d Nkr895-995; 🛜) Modern and slickly run, this utterly immaculate hostel has stylish, functional rooms, a big

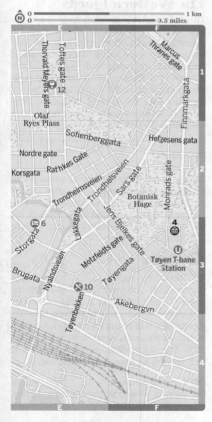

sociable lounge area, good internet access, lots of travel info and a very central location.

Anker Hostel
HOSTEL €

(☑22 99 72 00; www.ankerhostel.no; Storgata 55; dm Nkr250-290, r Nkr640; 🛜) This huge traveller-savvy hostel boasts an international atmosphere, rather sterile rooms, a laundry, luggage room, kitchens (some rooms also contain kitchens) and a small bar. Linen costs an extra Nkr70. The location isn't very scenic, but it's convenient, with Grünerløkka and the city centre only a five-minute walk away.

★ Ellingsens Pensjonat
PENSION €€

(☑22 60 03 59; www.ellingsenspensjonat.no; Holtegata 25; s/d from Nkr700/990, without bathroom Nkr550/800, apt s/d Nkr700/1200; 🛜) Located in a quiet, pleasant neighbourhood, this homey pension offers one of the best deals in the capital. The building dates from 1890 and many of the original features (high ceilings, rose designs) remain. Rooms are bright, airy and beautifully decorated, with fridges and kettles, and there's a small garden to lounge about in on sunny days.

🍴 Eating

★ Kasbah
MIDDLE EASTERN €

(☑21 94 90 99; www.thekasbah.no; Kingosgate 1b; mezes Nkr47-80, mains Nkr80-170; ⊙11am-1am Mon-Fri) Graze on mezes or tuck into a more substantial lunch, including such tummy pleasers as homemade felafels and a veggie couscous soup, at this totally chilled Norwegian-run, Middle East–flavoured restaurant bursting with colour.

★**Punjab Tandoori**   INDIAN €
(☎ 22 17 20 86; www.punjabtandoori.no; Grønlandsleiret 24; lunch special Nkr69, mains Nkr80-130; ⊙11am-11pm Mon-Sat, noon-10pm Sun) Full of the richness and flavours of the north of the subcontinent, this simple canteen-style affair is a real neighbourhood institution for the local Asian community and Norwegians in the know.

Fisherman's Coop   SEAFOOD €
(Rådhusbrygge 3/4; shrimp per kg Nkr150; ⊙7am-5pm Tue-Sat) If the weather is nice, the local meal of choice is peel-and-eat shrimp, eaten dockside with a fresh baguette, mayonnaise and just a touch of lemon. In the summer, you can buy shrimp from the Fisherman's Coop.

🍸 Drinking & Entertainment

The city's best neighbourhood bar scene is along Thorvald Meyers gate and the surrounding streets in Grünerløkka. The Youngstorget area has some of the most popular places close to the city centre, while the Grønland neighbourhood has a more alternative feel.

Bar Boca   BAR
(Thorvald Meyers gate 30; ⊙11am-1am Mon-Thu, to 3am Fri & Sat, noon-1am Sun) Squeeze into what is quite possibly the smallest bar in Oslo and you'll find that you have slid back in time to the 1960s. It's retro cool and has a cocktail selection as great as its atmosphere.

★**Blå**   JAZZ
(www.blaaoslo.no; Brenneriveien 9c; admission Nkr100-270) It would be a pity to leave Oslo without checking out Blå, which features on a global list of 100 great jazz clubs compiled by the savvy editors at the US jazz magazine *Down Beat*. As one editor put it, 'To get in this list means that it's quite the club'.

ℹ Information

Oslo Tourist Office (☎ 81 53 05 55; www.visitoslo.com; Fridtjof Nansens plass 5; ⊙9am-6pm) The main tourist office is located just north of the Rådhus and can provide masses of information. Look out for its useful *Oslo Guide* or the monthly *What's On in Oslo* (both are available at all tourist offices in and around the city, as well as at many sights and hotels).

ℹ Getting There & Away

➧ Oslo Gardermoen International Airport (www.osl.no), 50km north of town, is the city's principal airport. Some airlines also operate 'Oslo' services to/from Torp, some 123km southwest of Oslo, and Rygge, around 60km southeast of the centre.

➧ Ferries run daily to Copenhagen and Fredrikshavn in Denmark, and to Kiel in Germany in summer.

➧ All trains arrive and depart from Oslo S in the city centre. Long-distance trains arrive and depart from the adjacent Galleri Oslo Bus Terminal.

ℹ Getting Around

➧ Oslo has an efficient public-transport system with an extensive network of buses, trams, underground trains (T-bane) and ferries. In addition to single-trip tickets, one-day and transferable eight-trip tickets are also available.

➧ Gardermoen airport is linked to the centre by bus and train.

The Western Fjords

This spectacular region has truly indescribable scenery. Lysefjord, Hardangerfjord, Sognefjord and Geirangerfjord are all variants on the same theme: steep crystalline rock walls dropping with sublime force straight into the sea, often decorated with waterfalls, and small farms harmoniously blending into the natural landscape. Bergen and Stavanger are engaging, lively cities with attractive historic quarters.

Stavanger

POP 124,940

Said by some to be the largest wooden city in Europe, Stavanger's old quarter climbs up the slopes around a pretty harbour. Stavanger is also one of Norway's liveliest urban centres and an excellent base to explore stunning Lysefjord.

◎ Sights

★**Gamle Stavanger**   AREA
Gamle (Old) Stavanger, above the western shore of the harbour, is a delight. The Old Town's cobblestone walkways pass between rows of late-18th-century whitewashed wooden houses, all immaculately kept and adorned with cheerful, well-tended flowerboxes. It well rewards an hour or two's ambling.

★**Norsk Oljemuseum**   MUSEUM
(Oil Museum; www.norskolje.museum.no; Kjeringholmen; adult/child Nkr120/60; ⊙10am-7pm daily

Jun-Aug, 10am-4pm Mon-Sat, to 6pm Sun Sep-May) You could spend hours in this state-of-the-art, beautifully designed museum, one of Norway's best. Focusing on oil exploration in the North Sea from discovery in 1969 to the present, it's filled with high-tech interactive displays and authentic reconstructions.

Sleeping

★ **Thompsons B&B** B&B €
(☑ 51 52 13 29; www.thompsons-bed-and-breakfast.com; Muségata 79; s/d with shared bathroom Nkr400/500; P) Housed in a 19th-century villa in a peaceful residential area, this four-bed B&B has a home-away-from-home vibe engendered by the warm and welcoming owner, Sissel Thompson. Rooms are cosy and comfortable, and traditional Norwegian breakfast, taken around the downstairs dining table, is generous.

Eating & Drinking

★ **Renaa Matbaren** INTERNATIONAL €€
(☑ 51 55 11 11; http://restaurantrenaa.no; Breitorget 6, enter from Bakkegata; small dishes Nrk135-189, mains Nkr195-335; ⊙ 11am-1am Mon-Sat, 1pm-midnight Sun) Yes, that's a proper Tracey Emin on the far wall and an actual Anthony Gormley in the middle of the room. This perpetually bustling bistro is testament to just how cashed-up and cultured this North Sea port is. You'd be happy to be here just for the buzz, but the food is fabulous, too.

★ **Bøker & Børst** BAR
(www.bokerogborst.webs.com; Øvre Holmegate 32; ⊙ 10am-2am) There are many little cafes beckoning in the lanes climbing the hillside west of the oil museum, but our favourite is book-clad Bøker & Børst, with its bohemian decor, good coffee and Stavanger's most interesting crowd, day or night.

Information

Tourist Office (☑ 51 85 92 00; www.regionstavanger.com; Domkirkeplassen 3; ⊙ 9am-8pm Jun-Aug, 9am-4pm Mon-Fri, to 2pm Sat Sep-May) Local information and advice on Lysefjord and Preikestolen.

Getting There & Away

➤ Bus destinations include Bergen (Nkr550, 5½ hours, six daily) and Oslo (Nkr820, 9½ hours, three daily) via Kristiansand.

➤ Trains run to Oslo (Nkr929, eight hours, up to five daily) via Kristiansand.

➤ Fjord Line ferries run daily to Hirtshals in Denmark (10½ hours).

DON'T MISS

LYSEFJORD

All along the 42km-long Lysefjord, the granite glows with an ethereal, ambient light, even on dull days. This is many visitors' favourite fjord, and there's no doubt that it has a captivating beauty. Boat trips run from Stavanger along the fjord, but the area's most popular outing is the hike (think two hours) to the top of incredible Preikestolen (Pulpit Rock), 25km east of Stavanger. You can inch up to the edge of its flat top and peer 604m straight down a sheer cliff into the blue water for some intense vertigo. Boat-bus-hike combinations run here from Stavanger May to mid-September; book tickets from Tide Reiser (www.tidereiser.com), the tourist office or Fiskespiren Quay.

Bergen
POP 258,500

Surrounded by seven hills and fjords, Bergen is a charming city. With the World Heritage–listed Bryggen and buzzing Vågen harbour as its centrepiece, Bergen climbs the hillsides with timber-clad houses, while cable cars offer stunning views from above.

Sights

★ **Bryggen** HISTORIC SITE
Bergen's oldest quarter runs along the eastern shore of Vågen Harbour in long, parallel and often leaning rows of gabled buildings. The wooden alleyways of Bryggen have become a haven for artists and craftspeople, and there are bijou shops and boutiques at every turn. The atmosphere of an intimate waterfront community remains intact, and losing yourself in Bryggen is one of Bergen's pleasures.

Sleeping

Citybox HOSTEL €
(☑ 55 31 25 00; www.citybox.no; Nygårdsgaten 31; s/d from Nkr500/700, without bathroom from Nkr450/500; ⊛) The Citybox mini-chain began in Bergen and is one of the best of the hostel–budget hotel hybrids. Colour-splashed modern rooms make use of the original historic features and are blissfully high-ceilinged. Communal spaces, including a shared laundry room, can be hectic, but staff are friendly and helpful.

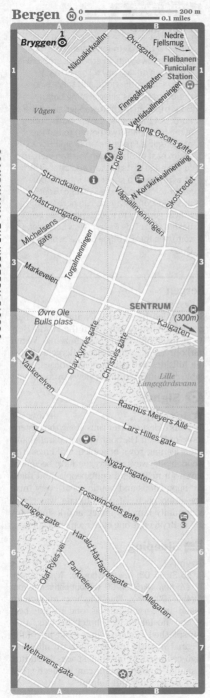

Bergen

⊙ Top Sights
1 Bryggen...A1

⊜ Sleeping
2 Bergen Vandrerhjem YMCA...............B2
3 Citybox..B6

⊗ Eating
4 Pingvinen...A4
5 Torget Fish Market.............................B2

⊙ Drinking & Nightlife
6 Garage...A5

⊛ Entertainment
7 Hulen...B7

Bergen Vandrerhjem YMCA HOSTEL €
(☑ 55 60 60 55; www.bergenhostel.no; Nedre Korskirkealmenning 4; dm Nkr205-330, s/d Nkr600/980) Gone are the days when staying in a hostel meant a long hike into town: this friendly place could be Norway's most central budget choice. While it's a standard hostel – same-sex or mixed dorms, large kitchen facilities etc – the terrace is extraordinary and staff are great. Bookings are essential year-round and, unusually, bed linen is included in the price.

✕ Eating

Pingvinen NORWEGIAN €
(☑ 55 60 46 46; www.pingvinen.no; Vaskerelven 14; daily specials Nkr119, mains Nkr159-249; ⊙ noon-3am) Devoted to Norwegian home cooking, and with a delightfully informal ambience, Pingvinen is the old favourite of *everyone* in Bergen. They come for meals their mothers and grandparents used to cook, and although the menu changes regularly, there'll be one or more of the following: fish-cake sandwiches, reindeer, fish pie, whale, salmon, lamb shank and *raspeballer* (aka *komle*), west-coast potato dumplings.

Torget Fish Market SEAFOOD €
(Torget; ⊙ 7am-7pm Jun-Aug, 7am-4pm Mon-Sat Sep-May) For atmosphere, it's hard to beat the fish market. Right alongside the harbour and a stone's throw from Bryggen, you'll find everything from salmon to calamari, fish and chips, fish cakes, prawn baguettes, seafood salads, local caviar and, sometimes, reindeer and elk.

☆ Entertainment

Garage   LIVE MUSIC
(www.garage.no; Christies gate 14; ⊙3pm-3am Mon-Sat, 5pm-3am Sun) Garage has taken on an almost mythical quality for music lovers across Europe. It does have the old jazz and acoustic act, but this is a rock and metal venue at heart, with well-known Norwegian and international acts drawn to the cavernous basement. Stop by for the Sunday jam sessions in summer.

Hulen   LIVE MUSIC
(www.hulen.no; Olaf Ryes vei 48; ⊙9pm-3am Thu-Sat mid-Aug–mid-Jun) A veteran of 1968, this is the oldest rock club in northern Europe and one of the classic indie stages of the world. Come here to hear the best up-and-coming west-coast bands, or catch an international act. Hulen means 'cave' and the venue is indeed underground, in a converted bomb shelter.

❶ Information

Tourist Office (☏ 55 55 20 00; www.visit-bergen.com; Strandkaien 3; ⊙8.30am-10pm Jun-Aug, 9am-8pm May & Sep, 9am-4pm Mon-Sat Oct-Apr) One of the best and busiest in the country, Bergen's tourist office distributes the free and worthwhile *Bergen Guide* booklet, as well as a huge stock of information on the entire region. It also sells rail tickets. If booking or making an enquiry, come early or be prepared to queue.

---

❶ FJORD TOURS FROM BERGEN

Fjord Tours (☏81 56 82 22; www.fjord-tours.com) has mastered the art of making the most of limited time with a series of tours into the fjords. Its popular and year-round 'Norway in a Nutshell' tour is a great way to see far more than you thought possible in a single day.

The day ticket from Bergen combines a morning train to Voss, a bus to the Stalheim Hotel and then on to Gudvangen, from where a ferry takes you up the spectacular Nærøyfjord to Flåm, joining the stunning mountain railway to Myrdal, and then taking a train back to Bergen in time for a late dinner (or continue on to Oslo to arrive at around 10pm).

From May to September, Fjord Tours also runs 'Hardangerfjord in a Nutshell' and 'Sognefjord in a Nutshell' day trips.

WORTH A TRIP

THE HURTIGRUTEN

Norway's legendary **Hurtigruten** (☏81 00 30 30; www.hurtigruten.com) coastal ferry has been a lifeline linking coastal towns and villages and is now one of the most popular ways to explore Norway. A Hurtigruten ferry heads north from Bergen nightly, pulling into 35 ports on its six-day journey to Kirkenes, where it then turns around and heads back south. The return journey takes 11 days and covers a distance of 5200km. In agreeable weather (by no means guaranteed) the fjord and mountain scenery along the way is nothing short of spectacular.

❶ Getting There & Away

➡ There are ferry services to Hirtshals in Denmark. This is also the southernmost point of the Hurtigruten coastal ferry that runs right up to the Norwegian Arctic.

➡ Bus destinations include Oslo (Nkr680, 11 hours, three daily), Stavanger (Nkr550, 5½ hours, six daily) and Trondheim (Nkr848, 14½ hours, one daily).

➡ The spectacular train journey between Bergen and Oslo (Nkr349 to Nkr829, 6½ to eight hours, five daily) runs through the heart of Norway.

Sognefjorden

Sognefjorden, the country's longest (204km) and deepest (1308m) fjord, cuts a deep slash across the map of western Norway. In places, sheer walls rise more than 1000m above the water.

FLÅM
POP 450

Scenically set at the head of Aurlandsfjorden, Flåm is a tiny village that's a jumping-off spot to explore the Sognefjorden area. It gets a little overrun with people when a cruise ship's in port, and sees an amazing 500,000 visitors every summer.

❍ Sights

Flåmsbana Railway   SCENIC RAILWAY
(www.flaamsbana.no; adult/child one-way Nkr340/170, return Nkr440/170) A 20km-long engineering wonder hauls itself up 864m of altitude gain through 20 tunnels. At a gradient of 1:18, it's the world's steepest railway that runs without cable or rack wheels. It takes a full 45 minutes to climb to Myrdal on the bleak,

DON'T MISS

SOGNEFJORDEN BY BOAT

It may get overrun in summer, but the classic boat trip from Flåm to Gudvangen is one of the most beautiful on earth. Ferries (one way/return Nkr295/400) leave Flåm at 3.10pm year-round and up to five times daily between May and September. In Gudvangen, buses to Voss connect with the ferry arrival; from Voss you can get the train to Bergen or Oslo. Boat and bus tickets can be bought at the tourist offices in Flåm and Gudvangen.

Norled (☎ 51 86 87 00; www.norled.no; Kong Christian Frederiks plass 3) operates a daily express boat between Bergen and both Flåm (Nkr750, 5½ hours) and Sogndal (Nkr645, 4¾ hours), stopping along the way.

treeless Hardangervidda plateau, past thundering waterfalls (there's a photo stop at awesome Kjosfossen). The railway runs year-round, with up to 10 departures daily in summer.

🛏 Sleeping

⭐**Flåm Camping & Hostel**　　　　HOSTEL, CAMPGROUND €
(☎ 94 03 26 81; www.flaam-camping.no; 1-/2-person tent Nkr120/205, dm/s/tw/q Nkr325/550/905/1290, with shared bathroom Nkr250/400/700/985; ☺ Mar-Nov; 🛜) Family-run and built on the site of their old family farm, a lot of love has gone into every aspect of this operation. Rooms, from dorms to en-suite doubles, are spread across the lush site, each with a stylish simplicity of its own. Campsites are idyllically located, too. In a gorgeous spot a few minutes' walk from the station.

🍷 Drinking & Nightlife

Ægir Bryggeri　　　　　　　　BREWERY
(www.flamsbrygga.no/bryggeri; ☺ noon-10pm May–mid-Sep, 6-10pm mid-Sep–Apr) Looking for all the world like a stave church, Ægir Brewery, all appealing woodwork and flagstones, offers six different kinds of draught beer, all brewed on the spot. It also does a tasty, creative take on Norwegian comfort food as well as burgers and pizzas (Nkr160 to Nkr210).

ℹ Getting There & Away

➡ Flåm is the only Sognefjorden village with a rail link, via the magnificent Flåmsbana railway.

There are train connections to Oslo and Bergen at Myrdal.
➡ Buses run to Bergen (Nkr330, three hours), among other local destinations.

Geirangerfjorden

Scattered cliffside farms, most long abandoned, still cling to the towering, near-sheer walls of twisting, 20km-long emerald-green Geirangerfjord, a Unesco World Heritage Site. Geiranger village has a fabulous location at the head of the fjord, but gets overrun by visitors and cruise ships. The one-hour scenic ferry trip along the fjord between Geiranger and Hellesylt is as much mini-cruise as means of transport – take it even if you've no particular reason to get to the other end.

◉ Sights & Activities

Flydalsjuvet　　　　　　　　VIEWPOINT
Somewhere you've seen that classic photo, beloved of brochures, of the overhanging rock Flydalsjuvet, usually with a figure gazing down at a cruise ship in Geirangerfjord. The car park about 5km uphill from Geiranger on the Stryn road, offers a great view of the fjord and the green river valley, but doesn't provide the postcard view down to the last detail.

For that, you'll have to walk about 150m down the hill, then descend a slippery and rather indistinct track to the edge. Your intrepid photo subject will have to scramble down gingerly to the overhang about 50m further along, or if it's a selfie, we advise extreme care.

Kayak More Tomorrow　　KAYAKING, HIKING
(☎ 95 11 80 62; www.kmtgeiranger.com; sea kayaks per hour/half-day/day Nkr150/450/800, kayaking-hiking trips Nkr800-1250) 🛶 Based at Geiranger Camping (a short walk from the ferry terminal) this much recommended company rents sea-kayaks and does daily hiking and canoeing trips to four of the finest destinations around the fjord.

☞ Tours

Geiranger Fjordservice　　　　BOAT TOUR
(☎ 70 26 30 07; www.geirangerfjord.no; tours adult/child Nkr110/45) This operation offers 1½-hour sightseeing boat tours (sailing four times daily June to August). Its kiosk is within the Geiranger tourist office. From mid-June to August, it also operates a smaller, 15-seater boat (adult/child Nkr390/190) that scuds deeper and faster into the fjord.

🛏 Sleeping

Geirangerfjorden Feriesenter CAMPGROUND €
(☏ 95 10 75 27; www.geirangerfjorden.net; Grande; campsites Nkr160-190 plus per adult/child Nkr30/15, cabins from Nkr1050; ⊙ late Apr–mid-Sep; @ 🛜) An excellent camping option with well-maintained facilities and particularly pretty, well-decorated cabins. Good longer-stay rates are available.

❶ Getting There & Away

➡ From mid-June to mid-August two buses daily make the spectacular run to/from Geiranger to Åndalsnes (Nkr265, three hours) via Valldal (Nkr85, 1½ hours). For Molde, change buses in Åndalsnes; for Ålesund, change at Linge.

➡ For Hellesylt, some ferries connect with buses to/from Stryn (Nkr115, one hour) and Ålesund (Nkr195, 2¾ hours).

Northern Norway

With vibrant cities and some wondrous natural terrain, you'll be mighty pleased with yourself for undertaking an exploration of this huge territory that spans the Arctic Circle.

Trondheim

POP 182,035

Trondheim, Norway's original capital, is nowadays the country's third-largest city after Oslo and Bergen. With wide streets and a partly pedestrianised heart, it's a simply lovely city with a long history. Fuelled by a large student population, it buzzes with life, has some good cafes and restaurants, and is rich in museums.

⊙ Sights

⭐ **Nidaros Domkirke** CATHEDRAL
(www.nidarosdomen.no; Kongsgårdsgata; adult/child/family Nkr90/40/220, tower Nkr40; ⊙ 9am-6pm Mon-Fri, to 2pm Sat, to 5pm Sun mid-Jun–mid-Aug, shorter hours rest of year) Nidaros Cathedral is Scandinavia's largest medieval building, with a striking facade of niched statues. The altar sits over the original grave of St Olav, the Viking king who replaced the Nordic pagan religion with Christianity. In summer, you can climb the tower for views.

🛏 Sleeping

⭐ **Pensjonat Jarlen** GUESTHOUSE €
(☏ 73 51 32 18; www.jarlen.no; Kongens gate 40; s/d Nkr540/690; 🛜) Price, convenience and value for money are a winning combination here.

> **WORTH A TRIP**

> ## HARDANGERFJORD

> Running from the Atlantic to the steep wall of central Norway's Hardangervidda Plateau, Hardangerfjord is classic Norwegian fjord country. There are many beautiful corners, although our picks would take in Eidfjord, Ulvik and Utne, while Folgefonna National Park offers glacier walks and top-level hiking. You can easily explore Hardangerfjord from Bergen (p189); www.hardangerfjord.com is a good resource.

After a recent overhaul, the rooms at this central spot have a contemporary feel and are outstanding value, although some bathrooms could do with a fresh look. Some rooms have polished floorboards, others carpet, and most have a hot plate and fridge thrown in.

🍴 Eating & Drinking

⭐ **Ravnkloa Fish Market** SEAFOOD €
(☏ 73 52 55 21; www.ravnkloa.no; Munkegata; snacks from Nkr45, mains Nkr150-185; ⊙ 10am-5pm Mon-Fri, to 4pm Sat) Everything looks good at this fish market that doubles as a cafe with quayside tables out front. The fish cakes are fabulous, and it also does shrimp sandwiches, mussels and a fine fish soup. In addition to seafood, it sells an impressive range of cheeses and other gourmet goods.

⭐ **Baklandet Skydsstasjon** NORWEGIAN €€
(☏ 73 92 10 44; www.skydsstation.no; Øvre Bakklandet 33; mains Nkr138-245; ⊙ 11am-1am Mon-Fri, noon-1am Sat & Sun) Within what began life as an 18th-century coaching inn are several cosy rooms with poky angles and listing floors. It's a hyperfriendly place where you can tuck into tasty dishes, such as its renowned fish soup ('the best in all Norway', a couple of diners assured us) or the lunchtime herring buffet (Nkr178) from Thursday to Saturday. Always leave room for a homemade cake.

⭐ **Trondheim Microbryggeri** MICROBREWERY
(www.tmb.no; Prinsens gate 39; ⊙ 5pm-midnight Mon, 3pm-2am Tue-Fri, noon-2am Sat) This splendid home-brew pub deserves a pilgrimage as reverential as anything accorded to St Olav from all committed øl (beer) quaffers. With up to eight of its own brews on tap and good light meals coming from the kitchen, it's a place to linger, nibble and tipple. It's down a short lane, just off Prinsens gate.

SCANDINAVIA NORTHERN NORWAY

ℹ️ Information

Tourist Office (📞 73 80 76 60; www.visittrond-heim.no; Nordre gate 11; ⏰ 9am-6pm daily mid-Jun–mid-Aug, 9am-6pm Mon-Sat rest of year) In the heart of the city with an accommodation booking service.

ℹ️ Getting There & Away

➡ The bus and train stations are adjoining.

➡ Bus services include Alesund (Nkr587, seven hours, two to three daily) and Bergen (Nkr848, 14½ hours, one overnight).

➡ There are two to four trains daily to/from Oslo (Nkr899, 6½ hours). Two head north to Bodø (Nkr1059, 9¾ hours).

Lofoten

You'll never forget your first approach to the Lofoten Islands by ferry. The islands spread their tall, craggy physique against the sky like some spiky sea dragon and you wonder how humans eked out a living in such inhospitable surroundings. The four main islands are all linked by bridges or tunnels, with buses running the entire length of the Lofoten road (E10) from Fiskebøl in the north to Å at road's end in the southwest.

◉ Sights & Activities

Lofoten's principal settlement, Svolvær, makes a pretty spot from which to base your explorations, with steep mountains rising sharply in the background and a busy harbour. The still-active fishing village of Henningsvær, perched at the end of a thin promontory, is the lightest, brightest and trendiest village in the archipelago, while Å is a very special place at what feels like the end of the world on the western tip of Lofoten. Its shoreline is lined with red-painted fisherfolk's shanties on stilts over the water.

★ **Svolværgeita**   HIKING, CLIMBING

You'll see it on postcards all over Lofoten – some daring soul leaping between two fingers of rock high above Svolvær. To hike up to a point just behind the two pinnacles (355m), walk northeast along the E10 towards Narvik, pass the marina, and then turn left on Nyveien, then right on Blatind veg – the steep climb begins just behind the children's playground.

To actually climb Svolværgeita and take the leap, you'll need to go with a climbing guide: try **Northern Alpine Guides** (📞 94 24 91 10; alpineguides.no; Havnegata 3).

🛏️ Sleeping

Å-Hamna Rorbuer & Vandrerhjem HOSTEL € (📞 76 09 12 11; www.lofotenferie.com; Å; hostel dm/s/d/tr Nkr250/300/570/750, 4- to 8-bed rorbu with bathroom Nkr1000-1400) Sleep simple or sleep in more comfort in peaceful Å – either

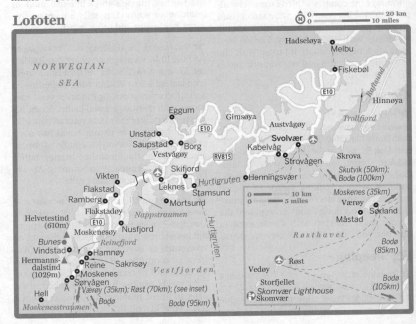

Lofoten

way, this is an attractive choice This place has dorms above a fishing museum and in a quiet villa, set in its garden. For more space and privacy, choose one of the restored *rorbuer* (fishing huts), the prices of which drop significantly outside high summer.

⭐ **Svinøya Rorbuer**   CABIN €€

(📞 76 06 99 30; www.svinoya.no; Gunnar Bergs vei 2; cabins & ste Nkr1150-3200) Across a bridge on the islet of Svinøya, site of Svolvær's first settlement, are several cabins, some historic, most contemporary, and all cosy and comfortable. Reception is a veritable museum, a restored and restocked *krambua* (general store), constructed in 1828, which was Svolvær's first shop. The company has properties all over the area, including some of the best *rorbuer* in Lofoten.

ⓘ Information

Tourist Office (📞 76 07 05 75; www.lofoten. info; Torget; ⏰9am-9pm Mon-Sat, 10am-9pm Sun mid-Jun–mid-Aug, shorter hours rest of year) In Svolvær. Provides information on the entire archipelago.

ⓘ Getting There & Around

→ From the south, the easiest way for non-drivers to reach Lofoten is the foot-passenger-only express boat between Bodø and Svolvær (3¾ hours).

→ Getting around is easy. Buses run the entire E10 from the Fiskebøl–Melbu ferry in the north to Å at road's end in the southwest. Tourist offices sell an excellent Lofoten cycling guide (Nkr298).

Tromsø

POP 67,300

Simply put, Tromsø parties. By far the largest town in far-northern Norway and administrative centre of Troms county, it's lively with an animated street scene, a respected university, the hallowed Mack Brewery, and more pubs per capita than any other Norwegian town. Its corona of snow-topped peaks provides arresting scenery, excellent summer hiking and great winter skiing and dog-sledding.

◉ Sights & Activities

Winter activities include chasing the northern lights, cross-country skiing, reindeer- and dog-sledding, snowshoe safaris, ice fishing and snowmobiling. In summer try hiking, fishing, glacier trekking and sea-kayaking. The tourist office can book things for you.

⭐ **Polaria**   MUSEUM, AQUARIUM

(www.polaria.no; Hjalmar Johansens gate 12; adult/child Nkr125/60; ⏰10am-7pm mid-May–Aug, to 5pm Sep–mid-May) Daringly designed Polaria is an entertaining multimedia introduction to northern Norway and Svalbard. After an excellent 14-minute film about the latter (screened every 30 minutes), plus another about the northern lights, an Arctic walk leads to displays on shrinking sea ice, a northern lights display and an aquarium.

⭐ **Arctic Cathedral**   CHURCH

(Ishavskatedralen; www.ishavskatedralen.no; Hans Nilsensvei 41; adult/child Nkr40/free, organ recitals Nkr70-150; ⏰9am-7pm Mon-Sat, 1-7pm Sun Jun–mid-Aug, 3-6pm Apr, May & mid-Aug–Jan, 2-6pm Feb & Mar) The 11 arching triangles of the Arctic Cathedral (1965), as the Tromsdalen Church is more usually called, suggest glacial crevasses and auroral curtains. The magnificent glowing stained-glass window that occupies almost the whole of the east end depicts Christ descending to earth. Take bus 20 or 24.

🛏 Sleeping

Tromsø Camping   CAMPGROUND €

(📞 77 63 80 37; www.tromsocamping.no; Tromsdalen; tent/caravan sites Nkr165/360, cabins Nkr590-1690; 🅿 @) Tent campers enjoy leafy green campsites beside a slow-moving stream. However, bathroom and cooking facilities at this veritable village of cabins are stretched to the limit. Take bus 20 or 24.

🍴 Eating & Drinking

Driv   CAFE €

(www.driv.no; Tollbodgata 3; mains Nkr115-185; ⏰noon-1.30am Mon-Thu, to 3am Fri & Sat, kitchen shuts 9pm) This student-run converted warehouse serves meaty burgers (try its renowned Driv burger) and great salads. It organises musical and cultural events and has a disco every Saturday. In winter you can steep yourself in good company within its open-air hot tub.

⭐ **Emma's Under**   NORWEGIAN €€

(📞 77 63 77 30; www.emmas.as; Kirkegata; mains Nkr155-365; ⏰11am-10pm Mon-Fri, noon-10pm Sat) Intimate and sophisticated, this is one of Tromsø's most popular lunch spots, where mains include northern Norwegian staples such as reindeer fillet, lamb and stockfish. Upstairs is the more formal Emma's Drømmekjøkken, a highly regarded gourmet restaurant where advance booking is essential.

Ølhallen Pub　　　　　　　　　　PUB

(www.olhallen.no; Storgata 4; ⊗10am-7.30pm Mon-Wed, to 12.30am Thu-Sat) At Mack Brewery's Ølhallen Pub you can sample its fine ales right where they're brewed. It carries eight varieties on draught.

ℹ Information

Tourist Office (⌖77 61 00 00; www.visittromso.no; Kirkegata 2; ⊗9am-7pm Mon-Fri, 10am-6pm Sat & Sun mid-May–Aug, shorter hours rest of year) Produces the comprehensive *Tromsø Guide*. Has two free internet points.

ℹ Getting There & Away

➡ SAS and Norwegian have direct flights to many Scandinavian cities.

➡ There are up to three daily express buses to/from Narvik (Nkr240, 4¼ hours) and one to/from Alta (Nkr560, 6½ hours), where you can pick up a bus for Honningsvåg, and from there, on to Nordkapp, Europe's northernmost mainland point.

Norway Survival Guide

ℹ Directory A–Z

ACCOMMODATION

Staying within a tight budget is difficult in Norway, and you'll either need to stay at campsites (in a tent or a simple cabin), hostels or guesthouses; within the budget category, it's rare that you'll have your own private bathroom.

LGBT TRAVELLERS

Norwegians are generally tolerant of alternative lifestyles, though attitudes aren't quite as liberal as Denmark or Sweden. Oslo has the liveliest gay scene.

ℹ PRICE RANGES

The following price ranges relate to a double room with private bathroom in high season:

€ less than Nkr750

€€ Nkr750–1400

€€€ more than Nkr1400

For eating choices, the following prices refer to a standard main course:

€ less than Nkr125

€€ Nkr125

€€€ more than Nkr200

MONEY

➡ Credit and debit cards are widely used, even for small transactions.

➡ One Norwegian krone (Nkr1) equals 100 øre.

➡ Service charges and tips are included in restaurant bills and taxi fares; tipping on a North American scale is not expected. It is, however, customary to round up the bill.

OPENING HOURS

Banks 8.15am to 3pm Monday to Wednesday and Friday, 8.15am to 5pm Thursday

Post Offices 9am to 5pm Monday to Friday, 10am to 2pm Saturday

Restaurants noon to 3pm and 6pm to 11pm

Shops 10am to 5pm Monday to Wednesday and Friday, 10am to 7pm Thursday, 10am to 2pm Saturday

Supermarkets 9am to 9pm Monday to Friday, 9am to 6pm Saturday

PUBLIC HOLIDAYS

New Year's Day (Nyttårsdag) 1 January

Maundy Thursday (Skjærtorsdag) March/April

Good Friday (Langfredag) March/April

Easter Monday (Annen Påskedag) March/April

Labour Day (Første Mai, Arbeidsdag) 1 May

Constitution Day (Nasjonaldag) 17 May

Ascension Day (Kristi Himmelfartsdag) May/June, 40th day after Easter

Whit Monday (Annen Pinsedag) May/June, 8th Monday after Easter

Christmas Day (Første Juledag) 25 December

Boxing Day (Annen Juledag) 26 December

TELEPHONE

➡ All telephone numbers in Norway have eight digits; there are no separate area codes.

➡ Country code: ⌖47.

➡ International access code: ⌖00.

➡ Local SIM cards with data packages are easily available and cheap.

ℹ Getting There & Around

AIR

➡ Norway is well linked to other European countries by air. Norwegian (www.norwegian.com) is Europe's best budget airline, with a wide network. The country's principal airport is Oslo Gardermoen.

➡ Due to the time and distances involved in overland travel within Norway, even budget travellers may want to consider a segment or two by air. The major Norwegian domestic routes are quite competitively priced.

BUS

Swebus Express (⌖0200 218 218; www.swebusexpress.se) has the cheapest buses between Oslo and Swedish cities. Eurolines

THE AURORA

The aurora borealis (Northern Lights), an utterly haunting and exhilarating sight, is often visible to observers above the Arctic Circle. It's particularly striking during the dark winter; in summer the sun more or less renders it invisible.

To see the lights, you'd best have a dark, clear night with high auroral activity. October, November and March are often optimal for this. Then it's a question of waiting patiently outside, preferably between the hours of 9pm and 2am, and seeing if things kick off. The Aurora Forecast app helps you predict auroral activity on the hoof.

(www.eurolines.com) also has many international routes. In the north, cross-border buses link Norway with Russia and Finland.

Within Norway, there's an excellent network of long-distance buses. Nor-Way Bussekspress (www.nor-way.no) operates the largest network. Lavprisekspressen (www.lavprisekspressen. no) operates the cheapest services if you get the right moment online. Nettbuss (www.nettbuss. no) also has a large network.

FERRY

International ferry connections are possible between Norway and Denmark, Germany and Sweden. Check www.directferries.com for all routes.

A great way to explore the coast is the **Hurtigruten coastal ferry** (p191).

TRAIN

→ Norway is connected to Sweden by train at several points. There are regular connections to Oslo from Stockholm and Göteborg. Rail services between Sweden and Norway are operated by **Norwegian State Railways** (NSB; ☑ 81 50 08 88; www.nsb.no) or **Swedish Railways** (SJ; ☑ in Sweden 0771-75 75 99; www.sj.se).
→ Within Norway, Norwegian State Railways runs an excellent, though limited system of lines connecting Oslo with Stavanger, Bergen, Trondheim and other southern cities. Rail lines reach as far north as Bodø (you can also reach Narvik by rail from Sweden); further north you're limited to buses and ferries.

ICELAND

Reykjavík

POP 204,775

The world's most northerly capital combines colourful buildings, wild nightlife and a capricious soul to brilliant effect. You'll find Viking history, captivating museums, cool music, and offbeat cafes and bars. And it's a superb base for touring Iceland's natural wonders. Reykjavík's heart lies between Tjörnin (the Pond) and the harbour, and along Laugavegur, with nearly everything for visitors within walking distance.

⊙ Sights

★ Old Reykjavík
AREA

With a series of sights and interesting historic buildings, the area dubbed Old Reykjavík is the heart of the capital, and the focal point of many historic walking tours. The area is anchored by Tjörnin, the city-centre lake, and sitting between it and Austurvöllur park to the north are the Raðhús (city hall) and Alþingi (parliament).

★ National Museum
MUSEUM

(Þjóðminjasafn Íslands; ☑ 530 2200; www.nationalmuseum.is; Suðurgata 41; adult/child Ikr1500/free; ⊙10am-5pm May–mid-Sep, closed Mon mid-Sep–Apr; 🚌1, 3, 6, 12 or 14) This superb museum displays artefacts from Settlement to the modern age. Exhibits give an excellent overview of Iceland's history and culture, and the audio guide adds loads of detail. The strongest section describes the Settlement Era – including how the chieftains ruled and the introduction of Christianity – and features swords, drinking horns, silver hoards and a powerful little bronze figure of Thor. The priceless 13th-century **Valþjófsstaðir church door** is carved with the story of a knight, his faithful lion and a passel of dragons.

★ Hallgrímskirkja
CHURCH

(☑510 1000; www.hallgrimskirkja.is; Skólavörðustígur; tower adult/child Ikr900/100; ⊙9am-9pm Jun-Sep, 9am-5pm Oct-May) Reykjavík's immense white-concrete church (1945–86), star of a thousand postcards, dominates the skyline, and is visible from up to 20km away. Get an unmissable view of the city by taking an elevator trip up the 74.5m-high **tower**. In contrast to the high drama outside, the Lutheran church's interior is quite plain. The most eye-catching feature is the vast 5275-pipe **organ** installed in 1992. The church's size and radical design caused controversy, and its architect, Guðjón Samúelsson (1887–1950), never saw its completion.

★ Icelandic Phallological Museum
MUSEUM

(Hið Íslenzka Reðasafn; ☑561 6663; www.phallus.is; Laugavegur 116; adult/child Ikr1250/free;

Central Reykjavík

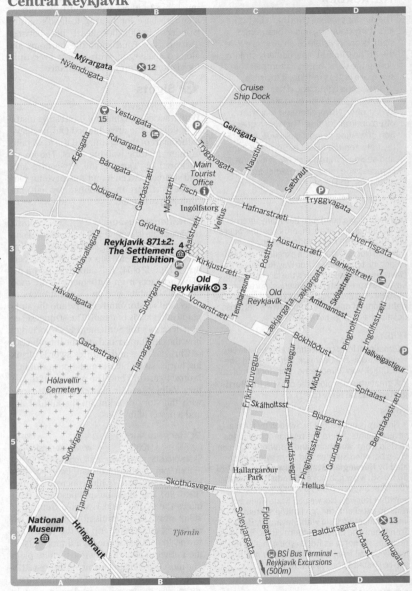

⊙10am-6pm May-Sep, 11am-6pm Oct-Apr) Oh, the jokes are endless here, but though this unique museum houses a huge collection of penises, it's actually very well done. From pickled pickles to petrified wood, there are 283 different members on display, representing all Icelan-dic mammals and beyond. Featured items include contributions from sperm whales and a polar bear, minuscule mouse bits, silver cast-ings of each member of the Icelandic handball team and a single human sample – from de-ceased mountaineer Páll Arason.

house unearthed here from 2001 to 2002, and the other settlement-era finds from central Reykjavík. It imaginatively combines technological wizardry and archaeology to give a glimpse into early Icelandic life.

✳ Festivals & Events

Iceland Airwaves   MUSIC
(www.icelandairwaves.is) You'd be forgiven for thinking Iceland is just one giant music-producing machine. Since the first edition of Iceland Airwaves was held in 1999, this fab November festival has become one of the world's premier annual showcases for new music (Icelandic and otherwise).

☞ Tours

Reykjavík is the hub for tours to amazing landscapes and activities around Iceland.

Elding Adventures at Sea   WHALE WATCHING
(☑519 5000; www.whalewatching.is; Ægisgarður 5; adult/child Ikr9900/4950; ⊙harbour kiosk 8am-9pm) 🐾 The city's most established and eco-friendly outfit, with an included whale exhibition and refreshments sold on-board. Elding also offers angling and puffin-watching trips, combo tours, and runs the ferry to Viðey.

⊗ **Reykjavík 871±2:**
The Settlement Exhibition   MUSEUM
(☑411 6370; www.reykjavikmuseum.is; Aðalstræti 16; adult/child Ikr1500/free; ⊙9am-8pm) This fascinating archaeological ruin/museum is based around a 10th-century Viking long-

DON'T MISS

THE BLUE LAGOON

As the Eiffel Tower is to Paris, so the **Blue Lagoon** (Bláa Lónið; ✆ 420 8800; www.bluelagoon. com; adult/child 14-15yr/child under 14yr Jun-Aug from €50/25/free, Sep-May from €40/25/free; ◷ 8am-midnight Jun–mid-Aug, 9am-8pm mid-Aug–May) is to Iceland...with all the positive and negative connotations implied. Those who say it's too expensive, too commercial, too crowded aren't wrong, but you'll be missing something special if you don't go.

In a magnificent black-lava field, the milky-teal spa is fed water from the futuristic Svartsengi geothermal plant; with its silver towers, the roiling clouds of steam, and people daubed in white silica mud, it's an otherworldly place.

The superheated water (70% sea water, 30% fresh water, at a perfect 38°C) is rich in blue-green algae, mineral salts and fine silica mud, which condition and exfoliate the skin – sounds like advertising speak, but you really do come out as soft as a baby's bum. The water is hottest near the vents where it emerges, and the surface is several degrees warmer than the bottom. Bus services run year-round, as do tours (which sometimes offer better deals than a bus ticket plus lagoon admission). You must book in advance.

Arctic Adventures   ADVENTURE TOUR
(✆ 562 7000; www.adventures.is; Laugavegur 11; ◷ 8am-10pm) With young and enthusiastic staff, this company specialises in action-filled tours: kayaking, rafting, horse riding, quad-biking, glacier walking and so on. It has a booking office with gear shop **Fjallakofinn** (✆ 510 9505; www.fjallakofinn.is; Laugavegur 11; ◷ 9am-7pm Mon-Fri, 10am-4pm Sat, noon-5pm Sun) in central Reykjavík.

Reykjavík Excursions   BUS TOUR
(Kynnisferðir; ✆ 580 5400; www.re.is; Vatnsmýrarvegur 10, BSÍ Bus Terminal) The most popular bus-tour operator (with large groups) has an enormous booklet full of summer and winter programs. Extras include horse riding, snowmobiling and themed tours tying in with festivals. Also offers 'Iceland on Your Own' bus tickets and passports for transport.

🛏 Sleeping

⭐ **Reykjavík Downtown Hostel**   HOSTEL €
(✆ 553 8120; www.hostel.is; Vesturgata 17; dm 4-/10-bed Ikr8400/5750, d with/without bathroom Ikr25,000/21,000; @) Squeaky clean and well run, this effortlessly charming hostel gets such good reviews that it regularly lures large groups and the non-backpacker set. Enjoy friendly service, guest kitchen and excellent rooms. Discount Ikr700 for HI members.

⭐ **KEX Hostel**   HOSTEL €
(✆ 561 6060; www.kexhostel.is; Skúlagata 28; dm 4-/16-bed Ikr8900/4900, d with/without bathroom Ikr29,700/24,600; @ 🛜) An unofficial headquarters of backpackerdom and popular local gathering place, KEX is a mega-hostel with heaps of style (think retro Vaudeville meets rodeo) and sociability. Overall it's not as prim as the other hostels – and bathrooms are shared by many – but KEX is a perennial favourite for its friendly vibe and booming restaurant-bar with water views and interior courtyard.

Loft Hostel   HOSTEL €
(✆ 553 8140; www.lofthostel.is; Bankastræti 7; dm Ikr6900-8000, d Ikr25,000-32,000; @ 🛜) Perched high above the action on bustling Bankastræti, this modern hostel attracts a decidedly younger crowd, including locals who come for its trendy bar and cafe terrace. This sociable spot comes with prim dorms, linen included and en-suite bathrooms in each. HI members discount dorm/double Ikr700/2800.

Salvation Army Guesthouse   HOSTEL €
(✆ 561 3203; www.guesthouse.is; Kirkjustræti 2; dm/s/tw/d Ikr4500/10,000/10,500/15,500; ◷ Jun-Aug; 🛜) Simple, clean rooms come in loads of sizes. Step outside and the whole of Reykjavík is at your feet. Linen Ikr900.

🍴 Eating

⭐ **Gló**   ORGANIC, VEGETARIAN €
(✆ 553 1111; www.glo.is; Laugavegur 20b; mains Ikr1700-2500; ◷ 11am-9pm; 🛜 🍽) Join the cool cats in this upstairs, airy restaurant serving fresh, large daily specials loaded with Asian-influenced herbs and spices. Though not exclusively vegetarian, it's a wonderland of raw and organic foods, with your choice from a broad bar of elaborate salads, from root veggies to Greek.

⭐ **Sægreifinn**   SEAFOOD €
(Seabaron; ✆ 553 1500; www.saegreifinn.is; Geirsgata 8; mains Ikr1350-1900; ◷ 11.30am-11pm

mid-May–Aug, 11.30am-10pm Sep–mid-May) Sidle into this green harbour-side shack for the most famous lobster soup (Ikr1300) in the capital, or to choose from a fridge full of fresh fish skewers to be grilled on the spot. Though the original sea baron sold the restaurant a few years ago, the place retains a homey, laid-back feel.

★ **Bakarí Sandholt** BAKERY €
(☑551 3524; www.sandholt.is; Laugavegur 36; mains Ikr250-980; ⏱7am-9pm) Reykjavík's favourite bakery is usually crammed with folks hoovering up the generous assortment of fresh baguettes, croissants, pastries and sandwiches. The soup of the day (Ikr1300) comes with delicious sourdough bread.

★ **Þrír Frakkar** ICELANDIC, SEAFOOD €€
(☑552 3939; www.3frakkar.com; Baldursgata 14; mains Ikr4200-6000; ⏱11.30am-2.30pm & 6-10pm Mon-Fri, 6-11pm Sat & Sun) Owner-chef Úlfar Eysteinsson has built up a consistently excellent reputation at this snug little restaurant – apparently a favourite of Jamie Oliver's. Specialities range throughout the aquatic world from salt cod and halibut to *plokkfiskur* (fish stew) with black bread. Non-fish items run toward guillemot, horse, lamb and whale.

Drinking & Nightlife

Reykjavík is renowned for its weekend *djammið,* when folks buy booze from Vínbúðin (state alcohol shop), have a pre-party at home, then hit the town at midnight. Many of the cafes around town morph into bars at night. Minimum drinking age is 20.

★ **Kaffibarinn** BAR
(www.kaffibarinn.is; Bergstaðastræti 1; ⏱3pm-1am Sun-Thu, to 4.30am Fri & Sat) This old house with the London Underground symbol over the door contains one of Reykjavík's coolest bars; it even had a starring role in the cult movie *101 Reykjavík* (2000). At weekends you'll feel like you need a famous face or a battering ram to get in. At other times it's a place for artistic types to chill with their MacBooks.

★ **Micro Bar** BAR
(Vesturgata 2; ⏱2pm-midnight Sun-Thu, 2pm-2am Fri & Sat Jun-Sep, from 4pm Oct-May) Boutique brews is the name of the game at this low-key spot near Austurvöllur. Bottles of beer represent a slew of brands and countries, but more importantly you'll discover ten local draughts on tap from the island's top microbreweries: the best selection in Reykjavík. Its five-beer minisampler costs Ikr2500; happy hour (5pm to 7pm) offers Ikr600 beers.

★ **Kaldi** BAR
(www.kaldibar.is; Laugavegur 20b; ⏱noon-1am Sun-Thu, to 3am Fri & Sat) Effortlessly cool with mismatched seats and teal banquettes, plus a popular smoking courtyard, Kaldi is awesome for its full range of Kaldi microbrews, not available elsewhere. Happy hour (4pm to 7pm) gets you one for Ikr650. Anyone can play the in-house piano.

★ **KEX Bar** BAR
(www.kexhostel.is; Skúlagata 23; ⏱noon-11pm; 🛜) Believe it or not, locals flock to this hostel bar-restaurant (mains Ikr1700 to Ikr2500) in an old cookie factory (*kex* means cookie) with broad windows facing the sea, an inner courtyard and loads of happy hipsters. The vibe is 1920s Vegas, with saloon doors, an old-school barber station, scuffed floors and cheerful chatter.

ⓘ Information

Main Tourist Office (Upplýsingamiðstöð Ferðamanna; ☑590 1550; www.visitreykjavik. is; Aðalstræti 2; ⏱8am-7pm) Friendly staff and mountains of free brochures, plus maps and Strætó city bus tickets for sale. Book accommodation, tours and activities. Also one site for getting your duty-free refund.

ⓘ Getting There & Around

➡ International flights operate through Keflavík International Airport, 48km west of Reykjavík.

➡ Flybus, Airport Express and discount operator K-Express have buses connecting the airport with Reykjavík. Flybus offers pick-up/drop-off at many accommodations (Ikr1950 to Reykjavík, Ikr2500 to hotel).

➡ Strætó (www.straeto.is) operates regular, easy buses around Reykjavík and its suburbs; it also operates long distance buses.

The Golden Circle

The Golden Circle takes in three popular attractions all within 100km of the capital: Þingvellir, Geysir and Gullfoss. It is a tourist circuit loved (and marketed) by thousands. The Golden Circle offers the opportunity to see a meeting-point of the continental plates and site of the ancient Icelandic parliament (Þingvellir), a spouting hot spring (Geysir) and a roaring waterfall (Gullfoss), all in one doable-in-a-day loop. Visiting under your own steam – by bike or hire car – allows you to visit at off-hours and explore exciting attractions further afield. Almost every tour company in the Reykjavík area offers a Golden Circle excursion (from bus to bike to super-Jeep), often combinable with other sights as well.

◉ Sights

★ Tectonic Plates   CANYONS, WATERFALLS
The Þingvellir plain is situated on a tectonic plate boundary where North America and Europe are tearing away from each other at a rate of 1mm to 18mm per year. As a result, the plain is scarred by dramatic fissures, ponds and rivers, including the great rift **Almannagjá**. A path runs along the fault between the cliff-top visitors centre and the Alþingi site.

★ Alþingi   LANDMARK
Near the dramatic Almannagjá fault and fronted by a boardwalk is the **Lögberg** (Law Rock), where the Alþing convened annually. Here the *lögsögumaður* (law speaker) recited the existing laws to the assembled parliament (one third each year). After Iceland's conversion to Christianity, the site shifted to the foot of the Almannagjá cliffs, which acted as a natural amplifier, broadcasting the speakers across the assembled crowds. That site is marked by the Icelandic flag.

Geysir   GEYSER
FREE One of Iceland's most famous tourist attractions, Geysir (gay-zeer; which

---

OFF THE BEATEN TRACK

THE WESTFJORDS

The Westfjords is where Iceland's dramatic landscapes come to a riveting climax and where mass tourism disappears – only about 14% of Iceland's visitors ever see the region. Jagged bird cliffs and broad multihued dream beaches flank the south. Rutted dirt roads snake north along jaw-dropping coastal fjords and over immense central mountains, revealing tiny fishing villages embracing traditional ways of life. In the far north, the Hornstrandir hiking reserve crowns the quiet region. Ísafjörður is the major bus hub in the Westfjords and accessible from Reykjavík. West Travel (www.westfjordsadventure.is) run limited bus services in the region. Local ferries also zip around the area.

---

literally means gusher) is the original hot-water spout after which all other geysers are named. Earthquakes can stimulate activity, though eruptions are rare. Luckily for visitors, the very reliable geyser, Strokkur, sits alongside. You rarely have to wait more than five to 10 minutes for the hot spring to shoot an impressive 15m to 30m plume before vanishing down its enormous hole.

Gullfoss   WATERFALL
(www.gullfoss.is) **FREE** Iceland's most famous waterfall, Gullfoss ('Golden Falls') is a spectacular double cascade dropping a dramatic 32m. As it descends, it kicks up magnificent walls of spray before thundering down a rocky ravine. On sunny days the mist creates shimmering rainbows, and in winter the falls glitter with ice. Although it's a popular sight, the remote location still makes you feel the ineffable forces of nature that have worked this landscape for millennia.

The South

As you work your way east from Reykjavík, Rte 1 (the Ring Road) emerges into austere volcanic foothills punctuated by surreal steam vents, around Hveragerði, then swoops through a flat, wide coastal plain, full of verdant horse farms and greenhouses, before the landscape suddenly begins to grow wonderfully jagged, after Hella and Hvolsvöllur. Mountains thrust upward on the inland side, some of them volcanoes wreathed by mist (Eyjafjallajökull, site of the 2010 eruption), and the first of the awesome glaciers appears, as enormous rivers like the Þjórsá cut their way to the black-sand beaches rimming the Atlantic.

Throughout, roads pierce deep inland, to realms of lush waterfall-doused valleys and awe-inspiring volcanoes. Public transport (and traffic) is solid along the Ring Road, which is studded with interesting settlements.

Vestmannaeyjar

Jagged and black, the Vestmannaeyjar (sometimes called the Westman Islands) form 15 eye-catching silhouettes off the southern shore. The islands were formed by submarine volcanoes around 11,000 years ago, except for Surtsey, the archipelago's newest addition, which rose from the waves in 1963. Surtsey was made a Unesco World Heritage Site in 2008, but its unique scientific status means that it is not possible to land there except for scientific study.

> DON'T MISS
>
> ## JÖKULSÁRLÓN
>
> Spectacular, luminous-blue icebergs drift through **Jökulsárlón** glacier lagoon (⊙24hr), right beside the Ring Road between Höfn and Skaftafell. It's one of Iceland's top visual treats: take in wondrous ice sculptures (some of them striped with ash layers from volcanic eruptions) calved off enormous Breiðamerkurjökull glacier, scout for seals, take a boat trip, or track the icebergs to the black-sand beach where they head out to sea.
>
> The lagoon boat trips are excellent, but you can get almost as close to those cool-blue masterpieces by walking along the shore, and you can taste ancient ice by hauling it out of the water. On the Ring Road west of the car park, there are designated parking areas where you can walk over the mounds to visit the lake at less-touristed stretches of shoreline.
>
> It's also highly recommended that you visit the rivermouth (there are car parks on the ocean side of the Ring Road), where you'll see ice boulders resting photogenically on the black-sand beach as part of their final journey out to sea.
>
> Several bus services and tours between Reykjavík and Höfn stop at Jökulsárlón.

Heimaey is the only inhabited island. Its little town and sheltered harbour lie between dramatic *klettur* (escarpments) and two ominous volcanoes – blood-red Eldfell and conical Helgafell. These days Heimaey is famous for its puffins (around 10 million birds come here to breed); Þjóðhátíð, Iceland's biggest outdoor festival, held in August; and its new volcano museum.

◉ Sights

★ **Eldheimar**   MUSEUM
(Pompeii of the North; ☑488 2700; www.eldheimar.is; Gerðisbraut 10; adult/child 10-18yr/child under 10yr Ikr2300/1200/free; ⊙11am-6pm May–mid-Oct, 1-5pm Wed-Sun rest of year) More than 400 buildings lie buried under lava from the 1973 eruption, and on the edge of the flow 'Pompeii of the North' is a new museum revolving around one house excavated from 50m of pumice, along what was formerly Suðurvegur. The modern volcanic-stone building allows a glimpse into the home with its crumbling walls and intact but toppled knick-knacks, and is filled with multimedia exhibits on the eruption and its aftermath, from compelling footage and eyewitness accounts to the homeowners' story.

★ **Eldfell**   VOLCANO
The 221m-high volcanic cone Eldfell appeared from nowhere in the early hours of 23 January 1973. Once the fireworks finished, heat from the volcano provided Heimaey with geothermal energy from 1976 to 1985. Today the ground is still hot enough in places to bake bread or char wood. Eldfell is an easy climb from town, up the collapsed northern wall of the crater; stick to the path,

as the islanders are trying to save their latest volcano from erosion.

★ **Eldfellshraun**   LAVA FIELD
Known as Eldfellshraun, the new land created by the 1973 lava flow is now criss-crossed with a maze of otherworldly hiking tracks that run down to the fort at Skansinn and the house graveyard, and all around the bulge of the raw, red eastern coast. Here you'll find small black-stone beaches, Gaujulundur lava garden, and a lighthouse.

✦✦ Festivals & Events

★ **Þjóðhátíð**   MUSIC
(National Festival; www.dalurinn.is; admission Ikr18,900) Three-day Þjóðhátíð is the country's biggest outdoor festival. Held at Herjólfsdalur festival ground over the last weekend in July or the first weekend in August, it involves music, dancing, fireworks, a big bonfire, gallons of alcohol and, as the night progresses, lots of drunken sex (it's something of a teen rite of passage), with upwards of 17,000 people attending.

🛏 Sleeping & Eating

Aska Hostel   HOSTEL €
(☑662 7266; www.askahostel.is; Bárustigur 11; dm/d/q without bathroom Ikr5600/19,000/28,900; 🛜) This excellent modern hostel is set in a cheery yellow historic building in the village centre.

★ **Slippurinn**   ICELANDIC €€
(☑481 1515; www.slippurinn.com; Strandvegur 76; mains Ikr2000-3900; ⊙5-10pm mid-May–mid-Sep; 🛜) Lively Slippurinn fills the upper storey of a beautifully remodeled old machine workshop that once serviced the ships in the harbour and now has great views to it. The

tool shelves are still in their original positions, with tables made from old boat scraps beneath them. The food is delicious Icelandic with a few bright flavours from the Med.

ℹ Getting There & Away

Eimskip's ferry **Herjólfur** (☑ 481 2800; www.eimskip.is; adult/child/car/bicycle Ikr1260/630/2030/630) sails from Landeyjahöfn (about 12km off the Ring Road between Hvolsvöllur and Skógar) to Heimaey year-round. The journey takes about 30 minutes. Passengers should book ahead in high season.

Getting to or from Landeyjahöfn, Strætó (p208) bus 52 runs from Reykjavík (Ikr3500, 2¼ hours, three daily in summer).

Skógar

POP 20

Skógar nestles under the Eyjafjallajökull ice cap just off the Ring Road. This little tourist settlement is the start (or occasionally end) of the fantastic 23km day hike over the Fimmvörðuháls Pass to Þórsmörk, and is one of the busiest activities centres in the southwest. At its western edge, you'll see the dizzyingly high waterfall, Skógafoss, and on the eastern side you'll find a fantastic folk museum.

◎ Sights

⭐ **Skógar Folk Museum**　　　　MUSEUM
(Skógasafn; ☑ 487 8845; www.skogasafn.is; adult/child Ikr2000/free; ⊙9am-6pm Jun-Aug, 10am-5pm Sep-May) The highlight of little Skógar is the wonderful Skógar Folk Museum, which covers all aspects of Icelandic life. The vast collection was put together by 91-year-old Þórður Tómasson over more than 75 years. There are also restored buildings (church, turf-roofed farmhouse, cowsheds etc), and a huge, modern building houses an interesting transport and communication museum, cafe and shop.

⭐ **Skógafoss**　　　　　　WATERFALL
This 62m-high waterfall topples over a rocky cliff at the western edge of Skógar in dramatic style. Climb the steep staircase alongside for giddy views, or walk to the foot of the falls, shrouded in sheets of mist and rainbows. Legend has it that a settler named Þrasi hid a chest of gold behind Skógafoss...

🛏 Sleeping

Skógar HI Hostel　　　　HOSTEL €
(☑ 487 8801; www.hostel.is; dm/d Ikr4400/12,000; ⊙late May–mid-Sep; 🛜) A solid link in the HI

chain, this spot is located a stone's throw from Skógafoss in an old school with utilitarian rooms. There's a guest kitchen and a laundry (Ikr800). The nearby campsite is excellent.

ℹ Getting There & Away

Strætó bus 51 runs here from Reykjavík twice daily (Ikr4200, 2½ hours). Sterna and Reykjavík Excursions services also pass through in summer.

Landmannalaugar & Þórsmörk

Two of the most renowned inland spots of southern Iceland are Landmannalaugar, where vibrantly coloured rhyolite peaks

Skaftafell

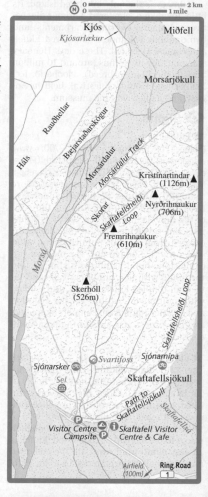

meet bubbling hot springs, and Þórsmörk, a gorgeous, forested valley tucked away from the brutal northern elements under a series of ice caps. They are linked by the rightly famous 55km Laugavegurinn hike, Iceland's most popular trek (for more information, check Ferðafélag Íslands' website, www.fi.is). Since these areas lie inland on roads impassable by standard vehicles, most visitors access them on tours or amphibious buses from the southern Ring Road. Þórsmörk, one of Iceland's most popular hiking destinations, can be done as a day trip from Reykjavík.

Skaftafell & Vatnajökull National Park (Jökulsárgljúfur)

Skaftafell, the jewel in the crown of Vatnajökull National Park (Jökulsárgljúfur), encompasses a breathtaking collection of peaks and glaciers. It's the country's favourite wilderness: hundreds of thousands come yearly to marvel at thundering waterfalls, twisted birch woods, the tangled web of rivers threading across the sandar (sand deltas) and brilliant blue-white Vatnajökull with its myriad ice tongues.

Icelandic Mountain Guides (IMG; ☑ Reykjavík office 587 9999, Skaftafell 894 2959; www.mountainguide.is) and **Glacier Guides** (☑ Reykjavík office 571 2100, Skaftafell 659 7000; www.glacierguides.is) lead glacier walks and adventure tours.

The **visitor centre** (Skaftafellsstofa; ☑ 470 8300; www.vjp.is; ⊙ 9am-7pm May-Sep, 10am-5pm Feb-Apr & Oct-Nov, 11am-5pm Dec, 10am-4pm Jan; ☏) has a **campsite** (☑ 470 8300; www.vjp.is; sites per adult/teen/child Ikr1600/750/free; ⊙ May-Sep; ☏) and summertime cafe. Various buses and transports travelling between Reykjavík and Höfn stop here.

The North

Iceland's mammoth and magnificent north is a wonderland of moon-like lava fields, belching mudpots, epic waterfalls, snow-capped peaks and whale-filled bays. The region's top sights are variations on one theme: a grumbling, volcanically active earth.

Akureyri

POP 17,930

Little Akureyri, with its surprising moments of big-city living, is the best base in the north. From here you can explore by car or bus, and tour the region's highlights.

◉ Sights

★ Akureyrarkirkja CHURCH
(www.akureyrarkirkja.is; Eyrarlandsvegur; ⊙ generally 10am-4pm Mon-Fri) Dominating the town from high on a hill, Akureyri's landmark church was designed by Guðjón Samúelsson, the architect responsible for Reykjavík's Hallgrímskirkja. Although the basalt theme connects them, Akureyrarkirkja looks more like a stylised 1920s US skyscraper than its big-city brother.

Jökulsárgljúfur

Húsavík (58km)
Keldhverfi
Kópasker (33km)
85
Bakkahlaup
Kallbjörg
Landgræðslusvæði
Fjöllin
85
Ásbyrgi
Petrol Station & Grill
Active North
Campsite
Ásheiði
Tófugjá
Eyjan
Klappir
Botnstjörn
Kúahvammur
862
Ásbyrgi
Ásheiði
Kvíar
Kjalarás
Rauðhólar
Lambafell
Hallhöfði
864
Hljóðaklettar
Ranger Station
Campsite
Hafurssstaðavatn
Tröllahellir
Hafersstaðir
Karl og
Vesturdalur
Kerling
Skógarskinnshæð
Svínadalur
Kallbjarg
Miðaftansfjall
Gloppa
Hólmáfossar
Hólmatungur
Hólma
Urriðafossar
862
Katlar
Saudafell
Ytra-Þórunnarfjall
Rauðhólar
Hvannstóð
Syðra-Þórunnarfjall
Hafragil
Svínadalsháls
Gróthals
Sjónnípa
Hafragilsfoss
Eilífur (698m)
Rauðhóll
Jökulsá á Fjöllum
Hikers Campsite
Dettifoss
Krafla (12km)
Walking Route Only
Selfoss
Ring Road (24km)

Ⓝ C ▬▬▬ 2 km
   C ▬▬▬ 1 mile

☞ Tours

★ Saga Travel　　　ADVENTURE TOUR
(☑ 558 8888; www.sagatravel.is; Kaupvangsstræti 4; ⊙ 7.30am to 10pm in summer, reduced hours rest of year) Offers a rich and diverse year-round program of excursions and activities throughout the north – obvious destinations such as Mývatn, Húsavík (for whale watching) and Askja in the highlands, but also innovative tours along themes such as food or art and design. Check out Saga's full program online, or drop by its office.

🛏 Sleeping & Eating

Akureyri Backpackers　　　HOSTEL €
(☑ 571 9050; www.akureyribackpackers.com; Hafnarstræti 98; dm Ikr5300-6300; d without bathroom Ikr23,000; @ 🛜) Supremely placed in the town's heart, this backpackers has a chilled travellers vibe and includes a tour-booking service and popular bar.

Blaá Kannan　　　CAFE €
(Hafnarstræti 96; lunchtime buffet Ikr1490; ⊙ 9am-11.30pm Mon-Fri, from 10am Sat & Sun) Prime people-watching is on offer at this much-loved cafe (the 'Blue Teapot', in the dark-blue Cafe Paris building) on the main drag. The interior is timber-lined and blinged up with chandeliers; the menu offers panini and bagels, and there's a cabinet full of sweet treats.

ℹ Information

Tourist Office (☑ 450 1050; www.visitakureyri. is; Hof, Strandgata 12; ⊙ 8am-6.30pm mid-Jun–Sep, shorter hours rest of year; 🛜) This friendly, efficient office has loads of brochures, maps, internet access and a great design store. Knowledgable staff can book tours and transport, and accommodation in the area (Ikr500).

ℹ Getting There & Away

Akureyri's **bus station** (Hafnarstræti 82) is the hub for bus travel in the north provided by SBA-Norðurleið and Sterna; Strætó operates from a stop in front of Hof. If you need to return to Reykjavík, consider taking an all-terrain bus route through the interior highlands, rather than along Rte 1. Buses run to Mývatn, Egilsstaðir, Húsavik, Reykjavík and other destinations.

Mývatn Region

Undisputed gem of the northeast, Mývatn (*mee*-vaht) lake and the surrounding area are starkly beautiful, an otherworldly landscape of spluttering mudpots, weird lava formations, steaming fumaroles and volcanic craters.

Reykjahlíð, at the northern end of the lake, is more an assortment of accommodation than a true town, but it makes the best base.

👁 Sights

Krafla　　　VOLCANIC AREA
Steaming vents and craters await at Krafla, an active volcanic region 7km north of the Ring Road. Technically, Krafla is just an 818m-high mountain, but the name is now used for the entire area as well as a geothermal power station and the series of eruptions that created Iceland's most awesome lava field. From Reykjahlíð, a reasonably easy hike of around 13km leads into Leirhnjúkur, the most impressive smouldering crater.

Dimmuborgir　　　LAVA FIELD
The giant jagged lava field at Dimmuborgir (literally 'Dark Castles') is one of the most fascinating flows in the country. A series of nontaxing, colour-coded walking trails runs through the easily anthropomorphised landscape. The most popular path is the easy Church Circle (2.3km).

🛏 Sleeping

Vógar　　　GUESTHOUSE, CAMPGROUND €€
(☑ 464 4399; www.vogahraun.is; Vógar; tents per person Ikr1500; d with/without bathroom Ikr27,700/15,400) A range of decent options here, 2.5km south of Reykjahlíð: camping, sleeping-bag accommodation in utilitarian prefab huts, and a newer block of compact guesthouse rooms, with and without bathroom. Sleeping bags reduce the price, as does staying a second night.

ℹ Getting There & Away

All buses pick up/drop off passengers at the information centre in Reykjahlíð. Tourist bus services run to Akureyri, Reykjavík, Egilsstaðir and more.

Húsavík

POP 2205

Húsavík, Iceland's whale-watching capital, has become a firm favourite on travellers' itineraries – and with its colourful houses, unique museums and stunning snowcapped peaks across the bay, it's easily the northeast's prettiest fishing town.

👁 Sights

★ Húsavík Whale Museum　　　MUSEUM
(Hvalasafnið; ☑ 414 2800; www.whalemuseum.is; Hafnarstétt; adult/child Ikr1800/500; ⊙ 8.30am-

6.30pm May-Sep, 9am-2pm Mon-Fri Oct-Apr) This excellent museum tells you all you ever needed to know about the impressive creatures that come a-visiting Skjálfandi Bay. Housed in an old harbourside slaughterhouse, the museum interprets the ecology and habits of whales, and covers conservation and the history of whaling in Iceland through beautifully curated displays, including several huge skeletons soaring high above (they're real!).

☞ Tours

Gentle Giants WHALE WATCHING
(☑ 464 1500; www.gentlegiants.is; Hafnarstétt; 3hr tour adult/child Ikr10,300/4200) Gentle Giants has a flotilla of old fishing vessels, plus recent additions of high-speed rigid inflatable boats (RIBs) and Zodiacs, offering a way to cover more ground in the bay. Gentle Giants also runs special trips to Flatey (Flat Island) for birdwatching, and fast (and pricey) RIB trips to Grímsey.

North Sailing WHALE WATCHING
(☑ 464 7272; www.northsailing.is; Hafnarstétt 9; 3hr tour adult/child Ikr10,500/4200, 4hr tour Ikr14,000/5600) The original operator, with a fleet of lovingly restored traditional boats, including the oak schooners *Haukur* and *Hildur*. Its four-hour 'Whales, Puffins & Sails' tour is onboard an old schooner; when conditions are right, there may be some sailing without the engine. Overnight sailing adventures to Grímsey are available in summer.

🛏 Sleeping & Eating

Húsavík Hostel HOSTEL €
(☑ 463 3399; www.husavikhostel.com; Vallholtsvegur 9; dm without/with linen Ikr6500/7500, s/d without bathroom Ikr11,350/15,840; 🖥) The only in-town budget option, this small hostel fills fast. There are bunk-filled dorm rooms and a couple of private rooms (rates without linen are much cheaper for these), plus kitchen.

★ Naustið SEAFOOD €€
(www.facebook.com/naustid; Naustagarði 4; mains Ikr1700-3500; ⊙ noon-10pm) Quietly going about its business at the end of the harbour, sweetly rustic Naustið wins praise for its super-fresh fish and a fun, simple concept: skewers of fish and vegetables, grilled to order. There's also fish soup (natch), salmon and langoustine, plus home-baked pie for dessert.

❶ Information

Tourist Information Centre (☑ 464 4300; www.visithusavik.is; Hafnarstétt; ⊙ 8.30am-6.30pm May-Sep, 9am-2pm Mon-Fri Oct-Apr) At the Whale Museum, with plentiful maps and brochures.

❶ Getting There & Away

SBA-Norðurleið (☑ 550 0700; www.sba.is) services (depart from in front of Gamli Baukar restaurant, on the waterfront) include Bus 641a to Akureyri (Ikr3700, 1½ hours, two daily mid-June to August), Bus 650a to Mývatn (Ikr3100, 40 minutes, two daily mid-June to August).
Strætó (☑ 540 2700; www.straeto.is) services (depart from N1 service station) include Bus 79 to Akureyri (Ikr2100, 1¼ hours, three daily).

Iceland Survival Guide

❶ Directory A–Z

ACCOMMODATION

For visits between June and August travellers should book accommodation well in advance (no need to prebook campsites). All hostels and some guesthouses and hotels offer cheaper rates if guests use their own sleeping bags. Generally, accommodation prices are very high compared to mainland European lodging.

Iceland has 32 well-maintained hostels administered by Hostelling International Iceland (www.hostel.is). In Reykjavík and Akureyri, there are also independent backpacker hostels. Bookings are recommended at all of them, especially from June to August.

LGBT TRAVELLERS

Icelanders have a very open, accepting attitude towards homosexuality, though the gay scene is quite low-key, even in Reykjavík.

---

❶ PRICE RANGES

Sleeping price categories are based on the high-season price of a double room:

€ less than Ikr15,000

€€ Ikr15,000–30,000

€€€ more than Ikr30,000

Eating categories are based on the cost of an average main course:

€ less than Ikr2000

€€ Ikr2000–5000

€€€ more than Ikr5000

ℹ ARRIVING AT SEYÐISFJÖRÐUR

The Norröna ferry from Denmark arrives at Seyðisfjörður in the east. It's a good introduction to the country: made up of multicoloured wooden houses and surrounded by snowcapped mountains and cascading waterfalls, it's picturesque and the most historically and architecturally interesting town in east Iceland.

There's tourist information in the ferry terminal. From here, buses run to the transport hub of Egilsstaðir (Ikr1100, 45 minutes), from where you can get onward transport to Rekyjavík and elsewhere.

MONEY

→ The Icelandic unit of currency is the króna (plural krónur), written as Ikr here, and often written elsewhere as ISK.

→ Coins come in denominations of Ikr1, Ikr5, Ikr10, Ikr50 and Ikr100.

→ Notes come in denominations of Ikr500, Ikr1000, Ikr2000, Ikr5000 and Ikr10,000.

→ Credit cards reign supreme, even in the most rural reaches of the country (PIN required for purchases). ATMs are available in all towns.

→ As service and VAT are always included in prices, tipping isn't required in Iceland.

OPENING HOURS

Standard opening hours:

Banks 9am to 4pm Monday to Friday

Cafe-bars 10am to 1am Sunday to Thursday, 10am to between 3am and 6am Friday and Saturday

Cafes 10am to 6pm

Post offices 9am to 4pm or 4.30pm Monday to Friday (to 6pm in larger towns)

Restaurants 11.30am to 2.30pm and 6pm to 9pm or 10pm

Shops 10am to 6pm Monday to Friday, 10am to 4pm Saturday; some Sunday opening in Reykjavík malls and major shopping strips

Supermarkets 9am to 8pm (later in Reykjavík)

Vínbúðin (government-run alcohol stores) Variable; many outside Reykjavík only open for a couple of hours per day

PUBLIC HOLIDAYS

National public holidays in Iceland:

New Year's Day 1 January

Easter Maundy Thursday and Good Friday to Easter Monday (changes annually; March or April)

First Day of Summer First Thursday after 18 April

Labour Day 1 May

Ascension Day May or June (changes annually)

Whit Sunday and Whit Monday May or June (changes annually)

National Day 17 June

Commerce Day First Monday in August

Christmas 24 to 26 December

New Year's Eve 31 December

TELEPHONE

→ All telephone numbers in Iceland have seven digits; there are no area codes.

→ Country code: ☑ 354.

→ International access code: ☑ 00.

→ Local SIM cards with data packages are easily available and cheap.

ℹ Getting There & Away

AIR

A growing number of airlines fly to Iceland (including budget carriers) from destinations in Europe and North America. Some airlines have services only from June to August.

FERRY

Smyril Line (www.smyrilline.com) operates a pricey but well-patronised weekly car ferry, the *Norröna*, from Hirsthals (Denmark) through Tórshavn (Faroe Islands) to Seyðisfjörður in east Iceland from late March until October. Limited winter passage is possible (departures are weather-dependent) – see the website. Fares vary widely.

ℹ Getting Around

Iceland has an extensive network of long-distance bus routes, with services provided by a number of companies. The free *Public Transport in Iceland* map has an overview of routes.

From roughly mid-May to mid-September there are regular scheduled buses to most places on the Ring Road, into the popular hiking areas of the southwest, and to larger towns in the Westfjords. Many bus services can be used as day tours (the bus spends a few hours at the final destination and stops at points of interest en route. Main bus companies include the following:

Reykjavík Excursions (☑ 580 5400; www.re.is)

SBA-Norðurleið (☑ 550 0700; www.sba.is)

Sterna (☑ 551 1166; www.sternatravel.com)

Strætó (☑ 540 2700; www.straeto.is)

Germany & Benelux

Best Places to Eat

➡ Cafe Jacques (p223)

➡ Restaurant Elmar (p282)

➡ Brauerei im Füchschen (p251)

➡ Fenix Food Factory (p288)

➡ Saint-Boniface (p261)

Best Places to Sleep

➡ King Kong Hostel (p288)

➡ Cocomama (p279)

➡ Captaincy Guesthouse (p260)

➡ Superbude St Pauli (p254)

➡ Grand Hostel Berlin (p221)

Why Go?

Tradition and modernity combine to dazzling effect in this sizeable chunk of old Europe, home to a hundred million people and several of the continent's classic landscapes and most enticing cities.

Castles and chocolate, tulips and cuckoo-clocks, Alps and rivers and canals; all the icons are here to be discovered along with the region's architecturally glorious villages, towns and cities, with their noble cathedrals, art galleries full of Old Masters and superbly traditional cafes, beer halls and pubs. Munich, Amsterdam, Bruges, Berlin and Cologne are high on the list of Europe's must-see places.

But these countries aren't museums. From the devastation of war came opportunities for regrowth and innovation and cities like Leipzig, Düsseldorf, Rotterdam and Antwerp are hotbeds of modern architecture, edgy cultural happenings and contemporary zeitgeist, real drivers of the exciting 21st-century scene in northern Europe.

Fast Facts

Capitals Berlin (Germany), Brussels (Belgium), Luxembourg (Luxembourg), Amsterdam (Netherlands)

Emergency ☑ 112

Currency Euro (€)

Languages German, Dutch, French, Letzeburgesch

Time zone Central European (UTC/GMT plus one hour)

Country codes ☑ 49 (Germany), ☑ 32 (Belgium), ☑ 352 (Luxembourg), ☑ 31 (Netherlands)

Population 81.2 million (Germany), 11.2 million (Belgium), 560,000 (Luxembourg), 16.9 million (Netherlands)

Germany & Benelux Highlights

1 Berlin Prepare for a full-on cultural and party scene in Europe's capital of alternative cred. (p218)

2 Dresden Discover how a bombed city rose from the ashes to become an icon of the east. (p228)

3 Munich Jump onboard for beer fests, BMWs, Alpine excursions and more. (p231)

4 The Black Forest Breathe in the mist and experience the lakes and trees, cherry cake and cuckoo clocks. (p241)

5 The Romantic Rhine Snap a postcard-perfect village along this beautiful stretch of river. (p243)

6 Luxembourg City Stroll with Eurocrats in this stunningly beautiful small city. (p275)

7 Brussels Imbibe atmosphere and your fill of beers in Belgium's stylish capital. (p257)

8 Bruges Appreciate the picture-perfect canal scenes of this heart-winning town. (p268)

9 Delft Wander the townscapes while admiring the elegant ceramics of this pretty town. (p287)

10 Amsterdam Rejoice in your urbanity in this sophisticated, fun and handsome icon of cool. (p278)

WORTH A TRIP: DÜSSELDORF

Vibrant, stylish and hedonistic; Germany's most underrated city. (p249)

WORTH A TRIP: MAASTRICHT

Much more than a treaty; treat yourself to its charms. (p292)

OFF THE BEATEN TRACK: BOUILLON

Picture-perfect village with a craggy, tough and dramatic castle. (p273)

OFF THE BEATEN TRACK: VIANDEN

Luxembourg's pretty castle villages are many: this is the best. (p277)

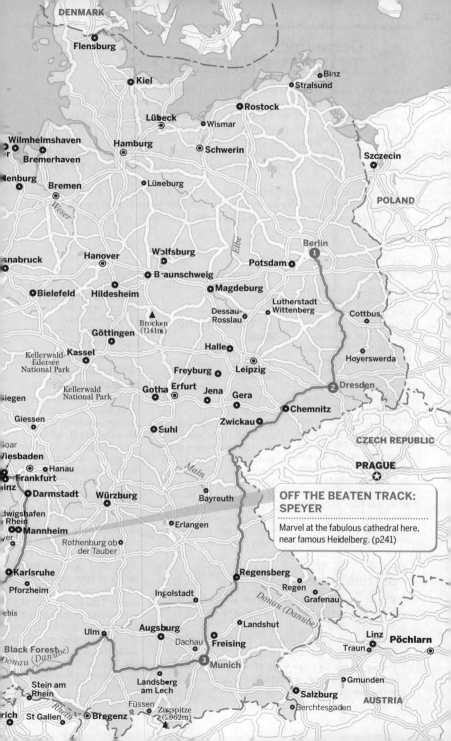

DENMARK

Flensburg

Kiel

Lübeck

Wismar

Rostock

Binz

Stralsund

Wilmhelmshaven

Bremerhaven

Hamburg

Schwerin

Szczecin

enburg

Bremen

Lüneburg

POLAND

Weser

snabruck

Hanover

Wolfsburg

Braunschweig

Potsdam

Berlin 1

Bielefeld

Hildesheim

Magdeburg

Elbe

Dessau-
Rosslau

Lutherstadt
Wittenberg

Cottbus

Brocken
(1141m)

Göttingen

Halle

Leipzig

Hoyerswerda

Kellerwald-
Edersee
National Park

Kassel

Freyburg

Dresden 2

iegen

Kellerwald
National Park

Gotha

Erfurt

Jena

Gera

Giessen

Suhl

Zwickau

Chemnitz

CZECH REPUBLIC

oar

Main

PRAGUE

iesbaden

Hanau

Frankfurt

inz

Darmstadt

Würzburg

Bayreuth

**OFF THE BEATEN TRACK:
SPEYER**

Marvel at the fabulous cathedral here,
near famous Heidelberg. (p241)

dwigshafen

Rhein

Mannheim

er

Erlangen

Rothenburg ob
der Tauber

Karlsruhe

Pforzheim

Regensberg

Regen

Grafenau

Donau (Danube)

ebis

Ingolstadt

Landshut

Ulm

Augsburg

Dachau

Freising

Munich 3

Black Forest

Donau (Danube)

Linz

Pöchlarn

Traun

Gmunden

Stein am
Rhein

Landsberg
am Lech

Salzburg

AUSTRIA

Füssen

Zugspitze
(2962m)

Berchtesgaden

rich

St Gallen

Bregenz

Germany's
TOP EXPERIENCES

Prepare for a roller coaster of feasts, treats and temptations as you take in Germany's soul-stirring scenery, spirit-lifting culture, old and bold architecture, big-city beauties, romantic castles and towns with half-timbered buildings.

Few countries have had as much impact on the world as Germany (p218), which has given us the printing press, the automobile, aspirin and MP3 technology. This is the birthplace of Martin Luther, Albert Einstein and Karl Marx, of Bach, Beethoven, the Brothers Grimm and other heavyweights who have left their mark on human history.

Germany's story-book landscapes will likely leave an even bigger imprint on your memories. There's something undeniably artistic in the way the scenery unfolds from the windswept maritime north to the off-the-charts splendour of the Alps.

⭐ Berlin

Berlin's glamour and grit will mesmerise anyone keen on exploring its vibrant culture, edgy architecture, fabulous food, intense parties and palpable history. Over a quarter-century after the Wall's collapse, the capital is increasingly grown up without relinquishing its indie spirit and penchant for creative improvisation. There's haute cuisine in a former brewery, all-night parties in power stations and world-class art in a WWII bunker. Visit major historical sites – the Reichstag, Brandenburger Tor and Checkpoint Charlie among them – then feast on a smorgasbord of culture in myriad museums. (p218)

⭐ The Romantic Rhine

As the mighty Rhine flows from Rüdesheim to Koblenz, the landscape's unique face-off between rock and water creates a magical mix of the wild (churning whirlpools, dramatic cliffs), the agricultural (near-vertical vineyards), the medieval (hilltop castles, half-timbered hamlets), the legendary (Loreley) and the modern (in the 19th-century sense: barges, ferries, passenger steamers and trains). From every riverside village, trails take you through vineyards and forests, up to panoramic viewpoints and massive stone fortresses, and back to a romantic evening spent sampling the local wines. (p243)

⭐ Schloss Neuschwanstein

Commissioned by Bavaria's most celebrated (and loopiest) 19th-century monarch, King Ludwig II, Schloss Neuschwanstein rises from the mysterious Alpine forests like a bedtime-storybook illustration. Inside, the make-believe continues, with chambers and halls reflecting Ludwig's obsession with the mythical Teutonic past – and his admiration of composer Wagner – in a confection that puts even the flashiest oligarch's *palazzo* in the shade. This sugary folly is said to have inspired Walt's castle at Disney World; now it inspires tourist masses to make the pilgrimage along the Romantic Road, which culminates at its gates. (p236)

GETTING AROUND

Bus A growing network of good-value, high-quality bus routes connect major cities. Routes are easily searched online.

Train Germany's main transport system covers the country comprehensively.

Urban Transport Major cities have underground/subway networks known as the U-Bahn. Trams and suburban trains (S-Bahn) add to urban networks.

⭐ Munich

If you're looking for Alpine clichés, Munich will hand them to you in one chic and compact package. But the Bavarian capital also has plenty of unexpected trump cards under its often bright-blue skies. Folklore and age-old traditions exist side by side with sleek BMWs, designer boutiques and high-powered industry. The city's museums showcase everything from artistic masterpieces to technological treasures and Oktoberfest history, while its music and cultural scenes are second only to Berlin's. (p231)

⭐ Hamburg

Anyone who thinks Germany doesn't have round-the-clock delights hasn't been to Hamburg. This ancient, wealthy city on the Elbe River traces it roots back to the Hanseatic League and beyond. By day you can tour its magnificent port, explore its history in restored quarters and discover shops selling goods you didn't think were sold. By night, some of Europe's best music clubs pull in the punters, and diversions for virtually every other taste are plentiful as well. And then, another Hamburg day begins. (p251)

⭐ The Black Forest

Mist, snow or shine, the deep, dark Black Forest is just beautiful. If it's back-to-nature moments you're after, this sylvan slice of southwestern Germany is the place to linger. Every valley reveals new surprises: half-timbered villages looking every inch

the fairy-tale fantasy, thunderous waterfalls, cuckoo clocks the size of houses. Breathe in the cold, sappy air, drive roller-coaster roads to middle-of-nowhere lakes, have your cake, walk it off on trail after gorgeously wooded trail, then hide away in a heavy-lidded farmhouse. Hear that? Silence. What a wonderful thing. (p241)

⭐ Oktoberfest

Anyone with a taste for hop-scented froth knows that the daddy of all beer festivals, Oktoberfest, takes place annually in Munich. The world's favourite sud fest actually begins in mid-September and runs for 16 ethanol-fuelled days on the Theresienwiese (Theresa's Meadow), with troops of crimson-faced oompah bands entertaining revellers; armies of traditionally garbed locals and foreigners guzzling their way through seven million litres of lager; and entire farms of chickens hitting the grill. So find your favourite tent and raise your 1L stein. *Ozapft ist's!* (The tap is in!) (p235)

if Germany were 100 people

92 would be German
2 would be Turkish
6 would be other

belief systems
(% of population)

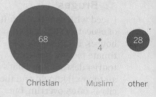

68 Christian · 4 Muslim · 28 other

population per sq km

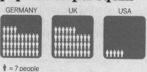

GERMANY · UK · USA

⭐ = 7 people

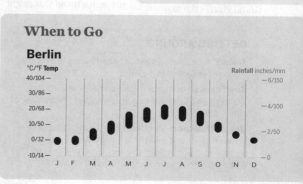

When to Go
Berlin

Belgium & Luxembourg's
TOP EXPERIENCES

Fabulously historic yet flush with the new, these compact, gentle and multilingual little countries are packed with wonderful surprises. Stereotypes of comic books, chips and sublime chocolates are just the start in eccentric little Belgium (p257); its people have quietly spent centuries producing some of Europe's finest art and architecture. Bilingual Brussels is the dynamic yet personable EU capital, with what's arguably the world's most beautiful city square. Flat, Flemish Flanders has many other alluring medieval cities, all easily linked by regular trains. In hilly, French-speaking Wallonia, there's a tranquil, rural feel and some marvellous castle villages, as there are in independent Luxembourg (p275), the EU's richest country, famed for banking but also sporting a fairy-tale historic old town. And from the beers of Belgium to the wines of Luxembourg's Moselle Valley, there's plenty to lubricate some of Europe's best dining.

★ Bruges

Laced with canals and full of evocative step-gabled houses, Bruges is the ultimate picture-postcard tourist destination. That's all too well known and the city is often overrun, but come midweek in February you may have it largely to yourself. Year-round you can escape the crowds by dipping into some majestic art collections. The Groeningemuseum is hard to beat, offering a history of Belgian art, with an outstanding selection of works by the Flemish Primitives. (p268)

★ Grand Place

Brussels' heart beats in the Grand Place – the most theatrically beautiful medieval square in Europe. It is ringed by gold-trimmed, gabled guildhouses and flanked by the 15th-century Gothic town hall. The cobblestones were laid in the 12th century, when the square was a marketplace; the names of the surrounding lanes evoke herbs, cheese and poultry. The Grand Place still hosts a flower market, as well as Christmas stalls, concerts and – every two years – a dazzlingly colourful 'carpet' of flower petals. (p257)

★ Belgian Beer

Ordering in a classic Belgian pub requires you to trawl through a menu that might have 200 choices. Each brew is served in its own special glass. Exports of Hoegaarden, Leffe and Stella Artois have introduced mainstream Belgian brewing into bars worldwide, but what really excites are the abbey-brewed Trappists, locally crafted dark ales, crisp golden triples and so much more. Go easy – many are over 8% alcohol. For the adventurous there's a range of sharp, spontaneously fermented lambics, often blended or flavoured with soft fruit. (p269)

★ Luxembourg City

No it's not just banks and Eurocrats. Wealthy Luxembourg City is one of Europe's most underestimated capitals, with a fine range of museums and galleries and a brilliant dining scene. But most impressive is the town centre's spectacular setting, straddling a deep-cut river gorge whose defences were the settlement's original raison d'être. Come on a summer weekend when accommodation prices drop, the streets are often full of music and there's an ample

GETTING AROUND

Train The best way to get between towns, trains are frequent and offer good value.

Bus There's a comprehensive network in Flanders, Wallonia and Luxembourg. Buses cover places where trains don't reach.

Urban Transport The major cities in both countries have efficient and reliable bus networks. Trams are also used in some Belgian cities, and Brussels and Antwerp also have metro systems.

flow of inexpensive local bubbly. (p275)

⭐ Flanders Fields

Flanders' fields, once known for potato and hop production, became synonymous with death in the wake of the trench warfare of WWI. The area around Ypres remains dotted with graveyards where white memorial crosses movingly bear silent witness in seemingly endless rows. Museums vividly evoke the context and conditions for everyday soldiers, and the rebuilt central square of Ypres is a wonder in itself. (p271)

⭐ Castles

From French-style *châteaux* to Crusader-era ruins, Belgium is overloaded with spectacular castles. Antwerp and Ghent both retain dinky medieval ones right in their city centres. But our personal favourites are further south. The gnarled fortress overlooking Bouillon is everything a medieval castle should be, while Vianden's brooding masterpiece is the focal point of one of the Grand Duchy of Luxembourg's most delightful country getaways.

⭐ War Museums

The 100th anniversary of WWI's first salvo in 2014 and the bicentenary of the battle of Waterloo in 2015 saw the opening of some compelling, state-of-the-art museums around Belgium. The Mons Memorial Museum (p273) explores the city's experience of world wars, getting the balance just right between military history and personal testimony; indulging in a little toy-soldier fantasy at Waterloo (p261) can now

be done in totally revamped surrounds, with a spectacular wraparound audiovisual as the climax.

⭐ Art Cities

If you love the medieval appeal of Bruges but want to be a little more original, a great choice is Ghent (p266). This historic city has its share of canalside splendour but also has a great arts scene and a grittier charm that many visitors find refreshing. Or try Leuven (p262), Belgium's ancient university city, whose centre is graced by a brilliantly flamboyant, statue-festooned town hall.

⭐ Chocolate

In 1857 Swiss confectioner Jean Neuhaus opened a 'medicinal sweet shop' in Brussels' Galeries St-Hubert – it's still there. In 1912 Neuhaus' son was credited with creating that most Belgian of morsels, the praline, by filling a chocolate shell with flavoured centres. Belgian chocolates remain world beaters due to the local insistence on 100% cocoa butter, and every town has its selection of chocolatier shops, hushed, hallowed temples where glove-handed assistants patiently load up *ballotin* boxes with your individual selection.

if Belgium were 100 people

60 would speak Dutch
39 would be speak French
1 would speak German

belief systems
(% of population)

75 Roman Catholic

25 other

population per sq km

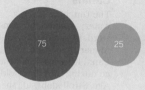

BELGIUM LUXEMBOURG USA

🧍 = 30 people

When to Go

Brussels

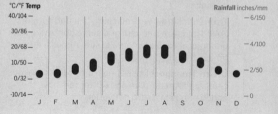

°C/°F Temp
40/104 —
30/86 —
20/68 —
10/50 —
0/32 —
-10/14 —

Rainfall inches/mm
— 6/150
— 4/100
— 2/50
— 0

J F M A M J J A S O N D

Netherlands'
TOP EXPERIENCES

Old and new intertwine in the Netherlands (p278). The legacies of great Dutch artists, beautiful 17th-century canals, windmills, tulips and quaint cafes lit by candles coexist with ground-breaking contemporary architecture, cutting-edge fashion, design and food scenes, phenomenal nightlife and a progressive mindset. Much of the Netherlands is famously below sea level and the flat landscape offers idyllic cycling. Locals live on bicycles and you can too. Rental outlets are found throughout the country, which is criss-crossed with cycling paths. Allow plenty of time to revel in magical, multifaceted Amsterdam, to visit charming canal-laced towns such as Leiden and Delft, and to check out cities like exquisite Maastricht, with its city walls, ancient churches and grand squares, and the pulsing port city of Rotterdam, currently undergoing an urban renaissance. It's a very big small country.

⭐ Amsterdam's Canals

The Dutch capital is a watery wonderland. Amsterdam made its fortune in maritime trade, and its Canal Ring was constructed during the city's Golden Age. Stroll alongside the canals and check out the narrow, gabled houses and thousands of houseboats; relax on a canal-side *café* (pub) terrace; or, better still, go for a ride. Cruises and boat rentals abound. From boat level you'll see a whole new set of architectural details, such as the or-namentation bedecking the bridges and, come nightfall, glowing lights reflecting in the ripples. (p278)

⭐ Cycling

Grab a bike and go. You can rent them anywhere and no nation on earth is better suited for cycling. Not only is it as flat as a classic Dutch pancake but there are thousands of kilometres of bike lanes and paths linking virtually every part of the country. You can see *polders* (areas surrounded by dykes where water can be artificially controlled) and creaking traditional windmills (as well as tulips blooming in springtime), and hear cows lowing in expansive green fields before arriving at the next enchanting village.

⭐ Brown Cafes

Gezelligheid has no English translation but is better experienced than defined. It refers to the uniquely Dutch state of conviviality, cosiness, warmth, good humour and sense of togetherness that is a hallmark of the country's famous brown cafés. Named for their aged, tobacco-stained walls from centuries past, these small, snug, history-steeped pubs are filled with good cheer. There are around a thousand in Amsterdam alone, and countless others throughout the country. It takes little time, on even your first visit, to be drawn into their welcoming atmosphere.

⭐ Delft

The Netherlands has no shortage of evocative old towns that bring the beauty of the Golden Age

GETTING AROUND

Bike Any Dutch town you visit is liable to be blanketed with bicycle paths. They're either on the streets or in the form of smooth off-road routes.

Bus Used for regional transport rather than long distances.

Train Dutch trains are efficient, fast and comfortable. Trains are frequent and serve domestic destinations at regular intervals, sometimes five or six times an hour.

Urban Transport Buses and trams operate in most cities, and Amsterdam and Rotterdam have the added bonus of metro networks.

into the present day. Haarlem, Leiden and Utrecht are some of the more well-known; other historic gems include Enkhuizen and Hoorn. One of the most exquisite (and accessible) of them all is Vermeer's home town, Delft. It's essential to spend an afternoon enjoying the canals, churches and museums, and sitting in a *café* soaking it all in. But Delft is at its most romantic in the evening after the day trippers have left. (p287)

⭐ Artistic Masterpieces

The Netherlands has produced a wealth of famous artists. In Amsterdam, Rembrandt's *The Night Watch,* Vermeer's *Kitchen Maid* and other Golden Age treasures fill the mighty Rijksmuseum, the Van Gogh Museum hangs the world's largest collection by tortured native son Vincent, while the Stedelijk Museum shows Mondrian, de Kooning and other Dutch visionaries among its modern stock. Outside the capital, Haarlem's Frans Hals Museum collects the painter's works, Rotterdam's Museum Boijmans van Beuningen spans all eras, and Den Haag's Mauritshuis unfurls a who's who of Dutch Masters. (p278)

⭐ Maastricht

The city where Europe's common currency began has been a meeting place for centuries. The Romans built underground forts here that you can still explore, and every generation since has left its mark. But 2000 years of history, magnificent monuments, mighty ruins, soaring churches and sublime museums aside, where Maastricht really shines is in how it embraces the moment. Few places in the Netherlands have such a dense concentration of *cafés* and restaurants, filled with people coming together to enjoy every minute of life. (p292)

⭐ Architecture, Rotterdam

Unlike many European cities that emerged from the ashes of WWII with hastily reconstructed city centres, Rotterdam pursued a different path from the start. Its architecture is striking rather than simply functional and contributes to its glittering, skyscraper-defined skyline. The world's best architects compete here for commissions that result in eye-popping, one-of-a-kind designs, such as a 'vertical city' (the country's largest building), a forest of cube houses, a pencil-shaped residential tower, a swooping white cable-stayed bridge, a fantastical horseshoe-shaped covered market, and an ethereal 'cloud-like' building housing the city's history museum. (p288)

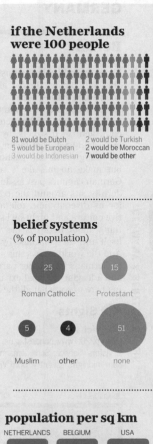

if the Netherlands were 100 people

81 would be Dutch
5 would be European
3 would be Indonesian
2 would be Turkish
2 would be Moroccan
7 would be other

belief systems
(% of population)

25 Roman Catholic

15 Protestant

5 Muslim

4 other

51 none

population per sq km

NETHERLANDS   BELGIUM   USA

👤 ≈ 35 people

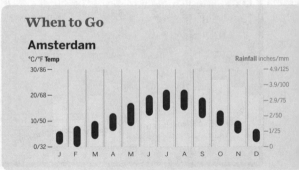

When to Go

Amsterdam

°C/°F **Temp**

30/86 —
20/68 —
10/50 —
0/32 —

Rainfall inches/mm

— 4.9/125
— 3.9/100
— 2.9/75
— 2/50
— 1/25
— 0

J F M A M J J A S O N D

GERMANY

Berlin

📖 030 / POP 3.6 MILLION

Bismarck and Marx, Einstein and Hitler, JFK and Bowie, they've all shaped – and been shaped by – Berlin, whose richly textured history stares you in the face at every turn. You might be distracted by the trendy, edgy, gentrified streets, by the bars bleeding a laid-back cool factor, by the galleries sprouting talent and pushing the envelope, but make no mistake – reminders of the German capital's past assault you while modernity sits around the corner. Renowned for its diversity and tolerance, its alternative culture and night-owl stamina, the best thing about Berlin is the way it reinvents itself and isn't shackled by its unique past. And the world knows this – a steady stream of Germans from other parts of the country and a league of global expatriates are flocking here to see what all the fuss is about.

⊙ Sights

★**Reichstag**   HISTORIC BUILDING
(Map p220; www.bundestag.de; Platz der Republik 1, Vistors' Service: Scheidemannstrasse; ⊙lift ride 8am-midnight, last entry 10pm, Visitors' Service 8am-

8pm Apr-Oct, to 6pm Nov-Mar; 🚌100, ⑤Bundestag, 🚉Hauptbahnhof, Brandenburger Tor) FREE It's been burned, bombed, rebuilt, buttressed by the Wall, wrapped in fabric and finally turned into the modern home of the German parliament by Norman Foster: the 1894 Reichstag is indeed one of Berlin's most iconic buildings. Its most distinctive feature, the glittering glass dome, is serviced by lift and affords fabulous 360-degree city views. For guaranteed access, make free reservations online, otherwise try scoring tickets at the Visitors' Service for the same or next day. Bring ID.

★**Brandenburger Tor**   LANDMARK
(Map p220; Pariser Platz; ⊙24hr; ⑤Brandenburger Tor, 🚉Brandenburger Tor) FREE A symbol of division during the Cold War, the landmark Brandenburg Gate now epitomises German reunification. Carl Gotthard Langhans found inspiration in Athens' Acropolis for the elegant triumphal arch, completed in 1791 as the royal city gate. It stands sentinel over Pariser Platz, a harmoniously proportioned square once again framed by banks as well as the US, British and French embassies, just as it was during its 19th-century heyday.

★**Deutsches Historisches Museum**   MUSEUM
(Map p222; 📖 030 203 040; www.dhm.de; Unter den Linden 2; adult/concession/under 18yr €8/4/

Berlin

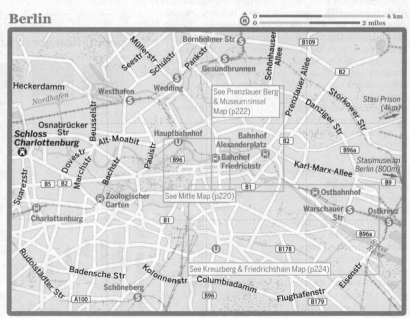

free; ⊗10am-6pm; 🚇100, 200, ⑤Hausvogteiplatz, 🚉Hackescher Markt) This engaging museum zeroes in on 1500 years of German history in all its gore and glory – not in a nutshell, but on two floors of a Prussian-era armoury. Check out the Nazi globe, the pain-wracked faces of dying warrior sculptures in the courtyard, and the temporary exhibits in the boldly modern annex designed by IM Pei.

Hitler's Bunker   HISTORIC SITE
(Map p220; cnr In den Ministergärten & Gertrud-Kolmar-Strasse; ⊗24hr; ⑤Brandenburger Tor, 🚉Brandenburger Tor) Berlin was burning and Soviet tanks advancing relentlessly when Adolf Hitler committed suicide on 30 April 1945, alongside Eva Braun, his long-time female companion, hours after their marriage. Today, a parking lot covers the site, revealing its dark history only via an information panel with a diagram of the vast bunker network, construction data and the site's post-WWII history.

Holocaust Memorial   MEMORIAL
(Memorial to the Murdered European Jews; Map p220; ☎030 2639 4336; www.stiftung-denkmal.de; Cora-Berliner-Strasse 1; audioguide adult/concession €4/2; ⊗field 24hr, information centre 10am-8pm Tue-Sun Apr-Sep, to 7pm Oct-Mar, last entry 45min before closing; ⑤Brandenburger Tor, 🚉Brandenburger Tor) FREE Inaugurated in 2005, this football-field-sized memorial by American architect Peter Eisenman consists of 2711 sarcophagi-like concrete columns rising in sombre silence from undulating ground. You're free to access this maze at any point and make your individual journey through it. For context visit the subterranean **Ort der Information** (Information Centre), the exhibits of which will leave no one untouched. Audioguides are available.

★Pergamonmuseum   MUSEUM
(Map p222; ☎030-266 424 242; www.smb.museum; Bodestrasse 1-3; adult/concession €12/6; ⊗10am-6pm, to 8pm Thu; 🚇100, 200, TXL, 🚉Hackescher Markt, Friedrichstrasse) Opening a fascinating window onto the ancient world, this palatial three-wing complex unites a rich feast of classical sculpture and monumental architecture from Greece, Rome, Babylon and the Middle East, including the radiant-blue Ishtar Gate from Babylon, the Roman Market Gate of Miletus and the Caliph's Palace of Mshatta. Renovations put the namesake Pergamon Altar off limits until 2019. Budget at least two hours for this

amazing place and be sure to pick up the free and excellent audioguide.

★Neues Museum   MUSEUM
(New Museum; Map p222; ☎030-266 424 242; www.smb.museum; Bodestrasse 1-3; adult/concession €12/6; ⊗10am-6pm, to 8pm Thu; 🚇100, 200, TXL, 🚉Hackescher Markt) David Chipperfield's reconstruction of the bombed-out Neues Museum is now the residence of Queen Nefertiti, the show-stopper of the Egyptian Museum that also features mummies, sculptures and sarcophagi. Pride of place of the Museum of Pre- and Early History in the same building goes to Trojan antiquities, a Neanderthal skull and the 3000-year-old 'Berliner Goldhut', a golden conical hat. Skip the queue by buying your timed ticket online.

★Potsdamer Platz   AREA
(Map p220; Alte Potsdamer Strasse; 🚇200, ⑤Potsdamer Platz, 🚉Potsdamer Platz) The rebirth of the historic Potsdamer Platz was Europe's biggest building project in the 1990s, a showcase of urban renewal masterminded by such top international architects as Renzo Piano and Helmut Jahn. An entire city quarter sprouted on terrain once bifurcated by the Berlin Wall and today houses offices, theatres and cinemas, hotels, apartments and museums. Highlights include the glass-tented Sony Center and the Panoramapunkt observation deck.

★Gemäldegalerie   GALLERY
(Gallery of Old Masters; Map p220; ☎030-266 424 242; www.smb.museum/gg; Matthäikirchplatz; adult/concession €10/5; ⊗10am-6pm Tue, Wed &

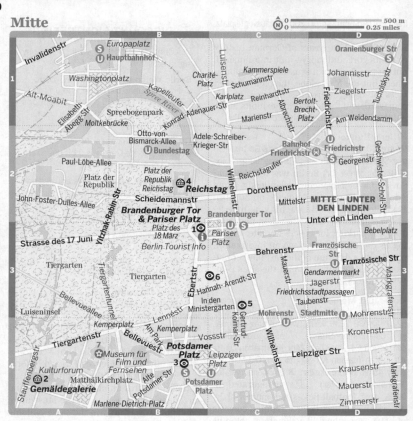

Fri, 10am-8pm Thu, 11am-6pm Sat & Sun; 🚌M29, M41, 200, Ⓢ Potsdamer Platz, ⓇPotsdamer Platz) The principal Kulturforum museum boasts one of the world's finest and most comprehensive collections of European art from the 13th to the 18th centuries. Wear comfy shoes when exploring the 72 galleries: a walk past masterpieces by Rembrandt, Dürer, Hals, Vermeer, Gainsborough and many more Old Masters covers almost 2km.

★ Gedenkstätte Berliner Mauer MEMORIAL
(Berlin Wall Memorial; Map p222; 🕿030-467 986 666; www.berliner-mauer-gedenkstaette.de; Bernauer Strasse btwn Schwedter Strasse & Gartenstrasse; ⊙visitor centre & documentation centre 10am-6pm Tue-Sun, open-air exhibit 8am-10pm daily; ⓇNordbahnhof, Bernauer Strasse, Eberswalder Strasse) FREE The outdoor Berlin Wall Memorial extends for 1.4km along Bernauer Strasse and integrates an original section of Wall, vestiges of the border installations and escape tunnels, a chapel and a monument.

Multimedia stations, panels, excavations and a Documentation Centre provide context and explain what the border fortifications looked like and how they shaped the everyday lives of people on both sides of it. There's a great view from the centre's viewing platform.

★ Schloss Charlottenburg PALACE
(🕿030-320 910; www.spsg.de; Spandauer Damm 10-22; day pass to all 4 buildings adult/concession €12/9; ⊙hours vary by building; Ⓟ; 🚌M45, 109, 309, Ⓢ Richard-Wagner-Platz, Sophie-Charlotte-Platz) Charlottenburg Palace is one of the few sites in Berlin that still reflects the one-time grandeur of the Hohenzollern clan that ruled the region from 1415 to 1918. Originally a petite summer retreat, it grew into an exquisite baroque pile with opulent private apartments, richly festooned festival halls, collections of precious porcelain and paintings by French 18th-century masters. It's lovely in summer when you can fold a

Mitte

stroll in the palace park into a cay of peeking at royal treasures.

Tours

Alternative Berlin Tours   WALKING TOUR
(☑ 0162 819 8264; www.alternativeberlin.com; tours €10-20) Pay-what-you-wish subculture tours that get beneath the skin of the city, plus a street-art workshop, an alternative pub crawl, the surreal 'Twilight Tour', an eco-tour, and a food and drink tour.

Sleeping

★**Grand Hostel Berlin**   HOSTEL €
(Map p224; ☑ 030-2009 5450; www.grandhostel-berlin.de; Tempelhofer Ufer 14; dm from €14, d with/without bathroom €58/44; @ 🛜; ⑤ Möckernbrücke) Afternoon tea in the library bar? Check. Rooms with stucco-ornamented ceilings? Got 'em. Canal views? Yup. OK, the Grand Hostel may be no five-star hotel, but it is one of Berlin's most supreme y comfortable and atmospheric hostels. Ensconced in a fully renovated 1870s building are private rooms and dorms with quality single beds (linen costs €3.60) and large lockers. Optional buffet breakfast is €6.20.

EastSeven Berlin Hostel   HOSTEL €
(Map p222; ☑ 030-9362 2240; www.eastseven.de; Schwedter Strasse 7; dm €14-23, d €52; ☺ @ 🛜; ⑤ Senefelderplatz) Staff at this personable, delightful hostel close to hip hang-outs and public transport go out of their way to make all feel welcome. Make new friends at garden barbecues, spaghetti dinners or chilling in the lounge, then retreat to comfy pine beds in brightly painted dorms with lockers, or a private room. Baths are shared, linen is free and breakfast is €3.

Wombat's Berlin   HOSTEL €
(Map p222; ☑ 030-8471 0820; www.wombats-hostels.com; Alte Schönhauser Strasse 2; dm €13-24, d €58-78; @ 🛜; ⑤ Rosa-Luxemburg-Platz) Sociable and central, Wombats gets hostelling right. From backpack-sized in-room lockers to individual reading lamps and a guest kitchen with dishwasher, the attention to detail here is impressive. Spacious en-suite rooms are as much part of the deal as free linen and a welcome drink, best enjoyed with fellow party pilgrims at sunset on the rooftop.

Eastern Comfort Hostelboat   HOSTEL €
(Map p224; ☑ 030-6676 3806; www.eastern-comfort.com; Mühlenstrasse 73-77; dm €16, d €55-78; ☺ reception 8am-midnight; @ 🛜; ⑤ Warschauer Strasse, ☒ Warschauer Strasse) Let the Spree River murmur you to sleep while you're snugly ensconced in this two-boat floating hostel right by the East Side Gallery. Cabins are carpeted and trimmed in wood, but sweetly snug (except for 'first-class') must have their own shower and toilet. The party zones of Kreuzberg and Friedrichshain are handily within staggering distance.

★**Circus Hotel**   HOTEL €€
(Map p222; ☑ 030-2000 3939; www.circus-berlin.de; Rosenthaler Strasse 1; d €85-120, apt €120-190; @ 🛜; ⑤ Rosenthaler Platz) At this superb budget boutique hotel, none of the mod rooms are alike, but all feature upbeat colours, thoughtful design touches, sleek oak floors and quality baths. Baths have walk-in rain showers. Unexpected perks include a roof terrace with summertime yoga, bike rentals and a fabulous breakfast buffet (€9) served until 1pm. Simply good value all-round.

Eating

Berlin is a snacker's paradise, with Turkish, wurst (sausage), Greek, Italian and Chinese Imbiss (snack) stalls throughout the city. For a local snack, try a ubiquitous *Currywurst* (slivered sausage drizzled with ketchup and curry powder).

FARMERS MARKETS

Excellent farmers markets include those at **Kollwitzplatzmarkt** (Map p222; Kollwitzstrasse; ☺ noon-7pm Thu, 9am-4pm Sat; ⑤ Senefelderplatz) in Prenzlauer Berg and the **Türkischer Markt** (Turkish Market; Map p224; www.tuerkenmarkt.de; Maybachufer; ☺ 11am-6.30pm Tue & Fri; ⑤ Schönleinstrasse) in Kreuzberg.

GERMANY & BENELUX BERLIN

Habba Habba MIDDLE EASTERN €
(Map p222; ☎030-3674 5726; www.habba-habba
.de; Kastanienallee 15; dishes €4.50-9; ⊙10am-
10pm; ⚑; 🚊M1, 12, 🚆Eberswalder Strasse) This
tiny Imbiss makes the best wraps in town,
especially the one stuffed with pomegran-
ate-marinated chicken and nutty buckwheat

dressed in a minty yoghurt sauce. One bite
and you're hooked. Also served as low-carb
bowls and as vegetarian and vegan versions.

Masaniello ITALIAN €
(Map p224; ☎030-692 6657; www.masaniello.de;
Hasenheide 20; pizza €6-9.50; ⊙noon-midnight;

Prenzlauer Berg & Museumsinsel

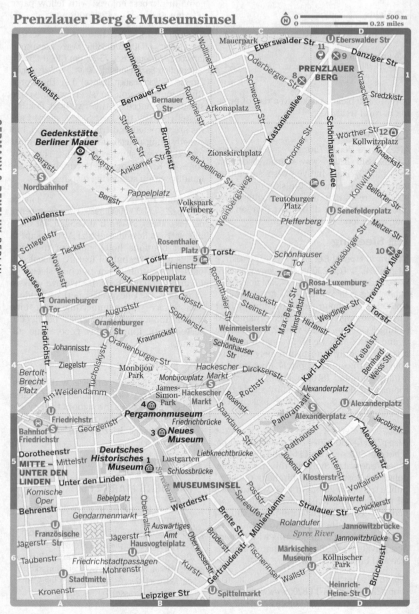

Prenzlauer Berg & Museumsinsel

Ⓢ Hermannplatz) Tables are almost too small for the wagon-wheel-size certified Neapolitan pizzas tickled by wood fire at this low-key pizzeria, whose spacious flowery terrace transports you to the boot on a balmy summer night. A vegan fave is the Pizza Contadina with eggplant, peppers, zucchini, mushrooms and artichokes.

Konnopke's Imbiss   GERMAN €
(Map p222; ☎030-442 7765; www.konnopke-imbiss.de; Schönhauser Allee 44a; sausages €1.30-2; ⊙9am-8pm Mon-Fri, 11.30am-8pm Sat; Ⓢ Eberswalder Strasse, ☒M1, M10) Brave the inevitable queue at this famous sausage kitchen, ensconced in the same spot below the elevated U-Bahn track since 1930, but now equipped with a heated pavilion and an English menu. The 'secret' sauce topping its classic *Currywurst* comes in a four-part heat scale from mild to wild.

★**Cafe Jacques**   INTERNATIONAL €€
(Map p224; ☎030-694 1048; Maybachufer 14; mains €12-20; ⊙6pm-late; Ⓢ Schönleinstrasse) A favourite with off-duty chefs and loyal foodies, Jacques infallibly charms with flattering candlelight, arty-elegant decor and fantastic wine. It's the perfect date spot but, quite frankly, you only have to be in love with good food to appreciate the French- and North African–inspired blackboard menu. Fish and meat are always tops and the pasta is homemade. Reservations essential.

La Soupe Populaire   GERMAN €€
(Map p222; ☎030-4431 9680; www.lasoupepopulaire.de; Prenzlauer Allee 242; mains €14-21; ⊙noon-2.30pm & 5.30-10.10pm Thu-Sat; Ⓢ Senefelder Platz, ☒M2) Helmed by local top toque Tim Raue, this industrial-chic gastro destination inside a defunct 19th-century brewery embraces the soulful goodness of German home cooking. The star of the regular menu is Raue's riff on *Königsberger Klopse* (veal meatballs in caper sauce)

but there's also a separate one inspired by changing art exhibits in the hall overlooked by the dining room.

🍷 Drinking & Nightlife

With no curfew, Berlin is a notoriously late city, where bars stay packed from dusk to dawn and beyond and some clubs don't hit their stride until 6am. Kreuzberg and Friedrichshain are currently the edgiest bar-hopping grounds.

Madame Claude   PUB
(Map p224; ☎030-8411 0859; www.madameclaude.de; Lübbener Strasse 19; ⊙from 7pm; Ⓢ Schlesisches Tor, Görlitzer Bahnhof) Gravity is literally upended at this David Lynchian booze burrow where the furniture dangles from the ceiling and the moulding is on the floor. There are concerts, DJs and events every night, including eXperimondays, Wednesday's music quiz night and open-mike Sundays. The name honours a famous French prostitute – *très apropos* given the place's bordello pedigree.

LOCAL KNOWLEDGE

LGBT BERLIN

Berlin's legendary liberalism has spawned one of the world's biggest and most diverse LGBT playgrounds. The historic 'gay village' is near Nollendorfplatz in Schöneberg (Motzstrasseand Fuggerstrasse especially), where the crowds skew older and leather. Current hipster central is Kreuzberg, where freewheeling party pens cluster around Mehringdamm and Oranienstrasse. Check Siegessäule (www.siegesaeule.de), the weekly freebie 'bible' to all things gay and lesbian in town, for the latest happenings.

GERMANY & BENELUX BERLIN

Kreuzberg & Friedrichshain

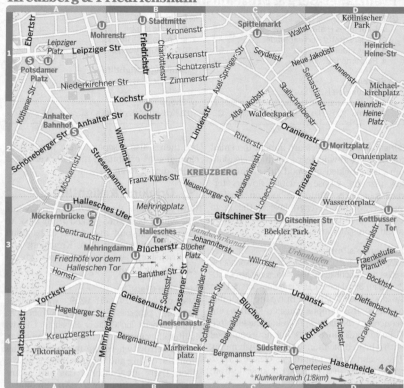

Prater Biergarten BEER GARDEN
(Map p222; ☎030-448 5688; www.pratergarten.
de; Kastanienallee 7-9; snacks €2.50-6; ⊙noon-
late Apr-Sep, weather permitting; Ⓢ Eberswalder
Strasse) Berlin's oldest beer garden has
seen beer-soaked nights since 1837 and is
still a charismatic spot for guzzling a cus-
tom-brewed Prater Pilsner beneath the ancient chestnut trees (self-service). Kids can
romp around the small play area. In foul
weather, and in winter, the adjacent beer
hall is a fine place to sample classic Berlin
dishes (mains €8 to €20).

Berghain/Panorama Bar CLUB
(Map p224; www.berghain.de; Am Wriezener Bahnhof; ⊙midnight Fri-Mon morning; Ⓡ Ostbahnhof)
Only world-class spinmasters heat up this
hedonistic bass junkie hellhole inside a labyrinthine ex-power plant. Hard-edged minimal techno dominates the ex-turbine hall
(Berghain) while house dominates at Panorama Bar one floor up. Strict door, no camer-

as. Check the website for midweek concerts
and record-release parties at the main venue and the adjacent **Kantine am Berghain**
(Map p224; ☎030-2936 0210; www.berghain.
de; Am Wriezener Bahnhof; varies; ⊙hours vary;
Ⓡ Ostbahnhof).

☆ Entertainment

Berliner Philharmonie CLASSICAL MUSIC
(Map p220; ☎tickets 030-254 888 999; www.
berliner-philharmoniker.de; Herbert-von-Kara-
jan-Strasse 1; tickets €30-100; 🚌200, Ⓢ Potsdamer Platz, Ⓡ Potsdamer Platz) This world-famous
concert hall has supreme acoustics and,
thanks to Hans Scharoun's clever terraced
vineyard design, not a bad seat in the house.
It's the home turf of the Berliner Philharmoniker, who will be led by Sir Simon Rattle
until 2018 when Russia-born Kirill Petrenko
will pick up the baton as music director.
Chamber music concerts take place at the
adjacent Kammermusiksaal.

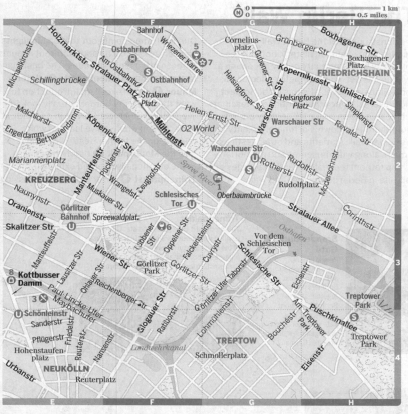

Kreuzberg & Friedrichshain

ℹ️ Information

Berlin Tourist Info - Brandenburger Tor (Map p220; ☑ 030 250 025; www.visitberlin.de; Brandenburger Tor, south wing, Pariser Platz; ⏱ 9.30am-7pm Apr-Oct, to 6pm Nov-Mar; Ⓢ Brandenburger Tor, Ⓡ Brandenburger Tor) Official tourist office. Has maps, information, tickets and souvenirs. Staff can also help with finding accommodation. There's another branch at the train station.

ℹ️ Getting There & Away

AIR

The opening of Berlin's new central airport, located about 24km southeast of the city center, has been delayed indefinitely. Check www.berlinairport.de for the latest. Flights continue to land at the city's Tegel and Schönefeld airports.

BUS

Most long-haul buses arrive at the **Zentraler Omnibusbahnhof** (ZOB; www.iob-berlin.de;

The Berlin Wall

The construction of the Berlin Wall was a unique event in human history, not only for physically bisecting a city but by becoming a dividing line between competing ideologies and political systems. It's this global impact and universal legacy that continue to fascinate people more than a quarter century after its triumphant tear-down. Fortunately, plenty of original Wall segments and other vestiges remain, along with museums and memorials, to help fathom the realities and challenges of daily life in Berlin during the Cold War.

Our illustration points out the top highlights you can visit to learn about different aspects of these often tense decades. The best place to start is at the **Gedenkstätte Berliner Mauer ❶** for an excellent introduction to what the inner-city border actually looked liked and what it meant to live in its shadow. Reflect upon what you've learned while relaxing on the former death strip that is now the **Mauerpark ❷** before heading to the emotionally charged exhibit at the **Tränenpalast ❸**, an actual border crossing

Brandenburg Gate

People around the world cheered as East and West Berliners partied together atop the Berlin Wall in front of the iconic city gate which today is a photogenic symbol of united Germany.

Tränenpalast

This modernist 1962 glass-and-steel border pavilion was dubbed 'Palace of Tears' because of the many tearful farewells that took place outside the building as East Germans and their western visitors had to say goodbye.

Potsdamer Platz

Nowhere was the death strip as wide as on the former no-man's-land around Potsdamer Platz from which sprouted a new postmodern city quarter in the 1990s. A tiny section of the Berlin Wall serves as a reminder.

Checkpoint Charlie

Only diplomats and foreigners were allowed to use this border crossing. Weeks after the Wall was built, US and Soviet tanks faced off here in one of the hottest moments of the Cold War.

Bernauer Stras

Chausseestr

Unter den Linden

Leipziger Str

pavilion. Relive the euphoria of the Wall's demise at the **Brandenburg Gate ❹**, then marvel at the revival of **Potsdamer Platz ❺** that was nothing but death strip wasteland until the 1990s. The Wall's geopolitical significance is the focus at **Checkpoint Charlie ❻**, which saw some of the tensest moments of the Cold War. Wrap up with finding your favourite mural motif at the **East Side Gallery ❼**.

It's possible to explore these sights by using a combination of walking and public transport, although a bike ride is actually the best method for getting a sense of the former Wall's erratic flow through the central city.

FAST FACTS

» **Beginning of construction:** 13 August 1961
» **Total length:** 155km
» **Height:** 3.6m
» **Weight of each segment:** 2.6 tonnes
» **Number of watchtowers:** 300

Mauerpark
Famous for its flea market and karaoke, this popular park actually occupies a converted section of death strip. A 30m segment of surviving Wall is now an official practice ground for budding graffiti artists.

JOHN FREEMAN/GETTY IMAGES ©

remnants of the Wall →

DAVID PEEVERS/GETTY IMAGES ©

Gedenkstätte Berliner Mauer
Germany's central memorial to the Berlin Wall and its victims exposes the complexity and barbaric nature of the border installation along a 1.4km stretch of the barrier's course.

Alexanderplatz

Alexander Str

East Side Gallery
Paralleling the Spree for 1.3km, this is the longest Wall vestige. After its collapse, more than a hundred international artists expressed their feelings about this historic moment in a series of colourful murals.

MEIN GOTT HILF MIR DIESE TÖDLICHE LIEBE ZU ÜBERLEBEN

DMITRY VRUBEL ©

Engelbecken

❼

WORTH A TRIP

POTSDAM

Easily reached in half an hour from central Berlin, the former royal Prussian seat of Potsdam lures visitors to its splendid Unesco-recognised palaces and parks dreamed up by 18th-century King Friedrich II (Frederick the Great). Headlining the roll call of royal pads is **Schloss Sanssouci** (☑0331-969 4200; www.spsg.de; Maulbeerallee; adult/ concession incl audioguide €12/8; ☉10am-6pm Tue-Sun Apr-Oct, to 5pm Nov-Mar; 🚌650, 695), a celebrated rococo palace and the king's favourite summer retreat. Standouts on the audioguided tour include the whimsically decorated concert hall, the intimate library and the domed Marble Hall. Admission is limited and by timed ticket only; book online (http://tickets.spsg.de) to avoid wait times and/or disappointment. The castle is surrounded by a sprawling park dotted with numerous other palaces, pavilions, fountains, statues and romantic corners.

Masurenallee 4-6; ⑤Kaiserdamm, 🚊Messe/ ICC Nord) in far western Berlin. The U2 U-Bahn line links to the centre.

TRAIN

Berlin's **Hauptbahnhof** (Main Train Station; www.berlin-hauptbahnhof.de; Europaplatz, Washingtonplatz; ⑤Hauptbahnhof, 🚊Hauptbahnhof) is in the heart of the city. From here, the U-Bahn, S-Bahn, trams and buses provide links to all parts of town.

ⓘ Getting Around

TO/FROM THE AIRPORT

From Tegel, TXL bus runs to Alexanderplatz (€2.60, 40 minutes) via Haupbahnhof every 10 minutes.

From Schönefeld, regular regional trains go to central Berlin twice hourly (€3.20, 30 minutes). S-Bahn S9 runs every 20 minutes and is handy for Friedrichshain or Prenzlauer Berg.

PUBLIC TRANSPORT

One ticket is valid on all forms of public transport. Most trips within Berlin require an AB ticket (€2.60), valid for two hours (transfers allowed, but not round trips).Tickets are available from bus drivers, vending machines at stations and aboard trams. Expect to pay cash (change given) and be sure to validate (stamp) your ticket. Plan routes at www.bvg.de.

Dresden

☑0351 / POP 512,000

There are few city silhouettes more striking than Dresden's. The classic view from the Elbe's northern bank takes in spires, towers and domes belonging to palaces, churches and stately buildings, and indeed it's hard to believe that the city was all but wiped off the map by Allied bombings in 1945.

◉ Sights

Frauenkirche   CHURCH
(www.frauenkirche-dresden.de; Neumarkt; audio guide €2.50, cupola adult/student €8/5; ☉10am-noon & 1-6pm) **FREE** The domed Frauenkirche – Dresden's most beloved symbol – has literally risen from the city's ashes. The original graced its skyline for two centuries before collapsing after the February 1945 bombing, and was rebuilt from a pile of rubble between 1994 and 2005. A spitting image of the original, it may not bear the gravitas of age but that only slightly detracts from its festive beauty inside and out. The altar, reassembled from nearly 2000 fragments, is especially striking.

★**Historisches Grünes Gewölbe**   MUSEUM
(Historic Green Vault; ☑0351-4914 2000; www.skd. museum; Residenzschloss; admission incl audioguide €14; ☉10am-6pm Wed-Mon) The Historic Green Vault displays some 3000 precious items in the same fashion as during the time of August der Starke, namely on shelves and tables without glass protection in a series of increasingly lavish rooms. Admission is by timed ticket only, and only a limited number of visitors per hour may pass through the 'dust lock'. Get advance tickets online or by phone since only 40% are sold at the palace box office for same-day admission.

★**Gemäldegalerie Alte Meister**   MUSEUM
(www.skd.museum; Zwinger, Theaterplatz 1; adult/ student €10/7.50, audioguide €3; ☉10am-6pm Tue-Sun) This astounding collection of European art from the 16th to 18th centuries boasts an incredible number of masterpieces, including Rafael's famous *Sistine Madonna*, which dominates the enormous main hall on the ground floor, as well as works by Titian, Tintoretto, Holbein, Dürer and Cranach, whose *Paradise* (1530) is particularly arresting. Upstairs you'll find an exquisite display of Rembrandt, Botticelli, Veronese, Van Dyck, Vermeer, Brueghel and Poussin. Finally, don't miss Canaletto's sumptuous portrayals of 18th-century Dresden on the top floor.

Dresden

Map scale: 0 — 500 m / 0 — 0.25 miles

Dresden

🛏 Sleeping

Hostel Mondpalast   HOSTEL €
(☎0351-563 4050; www.mondpalast.de; Louisen-strasse 77; dm/d from €15/56, liner €2; @🛜) A funky location in the thick of the Äussere Neustadt is the main draw of this out-of-this-world hostel-bar-cafe (with cheap drinks). Each funky and playful room is designed to reflect a sign of the zodiac. Bonus points for the bike rentals and the well-equipped kitchen. Breakfast is €7.

🍴 Eating

Cafe Continental   INTERNATIONAL €
(☎0351-272 1722; www.cafe-continental-dresden.de; Görlitzer Strasse 1; dishes €4-15; ⊙24hr) If the greenly lit openings behind the bar remind you of aquariums, you've hit the nail on the head, for buzzy 'Conti' was a pet store back in GDR days. Today, it's a great place to hit no matter the hour for anything from cappuccinos and cocktails to homemade cakes or a full meal. Breakfast is served until 4pm.

Zum Schiesshaus   SAXON €€
(☎0351-484 5990; www.zum-schiesshaus.de; Am Schiesshaus 19; mains €10-25; ⊙11am-1am) If you're yearning for something traditional, meaty and quintessentially Saxon, then this is the place for you. Oozing old-world atmosphere despite having been destroyed in both the Thirty Years War and WWII, this former medieval shooting range has been rebuilt

and now caters for those wanting a hearty meal washed down with plenty of local beer.

ℹ Information

Tourist Office – Frauenkirche (☑ 0351-501 501; www.dresden.de; QF Passage, Neumarkt 2; ⏰10am-7pm Mon-Fri, to 6pm Sat, to 3pm Sun) Go to the basement of the shopping mall to find the city's most central tourist office. Helpful English-speaking staff can give you advice, book rooms and tours, rent out audioguides and sell the excellent-value Dresden Cards.

ℹ Getting There & Away

Fast trains make the trip to Dresden from Berlin-Hauptbahnhof in two hours (€40) and Leipzig in 1¼ hours (€24.50).

Leipzig

☑ 0341 / POP 532,000

Hypezig! cry the papers; The New Berlin, says just about everybody. Yes, Leipzig is Saxony's coolest city, a playground for nomadic young creatives who have been displaced even by the fast-gentrifying German capital, but it's also a city of enormous history, a trade-fair mecca and solidly in the sights of music lovers due to its intrinsic connection to the lives and work of Bach, Mendelssohn and Wagner.

◉ Sights

★**Museum der Bildenden Künste**   MUSEUM
(☑ 0341-216 990; www.mdbk.de; Katharinenstrasse 10; adult/concession €5/4; ⏰10am-6pm Tue & Thu-Sun, noon-8pm Wed) This imposing modernist glass cube is the home of Leipzig's fine arts museum and its world-class collection of paintings from the 15th century to today, including works by Caspar David Friedrich, Cranach, Munch and Monet. Highlights include rooms dedicated to native sons Max Beckmann, Max Klinger and Neo Rauch. Exhibits are playfully juxtaposed and range from sculpture and installation to religious art. The collection is enormous, so set aside at least two hours to do it justice.

Zeitgeschichtliches Forum   MUSEUM
(Forum of Contemporary History; ☑ 0341-222 00; www.hdg.de/leipzig; Grimmaische Strasse 6; ⏰9am-6pm Tue-Fri, 10am-6pm Sat & Sun) FREE This fascinating, enormous and very well curated exhibit tells the political history of the GDR, from division and dictatorship to fall-of-the-Wall ecstasy and post-*Wende* blues.

It's essential viewing for anyone seeking to understand the late country's political power apparatus, the systematic oppression of regime critics, milestones in inter-German and international relations, and the opposition movement that led to its downfall.

Bach-Museum Leipzig   MUSEUM
(☑ 0341-913 70; www.bachmuseumleipzig.de; Thomaskirchhof 16; adult/concession/under 16yr €8/6/free; ⏰10am-6pm Tue-Sun) This interactive museum does more than tell you about the life and accomplishments of Johann Sebastian Bach. Learn how to date a Bach manuscript, listen to baroque instruments or treat your ears to any composition he ever wrote. The 'treasure room' downstairs displays rare original manuscripts.

🛏 Sleeping

Hostel Sleepy Lion   HOSTEL €
(☑ 0341-993 9480; www.hostel-leipzig.de; Jacobstrasse 1; dm/s/d/apt from €13.50/40.50/49/60, linen €2.50, breakfast €4; @🕿) This top-rated hostel gets our thumbs up with its clean and cheerfully painted en-suite rooms, a super-central location and clued-in staff. Every budget can be catered for in dorms sleeping four to 10, as well as private rooms and spacious 4th-floor apartments with killer views. The kitchen is very basic, however, and not really suitable for self-caterers.

🍴 Eating

Aside from locations listed here, another good place to head to is restaurant row on popular Münzgasse, just south of the city centre. Take tram 10 or 11 to 'Hohe Strasse'.

★**Reisladen**   INTERNATIONAL €
(Karl-Heine-Strasse 49; mains €3.50-4.50; ⏰11.30am-2.30pm; 🌱) If you're exploring funky Plagwitz, then this lunch-only joint will surely be top of your list for a wonderfully good value, healthy and tasty lunch. Normally with a line out the door, this local establishment has daily changing specials of rice dishes that can be taken away or eaten in; it's a great choice for vegetarians and vegans.

★**Auerbachs Keller**   GERMAN €€€
(☑ 0341-216 100; www.auerbachs-keller-leipzig.de; Mädlerpassage, Grimmaische Strasse 2-4; mains Keller €10-27, Weinstuben €33-35; ⏰Keller noon-11pm daily, Weinstuben 6-11pm Mon-Sat) Founded in 1525, Auerbachs Keller is one of Germany's best-known restaurants. It's cosy and touristy but the food's actually quite good and the

Central Leipzig

setting memorable. There are two sections: the vaulted Grosser Keller for hearty Saxonian dishes and the four historic rooms of the Historische Weinstuben for upscale German fare. Reservations highly advised.

In Goethe's *Faust*, Part I, Mephistopheles and Faust carouse here with students before riding off on a barrel.

🍷 Drinking & Nightlife

Party activity centres on three main areas: the boisterous Drallewatsch pub strip, the more upmarket theatre district around Gottschedstrasse, and the mix of trendy and alt-vibe joints along Karl-Liebknecht-Strasse (aka 'Südmeile').

ℹ Information

Tourist Office (☎ 0341-710 4260, room referral 0341-710 4255; www.leipzig.travel; Katharinenstrasse 8; ⏰ 9.30am-6pm Mon-Fri, to 4pm Sat, to 3pm Sun) Room referral, ticket sales, maps and general information. Also sells the Leipzig Card (one/three days €10.90/21.90).

ℹ Getting There & Away

Deutsche Bahn has frequent services to Frankfurt (€76, 3¾ hours), Dresden (€24.50, 1¼ hours) and Berlin (€47, 1¼ hours), though all of these can be had for considerably less by booking online several days in advance.

Central Leipzig

◎ **Top Sights**
1 Museum der Bildenden Künste B2

◎ **Sights**
2 Bach-Museum Leipzig B3
3 Zeitgeschichtliches Forum.................C3

🛏 **Sleeping**
4 Hostel Sleepy Lion...............................A1

🍴 **Eating**
5 Auerbachs Keller.................................B3

Munich

📷 089 / POP 1.38 MILLION

If you're looking for Alpine clichés, they're all here, but Munich also has plenty of unexpected cards down its dirndl. Folklore and age-old traditions exist side by side with sleek BMWs, designer boutiques and high-powered industry. Its museums include world-class collections of artistic masterpieces, and its music and cultural scenes are second only to Berlin's.

◎ Sights

Marienplatz SQUARE
(Ⓢ Marienplatz, Ⓤ Marienplatz) The epicentral heart and soul of the Altstadt, Marienplatz

Central Munich

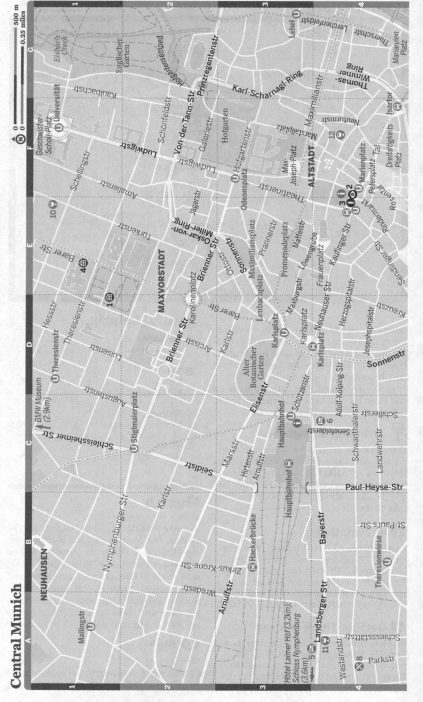

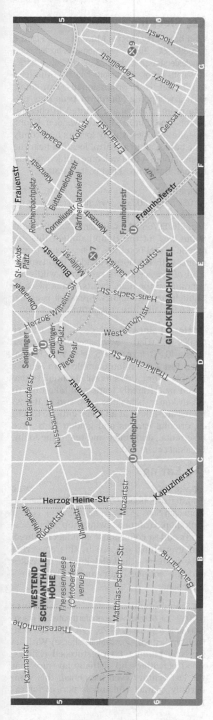

Central Munich

is a popular gathering spot and packs a lot of personality into a compact frame. It's anchored by the **Mariensäule** (Mary's Column), built in 1638 to celebrate victory over Swedish forces during the Thirty Years' War. This is the busiest spot in all Munich: throngs of tourists swarm across its expanse from early morning till late at night.

Alte Pinakothek   MUSEUM
(☎089-238 0526; www.pinakothek.de; Barer Strasse 27; adult/child €4/2, Sun €1, audioguide €4.50; ☺10am-8pm Tue, to 6pm Wed-Sun; 🚋Pinakotheken, 🚇Pinakotheken) Munich's main repository of Old European Masters is crammed with all the major players that decorated canvases between the 14th and 18th centuries. This neoclassical temple was masterminded by Leo von Klenze and is a delicacy even if you can't tell your Rembrandt from your Rubens. The collection is world famous for its exceptional quality and depth, especially when it comes to German masters.

The Alte Pinakothek is under much-needed renovation until mid-2018, with parts of the building taking turns to close while work is carried out.

Neue Pinakothek   MUSEUM
(☎089-2380 5195; www.pinakothek.de; Barer Strasse 29; adult/child €7/5, Sun €1; ☺10am-6pm Thu-Mon, to 8pm Wed; 🚋Pinakotheken, 🚇Pinakotheken) The Neue Pinakothek harbours a well-respected collection of 19th- and early-20th-century paintings and sculpture, from rococo to *Jugendstil* (art nouveau). All the world-famous

GERMANY & BENELUX MUNICH

household names get wall space here, including crowd-pleasing French impressionists such as Monet, Cézanne and Degas as well as Van Gogh, whose boldly pigmented *Sunflowers* (1888) radiates cheer.

Schloss Nymphenburg   PALACE
(www.schloss-nymphenburg.de; adult/concession €6/5; ⊘9am-6pm Apr–mid-Oct, 10am-4pm mid-Oct–Mar; ⊜Schloss Nymphenburg) This commanding palace and its lavish gardens sprawl around 5km northwest of the Altstadt. Begun in 1664 as a villa for Electress Adelaide of Savoy, the stately pile was extended over the next century to create the royal family's summer residence. Franz Duke of Bavaria, head of the once-royal Wittelsbach family, still occupies an apartment here.

BMW Museum   MUSEUM
(www.bmw-welt.de; Am Olympiapark 2; adult/concession €10/7; ⊘10am-6pm Tue-Sun; ⊍Olympiazentrum) This silver, bowl-shaped museum comprises seven themed 'houses' that examine the development of BMW's product line and include sections on motorcycles and motor racing. Even if you can't tell a head gasket from a crankshaft, the interior design – with its curvy retro feel, futuristic bridges, squares and huge backlit wall screens – is reason enough to visit.

WORTH A TRIP

DACHAU

KZ-Gedenkstätte Dachau (Dachau Concentration Camp Memorial Site; ☑08131-669 970; www.kz-gedenkstaette-dachau.de; Peter-Roth-Strasse 2a, Dachau; museum admission free; ⊘9am-5pm Tue-Sun) was the Nazis' first concentration camp, built by Heinrich Himmler in March 1933 to house political prisoners. All in all, it 'processed' more than 200,000 inmates, killing at least 43,000, and is now a haunting memorial. Expect to spend two to three hours here to fully absorb the exhibits.

Dachau is about 16km northwest of central Munich. The S2 makes the trip from Munich Hauptbahnhof to the station in Dachau in 21 minutes. You'll need a two-zone ticket (€5.20). Here change to frequent bus 726 (direction Saubachsiedlung) to get to the camp.

🛏 Sleeping

Wombats City Hostel Munich   HOSTEL €
(☑089-5998 9180; www.wombats-hostels.com; Senefelderstrasse 1; dm €23-32, d €84; ⊡@🛜; ⊜Hauptbahnhof, ⊍Hauptbahnhof) Munich's top hostel is a professionally run affair with a whopping 300 dorm beds plus private rooms. Dorms are painted in cheerful pastels and outfitted with wooden floors, en-suite facilities, sturdy lockers and comfy pine bunks, all in a central location near the train station. A free welcome drink awaits in the bar. Buffet breakfast costs €4.30.

Meininger's   HOSTEL, HOTEL €
(☑089-5499 8023; www.meininger-hostels.de; Landsbergerstrasse 20; dm/s/d without breakfast from €16/50/66; 🛜; ⊜Holzapfelstrasse) About 800m west of the Hauptbahnhof, this energetic hostel-hotel has basic, clean, bright rooms with big dorms divided into two for a bit of privacy. Room rates vary wildly depending on the date, events taking place in Munich, and occupancy. Breakfast is an extra €6.90; bike hire costs from €8 per day.

★Hotel Laimer Hof   HOTEL €€
(☑089-178 0380; www.laimerhof.de; Laimer Strasse 40; s/d from €65/75; ⊡@🛜; ⊜Romanplatz) Just a five-minute amble from Schloss Nymphenburg, this superbly tranquil refuge is run by a friendly team who take time to get to know their guests. No two of the 23 rooms are alike, but all boast antique touches, oriental carpets and golden beds. Free bike rental, and coffee and tea in the lobby. Breakfast costs €10.

🍴 Eating

★Marais   CAFE €
(Parkstrasse 2; dishes €5-13; ⊘8am-8pm Tue-Sat, 10am-6pm Sun; �; ⊜Holzapfelstrasse) Is it a junk shop, a cafe or a sewing shop? Well, Westend's oddest coffeehouse is in fact all three, and everything you see in this converted haberdashery – the knick-knacks, the cakes and the antique chair you're sitting on – is for sale.

★Fraunhofer   BAVARIAN €€
(☑089-266 460; www.fraunhofertheater.de; Fraunhoferstrasse 9; mains €7-25; ⊘4.30pm-1am Mon-Fri, 10am-1am Sat; ⊘; ⊜Müllerstrasse) With its screechy parquet floors, stuccoed ceilings, wood panelling and virtually no trace that the last century even happened, this wonderfully characterful inn is perfect for exploring the region with a fork. The menu is

a seasonally adapted checklist of southern German favourites but also features at least a dozen vegetarian dishes and the odd exotic ingredient.

Wirtshaus in der Au   BAVARIAN €€

(📞089-448 1400; Lilienstrasse 51; mains €10-16; ⏲5pm-midnight Mon-Fri, from 10am Sat & Sun; 🚋Deutsches Museum) This Bavarian tavern's simple slogan is 'Beer and dumplings since 1901', and it's that time-honoured staple (the dumpling) that's the speciality here (the tavern even runs a dumpling-making course in English). Once a brewery, the space-rich dining area has chunky tiled floors, a lofty ceiling and a crackling fireplace in winter. When spring springs, the beer garden fills.

🍸 Drinking & Nightlife

⭐ Alter Simpl   PUB

(www.eggerlokale.de; Türkenstrasse 57; ⏲11am-3am Mon-Fri, to 4am Sat & Sun; 🚋Schellingstrasse) Thomas Mann and Hermann Hesse used to knock 'em back at this well-scuffed and wood-panelled thirst parlour. A bookish ambience still pervades, making this an apt spot to curl up with a weighty tome over a few Irish ales. The curious name is an abbreviation of the satirical magazine *Simplicissimus*.

Hofbräuhaus   BEER HALL

(📞089-290 136 100; www.hofbraeuhaus.de; Am Platzl 9; 1L beer €8, mains €10-20; ⏲9am-11.30pm; 🚋Kammerspiele, Ⓢ Marienplatz, Ⓛ Marienplatz) Every visitor to Munich should make a pilgrimage to this mothership of all beer halls, if only once. There is a range of spaces in which to do your *Maß* lifting: the horse chestnut-shaded garden, the main hall next to the oompah band, tables opposite the industrial-scale kitchen and quieter corners.

⭐ Augustiner Bräustuben   BEER HALL

(📞089-507 047; www.braeustuben.de; Landsberger Strasse 19; ⏲10am-midnight 🚋Holzapfelstrasse) Depending on the wind, an aroma of hops envelops you as you approach this traditional beer hall inside the Augustiner brewery. The Bavarian fare is superb, especially the *Schweinshaxe* (pork knuckle). Due to the location the atmosphere in the evenings is slightly more authentic than that of its city-centre cousins, with fewer tourists at the long tables.

OKTOBERFEST

Hordes come to Munich for **Oktoberfest** (www.oktoberfest.de), running the 15 days before the first Sunday in October. Reserve accommodation well ahead and go early in the day so you can grab a seat in one of the hangar-sized beertents spread across the Theresienwiese grounds, about 1km southwest of the Hauptbahnhof. While there is no entrance fee, those €11 1L steins of beer (called *Maß*) add up fast. Although its origins are in the marriage celebrations of Crown Prince Ludwig in 1810, there's nothing regal about this beery bacchanal now: expect mobs, expect to meet new and drunken friends, expect decorum to vanish as night sets in and you'll have a blast.

🛈 Information

Tourist Office – Marienplatz (📞089-2339 6500; www.muenchen.de; Marienplatz 2; ⏲10am-8pm Mon-Fri, to 4pm Sat, to 2pm Sun Apr-Dec, closed Sun Jan-Mar; Ⓤ Marienplatz, Ⓢ Marienplatz) There's another branch at the Hauptbahnhof (📞089-2339 6500; Bahnhofplatz 2; ⏲9am-8pm Mon-Sat, 10am-6pm Sun; 🚋Hauptbahnhof, Ⓤ Hauptbahnhof, Ⓢ Hauptbahnhof).

🛈 Getting There & Away

Frequent fast and direct service include trains to Nuremberg (€55, 1¼ hours), Frankfurt (€101, 3¼ hours), Berlin (€130, six hours) and Vienna (€91.20, four hours), as well as twice-daily trains to Prague (€69.10 six hours).

Berchtesgaden

📞08652 / POP 7800

Steeped in myth and legend, Berchtesgaden and the surrounding countryside is almost preternaturally beautiful. Framed by six formidable mountain ranges and home to Germany's second-highest mountain, the Watzmann (2713m), its dreamy, fir-lined valleys are filled with gurgling streams and peaceful Alpine villages. Alas, Berchtesgaden's history is also indelibly tainted by the Nazi period. The area is easily visited on a day trip from Salzburg, Austria.

DON'T MISS

GERMANY'S HIGHEST PEAK

An outdoor paradise for skiers and hikers, Garmisch-Partenkirchen is blessed with a fabled setting a snowball's throw from Germany's highest peak, 2962m-high **Zugspitze** (www.zugspitze. de; return adult/child €51/29.50; ☺ train 8.15am-2.15pm). On good days, views from Germany's rooftop extend into four countries. The round trip starts in Garmisch aboard a cogwheel train (Zahnradbahn) that chugs along the mountain base to the Eibsee, an idyllic forest lake. From here, the Eibsee-Seilbahn, a super-steep cable car, swings to the top at 2962m. When you're done admiring the views, the Gletscherbahn cable car takes you to the Zugspitze glacier at 2600m, from where the cogwheel train heads back to Garmisch.

Numerous tour operators run day trips to Garmisch-Partenkirchen from Munich but there's also at least hourly direct train service (€20.10,1¼ hour).

⊙ Sights

Eagle's Nest   HISTORIC SITE
(Kehlsteinhaus; ☐ 08652-2969; www.kehlstein-haus.de; Obersalzberg; adult/child €16.10/9.30; ☺ buses 7.40am-4pm mid-May–Oct) The Eagle's Nest was built as a mountaintop retreat for Hitler, and gifted to him on his 50th birthday. It took some 3000 workers only two years to carve the precipitous 6km-long mountain road, cut a 124m-long tunnel and a brass-panelled lift through the rock, and build the lodge itself (now a restaurant). It can only be reached by special shuttle bus from the Kehlsteinhaus bus station.

Königssee   LAKE
Crossing the serenely picturesque, emerald-green Königssee makes for some unforgettable memories and once-in-a-lifetime photo opportunities. Cradled by steep mountain walls some 5km south of Berchtesgaden, the Königssee is Germany's highest lake (603m), with drinkably pure waters shimmering into fjordlike depths. Bus 841/842 makes the trip out here from the Berchtesgaden train station roughly every hour.

❶ Getting There & Away

Bus 840 connects the train stations in Berchtesgaden and Salzburg twice hourly (50 minutes).Travelling from Munich by train involves a change to a bus at Freilassing (€32.80, 2½ hours).

Romantic Road

Stretching 400km from the vineyards of Würzburg to the foot of the Alps, the Romantic Road (Romantische Strasse) is by far the most popular of Germany's themed holiday routes. It passes through more than two-dozen cities and towns, most famously Rothenburg ob der Tauber.

❶ Getting There & Around

Frankfurt and Munich are the most popular gateways for exploring the Romantic Road, especially if you decide to take the **Romantic Road Coach** (www.romanticroadcoach.de). From April to October this special service runs one coach daily in each direction between Frankfurt and Füssen (for Neuschwanstein) via Munich; the entire trip takes around 12 hours. There's no charge for breaking the journey and continuing the next day. Buses get incredibly crowded in summer. Tickets are available for the entire route or for segments. Buy them online or from travel agents or Reisezentrum offices in larger train stations.

Füssen

Nestled at the foot of the Alps, tourist-busy Füssen is the southern climax of the Romantic Road, with the nearby castles of Neuschwanstein and Hohenschwangau the highlight of many a southern Germany trip.

⊙ Sights

★**Schloss Neuschwanstein**   CASTLE
(☐ tickets 08362-930 830; www.neuschwanstein. de; Neuschwansteinstrasse 20; adult/concession €12/11, incl Hohenschwangau €23/21; ☺ 9am-6pm Apr–mid-Oct, 10am-4pm mid-Oct–Mar) Appearing through the mountaintops like a mirage, Schloss Neuschwanstein was the model for Disney's *Sleeping Beauty* castle. King Ludwig II planned this fairy-tale pile himself, with the help of a stage designer rather than an architect. He envisioned it as a giant stage on which to re-create the world of Germanic mythology, inspired by the operatic works of his friend Rich-

ard Wagner. The most impressive room is the **Sängersaal** (Minstrels' Hall), whose frescos depict scenes from the opera *Tannhäuser*.

Built as a romantic medieval castle, work started in 1869 and, like so many of Ludwig's grand schemes, was never finished.

Schloss Hohenschwangau CASTLE
(📞08362-930 830; www.hohenschwangau.de; Alpseestrasse 30; adult/concession €12/11, incl Neuschwanstein €23/21; ⊙8am-5.30pm Apr–mid-Oct, 9am-3.30pm mid-Oct–Mar) King Ludwig II grew up at the sun-yellow Schloss Hohenschwangau and later enjoyed summers here until his death in 1886. His father, Maximilian II, built this palace in a neo-Gothic style atop 12th-century ruins left by Schwangau knights. Far less showy than Neuschwanstein, Hohenschwangau has a distinctly lived-in feel where every piece of furniture is a used original. After his father died, Ludwig's main alteration was having stars, illuminated with hidden oil lamps, painted on the ceiling of his bedroom.

Rothenburg ob der Tauber

📞 09861 / POP 10,900

With its jumble of half-timbered houses enclosed by Germany's best-preserved ramparts, Rothenburg ob der Tauber lays on the medieval cuteness with a trowel. It's an essential stop on the Romantic Road but, alas, overcrowding can detract from its charm. Visit early or late in the day (or, ideally, stay overnight) to experience this historic wonderland sans crowds.

⊙ Sights

Jakobskirche CHURCH
(Church of St Jacob; Klingengasse 1; adult/concession €2.50/1.50; ⊙9am-5.15pm Mon-Sat, 10.45am-5.15pm Sun) One of the few places of worship in Bavaria to charge admission, Rothenburg's Lutheran parish church was begun in the 14th century and finished in the 15th. The building sports some wonderfully aged stained-glass windows but the top attraction is Tilman Riemenschneider's **Heilig Blut Altar** (Altar of the Holy Blood). The gilded cross above the main scene depicting the Last Supper incorporates Rothenburg's most treasured reliquary – a rock crystal capsule said to contain three drops of Christ's blood.

ℹ CASTLE TICKETS

Both Hohenschwangau and Neuschwanstein must be seen on guided 35-minute tours (in German or English). Timed tickets are only available from the **Ticket-Center** (📞08362-930 830; www.hohenschwangau.de; Alpenseestrasse 12; ⊙8am-5.30pm Apr–mid-Oct, 9am-3.30pm mid-Oct–Mar) at the foot of the castles and may be reserved online until two days prior to your visit (recommended). If visiting both castles on the same day, the Hohenschwangau tour is scheduled first, with enough time for the steep 30- to 40-minute walk between the castles. The footsore can travel by bus or by horse-drawn carriage.

Rathausturm HISTORIC BUILDING
(Town Hall Tower; Marktplatz; adult/concession €2/0.50; ⊙9.30am-12.30pm & 1-5pm daily Apr-Oct, 10.30am-2pm & 2.30-6pm daily Dec, noon-3pm Sat & Sun rest of year) The Rathaus on Marktplatz was begun in Gothic style in the 14th century and was completed during the Renaissance. Climb the 220 steps of the medieval town hall to the viewing platform of the Rathausturm to be rewarded with widescreen views of the Tauber.

🛏 Sleeping

Pension Birgit B&B €
(📞09861-6107; www.birgit-pension.de; Wenggasse 16; s/d from €30/40; 🛜) Basic owner-run pension that offers Rothenburg's cheapest rooms in an epicentral location. Rates include a modest buffet breakfast.

✗ Eating

Gasthof Butz GERMAN €
(📞09861-2201; Kapellenplatz 4; mains €7-15; ⊙noon-11pm Fri-Wed; 🛜) For a quick, no-nonsense goulash, schnitzel or roast pork, lug your weary legs to this locally adored, family-run inn in a former brewery. In summer two flowery beer gardens beckon. It also rents a dozen simply furnished rooms (double €36 to €75).

ℹ Getting There & Away

The Romantic Road Coach pauses in town for 45 minutes. There are hourly trains to/from Steinach, a transfer point for service to Würzburg (€12.90, 1¼ hours).

Würzburg

☎ 0931 / POP 133,800

Tucked in among river valleys lined with vineyards, Würzburg beguiles long before you reach the city centre and is renowned for its art, architecture and delicate wines. Its crowning architectural glory is the Residenz, one of the finest baroque structures in Germany and a Unesco World Heritage Site.

◉ Sights

★ **Würzburg Residenz**   PALACE

(www.residenz-wuerzburg.de; Balthasar-Neumann-Promenade; adult/concession/under 18yr €7.50/6.50/free; ⏰ 9am-6pm Apr-Oct, 10am-4.30pm Nov-Mar, 45min English tours 11am & 3pm, also 4.30pm Apr-Oct) The vast Unesco-listed Residenz, built by 18th-century architect Balthasar Neumann as the home of the local prince-bishops, is one of Germany's most important and beautiful baroque palaces. Top billing goes to the brilliant zigzagging **Treppenhaus** (Staircase) lidded by what still is the world's largest fresco, a masterpiece by

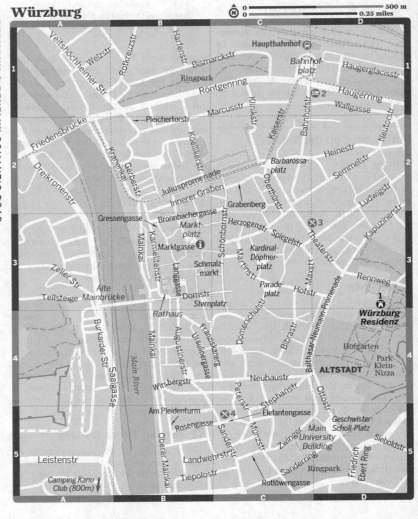

Würzburg

Giovanni Battista Tiepolo depicting allegories of the four then-known continents.

🛏 Sleeping & Eating

Babelfish   HOSTEL €
(☑0931-304 0430; www.babelfish-hostel.de; Haugerring 2; dm €17-23, s/d €45/70) With a name inspired by a creature in Douglas Adams' novel *The Hitchhiker's Guide to the Galaxy*, this uncluttered and spotlessly clean hostel has 74 beds spread over two floors and a sunny rooftop terrace. The communal areas are an inviting place to down a few beers in the evening and there's a well-equipped guest kitchen.

Capri & Blaue Grotto   ITALIAN €
(Elefantengasse 1; pizzas €5.90-8.30, other mains €6.90-10.90; ⊙11.30am-2pm & 6-10.30pm) This outpost of the *bel paese* has been plating up pronto pasta and pizza since 1952 – it was in fact Germany's first ever pizzeria.

★ Bürgerspital Weinstube   WINE RESTAURANT €€
(☑0931-352 880; Theaterstrasse 19; mains €13-24; ⊙10am-11pm) If you are going to eat out just once in Würzburg, the aromatic and cosy nooks of this labyrinthine medieval place probably provide the top local experience. Choose from a broad selection of Franconian wines (some of Germany's best) and wonderful regional dishes and snacks, including *Mostsuppe* (a tasty wine soup).

ℹ Information

Tourist Office (☑0931-372 398; www.wuerzburg.de; Marktplatz 9; ⊙10am-5pm Mon-Fri, 10am-2pm Sat & Sun, closed Sun Nov-Apr) Within the attractive Falkenhaus this efficient office can help you with room reservations and tour booking.

ℹ Getting There & Away

The Romantic Road Coach stops next to the Hauptbahnhof. Frequent trains run to Bamberg

Würzburg

◎ Top Sights

(€20.10, one hour), Frankfurt (€35, 1¼ hours), Nuremberg (from €20.30, one hour) and Rothenburg ob der Tauber (€12.90, 1¼ hour).

Nuremberg
☑0911 / POP 510,600

Nuremberg (Nürnberg) woos visitors with its wonderfully restored medieval Altstadt, its grand castle and, in December, its magical *Christkindlmarkt* (Christmas market). The town played a key role during the Nazi years. It was here that the fanatical party rallies were held, the boycott of Jewish businesses began and the anti-Semitic Nuremberg Laws were enacted. After WWII the city was chosen as the site of the Nuremberg Trials of Nazi war criminals.

◉ Sights

The city centre is best explored on foot but the Nazi-related sights are a tram ride away.

★ Kaiserburg   CASTLE
(Imperial Castle; ☑0911-244 6590; www.kaiserburg-nuernberg.de; Auf der Burg; adult/concession incl Sinwell Tower €7/6, Palas & Museum €5.50/4.50; ⊙9am-6pm Apr-Sep, 10am-4pm Oct-Mar) This enormous castle complex above the Altstadt poignantly reflects Nuremberg's medieval might. The main attraction is a tour of the newly renovated residential wing (**Palas**) to see the lavish Knights' and Imperial Hall, a Romanesque double chapel and an exhibit on the inner workings of the Holy Roman Empire. This segues to the **Kaiserburg Museum**, which focuses on the castle's military and building history. Elsewhere, enjoy panoramic views from the **Sinwell Tower** or peer 48m down into the **Deep Well**.

Memorium Nuremberg Trials   MEMORIAL
(☑0911-3217 9372; www.memorium-nuremberg.de; Bärenschanzstrasse 72; adult/concession incl audioguide €5/3; ⊙10am-6pm Wed-Mon) Göring, Hess, Speer and 21 other Nazi leaders were tried for crimes against peace and humanity by the Allies in **Schwurgerichtssaal 600** (Court Room 600) of this still-working courthouse. Today the room forms part of an engaging exhibit detailing the background, progression and impact of the trials using film, photographs, audiotape and even the original defendants' dock. To get here, take the U1 towards Bärenschanze and get off at Sielstrasse.

Reichsparteitagsgelände HISTORIC SITE
(Luitpoldhain; ☏0911-231 5666; www.museen-nuernberg.de; Bayernstrasse 110; grounds free, documentation centre adult/concession incl audioguide €5/3; ⏰grounds 24hr, documentation centre 9am-6pm Mon-Fri, 10am-6pm Sat & Sun) If you've ever wondered where the infamous black-and-white images of ecstatic Nazi supporters hailing their Führer were taken, it was here in Nuremberg. Much of the grounds were destroyed during Allied bombing raids, but enough remain to get a sense of the megalomania behind it, especially after visiting the excellent **Dokumentationszentrum** (Documentation Centre) served by tram 9 from the Hauptbahnhof.

🛏 Sleeping

DJH Hostel HOSTEL €
(☏0911-2309360; www.nuernberg.jugendherberge.de; Burg 2; dm from €31.90) Open year round, this youth hostel is a real trip-stopper with a standard of facilities many four-star hotels would envy. Fully revamped a few years ago, the old Kornhaus is a dramatic building itself, but now sports funky corridors, crisply maintained dorms with super-modern bathrooms, a canteen, a bar and very helpful staff.

Five Reasons HOSTEL €
(☏0911-9928 6625; www.five-reasons.de; Frauentormauer 42; dm/d from €23/69; @🛜) Crisply appointed, newly renovated and rebranded 90-bed hostel with spotless dorms, the trendiest hostel bathrooms you are ever likely to encounter, pre-made beds, card keys, a fully equipped kitchen, a small bar and very nice staff. Breakfast is an extra €3.10 to €5.80 depending on what option you choose. Overall a great place to lay your head.

🍴 Eating

Don't leave without trying the famous finger-sized *Nürnberger Bratwürste* sausages.

Café am Trödelmarkt CAFE €
(Trödelmarkt 42; dishes €4-8.50; ⏰9am-6pm Mon-Sat, 11am-6pm Sun) A gorgeous place on a sunny day, this multilevel waterfront cafe overlooks the covered Henkersteg bridge. It's especially popular for its continental breakfasts, and has fantastic cakes, as well as good blackboard lunchtime specials between 11am and 2pm.

⭐Albrecht Dürer Stube FRANCONIAN €€
(☏0911-227 209; www.albrecht-duerer-stube.de; cnr Albrecht-Dürer-Strasse & Agnesgasse; mains €7-15; ⏰6pm-midnight Mon-Sat, 11.30am-2.30pm Fri & Sun) This unpretentious and intimate restaurant has a Dürer-inspired dining room, prettily laid tables, a ceramic stove keeping things toasty when they're not outside and a menu of Nuremberg sausages, steaks, sea fish, seasonal specials, Franconian wine and *Landbier* (regional beer). There aren't many tables so booking ahead at weekends is recommended.

ℹ Information

Tourist Office (☏0911-233 60; www.tourismus.nuernberg.de; Hauptmarkt 18; ⏰9am-6pm Mon-Sat year round, plus 10am-4pm Sun Apr-Oct)

ℹ Getting There & Away

Rail connections from Nuremberg include Frankfurt (€55, two hours) and Munich (€55, 1½ hours).

Heidelberg

☏06221 / POP 152,435

Surrounded by forest 93km south of Frankfurt, Germany's oldest and most famous university town is renowned for its baroque Altstadt, spirited student atmosphere, beautiful riverside setting and evocative half-ruined hilltop castle, which draw 11.8 million visitors a year. They follow in the footsteps of the late-18th- and early-19th-century romantics, most notably the poet Goethe.

◎ Sights

⭐Schloss Heidelberg CASTLE
(☏06221-658 880; www.schloss-heidelberg.de; adult/child incl Bergbahn €6/4, tours €4/2, audioguide €4; ⏰grounds 24hr, castle 8am-6pm, English tours hourly 11.15am-4.15pm Mon-Fri, 10.15am-4.15pm Sat & Sun Apr-Oct, reduced tours Nov-Mar) Towering over the Altstadt, Heidelberg's ruined Renaissance castle cuts a romantic figure, especially across the Neckar River when illuminated at night. Attractions include the world's largest wine cask and fabulous views. It's reached either via a steep, cobbled trail in about 10 minutes or by taking the **Bergbahn** (cogwheel train) from Kornmarkt station. The only way to see the less-than-scintillating interior is by tour, which can be safely skipped. After 6pm you can stroll the grounds for free.

⭐Philosophenweg TRAIL
(Philosophers' Walk; south bank of the Neckar River) Winding past monuments, towers, ruins, a

beer garden and an enormous Thingstätte (amphitheatre; built by the Nazis in 1935), the 2.5km-long Philosophers' Walk has captivating views of Heidelberg's Schloss, especially at sunset when the city is bathed in a reddish glow. Access is easiest via the steep Schlangenweg from **Alte Brücke** (Karl-Theodor-Brücke).

🛏 Sleeping

Steffis Hostel   HOSTEL €
(☑06221-778 2772; www.hostel-heidelberg.de; Alte Eppelheimer Strasse 50; dm from €18, s/d/f without bathroom from €45/56/100; ☺reception 8am-10pm; P@🛜) In a 19th-century tobacco factory a block north of the Hauptbahnhof, accessed via an industrial-size lift (elevator), Steffis offers bright, well-lit dorms and rooms (all with shared bathrooms), a colourful lounge that's great for meeting fellow travellers, a spacious kitchen and an old-school hostel vibe. Breakfast costs €3. Perks include tea, coffee and free bike rental.

🍴 Eating & Drinking

Die Kuh Die Lacht   BURGERS €
(www.diekuhdielacht.com; Hauptstrasse 133; mains €6.50-10; ☺11am-11pm Mon-Sat, noon-10pm Sun; 🏠) Since it opened in 2015, this sleek burger joint has been packed to the rafters. Its 18 different, all-natural burgers are handmade on the premises, with choices like chicken caesar, barbecued beef, a Mexican burger with beans and corn, as well as veggie options including a tofu burger and a falafel burger. Sides include onion rings or fried bacon.

KulturBrauerei   MICROBREWERY
(www.heidelberger-kulturbrauerei.de; Leyergasse 6; ☺7am-midnight) With its wood-plank floor, chairs from a Spanish monastery and black iron chandeliers, this brewpub is an atmospheric spot to quaff the house brews (including many seasonal specialities) in the enchanting beer garden. Soak them up with time-tested local dishes such as homemade sausages with cream cheese, radish and dark bread. It also has some lovely **hotel rooms** (☑06221-502 980; d €120-180; 🛜).

❶ Information

Tourist Office (☑06221-584 4414; www.heidelberg-marketing.de) There are branches at Hauptbahnhof (☑06221-584 4444; www.heidelberg-marketing.de; Willy-Brandt-Platz 1; ☺9am-7pm Mon-Sat, 10am-6pm Sun Apr-Oct,

OFF THE BEATEN TRACK

SPEYER'S CATHEDRAL

Begun in 1030 by Emperor Konrad II of the Salian dynasty, the extraordinary Romanesque cathedral **Kaiserdom** (http://bistum-speyer.de; Domplatz; crypt adult/child €3.50/1, tower €6/3; ☺cathedral & crypt 9am-7pm Apr-Oct, to 5pm Nov-Mar, tower 10am-5pm Mon-Sat, noon-5pm Sun Apr-Oct)in the town of Speyer is a World Heritage Site. Its square red towers and green copper dome float majestically above Speyer's rooftops; you can climb the 304 steps of the **southwest tower** to reach the 60m-high viewing platform for a spectacular panorama. Other highlights include the fascinating crypt and 19th-century paintings in the **Kaisersaal**.

Speyer, which also has some fine museums and the remains of a medieval synagogue, is easily reached by S-Bahn from Heidelberg (€12, 50 minutes).

9am-6pm Mon-Sat Nov-Mar), right outside the main train station, and on Marktplatz (Marktplatz 10; ☺8am-5pm Mon-Fri, 10am-5pm Sat), in the old town.

❶ Getting There & Away

From the station, 3km west of the castle, there are at least hourly train services to/from Frankfurt (€18 to €29, one hour to 1½ hours) and Stuttgart (€19 to €39, 40 minutes to 1½ hours).

Black Forest

The Black Forest (Schwarzwald) gets its name from its dark canopy of evergreens. Let winding backroads take you through misty vales, fairy-tale woodlands and villages that radiate earthy authenticity. It's not nature wild and remote, but bucolic and picturesque. And, yes, there are many, many places to buy cuckoo clocks.

Triberg

☑07722 / POP 5000
Cuckoo-clock capital, black forest–cake pilgrimage site and Germany's highest waterfall – Triberg is a torrent of Schwarzwald superlatives and attracts a ton of guests.

◉ Sights

★ **Triberger Wasserfälle**   WATERFALL
(adult/concession/family €4/3.50/9.50; ⏰9am-7pm Mar-early Nov, 25-30 Dec) Niagara they ain't but Germany's highest waterfalls do exude their own wild romanticism. The Gutach River feeds the seven-tiered falls, which drop a total of 163m and are illuminated until 10pm.

✕ Eating

★ **Café Schäfer**   CAFE €
(☎07722-4465; www.cafe-schaefer-triberg.de; Hauptstrasse 33; cake €3-4; ⏰9am-6pm Mon, Tue,

Black Forest

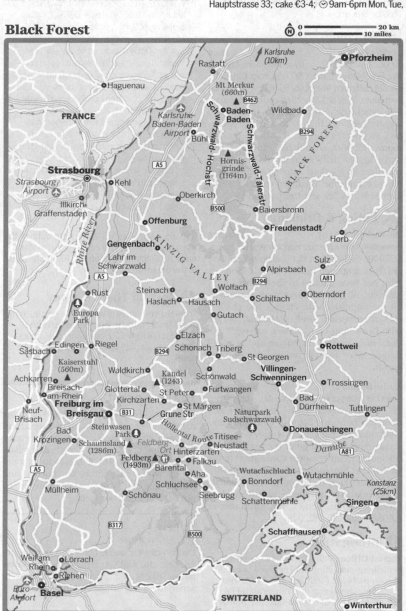

0 ————— 20 km
0 ————— 10 miles

Karlsruhe (10km)
Pforzheim
Rastatt
Haguenau
Mt Merkur (660m)
Wildbad
FRANCE
Karlsruhe-Baden-Baden Airport
Baden-Baden
Bühl
Schwarzwald-Hochstr
Schwarzwald-Talerstr
Hornisgrinde (1164m)
BLACK FOREST
Strasbourg
Strasbourg Airport
Kehl
Oberkirch
Baiersbronn
Illkirch-Graffenstaden
Rhine River
Offenburg
Freudenstadt
Horb
Gengenbach
KINZIG VALLEY
Lahr im Schwarzwald
Alpirsbach
Sulz
Rust
Steinach
Wolfach
B294
Oberndorf
Haslach
Hausach
Schiltach
A81
Europa Park
Gutach
Säsbach
Edingen
Riegel
Elzach
Rottweil
Schonach
Triberg
Kaiserstuhl (560m)
Waldkirch
Kandel (1243)
Schönwald
St Georgen
Villingen-Schwenningen
Achkarren
Breisach-am-Rhein
Glottertal
St Peter
Furtwangen
Trossingen
Kirchzarten
Bad Dürrheim
Tuttlingen
Neuf-Brisach
Freiburg im Breisgau
B31
St Märgen
Grune Str
Naturpark Sudschwarzwald
Donaueschingen
Bad Krozingen
Steinwasen Park
Höllental Route
Titisee-Neustadt
Danube
A81
Schauinsland (1286m)
Feldberg-Ort
Hinterzarten
Müllheim
Feldberg (1493m)
Bärental
Falkau
Konstanz (25km)
A5
Aha
Wutachschlucht
Wutachmühle
Schönau
Schluchsee
Bonndorf
Seebrugg
Schattenmühle
Singen
B317
B500
Schaffhausen
Weil am Rhein
Lörrach
Riehen
Euro-Airport
Basel
SWITZERLAND
Winterthur
A5
B462
B294
B500
A5

Thu & Fri, 8am-6pm Sat, 11am-6pm Sun) Confectioner Claus Schäfer uses the original 1915 recipe for Black Forest gateau to prepare this sinful treat that layers chocolate cake perfumed with cherry brandy whipped cream and sour cherries and wraps it all in more cream and shaved chocolate. Trust us, it's worth the calories.

ℹ Getting There & Away

The Schwarzwaldbahn train line loops southeast to Konstanz (€23.50, 1½ hours, hourly), and northwest to Offenburg (€12.10, 46 minutes, hourly), from where you can connect to other cities.

Freiburg

☎ 0761 / POP 224,200

Sitting at the foot of the Black Forest's wooded slopes and vineyards, Freiburg is a sunny, cheerful university town, its medieval Altstadt a story-book tableau of gabled town houses, cobblestone lanes and cafe-rimmed plazas. Party-loving students spice up the local nightlife.

◉ Sights

★ **Freiburger Münster**   CATHEDRAL
(Freiburg Minster; ☎ 0761-202 790; www.freiburgermuenster.info; Münsterplatz; tower adult/concession €2/1.50; ⊙ 9.30am-5pm, tower 9.30am-4.45pm Mon-Sat, 1-5pm Sun) With its lacy spires, cheeky gargoyles and intricate entrance portal, Freiburg's 11th-century minster cuts an impressive figure above the central market square. It has dazzling kaleidoscopic stained-glass windows that were mostly financed by medieval guilds and a high altar with a masterful triptych by Dürer protege Hans Baldung Grien. Square at the base, the tower becomes an octagon higher up and is crowned by a filigreed 116m-high spire.

On clear days you can spy the Vosges Mountains in France.

🛏 Sleeping

Black Forest Hostel   HOSTEL €
(☎ 0761-881 7870; www.blackforest-hostel.de; Kartäuserstrasse 33; dm €17-27, s/d €35/58, linen €4; ⊙ reception 7am-1am; @) Boho budget digs with chilled common areas, a shared kitchen, bike rental and spacey stainless-steel showers. It's a five-minute walk from the town centre.

✗ Eating & Drinking

Markthalle   MARKET €
(www.markthalle-freiburg.de; Martinsgasse 235; light meals €4-8; ⊙ 8am-8pm Mon-Thu, to midnight Fri & Sat) Eat your way around the world – from curry to sushi, oysters to antipasti – at the food counters in this historic market hall, nicknamed 'Fressgässle'.

Hausbrauerei Feierling   BEER GARDEN
(Gerberau 46; ⊙ 11am-midnight, to 1am Fri & Sat Mar-Oct) Thumbs up for the Feierling housebrew which has kept beer lovers lubricated for over a quarter century. In summer grab a table in the lovely beer garden and stave off a hangover with honest-to-goodness German classics or try one of the flavour-packed vegetarian alternatives.

ℹ Information

Tourist Office (☎ 0761-388 1880; www.freiburg.de; Rathausplatz 2-4; ⊙ 8am-8pm Mon-Fri, 9.30am-5pm Sat, 10.30am-3.30pm Sun) Pick up the three-day WelcomeKarte discount card at Freiburg's central tourist office.

ℹ Getting There & Away

Freiburg is on a major north–south rail corridor, with frequent departures for destinations such as Basel (€19 to €24.20, 45 minutes) and Baden-Baden (€18.10 to €25.80, 45 minutes to one hour).

The Romantic Rhine

Between Koblenz and Bingen, the Rhine cuts deeply through the Rhenish slate mountains. Nicknamed the 'Romantic Rhine', the stretch is justifiably a highlight for many Germany explorers. Hillsides cradle craggy cliffs and nearly vertical terraced vineyards. Idyllic villages appear around

---

ℹ FLYING INTO FRANKFURT

Frankfurt Airport (FRA; www.frankfurt-airport.com), 12km southwest of the major metropolis of Frankfurt-am-Main, is Germany's busiest. S-Bahn lines S8 and S9 shuttle between the airport's train station (Regionalbahnhof) and the city centre (€4.35, 11 minutes) several times hourly. Note that Frankfurt-Hahn Airport (HHN; www.hahn-airport.de), served by Ryanair, is actually 125km west of Frankfurt.

Romantic Rhine Valley

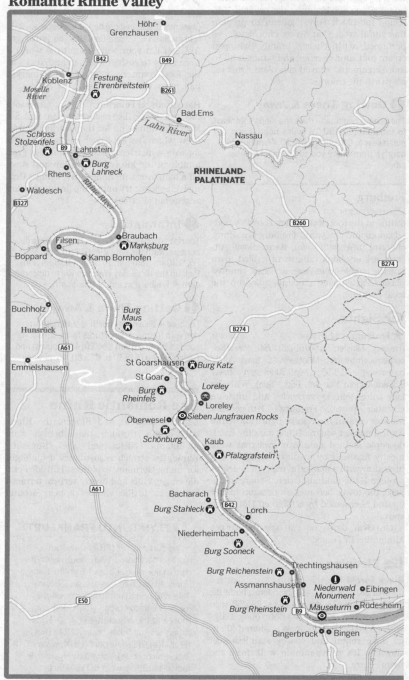

Höhr-
Grenzhausen

B42

B49

Koblenz

Festung
Ehrenbreitstein

B261

Moselle
River

Bad Ems

Lahn River

Nassau

Schloss
Stolzenfels

B9

Lahnstein

Burg
Lahneck

RHINELAND-
PALATINATE

Rhens

Waldesch

Rhine River

B327

B260

Braubach

Marksburg

Filsen

B274

Boppard

Kamp Bornhofen

Buchholz

Burg
Maus

Hunsrück

B274

A61

Emmelshausen

St Goarshausen

Burg Katz

St Goar

Loreley

Burg
Rheinfels

Loreley

Oberwesel

Sieben Jungfrauen Rocks

Schönburg

Kaub

Pfalzgrafstein

A61

Bacharach

Burg Stahleck

B42

Lorch

Niederheimbach

Burg Sooneck

Trechtingshausen

Burg Reichenstein

Niederwald
Monument

Eibingen

Assmannshausen

Burg Rheinstein

B9

Mäuseturm

Rüdesheim

E50

Bingerbrück

Bingen

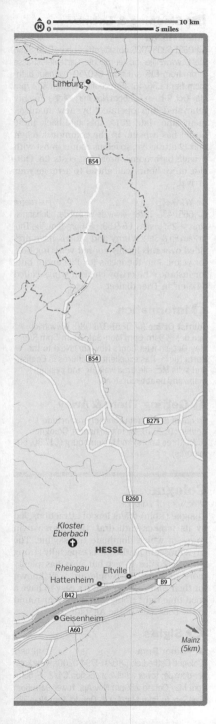

each bend, their neat half-timbered houses and church steeples seemingly plucked from the world of fairy tales. High above the river, busy with barge traffic, are famous medieval castles, some ruined, some restored, all vestiges from a mysterious past. Although Koblenz and Mainz are logical starting points, the area can also be explored on a long day trip from Frankfurt.

❶ Getting There & Around

From about Easter to October, passenger ships run by **Köln-Düsseldorfer** (☑ 0221-208 8318; www.k-d.com) link Rhine villages on a set timetable.

Villages on the Rhine's left bank are served regularly by local trains on the Koblenz–Mainz run.

Right-bank villages are linked hourly to Koblenz' Hauptbahnhof and Wiesbaden by the RheingauLinie.

Various ferry services cross the river.

Bacharach

One of the prettiest of the Rhine villages, tiny Bacharach conceals its considerable charms behind a 14th-century wall. Beyond the thick arched gateways awaits a beautiful medieval old town graced with half-timbered townhouses. There's no shortage of atmospheric places to eat and sample the local vintages. In a dream setting inside a medieval castle, **DJH Burg Stahleck** (☑ 06743-1266; www.jugendherberge.de; Burg Stahleck; dm/s/d €21.50/27/54; ℗ @) is a hillside hostel with beds in rooms for one to six people, almost all with private bathrooms.

St Goar & St Goarshausen

These twin towns face each other across the Rhine. On the left bank, St Goar is lorded over by **Burg Rheinfels** (www.st-goar.de; adult/child €5/2.50; ⊙ 9am-6pm mid-Mar–late Oct, 11am-5pm late Oct–mid-Nov), one of the largest and most impressive river castles. Its labyrinthine ruins reflect the greed and ambition of the local count who built the behemoth in 1245 to levy tolls on passing ships. Today an inexpensive ferry links St Goar with St Goarshausen and the most fabled spot along the Romantic Rhine, the **Loreley Rock**. This vertical slab of slate owes its fame to a mythical maiden whose siren songs are said to have lured sailors to their death in the river's treacherous currents.

Braubach

Framed by forested hillsides, vineyards and Rhine-side rose gardens, the 1300-year-old town of Braubach, on the right bank, is centred on the small, half-timbered market square. High above are the dramatic towers, turrets and crenellations of the 700-year-old **Marksburg** (www.marksburg.de; adult/child €6/4; ⊙ 10am-5pm mid-Mar–Oct, 11am-4pm Nov–mid-Mar) which – unique among the Rhine fortresses – was never destroyed.

Trier

📞 0651 / POP 106,500

This handsome, leafy Moselle town is home to Germany's finest ensemble of Roman monuments – including thermal baths and an amphitheatre – as well as architectural gems from later ages.

◉ Sights

★ **Amphitheater**   HISTORIC SITE
(Olewiger Strasse; adult/child €3/2; ⊙ 9am-6pm Apr-Sep, to 5pm Mar & Oct, to 4pm Nov-Feb) Trier's Roman amphitheatre could accommodate 20,000 spectators for gladiator tournaments and animal fights. Beneath the arena are dungeons where prisoners sentenced to death waited next to starving beasts for the final showdown.

★ **Kaiserthermen**   HISTORIC SITE
(Imperial Baths; Weberbachstrasse 41; adult/child €3/2; ⊙ 9am-6pm Apr-Sep, to 5pm Mar & Oct, to 4pm Nov-Feb) Get a sense of the layout of this vast Roman thermal bathing complex with its striped brick-and-stone arches from the corner lookout tower, then descend into an underground labyrinth consisting of cavernous hot- and cold-water baths, boiler rooms and heating channels.

★ **Konstantin Basilika**   CHURCH
(📞 0651-425 70; www.konstantin-basilika.de; Konstantinplatz 10; ⊙ 10am-6pm Mon-Sat, 1-4pm Sun Apr-Oct, 10am-noon & 2-4pm Mon-Sat, 1-4pm Sun Nov-Mar) Constructed around AD 310 as Constantine's throne room, the brick-built basilica is now an austere Protestant church. With built-to-impress dimensions (some 67m long, 27m wide and 33m high), it's the largest single-room Roman structure still in existence. A new organ, with 87 registers and 6500 pipes, generates a seven-fold echo.

🛏 Sleeping & Eating

Hille's Hostel   HOSTEL €
(📞 0651-6998 7026, outside office hours 0157 8856 9594; www.hilles-hostel-trier.de; Gartenfeldstrasse 7; dm from €15, s/d from €40/50, without bathroom from €36/46; ⊙ reception 8-11am & 2-7pm May-Oct, 9-11am & 3-6pm Nov-Apr; @ 🛜) Freshly renovated and operated by new management since late 2014, this laid-back indie hostel has a piano in the common kitchen and 12 attractive, spacious rooms, most with private bathrooms. Breakfast costs €6. Outside office hours, call ahead to arrange your arrival.

de Winkel   PUB FOOD €
(📞 0651-436 1878; www.de-winkel.de; Johannisstrasse 25; mains €6-9.50; ⊙ 6pm-1am Tue-Thu, to 2am Fri & Sat) Winny and Morris have presided over this locally adored watering hole for years. Join the locals for Pils and a bite, for instance the crispy chicken wings called 'Flieten' in Trier dialect.

ⓘ Information

Tourist Office (📞 0651-978 080; www.trier-info.de; ⊙ 9am-6pm Mon-Sat, 10am-5pm Sun May-Oct, shorter hours Nov-Apr) Next to the Porta Nigra. Has excellent brochures in English and sells Moselle-area walking and cycling maps and boat excursions.

ⓘ Getting There & Away

Frequent direct train connections include Koblenz (€22.10, 1½ to two hours), Cologne (€33, three hours) and Luxembourg (€17.30, 50 minutes).

Cologne

📞 0221 / POP 1 MILLION

Cologne (Köln) offers lots of attractions, led by its famous cathedral, the filigree twin spires of which dominate the skyline. The city's museum landscape is especially strong when it comes to art but also has plenty more in store. Its people are well known for their *joie de vivre* and it's easy to have a good time right along with them year-round in the beer halls of the Altstadt.

◉ Sights

★ **Kölner Dom**   CATHEDRAL
(Cologne Cathedral; 📞 0211-1794 0200; www.koelner-dom.de; tower adult/concession €4/2; ⊙ 6am-9pm May-Oct, to 7.30pm Nov-Apr, tower 9am-6pm May-Sep, to 5pm Mar-Apr & Oct, to 4pm Nov-Feb)

Cologne's geographical and spiritual heart – and its single-biggest tourist draw – is the magnificent Kölner Dom. With its soaring twin spires, this is the Mt Everest of cathedrals, jam-packed with art and treasures. For an exercise fix, climb the 533 steps up the Dom's south tower to the base of the steeple that dwarfed all buildings in Europe until Gustave Eiffel built a certain tower in Paris. The underground Domforum visitor centre is a good source of info and tickets.

★ Römisch-Germanisches Museum
MUSEUM

(Roman Germanic Museum; ☑ 0221-2212 4438; www.museenkoeln.de; Roncalliplatz 4; adult/concession €9/5; ☉ 10am-5pm Tue-Sun) Sculptures and ruins displayed outside the entrance are merely the overture to a full symphony of Roman artefacts found along the Rhine. Highlights include the giant Poblicius tomb (AD 30–40), the magnificent 3rd-century Dionysus mosaic, and astonishingly well-preserved glass items. Insight into daily Roman life is gained from toys, tweezers, lamps and jewellery, the designs of which have changed surprisingly little since Roman times.

Museum Ludwig
MUSEUM

(☑ 0221-2212 6165; www.museum-ludwig.de; Heinrich-Böll-Platz; adult/concession €11/7.50, more during special exhibits; ☉ 10am-6pm Tue-Sun) A mecca of contemporary art, Museum Ludwig presents a tantalising mix of works from all major phases. Fans of German expressionism (Beckmann, Dix, Kirchner) will get their fill here as much as those with a penchant for Picasso, American pop art (Warhol, Lichtenstein) and Russian avant-garde painter Alexander Rodchenko. Rothko and Pollock are highlights of the abstract collection, while Gursky and Tillmanns are among the reasons the photography section is a must stop.

★☆ Festivals

★ Karneval
PARADE

(Carnival; www.koelnerkarneval.de) Ushering in Lent in late February or early March, Cologne's Carnival is one of Europe's most raucous, as people dress in creative costumes and party in the streets. Things kick off the Thursday 52 days before Easter Sunday, culminate on Monday (Rosenmontag), when there are televised street parades, and end on Ash Wednesday.

🛌 Sleeping

Meininger Hotel Cologne City Center
HOSTEL, HOTEL €

(☑ 0221-9976 0965; www.meininger-hotels.com; Engelbertstrasse 33-35; dm/s/d from €20/50/80; @ 🛜) In a former hotel, this flashpacker hostel and hotel in the cool Zülpicher Viertel is loaded with retro appeal. The 52 modern rooms feature lockers, reading lamps, a small TV and private bathrooms. Freebies include linen and towels in the dorms. It's got six floors served by one lift and you can rent a bike.

Station Hostel for Backpackers
HOSTEL €

(☑ 0221-912 5301; www.hostel-cologne.de; Marzellenstrasse 44-56; dm €17-20, s/d from €32/50; @ 🛜) Near the Hauptbahnhof, this is a hostel as hostels should be: central, convivial and economical. A lounge gives way to clean, colourful rooms sleeping one to six people. There's lots of free stuff, including linen, internet, lockers, city maps and guest kitchen. Some private rooms have their own bathrooms.

🍴 Eating

Engelbät
EUROPEAN €

(☑ 0221-246 914; www.engelbaet.de; Engelbertstrasse 7; crepes €5-8.50; ☉ 11am-1am) 🌱 This cosy restaurant-pub is famous for its habit-forming crepes, which come in 40 varieties – sweet, meat or vegetarian. Also popular for weekend breakfast (served until 3pm). Outside of summer, there's often live jazz at night. The sidewalk tables are popular.

★ Salon Schmitz
MODERN EUROPEAN €€

(☑ 0221-9229 9594; www.salonschmitz.com; Aachener Strasse 28; mains from €10; ☉ 9am-late, hours vary by venue) Spread over three historic row houses, the Schmitz empire is your one-stop for excellent food and drink. From the casual bistro to excellent seasonal meals in the restaurant to the takeaway deli, you'll find something you like at Schmitz almost any time of day. Wash it all down with the house-brand *Kölsch*.

🍺 Drinking & Nightlife

There are plenty of beer halls in the tourist-adored Altstadt, but for a more local vibe head to student-flavoured Zülpicher Viertel or the Belgisches Viertel, both in the city centre. Local breweries turn out a variety

Cologne

Map labels:
Christophstr/Mediapark, Kyotostr, Brüsseler Str, Gereonstr, Kardinal-Frings-Str, Tunisstr, Stolkgasse, Bismarckstr, Appelhofplatz, Zeughaus, Komödienstr, Friesenplatz, Zeughausstr, Burgmauer, Burgmauer, Antwerpener Str, Am Römerturm, Burgmauer, Elisenstr, Appelhofplatz, Appelhofplatz, Breite Str, Drususgasse, Maastrichter Str, Hohenzollernring, Friesenwall, Breite Str, Morsergasse, Kolumbastr, Glockengasse, Brückenstr, Ludwigstr, Wolfstr, Richmodstr, Hämergasse, Ottenbachplatz, Tunisstr, Herzogstr, Zeppelinstr, Brüderstr, Rudolfplatz, Mittelstr, Aachener Str, Schilderstr, Neumarkt, Kronengasse, Nord-Sud-Fahrt, Cäcilienstr, Handelstr, Hohenzollernring, Mauritiussteinweg, Neumarkt, Cäcilienstr, Jabachstr, Cäcilienstr, Schaafenstr, Fleischmengergasse, Mozartstr, Engelbertstr, Mauritiuswall, Agrippastr, Rathenau-platz, Roonstr, Thieboldsgasse, Kleiner Griechenmarkt, Poststr, Grosser Griechenmarkt, Tel-Aviv-Str, Poststr, Blaubach

called Kölsch, which is relatively light and served in skinny 200mL glasses.

⭐ **Päffgen**   BEER HALL
(☎0221-135 461; www.paeffgen-koelsch.de; Friesenstrasse 64-66; mains €6-20; ⊙10am-midnight Sun-Thu, to 12.30am Fri & Sat) Busy, loud and boisterous, Päffgen has been pouring *Kölsch* since 1883 and hasn't lost a step since. In summer you can enjoy the refreshing brew and local specialities (€1.10 to €10.70) beneath starry skies in the beer garden.

⭐ **Biergarten Rathenauplatz**   BEER GARDEN
(☎0221-801 7349; www.rathenauplatz.de; Rathenauplatz; ⊙noon-11pm Apr-Oct) A large, leafy park has one of Cologne's best places for a drink: a community-run beer garden. Tables sprawl under huge, old trees, while simple snacks such as salads and very good *frikadelle* (spiced hamburger) issue forth from a cute little hut. Prices are cheap; beers come from nearby Hellers Brewery – try the organic lager. Proceeds help maintain the park.

ⓘ Information

Tourist Office (☑0221-346 430; www.cologne-tourism.com; Kardinal-Höffner-Platz 1; ◷9am-8pm Mon-Sat, 10am-5pm Sun) Excellent; near the cathedral. The app is well done.

ⓘ Getting There & Around

Services to and from Cologne are fast and frequent in all directions. A sampling: Berlin (€117, 4¼ hours), Frankfurt (€71, 1¼ hours), Düsseldorf (€11.30, 30 minutes). ICE trains leave for Brussels to connect with the Eurostar for London or Paris.

For public transport information, see www.vrs.de.

Düsseldorf

☑0211 / POP 594,000

Düsseldorf dazzles with boundary-pushing architecture, zinging nightlife and an art scene to rival many a metropolis. It's a posh and modern city whose economy is dominated by banking, advertising, fashion and telecommunications. However, a couple of hours of partying in the boisterous pubs of the Altstadt, the historical quarter along the Rhine, is all you need to realise that locals have no problem letting their hair down once they slip out of those Boss jackets.

◎ Sights

K20 Grabbeplatz　　　　　　　MUSEUM

(☑0211-838 1130; Grabbeplatz 5; adult/child €12/2.50; ◷10am-6pm Tue-Fri, 11am-6pm Sat & Sun) A collection that spans the arc of 20th-century artistic vision gives the K20 an enviable edge in the art world. It encompasses major works by Picasso, Matisse and Mondrian and more than 100 paintings and drawings by Paul Klee. Americans represented include Jackson Pollock, Andy Warhol and Jasper John. Düsseldorf's own Joseph Beuys has a major presence as well.

K21 Ständehaus　　　　　　　MUSEUM

(☑0211-838 1630; Ständehausstrasse 1; adult/child €12/2.50; ◷10am-6pm Tue-Fri, 11am-6pm Sat & Sun) A stately 19th-century parliament building forms a fabulous dichotomy to the cutting-edge art of the K21 – a collection showcasing only works created after the

Düsseldorf

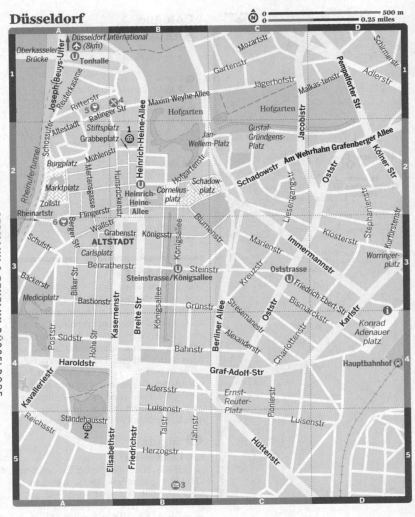

Düsseldorf

1980s. Large-scale film and video installations and groups of works share space with site-specific rooms by an international cast of artists including Andreas Gursky, Candida Höfer, Bill Viola and Nam June Paik.

🛏 Sleeping

Backpackers-Düsseldorf HOSTEL €
(📞0211-302 0848; www.backpackers-duesseldorf.
de; Fürstenwall 180; dm €19-25; ⊙reception
8am-10pm; 🅿@🛜) Düsseldorf's adorable
indie hostel sleeps 60 in clean four- to 10-
bed dorms outfitted with individual backpack-sized lockers. It's a low-key place with

a kitchen and a relaxed lounge where cultural and language barriers melt quickly. The vending machine is filled with beer. Rates include a small breakfast; linen costs €3.

✗ Eating & Drinking

The local beverage of choice is *Altbier*, a dark and semisweet beer typical of Düsseldorf.

★ Brauerei im Füchschen — GERMAN €€
(☑ 0211-137 470; www.fuechschen.de; Ratinger Strasse 28; mains €6-16; ☺ 9am-1am Mon-Thu, to 2am Fri & Sat, to midnight Sun) Boisterous, packed and drenched with local colour – the 'Little Fox' in the Altstadt is all you expect a Rhenish beer hall to be. The kitchen makes a mean *Schweinshaxe* (roast pork leg). The high-ceilinged interior echoes with the mirthful roar of people enjoying their meals. This is one of the best *Altbier* breweries in town.

★ Zum Uerige — BEER HALL
(☑ 0211-866 990; www.uerige.de; Berger Strasse 1; ☺ 10am-midnight) This cavernous brew pub is the quintessential Düsseldorf haunt to try the city's typical *Altbier*. The suds flow so quickly from giant copper vats that the waiters – called *Köbes* – simply carry huge trays of brew and plonk down a glass whenever they spy an empty. Even on a cold day, the outside tables are alive with merriment.

★ Stone Im Ratinger Hof — CLUB
(☑ 0211-210 7828; www.stone-club.de; Ratinger Strasse 10; cover varies; ☺ Wed, Fri & Sat) The venerable Ratinger Hof is the place for indie and alt sounds. Depending on the night, tousled boho types, skinny-jean emos and sneaker-wearing students thrash it out to everything from noise pop to indietronic to punk and roll.

❶ Information

Tourist Office – Hauptbahnhof (☑ 0211-1720 2844; www.visitduesseldorf.de; Immermannstrasse 65b; ☺ 9.30am-7pm Mon-Fri, to 5pm Sat) The main tourist office, across from the train station.

❶ Getting There & Away

Düsseldorf International Airport (DUS; www.dus-int.de) is linked to the city centre by the S-Bahn line 1 (€2.50, 10 minutes).

Regional trains travel to Cologne (€11.30, 30 minutes) and Aachen (€20.70, 1½ hours). Fast ICE train links include Berlin (€111, 4-4 hours),

AACHEN

A spa town with a hopping student population and tremendous amounts of character, Aachen makes for an excellent day trip from Cologne or Düsseldorf or a worthy overnight stop en route to nearby Netherlands or Belgium.

It's impossible to overestimate the significance of Aachen's magnificent **cathedral** (☑ 0241-447 090; www.aachendom.de; Münsterplatz; ☺ 7am-7pm Apr-Dec, to 6pm Jan-Mar). The burial place of Charlemagne, it's where more than 30 German kings were crowned and where pilgrims have flocked since the 12th century. Before entering the church, stop by Dom Information for info and tickets for tours and the cathedral treasury.

Regional trains frequently head to Cologne (€16.80, 55 minutes), Düsseldorf (€20.70, 1½ hours) and beyond.

Hamburg (€82, 3½ hours) and Frankfurt (€82, 1½ hours).

Hamburg

☑ 040 / POP 1.8 MILLION

'The gateway to the world' might be a bold claim, but Germany's second-largest city and biggest port has never been shy. Hamburg has engaged in business with the world ever since it joined the Hanseatic League trading bloc back in the Middle Ages. Hamburg's maritime spirit infuses the entire city: from architecture to menus to the cry of gulls, you always know you're near the water. The city has vibrant neighbourhoods awash with multicultural eateries, as well as the gloriously seedy Reeperbahn party and red-light district.

❶ CHEAP CRUISING

This maritime city offers a bewildering array of boat trips, but there's no need to fork over €18 for a cruise to see the port. Instead, hop on one of the public ferries for the price of a standard public transport ticket (€3). The handiest line is ferry 62, which leaves from Landungsbrücken (pier 3) and travels west to Finkenwerder.

Hamburg

◉ Sights

Rathaus
HISTORIC BUILDING

(☏040-428 312 064; Rathausmarkt 1; tours adult/under 14yr €4/free; ⊙tours half-hourly 10am-3pm Mon-Fri, to 5pm Sat, to 4pm Sun, English tours depend on demand; Ⓢ Rathausmarkt, Jungfernstieg) With its spectacular coffered ceiling, Hamburg's baroque Rathaus is one of Europe's most opulent, and is renowned for its Emperor's Hall and Great Hall. The 40-minute tours take in only a fraction of this beehive of 647 rooms. A good secret to know about is the inner courtyard, where you can take a break from exploring the Rathaus on comfy chairs with tables.

★ Hamburger Kunsthalle
MUSEUM

(☏040-428 131 200; www.hamburger-kunsthalle.de; Glockengiesserwall; adult/child €12/free; ⊙10am-6pm Tue, Wed & Fri-Sun, to 9pm Thu; Ⓢ Hauptbahnhof) A treasure trove of art from the Renaissance to the present day, the Kunsthalle spans two buildings linked by an underground passage. The main building houses works ranging from medieval portraiture to 20th-century classics, such as Klee and Kokoschka. There's also a memorable room

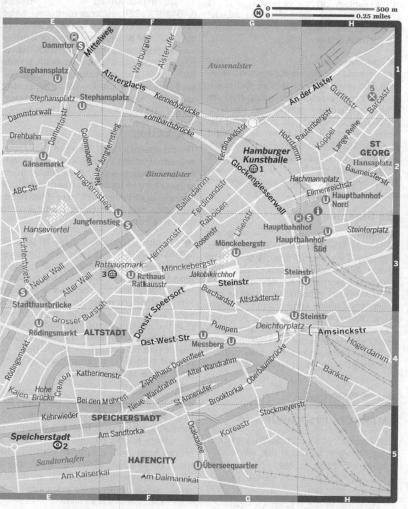

GERMANY & BENELUX HAMBURG

Hamburg

of 19th-century landscapes by Caspar David Friedrich. Its stark white modern cube, the Galerie der Gegenwart, showcases contemporary German artists.

★ Speicherstadt
AREA

(Am Sandtorkai; ⊘24hr; Ⓢ Rödingsmarkt, Messberg) The seven-storey red-brick warehouses lining the Speicherstadt archipelago are a famous Hamburg symbol and the largest continuous warehouse complex in the world, recognised by Unesco as a World Heritage Site. Its distinctive architecture is best appreciated on a leisurely wander or a ride on a flat tour boat (called *Barkasse*). Many buildings contain shops, cafes and small museums.

🛏 Sleeping

★ Superbude St Pauli
HOTEL, HOSTEL €

(☑040-807 915 820; www.superbude.de; Juliusstrasse 1-7; dm/r from €20/60; @ 🛜; Ⓢ Sternschanze, Ⓡ Sternschanze, Holstenstrasse) The young and forever-young mix and mingle without a shred of prejudice at this rocking design hotel-hostel combo that's all about living, laughing, partying and, yes, even sleeping well. All rooms have comfy beds and sleek private baths, breakfast is served until noon and there's even a 'rock star suite' with an Astra beer as a pillow treat.

DON'T MISS

MARKETS IN HAMBURG

. . . .

St Pauli Nachtmarkt (Spielbudenplatz; ⊘4-10pm Wed; Ⓢ St Pauli) This after-dark farmers and gourmet market with fun snack stands lures locals and visitors to the heart of St Pauli.

Flohschanze (Neuer Kamp 30; ⊘8am-4pm Sat; Ⓢ Feldstrasse) Hamburg's best flea market is nirvana for thrifty trinket hunters and vintage junkies, with hundreds of vendors holding forth outdoors in the hip Karolinenviertel.

Isemarkt (www.isemarkt.com; btwn U-Bahn stations Hoheluft & Eppendorfer Baum; ⊘8.30am-2pm Tue & Fri; Ⓢ Eppendorfer Baum, Hoheluft) Winding for over 1km beneath the elevated U-Bahn tracks, the twice-weekly Isemarkt in Eppendorf is literally the longest farmers market in Germany with some 200 vendors offering quality anything.

Schanzenstern Altona
PENSION €

(☑040-3991 9191; schanzenstern.com; Kleine Rainstrasse 24-26; dm/s/d from €20/50/75, apt from €85; ❤ @ 🛜; Ⓡ Altona) A mix of families and slightly more grown-up backpackers inhabit these sparkling rooms (with private bathrooms) and self-catering apartments. Staff are wired into what's happening around Hamburg. Dorms have two to seven beds. There is another property in St Pauli.

🍴 Eating

The Schanzenviertel (U-Bahn to Feldstrasse or Schanzenstern) swarms with cheap eateries; try Schulterblatt for Portuguese outlets or Susannenstrasse for Asian and Turkish. St Georg's Lange Reihe (U-Bahn to Hauptbahnhof) offers many characterful eating spots to suit every budget.

★ Fischbrötchenbude Brücke 10
SEAFOOD €

(☑040-3339 9339; www.bruecke-10.de; Landungsbrücken, Pier 10; sandwiches €2.50-7.50; ⊘10am-10pm Apr-Oct, to 8pm Nov-Mar; Ⓢ Landungsbrücken, Ⓡ Landungsbrücken) There are a gazillion fish sandwich vendors in Hamburg, but we're going to stick our neck out and say that this vibrant, clean and contemporary outpost makes the best. Try a classic *Bismarck* (pickled herring) or *Matjes* (brined), or treat yourself to a bulging shrimp sandwich. Lovely tables outside.

Café Koppel
VEGETARIAN €

(☑040-249 235; www.cafe-koppel.de; Lange Reihe 66; mains €5-10; ⊘10am-11pm; ; Ⓢ Hauptbahnhof) Set back from busy Lange Reihe in the gallery Koppel 66, this veggie cafe is a refined oasis (with a summer garden). The menu could be an ad for the fertile fields of northern Germany, as there are baked goods, salads, soups and much more made with fresh seasonal ingredients.

🍷 Drinking & Nightlife

No discussion of Hamburg is complete without mentioning St Pauli, home to one of Europe's most (in)famous red-light districts. Sex shops, table-dance bars and strip clubs still line its main drag, the Reeperbahn, and side streets, but prostitution has declined dramatically, being concentrated mainly on gated Herbertstrasse (no women or under-18s allowed). St Pauli is Hamburg's main nightlife district, drawing people of all ages and walks of life to live-music and dance clubs, chic bars and theatres.

★ **Strandperle** BAR

(☑040-880 1112; www.strandperle-hamburg.de; Oevelgönne 60; ⊙10am-11pm Mon-Fri, 9am-11pm Sat & Sun May-Sep, shorter hours Oct-Apr; ☐112) Hamburg's original beach bar is a must for primo beer, burgers and people-watching. All ages and classes gather, mingle and wriggle their toes in the sand, especially at sunset, right on the Elbe as huge freighters glide past. Get here by taking ferry 62 from Landungsbrücken or bus 112 from Altona station to Neumühlen/Oevelgönne.

★ **Golden Pudel Club** LIVE MUSIC

(☑040-3197 9930; www.pudel.com; St-Pauli-Fischmarkt 27; ⊙11pm-6am; ☒Reeperbahn) In a 19th-century bootleggers' jail, this tiny bar-club is run by members of the legendary ex-punk band Die Goldenen Zitronen and is an essential stop on the St Pauli party circuit. Night after night it gets packed to the rafters for its countercultural vibe, quality bands and DJs, and relaxed crowd.

❶ Information

Tourist Information Hauptbahnhof (Hauptbahnhof, near Kirchenallee exit; ⊙9am-7pm Mon-Sat, 10am-6pm Sun; ⑤Hauptbahnhof, ☒Hauptbahnhof) Busy all the time.

❶ Getting There & Around

Hamburg is a major train hub with four mainline train stations. Frequent trains serve Lübeck (€13.70, 45 minutes), Bremen (from €28, 55 minutes), Berlin (€78, 1¾ hours), Copenhagen (€85.40, 4¾ hours) and many other cities.

For public transport information, go to www. hvv.de. The city is divided into zones. Fare zone A covers the city centre, inner suburbs and airport.

Bremen

☑0421 / POP 546,450

This little city is big on charm, from the statue of Grimm's *Musicians of Bremen* to a jaw-dropping expressionist laneway and impressive town hall. On top of that, the Weser riverside promenade is a relaxing bistro-and-beer-garden–lined refuge and the lively student district ('Das Viertel') along Ostertorsteinweg is filled with indie boutiques, cafes, art-house cinemas and alternative cultural venues.

WORTH A TRIP

LÜBECK

Compact and charming Lübeck makes for a great day trip from Hamburg. Looking like a pair of witches' hats, the pointed towers of its landmark Holstentor (Holsten Gate) form the gateway to its historic centre that sits on an island embraced by the arms of the Trave River. The Unesco-recognised web of cobbled lanes flanked by gabled merchants' homes and spired churches is an enduring reminder of Lübeck's role as the one-time capital of the medieval Hanseatic League trading power. Today it enjoys fame as Germany's marzipan capital.

Regional trains connect to Hamburg twice hourly (€13.50, 45 minutes).

◉ Sights

Markt SQUARE

Bremen's World Heritage–protected Markt is striking, especially for its ornate, gabled and sculpture-festooned Rathaus (town hall; 1410). In front stands a 5.5m-high medieval statue of the knight Roland (1404), symbolic protector of Bremen's civic rights and freedoms. On the town hall's western side is a sculpture of the *Town Musicians of Bremen* (1951).

★ **Beck's Brewery** BREWERY

(☑0421-5094 5555; www.becks.de/besucherzentrum; Am Deich 18/19; tours €10.90; ⊙tours 10am, 11.30am, 1pm, 3pm, 4.30pm & 6pm Thu-Sat) Two-hour tours of one of Germany's most internationally famous breweries must be booked online. The 3pm tour is also in English. Minimum age 16. Meet at the brewery's visitor centre, reached by taking tram 1, 2 or 3 to Am Brill.

🛏 Sleeping

Townside Hostel Bremen HOSTEL €

(☑0421-780 15; www.townside.de; Am Dobben 62; dm from €15, s/d with bathroom from €46/64; ☜) This bright, professionally run hostel is right in the middle of Bremen's nightlife quarter and handy to Werder Bremen's stadium. Breakfast costs €5.50. Take tram 10 from Hauptbahnhof to Humboldtstrasse or tram 2 or 3 to Sielwall.

✕ Eating, Drinking & Nightlife

Engel Weincafe CAFE €

([☎]0421-6964 2390; www.engelweincafe-bremen. de; Ostertorsteinweg 31; dishes €4-13; [⏰]8am-1am Mon-Fri, 10am-1am Sat & Sun; [📶][♿]) Exuding the nostalgic vibe of a former pharmacy, this popular hang-out gets a good crowd no matter where the hands on the clock. Come for breakfast, a hot lunch special, crispy *Flammekuche* (French pizza), carpaccio or pasta, or just some cheese and a glass of wine.

★ Lila Eule LIVE MUSIC

(www.lilaeule.de; Bernhardstrasse 10; [⏰]from 8pm) A decade or more is a long time to be a hot tip, but this gem off Sielwall has pulled it off. A student crowd gathers here for parties and events; Thursday night is the legendary bash.

ℹ Information

Tourist Office Markt ([☎]0421-308 0010; www.bremen-tourism.de; Langenstrasse 2-4; [⏰]10am-4pm, extended hours in summer) Bremen's full-service tourist office has friendly staff who can help you navigate through the multitude of excellent English-language maps, pamphlets and programs. A wide range of tours are available.

ℹ Getting There & Away

Trains include InterCity (IC) services to Hamburg (€28, one hour) and Cologne (€67, three hours).

Germany Survival Guide

ℹ Directory A–Z

ACCOMMODATION

Reservations are a good idea, especially between June and September, around major holidays and events. Local tourist offices can help.

LGBT TRAVELLERS

Germany is a magnet for *schwule* (gay) and *lesbische* (lesbian) travellers, with the rainbow flag flying especially proudly in Berlin and Cologne, and with sizeable communities in Hamburg, Frankfurt and Munich.

MONEY

➡ Cards aren't as widely accepted as some European countries, so always carry cash too.

➡ Restaurant bills include a *Bedienung* (service charge), but most people add 5% or 10%, unless service was awful. Don't leave the tip on the table; tell the server how much you want to pay in total.

ℹ PRICE RANGES

Sleeping price ranges refer to a double room with private bathroom and breakfast in high season:

€ less than €80

€€ €80–€160

€€€ more than €160

Eating price ranges are for the cost of a main course:

€ less than €8

€€ €8–€18

€€€ more than €18

OPENING HOURS

Banks 9am to 4pm Monday to Friday, extended hours usually on Tuesday and Thursday, some open Saturday

Bars 6pm to 1am

Cafes 8am to 8pm

Clubs 11pm to early morning

Restaurants 11am to 11pm (food service often stops at 9pm in rural areas)

Major stores and supermarkets 9.30am to 8pm Monday to Saturday (shorter hours outside city centres)

PUBLIC HOLIDAYS

The following are *gesetzliche Feiertage* (public holidays). Individual states add some others.

Neujahrstag (New Year's Day) 1 January

Ostern (Easter) March/April; Good Friday, Easter Sunday and Easter Monday

Christi Himmelfahrt (Ascension Day) Forty days after Easter

Maifeiertag/Tag der Arbeit (Labour Day) 1 May

Pfingsten (Whit/Pentecost Sunday & Monday) Fifty days after Easter

Tag der Deutschen Einheit (Day of German Unity) 3 October

Weihnachtstag (Christmas Day) 25 December

Zweiter Weihnachtstag (Boxing Day) 26 December

TELEPHONE

➡ Country code [☎]49. International access code [☎]00.

➡ Pay-as-you-go SIM cards with data deals are easily available and cheap.

ℹ Getting There & Around

AIR

Frankfurt Airport is the main gateway for transcontinental flights, although Berlin, Düsseldorf and Munich also receive their share. Budget airlines also hit numerous regional airports.

BUS

Bus travel is becoming increasingly popular in Germany thanks to a new crop of companies offering good-value connections within Germany and beyond. For routes, times and prices, check www.busliniensuche.de.

FERRY

Ferries to Scandinavian and Baltic destinations leave from several northern ports; check www.directferries.com for route info.

TRAIN

➡ Germany's train network is almost entirely run by Deutsche Bahn (www.bahn.com).

➡ Of the several train types, ICE trains are the fastest and most comfortable. IC trains (EC if they cross borders) are almost as fast but older. Regional Express (RE) and Regionalbahn (RB) trains are regional. S-Bahn are suburban trains operating in large cities and conurbations.

➡ Buy tickets online (www.bahn.com) or at stations from vending machines or a Reisezentrum (ticket office).

➡ Eurail and Interrail passes are valid on all German national trains.

BELGIUM

Brussels

☑ 02 / POP 1.2 MILLION

Belgium's fascinating capital, and the administrative capital of the EU, Brussels is historic yet hip, bureaucratic yet bizarre, self-confident yet unshowy, and multicultural to its roots. These contrasts are multilayered – Francophone alongside Flemish, and Eurocrats cheek-by-jowl with immigrants. And all this plays out in a cityscape that swings from majestic to quirky to rundown and back again, swirling out from Brussels' medieval core, where the Grand Place is one of the world's most beautiful squares.

One constant is the enviable quality of everyday life, with a *café*/bar scene that could keep you drunk for years.

◉ Sights

★ Grand Place   SQUARE
(Ⓜ Gare Centrale) Brussels' magnificent Grand Place is one of the world's most unforgettable urban ensembles. Oddly hidden, the enclosed cobblestone square is only revealed as you enter on foot from one of six narrow side alleys: Rue des Harengs is the best first approach. The focal point is the spired 15th-century city hall, but each of the antique guildhalls (mostly 1697–1705) has a charm of its own. Most are unashamed exhibitionists, with fine baroque gables, gilded statues and elaborate guild symbols.

Manneken Pis   MONUMENT
(cnr Rue de l'Étuve & Rue du Chêne; Ⓜ Gare Centrale) Rue Charles Buls – Brussels' most unashamedly touristy shopping street, lined with chocolate and trinket shops – leads the hordes three blocks from the Grand Place to the Manneken Pis. This fountain-statue of a little boy taking a leak is comically tiny and a perversely perfect national symbol for surreal Belgium. Most of the time the statue's nakedness is hidden beneath a costume relevant to an anniversary, national day or local event: his ever-growing wardrobe is partly displayed at the **Maison du Roi** (Musée de la Ville de Bruxelles; Grand Place; Ⓜ Gare Centrale).

Musées Royaux des Beaux-Arts   GALLERY
(Royal Museums of Fine Arts; ☑ 02-508 32 11; www.fine-arts-museum.be; Rue de la Régence 3; adult/6-25yr/BrusselsCard €8/2/free with Magritte Museum €13; ⊙ 10am-5pm Tue-Fri, 11am-6pm Sat & Sun; Ⓜ Gare Centrale, Parc) This prestigious museum incorporates the Musée d'Art Ancien (ancient art); the Musée d'Art Moderne (modern art), with works by surrealist Paul Delvaux and fauvist Rik Wouters; and the purpose-built Musée Magritte. The 15th-century Flemish Primitives are wonderfully represented in the Musée d'Art Ancien: there's Rogier Van der Weyden's *Pietà* with its hallucinatory sky, Hans Memling's refined portraits, and the richly textured *Madonna With Saints* by the Master of the Legend of St Lucy.

Musée Magritte   MUSEUM
(www.musee-magritte-museum.be; Place Royale; adult/under 26yr/BrusselsCard €8/2/free; ⊙ 10am-5pm Tue-Fri, 11am-6pm Sat & Sun; Ⓜ Gare Centrale, Parc) The beautifully presented Magritte Museum holds the world's largest collection of the surrealist pioneer's paintings and drawings. Watch his style develop from colourful Braque-style cubism in 1920 through a Dalí-esque phase and a late-1940s period of Kandinsky-like brushwork to his trademark bowler hats of the 1960s. Regular screenings of a 50-minute documentary provide insights into the artist's unconventionally conventional life.

Central Brussels

200 m
0.1 miles

Pl Ste Gudule
Pl de Louvain
Blvd Pacheco
R de la Loi
R de la Ligne
R Royale
Parc
R des Colonies
R du Bois Sauvage
R des Sables
R du Meiboom
R de Berlaimont
Gare Centrale
R Ravenstein
R des Marais
R du Persil
R des Comédiens
R des Boiteux
R de Montagne aux Herbes Potagères
R de Loxum
Pl Ste Gudule
Bruxelles-Central
R Cardinal Mercier
Blvd de l'Impératrice
Pl des Martyrs
R d'Argent
R du Fossé aux Loups
R des Princes
R d'Arenberg
R de la Montagne
R de l'Infante Isabelle
R de la Madeleine
R Neuve
R L Léopold
Galerie des Princes
Galerie du Roi
R des Dominicains
Galerie de la Reine
Pl d'Espagne
R des Harengs
ÎLOT SACRÉ
Galerie Agora
R des Éperonniers
R du Marché aux Fromages
Pl de la Monnaie
R de la Reine
R de l'Écuyer
petite R des Bouchers
R des Bouchers
R de la Colline
Grand Place
R des Brasseurs
Pl de Brouckère
De Brouckère
R des Augustins
R Grétry
R des Fripiers
R de la Fourche
R du Marché aux Herbes
R au Beurre
Visit Brussels
R de la Tête d'Or
R Charles Buls
R de la Violette
R de l'Amigo
STE-CATHERINE
R de l'Évêque
Blvd Anspach
R du Marché au Charbon
R des Halles
R de la Bourse
R du Midi
R de Tabora
R du Marché aux Grands Carmes
Eurolines (1km)
Bruxelles-Nord (1.1km)
Pl du Samedi
Bourse
R Henri Maus
Pl de la Bourse
R des Pierres
R Paul Devaux
R des Grands Carmes
R des Teinturiers
R Plattesteen
R du Marché au Charbon
Captaincy Guesthouse (450m)
Pl Ste Catherine
R Ste-Catherine
R Melsens
R de la Vierge Noire
R des Poissonniers
ST-GÉRY
R J van Praet
Borgval
Pl St Géry
R St-Géry
ST-GÉRY
R des Riches Claires
Blvd Anspach
Pl Fontainas
Pl des 6 Jetons
Marché aux Poissons
R Antoine Dansaert
R du Vieux Marché aux Grains
R des Chartreux
R Van Artevelde
R St-Christophe
R Pletinckx
R de la Grande Île
Cantillon Brewery (1km)
R de la Braie

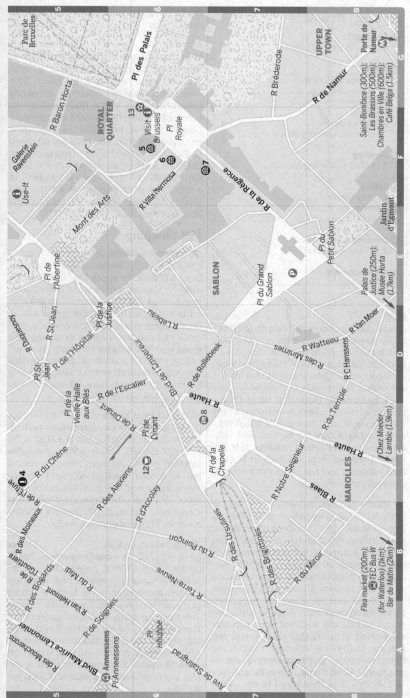

GERMANY & BENELUX BRUSSELS

Parc de Bruxelles

Pl des Palais

ROYAL QUARTER

13
Visit Brussels
5
6
Pl Royale

UPPER TOWN

Porte de Namur Ⓜ

R Brédérode

R de Namur

Saint-Boniface (300m);
Les Brassins (500m);
Chambres en Ville (600m);
Café Belga (1.5km)

Galerie Ravenstein

Use-It

R Baron Horta

Galerie Ravenstein

7

R de la Régence

R Villa Hermosa

Mont des Arts

Pl de l'Albertine

SABLON

Pl du Grand Sablon

Pl du Petit Sablon

Jardin d'Egmont

Palais de Justice (250m);
Musée Horta (1.7km)

R St-Jean

R de l'Hôpital

R Duquesnoy

Pl St-Jean

Pl de la Justice

R Lebeau

Bld de l'Empereur

R de Rollebeek

R des Minimes

R Watteau

R C Hanssens

R Van Moer

Pl de la Vieille Halle aux Blés

R de l'Escalier

R du Chêne

R de Dinant

Pl de Dinant

R Haute

8

Pl de la Chapelle

R du Temple

R Notre Seigneur

Chez Moeder Lambic (1.9km)

R Haute

MAROLLES

4

R de l'Étuve

R des Moineaux

R des Alexiens

R d'Accolay

12

R des Ursulines

R Blaes

R des Brigittines

R du Miroir

Flea market (200m);
TEC Bus W
(for Waterloo) (1km);
Bar du Matin (2km)

R Goutière

R de Bogards

R Van Helmont

R du Midi

R des Soignies

R Terre-Neuve

R du Poinçon

Blvd Maurice Lemonnier

R des Moucherons

Anneessens Ⓜ
Pl Anneessens

Pl Rouppe

Ave de Stalingrad

Central Brussels

◉ Top Sights

◎ Sights

⌂ Sleeping

✖ Eating

◉ Drinking & Nightlife

✦ Entertainment

MIM
MUSEUM

(Musée des Instruments de Musique; ☑02-545 01 30; www.mim.be; Rue Montagne de la Cour 2; adult/concession €8/6; ⏰9.30am-5pm Tue-Fri, 10am-5pm Sat & Sun; Ⓜ Gare Centrale, Parc) Strap on a pair of headphones, then step on the automated floor panels in front of the precious instruments (including world instruments and Adolphe Sax's inventions) to hear them being played. As much of a highlight as the museum itself are the premises – the art-nouveau Old England Building. This former department store was built in 1899 by Paul Saintenoy and has a panoramic rooftop *café* and outdoor terrace.

★ Musée du Cinquantenaire
MUSEUM

(☑02-741 72 11; www.kmkg-mrah.be; Parc du Cinquantenaire 10; adult/child/BrusselsCard €5/€1.50/free; ⏰9.30am-5pm Tue-Fri, from 10am Sat & Sun; Ⓜ Mérode) This astonishingly rich collection ranges from ancient Egyptian sarcophagi to Meso-American masks to icons to wooden bicycles. Decide what you want to see before coming or the sheer scope can prove overwhelming. Visually attractive spaces include the medieval stone carvings set around a neo-Gothic cloister and the soaring Corinthian columns (convincing fibreglass props) that bring atmosphere to an original AD 420 mosaic from Roman Syria. Labelling is in French and Dutch, so the

English-language audioguide (€3) is worth considering.

Atomium
MONUMENT, MUSEUM

(www.atomium.be; Sq de l'Atomium; adult/student/BrusselsCard €11/8/9; ⏰10am-6pm; Ⓜ Heysel, ☒51) The space-age Atomium looms 102m over north Brussels' suburbia, resembling a steel alien from a '60s Hollywood movie. It consists of nine house-sized metallic balls linked by steel tube-columns containing escalators and lifts. The balls are arranged like a school chemistry set to represent iron atoms in their crystal lattice...except these are 165 billion times bigger. It was built as a symbol of postwar progress for the 1958 World's Fair and became an architectural icon, receiving a makeover in 2006.

🛏 Sleeping

★ Captaincy Guesthouse
HOSTEL €

(☑0496 59 93 79; www.thecaptaincybrussels.com; Quai à la Chaux 8; per person €34-50; Ⓜ Ste-Catherine) An idiosyncratic, warmly friendly venture, housed in a 17th-century mansion with a hip Ste-Catherine location and a mix of dorms (some mixed sex) and rooms. A generous €5 breakfast is served in the spacious living area. The wooden attic housing an ensuite four-bed female dorm has a fabulous boutique-hotel feel, and the attic double is a winner too. Dorms have antique chests to lock your belongings in.

HI Hostel John Bruegel
HOSTEL €

(☑02-511 04 36; www.jeugdherbergen.be/brussel.htm; Rue du St-Esprit 2; dm/tw €27.20/63.30, youth €24.45/57.90; ⏰lockout 10am-2pm, curfew 1am-7am; ⊖@☎; Ⓜ Louise) Superbly central but somewhat institutional with limited communal space. The attic singles are a cut above singles at other hostels. Internet costs €2 per hour, lockers €1.50. There's a 10% discount for HI members. Free wi-fi.

★ Chambres en Ville
B&B €€

(☑02-512 92 90; www.chambresenville.be; Rue de Londres 19; s/d €80/100, 2 nights €140/180; ☎; Ⓜ Porte de Namur) Impressive B&B in an unmarked 19th-century town house featuring partly stripped wooden floors, high ceilings and large, tastefully appointed guestrooms. Furniture new and old combined with striking artwork and curiosities from all over the world (notably antique African statuettes) gives the place a unique character. A duplex top-floor studio is available (€1000 per month).

Eating

★ Saint-Boniface · FRENCH, BASQUE €
(02-511 53 66; www.saintboniface.be; Rue St-Boniface 9; mains €12-17; noon-2.30pm & 7-10pm Mon-Fri; Porte de Namur) Enchanting old-world restaurant near the eponymous church, featuring gingham tablecloths, walls jammed with framed pictures and authentic dishes from France's southwestern and Basque regions, notably *cassoulet*, Périgord duck, foie gras and *andouillette* (strongly flavoured tripe sausage – very much an acquired taste).

Fin de Siècle · BELGIAN €
(Rue des Chartreux 9; mains €11.25-20; bar 4.30pm-1am, kitchen 6pm-12.30am; Bourse) From *carbonade* (beer-based hot pot) and *kriek* (cherry beer) chicken to mezzes and tandoori chicken, the food is as eclectic as the decor in this low-lit cult place. Tables are rough, music constant and ceilings purple. To quote the barman, 'there's no phone, no bookings, no sign on the door...we do everything to put people off but they still keep coming'.

Viva M'Boma · BELGIAN €
(02-512 15 93; Rue de Flandre 17; mains €12-19; noon-2.30pm & 7-10pm Thu-Sat, noon-2pm Mon & Tue; Ste-Catherine) Hefty Belgian classics served in a long, narrow bistro entirely walled in gleaming white tiles like the butchers' shop it once was. Stuffed sheeps' and pigs' heads meet and greet.

Mer du Nord · SEAFOOD €
(www.vishandelnoordzee.be; Rue Ste-Catherine 1; 8am-6pm Tue-Fri, 8am-5pm Sat; Ste-Catherine) Well-reputed fishmonger's window catering to a queue of stand-and-snack lunch-grabbers around bare metal outdoor tables.

Les Brassins · BELGIAN €
(02-512 69 99; www.lesbrassins.be; Rue Keyenveld 36; mains €13.50-23; noon-midnight; Louise) On a quiet, unpromising backstreet, this unpretentious brasserie is decorated with old enamel brewery adverts and serves reliable, well-priced Belgian home-cooked classics such as *carbonade* (beer-based hot pot), *filet américain* and *boulettes* (meatballs), accompanied by perfect *frites* (or *stoemp*; you choose) and washed down by an excellent range of Belgian beers. No credit cards.

Drinking & Nightlife

Cafe culture is one of Brussels' greatest attractions. On the Grand Place itself, 300-year-old gems, like Le Roy d'Espagne and Chaloupe d'Or, are magnificent but predictably pricey. Go out of the centre a little to explore the city's new brand of laid-back hipster bars, most decorated in minimal upcycled style, and hosting DJ nights and live-music events.

★ Chez Moeder Lambic · PUB
(02-539 14 19; www.moederlambic.com; Rue de Savoie 68; 4pm-4am; Horta) An institution. Behind windows plastered with beer stickers, this tattered, quirky old brown cafe is the ultimate beer spot in Brussels. Sample some of its hundreds of brews while flipping through its collection of dog-eared comics.

GERMANY & BENELUX BRUSSELS

DON'T MISS

WATERLOO

Tourists have been swarming to Waterloo ever since Napoleon's 1815 defeat, a seminal event in European history.

Inaugurated for the 2015 bicentenary, **Memorial 1815** (02-385 19 12; www.waterloo1815.be; Rte du Lion, Hameau du Lion; adult/child €16/13, with Wellington & Napoleon headquarters museums €19/15; 9.30am-6.30pm Apr-Sep, 10am-5pm Oct-Mar) is a showpiece underground museum and visitor centre at the main battlefield area (known as Hameau du Lion). There's a detailed audioguide and some enjoyable technological effects. The climax is an impressive 3D film that sticks you right into the middle of the cavalry charges. It includes admission to various other battlefield attractions, including the Butte du Lion, a memorial hill from which you can survey the terrain, and the recently restored Hougoumont farmhouse that played a key part in the battle.

TEC bus W runs every 30 minutes from Ave Fonsny at Brussels-Midi to Braine-l'Alleud train station, passing through Waterloo town and stopping near Hameau du Lion (€3.20, one hour). If coming by train, get off at Braine-l'Alleud rather than awkwardly located Waterloo station, then switch to bus W to reach the battlefield.

★ **Café Belga** BAR
(📞 02-640 3508; www.cafebelga.be; Place Flagey 18; ⏰ 8am-2am Sun-Thu, to 3am Fri & Sat; 🚊 81, 82)
This hip brasserie in a corner of the art-deco Flagey 'liner' building is mellow by day, but the beats grow ever louder towards closing time. There's live jazz on a Sunday twice a month (at 5pm).

La Fleur en Papier Doré CAFE
(www.goudblommekeinpapier.be; Rue des Alexiens 53; ⏰ 11am-midnight Tue-Sat, to 7pm Sun; Ⓜ Bruxelles Central) The nicotine-stained walls of this tiny cafe, adored by artists and locals, are covered with writings, art and scribbles by Magritte and his surrealist pals, some of which were reputedly traded for free drinks. 'Ceci n'est pas un musée', quips a sign on the door reminding visitors to buy a drink and not just look around.

ℹ Information

Use-It (📞 02-218 39 06; http://use-it.travel/cities/detail/brussels; Galerie Ravenstein 17; ⏰ 10am-6.30pm Mon-Sat; 📶; Ⓜ Gare Central) Meeting place for young travellers, with free coffee and tea and a list of live-music events written up by the door. It does a free alternative city tour at 2pm on Monday, with an emphasis on social history and nightlife. The printed material is first rate, with a quirky city map, a guide for wheelchair users and a beer pamphlet.

Visit Brussels (📞 02-513 89 40; www.visit brussels.be; Hôtel de Ville, Grand Place; ⏰ 9am-6pm; 🚇 Bourse) Visit Brussels has stacks of city-specific information as well as handy fold-out guides (independently researched) to the best shops, restaurants and pubs in town. The Rue Royale (📞 02-513 89 40; rue Royale 2; ⏰ 9am-6pm Mon-Fri, 10am-6pm Sat-Sun; Ⓜ Parc) office is much less crowded than the Grand Place one. Here you'll also find the Arsène50 (📞 02-512 57 45; www.arsene50.be; ⏰ 12.30-5.30pm Tue-Sat; Ⓜ Parc) desk, which provides great discounts for cultural events.

ℹ Getting There & Away

International bus service Eurolines has buses departing from Bruxelles-Nord train station.

Brussels has three major stations. High-speed trains stop only at Bruxelles-Midi (Brussel-Zuid). From there, jump straight onto any local service for the four-minute hop to more conveniently central Bruxelles-Central.

Regular services include the following:

DESTINATION	FARE (€)	DURATION (MIN)
Antwerp	7.30	35-49
Bruges	14.10	62
Ghent	8.90	36
Leuven	5.30	24-36
Luxembourg City	37.80	180
Mons	9.40	55
Ypres	17.50	105

ℹ Getting Around

Airport City Express (tickets €5.60; ⏰ 5.30am-12.20am) trains run four times hourly between Brussels Airport and the city's three main train stations, Bruxelles-Nord (15 minutes), Bruxelles-Central (€8.50, 20 minutes) and Bruxelles-Midi (25 minutes).

Brussels' integrated bus-tram-metro system is operated by **STIB/MIVB** (📞 02-515 2000; www.stib.be; Rue de l'Évêque 2; ⏰ 10am-6pm Mon-Sat). Single-/five-/10-journey STIB/MIVB tickets cost €2.10/8/14 including transfers. Unlimited one-day passes cost €6.

Leuven

📞 016 / POP 97,600
Lively Leuven (Louvain in French) is an ancient capital, a prominent brewing centre and Flanders' oldest university town. In term time, and even during holidays, some 25,000 students give the city an upbeat, creative air. The picturesque core is small enough that you could easily see the sights in a short day trip from Brussels or Antwerp, but characterful pubs and good-value dining could keep you here for weeks.

⊙ Sights

★ **Stadhuis** ARCHITECTURE
(Grote Markt 9; tours €4; ⏰ tours 3pm) Leuven's most iconic sight, the incredible 15th-century stadhuis is a late-Gothic architectural wedding cake flamboyantly overloaded with terraced turrets, fancy stonework and colourful flags. Added in the mid-19th century, a phenomenal 236 statues smother the exterior, each representing a prominent local scholar, artist or noble from the city's history. Somehow the stadhuis survived the numerous wars that devastated the rest of the town. A WWII bomb that scoured part of the facade miraculously failed to explode. The interior is less dramatic.

Stella Artois
BREWERY

(www.breweryvisits.com; Vuurkruisenlaan; adult/ concession €8.50/7.50; ⊘9am-7.30pm Tue-Sat) There are two tour options at this world-famous, highly automated brewery. Book online at least two days ahead if possible: choose 'last minute' and find a slot according to the flagged language of the available tours. Alternatively, from May to October, 90-minute tours in English are available at 3.30pm on Saturday and Sunday, with tickets sold through the tourist office. The brewery is just off the main inner ring road around 800m northwest of the train station.

🛏 Sleeping

Leuven City Hostel
HOSTEL €

(☑016-84 30 33; www.leuvencityhostel.com; Ravenstraat 37; dm/d €23/54; ⊘reception 4-8pm; @🛜) This new hostel tucked away behind KUL comes with a comfy games lounge, a quality kitchen and a sweet little courtyard-garden area. There are no membership requirements, and breakfast and linen are included in the price.

🍴 Eating & Drinking

Terrace cafes surround the stadhuis, and perpetually packed, casually stylish restaurants and bars spill tables onto a cosy flag-decked medieval alley called Muntstraat. For cheap Asian food, pizza and snacks, stroll pedestrianised Parijsstraat, Tiensestraat or Naamsestraat.

Lukemieke
VEGETARIAN €

(☑016-22 97 05; www.lukemieke.be; Vlamingenstraat 55; menus €14 & €12; ⊘noon-2pm & 6-8.30pm Mon-Fri; 🍴) This sweet vegetarian eatery with garden terrace is hidden in a pretty residential street facing Stadspark. The menu changes daily; add €2 for a glass of wine.

Domus
PUB FOOD €

(☑016-20 14 49; www.domusleuven.be; Tiensestraat 8; snacks €6-8, mains €11-18; ⊘9am-1am Tue-Sun, kitchen to 10.30pm; 🛜) Reminiscent of a rambling old-English country pub, this brewery-*café* has heavy beams and rough-plastered part-brick walls generously adorned with photos, paintings and assorted knick-knacks. It's great for sandwiches, fairly priced Flemish meals or one of its own brews: try Nostra Domus, a gentle but balanced 5.8% amber beer.

Capital
BEER HALL

(www.thecapital.be; Grote Markt 14; ⊘noon-3am daily) Leuven's bars and pubs like to advertise how many beers they offer, with the average about 300 to 400. But the Capital – a relative newcomer despite looking as though it's been here for centuries – has upped the ante: 2000 brews on offer, with 20 or so on tap at any given time.

ℹ Information

Tourist Office (☑016-20 30 20; www.visitleuven.be; Naamsestraat 1; ⊘10am-5pm Mon-Sat) Located around the side of the stadhuis. It produces a handy app called *Leuven Walk*.

ℹ Getting There & Away

Very regular train services:
Antwerp (€7.90, fast/slow 50/65 minutes)
Brussels (€5.30, fast/slow 24/36 minutes)
Brussels Airport (€8.80, 16 minutes)

Antwerp

☑03 / POP 503,200

Belgium's second city and biggest port, Antwerp (Antwerpen/Anvers in Dutch/French) is the country's capital of cool, a powerful magnet for mode moguls, club queens, art lovers and diamond dealers. In the mid-16th century it was one of Europe's most important cities and home to baroque superstar painter Pieter Paul Rubens, as you'll be regularly reminded. Despite historical travails and WWII bombing, the city retains an intriguing medieval heart with *café*-filled cobbled lanes, a riverside fortress and a truly impressive cathedral.

◉ Sights

As with every great Flemish city, Antwerp's medieval heart is a classic Grote Markt (market square).

Onze-Lieve-Vrouwekathedraal CATHEDRAL
(www.dekathedraal.be; Handschoenmarkt; adult/reduced €6/4; ⊘10am-5pm Mon-Fri, to 3pm Sat, 1-4pm Sun) Belgium's finest Gothic cathedral was 169 years in the making (1352–1521). Wherever you wander in Antwerp, its gracious, 123m-high spire has a habit of popping unexpectedly into view and it rarely fails to prompt a gasp of awe. The sight is particularly well framed when looking up Pelgrimstraat in the afternoon light.

GERMANY & BENELUX ANTWERP

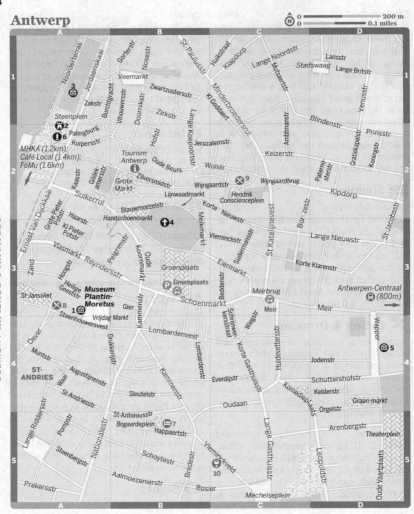

Het Steen CASTLE

(Steenplein) On a riverside knoll, Het Steen is a dinky but photogenic castle dating from 1200 and occupying the site of Antwerp's original Gallo-Roman settlement. Outside is a humorous **statue of Lange Wapper**, a tall folkloric 'peeping Tom' figure showing off his codpiece to two diminutive onlookers. Directly north, the misnamed **Maritime Park** is a long, open-sided wrought-iron shed displaying a historic barge collection. There is nothing to see inside the castle.

★**Museum Plantin-Moretus** HISTORIC BUILDING

(www.museumplantinmoretus.be; Vrijdag Markt 22; adult/reduced €8/6; ⊙10am-5pm Tue-Sun) Giving a museum Unesco World Heritage status might seem odd – until you've seen this astonishing place. Once home to the world's first industrial printing works, it's been a museum since 1876. The medieval building and 1622 courtyard garden alone would be worth a visit, but the world's oldest printing press, priceless manuscripts and original type sets make for a giddy experience indeed. Other highlights include the 1640 li-

Antwerp

brary, a bookshop dating to 1700 and rooms lined with gilt leather.

Rubenshuis MUSEUM
(www.rubenshuis.be; Wapper 9-11; adult/concession €8/6, audioguide €2; ⊗10am-5pm Tue-Sun) The 1611 building was built as home and studio by celebrated painter Pieter Paul Rubens. Rescued from ruins in 1937, and extensively and sensitively restored, the building is a delightfully indulgent one, with baroque portico, rear facade and exquisite formal garden. The furniture all dates from Rubens' era, although it's not part of the original decor. Fourteen Rubens canvases are displayed, along with some wonderful period ephemera, such as the metal frame of a ruff collar and a linen press.

🛏 Sleeping

ABhostel HOSTEL €
(☑0473 57 01 66; www.abhostel.com; Kattenberg 110; dm/tw €20/50; ⊗reception noon-3pm & 6-8pm; 🔊; 🚊10, 24 to Drink) This adorable, brightly decorated and family-run hostel has lots of little added extras. Its Borgerhout setting is 20 minutes' walk east of Antwerp-en-Centraal station. Across the street is the brilliantly unpretentious local pub **Plaza Real** (http://plazareal.be/; Kattenberg 89; ⊗from 8pm Wed-Sun; 🚊10, 24 to Drink), owned by a member of Antwerp band dEUS, and there are lots of cheap ethnic eats nearby too.

Pulcinella HOSTEL €
(☑03-234 03 14; www.jeugdherbergen.be; Bogaardeplein 1; dm/tw €27/32; @🔊) This giant,

tailor-made HI hostel is hard to beat for its Fashion District location and cool modernist decor. HI members and under-30s save €3; breakfast is included.

✖ Eating

For cheap, central snacks, stroll Hoogstraat, near the cathedral.

Domestic CAFE, BAKERY €
(☑03-239 98 90; www.domeweb.be; Steenbokstraat 37; ⊗7.30am-6pm Mon-Sat, to 2.30pm Sun; 🚊9 to Zurenborg) Julien Burlat from the Dôme Sur Mer and its fine-dining original Dôme is one of Antwerp's best bakers. This marble-lined cafe is the perfect pit stop if you're exploring Zurenborg's architecturally stunning streets, with a wonderful range of breads, brioche, tarts and quiches to have by the evocative railway bridge or to take away.

LOA INTERNATIONAL, FAST FOOD €
(☑03-291 64 85; www.loa.be; Hoogstaat 77; dishes €5-10; ⊗noon-10pm Wed-Thu, to midnight Fri & Sat, to 8pm Sun) International 'street food' – pad thai, Moroccan pancakes, tortillas, croquettes – are made with love and care in this bright cafe. There's complimentary mint tea to sip with your meal and front-row seats onto the square.

't Brantyser EUROPEAN €€
(☑03-233 18 33; www.brantyser.be; Hendrik Conscienceplein 7; snacks €6-12.50, mains €17-26; ⊗11.15am-10pm) The cosy, double-level Brantyser gets the antique-clutter effect just right, while its enviable terrace surveys one of old Antwerp's most appealing pedestrian squares. Portions are generous.

🍷 Drinking & Nightlife

To sound like a local, stride into a pub and ask for a *bolleke*. It means a 'little bowl' (ie glass) of De Koninck, the city's favourite ale.

Bierhuis Kulminator PUB
(☑03-232 45 38; Vleminckveld 32; ⊗4pm-midnight Tue-Sat, from 8pm Mon) Classic beer pub boasting 800 mostly Belgian brews, including notably rare 'vintage' bottles laid down to mature for several years like fine wine.

ⓘ Information

Tourism Antwerp (☑03-232 01 03; www.visitantwerpen.be; Grote Markt 13; ⊗9am-5.45pm Mon-Sat, to 4.45pm Sun & holidays) Tourism Antwerp has a large, central office with helpful staff – pick up maps, buy tram/bus passes and book tickets here. There is also a booth on the ground floor of Antwerpen-Centraal station.

ℹ️ Getting There & Away

The gorgeous main train station, **Antwerpen-Centraal** (Koningin Astridplein 27), is an attraction in itself. High-speed services to Amsterdam (Fyra; €31.40, 84 minutes) and Thalys (€71, 71 minutes) go via Rotterdam and Schiphol Airport. To reach the Netherlands more cheaply without reservations, take the hourly local service to Rosendaal (€9, 48 minutes), then change.

Domestic services:

DESTINATION	FARE (€)	DURATION (MIN)
Bruges	14.80	75
Brussels	7.30	35-49
Ghent-Dampoort	9.40	46
Leuven	7.30	fast/slow 42/63

Ghent

📞 09 / POP 247,500

Ghent (Gent in Dutch, Gand in French) is one of Europe's great discoveries – small enough to feel cosy but big enough to stay vibrant. It has enough medieval frivolity to create a spectacle but retains a gritty industrial edge that keeps things 'real'. Tourists remain surprisingly thin on the ground, yet with its fabulous canalside architecture, wealth of quirky bars and some of Belgium's most fascinating museums, this is a city you really won't want to miss.

👁 Sights

⭐ Patershol
AREA

(www.patershol.be) Dotted with half-hidden restaurants, enchanting Patershol is a web of twisting cobbled lanes whose old-world houses were once home to leather tradesmen and to the Carmelite Fathers (Paters), hence the name. An aimless wander here is one of the city's great pleasures; the low key restaurants and bars make it a popular hangout for students.

St-Baafskathedraal
CATHEDRAL

(www.sintbaafskathedraal.be; St-Baafsplein; ⊙8.30am-6pm Apr-Oct, to 5pm Nov-Mar) St-Baafs cathedral's towering interior has some fine stained glass and an unusual combination of brick vaulting with stone tracery. A €0.20 leaflet guides you round the cathedral's numerous art treasures, including a big original Rubens opposite the stairway that leads down into the partly muralled crypts. However, most visitors come to see just one magnificent work – the Van Eycks'

1432 'Flemish Primitive' masterpiece, *The Adoration of the Mystic Lamb* (adult/child/audioguide €4/1.50/1).

Belfort
HISTORIC BUILDING

(www.belfortgent.be; Botermarkt; adult/concession/child €6/2/free; ⊙10am-5.30pm) Ghent's soaring, Unesco-listed, 14th-century belfry is topped by a large dragon. That's a weathervane not a fire breather and it's become something of a city mascot. You'll meet two previous dragon incarnations on the climb to the top (mostly by lift) but other than some bell-making exhibits, the real attraction is the view. Enter through the **Lakenhalle**, Ghent's cloth hall that was left half-built in 1445 and only completed in 1903.

Gravensteen
CASTLE

(www.gravensteengent.be; St-Veerleplein; adult/concession/child €10/7.50/6; ⊙10am-6pm Apr-Oct, 9am-5pm Nov-Mar) The counts of Flanders' quintessential 12th-century stone castle comes complete with moat, turrets and arrow slits. It's all the more remarkable considering that during the 19th century the site was converted into a cotton mill. Meticulously restored since, the interior sports the odd suit of armour, a guillotine and torture devices. The relative lack of furnishings is compensated with a hand-held 45-minute movie guide, which sets a tongue-in-cheek historical costumed drama in the rooms, prison pit and battlements.

🛏 Sleeping

⭐ Uppelink
HOSTEL €

(📞09-279 44 77; www.hosteluppelink.com; Sint-Michielsplein 21; dm €19-35, s/tw €50/60)

Ghent Centre

◎ Top Sights

◎ Sights

🛏 Sleeping

✖ Eating

◎ Drinking & Nightlife

Within a classic step-gabled canalside house, the show-stopping attraction at this super-central new hostel is the unbeatable view of Ghent's main towers as seen from the breakfast room and from the biggest, cheapest dorms. Smaller rooms have little view, if any.

Hostel 47   HOSTEL €
(☑0478 71 28 27; www.hostel47.com; Blekerijstraat 47-51; dm €26.50-29.50, d/tr €66/€90; ☏) Unusually calm yet pretty central, this inviting hostel has revamped a high-ceilinged historic house with virginal white walls, spacious bunk rooms and designer fittings. Free lockers and cursory breakfast with Nespresso coffee; no bar.

✗ Eating

There's fast food around Korenmarkt and great-value Turkish options along Sleepstraat. Numerous vegetarian and organic choices feature on the tourist office's free Veggieplan Gent guide map.

't Oud Clooster   TAVERNA €
(☑09-233 78 02; www.toudclooster.be; Zwartezusterstraat 5; mains €9-18; ⊗noon-2.30pm & 6-10.30pm Mon-Fri, noon-2.30pm & 5-10.30pm Sat, 5-10.30pm Sun) Mostly candlelit at night, this

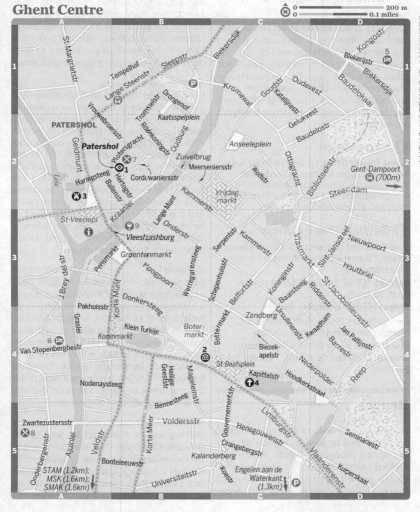

Ghent Centre

atmospheric double-level 'pratcafe' is built into sections of what was long ago a nunnery, hence the sprinkling of religious statues and cherub lamp-holders. Well-priced *café* food is presented with unexpected style and the kitchen works until midnight. Try the original curry-cream *Spaghetti Oud Clooster* (€9).

Amadeus RIBS **€**
(☑ 09-225 13 85; www.amadeussparerribrestaurant. be; Plotersgracht 8/10; mains €13.75-18.75; ☺ 6.30-11pm) All-you-can-eat spare ribs (€15.95) at four Ghent addresses, all within ancient buildings that are full of atmosphere, bustle and cheerful conversation.

Drinking & Nightlife

★ **'t Dreupelkot** BAR
(☑ 09 224 21 20; www.dreupelkot.be; Groenten-markt 12; ☺ 4pm-late) A traditional *jenever* bar, serving 100 Belgian concoctions – including the owner's homemade prune and raisin versions – and one north French. Traditionally *jenever* is made from grain and malt and packs a punch at 40% proof. The bare brick and tiled interior is warmly atmospheric.

ℹ️ Information

Ghent Tourist Office (☑ 09-266 56 60; www. visitgent.be; Oude Vismijn, St-Veerleplein 5; ☺ 9.30am-6.30pm mid-Mar–mid-Oct, to 4.30pm mid-Oct–mid-Mar) Very helpful for free maps and accommodation bookings.

ℹ️ Getting There & Away

Gent-Dampoort, 1km west of the old city, is the handiest station with useful trains to the following destinations:

Antwerp (€9.40, fast/slow 42/64 minutes, three per hour)

Bruges (€6.50, 36 minutes, hourly)

Gent-St-Pieters, 2.5km south of centre and Ghent's main station, has more choices:

Brussels (€8.90, 36 minutes, twice hourly)

Bruges (€6.50 fast/slow 24/42 minutes, five per hour)

Bruges

☑ 050 / POP 117,000
If you set out to design a fairy-tale medieval town, it would be hard to improve on central Bruges (Brugge in Dutch). Picturesque cobbled lanes and dreamy canals link photogenic market squares lined with soaring towers, historic churches and old white-washed almshouses. And there's plenty of it. The only downside is that everyone knows. That means that there's a constant crush of tourists in the centre, especially through the summer months. So to really enjoy Bruges stay overnight and try to visit midweek.

◉ Sights

The real joy of Bruges is simply wandering alongside the canals, soaking up the atmosphere. To avoid the worst crowds, explore east of pretty Jan van Eyckplein.

Belfort HISTORIC BUILDING
(Belfry; adult/child €8/5; ☺ 9.30am-5pm, last tickets 4.15pm) Towering 83m above the square like a gigantic medieval rocket is the fabulous 13th-century belfort. There's relatively little to see inside, but it's worth the mildly claustrophobic 366-step climb for the fine views. Visitor numbers are limited to 70 at once, which can cause queues at peak times.

★ **Groeningemuseum** GALLERY
(www.brugge.be; Dijver 12; adult/concession €8/6; ☺ 9.30am-5pm Tue-Sun) Bruges' most celebrated art gallery boasts an astonishingly rich collection whose strengths are in superb Flemish Primitive and Renaissance works, depicting the conspicuous wealth of the city with glitteringly realistic artistry. In room 2 are meditative works including Jan Van Eyck's 1436 radiant masterpiece *Madonna with Canon George Van der Paele* (1436) and the *Madonna* by the Master of the Embroidered Foliage, where the rich fabric of the Madonna's robe meets the 'real' foliage at her feet with exquisite detail.

Begijnhof HISTORIC BUILDING
(Wijngaardstraat; ☺ 6.30am-6.30pm) **FREE** Bruges' delightful *begijnhof* (building that housed a community of lay religious women) originally dates from the 13th century. Although the last *begijn* has long since passed away, today residents of the pretty, whitewashed garden complex include a convent of Benedictine nuns. Despite the hordes of summer tourists, the *begijnhof* remains a remarkably tranquil haven. In spring, a carpet of daffodils adds to the quaintness of the scene.

★ **Museum St-Janshospitaal** MUSEUM
(Memlingmuseum; Mariastraat 38; adult/concession/child €8/€6/free; ☺ 9.30am-5pm Tue-Sun) In the restored chapel of a 12th-century hospital building with superb timber beamwork, this museum shows various torturous-looking medical implements,

hospital sedan chairs and a gruesome 1679 painting of an anatomy class. But it is much better known for six masterpieces by 15th-century artist Hans Memling, including the enchanting reliquary of St Ursula. This gilded oak reliquary looks like a mini Gothic cathedral, painted with scenes from the life of St Ursula, including highly realistic Cologne cityscapes.

🛏 Sleeping

Bauhaus HOSTEL €
(☑050 34 10 93; www.bauhaus.be; Langestraat 145; hostel dm/tw €16/50, hotel s/c €16/50, 2-4 person apt per weekend from €240; @ 🖥) One of Belgium's most popular hang-outs for young travellers, this backpacker 'village' incorporates a hostel, apartments, a nightclub, an internet cafe and a little chill-out room that's well hidden behind the reception and laundrette section at Langestraat 145. Simple and slightly cramped dorms are operated with key cards; hotel-section double rooms have private shower cubicles; bike hire is also available.

Take bus 6 or 16 from the train station.

Passage Bruges HOSTEL €
(☑050 34 02 32; www.passagebruges.com; Dweersstraat 26-28; dm/tw/tr €25/50/75) Located above an invitingly old-fashioned cafe-restaurant is a recently renovated hostel; the next-door building houses spartan but large and well-priced hotel rooms.

't Keizershof HOTEL €
(☑050 33 87 28; www.hotelkeizershof.be; Oostermeers 126; s €35-47, d €47; P 🖥) Remarkably tasteful and well kept for this price, the seven simple rooms with shared bathrooms are above a former brasserie-cafe decorated with old radios (now used as the breakfast room). Free parking.

★ B&B Dieltiens B&B €€
(☑050 33 42 94; www.bedandbreakfastbruges.be; Waalsestraat 40; s €60-80, d €70-90, tr €90-100) Old and new art fills this lovingly restored classical mansion, which remains an appealingly real home run by charming musician hosts. Superbly central yet quiet. It also operates a holiday flat (from €75 per night) nearby in a 17th-century house.

🍴 Eating

Den Gouden Karpel SEAFOOD €
(☑050 33 33 89; www.dengoudenkarpel.be; Vismarkt 9-11; mains from €4; ⊙11am-6pm Tue-Sat)

Takeaway or eat in, this sleek little café-bar is a great location for a jumpingly fresh seafood lunch, right by the fish market. Crab sandwiches, smoked salmon salads, shrimp croquettes and oysters are on the menu.

Est Wijnbar TAPAS €
(☑050 33 38 39; www.wijnbarest.be; Braambergstraat 7; mains €10-14, tapas €4-10; ⊙4pm-midnight Fri-Mon; 🎵) This attractive little wine bar – the building dates back to 1637 – is a pleasantly informal supper spot, with raclette, pasta, snacks and salads on the menu, and tasty desserts. It's especially lively on Sunday nights, when you can catch live jazz, blues and occasionally other musical styles from 8.30pm.

🍷 Drinking & Entertainment

De Garre PUB
(☑050 34 10 29; www.degarre.be; Garre 1; ⊙noon-midnight Mon-Thu, to 1am Fri & Sat) Try its very own and fabulous Garre draught beer, which comes with a thick floral head in a glass that's almost a brandy balloon; they'll only serve you three of these due to the head-spinning 11% alcohol percentage. The hidden two-floor estaminet (tavern) also stocks dozens of other fine Belgian brews, including remarkable Struise Pannepot (€3.50).

Herberg Vlissinghe CAFE
(☑050 34 37 37; www.cafevlissinghe.be; Blekerstraat 2; ⊙11am-10pm Wed & Thu, to midnight Fri & Sat, to 7pm Sun) Luminaries have frequented Bruges' oldest pub for 500 years; local legend has it that Rubens once painted an imitation coin on the table here and then did a runner. The interior is gorgeously preserved

Bruges

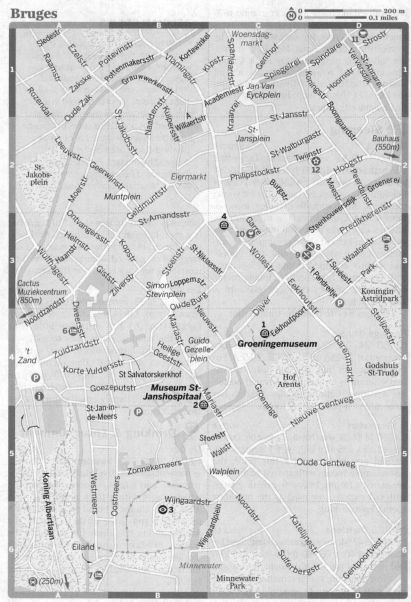

with wood panelling and a wood-burning stove, but in summer the best seats are in the shady garden where you can play boules.

★ **Retsin's Lucifernum** LIVE MUSIC
(☎ 0476 35 06 51; www.lucifernum.be; Twijnstraat 6-8; admission incl drink €10; ☺ 8-11pm Sun) A former Masonic lodge owned by a self-proclaimed vampire: ring the bell on a Sunday night, pass the voodoo temple and hope you're invited inside where an otherworldly candle-lit bar may be serving potent rum cocktails and serenading you with live Latin

Bruges

◉ **Top Sights**

◉ **Sights**

🛏 **Sleeping**

✖ **Eating**

🍷 **Drinking & Nightlife**

🎭 **Entertainment**

music. Or maybe not. It's always a surprise. Don't miss the graves in the tropical garden.

In case you're wondering, the permanent scaffolding is an artwork – and a thorn in the side of the local council.

❶ Information

Tourist Office (In&Uit Brugge; 't Zand 34; ⊙10am-5pm Mon-Sat, 10am-2pm Sun) The tourist office is situated at street level of the big, red Concertgebouw concert hall with a branch at the train station. Excellent Use-It guide-maps (www.use-it.be) are free if you ask.

❶ Getting There & Away

Bruges' **train station** (📞 050 30 24 24) is 1.5km south of the Markt. Twice-hourly trains run to Brussels (€14.10, 62 minutes via Ghent (€6.50, 23 minutes). Hourly trains go to Antwerp (€14.80, 80 minutes). For Ypres (Ieper), take the train to Roeselare then bus 95 via Langemark or 94 via Passendale, Tyne Cot and Zonnebeke.

Ypres

📞 057 / POP 35,100

Only the hardest of hearts are unmoved by historic Ypres (Ieper in Dutch). In the Middle Ages it was an important cloth town ranking alongside Bruges and Ghent. In WWI some 300,000 Allied soldiers died in the 'Salient', a bow-shaped bulge that formed the front line around town. Ypres remained unoccupied

by German forces, but was utterly flattened by bombardment. After the war, the beautiful medieval core was convincingly rebuilt and the restored Ypres Lakenhalle is today one of the most spectacular buildings in Belgium. Most tourism still revolves around WWI; the Salient is dotted with cemeteries, memorials, bunkers and war museums.

◉ Sights

★**In Flanders Fields**   MUSEUM
(www.inflandersfields.be; Lakenhalle, Grote Markt 34; adult/under 26 yr/child €9/5/4; ⊙10am-6pm Apr–mid-Nov, to 5pm Tue-Sun mid-Nov–Mar) This standout museum gives a balanced yet moving and user-friendly introduction to WWI history. It's a multi-sensory experience combining soundscapes, videos, well-chosen exhibits and interactive learning stations at which you 'become' a character and follow his/her progress through the wartime period. An electronic 'identity' bracelet activates certain displays.

Lakenhalle   HISTORIC BUILDING
(Cloth Hall; Grote Markt 34) Dominating the Grote Markt, the enormous reconstructed Lakenhalle is one of Belgium's most impressive buildings. Its 70m-high belfry has the vague appearance of a medieval Big Ben. The original version was completed in 1304 beside the Ieperslee, a river that, now covered over, once allowed ships to sail right up to the Lakenhalle to unload their cargoes of wool. These were stored beneath the high gables of the 1st floor, where you'll find the unmissable In Flanders Fields Museum.

Menin Gate   MEMORIAL
(Menenpoort) A block east of Grote Markt, the famous Menin Gate is a huge stone gateway straddling the main road at the city moat. It's inscribed with the names of 54,896 'lost' British and Commonwealth WWI troops whose bodies were never found. At 8pm daily, traffic is halted while buglers sound the Last Post in remembrance of the WWI dead, a moving tradition begun in 1928.

☞ Tours

Over the Top   BUS TOUR
(📞0472 34 87 47; www.overthetoptours.be; Meensestraat 41; tours €40; ⊙tours 9am-1pm, 2.30-5.30pm & 7.30-8.30pm) This WWI specialist bookshop towards the Menin Gate offers twice-daily, half-day guided minibus tours of the Ypres Salient. The north salient tour is in the morning, the south in the afternoon.

VISITING THE YPRES SALIENT

Many WWI sites are in rural locations that are awkward to reach without a car or tour. These sights are all within 600m of Ypres–Roeselare bus routes 94 and 95 (once or twice hourly weekdays, five daily weekends), so could be visited en route between Ypres and Bruges.

Memorial Museum Passchendaele 1917 (www.passchendaele.be; Ieperstraat 5; admission €7.50; ⏱9am-6pm Feb-Nov; 🚌94) In central Zonnebeke village, Kasteel Zonnebeke (www.zonnebeke.be) is a lake-fronted Normandy chalet-style mansion built in 1922 to replace a castle bombarded into rubble during WWI. It hosts a tourist office, a cafe and a particularly polished WWI museum charting local battle progressions with plenty of multilingual commentaries. The big attraction here is descending into its multiroom 'trench experience' with low-lit, wooden-clad subterranean bunk rooms and a soundtrack. Explanations are more helpful here than in 'real' trenches elsewhere.

Tyne Cot (⏱24hr, visitor centre 9am-6pm Feb-Nov; 🚌94) Probably the most visited Salient site, this is the world's biggest British Commonwealth war cemetery, with 11,956 graves. A huge semicircular wall commemorates another 34,857 lost-in-action soldiers whose names wouldn't fit on Ypres' Menin Gate. The name Tyne Cot was coined by Northumberland Fusiliers who fancied that German bunkers on the hillside here looked like Tyneside cottages. Two such dumpy concrete bunkers sit amid the graves, with a third visible through the metal wreath beneath the white Cross of Sacrifice.

Deutscher Soldatenfriedhof The area's main German WWI cemetery is memorable, amid oak trees and trios of squat, mossy crosses. Some 44,000 corpses were grouped together here, up to 10 per granite grave slab, and four eerie silhouette statues survey the site. Entering takes you through a black concrete 'tunnel' that clanks and hisses with distant war sounds, while four short video montages commemorate the tragedy of war. It's beyond the northern edge of Langemark on bus route 95.

British Grenadier BUS TOUR
(📞057 21 46 57; www.salienttours.be; Meensestraat 5; short/long tour €30/38; ⏱10am-2pm & 2.30-5pm) Two Ypres tours – the 2½-hour option takes in Hill 60, the Caterpillar Crater and the German Bayernwald trench complex, while the standard four-hour tour covers every site on the Salient.

🛏 Sleeping & Eating

B&B Ter Thuyne B&B €€
(📞057 36 00 42; www.terthuyne.be; Gustave de Stuersstraat 19; d €95; @) Three comfortable rooms that are luminously bright and scrupulously clean, but not overly fashion-conscious.

't Leedvermaak BISTRO €
(📞057 216 385; Korte Meersstraat 2; mains €7-17; ⏱11.30am-1.30pm & 6-11pm Tue-Sun) Low-key theatrically themed bistro serving fair-priced pastas, vegie dishes and tapas.

⭐ De Ruyffelaer FLEMISH €€
(📞057 36 60 06; www.deruyffelaer.be; Gustave de Stuersstraat 9; mains €15-21, menus €26-34; ⏱11.30am-3.30pm Sun, 5.30-9.30pm Thu-Sun) Traditional local dishes served in an adorable, wood-panelled interior with old checkerboard floors and a brocante decor, including dried flowers, old radios and antique biscuit tins.

ℹ Information

Tourist Office (📞057 23 92 20; www.toerismeieper.be; Lakenhalle; ⏱9am-6pm Mon-Fri, 10am-6pm Sat & Sun Apr–mid-Nov, to 5pm mid-Nov–Mar) Tourist office for Ypres and surrounds with an extensive bookshop.

ℹ Getting There & Away

For Bruges, take bus 94 or 95 to Roeselare from the train station or Grote Markt, then swap to a train. Trains run at least hourly to Brussels (1¾ hours).

Mons

📞065 / POP 93,400

With a characterful medieval centre climbing up a hill and a fine Grand Place, Mons (Bergen in Dutch), in French-speaking Wallonia, had a substantial facelift in 2015, when it was a European Capital of Culture.

The legacy is a handful of entertaining modern museums that make Mons an excellent visit, with plenty to keep you busy for two or three days.

◉ Sights

★ Mons Memorial Museum   MUSEUM
(☑065-40 53 12; www.monsmemorialmuseum.mons.be; Blvd Dolez 51; adult/child €9/2; ☺10am-6pm Tue-Sun) A superb new museum, this extensive display mostly covers Mons' experience of the two world wars, though the constant sieges of this town's turbulent history are also mentioned. It gets the balance just right between military history, personal testimony of civilians and soldiers, and thought-provoking items on display. Some seriously good visuals make the to-and-fro (and stuck for years in the mud) of WWI instantly comprehensible, and there's an animated 3D film on the legend of the Angels of Mons.

Musée du Doudou   MUSEUM
(www.museedudoudou.mons.be; Jardin du Mayeur; adult/child €9/2; ☺10am-6pm Tue-Sun) Head through the Hôtel de Ville on the Grand Place to reach this museum dedicated to Mons' riotous **Ducasse festival** (www.ducassedemons.be). All aspects of this curious event, as well as background on St George, Ste Waudru and dragons, are covered in entertaining interactive fashion, and there are interesting cultural musings on the festival's changing nature over time. At the audiovisual showing the climactic Lumeçon battle, you can almost smell the beer and sweat. There's audio content in French, Dutch and English.

🛏 Sleeping & Eating

Auberge de Jeunesse   HOSTEL €
(☑065-87 55 70; www.lesaubergesdejeunesse.be; Rampe du Château 2; dm/s/d €28/46/68; P@🛜) Just before the base of the belfry, this modern, well-equipped HI hostel has an attractive tiered design making good use of the sloping terrain. Worth booking ahead. Prices drop significantly in quieter months. Rates are €2 less per person for those 26 and under; 10% HI discount.

La Vie est Belle   BELGIAN €
(☑065-56 58 45; Rue d'Havré 39; mains €8-18; ☺noon-3pm & 6-11pm Tue-Sat, noon-3pm Sun) This family-style restaurant is superb value for home-style Belgian food that's filling rather than gourmet (think meatballs, mashed potatoes, rabbit or mussels). The naive puppet models adorning the decorative mirrors add character.

ℹ Information

Maison du Tourisme (☑065-33 55 80; www.visitmons.be; Grand Place 27; ☺9am-7pm daily; 🛜) On the main square, with lots of booklets and information, and bike rental.

ℹ Getting There & Away

Mons' **train station** (Place Léopold), which is provisional until the new Calatrava design is finally finished, and neighbouring **TEC bus station** (☑065-38 88 15) are 700m west of the Grand Place. There are very regular services to Brussels (€9.40, 50 minutes), as well as other Belgian destinations.

OFF THE BEATEN TRACK

BOUILLON

Dreamily arrayed around a tight loop of the Semois River, pretty Bouillon is protected by its gloriously medieval castle, gnarled and grim up on the hill. On a summer evening, limpid light and reflections in the water can make this one of Belgium's prettiest towns.

The **Château de Bouillon** (☑061 46 62 57; www.bouillon-initiative.be; Rue du Château; adult/child €7/5; ☺10am-7pm Jul & Aug, 10am-5pm or 6pm Feb-Jun & Sep-Dec, weekends only Jan; P🛜) Belgium's finest feudal castle, accessed by two stone bridges between crags, harks back to 988, but is especially associated with Crusader knight Godefroid (Godefroy) de Bouillon. The super-atmospheric castle still has everything you might wish for – dank dripping passageways tunnelling into the hillside, musty half-lit cell rooms, rough-hewn stairwells and many an eerie nook and cranny to discover.

To reach Bouillon, catch a train to Libramont, then take bus 8 (€3.20, 45 minutes, roughly hourly weekdays, two-hourly weekends).

Belgium Survival Guide

ℹ Directory A–Z

ACCOMMODATION

Availability varies markedly by season and area. May to September occupancy is very high (especially at weekends) in Bruges, for example.

Hostels (*jeugdherbergen* in Dutch, *auberges de jeunesse* in French) generally charge from €18 to €28 for a dorm bed. Rates are cheaper for under-30s in Flanders, or under-26s in Wallonia.

LGBT TRAVELLERS

Attitudes to homosexuality are pretty laid-back. Same-sex couples have been able to wed legally since 2003, and since 2006 have had the same rights enjoyed by heterosexual couples, including inheritance and adoption. Brussels has a decent gay scene.

MONEY

➡ Credit cards are widely accepted. ATMs are very common and are the best way of accessing cash.

➡ Tipping is not required for taxis, restaurants or bars, though some locals round up a bill.

OPENING HOURS

Many sights close on Monday. Restaurants normally close one full day per week.

Banks 8.30am to 3.30pm or later Monday to Friday, some also Saturday morning

Bars 10am to 1am, but hours very flexible

Restaurants noon to 2.30pm and 7pm to 9.30pm

Shops 10am to 6.30pm Monday to Saturday, sometimes closed for an hour at lunchtime

PUBLIC HOLIDAYS

New Year's Day 1 January

Easter Monday March/April

Labour Day 1 May

Iris Day 8 May (Brussels region only)

Ascension Day 39 days after Easter Sunday (always a Thursday)

Pentecost Monday 50 days after Easter Sunday

Flemish Community Day 11 July (Flanders only)

Belgium National Day 21 July

Assumption Day 15 August

Francophone Community Day 27 September (Wallonia only)

All Saints' Day 1 November

Armistice Day 11 November

Christmas Day 25 December

TELEPHONE

➡ Country code ☑ 32. International access code ☑ 00.

➡ If you've got an unlocked smartphone, you can pick up a local SIM card for a few euros and charge it with a month's worth of data at a decent speed for under €20.

ℹ Getting There & Around

AIR

Brussels is the major airport and is pretty well connected. Charleroi airport is a budget hub.

BUS

Useful Eurolines bus routes include London–Brussels (seven to eight hours), London–Bruges/Ghent (six to seven hours), Brussels–Paris (four hours), Brussels–Amsterdam (three to four hours) and Brussels–Berlin (10 hours).

Within Belgium, the train is normally more convenient, but the route planner at www.belgianrail.be gives useful bus suggestions where that's the logical choice.

FERRY

At the time of research, there was only one ferry service operating from Belgium: the P&O (www.poferries.com) service Zeebrugge–Hull (14 hours, overnight).

TRAIN

➡ Thalys (www.thalys.com) operates high speed trains from Brussels to Cologne (1¾ hours, five daily), Paris (82 minutes, 16 daily) and Amsterdam via Rotterdam (110 minutes, 11 daily).

➡ Eurostar (www.eurostar.com) runs Brussels Midi–Lille–London (two hours) seven to 10 times daily.

➡ Deutsche Bahn (www.bahn.com) has ICE trains running Brussels Midi–Aachen–Frankfurt (three hours, four daily) via Cologne (1¾ hours) and Frankfurt airport.

> ### ℹ PRICE RANGES: BELGIUM & LUXEMBOURG
>
> Sleeping price ranges refer to a double room with private bathroom and breakfast in high season:
>
> **€** less than €60
>
> **€€** €60–140
>
> **€€€** more than €140
>
> Eating price ranges are for the cost of a main course:
>
> **€** less than €15
>
> **€€** €15–25
>
> **€€€** more than €25

→ SNCF (http://voyages-sncf.com), the French rail operator, runs TGV trains Bruxelles Midi–Paris CDG Airport (1½ hours) and direct to several other French cities.

→ There's a comprehensive domestic network. Belgium's trains are run by **SNCB** (Belgian Railways; ☑ 02-528 28 28; www.belgianrail.be).

LUXEMBOURG

Luxembourg City

POP 111.300

If you thought that the Grand Duchy's capital was nothing more than banks and EU offices, you'll be delighted at discovering the attractive reality. The Unesco-listed Old Town is one of Europe's most scenic capitals, thanks largely to its unusual setting, draped across the deep gorges of the Alzette and Pétrusse rivers. It's full of weird spaces, tunnels, and surprising nooks to explore. Good museums and a great dining scene makes this a top city to visit. It's worth visiting on a weekend, when hotel prices drop and on-street parking is free.

◉ Sights

The Old Town counterpoints some fine old buildings with modern museums and an offering of high-end restaurants. The picturesque Grund area lies riverside, at the base of a dramatic fortified escarpment.

★ **Chemin de la Corniche** AREA
This pedestrian promenade has been hailed as 'Europe's most beautiful balcony'. It winds along the course of the 17th-century city ramparts with views across the river canyon towards the hefty fortifications of the Wenzelsmauer (Wenceslas Wall). The rampart-top walk continues along Blvd Victor Thorn to the Dräi Tier (Triple Gate) tower.

★ **Bock Casemates** FORTRESS
(Montée de Clausen; adult/child €4/2; ⊙10am-5.30pm Mar-Oct, last entry 5pm) Beneath the Montée de Clausen, the cliff-top site of Count Sigefroi's once-mighty fort, the Bock Casemates are a picturesque, atmospheric honeycomb of rock galleries and passages – yes, kids will love it – initially carved by the Spaniards between 1737 and 1746. Over the years the casemates have housed everything from garrisons to bakeries to slaughterhous-

> ⓘ **GETTING AROUND LUXEMBOURG**
>
> Luxembourg has a one-price domestic ticket system. Wherever you go by public transport within Luxembourg the price is the same, €2 for up to two hours, €4 for the day.

es; during WWI and WWII they sheltered 35,000 locals.

★ **Musée d'Histoire de la Ville de Luxembourg** MUSEUM
(Luxembourg City History Museum; ☑ 47 96 45 00; www.mhvl.lu; 14 Rue du St-Esprit; acult/under 21 yr €5/free; ⊙10am-6pm Tue-Sun, to 8pm Thu) This remarkably engrossing and interactive museum hides within a series of 17th-century houses, including a former 'holiday home' of the Bishop of Orval. A lovely garden and open terrace offers great views.

★ **US Military Cemetery** CEMETERY
(www.abmc.gov; 50 Val du Scheid; ⊙9am-5pm) In a beautifully maintained graveyard near Hamm lie over 5000 US WWII war dead, including George Patton, the audacious general of the US Third Army who played a large part in Luxembourg's 1944 liberation. It's a humbling sight, with its long rows of white crosses (and the odd Star of David). It's just near the airport off the N2; bus 15 gets you close. Take it to the second-last stop, Käschtewee.

🛏 Sleeping

There's only one city youth hostel, but rural HI hostels are relatively accessible at Bourglinster (17km) and Larochette (28km), both on Luxembourg–Diekirch bus route 100.

Auberge de Jeunesse HOSTEL €
(☑22 68 89; www.youthhostels.lu; 5 Rue du Fort Olisy; dm/s/d €25/40/60, €3 per person off for HI members; P ✳ @ 🛜) This state-of-the-art hostel has very comfortable, sex-segregated dorms with electronic entry. There are good-sized lockers (bring padlock), laundry facilities and masses of space including a great terrace from which to admire views to the old city. En-suite dorms cost €1 more.

It's a short but steep walking descent from the Casemates area down stairs near 'Clausen Plateau Altmunster' bus stop. The cafe does a decent two-course dinner for €10.90.

GERMANY & BENELUX LUXEMBOURG CITY

Luxembourg City

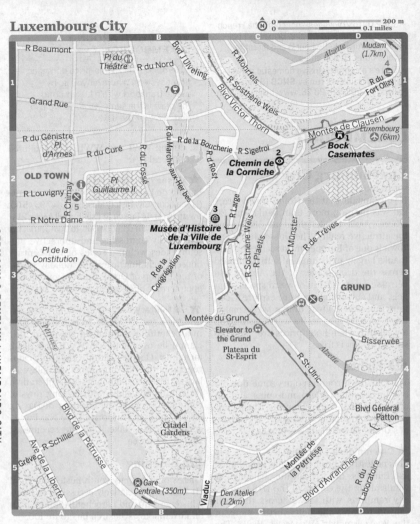

GERMANY & BENELUX LUXEMBOURG CITY

Luxembourg City

✗ Eating & Drinking

Eating is expensive in Luxembourg, but there's a lively dining scene. Inexpensive but mostly characterless places for Asian food are in the train station area.

Á la Soupe   CAFE €
(www.alasoupe.net; 9 Rue Chimay; breakfast €3.50-7, soup €4.90-7.30; ⊙10am-7pm Mon-Fri, 10am-6pm Sat) Central and minimally stylish soup station serving Moroccan and detox soups, as well as classic chicken.

Bosso   ALSATIAN, GERMAN €
(www.bosso.lu; 7 Bisserwée; mains €9-17; ⊙5.30-11.30pm Tue-Thu, 11.30am-11.30pm Fri-Sun; 🛜)

VIANDEN

Palace, citadel, fortified cathedral? At first glance it's hard to tell just what it is towering so grandly amid the mists and wooded hills above historic Vianden. In fact it's a vast slate-roofed **castle complex** (☑ 83 41 08 1; www.castle-vianden.lu; adult/child €6/2; ☺ 10am-4pm Nov-Feb, to 5pm Mar & Oct, to 6pm Apr-Sep) whose impregnable white stone walls glow golden in the evening's floodlights, creating one of Luxembourg's most photogenic scenes. Vianden's appealing old town is essentially one road, cobbled Grand Rue that rises 700m to the castle gates from a bridge across the River Our. Newer sections of town follow the riverbanks in either direction.

For somewhere special to stay, with a delicious grill restaurant to boot, try **Auberge Aal Veinen** (☑ 83 43 68; http://vianden.beimhunn.lu; 114 Grand Rue; s/d €60/80; ☺ closed mid-Dec–mid-Jan; ☏) on the main street.

From Luxembourg City, bus or train it to Diekirch or Ettelbrück, from where half-hourly buses hit Vianden (€2, up to 25 minutes).

In summer, the biggest attraction of this good-value Grund restaurant is the hidden courtyard garden where seating is attractively tree-shaded. Try the *flammeküeche*, wafer-thin Alsatian 'pizzas' or various takes on potato rösti, or just linger over a drink.

Konrad Cafe BAR
(www.facebook.com/Konradcafe; 7 Rue du Nord; ☺ 10am-midnight Mon-Thu, 10am-1am Fri & Sat, 11am-midnight Sun; ☏) Relaxed and happily bohemian, this sweet cafe is a cordial spot to drop in at any time of day for juices, light meals (€4 to €10) or a coffee and something sweet. At night it becomes more of a bar, with a downstairs space hosting regular comedy and live music.

ℹ Information

Luxembourg City Tourist Office (LCTO; ☑ 22 28 09; www.lcto.lu; Place Guillaume II; ☺ 9am-6pm Mon-Sat, 10am-6pm Sun) Sells city guides (€2), and has maps, walking-tour pamphlets and event guides.

Luxembourg Survival Guide

ℹ Directory A–Z

ACCOMMODATION
Luxembourg has an excellent network of Hostelling International (HI) youth hostels (http://youthhostels.lu).

Hotel accommodation in Luxembourg City is very expensive midweek but drops markedly at weekends. See p274 for price ranges.

DISCOUNT CARDS
The Luxembourg Card (www.visitluxembourg.com; one-/two-/three-day adult €13/20/28, family €28/48/68) offers excellent value.

LGBT TRAVELLERS
No worries here. Luxembourg legalised same-sex marriage in 2015, and prime minister Xavier Bettel soon took advantage to tie the knot himself.

MONEY
Credit cards are widely accepted. ATMs are very common and are the best way of accessing cash.

Tipping is not required for taxis, restaurants or bars, though some locals round up a bill.

For price ranges used for Luxembourg in this book, see p274.

OPENING HOURS
Banks 8.30am to 3.30pm or later Monday to Friday, some also Saturday morning
Bars 10am to 1am, but hours very flexible
Restaurants noon to 2.30pm and 7pm to 9.30pm
Shops 10am to 6.30pm Monday to Saturday, sometimes closed for an hour at lunchtime

PUBLIC HOLIDAYS
➡ **New Year's Day** 1 January
➡ **Easter Monday** March/April
➡ **Labour Day** 1 May
➡ **Ascension Day** 39 days after Easter Sunday (always a Thursday)
➡ **Pentecost Monday** 50 days after Easter Sunday
➡ **Luxembourg National Day** 23 June
➡ **Assumption Day** 15 August
➡ **All Saints' Day** 1 November
➡ **Christmas Day** 25 December

TELEPHONE
➡ Country code ☑ 352.
➡ International access code ☑ 00.
➡ Roaming with an EU SIM card is cheap these days, so you're probably better buying a local SIM.

ℹ Getting There & Away

AIR

Luxembourg has its own airport, but it's often cheaper to fly to Frankfurt, Brussels or Paris, for example, and connect from there.

BUS

Long-distance – the term is relative – buses pick up from a variety of central points. Several routes head into Germany and France, where you can connect with local networks. Consult timetables at www.mobiliteit.lu.

TRAIN

Trains are run by CFL (📞 24 89 24 89; www.cfl.lu), with good connections all through northern Europe. Fares from Luxembourg City include:

Brussels (€39, three hours, hourly)

Paris (2¼ hours, €82 to €104) Direct TGV five to six times daily via Metz.

Trier (€18, one hour, hourly) Continuing to Koblenz (€46.20, 2½ hours).

NETHERLANDS

Amsterdam

🌐 020 / POP 811,200

World Heritage–listed canals lined by gabled houses, candlelit cafes, whirring bicycles, lush parks, monumental museums, colourful markets, diverse dining, quirky shopping and legendary nightlife make the free-spirited Dutch capital one of Europe's great cities. Amsterdam has been a liberal place since the Netherlands' Golden Age, when it was at the forefront of European art and trade. Centuries later, in the 1960s, it again led the pack – this time in the principles of tolerance, with broad-minded views on drugs and same-sex relationships taking centre stage. Explore its many worlds-within-worlds, where nothing ever seems the same twice.

ℹ GAY AMSTERDAM

Amsterdam's gay scene is one of the largest in the world. Hubs include Warmoesstraat and Zeedijk in the Red Light District and Reguliersdwarsstraat in the Southern Canal Ring. Gay Amsterdam (www.gayamsterdam.com) lists hotels, bars, clubs and more.

◉ Sights

★ Rijksmuseum MUSEUM

(National Museum; Map p282; 📞 674 70 00; www.rijksmuseum.nl; Museumstraat 1; adult/child €17.50/free; ⏱ 9am-5pm; 🚊 2/5 Rijksmuseum) The Rijksmuseum is the Netherlands' premier art trove, splashing Rembrandts, Vermeers and 7500 other masterpieces over 1.5km of galleries. To avoid the biggest crowds, come after 3pm. Or prebook tickets online, which provides fast-track entry.

The Golden Age works are the highlight. Feast your eyes on still lifes, gentlemen in ruffled collars and landscapes bathed in pale yellow light. Rembrandt's *The Night Watch* (1642) takes pride of place.

★ Van Gogh Museum MUSEUM

(Map p282; 📞 570 52 00; www.vangoghmuseum.nl; Paulus Potterstraat 7; adult/child €17/free, audioguide €5; ⏱ 9am-6pm Sun-Thu, to 10pm Fri & Sat Jul-Oct, 9am-5pm Sat-Thu, to 10pm Fri Nov-Jun; 🚊 2/3/5/12 Van Baerlestraat) Framed by a gleaming new glass entrance hall, the world's largest Van Gogh collection offers a superb line-up of masterworks. Trace the artist's life from his tentative start through his giddy-coloured sunflower phase, and on to the black cloud that descended over him and his work. There are also paintings by contemporaries Gauguin, Toulouse-Lautrec, Monet and Bernard.

Queues can be huge; pre-booked e-tickets and discount cards expedite the process with fast-track entry.

★ Anne Frank Huis MUSEUM

(Map p280; 📞 556 71 00; www.annefrank.org; Prinsengracht 267; adult/child €9/4.50; ⏱ 9am-9pm, hours vary seasonally; 🚊 13/14/17 Westermarkt) The Anne Frank Huis draws almost one million visitors annually (prepurchase tickets online to minimise the queues). With its reconstruction of Anne's melancholy bedroom and her actual diary – sitting alone in its glass case, filled with sunnily optimistic writing tempered by quiet despair – it's a powerful experience.

The focus of the museum is the *achterhuis* (rear house), also known as the **Secret Annexe**, a dark and airless space where the Franks and others observed complete silence during the daytime.

★ Museum het Rembrandthuis MUSEUM

(Rembrandt House Museum; Map p280; 📞 520 04 00; www.rembrandthuis.nl; Jodenbreestraat 4; adult/child €12.50/4; ⏱ 10am-6pm; 🚊 9/14 Waterlooplein) You almost expect to find the master himself at the Museum het Rembrandthuis, where Rembrandt van Rijn ran the Netherlands' largest painting studio, only to lose the lot when profligacy set in, enemies swooped and bankruptcy came a-knocking. The museum has scores of etchings and sketches. Ask for the free audioguide at the entrance. You can buy advance tickets online, though it's not as vital here as at some of the other big museums.

★**Heineken Experience**　　　BREWERY
(Map p282; ☑ 523 92 22; www.heinekenexperience.com; Stadhouderskade 78; adult/child €18/12.50; ⏰ 10.30am-9pm Jul & Aug, to 7.30pm Mon-Thu, to 9pm Fri-Sun Sep-Jun; ☐ 16/24 Stadhouderskade) On the site of the company's old brewery, the crowning glory of this self-guided 'Experience' (samples aside) is a multimedia exhibit where you 'become' a beer by getting shaken up, sprayed with water and subjected to heat. True beer connoisseurs will shudder, but it's a lot of fun. Admission includes a 15-minute shuttle boat ride to the **Heineken Brand Store** (Map p280; www.heinekenthecity.nl; Amstelstraat 31; ⏰ noon-6pm Mon, from 10am Tue-Sun; ☐ 4/9/14 Rembrandtplein) near Rembrandtplein. Prebooking tickets online saves you €2 on the entry fee and allows you to skip the ticket queues.

★**Vondelpark**　　　PARK
(Map p282; www.vondelpark.nl; ☐ 2/5 Hobbemastraat) The lush urban idyll of the Vondelpark is one of Amsterdam's most magical places – sprawling, English-style gardens, with ponds, lawns, footbridges and winding footpaths. On a sunny day, an open-air party atmosphere ensues when tourists, lovers, cyclists, in-line skaters, pram-pushing parents, cartwheeling children, football-kicking teenagers, spliff-sharing friends and champagne-swilling picnickers all come out to play.

🏃 Activities & Tours

Canal Motorboats　　　BOATING
(☑ 422 70 07; www.canalmotorboats.com; Zandhoek 10a; rental 1st hour €50; ⏰ 10am-10pm; ☐ 48 Barentszplein) Has small, electric aluminium boats (maximum seven passengers) that are easy to drive (no boat licence required). Staff give you a map and plenty of advice, and will come and rescue you if need be. Credit-card imprint or €150 cash deposit required. Reduced rates after the first hour.

THE RED LIGHT DISTRICT

Just southeast of Centraal Station, the warren of medieval alleyways making up Amsterdam's Red Light District (locally known as De Wallen) is a carnival of vice, seething with skimpily clad prostitutes in brothel windows, raucous bars, haze-filled *coffeeshops*, sex shows, mind-boggling museums and shops. The area is generally safe, but keep your wits about you and don't photograph or film prostitutes in the windows – out of respect, and to avoid having your camera flung in a canal by the women's enforcers. Seriously.

Blue Boat Company　　　BOAT TOUR
(Map p280; ☑ 679 13 70; www.blueboat.nl; Stadhouderskade 30; 75min tour adult/child €16/8.50; ⏰ half-hourly 10am-6pm Mar-Oct, hourly Nov-Feb; ☐ 1/2/5/7/10 Leidseplein) Blue Boat's 75-minute main tour glides by the top sights. Ninety-minute evening cruises (adult/child €19.50/15.50) are offered at 8pm, 9pm and 10pm from March to October and at 8pm November to February. Other cruises include a children's pirate-themed tour, a dinner cruise and a tour in a smaller, open-top boat. The dock is near the Max Euweplein.

🛏 Sleeping

Book ahead for summer and weekends year-round. Many cheaper places cater specifically to party animals with general mayhem around the clock.

★**Cocomama**　　　HOSTEL €
(Map p282; ☑ 627 24 54; www.cocomama.nl; Westeinde 18; dm/d/tr from €38/109/146; @ 🛜; ☐ 4/25 Stadhouderskade) Amsterdam's first self-proclaimed 'boutique hostel' plays up its salacious past (the building was once home to a high-end brothel in some themed bunk rooms, while others are more demure, with Delftware or windmill themes. Private rooms (check out the monarchy-themed 'Royal' room) have iPod docking stations and flat-screen TVs.

★**ClinkNOORD**　　　HOSTEL €
(Map p280; ☑ 214 97 30; www.clinkhostels.com; Badhuiskade 3; dm €30-55, d from €100; ❄🛜; 🚢 Buiksloterweg) Clink is a European designer hostel chain that opened this Amsterdam

Central Amsterdam

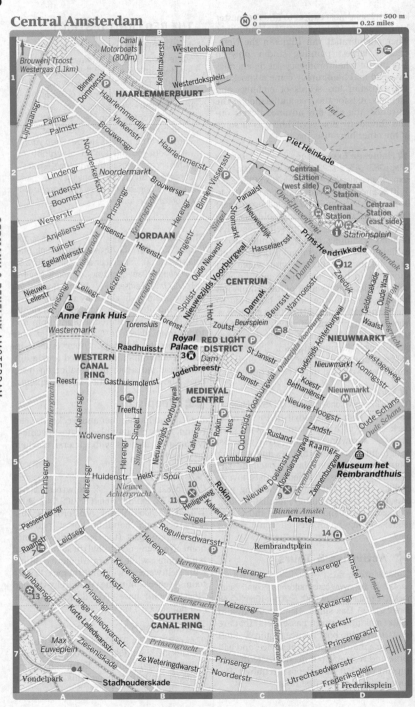

N 0   500 m
0   0.25 miles

Brouwerij Troost
Westergas (1.1km)

Canal
Motorboats
(800m)

HAARLEMMERBUURT

Westerdokseiland

Westerdoksplein

Het IJ

Piet Heinkade

Centraal
Station
(west side)

Centraal
Station

Centraal
Station
(east side)

Stationsplein

Prins-Hendrikkade

JORDAAN

CENTRUM

NIEUWMARKT

Nieuwmarkt

Anne Frank Huis

Westermarkt

Royal
Palace

RED LIGHT
DISTRICT

WESTERN
CANAL
RING

Raadhuisstr

MEDIEVAL
CENTRE

Museum het
Rembrandthuis

Rembrandtplein

Amstel

Binnen Amstel

SOUTHERN
CANAL
RING

Leidsegr

Max
Euweplein

Vondelpark

Stadhouderskade

Frederiksplein

Central Amsterdam

outpost in summer 2015. While it's a bit off the beaten path in Amsterdam-Noord, it's just a five-minute ferry ride from Centraal Station (the ferry is free and runs 24/7, incidentally). Dorms are done up in minimalist-industrial style, with four to 15 beds and en-suite facilities.

International Budget Hostel HOSTEL €
(Map p280; ☑ 624 27 84; www.internationalbudgethostel.com; Leidsegracht 76; dm €25-45; @☎; ☒1/2/5 Prinsengracht/Leidsestraat) So what if it's a bit grungy? Here are the selling points: canal-side location in a former warehouse; close to Leidseplein nightlife; cool mix of backpackers from around the world; bike rental; and staff who are more pleasant than they need to be. There are eight beds per dorm; two-night minimum stay on weekends.

St Christopher's at the Winston HOSTEL, HOTEL €
(Map p280; ☑ 623 13 80; www.winston.nl; Warmoesstraat 129; dm €40-45, s €95, d €124-144; ☎; ☒4/9/16/24 Dam) This place hops 24/7 with rock 'n' roll rooms, and a busy club, bar, beer garden and smoking deck downstairs. En-suite dorms sleep up to eight. Most private rooms are 'art' rooms: local artists were giv-

en free rein, with super-edgy (entirely stainless steel) to questionably raunchy results. Rates include breakfast (and ear plugs!).

★**Collector** B&B €€
(Map p282; ☑ 673 67 79; www.the-collector.nl; De Lairessestraat 46; s/d/tr from €80/95/115; @☎; ☒5/16/24 Museumplein) This spotless B&B near the Concertgebouw is furnished with museum-style displays of clocks, wooden clogs and ice skates – things the owner, Karel, collects. Each of the three rooms has balcony access and a TV. Karel stocks the kitchen for guests to prepare breakfast at their leisure (the eggs come from his hens in the garden).

The kitchen is open all day if you want to cook your own dinner. There are also a couple of bikes Karel lends out to guests.

★**Hoxton Amsterdam** DESIGN HOTEL €€
(Map p280; ☑ 888 55 55; www.thehoxton.com; Herengracht 255; r €120-200; ❄☎; ☒13/14/17 Westermarkt) Part of a European-based chain known for high style at affordable prices, the Hoxton opened in 2015 to great hipster fanfare. The 111 rooms splash through five canal houses and come in sizes from 'shoebox' to 'roomy'. The breakfast snack, speedy wi-fi, free international calls and low-priced canteen items are nice touches.

✕ Eating

★**Bakers & Roasters** CAFE €
(Map p282; www.bakersandroasters.com; 1e Jacob van Campenstraat 54; dishes €7.50-15.50; ☺8.30am-4pm; ☒16/24 Stadhouderskade) Sumptuous brunch dishes served up at Brazilian-Kiwi-owned Bakers & Roasters include banana nutbread French toast with homemade banana marmalade and crispy bacon; Navajo eggs with pulled pork, avocado, mango salsa and chipotle cream; and a smoked salmon stack with poached eggs, potato cakes and hollandaise. Wash them down with a fiery Bloody Mary. Fantastic pies, cakes and slices, too.

★**Vleminckx** FAST FOOD €
(Map p280; http://vleminckxdesausmeester.nl; Voetboogstraat 31; fries €2.10-4.10, sauces €0.60; ☺noon-7pm Sun & Mon, 11am-7pm Tue, Wed, Fri & Sat, to 8pm Thu; ☒1/2/5 Koningsplein) Vleminckx has been frying up *frites* (French fries) since 1887, and doing it at this hole-in-the-wall takeaway shack near the Spui for more than 50 years. The standard is smothered in mayonnaise, though you can also ask for

Southern Canal Ring

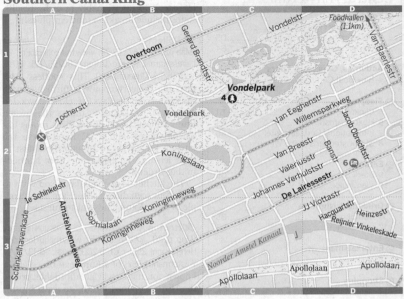

ketchup, peanut sauce or a variety of spicy toppings.

★ Sterk Staaltje   DELI €

(Map p280; www.sterkstaaltje.com; Staalstraat 12; dishes €4-7.60; ⊙8am-7pm Mon-Fri, 8am-6pm Sat, 11am-5pm Sun; ⊠4/9/14/16/24 Muntplein) From the fruit stacked up in crates on the pavement, Sterk Staaltje looks like an unassuming greengrocer's, but inside it's a veritable treasure chest of ready-to-eat treats: Teriyaki meatballs, feta and sundried tomato quiche, pumpkin-stuffed wraps, a soup of the day, and fantastic sandwiches (roast beef, horseradish and rucola; marinated chicken with guacamole and sour cream) plus salads and pastas.

★ Braai BBQ Bar   BARBECUE €

(Map p282; www.braaiamsterdam.nl; Schinkelhavenkade 1; dishes €5-11; ⊙11am-10pm; ⊠1 Overtoomsesluis) A canal-side *haringhuis* (herring stand) has been brilliantly converted into a street-food-style barbecue bar. Snacks span sandwiches such as hummus and grilled veggies or smoked *ossenworst* (raw-beef sausage originating from Amsterdam), a cheese and bacon burger and Braai's speciality – marinated, barbecued ribs (half or full rack). PIN cards are preferred, but it accepts cash. Tables scatter under the trees.

★ Foodhallen   FOOD HALL €

(www.foodhallen.nl; Hannie Dankbaar Passage 3, De Hallen; dishes €5-15; ⊙11am-8pm Sun-Wed, to 9pm Thu-Sat; ⊠17 Ten Katestraat) Inside De Hallen, this glorious international food hall has 21 stands surrounding an airy open-plan eating area. Some are offshoots of popular Amsterdam eateries, such as the **Butcher** (Map p282; ⊉470 78 75; www.the-butcher.com; Albert Cuypstraat 129; burgers €6.50-12.50; ⊙11am-late; ⊡; ⊠16/24 Albert Cuypstraat) and **Wild Moa Pies** (Map p282; Van Ostadestraat 147; dishes €3-4; ⊙10am-6.30pm Tue-Sat; ⊛⊉; ⊠3 2e Van der Helststraat); also look out for Viet View Vietnamese street food, Jabugo Iberico Bar ham, Pink Flamingo pizza, Bulls & Dogs hot dogs, Rough Kitchen ribs and De Ballenbar *bitterballen* (croquettes).

★ Restaurant Elmar   MODERN DUTCH €€

(Map p282; ⊉664 66 29; www.restaurantelmar.nl; Van Woustraat 110; mains lunch €7.50-12.50, dinner €19.50-24.50; ⊙noon-3pm & 6-10pm Tue-Sat; ⊠4 Ceintuurbaan) ⊘ Seriously good cooking at this charming little locavore restaurant utilises organic Dutch produce (Flevopolder beef, Texel lamb, Noord-Holland pigs, *polder* chickens and locally milled flour, along with seasonal fruit and vegetables). Original flavour combinations include ham-wrapped

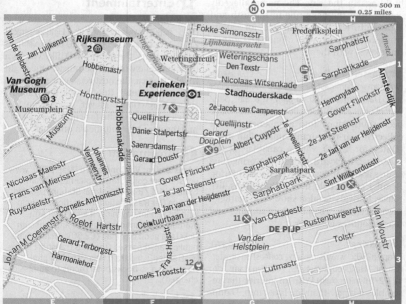

chicken stuffed with liver and sage in marsala jus, and bitter-chocolate mousse with apple compote and iced-coffee foam. There's a delightful courtyard garden.

Drinking & Nightlife

In addition to the Medieval Centre and Red Light District, party hotspots include Rembrandtplein and Leidseplein, both awash with bars, clubs and pubs. *Coffeeshops*, where you can buy and smoke marijuana, are also plentiful. They don't serve alcohol.

★ Brouwerij Troost BREWERY
(Map p282; 737 10 28; www.brouwerijtroost. nl; Cornelis Troostplein 21; 4pm-1am Mon-Thu, 4pm-3am Fri, 2pm-3am Sat, 2pm-midnight Sun; ; 12 Cornelis Troostplein) Watch beer being brewed in copper vats behind a glass wall at this outstanding craft brewery. Its dozen beers include a summery blonde, smoked porter, strong tripel, and deep-red Imperial IPA; it also distils gin from its beer and serves fantastic bar food including humongous burgers. Troost's popularity (book ahead on weekend evenings) saw its second premises (737 10 28; www.brouwerijtroost westergas.nl; Pazzanistraat 27, Westergasfabriek;

4pm-1am Mon-Thu, 4pm-3am Fri, noon-3am Sat, noon-midnight Sun; ; 10 Van Limburg Stirumstraat) open in Westergasfabriek.

★ In 't Aepjen BROWN CAFE
(Map p280; Zeedijk 1; noon-1am Mon-Thu, to 3am Fri & Sat; 4/9/16/24 Centraal Station) Candles burn even during the day at this bar based in a mid-16th-century house, which is one of two remaining wooden

buildings in the city. The name allegedly comes from the bar's role in the 16th and 17th centuries as a crash pad for sailors from the Far East, who often toted *aapjes* (monkeys) with them.

★ **Amsterdam Roest** BEER GARDEN
(www.amsterdamroest.nl; Jacob Bontiusplaats 1; ◷11am-1am Sun-Thu, to 3pm Fri & Sat; 🚊22 Wittenburgergracht) Derelict shipyards have been transformed into a super-cool artist collective–bar-restaurant, Amsterdam Roest (Dutch for 'Rust'), with a canal-facing terrace, huge backyard beneath towering blue cranes and an industrial warehouse interior. Regular events held here include films, live music, festivals, fashion shows and markets; there's a sandy urban beach in summer and toasty bonfires in winter.

Dampkring COFFEE
(Map p280; www.dampkring-coffeeshop-amsterdam.nl; Handboogstraat 29; ◷10am-1am; 📶; 🚊1/2/5 Koningsplein) With an interior that resembles a larger-than-life lava lamp, Dampkring is a consistent Cannabis Cup winner, and known for having the most comprehensive menu in town (including details about smell, taste and effect). Its name references the ring of the earth's atmosphere where smaller items combust.

DON'T MISS

TULIPS IN SPRING

One of the Netherlands' top attractions, **Keukenhof Gardens** (www.keukenhof.nl; Lisse; adult/child €16/8, parking €6; ◷8am-7.30pm mid-Mar–mid-May, last entry 6pm), 1km west of Lisse, is the world's largest bulb-flower garden. It attracts nearly 800,000 visitors during its eight-week season, which is almost as short-lived as the blooms on the millions of multicoloured tulips, daffodils and hyacinths.

Special buses (€9, every 15 minutes, 30 minutes) link Keukenhof with Leiden's Centraal Station; combination tickets covering entry and transport are available (adult/child €23.50/12.50). Pre-purchase tickets online to help avoid huge queues.

☆ **Entertainment**

Melkweg LIVE MUSIC
(Map p280; www.melkweg.nl; Lijnbaansgracht 234a; ◷6pm-1am; 🚊1/2/5/7/10 Leidseplein) In a former dairy, the nonprofit 'Milky Way' is a dazzling galaxy of diverse music. One night it's electronica, the next reggae or punk, and next heavy metal. Roots, rock and mellow singer-songwriters all get stage time too. Check out the website for cutting-edge cinema, theatre and multimedia offerings.

ℹ **Information**

I Amsterdam Visitor Centre (Map p280; www.iamsterdam.com; Stationsplein 10; ◷9am-6pm; 🚊4/9/16/24 Centraal Station) Located outside Centraal Station, this office can help with just about anything: it sells the I Amsterdam discount card; theatre and museum tickets; a good city map (€2.50); cycling maps; public transit passes (the GVB transport office is attached); and train tickets to Schiphol Airport. It also books hotel rooms (commission charged).

ℹ **Getting There & Away**

Most major airlines serve Schiphol airport,18km southwest of the city centre.

Eurolines buses connect with all major European capitals. Buses arrive at Amsterdam Duivendrecht train station, 7.5km southeast of the centre, which has an easy 15-minute metro link to Centraal Station

Amsterdam's main train station is fabled Centraal Station, with extensive services to the rest of the country and major European cities.

ℹ **Getting Around**

To/From the Airport Trains to Centraal Station leave every few minutes, take 15 to 20 minutes, and cost €4.

Public Transport Buy scan-on scan-off chipcards at visitor centres or from tram conductors. Trams are handy for the centre; bus, ferry and metro primarily serve outer districts.

Bike The locals' main mode of getting around. Rental companies are all over town; bikes cost about €11 per day.

Leiden

📳 071 / POP 121,249

Vibrant Leiden is renowned for being Rembrandt's birthplace, the home of the Netherlands' oldest university (and 20,000 students) and the place America's pilgrims raised money to lease the leaky Mayflower that took them to the New World in 1620. Beautiful 17th-century buildings line its canals. It's an easy day trip from Amsterdam but also appeals as a place to stay.

◎ Sights

Pieterskerk   CHURCH
(www.pieterskerk.com; Pieterskerkhof 1; admission €2; ⊙11am-6pm) Crowned by its huge steeple, Pieterskerk is often under restoration – a good thing as it has been prone to collapse since it was built in the 14th century. The precinct here is as old Leiden as you'll get and includes the gabled old Latin School, which – before it became a commercial building – was graced by a pupil named Rembrandt from 1616 to 1620. Across the plaza, look for the Gravensteen, which dates to the 13th century and was once a prison.

★ Rijksmuseum van Oudheden   MUSEUM
(National Museum of Antiquities; www.rmo.nl; Rapenburg 28; adult/child €9.50/3; ⊙10am-5pm Tue-Sun) This museum has a world-class collection of Greek, Roman and Egyptian artefacts, the pride of which is the extraordinary **Temple of Taffeh**, a gift from former Egyptian president Anwar Sadat to the Netherlands for helping to save ancient Egyptian monuments from flood.

✗ Eating

Vishandel Atlantic   SEAFOOD €
(http://vishandelatlantic.nl; Levendaal 118; dishes €3-12.50; ⊙9am-8pm) Two Turkish brothers opened this fish stand in 1989 and their attention to quality has propelled them to the Netherlands' top ranks of seafood vendors. Their raw herring rates 10 out of 10 in contests where 5.5 is considered a good score. You can also try all types of smoked fish as well as dishes like fish and chips

Oudt Leyden   PANCAKES €
(www.oudtleyden.nl; Steenstraat 49; pancakes €6.50-15.50, mains €16-24.50; ⊙11.30am-9.30pm; ⚑🏍) The giant Dutch-style pancakes here make kids and adults alike go wide-eyed. Whether you're after something savoury (marinated salmon, sour cream and capers), sweet (apple, raisins, almond paste, sugar and cinnamon) or simply adventurous (ginger and bacon), this welcoming place hits the spot every time. Pancakes as de, choices include mushroom lasagne, sirloin with red-wine jus and salmon fillets.

THE NETHERLANDS BY BIKE

The Netherlands has more than 32,000km of dedicated bike paths (*fietspaden*), which makes it the most bike-friendly place on the planet. You can criss-cross the country on the motorways of cycling: the LF routes, well marked by distinctive green-and-white signs.

➡ Comprehensive cycling website Nederland Fietsland (www.nederlandfietsland.nl) has route planners and downloadable GPS tracks.

➡ Bicycle hire is available all over the Netherlands at hotels, independent rental outlets and train stations. Prices average around €15 per 24 hours. You'll need to show ID and leave a deposit (€50 to €150).

➡ You may bring your bicycle onto any train outside peak hours as long as there is room. Bicycles require a day pass (*dagkaartfiets*; €6).

❶ Information

Tourist Office (☑071-516 60 00; www.visitleiden.nl; Stationsweg 41; ⊙7am-7pm Mon-Fri, 10am-4pm Sat, 11am-3pm Sun) Across from the train station.

❶ Getting There & Away

Buses leave from directly in front of Centraal Station. Train destinations include: Amsterdam (€8.80, 34 minutes, six per hour); Den Haag (€3.40, 10 minutes, six per hour); Schiphol airport (€5.70, 15 minutes, six per hour).

Den Haag
☑070 / POP 515,880

Flanked by wide, leafy boulevards, Den Haag (The Hague), officially known as 's-Gravenhage (Count's Hedge), is the Dutch seat of government (although Amsterdam is defined as the capital). Embassies and various international courts of justice give the city a worldly air and some standout attractions make it worth a stop. Around 5km northwest, the long beach at Scheveningen is overdeveloped.

◉ Sights

★ Binnenhof
PALACE

The Binnenhof's central courtyard (once used for executions) is surrounded by parliamentary buildings. The splendid 17th-century North Wing is still home to the Upper Chamber of the **Dutch Parliament**. The Lower Chamber formerly met in the ballroom, in the 19th-century wing; it now meets in a modern building on the south side. A highlight of the complex is the restored 13th-century **Ridderzaal** (Knights' Hall).

To see the buildings you need to join a tour through visitor organisation **ProDemos** (☑ 070-757 02 00; www.prodemos.nl; Hofweg 1; 45min Ridderzaal tour €5, 90min Ridderzaal & House of Representative tour €8.50, 75min Ridderzaal & Senate tour €8.50, 90min Ridderzaal, House of Representative & Senate tour €10; ☺ office 10am-5pm Mon-Sat, tours by reservation).

★ Escher in Het Paleis Museum
MUSEUM

(www.escherinhetpaleis.nl; Lange Voorhout 74; adult/child €9/6.50; ☺ 11am-5pm Tue-Sun) The Lange Voorhout Palace was once Queen Emma's winter residence. Now it's home to the work of Dutch graphic artist MC Escher. The permanent exhibition features notes, letters, drafts, photos and fully mature works covering Escher's entire career, from his early realism to the later phantasmagoria. There are some imaginative displays, including a virtual reality reconstruction of Escher's impossible buildings.

★ Mauritshuis
MUSEUM

(www.mauritshuis.nl; Plein 29; adult/child €14/free, combined ticket with Galerij Prins Willem V €17.50; ☺ 1-6pm Mon, 10am-6pm Tue, Wed & Fri-Sun, 10am-8pm Thu) For a comprehensive introduction to Dutch and Flemish Art, visit the Mauritshuis, a jewel-box of a museum in an old palace and brand-new wing. Almost every work is a masterpiece, among them Vermeer's *Girl with a Pearl Earring,* Rembrandts including a wistful self-portrait from the year of his death, 1669, and *The Anatomy Lesson of Dr Nicolaes Tulp.* A five-minute walk southwest, the recently restored **Galerij Prins Willem V** (www.mauritshuis.nl; Buitenhof 35; adult/child €5/2.50, combined ticket with Mauritshuis €17.50; ☺ noon-5pm Tue-Sun) contains 150 old masters (Steen, Rubens, Potter, et al).

⌂ Sleeping & Eating

Stayokay Den Haag
HOSTEL €

(☑ 070-315 78 88; www.stayokay.com; Scheepmakerstraat 27; dm/d from €19/49; ☎) This Stayokay HI hostel in an Amsterdam School–style building has four- to eight-bed dorms and good facilities including a bar, a restaurant and board games. Towel rental costs €4.50. It's a 500m walk northeast of HS station.

Brasserie 't Ogenblik
CAFE €

(www.t-ogenblik.nl; Molenstraat 4c; mains €6-15; ☺ 10am-5pm Mon-Fri, to 6pm Sat & Sun) Staff zip about this hopping cafe at the nexus of several pedestrianised shopping streets, which have summertime tables along Hoogstraat for people-watching. Coffees and teas offer refreshment, and a creative line-up of salads, sandwiches, soups and more offer sustenance.

★ Restaurant Allard
BISTRO €€

(☑ 070-744 79 00; www.restaurantallard.nl; Jagerstraat 6; mains €16-24, 2-/3-/4-course menu €32/39/46; ☺ 4-11pm Tue-Sun) Tucked down a charming alleyway with outdoor tables, Allard is a diamond find for flavour-packed creations such as tuna tartare with sundried tomato crème, lamb fillet with honey and fig jus, truffle risotto with wild mushrooms, and grilled sea bass with spinach and potato gratin. It's a cosy, cellar-like space with exposed brick walls, low-lit chandeliers and black-and-white chessboard-tiled floors.

☆ Entertainment

★ Paard van Troje
LIVE MUSIC

(www.paard.nl; Prinsegracht 12; ☺ hours vary) This emporium has an eclectic program of live music – from classical concerts to metal, blues, roots, reggae and soul – as well as Dutch spoken-word poetry, and club nights, such as hip hop and dance. Check the online agenda to find out what's happening.

❶ Information

Tourist Office (VVV; ☑ 070-361 88 60; http://denhaag.com; Spui 68; ☺ noon-8pm Mon, 10am-8pm Tue-Fri, 10am-5pm Sat & Sun; ☎) On the ground floor of the public library in the landmark New Town Hall (Spui 170).

❶ Getting There & Away

Most trains use Den Haag Centraal Station (CS), but some through trains only stop at Den Haag HS station just south of the centre. Very regular services include: Amsterdam (€11.20, 50 minutes); Rotterdam (€4.70, 25 minutes; also accessible by metro) and Schiphol airport (€8.20, 30 minutes).

Delft

📋 015 / POP 98,700

Compact and charming, Delft makes a perfect Dutch day trip. Founded around 1100, and renowned for its blue-and-white ceramics, it maintains tangible links to its romantic past despite the pressures of modernisation and tourist hordes. Many of the canal-side vistas could be scenes from the work of Delft-born Golden Age painter Johannes Vermeer.

⊙ Sights

★ Oude Kerk   CHURCH
(Old Church; http://oudeennieuwekerkdelft.nl; Heilige Geestkerkhof 25; adult/child incl Nieuwe Kerk €3.75/2.25; ⊙9am-6pm Apr-Oct, 11am-4pm Nov-Mar, closed Sun) The Gothic Oude Kerk, founded in 1246, is a surreal sight: its 75m-high tower leans nearly 2m from the vertical due to subsidence caused by its canal location, hence its nickname Scheve Jan ('Leaning Jan'). One of the tombs inside the church is Vermeer's.

★ Nieuwe Kerk   CHURCH
(New Church; http://oudeennieuwekerkdelft.nl; Markt 80; adult/child incl Oude Kerk €3.75/2.25, Nieuwe Kerk tower additional €3.75/2.25; ⊙9am-6pm Mon-Sat Apr-Oct, 11am-4pm Mon-Fri, 10am-5pm Sat Nov-Jan, 10am-5pm Mon-Sat Feb & Mar) Construction on Delft's Nieuwe Kerk began in 1381; it was finally completed in 1655. Amazing views extend from the 108.75m-high tower: after climbing its 376 narrow, spiralling steps you can see as far as Rotterdam and Den Haag on a clear day. It's the resting place of William of Orange (William the Silent), in a mausoleum designed by Hendrick de Keyser.

★ Vermeer Centrum Delft   MUSEUM
(www.vermeerdelft.nl; Voldersgracht 21; adult/child €8/4; ⊙10am-5pm) As the place where Vermeer was born, lived and worked, Delft is 'Vermeer Central' to many art-history and old-masters enthusiasts. Along with viewing life-sized images of Vermeer's oeuvre, you can tour a replica of Vermeer's studio, which reveals the way the artist approached the use of light and colour in his craft. A 'Vermeer's World' exhibit offers insight into his environment and upbringing, while temporary exhibits show how his work continues to inspire other artists.

De Candelaer   PORCELAIN STUDIO
(www.candelaer.nl; Kerkstraat 13; ⊙9.30am-5.30pm Mon-Fri, to 5pm Sat May-Sep, shorter hours Oct-Mar) FREE The most central and modest Delftware outfit is de Candelaer, just off the Markt. It has five artists, a few of whom work most days. When it's quiet they'll give you a detailed tour of the manufacturing process.

🛏 Sleeping

Hostel Delft   HOSTEL €
(📋06 1649 6621; www.hosteldelft.nl; Voldersgracht 17a; ⊙dm from €22; 🛜) In the heart of town a block from the Markt, this 2015-opened independent hostel has roof terraces, a self-catering kitchen and a cosy lounge. Its 43 beds are spread across en-suite dorms sleeping between four and 16, with secure lockers.

Soul Inn   B&B €
(📋015-215 72 46; www.soul-inn.nl; Willemstraat 55; s/d/f from €110/135/145, s/d without bathroom from €65/95; 🛜) This quirky B&B is an antidote for those who've experienced an overload of Delft quaintness; rooms play with colour schemes (such as hot pink) and themes (retro 1970s; Africa). It's 400m west of the centre.

🍴 Eating & Drinking

De Visbanken   SEAFOOD €
(www.visbanken.nl; Camaretten 2; dishes €3-8.50; ⊙10am-6pm Mon, 9am-6pm Tue-Fri, 9am-5pm Sat, 10am-5pm Sun) Fish has been sold on this spot since 1342. Display cases in the old open-air pavilion entice with fresh, marinated, smoked and fried fishy treats.

Stads-Koffyhuis   CAFE €
(http://stads-koffyhuis.nl; Oude Delft 133; mains €8-16.50; ⊙9am-8pm Mon-Fri, to 6pm Sat) The most coveted seats at this delightful cafe are on the terrace, aboard a barge moored out the front. Tuck into award-winning bread rolls, with fillings such as aged artisan Gouda with apple sauce, mustard, fresh figs and walnuts, or house-speciality pancakes, while admiring possibly the best view of the Oude Kerk, just ahead at the end of the canal.

Locus Publicus
BROWN CAFE

(www.locuspublicus.nl; Brabantse Turfmarkt 67; ⊙11am-1am Mon-Thu, 11am-2am Fri & Sat, noon-1am Sun) Cosy little Locus Publicus is filled with cheery locals quaffing their way through the 175-strong beer list. There's great people-watching from the front terrace.

ⓘ Information

Tourist Office (VVV; ☑ 015-215 40 51; www.delft.nl; Kerkstraat 3; ⊙10am-4pm Sun & Mon, 10am-5pm Tue-Sat Apr-Oct, noon-4pm Mon, 10am-4pm Tue-Sat, 11am-3pm Sun Nov-Mar) Sells excellent walking-tour brochures.

ⓘ Getting There & Away

Very regular trains run to: Amsterdam (€12.70, one hour), Den Haag (€2.40, 12 minutes), Rotterdam (€3.20, 12 minutes).

Den Haag is also linked to Delft by tram 1, which takes 30 minutes.

Rotterdam

☑ 010 / POP 616,000

Bold new initiatives, myriad urban regeneration projects, and electrifying dining and nightlife all make Rotterdam one of the most happening cities in Europe right now. The Netherlands' exhilarating 'second city' has a diverse, multi-ethnic community, an absorbing maritime tradition centred on Europe's busiest port, and a wealth of top-class museums.

◎ Sights & Activities

Rotterdam is a veritable open-air gallery of modern, postmodern and contemporary architecture, with mind-bending late-20th-century icons and eye-popping new additions.

★ Museum Boijmans van Beuningen
MUSEUM

(www.boijmans.nl; Museumpark 18-20; adult/child €15/free; ⊙11am-5pm Tue-Sun) Among Europe's finest museums, the Museum Boijmans van Beuningen has a permanent collection spanning all eras of Dutch and European art, including superb old masters. Among the highlights are *The Marriage Feast at Cana* by Hieronymus Bosch, *Three Maries at the Open Sepulchre* by Van Eyck, the minutely detailed *Tower of Babel* by Pieter Brueghel the Elder, and *Portrait of Titus* and *Man in a Red Cap* by Rembrandt.

Maritiem Museum Rotterdam
MUSEUM

(Maritime Museum; www.maritiemmuseum.nl; Leuvehaven 1; adult/child €8.50/4.50; ⊙10am-5pm Tue-Sat, 11am-5pm Sun, plus Mon during school holidays) This comprehensive, kid-friendly museum looks at the Netherlands' rich maritime traditions through an array of models. There are great explanatory displays such as Mainport Live, giving a 'real time' view of the port's action in miniature, and a raft of fun temporary exhibitions.

Spido
BOAT TOUR

(www.spido.nl; Willemsplein 85; adult/child €11.75/7.25) Harbour tours lasting 75 minutes depart from the pier at Leuvehoofd near the Erasmusbrug (by the Leuvehaven metro station). There are up to 10 departures daily in July and August, fewer during the rest of the year.

⌕ Sleeping

★ King Kong Hostel
HOSTEL €

(☑ 010-818 87 78; www.kingkonghostel.com; Witte de Withstraat 74; dm/d/q from €22.50/75/110; @⎙) Outdoor benches made from salvaged timbers and garden hoses by Sander Bokkinga sit outside King Kong, a design haven on Rotterdam's coolest street. Artist-designed rooms and dorms are filled with vintage and industrial furniture; fab features include hammocks, lockers equipped with device-charging points, a gourmet self-catering kitchen, roof garden and barbecue area, and Netflix.

Stayokay Rotterdam
HOSTEL €

(☑010-436 57 63; www.stayokay.com; Overblaak 85-87; dm/d from €21/59; ⎙) Inside the landmark Overblaak development, marked by its pencil-shaped tower and 'forest' of 45-degree-tilted, cube-shaped apartments on hexagonal pylons, this HI hostel has 245 beds in oddly shaped rooms that sleep two to eight.

✗ Eating

★ Fenix Food Factory
MARKET €

(www.fenixfoodfactory.nl; Veerlaan 19d; ⊙10am-7pm Wed-Fri, 10am-6pm Sat, noon-5pm Sun) Everything in this vast former warehouse is made locally and sold by separate vendors making their mark on the food scene. They include Booij Kaasmakers (cheese), Cider Cider (cider), Jordy's Bakery (bread and baked goods), Stielman Koffiebranders (coffee roasters), Kaapse Brouwers (craft beer) and Rechtstreex (locally grown fruit and

Rotterdam

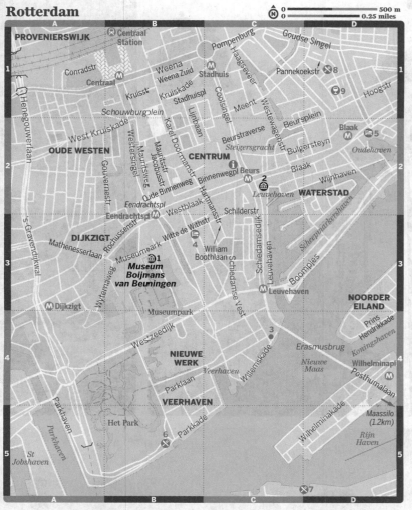

GERMANY & BENELUX ROTTERDAM

Vienna, Austria
altz into one of Europe's most romantic cities
367).

Romantic Rhine, Germany
uise, sip and relax along the Rhine River
243).

Bern, Switzerland
ern's most famous sight, the Zytglogge (p356),
ce formed part of the city's western gate.

Chamonix, France
ake to the slopes around Mont Blanc (p335).

veggies). There's also a bar here that stays open until 11pm.

De Ballentent CAFE €
(www.deballentent.nl; Parkkade 1; mains €6-16.50; ⊙9am-11pm) Rotterdam's best waterfront pub-café is also a great spot for a meal. Dine on one of two terraces or inside. Mussels, schnitzels and more line the menu but the real speciality here are *bals*, huge home-made meatloafy meatballs. Plain ones are tremendous, but go for the house style with a piquant sauce of fresh peppers, mushrooms and more. Waiters and customers alike enjoy a good laugh.

⭐**Tante Nel** FAST FOOD €
(www.tante-nel.com; Pannekoekstraat 53a; dishes €2.25-7.75; ⊙noon-10pm Tue-Sat, to 9pm Sun) New-generation Tante Nel is as tiny as a traditional *frites* (fries) stand but decked out with a stunning Dutch-design painted brick interior and marquee-style canopied terrace for savouring its organic, hand-cut fries (topped with nine different sauces), along with house-speciality milkshakes, beer, wine and 13 different gins.

🍷 Drinking & Nightlife

⭐**Bokaal** BAR
(http://bokaalrotterdam.nl; Nieuwemarkt 11; ⊙noon-1pm Sun-Thu, to 2am Fri & Sat) In a *bokaal* (trophy) location at the heart of the enclave around pedestrian Nieuwmarkt and Pannekoekstraat locally dubbed 'Soho Rotterdam', Bokaal's spectacularly designed bar has butcher-shop tiling, raw concrete floors, and an oak bar and huge all-day-sun terrace. Beer (craft and Trappist) is its speciality, with nine types on tap, and more than 80 in bottles, along with charcuterie and cheese.

ℹ Information

Tourist Office (📞010-790 01 85; www.rotterdam.info; Coolsingel 197; ⊙9.30am-6pm; 🛜) Main tourist office.

ℹ Getting There & Away

Rotterdam's stunning Centraal Station has direct services to Brussels and Paris, as well as Eurostar to London. Major services include: Amsterdam via Leiden (€14.80, 65 minutes); Amsterdam high speed (€17.10, 42 minutes); Schiphol airport (€11.90 to €14.20, 20 to 50 minutes).

ℹ Getting Around

Rotterdam's trams, buses and metro are operated by RET (www.ret.nl). Most converge in front of Centraal Station, where there's an info and ticket booth.

Maastricht
📞043 / POP 122,397

In the far-flung south, the grand old city of Maastricht is well worth the journey from Amsterdam and the pearls of the Ranstad, and you can easily continue to Belgium and Germany. Among Maastricht's 1650 listed historic buildings, look for Spanish and Roman ruins, French and Belgian architectural twists, splendid food and the cosmopolitan flair that made Maastricht the location for the signing of the namesake treaty, which created the modern EU in 1992.

◉ Sights

Maastricht's delights are scattered along both banks of the Maas and reward walkers.

⭐**Sint Servaasbasiliek** CHURCH
(www.sintservaas.nl; Keizer Karelplein 6; basilica free, treasury adult/child €4.50/free; ⊙10am-5pm, till 6pm Jul & Aug) Built around the shrine of St Servatius, the first bishop of Maastricht, the basilica presents an architectural pastiche dating from 1000. Its beautiful curved brick apse and towers dominate the Vrijthof. The **Treasury** is filled with medieval gold artwork. Be sure to duck around the back to the serene cloister garden.

⭐**Bonnefantenmuseum** MUSEUM
(📞329 01 90; www.bonnefanten.nl; Ave Cèramique 250; adult/child €9/4.50; ⊙11am-5pm Tue-Sun) Maastricht's star museum, in the Ceramique district east of the Maas, is easily recognisable by its rocket-shaped tower. Designed by the Italian Aldo Rossi, the distinctive E-shaped structure displays early European painting and sculpture on the 1st floor and contemporary works by Limburg artists on the next, linked by a dramatic sweep of stairs. The dome of the tower is reserved for large-scale installations.

Fort Sint Pieter FORTRESS
(📞325 21 21; www.maastrichtunderground.nl; Luikerweg 80; fort tour adult/child €6.20/5, combination tour €9.95/6.95; ⊙English tours 12.30pm) Looming atop a marlstone hill with commanding views of the Maas, the five-sided

Fort Sint Pieter formed the city's southern defense and is linked to a network of underground tunnels. It's been fully restored to its original 1701 appearance. Visit is by guided tour only, which can be combined with a tunnel tour. Purchase tickets at the visitor centre below the fort. It's a 2km walk south of Maastricht, or take bus No 4 and get off at 'Mergelweg.'

🛏 Sleeping

Stayokay Maastricht   HOSTEL €
(☑ 750 17 90; www.stayokay.com/maastricht; Maasboulevard 101; dm €21.50-35, d €59-89; @ 🛜) A vast terrace right on the Maas highlights this stunner of a hostel with 199 beds in dorms and private rooms. It's 1km south of the centre.

🍴 Eating & Drinking

★ **Bisschopsmolen**   BAKERY, CAFE €
(www.bisschopsmolen.nl; Stenebrug 3; vlaai €2.40, baguette sandwiches €6; ⊙ 9.30am 5.30pm Tue-Sat, 11am-5pm Sun) A working 7th-century water wheel powers a vintage flour mill that supplies its adjoining bakery. Spelt loaves and *vlaai* (seasonal fruit pies) come direct from the ovens out back. You can dine onsite at the cafe, and, if it's not busy, self-tour the mill and see how flour's been made for eons.

Marres Kitchen   MEDITERRANEAN €
(www.marres.org; Capucijnenstraat 98; mains €14-20) Adjunct to a gallery for contemporary art, the kitchen here is run by a Syrian who previously resided in Tuscany, and dishes span the Mediterranean spectrum. Facing a lush garden, the small dining hall consists of long tables conducive to interaction. Start your noshing from an array of Mideast appetisers.

★ **Take One**   BROWN CAFE
(www.takeonebiercafe.nl; Rechtstraat 23; ⊙ 4pm-2am Thu-Mon) This narrow, eccentric 1930s tavern has well over 100 beers from the most obscure parts of the Benelux. It's run by a husband-and-wife team who help you select the beer most appropriate to your taste. The Bink Blonde is sweet, tangy and very good.

ℹ Information

Tourist Office (VVV; ☑ 325 21 21; www.vvvmaastricht.nl; Kleine Straat 1; ⊙ 10am-6pm Mon-Sat, 11am-5pm Sun) In the 15th-century Dinghuis; cycling tours offered.

ℹ Getting There & Away

Trains to Brussels and Cologne require a change in Liège. Domestic services include Amsterdam (€25, 2½ hours, two per hour).

Netherlands Survival Guide

ℹ Directory A–Z

ACCOMMODATION

Always book accommodation ahead, especially during high season.

DISCOUNT CARDS

Many cities (eg Amsterdam, Den Haag and Rotterdam) offer discount-card schemes that are good for museums, attractions and local transport. Ask at tourist offices.

LEGAL MATTERS

Drugs are actually illegal in the Netherlands. Possession of soft drugs up to 5g is tolerated but larger amounts can get you jailed. Hard drugs are treated as a serious crime. Smoking is banned in all public places. In a uniquely Dutch solution, you can still smoke tobacco-free pot in *coffeeshops*.

LGBT TRAVELLERS

Amsterdam is one of the gay capitals of Europe. In towns outside Amsterdam, however, the scene is less prominent. Rotterdam is an exception, as are university towns with large gay and lesbian student populations.

MONEY

→ Cards are widely accepted. Some businesses will only accept chip-and-pin cards though.

> ### ℹ PRICE RANGES
>
> Sleeping price ranges refer to a double room with private bathroom and breakfast in high season:
>
> € less than €80
>
> €€ €80–160
>
> €€€ more than €160
>
> Eating price ranges are for the cost of a main course:
>
> € less than €12
>
> €€ €12–€25
>
> €€€ more than €25

➜ The Dutch do tip, but modestly. In restaurants, round up, or tip 5% to 10%.

OPENING HOURS

Banks and government offices 9am to 4pm Monday to Friday, some Saturday morning

Bars and cafes 11am to 1am; some open longer at weekends and others won't open till late afternoon

Businesses 8.30am to 5pm Monday to Friday

Clubs Hours vary, but in general 10pm to 4am Friday and Saturday; some also open Wednesday, Thursday and Sunday

Museums 10am to 5pm daily, some close Monday

Restaurants 10am or 11am to 10pm, with an afternoon break from 3pm to 6pm

Shops Noon to 6pm Monday, and 8.30am or 9am to 6pm Tuesday to Saturday

PUBLIC HOLIDAYS

Many people treat Remembrance Day (4 May) as a day off.

Nieuwjaarsdag (New Year's Day) Parties and fireworks galore

Goede Vrijdag Good Friday

Eerste Paasdag Easter Sunday

Tweede Paasdag Easter Monday

Koningsdag (King's Day) 27 April (26 April if the 27th is a Sunday)

Bevrijdingsdag (Liberation Day) 5 May. Not a universal holiday: government workers have the day off, but almost everyone else has to work.

Hemelvaartsdag (Ascension Day) Fortieth day after Easter Sunday

Eerste Pinksterdag (Whit Sunday; Pentecost) Fiftieth day after Easter Sunday

Tweede Pinksterdag (Whit Monday) Fiftieth day after Easter Monday

Eerste Kerstdag (Christmas Day) 25 December

Tweede Kerstdag ('Second Christmas' aka Boxing Day) 26 December

TELEPHONE

➜ Country code: ☑ 31. International access code: ☑ 00.

➜ Pay-as-you-go SIM cards with data deals are easily available and cheap.

ⓘ Getting There & Around

AIR

Huge Schiphol airport (AMS; www.schiphol.nl) is the Netherlands' main international airport.

BUS

Eurolines (www.eurolines.com) serves the Netherlands' major cities.

LOCAL TRANSPORT

Public transport works with the OV-chipkaart (www.ov-chipkaart.nl). Visitors can buy a one-hour card, multiday cards or rechargeable cards. Purchase cards and top up at machines, newsagents or ticket windows.

TRAIN

Train connections are excellent. Amsterdam is linked to Cologne, Brussels, Paris and London by high-speed trains. Maastricht is right on the Belgian and German borders, with connections to Cologne and Brussels.

All Eurail and Inter-Rail passes are valid on the Dutch national train service, Nederlandse Spoorwegen (NS; www.ns.nl).

FERRY

Several companies operate car/passenger ferries between the Netherlands and the UK. Check www.directferries.com for routes.

France, Switzerland & Austria

Best Places to Eat

➡ Du Pain et des Idées (p314)

➡ Magasin Général (p337)

➡ Gasthof Schloss Aigen (p380)

➡ Bistro Autour du Beurre (p325)

➡ Buvette des Bains (p352)

➡ Les Halles de Lyon Paul Bocuse (p334)

Best Places to Sleep

➡ Nepomuk's (p384)

➡ Haus Ballwein (p379)

➡ Mountain Hostel (p358)

➡ Generator Hostel (p309)

➡ Nice Pebbles (p343)

Why Go?

Monumental cities rammed with architectural icons and opulence, storybook villages, vine-stitched valleys and Alpine landscapes so hallucinatory beautiful they must be seen to be believed. Travelling through this French and Germanic wedge of Western Europe is a kaleidoscope of top-of-the-world landscapes and experiences.

Visiting France is about lapping up French *art de vivre* between celebrity sights. Think wine, food and excessive *dégustation* (tasting), indulged in at an escargot-slow pace.

Moving east, across Europe's largest lake shared by France and Switzerland, is a picture-perfect country that has seduced since Grand Tour days. The only tricky part about Switzerland is deciding where to snap that perfect selfie – with edgy urbanite Zürich, chocolate-box Bern, adventure-sports hub Innsbruck or Italianate lake-laced Ticino?

Then there's Austria, a German-speaking country that shares Switzerland's national passion for the great outdoors – and perfection – with its museum cities, ravishing *Kaffeehäuser* culture and unforgettable mountains.

Fast Facts

Capitals Paris (France), Bern (Switzerland), Vienna (Austria)

Emergency ☑ 112 (France), ☑ 117 (Switzerland), ☑ 112 (Austria)

Currency Euro € (France & Austria), Swiss franc CHF or Sfr (Switzerland)

Languages French (France), French, German, Italian, Romansch (Switzerland), German (Austria)

Visas Not required for stays of up to 90 days (or at all for EU citizens); some nationalities need a Schengen visa.

Mobile Phones European and Australian phones work, but only American cells with 900 and 1800 Mhz are compatible; slip in a local SIM card to call with a cheaper local number.

Time Zone Central European Time (GMT/UTC plus one hour)

ENGLAND

THE CHANNEL
(LA MANCHE)

PAS-
DE-CALAIS

Antwerp

BRUSSELS

BELGIUM

LUXEMBOURG
CITY

Dieppe

SOMME

Péronne

AISNE

Reims

Cherbourg

Bayeux

Honfleur

Rouen

OISE

St-Lô

Ouistreham

Caen

Evreux

MARNE

Mont
St-Michel

Falaise

Paris

Morlaix

ORNE

Provins

Troyes

St-Malo

Fougères

Alençon

Dinan

Chartres

HAUTE-
MARNE

Quimper

Rennes

LOIRET

Vitre

Le Mans

Loire Valley

Orléans

Auxerre

Abbaye
de Fontenay

ANJOU

Chambord

Vézelay

Dijon

Nantes

Tours

Blois

CHER

Chinon

Bourges

NIÈVRE

Châteauroux

Chalon-
sur-Saône

INDRE

Poitiers

Montluçon

VIENNE

La Rochelle

Guéret

Limoges

CREUSE

LOIRE

Bourgoin

ATLANTIC
OCEAN

Saintes

Cognac

Lyon

Jalliet

Clermont-
Ferrand

ISÈRE

Bay of
Biscay

Valence

Greno

Bordeaux

Sarlat-
la-Canéda

LOT

Figeac

ARDÈCHE

Agen

Albi

Avignon

LANDES

GERS

Nîmes

PROVEN

OFF THE BEATEN TRACK:
DUNE DE PILAT

Scamper, merry as a sand boy, up
Europe's biggest sand dune.
(p338)

Toulouse

TARN

Arles

Montpellier

Pau

Carcassonne

AUDE

Narbonne

Marseille

Golfe de
Beauduc

Burgos

SPAIN

Tarascon-
sur-Ariège

ANDORRA LA
VELLA

Perpignan

France, Switzerland & Austria Highlights

1 Paris Enjoy a whirlwind
romance with one of the
world's greatest cities. (p304)

2 Mont St-Michel Follow
pilgrims across the sand to this
ancient island abbey. (p323)

3 Loire Valley Relive the
Renaissance in royal châteaux.
(p325)

4 French Riviera Corniches
Motor a trio of coastal
cliffhangers near Nice. (p344)

5 Lake Geneva Admire Mont
Blanc and live the good life
ashore Europe's largest lake.
(p350)

6 Matterhorn Pander to
every last topographic need of

OFF THE BEATEN TRACK: GROSSGLOCKNER ROAD

Gorge on spectacular views of the Alps on Austria's legendary roller-coaster mountain road. (p386)

Cologne

Erfurt

GERMANY

Frankfurt-am-Main

Mainz

Bamberg

Brno

Saarbrücken

MOSELLE

Stuttgart

Linz

BRATISLAVA

St Pölten

Vienna

Nancy

Strasbourg

Regensburg

Pöchlarn

VOSGES

Colmar

Munich

Salzburg

Kapfenberg

HAUTE-SÔNE

Bregenz

Kitzbühel

Graz

Besançon

Zürich

VADUZ

Klagenfurt

Maribor

BERN

Cortina d'Ampezzo

Jesenice

Lake Geneva

Belluno

Udine

LJUBLJANA

ZAGREB

Geneva

Zermatt

Pordenone

Trieste

Karlovac

Chamonix

Matterhorn

Treviso

Venice

Rijeka

Annecy

Courmayeur

Padua

Krk

Milan

Pula

Sestriere

Ferrara

Zadar

HAUTES-ALPES

Ravenna

ITALY

Rapallo

SAN MARINO

French Riviera

Ligurian Sea

Ancona

Arezzo

Macerata

Nice

MONACO

Siena

Perugia

Antibes

Cannes

Terni

Pescara

Toulon

Viterbo

L'Aquila

Civitavecchia

ROME

Ajaccio

Isernia

Latina

Caserta

this iconic peak in uber-cool Zermatt. (p355)

7 Zürich Shop, party and kick back with wild lake swimming in this Swiss ode to urban innovation. (p361)

8 Kitzbühel Snuggle up to the Austrian Alps' staggering beauty in a glitzy mountain resort. (p385)

9 Salzburg Acquaint yourself with Mozart in this

storybook city of *Sound of Music* fame. (p377)

10 Vienna Roam Habsburg palaces between coffee stops in Austria's magnificent capital. (p367)

France's
TOP EXPERIENCES

France (p304) has so much to entice travellers – renowned gastronomy, iconic sights, splendid art heritage, a fabulous outdoors. You could sample it all in a week, but you'll invariably feel as though you've only scratched the surface of this big country.

Visiting France is certainly about seeing the major sights, but it's just as much about savouring life's little pleasures: a stroll through an elegant city square, a coffee on a sunny pavement terrace, a meal that lasts well into the afternoon or night, a scenic drive punctuated with photo stops and impromptu farm or vineyard visits. The French are big on their art de vivre (art of living) and you should embrace it, too.

 Eiffel Tower

More than seven million people annually visit the Eiffel Tower, one of a bounty of iconic sights in Paris, Europe's most hopelessly romantic and sophisticated city. Pedal or picnic beneath it, skip the lift and hike up it, snap a selfie in front of it, ice-skate on the 1st floor in winter or visit at night when all 320m of the iconic tower twinkle with pretty lights: every visit is fabulous and utterly unique. (p304)

 Mont St-Michel

Dodge tides, stroll moonlit sand and immerse yourself in legend at this magical and mysterious abbey-island in Normandy. Said by Celtic mythology to be a sea tomb to which souls of the dead were sent, Mont St-Michel sizzles with legend and history, keenly felt as you make your way barefoot across rippled sand to the stunning architectural ensemble. Walk around it alone or, better still, hook up with a guide for a dramatic day hike across the bay. (p323)

 Loire Valley Châteaux

If it's aristocratic pomp and architectural splendour you're after, this regal valley near Paris is the place to linger. Flowing for more than 1000km into the Atlantic Ocean, the Loire is one of France's last *fleuves sauvages* (wild rivers) and its banks provide a 1000-year snapshot of French high society. During the Renaissance, it was here that kings and queens built gobsmackingly beautiful châteaux sporting glittering turrets, cupolas and chapels et al. Chambord, Chenonceau, Cheverny and Villandry are the big hitters. (p325)

The Corniches, Nice

It's impossible to drive this dramatic trio of *corniches* (coastal roads), each scarily higher and with more hairpin bends than the next, without conjuring up cinematic images of Grace Kelly, Hitchcock, the glitz of Riviera high life, and the glamour of the Monaco royal family – all while absorbing views of the sweeping blue sea fringing Europe's most mythical coastline. Make a perfect day out of it by shopping for a picnic at the cours Saleya morning market before leaving Nice. (p344)

GETTING AROUND

Train Run by the state-owned SNCF, France's rail network is first-class, with extensive country coverage and frequent departures; find timetables at www.sncf.com.

Car A pain to park and unnecessary in cities and large towns, but essential for getting to/from villages and landscapes in rural France not served by public transport. Drive on the right. Be aware of France's potentially hazardous 'priority to the right' rule.

Bus Cheaper, slower and less frequent than trains.

Bicycle Certain regions – the Loire Valley, Provence and Burgundy – beg to be explored by two wheels and have dedicated cycling paths.

⭐ Dune du Pilat

This whopper of a sandcastle begs a windswept frolic or cartwheel at the very least. Not only is the panorama from the top of Europe's largest sand dune a stunner – ogle at the Banc d'Arguin bird reserve and Cap Ferret across the bay – but nearby beaches have some of the Atlantic coast's best surf. Cycle here from Arcachon and feast on locally farmed oysters at a 1930s hunting lodge redesigned by Philippe Stark, aka place-to-be-seen La Co(o)rniche. (p338)

⭐ Chamonix

Birthplace of mountaineering and winter playground to the rich, famous and not-so-famous, this iconic ski resort in the French Alps has something for everyone. Snow-sport fiends fly down slopes on skis or boards amid breathtaking views of Mont Blanc by day, and party hard at night. For nonskiers (and/or tired legs), hop aboard the Aiguille du Midi cable car – and onwards to Italy aboard the Télécabine Panoramique Mont Blanc – for the ride of a lifetime above 3800m. (p335)

⭐ Champagne

Taste bubbly in ancient *caves* (cellars) inside world-famous Champagne houses in main towns Reims and Épernay. Our tip – grab a car and cruise along scenic driving routes in search of Champagne's finest liquid gold created by passionate, small-scale vignerons in drop-dead gorgeous countryside villages. (p328)

⭐ Marseille

Lap up urban buzz in this rich, pulsating port city on the Med, oozing history, cutting-edge drinking and dining, hip multicultural locals and bags of seaside fun. The ancient Greek city's maritime heritage thrives at the vibrant Vieux Port (Old Port), while swanky MuCEM is the stunning icon of contemporary Marseille. Along the coast, seaside roads and cycling tracks unfurl past sun-scorched coves and sandy beaches, packed in equal measure with traditional fishing boats and uber-cool beach volleyball players. (p338)

⭐ Monaco

Hit the world's second-smallest country – think concrete jungle with glitzy port, its own monarchy, throngs of VIPs and bags of high-octane glamour – to watch the changing of the palace guard, visit the Musée Océanographique and soak up the glitz and glamour of Riviera high life at the Casino de Monte Carlo. And when the razzmatazz gets too much, retreat to the world's largest floating dike where a designer sun deck, secret beach and postcard-perfect panorama of Monte Carlo await. (p346)

if France were 100 people

77 would live in urban areas
23 would live in rural areas

belief systems
(% of population)

| Roman Catholic | Jewish |
| 87 | 2 |

| Muslim | Protestant |
| 10 | 1 |

population per sq km

FRANCE   USA   UK

👤 ≈ 30 people

When to Go

Paris

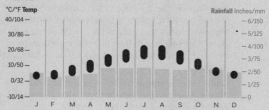

°C/°F Temp   Rainfall Inches/mm
40/104 — — 6/150
30/86 — — 5/125
20/68 — — 4/100
10/50 — — 3/75
0/32 — — 2/50
-10/14 — — 1/25
— 0

J F M A M J J A S O N D

Switzerland's
TOP EXPERIENCES

What giddy romance Zermatt, St Moritz and other glitterati-encrusted names evoke. This is Sonderfall Schweiz ('special-case Switzerland'), a privileged neutral country set apart from others, proudly idiosyncratic, insular and unique. It's blessed with gargantuan cultural diversity: its four official languages alone speak volumes.

The Swiss don't do half measures: Zürich, their most gregarious urban centre, has cutting-edge art, legendary nightlife and one of the world's highest living standards. The national passion for sharing the great outdoors provides access (by public transport, no less!) to some of the world's most inspiring panoramic experiences.

So don't depend just on your postcard images of Bern's and Lucerne's chocolate-box architecture, the majestic Matterhorn or those pristine lakes – Switzerland (p350) is a place so outrageously beautiful it simply must be seen to be believed.

⭐ Matterhorn

No mountain has so much pulling power or natural magnetism as this charismatic peak – a beauty from birth who demands to be admired, ogled and repeatedly photographed at sunset, sunrise, in different seasons and from every last infuriating angle. And there is no finer place to pander to Matterhorn's every last topographic need than Zermatt, one of Europe's most highly desirable Alpine resorts, in fashion with the skiing, climbing, hiking and hip hobnobbing set since the 19th century. (p355)

⭐ Zürich

One of Europe's most liveable cities, Zürich is an ode to urban renovation. (Yes, this is where Google employees shoot down a slide to work.) With something of a rough Berlin-esque edge, a visit to Zürich means drinking in waterfront bars, dancing until dawn in Züri-West, shopping for recycled fashion accessories in Kreis 5 and boogying with the best of them at Europe's largest street party, the city's wild and wacky, larger-than-life Street Parade in August. (p361)

⭐ Epic Outdoors

No trio are more immortalised in mountaineering legend than Switzerland's 'Big Three' – Eiger (Ogre), Mönch (Monk) and Jungfrau (Virgin) – peaks that soar to the sky above the traditional 19th-century resort of gorgeous old Grindelwald. And whether you choose to schuss around on skis, shoot down Europe's longest toboggan run on the back of an old-fashioned sledge, bungee-jump in the Gletscherschlucht or ride the train up to Europe's highest station at 3454m, your heart will thump. James Bond, eat your heart out.

⭐ Aletsch Glacier

One of the world's natural marvels, this mesmerising glacier of gargantuan proportions in the Upper Valais is tantamount to a 23km-long, five-lane highway of ice powering between mountain peaks at altitude. Its ice is glacial-blue and 900m thick at its deepest point. The view of Aletsch from Jungfraujoch will make your heart sing. (p358)

GETTING AROUND

Train An excellent rail network, run in the main by the Swiss Federal Railways, services urban Switzerland with regular, delightfully punctual trains; schedules and fares at www.sbb.ch.

Bus Regular, canary-yellow Post Buses supplement the rail network, following postal routes and linking towns to the less accessible mountain regions. Departures tie in with train arrivals, invariably from next to train stations; see www.postbus.ch for route details.

Car A set of wheels is useful in rural areas. Not all Alpine mountain passes are negotiable year-round; in winter, remember winter tyres and snow chains.

★ Swiss National Park

No country in Europe is more synonymous with magnificent and mighty hiking beneath eagle-dotted skies than Switzerland, and its high-altitude national park is the place to do it. Follow trails through flower-strewn meadows to piercing blue lakes, knife-edge ravines, rocky outcrops and Alpine huts where shepherds make summertime cheese with cows' milk, taken fresh that morning from the herd. This is a rare and privileged glimpse of Switzerland before the dawn of tourism. (p364)

★ Lake Geneva

The shores of Lake Geneva in wine-tasting Lavaux are stunning. But the urban viewpoint from which to experience Europe's largest lake is Geneva (p350), French-speaking Switzerland's most cosmopolitan city, where canary-yellow shuttle boats ferry locals across the water and Mont Blanc peeps in on the action. Strolling Old Town streets, paddle-boarding and making the odd dash beneath its iconic pencil fountain is what life's about for the 180 nationalities living here.

★ Glacier Express

It's among the world's most mythical train rides, linking two of Switzerland's glitziest Alpine resorts. Hop aboard the red train in St Moritz or Zermatt, and savour shot after cinematic shot of green peaks, glistening Alpine lakes and glacial ravines. Pulled by steam engine when it first puffed out of the station in 1930, the Glacier Express traverses 91 tunnels and 291 bridges on its famous journey. Bring your own Champagne picnic. (p352)

★ Basel

Contemporary architecture of world-class standing is Basel's golden ticket – seven winners of the Pritzker Prize have a living design that can be ogled in or around this city on the Rhine. Kick off with a hop across the German border to the Vitra Design Museum, designed by architect Frank Gehry, and devote the rest of the day to Switzerland's best private collection of modern art in a long, light-flooded building by Renzo Piano – the dream fusion of art and architecture at Fondation Beyeler. (p360)

★ Lago di Lugano

No Swiss spot exalts the country's Italianate soul with such gusto as Lugano Lake in Ticino, a shimmering Alpine lake fringed with palm-tree promenades and pastel-hued villages. Lugano, the biggest town on the lake, is vivacious and sassy with porticoed alleys, cafe-packed piazzas and boats yo-yoing around the lakeside destinations. (p363)

if Switzerland was 100 people

64 would speak German
20 would speak French
8 would speak another language
7 would speak Italian
1 would speak Romansch

belief systems
(% of population)

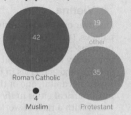

42 Roman Catholic
19 other
35 Protestant
4 Muslim

population per sq km

SWITZERLAND   USA   UK

👤 = 32 people

When to Go

Geneva

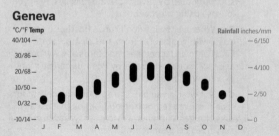

°C/°F **Temp**   Rainfall inches/mm
40/104 —   — 6/150
30/86 —
20/68 —   — 4/100
10/50 —
0/32 —   — 2/50
-10/14 —   — 0
        J F M A M J J A S O N D

Austria's
TOP EXPERIENCES

For such a small country, Austria (p367) has made it big. This is, after all, the land where Mozart was born, Strauss taught the world to waltz and Julie Andrews grabbed the spotlight with her twirling entrance in The Sound of Music. *This is where the Habsburgs built their 600-year empire, and where past glories still shine in the resplendent baroque palaces and chandelier-lit coffee houses of Vienna, Innsbruck and Salzburg. This is a perfectionist of a country and whatever it does – mountains, classical music, new media, castles, cake, you name it – it does exceedingly well.*

Beyond its grandiose cities, Austria's allure lies outdoors. And whether you're schussing down the legendary slopes of Kitzbühel, climbing high in the Alps of Tyrol or pedalling along the banks of the sprightly Danube (Donau), you'll find the kind of inspiring landscapes that no well-orchestrated symphony, camera lens or singing nun could ever quite do justice to.

⭐ Vienna

Discover opulent Habsburg palaces, traditional coffee houses, exciting contemporary museums and cutting-edge galleries in the Austrian capital, one of the most musical cities in the world with a rash of world-famous composers under its belt to boot. Packed with imperial history, the monumentally graceful Hofburg whisks you back to the age of empires, rivalled in grandeur only by the 1441-room Schloss Schönbrunn, a Unesco World Heritage Site. (p367)

⭐ Salzburg

No country can outshine Austria when it comes to classical music and this movie star of a city is the place to really sink your teeth into it. Hometown of 18th-century classical composer Mozart no less, Salzburg of *The Sound of Music* fame is a storybook mirage of baroque Old Town architecture, opulent palaces, soul-stirring concert halls and brilliant museums. The city's eclectic dining scene skips from the traditional to supertrendy to downright touristy, cafe culture is huge and then there's the call of the mountains beyond, kept in check by the glorious hilltop fortress of Festung Hohensalzburg. (p377)

⭐ Kitzbühel

In a country where three-year-olds can snowplough, 70-year-olds still slalom and the tiniest speck of a village has its own lift system, skiing is more than just a sport – it's a way of life. And there is no finer spot to immerse yourself in the full ski-hard-all-day, party-at-night winter-sports culture than Kitzbühel, one of Europe's foremost ski resorts where Franz Reisch slipped on skis and whizzed down the slopes of Kitzbüheler Horn way back when in 1893. (p385)

⭐ Grossglockner Road

Hairpin bends: 36. Length: 48km. Average slope gradient: 9%. Highest viewpoint: Edelweiss Spitze (2571m). Grossglockner Road is one of Europe's greatest drives and the showpiece

---

GETTING AROUND

Train Austria's main rail provider is the highly efficient, highly developed ÖBB (Austrian Federal Railway), with an extensive countrywide rail network supplemented by several private railways. Plan your journey using www.oebb.at.

Bus Wherever trains don't run, a Postbus usually does, with departures from outside train stations. Find *Fahrplan* (schedules) and fares at www.postbus.at or www.oebb.at. Travel by Postbus can be more expensive than train.

Car Not vital, given public transport is excellent for reaching even remote regions, although it usually takes longer. Winter or all-weather tyres are compulsory from 1 November to 15 April.

of Hohe Tauern National Park. The scenery unfolds as you climb higher on this serpentine road. And what scenery! Snowcapped mountains, plunging waterfalls and lakes scattered like gemstones are just the build-up to Grossglockner (3798m), Austria's highest peak, and the Pasterze Glacier. (p386)

★ Salzkammergut

Austria's jewel-coloured lake region is perfect for peeling off the city clothing and diving into spectacular, crystal-clear Alpine waters in Austria's summer playground. The Hallstätter See, set at the foot of the abrupt and monumentally rugged Dachstein Mountains, is the spot to linger – or swim, sail, fish and hike. With pastel-hued homes, swans and towering mountains on either side of a glassy green lake, main town Hallstatt is a Unesco World Heritage Site to boot. (p381)

★ Innsbruck

Set against a backdrop of the Nordkette range, Tyrol's capital has you celebrating cultural achievement in elegant state apartments or the Gothic Hofkirche one moment, and the next whizzing up into the mountain inside Zaha Hadid's futuristic funicular, clinging to a fixed rope on the Innsbrucker Klettersteig or tackling the less vertiginous Nordkette Singletrail on the back of a mountain bike. Then there's the cafe culture and student-fuelled bars in the picture-book medieval Old Town. (p382)

★ Eisriesenwelt

The twinkling chambers and passageways of Eisriesenwelt are like something out of Narnia under the White Witch. Sculpted drip by drip over millennia, the icy underworld of the limestone Tennengebirge range is billed as the world's largest accessible ice cave. Otherworldly sculptures, shimmering lakes and a cavernous *Eispalast* (ice palace) appear as you venture deep into the frozen heart of the mountain, carbide lamp in hand. (p381)

★ Graz

Austria's largest city after Vienna is also one of the country's most relaxed. After you have visited Schloss Eggenberg and climbed the Schlossberg for magnificent views over the red rooftops of town – perhaps sipping a long drink or two on a warm afternoon at the Aiola Upstairs – set your sights upon the south Styrian wine roads. This wine-growing region, about 50km south of Graz, is a visual treat of rolling, verdant hills and picturesque vineyards unfolding to the Slovenian border. (p374)

if Austria were 100 people

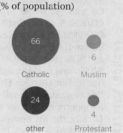

77 would be Austrian
23 would be foreign citizens

belief systems
(% of population)

66 Catholic
6 Muslim
24 other
4 Protestant

population per sq km

AUSTRIA   USA   GERMANY

🧍 ≈ 30 people

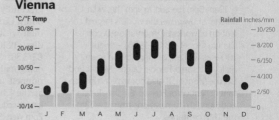

When to Go

Vienna

°C/°F Temp
30/86 —
20/68 —
10/50 —
0/32 —
-10/14 —

Rainfall inches/mm
— 10/250
— 8/200
— 6/150
— 4/100
— 2/50
— 0

J F M A M J J A S O N D

FRANCE

Paris

POP 2.2 MILLION

What can be said about the sexy, sophisticated City of Light that hasn't already been said myriad times before? Quite simply, this is one of the world's great metropolises – a trendsetter, market leader and cultural capital for over a thousand years and still going strong.

◉ Sights

◉ Left Bank

★ Eiffel Tower
LANDMARK

(Map p306; ☎ 08 92 70 12 39; www.tour-eiffel. fr; Champ de Mars, 5 av Anatole France, 7e; lift to top adult/youth/child €17/14.50/8, lift to 2nd fl €11/8.50/4, stairs to 2nd fl €7/5/3, lift 2nd fl to top €6; ◷ lifts & stairs 9am-12.45am mid-Jun–Aug, lifts 9.30am-11.45pm, stairs 9.30am-6.30pm Sep–mid-Jun; Ⓜ Bir Hakeim or RER Champ de Mars–Tour Eiffel) No one could imagine Paris today without it. But Gustave Eiffel only constructed this elegant, 320m-tall signature spire as a temporary exhibit for the 1889 World Fair. Luckily, the art nouveau tower's popularity assured its survival. Prebook tickets online to avoid long ticket queues. Lifts ascend to the tower's three floors; change lifts on the 2nd floor for the final ascent to the top. Energetic visitors can walk as far as the 2nd floor using the south pillar's 704-step stairs.

★ Musée du Quai Branly
MUSEUM

(Map p306; ☎ 01 56 61 70 00; www.quaibranly.fr; 37 quai Branly, 7e; adult/child €9/free; ◷ 11am-7pm Tue, Wed & Sun, 11am-9pm Thu-Sat; Ⓜ Alma

Marceau or RER Pont de l'Alma) No other museum in Paris so inspires travellers, armchair anthropologists and those who simply appreciate the beauty of traditional artisanship. A tribute to the diversity of human culture, Musée du Quai Branly presents an overview of indigenous and folk art. Its four main sections focus on Oceania, Asia, Africa and the Americas.

★ Hôtel des Invalides
MONUMENT, MUSEUM

(Map p306; www.musee-armee.fr; 129 rue de Grenelle, 7e; adult/child €11/free; ◷ 10am-6pm Apr-Oct, to 5pm Nov-Mar, hours can vary; Ⓜ Varenne) Flanked by the 500m-long Esplanade des Invalides lawns, the Hôtel des Invalides was built in the 1670s by Louis XIV to house 4000 *invalides* (disabled war veterans). On 14 July 1789, a mob broke into the building and seized 32,000 rifles before heading on to the prison at Bastille and the start of the French Revolution.

★ Musée Rodin
MUSEUM, GARDEN

(Map p306; www.musee-rodin.fr; 79 rue de Varenne, 7e; adult/child museum incl garden €10/7, garden only €4/2; ◷ 10am-5.45pm Tue & Thu-Sun, to 8.45pm Wed; Ⓜ Varenne) Sculptor, painter, sketcher, engraver and collector Auguste Rodin donated his entire collection to the French state in 1908 on the proviso that they dedicate his former workshop and showroom, the beautiful 1730 Hôtel Biron, to displaying his works. They're now installed not only in the magnificently restored mansion itself, but in its rose-filled garden – one of the most peaceful places in central Paris and a wonderful spot to contemplate his famous work *The Thinker*. Prepurchase tickets online to avoid queuing.

Jardin du Luxembourg
PARK

(Map p312; www.senat.fr/visite/jardin; numerous entrances; ◷ vary; Ⓜ Mabillon, St-Sulpice, Rennes, Notre Dame des Champs or RER Luxembourg) This inner-city oasis of formal terraces, chestnut groves and lush lawns has a special place in Parisians' hearts. Napoléon dedicated the 23 gracefully laid-out hectares of the Luxembourg Gardens to the children of Paris, and many residents spent their childhood prodding 1920s wooden **sailboats** (30/60 min €2/3.30; ◷ Apr-Oct) with long sticks on the octagonal **Grand Bassin** pond; watching puppets perform *Punch & Judy*-type shows at the **Théâtre du Luxembourg** (www.marionnettesduluxembourg.fr; tickets €6; ◷ usually 2pm Wed, Sat & Sun, plus 4pm daily during school

---

MUSÉE MARMOTTAN MONET

The **Musée Marmottan Monet** (Map p306; ☎ 01 44 96 50 33; www.marmottan.fr; 2 rue Louis Boilly, 16e; adult/child €11/6.50; ◷ 10am-6pm Tue-Sun, to 9pm Thu; Ⓜ La Muette) showcases the world's largest collection of works by impressionist painter Claude Monet (1840–1926) – about 100 – as well as paintings by Gauguin, Sisley, Pissarro, Renoir, Degas, Manet and Berthe Morisot. It also contains an important collection of French, English, Italian and Flemish illuminations from the 13th to the 16th centuries.

holidays); and riding the *carrousel* (merry-go-round) or **ponies** (rides €3.50; ⏱3-6pm Wed, Sat, Sun & school holidays).

Les Catacombes
CEMETERY
(Map p306; www.catacombes.paris.fr; 1 av Colonel Henri Roi-Tanguy, 14e; adult/child €12/free; ⏱10am-8pm Tue-Sun; M Denfert Rochereau) Paris' most macabre sight is its underground tunnels lined with skulls and bones. In 1785 it was decided to rectify the hygiene problems of Paris' overflowing cemeteries by exhuming the bones and storing them in disused quarry tunnels, and the Catacombes were created in 1810. After descending 20m (via 130 narrow, dizzying spiral steps) below street level, you follow the dark, subterranean passages to reach the ossuary (2km in all). Exit back up 83 steps onto rue Remy Dumoncel, 14e.

Musée d'Orsay
MUSEUM
(Map p306; www.musee-orsay.fr; 62 rue de Lille, 7e; adult/child €12/free; ⏱9.30am-6pm Tue, Wed & Fri-Sun, to 9.45pm Thu; M Assemblée Nationale or RER Musée d'Orsay) The home of France's national collection from the impressionist, postimpressionist and art nouveau movements spanning the 1848 to 1914 is the glorious former Gare d'Orsay railway station – itself an art nouveau showpiece – where a roll-call of masters and their world-famous works are on display.

Panthéon
MAUSOLEUM
(Map p312; www.monum.fr; place du Panthéon, 5e; adult/child €8.50/free; ⏱10am-6.30pm Apr-Sep, to 6pm Oct-Mar; M Maubert-Mutualité or RER Luxembourg) Overlooking the city from its Left Bank perch, the Panthéon's stately neoclassical dome stands out as one of the most recognisable icons on the Parisian skyline. An architectural masterpiece, the interior is impressively vast. Originally a church and now a mausoleum, it has served since 1791 as the resting place of some of France's greatest thinkers, including Voltaire, Rousseau, Braille and Hugo. Its four newest 'residents' are Resistance fighters Germaine Tillion, Genèvieve de Gaulle-Anthonioz, Pierre Brossolette and Jean Zay.

◉ The Islands

Paris' geographic and spiritual heart is here in the Seine, on inner-city islands Île de la Cité, dominated by Notre Dame, and serene eatery-clad Île St-Louis.

ⓘ PARIS MUSEUMS PASS

If you're a student, senior or EU citizen under 26 it's not worth buying a pass – you get hefty discounts or get in for free at most city museums. The **Paris Museum Pass** (www.parismuseumpass.com; 2/4/6 days €48/62/74) gets you into 50-odd venues in and around Paris; a huge advantage is that pass holders usually enter larger sights at a different entrance meaning you bypass (or substantially reduce) ridiculously long ticket queues.

★ Cathédrale Notre Dame de Paris
CATHEDRAL
(Map p312; ☎01 42 34 56 10; www.cathedraledeparis.com; 6 place du Parvis Notre Dame, 4e; cathedral free, towers adult/child €8.50/free, treasury €2/1; ⏱cathedral 8am-6.45pm Mon-Fri, to 7.15pm Sat & Sun, towers 10am-6.30pm Sun-Thu, to 11pm Fri & Sat Jul & Aug, 10am-6.30pm Apr-Jun & Sep, 10am-5pm Oct-Mar, treasury 9.30am-6pm Apr-Sep, 10am-5.30pm Oct-Mar; M Cité) Paris' most visited unticketed site, with upwards of 14 million visitors per year, is a masterpiece of French Gothic architecture. The focus of Catholic Paris for seven centuries, its vast interior accommodates 6000 worshippers.

Highlights include its three spectacular **rose windows, treasury,** and **bell towers** (www.monuments-nationaux.fr), which can be climbed. From the North Tower, 400-odd steps spiral to the top of the western facade, where you'll find yourself face-to-face with frightening gargoyles and a spectacular view of Paris.

Sainte-Chapelle
CHAPEL
(Map p312; ☎01 53 40 60 80, concerts 01 42 77 65 65; www.monuments-nationaux.fr; 4 bd du Palais, 1er; adult/child €8.50/free, joint ticket with Conciergerie €15; ⏱9.30am-6pm Thu-Tue, to 9pm Wed mid-May–mid-Sep, 9.30am-6pm Mar–mid-May & mid-Sep–Oct, 9am-5pm Nov-Feb; M Cité) Try to save Ste-Chapelle for a sunny day, when Paris' oldest, finest stained glass is at its dazzling best. Enshrined within the **Palais de Justice** (Law Courts), this gemlike Holy Chapel is Paris' most exquisite Gothic monument. Ste-Chapelle was built in just six years (compared with nearly 200 years for Notre Dame) and consecrated in 1248.

The chapel was conceived by Louis IX to house his personal collection of holy relics, including the famous Holy Crown (now in Notre Dame).

Greater Paris

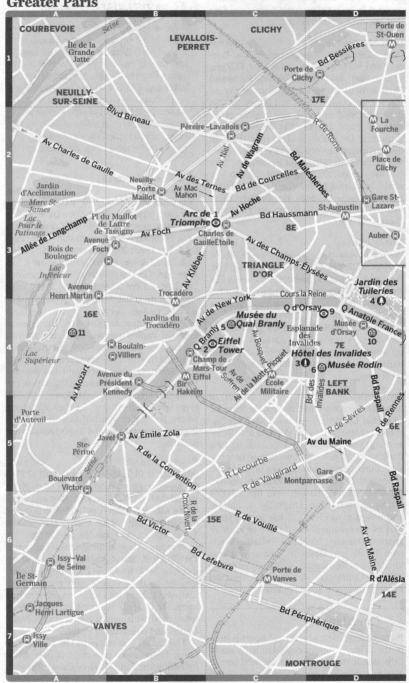

COURBEVOIE

Seine

Île de la
Grande Jatte

LEVALLOIS-
PERRET

CLICHY

Porte de
St-Ouen

Bd Bessières

Porte de
Clichy

17E

R de Rome

La
Fourche

Place de
Clichy

NEUILLY-
SUR-SEINE

Blvd Bineau

Av Charles de Gaulle

Péreire–Lavallois

Av Niel

Av de Wagram

Bd de Courcelles

Bd Malesherbes

Av des Ternes

Jardin
d'Acclimatation

Mare St-
James

Lac
Pour le
Patinage

Neuilly-
Porte
Maillot

Av Mac
Mahon

Pl du Maillot
de Lattre
de Tassigny

Av Foch

Allée de Longchamp

Avenue
Foch

Bois de
Boulogne

Lac
Inférieur

Arc de 1
Triomphe

Charles de
GaulleÉtoile

Av Hoche

Bd Haussmann

St-Augustin

Gare St-
Lazare

8E

Auber

Av des Champs-Élysées

Av Kléber

TRIANGLE
D'OR

Avenue
Henri Martin

Trocadéro

Cours la Reine

Jardin des
Tuileries
4

16E

11

Jardins du
Trocadéro

Av de New York

Q d'Orsay
9

Q Anatole France

Musée du
Quai Branly

Q Branly 5

Esplanade
des
Invalides

Musée
d'Orsay
10

Lac
Supérieur

Boulain-
Villiers

Eiffel
Tower

Champ de
Mars-Tour
Eiffel

Av de Suffren

Av Bosquet

Av de la Motte Picquet

Hôtel des Invalides

Musée Rodin

7E

3

6

Av Mozart

Avenue du
Président
Kennedy

Bir
Hakeim

École
Militaire

Bd des
Invalides

LEFT
BANK

Bd Raspail

Porte
d'Auteuil

Ste-
Périne

Javel

Av Émile Zola

Seine

R de la Convention

R Lecourbe

R de Vaugirard

R de Sèvres

Av du Maine

R de Rennes

6E

Bd Raspail

Boulevard
Victor

Gare
Montparnasse

Bd Victor

R de la
Croix Nivert

15E

R de Vouillé

Av du Maine

Issy–Val
de Seine

Bd Lefebvre

Porte de
Vanves

R d'Alésia

Île St-
Germain

14E

Jacques
Henri Lartigue

VANVES

Bd Périphérique

Issy
Ville

MONTROUGE

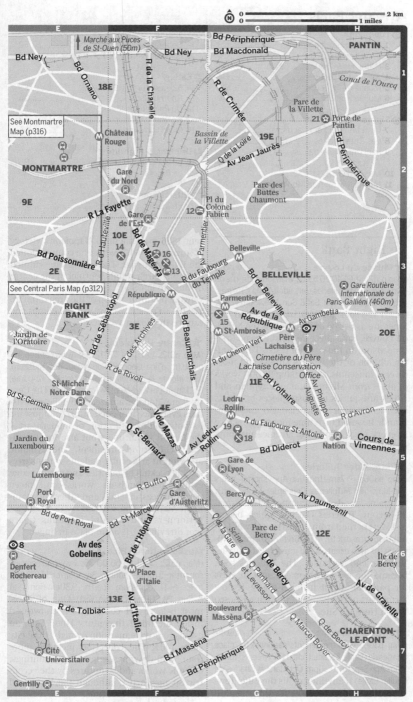

N
0 — 2 km
0 — 1 miles

Bd Périphérique
Bd Macdonald
Bd Ney

Marché aux Puces
de St-Ouen (50m)

PANTIN

Bd Ney

Bd Ney

Bd Ornano

R de la Chapelle

R de Crimée

Canal de l'Ourcq

18E

Parc de
la Villette

21 ⭐ Porte de
Pantin

See Montmartre
Map (p316)

Ⓜ Château
Rouge

Bassin de
la Villette

19E

Q de la Loire

Av Jean Jaurès

Bd Périphérique

MONTMARTRE

Ⓜ Gare
du Nord

9E

R La Fayette

Parc des
Buttes Chaumont

Ⓜ Gare
de l'Est

12 🏛

Pl du
Colonel
Fabien

10E

Bd de Magenta

R d'Hauteville

14 ✕

17 ✕

16 ✕

Belleville
Ⓜ

BELLEVILLE

Ⓡ Gare Routière
Internationale de
Paris-Galliéni (460m)

Bd Poissonnière

2E

13 🏛

R du Faubourg
du Temple

R du Faubourg

Bd de Belleville

See Central Paris Map (p312)

République Ⓜ

**RIGHT
BANK**

Bd de Sébastopol

3E

Parmentier
Ⓜ

15 ✕

Av de la
République

Ⓜ St-Ambroise

Père
Lachaise

Av Gambetta

7 ◎

Jardin de
l'Oratoire

R des Archives

R de Rivoli

R de Rivoli

Bd Beaumarchais

R du Chemin Vert

Père
Lachaise

ℹ

Cimetière du Père
Lachaise Conservation
Office

20E

St-Michel–
Notre Dame
Ⓜ

Bd St-Germain

4E

Voie Mazas

Q St-Bernard

Av Ledru-
Rollin

Ledru-
Rollin
Ⓜ

11E

Bd Voltaire

Av Philippe
Auguste

R du Faubourg St-Antoine

R d'Avron

Jardin du
Luxembourg

5E

19 ✕
18 ✕

Bd Diderot

Nation
Ⓡ

**Cours de
Vincennes**

Ⓡ
Luxembourg

R Buffo

Gare de
Lyon
Ⓜ

Port
Ⓡ Royal

Gare
d'Austerlitz

Bercy
Ⓜ

Av Daumesnil

Bd de Port Royal

Bd St-Marcel

Bd de l'Hôpital

Q de la Gare

Parc de
Bercy

12E

Q de Bercy

Île de
Bercy

8 ◎
Ⓡ

Av des
Gobelins

20

Q Panhard
et Levassor

Q Panhard
et Levassor

Av de Gravelle

Denfert
Rochereau

Ⓜ Place
d'Italie

13E

Av d'Italie

R de Tolbiac

CHINATOWN

Boulevard
Massèna

Q Marcel Boyer

Q de Bercy

**CHARENTON-
LE-PONT**

Ⓡ Cité
Universitaire

B.J Masséna

Bd Périphérique

Gentilly Ⓡ

FRANCE, SWITZERLAND & AUSTRIA PARIS

Greater Paris

FRANCE, SWITZERLAND & AUSTRIA PARIS

◉ Right Bank

★ **Musée du Louvre**   MUSEUM
(Map p312; ☎ 01 40 20 53 17; www.louvre.fr; rue de Rivoli & quai des Tuileries, 1er; adult/child €15/free; ⊙ 9am-6pm Mon, Thu, Sat & Sun, to 9.45pm Wed & Fri; M Palais Royal–Musée du Louvre) Few art galleries are as prized or daunting as the Musée du Louvre, Paris' pièce de résistance no first-time visitor to the city can resist. This is, after all, one of the world's largest and most diverse museums, showcasing 35,000 works of art – from Mesopotamian, Egyptian and Greek antiquities to masterpieces by artists such as Da Vinci, Michelangelo and Rembrandt It would take nine months to glance at every piece, rendering advance planning essential.

★ **Jardin des Tuileries**   PARK
(Map p306; ⊙ 7am-11pm Jun-Aug, shorter hours Sep-May; 🚼; M Tuileries, Concorde) Filled with fountains, ponds and sculptures, the formal 28-hectare Tuileries Garden, which begins just west of the Jardin du Carrousel, was laid out in its present form in 1664 by André Le Nôtre, who also created the gardens at Vaux-le-Vicomte and Versailles. The Tuileries soon became the most fashionable spot in Paris for parading about in one's finery. It now forms part of the Banks of the Seine Unesco World Heritage Site.

★ **Arc de Triomphe**   LANDMARK
(Map p306; www.monuments-nationaux.fr; place Charles de Gaulle, 8e; adult/child €12/free; ⊙ 10am-11pm Apr-Sep, to 10.30pm Oct-Mar; M Charles de Gaulle–Étoile) If anything rivals the Eiffel Tower as the symbol of Paris, it's this magnificent 1836 monument to Napoléon's victory at Austerlitz (1805), which he commissioned the following year. The intricately sculpted triumphal arch stands sentinel in the centre of the Étoile ('Star') roundabout. From the viewing platform on top of the arch (50m up via 284 steps and well worth the climb) you can see the dozen avenues.

★ **Centre Pompidou**   MUSEUM
(Map p312; ☎ 01 44 78 12 33; www.centrepompidou.fr; place Georges Pompidou, 4e; museum, exhibitions & panorama adult/child €14/free; ⊙ 11am-10pm Wed-Mon; M Rambuteau) The Centre Pompidou has amazed and delighted visitors ever since it opened in 1977, not just for its outstanding collection of modern art – the largest in Europe – but also for its radical architectural statement. The dynamic and vibrant arts centre delights with its irresistible cocktail of galleries and cutting-edge exhibitions, hands-on workshops, dance performances, cinemas and other entertainment venues. The exterior, with its street performers and fanciful fountains (place Igor Stravinsky), is a fun place to linger.

Musée National Picasso   MUSEUM
(Map p312; ☎ 01 85 56 00 36; www.museepicassoparis.fr; 5 rue de Thorigny, 3e; adult/child €12.50/free; ⊙ 10.30am-6pm Tue-Fri, 9.30am-6pm Sat & Sun; M St-Paul, Chemin Vert) One of Paris' most beloved art collections is showcased inside the mid-17th-century Hôtel Salé, an exquisite private mansion owned by the city since 1964. The collection includes more than 5000 drawings, engravings, paintings, ceramic works and sculptures by the eccentric Spanish artist, although they're not all displayed at the same time.

Cimetière du Père Lachaise CEMETERY
(Map p306; ☎ 01 55 25 82 10; www.pere-lachaise.com; 16 rue du Repos & 8 bd de Ménilmontant, 20e; ⊙8am-6pm Mon-Fri, 8.30am-6pm Sat, 9am-6pm Sun, shorter hours winter; ⓂPère Lachaise, Gambetta) The world's most visited cemetery, Père Lachaise, opened in 1804. Its 70,000 ornate, even ostentatious, tombs of the rich and/or famous form a verdant 44-hectare sculpture garden. The most visited are those of 1960s rock star Jim Morrison (division 6) and Oscar Wilde (division 89). Pick up cemetery maps at the **conservation office** (Bureaux de la Conservation; ⊙8.30am-12.30pm & 2-5pm Mon-Fri) near the main bd de Ménilmontant entrance. Other notables buried here include composer Chopin; playwright Molière; poet Apollinaire; and writers Balzac, Proust, Gertrude Stein and Colette.

Basilique du Sacré-Cœur BASILICA
(Map p316; ☎ 01 53 41 89 00; www.sacre-coeur-montmartre.com; place du Parvis du Sacré-Cœur; dome adult/child €6/4, cash only; ⊙6am-10.30pm, dome 8.30am-8pm May-Sep, to 5pm Oct-Apr; ⓂAnvers) Although some may poke fun at Sacré-Cœur's unsubtle design, the view from its parvis is one of those perfect Paris postcards. More than just a basilica, Sacré-Cœur is a veritable experience, from the musicians performing on the steps to the groups of friends picnicking on the hillside park. Touristy, yes. But beneath it all, Sacré-Cœur's heart is gold.

Le Mur des je t'aime PUBLIC ART
(Map p316; www.lesjetaime.com; Sq Jehan Rictus, place des Abbesses 18e; ⊙8am-8.30pm Mon-Fri, 9am-8.30pm Sat & Sun May-Aug, to 7.30pm Sep-Apr; ⓂAbbesses) Few visitors to Paris can resist a selfie in front of Montmartre's 'I Love You' wall, a public art work created in a small city-square park by artists Frédéric Baron and Claire Kito in the year 2000. The striking wall mural made from dark-blue enamel tiles features the immortal phrase 'I love you!' 311 times in 250 different languages. Find a bench beneath a maple tree and brush up your language skills romantic Paris-style.

🛏 Sleeping

★ Generator Hostel HOSTEL €
(Map p306; ☎ 01 70 98 84 00; www.generatorhostels.com; 11 place du Colonel Fabien, 10e; dm €23-42, d €112-218; ❄@🛜; ⓂColonel Fabien) A short walk from the water, this buzzing hostel is a shout-out to design, street art and French *art de vivre*. From the stylish

EUROPE'S BIGGEST FLEA MARKET

A metro ride to Porte de Clignancourt in northern Paris unveils the fabulous **Marché aux Puces de St-Ouen** (www.marcheauxpuces-saintouen.com; rue des Rosiers; ⊙varies; ⓂPorte de Clignancourt). This vast flea market, founded in the late 19th century and said to be Europe's largest, has more than 2500 stalls grouped into 15 *marchés* (markets). Each has its own specialty.

ground-floor cafe-restaurant and 9th-floor rooftop bar (spot Montmartre!) to the basement club and super-cool bathrooms with 'I love you' tiling, this overwhelmingly contemporary hostel is sharp. Dorms have USB sockets, and the best doubles have fabulous terraces with views.

Hôtel St-André des Arts HOTEL €
(Map p312; ☎ 01 43 26 96 16; www.hotel-saintandredesarts.fr; 66 rue St-André des Arts, 6e; s/d/tr/q €95/115/156/181; 🛜; ⓂOdéon) Located on a lively, restaurant-lined thoroughfare, this 31-room hotel is a veritable bargain in the centre of the action opposite the beautiful glass-roofed passage Cour du Commerce St André. The rooms are basic and there's no lift (elevator), but the public areas are very evocative of *vieux Paris* (old Paris), with beamed ceilings and ancient stone walls, and rates include breakfast.

Hôtel du Nord – Le Pari Vélo HOTEL €
(Map p306; ☎ 01 42 01 66 00; www.hotel-dunord-leparivelo.com; 47 rue Albert Thomas, 10e; s/d/q €73/86/125; 🛜; ⓂRépublique) This quaint address has 24 rooms decorated with flea-market antiques and 10 bikes for guests to borrow to ride around town. Beyond the bric-a-brac charm, Hôtel du Nord's other winning attribute is its prized location near place République. Ring and wait to enter. Breakfast costs €8.

🍴 Eating

Paris cooks up the whole gambit of cuisines, in every budget and genre. On the Left Bank, cheap-eat student spots are particularly rife in the Latin Quarter; rue Mouffetard here is famed for its food market and food shops.

On the Right Bank, Le Marais is the premier foodie destination; rue Rosiers, 4e, is

The Louvre

A HALF-DAY TOUR

Successfully visiting the Louvre is a fine art. Its complex labyrinth of galleries and staircases spiralling three wings and four floors renders discovery a snakes-and-ladders experience. Initiate yourself with this three-hour itinerary – a playful mix of Mona Lisa obvious and up-to-the-minute unexpected.

Arriving by the stunning main entrance, pick up colour-coded floor plans at the lower-ground-floor **information desk ❶** beneath IM Pei's glass pyramid, ride the escalator up to the Sully Wing and swap passport for multimedia guide (there are limited descriptions in the galleries) at the wing entrance.

The Louvre is as much about spectacular architecture as masterly art. To appreciate this zip up and down Sully's Escalier Henri II to admire **Venus de Milo ❷**, then up parallel Escalier Henri IV to the palatial displays in **Cour Khorsabad ❸**. Cross room 1 to find the escalator up to the 1st floor and staircase-as-art **L'Esprit d'Escalier ❹**. Next traverse 25 consecutive galleries (thank you, floor plan!) to flip conventional contemplation on its head with Cy Twombly's **The Ceiling ❺**, and the hypnotic **Winged Victory of Samothrace sculpture ❻** – just two rooms away – which brazenly insists on being admired from all angles. End with the impossibly famous **The Raft of Medusa ❼**, **Mona Lisa ❽** and **Virgin & Child ❾**.

TOP TIPS

» **Floor Plans** Don't even consider entering the Louvre's maze of galleries without a Plan/Information Louvre brochure, free from the information desk in the Hall Napoléon

» **Crowd dodgers** The Denon Wing is always packed; visit on late nights Wednesday or Friday or trade Denon in for the notably quieter Richelieu Wing

» **2nd floor** Not for first-timers: save its more specialist works for subsequent visits

MISSION MONA LISA

If you just want to venerate the Louvre's most famous lady, use the Porte des Lions entrance (closed Tuesday and Friday), from where it's a five-minute walk. Go up one flight of stairs and through rooms 26, 14 and 13 to the Grande Galerie and adjoining room 6.

Mona Lisa
Room 6, 1st Floor, Denon

No smile is as enigmatic or bewitching as hers. Da Vinci's diminutive *La Joconde* hangs opposite the largest painting in the Louvre – sumptuous, fellow Italian Renaissance artwork *The Wedding at Cana*.

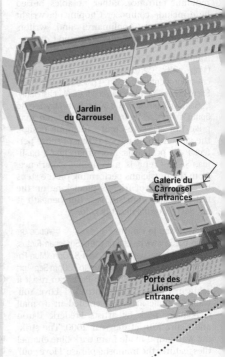

Rue de Rivoli Entrance

Jardin du Carrousel

Galerie du Carrousel Entrances

Porte des Lions Entrance

The Raft of the Medusa
Room 77, 1st Floor, Denon

Decipher the politics behind French romanticism in Théodore Géricault's *Raft of the Medusa*.

DEA/G DAGLI ORTI/GETTY IMAGES ©

L'Esprit d'Escalier
Escalier Lefuel, Richelieu
Discover the 'Spirit of the Staircase' through François Morellet's contemporary stained glass, which casts new light on old stone. **DETOUR»** Napoleon III's gorgeous gilt apartments.

Cour Khorsabad
Ground Floor, Richelieu
Time travel with a pair of winged human-headed bulls to view some of the world's oldest Mesopotamian art. **DETOUR»** Night-lit statues in Cour Puget.

The Ceiling
Room 32, 1st Floor, Sully
Admire the blue shock of Cy Twombly's 400-sq-metre contemporary ceiling fresco – the Louvre's latest, daring commission. **DETOUR»** *The Braque Ceiling*, room 33.

CY TWOMBLY FOUNDATION/GETTY IMAGES ©

Cour Khorsabad

③

Cour Puget

④ **Cour Marly**

Cour Carrée

RICHELIEU WING

SULLY WING

Cour Napoléon

①

⑤

Pyramid Main Entrance

②

Inverted Pyramid

⑥

⑦ **⑧** **Cour Visconti**

⑨

Pont des Arts

DENON WING

Pont du Carrousel

Virgin & Child
Room 5, Grande Galerie, 1st Floor, Denon
In the spirit of artistic devotion save the Louvre's most famous gallery for last: a feast of Virgin-and-child paintings by Raphael, Domenico Ghirlandaio, Giovanni Bellini and Francesco Botticini.

Winged Victory of Samothrace
Escalier Daru, 1st Floor, Sully
Draw breath at the aggressive dynamism of this headless, handless Hellenistic goddess. **DETOUR»** The razzle-dazzle of the Apollo Gallery's crown jewels.

Venus de Milo
Room 16, Ground Floor, Sully
No one knows who sculpted this seductively realistic goddess from Greek antiquity. Naked to the hips, she is a Hellenistic masterpiece.

JOHN SONES SINGING BOWL MEDIA/ GETTY IMAGES ©

Central Paris

500 m
0.25 miles

A **B** **C** **D** **E** **F** **G**

1 **2** **3** **4**

R de la Pierre Levée

Bd Jules Ferry

Bd Richard Lenoir

Bd Voltaire

11E

R Alphonse Baudin

Allée Verte

Bd Richard Lenoir

Breguet Sabin

R Daval

Bastille

Av de la République

Oberkampf

République

R St-Sébastien

R Amelot

Chemin Vert

Bd Beaumarchais

R des Tournelles

10E

Pl de la République

Bd du Temple

R Béranger

R de Turenne

Filles du Calvaire

16

St-Sébastien Froissart

R St-Sébastien

R St-Claude

Jardin St-Gilles Grand Veneur

R St-Gilles

R de Béarn

R du Pas de la Mule

Pl du Marché Ste-Catherine

Bd St-Martin

R Meslay

R Notre Dame de Nazareth

Temple

R Dupetit Thouars

R Perrée

Sq du Temple

3E

R de Bretagne

R de Poitou

13

12

R Charlot

R de Saintonge

11

Jardin de l'Hôtel Salé

5

R Ste-Anastase

R du Parc Royal

Sq G.Cain

R Barbette

R des Francs Bourgeois

R Malher

R St-Paul

R de Turbigo

R de Vertbois

R Réaumur

R des Gravilliers

R du Temple

R Pastourelle

R des Archives

R des Fils

R des Rosiers

R du Roi de Sicile

R du Bourg

R de la Verrerie

LE MARAIS

R des Blancs Manteaux

R Ste-Croix de la Bretonnerie

4E

R François Miron

R de Fourcy

R du Roi de Sicile

R de Rivoli

R Denis

St-Denis

Réaumur Sébastopol

Arts et Métiers

Sq Émile Chautemps

R des Vertus

R Beaubourg

R de Montmorency

R Michel le Comte

Rambuteau

R Rambuteau

R St-Martin

Pl Georges Pompidou

Centre Pompidou 2

R St-Merri

R Ste-Croix de la Bretonnerie

R du Renard

Q de l'Hôtel de Ville

Pont Louis-Philippe

R de Cléry

R d'Aboukir

R du Caire

R St-Sauveur

R Greneta

Étienne Marcel

R de Turbigo

R du Cygne

Châtelet – Les Halles

Les Halles

R Pierre Lescot

R Berger

R du Jour

R St-Honoré

Pl Joachim du Bellay

Sq de la Tour St-Jacques

St-Jacques

R de la Tour

Pont Notre Dame

Pont au Change

Q de l'Hôtel de Ville

Pl de l'Hôtel de Ville

Pont d'Arcole

R de Lutèce

Q de la Corse

Pont St-Louis

Ile de la Cité

Santier

2E

R Montmartre

R Montorgueil

R Étienne Marcel

Les Halles

R Jean-Jacques Rousseau

Pl René Cassin

R Berger

R Berger

1ER

R de Rivoli

Châtelet

R Jean Lantier

Châtelet

Q de la Mégisserie

Pont Neuf

Q de l'Horloge

Cité

Pl du Palais

Bd du Palais

Q des Orfèvres

7

R de Réaumur

R du Mail

R Paul Lelong

Pl des Victoires

R Croix des Petits Champs

R Croix des Petits Champs

RIGHT BANK

Jardin du Palais Royal

R du Louvre

Pl du Palais Royal

Louvre Rivoli

R du Faubourg St-Honoré

R du Pont Neuf

Pont Neuf

Sq du Vert Galant

Q des Grands Augustins

R de Savoie

R de Richelieu

R Vivienne

R de Richelieu

Pyramides

Av de l'Opéra

R des Pyramides

Pl des Pyramides

Paris Convention & Visitors Bureau

Palais Royal – Musée du Louvre

Jardin du Palais Royal

Pl du Palais Royal

R de l'Oratoire

Musée du Louvre 3

Pl du Louvre

Jardin de l'Infante

Q du Louvre

Q de Conti

Q des Grands Augustins

R Dauphine

R Mazarine

R de Seine

R de Buci

Palais Royal – Musée

Jardin des Tuileries

Pl du Carrousel

Cour Napoléon

Pont du Carrousel

Q du Louvre

Pont des Arts

Seine

Q Malaquais

7E

École des Beaux-Arts

R Bonaparte

R des Sts-Pères

R Jacob

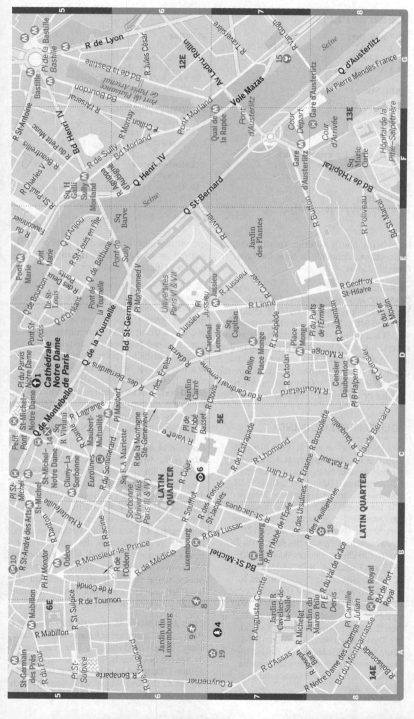

Central Paris

FRANCE, SWITZERLAND & AUSTRIA PARIS

lined with cheap eateries (many kosher). Multi-ethnic Belleville is tops for tasty, affordable Asian.

★ **Breizh Café**   CRÊPERIE €
(Map p312; www.breizhcafe.com; 109 rue Vieille du Temple, 3e; crêpes & galettes €6.50-18; ⊙11.30am-11pm Wed-Sat, to 10pm Sun; Ⓜ St-Sébastien-Froissart) It is a well-known fact among Parisians: everything at the Breton Café (breizh is 'Breton' in Breton) is 100% authentic, rendering it the top spot in the city for authentic crêpes. Be it the Cancale oysters, 20 types of cider or the buttery organic-flour crêpes,

---

GLUTEN-FREE DINING

For gluten-free dining, sit down to a light lunch or exceptional breads and cakes to go from stunning gluten-free bakery **Chambelland** (Map p306; ☏01 43 55 07 30; www.chambelland.com; 14 rue Ternaux, 11e; lunch menu €12; ⊙9am-8pm Tue-Sun; Ⓜ Parmentier) in Le Marais. Near the Louvre, **Noglu** (Map p316; ☏01 40 26 41 24; www.noglu.fr; 16 Passage des Panoramas, 2e; mains €16-25; ⊙noon-3pm Mon-Sat, 7.30-10.30pm Tue-Sat; ✐; Ⓜ Richelieu-Drouot, Grands Boulevards) is the GF address, to dine in style or takeaway. By Notre Dame, **Shakespeare & Company Café** (Map p312; www.shakespeareandcompany.com; 2 rue St-Julien le Pauvre, 5e; dishes €4-9.50; ⊙10am-6.30pm Mon-Fri, to 7.30pm Sat & Sun; 🕿✐📶; Ⓜ St-Michel) ✐, next to the legendary bookshop of the same name, usually has a couple of vegan and gluten-free dishes.

---

everything here is cooked to perfection. If you fail to snag a table in the main restaurant, try L'Épicerie next door.

★ **52 Faubourg St-Denis**   MODERN FRENCH €
(Map p306; www.faubourgstdenis.com; 52 rue du Faubourg St-Denis, 10e; mains €16-20; ⊙8am-midnight, kitchen noon-2.30pm & 7-11pm; 🕿; Ⓜ Château d'Eau) This thoroughly contemporary, neighbourhood cafe-restaurant is simply a brilliant space to hang out in at any time of day. Be it for breakfast, coffee, a zingy fresh-sage infusion, dinner or drinks, 52 Faubourg, as locals call it, gets it just right. Cuisine is modern and creative, and the chef is not shy in mixing veg with fruit in every course – including dessert. No reservations.

Du Pain et des Idées   BOULANGERIE €
(Map p306; www.dupainetdesidees.com; 34 rue Yves Toudic, 10e; pastries from €1.50; ⊙6.45am-8pm Mon-Fri; Ⓜ Jacques Bonsergent) This traditional bakery with exquisite interior from 1889 is famed for its naturally leavened bread, orange-blossom brioche and decadent escargots ('snails', like cinnamon rolls) in four sweet flavours. Its mini savoury pavés (breads) flavoured with reblochon cheese and fig, or goat's cheese, sesame and honey, make for the perfect lunch on the hoof. Top marks for the wooden picnic table on the pavement outside.

Chez Alain Miam Miam   SANDWICHES, CRÊPERIE €
(Map p312; www.facebook.com/ChezAlainMiamMiam; 39 rue de Bretagne & 33bis rue Charlot, 3e, Marché des Enfants Rouges; sandwiches €8; ⊙9am-3.30pm Wed-Fri, to 5.30pm Sat, to 3pm Sun; Ⓜ Filles du Calvaire) Weave your way through

the makeshift kitchens inside Marché des Enfants Rouges to find Alain, a retired baker with grey surfer locks and T-shirt with attitude. Watch him prepare you a monster sandwich or *galette* (savoury pancake) on a sizzling crêpe griddle from a bespoke combo of fresh, organic ingredients – grated fennel, smoked air-dried beef, avocado, sesame salt and carefully curated honeys.

Holybelly
INTERNATIONAL €
(Map p306; www.holybel.ly; 19 Rue Lucien Sampaix, 10e; breakfast €5-11.50, lunch mains €13.50-16.50; ⊙9am-6pm Thu, Fri, Mon, from 10am Sat & Sun; M Jacques Bonsergent) This outstanding barista-run coffee shop and kitchen is always rammed with a buoyant crowd, who never tire of Holybelly's exceptional service, Belleville-roasted coffee and cuisine. Sarah's breakfast pancakes served with egg, bacon, homemade bourbon butter and maple syrup are legendary, while her lunch menu features everything from traditional braised veal shank to squid *à la plancha*.

🍸 Drinking & Nightlife

The line between bars, cafes and bistros is blurred at best. It costs more to sit at a table than to stand at the counter, more on a fancy square than a backstreet, more in the 8e than in the 18e. After 10pm many cafes charge a pricier *tarif de nuit* (night rate).

★ Lockwood
CAFE
(Map p312; ☑ 01 77 32 97 21; 73 rue d'Aboukir, 2e; ⊙8am-2am Mon-Sat, 10am-4pm Sun; M Sentier) A happening address for hip coffee lovers. Savour beans from the Belleville Brûlerie during the day, brunch on weekends and well-mixed cocktails in the subterranean candle-lit *cave* at night.

★ Le Mary Céleste
COCKTAIL BAR
(Map p312; www.lemaryceleste.com; 1 rue Commines, 3e; ⊙6pm-1.30am; M Filles du Calvaire) Predictably there's a distinct nautical feel to this fashionable, ubercool cocktail bar in the Marais. Snag a stool at the central circular bar or play savvy and reserve one of a handful of tables (in advance online). Cocktails (€12 to €13) are creative and the perfect pairer to a dozen oysters or your pick of tapas-style 'small plates' designed to be shared (€8 to €15).

Le Baron Rouge
WINE BAR
(Map p306; ☑01 43 43 14 32; 1 rue Théophile Roussel, 12e; ⊙10am-2pm & 5-10pm Tue-Fri, 10am-10pm Sat, 10am-4pm Sun; M Ledru-Rollin)

Just about the ultimate Parisian wine-bar experience, this place has barrels stacked against the bottle-lined walls. As unpretentious as you'll find, it's a local meeting place where everyone is welcome and it's especially busy on Sunday after the Marché d'Aligre wraps up. All the usual suspects – cheese, charcuterie and oysters – will keep your belly full.

For a small deposit, you can fill up 1L bottles straight from the barrel for under €5.

Concrete
CLUB
(Map p312; www.concreteparis.fr; 60 Port de la Rapée, 12e; ⊙10pm-7am; M Gare de Lyon) This hugely popular, wild-child club with different dance floors lures a young international set to a boat on the Seine, firmly moored by Gare de Lyon. Notorious for introducing an 'after-hours' element to Paris' somewhat staid clubbing scene, Concrete is the trendy place to party all night until sunrise and beyond. Watch for all-weekend events, aka electronic dance music around the clock.

Le Batofar
CLUB
(Map p306; www.batofar.org; opp 11 quai François Mauriac, 13e; ⊙bar noon-midnight, club 11.30pm-6am; M Quai de la Gare, Bibliothèque) This much-loved, red-metal tugboat has a rooftop bar that's terrific in summer, and a respected restaurant, while the club underneath provides memorable underwater acoustics between its metal walls and portholes. Le Batofar is known for its edgy, experimental music policy and live performances from 7pm, mostly electro-oriented but also incorporating hip-hop, new wave, rock, punk or jazz.

Montmartre

☆ Entertainment

Paris' two top listings guides *Pariscope* (€0.70 or free smartphone app) and *L'Officiel des Spectacles* (www.offi.fr; €0.70), both in French but easy to navigate, are available from newsstands on Wednesday, and are crammed with everything that's on in the capital. Online check Paris Nightlife (www.parisnightlife.fr) or, for club and live gig listings, LYLO (www.lylo.fr). On the day of performance, theatre, opera and ballet tickets are sold for half price (plus €3 commission) at the **Kiosque Théâtre Madeleine** (Map p316; opposite 15 place de la Madeleine, 8e; ⊙12.30-8pm Tue-Sat, to 4pm Sun; Ⓜ Madeleine).

★ Philharmonie de Paris

CONCERT VENUE

(Map p306; ☏ 01 44 84 44 84; www.philharmoniedeparis.fr; 221 av Jean Jaurès, 19e; ⊙ box office noon-6pm Tue-Fri, 10am-6pm Sat & Sun; Ⓜ Porte de Pantin) This major complex, comprising the new Philharmonie 1 building by Jean Nouvel and neighbouring Philharmonie 2 building (previously called Cité de la Musique), hosts an eclectic range of concerts in its main 1200-seat Grande Salle and smaller concert halls. There's every imaginable type of music and dance, from classical to North African to Japanese.

Montmartre

★ **Café Universel**   JAZZ, BLUES
(Map p312; ☑ 01 43 25 74 20; www.cafeuniversel.
com; 267 rue St-Jacques, 5e; ⊙ 9pm-2am Mon-
Sat; ☎; Ⓜ Censier Daubenton or RER Port Royal)
Café Universel hosts a brilliant array of live
concerts with everything from bebop and
Latin sounds to vocal jazz sessions. Plenty
of freedom is given to young producers and
artists, and its convivial relaxed atmosphere
attracts a mix of students and jazz lovers.
Concerts are free, but tip the artists when
they pass the hat around.

Palais Garnier   OPERA, BALLET
(Map p316; ☑ 08 92 89 90 90; www.operadeparis.fr;
place de l'Opéra, 9e; Ⓜ Opéra) The city's original
opera house is smaller than its Bastille counterpart, but has perfect acoustics Due to its
odd shape, some seats have limited or no
visibility – book carefully. Ticket prices and
conditions (including last-minute discounts)
are available from the **box office** (Map p316;
cnr rues Scribe & Auber; ⊙ 11am-6.30pm Mon-Sat;
Ⓜ Opéra).

ℹ Information

Paris Convention & Visitors Bureau (Office
du Tourisme et des Congrès de Paris; Map
p312; www.parisinfo.com; 27 rue des Pyramides, 1er; ⊙ 7am-7pm May-Oct, 10am-7pm
Nov-Apr; Ⓜ Pyramides) Main branch of the
Paris Convention & Visitors Bureau, about
500m northwest of the Louvre.

ℹ Getting There & Away

AIR
There are three main airports in Paris:
Aéroport de Charles de Gaulle (CDG; ☑ 01
70 36 39 50; www.aeroportsdeparis.fr) Most
international airlines fly to CDG, 28km northeast of central Paris.

Aéroport d'Orly (ORY; ☑ 01 70 36 39 50;
www.aeroportsdeparis.fr) Located 19 km south
of Paris but not as frequently used by international airlines.

Aéroport de Beauvais (BVA; ☑ 08 92 68 20
66; www.aeroportbeauvais.com) Not really in
Paris at all (it's 75km north); used by some
low-cost carriers.

BUS
Eurolines (Map p312; www.eurolines.fr; 55 rue
St-Jacques, 5e; ⊙ ticket office 9.30am-6.30pm
Mon-Fri, 10am-1pm & 2-5pm Sat; Ⓜ Cluny-La
Sorbonne) connects all major European cap-
itals to Paris' international bus terminal **Gare
Routiére Internationale de Paris-Galliéni**
(☑ 08 92 89 90 91; 28 av du Général de Gaulle;
Ⓜ Galliéni), a 15-minute metro ride to the more
central République station.

TRAIN
Paris has six major train stations serving both
national and international destinations. For
mainline train information, check **SNCF** (www.
sncf-voyages.com).

ℹ Getting Around

TO/FROM THE AIRPORT
Aéroport de Charles de Gaulle Trains (RER),
buses and night buses to the city centre €6 to
€17.50; taxi €50 to €55, 15% higher evenings
and Sundays.

Aéroport d'Orly Trains (Orlyval then RER),
buses and night buses to the city centre €7.50
to €12.50; T7 tram to Villejuif-Louis Aragon
then metro to centre (€3.60); taxi €30 to €35,
15% higher evenings and Sundays.

Aéroport de Beauvais Buses (€17) to Porte
Maillot then metro (€1.80); taxi at least €150
(probably more than the cost of your flight!).

BICYCLE
The **Vélib'** (☑ 01 30 79 79 30; http://en.velib.
paris.fr; day/week subscription €1.70/8, bike
hire up to 30/60/90/120min free/€1/2/4) bike
share scheme puts 23,600 bikes at the disposal
of Parisians and visitors for getting around the
city. There are some 1800 stations throughout
the city, each with anywhere from 20 to 70 bike
stands.

BOAT
Batobus (www.batobus.com; adult/child 1-day
pass €17/10, 2-day pass €19/10; ⊙ 10am-
9.30pm Apr-Aug, to 7pm Sep-Mar) runs
glassed-in trimarans that dock every 20 to 25
minutes at nine small piers along the Seine. Buy
tickets online, at ferry stops or at tourist offices.

PUBLIC TRANSPORT
Paris' public transit system is operated by the
RATP (www.ratp.fr). RATP tickets are valid on
the 14-line metro, RER (underground suburban
train line with five lines within the city limits),
buses, trams and Montmartre funicular. A single
ticket/carnet of 10 costs €1.80/14.10.

FRANCE, SWITZERLAND & AUSTRIA PARIS

Versailles
A DAY IN COURT

Visiting Versailles – even just the State Apartments – may seem overwhelming at first, but think of it as a house where people ate, drank, worked, slept and conspired and you'll be on the right path.

Some two decades into his long reign, Louis XIV began turning his father's hunting lodge into a palace large enough to house his entire court (to keep closer tabs on the 6000-strong army of courtiers). Sparing no expense, the Sun King employed the greatest artists and craftspeople of the day and by 1682 he'd created the most extravagant dormitory in history.

The royal schedule was as accurate and predictable as a Swiss watch. By following this itinerary of rooms you can recreate the king's day, starting with the **King's Bedchamber ❶** and the **Queen's Bedchamber ❷**, where the royal couple was roused at about the same time. The royal procession then leads through the **Hall of Mirrors ❸** to the **Royal Chapel ❹** for morning Mass and returns to the **Council Chamber ❺** for late-morning meetings with ministers. After lunch the king might ride or hunt or visit the **King's Library ❻**. Later he could join courtesans for an 'apartment evening' starting from the **Hercules Drawing Room ❼** or play billiards in the **Diana Drawing Room ❽** before supping at 10pm.

For more information on Versailles, see p320.

VERSAILLES BY NUMBERS

- ➡ **Rooms** 700 (11 hectares of roof)
- ➡ **Windows** 2153
- ➡ **Staircases** 67
- ➡ **Gardens and parks** 800 hectares
- ➡ **Trees** 200,000
- ➡ **Fountains** 50 (with 620 nozzles)
- ➡ **Paintings** 6300 (measuring 11km laid end to end)
- ➡ **Statues and sculptures** 2100
- ➡ **Objets d'art and furnishings** 5000
- ➡ **Visitors** 5.3 million per year

CHRISTOPHE LEHENAFF/GETTY IMAGES ©

Queen's Bedchamber
Chambre de la Reine
The queen's life was on constant public display and even the births of her children were watched by crowds of spectators in her own bedchamber. **DETOUR »** The Guardroom, with a dozen armed men at the ready.

LUNCH BREAK

Diner-style food at Sister's Café, crêpes at Le Phare St-Louis or picnic in the park.

Guardroom

South Wing

King's Library
Bibliothèque du Roi
The last resident, bibliophile Louis XVI, loved geography and his copy of *The Travels of James Cook* (in English, which he read fluently) is still on the shelf here.

DEA/G. DAGLI ORTI/GETTY IMAGES ©

SAVVY SIGHTSEEING

Avoid Versailles on Monday (closed), Tuesday (Paris' museums close, so visitors flock here) and Sunday, the busiest day. Also, book tickets online so you don't have to queue.

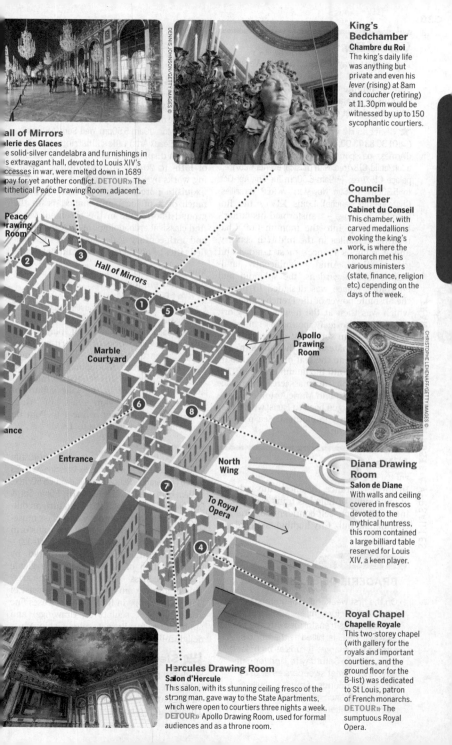

King's Bedchamber
Chambre du Roi
The king's daily life was anything but private and even his *lever* (rising) at 8am and *coucher* (retiring) at 11.30pm would be witnessed by up to 150 sycophantic courtiers.

Hall of Mirrors
Galerie des Glaces
The solid-silver candelabra and furnishings in this extravagant hall, devoted to Louis XIV's successes in war, were melted down in 1689 to pay for yet another conflict. DETOUR» The antithetical Peace Drawing Room, adjacent.

Peace Drawing Room

Hall of Mirrors

Marble Courtyard

Apollo Drawing Room

Entrance

North Wing

To Royal Opera

Council Chamber
Cabinet du Conseil
This chamber, with carved medallions evoking the king's work, is where the monarch met his various ministers (state, finance, religion etc) depending on the days of the week.

Diana Drawing Room
Salon de Diane
With walls and ceiling covered in frescos devoted to the mythical huntress, this room contained a large billiard table reserved for Louis XIV, a keen player.

Royal Chapel
Chapelle Royale
This two-storey chapel (with gallery for the royals and important courtiers, and the ground floor for the B-list) was dedicated to St Louis, patron of French monarchs. DETOUR» The sumptuous Royal Opera.

Hercules Drawing Room
Salon d'Hercule
This salon, with its stunning ceiling fresco of the strong man, gave way to the State Apartments, which were open to courtiers three nights a week. DETOUR» Apollo Drawing Room, used for formal audiences and as a throne room.

Versailles

The easiest way to get to/from Versailles is aboard RER line C5 (€4.20, 40 minutes, every 15 minutes) from Paris' Left Bank RER stations to Versailles-Château–Rive Gauche, 700m southeast of the château.

★ **Château de Versailles** PALACE
(☑ 01 30 83 78 00; www.chateauversailles.fr; place d'Armes; passport ticket incl estate-wide access adult/child €18/free, with musical events €25/free, palace €15/free; ⊙ 9am-6.30pm Tue-Sun Apr-Oct, to 5.30pm Tue-Sun Nov-Mar; M RER Versailles-Château–Rive Gauche) Louis XIV – the Roi Soleil (Sun King) – transformed his father's hunting lodge into the monumental Château de Versailles in the mid-17th century, and it remains France's most famous and grand palace. Amid magnificently landscaped formal gardens, the splendid and enormous palace was designed to project the absolute power of the French monarchy, which was then at the height of its glory. Situated in the leafy, bourgeois suburb of Versailles, 28km southwest of central Paris, the Baroque château was the kingdom's political capital and the seat of the royal court from 1682 up until the fateful events of 1789 when revolutionaries massacred the palace guard. Louis XVI and Marie Antoinette were ultimately dragged back to Paris, where they were ingloriously guillotined. See p318 for more information.

Lille

POP 231,500

In northern France, the once grimy industrial metropolis of Lille has transformed itself into a glittering, self-confident cultural and commercial hub. City highlights include an attractive Old Town with a strong Flemish accent, renowned art museums, stylish shopping and a cutting-edge nightlife.

◉ Sights

Palais des Beaux Arts ART MUSEUM
(Fine Arts Museum; ☑ 03 20 06 78 00; www.pba-lille.fr; place de la République; adult/child €7/4; ⊙ 2-5.50pm Mon, 10am-5.50pm Wed-Sun; ▥; M République Beaux-Arts) Lille's illustrious Fine Arts Museum displays a truly first-rate collection of 15th- to 20th-century paintings, including works by Rubens, Van Dyck and Manet. Exquisite porcelain and faience (pottery), much of it of local provenance, is on the ground floor, while in the basement you'll find classical archaeology, medieval statuary and 18th-century scale models of the fortified cities of northern France and Belgium.

Musée d'Art Moderne, d'Art Contemporain et d'Art Brut – LaM ART MUSEUM
(☑ 03 20 19 68 88; www.musee-lam.fr; 1 allée du Musée, Villeneuve-d'Ascq; adult/child €7/5; ⊙10am-6pm Tue-Sun) Colourful, playful and just plain weird works of modern and contemporary art by masters such as Braque, Calder, Léger, Miró, Modigliani and Picasso are the big draw at this renowned museum and sculpture park in the Lille suburb of Villeneuve-d'Ascq, 9km east of Gare Lille-Europe. Take metro line 1 to Pont de Bois, then bus L4 six stops to 'LAM'.

La Piscine Musée d'Art et d'Industrie ART MUSEUM
(☑ 03 20 69 23 60; www.roubaix-lapiscine.com; 23 rue de l'Espérance, Roubaix; adult/child €5.50/free; ⊙11am-6pm Tue-Thu, 11am-8pm Fri, 1-6pm Sat & Sun; M Gare Jean Lebas) If Paris can turn an outmoded train station into a world-class museum (the Musée d'Orsay), why not transform an art deco swimming pool (built 1927–32) – an architectural masterpiece inspired by a combination of civic pride and hygienic high-mindedness – into a temple of the arts? This innovative museum, 12km northeast of Gare Lille-Europe in Roubaix, showcases fine arts (paintings, sculptures, drawings) and applied arts (furniture, textiles, fashion) in a delightfully watery environment.

⌂ Sleeping & Eating

Students fill bars on rue Masséna and rue Solférino. In warm weather, cafe terraces on place du Général de Gaulle and place du Théâtre are tip-top beer-sipping spots.

DON'T MISS

BRADERIE DE LILLE

On the first weekend in September, Lille's entire city centre – 200km of footpaths – is transformed into the Braderie de Lille, billed as the world's largest flea market. It runs all night long from 2pm on Saturday to 11pm on Sunday, when street sweepers emerge to tackle the mounds of mussel shells and old *frites* (French fries) left behind by the merrymakers.

Auberge de Jeunesse
HOSTEL €

(☎ 03 20 57 08 94; www.hifrance.org; 235 bd Paul Painlevé; dm incl breakfast & sheets €25; @ ☎; M Porte de Valenciennes) The good news is that Lille has a new youth hostel, opened in 2015, with a facade sporting the colours of Europe. The bad news is that while all 55 rooms have showers, only 12 have attached toilets, and instead of taps the showers have annoying timer-buttons. Wi-fi is available only in the lobby.

★ Meert
PATISSERIE €

(☎ 03 20 57 93 93; www.meert.fr; 27 rue Esquermoise; waffles from €3; ⊙ shop 9.30am-7.30pm Tue-Sat, 9am-1pm & 3-7pm Sun, tearoom 9.30am-10pm Tue-Sat, 9am-6pm Sun; ☎; M Rihour) Famed for its *gaufres* (waffles) made with Madagascar vanilla, Meert has served kings, viceroys and generals since 1761. The sumptuous chocolate shop's coffered ceiling, painted wooden panels, wrought-iron balcony and mosaic floor date from 1839.

Au Vieux de la Vieille
FLEMISH €

(☎ 03 20 13 81 64; www.estaminetlille.fr; 2-4 rue des Vieux Murs; mains €12-15; ⊙ noon-2pm & 7-10pm daily, to 10.30pm Fri & Sat; ☎) Hops hang from the rafters at this *estaminet* (Flemish-style eatery), where specialities include *carbonade flamande* (braised beef slow-cooked with beer, onions, brown sugar and ginger bread) and *Welsh au Maroilles* (toast and ham smothered with Maroilles cheese melted in beer). From about March to October there's outdoor seating on picturesque place aux Oignons.

ⓘ Information

Tourist Office (☎ 03 59 57 94 00; www.lilletourism.com; place Rihour; ⊙ 9am-6pm Mon-Sat, 10am-4.30pm Sun & holidays; M Rihour)

ⓘ Getting There & Around

AIR
Aéroport de Lille (www.lille.aeroport.fr) is linked to destinations around France and southern Europe by a variety of low-cost carriers. To get to/from the city centre (Euralille shopping mall), take a shuttle bus (€8, 20 minutes, hourly).

TRAIN
Lille has two train stations: **Gare Lille-Flandres** (☎; M Gare Lille-Flandres) for regional services and Paris' Gare du Nord (€50 to €67, one hour, 16 to 24 daily), and ultra-modern **Gare Lille-Europe** (☎; M Gare Lille-Europe) for all other trains, including Eurostars to London and TGVs/

Eurostars to Brussels-Midi (€30, 35 minutes, at least a dozen daily).

The Somme

The Battle of the Somme has become a symbol of the meaningless slaughter of WWI, and its killing fields have since become sites of pilgrimage. Each year, thousands of visitors follow the **Circuit du Souvenir** (Remembrance Trail; www.somme-battlefields.com).

Convenient bases for exploring the area include Flemish-styled **Arras** (www.explorearras.com), 50km south of Lille, and former Picardy capital **Amiens** (www.amiens-tourisme.com), 60km further south again.

The battlefields and memorials are numerous and relatively scattered – joining a tour is an excellent option if you don't have your own transport. Respected operators include **Battlefields Experience** (☎ 03 22 76 29 60; www.thebattleofthesomme.co.uk), **Chemins d'Histoire** (☎ 06 31 31 85 02; www.cheminsdhistoire.com) and **Terres de Mémoire** (☎ 03 22 84 23 05; www.terresdememoire.com).

⊙ Sights

★ Historial de la Grande Guerre
MUSEUM

(Museum of the Great War; ☎ 03 22 83 14 18; www.historial.org; Château de Péronne, Péronne; adult/child incl audioguide €9/4.50; ⊙ 9.30am-5pm, closed Wed Oct-Mar, closed mid-Dec–mid-Feb) The best place to begin a visit to the Somme battlefields – especially if you're interested in WWI's historical and cultural context – is the outstanding Historial de la Grande Guerre in Péronne, about 60km east of Amiens. Located inside the town's fortified medieval château, this award-winning museum tells the story of the war chronologically, with equal space given to the German, French and British perspectives on what happened, how and why.

★ Beaumont-Hamel Newfoundland Memorial
MEMORIAL

(☎ 03 22 76 70 86; www.veterans.gc.ca; Beaumont-Hamel; ⊙ Welcome Centre 11am-5pm Mon, 9am-5pm Tue-Sun) This evocative memorial preserves part of the Western Front in the state it was in at fighting's end. The zigzag trench system, which still fills with mud in winter, is clearly visible, as are countless shell craters and the remains of barbed-wire barriers. Canadian students based at the Welcome Centre, which resembles a Newfoundland fisher's house, give free guided tours on the hour (except from mid-December to mid-January). Situated 9km north of Albert; follow the signs for 'Memorial Terreneuvien'.

★ Fromelles (Pheasant Wood) Cemetery & Museum CEMETERY, MUSEUM
(📞 03 59 61 15 14; www.musee-bataille-fromelles.fr; rue de la Basse Ville, Fromelles; museum adult/child €6.50/4; ⊙ cemetery 24hr, museum 9.30am-5.30pm Wed-Mon) The death toll was horrific – 1917 Australians and 519 Britons killed in just one day of fighting – yet the Battle of Fromelles was largely forgotten until 2008, when the remains of 250 of the fallen were discovered. They are now buried in the Fromelles (Pheasant Wood) Cemetery, the first new Commonwealth cemetery established in half a century. Next door, the excellent **Musée de la Bataille de Fromelles**, opened in 2014, evokes life in the trenches with reconstructed bunkers, photographs and biographies.

★ Ring of Remembrance MEMORIAL
(Anneau de la Mémoire; Ablain-St-Nazaire; ⊙ 9am-4.15pm, to 5.30pm or 6.30pm Apr-Sep) It's hard not to be overwhelmed by the waste and folly of the Western Front as you walk past panel after panel engraved with 580,000 tiny names: WWI dead from both sides who are listed in strict alphabetical order, without reference to nationality, rank or religion.

WORTH A TRIP

LENS

Long known mainly for its towering black slag heaps, the struggling former coal-mining town of Lens, 38km south of Lille, has little to offer visitors except for a brash new branch of Paris' renowned Louvre. The innovative **Louvre-Lens** (📞 03 21 18 62 62; www. louvrelens.fr; 99 rue Paul Bert; multimedia guide €3; ⊙ 10am-6pm Wed-Mon) **FREE** showcases hundreds of treasures from Paris' venerable Musée du Louvre in state-of-the-art exhibition spaces. The centrepiece, the 120m-long Galerie du Temps, displays a semi-permanent collection of 200-plus judiciously chosen objects – some of them true masterpieces – from the dawn of civilisation to the mid-1800s.

There are hourly trains from Lille-Flandres to/from Lens (€8.30, 45 minutes).

Normandy

Famous for cows, cider and Camembert, this largely rural region (www.normandie-tourisme.fr) is one of France's most traditional, and most visited thanks to a trio of world-renowned sights.

Bayeux

POP 13,900
Bayeux has become famous throughout the English-speaking world thanks to a 68.3m-long piece of painstakingly embroidered cloth: the 11th-century Bayeux Tapestry. With its delightful, flowery city centre crammed with 13th- to 18th-century buildings and a fine Norman Gothic cathedral, the town moreover is a great spot to soak up the gentile Norman atmosphere.

◉ Sights

★ Bayeux Tapestry TAPESTRY
(📞 02 31 51 25 50; www.bayeuxmuseum.com; rue de Nesmond; adult/child incl audioguide €9/4; ⊙ 9am-6.30pm Mar-Oct, to 7pm May-Aug, 9.30am-12.30pm & 2-6pm Nov–Feb) The world's most celebrated embroidery depicts the conquest of England by William the Conqueror in 1066 from an unashamedly Norman perspective. Commissioned by Bishop Odo of Bayeux, William's half-brother, for the opening of Bayeux' cathedral in 1077, the 68.3m-long cartoon strip tells the dramatic, bloody tale with verve and vividness.

★ Musée d'Art et d'Histoire Baron Gérard MUSEUM
(MAHB; 📞 02 31 92 14 21; www.bayeuxmuseum.com; 37 rue du Bienvenu; adult/child €7/4; ⊙ 9.30am-6.30pm May-Sep, 10am-12.30pm & 2-6pm Oct-Apr, closed Jan-mid-Feb) Exquisite exhibitions cover everything from Gallo-Roman archaeology to medieval art to paintings from the Renaissance to the 20th century, including a fine work by Gustave Caillebotte. Other highlights include impossibly delicate local lace and Bayeux-made porcelain. Housed in the former bishop's palace.

🛏 Sleeping & Eating

Les Logis du Rempart B&B €
(📞 02 31 92 50 40; www.lecornu.fr; 4 rue Bourbesneur; d €60-105, tr €110-130; 🐾) The three rooms of this delightful *maison de famille* ooze old-fashioned cosiness. Our favourite, the Bajocasse, has parquet flooring, a canopy bed and Toile de Jouy wallpaper.

D-DAY BEACHES

Early on 6 June 1944, Allied troops stormed 80km of beaches north of Bayeux, code-named (from west to east) Utah, Omaha, Gold, Juno and Sword. The landings on D-Day – called Jour J in French – ultimately led to the liberation of Europe from Nazi occupation.

The most brutal fighting on D-Day took place 15km northwest of Bayeux along the stretch of coastline now known as **Omaha Beach**, today a glorious stretch of fine golden sand partly lined with sand dunes and summer homes. **Circuit de la Plage d'Omaha**, a trail marked with a yellow stripe, is a self-guided tour along the beach, surveyed from a bluff above by the huge **Normandy American Cemetery & Memorial** (☑ 02 31 51 62 00; www.abmc.gov; Colleville-sur-Mer; ☺9am-6pm mid-Apr–mid-Sep, to 5pm mid-Sep–mid-Apr).

Caen's high-tech, hugely impressive **Le Mémorial – Un Musée pur la Paix** (Memorial – A Museum for Peace; ☑ 02 31 06 06 44; www.memorial-caen.fr; esplanade Général Eisenhower; adult/child €20/17; ☺9am-7pm daily early Feb-early Nov, 9.30am-6.30pm Tue-Sun early Nov-early Feb, closed 3 weeks in Jan) is one of Europe's premier WWII museums. Book online for the excellent year-round minibus tours it organises.

Bayeux tourist office handles reservations for other guided minibus tours – an excellent way to get a sense of the D-Day beaches and their place in history.

The shop downstairs is the perfect place to stock up on top-quality, homemade cider and *calvados* (apple brandy). Two-night minimum stay.

L'Assiette Normande FRENCH €
(☑ 02 31 22 04 61; 1-3 rue des Chanoines; lunch menu €10, other menus €15-36; ☺noon-3pm Tue-Sat & 7-11pm daily, closed Sun & Mon Dec-Mar) This rustic eatery is about straightforward French food – meat, fish and oysters – at reasonable prices.

ⓘ Information

Tourist Office (☑ 02 31 51 28 28; www.bayeux-bessin-tourisme.com; pont St-Jean; ☺9.30am-12.30pm & 2-6pm)

ⓘ Getting There & Away

Trains link Bayeux with Caen (€7, 20 minutes, hourly), from where there are connections to Paris' Gare St-Lazare and Rouen.

Mont St-Michel

On a rocky island opposite the coastal town of Pontorson, connected to the mainland by a narrow causeway, the sky-scraping turrets of the **Abbaye du Mont St-Michel** (☑ 02 33 89 80 00; www.monuments-nationaux.fr; adult/child incl guided tour €9/free; ☺9am-7pm, last entry 1hr before closing) provide one of France's iconic sights. The surrounding bay is notorious for its fast-rising tides: at low tide, the Mont is surrounded by bare sand for miles

around; at high tide, just six hours later, the bay is submerged.

From the **tourist office** (☑ 02 33 60 14 30; www.ot-montsaintmichel.com; ☺9am-12.30pm & 2-6pm Sep-Jun, 9am-7pm Jul & Aug) at the base of Mont St-Michel, a cobbled street winds up to the **Église Abbatiale** (Abbey Church), incorporating elements of both Norman and Gothic architecture.

The cheapest accommodation near the Mont is in **Pontorson**, 7km south of the shuttle stop in La Caserne, whose main street, rue Couësnon, is home to a number of small, simple, family-run hotels offering doubles for as little as €40. Pontorson is linked with Bayeux (€25, one hour 45 minutes, three daily) by train; and with La Caserne by bus (€3.20).

Brittany

Brittany, with its wild coastline, thick forests and the eeriest stone circles this side of Stonehenge, is for explorers. It's a land of prehistoric mysticism, proud tradition and culinary wealth, where Breton culture (and cider) is fiercely celebrated.

Quimper

POP 66,900
Small enough to feel like a village – with its slanted half-timbered houses and narrow cobbled streets – and large enough to buzz as the troubadour of Breton culture, Quimper (pronounced kam-pair) is the

thriving capital of Finistère (meaning 'land's end'). At the centre of the city is Quimper's Gothic **Cathédrale St-Corentin** (place St-Corentin; ⊙ 8.30am-noon & 1.30-6.30pm Mon-Sat, 8.30am-noon & 2-6.30pm Sun); the neighbouring **Musée Départemental Breton** (📱 02 98 95 21 60; www.museedepartementalbreton.fr; 1 rue du Roi Gradlon; adult/child €5/free; ⊙ 9am-12.30pm & 1.30-5pm Tue-Sat, 2-5pm Sun Sep-Jun, 9am-6pm daily Jul & Aug) showcases Breton history, crafts and archaeology in a former bishop's palace.

As a bastion of Breton culture, Quimper has some exceptional crêperies, all centred on, fittingly, place au Beurre. Covered market **Halles St-François** (www.halles-cornouaille.com; 16 quai du Steir; ⊙ 7am-7.30pm Mon-Sat, to 1pm Sun) has a slew of salad and sandwich options. Find hipsters listening to traditional Breton music over a Breton Coreff or a Telenn Du beer at **Le Ceili** (www.facebook.com/Ceili.Pub; 4 rue Aristide Briand; ⊙ 11am-1am Mon-Sat, 5pm-1am Sun).

The **tourist office** (📱 02 98 53 04 05; www.quimper-tourisme.com; place de la Résistance; ⊙ 9am-7pm Mon-Sat, 10am-12.45pm & 3-5.45pm Sun Jul-Aug, 9.30am-12.30pm & 1.30-6.30pm Mon-Sat Sep-Jun, plus 10am-12.45pm Sun Apr-Jun & Sep; 🖱) has accommodation lists, although Quimper has a chronic shortage of inexpensive sleeping options.

Frequent trains serve Paris' Gare Montparnasse (€30 to €96, four hours 45 minutes, nine daily).

St-Malo
POP 46,600

The mast-filled port of fortified St-Malo is inextricably tied up with the deep briny blue: the town became a key harbour during the 17th and 18th centuries, functioning as a base for merchant ships and government-sanctioned privateers. These days it's a busy cross-Channel ferry port and summertime getaway.

⊙ Sights

Exploring the tangle of streets in the walled city of St-Malo, known as **Intra-Muros** ('within the walls') is a highlight of a visit to Brittany – walking on top of the sturdy 17th-century ramparts (1.8km) ensnaring the city affords great views.

★**Château de St-Malo**   CASTLE
Château de St-Malo was built by the dukes of Brittany in the 15th and 16th centuries, and now holds the **Musée d'Histoire de St-Malo** (📱 02 99 40 71 57; www.ville-saint-malo.fr/culture/les-musees; adult/child €6/3; ⊙ 10am-12.30pm & 2-6pm daily Apr-Sep, Tue-Sun Oct-Mar)

OFF THE BEATEN TRACK

MORBIHAN MEGALITHS

Predating Stonehenge by around 100 years, Carnac (Garnag in Breton) safeguards the world's greatest concentration of megalithic sites. There are no fewer than 3000 of these upright stones, erected between 5000 and 3500 BC.

One kilometre north of **Carnac-Ville** a vast array of monoliths are set up in several distinct alignments, all visible from the road. The best way to appreciate the sheer numbers of stones is to walk or bike between the **Ménec** and **Kerlescan** groups, with menhirs almost continuously in view. Between June and September seven buses a day run between the two sites, as well as Carnac-Ville and Carnac-Plage. **A Bicyclette** (📱 02 97 52 75 08; www.velocarnac.com; 93bis av des Druides, bicycle per day from €10, buggy per hour from €8) near the beach rents bikes.

Near the stones, the **Maison des Mégalithes** (📱 02 97 52 29 81; www.menhirs-carnac.fr; rte des Alignements, D196; tour adult/child €6/free; ⊙ 9.30am-8pm Jul & Aug, 10am-5pm Sep-Apr, 9am-6pm May & Jun) explores the history of the site and offers guided visits. Due to severe erosion the sites are fenced off to allow the vegetation to regenerate. From October to March you can wander freely through parts – the Maison des Mégalithes has maps of what's open.

For background, visit Carnac's **Musée de Préhistoire** (📱 02 97 52 22 04; www.museedecarnac.fr; 10 place de la Chapelle; adult/child €6/2.50; ⊙ 10am-6.30pm Jul & Aug, 10am-12.30pm & 2-6pm Wed-Mon Apr-Jun & Sep, shorter hours Oct-Mar). The nearest useful train station is in Auray, 12km northeast.

which looks at the life and history of the city. The castle's lookout tower offers eye-popping views of the old city.

🛌 Sleeping & Eating

Le Nautilus   HOTEL €
(☑02 99 40 42 27; www.hotel-lenautilus-saint-malo.com; 9 rue de la Corne de Cerf; s €50-70, d €60-94; ☺Feb-Nov; ☎) With efficient, friendly service and comfortable albeit smallish rooms, this super central two-star abode offers excellent value. The decor has been freshened up with smartly finished bathrooms and light yellow walls.

★ Breizh Café   CRÊPERIE €
(☑02 99 56 96 08; www.breizhcafe.com; 6 rue de l'Orme; crêpes €9-13; ☺noon-2pm & 7-10pm Wed-Sun) This will be one of your most memorable meals in Brittany. The creative chef combines traditional Breton ingredients and *galette* and crêpe styles with Japanese flavours and brilliant textures and presentation. Seaweed and delightful seasonal pickles meets local ham, organic eggs and roast duck.

★ Bistro Autour du Beurre   BISTRO €€
(☑02 23 18 25 81; www.lebeurrebordier.com; 7 rue de l'Orme; lunch menu €19, mains €18-24; ☺noon-2pm Tue-Sat & 7-10pm Thu-Sat) This casual bistro showcases the cheeses and butters handmade by the world-famous Jean-Yves Bordier – you'll find his **shop** (☺9am-1pm & 3.30-7.30pm Tue-Sat, 9am-1pm Mon & Sun) next door. His products are shipped to renowned restaurants around the globe. At the bistro, the butter sampler (€15 in the shop, but included in meals) and bottomless bread basket are just the start to creative, local meals that change with the seasons.

ℹ Information

Tourist Office (☑08 25 13 52 00; www.saint-malo-tourisme.com; esplanade St-Vincent; ☺9am-7.30pm Mon-Sat, 10am-6pm Sun Jul & Aug, shorter hours Sep-Jun; ☎)

ℹ Getting There & Away

Brittany Ferries (www.brittany-ferries.com) sails between St-Malo and Portsmouth. **Condor Ferries** (www.condorferries.co.uk) runs to/from Poole via Jersey or Guernsey.

TGV train services serve Paris' Gare Montparnasse (€45 to €79, 3½ hours, three daily).

WORTH A TRIP

CANCALE OYSTERS

No day trip from St-Malo is tastier than **Cancale**, an idyllic Breton fishing port 14km east, famed for its offshore oyster beds.

Learn all about oyster farming at the **Ferme Marine** (☑02 99 89 69 99; www.ferme-marine.com; corniche de l'Aurore; adult/child €7/3.70; ☺guided tours in English 2pm, in French 11am, 3pm & 5pm Jul-mid-Sep, 3pm only mid-Feb–Jun & mid-Sep–Oct), then lunch on fresh oysters at the **Marché aux Huîtres** (12 oysters from €4; ☺9am-6pm), the daily oyster market atmospherically clustered around the Pointe des Crolles lighthouse.

Buses stop behind the church on place Lucidas and at Port de la Houle, next to the fish market. Keolis St-Malo (www.ksma.fr) has year-round services to/from St-Malo (€1.30, 30 minutes).

The Loire Valley

One step removed from the French capital, the Loire was historically the place where princes, dukes and notable nobles established their country getaways.

Blois

POP 47,500

Towering above the northern bank of the Loire, Blois' royal château, one-time feudal seat of the powerful counts of Blois, offers a great introduction to some key periods in French history and architecture.

◉ Sights

★ Château Royal de Blois   CHÂTEAU
(☑02 54 90 33 33; www.chateaudeblois.fr; place du Château; adult/child €10/5, audioguide €4/3; ☺9am-6pm or 7pm Apr-Oct, 9am-noon & 1.30-5.30pm Nov-Mar) Seven French kings lived in Blois' royal château, whose four grand wings were built during four distinct periods in French architecture: Gothic (13th century), Flamboyant Gothic (1498–1501), early Renaissance (1515–20) and classical (1630s). You can easily spend a half-day immersing yourself in the château's dramatic and bloody history and its extraordinary architecture. In July and August there are free tours in English.

ⓘ COMBO TICKETS

Billets jumelés (combo tickets; €11 to €16), sold at the château and Maison de la Magie, can save you some cash.

★ **Maison de la Magie**   MUSEUM
(✆02 54 90 33 33; www.maisondelamagie.fr; 1 place du Château; adult/child €9/5; ⊙10am-12.30pm & 2-6.30pm Apr-Aug & mid-Oct–2 Nov, 2-6.30pm 1st half Sep; ⚑) Across the square from the château, this museum of magic occupies the one-time home of watchmaker, inventor and conjurer Jean Eugène Robert-Houdin (1805–71), after whom the American magician Harry Houdini named himself. Dragons emerge roaring from the windows every half-hour, while inside the museum has exhibits on Houdin and the history of magic, displays of optical trickery, and several daily magic shows.

🛏 Sleeping & Eating

Hôtel Anne de Bretagne   HOTEL €
(✆02 54 78 05 38; www.hotelannedebretagne.com; 31 av du Dr Jean Laigret; s/d/q €60/69/95; Ⓟ🖙) This ivy-covered hotel, in a great location midway between the train station and the château, has friendly staff, a cosy piano-equipped *salon* and 29 brightly coloured rooms with bold bedspreads. A packed three-course picnic lunch costs €11.50. It also rents out bicycles.

Le Coup de Fourchette   BISTRO €
(✆02 54 55 00 24; 15 quai de la Saussaye; lunch menus €13-17, dinner menus €20; ⊙noon-2pm Tue-Sat, 7-9.30pm Thu-Sat; 🖙) Simple, delectable French cuisine is dished up with a smile in this mod eatery with a warm-season terrace. Popular with locals, it offers some of Blois' best cheaper eats.

ⓘ Information

Tourist Office (✆02 54 90 41 41; www.bloischambord.co.uk; 23 place du Château; ⊙9am-7pm Easter-Sep, 10am-7pm Oct-Easter)

ⓘ Getting There & Away

A *navette* (shuttle bus; €6) run by **Route 41** (TLC; ✆02 54 58 55 44; www.route41.fr) makes it possible to do a Blois–Chambord–Cheverny–Beauregard–Blois circuit on Wednesday, Saturday and Sunday from early April to 1 November.

A *navette* (one way/return €2.15/4.15) operated by **Azalys** (✆09 69 36 93 41; www.azalys-blois.fr) links Blois' train station and château with Château de Chaumont twice a day on Saturday, Sunday and holidays from April to October (daily in July and August).

From **Blois-Chambord train station** (av Dr Jean Laigret), 600m west from Blois' château, there are trains to Amboise (€7.20, 15 minutes, 16 to 25 daily) and Paris Gare d'Austerlitz (€29.40, 1½ hours, five daily).

DON'T MISS

BLÉSOIS CHÂTEAUX

The peaceful, verdant countryside around the former royal seat of Blois is home to some of France's finest châteaux.

Château de Chambord (✆info 02 54 50 40 00, tour & spectacle reservations 02 54 50 50 40; www.chambord.org; adult/child €11/9, parking near/distant €6/4; ⊙9am-5pm or 6pm; ⚑) One of the crowning achievements of French Renaissance architecture, this châteaux is 16km east of Blois, with 440 rooms, 365 fireplaces and 84 staircases. Begun in 1519 by François I (r 1515–47) as a weekend hunting lodge, it quickly grew into one of the most ambitious – and expensive – architectural projects ever attempted by a French monarch.

Château de Cheverny (✆02 54 79 96 29; www.chateau-cheverny.fr; av du Château, Cheverny; château & gardens adult/child €10.50/7.50; ⊙9.15am-7pm Apr-Sep, 10am-5.30pm Oct-Mar) Located 18km south of Chambord, this represents the zenith of French classical architecture: the perfect blend of symmetry, geometry and aesthetic order. Inside, sumptuous and elegantly furnished rooms remain virtually unchanged for generations thanks to the Hurault family who has lived here since the château's construction in the early 1600s.

TOURAINE CHATEAUX

Often dubbed the 'Garden of France', the Touraine region is known for its rich food, famously pure French accent and glorious châteaux.

Château de Chenonceau (☑ 02 47 23 90 07; www.chenonceau.com; adult/child €13/10, with audioguide €17.50/14; ☺ 9am-7pm or later Apr-Sep, to 5pm or 6pm Oct-Mar) Spanning the languid Cher River atop a supremely graceful arched bridge, this is one of France's most elegant châteaux with formal gardens and a fascinating history shaped by a series of powerful women. Its art collection that includes works by Tintoretto, Correggio, Rubens, Murillo and Van Dyck. The château is 13km southeast of Amboise and 40km southwest of Blois. From the town of Chenonceaux (spelt with an x), just outside the château grounds, trains go to Tours (€7, 25 minutes, nine to 12 daily).

Château de Villandry (☑ 02 47 50 02 09; www.chateauvillandry.com; 3 rue Principale, Villandry; chateau & gardens adult/child €10.50/6.50, gardens only €6.50/4.50, audioguides €4; ☺ 9am-btwn 5pm & 7pm year-round, château interior closed mid-Nov–mid-Dec & early Jan-early Feb) Six themed landscaped gardens with over 6 hectares of cascading flowers, ornamental vines, manicured lime trees, razor-sharp box hedges and tinkling fountains are the highlight here. Try to visit when the gardens are blooming, between April and October; midsummer is most spectacular.

Amboise

POP 13,200

The childhood home of Charles VIII and the final resting place of Leonardo da Vinci, elegant Amboise, 35km southwest of Blois, is pleasantly perched along the southern bank of the Loire and overlooked by its fortified château.

☉ Sights

★ Château Royal d'Amboise   CHÂTEAU

(☑ 02 47 57 00 98; www.chateau-amboise.com; place Michel Debré; adult/child €11.20/7.50, incl audioguide €15.20/10.50; ☺ 9am-6pm or 7.30pm Mar–mid-Nov, 9am-12.30pm & 2-5.15pm mid-Nov–Feb) Perched on a rocky escarpment above town, Amboise's castle was a favoured retreat for all of France's Valois and Bourbon kings. Only a few of the château's original structures survive, but you can still visit the furnished Logis (Lodge) – Gothic except for the top half of one wing, which is Renaissance – and the Flamboyant Gothic Chapelle St-Hubert (1493), where Leonardo da Vinci's presumed remains have been buried since 1863. The ramparts afford thrilling views of the town and river.

★ Le Clos Lucé   HISTORIC BUILDING

(☑ 02 47 57 00 73; www.vinci-closluce.com; 2 rue du Clos Lucé; adult/child €15/10.50; ☺ 9am-7pm or 8pm Feb-Oct, 9am or 10am-5pm or 6pm Nov-Jan; ⛲) It was on the invitation of François I that Leonardo da Vinci (1452–1519), aged 64, took up residence at this grand manor house (built 1471). An admirer of the Italian Renaissance, the French monarch named Da Vinci 'first painter, engineer and king's architect', and the Italian spent his time here sketching, tinkering and dreaming up ingenious contraptions. Fascinating models of his many inventions are on display inside the home and around its lovely 7-hectare gardens.

⛺ Sleeping & Eating

Hôtel Chaptal   HOTEL €

(☑ 02 47 57 14 46; www.hotel-chaptal-amboise. fr; 11-13 rue Chaptal; s/d/q €54/67/91; ☺ reception 7.30am-9pm, closed Dec & Jan; ⊛☎) You don't have to have a big budget to enjoy the charms of Amboise. This friendly and very central hotel has 26 simple, clean rooms – great value! No lift.

★ Food Market   FOOD MARKET €

(quai du Général de Gaulle; ☺ 8am-1pm Sun) Voted France's *marché préféré* (favourite market) in 2015, this riverfront extravaganza, 400m southwest of the château, draws 200 to 300 stalls selling both edibles and durables.

❶ Information

Tourist Office (☑ 02 47 57 09 28; www. amboise-valdeloire.co.uk; cnr quai du Général de Gaulle & allée du Sergent Turpin; internet access per 30min €4; ☺ 9am or 10am-6pm or 7pm Mon-Sat, 10am-12.30pm Sun Apr-Oct, 10am-12.30pm & 2-5pm Mon-Sat Nov-Mar; ☎)

ⓘ Getting There & Away

Touraine Fil Vert (☑ 02 47 31 14 00; www.
tourainefilvert.com) bus line C links Amboise
with Chenonceau (€2.40, 18 minutes, one or
two daily Monday to Saturday).

From the **train station** (bd Gambetta), 1.5km
north of the château, services include Blois
(€7.20, 15 minutes, 16 to 25 daily) and Paris Gare
d'Austerlitz (€33.20, 1¾ hours, four direct daily).

Champagne

Known in Roman times as Campania, meaning 'plain', the agricultural region of Champagne is synonymous these days with its
world-famous bubbly. The self-drive **Champagne Route** (www.tourisme-en-champagne.
com) wends its way through the region's
most celebrated vineyards.

Reims

POP 186,500

Over the course of a millennium (from
816 to 1825), some 34 sovereigns – among
them two dozen kings – began their reigns
in Reims' famed cathedral. Meticulously reconstructed after WWI and again following
WWII, the city – whose name is pronounced
something like 'rance' and is often anglicised
as Rheims – is endowed with handsome pedestrian zones, well-tended parks and lively
nightlife.

◉ Sights

The musty *caves* (cellars) of several Champagne houses can be visited on guided tours
which end with tasting. Cellar temperatures
hover at 10°C so bring warm clothes!

★**Cathédrale Notre Dame**   CATHEDRAL
(www.cathedrale-reims.culture.fr; place du Cardinal
Luçon; tower adult/child €7.50/free, incl Palais du
Tau €11/free; ⊙ 7.30am-7.15pm, tower tours hourly
10am-4pm Tue-Sat, 2-4pm Sun May-Sep, 10am-4pm
Sat, 2-4pm Sun mid-Mar–Apr) Imagine the egos
and extravagance of a French royal coronation. The focal point of such bejewelled

ⓘ PACKAGE DEAL

The great-value **Pass Reims** (€9),
available at the tourist office, gives you
entry to a museum of your choice and
an audioguide tour of the city, plus discounts on activities such as Champagne
house visits.

pomposity was Reims' resplendent Gothic
cathedral, begun in 1211 on a site occupied
by churches since the 5th century. The interior is a rainbow of stained-glass windows;
the finest are the western facade's 12-petalled
great rose window – under restoration at
the time of research – the north transept's
rose window and the vivid **Chagall** creations (1974) in the central axial chapel.

★**Basilique St-Rémi**   BASILICA
(place du Chanoine Ladame; ⊙ 8am-7pm) FREE
This 121m-long former Benedictine abbey
church, a Unesco World Heritage Site, mixes Romanesque elements from the mid-11th
century (the worn but stunning nave and
transept) with early Gothic features from
the latter half of the 12th century (the choir,
with a large triforium gallery and, way up
top, tiny clerestory windows).

★**Palais du Tau**   MUSEUM
(www.palais-du-tau.fr; 2 place du Cardinal Luçon;
adult/child €7.50/free, incl cathedral tower €11/
free; ⊙ 9.30am-12.30pm & 2-5.30pm Tue-Sun)
A Unesco World Heritage Site, this lavish
former archbishop's residence, redesigned
in neoclassical style between 1671 and 1710,
was where French princes stayed before
their coronations – and where they threw
sumptuous banquets afterwards. Now a museum, it displays truly exceptional statuary,
liturgical objects and tapestries from the cathedral, some in the impressive, Gothic-style
Salle de Tau (Great Hall).

★**Taittinger**   CHAMPAGNE HOUSE
(☑ 03 26 85 45 35; www.taittinger.com; 9 place
St-Nicaise; tours €17-45; ⊙ 9.30am-5.30pm,
shorter hours & closed weekends Oct-Mar) The
headquarters of Taittinger are an excellent
place to come for a clear, straightforward
presentation on how Champagne is actually
made – there's no claptrap about 'the Champagne mystique' here. Parts of the cellars
occupy 4th-century Roman stone quarries;
other bits were excavated by 13th-century
Benedictine monks. No need to reserve. Situated 1.5km southeast of Reims centre; take
the Citadine 1 or 2 bus to the St-Nicaise or
Salines stops.

🛏 Sleeping & Eating

Chambre d'Hôte Cathédrale   B&B €
(☑ 03 26 91 06 22; 21 place du Chapitre; s/d/tr
without bathroom €55/65/80) The cathedral
bells are your wake-up call at this sweet and
simple B&B. Rooms are immaculate and

old-fashioned, with stripy wallpaper, heavy wood furnishings and shared bathrooms.

à l'ère du temps   CRÊPERIE €
(☑ 03 26 06 16 88; www.aleredutemps.com; 123 ave de Laon; lunch menu €10, mains €7-14; ⏱ 11.45am-2pm & 6.45-9.30pm Tue-Sat) A short stroll north of place de la République brings you to this sweet and simple crêperie. It does a roaring trade in homemade crêpes, buckwheat *galettes* and gourmet salads.

ℹ Information

Tourist Office (☑ 03 26 77 45 00; www.reims-tourisme.com; 6 rue Rockefeller; ⏱ 10am-6pm Mon-Sat, 10am-12.30pm & 1.30-5pm Sun)

ℹ Getting There & Away

From Reims train station, 1km northwest of the cathedral, at least hourly services run to Paris Gare de l'Est (€19 to €63, 46 minutes to one hour) and Épernay (€7, 20 to 42 minutes).

Épernay

POP 23,500

Prosperous Épernay, 25km south of Reims, is the self-proclaimed *capitale du Champagne* and home to many of the world's most celebrated Champagne houses. Beneath the town's streets, some 200 million bottles of Champagne are slowly being aged in 110km of subterranean cellars. In 1950 one such cellar – owned by the irrepressible Mercier family – hosted a car rally without the loss of a single bottle!

◉ Sights

Numerous *maisons de Champagne* offer informative and engaging cellar tours, followed by a *dégustation* (tasting) and a visit to the factory-outlet shop. The tourist office can point you in the right direction.

★ **Avenue de Champagne**   STREET
Épernay's handsome ave de Champagne fizzes with *maisons de champagne* (Champagne houses). The boulevard is lined with mansions and neoclassical villas, rebuilt after WWI. Peek through wrought-iron gates at Moët's private **Hôtel Chandon**, an early 19th-century pavilion-style residence set in landscaped gardens, which counts Wagner among its famous past guests. The haunted-looking **Château Perrier**, a red-brick mansion built in 1854 in neo-Louis XIII style, is aptly placed at number 13! The

CHAMPAGNE SPLURGE

There is no finer spot to splurge on chargrilled meats and French dishes using the local fire water such as crayfish pan-fried in Champagne than **La Grillade Gourmande** (☑ 03 26 55 44 22; www.lagrilladegourmande.com; 16 rue de Reims; menus €19-59; ⏱ noon-2pm & 7.30-10pm Tue-Sat), a chic bistro with wonderful alfresco terrace dining in the warm months. And to drink? Champagne, *naturellement*.

roundabout presents photo ops with its giant cork and bottle-top.

★ **Moët & Chandon**   CHAMPAGNE HOUSE
(☑ 03 26 51 20 20; www.moet.com; 20 av de Champagne; adult incl 1/2 glasses €23/28, 10-18yr €10; ⏱ tours 9.30-11.30am & 2-4.30pm Apr–mid-Nov, 9.30-11.30am & 2-4.30pm Mon-Fri mid-Nov–Mar) Flying the Moët, French, European and Russian flags, this prestigious *maison* offers frequent one-hour tours that are among the region's most impressive, offering a peek at part of its 28km labyrinth of *caves* (cellars).

🛏 Sleeping

La Villa St-Pierre   HOTEL €
(☑ 03 26 54 40 80; www.villasaintpierre.fr; 1 rue Jeanne d'Arc; d €57-95, q €105-115; 🛜) Expect a warm, family-style *bienvenue* and a friendly yap from the shih tzus at this early-20th-century town house turned B&B. The 11 simple rooms retain some yesteryear charm, with chintzy florals and wooden furnishings. Breakfast (€8) includes a tantalising array of pastries.

🍴 Eating & Drinking

Pâtisserie Vincent Dallet   PATISSERIE €
(www.chocolat-vincentdallet.fr; 26 rue du Général Leclerc; pastries €2.70-4.50, light meals €8-18; ⏱ 7.30am-7.45pm Tue-Sun) A sweet dream of a chocolaterie, patisserie and tearoom, with delectable pralines, macarons and pastries. A *champenoise* speciality is the 'Baba', vanilla cream topped by a cork-shaped pastry flavoured with Champagne. *Café gourmand*, coffee with a selection of mini desserts, costs €8.90.

★ **C. Comme**   WINE BAR
(www.c-comme.fr; 8 rue Gambetta; light meals €7.50-14.50, 6-glass Champagne tasting €33-39;

FRANCE, SWITZERLAND & AUSTRIA CHAMPAGNE

⊘10am-8.30pm Sun-Wed, to 11pm Thu, to midnight Fri & Sat) The downstairs cellar has a stash of 300 different varieties of Champagne; sample them (from €6 a glass) in the softly lit bar-bistro upstairs. Accompany with a tasting plate of regional cheese, charcuterie and *rillettes* (pork pâté). We love the funky bottle-top tables and relaxed ambience.

❶ Information

Tourist Office (☑03 26 53 33 00; www.ot-epernay.fr; 7 av de Champagne; ⊘9am-12.30pm & 1.30-7pm Mon-Sat, 10.30am-1pm & 2-4.30pm Sun, closed Sun mid-Oct–mid-Apr; ⊛)

❶ Getting There & Away

The **train station** (place Mendès-France) has direct services to Reims (€7, 24 to 37 minutes, 14 daily) and Paris Gare de l'Est (€24 to €65, 1¼ hours to 2¾ hours, eight daily).

Burgundy

If there's one place in France where you're really going to find out what makes the nation tick, it's Burgundy. Two of the country's enduring passions – food and wine – come together in this gorgeously rural region stiched from rolling green hills, mustard fields, ancient vineyards, medieval villages and handsome towns.

MAD ABOUT MUSTARD

If there is one pilgrimage to be made in Dijon it is to **Moutarde Maille** (☑03 80 30 41 02; www.maille.com; 32 rue de la Liberté; ⊘10am-7pm Mon-Sat), the factory boutique of the company that makes Dijon's most famous mustard. The tangy odours of the sharp sauce assault your nostrils instantly upon entering and there are 36 kinds to buy, including cassis-, truffle- or celery-flavoured; sample three on tap.

In Beaune head to **Moutarderie Fallot** (Mustard Mill; ☑03 80 22 10 10; www.fallot.com; 31 rue du Faubourg Bretonnière; adult/child €10/8; ⊘tasting room 9.30am-6pm Mon-Sat, tours by arrangement) where Burgundy's last family-run, stone-ground mustard company offers tours of its facilities and mustard museum. Reserve ahead at Beaune tourist office (p332).

Dijon

POP 157,200

Dijon is one of France's most appealing cities. Filled with elegant medieval and Renaissance buildings, the lively centre is wonderful for strolling, especially if you like to leaven your cultural enrichment with excellent food, fine wine and shopping.

◉ Sights & Activities

★ **Musée des Beaux-Arts**   MUSEUM
(☑03 80 74 52 09; http://mba.dijon.fr; 1 rue Rameau; audioguide €4, guided tour €6; ⊘9.30am-6pm May-Oct, 10am-5pm Nov-Apr, closed Tue year-round) FREE Housed in the monumental **Palais des Ducs** (Palace of the Dukes & States of Burgundy; place de la Libération), these sprawling galleries (works of art in themselves) constitute one of France's most outstanding museums. The star attraction is the wood-panelled **Salle des Gardes**, which houses the ornate, carved late-medieval sepulchres of dukes John the Fearless and Philip the Bold.

Tour Philippe le Bon   TOWER
(place de la Libération; adult/child €3/free; ⊘guided tours every 45min 10.30am-noon & 1.45-5.30pm daily Apr–mid-Nov, hourly 2-4pm Tue, 11am-4pm Sat & Sun mid-Nov–Mar) Adjacent to the ducal palace, this 46m-high, mid-15th-century tower affords fantastic views over the city. On a clear day you can see all the way to Mont Blanc. Dijon's tourist office handles reservations.

Authentica Tours   VINEYARD TOUR
(☑06 87 01 43 78; www.authentica-tours.com; tours €65-130) Offers half- and full-day tours through the vineyards surrounding Dijon and Beaune.

🛏 Sleeping & Eating

Find loads of restaurants on buzzy rue Berbisey, around place Émile Zola, on rue Amiral Roussin and around Dijon's fabulous covered food market, **Les Halles** (rue Quentin; ⊘8am-1pm Tue & Thu-Sat) – a one-stop shop for the perfect picnic.

Hôtel Le Chambellan   HOTEL €
(☑03 80 67 12 67; www.hotel-chambellan.com; 92 rue Vannerie; s €50-55, d €55-60, s/d with shared bathroom €35/38; ⊛) For budget digs in the heart of medieval Dijon, it's hard to beat this small, unpretentious hotel in a building dating to 1730. Top-floor rooms under the rafters are a steal if you don't mind sharing a bathroom and climbing three flights of stairs. Breakfast €7.50.

Dijon

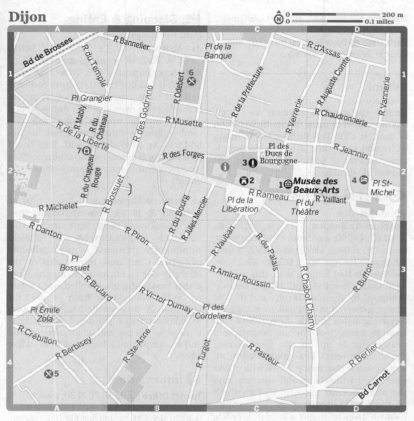

Chez le Bougnat BURGUNDIAN €
(☑ 03 80 43 31 17; www.facebook.com/chezle
bougnat; 53 rue Berbisey; menus €10.50-18;
☺ noon-2.30pm & 7pm-1am) Chef-owner (and
former TV scriptwriter) Cyrille Doudies
serves up copious plates of authentic Burgundian food at insanely low prices in this
one-room eatery decorated with concert
posters and old 45 RPM records.

❶ Information

Tourist Office (☑ 08 92 70 05 58; www.visitdi-
jon.com; 11 rue des Forges; ☺ 9.30am-6.30pm
Mon-Sat, 10am-6pm Sun Apr-Sep, 9.30am-1pm
& 2-6pm Mon-Sat, 10am-4pm Sun Oct-Mar; ☎)

❶ Getting There & Away

BUS

Transco (☑ 03 80 11 29 29; www.cotedor.fr/
cms/transco-horaires) buses stop in front of
the train station. Tickets are sold on board
(€1.50). Bus 44 goes to Nuits-St-Georges (45
minutes) and Beaune (1¼ hours).

Dijon

◎ Top Sights
1 Musée des Beaux-Arts	C2

◎ Sights
2 Palais des Ducs et des États de Bourgogne	C2
3 Tour Philippe le Bon	C2

⬤ Sleeping
4 Hôtel Le Chambellan	D2

⊗ Eating
5 Chez le Bougnat	A4
6 Les Halles	B1

⬤ Shopping
7 Moutarde Maille	A2

TRAIN

Connections from Dijon's train station include:
Lyon-Part Dieu Regional train/TGV from
€32/39, 2/1½ hours, 25 daily.

Marseille TGV from €82, 3½ hours, six direct daily.

Paris Gare de Lyon Regional train/TGV from €46/59, 3/1½ hours, 25 daily.

Beaune

POP 22,500

Beaune (pronounced similarly to 'bone'), 44km south of Dijon, is the unofficial capital of the Côte d'Or. This thriving town's raison d'être and the source of its *joie de vivre* is wine: making it, tasting it, selling it, but most of all, drinking it.

◉ Sights & Activities

Hôtel-Dieu des Hospices de Beaune   HISTORIC BUILDING

(☑ 03 80 24 45 00; www.hospices-de-beaune.com; rue de l'Hôtel-Dieu; adult/child €7.50/3; ⊙ 9am-6.30pm mid-Mar–mid-Nov, 9-11.30am & 2-5.30pm mid-Nov–mid-Mar) Built in 1443, this magnificent Gothic hospital (until 1971) is famously topped by stunning turrets and pitched rooftops covered in multicoloured tiles. Interior highlights include the barrel-vaulted **Grande Salle** (look for the dragons and peasant heads up on the roof beams); the mural-covered **St-Hughes Room**; an 18th-century **pharmacy** lined with flasks once filled with elixirs and powders; and the multipanelled masterpiece **Polyptych of the Last Judgement** by 15th-century Flemish painter Rogier van der Weyden, which depicts Judgment Day in glorious technicolour.

Patriarche Père et Fils   WINE TASTING

(☑ 03 80 24 53 01; www.patriarche.com; 7 rue du Collège; audioguide tour €17; ⊙ 9.30-11.30am & 2-5.30pm) Spanning 2 hectares and in business since 1780, Burgundy's largest cellars have 5km of corridors lined with about five million bottles of wine. (The oldest is a Beaune Villages AOC from 1904!) Visitors armed with multilingual audioguides can tour the premises in 60 to 90 minutes, tasting 13 wines along the way and taking the *tastevin* (tasting cup) home.

Bourgogne Evasion   CYCLING

(☑ 06 64 68 83 57; www.bourgogne-evasion.fr) Offers half-day, full-day and multi-day cycling tours through the vineyards, along with bike and trailer rentals. Tours meet at Beaune's tourist office on bd Perpreuil.

🛌 Sleeping & Eating

Café-Hôtel-Restaurant de l'Abattoir   HOTEL €

(☑ 03 80 22 21 46; www.hotel-abattoir.fr; 19 rue du Faubourg Perpreuil; r €29, s/d with half board €48/78) If you don't need creature comforts and just want a central location at an unbeatable price, consider this unfussy hotel catering to local workers, with small, tidy rooms only a five-minute walk from the Hôtel-Dieu. Accommodation with half board (breakfast and dinner) is also available. Note that reception is intermittently closed; call ahead.

La Maison du Colombier   TAPAS €

(☑ 03 80 26 16 26; www.maisonducolombier.com; 1 rue Charles Cloutier; tapas from €8) This supremely cosy 'gastro-bar' in candlelit 16th-century surrounds is the brainchild of Roland Chanliaud, former chef at the Michelin-starred Jardin des Remparts. Grab a seat beside the brick-walled open kitchen, on the sidewalk out front, or amid the labyrinth of stone-vaulted interior rooms to enjoy *tartines* (open-faced sandwiches), tapas-style cheese and charcuterie plates and an exceptional selection of Burgundian wines.

ⓘ Information

Tourist Office (☑ 03 80 26 21 30; www.beaune-tourisme.fr; 6 bd Perpreuil; ⊙ 9am-6.30pm Mon-Sat, to 6pm Sun Apr-Oct, shorter hours Nov-Mar)

ⓘ Getting There & Away

Bus 44 links Beaune with Dijon (€1.50, 1½ hours, two to seven daily), stopping at Côte d'Or villages such as Nuits-St-Georges.

Trains connect the following places:

Dijon €8, 20 to 30 minutes, 40 daily
Lyon-Part Dieu from €27.20, 1¾ hours, 16 daily
Paris €50, 3½ hours, seven direct daily

Lyon

POP 509,000

Gourmets, eat your heart out: Lyon is the gastronomic capital of France, with a lavish table of piggy-driven dishes and delicacies to tuck into. This is France's third-largest city, with outstanding museums, a dynamic nightlife, green parks and a Unesco-listed old town known as Vieux Lyon.

⊙ Sights

Over two millennia ago, the Romans built the city of Lugdunum on the slopes of Fourvière, on the Saône's western bank. Footpaths and a less-taxing funicular wind uphill from Vieux Lyon.

Basilique Notre Dame de Fourvière
CHURCH

(www.fourviere.org; place de Fourvière, 5e; rooftop tour adult/child €7/4; ⊙8am-6.45pm, guided tours Apr-Nov; funicular Fourvière) Crowning Fourvière hill, with stunning city panoramas from its terrace, this superb example of late-19th-century French ecclesiastical architecture is lined with intricate mosaics. One-hour **discovery visits** take in the main features of the basilica and crypt; 75-minute **rooftop tours** ('Visite Insolite') climax on the stone-sculpted roof.

Cathédrale St-Jean
CATHEDRAL

(place St-Jean, 5e; ⊙8.15am-7.45pm Mon-Fri, to 7pm Sat & Sun; M Vieux Lyon) Lyon's partly Romanesque cathedral was built between the late 11th and early 16th centuries. The portals of its Flamboyant Gothic facade, completed in 1480 (and recently renovated), are decorated with 280 square stone medallions. Inside, the highlight is the **astronomical clock** in the north transept.

Musée des Beaux-Arts
MUSEUM

(☏04 72 10 17 40; www.mba-lyon.fr; 20 place des Terreaux, 1er; adult/child €8/free; ⊙10am-6pm Wed, Thu & Sat-Mon, 10.30am-6pm Fri; M Hôtel de Ville) This stunning and eminently manageable museum showcases France's finest collection of sculptures and paintings outside of Paris from antiquity onwards. Highlights include works by Rodin, Rubens, Rembrandt, Monet, Matisse and Picasso.

ⓘ CENT SAVER

The excellent-value **Lyon City Card** (www.lyon-france.com; 1/2/3 days adult €22/32/42, child €13.50/18.50/23.50) offers free admission to every Lyon museum, the roof of Basilique Notre Dame de Fourvière, guided city tours, Guignol puppet shows and river excursions (April to October). It also includes unlimited travel on public transport. Buy one at the tourist office or online (10% cheaper).

DRINKS AFLOAT

Along **quai Victor Augagneur** on the Rhône's left bank, a string of *péniches* (barges with onboard bars) serve drinks from mid-afternoon onwards, many of them rocking until the wee hours with DJs and/or live bands. To study your options, stroll the quayside between Pont Lafayette and Pont de la Guillotière.

Musée des Confluences
MUSEUM

(☏04 28 38 11 90; www.museedesconfluences.fr; 86 quai Perrache, 6e; adult/child €9/free; ⊙11am-6.15pm Tue, Wed & Fri, 11am-9.15pm Thu, 10am-6.15pm Sat & Sun; ⛟T1) Lying at the confluence of the Rhône and Saône rivers, this ambitious science and humanities museum is the crowning glory of Lyon's newest neighbourhood, the Confluence. Four permanent exhibitions (exploring the origins of the universe, humankind's place in the living world, societies and death in different civilisations) and a fabulous array of temporary exhibitions are housed in a futuristic, steel-and-glass transparent crystal and cloud, set on a concrete base on the water's edge.

🛏 Sleeping

Auberge de Jeunesse du Vieux Lyon
HOSTEL €

(☏04 78 15 05 50; www.hifrance.org; 41-45 montée du Chemin Neuf, 5e; dm incl breakfast €19.50-25.60; ⊙reception 7am-1pm, 2-8pm & 9pm-1am; @🛜; M Vieux Lyon, funicular Minimes) Stunning city views unfold from the terrace of Lyon's HI-affiliated hostel, and from many of the (mostly four- and six-bed) dorms. Bike parking and kitchen facilities are available, and there's an on-site bar. Try for a dorm with city views.

Hôtel Le Boulevardier
HOTEL €

(☏04 78 28 48 22; www.leboulevardier.fr; 5 rue de la Fromagerie, 1er; s €69-79, d €79; ❄🛜; M Hôtel de Ville, Cordeliers) Le Boulevardier is a bargain 14-room hotel with snug, spotless rooms, and sports quirky touches such as old skis and tennis racquets adorning the hallways. No two rooms are alike; some have exposed brick walls and wooden ceilings. It's up a steep spiral staircase above a cool little cafe, which doubles as reception.

Lyon

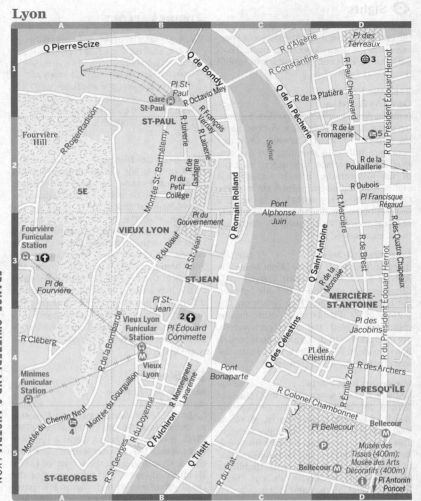

✖ Eating

On the Presqu'Île, cobbled rue Mercière and rue des Marronniers – both in the 2e (metro Bellecour) – are chock-a-block with sidewalk terraces in summer. In the 1er, the tangle of streets south of the opera house, including rue du Garet, rue Neuve and rue Verdi, is equally jam-packed with eateries.

★ Les Halles de Lyon Paul Bocuse

MARKET €

(📞 04 78 62 39 33; www.hallespaulbocuse.lyon.fr; 102 cours Lafayette, 3e; ⏰ 7am-10.30pm Tue-Sat, to 4.30pm Sun; Ⓜ Part-Dieu) Lyon's famed indoor food market has nearly five-dozen stalls selling countless gourmet delights. Pick up a round of runny St-Marcellin from legendary cheesemonger **Mère Richard**, and a knobbly Jésus de Lyon from **Charcuterie Sibilia**. Or enjoy a sit-down lunch of local produce, especially enjoyable on Sundays when local families congregate for shellfish and white-wine brunches.

Le Bistrot du Potager

NEOBISTRO, TAPAS €

(📞 04 78 29 61 59; www.lebistrotdupotager.com; 3 rue de la Martinière, 1er; mains €12-17; ⏰ noon-2pm & 7.30-9.30pm Tue-Sat; Ⓜ Hôtel de Ville) An

ℹ Getting There & Around

AIR
Lyon-St-Exupéry Airport (www.lyonaero-ports.com), 25km east of the city, is linked to Part-Dieu train station by the **Rhônexpress** (www.rhonexpress.fr; adult/youth/child €15.90/13.20/free) tramway (30 minutes, every 15 minutes).

BUS
Eurolines (☑ 04 72 56 95 30, 08 92 89 90 91; www.eurolines.fr; Gare de Perrache, 2e; Ⓜ Perrache) and **Linebús** (☑ 04 72 41 72 27; www.linebus.com; Gare de Perrache) offer service to Spain, Portugal, Italy and Germany from the Centre d'Échange building at the north end of the Perrache train complex.

PUBLIC TRANSPORT
Buses, trams, a four-line metro and two funiculars linking Vieux Lyon to Fourvière are run by **TCL** (www.tcl.fr). Public transport runs from around 5am to midnight. Tickets cost €1.80 (€16.20 for *carnet* of 10).

TRAIN
Lyon has two main-line train stations with direct TGV services: **Gare de la Part-Dieu** (place Charles Béraudier, 3e; Ⓜ Part-Dieu) and **Gare de Perrache** (cours de Verdun Rambaud, 2e; Ⓜ Perrache). Frequent TGV services include the following:

Dijon €37, 1½ hours, at least six daily
Marseille €53, 1¾ hours, every 30 to 60 minutes
Paris Charles de Gaulle Airport €97, two hours, at least 11 daily
Paris Gare de Lyon €75, two hours, every 30 to 60 minutes

offshoot of the renowned Potager des Halles restaurant, this gourmet bistro and tapas bar is a dreamy spot for a tasty lunch or to while away an evening. Happy diners throng the high-ceilinged main dining room, cosy upstairs balcony and sidewalk tables opposite the Fresque des Lyonnais, lingering over wine and creative seasonal dishes.

ℹ Information
Tourist Office (☑ 04 72 77 69 69; www.lyon-france.com; place Bellecour, 2e; ◷ 9am-6pm; Ⓜ Bellecour)

Chamonix
POP 9300

With the pearly white peaks of the Mont Blanc massif as a sensational backdrop, being an icon comes naturally to Chamonix in the French Alps. First 'discovered' by Brits

FRANCE, SWITZERLAND & AUSTRIA CHAMONIX

William Windham and Richard Pococke in 1741, this mountain resort is the mecca of mountaineering. Its knife-edge peaks, plunging slopes and massive glaciers have enthralled generations of adventurers and thrill-seekers ever since. Its après-ski scene is equally pumping.

◉ Sights & Activities

★ Aiguille du Midi   VIEWPOINT

A great broken tooth of rock rearing amongst the Alpine fastness of the Mont Blanc massif, the Aiguille du Midi (3842m) is one of Chamonix' most distinctive geographical features. If you can handle the altitude, the 360-degree views of the French, Swiss and Italian Alps from the summit are (quite literally) breathtaking. Year-round, you can float in a cable car from Chamonix to the Aiguille du Midi on the vertiginous **Téléphérique de l'Aiguille du Midi** (www.compagniedumontblanc. co.uk; place de l'Aiguille du Midi; adult/child return to Aiguille du Midi €58.50/49.70, to Plan de l'Aiguille summer €31/26.40, winter €17/14.50; ◔1st ascent btwn 7.10am & 8.30am, last btwn 3.30pm & 5pm).

Mer de Glace   VIEWPOINT

France's largest glacier, the 200m-deep 'Sea of Ice', flows 7km down the northern side of Mont Blanc, moving up to 1cm an hour (about 90m a year). The **Train du Montenvers** (☑04 50 53 22 75; www.compagniedumontblanc.fr; 35 place de la Mer de Glace; adult/child return €31/26.40; ◔10am-4.30pm), a picturesque, 5km-long cog railway opened in 1909, links Gare du Montenvers with Montenvers (1913m), from where a cable car takes you down to the glacier and the **Grotte de Glace** (◔closed last half of May & late Sep–mid-Oct). Your ticket also gets you into the Glaciorium, which looks at the birth, life and future of glaciers.

SkyWay Monte Bianco   OUTDOORS

(www.montebianco.com; Pointe Helbronner; one-way adult/child €36/25.20; ◔8.30am-4.30pm, earlier starts in summer) Three years in the making, this spectacular, international cable car links France with Italy, from Pointe Helbronner to Courmayeur in the Val d'Aosta. The cars rotate a full 360 degrees, affording peerless views of Mont Blanc, the Matterhorn and Gran Paradiso. To get there, take the Aiguille du Midi and **Télécabine Panoramique Mont Blanc** (☑04 50 53 22 75; Aiguille du Midi; adult/child return from Chamonix €80/68; ◔last departure from Aiguille du Midi 2.30pm) cable cars.

🛏 Sleeping & Eating

In the centre, riverside rue des Moulins boasts a line-up of après-ski joints serving food as well as booze into the wee hours.

Gîte Le Vagabond   HOSTEL €

(☑04 50 53 15 43; www.gitevagabond.com; 365 av Ravanel-le-Rouge; dm/sheets €21/5.50, d incl breakfast €101; ◔reception 8-10am & 4.30-10.30pm; 🛜) In the 150-year-old Le Brévent, once a stagecoach inn for travellers to Switzerland, Le Vagabond is Chamonix' hippest bunkhouse. It has rooms with four to six beds and a buzzing bar with a great log fire in winter, and can be found 850m southwest of the town centre.

Hôtel du Buet   HOTEL €

(☑04 50 54 60 05; www.hotelbuet.com; D1506, Vallorcine-Le Buet; d/q €66/109; ◔7.30am-10.30pm daily mid-Dec–Apr & mid-Jun–Sep) Another of the Chamonix-Mont Blanc Valley's long-standing family concerns (this one's been handed down from Chamel to Chamel since 1889) the Hôtel du Buet has 25 basic rooms and a restaurant serving the best-value fondue in the area.

ⓘ Information

Tourist Office (☑04 50 53 00 24; www.chamonix.com; 85 place du Triangle de l'Amitié; ◔8.30am-7pm winter & summer, 9am-12.30pm & 2-6pm in low season; 🛜)

ⓘ Getting There & Away

BUS

Services to/from Chamonix' **bus station** (☑04 50 53 01 15; 234 av Courmayeur, Chamonix Sud; ◔8am-noon & 1.15-6.30pm in winter, shorter hours rest of year).

Geneva (airport and bus station) One-way/return €25/50, 1½ to two hours, six to eight daily. Operated by **Starshipper** (☑04 56 12 40 59; www.starshipper.com; ◔phone line open 8.30am-noon & 2-6pm Mon-Fri).

Courmayeur One-way/return €15/21, 45 minutes, four daily. Run by **Savda** (☑+39 01 65 36 70 11; www.savda.it), with onward connections to Aosta and Milan.

TRAIN

The Mont Blanc Express narrow-gauge train trundles from St-Gervais-Le Fayet station, 23km west of Chamonix, to Martigny in Switzerland, stopping in Chamonix (45 minutes) en route. From St-Gervais-Le Fayet, there are trains to major French cities.

Bordeaux

POP 243,000

The southern city of Bordeaux is among France's most exciting, vibrant and dynamic cities. Half the city (18 sq km) is Unesco-listed, making it the largest urban World Heritage Site, and its pedestrian boulevards and squares are a delight to explore. Bolstered by its high-spirited university-student population and 5.5 million visitors annually, Belle Bordeaux scarcely sleeps: think barista-run coffee shops, super-food food trucks, an exceptional dining scene and more fine wine than you could ever possibly drink. *Santé!*

Sights

Cathédrale St-André   CATHEDRAL
(www.cathedrale-bordeaux.fr; place Jean Moulin; ⊙2-6pm Mon, 10am-noon & 2-6pm Tue-Sun) Lording over the city, and a Unesco World Heritage site prior to the city's classification, the cathedral's oldest section dates from 1096; most of what you see today was built in the 13th and 14th centuries. Enjoy exceptional masonry carvings in the north portal. Even more imposing than the cathedral itself is the gargoyled, 50m-high Gothic belfry, **Tour Pey-Berland** (adult/child €5.50/free; ⊙10am-1.15pm & 2-6pm Jun-Sep, 10am-12.30pm & 2-5.30pm Oct-May), erected between 1440 and 1466.

★ **La Cité du Vin**   MUSEUM
(☑05 56 81 38 47; www.laciteduvin.com; 1 Esplanade de Pontac; adult/child €20/free ⊙9.30am-7.30pm daily Apr-Oct, 9.30am-7.30pm Tue-Sun Nov-Mar) The complex world of wine is explored in depth at ground-breaking La Cité du Vin, a stunning piece of contemporary architecture resembling a wine decanter on the banks of the Garonne River. The curvaceous gold building glitters in the sun and its 3000 sq metres of exhibits are equally sensory and sensational. Digital guides lead visitors around 20 different themed sections covering everything from vine cultivation, grape varieties and wine production to ancient wine trade, 21st-century wine trends and celebrated personalities.

★ **Miroir d'Eau**   FOUNTAIN
(Water Mirror; place de la Bourse; ⊙10am-10pm summer) FREE A fountain of sorts, the Miroir d'Eau is the world's largest reflecting pool. Covering an area of 3450 sq metres of black granite on the quayside opposite the imposing Palais de la Bourse, the 'water mirror' provides hours of entertainment on warm sunny days when the reflections in its thin slick of water – drained and refilled every half-hour – are stunning. Every 23 minutes a dense fog-like vapor is ejected for three minutes to add to the fun (and photo opportunities).

Sleeping

Hôtel Notre Dame   HOTEL €
(☑05 56 52 88 24; 36-38 rue Notre Dame; s/d €54/63; ☎) Location is the key selling point of this good-value hotel. It's within an easy stroll of the town centre, just back from the river and in the middle of a trendy village-like neighbourhood of antique shops, fashion boutiques, cafes and restaurants. It also has a wheelchair-accessible room. Breakfast €8.

Eating & Drinking

Iconic addresses mingle with new openings in the tasty tangle of pedestrian streets around place du Parlement; place St-Pierre is perfect for cheaper eats alfresco. North along the river, quai des Chartons is laced with waterfront restaurants and bars. Student pubs, coffee shops and wine bars pepper rue St-James.

★ **Magasin Général**   INTERNATIONAL €
(☑05 56 77 88 35; www.magasingeneral.camp/; 87 quai des Queyries; 2-/3-course menu €14/18, mains €9-19; ⊙8.30am-6pm Wed-Fri, 8.30am-midnight Sat, 10am-midnight Sun, kitchen noon-2.15pm & 7-10pm; ☎) Follow the hip crowd across the river to this huge industrial hangar on the right bank, France's biggest and best organic restaurant with gargantuan terrace complete with vintage sofa seating, ping-pong table and table football. Everything here, from the vegan burgers and super-food salads to smoothies, pizzas, wine and French bistro fare, is *bio* (organic) and sourced locally. Sunday brunch (€24) is a bottomless feast.

★ **Utopia**   CAFE, BAR
(www.cinemas-utopia.org; 3 place Camille Jullian; ⊙10am-1am summer, to 10.30pm winter) At home in an old church, this much-venerated art

FRANCE, SWITZERLAND & AUSTRIA BORDEAUX

ⓘ CENT SAVER

Consider investing in a **Bordeaux City Pass** (www.bordeauxcitypass.com; 1/2/3 days €26/33/40), which covers admission to many museums and monuments, unlimited public transport and various other discounts. The tourist office sells it.

DUNE DU PILAT

This colossal sand dune (sometimes referred to as the Dune de Pyla because of its location 4km from the small seaside resort town of Pyla-sur-Mer), 60km south of Bordeaux, stretches from the mouth of the Bassin d'Arcachon southwards for 2.7km. Already Europe's largest, the dune is growing eastwards 1.5m a year – it has swallowed trees, a road junction and even a hotel, so local lore claims.

The view from the top – approximately 115m above sea level – is magnificent. To the west you see the sandy shoals at the mouth of the Bassin d'Arcachon, including Cap Ferret and the **Banc d'Arguin** bird reserve where up to 6000 couples of Sandwich terns nest each spring.

Although an easy day trip from Bordeaux (the dune is 8km from Arcachon train station, with local bus line 1 linking the two), the area around the dune is an enjoyable place to kick back for a while. For a splurge to remember, head downhill into Pyla-sur-Mer after the dune for a stylish drink with awesome dune view at **La Co(o)rniche** (☏05 56 22 72 11; www.lacoorniche-pyla.com; 46 av Louis Gaume; 2-/3-course lunch menu €53/58, seafood platters €40-85). Should you decide to kip the night, there's a swag of seasonal campgrounds listed at www.bassin-arcachon.com.

address is a local institution. Art-house cinema, mellow cafe, hot lunch spot and bar rolled into one, it is one of the top addresses in the city to mingle over a drink, *tartine* (open sandwich, €7) or good-value meal (mains €13 to €15) with local Bordelais at any time of day. Its atmospheric pavement terrace on a car-free square catches the morning sun.

ℹ Information

Tourist Office (☏05 56 00 66 00; www.bordeaux-tourisme.com; 12 cours du 30 Juillet; ⊙9am-7.30pm Mon-Sat, 9.30am-6.30pm Sun Jul & Aug, shorter hours Sep-Jun)

ℹ Getting There & Around

Aéroport de Bordeaux (www.bordeaux.aeroport.fr) is in Mérignac, 10km southwest of the city centre. Hourly shuttle buses (www.navette aeroport-bordeaux.com; €7.20, 30 minutes) and public bus line 1 (€1.50, 40 minutes) link it with the train station.

Bordeaux is one of France's major rail-transit points with trains to dozens of destinations from **Gare St-Jean** (cours de la Marne), about 3km from the city centre. Tram line C (www.infotbc.com) links the two via the riverside; buy a ticket (€1.50) from machines at tram stops and timestamp on board.

Provence

Provence conjures up images of rolling lavender fields, blue skies, gorgeous villages, wonderful food and superb wine. It certainly delivers on all those fronts, but it's not just worth visiting for its good looks – dig a little

deeper to find extraordinary art, culture and a party vibe.

Marseille

POP 858,900

Marseille grows on you with its fusion of cultures, souk-like markets, vibrant millennia-old port and *corniches* (coastal roads) along rocky inlets and sun-baked beaches. Founded by Greek settlers who came ashore here around 600 BC, this is France's second-largest city.

◉ Sights

★**Vieux Port**   HISTORIC SITE
(Ⓜ Vieux Port) Ships have docked for more than 26 centuries at the city's birthplace, the colourful Old Port. The main commercial docks were transferred to the Joliette area north of here in the 1840s, but the Old Port remains a thriving harbour for fishing boats, pleasure yachts and tourists.

★**Musée des Civilisations de l'Europe et de la Méditerranée**   MUSEUM
(MuCEM, Museum of European & Mediterranean Civilisations; ☏04 84 35 13 13; www.mucem.org; 7 Promenade Robert Laffont; adult/family/child incl all exhibitions €9.50/14/free, 1st Sun of month free; ⊙10am-8pm Wed-Mon Jul & Aug, 11am-7pm Wed-Mon Sep, Oct, May & Jun, 11am-6pm Wed-Mon Nov-Apr; ♿; Ⓜ Vieux Port or Joliette) The icon of modern Marseille, this stunning museum explores the history, culture and civilisation of the Mediterranean region through anthropological exhibits, rotating art ex-

hibitions and film. The collection sits in a bold, contemporary building, J4, designed by Algerian-born, Marseille-educated architect Rudi Ricciotti. It is linked by a vertigo-inducing footbridge to the 13th-century **Fort St-Jean**, from which there are stupendous views of the Vieux Port and the Mediterranean. The fort grounds and their gardens are free to explore.

★**Le Panier**   HISTORIC SITE

(M Vieux Port) From the Vieux Port, hike north up to this fantastic history-woven quarter, which is fabulous for a wander with its artsy ambience, cool hidden squares and sun-baked cafes. In Greek Massilia it was the site of the *agora* (marketplace), hence its name, which means 'the basket'. During WWII the quarter was dynamited and afterwards rebuilt. Today it's a mishmash of lanes hiding artisan shops, *ateliers* (workshops) and terraced houses strung with drying washing.

Its centrepiece is **Centre de la Vieille Charité** (www.vieille-charite-marseille.com; 2 rue de la Charité; ⊙10am-6pm Tue-Sun M Joliette) FREE. Nearby **Cathédrale de Marseille Notre Dame de Major** (⊙10am-6.30pm Wed-Sun Apr-Sep, to 5.30pm Oct-Mar; M Joliette) stands guard between the old and new ports.

🛏 Sleeping & Eating

Vieux Port and the surrounding pedestrian streets teem with cafe terraces, but choose carefully. For world cuisine, try cours Julien and nearby rue des Trois Mages. For pizza, roast chickens, and Middle Eastern food under €10, nose around the streets surrounding **Marché des Capucins** (place des Capucins; ⊙8am-7pm Mon-Sat; M Noailles, 🚊 Canebière Garibaldi).

Vertigo Vieux-Port   HOSTEL €

(🗷 04 91 54 42 95; www.hotelvertigo.fr; 38 rue Fort Notre Dame; dm €29-33, tw €70; 🛜; M Vieux Port) One of two Vertigo hostels in Marseille, this place shows a swanky sleep is possible on a shoestring budget – street-art murals, vintage furniture, stripped wooden floors and lots of original architectural details (some dorms have wooden beams, others exposed stone arches). All rooms have their own modern bathroom, and there's a good kitchen, lockers and a TV lounge.

★**Les Buffets du Vieux Port**   FRENCH €

(🗷 04 13 20 11 32; www.clubhousevieuxport. com; 158 quai du Port; adult/child menu €23/13; ⊙noon-2.30pm & 7.30-10.30pm; 🍴; M Vieux Port) What a great idea – a high-class, on-trend self-service canteen, with a vast array of starters, mains, salads and desserts laid out like a banquet for diners to help themselves to. Premium cold cuts, fresh seafood, bouillabaisse, mussels, fish soup – it's all here and more. Portside tables go fast, but there's plenty of room inside.

ⓘ Information

Tourist Office (🗷 04 91 13 89 00; www. marseille-tourisme.com; 11 La Canebière; ⊙9am-7pm Mon-Sat, 10am-5pm Sun; M Vieux Port)

ⓘ Getting There & Around

AIR

Aéroport Marseille-Provence (Aéroport Marseille-Marignane; MRS; 🗷 04 42 14 14 14; www.marseille.aeroport.fr), 25km northwest of Marseille in Marignane, is linked to the main train station by **Navette Marseille** (www. navettemarseilleaeroport.com; ⊙4.30am-11.30pm).

LES CALANQUES

Marseille abuts the wild and spectacular **Parc National des Calanques** (www. calanques-parcnational.fr), a 20km stretch of high, rocky promontories rising from brilliant-turquoise Mediterranean waters.

The sheer cliffs are occasionally interrupted by small idyllic beaches, some impossible to reach without a kayak. Among the most famous are the calanques of Sormiou, Port-Miou, Port-Pin and En-Vau.

From October to June, the best way to see the calanques is to hike. The best access is from the small town of **Cassis**. Its **tourist office** (🗷 08 92 39 01 03; www.ot-cassis.com; quai des Moulins; ⊙9am-7pm Mon-Sat, 9.30am-12.30pm & 3-6pm Sun Jul & Aug, shorter hours rest of year; 🛜) has maps. In July and August, trails close because of fire danger: take a boat tour from Marseille or Cassis, sea kayak with **Raskas Kayak** (www.raskas-kayak. com); drive; or take a bus.

BOAT

The **passenger ferry terminal** (www.marseille-port.fr; Ⓜ Joliette) is 250m south of place de la Joliette, 1er. **SNCM** (☑ 08 91 70 18 01; www.sncm.fr; 61 bd des Dames; Ⓜ Joliette) boats sail to Corsica, Sardinia and North Africa.

TRAIN

From Marseille's Gare St-Charles, trains go all over France and Europe. Services include the following:

Avignon €29.50, 35 minutes
Lyon €65, 1¾ hours
Nice €37, 2½ hours
Paris Gare de Lyon €113, three hours

Aix-en-Provence

POP 145,300

A pocket of left-bank Parisian chic deep in Provence, the student town of Aix (pronounced like the letter X) is all class. Haughty stone lions guard its grandest avenue, cafe-laced **cours Mirabeau**, where fashionable Aixois pose on polished pavement terraces sipping espresso.

A stroller's paradise, Aix' highlight is the mostly pedestrian old city, **Vieil Aix**. South of cours Mirabeau, the **Quartier Mazarin** was laid out in the 17th century, and is home to some of Aix' finest buildings. The town's most famous son is Cézanne, whose last studio, the **Atelier Cézanne** (☑ 04 42 21 06 53; www.atelier-cezanne.com; 9 av Paul Cézanne; adult/child €6/free; ⊙ 10am-6pm Jul & Aug, shorter hours Sep-Jun), was preserved as it was at the time of his death. Take bus 1 or 20 to the Atelier Cézanne stop or walk the 1.5km from town. None of his paintings hang here, but there are nine in the town's world-class art museum, **Musée Granet** (☑ 04 42 52 88 32;

SPLURGE IN AIX

When in Aix, treat yourself to slow-braised meats, seasonal veg, sinful desserts and some super wines over lunch at **Le Petit Verdot** (☑ 04 42 27 30 12; www.lepetitverdot.fr; 7 rue d'Entrecasteaux; mains €19-25; ⊙ 7pm-midnight Mon-Sat). Great Provençal food, great Provençal wines - really, what more do you want from a meal in this part of France? It's all about hearty, honest dining here, with table-tops made out of old wine crates, and a lively chef-patron who runs the place with huge enthusiasm.

www.museegranet-aixenprovence.fr; place St-Jean de Malte; adult/child €5/free; ⊙ 11am-7pm Tue-Sun), to compensate.

From Aix' **bus station** (☑ 04 42 91 26 80, 08 91 02 40 25; place Marius Bastard) buses shuttle to Marseille (€5.60, 25 minutes, every 10 minutes, up to five daily). Alternatively, catch a Marseille train (€6.50, 45 minutes) from the tiny **city-centre train station** (av Victor Hugo).

Aix' **TGV station**, 15km from the centre, is a stop on the high-speed Paris–Marseille line. Bus 40 runs from the TGV station to Aix' bus station (€4.10, 15 minutes, every 15 minutes).

Avignon

POP 92,200

Hooped by 4.3km of superbly preserved stone ramparts, this graceful city is the belle of Provence's ball. Its turn as the papal seat of power has bestowed Avignon with a treasury of magnificent art and architecture. Famed for its annual performing arts festival, these days Avignon is a lively student city and an ideal spot from which to step out into the surrounding region.

◉ Sights

★**Palais des Papes**   PALACE
(Papal Palace; www.palais-des-papes.com; place du Palais; adult/child €11/9, with Pont St-Bénezet €13.50/10.50; ⊙ 9am-8pm Jul, to 8.30pm Aug, shorter hours Sep-Jun) The largest Gothic palace ever built, the Palais des Papes was built by Pope Clement V, who abandoned Rome in 1309 as a result of violent disorder following his election. It served as the seat of papal power for seven decades, and its immense scale provides ample testament to the medieval might of the Roman Catholic church. Ringed by 3m-thick walls, its cavernous halls, chapels and antechambers are largely bare today, but an audioguide (€2) provides a useful backstory.

★**Pont St-Bénezet**   BRIDGE
(bd du Rhône; adult/child 24hr ticket €5/4, with Palais des Papes €13.50/10.50; ⊙ 9am-8pm Jul, to 8.30pm Aug, shorter hours Sep-Jun) Legend says Pastor Bénezet had three saintly visions urging him to build a bridge across the Rhône. Completed in 1185, the 900m-long bridge with 20 arches linked Avignon with Villeneuve-lès-Avignon. It was rebuilt several times before all but four of its spans were washed away in the 1600s.

PONT DU GARD

An icon of Roman France, this extraordinary three-tiered **aqueduct** (☎ 04 66 37 50 99; www.pontdugard.fr; car & up to 5 passengers €18, after 8pm €10, by bicycle or on foot €7, after 8pm €3.50; ☺ site 24hr year-round, visitor centre & museum 9am-8pm Jul & Aug, shorter hours Sep–mid-Jan & mid-Feb–Jun), 45km southwest of Avignon, was once part of a 50km-long system of channels built around 19 BC to transport up to 20,000 cu metres of water per day from Uzès to Nîmes. The scale is huge: the bridge is 48.8m high, 275m long and graced with 35 precision-built arches.

You can walk across the tiers for panoramic views over the Gard River, but the best perspective on the bridge is from downstream, along the 1.4km **Mémoires de Garrigue** walking trail. Early evening is a good time to visit, as admission is cheaper and the bridge is stunningly illuminated after dark.

If you don't want to pay to visit the bridge, admire it for free from Rocher des Doms park or Pont Édouard Daladier or on Île de la Barthelasse's chemin des Berges.

Festivals & Events

Hundreds of artists take to the stage and streets during the world-famous **Festival d'Avignon** (www.festival-avignon.com; ☺ Jul) and fringe **Festival Off** (www.avignonleoff.com; ☺ Jul).

Sleeping & Eating

Le Colbert HOTEL €
(☎ 04 90 86 20 20; www.lecolbert-hotel.com; 7 rue Agricol Perdiguier; s €72-92, d €82-112; ❄) As bright and sunny as a Provençal summer day, this pleasant little hotel has 15 rooms decked out in art posters and zingy shades of yellow, terracotta and tangerine. Rooms are fairly standard, but it's the sweet little interior patio that sells it – with a palm tree and a tinkling fountain, it's a dreamy setting for breakfast.

Le Potard BURGERS €
(☎ 04 90 82 34 19; www.lepotard.com; 19-21 place de la Principale; burgers €14-18; ☺ noon-2.30pm Tue-Sat, 6.30-10pm Wed-Sat) Gourmet brioche-based burgers in a multitude of guises, loaded with tempting goodies from smoked bacon and St-Nectaire cheese to caramelised onions, crunchy rocket and sundried tomato caviar. There's also a range of salad plates served with mini-burgers.

❶ Information

Tourist Office (☎ 04 32 74 32 74; www.avignon-tourisme.com; 41 cours Jean Jaurès; ☺ 9am-6pm Mon-Sat, 10am-5pm Sun Apr-Oct, shorter hours Nov-Mar)

❶ Getting There & Away

Avignon has two stations: **Gare Avignon TGV**, 4km southwest in Courtine, and **Gare Avignon Centre** (42 bd St-Roch), with services to/from Arles (€6.50, 20 minutes) and Nîmes (€8, 30 minutes).

Destinations served by TGV include Paris Gare du Lyon (€35 to €80, 3½ hours), Marseille (€17.50, 35 minutes) and Nice (€31 to €40, 3¼ hours). Eurostar services operate up to five times weekly between Avignon TGV and London (from €59.50, 5¾ hours) en route to/from Marseille.

French Riviera

With its glistening seas, idyllic beaches and fabulous weather, the French Riviera (Côte d'Azur in French) screams exclusivity, extravagance and excess. It has been a favourite getaway for the European jet set since Victorian times.

Nice

POP 346,300

Riviera queen Nice is what good living is all about – shimmering shores, the very best of Mediterranean food, a unique historical heritage, free museums, a charming Old Town and exceptional art.

◉ Sights

★**Vieux Nice** HISTORIC SITE
Getting lost among the dark, narrow, winding alleyways of Nice's Old Town is a highlight. The layout has barely changed since the 1700s, and it's now packed with delis, restaurants, boutiques and bars, but the centrepiece remains **cours Saleya**: a massive market square that's permanently thronged in summer. The **food market** (☺ 6am-1.30pm Tue-Sun) is perfect for fresh produce and foodie souvenirs, while the flower market is

Nice

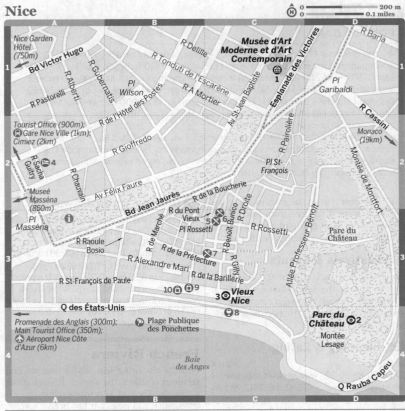

Nice

◎ Top Sights

1 Musée d'Art Moderne
  et d'Art
  Contemporain C1
2 Parc du Château D4
3 Vieux Nice C3

🛏 Sleeping

4 Villa Saint-Exupéry
  Beach Hostel A2

✴ Eating

5 Fenocchio C3
6 La Rossettisserie C3
7 Olive et Artichaut C3

🍷 Drinking & Nightlife

8 Ark C4

🛍 Shopping

9 Flea Market B3
10 Food Market B3

worth visiting just for the colours and fragrances. A **flea market** (⊙8am-5pm Mon) is held on Monday.

★ Promenade des Anglais ARCHITECTURE

The most famous stretch of seafront in Nice – if not France – is this vast paved promenade, which gets its name from the English expat patrons who paid for it in 1822. It runs for the whole 4km sweep of the Baie des Anges with a dedicated lane for cyclists and skaters.

★ Parc du Château GARDENS

(⊙8.30am-8pm Apr-Sep, to 6pm Oct-Mar) FREE
For the best views over Nice's red-tiled rooftops, climb the winding staircases up to this wooded outcrop on the eastern edge of the Old Town. There are various entrances, including one beside the tower – or you can cheat ride the free **lift** (Ascenseur du Château; rue des Ponchettes; ⊙9am-8pm Jun-Aug, 9am-7pm Apr, May & Sep, 10am-6pm Oct-Mar).

★ Musée Masséna
MUSEUM

(☑ 04 93 91 19 10; 65 rue de France; adult/child €6/
free; ⊙ 10am-6pm Wed-Mon) Originally built as
a holiday home for Prince Victor d'Essling
(the grandson of one of Napoléon's favourite generals, Maréchal Massena), this lavish belle époque building is another of the
city's iconic architectural landmarks. Built
between 1898 and 1901 in grand neoclassical style with an Italianate twist, it's now a
fascinating museum dedicated to the history
of the Riviera – taking in everything from
holidaying monarchs to expat Americans,
the boom of tourism and the enduring importance of Nice carnival.

★ Musée d'Art Moderne et d'Art Contemporain
ART MUSEUM

(MAMAC; ☑ 04 97 13 42 01; www.mamac-nice.org;
place Yves Klein; ⊙ 10am-6pm Tue Sun) **FREE**
European and American avant-garde works
from the 1950s to the present are the focus
of this museum. Highlights include many
works by Christo and Nice's New Realists:
Niki de Saint Phalle, César, Arman and Yves
Klein. The building's rooftop also works as
an exhibition space (with knockout panoramas of Nice to boot).

Musée Matisse
ART MUSEUM

(☑ 04 93 81 08 08; www.musee-matisse-nice.org;
164 av des Arènes de Cimiez; ⊙ 10am-6pm Wed-
Mon) **FREE** This museum, 2km north in the
leafy Cimiez quarter, houses a fascinating
assortment of works by Matisse, including
oil paintings, drawings, sculptures, tapestries and Matisse's famous paper cut-outs.
The permanent collection is displayed in
a red-ochre 17th-century Genoese villa in
an olive grove. Temporary exhibitions are
in the futuristic basement building. Matisse is buried in the **Monastère de Cimiez cemetery**, across the park from the
museum.

🛏 Sleeping

Villa Saint-Exupéry Beach Hostel
HOSTEL €

(☑ 04 93 16 13 45; www.villahostels.com; 6 rue Sa-
cha Guitry; dm €40-50, d/tr €120/150; 🅿@🛜)
It's actually a few blocks from the beach,
but this longstanding city hostel has plenty
of other pluses: bar, kitchen, free wi-fi, gym,
games room etc, plus friendly multilingual
staff and a great location. The downside?
High prices (at least for a hostel) and occasionally drab decor. All dorms have a private
ensuite bathroom, and sleep from three
to 14.

THE BEST ICE IN TOWN

Loads of places sell it, but the best ice
cream in Nice is made by *maître glacier*
Fenocchio (☑ 04 93 80 72 52; www.
fenocchio.fr; 2 place Rossetti; 1/2 scoops
€2.50/4; ⊙ 9am-midnight Feb-Oct), in
the biz since 1966. Dither too long over
the 70-plus flavours of ice cream and
sorbet and you'll never make it to the
front of the queue. Eschew predictable
favourites and indulge in a new taste
sensation: black olive, thyme, rosemary,
lavender, ginger chocolate, violet or
typical Niçois *tourte de blette* (a sweet
Swiss Chard tart made with raisins, pine
nuts and Parmesan cheese).

★ Nice Pebbles
SELF-CONTAINED €€

(☑ 04 97 20 27 30; www.nicepebbles.com;
1-/2-/3-bedroom apt from €110/130/200; 🅿🛜)
Nice Pebbles offers nearly a hundred apartments and villas to choose from, from one
to five bedrooms: all chosen for quirkiness
and design, though sizes and location vary.
Wi-fi, DVD players and proper kitchens are
standard, and some also have luxuries like a
swimming pool, patio or garden. Rates vary
widely; off-season deals can be very good.

🍴 Eating & Drinking

Vieux Nice's streets are stuffed with bars, cafes and restaurants. Nice nightlife – vibrant
live-music scene – likewise rocks.

★ La Rossettisserie
FRENCH €

(☑ 04 93 76 18 80; www.larossettisserie.com; 8
rue Mascoïnat; mains €13.50-14.50; ⊙ noon-2pm
& 7.30-10pm Mon-Sat) Roast meat is the order of the day here: make your choice from
beef, chicken, veal or lamb, and pair it with
a choice of mashed or sautéed potatoes and
ratatouille or salad. Simple and sumptuous –
and the vaulted cellar is a delight.

★ Olive et Artichaut
PROVENCAL €€

(☑ 04 89 14 97 51; www.oliveartichaut.com; 6 rue
Ste-Réparate; 3-course menu €32, mains €16-22;
⊙ noon-2pm & 7.30-10pm Wed-Sun) There's barely enough room to swing a pan in this tiny
street bistro, especially when it's full of diners (as it often is), but it doesn't seem to faze
young Niçois chef Thomas Hubert and his
friendly team. He sources as much produce
as possible from close-to-home suppliers
(Sisteron lamb, Niçois olives, locally caught

WORTH A TRIP

THE CORNICHES

Some of the Riviera's most spectacular scenery stretches east between Nice and Monaco. A trio of *corniches* (coastal roads) hugs the cliffs between the two seaside towns, each higher up the hill than the last. The middle corniche ends in Monaco; the upper and lower continue to Menton near the France–Italy border.

Corniche Inférieure Skimming the glittering, villa-studded shoreline, this road is all about belle époque glamour, the height of which can be seen at the extravagant **Villa Ephrussi de Rothschild** (☑ 04 93 01 33 09; www.villa-ephrussi.com/en; adult/child €13/10; ⊙ 10am-7pm Jul & Aug, 10am-6pm Feb, Mar, Sep & Oct, 2-6pm Mon-Fri, 10am-6pm Sat & Sun Nov-Jan) in St-Jean-Cap Ferrat.

Moyenne Corniche The jewel in the Riviera crown undoubtedly goes to Èze, a medieval village spectacularly clinging to a rocky outcrop with dazzling views of the Med.

Grande Corniche The epitome of 'scenic drive', with sublime panoramas unfolding at every bend. Stop in La Turbie for dramatic views of Monaco.

fish) and likes to give the old classics his own individual spin. Wise diners reserve.

★ **Ark**　　　　　　　　　LOUNGE
(☑ 03 34 93 80 04; 41 quai des États-Unis; ⊙ 11am-1am) Nice's drinking scene became a whole load more glamorous with the 2015 opening of Ark, a super-chic lounge bar wedged between the sea and Cours Saleya. Snag a seat on one of the drop-dead-gorgeous 2nd-floor balconies gazing out at the Med and you'll know you've hit Nice's jetsetter jackpot.

❶ Information

Main Tourist Office (Promenade des Anglais; ☑ 08 92 70 74 07; www.nicetourisme.com) Nice's main tourist office on the Promenade des Anglais was undergoing renovations in 2016. There are smaller branches in front of the train station (Gare de Nice; av Thiers; ⊙ 9am-7pm daily Jun-Sep, 9am-6pm Mon-Sat & 10-5pm Oct-May) and on Promenade du Paillon (⊙ 9am-6pm Mon-Sat).

❶ Getting There & Around

AIR
Nice Côte d'Azur Airport (☑ 08 20 42 33 33; www.nice.aeroport.fr; 🛜) is 6km west of Nice, by the sea. Buses 98 and 99 link the airport terminal with Promenade des Anglais and Nice train station respectively (€6, 35 minutes, every 20 minutes). Bus 110 (€20, hourly) links the airport with Monaco (40 minutes).

BUS
There is an excellent intercity bus service from Nice; tickets cost just €1.50. Bus 100 goes to Menton (1½ hours) and Monaco (40 minutes); bus 200 serves Cannes (1½ hours).

TRAIN
From Nice's train station, 1.2km north of the beach, there are frequent services to Cannes (€5.90, 40 minutes) and Monaco (€3.30, 25 minutes).

Cannes
POP 74,600

Most have heard of Cannes and its celebrity film festival. The latter only lasts for two weeks in May, but the buzz and glitz linger all year thanks to regular visits from celebrities who come here to indulge in designer shopping, beaches and the palace hotels of the Riviera's most glam seafront.

◉ Sights & Activities

★ **La Croisette**　　　　ARCHITECTURE
The multi-starred hotels and couture shops lining the iconic bd de la Croisette (aka La Croisette) may be the preserve of the rich and famous, but anyone can enjoy strolling the palm-shaded promenade – a favourite pastime among Cannois at night, when it twinkles with bright lights. Views of the Baie de Cannes and nearby Estérel mountains are beautiful, and seafront hotel palaces dazzle in all their stunning art deco glory.

Îles de Lérins　　　　ISLAND
Although just 20 minutes away by boat, these tranquil islands feel far from the madding crowd. **Île Ste-Marguerite**, where the mysterious Man in the Iron Mask was incarcerated during the late 17th century, is known for its bone-white beaches, eucalyptus groves and small marine museum. Tiny **Île St-Honorat** has been a monastery since the 5th century: you can visit the church

and small chapels and stroll through the monks' vineyards.

Boats leave Cannes from quai des Îles on the western side of the harbour. **Riviera Lines** (📞 04 92 98 71 31; www.riviera-lines.com; quai Max Laubeuf) runs ferries to Île Ste-Marguerite and **Compagnie Planaria** (www.cannes-ilesdelerins.com; quai Max Laubeuf) covers Île St-Honorat.

🛏 Sleeping & Eating

Hôtel Alnea   HOTEL €
(📞04 93 68 77 77; www.hotel-alnea.com; 20 rue Jean de Riouffe; s €61-75, d €70-99; 🅿🛜) At this breath of fresh air in a town of stars, Noémi and Cédric have put their heart and soul into this hotel, offering bright, colourful two-star rooms, original paintings and numerous little details, such as the afternoon coffee break, the honesty bar, and the bike or boules (to play *pétanque*) loans. Breakfast €8.50.

⭐PhilCat   SANDWICHES €
(Promenade de la Pantiéro; sandwiches & salads €3.50-6; ⏱ 7am-7pm Mar-Oct; 🖉) Phillipe and Catherine's prefab cabin on the waterfront is a perfect lunch spot. This is fast-food, Cannes-style – giant salads, toasted panini and the best *pan bagna* (€5; a gargantuan bun filled with tuna, onion, red pepper, lettuce and tomato, and dripping in olive oil) on the Riviera. The 'super' version (€5.30) throws anchovies into the mix.

⭐Bobo Bistro   MEDITERRANEAN €
(📞 04 93 99 97 33; 21 rue du Commandant André; pizza €12-16, mains €15-20; ⏱ noon-3pm & 7-11pm Mon-Sat, 7-11pm Sun) Predictably, it's a 'bobo' (bourgeois bohemian) crowd that gathers at this achingly cool bistro in Cannes' fashionable Carré d'Or (Golden Sq). Decor is stylishly retro, with attention-grabbing objets d'art like a tableau of dozens of spindles of coloured yarn. Cuisine is local, seasonal and invariably organic: artichoke salad, tuna carpaccio with passionfruit, roasted cod with mash *fait masion* (homemade).

ℹ Information

Tourist Office (📞 04 92 99 84 22; www cannes-destination.fr; 1 bd de la Croisette; ⏱ 9am-8pm Jun-Aug, 9am or 10am-7pm Sep-May; 🛜)

ℹ Getting There & Away

Cannes' gleaming white train station is well connected with other towns along the coast including Marseille (€25, two hours, half-hourly),

Monaco (€8, one hour, at least twice hourly) and Nice (€6, 40 minutes, every 15 minutes).

St-Tropez
POP 4900

In the soft autumn or winter light, it's hard to believe the pretty terracotta fishing village of St-Tropez is a stop on the Riviera celebrity circuit. It seems far removed from its glitzy siblings further up the coast, but come spring or summer, it's a different world: the population increases tenfold, prices triple and fun-seekers pile in to party till dawn.

⊙ Sights & Activities

For St-Tropez' fabled beach scene, head to **Plage de Pampelonne**, a glorious 9km stretch of golden sand peppered with A-lister beach bars and restaurants.

Vieux Port   PORT
Yachts line the harbour and visitors stroll the quays at the picturesque old port. In front of the sable-coloured town houses, the **Bailli de Suffren statue** (quai Suffren), cast from a 19th-century cannon, peers out to sea. The bailiff (1729–88) was a sailor who fought with a Tropezien crew against Britain and Prussia during the Seven Years' War.

Duck beneath the archway, next to the tourist office, to uncover St-Tropez' daily morning **fish market**, on place aux Herbes.

Place des Lices   SQUARE
St-Tropez' legendary and very charming central square is studded with plane trees, cafes and *pétanque* players. Simply sitting on a cafe terrace watching the world go by or jostling with the crowds at its extravaganza of a twice-weekly **market** (⏱8am-1pm Tue & Sat), jam-packed with everything from fruit and veg to antique mirrors and sandals, is an integral part of the St-Tropez experience.

Artists and intellectuals have met for decades in St-Tropez' famous Café des Arts, now simply called **Le Café** (📞04 94 97 44 69; www.lecafe.fr; lunch/dinner menus €18/32; ⏱8am-11pm) – not to be confused with the newer, green-canopied Café des Arts on the corner of the square. Aspiring *pétanque* players can borrow a set of boules from the bar.

⭐Musée de l'Annonciade   ART MUSEUM
(place Grammont; adult/child €6/free; ⏱10am-1pm & 2-6pm Wed-Mon) In a gracefully converted 16th-century chapel, this small but famous museum showcases an impressive collection of modern art infused with that

legendary Côte d'Azur light. Pointillist Paul Signac bought a house in St-Tropez in 1892 and introduced other artists to the area.

🛏 Sleeping & Eating

Multi-star campgrounds abound on the road to Plage de Pampelonne. Quai Jean Jaurès at the Vieux Port is littered with restaurants and cafes.

Hôtel Lou Cagnard   HOTEL €€
(📞 04 94 97 04 24; www.hotel-lou-cagnard.com; 18 av Paul Roussel; d €83-176; ⊗Mar-Oct; ❄🛜) This old-school hotel stands out in stark contrast against most of the swanky hotels around St-Tropez. Located in an old house shaded by lemon and fig trees, its rooms are unashamedly frilly and floral, but some have garden patios, and the lovely jasmine-scented garden and welcoming family feel make it a home away from home.

★La Tarte Tropézienne   CAFE, BOULANGERIE €
(📞 04 94 97 04 69; www.latartetropezienne.fr; place des Lices; mains €13-15, cakes €3-5; ⊗6.30am-7.30pm & noon-3pm) This cafe-bakery is the creator of the eponymous sugar-crusted, orange-perfumed cake. Find a smaller branch on **rue Clemenceau** (📞 04 94 97 71 42; 36 rue Clémenceau; ⊗7am-7pm).

ℹ Information

Tourist Office (📞 08 92 68 48 28; www.sainttropeztourisme.com; quai Jean Jaurès; ⊗9.30am-1.30pm & 3-7.30pm Jul & Aug, 9.30am-12.30pm & 2-7pm Apr-Jun, Sep & Oct, to 6pm Mon-Sat Nov-Mar)

ℹ Getting There & Away

During high season, avoid horrendous four-hour traffic bottlenecks on the one road into St-Tropez (or €40 parking, impossible to find) by parking in **Port Grimaud** or **Ste-Maxime** and taking a **Les Bateaux Verts shuttle boat** (📞 04 94 49 29 39; www.bateauxverts.com; quai Jean Jaurès).

By train, the most convenient station is in St-Raphaël, served by **Les Bateaux de St-Raphaël** (📞 04 94 95 17 46; www.bateauxsaintraphael.com) boats in high season, or bus.

Monaco

POP 37,800

Squeezed into just 200 hectares, this confetti principality may be the world's second-smallest country (the Vatican is smaller), but what it lacks in size it makes up for in attitude. Glitzy, glam and screaming hedonism, skyscraper Monaco is truly beguiling.

Accommodation in Monaco is expensive; day-trip it from Nice, a short train ride away. Include Monaco's country code (📞377) when calling Monaco from outside the principality.

⦿ Sights & Activities

★Le Rocher   HISTORIC SITE
Monaco Ville, also called Le Rocher, is the only part of Monaco to have retained its original old town, complete with small, winding medieval lanes. The old town thrusts skywards on a pistol-shaped rock, its strategic location overlooking the sea that became the stronghold of the Grimaldi dynasty.

Palais Princier de Monaco   PALACE
(📞 93 25 18 31; www.palais.mc; place du Palais; adult/child €8/4, incl Car Museum €11.50/5; ⊗10am-6pm Apr-Oct, to 7pm Jul & Aug) Built as a fortress atop Le Rocher in the 13th century, this palace is the private residence of the Grimaldi family. It is protected by the blue-helmeted, white-socked Carabiniers du Prince; **changing of the guard** takes place daily at 11.55am, when crowds gather outside the gates to watch.

★Musée Océanographique de Monaco   AQUARIUM
(📞 93 15 36 00; www.oceano.mc; av St-Martin; adult €11-16, child €7-12 depending on season; ⊗9.30am-8pm Jul & Aug, 10am-7pm Apr, May, Jun & Sep, to 6pm Oct-Mar) Stuck dramatically to the edge of a cliff since 1910, the world-renowned Musée Océanographique de Monaco, founded by Prince Albert I (1848–1922), is a stunner. Its centrepiece is its **aquarium** with a 6m-deep lagoon where sharks and marine predators are separated from colourful tropical fishes by a coral reef.

★Casino de Monte Carlo   CASINO
(📞 98 06 21 21; www.montecarlocasinos.com; place du Casino; 9am-noon €10, admission from 2pm Salons Ordinaires/Salons Privées €10/20; ⊗visits 9am-noon, gaming 2pm-2am or 4am or when last game ends) Peeping inside Monte Carlo's legendary marble-and-gold casino is a Monaco essential. The building, open to visitors every morning, is Europe's most lavish example of belle époque architecture. Prince Charles III came up with the idea of the casino and in 1866, three years after its inauguration, the name 'Monte Carlo' – Ligurian for 'Mount Charles' in honour of the prince – was coined. To gamble or watch the poker-faced play, visit after 2pm (when a strict over-18s-only admission rule kicks in).

Monaco

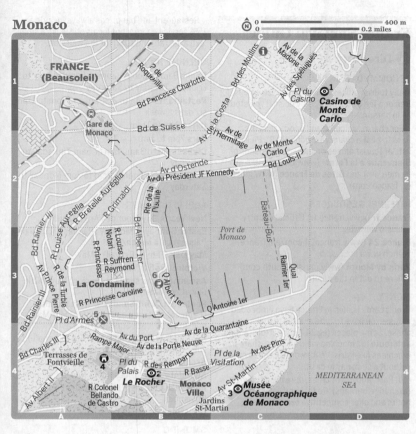

✖ Eating & Drinking

★ **Marché de la Condamine** FOOD COURT
(www.facebook.com/marche.condamine; 15 place
d'Armes; ⊘7am-3pm Mon-Sat, to 2pm Sun) For
tasty, excellent-value fare around shared
tables hit Monaco's fabulous market food
court, tucked beneath the arches behind the
open-air market stalls on place d'Armes.

Brasserie de Monaco MICROBREWERY
(☏97 98 51 20; www.brasseriedemonaco.com; 36
rte de la Piscine; ⊘noon-2pm) Having Monaco's
only microbrewery gives this ports de bar an
edge, and its organic lagers and ales seems
to pack the punters in. Inside it's all chrome,
steel and big-screen TVs, and live sports and
DJs keep the weekends extra busy.

❶ Information

Tourist Office (www.visitmonaco.com; 2a bd
des Moulins; ⊘9am-7pm Mon-Sat, 11am-1pm
Sun)

Monaco

◎ Top Sights
1 Casino de Monte Carlo	D1
2 Le Rocher	B4
3 Musée Océanographique de Monaco	C4

◎ Sights
4 Palais Princier de Monaco	A4

⊗ Eating
5 Marché de la Condamine	A3

⊜ Drinking & Nightlife
6 Brasserie de Monaco	B3

❶ Getting There & Away

Services run about every 20 minutes to Nice
(€3, 25 minutes); the last trains leave around
11pm.

France Survival Guide

Directory A–Z

ACCOMMODATION

Many tourist offices make room reservations, for free or a fee of €5; many only do so if you stop by in person.

For charm, welcome and good value, it's hard to beat a *chambre d'hôte* (B&B). Pick up lists at tourist offices or check the websites of **Bienvenue à la Ferme** (www.bienvenue-a-la-ferme-com) and **Gîtes de France** (www.gites-de-france.com).

INTERNET RESOURCES

France.fr (www.france.fr) Official country tourism website.

France 24 (www.france24.com/en/france) French news in English.

Paris by Mouth (www.parisbymouth.com) Where to eat in the capital.

MONEY

Credit cards issued in France have embedded chips – you have to type in a PIN to make a purchase. Some places (eg 24-hour petrol stations, autoroute toll machines and city bike-share pay machines like Paris' Vélib) won't accept a card without a chip; pay in cash.

In Paris and major cities, *bureaux de change* (exchange bureaus) are fast and easy, open long hours and offer competitive exchange rates.

ℹ️ PRICE RANGES

Price indicators for accommoation refer to the cost of a double hotel room with bathroom, excluding breakfast, in high season.

€ less than €90 (less than €130 in Paris)

€€ €90 to €190 (€130 to €250 in Paris)

€€€ more than €190 (more than €250 in Paris)

Price indicators for restaurants/eateries refer to the average cost of a two-course meal. Lunchtime *formules* (two courses) and *menus* (three courses) are a snip of the price of evening dining.

€ less than €20

€€ €20 to €40

€€€ more than €40

Restaurant and bar prices always include a 15% service charge, but locals still leave a small 'extra' tip (around 10%) for the waitstaff.

OPENING HOURS

Banks 9am to noon & 2pm to 5pm Monday to Friday or Tuesday to Saturday

Restaurants Noon to 2.30pm and 7pm to 11pm six days a week

Cafes 7am to 11pm

Bars 7pm to 1am

Clubs 10pm to 3am, 4am or 5am Thursday to Saturday

Shops 10am to noon & 2pm to 7pm Monday to Saturday

PUBLIC HOLIDAYS

New Year's Day (Jour de l'An) 1 January

Easter Sunday & Monday (Pâques & Lundi de Pâques) Late March/April

May Day (Fête du Travail) 1 May

Victoire 1945 8 May

Ascension Thursday (Ascension) May; 40th day after Easter

Pentecost/Whit Sunday & Whit Monday (Pentecôte & Lundi de Pentecôte) Mid-May to mid-June; seventh Sunday after Easter

Bastille Day/National Day (Fête Nationale) 14 July – *the* national holiday

Assumption Day (Assomption) 15 August

All Saints' Day (Toussaint) 1 November

Remembrance Day (L'onze Novembre) 11 November

Christmas (Noël) 25 December

SMOKING

Smoking is illegal in all indoor public spaces, including restaurants and pubs (though, of course, smokers still light up on the terraces outside).

TELEPHONE

➤ Area codes do not exist in France.

➤ The country code for France is ☏ 33. When calling France from abroad, drop the initial '0' from the 10-digit telephone number.

➤ To call abroad from France, use the international access code ☏ 00.

➤ Buy prepaid SIM cards from a French provider such as Orange, SFR, Bouygues and Free Mobile.

➤ French mobile telephone numbers begin with ☏ 06 or ☏ 07.

➤ Save up to 60% on the normal international rate by buying a prepaid Ticket Téléphone (phonecard) from tobacconists) or online at www.topengo.fr.

VISAS

For up-to-date details on visa requirements, check the **Ministry of Foreign Affairs** (Map p306; www.diplomatie.gouv.fr; 37 quai d'Orsay, 7e; M Assemblée Nationale).

ℹ Getting There & Away

AIR

International airports include the following; there are many smaller ones serving European destinations only.

Aéroport de Charles de Gaulle (p317)
Aéroport Marseille-Provence (p339)
Aéroport Nice Côte d'Azur (p344)

LAND

Car & Motorcycle

A right-hand-drive vehicle brought to France from the UK or Ireland must have deflectors affixed to the headlights to avoid dazzling oncoming traffic.

Departing from the UK, **Eurotunnel Le Shuttle** (☑ in France 08 10 63 03 04, in UK 08443 35 35 35; www.eurotunnel.com) trains whisk bicycles, motorcycles, cars and coaches in 35 minutes from Folkestone through the Channel Tunnel to Coquelles, 5km southwest of Calais. Shuttles run 24 hours a day, with up to three departures an hour during peak periods. The earlier you book, the less you pay. Fares for a car, including up to nine passengers, start at UK£23/€32.

Train

Rail services – including **Eurostar** (☑ in France 08 92 35 35 39, in UK 08432 186 186; www.eurostar.com) services to/from the UK – link France with virtually every country in Europe.

Book tickets and get information from **Rail Europe** (www.raileurope.com). In France ticketing is handled by **SNCF** (www.voyages-sncf.com); internet bookings are possible, but SNCF won't post tickets outside France.

SEA

Regular ferries travel to France from the UK, Ireland and Italy.

Brittany Ferries (www.brittany-ferries.co.uk) Links between England/Ireland and Brittany and Normandy.

P&O Ferries (www.poferries.com) Ferries between England and northern France

SNCM (www.sncm.fr) Ferries between France and Sardinia.

ℹ **DISCOUNT TICKETS**

The SNCF's most heavily discounted tickets are **Prem's**, available online, at ticket windows and from ticket machines: 100% Prem's are available from Thursday evening to Monday night, for last-minute travel that weekend; Saturday-return Prem's are valid for return travel on a Saturday; and three-month Prem's can be booked a maximum of 90 days in advance. Prem's are nonrefundable and nonchangeable.

Bons Plans fares, a grab bag of really cheap options, are advertised on the SNCF website (www.sncf.com) under Fares & Cards/Special Deals.

ℹ Getting Around

Transport in France is comfortable, quick, usually reliable and reasonably priced.

BICYCLE

The Loire Valley, Provence and Burgundy beg to be explored by two wheels and have dedicated cycling paths, some along canal towpaths or between fruit orchards and vineyards.

Online see **Voies Vertes** (www.voievertes.com).

BUS

Cheaper and slower than trains. Useful for more remote villages that aren't serviced by trains.

CAR & MOTORCYCLE

➡ Cars can be hired at airports and train stations. All vehicles driven in France must carry a high-visibility reflective safety vest (stored inside the vehicle, not in the trunk/boot), a reflective triangle, and a portable, single-use breathalyser kit.

➡ Drive on the right; be aware of France's potentially hazardous 'priority to the right' rule.

➡ Speed limits are 50km/h in built-up areas, 130km/h on motorways and 90km/h on other roads.

➡ Pay tolls (*péages*) to use motorways (*autoroutes*). For info on tolls, rest areas, traffic and weather, see www.autoroutes.fr.

➡ **Bison Futé** (www.bison-fute.equipement.gouv.fr) is an excellent source of information about traffic conditions.

TRAIN

Run by the state-owned SNCF, France's rail network is truly first-class, with extensive coverage of the country and frequent departures.

Check timetables on www.sncf.com.

SWITZERLAND

Geneva

POP 189,000

The whole world seems to be in Geneva, Switzerland's second city. The UN, the International Red Cross, the World Health Organization – 200-odd governmental and nongovernmental international organisations fill the city's plush hotels with big-name guests, who feast on an extraordinary choice of cuisine and help prop up the overload of banks, jewellers and chocolate shops for which Geneva is known.

◉ Sights

★ Jet d'Eau   FOUNTAIN

(Quai Gustave-Ador) When landing by plane, this lakeside fountain is the first dramatic glimpse you get of Geneva. The 140m-tall structure shoots up water with incredible force – 200km/h, 1360HP – to create the sky-high plume, kissed by a rainbow on sunny days. At any one time, 7 tonnes of water is in the air, much of which sprays spectators on the pier beneath. Two or three times a year it is illuminated pink, blue or another colour to mark a humanitarian occasion.

Jardin Anglais   GARDENS

(Quai du Général-Guisan) Before tramping up the hill, join the crowds getting snapped in front of the flower clock in Geneva's flowery waterfront garden, landscaped in 1854 on the site of an old lumber-handling port and merchant yard. The **Horloge Fleurie** (Flower Clock), Geneva's most photographed clock, is crafted from 6500 plants and has ticked since 1955 in the garden. Its second hand, 2.5m long, is claimed to be the world's longest.

★ Cathédrale St-Pierre   CATHEDRAL

(http://www.cathedrale-geneve.ch; Cour St-Pierre; towers adult/child Sfr5/2; ⊙9.30am-6.30pm Mon-Sat, noon-6.30pm Sun Jun-Sep, 10am-5.30pm Mon-Sat, noon-5.30pm Sun Oct-May) Begun in the 11th century, Geneva's cathedral is predominantly Gothic with an 18th-century neoclassical facade. Between 1536 and 1564 Protestant John Calvin preached here; see his seat in the north aisle. Inside the cathedral, 77 steps spiral up to the attic – a fascinating glimpse at its architectural construction – from where another 40 lead to the top of the panoramic northern and southern towers.

In summer, free carillon (5pm) and organ (6pm) concerts fill the cathedral and its surrounding square with soul.

Musée International de la Croix-Rouge et du Croissant-Rouge   MUSEUM

(International Red Cross & Red Crescent Museum; www.redcrossmuseum.ch; Av de la Paix 17; adult/child Sfr15/7; ⊙10am-6pm Tue-Sun Apr-Oct, to 5pm Nov-Mar) Compelling multimedia exhibits at this fascinatingmuseum trawl through atrocities perpetuated by humanity. The litany of war and nastiness, documented in films, photos, sculptures and soundtracks, is set against the noble aims of the organisation created by Geneva businessmen and philanthropists Henri Dunant and Henri Dufour in 1864. Excellent temporary exhibitions command an additional entrance fee. Take bus 8 from Gare de Cornavin to the Appia stop.

⌸ Sleeping

When checking in, be sure to get your free Public Transport Card – your ticket to unlimited city bus and tram travel for the duration of your stay.

★ Hôtel Bel'Esperance   HOTEL €

(☑022 818 37 37; www.hotel-bel-esperence.ch; Rue de la Vallée 1; s/d/tr/q from Sfr150/170/210/250; ⊙reception 7am-10pm; @🛜) This two-star hotel is extraordinary value. Rooms are quiet and cared for, those on the 1st floor share a kitchen, and there are fridges for guests to store picnic supplies – or sausages – in! Ride the lift to the 5th floor to flop on the wonderful flower-filled rooftop terrace, complete with barbecue that can be rented.

City Hostel   HOSTEL €

(☑022 901 15 00; www.cityhostel.ch; Rue de Ferrier 2; dm/s/d from Sfr33/65/89; ⊙reception 7.30am-

---

Geneva

noon & 1pm-midnight; P@��) This clean, well-organised hostel near the train station feels more like a hotel than a hostel. It does not serve breakfast but guests are welcome to make their own in the communal kitchen or nip to a neighbouring cafe.

✕ Eating

Geneva flaunts ethnic cuisines galore. If it's local and traditional you're after, dip into a cheese fondue or platter of pan-fried *filets de perche* (perch fillets). Find cafes serving decent food too in the Old Town and along the lakeside quays.

Geneva

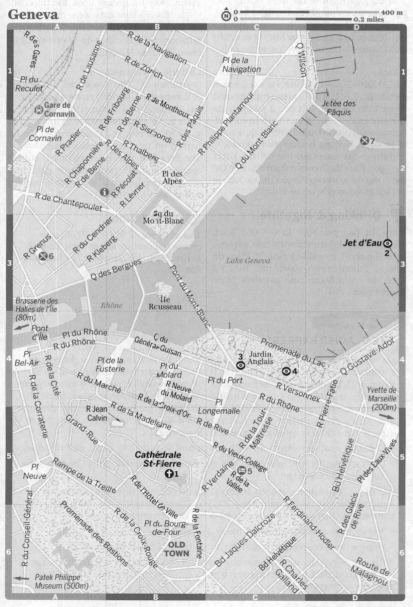

FRANCE, SWITZERLAND & AUSTRIA GENEVA

★ **Buvette des Bains** CAFETERIA €

(☑ 022 738 16 16; www.bains-des-paquis.ch; Quai du Mont-Blanc 30, Bains des Pâquis; mains Sfr14-20; ⊙7am-10.30pm) Meet Genevans at this earthy beach bar – rough and hip around the edges – at lakeside pool, Bains des Pâquis. Grab breakfast, a salad or the *plat du jour* (dish of the day), or dip into a *fondue au crémant* (Champagne fondue). Dining is self-service on trays and alfresco in summer. In summer pay Sfr2/1 per adult/child to access the canteen, inside the pub.

À Table FOOD TRUCK €

(☑ 022 731 68 57; www.a-table.ch; Place de Grenus 4; pasta Sfr18-22; ⊙11.30am-2pm Mon-Fri) A hip and nippy little number, this *bar à pâtes* (pasta bar) cooks delicious homemade pasta and, occasionally, risotto loaded with fresh, seasonal produce. Nothing is industrially produced and gluten-free eaters can dine well too. Eat at the *bijou* Place de Grenus restaurant or on the move thanks to its two Piaggio trucks that are parked at different spots each day.

 Drinking & Nightlife

Place du Bourg-de-Four in the Old Town and Carouge are strewn with cafe terraces, as is the short riverside length of Place du Rhône. Summertime waterfront bars on Quai du Mont-Blanc have priceless Mont Blanc views.

★ **Yvette de Marseille** BAR

(Rue Henri Blanvalet 13; ⊙5.30pm-midnight Mon & Tue, 5.30pm-1am Wed & Thu, 5.30pm-2am Fri, 6.30pm-2am Sat) No bar begs the question 'what's in the name?' more than this buzzy drinking hole. Urban and edgy, it occupies a mechanic's workshop once owned by Yvette. Note the garage door, the trap door in the floor where cars were repaired and the street number 13 (aka the departmental number of the Bouches-du-Rhône *département*, home to Marseille).

La Barje des Lavandières BAR

(www.labarje.ch; Promenade des Lavandières; ⊙11am-midnight Mon-Fri, noon-midnight Sat & Sun May-Sep) This summertime address is not a barge at all, but rather a vintage caravan with tin roof and candy-striped facade, parked on the grassy banks of the Rhône. The beer and music are plentiful, outside concerts and art performances pull huge crowds, and proceeds go towards helping young people in difficulty.

ℹ **Information**

Tourist Office (☑ 022 909 70 00; www.geneve-tourisme.ch; Rue du Mont-Blanc 18; ⊙10am-6pm Mon, 9am-6pm Tue-Sat, 10am-4pm Sun)

DON'T MISS

THE GLACIER EXPRESS

Marketed as the world's slowest express train, the **Glacier Express** (www.glacierexpress.ch; adult/child one-way St Moritz–Zermatt Sfr149/74.50, obligatory seat reservation summer/winter Sfr33/13, on-board 3-course lunch Sfr43; ⊙three trains daily May-Oct, one train daily mid-Dec–Feb) is one of Europe's mythical train journeys. It links two of Switzerland's oldest, glitziest mountain resorts – Zermatt (p355) and **St Moritz** (www.stmoritz.ch), 290km away in Graubünden in far eastern Switzerland. The Alpine scenery is truly magnificent in parts, but a ticket is not cheap. To avoid disappointment:

➡ Check the weather forecast. Beneath a china-blue sky is the *only* way to do this journey.

➡ Don't assume it's eight hours and 290km of hard-core mountain porn: views inside the 91 tunnels are non-existent.

➡ Opt for just a section of the trip: the best bit is the one-hour ride from Disentis to Andermatt across the **Oberalp Pass** (2033m). The celebrity six-arch, 65m-high **Landwasser Viaduct** dazzles during the 50km leg from Chur to Filisur.

➡ The southern side of the train has the best views.

➡ Skip the three-course lunch served on board; bring a Champagne picnic.

➡ Panoramic carriage windows can't be opened. If photography or video is the reason you're aboard, ditch the direct glamour train for (cheaper) regional express SBB trains along the same route.

ℹ️ Getting There & Away

AIR

Geneva Airport (www.gva.ch) is 4km from the centre.

TRAIN

International daily rail connections from **Gare de Cornavin** (Place de Cornavin) include Paris by TGV (3¼ hours) and Milan (four hours). Hourly connections run to most Swiss towns including Lausanne (Sfr21.80, 30 minutes), Bern (Sfr49, 1¾ hours) and Zürich (Sfr84, 2¾ hours).

ℹ️ Getting Around

TO/FROM THE AIRPORT

Getting from the airport is easy with regular trains into Gare de Cornavin (Sfr2, 10 minutes, half-hourly). Slower TPG bus 10 (www.tpg.ch; Sfr3) to Rive does the same 4km trip. A metered taxi costs Sfr35 to Sfr50.

BOAT

Yellow shuttle boats called Les Mouettes (Seagulls) cross the lake every 10 minutes between 7.30am and 6pm. Public-transport tickets from the machines at boat bays are valid.

PUBLIC TRANSPORT

Tickets for buses, trolley buses and trams run by TPG are sold at dispensers at stops and at the **TPG office** (www.tpg.ch; Rue de Montbrillant; ⏰7am-7pm Mon-Fri, 9am-6pm Sat) inside the train station. A one-hour ticket for multiple rides in the city costs Sfr3; a ticket valid for three stops in 30 minutes is Sfr2.

Lausanne

POP 130.400

In a fabulous location overlooking Lake Geneva, Lausanne is an enchanting beauty with several distinct personalities: the former fishing village of Ouchy, with its lakeside bustle; the Vieille Ville (Old Town), with charming cobblestone streets and covered staircases; and Flon, a warehouse district of bars and boutiques.

👁️ Sights

⭐ **Cathédrale de Notre Dame**   CATHEDRAL
(Place de la Cathédrale; ⏰9am-7pm Apr-Sep, to 5.30pm Oct-Mar) Lausanne's Gothic cathedral, Switzerland's finest, stands proudly at the heart of the Old Town. Raised in the 12th and 13th centuries on the site of earlier, humbler churches, it lacks the lightness of French Gothic buildings but is remarkable nonetheless. Pope Gregory X, in the pres-

---

WORTH A TRIP

LAVAUX WINE REGION

East of Lausanne, serried ranks of lush, pea-green vineyards stagger up the steep terraced slopes above Lake Geneva to form the Lavaux wine region – a Unesco World Heritage site. One-fifth of the Canton of Vaud's wine is produced on these steep, gravity-defying slopes.

Walking between vines and wine tasting are key reasons to explore the string of 14 villages beaded along this 40km stretch of fertile and wealthy shore. The **tourist office** (📞0848 86 84 84; www.montreux-vevey.com; Place de l'Eurovision; ⏰9am-6pm Mon-Fri, 9.30am-5pm Sat & Sun May-Sep, 9am-noon & 1-5.30pm Mon-Fri, 10am-2pm Sat & Sun Oct-Apr) in nearby Montreux (yes, of jazz-festival fame) is the best place to pick up detailed information and maps.

---

ence of Rudolph of Habsburg (the Holy Roman Emperor) and an impressive following of European cardinals and bishops, consecrated the church in 1275.

Free 40-minute guided tours run July through September.

Place de la Palud   SQUARE
In the heart of the Old Town, this 9th-century medieval market square – pretty as a picture – was originally bogland. For five centuries it has been home to the city government, now housed in the 17th-century **Hôtel de Ville** (town hall). A fountain pierces one end of the square, presided over by a brightly painted column topped by the allegorical figure of Justice, clutching scales and dressed in blue.

⭐ **Musée Olympique**   MUSEUM
(Olympic Museum; 📞021 621 65 11; www.olympic.org/museum; Quai d'Ouchy 1; adult/child Sfr18/10; ⏰9am-6pm daily May–mid-Oct, 10am-6pm Tue-Sun mid-Oct–Apr) Musée Olympique is easily Lausanne's most lavish museum and an essential stop for sports buffs (and kids). Its tiered landscaped gardens and site-specific sculptural are super stylish, as is the top-floor TOM Café with terrace and champion lake view. The state-of-the-art museum recounts the Olympic story from its inception to the present day through video, interactive displays, memorabilia and temporary themed exhibitions.

Lausanne

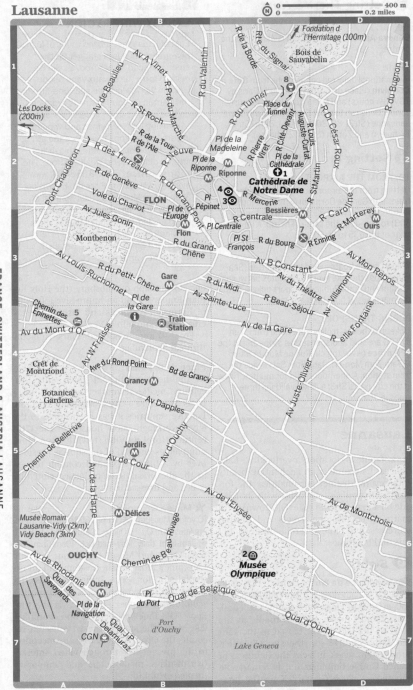

N

0   400 m
0   0.2 miles

Fondation d'
l'Hermitage (100m)

Bois de
Sauvabelin

Les Docks
(200m)

Av A Vinet

R du Valentin

R de la Borde

Rte du Signal

R du Bugnon

R St Roch

R Pré-du-Marché

R du Tunnel

Place du
Tunnel

8

R-Dr-César-Roux

Av de Beaulieu

R de la Tour

R de l'Ale

6

Pl de la
Madeleine

R Pierre Viret

R Cité-Devant

R.Louis-Auguste Curtat

Pl de la
Cathédrale

R des Terreaux

R Neuve

Pl de la
Riponne

Riponne

4

3

Cathédrale de
Notre Dame

1

St-Martin

R de Genève

R du Grand Pont

Pl
Pépinet

R Mercerie

R Caroline

Voie du Chariot

FLON

Pl de
l'Europe

R Centrale

Bessières

R Marterey

Pont Chauderon

Av Jules Gonin

Flon

Pl Centrale

7

R Enning

Ours

Montbenon

R du Grand-
Chêne

Pl St
François

R du Bourg

Av Mon Repos

Av Louis-Ruchonnet

R du Petit-Chêne

Gare

R du Midi

Av B Constant

Av du Théâtre

Av -Villamont

Pl de
la Gare

Av Sainte-Luce

R Beau-Séjour

R elle Fontaine

Chemin des
épinettes

5

Train
Station

Av de la Gare

Av Juste-Olivier

Av du Mont d'Or

Av W Fraisse

Ave du Rond Point

Bd de Grancy

Crêt de
Montriond

Grancy

Botanical
Gardens

Av Dapples

Chemin de Bellerive

Jordils

Av de Cour

Av d'Ouchy

Av de l'Élysée

Av de Montchoisi

Av de la Harpe

Musée Romain
Lausanne-Vidy (2km);
Vidy Beach (3km)

Délices

OUCHY

Chemin de Beau-Rivage

2

Musée
Olympique

Av de Rhodanie

Ouchy

Quai des Savoyards

Pl de la
Navigation

Pl
du Port

Quai de Belgique

Quai d'Ouchy

Quai J-P
Delamuraz

CGN

Port
d'Ouchy

Lake Geneva

Lausanne

🛏 Sleeping

Pick up a Lausanne Transport Card when you check in – it gives you unlimited use of public transport for the duration of your stay.

Lausanne Guest House　HOSTEL €
(☑ 021 601 80 00; www.lausanne-guesthouse.ch; Chemin des Épinettes 4; dm/s/d/q from Sfr35/68/80/148; ⊙ reception 7.30am-noon & 3-10pm; P@🛜) An attractive mansion converted into quality backpacking accommodation near the train station. Many rooms have lake views and you can hang out in the garden or on the terrace. There's a 24-hour laundry and room to leave your bike. Some of the building's energy is solar.

🍴 Eating & Drinking

Where there's a bridge, there's a bar. At least that's how it works in artsy Lausanne where the monumental arches of its bridges shelter the city's most happening summertime bars.

⭐ **Holy Cow**　BURGERS €
(www.holycow.ch; Rue Cheneau-de-Bourg 17; burger with chips & drink Sfr16-20; ⊙ 11am-10pm Mon & Tue, to 11pm Wed-Sat; 🍴) Holy Cow is a Lausanne success story, with branches in Geneva, Zürich and other Swiss cities; its burgers (beef, chicken or vegie) feature local ingredients, creative toppings and witty names. Grab an artisanal beer, sit at a shared wooden table, and wait for your burger and fab fries to arrive in a straw basket. A second outlet can be found at **Rue des Terreaux** (Rue des Terreaux 10; ⊙ 11am-11pm Mon-Sat).

Caffè Bellini　BAR
(☑ 021 351 24 40; www.caffebellini.ch; Rue de la Barre 5; ⊙ 10am-1am Mon-Thu, to 2am Fri & Sat) Lausanne's most charming terrace is tucked away in the Old Town and is *the* spot for summertime drinks, with fairy lights, a cool crowd and a retro-influenced interior. Antipasto platters and pizzas are good, and service chipper but occasionally forgetful. Call to reserve your spot.

ⓘ Information

Tourist Office (☑ 021 613 73 73; www.lausanne-tourisme.ch; Place de la Gare 9; ⊙ 9am-7pm)

ⓘ Getting There & Away

BOAT
CGN (Compagnie Générale de Navigation; www.cgn.ch) runs passenger boats from Ouchy to destinations around Lake Geneva (including France) including Montreux (Sfr26, 1½ hours, up to six daily) and Geneva (Sfr43, 3½ to four hours, up to five daily).

TRAIN
Travel by train to/from Geneva (Sfr22.40, 33 to 50 minutes, up to six hourly), Geneva Airport (Sfr27, 45 minutes, up to four hourly) and Bern (Sfr33, 70 minutes, one or two an hour).

Valais

This is Matterhorn country, an intoxicating land that seduces the toughest of critics with its endless panoramic vistas and breathtaking views. Switzerland's 10 highest mountains rise to the sky here, while snow fiends get high in top European resort Zermatt.

Zermatt
POP 6000

Since the mid-19th century, Zermatt has starred among Switzerland's glitziest resorts. Today it attracts intrepid mountaineers and hikers, skiers and boarders, all spellbound by the scenery and the Matterhorn (4478m) – an unfathomable monolith synonymous with Switzerland that you simply can't quite stop looking at.

◉ Sights & Activities

⭐ **Matterhorn Glacier Paradise**　CABLE CAR
(www.matterhornparadise.ch; adult/child return Sfr100/50; ⊙ 8.30am-4.20pm) Views from Zermatt's cable cars are all remarkable, but

the Matterhorn Glacier Paradise is the icing on the cake. Ride Europe's highest-altitude cable car to 3883m and gawp at 14 glaciers and 38 mountain peaks over 4000m from the **Panoramic Platform** (only open in good weather). Don't miss the **Glacier Palace**, an ice palace complete with glittering ice sculptures and an ice slide to swoosh down bum first. End with some exhilarating **snow tubing** outside in the snowy surrounds.

★**Gornergratbahn** RAILWAY
(www.gornergrat.ch; Bahnhofplatz 7; adult/child one way Sfr45/22.50; ☉7am-9.50pm) Europe's highest cogwheel railway has climbed through picture-postcard scenery to **Gornergrat** (3089m) – a 30-minute journey – since 1898. Sit on the right-hand side of the little red train to gawp at the Matterhorn. Tickets allow you to get on and off en route; there are restaurants at Riffelalp (2211m) and Riffelberg (2582m). In summer an extra train runs once a week at sunrise and sunset – the most spectacular trips of all.

★**Matterhorn Museum** MUSEUM
(☏027 967 41 00; www.matterhornmuseum.ch; Kirchplatz; adult/child Sfr10/5; ☉11am-6pm Jul-Sep, 3-6pm Oct–mid-Dec, 3-7pm mid-Dec–Mar, 2-6pm Apr-Jun) This crystalline, state-of-the-art museum provides fascinating insight into Valaisian village life, mountaineering, the dawn of tourism in Zermatt and the lives the Matterhorn has claimed. Short films portray the first successful ascent of the Matterhorn on 13 July 1865 led by Edward Whymper, a feat marred by tragedy on the descent when four team members crashed to their deaths in a 1200m fall down the North Wall. The infamous rope that broke is exhibited. No credit cards.

🍴 Sleeping & Eating

★**Hotel Bahnhof** HOTEL€
(☏027 967 24 06; www.hotelbahnhof.com; Bahnhofstrasse; dm/s/d/q from Sfr35/65/100/195; ☉reception 8-11.30am & 4-7pm, hotel closed May, Oct & Nov; ☜) Opposite the train station, these five-star budget digs have comfy beds, spotless bathrooms and family-perfect rooms for four. Dorms (Sfr5 liner obligatory) are cosy and there's a stylish lounge with armchairs to flop in and books to read. No breakfast, but feel free to prepare your own in the snazzy, open-plan kitchen.

★**Snowboat** INTERNATIONAL€
(☏027 967 43 33; www.snowboat.ch; Vispastrasse 20; mains Sfr26-49; ☉2.30pm-midnight) This hybrid eating-drinking (food from 6pm), riverside address with marigold-yellow deckchairs sprawled across its rooftop sun terrace, is a blessing. When fondue tires, head here for barbecue-sizzled burgers, veggie mains, super-power creative salads (the Omega 3 buster is a favourite) and great cocktails. The vibe? 100% fun and funky.

ℹ Information

Tourist Office (☏027 966 81 00; www.zermatt.ch; Bahnhofplatz 5; ☉8.30am-6pm; ☜)

ℹ Getting There & Around

Zermatt is car-free. Park in Täsch and ride the Zermatt Shuttle train (adult/child Sfr8.20/4.10, 12 minutes, every 20 minutes) the last 5km up to Zermatt. From Täsch there are trains roughly every 20 minutes to/from Brig (Sfr33, 1½ hours), a major rail hub.

Mittelland & Bernese Oberland

At first glance it may seem funny that this flat, unassuming 'middle ground', as its straight-talking name states, should have Switzerland's delightfully languid and laid-back capital at its heart. Moving south, nature works on an epic scale in the Bernese Oberland where the Swiss Alps make hearts skip a beat.

Bern

POP 127,500
One of the planet's most underrated capitals, riverside Bern is a medieval and modern city, with the genteel old soul of a Renaissance man and the heart of a high-flying 21st-century gal. Its 15th-century Old Town, with striking Gothic cathedral, is definitely worthy of its Unesco World Heritage Site status.

◉ Sights & Activities

★**Zytglogge** CLOCK TOWER
(Marktgasse) Bern's most famous Old Town sight, this ornate clock tower once formed part of the city's western gate (1191–1256). Crowds congregate to watch its revolving figures twirl at four minutes before the hour, after which the chimes begin. Tours enter

the tower to see the clock mechanism from May to October; contact the tourist office for details. The clock tower supposedly helped Albert Einstein hone his special theory of relativity, developed while working as a patent clerk in Bern.

⭐ **Historisches Museum Bern** MUSEUM
(Bern Historical Museum; ☑ 031 350 77 11; www.bhm.ch; Helvetiaplatz 5; adult/child Sfr13/4, incl Einstein Museum Sfr18/8; ⊘ 10am-5pm Tue-Sun) Tapestries, diptychs and other treasures vividly illustrate Bernese history from the Stone Age to the 20th century in this marvellous castle-like edifice, the best of several museums surrounding Helvetiaplatz. The highlight for many is the 2nd floor, devoted to a superb permanent exhibition on Einstein.

⭐ **Zentrum Paul Klee** MUSEUM
(☑ 031 359 01 01; www.zpk.org; Monument im Fruchtland 3; adult/child Sfr24/7; ⊘ 10am-5pm Tue-Sun) Bern's answer to the Guggenheim, Renzo Piano's architecturally bold 150m-long wave-like edifice houses an exhibition space that showcases rotating works from Paul Klee's prodigious and often playful career. Interactive computer displays and audioguides help interpret the Swiss-born artist's work. Next door, the fun-packed **Kindermuseum Creaviva** (☑ 031 359 01 61; www.creaviva-zpk.org; ⊘ 10am-5pm Tue-Sun) FREE lets kids experiment with hands-on art exhibits or create original artwork with the atelier's materials during the weekend **Five Franc Studio** (www.creaviva-zpk.org/5-franc-studio; Sfr5; ⊘ 10am-4.30pm Sat & Sun).

Bus 12 runs from Bubenbergplatz direct to the museum.

🛏 Sleeping & Eating

Look for interesting cafes and bistros scattered amid the arcades on Old Town streets including Zeughausgasse, Rathausgasse, Marktgasse and Kramgasse.

Hotel Landhaus HOTEL €
(☑ 031 348 03 05; www.landhausbern.ch; Altenbergstrasse 4; dm Sfr38, s Sfr80-130, d Sfr120-180, t/q Sfr200/220; P❤@🛜) Fronted by the river and Old Town spires, this well-run boho hotel offers a mix of stylish six-bed dorms, family rooms and doubles. Its buzzing ground-floor cafe and terrace attracts a cheery crowd. Breakfast (included with private rooms) costs Sfr8 extra for dorm-dwellers.

ℹ Information

Tourist Office (☑ 031 328 12 12; www.bern.com; Bahnhoftplatz 10a; ⊘ 9am-7pm Mon-Sat, to 6pm Sun)

ℹ Getting There & Away

Trains run at least hourly to Geneva (Sfr50, 1¾ hours), Basel (Sfr40, 55 minutes), Interlaken Ost (Sfr28, 55 minutes) and Zürich (Sfr50, one to 1¼ hours).

Interlaken

POP 5700 / ELEV 570M

Once Interlaken made the Victorians swoon with mountain vistas from the chandelier-lit confines of grand hotels; today it makes daredevils scream with adrenalin-loaded adventures. Straddling the glittering Lakes Thun and Brienz and dazzled by the pearly whites of Eiger, Mönch and Jungfrau, scenery here is mind-blowing.

👁 Sights & Activities

Interlaken is Switzerland's adventure-sports hub. Sample prices: Sfr120 for rafting or canyoning, Sfr140 for hydro-speeding, Sfr130 to Sfr180 for bungee or canyon jumping, Sfr170 for tandem paragliding, Sfr180 for ice climbing, Sfr220 for hang-gliding and Sfr430 for skydiving. A half-day mountain-bike tour will set you back around Sfr25.

Harder Kulm MOUNTAIN
(www.harderkulm.ch) For far-reaching views to the 4000m giants, ride the **funicular** (adult/child return Sfr30/15) to 1322m Harder Kulm. Many hiking paths begin here, and the vertigo-free can enjoy the panorama from the **Zweiseensteg** (Two Lake Bridge) jutting out above the valley. The wildlife park near the valley station is home to Alpine critters, including marmots and ibex.

🛏 Sleeping & Eating

⭐ **Rugenpark B&B** B&B €
(☑ 033 822 36 61; www.rugenpark.ch; Rugenparkstrasse 19; s Sfr87, d Sfr100-130, tr Sfr126-165, q Sfr154-200; P🛜) Chris and Ursula have worked magic to transform this into an incredibly sweet B&B. Rooms remain humble, but the place is spotless and has been enlivened with colourful butterflies, beads and travel trinkets. You'll feel right at home in the shared kitchen and garden, and your knowledgeable hosts are always ready to help with local tips.

DON'T MISS

JUNGFRAUJOCH

Jungfraujoch (3471m) is a once-in-a-lifetime trip and there's good reason why two million people a year visit Europe's highest train station: the icy wilderness of swirling glaciers and 4000m turrets that unfolds at the top is staggeringly beautiful. The highlight is the 23km-long Aletsch Glacier.

Clear good weather is essential; check www.jungfrau.ch or call ☑ 033 828 79 31, and don't forget warm clothing, sunglasses and sunscreen.

From Interlaken Ost, the journey time is 2½ hours each way (Sfr204.40 return, discounts with rail passes). The last train back sets off at 5.45pm in summer and 4.45pm in winter. However, from May to October there's a cheaper Good Morning Ticket costing Sfr145 if you take the first train (which departs at 6.35am from Interlaken Ost) and leave the summit by 1pm; buy it online at https://shop.jungfrau.ch.

Backpackers Villa Sonnenhof HOSTEL €
(☑ 033 826 71 71; www.villa.ch; Alpenstrasse 16; dm from Sfr34.50, s/d/tr/q Sfr87/130/165/200; P@⑤) Sonnenhof is a slick combination of ultramodern chalet and elegant art nouveau villa. Dorms are immaculate, and some have balconies with Jungfrau views. There's also a relaxed lounge, a well-equipped kitchen, a kids' playroom and a leafy garden for mountain gazing. Special family rates are available.

★ **WineArt** MEDITERRANEAN €€
(☑ 033 823 73 74; www.wineart.ch; Jungfraustrasse 46; mains Sfr25-60, 4-course menu Sfr75; ⊙4pm-12.30am Mon-Sat) This is a delightful wine bar, lounge, restaurant and deli rolled into one. High ceilings, chandeliers and wood floors create a slick, elegant backdrop for season-driven Mediterranean food. Pair one of 600 wines with dishes as simple as buffalo mozzarella and rocket salad and corn-fed chicken with honey-glazed vegetables – quality and flavour is second to none.

① Information

Tourist Office (☑ 033 826 53 00; www.interlakentourism.ch; Höheweg 37; ⊙8am-7pm Mon-Fri, to 5pm Sat, 10am-4pm Sun Jul & Aug, shorter hours Sep-Jun)

① Getting There & Away

There are two train stations: **Interlaken West** is slightly closer to the centre and is a stop for trains to Bern (Sfr28, one hour). **Interlaken Ost** is the rail hub for all lines, including the scenic ones up into the Jungfrau region and the lovely GoldenPass Line to Lucerne (Sfr32, two hours).

Grindelwald

POP 3800 / ELEV 1034M

Grindelwald's sublime natural assets are film-set stuff – the chiselled features of Eiger north face, the glinting tongues of Oberer and Unterer Glaciers and the crown-like peak of Wetterhorn will make you stare, swoon and lunge for your camera. Skiers and hikers cottoned onto its charms in the late 19th century and it's lost none of its appeal, with geranium-studded Alpine chalets and verdant pastures set against an Oscar-worthy backdrop.

🏃 Activities

★ **Kleine Scheidegg Walk** HIKING
One of the region's most stunning day hikes is this 15km trek from Grindelwald Grund to Wengen via Kleine Scheidegg, which heads up through wildflower-freckled meadows to skirt below the Eiger's north face and reach Kleine Scheidegg, granting arresting views of the 'Big Three'. Allow about 5½ to six hours. The best map is SAW *1:50,000 Interlaken*.

Grindelwald Sports ADVENTURE SPORTS
(☑ 033 854 12 80; www.grindelwaldsports.ch; Dorfstrasse 103; ⊙8.30am-6.30pm, closed Sat & Sun in low season) Opposite the tourist office, this outfit arranges mountain climbing, ski and snowboard instruction, canyon jumping and glacier bungee jumping at the Gletscherschlucht. It also houses a cosy cafe and sells walking guides.

🛏 Sleeping & Eating

Mountain Hostel HOSTEL €
(☑ 033 854 38 38; www.mountainhostel.ch; Grundstrasse 58; dm Sfr35-39, d Sfr98; P⑤) Near Männlichen cable-car station, this is an ideal base for sports junkies, with well-kept dorms and a helpful crew. There's a beer garden, ski storage, TV lounge and mountain and e-bike rental. Take at least one soak in the glorious hot tub, glass of prosecco in hand.

★ **Cafe 3692** CAFE €
(☑ 033 853 16 54; www.cafe3692.ch; Terrassenweg 61; snacks & light meals Sfr7-25; ⊙8.30am-

6pm Sun-Tue, 8.30am-midnight Fri & Sat) Run by dream duo Myriam and Bruno, Cafe 3692 is a delight. Bruno is a talented carpenter and has let his imagination run riot – a gnarled apple tree is an eye-catching artwork, a minecart trolley cleverly transforms into a grill, the ceiling is a wave of woodwork. Garden herbs and Grindelwald-sourced ingredients are knocked up into tasty day specials.

ℹ️ Information

Tourist Office (☎ 033 854 12 12; www.grindelwald.ch; Dorfstrasse 110; ⊙ 8am-noon & 1.30-6pm Mon-Fri, 9am-noon & 1.30-5pm Sat & Sun; 📶)

ℹ️ Getting There & Away

Hourly trains depart for Grindelwald (Sfr11) from Interlaken Ost station; sit in the back half of the train.

Lucerne

POP 79,500 / ELEV 435M

Recipe for a gorgeous Swiss city: take a cobalt lake ringed by mountains of myth, add a well-preserved medieval Altstadt (Old Town) and a reputation for making beautiful music, then sprinkle with covered bridges, sunny plazas, candy-coloured houses and waterfront promenades. Lucerne in central Switzerland is stunning, and deservedly popular since the likes of Goethe, Queen Victoria and Wagner savoured her views in the 19th century.

⦿ Sights & Activities

Lake Lucerne boat trips depart from the quays around Bahnhofplatz and Europaplatz.

Old Town   HISTORIC SITE
(Altstadt) Your first port of call should be the medieval Old Town, with its ancient rampart walls and towers, 15th-century buildings with painted facades and the two much-photographed covered bridges. **Kapellbrücke** (Chapel Bridge), dating from 1333, is Lucerne's best-known landmark. It's famous for its distinctive water tower and the spectacular 1993 fire that nearly destroyed it. Though it has been rebuilt, fire damage is still obvious in the 17th-century pictorial panels under the roof.

★ Museum Sammlung Rosengart   MUSEUM
(☎ 041 220 16 60; www.rosengart.ch; Pilatusstrasse 10; adult/child Sfr18/10; ⊙ 10am-6pm Apr-Oct, 11am-5pm Nov-Mar) Lucerne's block-buster cultural attraction is the Sammlung Rosengart, occupying a graceful neoclassical pile. It showcases the outstanding stash of Angela Rosengart, a Swiss art dealer and close friend of Picasso. Alongside works by the great Spanish master are paintings and sketches by Cézanne, Klee, Kandinsky, Miró, Matisse and Monet. Standouts include Joan Miró's electric-blue *Dancer II* (1925) and Paul Klee's childlike *X-chen* (1938).

🛏️ Sleeping & Eating

Backpackers Lucerne   HOSTEL €
(☎ 041 360 04 20; www.backpackerslucerne.ch; Alpenquai 42; dm/d/tr Sfr33/84/111; ⊙ reception 7-10am & 4-11pm; @📶) Could this be backpacker heaven? Just opposite the lake, this is a soulful place to crash with art-slung walls, bubbly staff, a well-equipped kitchen and immaculate dorms with balconies. It's a 15-minute walk southeast of the station. There's no breakfast, but guests have kitchen access.

★ Wirtshaus Galliker   SWISS €€
(☎ 041 240 10 01; Schützenstrasse 1; mains Sfr21-51; ⊙ 9.30am-11.45pm Tue-Sat) Passionately run by the Galliker family for over four generations, this old-style, wood-panelled tavern attracts a lively bunch of regulars. Motherly waitresses dish up Lucerne soul food (rösti, *chögalipaschtetli* and the like) that is batten-the-hatches filling.

ℹ️ Information

Tourist Office (☎ 041 227 17 17; www.luzern.com; Zentralstrasse 5; ⊙ 8.30am-7pm Mon-Fri, 9am-7pm Sat, 9am-5pm Sun May-Oct, shorter hours Nov-Apr)

ℹ️ KIP WITH THE COWS

A unique way to experience life on a Swiss farm is Switzerland's **Aventure sur la paille/Schlaf im Stroh** (Agrotourismus Schweiz; ☎ 031 359 50 30; www.schlaf-im-stroh.ch) – the ultimate roll in the hay. Swiss farmers charge travellers Sfr20 to Sfr30 per adult and Sfr10 to Sfr20 per child under 15 to sleep on straw in their hay barns. Guests need their own sleeping bags and – strongly advisable – pocket torch. Nightly rates include a farmhouse breakfast; a morning shower and evening meal are usually available for an extra Sfr2 and Sfr20 to Sfr30, respectively.

---

❶ Getting There & Away

Frequent trains connect Lucerne to Interlaken Ost (Sfr32, 1¾ hours), Bern (Sfr35, one hour), Lugano (Sfr60, 2½ hours) and Zürich (Sfr25, 45 to 55 minutes).

Basel

POP 165,566

Tucked up against the French and German borders in Switzerland's northwest corner, Basel straddles the majestic Rhine. The town is home to art galleries, 30-odd museums and avant-garde architecture, and it boasts an enchanting old town centre.

◉ Sights

Old Town   AREA

(Altstadt) Begin exploring Basel's delightful medieval Old Town in **Marktplatz**, dominated by the astonishingly vivid red facade of the 16th-century **Rathaus** (Town Hall). From here, climb 400m west along Spalenberg through the former artisans' district to the 600-year-old **Spalentor** city gate, one of only three to survive the walls' demolition in 1866. Along the way, linger in captivating lanes such as Spalenberg, Heuberg and Leonhardsberg, lined by impeccably maintained, centuries-old houses.

★ Fondation Beyeler   MUSEUM

(☑ 061 645 97 00; www.fondationbeyeler.ch; Baselstrasse 101, Riehen; adult/child Sfr25/6; ☺10am-6pm, to 8pm Wed) This astounding private turned public collection, assembled by former art dealers Hildy and Ernst Beyeler, is housed in a long, low, light-filled, open-plan building designed by Italian architect Renzo Piano. The varied exhibits juxtapose 19th- and 20th-century works by Picasso and Rothko against sculptures by Miró and Max Ernst and tribal figures from Oceania. Take tram 6 to Riehen from Barfüsserplatz or Marktplatz.

---

❶ BASEL CARD

The good-value **BaselCard** (24/48/72hr Sfr20/27/35) gets you half-price tickets to all museums within the city limits, plus a free city walking tour and ferry crossing, and free admission to Basel Zoo (www.zoobasel.ch).

★ Museum Jean Tinguely   MUSEUM

(☑ 061 681 93 20; www.tinguely.ch; Paul Sacher-Anlage 2; adult/child Sfr18/free; ☺11am-6pm Tue-Sun) Built by leading Ticino architect Mario Botta, this museum showcases the playful, mischievous and downright wacky artistic concoctions of sculptor turned mad scientist Jean Tinguely. Push-buttons next to some of Tinguely's 'kinetic' sculptures allow visitors to set them in motion. It's great fun to watch them rattle, shake and twirl, with springs, feathers and wheels radiating at every angle, or to hear the haunting musical sounds produced by the gigantic *Méta-Harmonies* on the upper floor. Catch bus 31 from Claraplatz.

🛌 Sleeping & Eating

When checking in, ask for your 'mobility ticket', which entitles all Basel hotel guests to free use of public transport.

★ SYHA Basel St Alban
Youth Hostel   HOSTEL €

(☑ 061 272 05 72; www.youthhostel.ch; St Alban-Kirchrain 10; dm Sfr42, s Sfr97-120, d Sfr132; 🛜) Designed by Basel-based architects Buchner & Bründler, this swank modern hostel in a very pleasant neighbourhood is flanked by tree-shaded squares and a rushing creek. It's only a stone's throw from the Rhine, and 15 minutes on foot from the SBB Bahnhof (or take tram 2 to Kunstmuseum and walk five minutes downhill).

Druck Punkt   BISTRO €

(☑ 061 261 50 22; St Johanns Vorstadt 19; mains Sfr15-30; ☺noon-2pm & 6.30-10pm Mon-Fri, 6.30-10pm Sat) This converted print shop makes an unpretentious bistro, with chalky walls and heavy wooden tables. Filling meals, including a super salad (Sfr19), come at affordable prices.

❶ Information

Basel Tourismus (☑ 061 268 68 68; www.basel.com) Branches at the train station SBB Bahnhof (☺8-6pm Mon-Fri, 9am-5pm Sat, 9am-3pm Sun) and in town (Steinenberg 14; ☺9am-6.30pm Mon-Fri, to 5pm Sat, 10am-3pm Sun).

❶ Getting There & Away

Basel has two main train stations: Swiss/French train station **SBB Bahnhof** to the south, and the German train station **BBF Bahnhof** in the north.

RHEINFALL

Ensnared in wispy spray, the thunderous Rheinfall in Schloss Laufen am Rheinfall might not give Niagara much competition in height (23m), width (150m) or even flow of water (700 cu metre per second in summer), but Europe's largest plain waterfall is stunning nonetheless. Trails thread up and along its shore, with viewpoints providing abundant photo ops. Or ride the panoramic lift down to the Känzeli viewing platform at neighbouring medieval castle, **Schloss Laufen** (www.schlosslaufen.ch; adult/child Sfr5/3.50; ⊘8am-7pm Jun-Aug, shorter hours Sep-May), to enjoy the full-on crash-bang spectacle of the falls. For an above-the-treetops perspective of the falls, hit **Adventure Park** (www.ap-rheinfall. ch; adult/child Sfr40/26; ⊘10am-7pm Apr Oct), one of Switzerland's biggest rope parks, with routes graded according to difficulty. From Schloss Laufen am Rheinfall train station, walk up the hill to the falls and castle.

Two or three trains an hour run from SBB Bahnhof to Geneva (Sfr75, 2¾ hours). At least four, mostly direct, leave every hour for Zürich (Sfr33, 55 minutes to 1¼ hours). There's also fast TGV service to Paris (Sfr158, three hours) every other hour.

Zürich

POP 380,800

Zürich, Switzerland's largest city, is an enigma. A savvy financial centre with the densest public transport system in the world, it also has a gritty, postindustrial edge that always surprises and an evocative Old Town, not to mention a lovely lakeside location.

◉ Sights & Activities

The city spreads around the northwest end of Zürichsee (Lake Zürich), from where the Limmat River runs further north still, splitting the medieval city centre in two.

Old Town   HISTORIC SITE

Explore the cobbled streets of the pedestrian Old Town lining both sides of the river. The bank vaults beneath **Bahnhofstrasse**, the city's most elegant street, are said to be crammed with gold and silver. Indulge in affluent Züricher-watching and ogle at the luxury shops selling watches, clocks, chocolates, furs, porcelain and fashion labels galore.

★ Fraumünster   CATHEDRAL

(www.fraumuenster.ch; Münsterhof; ⊘10am-6pm Mar-Oct, to 4pm Nov-Dec, to 5pm Jan & Feb) The 13th-century cathedral is renowned for its stunning, distinctive stained-glass windows, designed by the Russian-Jewish master Marc Chagall (1887–1985). He did a series of

five windows in the choir stalls in 1971 and the rose window in the southern transept in 1978. The rose window in the northern transept was created by Augusto Giacometti in 1945.

★ Kunsthaus   MUSEUM

(☑044 253 84 84; www.kunsthaus.ch; Heimplatz 1; adult/child Sfr15/free, Wed free; ⊘10am-8pm Wed & Thu, to 6pm Tue & Fri-Sun) Zürich's impressive fine-arts gallery boasts a rich collection of largely European art. It stretches from the Middle Ages through a mix of Old Masters to Alberto Giacometti stick figures, Monet and Van Gogh masterpieces, Rodin sculptures, and other 19th- and 20th-century art. Swiss Rail and Museum Passes don't provide free admission but the ZürichCard does.

Letten   SWIMMING

(☑044 362 92 00; Lettensteg 10) **FREE** North of the train station on the east bank of the Limmat (just south of Kornhausbrücke), this is where Züri-West trendsetters swim, dive off bridges, skateboard, play volleyball, or just drink at the riverside bars and chat on the grass and concrete steps.

⌸ Sleeping

Finding a room on the weekend of the Street Parade is tough and prices skyrocket.

DON'T MISS

STREET PARADE

This techno celebration (www.streetparade.com) in the middle of August has established itself as one of Europe's largest and wildest street parties since its first festive outing in 1992.

FRANCE, SWITZERLAND & AUSTRIA ZÜRICH

SYHA Hostel   HOSTEL €

(☑ 043 399 78 00; www.youthhostel.ch; Mutschellenstrasse 114; dm Sfr43-49, s/d Sfr120/144; @ 🛜) A bulbous, Band-Aid-pink 1960s landmark houses this busy hostel with 24-hour reception, dining hall, sparkling modern bathrooms and dependable wi-fi in the downstairs lounge. The included breakfast features miso soup and rice alongside all the Swiss standards. It's about 20 minutes south of the Hauptbahnhof. Take tram 7 to Morgental, or the S-Bahn to Wollishofen, then walk five minutes.

Kafischnaps   HOTEL €

(☑ 043 538 81 16; www.kafischnaps.ch; Kornhausstrasse 57; r Sfr88-118) Set in a one-time butcher's shop, this cool, bustling neighbourhood cafe has a collection of five cheerful little rooms upstairs, each named and decorated after a fruit-based liquor. Book ahead online; they fill up fast. The bar (8am or 9am to midnight daily) is grand for a coffee, beer or brunch. Take tram 11 or 14 to Schaffhauserplatz.

✗ Eating & Drinking

The narrow streets of the Niederdorf quarter on the river's east bank are crammed with restaurants, bars and shops. The bulk of the more animated drinking dens are in Züri-West, especially along Langstrasse in Kreis 4 and Hardstrasse in Kreis 5.

★ Haus Hiltl   VEGETARIAN €

(☑ 044 227 70 00; www.hiltl.ch; Sihlstrasse 28; per 100g take-away/cafe/restaurant Sfr3.50/4.50/5.50; ☺ 6am-midnight Mon-Sat, 8am-midnight Sun; 🍴) Certified by Guinness World Records as the oldest vegetarian restaurant in the world (established 1898), Hiltl proffers an astounding smorgasbord of meatless delights, from Indian and Thai curries to Mediterranean grilled veggies to salads and desserts. Browse to your heart's content, fill your plate and weigh it, then choose a seat

in the informal cafe or the spiffier adjoining restaurant (economical take-away service is also available).

★ Alpenrose   SWISS €€

(☑ 044 271 39 19; Fabrikstrasse 12; mains Sfr25-45; ☺ 11am-midnight Wed-Fri, 6.15pm-midnight Sat, 6.15-11pm Sun) With its timber-clad walls, 'No Polka Dancing' warning and multiregional Swiss cuisine, the Alpenrose exudes cosy charm. Specialities include Ticinese risotto and *Pizokel,* a savoury kind of *Spätzli* from Graubünden – as proudly noted on the menu, more than 20,000kg of the stuff has been served over the past 20 years! Save room for creamy cognac parfait and other scrumptious desserts.

★ Frau Gerolds Garten   BAR

(www.fraugerold.ch; Geroldstrasse 23/23a; ☺ bar-restaurant 11am-midnight Mon-Sat, noon-10pm Sun Apr-Sep, 6pm-midnight Mon-Fri, 5pm-midnight Sat Oct-Mar, market & shops 11am-7pm Mon-Fri, to 6pm Sat year-round; 🚼) Hmm, where to start? The wine bar? The margarita bar? The gin bar? Whichever poison you choose, this wildly (and deservedly) popular contribution to Zürich's drinking scene is pure unadulterated fun and one of the best grown-up playgrounds in Europe.

ℹ Information

Zürich Tourism (☑ 044 215 40 00, hotel reservations 044 215 40 40; www.zuerich.com; train station; ☺ 8am-8.30pm Mon-Sat, 8.30am-6.30pm Sun May-Oct, 8.30am-7pm Mon-Sat, 9am-6pm Sun Nov-Apr)

ℹ Getting There & Away

Zürich Airport (ZRH; ☑ 043 816 22 11; www.zurich-airport.com) is 9km north of the centre.

Direct trains run to Stuttgart (Sfr64, three hours), Munich (Sfr97, 4¼ hours), Innsbruck (Sfr77, 3½ hours) and other international destinations, plus regular direct departures to most major Swiss towns.

ℹ Getting Around

Up to nine trains an hour connect the airport with the Hauptbahnhof between around 6am and midnight (Sfr6.60, nine to 14 minutes).

The comprehensive, unified bus, tram and S-Bahn public transit system **ZVV** (www.zvv.ch) includes boats plying the Limmat River. Short trips under five stops are Sfr2.60, typical trips are Sfr4.20. A 24-hour pass for the city centre is Sfr8.40.

ℹ CENT SAVER

Available from the tourist office and the airport train station, the **Zürich-Card** (www.zuerichcard.ch; adult/child 24hr Sfr24/16, 72hr Sfr48/32) is your cent-saver ticket to free public transport, free museum admission and other discounts.

RECYCLED FASHION

Switzerland's Freitag brothers recycle colourful truck tarps into water-resistant, carry-all chic in their zany Zürich **factory** (☑ 043 366 95 20; www.freitag. ch; Geroldstrasse 17; ⊙ 11am-7.30pm Mon-Fri, 10am-6pm Sat). Every item, from purses to laptop bags, is original. The Freitag outlet is pure whimsy – a pile of shipping containers that's been dubbed Kreis 5's first skyscraper. Shoppers can climb to the rooftop terrace for spectacular city views. Take the train from Hauptbahnhof to Hardbrücke.

Ticino

Switzerland meets Italy: in Ticino the summer air is rich and hot, peacock-proud posers propel their scooters in and out of traffic, then there's the Italian gelato, Italian pizza, Italian architecture and Italian language.

Locarno

POP 15,500

Italianate architecture and the northern end of Lago Maggiore, plus more hours of sunshine than anywhere else in Switzerland, give this laid-back town a summer resort atmosphere.

Locarno is on the northeastern corner of Lago Maggiore, which mostly lies in Italy's Lombardy region. **Navigazione Lago Maggiore** (www.navigazionelaghi.it) operates boats across the entire lake.

◉ Sights & Activities

Locarno's Italianate **Città Vecchia** (Old Town) fans out from Piazza Grande, a photogenic ensemble of arcades and Lombard-style houses.

★**Castello Visconteo**   MUSEUM, CASTLE
(Piazza Castello; adult/student Sfr7/5; ⊙ 10am-noon & 2-5pm Tue-Sun Apr-Oct) Named after the Visconti clan that long ruled Milan, this stout 15th-century castle's nucleus was raised around the 10th century. It now houses a museum with Roman and Bronze Age exhibits and also hosts a small display (in Italian) on the Locarno Treaty.

★**Giardini Pubblici**   GARDENS
(Lungolago Motta) Locarno's climate is perfect for lolling about the lake. Bristling with palms and banana trees, these botanic gardens are a scenic spot for a picnic or swim, and tots can let off steam in the adventure playground.

★**Santuario della Madonna del Sasso**   CHURCH
(⊙ 6.30am-6.30pm) FREE Overlooking the town, this sanctuary was built after the Virgin Mary supposedly appeared in a vision to a monk, Bartolomeo d'Ivrea, in 1480. There's a highly adorned church and several rather rough, near-life-size statue groups (including one of the Last Supper) in niches on the stairway. The best-known painting in the church is *La Fuga in Egitto* (Flight to Egypt), painted in 1522 by Bramantino.

A **funicular** (one-way/return adult Sfr4.80/7.20, child Sfr2.20/3.60; ⊙ 8am-10pm) runs every 15 minutes from the town centre past the sanctuary to Orselina, but a more scenic, pilgrim-style approach is the 20-minute walk up the chapel-lined Via Crucis (take Via al Sasso off Via Cappuccini).

ⓘ Getting There & Away

Locarno is well linked to Ticino and the rest of Switzerland via Bellinzona, or take the scenic **Centovalli Express** (www.centovalli.ch) to Brig via Domodossola in Italy.

Lugano

POP 61,800

Lugano is the country's third-most-important banking centre. Suits aside, it's a vivacious city, with bars and pavement cafes huddling in the spaghetti maze of steep cobblestone streets that untangle at the edge of the lake and along the flowery promenade.

◉ Sights & Activities

The Old Town, an ancient patchwork of interlocking piazze, is a 10-minute walk downhill from the train station; take the stairs or the **funicular** (Sfr1.10).

★**Cattedrale di San Lorenzo**   CATHEDRAL
(St Lawrence Cathedral; Via San Lorenzo; ⊙ 6.30am-6pm) Lugano's early-16th-century cathedral conceals some fine frescoes and ornate baroque statues behind its Renaissance facade. Out front are far-reaching

SWISS NATIONAL PARK

The almost-3000km-long Inn River (En in Romansch) springs up from the snowy Graubünden Alps in eastern Switzerland and gives its name to the **Engadine Valley**, home to the Swiss National Park. Spanning 172 sq km, Switzerland's only national park is a nature-gone-wild swath of dolomitic peaks, shimmering glaciers, larch woodlands, pastures, waterfalls and high moors strung with topaz-blue lakes.

The park is a glimpse of the Alps before the dawn of tourism. There are some 80km of well-marked hiking trails, where, with a little luck and a decent pair of binoculars, ibex, chamois, marmots and golden eagles can be sighted. The **Swiss National Park Centre** (☑081 851 41 41; www.nationalpark.ch; exhibition adult/child Sfr7/3; ⊙8.30am-6pm Jun-Oct, 9am-noon & 2-5pm Nov-May) in Zernez should be your first port of call for information on activities and accommodation, including guided wildlife-spotting treks and high-alpine hikes.

views over the Old Town's jumble of terracotta rooftops to the lake and mountains.

★**Chiesa di Santa Maria degli Angioli**   CHURCH
(St Mary of the Angel; Piazza Luini; ⊙7am-6pm) This simple Romanesque church contains two frescoes by Bernardino Luini dating from 1529. Covering the entire wall that divides the church in two is a grand didactic illustration of the crucifixion of Christ. The power and vivacity of the colours are astounding.

Società Navigazione del Lago di Lugano   BOAT TOUR
(www.lakelugano.ch; Riva Vela 12; ⊙Apr-Oct) A relaxed way to see the lake's highlights is on one of these cruises, including one-hour bay tours and three-hour morning cruises. Visit the website for timetables.

🛏 Sleeping & Eating

For pizza or pasta, try any of the places around Piazza della Riforma.

SYHA Hostel   HOSTEL €
(☑091 966 27 28; www.luganoyouthhostel.ch; Via Cantonale 13, Savosa; dm Sfr29-43, s Sfr59-89, d Sfr78-98; ⊙Mar-Oct; ▣) Housed in the Villa Savosa, this is one of the more enticing youth hostels in the country, with bright well-kept dorms, a barbecue area, a swimming pool and lush gardens. Take bus 5 from the train station to Crocifisso.

Hotel & Hostel Montarina   HOTEL, HOSTEL €
(☑091 966 72 72; www.montarina.ch; Via Montarina 1; dm/s/d Sfr29/105/140; ▣�🌐▣) Occupying a pastel-pink villa dating to 1860, this hotel-hostel duo extends a heartfelt welcome. Mosaic floors, high ceilings and

wrought-iron balustrades are lingering traces of old-world grandeur. There's a shared kitchen-lounge, toys to amuse the kids, a swimming pool set in palm-dotted gardens and even a tiny vineyard. Breakfast costs an extra Sfr15.

ℹ Information

Tourist Office (☑058 866 66 00; www.lugano-tourism.ch; Piazza Riforma, Palazzo Civico; ⊙9am-7pm Mon-Fri, 9am-6pm Sat, 10am-5pm Sun mid-Mar–Oct, shorter hours Nov–mid-Mar) There is also a tourist information booth at the main railway station (2pm to 7pm Monday to Saturday).

ℹ Getting There & Away

Lugano is on the main line connecting Milan to Zürich and Lucerne. Services from Lugano include Milan (Sfr17, 75 minutes), Zürich (Sfr64, 2¾ hours) and Lucerne (Sfr60, 2½ hours).

Switzerland Survival Guide

ℹ Directory A–Z

ACCOMMODATION

➤ Switzerland sports traditional and creative accommodation in every price range. Many budget hotels have cheaper rooms with shared toilet and shower facilities.

➤ Breakfast buffets can be extensive and tasty but are not always included in room rates.

➤ Rates in cities and towns stay constant most of the year. In mountain resorts prices are seasonal (and can fall by 50% or more outside high season).

➤ High season translates as July to August, plus Christmas and mid-February to Easter in mountain resorts.

ELECTRICITY

The electricity current is 220V, 50Hz. Swiss sockets are recessed, three-holed hexagonally shaped and incompatible with many plugs from abroad.

INTERNET RESOURCES

My Switzerland (www.myswitzerland.com) Swiss tourism.

ch.ch (www.ch.ch) Swiss authorities online.

Swiss Info (www.swissinfo.ch) Swiss news and current affairs.

MONEY

➡ Swiss francs are divided into 100 centimes (*Rappen* in German-speaking Switzerland). There are notes for 10, 20, 50, 100, 200 and 1000 francs, and coins for 5, 10, 20 and 50 centimes, as well as for one, two and five francs.

➡ Businesses throughout Switzerland, including most hotels and some restaurants and souvenir shops, will accept payment in euros.

➡ Automated teller machines (ATMs) – called Bancomats in banks and Postomats in post offices – are widespread and accessible 24 hours. They accept most international bank or credit cards.

➡ The use of credit cards is less widespread than in the UK or USA and not all shops, hotels or restaurants accept them. EuroCard/Master-Card and Visa are the most popular

OPENING HOURS

Each Swiss canton decides how long shops and businesses can stay open for. Shops in Lucerne, for example, must close by 4pm on Saturdays while those in Zürich can stay open until 8pm.

Listed hours are high-season opening hours for sights and attractions; hours are almost always shorter during low season.

Shops With the exception of souvenir shops and supermarkets at some train stations, shops are shut on Sunday. Many close Monday too.

Service stations Open 24 hours a day; stock basic groceries.

Restaurants Open noon to 2pm and 6pm to 10pm five or six days a week.

Museums Closed Monday or Tuesday. Many have a late-night opening one day a week (often Thursday).

PUBLIC HOLIDAYS

New Year's Day 1 January
Good Friday March/April
Easter Sunday & Monday March/April

ⓘ PRICE RANGES

Price indicators for accommodation refer to the cost of a double hotel room in high season, with bathroom and including breakfast unless noted otherwise.

€ less than Sfr170

€€ Sfr170 to Sfr350

€€€ more than Sfr350

Price indicators for restaurants/ eateries refer to the average cost of a main course; 2- or 3-course *menus* (pre-set meals at a fixed price) yield best-value, especially at lunchtime.

€ less than Sfr25

€€ Sfr25 to Sfr50

€€€ more than Sfr50

Ascension Day 40th day after Easter
Whit Sunday & Monday 7th week after Easter
National Day 1 August
Christmas Day 25 December
St Stephen's Day 26 December

Some cantons observe their own special holidays and religious days, eg 2 January, Labour Day (1 May), Corpus Christi, Assumption (15 August) and All Saints' Day (1 November).

TELEPHONE

➡ Area codes do not exist in Switzerland. Numbers in a particular city or town share the same three-digit prefix (Bern 🕽 031, Geneva 🕽 022 etc) which must always be dialled, even when calling locally.

➡ The country code for Switzerland is 🕽 41. When calling Switzerland from abroad, drop the initial zero from the local telephone number.

➡ To call abroad from Switzerland, use the international access code 🕽 00.

➡ Buy prepaid SIM cards online from **Mobile Zone** (www.mobilezone.ch).

➡ Swiss mobile telephone numbers begin with 🕽 076, 078 or 079.

➡ Save money on the normal international rate by buying a prepaid Swisscom card worth Sfr10 to Sfr100.

VISAS

For up-to-date details on visa requirements, go to www.sem.admin.ch.

Visas are not required for passport holders from the UK, the EU, Ireland, the USA, Canada, Australia, New Zealand, Norway and Iceland.

ℹ️ Getting There & Away

AIR

The main international airports, with flights to most European capitals as well as some in Africa, Asia and North America:

Geneva Airport (p353)
Zürich Airport (p362)

LAND

Switzerland is a hub of train connections to the rest of the Continent. Zürich is the busiest international terminus, with service to all neighbouring countries. Destinations include München (four hours), and Vienna (eight hours), from where there are extensive onward connections to cities in Eastern Europe.

➡ Numerous TGV trains daily connect Paris to Geneva (three hours), Lausanne (3¾ hours), Basel (three hours) and Zürich (four hours).

➡ Nearly all connections from Italy pass through Milan before branching off to Zürich, Lucerne, Bern or Lausanne.

➡ Most connections from Germany pass through Zürich or Basel.

➡ **Swiss Federal Railways** (SBB CFF FFS; www. sbb.ch) accepts internet bookings but does not post tickets outside of Switzerland; print off an e-ticket or save it on your smartphone.

ℹ️ Getting Around

Swiss public transport is an efficient, fully integrated and comprehensive system, incorporating rains, buses, boats and funiculars.

Marketed as the **Swiss Travel System** (www. swisstravelsystem.com), the network has a useful website, and excellent free maps covering the country are available at train stations and tourist offices.

PASSES & DISCOUNTS

For extensive travel within Switzerland, the following national travel passes (www.swiss-pass. ch) generally offer better savings than Eurail or InterRail passes.

Swiss Pass Unlimited travel on almost every train, boat and bus countrywide, and on trams and buses in 41 towns, plus free entry to 400-odd museums. Reductions of 50% apply on funiculars, cable cars and private railways. Different passes are available, valid from three days (Sfr210) to 15 days.

Swiss Flexi Pass Unlimited travel during a certain number of days – from three (Sfr239) to 15 (Sfr484) – during one month.

Swiss Half-Fare Card Pay half the fare on trains with this card (Sfr120 for one month), plus discounts on local-network buses, trams and cable cars.

BICYCLE

SBB Rent a Bike (☎ 041 925 11 70; www. rentabike.ch; half/full day from Sfr27/35), the super-efficient bike-rental service run by Swiss railways, offers bike hire at 80-odd train stations. Wheels can be reserved in advance online or by telephone and – for an Sfr8 surcharge – can be collected at one station and returned to another. Rates include helmets.

BOAT

Ferries and steamers link towns and cities on many lakes, including Geneva, Lucerne, Lugano and Zürich.

BUS

Canary-yellow Post Buses (www.postbus.ch) supplement the rail network, linking towns to less accessible mountain regions. Fares are comparable to train fares.

Swiss national travel passes are valid on postal buses; a few tourist-oriented Alpine routes levy a surcharge.

CAR & MOTORCYCLE

➡ Headlights must be on at all times, and dipped in tunnels.

➡ The speed limit is 50km/h in towns, 80km/h on main roads outside towns, 100km/h on single-lane freeways and 120km/h on dual-lane freeways.

➡ There's an annual one-off charge of Sfr40 to use Swiss freeways and semi-freeways. Buy the required sticker ('vignette' in French and German, 'contrassegno' in Italian) to display on your windscreen at the border (in cash, including euros), at petrol stations and from Swiss tourist offices abroad. For more details, see www.vignette.ch.

➡ Some Alpine passes are closed from November to May – check with the local tourist offices before setting off.

➡ In winter, your car must be equipped with winter tyres and a set of snow chains.

TRAIN

➡ The **Swiss Federal Railway** (www.sbb.ch) is abbreviated to SBB in German, CFF in French and FFS in Italian. Power points for laptops let you work or play aboard and some seats are in wi-fi hotspots.

➡ All major train stations are connected to each other by hourly departures, at least between 6am and midnight.

➡ Seat reservations (Sfr5) are advisable for longer journeys in high season.

➡ Ticket vending machines accept most major credit cards.

➡ The SBB smartphone app is an excellent resource and can be used to store your tickets electronically.

AUSTRIA

Vienna

01 / POP 1.79 MILLION

Few cities in the world waltz so effortlessly between the present and the past like Vienna. Its splendid historical face is easily recognised: grand imperial palaces and bombastic baroque interiors, revered opera houses and magnificent squares.

But Vienna is also one of Europe's most dynamic urban spaces. Provocative contemporary art hides behind striking basalt facades, design stores sidle up to old-world confectioners, and Austro-Asian fusion restaurants stand alongside traditional *Beisl* (small taverns).

Throw in the mass of green space within the confines of the city limits and the 'blue' Danube (Donau) cutting a path east of the historical centre, and this is a capital that is distinctly Austrian.

◉ Sights

Heading into the Innere Stadt will take you to a different age. Designated a Unesco World Heritage Site, the heart of the city is blessed with a plethora of architectural wonders evocative of Vienna's long and brilliant history.

◉ The Hofburg & Around

★ **Hofburg** PALACE
(Imperial Palace; www.hofburg-wien.at; 01, Michaelerkuppel; 1A, 2A Michaelerplatz, Herrengasse, D, 1, 2, 71, 46, 49 Burgring) FREE Nothing symbolises the culture and heritage of Austria more than its Hofburg, home base of the Habsburgs from 1273 to 1918. The oldest section is the 13th-century **Schweizerhof** (Swiss Courtyard), named after the Swiss guards who used to protect its precincts. The Renaissance **Swiss gate** dates from 1553. The courtyard adjoins a larger courtyard, **In der Burg**, with a monument to Emperor Franz II adorning its centre. The palace now houses the Austrian president's offices and a raft of museums.

★ **Kaiserappartements** PALACE
(Imperial Apartments; www.hofburg-wien.at; 01, Michaelerplatz; adult/child €13/8, with guided tour €16/9; 9am-6pm Jul & Aug, to 5.30pm Sep-Jun; Herrengasse) The Kaiserappartements, once the official living quarters of Franz Josef I and Empress Elisabeth, are dazzling in

their chandelier-lit opulence. One section, known as the **Sisi Museum**, is devoted to Austria's most beloved empress. It has a strong focus on the clothing and jewellery of Austria's monarch. Audioguides – available in 11 languages – are also included in the admission price. Admission on guided tours includes the Kaiserappartements plus the Sisi Museum.

★ **Kaiserliche Schatzkammer** MUSEUM
(Imperial Treasury; www.kaiserliche-schatzkammer.at; 01, Schweizerhof; adult/under 19yr €12/free; 9am-5.30pm Wed-Mon; Herrengasse) The Schatzkammer contains secular and ecclesiastical treasures of priceless value and splendour – the sheer wealth of this collection of crown jewels is staggering. As you walk through the rooms you see magnificent treasures such as a golden rose, diamond-studded Turkish sabres, a 2680-carat Colombian emerald and, the highlight of the treasury, the imperial crown.

★ **Albertina** GALLERY
(www.albertina.at; 01, Albertinaplatz 3; adult/under 19yr €13/free; 10am-6pm Thu-Tue, to 9pm Wed; ; Karlsplatz, Stephansplatz, D, 1, 2, 71 Kärntner Ring/Oper) Once used as the Habsburg's imperial apartments for guests, the Albertina is now a repository for the greatest collection of graphic art in the world. The permanent Batliner Collection – with paintings covering the period from Monet to Picasso – and the high quality of changing exhibitions are what really make the Albertina so worthwhile visiting.

◉ Stephansdom & the Historic Centre

★ **Stephansdom** CATHEDRAL
(St Stephan's Cathedral; www.stephanskirche.at; 01, Stephansplatz; 6am-10pm Mon-Sat, from 7am Sun, main nave & Domschatz audio tours 9-11.30am & 1-4.30pm Mon-Sat, 1-3.30pm Sun; Stephansplatz) Vienna's Gothic masterpiece Stephansdom, or Steffl (Little Stephan) as it's nicknamed, is the city's

Central Vienna

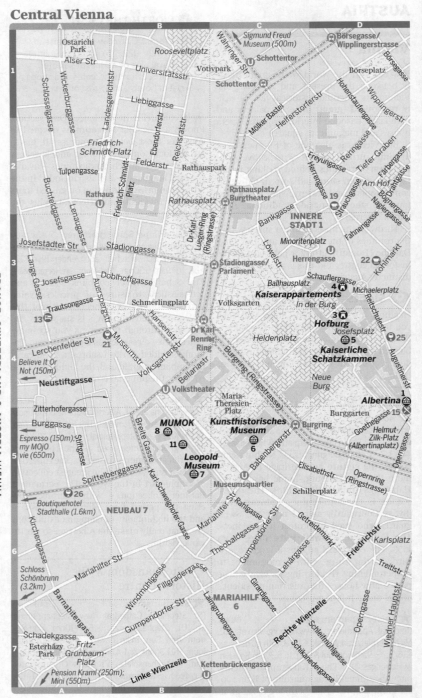

Sigmund Freud Museum (500m)

Börsegasse/Wipplingerstrasse

Ostarichi Park

Alser Str

Rooseveltplatz

Schlösselgasse

Wickenburggasse

Landesgerichtsstr

Universitätsstr

Schottentor

Börsegasse

Börseplatz

Wipplingerstr

Votivpark

Schottentor

Hohenstaufengasse

Liebiggasse

Ebendorferstr

Reichsratsstr

Rathauspark

Helferstorferstr

Renngasse

Färbergasse

Drahtgasse

Tiefer Graben

Mölker Bastei

Tulpengasse

Friedrich-Schmidt-Platz

Felderstr

Rathausplatz

Freyungasse

Am Hof

Buchfeldgasse

Lenaugasse

Rathaus

Friedrich-Schmidt-Platz

Herrengasse

Strauchgasse

Bognergasse

Naglergasse

Rathausplatz/Burgtheater

Bankgasse

19

INNERE STADT 1

Kohlmarkt

Josefstädter Str

Stadiongasse

Minoritenplatz

Lange Gasse

Josefsgasse

Doblhoffgasse

Löwelstr

Herrengasse

22

Fähnrengasse

Reitschulstr

Trautsongasse

Auerspergstr

Hansenstr

Schmerlingplatz

Volksgarten

Ballhausplatz

Schauflergasse

Kaiserappartements

In der Burg

Michaelerplatz

13

Lerchenfelder Str

21

Museumstr

Volksgartenstr

Dr Karl-Renner-Ring

Burgring (Ringstrasse)

Heldenplatz

3

Hofburg

Josefsplatz

5

Kaiserliche Schatzkammer

25

Believe It Or Not (150m)

Neustiftgasse

Zitterhofergasse

Bellariastr

Volkstheater

Maria-Theresien-Platz

Neue Burg

Albertina

1

Burggarten

Espresso (150m); my MOjO vie (650m)

Burggasse

Stiftgasse

Breite Gasse

MUMOK

8

11

Kunsthistorisches Museum

6

Babenbergerstr

Burgring

15

Helmut-Zilk-Platz (Albertinaplatz)

Spittelberggasse

Karl-Schweighofer-Gasse

Leopold Museum

7

Museumsquartier

Elisabethstr

Schillerplatz

Opernring (Ringstrasse)

26

Boutiquehotel Stadthalle (1.6km)

NEUBAU 7

Mariahilfer Str

Rahlgasse

Theobaldgasse

Getreidemarkt

Friedrichstr

Karlsplatz

Schloss Schönbrunn (3.2km)

Kirchengasse

Mariahilfer Str

Windmühlgasse

Fillgradergasse

Gumpendorfer Str

Lehargasse

Girardigasse

Treitlstr

Barnabitengasse

Gumpendorfer Str

Laimgrubengasse

MARIAHILF

6

Opengasse

Scheiffmühlgasse

Wiedner Hauptstr

Schadekgasse

Esterházy Park

Fritz-Grünbaum-Platz

Linke Wienzeile

Kettenbrückengasse

Rechte Wienzeile

Schikanedergasse

Pension Kraml (250m); Mini (550m)

△ 0 _____ 500 m
Ⓝ 0 _____ 0.25 miles

Karmelitermarkt
(300m)

Werdertorgasse

Heinrichsgasse

Salztorbrücke

Nestroyplatz Ⓤ

Prater
(1km);
Pratersauna
(1.9km)

Rudolfsplatz

LEOPOLDSTADT
2

Gredlerstr

Grosse Mohrengasse

Salzgries

INNERE
STADT 1

Salztorgasse

Franz-Josefs-Kai (Ringstrasse)

Obere Donaustr

Danube Canal

Taborstr

Praterstr

Aspernbrückengasse

Passauer Platz

Marc-Aurel-Str

Morzinplatz

Untere Donaustr

Judenplatz

Lichtensteg

Ruprechtsstiege

Rabenstieg

✕16

Schwedenplatz Ⓤ

Julius-Raab-
Platz Ⓤ

Kurrentgasse

Bauernmarkt

Rotgasse

Rotenturmstr

Hafnersteig

Schwedenplatz

Postgasse

Wiesingerstr

Vordere Zollamtstr

Tuchlauben

Brandstätte

Fleischmarkt

Sonnenfelsgasse

Bäckerstr

✕14

Dominikanerbastei

Rosenbursenstr

Graben

Braunerstr

Stock-im-
Eisen-
Platz

10
✚Stephansdom

Domgasse

Wollzeile

Falkestr

Stubenring (Ringstrasse)

Marxergasse

17✕

Ⓤ18
Stephansplatz

☕23

Weiskirchnerstr

Landstrasser
Hauptstr

Wien
Mitte
🚆

Dorotheergasse

Spiegelgasse

Seilergasse

Kärntner-Str

Stephansplatz

Weihburggasse

Blutgasse

Singerstr

Schulerstr

Grünangergasse

Kumpfgasse

Riemergasse

Jakobergasse

Stubentor Ⓤ

Stubentor

Landstrasse

Plankengasse

Franziskanerplatz

Seilerstätte

Parkring (Ringstrasse)

Ungargasse

Maysedergasse

Führichgasse

ℹ

Johannesgasse

Himmelpfortgasse

Coburgbastei

Weihburggasse

🍽20

☕24

Annagasse

2
🏛Haus der Musik

Seilerstätte

Schellinggasse

Hegelgasse

Johannesgasse

Stadtpark

Am Stadtpark

Linke Bahngasse

🍽12

Krugerstr

Philharmonikerstr

Walfischgasse

Schubertring (Ringstrasse)

Fichtegasse

Beethovenplatz

Stadtpark Ⓤ

Beatrixgasse

Rechte Bahngasse

Mahlerstr

Schwarzenbergstr

Kärntner
Ring/Oper Ⓤ

Bösendorferstr

Kärntner Ring
(Ringstrasse)

Schwartzenbergstrasse

Lothringerstr

Am Heumarkt

Marokkanergasse

Lagergasse

Salesianergasse

Reisnerstr

Karlsplatz Ⓤ

Lothringerstr

Schwarzenbergplatz

Lisztstr

Neulinggasse

Resselpark

Resselpark

Stadt
Wien

Zaunergasse

Strohgasse

Paniglgasse

Karlsgasse

Mattiellistr

Gusshausstr

Schwindgasse

Oberes
Belvedere
(650m)

Rennweg

Schloss
Belvedere
🏛9

Reisnerstr

FRANCE, SWITZERLAND & AUSTRIA VIENNA

Central Vienna

FRANCE, SWITZERLAND & AUSTRIA VIENNA

pride and joy. A church has stood here since the 12th century, and reminders of this are the Romanesque **Riesentor** (Giant Gate) and **Heidentürme**. From the exterior, the first thing that will strike you is the glorious tiled **roof**, with its dazzling row of chevrons and Austrian eagle. Inside, the magnificent Gothic stone **pulpit** presides over the main nave, fashioned in 1515 by an unknown artisan.

★**Haus der Musik**   MUSEUM
(www.hdm.at; 01, Seilerstätte 30; adult/child €13/6, after 8pm €6.50, with Mozarthaus Vienna €18/8; ⊙10am-10pm; 👶; Ⓜ Karlsplatz, ⊡ D, 1, 2 Kärntner Ring/Oper) The Haus der Musik is an interesting and unusual museums as it manages to explain the world of sound in an amusing and highly interactive way (in English and German) for both children and adults. Exhibits are spread over four floors and cover everything from how sound is created through to Vienna's Philharmonic Orchestra and street noises.

> **DON'T MISS**
>
> ### A BIRD'S-EYE VIEW
>
> One of the city's most visible icons is the **Riesenrad**. Built in 1897, this 65m-high Ferris wheel of *The Third Man* fame affords far-reaching views of Vienna. Find it in **Prater** (www.wiener-prater.at; Ⓜ Praterstern), a large city park encompassing meadows, woodlands and an amusement park (the Würstelprater).

◉ Museum District & Neubau

MuseumsQuartier   MUSEUM
(Museum Quarter; www.mqw.at; 07, Museumsplatz; ⊙information & ticket centre 10am-7pm; Ⓜ Museumsquartier, Volkstheater) The MuseumsQuartier is a remarkable ensemble of museums, cafes, restaurants and bars inside former imperial stables designed by Fischer von Erlach. This breeding ground of Viennese cultural life is the perfect place to hang out and watch or meet people on warm evenings. With over 60,000 sq metres of exhibition space, the complex is one of the world's most ambitious cultural spaces.

★**Leopold Museum**   MUSEUM
(www.leopoldmuseum.org; 07, Museumsplatz 1; adult/child €13/8; ⊙10am-6pm Wed-Mon, to 9pm Thu; Ⓜ Museumsquartier, Volkstheater) The undoubted highlight of a visit to the MuseumsQuartier is the Leopold Museum, a striking white limestone gallery that showcases the world's largest collection of Egon Schiele paintings, alongside some fine Klimts and Kokoschkas.

★**MUMOK**   GALLERY
(Museum Moderner Kunst, Museum of Modern Art; www.mumok.at; 07, Museumsplatz 1; adult/child €10/free; ⊙2-7pm Mon, 10am-7pm Tue, Wed & Fri-Sun, 10am-9pm Thu; Ⓜ Museumsquartier, Volkstheater, ⊡ 49 Volkstheater) The dark basalt edifice and sharp corners of the Museum Moderner Kunst are a complete contrast to the MuseumsQuartier's historical sleeve. Inside, MUMOK is crawling with Vienna's finest collection of 20th-century art, cen-

tred on fluxus, nouveau realism, pop art and photo-realism.

★ **Kunsthistorisches Museum**   MUSEUM
(KHM, Museum of Art History; www.khm.at; 01, Maria-Theresien-Platz; adult/under 19yr incl Neue Burg museums €15/free; ⊙10am-6pm Fri-Wed, to 9pm Thu Jun-Aug, closed Mon Sep-May; ▦; Ⓜ Museumsquartier, Volkstheater) One of the unforgettable experiences of being in Vienna will be a visit to the Kunsthistorisches Museum, brimming with works by Europe's finest painters, sculptors and artisans. Occupying a neoclassical building as sumptuous as the art it contains, the museum takes you on a time-travel treasure hunt from Classical Rome to Egypt and the Renaissance. If time is an issue, skip straight to the **Picture Gallery**, where you'll want to dedicate at least an hour or two to the Old Masters.

◉ Hietzing

★ **Schloss Schönbrunn**   PALACE
(www.schoenbrunn.at; 13, Schönbrunner Schlossstrasse 47; adult/child Imperial Tour €13.30/9.80, Grand Tour €16.40/10.80; ⊙8.30am-6.30pm Jul & Aug, to 5.30pm Sep-Oct & Apr-Jun, to 5pm Nov-Mar; Ⓜ Hietzing) The Habsburgs' overwhelmingly opulent summer palace is now a Unesco World Heritage site. Of its 1441 rooms, 40 are open to the public; the Imperial Tour takes you into 26 of these.

★ **Klimt Villa**   MUSEUM
(www.klimtvilla.at; 13, Feldmühlgasse 11; adult/child €10/5; ⊙10am-6pm Thu-Sat Apr-Dec; Ⓜ Unter St Veit) The Klimt Villa immerses you in the sensual world of Vienna's most famous Secessionist. Set in landscaped grounds in a leafy corner of Hietzing, the 1920s neo-baroque villa was built on and around the site of the artist's last studio (1911–18), which opened to the public in September 2012 following a complete makeover.

✷ Festivals & Events

Opernball   CULTURAL
(www.wiener-staatsoper.at; ⊙Jan/Feb) Of the 300 or so balls held in January and February, the Opernball (Opera Ball) is number one. Held in the Staatsoper, it's a supremely lavish affair, with the men in tails and women in shining white gowns.

Christkindlmärkte   CHRISTMAS MARKET
(www.christkindlmarkt.at; ⊙mid-Nov–25 Dec) Vienna's much-loved Christmas market.

THE KISS

For exquisite baroque architecture and masterpiece art, visit the **Schloss Belvedere** (www.belvedere.at; adult/child Oberes Belvedere €14/free, Unteres Belvedere €12/free, combined ticket €20/free; ⊙10am-6pm; ▦ Taubstummengasse, Südtiroler Platz, ▣D, 71 Schwarzenbergplatz). One of the world's finest baroque palaces, it was designed by Johann Lukas von Hildebrandt (1668–1745) for Prince Eugene of Savoy. The first of the palace's two buildings is the **Oberes Belvedere** (Upper Belvedere), showcasing Gustav Klimt's *The Kiss* (1908), the perfect embodiment of Viennese art nouveau, alongside other late-19th- to early-20th-century Austrian works. The lavish **Unteres Belvedere** (Lower Belvedere), with its richly frescoed Marmorsaal (Marble Hall), sits at the end of sculpture-dotted gardens.

🛏 Sleeping

my MOjO vie   HOSTEL €
(🕿0676-551 11 55; www.mymojovie.at; 07, Kaiserstrasse 77; dm €28, d/tr/q with shared bathroom €60/90/120, with private bathroom €80/120/160; @🛜; Ⓜ Burggasse Stadthalle) An old-fashioned cage lift rattles up to these incredible backpacker digs. Everything you could wish for is here – design-focused dorms, kitchen with free supplies, netbooks for surfing, guidebooks for browsing, even musical instruments for your own jam session. No breakfast.

Pension Wild   PENSION €
(🕿406 51 74; www.pension-wild.com; 08, Lange Gasse 10; s €44-69, d €49-99, tr €69-119, q €99-129; Ⓜ Rathaus, Volkstheater) Wild is one of the few openly gay-friendly *Pensionen* in Vienna, but the warm welcome extends to all walks of life. The top-floor 'luxury' rooms are simple yet appealing, with light-wood furniture and private bathrooms, and are a big advantage over Wild's other two categories. All, however, are spotlessly clean and kitchens are there for guests to use.

★ **Opera Suites**   PENSION €€
(🕿512 93 10; www.operasuites.at; 01, Kärntner Strasse 47; s/d €99/139; @🛜; Ⓜ Karlsplatz, ▣D, 1, 2 Kärntner Ring/Oper) Located directly across from the famous Hotel Sacher and close to the major sights, Opera Suites offers

well-priced and comfortable standard and superior rooms, some of which have cooking facilities and are more like apartments or holiday flats. Book well ahead, and expect to pay from €5.80 to €11.80 for breakfast if you want it.

✕ Eating

Self-caterers can stock up at central Hofer, Billa and Spar supermarkets. Some have delis that make sandwiches to order. *Würstel Stand* (sausage stands) are great for a cheap bite on the run.

Trzesniewski SANDWICHES €
(www.trzesniewski.at; 01, Dorotheergasse 1; bread & spread €1.20; ⊘8am-7pm Mon-Fri, 9am-5pm Sat; ⊞Stephansplatz) Possibly the finest sandwich shop in Austria, Trzesniewski has been serving spreads and breads to the entire spectrum of munchers for over 100 years.

Bitzinger Würstelstand am Albertinaplatz SAUSAGE STAND €
(01, Albertinaplatz; sausages €1.50-5; ⊘8am-4am; ⊞Karlsplatz, Stephansplatz, ⊟Kärntner Ring/Oper) Vienna has many sausage stands but this one located behind the Staatsoper is hands down one of the best.

★Maschu Maschu MIDDLE EASTERN €
(☏533 29 04; www.maschu-maschu.at; 01, Rabensteig 8; mains €5-9; ⊘11.30am-11.30pm; 🖉; ⊞Schwedenplatz, ⊟1, 2 Schwedenplatz) Deli-cious falafels, hummus and salads are the keys to Maschu Maschu's success. This branch on Rabensteig, with its meagre number of tables, is better used as a take-away joint, while another branch in **Neubau** (☏01 990 47 13; 07, Neubaugasse 20; falafel €4.50-7, mains €9.80-18.20; ⊘10.30am-midnight; 🖉; ⊞Neubaugasse) is best for sit-down meals.

★Beim Czaak BISTRO PUB €
(☏513 72 15; www.czaak.com; 01, Postgasse 15; mains €10-19; ⊘11am-midnight Mon-Sat; ⊞Schwedenplatz, ⊟1, 2 Schwedenplatz) Beim Czaak has a genuine and relatively simple interior. As you would expect, classic Viennese meat dishes dominate the menu, with long-time favourites like Wiener Schnitzel, *Tafelspitz* (prime boiled beef), the *Haus Schnitzel* (weighted down with ham, cheese, mushrooms and onions – yum) and Styrian chicken.

Drinking & Nightlife

Pulsating bars cluster north and south of the Naschmarkt, around Spittelberg and along the Gürtel (mainly around the U6 stops of Josefstädter Strasse and Nussdorfer Strasse).

Vienna's *Heurigen* (wine taverns) cluster in the wine-growing suburbs to the north, southwest, west and northwest of the city.

DON'T MISS

COFFEE HOUSE CULTURE

Vienna's legendary *Kaffeehauser* (coffee houses) are hot spots for people-watching, daydreaming, chatting and browsing the news. Most serve light meals alongside mouth-watering cakes and tortes. Expect to pay around €8 for a coffee with a slice of cake at these iconic addresses:

Demel (www.demel.at; 01, Kohlmarkt 14; ⊘9am-7pm; ⊟1A, 2A Michaelerplatz, ⊞Herrengasse, Stephansplatz) One-time purveyor to the imperial and royal court, famous for its chocolate-nougat *Annatorte* and fragrant candied violets.

Café Sacher (www.sacher.com; 01, Philharmonikerstrasse 4; ⊘8am-midnight; ⊞Karlsplatz, ⊟D, 1, 2, 71 Kärntner Ring/Oper) King of the Sacher Torte (rich iced chocolate cake filled with apricot jam).

Aida (☏512 29 77; www.aida.at; 01, Singerstrasse 1; ⊘7am-10pm Mon-Sat, 8am-10pm Sun; ⊞Stephansplatz) Pink-kissed 1950s decor and delectable cakes.

Diglas (☏512 57 65; www.diglas.at; 01, Wollzeile 10; ⊘8am-10.30pm; ⊞Stephansplatz) Legendary Apfelstrudel that flakes just so.

Café Central (www.palaisevents.at; 01, Herrengasse 14; ⊘7.30am-10pm Mon-Sat, 10am-10pm Sun; 🖥; ⊞Herrengasse) Trotsky's old haunt, perfect for a *Melange* and a slice of chocolate-truffle *Altenbergtorte*.

WORTH A TRIP

THE DANUBE VALLEY

The Danube (Donau), which enters Lower Austria from the west near **Ybbs** and exits in the east near Bratislava, Slovakia's capital, carves a picturesque path through the province's hills and fields.

Austria's most spectacular section of the Danube is the dramatic stretch of river between **Krems an der Donau**, with its atmospheric historical centre and gallery-dotted **Kunstmeile** (Art Mile; www.kunstmeile.at), and **Melk**, dominated by a spectacular abbey fortress called **Stift Meik** (Benedictine Abbey of Melk; www.stiftmelk.at; Abt Berthold Dietmayr Strasse 1; adult/child €11/6, with guided tour €13/8; ⏱9am-5.30pm, tours 10.55am & 2.55pm May-Sep, tours only 11am and 2pm Nov-Mar). The landscape here – known as Wachau and a Unesco World Heritage Site – is characterised by vineyards, forested slopes, wine-producing villages and imposing fortresses at nearly every bend. Modern art lovers will enjoy the town of **Linz** with its exceptional art museum and digital-savvy **Ars Electronica Center** (www.aec.at; Ars Electronica Strasse 1; adult/child €9.50/7.50; ⏱9am-5pm Tue, Wed & Fri, to 9pm Thu, 10am-6pm Sat & Sun).

Contact **Tourismusverband Wachau Nibelungengau** (📞02713-300 60 60; www.wachau.at; Schlossgasse 3, Spitz an der Donau; ⏱9am-4.30pm Mon-Thu, to 2.30pm Fri) for comprehensive information on the Wachau and surrounding area.

Opening times are approximately from 4pm to 11pm, and wine costs around €3 per *Viertel* (250mL).

★ Dachboden
BAR

(www.25hours-hotels.com; 07, Lerchenfelder Strasse 1-3; ⏱3pm-1am; 📶; Ⓜ Volkstheater) Housed in the circus-themed 25hours Hotel, Dachboden has big-top views of Vienna's skyline from its decked terrace. DJs spins jazz, soul and funk on Wednesday and Friday nights.

★ Kruger's American Bar
BAR

(www.krugers.at; 01, Krugerstrasse 5; ⏱from 6pm Mon-Sat; Ⓜ Stephansplatz, 🚋D, 1, 2, 71 Kärntner Ring/Oper) This wood-panelled American-style bar is a legend in Vienna, retaining some of its original furnishings from the 1930s and complete with a separate cigar and smoker's lounge.

Siebensternbräu
MICROBREWERY

(www.7stern.at; 07, Siebensterngasse 19; ⏱11am-midnight; Ⓜ Neubaugasse) You can guzzle some of Vienna's finest microbrews at this lively, no-nonsense brewpub. Besides hoppy lagers and malty ales, there are unusual varieties like hemp, chilli and wood-smoked beer. Try them with pretzels or meaty pub grub like schnitzel, goulash and pork knuckles (mains €9 to €16.50). The courtyard garden fills quickly with Wiener beer-lovers in the warmer months.

★ Palffy Club
CLUB

(www.palffyclub.at; 01, Josefsplatz 6; cover €12; ⏱from 10pm Fri & Sat; 🚌1A, 2A Michaelerplatz, Ⓜ Herrengasse, 🚋D, 1, 2, 71 Burgring) This 550-sq-metre club occupies two floors (right as you enter) of an illustrious old building used for live-music performances. The 1st-floor lounge bar is set with thousands of miniature glittering gemstones below a 12m chandelier with 80,000 Swarovski crystals. The 1st floor has R&B and '70s and '80s, while the 2nd floor opens at 1am with house and techno beats.

ⓘ Information

Tourist Info Wien (📞245 55; www.wien.info; 01, Albertinaplatz; ⏱9am-7pm; 📶; Ⓜ Stephansplatz, 🚋D, 1, 2, 71 Kärntner Ring/Oper)

ⓘ Getting There & Away

AIR

Vienna International Airport (VIE; www.viennaairport.com), 20km southwest of the city centre, has good connections worldwide, but some travellers might find it more convenient to use international flights to Frankfurt am Main or Munich (Germany), Budapest (Hungary) or Zürich (Switzerland) and travel on by train.

BUS

Vienna has no central bus station. Südtiroler Platz (alongside Wien Hauptbahnhof) is the closest thing to one. **Eurolines** (📞0900 128

712; www.eurolines.com; Erdbergstrasse 200; ☉6.30am-9pm Mon-Fri; Ⓜ Erdberg) uses its own terminal at the U3 U-Bahn station Erdberg, along with Südtiroler Platz and a few other stops. It has bus connections with the rest of Europe.

TRAIN

Vienna is one of central Europe's main rail hubs, with direct services to many European cities from its sparkling new central station, Wien Hauptbahnhof. For train timetables and prices, see the ÖBB website (Austrian Federal Railway; www.oebb.at).

❶ Getting Around

TO/FROM THE AIRPORT

The **City Airport Train** (CAT; www.cityairport-train.com; single/return €11/17) links the airport and centre every 30 minutes; journey time is 16 minutes. Book online for a €2 discount. The S-Bahn (S7) does the same journey (single €4.40) but in 25 minutes.

BICYCLE

Vienna is a fabulous place to get around by bike. Vienna's city bike scheme is called **Citybike Wien** (Vienna City Bike; www.citybikewien.at; 1st hour free, 2nd/3rd hour €1/2, per hour thereafter €4), with more than 120 bicycle stands across the city. A credit card is required to rent bikes – just swipe your card in the machine and follow the instructions.

PUBLIC TRANSPORT

A single ticket for Vienna's trains, trams, buses, underground (U-Bahn) and suburban (S-Bahn) trains cost €2.30 (€7.60/ €13.30 for a 24-/48-hour pass). Validate at the entrance to U-Bahn stations or aboard buses and trams. Buy at tobacconists or online (then display on your smartphone) at https://shop.wienerlinien.at.

Graz

📱 0316 / POP 265,300

Austria's second-largest city is probably its most relaxed and, after Vienna, its liveliest for after-hours pursuits. Capital of the southern province of Styria, Graz is an attractive place with bristling green parkland, red rooftops and a small, fast-flowing river gushing through its centre. Architecturally, it has Renaissance courtyards and provincial baroque palaces complemented by innovative modern designs. The surrounding countryside, a mixture of vineyards, mountains, forested hills and thermal springs, is within easy striking distance.

◉ Sights

Graz is a city easily enjoyed by simply wandering aimlessly. Admission to all of the Joanneum museums with a 24-hour ticket costs €11/4 for adults/children.

★**Schlossberg**　　　　　　VIEWPOINT
(1hr ticket for lift or funicular €2.10; 🚋4, 5 Schlossbergplatz) FREE Rising to 473m, Schlossberg is the site of the original fortress where Graz was founded and is topped by the city's most visible icon – the Uhrturm. Its wooded slopes can be reached by a number of bucolic and strenuous paths, but also by lift or Schlossbergbahn funicular. Take tram 4 or 5 to Schlossplatz/Murinsel for the lift.

★**Kunsthaus Graz**　　　　　　GALLERY
(www.kunsthausgraz.at; Lendkai 1; adult/child €9/3; ☉10am-5pm Tue-Sun; 🚋1, 3, 6, 7 Südtiroler Platz) Designed by British architects Peter Cook and Colin Fournier, this world-class contemporary-art space is a bold creation that looks something like a space-age sea slug. Exhibitions change every three to four months.

Neue Galerie Graz　　　　　　GALLERY
(www.museum-joanneum.at; Joanneumsviertel; adult/child €9/3; ☉10am-5pm Tue-Sun; 🚋1, 3, 4, 5, 6, 7 Hauptplatz) The Neue Galerie is the crowning glory of the three museums inside the Joanneumsviertel museum complex. The stunning collection on level 0 is the highlight. Though not enormous, it showcases richly textured and colourful works by painters such as Ernst Christian Moser, Ferdinand Georg Waldmüller and Johann Nepomuk Passini. Egon Schiele is also represented here.

Schloss Eggenberg　　　　　　PALACE
(Eggenberger Allee 90; adult/child €11.50/5.50; ☉tours 10am-4pm Tue-Sun Palm Sun-Oct; 🚋1 Schloss Eggenberg) Graz' elegant palace was created for the Eggenberg dynasty in 1625 by Giovanni Pietro de Pomis (1565–1633) at the request of Johann Ulrich (1568–1634). Admission is on a highly worthwhile guided tour during which you learn about the idiosyncrasies of each room, the stories told by the frescoes and about the Eggenberg family itself.

🛏 Sleeping

★**Hotel Daniel**　　　　　　HOTEL €
(📱711 080; www.hoteldaniel.com; Europaplatz 1; d €87-104; ▣☀@🛜; 🚋1, 3, 6, 7 Hauptbahnhof)

Graz

The Daniel is a design hotel with slick, minimalist-style rooms, a 'loft cube' on its roof and a seriously funky style. Rent a Vespa or bike for €15 or €5 respectively to cruise around town in style. Breakfast €12.

★ **Hotel Weitzer**   HOTEL €
(2 7030; www.hotelweitzer.com; Grieskai 12; d €112-161; P @ 🛜; 🚊1, 3, 6, 7 Südtiroler Platz) Favoured by tour groups as well as individual travellers on limited budgets, this hotel offers good-value rooms in three comfort categories. Most have been renovated. There are a couple of eateries in the building, as well as sauna and fitness facilities. Breakfast from €15.

✘ Eating & Drinking

Cheap eats abound near Universität Graz, particularly on Halbärthgasse, Zinzendorfgasse and Harrachgasse. Stock up for a picnic at the farmers markets on **Kaiser-Josef-Platz**

(⊙ 6am-noon, closed Sun; 🚊1, 7 Kaiser-Josef-Platz) and **Lendplatz** (⊙ 6am-1pm, closed Sun; 🚊1, 3, 6, 7 Südtiroler Platz). For fast food, hit Hauptplatz and Jakominiplatz.

★ **Thomawirt** BISTRO PUB €€
(☑ 328 637; www.thomawirt.at; Leonhardstrasse 40-42; lunch menu €8, mains €9-16; ⊙ 9am-1am; ☑; 🚌 7 Merangasse) This neo-*Beisl* (bistro pub) in the uni quarter serves a lunch special weekdays from 11am, and other excellent lunch and dinner dishes ranging from Styrian classics to steaks and vegetarian mains until 1am. Chill out with occasional music in the bar; the place is divided up into cafe, restaurant and lounge-bar areas.

★ **Der Steirer** AUSTRIAN, TAPAS €€
(☑ 703 654; www.dersteirer.at; Belgiergasse 1; lunch menu €9, mains €11-16; ⊙ 11am-midnight; ☑; 🚌 1, 3, 6, 7 Südtiroler Platz) This Styrian neo-*Beisl* and wine bar has a small but fantastic selection of local dishes, including a great goulash, and Austrotapas if you just feel like nibbling.

❶ Information

Graz Tourismus (☑ 8075; www.graztourismus. at; Herrengasse 16; ⊙ 10am-7pm Apr-Oct & Dec, to 6pm Nov & Jan-Mar; 📶; 🚌 1, 3, 4, 5, 6, 7 Hauptplatz)

❶ Getting There & Away

AIR
Graz Airport (GRZ; ☑ 29 020; www.flughafen-graz.at), 10km south of town, is served by carriers including **Air Berlin** (www.airberlin. com), which connects the city with Berlin.

TRAIN
Trains to Vienna depart hourly (€37.30, 2½ hours), and six daily go to Salzburg (€48.80, four hours). International train connections from Graz include Zagreb, Croatia (€46.60, four hours); Ljubljana, Slovenia (€28.30 to €41.30, four hours); and Budapest, Hungary (€76.60, 5½ hours).

Klagenfurt
☑ 0463 / POP 94,800

With its captivating location on Wörthersee and more Renaissance than baroque beauty, Klagenfurt has a distinct Mediterranean feel. As capital to the southern state of Carinthia, it makes a handy base for exploring Wörthersee's lakeside villages and elegant medieval towns to the north.

⊙ Sights & Activities

Boating and swimming in the lake are usually possible May to September. Summertime operas, ballets and pop concerts take place on an offshore stage on Wörthersee during the summer-long **Wörthersee Festspiele**.

★ **Eboard Museum** MUSEUM
(☑ 0699-1914 41 80; www.eboardmuseum.com; Florian Gröger Strasse 20; adult/family €10/20; ⊙ 2-7pm Sun-Fri, call ahead Sat) With the largest collection of keyboard instruments in Europe (more than 1300), this quirky museum is literally a 'fingers-on' museum: you are able play most of the organs, including rare items such as a Model A Hammond from 1934 and many more. Live bands perform on Friday (except July and August) nights at 8pm (€10).

★ **Strandbad** SWIMMING
(www.stw.at; Metnitzstrand 2; adult/child €4.50/1.80; ⊙ 8am-8pm Jun-Aug, to 7pm May & Sep, closed Oct-Apr; 🚼) Klagenfurt's wonderful lakeside beach has cabins, restaurants and piers for basking like a seal. There's also good swimming outside the buoys further south, past the Maria Loretto beach. You can indulge in paddle or electric boat escapades alongside the *Strandbad*.

WORTH A TRIP

STYRIA EXPLORER

The southern state of Styria (Steiermark) is a blissful amalgamation of genteel architecture, rolling green hills, vine-covered slopes and soaring mountains.

East of Graz, eastern Styria unfolds in an undulating scape of rejuvenating thermal springs and centuries-old castles. If you're a fan of the former (and/or of Friedensreich Hundertwasser's playful architectural style), **Rogner-Bad Blumau** (☑ 03383-51 00; www.blumau.com; adult/child Mon-Fri €43/24, Sat & Sun €52/29, admission after 5pm €30.90/20.90; ⊙ 9am-11pm), 50km east of Graz, is a mandatory stop. Call ahead to book treatments from sound meditation to invigorating Styrian elderberry wraps. If you prefer castles, **Schloss Riegersburg** (☑ 3153-82 131; www.veste-riegersburg.at; Riegersburg 1; adult/child €12.50/7.50; ⊙ 9am-6pm May-Sep, 10am-6pm Apr & Oct) is one of Austria's best.

🛏 Sleeping & Eating

★ Hotel Palais Porcia   HOTEL €€
(☑ 511 5900; www.palais-porcia.at; Neuer Platz 13;
s/ from €75/119; P☺❄@☎) This marvellously ornate and old-fashioned hotel has
gilt, mirrors and red-velvet couches, with
pink marble and gold taps in the bathrooms.
It also has a private beach that guests can
use near its other hotel in Pörtschach.

Bierhaus zum Augustin   BISTRO PUB €€
(Pfarrhofgasse 2; mains €8-26; ☺ 11am-midnight
Mon-Sat) Bierhaus zum Augustin is one of
Klagenfurt's liveliest haunts for imbibers,
thanks especially to its traditional pub atmosphere. There's a cobbled courtyard at
the back for alfresco eating.

ℹ Information

Tourist Office (☑ 53 722 23; www.klagenfurt-
tourismus.at; Neuer Platz 1, Rathaus; ☺ 8am-
6pm Mon-Fri, 10am-5pm Sat, 10am-3pm Sun)

ℹ Getting There & Around

AIR
Klagenfurt's **airport** (www.klagenfurt-airport.
com; Flughafenstrasse 60-66) is 3km north of
town. Ryanair connects Klagenfurt with London
Stansted; Germanwings flies to Cologne-Bonn
in Germany.

BUS
Bus 40/42 shuttles between the Hauptbahnhof
and the airport; drivers sell tickets (€2.10).

TRAIN
Two-hourly direct trains run from Klagenfurt
to Vienna (€52.60, 3¾ hours) and Salzburg
(€39.50, three hours). Trains to Graz depart
every two to three hours (€28.60 to €40.30, 2¾
hours). Trains to western Austria, Italy, Slovenia
and Germany go via Villach (€7.60, 25 to 40
minutes, two to four per hour).

Salzburg

☑ 0662 / POP 150,000

The joke 'If it's baroque, don't fix it' is a perfect
maxim for Salzburg; the tranquil Old Town
burrowed below steep hills looks much as it
did when Mozart lived here 250 years ago.

A Unesco World Heritage Site, Salzburg's
overwhelmingly baroque Old Town is entrancing, both at ground level and from Hohensalzburg fortress high above. Across the
fast-flowing Salzach River rests Schloss Mirabell, surrounded by gorgeous manicured
gardens.

If this doesn't whet your appetite, then
bypass the grandeur and head straight
for kitsch-country by joining a tour of *The
Sound of Music* film locations.

◉ Sights

★ Dom   CATHEDRAL
(Cathedral; Domplatz; ☺ 8am-7pm Mon-Sat, 1-7pm
Sun) Gracefully crowned by a bulbous copper dome and twin spires, the Dom stands
out as a masterpiece of baroque art. Bronze
portals symbolising faith, hope and charity
lead into the cathedral. In the nave, intricate
stucco and Arsenio Mascagni's ceiling frescoes recounting the Passion of Christ guide
the eye to the polychrome dome.

Residenzplatz   SQUARE
With its horse-drawn carriages, palace and
street entertainers, this stately baroque
square is the Salzburg of a thousand postcards. Its centrepiece is the **Residenzbrun-
nen**, an enormous marble fountain ringed
by four water-spouting horses and topped
by a conch shell–bearing Triton. The plaza
is the late-16th-century vision of Prince-
Archbishop Wolf Dietrich von Raitenau
who, inspired by Rome, enlisted Italian architect Vincenzo Scamozzi.

★ Residenz   PALACE
(www.domquartier.at; Residenzplatz 1; DomQuartier ticket adult/child €12/5; ☺ 10am-5pm Thu-Tue,
to 8pm Wed Jul & Aug, 10am-5pm Wed-Mon Sep-
Jun) The crowning glory of Salzburg's new
DomQuartier, the Residenz is where the
prince-archbishops held court until Salzburg became part of the Habsburg empire
in the 19th century. An audioguide tour
takes in the exuberant **state rooms**, lavishly
adorned with tapestries, stucco and frescoes
by Johann Michael Rottmayr. The 3rd floor
is given over to the **Residenzgalerie**, where
the focus is on Flemish and Dutch masters.
Must-sees include Rubens' *Allegory on Emperor Charles V* and Rembrandt's chiaro-
scuro *Old Woman Praying*.

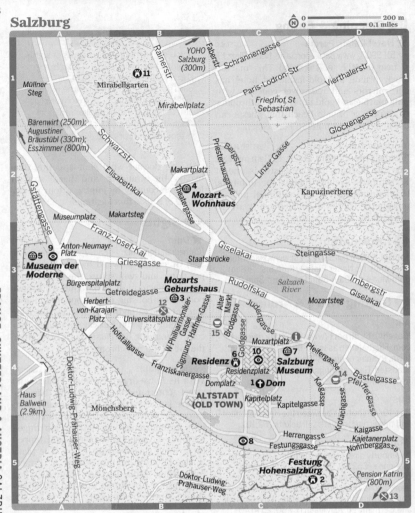

★**Salzburg Museum**   MUSEUM
(www.salzburgmuseum.at; Mozartplatz 1; adult/
child €8.50/3; ⊙9am-5pm Tue-Sun, to 8pm Thu;
📷) Housed in the baroque Neue Residenz
palace, this flagship museum takes you
on a fascinating romp through Salzburg
past and present. Ornate rooms showcase
everything from Roman excavations to
prince-archbishop portraits. There are free
guided tours at 6pm every Thursday.

★**Festung Hohensalzburg**   FORT
(www.salzburg-burgen.at; Mönchsberg 34; adult/
child/family €12/6.80/26.20, incl Festungsbahn
funicular €15.20/8.70/33.70; ⊙9am-7pm) Salzburg's most visible icon is this mighty
900-year-old clifftop fortress, one of the
biggest and best preserved in Europe. It's
easy to spend half a day up here, roaming
the ramparts for far-reaching views over
the city's spires, the Salzach River and the
mountains. The fortress is a steep 15-minute
jaunt from the centre or a speedy ride in the
glass **Festungsbahn funicular** (Festungs-
gasse 4; one way/return adult €6.70/8.30, child
€3.70/4.50; ⊙9am-8pm).

★**Mozarts Geburtshaus**   MUSEUM
(Mozart's Birthplace; www.mozarteum.at; Getreidegasse 9; adult/child €10/3.50, incl Mozart-

Salzburg

Wohnhaus €17/5; ⊘8.30am-7pm Jul & Aug, 9am-5.30pm Sep-Jun) Wolfgang Amadeus Mozart, Salzburg's most famous son, was born in this bright-yellow townhouse in 1756 and spent the first 17 years of his life here.

★**Mozart-Wohnhaus**   MUSEUM
(Mozart's Residence; www.mozarteum.at; Makartplatz 8; adult/child €10/3.50, incl Mozarts Geburtshaus €17/5; ⊘9am-8.30pm Jul & Aug, to 5.30pm Sep-Jun) Tired of the cramped living conditions on Getreidegasse, the Mozart family moved to this more spacious abode in 1773, where a prolific Mozart composed works such as the *Shepherd King* (K208) and *Idomeneo* (K366). Emanuel Schikaneder, a close friend of Mozart and the librettist of *The Magic Flute*, was a regular guest here. An audioguide accompanies your visit, serenading you with opera excerpts. Alongside family portraits and documents you'll find Mozart's original fortepiano.

★**Museum der Moderne**   GALLERY
(www.museumdermoderne.at; Mönchsberg 32; adult/child €8/6; ⊘10am-6pm Tue-Sun, to 8pm Wed) Straddling Mönchsberg's cliffs, this contemporary glass-and-marble oblong of a gallery stands in stark contrast to the fortress. The gallery shows first-rate temporary exhibitions of 20th- and 21st-century art. The works of Alberto Giacometti, Dieter Roth, Emil Nolde and John Cage have previously featured. There's a free guided tour of the gallery at 6.30pm every Wednesday. The **Mönchsberg Lift** (Gstättengasse 13; one-way/return €2.10/3.40, incl gallery €9.70/6.80; ⊘8am-7pm Thu-Tue, to 9pm Wed) whizzes up to the gallery year-round.

Schloss Mirabell   PALACE
(Mirabellplatz 4; ⊘Marble Hall 8am-4pm Mon, Wed & Thu, 1-4pm Tue & Fri, gardens 6am-dusk) `FREE`
Prince-Archbishop Wolf Dietrich built this splendid palace in 1606 to impress his beloved mistress Salome Alt. It must have done the trick because she went on to bear the archbishop some 15 children; sources disagree on the exact number – poor Wolf was presumably too distracted by spiritual matters to keep count himself. Johann Lukas von Hildebrandt, of Schloss Belvedere fame, remodelled the palace in baroque style in 1721. The lavish baroque interior, replete with stucco, marble and frescoes, is free to visit.

★ Festivals & Events

Mozartwoche   MUSIC
(Mozart Week; www.mozarteum.at; ⊘late Jan) World-renowned orchestras, conductors and soloists celebrate Mozart's birthday with a feast of his music in late January.

Salzburg Festival   ART
(Salzburger Festspiele; www.salzburgerfestspiele.at; ⊘late Jul-Aug) You'll need to book tickets months ahead for this venerable summer festival, running since 1920.

⌁ Sleeping

★**Haus Ballwein**   GUESTHOUSE €
(☑82 40 29; www.haus-ballwein.at; Moosstrasse 69a; s/d/q from €45/65/90; ℗☎) With its bright, pine-filled rooms, mountain views, free bike hire and garden, this place is big on charm. The largest, quietest rooms face the back and have balconies and kitchenettes. It's a 10-minute trundle from the Altstadt; take bus 21 to Gsengerweg. Breakfast is a wholesome spread of fresh rolls, eggs, fruit, muesli and cold cuts. No credit cards.

YOHO Salzburg   HOSTEL €
(☑87 96 49; www.yoho.at; Paracelsusstrasse 9; dm €18-22, s/d €40/70; @☎) Free wi-fi, secure lockers, comfy bunks, plenty of cheap beer and good-value schnitzels – what more

could a backpacker ask for? Except, perhaps, a merry singalong with *The Sound of Music* screened daily (yes, *every* day) at 8pm. The friendly crew can arrange tours, adventure sports such as rafting and canyoning, and bike hire. Breakfast is a bargain €4 (€3.50 if ordered the evening before).

✕ Eating

Pick up regional cheese, ham, fruit, bread, gigantic pretzels and other picnic-perfect fodder at food market, **Grünmarkt** (Green Market; Universitätsplatz; ⊘ 7am-7pm Mon-Fri, to 3pm Sat), on one of Salzburg's grandest squares.

Bärenwirt   AUSTRIAN €€
(☑ 42 24 04; www.baerenwirt-salzburg.at; Müll-ner Hauptstrasse 8; mains €9-14; ⊘ 11am-11pm) Sizzling and stirring since 1663, Bärenwirt is Austrian through and through. Go for hearty *Bierbraten* (beer roast) with dumplings, locally caught trout or organic wild boar bratwurst. A tiled oven warms the woody, hunting-lodge-style interior in winter, while the river-facing terrace is a summer crowd-puller. The restaurant is 500m north of Museumplatz.

The Green Garden   VEGETARIAN €€
(☑ 84 12 01; www.thegreengarden.at; Nonntaler Hauptstrasse 16; mains €9-15; ⊘ noon-2pm & 5.30-9pm Tue-Sat; ⓓ) 🌱 The Green Garden is a breath of fresh air for vegetarians and vegans. Locavore is the word at this bright, modern cottage-style restaurant, pairing dishes like wild herb salad, saffron risotto

---

SALZBURG SPLURGE
. . . .
A country manor with an elegantly rustic interior and a chestnut-shaded courtyard, **Gasthof Schloss Ai-gen** (☑ 62 12 84; www.schloss-aigen.at; Schwarzenbergpromenade 37; mains €17.90-24.50, 3-/4course menu €46/56; ⊘ 11.30am-2pm & 5.30-9.30pm Thu & Fri, 11.30am-9.30pm Sat & Sun) is Austrian dining at its finest. The Forstner family's house speciality is *Wiener Melange*, different cuts of meltingly tender Pinzgauer beef, served with apple horseradish, chive sauce and roast potatoes, best matched with robust Austrian wines. Bus 7 stops at Bahnhof Aigen, a 10-minute stroll away.

---

with braised fennel, and vegan fondue with organic wines in a totally relaxed setting.

Drinking & Nightlife

Bars are concentrated along both banks of the Salzach and some of the most upbeat around Gstättengasse. Rudolfskai can be on the rough side of rowdy at weekends.

★ **Augustiner Bräustübl**   BREWERY
(www.augustinerbier.at; Augustinergasse 4-6; ⊘ 3-11pm Mon-Fri, from 2.30pm Sat & Sun) Who says monks can't enjoy themselves? Since 1621, this cheery monastery-run brewery has been serving potent homebrews in Stein tankards in the vaulted hall and beneath the chestnut trees in the 1000-seat beer garden.

Café Tomaselli   CAFE
(www.tomaselli.at; Alter Markt 9; ⊘ 7am-7pm Mon-Sat, from 8am Sun) Going strong since 1705, this marble and wood-panelled cafe is a former Mozart haunt. It's famous for having Salzburg's flakiest strudels, best *Einspänner* (coffee with whipped cream) and grumpiest waiters.

220 Grad   CAFE
(www.220grad.com; Chiemseegasse 5; ⊘ 9am-7pm Tue-Fri, to 6pm Sat) Famous for freshly roasted coffee, this retro-chic cafe serves probably the best espresso in town and whips up superb breakfasts.

❶ Information

Tourist Office (☑ 88 987 0; www.salzburg.info; Mozartplatz 5; ⊘ 9am-6pm)

❶ Getting There & Around

AIR
Salzburg Airport (☑ 858 00; www.salzburg-airport.com; Innsbrucker Bundesstrasse 95), 5km west of the centre, is linked to the Altstadt fringe and Hauptbahnhof by bus 2 and 27 (€2.50) every 10 to 15 minutes.

BUS
Buses depart from just outside the Hauptbahn-hof on Südtiroler Platz. For bus timetables and fares, see www.svv-info.at and www.postbus.at.

TRAIN
Fast trains leave frequently for Vienna (€51.90, three hours) and Linz (€26, 1¼ hours). There is a two-hourly express service to Klagenfurt (€39.50, three hours) and hourly trains to Innsbruck (€45.50, two hours).

EIRIESENWELT

The world's largest accessible ce caves, the soaring limestone turrets of the Ten-nengebirge range and a formidable medieval fortress are but the tip of the superlative iceberg in **Werfen**, 45km south of Salzburg and a great day trip from the city. Such sala-cious natural beauty hasn't escaped Hollywood producers: Werfen stars in WWII action film *Where Eagles Dare* (1968) and makes a cameo appearance in the picnic scene of *The Sound of Music*.

Billed as the world's largest accessible ice caves, **Eisriesenwelt** (www.eisriesenwelt. at; adult/child €14/9, incl cable car €24/14; ⊗8am-4pm Jul & Aug, to 3pm May, Jun, Sep & Oct) is a glittering ice empire spanning 30,000 sq metres and 42km of narrow passages bur-rowing deep into the heart of the mountains. As you climb up wooden steps and down pitch-black passages, otherworldly ice sculptures emerge from the shadows. In summer, shuttlebuses link Werfen train station and the Eisriesenwelt car park, which is a 20-minute walk from the bottom station of the cable car.

Post-caves, catch an afternoon falconry show in the grounds of **Burg Hohen-werfen** (Hohenwerfen Fortress; ☑06468-76 03; www.salzburg-burgen.at; adult/child/family €12/6.50/28.50, incl lift €15.50/13.50/36.50; ⊗9am-6pm mid-Jul–mid-Aug, to 5pm May–mid-Jul & mid-Aug–Sep, 9.30am-4pm Tue-Sun Mar, Apr, Oct & Nov; ⊕), a fortress slung on a wood-ed clifftop with far-reaching views over Werfen from its 16th-century belfry.

Frequent trains link Werfen and Salzburg (€8.60, 40 minutes).

Salzkammergut

A wonderland of glassy blue lakes and tall craggy peaks, Austria's Lake District is a long-time favourite holiday destination. The peaceful lakes attract visitors in droves, who come to boat, fish, swim or just laze on the shore.

Bad Ischl is the region's transport hub, but Hallstatt is its true jewel. For info visit **Salzkammergut Touristik** (☑06132-24 000; www.salzkammergut.co.at; Götzstrasse 2; ⊗9am-7pm daily summer, 9am-6pm Mon-Fri, to 5am Sat rest of year).

The **Salzkammergut Card** (€4.90, avail-able May to October) provides up to 30% discounts on sights, ferries, cable cars and some buses.

Hallstatt

☑06134 / POP 800

With pastel-hued homes, swans and tow-ering mountains on either side of a glassy green lake, Hallstatt looks like some kind of greeting card for tranquillity. Now a Unesco World Heritage Site, Hallstatt was settled 4500 years ago and over 2000 graves have been discovered in the area, most of them dating from 1000 to 500 BC.

⊙ Sights & Activities

Salzwelten MINE
(☑06132-200-2400; www.salzwelten.at; Salzberg-strasse 21; funicular return plus tour adult/child/family €28/15/63, tour only €22/11/46; ⊗9.30am-4.30pm Apr-Sep, to 3pm Oct, to 2.30pm Nov) The fascinating Salzbergwerk is situated high above Hallstatt on Salzberg (Salt Mountain) and is the lake's major cultural attraction. The German-English tour details how salt is formed and the history of mining, and takes visitors down into the depths on miners' slides – the largest is 60m, during which you have your photo taken.

The **funicular** (one way adult/child €9/4.50) is the easiest way up to the mountain sta-tion, from where the mine is 15 minutes' walk; a switchback trail takes about 40 min-utes to walk.

Hallstätter See LAKE
(boat hire per hour from €11) You can hire boats and kayaks to get out on the lake, or scu-ba dive with the **Tauchclub Dachstein** (☑0664-88 600 481; www.dive-adventures.at; in-tro course from €35).

🛏 Sleeping & Eating

Pension Sarstein GUESTHOUSE €
(☑06134-8217; Gosaumühlstrasse 83; d €76-96 incl breakfast, apt 2/3/4 people excl breakfast €100/130/150; 🕾) The affable Fischer family

take pride in their little guesthouse, a few minutes' walk along the lakefront from central Hallstatt. The old-fashioned rooms are nothing flash, but they are neat and cosy, and have balconies with dreamy lake and mountain views. Family-sized apartments come with kitchenettes.

★ **Restaurant zum Salzbaron** EUROPEAN €€
(☑ 06134-82 63; www.gruenerbaum.cc; Marktplatz 104; mains €15-25; ⊘ 11.30am-10pm; 🛜 ☑) One of the best gourmet acts in town, the Salzbaron is perched alongside the lake inside the Seehotel Grüner Baum and serves a seasonal pan-European menu; local trout features strongly in summer.

❶ Information

Tourist Office (☑ 82 08; www.dachstein-salzkammergut.at; Seestrasse 99; ⊘ 9am-5pm Mon-Fri, to 1pm Sat)

❶ Getting There & Away

Hallstatt train station is across the lake from the village, and boat services coincide with train arrivals (€2.40, 10 minutes, last ferry to Hallstatt Markt 6.50pm). About a dozen trains daily connect Hallstatt and Bad Ischl (€4.20, 27 minutes).

Tyrol

With converging mountain ranges behind lofty pastures and tranquil meadows, Tyrol (also Tirol) captures a quintessential Alpine panoramic view. Occupying a central position is Innsbruck, the region's jewel, while in the northeast and southwest are superb ski resorts. In the southeast, separated somewhat from the main state since part of South Tyrol was ceded to Italy at the end of WWI, lies the protected natural landscape of the Hohe Tauern National Park, an Alpine wonderland of 3000m peaks, including the country's highest, the Grossglockner (3798m).

Innsbruck

☑ 0512 / POP 121,300 / ELEV 574M

Tyrol's capital is a sight to behold. The mountains are so close that within 25 minutes it's possible to travel from the heart of the city to over 2000m above sea level. Summer and winter outdoor activities abound, and it's understandable why some visitors only take a peek at Innsbruck proper before heading for the hills. But to do so is a shame, for Innsbruck has its own share of gems, including an authentic medieval Altstadt (Old Town), inventive architecture and vibrant student-driven nightlife.

⊙ Sights

★ **Hofkirche** CHURCH
(www.tiroler-landesmuseum.at; Universitätsstrasse 2; adult/child €5/free; ⊘ 9am-5pm Mon-Sat, 12.30-5pm Sun) Innsbruck's pride and joy is the Gothic Hofkirche, one of Europe's finest royal court churches. It was commissioned in 1553 by Ferdinand I, who enlisted top artists of the age such as Albrecht Dürer, Alexander Colin and Peter Vischer the Elder. Top billing goes to the empty **sarcophagus of Emperor Maximilian I** (1459–1519), a masterpiece of German Renaissance sculpture, elaborately carved from black marble.

★ **Goldenes Dachl Museum** MUSEUM
(Golden Roof Museum; Herzog-Friedrich-Strasse 15; adult/child €4.80/2.40; ⊘ 10am-5pm May-Sep, closed Mon Oct-Apr) Innsbruck's golden wonder is this Gothic oriel, built for Emperor Maximilian I and glittering with 2657 firegilt copper tiles. An audioguide whizzes you through the history in the museum; look for the grotesque tournament helmets designed to resemble the Turks of the rival Ottoman Empire.

★ **Hofburg** PALACE
(Imperial Palace; www.hofburg-innsbruck.at; Rennweg 1; adult/child €9/free; ⊘ 9am-5pm) Demanding attention with its imposing facade and cupolas, the Hofburg was built as a castle for Archduke Sigmund the Rich in the 15th century, expanded by Emperor Maximilian I in the 16th century and given a baroque makeover by Empress Maria Theresia in the 18th century. The centrepiece of the lavish rococo state apartments is the 31m-long **Riesensaal** (Giant's Hall).

★ **Tiroler Landesmuseum Ferdinandeum** GALLERY
(☑ 0512-594 89; www.tiroler-landesmuseum.at; Museumstrasse 15; adult/child €11/7; ⊘ 9am-5pm Tue-Sun) This treasure-trove of Tyrolean history and art moves from Bronze Age artefacts to the original reliefs used to design the Goldenes Dachl. Alongside brooding Dutch masterpieces of the Rembrandt ilk, the gallery displays an astounding collection of Austrian art including Gothic altarpieces, a handful of Klimt and Kokoschka paintings, and some shocking Viennese Actionist works.

FRANCE, SWITZERLAND & AUSTRIA TYROL

Bergisel VIEWPOINT
(www.bergisel.info; adult/child €9.50/4.50; ⊙9am-6pm) Rising above Innsbruck like a celestial staircase, this glass-and-steel ski jump was designed by much-lauded Iraqi architect Zaha Hadid. It's 455 steps or a two-minute funicular ride to the 50m-high **viewing platform**, with a breathtaking panorama of the Nordkette range, Innta and Innsbruck. Tram 1 trundles here from central Innsbruck.

🏃 Activities

Anyone who loves the great outdoors will be just itching to head up into the Alps in Innsbruck. Aside from skiing and walking, rafting, mountain biking, paragliding and bobsledding tempt the daring.

Nordkettenbahnen FUNICULAR
(www.nordkette.com; one way/return to Hungerburg €4.80/8, Seegrube €17.30/28.80, Hafelekar €19.20/32; ⊙Hungerburg 7am-7.15pm Mon-Fri, 8am-7.15pm Sat & Sun, Seegrube 8.30am-5.30pm daily, Hafelekar 9am-5pm daily) Zaha Hadid's space-age funicular runs every 15 minutes, whizzing you from the Congress Centre to the slopes in no time. Walking trails head off in all directions from **Hungerburg** and **Seegrube**. For more of a challenge, there is a downhill track for mountain bikers and two fixed-rope routes (Klettersteige) for climbers.

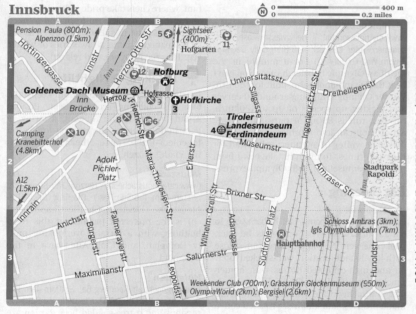

Innsbruck

⦿ Top Sights
1 Goldenes Dachl Museum................B1
2 Hofburg......................................B1
3 Hofkirche....................................B1
4 Tiroler Landesmuseum
   Ferdinandeum...........................C2

⊕ Activities, Courses & Tours
5 Nordkettenbahnen.......................B1

🛏 Sleeping
6 Hotel Weisses Kreuz B2

7 Nepomuk's...................................B2

✖ Eating
8 Die Wilderin.................................B2
9 Kröll...B1
10 Markthalle..................................A2

🍷 Drinking & Nightlife
11 Hofgarten..................................C1
12 Moustache.................................B1

FRANCE, SWITZERLAND & AUSTRIA TYROL

ℹ CENT SAVERS

The money-saving **Innsbruck Card** (24/48/72hr €39/48/55, children half price) allows one visit to Innsbruck's main sights and attractions, a return journey with any cable car or funicular, five hours' bike rental and unlimited use of public transport. The card also yields numerous discounts on tours and activities. It's available at the tourist office.

Stay overnight in Innsbruck and you'll receive a **guest card**, giving discounts on transport and activities and entry to a number of pools and lidos; it also allows you to join the tourist office's **free guided hikes** in summer.

Olympiabobbahn　　　　　　BOB RUN
(www.olympiaworld.at; Heiligwasserwiese, Igls; summer/winter €25/30; ⊙5-8pm daily Dec-Mar, 2-6pm Wed-Fri Jul-Aug) For a minute in the life of an Olympic bobsleigh racer, you can't beat the Olympiabobbahn, built for the 1976 Winter Olympics. Zipping around 10 curves and picking up speeds of up to 100km/h, the bob run is 800m of pure hair-raising action. You can join a professional bobsled driver in winter or summer; call ahead for the exact times. To reach it, take bus J from the Landesmuseum to Igls Olympiaexpress.

🛏 Sleeping

★Nepomuk's　　　　　　HOSTEL €
(☑584 118; www.nepomuks.at; Kiebachgasse 16; dm/d from €24/58; 🛜) Could this be the backpacker heaven? Nepomuk's sure comes close, with its Altstadt location, well-stocked kitchen and high-ceilinged dorms with homely touches like CD players. The delicious breakfast in attached Cafe Munding, with homemade pastries, jam and fresh-roasted coffee, gets your day off to a grand start.

★Hotel Weisses Kreuz　　HISTORIC HOTEL €€
(☑594 79; www.weisseskreuz.at; Herzog-Friedrich-Strasse 31; s/d from €77/119, with shared bathroom from €41-46/75-83; 🅿@🛜) Beneath the arcades, this atmospheric Altstadt hotel has played host to guests for 500 years, including a 13-year-old Mozart. With its wood-panelled parlours, antiques and twisting staircase, the hotel oozes history with every creaking beam. Rooms are supremely comfortable, staff charming and breakfast is a lavish spread.

🍴 Eating

Pick up fresh bread, Tyrolean cheese, organic fruit, smoked ham, salami and other tasty picnic supplies at **Markthalle** (www.markthalle-innsbruck.at; Herzog-Siegmund-Ufer 1-3; ⊙7am-6.30pm Mon-Fri, to 1pm Sat).

Kröll　　　　　　SNACKS €
(Hofgasse 6; snacks €3-5; ⊙6am-9pm) Forget plain apple, this hole-in-the-wall cafe's strudels include rhubarb, poppy, feta and plum. The fresh juices pack a vitamin punch.

★Die Wilderin　　　　AUSTRIAN €€
(☑562 728; www.diewilderin.at; Seilergasse 5; mains €9-18; ⊙5pm-2am Tue-Sat, 4pm-midnight Sun) 🍃 Take a gastronomic walk on the wild side at this modern-day hunter-gatherer of a restaurant, where chefs take pride in local sourcing and using top-notch farm-fresh and foraged ingredients. The menu sings of the seasons, be it asparagus, game, strawberries or winter veg. The vibe is urbane and relaxed.

🍷 Drinking & Nightlife

Innsbruck's student population keeps the bar and clubbing scene upbeat. Besides a glut of bars in the Altstadt, a string of bars huddles under the railway arches on Ingenieur-Etzel-Strasse, otherwise known as the Viaduktbögen.

Moustache　　　　　　BAR
(www.cafe-moustache.at; Herzog-Otto-Strasse 8; ⊙11am-2am Tue-Sun; 🛜) Playing Spot-the-Moustache (Einstein, Charlie Chaplin and co) is the preferred pastime at this retro bolthole, with a terrace overlooking pretty Domplatz and Club Aftershave in the basement.

Hofgarten　　　　　　BAR
(www.tagnacht.at; Rennweg 6a; ⊙10am-4am Tue, Fri & Sat, to 2am Wed & Thu, to midnight Sun) DJ sessions and a tree-shaded beer garden are crowd-pullers at this trendy cafe-cum-bar set in the greenery of Hofgarten.

ℹ Information

Innsbruck Information (☑53 56-0, 59 850; www.innsbruck.info; Burggraben 3; ⊙9am-6pm)

ℹ Getting There & Away

AIR

EasyJet flies to **Innsbruck Airport** (INN; ☑0512-22 525; www.innsbruck-airport.com; Fürstenweg 180), 4km west of the city centre.

TRAIN

Fast trains depart at least every two hours for Bregenz (€37.50, 2¾ hours), Salzburg (€45.50, two hours), Kitzbühel (€15.80, 1¾ hours) and Munich (€41.20, 1¾ hours).

ⓘ Getting Around

Bus F links the airport every 15 or 20 minutes with Maria-Theresien-Strasse. Single tickets on buses and trams (www.ivb.at) cost €2.30 and a day ticket is €4.10.

Kitzbühel

☏ 05356 / POP 8500 / ELEV 762M

Kitzbühel began life in the 16th century as a silver- and copper-mining town, and to-day preserves a charming car-free medieval centre despite its other persona – as a fashionable and prosperous winter resort. It's renowned for the white-knuckled Hahnen-kamm downhill ski race in January and the excellence of its 170km of groomed slopes.

🏃 Activities

In winter there's first-rate intermediate **skiing** and **freeriding** on Kitzbüheler Horn to the north and Hahnenkamm to the south of town.

Dozens of summer **hiking** trails thread through the Kitzbühel Alps; the tourist office gives walking maps and runs free guided hikes for guests staying in town.

🛏 Sleeping & Eating

Snowbunny's Hostel   HOSTEL €
(☏ 067-6794 0233; www.snowbunnys.co.uk; Bichl-strasse 30; dm €22-45, d €66-130; 🅿🛜) This friendly, laid-back hostel is a bunny-hop from the slopes. Dorms are fine, if a tad dark; breakfast is DIY-style in the kitchen. There's a TV lounge, ski storage room and cats to stroke.

Huberbräu Stüberl   AUSTRIAN €€
(☏ 656 77; Vorderstadt 18; mains €10-20; ⊙8am-midnight Mon-Sat, from 9am Sun) An old-world Tyrolean haunt with vaults and pine benches, this tavern favours substantial portions of Austrian classics, such as schnitzel, goulash and dumplings, cooked to perfection.

ⓘ Information

Tourist Office (☏ 666 60; www.kitzbuehel.com; Hinterstadt 18; ⊙8.30am-6pm Mon-Fri, 9am-1pm & 2-6pm Sat, 10am-noon & 4-6pm Sun)

ⓘ Getting There & Away

Trains run frequently from Kitzbühel to Innsbruck (€20.80, 1¾ hours) and Salzburg (€31.40, 2½ hours). It's quicker and cheaper to reach Lienz by bus (€15.80, two hours, every two hours).

Lienz

☏ 04852 / POP 11,800 / ELEV 673M

With the jagged Dolomites crowding its southern skyline, the capital of East Tyrol is a scenic staging point for travels through the Hohe Tauern National Park.

◉ Sights & Activities

A €36 day pass covers skiing on the nearby **Zettersfeld** and **Hochstein** peaks. However, the area is more renowned for its 100km of cross-country trails; the town fills up for the annual Dolomitenlauf cross-country skiing race in mid-January.

Schloss Bruck   CASTLE
(www.museum-schlossbruck.at; Schlossberg 1; adult/child €8.50/2.50; ⊙10am-6pm Jul & Aug, to 4pm Tue-Sun Sep & Oct, to 6pm Tue-Sun Nov-Jun) Lienz' famous medieval fortress has a museum chronicling the region's history, as well as Roman artefacts, Gothic winged altars and local costumes. The **castle tower** is used for changing exhibitions; a highlight for art enthusiasts is the **Egger-Lienz-Galerie** devoted to the emotive works of Albin Egger-Lienz.

🛏 Sleeping & Eating

Goldener Stern   PENSION €
(☏ 621 92; www.goldener-stern-lienz.at; Schweiz-ergasse 40; s/d from €45/80; 🅿) Framed by neat gardens, this 600-year-old *Pension* has spacious, old-fashioned rooms. Breakfast is served in the tiny courtyard in summer.

Da Leonardo   PIZZA €
(☏ 699 44; www.daleonardo.at; Tiroler Strasse 30; pizza €7-15; ⊙11am-11pm) Not many chefs can claim to be a world champion of pizza making, but Leonardo Granata can – he's picked up the award of World Champion, and many other awards, using dough he allows to stand for 24 to 48 hours.

ⓘ Information

Tourist Office (☏ 050-212 400; www.lienzer-dolomiten.net; Europaplatz 1; ⊙8.30am-6pm Mon-Fri, 9am-noon & 2-5pm Sat, 8.30-11am Sun)

HOHE TAUERN NATIONAL PARK

Straddling Tyrol, Salzburg and Carinthia, this national park is the largest in the Alps: a 1786-sq-km wilderness of 3000m peaks, Alpine meadows and waterfalls. At its heart lies **Grossglockner** (3798m), Austria's highest mountain, which towers over the 8km-long Pasterze Glacier, best seen from the outlook at **Kaiser-Franz-Josefs-Höhe** (2369m).

The 48km **Grossglockner Road** (www.grossglockner.at; Hwy 107; car/motorcycle day ticket €35/25, 30-day ticket €54/43; ☉ 6am-8.30pm May, 5am-9.30pm Jun-Aug, 6am-7.30pm Sep–mid-Nov) from Bruck in Salzburgerland to Heiligenblut in Carinthia is one of Europe's greatest Alpine drives. A feat of 1930s engineering, the road swings giddily around 36 switchbacks, passing jewel-coloured lakes, forested slopes and wondrous glaciers. The major village on the Grossglockner Road is **Heiligenblut**, famous for its 15th-century pilgrimage church. Bus 5002 links Lienz and Heiligenblut (€8.50, one hour).

A real crash-bang spectacle, the 380m-high, three-tier **Krimmler Wasserfälle** (Krimml Falls; ☑ 06564-72 12; www.wasserfaelle-krimml.at; adult/child €3/1; ☉ ticket office 8am-6pm mid-Apr–mid-Oct), the thunderous centrepiece of the tiny village of Krimml, is Europe's highest waterfall. From the tourist office in the village, the **Wasserfallweg** (Waterfall Trail) weaves uphill through mixed forest, with numerous viewpoints with photogenic close-ups of the falls.

ℹ️ Getting There & Away

Buses pull up in front of the train station, where you'll find the **Postbus information office** (☑ 930 00 187; Hauptbahnhof; ☉ 8am-12.30pm & 1-2.30pm Mon-Fri). There are bus connections to regional ski resorts and northwards to the Hohe Tauern National Park. Buses to Kitzbühel (€15.80, two hours, every two hours) are quicker than the train, but less frequent.

There are several daily services to Innsbruck (from €15.80, 3¼ to 4½ hours) and Salzburg (€41.20, 3½ hours).

Vorarlberg

Vorarlberg has always been a little different. Cut off from the rest of Austria by the snow-capped Arlberg massif, this westerly region has often associated itself more with nearby Switzerland than distant Vienna, and also provides a convenient gateway to Germany and Liechtenstein.

The capital, **Bregenz**, sits prettily on the shores of Lake Constance. But it is the wild and austerely beautiful Arlberg region, shared by Tyrol and neighbouring Vorarlberg, that steals the limelight with some of Austria's finest skiing. Heralded as the cradle of Alpine skiing, **St Anton am Arlberg** is undoubtedly the best known and most popular resort with downhill skiing, off-piste adventure and après-ski partying to die for. The **tourist office** (☑ 05446-226 90; www.stantonamarlberg.com; Dorfstrasse 8; ☉ 8am-6pm Mon-Fri, 9am-6pm Sat, 9am-noon & 2-5pm Sun)

has maps and information on accommodation and activities.

St Anton is on the main railway route between Bregenz (€21.40, 1½ hours) and Innsbruck (€24.20, 1¼ hours). It's close to the eastern entrance of the **Arlberg Tunnel**, the toll road connecting Vorarlberg and Tyrol (€9).

Austria Survival Guide

ℹ️ Directory A–Z

ACCOMMODATION

➡ From simple mountain huts to five-star hotels – you'll find the lot in Austria.

➡ Tourist offices keep lists and details; some arrange bookings for free or for a nominal fee.

➡ Book ahead for the high seasons: July and August, and December to April (in ski resorts).

➡ Some hostels and rock-bottom digs have an *Etagendusche* (communal shower).

➡ In mountain resorts, high-season prices can be up to double the prices charged in the low season (May to June and October to November).

➡ Some resorts issue a *Gästekarte* (guest card) when you stay overnight, offering discounts on things such as cable cars and admission.

INTERNET RESOURCES

Österreich Werbung (www.austria.info) National tourism authority.

Austrian Hotelreservation (www.austrian-hotelreservation.at) One-stop shop for hotel reservations.

ÖBB (www.oebb.at) Austrian Federal Railways.

MONEY

➡ Austria's currency is the euro.

➡ *Bankomaten* (ATMs) are widely available. Most hotels and midrange restaurants accept Maestro direct debit and Visa and MasterCard credit cards.

➡ An approximate 10% tip is expected in restaurants. Give it to the server; don't leave it on the table.

OPENING HOURS

Banks 8am to 3pm Monday to Friday, to 5.30pm Thursday

Restaurants 11am to 2.30pm and 6pm to 11pm or midnight

Shops 9am to 6.30pm Monday to Friday (often to 9pm Thursday or Friday in cities). 9am to 5pm Saturday

PUBLIC HOLIDAYS

New Year's Day (Neujahr) 1 January

Epiphany (Heilige Drei Könige) 6 January

Easter Monday (Ostermontag) March/April

Labour Day (Tag der Arbeit) 1 May

Whit Monday (Pfingstmontag) 6th Monday after Easter

Ascension Day (Christi Himmelfahrt) 6th Thursday after Easter

Corpus Christi (Fronleichnam) 2nd Thursday after Whitsunday

Assumption (Maria Himmelfahrt) 15 August

National Day (Nationalfeiertag) 26 October

All Saints' Day (Allerheiligen) 1 November

Immaculate Conception (Mariä Empfängnis) 8 December

Christmas Day (Christfest) 25 December

St Stephen's Day (Stephanitag) 26 December

TELEPHONE

➡ Austrian telephone numbers consist of an area code followed by the local number. Drop the initial '0' from the area code when calling from abroad. Drop the area code altogether when calling locally.

➡ Austria's country code is 43; the international access code is 00.

➡ Phone shops sell prepaid SIM cards for about €10.

➡ Austrian mobile (*Handy*) telephone numbers begin with 0650 or higher up to 0699.

VISAS

Schengen visa rules apply. The Austrian Foreign Ministry website (www.bmeia.gv.at) lists embassies.

 PRICE RANGES

Accommodation prices listed are for the high summer season and refer to a double room with a bathroom, including breakfast.

€ less than €80

€€ €80 to €200

€€€ more than €200

Price ranges for restaurants/eateries refer to a two-course meal, excluding drinks.

€ less than €15

€€ €15 to €30

€€€ more than €30

 Getting There & Away

AIR

Vienna is the main transport hub for Austria, but Graz, Linz, Klagenfurt, Salzburg and Innsbruck all receive international flights. Flights to these cities can be a cheaper option than those to the capital, as are flights to Airport Letisko (Bratislava Airport), just 60km east of Vienna, in Slovakia.

LAND

Train

Austria benefits from its central location within Europe by having excellent rail connections to all important destinations.

The main services in and out of the country from the west normally pass through Bregenz, Innsbruck or Salzburg en route to Vienna. From Vienna there are ample trains into Eastern Europe, including Bratislava, Budapest, Prague and Warsaw; there are also connections south to Italy via Klagenfurt, and north to Berlin.

For timetables and tickets, visit the website of **ÖBB** (Österreichische Bundesbahnen. Austrian Federal Railways; www. oebb.at).

SparSchiene (discounted tickets) are often available when you book online in advance.

RIVER & LAKE

Hydrofoils run to Bratislava and Budapest from Vienna; slower boats cruise the Danube between the capital and Passau. The **Danube Tourist Commission** (www.danube-river.org) has a country-by-country list of operators and agents who can book tours.

FRANCE, SWITZERLAND & AUSTRIA AUSTRIA SURVIVAL GUIDE

RAIL PASSES

Depending on the amount of travelling you intend to do in Austria, rail passes can be a good deal.

Eurail Austria Pass This handy pass is available to non-EU residents; prices start at €129 for three days' unlimited 2nd-class travel within one month. See the website at www.eurail.com for all options.

Interrail Passes For European residents, these passes include One Country Pass Austria (three/four/six/eight days €131/154/187/219). Youths under 26 receive substantial discounts. See www.interrail.eu for all options.

Getting Around

BICYCLE

All cities have at least one bike shop that doubles as a rental centre; you'll pay around €10 to €15 per day.

You can take bicycles on any train with a bicycle symbol at the top of its timetable. For regional and long-distance trains, you'll pay an extra 10% on your ticket price. It costs €12 to take your bike on international trains.

The Danube cycling trail is like a Holy Grail for cyclists, following the entire length of the river in Austria between the borders with Germany and Slovakia. Tourist offices have information.

BUS & TRAIN

Austria's national railway system is integrated with the Postbus services. Plan your route using the ÖBB (www.oebb.at) or Postbus (www.postbus.at) websites.

For telephone information inside Austria, call ☑ 05 1717. From outside Austria, call ☑ 43 5 17 17.

Reservations are usually unnecessary. It's possible to buy tickets in advance on some routes, but on others you can only buy tickets from the drivers.

CAR & MOTORCYCLE

Speed limits are 50km/h in built-up areas, 130km/h on motorways and 100km/h on other roads.

A *Vignette* (toll sticker) is imposed on all motorways; charges for cars/motorbikes are €8.70/5 for 10 days and €25.30/12.70 for two months. Purchase *vignettes* at border crossings, petrol stations and Tabak shops.

Some mountain tunnels command additional tolls (usually €2.50 to €10).

Spain & Portugal

Best Places to Eat

➡ El Celler de Can Roca (p427)

➡ Fangas Mercearia Bar (p480)

➡ Mercado de San Miguel (p400)

➡ Mercado da Ribeira (p464)

➡ La Cuchara de San Telmo (p406)

Best Places to Sleep

➡ Lisbon Destination Hostel (p461)

➡ Casa Gràcia (p422)

➡ Moon Hill Hostel (p467)

➡ Russafa Youth Hostel (p435)

➡ Casa Caracol (p453)

Why Go?

Beyond the Pyrenees is another Europe, a diverse and magical land surrounded by sea with cultures all of its own. It's scenically spectacular, with a staggering array of beaches, national parks and mountains, and a turbulent history has left a majestic range of architecture, from Roman remains to noble cathedrals, from Moorish palaces to Modernista gems and landmark modern buildings.

Some of the continent's best food is produced here; Portugal's excellent fish is famed, while Spain's legendary tapas culture is just one aspect of a country enthusiastically dedicated to sociable eating and drinking. The nightlife is superb, but adjust your body clock: when midnight strikes, things are often just beginning. Whether you're showing off your dance moves at a superclub, trying the astonishing variety of local wines or listening to fado's soulful strains or flamenco's anguished energy, many of your best moments in the region will come after dark.

Fast Facts

Capitals Madrid (Spain), Lisbon (Portugal)

Emergency ☎112

Currency Euro (€)

Languages Spanish, Portuguese, Catalan, Basque, Galician, Aranese

Time Zones Central European (Spain; UTC/GMT plus one hour); Western European (Portugal; UTC/GMT)

Country Codes ☎34 (Spain), ☎351 (Portugal)

Population 46.8 million (Spain), 10.5 million (Portugal)

Spain & Portugal Highlights

① Barcelona
Admire the genius of Gaudí and wallow in cultural riches and a glorious food culture. (p416)

② Mallorca Enjoy Mediterranean sunshine on the blessed Balearic beaches. (p428)

③ Madrid Spend your days in Europe's best art galleries and nights amid its best nightlife. (p396)

④ Toledo Explore Spain's multicultural past and staggering architectural legacy. (p402)

⑤ Granada See the exquisite Alhambra and wander the Albayzín's twisting lanes. (p448)

⑥ Seville Admire the architecture and surrender to the party atmosphere. (p439)

⑦ Lisbon Follow the sound of fado in the lamplit lanes of the enchanting old-world heart of the city. (p460)

⑧ Porto Sample velvety ports at riverside wine lodges in the Unesco World Heritage–listed centre. (p481)

⑨ Santiago de Compostela Join the pilgrims making their way to the magnificent cathedral. (p414)

⑩ San Sebastián Eat your way through the peninsula's foodie capital, a gourmand's paradise with an idyllic setting. (p404)

OFF THE BEATEN TRACK: SERRA DA ESTRELA

Glorious hiking in Portugal's highest mountains. (p480)

WORTH A TRIP: ASTURIAS

Cider, seafood and great hikes in the Picos de Europa. (p413)

OFF THE BEATEN TRACK: THE ALGARVE

The Algarve's western surf beaches are wild and undeveloped. (p475)

WORTH A TRIP: CÁDIZ

Vibrant Cádiz has a top town beach and unique ambience. (p452)

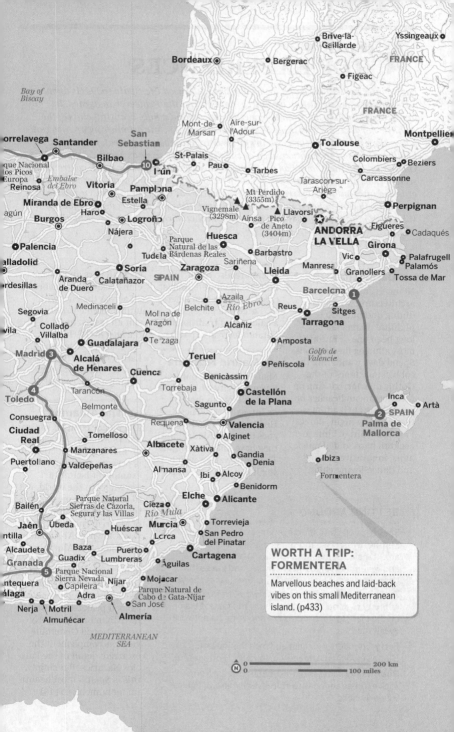

Bay of Biscay

FRANCE

Bordeaux ◉
Bergerac
Brive-la-Gaillarde ◉
Yssingeaux
Figeac ◉
FRANCE
Montpellier

Mont-de-Marsan
Aire-sur-l'Adour
Toulouse ◉
Colombiers ◉ ◉ Beziers
Carcassonne

orrelavega ◉ Santander
San Sebastian
St-Palais
Tarbes ◉
Tarascon-sur-Ariège
Perpignan

que Nacional os Picos Europa
10
I-ún
Pau
Pamplona
Mt Perdido (3355m) ▲
Vignemale (3298m)
Llavorsí
Figueres

Reinosa
Embalse del Ebro
Vitoria
Estella
Aínsa
Pico de Aneto (3404m) ▲
ANDORRA LA VELLA ★
Cadaqués

Miranda de Ebro
Haro
Logroño
Huesca
Barbastro
Vic
Girona

agún
Burgos
Nájera
Parque Natural de las Bárdenas Reales
Tudela
Sariñena
Manresa
Granollers
Palafrugell
Palamós

Palencia
Soria
Zaragoza
Lleida
Tossa de Mar

alladolid
Aranda de Duero
Calatañazor
SPAIN
Barcelona
1

rdesillas
Medinaceli
Azaila
Río Ebro
Reus
Sitges

Segovia
Mol na de Aragón
Belchite
Alcañiz
Tarragona

vila
Collado Villalba
Te·zaga
Amposta
Golfo de Valencie

Madrid
3
Guadalajara
Teruel
Peñíscola

Alcalá de Henares
Cuenca
Benicàssim

Toledo
4
Tarancón
Torrebaja
Castellón de la Plana
Inca
Artà

Consuegra
Belmonte
Sagunto
Palma de Mallorca
2
SPAIN

Ciudad Real
Tomelloso
Requena
Valencia

Puertol ano
Manzanares
Valdepeñas
Albacete
Xàtiva
Alginet
Gandia
Denia
Ibiza

Al·mansa
Ibi
Alcoy
Formentera

Bailén
Parque Natural Sierras de Cazorla, Segura y las Villas
Cieza
Río Mula
Benidorm

Jaén
Úbeda
Elche
Alicante

ntilla
Huéscar
Murcia

Alcaudete
Baza
Lorca
Torrevieja
San Pedro del Pinatar

Granada
5
Guadix
Puerto Lumbreras
Águilas
Cartagena

ntequera
Parque Nacional Sierra Nevada
Capileira
Níjar
Mojácar

álaga
Adra
Parque Natural de Cabo de Gata-Níjar
San José

Nerja
Motril
Almería

Almuñécar

MEDITERRANEAN SEA

WORTH A TRIP: FORMENTERA

....

Marvellous beaches and laid-back vibes on this small Mediterranean island. (p433)

0 ——— 200 km
0 ——— 100 miles
Ⓝ

Spain's
TOP EXPERIENCES

Passionate, sophisticated and devoted to living the good life, Spain (p396) is at once a stereotype come to life and a country more diverse than you ever imagined. Its landscapes stir the soul, from the jagged Pyrenees and wildly beautiful cliffs of the Atlantic northwest to charming Mediterranean coves, while astonishing architecture spans the ages at every turn. Spain's cities march to a beguiling beat, rushing headlong into the 21st century even as timeless villages serve as beautiful signposts to Old Spain. And then there's one of Europe's most celebrated (and varied) gastronomic scenes. Aove all, Spain lives very much in the present. Perhaps you'll sense it along a crowded after-midnight street when all the world has come out to play. Or maybe that moment will come when a flamenco performer touches something deep in your soul. Whenever it happens, you'll find yourself nodding in recognition: this is Spain.

Barcelona

Home to cutting-edge architecture, world-class dining and pulsating nightlife, Barcelona has long been one of Europe's most alluring destinations. Spend days wandering the cobblestone lanes of the Gothic quarter, basking on Mediterranean beaches or marvelling at Gaudí masterpieces. By night, Barcelona is a whirl of vintage cocktail bars, gilded music halls, innovative eateries and dance-loving clubs.

There are also colourful markets, hallowed arenas (such as Camp Nou where FC Barcelona plays), and a calendar of traditional Catalan festivals. (p416)

Madrid Nightlife

Madrid is not the only European city with nightlife, but few can match its intensity. As Ernest Hemingway said, 'Nobody goes to bed in Madrid until they have killed the night.' There are wall-to-wall bars, small clubs, live venues, cocktail bars and megaclubs beloved by celebrities all across the city, with unimaginable variety to suit all tastes. But it's in the *barrios* of Huertas, Malasaña, Chueca and La Latina that you'll really understand what we're talking about. (p400)

The Alhambra

The palace complex of Granada's Alhambra is close to architectural perfection. It is perhaps the most refined example of Islamic art anywhere in the world, not to mention the most enduring symbol of 800 years of Moorish rule in what was known as Al-Andalus. From afar, the Alhambra's red fortress towers dominate the Granada skyline, set against a backdrop of the Sierra Nevada's snow-capped peaks. Up close, the Alhambra's perfectly proportioned Generalife gardens complement the exquisite detail of the Palacios Nazaríes. Put simply, this is Spain's most beautiful monument. (p448)

GETTING AROUND

Spain's public transport system is one of the best in Europe, with a fast and super-modern train system, an extensive domestic air network, an impressive and well-maintained road network, and buses that connect villages in the country's remotest corners.

Train Extremely efficient rail network, from slow intercity regional trains to some of the fastest trains on the planet. More routes are added to the network every year.

Ferry Connects the mainland with the Balearic Islands of Mallorca, Menorca, Ibiza and Formentera.

Bus The workhorses of the Spanish roads, from slick express services to stop-everywhere village-to-village buses.

★ Córdoba's Mezquita

A church that became a mosque before reverting back to a church, Córdoba's Mezquita charts the evolution of Western and Islamic architecture over a 1000-year trajectory. Its most innovative features include some early horseshoe arches, an intricate mihrab, and a veritable 'forest' of 856 columns, many of them recycled from Roman ruins. The sheer scale of the Mezquita reflects Córdoba's erstwhile power as the most cultured city in 10th-century Europe. It was also inspiration for even greater buildings to come, most notably in Seville and Granada. (p443)

★ Camino de Santiago

Every year, tens of thousands of pilgrims and walkers set out to walk across northern Spain. Their destination, Santiago de Compostela, is a place of untold significance for Christians, but the appeal of this epic walk goes far beyond the religious. With numerous routes across the north, there is no finer way to get under Spain's skin and experience the pleasures and caprices of its natural world. And even completing one small stage will leave you with a lifetime of impressions. (p414)

★ Seville

Nowhere is as quintessentially Spanish as Seville, a city of capricious moods and soulful secrets, which has played a pivotal role in the evolution of flamenco, bullfighting, baroque art

and Mudéjar architecture. Blessed with year-round sunshine and fuelled culturally by a never-ending schedule of ebullient festivals, everything seems more amorous here, a feeling not lost on legions of 19th-century aesthetes, who used the city as a setting in their romantic works of fiction. Head south to the home of Carmen and Don Juan and take up the story. (p439)

★ A La Playa

It's easy to see why Spain's beaches are Europe's favourite summer playground, but the beach is also an obsession among Spaniards in summer, when the entire country seems to head for the coast. There's so much more to Spain's coastline than the overcrowded beaches of the south: the rugged coves of the Costa Brava near Girona, or Cabo de Gata in Andalucía, come close to the Mediterranean ideal, while the Atlantic beaches around Tarifa to the Portuguese frontier and the dramatic coastline of Spain's northwest are utterly spectacular.

if Spain were 100 people

74 would speak Castilian Spanish
17 would speak Catalan
7 would speak Galician
2 would speak Basque

belief systems
(% of population)

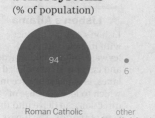

94
Roman Catholic

6
other (mostly Islam)

population per sq km

SPAIN   USA   UK

👤 ≈ 30 people

When to Go

Madrid

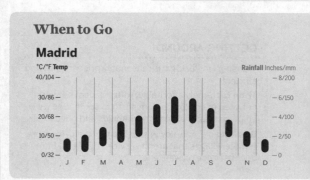

°C/°F Temp
40/104 —
30/86 —
20/68 —
10/50 —
0/32 —

Rainfall Inches/mm
— 8/200
— 6/150
— 4/100
— 2/50
— 0

J F M A M J J A S O N D

Portugal's
TOP EXPERIENCES

With medieval castles, frozen-in-time villages, captivating cities and golden-sand bays, the Portuguese experience can mean many things. History, terrific food and wine, lyrical scenery and all-night partying are just the beginning here (p460).

Portugal's beautiful capital, Lisbon, and its soulful northern rival, Porto, are two of Europe's most charismatic cities. Both are a joy to stroll, with gorgeous river views, rattling trams and tangled lanes hiding boutiques and vintage shops, new-wave bars and a seductive mix of restaurants, clubs and cafes. Beyond the cities, the landscape unfolds in all its beauty. Here, you can stay in converted hilltop fortresses fronting age-old vineyards, hike amid granite peaks or explore medieval villages. More than 800km of coast shelters some of Europe's best beaches with dramatic end-of-the-world cliffs, Atlantic breaks to surf and sandy islands to laze on.

 ## Lisbon's Alfama

Lisbon's Alfama district, with its labyrinthine alleyways, hidden courtyards and curving shadow-filled lanes, is a magical place in which to lose all sense of direction and delve into the soul of the city. You'll pass breadbox-sized grocers, brilliantly tiled buildings and cosy taverns filled with easygoing chatter, accompanied by the scent of chargrilled sardines and the mournful rhythms of fado drifting in the breeze. Round a bend and catch sight of steeply pitched rooftops leading down to the glittering Tejo, and you know you're hooked... (p460)

 ## Sintra

Less than an hour by train from the capital, Sintra feels like another world. Like something from a fairy tale, it's a quaint village sprinkled with stone-walled taverns, with a whitewashed palace looming over town. Forested hillsides form the backdrop to the storybook setting, with imposing castles, mystical gardens, strange mansions and centuries-old monasteries hidden among the woodlands. The fog that sweeps in by night adds another layer of mystery, and cool evenings are best spent fireside in one of Sintra's many charming B&Bs. (p466)

 ## Historic Évora

The Queen of the Alentejo and one of Portugal's most beautifully preserved medieval towns, Évora is an enchanting place to spend several days delving into the past. Inside the 14th-century walls, Évora's narrow, winding lanes lead to striking architectural works: an elaborate medieval cathedral and cloisters, Roman ruins and a picturesque town square. Historic and aesthetic virtues aside, Évora is also a lively university town, and its many attractive restaurants serve up excellent, hearty Alentejan cuisine. (p475)

 ## Porto

It would be hard to dream up a more romantic city than Portugal's second largest. Laced with narrow pedestrian laneways, it is blessed with countless baroque churches, epic theatres and sprawling plazas. Its Ribeira district – a Unesco World Heritage Site – is just a short walk across a landmark bridge from centuries-old port wineries in Vila Nova de

---

GETTING AROUND

Transport in Portugal is reasonably priced, quick and efficient.

Train Extremely affordable, with a decent network between major towns from north to south. See www.cp.pt/passageiros/en for schedules and prices.

Bus Cheaper and slower than trains. Useful for more remote villages that aren't serviced by trains. Infrequent service on weekends.

Gaia, where you can sip the world's best port. And though some walls are crumbling, renewal – in the form of spectacular modern architecture, cosmopolitan restaurants, burgeoning nightlife and a vibrant arts scene – is palpable. (p481)

⭐ Batalha, Alcobaça & Tomar

These medieval Christian monuments – all Unesco World Heritage Sites – constitute one of Portugal's greatest national treasures. Each has its own magic: the whimsy of Manueline adornments and the haunting roofless shell of the unfinished Capelas Imperfeitas at Batalha's monastery; the great kitchen at Alcobaça's monastery, where a multistorey chimney and fish-stocked river once stoked the appetites of countless monks; or the labyrinthine courtyards and mysterious 16-sided chapel of the Knights Templar at Tomar's Convento de Cristo. (p477)

⭐ Coimbra

Portugal's atmospheric college town, Coimbra rises steeply from the Rio Mondego to a medieval quarter housing one of Europe's oldest universities. Students roam the narrow streets clad in black capes, while strolling fado musicians give free concerts beneath the Moorish town gate or under the stained-glass windows of Café Santa Cruz. Kids can keep busy at Portugal dos Pequenitos, a theme park with miniature versions of Portuguese monuments; grown-ups will appreciate the upper town's student-driven nightlife and the new cluster of bars and restaurants in the riverside park below. (p478)

⭐ Pastries

One of the great culinary wonders of Portugal, the cinnamon-dusted *pastel de nata* (custard tart), with its flaky crust and creamy centre, lurks irresistibly behind counters across the country; the best are served hot in Belém. Of course, when it comes to dessert, Portugal is more than a one-hit wonder, with a dazzling array of regional sweets – from the jewel-like Algarve marzipan to Sintra's heavenly almond-and-egg *travesseiros* to Serpa's cheesecake-like *queijadas*.

⭐ Parque Nacional da Peneda-Gerês

The vast rugged wilderness of Portugal's northernmost park is home to dramatic peaks, meandering streams and rolling hillsides covered with wildflowers. Its age-old stone villages seem lost in time and, in remote areas, wolves still roam. As always, the best way to feel nature's power is on foot along one of more than a dozen hiking trails. Some scale peaks, a few link to old Roman roads, others lead to castle ruins or waterfalls. (p486)

if Portugal were 100 people

60 would work in services
28 would work in industry
12 would work in agriculture

belief systems
(% of population)

85
Roman Catholic

9
other

4
no religion

2
other Christian

population per sq km

PORTUGAL   USA   UK

🧍 ≈ 30 people

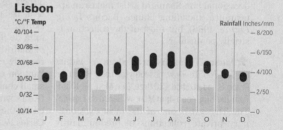

When to Go

Lisbon

°C/°F Temp   Rainfall Inches/mm

SPAIN

Madrid

POP 6.18 MILLION (URBAN AREA) / ELEV 667M

No city on earth is more alive than Madrid, a beguiling place whose sheer energy carries a simple message: *madrileños* (people from Madrid) know how to live. Explore the old streets of the centre, relax in the plazas, soak up the culture in Madrid's excellent art museums, and spend at least one night in the city's legendary nightlife scene.

👁 Sights

★ Museo del Prado   MUSEUM

(www.museodelprado.es; Paseo del Prado; adult/child €14/free, free 6-8pm Mon-Sat & 5-7pm Sun, audioguides €3.50, admission plus official guidebook €23; ⊙10am-8pm Mon-Sat, 10am-7pm Sun; MBanco de España) Welcome to one of the world's premier art galleries. The more than 7000 paintings held in the Museo del Prado's collection (although only around 1500 are currently on display) are like a window onto the historical vagaries of the Spanish soul, at once grand and imperious in the royal paintings of Velázquez, darkly tumultuous in *Las pinturas negras* (The Black Paintings) of Goya, and outward looking with sophisticated works of art from all across Europe.

★ Centro de Arte Reina Sofía   MUSEUM

(🖉91 774 10 00; www.museoreinasofia.es; Calle de Santa Isabel 52; adult/concession €8/free, free 1.30-7pm Sun, 7-9pm Mon & Wed-Sat; ⊙10am-9pm Mon & Wed-Sat, 10am-7pm Sun; MAtocha) Home to Picasso's *Guernica,* arguably Spain's most famous artwork, the Centro de Arte Reina Sofía is Madrid's premier collection of contemporary art. In addition to plenty of paintings by Picasso, other major drawcards are works by Salvador Dalí (1904–89) and Joan Miró (1893–1983). The collection principally spans the 20th century up to the 1980s. The occasional non-Spaniard artist makes an appearance (including Francis Bacon's *Lying Figure;* 1966), but most of the collection is strictly peninsular.

★ Museo Thyssen-Bornemisza   MUSEUM

(🖉902 760511; www.museothyssen.org; Paseo del Prado 8; adult/child €10/free, free Mon; ⊙10am-7pm Tue-Sun, noon-4pm Mon; MBanco de España) The Thyssen is one of the most extraordinary private collections of predominantly European art in the world. Where the Prado or Reina Sofía enable you to study the body of work of a particular artist in depth, the Thyssen is the place to immerse yourself in a breathtaking breadth of artistic styles. Most of the big names are here, sometimes with just a single painting, but the Thyssen's gift to Madrid and the art-loving public is to have them all under one roof.

★ Palacio Real   PALACE

(🖉91 454 88 00; www.patrimonionacional.es; Calle de Bailén; adult/concession €11/6, guide/audioguide €4/4, EU citizens free last two hours Mon-Thu; ⊙10am-8pm Apr-Sep, 10am-6pm Oct-Mar; MÓpera) Spain's lavish Palacio Real is a jewel box of a palace, although it's used only occasionally for royal ceremonies; the royal family moved to the modest Palacio de la Zarzuela years ago.

When the *alcázar* (Muslim-era fortress) burned down on Christmas Day 1734, Felipe V, the first of the Bourbon kings, decided to build a palace that would dwarf all its European counterparts. Felipe died before the palace was finished, which is perhaps why the Italianate baroque colossus has a mere 2800 rooms, just one-quarter of the original plan.

★ Plaza Mayor   SQUARE

(MSol) Madrid's grand central square, a rare but expansive opening in the tightly packed streets of central Madrid, is one of the prettiest open spaces in Spain, a winning combination of imposing architecture, picaresque historical tales and vibrant street life coursing across its cobblestones. At once beautiful in its own right and a reference point for so many Madrid days, it also hosts the city's main tourist office, a Christmas market in December and arches leading to laneways leading out into the labyrinth.

★ Ermita de San Antonio de la Florida   GALLERY

(🖉91 542 07 22; www.sanantoniodelaflorida.es; Glorieta de San Antonio de la Florida 5; ⊙10am-8pm Tue-Sun, hours vary Jul & Aug; MPríncipe Pío) FREE The frescoed ceilings of the Ermita de San Antonio de la Florida are one of Madrid's most surprising secrets. It's been recently restored and is also known as the Panteón de Goya. The southern of the two small chapels is one of the few places to see Goya's work in its original setting, as painted by the master in 1798 on the request of Carlos IV. Simply breathtaking.

🛏 Sleeping

★ Hostal Main Street Madrid   HOSTAL €
(📞 91 548 18 78; www.mainstreetmadrid.com; 5th fl, Gran Vía 50; r from €61; ✳️ 🛜; Ⓜ Callao, Santo Domingo) Excellent service is what travellers rave about here, but the rooms – modern and cool in soothing greys – are also some of the best *hostal* (budget hotel) rooms you'll find anywhere in central Madrid. It's an excellent package and not surprisingly they're often full, so book well in advance.

Life Hotel   HOTEL €
(📞 91 531 42 96; www.hotellifemadrid.es; Calle de Pizarro 16; s/d from €39/55; ✳️ 🛜; Ⓜ Noviciado) If only all places to stay were this good. This place inhabits the shell of an historic Malasaña building, but the rooms are slick and contemporary with designer bathrooms. You're also just a few steps up the hill from Calle del Pez, one of Malasaña's most happening streets. It's an exceptionally good deal, even when prices head upwards.

★ Lapepa Chic B&B   B&B €
(📞 648 474742; www.lapepa-bnb.com 7th fl, Plaza de las Cortes 4; s/d from €63/69; ✳️ 🛜; Ⓜ Banco de España) A short step off the Paseo del Prado and on a floor with an art nouveau interior, this fine little B&B has lovely rooms with a contemporary, clean-lined look so different from the dour *hostal* furnishings you'll find elsewhere – modern art or even a bedhead lined with flamenco shoes give this place personality in bucketloads.

Hostal Madrid   HOSTAL, APARTMENT €
(📞 91 522 00 60; www.hostal-madrid.info; Calle de Esparteros 6; s €35-62, d €45-78, d apt €45-150; ✳️ 🛜; Ⓜ Sol) The 24 rooms at this well-run *hostal* have been wonderfully renovated with exposed brickwork, brand-new bathrooms and a look that puts many three-star hotels to shame. There are also terrific apartments (some recently renovated, others ageing in varying stages of gracefulness, and ranging in size from 33 sq metres to 200 sq metres). The apartments have a separate website – www.apartamentosmayorcentro.com.

Mad Hostel   HOSTEL €
(📞 91 506 48 40; www.madhostel.com; Calle de la Cabeza 24; dm €20-24; ✳️ @ 🛜; Ⓜ Antón Martín) This vibrant hostel is filled with life. The 1st-floor courtyard – with retractable roof – recreates an old Madrid *corrala* (traditional internal or communal patio) and is a wonderful place to chill, while the four- to eight-bed rooms are smallish but clean. There's a small rooftop gym.

★ Posada del León de Oro   BOUTIQUE HOTEL €€
(📞 91 119 14 94; www.posadadelleondeoro.com; Calle de la Cava Baja 12; r from €105; ✳️ 🛜; Ⓜ La Latina) This rehabilitated inn has muted colour schemes and generally large rooms. There's a *corrala* in its core, and thoroughly modern rooms (some on the small side) along one of Madrid's best-loved streets. The downstairs bar is terrific.

🍴 Eating

Madrid has transformed itself into one of Europe's culinary capitals, not least because the city has long been a magnet for people (and cuisines) from all over Spain. Travel from one Spanish village to the next and you'll quickly learn that each has its own speciality; travel to Madrid and you'll find them all.

Almendro 13   TAPAS €
(📞 91 365 42 52; Calle del Almendro 13; mains €7-15; ⏰ 1-4pm & 7.30pm-midnight Sun-Thu, 1-5pm & 8pm-1am Fri & Sat; Ⓜ La Latina) Almendro 13 is a charming *taberna* (tavern) where you come for traditional Spanish tapas with an emphasis on quality rather than frilly elaborations. Cured meats, cheeses, omelettes and variations on these themes dominate the menu.

★ Casa Julio   SPANISH €
(📞 91 522 72 74; Calle de la Madera 37; 6/12 croquetas €5/10; ⏰ 1-3.30pm & 6.30-11pm Mon-Sat Sep-Jul; Ⓜ Tribunal) A city-wide poll for the best *croquetas* (croquettes) in Madrid would see half of those polled voting for Casa Julio and the remainder not doing so only because they haven't been yet. They're that good that celebrities and mere mortals from all over Madrid come here, along with the crusty old locals.

★ Casa Revuelta   TAPAS €
(📞 91 366 33 32; Calle de Latoneros 3; tapas from €2.80; ⏰ 10.30am-4pm & 7-11pm Tue-Sat, 10.30am-4pm Sun, closed Aug; Ⓜ Sol, La Latina) Casa Revuelta puts out some of Madrid's finest tapas of *bacalao* (cod) bar none – unlike elsewhere, *tajadas de bacalao* don't have bones in them and slide down the throat with the greatest of ease. Early on a Sunday afternoon, as the Rastro crowd gathers here, it's filled to the rafters.

Central Madrid

SPAIN & PORTUGAL MADRID

400 m
0.2 miles

Plaza de la Villa de París
C de Bárbara de Braganza
C de Piamonte
C del Almirante
C de Prim
Recoletos
Paseo de los Recoletos
Paseo del Prado

Plaza de las Salesas
C de Fernando VI
C de Santo Tomé
Paseo del Prado
Banco de España
C de Alcalá
C de Marqués de Cubas

C de la Santa Brígida
C de San Lucas
CHUECA
C de Augusto Figueroa
C de San Marcos
Plaza del Rey
C del Marqués del Valdeiglesias
C de Zorrilla

19
C de Belén
C de San Gregorio
C de Gravina
Plaza de Chueca
C de Barbieri
13
C de la Libertad
C de las Infantas
C del Caballero de Gracia
C de los Madrazo

Chueca
C de Pelayo
C de San Bartolomé
22
Plaza de Vásquez de Mella
C del Clavel
C de la Reina
Gran Vía
Sevilla
C del Caballero de Gracia
C de los Cedaceros
C de Artabán

C de la Farmacia
C de Hernán Cortés
C de Hortaleza
C del Clavel
C de la Virgen de los Peligros
Sevilla
C de Alcalá

C de la Santa Brígida
C de Fuencarral
17
C de los Jardines
CENTRO
C de la Aduana
C de San Jerónimo

C Santa Bárbara
C de Colón
C de Valverde
23
Gran Vía
Plaza de la Red de San Luis
C de la Montera
Carrera de San Jerónimo

C del Barco
C de la Puebla
C del Barco
C de la Salud
Plaza del Carmen
C de Tetuán
Plaza de la Puerta del Sol
Sol

15
C de la Madera
C del Molino de Viento
C de la Corredera Baja de San Pablo
Chinchilla
C del Carmen
C de Preciados
Travesía del Arenal

C del Pez
6
C de San Roque
C de San Andrés
Plaza de Santa María Soledad
C de la Abada
Plaza de las Descalzas
21

MALASAÑA
Noviciado
C de Andrés Borrego
C de las M
C de Pizarro
C de la Luna
Callao
Gran Vía
Plaza del Callao
C de Tudescos
Plaza de San Martín
Ópera

Pozas
C de Manzana
C de Antonio Grilo
C del Marqués de Leganés
C de la Flor Alta
7
C de Silva
C de Preciados
Plaza de San Martín
C del Maestro Victoria
C del Arenal

Plaza de España
C de los Reyes
C García Molinas
C de San Bernardo
C de Isabel la Católica
Plaza de Santo Domingo
Costanilla Los Ángeles
Plaza de las Descalzas
C de los Coloreros

Plaza de España
Gran Vía
Ermita de San Antonio de la Florida (1.6km)
C de Leganitos
C de Isabel la Católica
C de Fomento
Cuesta de Santo Domingo
C del Fomento
C de Campomanes
C de la Bola
C de Torija
C de Arrieta
C de Vergara

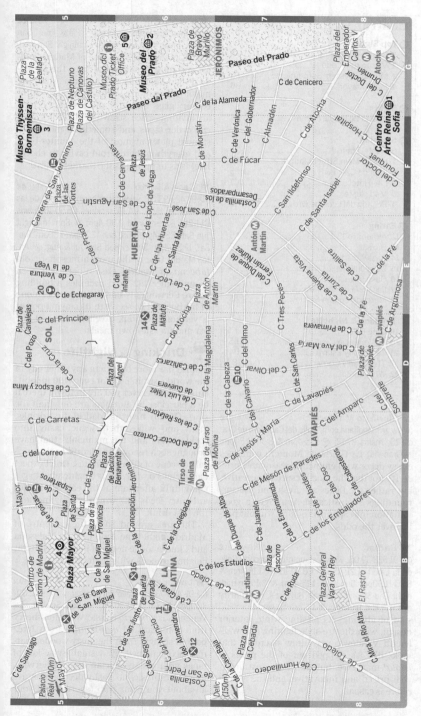

Central Madrid

La Gloria de Montera   SPANISH €

(www.grupandilana.com; Calle del Caballero de Gracia 10; mains €7-13; ⊙1.15-4pm & 8.30-11.30pm; ⓂGran Vía) La Gloria de Montera combines classy decor with eminently reasonable prices. It's not that the food is especially creative, but rather the tastes are fresh and the surroundings sophisticated. You'll get a good initiation into Spanish cooking without paying over the odds.

★Bazaar   MODERN SPANISH €

(☑91 523 39 05; www.restaurantbazaar.com; Calle de la Libertad 21; mains €6.50-10; ⊙1.15-4pm & 8.30-11.30pm Sun-Wed, 1.15-4pm & 8.15pm-midnight Thu-Sat; ⓂChueca) Bazaar's popularity among the well-heeled Chueca set shows no sign of abating. Its pristine white interior design, with theatre-style lighting and wall-length windows, may draw a crowd that looks like it's stepped out of the pages of *¡Hola!* magazine, but the food is extremely well priced and innovative, and the atmosphere is casual.

★Mercado de San Miguel   TAPAS €€

(www.mercadodesanmiguel.es; Plaza de San Miguel; tapas from €1; ⊙10am-midnight Sun-Wed, 10am-2am Thu-Sat; ⓂSol) One of Madrid's oldest and most beautiful markets, the Mercado de San Miguel has undergone a stunning major renovation. Within the early-20th-century glass walls, the market has become an inviting space strewn with tables. You can order tapas and sometimes more substantial plates at most of the counter-bars, and everything here (from caviar to chocolate) is as tempting as the market is alive.

★Casa Alberto   TAPAS €€

(☑91 429 93 56; www.casaalberto.es; Calle de las Huertas 18; tapas €4-10, raciónes €6.50-16, mains €14-21; ⊙restaurant 1.30-4pm & 8pm-midnight Tue-Sat, 1.30-4pm Sun, bar 12.30pm-1.30am Tue-Sat, 12.30-4pm Sun, closed Sun Jul & Aug; ⓂAntón Martín) One of the most atmospheric old *tabernas* of Madrid, Casa Alberto has been around since 1827 and occupies a building where Cervantes is said to have written one of his books. The secret to its staying power is vermouth on tap, excellent tapas at the bar and fine sit-down meals.

🍷 Drinking & Nightlife

Madrid has more bars than any other city in the world – six, in fact, for every 100 inhabitants – and, wherever you are in town, there'll be a bar close by. But bars are only half the story. On any night in Madrid, first drinks, tapas and wines then segue easily into cocktail bars and the nightclubs that have brought such renown to Madrid as the unrivalled scene of all-night fiestas. Don't expect dance clubs or *discotecas* (nightclubs) to get going until after 1am at the earliest. Standard entry fee is €12, which usually includes the first drink.

The area around Sol is the epicentre of Madrid's night-time action, while Malasaña and Chueca to the north of here are all-night neighbourhoods with great options.

★La Venencia   BAR

(☑91 429 73 13; Calle de Echegaray 7; ⊙12.30-3.30pm & 7.30pm-1.30am; ⓂSol, Sevilla) La Venencia is a *barrio* classic, with fine sherry from Sanlúcar and *manzanilla* from Jeréz poured straight from the dusty wooden barrels, accompanied by a small selection of tapas with an Andalucian bent. Otherwise, there's no music, no flashy decorations; it's all about you, your *fino* (sherry) and your friends. As one reviewer put it, it's 'a classic among classics'.

★ Café Belén   BAR
(☑ 91 308 27 47; www.elcafebelen.com; Calle de Belén 5; ☺ 3.30pm-3am Tue-Thu, 3.30pm-3.30am Fri, 1pm-3.30am Sat, 1-10pm Sun; Ⓜ Chueca) Café Belén is cool in all the right places – lounge and chill-out music, dim lighting, a great range of drinks (the mojitos are especially good) and a low-key crowd that's the height of casual sophistication. It's one of our preferred Chueca watering holes.

★ Delic   BAR
(☑ 91 364 54 50; www.delic.es; Costanilla de San Andrés 14; ☺ 11am-2am Sun & Tue-Thu, 11am-2.30am Fri & Sat; Ⓜ La Latina) We could go on for hours about this long-standing cafe-bar, but we'll reduce it to its most basic elements: nursing an exceptionally good mojito (€8) or three on a warm summer's evening at Delic's outdoor tables on one of Madrid's prettiest plazas is one of life's great pleasures. Bliss.

★ Teatro Joy Eslava   CLUB
(Joy Madrid; ☑ 91 366 37 33; www.joy-eslava.com; Calle del Arenal 11; ☺ 11.30pm-6am Ⓜ Sol) The only thing guaranteed at this grand old Madrid dance club (housed in a 19th-century theatre) are a crowd and the fact that it'll be open (it claims to have operated every single day for the past 29 years). The music and the crowd are a mixed bag, but queues are long and invariably include locals and tourists, and even the occasional *famoso* (celebrity). Every night's a little different. Admission is €12 to €15.

Ya'sta   CLUB
(☑ 91 521 88 33; www.yastaclub.net; Calle de Valverde 10; ☺ 11.45pm-6am Wed-Sat; Ⓜ Gran Vía) Going strong since 1985 and the height of *la movida madrileña* (Madrid's late-night partying scene), Ya'sta is a stalwart of the Malasaña night. Everything gets a run here, from techno, psychedelic trance and electronica to indie pop. Admission is €10; check the website for upcoming sessions.

Why Not?   CLUB
(☑ 91 521 80 34; www.whynotmadrid.com; Calle de San Bartolomé 7; ☺ 10.30pm-6am; Ⓜ Chueca) Underground, narrow and packed with bodies, gay-friendly Why Not? is the sort of place where nothing's left to the imagination (the gay and straight crowd who come here are pretty amorous) and it's full nearly every night of the week. Pop and top 40 music are

TAPAS

Too many travellers miss out on the joys of tapas because, unless you speak Spanish, the art of ordering can seem one of the dark arts of Spanish etiquette. Fear not – it's not as difficult as it first appears.

Tapas customs vary across the country, but there's often a mixture of tapas on display and others that are cooked or heated to order. Sometimes you get a free tapa with a drink, otherwise you can order from a list. Traditionally tapas are eaten standing up at the bar, but the distinction between tapas bars and restaurants is blurred, so you can often sit down to order *raciones* (literally 'rations'; full-plate-size tapas servings) or *media raciones* (half-rations; smaller tapas servings). Remember, however, that after a couple of *raciones* you'll almost certainly be full; the *media ración* is a good choice if you want to experience a broader range of tastes.

the standard here, and the dancing crowd is mixed and serious about having a good time.

We're not huge fans of the bouncers here, but once you get past them it's all good fun. Admission is €10.

☆ Entertainment

★ Estadio Santiago Bernabéu   STADIUM
(☑ tickets 902 324 324, tours 91 398 43 00/70; www.realmadrid.com; Av de Concha Espina 1; tour adult/child €19/13; ☺ tours 10am-7pm Mon-Sat, 10.30am-6.30pm Sun, except match days; Ⓜ Santiago Bernabéu) Football fans and budding Madridistas (Real Madrid supporters) will want to make a pilgrimage to the Estadio Santiago Bernabéu, a temple to all that's extravagant and successful in football. The self-guided tours take you up into the stands for a panoramic view of the stadium, then pass through the presidential box, press room, dressing rooms, players' tunnel and even onto the pitch itself. The tour ends in the extraordinary Exposición de Trofeos (trophy exhibit). Better still, attend a game alongside 80,000 delirious fans.

For bigger games, tickets are difficult to find unless you're willing to take the risk with scalpers. For less important matches, you shouldn't have too many problems. Tickets can be purchased online, by phone or in person from the ticket office.

ℹ Information

Centro de Turismo de Madrid (☑ 010, 91 454 44 10; www.esmadrid.com; Plaza Mayor 27; ⏱ 9.30am-8.30pm; Ⓜ Sol) The Madrid government's Centro de Turismo is terrific. Housed in the Real Casa de la Panadería on the north side of the Plaza Mayor, it allows free access to its outstanding website and city database, and offers free downloads of the metro map to your mobile; staff are helpful.

ℹ Getting There & Away

Madrid's Barajas Airport is one of Europe's busiest and is served by almost 100 airlines.

Within Spain, Madrid is the hub of the country's outstanding bus and train network.

Estación Sur de Autobuses (☑ 91 468 42 00; www.estaciondeautobuses.com; Calle de Méndez Álvaro 83; Ⓜ Méndez Álvaro), just south of the M-30 ring road, is the city's principal bus station.

Madrid's main train station, the **Puerta de Atocha** (www.renfe.es; Ⓜ Atocha Renfe), is at the southern edge of the city centre. This is where most international, national and local *cercanías* arrive, including many high-speed AVE services. North of the city centre, **Estación de Chamartín** (☑ 902 432 343; Ⓜ Chamartín) has numerous long-distance rail services, especially those to/from northern Spain. This is also where long-haul international trains arrive from Paris and Lisbon.

ℹ Getting Around

The easiest way into town from the airport is line 8 of the metro. A single ticket costs €4.50 including the €3 airport supplement.

Ten-trip Metrobús tickets cost €12.20 and are valid for journeys on Madrid's metro and bus network. Tickets can be bought from most newspaper kiosks and *estancos* (tobacconists), as well as in metro stations.

MENÚ DEL DÍA

The key to eating cheaply in Spain is to have your main meal at lunchtime, when the *menú del día* (daily set menu), a three-course meal with water, bread and wine, is offered. These meals tend to run from about €10 to €16. You'll be given a menu with five or six entrées, the same number of mains and a handful of desserts – choose one from each category. Prices go up at weekends – or the set menu disappears entirely.

Metro The quickest and easiest way to get around. Runs 6.05am to 1.30am.

Bus Extensive network but careful planning is needed to make the most of over 200 routes. Runs 6.30am to 11.30pm.

Taxi Cheap fares by European standards; plentiful.

Walking Compact city centre makes walking a good option, but hillier than first appears.

Around Madrid

Toledo
POP 85,600

Dramatically sited atop a gorge overlooking the Río Tajo, Toledo was known as the 'city of three cultures' in the Middle Ages, a place where – legend has it – Christian, Muslim and Jewish communities peacefully coexisted. Rediscovering the vestiges of this unique cultural synthesis remains modern Toledo's most compelling attraction. Horseshoe-arched mosques, Sephardic synagogues and one of Spain's finest Gothic cathedrals cram into its dense historical core. Toledo's other forte is art, in particular the haunting canvases of El Greco, the influential, impossible-to-classify painter with whom the city is synonymous.

⊙ Sights

★**Catedral**　　　　　　　　　　CATHEDRAL
(www.catedralprimada.es; Plaza del Ayuntamiento; adult/child €11/free; ⏱ 10am-6pm Mon-Sat, 2-6pm Sun) Toledo's illustrious main church ranks among the top 10 cathedrals in Spain. An impressive example of medieval Gothic architecture, its humongous interior is full of the classic characteristics of the style, rose windows, flying buttresses, ribbed vaults and pointed arches among them. Equally visit-worthy is the art. The cathedral's sacristy is a veritable art gallery of old masters with works by Velázquez, Goya and – of course – El Greco.

★**Sinagoga del Tránsito**　SYNAGOGUE, MUSEUM
(☑ 925 22 36 65; http://museosefardi.mcu.es; Calle Samuel Leví; adult/child €3/1.50, after 2pm Sat & all day Sun free; ⏱ 9.30am-7.30pm Tue-Sat Mar-Oct, 9.30am-6pm Tue-Sat Nov-Feb, 10am-3pm Sun year-round) This magnificent synagogue was built in 1355 by special permission from Pedro I. The synagogue now houses the **Museo Sefardí**. The vast main prayer hall has been expertly restored and the

Toledo

Toledo

◎ Top Sights

◎ Sights

◎ Sleeping

◎ Eating

◎ Drinking & Nightlife

Mudéjar decoration and intricately carved pine ceiling are striking. Exhibits provide an insight into the history of Jewish culture in Spain, and include archaeological finds, a memorial garden, costumes and ceremonial artefacts.

★ **Alcázar**   FORTRESS, MUSEUM
(Museo del Ejército; Calle Alféreces Provisionales; adult/child €5/free, Sun free; ⊙ 10am-5pm Thu-Tue) At the highest point in the city looms the foreboding Alcázar. Rebuilt under Franco, it has been reopened as a vast **military museum**. The usual displays of uniforms and medals are here, but the best part is the exhaustive historical section, with an in-depth overview of the nation's history in Spanish and English.

🛏 Sleeping

Oasis Backpackers Hostel   HOSTEL €
(☑ 925 22 76 50; www.hostelsoasis.com; Calle Cadenas 5; dm/d €14/34; ❀ 🐾) One of four Oasis hostels in Spain, this relatively new affair sparkles with what have become the chain's glowing hallmarks – laid-back but refreshingly well-organised service and an atmosphere that is fun without ever being loud or obnoxious. There are private rooms if you're not up for a dorm-share and lots of free information on city attractions.

Albergue San Servando   HOSTEL €
(☑ 925 22 45 58; www.reaj.com; Subida del Castillo; dm under/over 30 €14.05/16.90; ❀ ❀ 🐾 🐾) Occupying digs normally reserved for *paradores* (luxurious state-owned hotels) is this unusual youth hostel encased in a 14th-century castle built by the Knights Templar,

no less. Dorms have either two single beds or two double bunks, and there's a cafeteria serving meals as well as a summer pool. If you're not a HI member, you'll need to buy a card here.

🍴 Eating & Drinking

Kumera   MODERN SPANISH €
(☑ 925 25 75 53; www.restaurantekumera.com; Calle Alfonso X El Sabio 2; meals €9-10, set menus €20-35; ⊙ 8am-2.30am Mon-Fri, 11am-2.30am Sat & Sun) This place serves up innovative takes on local traditional dishes such as *cochinillo* (suckling pig), *rabo de toro* (bull's tail) or *croquetas* (croquettes, filled with *jamón*, squid, cod or wild mushrooms), alongside gigantic toasts and other creatively conceived dishes. The dishes with foie gras as the centrepiece are especially memorable.

ÁVILA

Ávila's old city, just over an hour from Madrid and a good day trip, is surrounded by imposing city walls comprising eight monumental gates, 88 watchtowers and more than 2500 turrets. It's one of the best-preserved medieval bastions in Spain. Two sections of the **walls** (www.murealladeavila.com; adult/under 12yr €5/free; ⊙10am-8pm Apr-Oct, to 6pm Nov-Mar; ♿) can be climbed – a 300m stretch that can be accessed from just inside the Puerta del Alcázar, and a longer (1300m) stretch from Puerta de los Leales that runs the length of the old city's northern perimeter. The admission price includes a multilingual audioguide.

Also worth a visit, Ávila's 12th-century **cathedral** (☎920 21 16 41; Plaza de la Catedral; admission incl audioguide €4; ⊙10am-7pm Mon-Fri, 10am-8pm Sat, noon-6.30pm Sun) is both a house of worship and an ingenious fortress: its stout granite apse forms the central bulwark in the historic city walls. The sombre, Gothic-style facade conceals a magnificent interior with an exquisite early-16th-century altar frieze showing the life of Jesus, plus Renaissance-era carved choir stalls and a museum with an El Greco painting and a splendid silver monstrance by Juan de Arfe.

There are train services to Madrid (from €8.95, 1¼ to two hours), Salamanca (from €12.25, 1¼ hours) and elsewhere. Buses run to Salamanca (€7.10, 1½ hours, five daily) and Madrid (€9.90, 1½ hours).

★**Libro Taberna El Internacional** BAR, CAFE
(Ciudad 15; ⊙8pm-1.30am Tue-Thu, noon-1.30am Fri & Sat, noon-4pm Sun) ♪ If you think Toledo is more touristy than trendy, you clearly haven't dipped your hipster detector into the cool confines of El Internacional, a proud purveyor of slow food, spray-painted tables, rescued 1970s armchairs, and beards.

ℹ Information

Main Tourist Office (☎925 25 40 30; www.toledo-turismo.com; Plaza Consistorio; ⊙10am-6pm) Within sight of the cathedral. There's another branch (Estación de Renfe; ⊙9.30am-3pm) at the train station.

ℹ Getting There & Away

From Toledo's bus station, buses depart for Madrid's Plaza Elíptica roughly every half-hour (from €5.40, one hour to 1¾ hours).

High-speed AVE trains run every hour or so to Madrid (€12.90, 30 minutes).

El Escorial

The imposing palace and monastery complex of **San Lorenzo de El Escorial** (☎91 890 78 18; www.patrimonionacional.es; adult/concession €10/5, guide/audioguide €4/4, EU citizens free last three hours Wed & Thu; ⊙10am-8pm Apr-Sep, 10am-6pm Oct-Mar, closed Mon) is an impressive place, rising up from the foothills of the mountains that shelter Madrid from the north and west. Built in the 16th century by King Felipe II, it became a symbol of Spanish imperial power. The project included a monastic centre, a decadent royal palace and a mausoleum for Felipe's parents, Carlos I and Isabel. Architect Juan de Herrera oversaw the works. The Escorial imposes by its sheer size; within, its sombre basilica, galleries and rooms are a treasure chest of Spanish and European art.

A few dozen Renfe C8 *cercanías* make the trip daily from Madrid's Atocha or Chamartín train station to El Escorial (€1.25, one hour).

San Sebastián

POP 186,100

San Sebastián (Basque: Donostia) is a city filled with people that love to indulge – and with Michelin stars apparently falling from the heavens onto its restaurants, not to mention an unmatched *pintxo* (tapas) culture, San Sebastián frequently tops lists of the world's best places to eat.

Just as good as the food is the summertime fun in the sun. For its setting, form and attitude, Playa de la Concha is the equal of any city beach in Europe.

◎ Sights

★**Aquarium** AQUARIUM
(www.aquariumss.com; Plaza Carlos Blasco de Imaz 1; adult/child €13/6.50; ⊙10am-9pm daily Jul & Aug, 10am-8pm Mon-Fri, 10am-9pm Sat & Sun Easter-Jun & Sep, shorter hours rest of year) Fear

San Sebastián

for your life as huge sharks bear down behind glass panes, or gaze in disbelief at tripped-out fluoro jellyfish. The highlights of a visit to the city's excellent aquarium are the cinema-screen-sized deep-ocean and coral-reef exhibits and the long tunnel, around which swim monsters of the deep. The aquarium also contains a maritime museum section. Allow at least 1½ hours for a visit.

San Telmo Museoa MUSEUM
(www.santelmomuseoa.com; Plaze Zuloaga 1; adult/student/child €6/3/free; ⊘10am-8pm Tue-Sun) Although it's one of the newest museums in the Basque Country, the San Telmo Museoa has actually been around since the 1920s. It was closed for many years, but after major renovation work it reopened in 2011. The displays range from historical artefacts to the squiggly lines of modern art, with all pieces reflecting Basque culture and society.

🛏 Sleeping

Prices are high and availability in peak season is very tight. Budget *pensiones* cluster in the old town.

Pensión Amaiur BOUTIQUE HOTEL €€
(📞943 42 96 54; www.pensionamaiur.com; Calle de 31 de Agosto 44; d with/without bathroom €60/75; @🛜) A top-notch guesthouse in a prime old-town location, Amaiur has bright floral wallpapers and bathrooms tiled in Andalucian blue and white. The best rooms are those that overlook the main street, where you can sit on a little balcony and be completely enveloped in blushing red flowers. Some rooms share bathrooms.

Pensión Donostiarra PENSIÓN €€
(📞943 42 61 67; www.pensiondonostiarra.com; Calle de San Martín 6; d from €70; 🛜) This no-frills *pensión*, accessible via an imposing old-fashioned stairway lined with stained-glass, has well-maintained rooms some of which have little balconies overlooking the city life below.

🍴 Eating

A Fuego Negro BASQUE €
(www.afuegonegro.com; Calle 31 de Agosto 31; pintxos from €2.50) Dark, theatrical and anything but traditional, A Fuego Negro is one of the leading designers of arty *pintxos*. Everything here is a surprise: expect white rabbit cut-outs popping out of *pintxos* and art-easel backdrops to molecular creations. This place is young, different and worth watching.

Bodega Donostiarra PINTXOS €
(www.bodegadonostiarra.com; Calle de Peña y Goñi 13; pintxos from €2.50, mains €9; ⊘9.30am-

PINTXOS

The Basque version of a tapa, the *pintxo* transcends the commonplace by the sheer panache of its culinary campiness. In San Sebastián especially, Basque chefs have refined the *pintxo* to such an art form that many people would say that there's simply no other city in Spain that can beat it.

Many *pintxos* are bedded on small pieces of bread upon which towering creations are constructed and pinned in place by large toothpicks. The choice isn't normally limited to what's on the bar top in front of you: many of the best *pintxos* are the hot ones you need to order. These are normally chalked up on a blackboard on the wall somewhere.

midnight Mon-Sat) The stone walls, potted plants and window ornaments give this place a real old-fashioned French bistro look, but at the same time it feels very up to date and modern. Although initial impressions make you think the food would be very snooty, it's actually best known for humble *jamón* (cured ham), chorizo and, most of all, tortilla.

★**La Cuchara de San Telmo**　CONTEMPORARY BASQUE €€
(www.lacucharadesantelmo.com; Calle de 31 de Agosto 28; pintxos from €2.50; ⊙ 7.30-11pm Tue, noon-3.30pm & 7.30-11pm Wed-Sun) This unfussy, hard-to-find bar offers miniature *nueva cocina vasca* (Basque nouvelle cuisine) from a supremely creative kitchen. Unlike many San Sebastián bars, this one doesn't have any *pintxos* laid out on the bar top; instead you must order from the blackboard menu behind the counter.

Bar Borda Berri　PINTXOS €€
(Calle Fermín Calbetón 12; pintxos from €2.50; ⊙noon-midnight) The mustard-yellow Bar Borda Berri is a *pintxo* bar that really stands out. The house specials are pig's ears served in garlic soup (much better than it sounds!), braised veal cheeks in wine, and a mushroom and *idiazábal* (a local cheese) risotto.

ℹ Information

Oficina de Turismo (☎ 943 48 11 66; www.sansebastianturismo.com; Alameda del Boulevard 8; ⊙ 9am-8pm Mon-Sat, 10am-7pm Sun Jul-Sep, shorter hours rest of year) This friendly office offers comprehensive information on the city and the Basque Country in general.

ℹ Getting There & Away

Trains run from the station, just across the river from the centre, to Madrid (from €27, 5½ hours) and Barcelona (€19.25, six hours) among other places. For France, change at Irún/Hendaye for French mainline services.

There are regular bus services to Bilbao (€9, one hour), Madrid (€36, five to six hours) and Pamplona (€7.80, one hour) from the new bus station adjacent to the train station. Cross-border services include buses to Biarritz.

Bilbao

POP 875,600 (URBAN AREA)

The commercial hub of the Basque Country, Bilbao (Bilbo in Basque) is best known for the magnificent Guggenheim Museum. An architectural masterpiece by Frank Gehry, the museum was the catalyst of a turnaround that saw Bilbao transformed from an industrial port city into a vibrant cultural centre. After visiting this must-see temple to modern art, spend time exploring Bilbao's Casco Viejo (Old Quarter), a grid of elegant streets dotted with shops, cafes, *pintxos* bars and several small but worthy museums.

◉ Sights

★ Museo Guggenheim GALLERY

(www.guggenheim-bilbao.es; Avenica Abandoibarra 2; adult/student/child €13/7.50/free; ☉10am-8pm, closed Mon Sep-Jun) Opened in September 1997, Bilbao's shimmering titanium Museo Guggenheim is one of modern architecture's most iconic buildings. It almost single-handedly lifted Bilbao out of its post-industrial depression and into the 21st century – and with sensation. It boosted the city's already inspired regeneration, stimulated further development and placed Bilbao firmly in the international art and tourism spotlight.

★ Museo de Bellas Artes GALLERY

(www.museobilbao.com; Plaza del Museo 2; adult/student/child €7/5/free, Wed free; ☉10am-8pm Wed-Mon) The Museo de Bellas Artes houses a compelling collection that includes everything from Gothic sculptures to 20th-century pop art. There are three main subcollections: classical art, with works by Murillo, Zurbarán, El Greco, Goya and van Dyck; 19th- and 20th-century art, featuring works by Paul Gauguin, Francis Bacon and Anthony Caro; and Basque art, with works of the great sculptors Jorge Oteiza and Eduardo Chillida, and strong paintings by the likes of Ignacio Zuloaga and Juan de Echevarría.

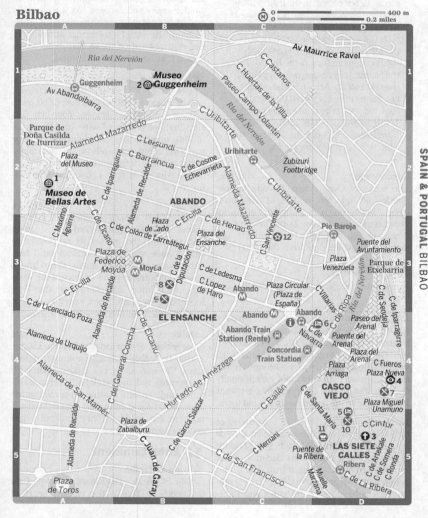

Bilbao

SPAIN & PORTUGAL BILBAO

DON'T MISS

LOS SANFERMINES

Immortalised by Ernest Hemingway in *The Sun Also Rises*, Pamplona (Iruña in Basque) is home of the wild Sanfermines festival, which features among astonishing general revelry – it's one of Spain's most vibrant fiestas – a daily *encierro* (running of the bulls). The festival is held from 6 to 14 July, when Pamplona is overrun with thrill-seekers, curious onlookers and, yes, bulls. The *encierro* begins at 8am, when bulls are let loose from the Coralillos Santo Domingo and run an 825m course to the bullring. Animal rights groups oppose bullrunning as a cruel tradition, and the participating bulls will almost certainly all be killed in the afternoon bullfight. The anti-bullfighting demonstration, the Running of the Nudes, takes place two days before the first bullrun. Accommodation for Los Sanfermines is priced through the roof and should be booked way before. There are frequent bus connections from Bilbao and San Sebastián though, which many partygoers opt for.

Casco Viejo
OLD TOWN

The compact Casco Viejo, Bilbao's atmospheric old quarter, is full of charming streets, boisterous bars and plenty of quirky and independent shops. At the heart of the Casco are Bilbao's original seven streets, Las Siete Calles, which date from the 1400s.

🛏 Sleeping

Numerous cheap *pensiones* dot the old town.

Casual Bilbao Gurea
PENSIÓN €

(944 16 32 99; www.casualhoteles.com; Calle de Bidebarrieta 14; s/d from €42/48; 🛜) The family-run Gurea has arty, modern rooms with wooden floors and large bathrooms (most of which have bath-tubs) and exceptionally friendly staff. Add it all up and you get what is easily one of the best deals in the old town.

Hostal Begoña
GUESTHOUSE €€

(944 23 01 34; www.hostalbegona.com; Calle de la Amistad 2; s/d from €46/60; P @ 🛜) Friendly Begoña has guest rooms decorated with modern artwork, wrought-iron beds, and colourful tiled bathrooms. The cozy common areas have plenty of books and information about local culture and attractions. It's a great place to meet other travellers, too.

🍴 Eating & Drinking

Café-Bar Bilbao
PINTXOS €

(Plaza Nueva 6; pintxos from €2.50; 🕖 7am-11pm Mon-Fri, 9am-11.30pm Sat, 10am-3pm Sun) Cool blue southern tiles, warm northern atmosphere and superb array of *pintxos*.

El Globo
PINTXOS €

(www.barelglobo.com; Calle de Diputación 8; pintxos from €2.50; 🕗 8am-11pm Mon-Thu, 8am-midnight Fri & Sat) This is a popular bar with a terrific range of *pintxos modernos,* including favourites such as *txangurro gratinado* (spider crab) and *hongos con su crema y crujiente de jamón* (mushrooms with crusted ham). Its variety, congenial atmosphere and central location mean that many locals regard it as one of the best around.

⭐ La Viña del Ensanche
PINTXOS €

(944 15 56 15; www.lavinadelensanche.com; Calle de la Diputación 10; pintxos from €2.50, menú €30; 🕗 8.30am-11pm Mon-Fri, noon-1am Sat) Hundreds of bottles of wine line the walls of this outstanding octogenarian *pintxos* bar. This could very well be the best place to eat *pintxos* in the entire city. If you can't decide what to sample, opt for the €30 tasting menu.

Rio-Oja
BASQUE €

(944 15 08 71; www.rio-oja.com; Calle de Perro 4; mains €7-12; 🕘 9am-11pm Tue-Sun) An institution that shouldn't be missed. It specialises in light Basque seafood and heavy inland fare, but for most visitors the snails, sheep brains or squid floating in pools of ink are the makings of a culinary adventure story they'll be recounting for years. Don't worry, though: it really does taste much better than it sounds.

Lamiak
CAFE

(Calle Pelota 8; 🕓 4pm-midnight Sun-Thu, 3.30pm-2.30am Fri & Sat) Lamiak, a long-standing Casco Viejo favourite, is a buzzing cafe with a cavernous red and black hall, cast iron columns and upstairs seating on a mezzanine floor. Good for coffees and cocktails, it exudes an arty, laid-back vibe and pulls in a cool weekend crowd.

☆ Entertainment

⭐ Kafe Antzokia
LIVE MUSIC

(944 24 46 25; www.kafeantzokia.com; Calle San Vicente 2) This is the vibrant heart of

contemporary Basque Bilbao, featuring international rock, blues and reggae, as well as the cream of Basque rock-pop. Weekend concerts run from 10pm to 1am, followed by DJs until 5am. During the day it's a cafe, restaurant and cultural centre all rolled into one and has frequent exciting events on.

❶ Information

Main Tourist Office (☑ 944 79 57 60; www.bilbaoturismo.net; Plaza Circular 1; ☺ 9am-9pm; ☎)

❶ Getting There & Around

A number of European airlines, including budget choices, serve Bilbao's airport.

Bilbao's main bus station, Termibus, has departures to Barcelona (€50, seven to eight hours), Madrid (€34, 4¾ hours) and San Sebastián (€9,1¼ hours) among other departures.

The very central train station has services to Barcelona (€65.40, 6¾ hours) and Madrid (€49.70, five to seven hours) among other destinations.

A metro and tram service with convenient stops make getting around central Bilbao a breeze.

Burgos

POP 177,800 / ELEV 859M

The extraordinary Gothic cathedral of Burgos is one of Spain's glittering jewels of religious architecture – it looms large over the city and skyline. Conservative Burgos seems to embody all the stereotypes of a north-central Spanish town, with sombre grey-stone architecture, the fortifying cuisine of the high *meseta* (plateau) and a climate of extremes. But this is a city that rewards deeper exploration.

◎ Sights

★ Catedral   CATHEDRAL
(☑ 947 20 47 12; www.catedraldeburgos.es; Plaza del Rey Fernando; adult/under 14yr inc audioguide €7/1.50, 4.30-6pm Tue free; ☺ 10am-5pm) This Unesco World Heritage–listed cathedral, once a modest Romanesque church, is a masterpiece. Work began on a grander scale in 1221; remarkably, within 40 years most of the French Gothic structure had been completed. You can enter from Plaza de Santa María for free for access to the **Capilla del Santísimo Cristo**, with its much-revered 13th-century crucifix, and the **Capilla de Santa Tecla**, with its extraordinary ceiling. However, we recommend that you visit the cathedral in its entirety.

★ Museo de la Evolución Humana   MUSEUM
(MEH; ☑ 902 02 42 46; www.museoevolucionhumana.com; Paseo Sierra de Atapuerca; adult/concession/child €6/4/free, 4.30-8pm Wed, 7-8pm Tue & Thu free; ☺ 10am-2.30pm & 4.30-8pm Tue-Fri, 10am-8pm Sat & Sun) This exceptional museum just across the river from the old quarter is a marvellously told story of human evolution. The basement exhibitions on **Atapuerca** (☑ 902 02 42 46; www.atapuerca.org; guided tours in Spanish €6; ☺ tours by appointment), an archaeological site north of Burgos where a 2007 discovery of Europe's oldest human fossil remains was made, are stunning; the displays on Charles Darwin and the extraordinary 'Human Evolution' section in the centre of the ground floor are simply outstanding. Even if you've no prior interest in the subject, don't miss it.

🛌 Sleeping & Eating

★ Rimbombín   HOSTAL €
(☑ 947 26 12 00; www.rimbombin.com; Calle Sombrería 6; d/tr/apt from €39/59/70; ✳ ☎) Opened in 2013, this 'urban *hostal*' has an upbeat, contemporary feel – its slick white furnishings and decor are matched with light-pine beams and modular furniture. Three of the rooms have balconies overlooking the pedestrian street. Conveniently, it's in the heart of Burgos' compact tapas district. The apartment is excellent value for longer stays, with the same chic modern look and two bedrooms.

★ Cervecería Morito   TAPAS €
(☑ 947 26 75 55; Calle de Diego Porcelos 1; tapas from €3.40, raciones from €5.10; ☺ 12.30-3.30pm & 7-11.30pm) Cervecería Morito is the undisputed king of Burgos tapas bars and as such it's always crowded. A typical order is *alpargata* (lashings of cured ham with bread, tomato and olive oil) or the *revueltos Capricho de Burgos* (scrambled eggs served with potatoes, blood sausage, red peppers, baby eels and mushrooms) – the latter is a meal in itself.

❶ Information

Municipal Tourist Office (☑ 947 28 88 74; www.aytoburgos.es/turismo; Plaza de Santa María; ☺ 9am-8pm daily Jun-Sep, 9.30am-2pm & 4-7pm Mon-Sat, 9.30am-5pm Sun Oct-May) Pick up its 24-hour, 48-hour and 72-hour guides to Burgos. These helpful itinerary suggestions can also be downloaded as PDFs from its website.

ⓘ Getting There & Around

Regular buses run to Madrid (from €17, three hours, up to 20 daily), Bilbao (€9 to €13.40, two hours, eight daily) and León (€5 to €15.50, two hours, three daily).

The train station is a considerable hike northeast of the town centre – bus 2 (€1.20) connects the train station with Plaza de España. Destinations include Madrid (from €27.75, 2½ to 4½ hours, seven daily), Bilbao (from €13.75, three hours, four daily), León (from €12.30, two hours) and Salamanca (from €17.50, 2½ hours, three daily).

Salamanca

POP 148,000 / ELEV 802M

Whether floodlit by night or bathed in late afternoon light, there's something magical about Salamanca. This is a city of rare beauty, awash with golden sandstone overlaid with ochre-tinted Latin inscriptions – an extraordinary virtuosity of plateresque and Renaissance styles. The monumental highlights are many, with the exceptional Plaza Mayor (illuminated to stunning effect at night) an unforgettable highlight. But this is also Castilla's liveliest city, home to a massive Spanish and international student population that throngs the streets at night and provides the city with so much vitality.

◉ Sights

★ Plaza Mayor   SQUARE

Built between 1729 and 1755, Salamanca's exceptional grand square is widely considered to be Spain's most beautiful central plaza. The square is particularly memorable at night when illuminated (until midnight) to magical effect. Designed by Alberto Churriguera, it's a remarkably harmonious and controlled baroque display. The medallions placed around the square bear the busts of famous figures.

★ Catedral Nueva   CATHEDRAL

(☑923 21 74 76; Plaza de Anaya; adult/child incl audioguide & admission to Catedral Vieja €4/3; ⊙10am-5.15pm Oct-Mar, 10am-8pm Apr-Sep) The tower of this late-Gothic cathedral lords over the city centre, its compelling *churrigueres-co* (an ornate style of baroque) dome visible from almost every angle. The interior is similarly impressive, with elaborate choir stalls, main chapel and retrochoir, much of it courtesy of the prolific José Churriguera.

The ceilings are also exceptional, along with the Renaissance doorways – particularly the **Puerta del Nacimiento** on the western face, which stands out as one of several miracles worked in the city's native sandstone.

The **Puerta de Ramos**, facing Plaza de Anaya, contains an encore to the 'frog spotting' challenge on the university facade. Look for the little astronaut and ice-cream cone chiselled into the portal by stonemasons during restoration work in 1992.

★ Catedral Vieja   CATHEDRAL

(Plaza de Anaya; adult/child €4/3 (includes audioguide & admission to Catedral Nueva); ⊙10am-5.15pm Oct-Mar, 10am-8pm Apr-Sep) The Catedral Nueva's largely Romanesque predecessor, the Catedral Vieja is adorned with an exquisite 15th-century **altarpiece**, one of the finest outside Italy. Its 53 panels depict scenes from the lives of Christ and Mary and are topped by a haunting representation of the Final Judgement. The cloister was largely ruined in an earthquake in 1755, but the **Capilla de Anaya** houses an extravagant alabaster sepulchre and one of Europe's oldest organs, a Mudéjar work of art from the 16th century.

★ Universidad Civil   HISTORIC BUILDING

(☑923 29 44 00, ext 1150; Calle de los Libreros; adult/concession €10/5, audioguide €2; ⊙10am-6.30pm Mon-Sat, to 1.30pm Sun) Founded initially in 1218, the university reached the peak of its renown in the 15th and 16th centuries. The visual feast of the entrance facade is a tapestry in sandstone, bursting with imag-

---

Salamanca

Salamanca

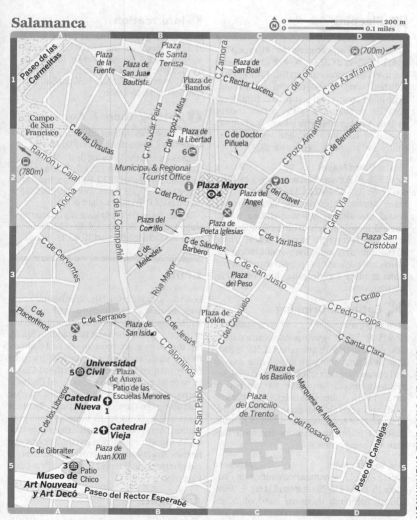

es of mythical heroes, religious scenes and coats of arms. A compulsory task for all visitors is to search out the frog sculpted into it. Behind the facade, the highlight of an otherwise modest collection of rooms lies upstairs: the extraordinary **university library**, the oldest one in Europe.

★ **Museo de Art**
Nouveau y Art Decó   MUSEUM
(Casa Lis; ☎923 12 14 25; www.museodecasalis.org; Calle de Gibralter; adult/under 12yr €4/free, Thu morning free; ⊙11am-2pm & 4-8pm Tue-Fri, 11am-8pm Sat & Sun Apr–mid-Oct plus Mon 11am-2pm & 4-8pm Aug, 11am-2pm & 4-7pm Tue-Fri, 11am-8pm Sat & Sun mid-Oct–Mar; ⛗) Utterly unlike any other Salamanca museum, this stunning collection of sculpture, paintings and art deco and art nouveau pieces inhabits a beautiful, light-filled Modernista (Catalan art nouveau) house. There's abundant stained glass and exhibits that include Lalique glass, toys by Steiff (inventor of the teddy bear), Limoges porcelain, Fabergé watches, fabulous bronze and marble figurines, and a vast collection of 19th-century children's dolls (some strangely macabre), which kids will love. There's also a cafe and an excellent gift shop.

🛏 Sleeping

Hostal Concejo
HOSTAL €

(☎ 923 21 47 37; www.hconcejo.com; Plaza de la Libertad 1; s €25-45, d €32-60; P ✳ ?) A cut above the average *hostal*, the stylish Concejo has polished-wood floors, tasteful furnishings, light-filled rooms and a superb central location. Try to snag one of the corner rooms, such as number 104, which has a traditional, glassed-in balcony, complete with a table, chairs and people-watching views.

Hostal Plaza Mayor
HOSTAL €

(☎ 923 26 20 20; www.hostalplazamayor.es; Plaza del Corrillo 20; s €30-40, d €33-66; ✳ @ ?) Near Plaza Mayor, this friendly, family owned *hostal* has simple but well-tended rooms washed in pale peach, with dark wood furniture and some with wooden beams. Three of the outside rooms have small balconies, which are pleasant for people watching but make it noisy for sleeping; interior rooms are far quieter.

🍴 Eating & Drinking

Mandala Café
MEDITERRANEAN €

(☎ 923 12 33 42; www.mandalasalamanca.com; Calle de Serranos 9-11; set menu €12.50; ☺ 8am-11pm; 🖫) Come here with an appetite, as cool and casual Mandala offers a three-course set menu (unusually available for lunch *and* dinner) with dishes like black rice with seafood, and vegetable lasagne. There are also 18 flavours of hot chocolate, 45 types of milkshake, 56 juice combinations and more teas than we could count.

Mesón Cervantes
CASTILIAN €€

(☎ 923 21 72 13; www.mesoncervantes.com; Plaza Mayor 15; mains €12-23, set menu €14.50; ☺ 10am-1.30am) Although there are outdoor tables on the square, the dark wooden beams and atmospheric buzz of the Spanish crowd on the 1st floor should be experienced at least once; if you snaffle a window table in the evening, you've hit the jackpot. The food's a mix of *platos combinados*, salads and *raciones*.

★ Tío Vivo
MUSIC BAR

(☎ 923 215 768; www.tiovivosalamanca.com; Calle del Clavel 3-5; ☺ 3.30pm-late) Sip drinks by flickering candlelight to a background of '80s music, enjoying the whimsical decor of carousel horses and oddball antiquities. There's live music Tuesday to Thursday from midnight, sometimes with a €5 cover charge.

ℹ Information

Municipal & Regional Tourist Office (☎ 923 21 83 42; www.salamanca.es; Plaza Mayor 14; ☺ 9am-2pm & 4.30-8pm Mon-Fri, 10am-8pm Sat, 10am-2pm Sun Easter–mid-Oct, 9am-2pm & 4-6.30pm Mon-Fri, 10am-6.30pm Sat, 10am-2pm Sun mid-Oct–Easter)

ℹ Getting There & Away

The bus and train stations are a 10- and 15-minute walk, respectively, from Plaza Mayor.

Buses include the following destinations: Madrid (regular/express €15.80/23, 2½ to three hours, hourly), Ávila (€7.10, 1½ hours, five daily), Segovia (€14.75, 2½ hours, four daily) and Valladolid (€8.60, 1½ hours, eight daily).

Regular trains depart to Madrid's Chamartín station (€24.10, 2½ hours), Ávila (€12.25, 1¼ hour) and Valladolid (from €10.45, 1½ hours).

León

POP 129,500 / ELEV 837M

León is a wonderful city, combining stunning historical architecture with an irresistible energy. Its standout attraction is the cathedral, one of the most beautiful in Spain, but there's so much more to see and do here. By day you'll encounter a city with its roots firmly planted in the soil of northern Castilla, with its grand monuments, loyal Catholic heritage and a role as an important staging post along the Camino de Santiago. By night León is taken over by its large student population, who provide it with a deep-into-the-night soundtrack of revelry that floods the narrow streets and plazas of the picturesque old quarter, the Barrio Húmedo. It's a fabulous mix.

⊙ Sights

★ Catedral
CATHEDRAL

(☎ 987 87 57 70; www.catedraldeleon.org; Plaza de Regla; adult/concession/under 12yr €5/4/free, combined ticket to the Claustro & Museo Catedralicio-Diocesano €8/6/free; ☺ 9.30am-1.30pm & 4-8pm Mon-Fri, 9.30am-noon & 2-6pm Sat, 9.30-11am & 2-8pm Sun Jun-Sep, 9.30am-1.30pm & 4-7pm Mon-Sat, 9.30am-2pm Sun Oct-May) León's 13th-century cathedral, with its soaring towers, flying buttresses and breathtaking interior, is the city's spiritual heart. Whether spotlit by night or bathed in glorious northern sunshine, the cathedral, arguably Spain's premier Gothic masterpiece, exudes a glorious, almost luminous quality. The show-stopping facade has a radiant **rose window**, three richly sculpted doorways and two muscular towers. The main entrance is lorded over by a scene of the Last Supper, while an extraordinary gallery of *vidrieras* (stained-glass windows) awaits you inside.

★ Panteón Real ▮ISTORIC BUILDING
(Plaza de San Isidoro; €5, 4-6.30pm Thu €1; ⏱10am-1.30pm & 4-6.30pm Mon-Sat, 10am-2pm Sun) Attached to the **Real Basílica de San Isidoro** (☑987 87 61 61; ⏱7.30am-11pm), the stunning Panteón Real houses royal sarcophagi, which rest with quiet dignity beneath a canopy of some of the finest Romanesque frescoes in Spain. Colourful motifs of biblical scenes drench the vaults and arches of this extraordinary hall, held aloft by marble columns with intricately carved capitals. The pantheon also houses a small **museum** where you can admire various treasures including a cup convincingly identified with what was in medieval times considered to be the Holy Grail.

🛏 Sleeping & Eating

The most atmospheric part of town for restaurants is the old town. You can easily fill up on tapas here – free with every drink. A good place to start is Plaza de San Martín, while on the other side of Calle Ancha, Plaza de Torres de Omaña is the epicentre of another good zone.

Hostal San Martín HOSTAL €
(☑987 87 51 87; www.sanmartinhostales.es; 2nd fl, Plaza de Torres de Omaña 1; s/d €30/43, with shared bathroom €23/30; 🛜) In a splendid central position occupying an 13th-century building, this is good old-fashioned budget value in the heart of town. The candy-coloured rooms are light and airy; all have small terraces. The spotless bathrooms have excellent water pressure and tubs, as well as showers, and there's a comfortable sitting area. The friendly owner can provide advice and a map.

La Trébede TAPAS €
(☑637 25 91 97; Plaza de Torres de Omaña; tapas from €2.50, raciones from €6.50; ⏱noon-4pm & 8pm-midnight Mon-Sat) As good for tapas (try the croquettes) as for first drinks (wines by the glass start at €1.50), La Trébede is always full. The decor is eclectic – deer's antlers, historic wirelesses and the scales of justice – and the sign outside declaring 350km to

WORTH A TRIP

ASTURIAS & THE PICOS DE EUROPA

Asturias, a Celtic province of cider, green valleys, industry and super cold-water beaches, is an enticing, hospitable place to explore for a few days, starting in its main cities Oviedo and Gijón. The jagged Picos de Europa in its southeast is some of the finest walking country in Spain. They comprise three limestone massifs (the highest peak rises 2648m). The 647-sq-km **Parque Nacional de los Picos de Europa** (www.picosdeeuropa.com) covers all three massifs and is Spain's second-biggest national park. There are numerous places to stay and eat all over the mountains. Getting here and around by bus can be slow-going but the Picos are accessible from Santander and Oviedo (the latter is easier) by bus.

Santiago may just prompt you to abandon the Camino and stay a little longer.

Ezequiel TAPAS €€
(☑987 00 19 61; www.restauranteezequiel.com; Calle Ancha 20; raciones €10-18; ⏱9am-midnight) It can be difficult to fight your way to the bar upstairs but it's worth doing so for the generous-sized *raciones*, which include all kind of cured meats straight from Ezequiel's own pig farm up in the province's north. In the downstairs restaurant, portions are huge and hearty. There's a *menú del día* that's great value, though it's not advertised.

ℹ Information

Regional Tourist Office (☑987 23 70 82; www.turismocastillayleon.com; Plaza de la Regla 2; ⏱9.30am-2pm & 5-8pm Mon-Sat, 9.30am-5pm Sun)

ℹ Getting There & Away

Buses depart to Madrid (€22.95, 3½ hours, eight daily), Burgos (€5 to €15.50, two hours, three daily) and Valladolid (€10.20, two hours, nine daily).

The AVE fast train runs to/from Madrid (€32.75, 2¼ hours), although there are cheaper and slower services. Other destinations include Burgos (from €9.85, two hours).

Santiago de Compostela

POP 80,000

Locals say the arcaded, stone streets of Santiago de Compostela – the final stop on the epic Camino de Santiago pilgrimage trail – are at their most beautiful in the rain, when the Old Town glistens. Most would agree, however, that it's hard to catch Santiago in a bad pose. Whether you're wandering the streets of the Old Town, nibbling on tapas in the taverns, or gazing down at the rooftops from atop the cathedral, Santiago seduces.

◉ Sights

★ Catedral de Santiago de Compostela
CATHEDRAL

(www.catedraldesantiago.es; Praza do Obradoiro; ⏰7am-8.30pm) The grand heart of Santiago, the cathedral soars above the city centre in a splendid jumble of spires and sculpture. Built piecemeal over several centuries, its beauty is a mix of the original Romanesque structure (constructed between 1075 and 1211) and later Gothic and baroque flourishes. The tomb of Santiago beneath the main altar is a magnet for all who come to the cathedral. The artistic high point is

Santiago de Compostela

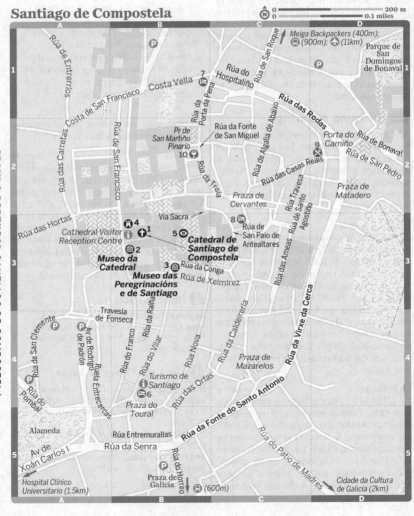

the Pórtico de la Gloria inside the west entrance, featuring 200 masterly Romanesque sculptures.

★ Museo das Peregrinacións e de Santiago

MUSEUM

(http://museoperegrinacions.xunta.gal; Praza das Praterías; adult/pilgrim & student/senior & child €2.40/1.20/free, Sat afternoon & Sun free; ⊙ 9.30am-8.30pm Tue-Sat, 10.15am-2.45pm Sun) Recently installed in a newly converted premises on Praza das Praterías, the brightly displayed Museum of Pilgrimages & Santiago gives fascinating insights into the phenomenon of Santiago (man and city) down the centuries. Much of the explanatory material is in English as well as Spanish and Galician. There are also great close-up views of some of the cathedral's towers from the 3rd-floor windows.

🛏 Sleeping

Hostal Suso

HOSTAL €

(☑981 586 611; www.hostalsuso.com; Rúa do Vilar 65; r €55-60; ⊛🐾) Stacked above a cafe, this family-run, 12-room *hostal* received a full makeover in 2016 and now boasts immaculate rooms in appealing greys and whites with up-to-date bathrooms and good, firm beds. Everything is thoroughly soundproofed too – the street outside is traffic-free but can get quite celebratory in summer.

Santiago de Compostela

The Last Stamp

HOSTEL €

(El Último Sello; ☑981 563 525; www.thelaststamp. es; Rúa Preguntoiro 10; dm €18-20; ⊙ closed approx late Dec-late Feb; ⊛@🐾) A purpose-designed hostel, the Last Stamp occupies a 300-year-old five-storey house (with lift) in the heart of the Old Town. The cleverly designed dorms feature semi-private modules with ultra-solid bunks, good mattresses and individual reading lights. Some rooms enjoy cathedral views. Bathrooms and kitchen are good and big – and Camino-themed murals add a bit of fun.

✖ Eating

Central Santiago is packed with eateries and most do their job pretty well. The many lining Rúa do Franco cater chiefly to a not particularly discriminating tourist market, and you'll find the most enticing options elsewhere. Don't leave Santiago without trying a *tarta de Santiago,* the city's famed almond cake.

★ Café Hotel Costa Vella

CAFE €

(Rúa da Porta da Pena 17; breakfast €2.60-4.30; ⊙ 8am-11pm; 🐾) The garden cafe of Hotel Costa Vella is the most delightful spot for breakfast (or a drink later in the day), with its fountain, a scattering of statuary, and beautiful flowering and fruit trees. And if the weather takes a Santiago-esque rainy turn, you can still enjoy it from the glass pavilion or the *galería.*

La Flor

SEAFOOD €

(Rúa das Casas Reais 25; dishes €7-10; ⊙ 11.30am-12.30am Mon-Thu, 11.30am-2.15am Fri-Sat; 🐾☑) La Flor is not just a fashionable, buzzy bar for drinks and good music but also a place where you can eat an eclectic range of creative and not-too-heavy dishes from vegetable lasagne to chicken fingers, homemade burgers or rocket-and-goat-cheese salad – all amid a uniquely random melange of art, *objets* and hanging lamps.

🍷 Drinking & Nightlife

★ Pub Atlántico

BAR

(☑981 572 152; Rúa da Fonte de San Miguel 9; ⊙ typically 5.30pm-3am or later, in winter may open 9pm & close Sun-Mon) This buzzing two-floor bar pulls in an artsy, mostly 20s and 30s crowd, with excellent gin tonics and cocktails, and a great soundtrack ranging from Cajun blues to Spanish indie.

SPAIN & PORTUGAL SANTIAGO DE COMPOSTELA

AROUND GALICIA

Galicia's dramatic Atlantic coastline is one of Spain's best-kept secrets, with wild and precipitous cliffs and isolated fishing villages. The lively port city of A Coruña has a lovely city beach and fabulous seafood (a recurring Galician theme). It's also the gateway to the stirring landscapes of the Costa da Morte and Rías Altas; the latter's highlight among many is probably Cabo Ortegal. Inland Galicia is also worth exploring, especially the old town of Lugo, surrounded by what many consider to be the world's best preserved Roman walls.

ⓘ Information

Turismo de Santiago (☑ 981 555 129; www.santiagoturismo.com; Rúa do Vilar 63; ⊙ 9am-9pm approx Apr-Oct, 9am-7pm Mon-Fri, 9am-2pm & 4-7pm Sat & Sun approx Nov-Mar) The efficient main municipal tourist office.

ⓘ Getting There & Away

The bus station is 1.5km northeast of the centre. Destinations include León (€30, 6 hours), Madrid (€46 to €57, eight hours), Porto, Portugal (€33, 3¼ hours).

The train station is about a kilometre south of the old town. High-speed AVE service to/from Madrid (currently €36, 5¼ hours) is due to start in 2018.

Barcelona

POP 4.7 MILLION (URBAN AREA)

Barcelona is one of Europe's coolest cities. Despite two millennia of history, it's a forward-thinking place, always on the cutting edge of art, design and cuisine. Whether you explore its medieval palaces and plazas, admire the Modernista masterpieces, shop for designer fashions along its bustling boulevards, sample its exciting nightlife or soak up the sun on the beaches, you'll find it hard not to fall in love with this vibrant city. As much as Barcelona is a visual feast, it will also lead you into culinary temptation. Anything from traditional Catalan cooking to the latest in avant-garde new Spanish cuisine will have your appetite in overdrive.

⊙ Sights

★**La Rambla**   STREET

(Map p424; Ⓜ Catalunya, Liceu, Drassanes) Barcelona's most famous street is both a tourist magnet and a window into Catalan culture, with cultural centres, theatres and intriguing architecture. Set between narrow traffic lanes and flanked by plane trees, the middle of La Rambla is a broad pedestrian boulevard, crowded every day until the wee hours with a wide cross-section of society. A stroll here is pure sensory overload, with souvenir hawkers, buskers, pavement artists, mimes and living statues all part of the ever-changing street scene.

★**Mercat de la Boqueria**   MARKET

(Map p424; ☑ 93 412 13 15; www.boqueria.info; La Rambla 91; ⊙ 8am-8.30pm Mon-Sat; Ⓜ Liceu) Mercat de la Boqueria is possibly La Rambla's most interesting building, not so much for its Modernista-influenced design (it was actually built over a long period, from 1840 to 1914, on the site of the former St Joseph Monastery), but for the action of the food market within.

★**MACBA**   MUSEUM

(Museu d'Art Contemporani de Barcelona; Map p420; ☑ 93 481 33 68; www.macba.cat; Plaça dels Àngels 1; adult/concession/under 12 €10/8/free; ⊙ 11am-7.30pm Mon & Wed-Fri, 10am-9pm Sat, 10am-3pm Sun & holidays; Ⓜ Universitat) Designed by Richard Meier and opened in 1995, MACBA has become the city's foremost contemporary art centre, with captivating exhibitions for the serious art lover. The permanent collection is on the ground floor and dedicates itself to Spanish and Catalan art from the second half of the 20th century, with works by Antoni Tàpies, Joan Brossa and Miquel Barceló, among others, though international artists, such as Paul Klee, Bruce Nauman and John Cage, are also represented.

★**La Catedral**   CATHEDRAL

(Map p424; ☑ 93 342 82 62; www.catedralbcn.org; Plaça de la Seu; admission free, 'donation entrance' €7, choir admission €3, roof admission €3; ⊙ 8am-12.45pm & 5.15-7.30pm Mon-Fri, to 8pm Sat & Sun, 'donation entrance' 1-5pm Mon-Sat, 2-5pm Sun; Ⓜ Jaume I) Barcelona's central place of worship presents a magnificent image. The richly decorated main facade, laced with gargoyles and the stone intricacies you would expect of northern European Gothic, sets it quite apart from other churches in the city. The facade was actually added in 1870, although the rest of the building was built between 1298 and 1460. The other facades are sparse in decoration, and the octagonal, flat-roofed towers are a clear reminder that, even here, Catalan Gothic architectural principles prevailed.

★ La Sagrada Família — CHURCH

(Map p420; ☎ 93 208 04 14; www.sagradafamilia. cat; Carrer de Mallorca 401; adult/concession/under 11 €15/13/free; ⊙9am-8pm Apr-Sep, to 6pm Oct-Mar; Ⓜ Sagrada Família) If you have time for only one sightseeing outing, this should be it. La Sagrada Família inspires awe by its sheer verticality, and in the manner of the medieval cathedrals it emulates it's still under construction after more than 100 years. When completed, the highest tower will be more than half as high again as those that stand today.

Unfinished it may be, but it attracts around 2.8 million visitors a year and is the most visited monument in Spain. The most important recent tourist was Pope Benedict XVI, who consecrated the church in a huge ceremony in November 2010.

The Temple Expiatori de la Sagrada Família (Expiatory Temple of the Holy Family) was Antoni Gaudí's all-consuming obsession. Given the commission by a conservative society that wished to build a temple as atonement for the city's sins of modernity, Gaudí saw its completion as his holy mission. As funds dried up, he contributed his own, and in the last years of his life he was never shy of pleading with anyone he thought a likely donor.

Gaudí devised a temple 95m long and 60m wide, able to seat 13,000 people, with a central tower 170m high above the transept (representing Christ) and another 17 of 100m or more. The 12 along the three facades represent the Apostles, while the remaining five represent the Virgin Mary and the four evangelists. With his characteristic dislike for straight lines (there were none in nature, he said), Gaudí gave his towers swelling outlines inspired by the weird peaks of the holy mountain Montserrat outside Barcelona, and encrusted them with a tangle of sculpture that seems an outgrowth of the stone. At Gaudí's death, only the crypt, the apse walls, one portal and one tower had been finished but construction has been mostly ongoing.

The roof is held up by a forest of extraordinary angled pillars. As the pillars soar towards the ceiling, they sprout a web of supporting branches, creating the effect of a forest canopy.

The **Nativity Facade** is the artistic pinnacle of the building, mostly created under Gaudí's personal supervision. You can climb high up inside some of the four towers by a combination of lifts and narrow spiral staircases – a vertiginous experience.

Basílica de Santa Maria del Mar — CHURCH

(Map p424; ☎ 93 310 23 90; Plaça de Santa Maria del Mar; incl guided tour noon-5pm €8; ⊙9am-8pm; Ⓜ Jaume I) At the southwest end of Passeig del Born stands the apse of Barcelona's finest Catalan Gothic church, Santa Maria del Mar (Our Lady of the Sea). Built in the 14th century with record-breaking alacrity for the time (it took just 54 years), the church is remarkable for its architectural harmony and simplicity.

Museu Picasso — MUSEUM

(Map p424; ☎ 93 256 30 00; www.museupicasso. bcn.cat; Carrer de Montcada 15-23; adult/concession/child all collections €14/7.50/free, permanent collection €11/7/free, temporary exhibitions €4.50/3/free, 3-7pm Sun & 1st Sun of month free; ⊙9am-7pm Tue, Wed & Fri-Sun, to 9.30pm Thu; Ⓜ Jaume I) The setting alone, in five contiguous medieval stone mansions, makes the Museu Picasso unique (and worth the probable queues). The pretty courtyards, galleries and staircases preserved in the first three of these buildings are as delightful as the collection inside.

Casa Batlló — ARCHITECTURE

(Map p420; ☎ 93 216 03 06; www.casabatllo.es; Passeig de Gràcia 43; adult/concession/under 7 €22.50/19.50/free; ⊙9am-9pm, last admission 8pm; Ⓜ Passeig de Gràcia) One of the strangest residential buildings in Europe, this is Gaudí at his hallucinatory best. The facade, sprinkled with bits of blue, mauve and green tiles and studded with wave-shaped window frames and balconies, rises to an uneven blue-tiled roof with a solitary tower.

Museu Nacional d'Art de Catalunya (MNAC) — MUSEUM

(Map p420; ☎ 93 622 03 76; www.museunacional. cat; Mirador del Palau Nacional; adult/student/child €12/€8.40/free, after 3pm Sat & 1st Sun of month free; ⊙10am-8pm Tue-Sat, to 3pm Sun May-Sep, to 6pm Tue-Sat Oct-Apr; Ⓜ Espanya) From across the city, the bombastic neobaroque

La Sagrada Família

A TIMELINE

1882 Francesc del Villar is commissioned to construct a neo-Gothic church.

1883 Antoni Gaudí takes over as chief architect, and plans a far more ambitious church to hold 13,000 faithful.

1926 Death of Gaudí; work continues under Domènec Sugrañes. Much of the **apse ❶** and **Nativity Facade ❷** is complete.

1930 Bell towers ❸ of the Nativity Facade completed.

1936 Construction is interrupted by Spanish Civil War; anarchists destroy Gaudí's plans.

1939-40 Architect Francesc de Paula Quintana i Vidal restores the crypt and meticulously reassembles many of Gaudí's lost models, some of which can be seen in the **museum ❹**.

1976 Completion of **Passion Facade ❺**.

1986-2006 Sculptor Josep Subirachs adds sculptural details to the Passion Facade including the panels telling the story of Christ's last days, amid much criticism for employing a style far removed from what was thought typical of Gaudí.

2000 Central nave vault ❻ completed.

2010 Church completely roofed over; Pope Benedict XVI consecrates the church; work begins on a high-speed rail tunnel that will pass beneath the church's **Glory Facade ❼**.

2020s–40s Projected completion date.

TOP TIPS

» **Light** The best light through the stained-glass windows of the Passion Facade bursts through into the heart of the church in the late afternoon.

» **Time** Visit at opening time on weekdays to avoid the worst of the crowds.

» **Views** Head up the Nativity Facade bell towers for the views, as long queues generally await at the Passion Facade towers.

Spiral staircase

Nativity Facade
Gaudí used plaster casts of local people and even of the occasional corpse from the local morgue as models for the portraits in the Nativity scene.

KRZYSZTOF DYDYNSKI/GETTY IMAGES ©

Central nave vault

Apse
Built just after the crypt in mostly neo-Gothic style, it is capped by pinnacles that show a hint of the genius that Gaudí would later deploy in the rest of the church.

JASON WALTMAN/500PX ©

Bell towers

The towers (eight completed) of the three facades represent the 12 Apostles. Lifts whisk visitors up one tower of the Nativity and Passion Facades (the latter gets longer queues) for fine views.

NIKADA/GETTY IMAGES ©

Completed church

Along with the Glory Facade and its four towers, six other towers remain to be completed. They will represent the four Evangelists, the Virgin Mary and, soaring above them all over the transept, a 170m colossus symbolising Christ.

Glory Facade

This will be the most fanciful facade of all, with a narthex boasting 16 hyperboloid lanterns topped by cones that will look something like an organ made of melting ice cream.

Museu Gaudí

Jammed with old photos, drawings and restored plaster models that bring Gaudí's ambitions to life, the museum also houses an extraordinarily complex plumb-line device he used to calculate his constructions.

Escoles de Gaudí

Crypt

The first completed part of the church, the crypt is in largely neo-Gothic style and lies under the transept. Gaudí's burial place here can be seen from the Museu Gaudí.

JEKATERINA NIKITINA/GETTY IMAGES ©

Passion Facade

See the story of Christ's last days from Last Supper to burial in an S-shaped sequence from bottom to top of the facade. Check out the cryptogram in which the numbers always add up to 33, Christ's age at his death.

STEPHEN SAKS/GETTY IMAGES ©

Barcelona

1 km
0.5 miles

SANT MARTÍ

EL CLOT

CAMP DE L'ARPA

LA DRETA DE L'EIXAMPLE

EL GUINARDÓ

Hospital de Sant Pau

Sagrada Família

La Sagrada Família

SAGRADA FAMÍLIA

L'EIXAMPLE

EL FORT PIENC

SANT GERVASI DE CASSOLES

EL CARMEL

GRÀCIA

Park Güell (200m)

Camp Nou (2km)

Via Augusta

Av Diagonal

Av Meridiana

Pg de Pujades

Parc de la Ciutadella

Ciutadella Vila Olímpica

Plaça de les Glòries Catalanes

Plaça de les Arts

Plaça de Joan Carles I

Plaça de Tetuan

Plaça de Raspall

Plaça del Sol

Plaça de la Torre

Plaça de Lesseps

Plaça de l'Hospital Militar

Hospital Clínic

Arc de Triomf

Monumental

C del Comerç

Av Tibidabo

Ronda del General Mitre

C de Balmes

C de Muntaner

Via Augusta

C de Pi i Margall

C de Ca l'Alegre de Dalt

C de l'Escorial

C de Sant Lluís

Travessera de Dalt

C de Verdi

C d'en Martí

C del Robí

C de l'Or

C de Sant Salvador

Travessera de Gràcia

C Gran de Gràcia

C de Tuset

C d'Enric Granados

C d'Aribau

C de Muntaner

C de Casanova

C de Londres

C de París

C de Viladomat

C de Loreto

C de Balmes

C d'Enric Granados

C de Borí i Fontestà

C de Calvet

C d'Amigó

C de Tavern

C de Saragossa

C de Vallirana

C de les Madrazo

C d'Alfons XII

Padua

La Bonanova

Vallcarca

Alfons X

Joanic

Fontana

Lesseps

Molina

Sant Gervasi

Muntaner

Provença

Gràcia

Diagonal

Urquinaona

Catalunya

Verdaguer

Girona

Glòries

Bogatell

Marina

C de Sardenya

C de Sicília

C de Nàpols

C de Roger de Flor

C del Bruc

C de Girona

C de Pau Claris

C de Roger de Llúria

Passeig de Gràcia

Pg de Gràcia

Av Diagonal

C d'Aragó

C de Provença

C del Rosselló

C de Còrsega

C de Sant Antoni Maria Claret

C d'Indústria

C de Còrsega

C del Rosselló

Pg de Sant Joan

C de Bailèn

C de Sant Joan

Mossèn Jacint Verdaguer

C del Consell de Cent

C de la Diputació

C de València

Ronda de Sant Pere

C d'Ausiàs Marc

C del Comerç

Pg de Sant Joan

C de Casp

C de la Marina

C de Sardenya

C d'Alí Bei

C de Pamplona

C de Zamora

C de Joan Miró

C de la Marina

C de Wellington

C de la Universitat

Pompeu Fabra

Parc de Carles I

Cascada

C d'Almogàvers

C dels Palais

C de Mallorca

C del Dos de Maig

C de la Independència

C del Rosselló

C de Cartagena

C de Padilla

C de Lepant

C de la Marina

C de València

18

15

9

4

6

5

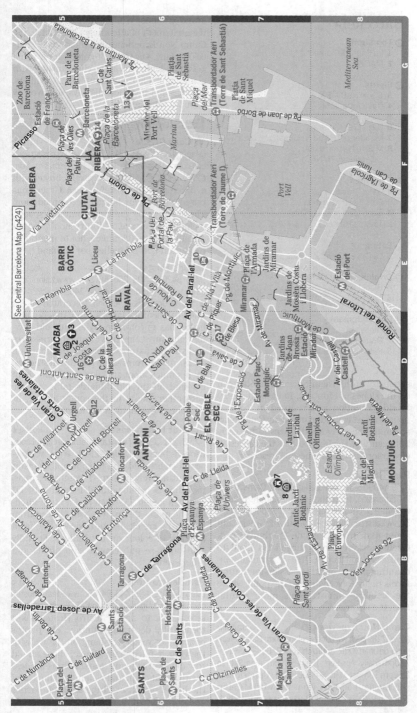

SPAIN & PORTUGAL BARCELONA

Barcelona

silhouette of the Palau Nacional can be seen on the slopes of Montjuïc. Built for the 1929 World Exhibition and restored in 2005, it houses a vast collection of mostly Catalan art spanning the early Middle Ages to the early 20th century. The high point is the collection of extraordinary Romanesque frescoes.

Park Güell　　　　　　　　　　　PARK
(☎93 409 18 31; www.parkguell.cat; Carrer d'Olot 7; admission to central area adult/child €8/6; ☺8am-9.30pm May-Aug, to 8pm Sep-Apr; ☐24, 32, Ⓜ Lesseps, Vallcarca) North of Gràcia and about 4km from Plaça de Catalunya, Park Güell is where Gaudí turned his hand to landscape gardening. It's a strange, enchanting place where his passion for natural forms really took flight – to the point where the artificial almost seems more natural than the natural.

Camp Nou Experience　　　　MUSEUM
(☎902 189900; www.fcbarcelona.com; Gate 9, Avinguda de Joan XXIII; adult/child €23/18; ☺9.30am-7.30pm daily Apr-Sep, 10am-6.30pm Mon-Sat, to 2.30pm Sun Oct-Mar; Ⓜ Palau Reial) A pilgrimage site for football fans from the world, Camp Nou (p426) is one of Barcelona's most hal-

lowed grounds. While nothing compares to the excitement of attending a live match, the Camp Nou Experience is a must for FC Barcelona fans. On this self-guided tour, you'll get an in-depth look at the club, starting with a museum filled with multimedia exhibits, trophies and historical displays, followed by a tour of the stadium.

🛏 Sleeping

★Casa Gràcia　　　　　　　　HOSTEL €
(Map p420; ☎93 174 05 28; www.casagracia-bcn.com; Passeig de Gràcia 116; dm/s/d from €27/90/103; ✳@☎; Ⓜ Diagonal) A hostel with a difference, the tasteful Casa Gràcia has raised the bar for budget accommodation. There are some enticing common spaces, including a terrace, a library nook and an artfully decorated lounge – not to mention a restaurant and DJ-fuelled bar on hand.

Tailor's Hostel　　　　　　　　HOSTEL €
(Map p420; ☎93 250 56 84; www.tailors-hostel.com; Carrer de Sepúlveda 146; dm €24-30; ✳☎; Ⓜ Urgell, Sant Antoni) Decorated like a mid-20th-century tailor's shop, this popular hostel has uncommon style, with old sewing machines, lovingly framed brassieres and vintage fixtures adorning the common areas. Aside from admiring the aesthetics, there's much afoot at Tailor's: you can shoot a round on the old billiards table, mingle with other guests in the comfy lounge, or join one of the many activities on offer.

Amistat Beach Hostel　　　　HOSTEL €
(☎93 221 32 81; www.amistatbeachhostel.com; Carrer de l'Amistat 21; dm €21-34; ✳☎; Ⓜ Poblenou) A stylish addition to Poblenou, Amistat has attractively designed common areas, including a beanbag-filled lounge with DJ set-up, a low-lit TV room and a guest kitchen. The rooms themselves, which sleep from four to 12, are clean, but basic – aside from a splash of colour on the ceilings. Friendly staff organise pub crawls, club nights and other events.

Pars Teatro Hostel　　　　　HOSTEL €
(Map p420; ☎93 443 94 66; www.teatrohostel.com; Carrer d'Albareda 12; dm €25-35; ☎; Ⓜ Drassanes) True to name, Teatro Hostel has a theatrically decorated interior: old photos of actors of yesteryear hang on the walls of the vintage-filled main lounge, above an old row of velvety theatre seats. Rooms are less exciting, but clean and well maintained, and the hostel organises dinners, beach parties and other activities. Friendly staff.

Alberg Hostel Itaca
HOSTEL €

(Map p424; 93 301 97 51; www.itacahostel.com; Carrer de Ripoll 21; dm €30, d without bathroom €76; ❄@🛜; Ⓜ Jaume I) A bright quiet hostel near the cathedral, Itaca has spacious dorms (sleeping six to 10 people) with parquet floors and spring colours, and two doubles. There's a lively vibe, and the hostel organises activities (pub crawls, flamenco concerts, free daily walking tours), making it a good option for solo travellers.

Sant Jordi Mambo Tango
HOSTEL €

(Map p420; 93 442 51 64; www.hostelmambo-tango.com; Carrer del Poeta Cabanyes 23; dm €29-35; ❄@🛜; Ⓜ Paral·lel) A fun, international hostel to hang out in, the Mambo Tango has basic but clean dorms (sleeping four to nine people) and a welcoming, somewhat chaotic atmosphere. The beds are a touch on the hard side, and light sleepers should bring earplugs. With pub crawls and other nightly activities, it's a good place to meet other travelers.

✖ Eating

Barcelona has a celebrated food scene fuelled by a combination of world-class chefs, imaginative recipes and magnificent ingredients fresh from farms and the sea. Catalan culinary masterminds like Ferran Adrià and Carles Abellan have become international icons, reinventing the world of haute cuisine, while classic old-world Catalan recipes continue to earn accolades in dining rooms and tapas bars across the city.

Bormuth
TAPAS €

(Map p424; 93 310 21 86; Carrer del Rec 31; tapas from €4; 1pm-midnight; 🛜; Ⓜ Jaume I) Opened on the pedestrian Carrer del Rec in 2013, Bormuth has tapped into the vogue for old-school tapas with modern-times service and decor, and serves all the old favourites – *patatas bravas* (potato chunks in a slightly spicy tomato sauce), *ensaladilla* (Russian salad), tortilla – along with some less predictable and superbly prepared numbers (try the chargrilled red pepper with black pudding).

★ La Cova Fumada
TAPAS €

(Map p420; 93 221 40 61; Carrer del Baluard 56; tapas €4-8; 9am-3.20pm Mon-Wed, 9am-3.20pm & 6-8.15pm Thu & Fri, 9am-1pm Sat; Ⓜ Barceloneta) There's no sign and the setting is decidedly downmarket, but this tiny, buzzing family-run tapas spot always packs in a crowd.

The secret? Mouthwatering *pulpo* (octopus), *calamar, sardinias* and 15 or so other small plates cooked to perfection in the small open kitchen. The *bombas* (potato croquettes served with *alioli*) and grilled *carxofes* (artichokes) are good, but everything is amazingly fresh.

Cervecería Taller de Tapas
TAPAS, CATALAN €

(Map p424; 93 481 62 33; www.tallerdetapas.com; Carrer Comtal 28; mains €7-10; 8.30am-1am Mon-Sat, noon-1am Sun; Ⓜ Urquinaona) Amid white stone walls and a beamed ceiling, this buzzing, easy-going place serves a broad selection of tapas as well as changing daily specials like *cochinillo* (roast suckling pig). A smattering of beers from across the globe – Leffe Blonde (Belgium), Guinness (Ireland), Brahma (Brazil) and Sol (Mexico) – add to the appeal.

Alcoba Azul
MEDITERRANEAN €

(Map p424; 93 302 81 41; Carrer de Sant Domènec del Call 14; mains €7-8.50; 6pm-2.30am winter, noon-2am Sun-Thu, to 3am Fri & Sat summer; 🛜; Ⓜ Jaume I) Peel back the centuries inside this remarkably atmospheric watering hole, with medieval walls, low ceilings, wooden floors and flickering candles. Grab one of the seats at the tiny bar in front or slide into one of the table booths at the back, where you can enjoy good wines by the glass, satisfying plates of stuffed peppers, salads, *tostas* (sandwiches) and blood sausage with caramelised onions.

Euskal Etxea
TAPAS €

(Map p424; 93 310 21 85; Placeta de Montcada 1; tapas €1.95; 10am-12.30am Sun-Thu, to 1am Fri & Sat; Ⓜ Jaume I) Barcelona has plenty of Basque and pseudo-Basque eateries, but this is the real deal. It captures the feel of San Sebastián better than many of its newer competitors. Choose your *pintxos* (tapas mounted on slices of bread), sip *txakoli* (Basque white wine), and keep the toothpicks so the staff can count them up and work out your bill.

Cat Bar
VEGAN €

(Map p424; Carrer de la Bòria 17; mains €6.50-8.50; 6-11.30pm Mon-Wed, 1-11pm Thu-Sat; 🛜🚼; Ⓜ Jaume I) This tiny little joint squeezes in a vegan kitchen, a great selection of local artisanal beers and a smattering of live music. The food mostly comprises different burgers, plus a gluten-free dish of the day, plus tapas and hummus. The beers change regularly, but there is always one wheat, one porter, one gluten-free and an IPA.

🍷 Drinking & Nightlife

Barcelona is a nightlife-lovers' town, with an enticing spread of candlelit wine bars, old-school taverns, stylish lounges and kaleidoscopic nightclubs where the party continues until daybreak. For something a little more sedate, the city's atmospheric cafes and tea-houses make a fine retreat when the skies turn grey.

★ La Caseta del Migdia   BAR
(☑ 617 956572; www.lacaseta.org; Mirador del Migdia; ⏰ 8pm-1am Wed-Fri, from noon Sat & Sun, weekends only in winter; 🚌 150) The effort of get-

ting to what is, for all intents and purposes, a simple *chiringuito* (makeshift cafe-bar) is worth it. Stare out to sea over a beer or coffee by day. As sunset approaches the atmosphere changes, as lounge music (from samba to funk) wafts out over the hillside. Drinks aside, you can also order barbecue, fired up on the outdoor grills.

El Born Bar   BAR
(Map p424; ☑ 93 319 53 33; Passeig del Born 26; ⏰ 10am-2am Mon-Sat, noon-1.30am Sun; 🛜; Ⓜ Jaume I) El Born Bar effortlessly attracts everyone from cool thirty-somethings from

Central Barcelona

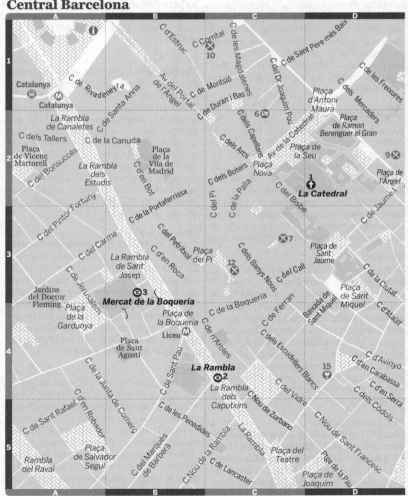

all over town to locals who pass judgement on Passeig del Born's passing parade. Its staying power depends on a good selection of beers, spirits, and *empanadas* and other snacks.

El Xampanyet
WINE BAR

(Map p424; ☑ 93 319 70 03; Carrer de Montcada 22; ⊙ noon-4pm & 7-11pm Tue-Sat, noon-4pm Sun; Ⓜ Jaume I) Nothing has changed for decades in this, one of the city's best-known *cava* (sparkling wine) bars. Plant yourself at the bar or seek out a table against the decoratively tiled walls for a glass or three of the cheap house *cava* and an assortment of tapas, such as the tangy *boquerones en vinagre* (fresh anchovies in vinegar).

BlackLab
MICROBREWERY

(Map p420; ☑ 93 221 83 60; www.blacklab.es; Plaça Pau Vila 1; ⊙ noon-1.30am; Ⓜ Barceloneta) Inside the historic Palau de Mar, BlackLab was Barcelona's first brewhouse to open way back in 2014. With 20 taps (including 18 housemade brews, including saisons, double IPAs and dry stouts), it's an impressive operation, and the brewmasters are constantly experimenting with new flavours.

Marula Cafè
BAR

(Map p424; ☑ 93 318 76 90; www.marulacafe.com; Carrer dels Escudellers 49; ⊙ 11pm-6am Wed-Sun; Ⓜ Liceu) A fantastic find in the heart of the Barri Gòtic, Marula will transport you to the 1970s and the best in funk and soul. James Brown fans will think they've died and gone to heaven. It's not, however, a monothematic place and DJs slip in other tunes, from breakbeat to house. Samba and other Brazilian dance sounds also penetrate here.

City Hall
CLUB

(Map p420; ☑ 93 238 07 22; www.cityhallbarcelona.com; Rambla de Catalunya 2-4; €10-15, incl 1 drink; ⊙ midnight-5am Wed & Thu, midnight-6am Fri & Sat, 11pm-5am Sun; Ⓜ Catalunya) A long corridor leads to the dance floor of this venerable

SPAIN & PORTUGAL BARCELONA

Central Barcelona

and popular club, located in a former theatre. House and other electro sounds dominate, with occasional funk nights, and – on Sundays – a gay night, Black Room. Check the website for details.

☆ Entertainment

Camp Nou   FOOTBALL
(☎902 189900; www.fcbarcelona.com; Carrer d'Arístides Maillol; MPalau Reial) The massive stadium of Camp Nou is home to the legendary Futbol Club Barcelona. Tickets to FC Barcelona matches are available at Camp Nou, online (through FC Barcelona's official website), and through various city locations. Tourist offices sell them as do FC Botiga stores. Tickets can cost anything from €39 to upwards of €250, depending on the seat and match.

★ Palau de la
Música Catalana   CLASSICAL MUSIC
(Map p420; ☎93 295 72 00; www.palaumusica.cat; Carrer de Palau de la Música 4-6; from €15; ☺box office 9.30am-9pm Mon-Sat, 10am-3pm Sun; MUrquinaona) A feast for the eyes, this Modernista confection is also the city's most traditional venue for classical and choral music, although it has a wide-ranging program, including flamenco, pop and – particularly – jazz. Just being here for a performance is an experience. In the foyer, its tiled pillars all a-glitter, sip a pre-concert tipple.

Gran Bodega Saltó   LIVE MUSIC
(Map p420; ☎93 441 37 09; www.bodegasalto.net; Carrer de Blesa 36; ☺7pm-2am Mon-Thu, noon-3am Fri & Sat, noon-midnight Sun; MParal·lel) The ranks of barrels give away the bar's history as a traditional bodega. Now, after a little homemade psychedelic redecoration with odd lamps, figurines and old Chinese beer ads, it's a magnet for an eclectic barfly crowd. The crowd is mixed and friendly, and gets pretty animated on nights when there is live music.

Gipsy Lou   LIVE MUSIC
(Map p420; www.gipsylou.com; Carrer de Ferlandina 55; ☺8pm-2.30am Sun-Thu, 8pm-3am Fri & Sat; MSant Antoni) A louche little bar that packs 'em in for live music from rumba to pop to flamenco, along with occasional storytelling events, and whatever else Felipe feels like putting on. There are decent bar snacks to keep you going on a long night of pisco sours, the house special.

❶ Information

Main Office (Map p424; ☎93 285 38 34; Plaça de Catalunya 17-S, underground; ☺8.30am-8.30pm; MCatalunya) The main tourist office is in Plaça de Catalunya. There are branches at the airport, train station and elsewhere.

❶ Getting There & Away

After Madrid, Barcelona is Spain's busiest international transport hub. A host of airlines, including many budget carriers, fly directly to Barcelona from around Europe. Some budget carriers use Girona and Reus airports (buses link Barcelona to both).

Long-distance trains arrive in Estació Sants, about 2.5km west of La Rambla. There are direct overnight trains from Paris, Geneva, Milan and Zürich. Fast train connections to Madrid run 18 times daily, some taking under three hours.

Long-haul buses arrive in Estació del Nord. A plethora of companies service different parts of Spain; many come under the umbrella of **Alsa** (☎902 422242; www.alsa.es). Eurolines and other operators service various European cities.

❶ Getting Around

From the airport, frequent buses make the 35-minute run into town (€5.90) from 6am to 1am.

The excellent metro can get you most places around town, with buses and trams filling in the gaps. Targeta T-10 (10-ride passes; €10.30) are the best value; otherwise, it's €2.15 per ride.

Girona
POP 97,200

Northern Catalonia's largest city is a jewellery box of museums, galleries and Gothic churches, strung around a tangle of cobbled lanes and medieval walls. Reflections of Modernista mansions shimmer in the Riu Onyar, which demarcates the historic centre on its right bank from the gleaming commercial centre on the left.

◉ Sights

★ Catedral   CATHEDRAL
(www.catedraldegirona.org; Plaça de la Catedral; adult/student incl Basílica de Sant Feliu €7/5, Sun free; ☺10am-7.30pm Apr-Oct, 10am-6.30pm Nov-Mar) Towering over a flight of 86 steps rising from Plaça de la Catedral, this edifice is far more ancient than its billowing baroque facade suggests. Built over an old Roman forum, parts of the cathedral's foundations date from the 5th century. Today, Gothic

ON THE DALÍ TRAIL

Figueres and the lovely seaside town of Cadaqués, easily accessible by train and bus respectively from Girona, have two excellent attractions intimately connected with the master artist and showman Salvador Dalí.

Teatre-Museu Dalí (www.salvador-dali.org; Plaça de Gala i Salvador Dalí 5; adult/under 9yr €12/free incl Museu de l'Empordà; ⊙ 9am-8pm Tue-Sun Jul-Sep, 10.30am-6pm Tue-Sun Oct-Jun, closed Mon) The first name that comes into your head when you lay your eyes on this red castle-like building in Figueres, topped with giant eggs and stylised Oscar-like statues and studded with plaster-covered croissants, is Dalí. An entirely appropriate final resting place for the master of surrealism, it has assured his immortality. Exhibits within these walls range from enormous installations - like *Taxi Plujós* (Rainy Taxi), an early Cadillac, surmounted by statues – to the more discreet, such as a tiny mysterious room with a mirrored flamingo.

Casa Museu Dalí (☎972 25 10 15; www.salvador-dali.org; adult/under 8yr €11/free; ⊙10.30am-6pm Tue-Sun, closed Jan–mid-Feb) Located by a peaceful cove in Port Lligat, a tiny fishing settlement a 20-minute walk from Cadaqués, the Casa Museu Dalí was the residence and sanctuary of Salvador Dalí. This splendid whitewashed structure is a mishmash of cottages and sunny terraces, linked together by narrow labyrinthine corridors and containing an assortment of offbeat furnishings. Access is by semi-guided tour only. It's essential to book ahead, by phone or via the website.

styling – built over the Romanesque church during the 14th century – dominates, though a fine, double-columned Romanesque **cloister** dates from the 12th century. It's a surprisingly formidable sight to explore, but an audioguide is included in the price.

★ **Museu d'Història dels Jueus de Girona**　MUSEUM
(www.girona.cat/call; Carrer de la Força 8; adult/child €4/free; ⊙10am-6pm Mon-Sat, to 2pm Sun) Until 1492 Girona was home to Catalonia's second most important medieval Jewish community (after Barcelona), and one of the finest Jewish quarters in the country. The Call (as the quarter is called) was centred on the narrow Carrer de la Força for 600 years, until relentless persecution forced the Jews out of Spain. This excellent museum shows genuine pride in Girona's Jewish heritage without shying away from the less salubrious aspects, such as persecution by the Inquisition and forced conversions.

🛏 Sleeping & Eating

Pensió Viladomat　PENSION €
(☎972 20 31 76; www.pensioviladomat.cat; Carrer dels Ciutadans 5; s/d without bathroom €24/40, d/tr with bathroom €50/68; 🛜) This is one of the nicest of the cheaper *pensiones* scattered about the southern end of the old town. It has simple, modernised, well-maintained rooms.

L'Alqueria　SPANISH, CATALAN €€
(☎972 22 18 82; www.restaurantalqueria.com; Carrer de la Ginesta 8; mains €14-20; ⊙1-4pm Tue-Sun, 9-11pm Wed-Sat) This smart minimalist *arrocería* serves the finest *arròs negre* (rice cooked in cuttlefish ink) and *arròs a la catalan* in the city, as well as around 20 other superbly executed rice dishes, including paellas. Eat your heart out, Valencia! It's wise to book ahead for dinner, though it also offers takeaway.

★ **El Celler de Can Roca**　CATALAN €€€
(☎972 22 21 57; www.cellercanroca.com; Calle Can Sunyer 48; degustation menus €150-180; ⊙1-4pm & 8.30-11pm Wed-Sat, 8.30-11pm Sun) Ever-changing avant-garde takes on Catalan dishes have catapulted El Celler to global fame. It was named best restaurant in the world in 2015 by The World's 50 Best Restaurants. Each year brings new innovations from molecular gastronomy to multi-sensory food-art interplay to sci-fi dessert trolleys, all with mama's home cooking as the core inspiration. Run by three brothers, El Celler de Can Roca is set in a refurbished country house, 2km northwest of central Girona. Book online 11 months in advance or join a standby list.

ℹ Information

Tourist Office (☎972 22 65 75; www.girona. cat/turisme; Rambla de la Llibertat 1; ⊙9am-

8pm Mon-Fri, 9am-2pm & 4-8pm Sat, 9am-2pm Sun) Multilingual and helpful tourist information spot by the river.

ℹ Getting There & Away

Girona is on the train line between Barcelona (€11.25 to €16.20, 40 minutes to 1¼ hours, up to 24 daily), Figueres (€4.10 to €5.45, 30 minutes, two to three daily) and Portbou, on the French border (€6.15 to €8.25, one hour, one daily).

The Balearic Islands

The Balearic Islands (Illes Balears in Catalan) adorn the glittering Mediterranean waters off Spain's eastern coastline. Beach tourism destinations par excellence, each of the islands has a quite distinct identity and they have managed to retain much of their individual character and beauty. All boast beaches second to none in the Med, but each offers reasons for exploring inland, too.

ℹ Getting There & Around

In summer, charter and regular flights converge on Palma de Mallorca and Ibiza from all over Europe.

Ferries are the other main way of getting to and between the islands. Barcelona, Dénia and Valencia are the principal mainland ports. Check www.directferries.com for all routes. Principal operators:

Acciona Trasmediterránea (📞 902 454645; www.trasmediterranea.es)

Baleària (📞 902 160180; www.balearia.com)

Mallorca

The sunny, warm hues of the medieval heart of Palma de Mallorca, the archipelago's capital, make a great introduction to the islands. The northwest coast, dominated by the Serra de Tramuntana mountain range, is a beautiful region of olive groves, pine forests and ochre villages, with a spectacularly rugged coastline. Most of Mallorca's best beaches are on the north and east coasts, and although many have been swallowed up by tourist developments, you can still find the occasional exception.

PALMA DE MALLORCA
POP 407,650

Nestled in the crook of the Badia de Palma, Mallorca's capital is the most agreeable of all Mediterranean towns. Shaped and defined by the sea and backed by not-so-distant mountains, it is a city of open horizons, oft-blue skies and a festive nature.

◉ Sights

★**Catedral**   CATHEDRAL
(La Seu; www.catedraldemallorca.org; Carrer del Palau Reial 9; adult/child €6/free; ⏰ 10am-6.15pm Mon-Fri, to 2.15pm Sat) Palma's vast cathedral is the city's major architectural landmark. Aside from its sheer scale and undoubted beauty, its stunning interior features, designed by Antoni Gaudí and renowned contemporary artist Miquel Barceló, make this unlike any cathedral elsewhere in the world. The awesome structure is predominantly Gothic, apart from the main facade, which is startling, quite beautiful and completely mongrel.

★**Palau de l'Almudaina**   PALACE
(Carrer del Palau Reial; adult/child €9/4, audioguide €4, guided tour €6; ⏰ 10am-8pm Apr-Sep, to 6pm Oct-Mar) Originally an Islamic fort, this mighty construction opposite the Catedral was converted into a residence for the Mallorcan monarchs at the end of the 13th century. The King of Spain resides here still, at least symbolically. The royal family are rarely in residence, except for the occasional ceremony, as they prefer to spend summer in the Palau Marivent (in Cala Major). At other times you can wander through a series of cavernous stone-walled rooms that have been lavishly decorated.

★**Palau March**   MUSEUM
(Carrer del Palau Reial 18; adult/child €4.50/free; ⏰ 10am-6.30pm Mon-Fri, to 2pm Sat) This house, palatial by any definition, was one of several residences of the phenomenally wealthy March family. Sculptures by 20th-century greats, such as Henry Moore, Auguste Rodin, Barbara Hepworth and Eduardo Chillida, grace the outdoor terrace. Within lie many more artistic treasures from some of Spain's big names in art, such as Salvador Dalí, and Barcelona's Josep Maria Sert and Xavier Corberó, as well as an extraordinary 18th-century Neapolitan baroque *belén* (nativity scene).

🛏 Sleeping & Eating

Hostal Pons   GUESTHOUSE €
(📞 971 72 26 58; www.hostalpons.com; Carrer del Vi 8; s €30, d €60-70, tr €85; 🛜) Bang in the heart of old Palma, this is a sweet, simple family-run guesthouse. Downstairs a cat slumbers

Mallorca

in a plant-filled patio, upstairs you'll find a book-lined lounge and rooms with rickety bedsteads and tiled floors. Cheaper rooms share communal bathrooms. The roof terrace offers peaceful respite.

Restaurant Celler Sa Premsa SPANISH €
(☎971 72 35 29; www.cellersapremsa.com; Plaça del Bisbe Berenguer de Palou 8; mains €9-14; ⏰12.30-4pm & 7.30-11.30pm Mon-Sat) A visit to this local institution is almost obligatory. It's a cavernous tavern filled with huge old wine barrels and has walls plastered with faded bullfighting posters – you find plenty such places in the Mallorcan interior but they're a dying breed here in Palma. Mallorcan specialities dominate the menu.

❶ Information

Consell de Mallorca Tourist Office (☎971 17 39 90; www.infomallorca.net; Plaça de la Reina 2; ⏰8am-6pm Mon-Fri, 8.30am-3pm Sat; ☎) Covers the whole island.

AROUND MALLORCA

Mallorca's northwestern coast is a world away from the high-rise tourism on the other side of the island. Dominated by the Serra de Tramuntana, it's a beautiful region of olive groves, pine forests and small villages with shuttered stone buildings. There are a couple of highlights for drivers: the hair-raising road down to the small port of Sa Calobra, and the amazing trip along the peninsula leading to the island's northern tip, Cap Formentor.

Menorca

Renowned for its pristine beaches and archaeological sites, tranquil Menorca was declared a Biosphere Reserve by Unesco in 1993.

Maó absorbs most of the tourist traffic. North of Maó, a drive across a lunar landscape leads to the lighthouse at Cap de Favàritx. South of the cape stretch some fine

Menorca

N
0 — 10 km
0 — 5 miles

Barcelona
(256km)

Palma de
Mallorca (187km);
Ibiza (282km);
Valencia (417km)

Cap de
Favàritx
Cala Presili
Platja d'en Tortuga

Illa
d'en Colom

Es Grau

Cala
Mesquida

Golden Farm Cap Negre
Collingwood House
Es Freus
Fortalesa de la Mola
Castell San Felipe
Cala de
Sant Esteve
Fort
Marlborough

Platja de
Punta Prima

Parc Natural
S'Albufera
d'es Grau

ME5

Maó
Es Castell ME6
Bodegas
Binifadet
Sant
Lluís

Binibèquer

Ecomuseu Cap
de Cavalleria

Far de
Cavalleria

Cap de
Cavalleria

Fornells

Platges de
Fornells

ME7

ME1

Talatí
de Dalt

Sant
Climent

Llucmaçanes
Aeropuerto
de Menorca

Es
Canutells

Cap
d'en
Font

Cala de
Binidalí

Platja
Cavalleria

Cala
Pregonda

ME15

Monte
El Toro
(357m)

Alaior
Torralba
d'en Salord

Cala'n
Porter

Cales
Coves

Torre d'en
Galmés

Cova
d'en
Xoroi

Es Mercadal

ME16

Es Migjorn
Gran

Son Bou

Cala en
Calderer

ME20

ME18

Cap
Gros

Cala
d'Algaiarens

Ferreries

ME22

Cala
Galdana

Cala
Mitjana

Cala
Morell

Cala en
Bosc

Naveta des
Tudons

ME1

Cala
Macarella

Cala
Turqueta

Cala
Mitjana

Cala es
Talaier

Ciutadella

Santandria

Son
Catlar

Arenal de
Son
Saura

Cala en
Bosc

Platja de
Son Xoriguer

Cala Blanca

Cap
d'Artrutx

Cala Ratjada (41km);
Port d'Alcúdia (63km)

sandy bays and beaches, including Cala Presili and Platja d'en Tortuga, reachable on foot. **Ciutadella**, with its smaller harbour and historic buildings, has a more distinctly Spanish feel to it and is the more attractive of the island's two main towns. A narrow country road leads south of Ciutadella (follow the 'Platges' sign from the *ronda*, or ring road) and then forks twice to reach some of the island's loveliest beaches: (from west to east) Arenal de Son Saura, Cala en Turqueta, Es Talaier, Cala Macarelleta and Cala Macarella. As with most beaches, you'll need your own transport. In the centre of the island, the 357m-high Monte Toro has great views; on a clear day you can see Mallorca. On the northern coast, the picturesque town of Fornells is on a large bay popular with windsurfers. The ports in both Maó and Ciutadella are lined with bars and restaurants.

Ibiza

Ibiza (Eivissa in Catalan) is an island of extremes. Its formidable party reputation is completely justified, with some of the world's greatest clubs attracting hedonists from the world over. The interior and northeast of the island, however, are another world. Peaceful country drives, hilly green territory, a sprinkling of mostly laid-back beaches and coves, and some wonderful inland accommodation and eateries are light years from the ecstasy-fuelled madness of the clubs that dominate the west.

IBIZA CITY
POP 49,400

Ibiza's capital is a vivacious, enchanting town with a captivating whitewashed old quarter topped by a cathedral. It's also a focal point for some of the island's best cafes, bars and clubs.

◉ Sights

★ **Ramparts** HISTORIC SITE
Encircling Dalt Vila, Ibiza's colossal protective walls reach over 25m in height and include seven bastions. Evocatively floodlit at night, these fortifications were constructed to safeguard Ibiza's residents against the threat of pirate attack. You can walk the entire perimeter of these impressive Renaissance-era ramparts, designed to withstand heavy artillery. Along the way, enjoy great views over the port area and south to Formentera.

CLUBBING IN IBIZA

From late May to the end of September, the west of the island is one big, nonstop dance party from sunset to sunrise and back again. The major clubs operate nightly from around midnight to 6am from mid-May or June to early October. Theme nights, fancy-dress parties and foam parties are regular features. Entertainment Ibiza-style doesn't come cheaply. Admission can cost anything from €20 to €65 (mixed drinks and cocktails then go for around €10 to €15).

Taxis are notorious for overcharging clubbers so use the **Discobus** (www.discobus.es; per person €3; ⊙midnight-6am Jun-Sep), which does an all-night whirl of the major clubs, bars and hotels.

🛏 Sleeping & Eating

Many of Ibiza City's hotels and *hostales* are closed in the low season and heavily booked between April and October. Make sure you book ahead.

Casa de Huéspedes Navarro HOTEL €
(☏ 971 31 07 71; Carrer de sa Creu 20; s/d without bathroom €32/62; ⊙May-Oct) Right in the thick of things, this simple option has eight rooms at the top of a long flight of stairs. The front rooms have harbour views, interior ones are quite dark (but cool in summer), and there's a sunny rooftop terrace. Bathrooms are shared but spotless.

★ **Comidas Bar San Juan** MEDITERRANEAN €
(Carrer de Guillem de Montgrí 8; mains €7-11; ⊙1-3.30pm & 8.30-11pm Mon-Sat) More traditional than trendy, this family-run operation, with two small dining rooms, harks back to the days before Ibiza became a byword for glam. It offers outstanding value, with fish dishes and steaks for around €10. It doesn't take reservations, so arrive early and expect to have other people at the same table as you.

🍷 Drinking & Nightlife

Sa Penya is the nightlife centre. Dozens of bars keep the port area jumping from sunset until the early hours. Alternatively, various bars at Platja d'en Bossa combine sounds, sand and sea with sangria and other tipples. After they wind down, you can continue at one of the island's world-famous nightclubs.

Ibiza

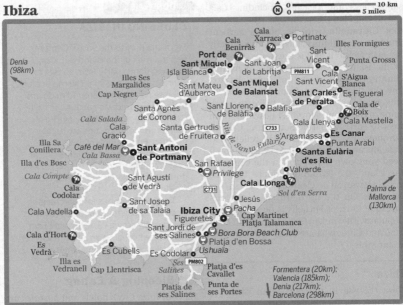

★ Pacha
CLUB

(www.pacha.com; Avinguda 8 d'Agost; admission €30-70, drinks from €12; ⊙11pm-6am daily May-Sep, 11pm-6am Sat Oct-Apr) Going strong since 1973, this is Ibiza's original and most classy nightclub. Built around the shell of a farmhouse, it has an amazing main dance floor, the Funky Room (for soul and disco sounds), a huge VIP section and myriad other places to groove or chill, including a fab open-air terrace and a Global Room for hip hop and R&B.

Privilege
CLUB

(www.privilegeibiza.com; Sant Rafel; admission €25-60; ⊙11pm-6am May-Sep) Welcome to the world's biggest club. Five kilometres along the road to San Rafael, Privilege is a mind-blowing space with 20 bars, an interior pool and capacity for 10,000 clubbers. The main domed dance temple is an enormous, pulsating area, where the DJ's cabin is suspended above the pool.

Ushuaïa
CLUB

(www.ushuaiabeachhotel.com; Platja d'en Bossa 10; admission €40-75; ⊙3pm or 5pm-midnight; ⏾) Queen of daytime clubbing, ice-cool Ushuaïa is an open-air megaclub. The party starts early with superstar DJs such as David Guetta, Luciano and Sven Väth, and poolside lounging by a lagoon with Bali beds. Check out the Sky Lounge for sparkling sea views, or stay the night in the minimalist-cool hotel (there are even swim-up rooms!).

Bora Bora Beach Club
BAR

(www.boraboraibiza.net; Carrer d'es Fumarell 1; ⊙noon-6am May-Sep) At Platja d'en Bossa, 4km from the old town, this is *the* place – a long beachside bar where sun and fun worshippers work off hangovers and prepare new ones. Entry's free and the ambience is chilled, with low-key club sounds wafting over the sand.

Soap at Dome
GAY

(☎971 19 18 38; Carrer de Santa Llúcia 21; ⊙10pm-3.30am Apr-Oct) A legendary gay bar, famous as the final destination for the club parades which so define the Ibiza night. Around midnight in the summer months, Soap at Dome's terrace is pure theatre as costumes are rated and there's a joyous buzz in the night air.

ⓘ Information

Main Tourist Office (☎971 30 19 00; www.ibiza.travel; Passeig de Vara de Rey 1; ⊙9am-8pm Mon-Sat, to 2pm Sun, shorter hours winter)

AROUND IBIZA

Ibiza has numerous unspoiled and relatively undeveloped beaches. Cala de Boix, on the northeastern coast, is the only black-sand beach on the island, while further north are the lovely beaches of S'Aigua Blanca. On the north coast near Portinatx, Cala Xarraca is in a picturesque, secluded bay, and near Port de Sant Miquel is the attractive Cala Benirrás. In the southwest, Cala d'Hort has a spectacular setting overlooking two rugged rock islets, Es Verda and Es Verdranell.

The best thing about rowdy Sant Antoni, the island's second-biggest town and north of Ibiza City, is heading to the small rock-and-sand strip on the north shore to join hundreds of others for sunset drinks at a string of chilled bars. The best known remains **Café del Mar** (www.cafedelmarmusic.com; Carrer Vara de Rey 27; ⊗ 4pm–midnight May–mid Oct), our favourite, but it's further north along the pedestrian walkway.

Local buses (www.ibizabus.com) run to most destinations between May and October.

Valencia

POP 786,200

Spain's third-largest city is a magnificent place, content for Madrid and Barcelona to grab the headlines while it gets on with being a wonderfully liveable city with thriving cultural, eating and nightlife scenes. Never afraid to innovate, Valencia diverted its flood-prone river to the outskirts of town and converted the former riverbed into a superb green ribbon of park winding right through the city. On it are the strikingly futuristic buildings of the Ciudad de las Artes y las Ciencias, designed by local boy Santiago Calatrava. The city also has great museums and a large, characterful old quarter. Valencia, surrounded by its *huerta,* a fertile fruit-and-veg farmland, is famous as the home of rice dishes like paella but its buzzy dining scene offers plenty more besides.

⊙ Sights

★ **Mercado Central**   MARKET
(Map p436; www.mercadocentralvalencia.es; Plaza del Mercado; ⊗ 7.30am-3pm Mon-Sat) Valencia's vast Modernista covered market, constructed in 1928, is a swirl of smells, movement and colour. Spectacular seafood counters display cephalopods galore and numerous fish species, while the fruit and vegetables, many produced locally in Valencia's *huerta* are of special quality. A tapas bar lets you sip a wine and enjoy the atmosphere.

WORTH A TRIP

FORMENTERA

If Ibiza is the party queen, her little sister, Formentera (population 10,757), is the shy, natural beauty, who prefers barefoot beach strolls by starlight to all-night raving in superclubs. Dangling off the south coast of Ibiza, a mere half an hour away by fast ferry, this 20km-long island is a place of lazy days spent lounging on some of Europe's (dare we say the world's?) most ravishing beaches. Nowhere is the lure of the sea more powerful in the Balearics than here, where enticing, frost-white slithers of sand are smoothed by water in unbelievable shades of azure, turquoise and lapis lazuli that will have you itching to leap in the moment you step off the boat. Ask people what they've done for the week here and watch them shrug their shoulders, shake the last sand out of their shoes, grin and reply: 'Nothing, it was awesome.'

★ **La Lonja**   HISTORIC BUILDING
(Map p436; ☑ 962 08 41 53; www.valencia.es; Calle de la Lonja; adult/child €2/1, free Sun; ⊗ 9.30am-7pm Mon-Sat, 9.30am-3pm Sun) This splendid building, a Unesco World Heritage Site, was originally Valencia's silk and commodity exchange, built in the late 15th century when Valencia was booming. It's one of Spain's finest examples of a civil Gothic building. Two main structures flank a citrus-studded courtyard; the magnificent Sala de Contratación, a cathedral of commerce with soaring twisted pillars, and the Consulado del Mar, where a maritime tribunal sat. The top floor boasts a stunning coffered ceiling brought here from another building.

★ **Catedral**   CATHEDRAL
(Map p436; ☑ 963 91 81 27; www.catedraldevalencia.es; Plaza de la Virgen; adult/child incl audioguide €5/3.50; ⊗ 10am-5.30pm or 6.30pm Mon-Sat, 2-5.30pm Sun, closed Sun Nov-Feb) Valencia's cathedral was built over the mosque after the 1238 reconquest. Its low, wide, brick-vaulted triple nave is mostly Gothic, with neoclassical side chapels. Highlights are the rich Italianate frescoes above the altarpiece, a pair of Goyas in the **Capilla de San Francisco de Borja**, and...ta-dah...in the flamboyant Gothic **Capilla del Santo Cáliz**, what's

claimed to be the **Holy Grail** from which Christ sipped during the Last Supper. It's a Roman-era agate cup, later modified, so at least the date is right.

★ Museo de Bellas Artes
GALLERY

(San Pío V; Map p434; www.museobellasartes valencia.gva.es; Calle de San Pío V 9; ☉10am-8pm Tue-Sun) FREE Bright and spacious, this gallery ranks among Spain's best. Highlights include a collection of magnificent late-medieval altarpieces, and works by several Spanish masters, including some great Goya portraits, a haunting Velázquez selfie, an El Greco *John the Baptist,* Murillos, Riberas

and works by the Ribaltas, father and son. Downstairs, an excellent series of rooms focuses on the great, versatile Valencian painter Joaquín Sorolla (1863–1923), who, at his best, seemed to capture the spirit of an age through sensitive portraiture.

★ Jardines del Turia
PARK

(Map p434; 🚲) Stretching the length of Río Turia's former course, this 9km-long lung of green is a fabulous mix of playing fields, cycling, jogging and walking paths, lawns and playgrounds. As it curves around the eastern part of the city, it's also a pleasant way of getting around. See Lilliputian kids

Valencia City

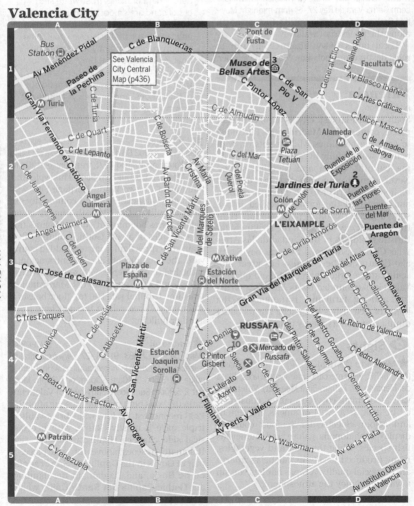

scrambling over a magnificent, ever-patient Gulliver (⊙10am-8pm Sep-Jun, 10am-2pm & 5-9pm Jul & Aug; 🚍19, 95) FREE south of the Palau de la Música.

★ **Ciudad de las Artes y las Ciencias**   BUILDING
(City of Arts & Sciences; Map p434; 📞 902 100031; www.cac.es; 🚻) The aesthetically stunning City of Arts & Sciences occupies a massive 350,000-sq-metre swath of the old Turia riverbed. A series of stunning modern buildings, it's mostly the work of world-famous, locally born architect Santiago Calatrava. He's a controversial figure for many Valen-

cians, who complain about the expense, and various design flaws. Nevertheless, if your taxes weren't involved, it's awe-inspiring stuff, and pleasingly family-oriented. The buildings include a striking concert hall, an IMAX cinema, a science museum and an aquarium.

Oceanogràfic   AQUARIUM
(Map p434; 📞902 10 00 31; www.cac.es/oceanografic; Camino de las Moreras; adult/child €28.50/21.50, audioguide €3.70, combined ticket with Hemisfèric & Museo de las Ciencias €36.90/28; ⊙10am-5pm Sun-Fri, 10am-7pm Sat low season, 10am-7pm busy times, 10am-midnight Jul & Aug; 🚻) Spain's most famous aquarium is the southernmost building of the City of Arts & Sciences. It's an impressive display; the complex is divided into a series of climate zones, reached overground or underground from the central hub building. The sharks, complete with tunnel, are an obvious favourite, while a series of beautiful tanks present species from temperate, Mediterranean, Red Sea and tropical waters. Less happily, the aquarium also keeps captive dolphins and belugas: research suggests that this is detrimental to their welfare.

🛌 **Sleeping**

★ **Russafa Youth Hostel**   HOSTEL €
(Map p434; 📞963 28 94 60; www.russafayouth hostel.com; Calle Padre Perera 5; dm/d incl

breakfast €20/44; @ 🛜) You'll feel instantly at home in this super-welcoming, cute hostel set over various floors of a venerable building in the heart of vibrant Russafa. It's all beds, rather than bunks, and with a maximum of three to a room, there's no crowd-

ing. Sweet rooms and spotless bathrooms make for a mighty easy stay.

Pensión París HOTEL €
(Map p436; 🖂 963 52 67 66; www.pensionparis. com; Calle de Salvà 12; s €26, d €34-46; 🛜) Welcoming, with spotless rooms – most with

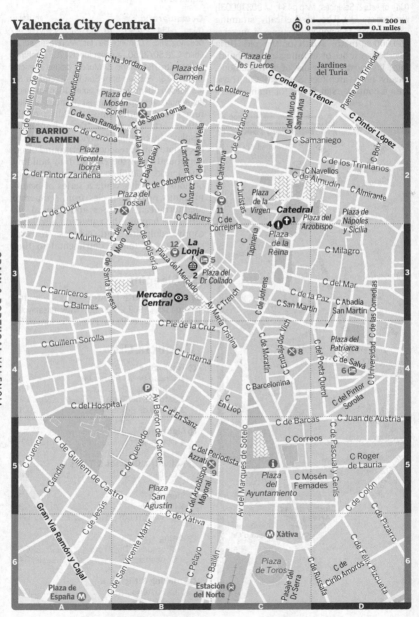

Valencia City Central

shared bathrooms, some with private facilities – is this family-run option on a quiet street. It's the antithesis of the crowded, pack-'em-in hostel. The best of the rooms have balconies and the original features of this stately old building.

Home Youth Hostel HOSTEL €
(Map p436; ☑963 91 62 29; www.homehostels valencia.com; Calle de la Lonja 4; dm €24-27, tw €60; ✳@🛜) Offering location, facilities and plenty more, this hostel sits right opposite the Lonja, a few steps from the central market. The rooms have happy retro decor and proper beds with decent sheets, with a minimum of room-mates. Kitchen, film library and cheery staff make this a top budget spot. Dorms are substantially cheaper outside high season.

Purple Nest HOSTEL €
(Map p434; ☑963 53 25 61; www.nesthostels valencia.com; Plaza de Tetuán 5; dm €15-20, tw €59-66; ✳@🛜) Well equipped and with plenty of events to help your Valencian social life along, this makes a pleasing base. There's a bar, kitchen and deck, and spacious, colourful rooms sleeping four to 10. If you value space, it's worth upgrading to the four-bed dorms. Breakfast is available for €2 extra.

✗ Eating

In the centre there are numerous traditional options, as well as trendy tapas choices. The main eating zones are the Barrio del Car-

Valencia City Central

LAS FALLAS

The exuberant, anarchic swirl of **Las Fallas de San José** (www.fallas.com; ☺March) – fireworks, music, festive bonfires and all-night partying – is a must if you're visiting Spain in mid-March.

The *fallas* themselves are huge sculptures of papier mâché on wood built by teams of local artists. Around-the-clock festivities include street parties, paella-cooking competitions, parades, open-air concerts and free firework displays. After midnight on the final day each *falla* goes up in flames – backed by yet more fireworks.

men, L'Eixample and, above all, the vibrant tapas-packed streets of Russafa.

¡¡Porque Lo Digo Yo!! TAPAS €
(Map p434; ☑657 56 28 01; www.facebook.com/sinpy.ruzafa; Calle de Cádiz 43; tapas €1-4; ☺7pm-12.30am Tue-Thu, 7pm-1.30am Fri-Sun; 🛜) Pretty tasty *montaditos* at just a euro a pop, accompanied by cheap beer and decent-sized *raciones* for a pittance make this the antithesis of the posher Russafa tapas bars. Art on the walls and a very eclectic crowd add atmosphere. Top value.

Copenhagen VEGETARIAN €
(Map p434; ☑963 28 99 28; www.grupocopenhagen.com; Calle del Literato Azorín 8; dishes €8-11; ☺1-4pm & 8-11.30pm; 🛜🍴) Bright and vibrant, the buzz from this popular vegetarian restaurant seems to spread a contagion of good cheer all along the street. They do a very toothsome soy burger as well as top homemade pasta, but the truth is it's all good here.

La Utielana VALENCIAN €
(Map p436; Calle de San Andrés 3; mains €4-12; ☺1.15-4pm & 9-11pm Mon-Fri, 1-4pm Sat) Not the easiest to track down, tucked-away La Utielana well merits a minute or two of sleuthing. Very Valencian, it packs in the crowds, drawn by the wholesome fare and exceptional value for money. Arrive early as it doesn't take reservations – if you have to wait, grab a numbered ticket from the dispenser.

SPAIN & PORTUGAL VALENCIA

PAELLA & MORE

There's something life-affirming about a proper Spanish paella, cheerily yellow like the sun and bursting with intriguing morsels. It seems to promise warm days and fine company. But there's more to this most Valencian of dishes than meets the eye. Traditional Valencian rices – always eaten for lunch by locals, never dinner – can have almost any ingredients, varying by region and season. The base always includes short-grain rice, garlic, olive oil and saffron. Paella should be cooked in a large shallow pan to enable maximum contact with flavour. And for the final touch of authenticity, the grains on the bottom (and only those) should have a crunchy, savoury crust known as the *socarrat*. Restaurants should take around 20 minutes or more to prepare a rice dish – beware if they don't – so expect to wait. Though rice dishes are usually for a minimum of two, many places will do one for a solo diner if asked. Paella has all the liquid evaporated, *meloso* rices are wet, and *caldoso* rices come with liquid.

La Pilareta   TAPAS €
(Bar Pilar; Map p436; ☑963 91 04 97; www.barla-pilareta.es; Calle del Moro Zeit 13; mussels €6.95; ⊙noon-midnight) Earthy, century-old and barely changed La Pilareta is great for hearty tapas and *clóchinas* (small, juicy local mussels), available between May and August. For the rest of the year it serves *mejillones* (mussels), altogether fatter if less tasty. A platterful comes in a spicy broth that you scoop up with a spare shell. It's got atmosphere in spades.

★**Navarro**   VALENCIAN €€
(Map p436; ☑963 52 96 23; www.restaurante-navarro.com; Calle del Arzobispo Mayoral 5; rices €11-18, set menu €22; ⊙1.30-4pm daily, plus 8.30-11pm Sat; 🔊) A byword in the city for decades for their quality rice dishes, Navarro is run by the grandkids of the original founders and it offers plenty of choice, outdoor seating and a set menu, including one of the rices as a main.

★**Refugio**   FUSION €€
(Map p436; ☑690 61 70 18; www.refugiorestau-rante.com; Calle Alta 42; mains €14-22, set menu €12-15; ⊙2-4pm & 9pm-midnight; 🔊) Named for the civil-war hideout opposite and simply decorated in whitewashed brick, Refugio preserves some of the Carmen *barrio*'s former revolutionary spirit. Excellent Med-fusion cuisine is presented in lunchtime menus of surprising quality: there are some stellar plates on show, though the veggie options aren't always quite as flavoursome. Evening dining is high quality and innovative.

🍷 Drinking & Nightlife

★**Café Negrito**   BAR
(Map p436; Plaza del Negrito; ⊙4pm-3am; 🔊) Something of a local legend, El Negrito has had a bit of a facelift in recent years and boasts a rather handsome interior. It hasn't changed its character though, with an intellectual, socially aware, left-wing clientele dominating and art exhibitions often focused on sustainable development or NGOs. The large terrace is a top spot to while away an evening.

Tyris on Tap   MICROBREWERY
(Map p436; ☑961 13 28 73; www.cervezatyris.com; Calle Taula de Canvis 6; ⊙6pm-1am or 1.30am Tue-Sun; 🔊) White-painted industrial brick, long-drop pendant lights and no-frills decor lend an air of warehouse chic to this bar. It's an outlet for a local microbrewery, and 10 taps issue some pretty tasty craft beers (half-pint/pint €3/5). There's one of our favourite central terraces out front to enjoy it too, and some bar food to soak it up.

La Fustería   BAR
(Map p434; www.lafusteriaruzafa.com; Calle de Cádiz 28; ⊙7-11pm Mon-Thu, 7pm-2.30am Fri & Sat; 🔊) This former carpentry workshop is now a likeably jumbled bar with mismatched furniture and bicycles bolted to the walls – they sell and repair them. It's a great venue for an after-dinner drink, with an amiable mix of folk, and regular events – flamenco when we were last there – out the back.

ℹ Information

Tourist Kiosk (Map p436; ☑963 52 49 08; www.turisvalencia.es; Plaza del Ayuntamiento; ⊙9am-7pm Mon-Sat, 10am-2pm Sun)

ℹ Getting There & Around

Valencia's **bus station** (Map p434; ☑963 46 62 66; Avenida Menéndez Pidal) is beside the riverbed. Bus 8 connects it to Plaza del Ayuntamiento.

There are very regular buses to/from Madrid (€29.75, four hours) and Barcelona (€29 to €35, four to five hours).

Trains run to Barcelona (€23 to €43, 3¼ to five hours) and Madrid (€21 to €71, 1¾ to seven hours). Fast trains run from the Valencia Joaquín Sorolla station, 800m south of the old town. Some slow trains still use Estación del Norte, between it and the old town.

Andalucía

Images of Andalucía are so potent, so quintessentially Spanish that it's sometimes difficult not to feel a sense of déjà vu. It's almost as if you've already been there in your dreams: a solemn Easter parade, an ebullient spring festival, exotic nights in the Alhambra. In the stark light of day, the picture is no less compelling.

Seville

POP 703,000

Some cities have looks, other cities have personality. The *sevillanos* – lucky devils – get both, courtesy of their flamboyant, charismatic, ever-evolving Andalucian metropolis founded, according to myth, 3000 years ago by the Greek god Hercules. Drenched for most of the year in spirit-enriching sunlight, this is a city of feelings as much as sights, with different seasons prompting vastly contrasting moods: solemn for Semana Santa, flirtatious for the spring fiesta and soporific for the gasping heat of summer.

◎ Sights & Activities

Seville's medieval *judería* (Jewish quarter), east of the cathedral and Alcázar, is today a tangle of atmospheric, winding streets and lovely plant-decked plazas perfumed with orange blossom. Among its most characteristic plazas is Plaza de Santa Cruz, which gives the *barrio* (district) its name. Nearby, Plaza de Doña Elvira is perhaps the most romantic small square in Andalucía, especially in the evening.

Catedral & Giralda   CATHEDRAL
(www.catedraldesevilla.es; adult/child €9/free; ⊙11am-3.30pm Mon, 11am-5pm Tue-Sat, 2.30-6pm Sun) Seville's immense cathedral, one of the largest Christian churches in the world, is awe-inspiring in its scale and sheer majesty. It stands on the site of the great 12th-century

Almohad mosque, with the mosque's minaret (the Giralda) still towering beside it.

★Alcázar   CASTLE
(⎙tours 954 50 23 24; www.alcazarsevilla.org; adult/child €9.50/free; ⊙9.30am-7pm Apr-Sep, to 5pm Oct-Mar) If heaven really *does* exist, then let's hope it looks a little bit like the inside of Seville's Alcázar. Built primarily in the 1300s during the so-called 'dark ages' in Europe, the castle's intricate architecture is anything but dark. Indeed, compared to our modern-day shopping malls, the Alcázar marks one of history's architectural high points. Unesco agreed, making it a World Heritage site in 1987.

Casa de Pilatos   PALACE
(⎙954 22 52 98; www.fundacionmedinaceli.org; Plaza de Pilatos; admission ground fl €6, whole house €8; ⊙9am-7pm Apr-Oct, to 6pm Nov-Mar) The haunting Casa de Pilatos, which is still occupied by the ducal Medinaceli family, is one of the city's most glorious mansions. It's a mixture of Mudéjar, Gothic and Renaissance styles, with some beautiful tilework and *artesonados* (ceilings of interlaced beams with decorative insertions). The overall effect is like a poor man's Alcázar.

★Hospital de los Venerables Sacerdotes   GALLERY
(⎙954 56 26 96; www.focus.abengoa.es; Plaza de los Venerables 8; adult/child €5.50/2.75, Sun afternoon free; ⊙10am-2pm & 4-8pm) Inside this 17th-century baroque mansion once used as a hospice for ageing priests, you'll find one of Seville's greatest and most admirable art collections. The on-site Centro Velázquez was founded in 2007 by the local Focus-Abengoa Foundation with the intention of reviving Seville's erstwhile artistic glory. Its collection of masterpieces anchored by Diego Velázquez' *Santa Rufina* is one of the best and most concise art lessons the city has to offer. The excellent audio commentary explains how medieval darkness morphed into Velázquezian realism.

Museo de Bellas Artes   GALLERY
(Fine Arts Museum; Plaza del Museo 9; €1.50, EU citizens free; ⊙10am-8.30pm Tue-Sat, to 5pm Sun) Housed in the beautiful former Convento de la Merced, Seville's Museo de Bellas Artes does full justice to Seville's leading role in Spain's 17th-century artistic Siglo de Oro (Golden Age). Much of the work here is of the dark, brooding religious type.

SPAIN & PORTUGAL ANDALUCÍA

Centro de Interpretación
Judería de Sevilla
MUSEUM

(☎954 04 70 89; www.juderiadesevilla.es; Calle Ximenez de Enciso; €6.50; ⏲10.30am-3.30pm & 5-8pm Mon-Sat, 10.30am-7pm Sun) A reinterpretation of Seville's weighty Jewish history has been long overdue and what better place to start than in the city's former Jewish quarter. This newish museum is in an old Sephardic Jewish house in the higgledy-piggledy Santa Cruz quarter, the one-time Jewish neighbourhood that never recovered from a brutal pogrom and massacre in 1391. The events of the pogrom and other historical happenings are catalogued inside, along with a few surviving mementos including documents, costumes and books. It's small but poignant.

Metropol Parasol
MUSEUM

(www.metropolsevilla.com; Plaza de la Encarnación; €3; ⏲10.30am-midnight Sun-Thu, to 1am Fri & Sat) Smarting with the audacity of a modern-day Eiffel Tower, the opinion-dividing Metropol Parasol claims to be the largest wooden building in the world. Its undulating honeycombed roof is held up by five giant mushroom-like pillars, earning it the local nickname *Las Setas* (the mushrooms). Roman ruins discovered during the building's

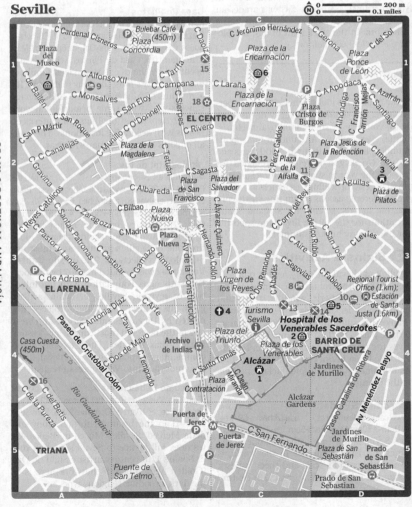

Seville

conception have been cleverly incorporated into a museum in the foundations, while upstairs on level 2 you can stroll along a surreal panoramic walkway with killer city views.

★ Pancho Tours
CULTURAL TOUR

(☑ 664 642 904; www.panchotours.com) FREE
The best walking tours in the city? Join in and see – they're free, although you're welcome to tip the hard-working guide who'll furnish you with an encyclopedia's worth of anecdotes, stories, myths and theories about Seville's fascinating past. Tours kick off daily, normally at 11am – check the website for exact details. Pancho also offers bike tours (€25) and nightlife tours (€10 to €15).

✿ Festivals & Events

Semana Santa
HOLY WEEK

(www.semana-santa.org; ☉ Mar/Apr) Every day from Palm Sunday to Easter Sunday, large, life-sized *pasos* (sculptural representations of events from Christ's Passion) are carried from Seville's churches through the streets

---

---

to the cathedral, accompanied by processions that may take more than an hour to pass. The processions are organised by more than 50 different *hermandades* or *cofradías* (brotherhoods, some of which include women).

The climax of the week is the *madrugá* (very early hours) of Good Friday, when some of the most respected brotherhoods file through the city. The costume worn by the marching penitents consists of a full robe and a conical hat with slits cut for the eyes. The regalia was incongruously copied by America's Ku Klux Klan.

Procession schedules are widely available during Semana Santa, or see the Semana Santa website. Arrive near the cathedral in the early evening for a better view.

Feria de Abril
SPRING FAIR

(☉ Apr) The April fair, held in the second half of the month (sometimes edging into May), is the jolly counterpart to the sombre Semana Santa. The biggest and most colourful of all Andalucía's ferias (fairs) is less invasive (and also less inclusive) than the Easter celebration. It takes place on El Real de la Feria, in the Los Remedios area west of the Río Guadalquivir.

The ceremonial lighting-up of the fairgrounds on the opening Monday night is the starting gun for six nights of *sevillanos'* favourite activities: eating, drinking, dressing up and dancing till dawn.

🛏 Sleeping

Oasis Backpackers' Hostel
HOSTEL €

(☑ 955 26 26 96; www.oasissevilla.com; Calle Almirante Ulloa 1; dm/d incl breakfast €15/50; ❀@🛜🏊) It's not often you get to backpack in a palace. A veritable oasis in the busy city-centre district, this place is a friendly welcoming hostel set in a palatial 19th-century mansion with some private room options, a cafe-bar and a rooftop deck with a small pool.

You can organise tonnes of activities here and meet plenty of multilingual fellow travellers in an atmosphere that's sociable but never over-the-top noisy.

Pensión San Pancracio
PENSIÓN €

(☑ 954 41 31 04; Plaza de las Cruces 9; d €50, s/d/tr with shared bathroom €33/36/52) A rare budget option in Santa Cruz, this old, rambling family house has plenty of different room options (all cheap) and a pleasant flower-bedizened patio-lobby. Friendly staff

---

make up for the lack of luxury. The compromise: shared bathrooms.

Hotel Goya   HOTEL €

(☑ 954 21 11 70; www.hotelgoyasevilla.com; Calle Mateos Gago 31; s/d €40/60; ❄@🛜❄) The gleaming Goya, close to the cathedral, remains a popular draw and accepts pets. It's clean, and good value considering its location.

✖ Eating

Seville produces Andalucía's most inventive tapas – end of story – and, if you're not enamoured with the new culinary alchemists, there are plenty of decent salt-of-the-earth tapas bars too.

Bodega Santa Cruz   TAPAS €

(Calle Mateos Gago; tapas €2; ☺ 11.30am-midnight) This forever crowded bodega is where eating tapas becomes a physical contact sport. Watch out for flying elbows and admire those dexterous waiters who bob and weave like prizefighters amid the chaos. The fiercely traditional tapas are best enjoyed alfresco with a cold beer as you watch marching armies of Santa Cruz tourists go squeezing past.

Bar Alfalfa   TAPAS €

(cnr Calles Alfalfa & Candilejo; tapas €3; ☺ 9am-midnight) It's amazing how many people, hams, wine bottles and knick-knacks you can stuff into such a small space. No matter, order through the window when the going gets crowded. You won't forget the tomato-tinged magnificence of the Italy-meets-Iberia *salmorejo* bruschetta.

Café Bar Las Teresas   TAPAS €

(Calle Santa Teresa 2; tapas €3; ☺ 10am-midnight) The hanging hams look as ancient as the bar itself, a sinuous wraparound affair with just enough room for two stout waiters to pass carrying precariously balanced tapas plates. The atmosphere is dark but not dingy, the food highly traditional, and the crowd an integrated mix of tourists and Santa Cruz locals.

Casa Cuesta   CONTEMPORARY SPANISH €

(☑ 954 33 33 37; www.casacuesta.net; Calle de Castilla 3-5; mains €10; ☺ 12.30-4.30pm & 8pm-12.30am) Massive glass windows look out onto a crowded plaza, mirrors artfully reflect framed bullfighting posters and flamenco iconography, and gleaming gold beer pumps furnish a wooden bar shielding bottles that

look older than most of the clientele. Casa Cuesta has that wonderful sensation of *sevillano* authenticity.

Bar Europa   TAPAS €

(☑ 954 22 13 54; www.bareuropa.info; Calle Siete Revueltas 35; tapas €3, media raciones €6-8; ☺ 8am-1am) An old-school bar with no pretensions that's been knocking out tapas since 1925. Notwithstanding, Europa isn't afraid to experiment. Its signature *tapa* is the *quesadilla los balanchares gratinada sobre manzana* which turns a boring old Granny Smith apple into a taste sensation by covering it in goat's cheese and laying it on a bed of strawberries.

★ La Pepona   TAPAS, MODERN €€

(☑ 954 21 50 26; Javier Lasso de la Vega 1; tapas €3.50-6.50; ☺ 1.30-4.30pm & 8pm-midnight Mon-Sat) One of the best newcomer restaurants of 2014, La Pepona gets all the basics right, from the bread (doorstop-sized rustic slices), to the service (fast but discreet), to the decor (clean Ikea lines and lots of wood). Oscar status is achieved with the food, which falls firmly into the nouveau tapas camp.

Try the goat with yoghurt, couscous and mint – an epic amalgamation of Iberia and Morocco.

T de Triana   ANDALUCIAN €€

(☑ 954 33 12 03; Calle Betis 20; ☺ 8pm-2am) The T is Triana being itself: simple fish-biased tapas, walls full of history, *fútbol* on the big screen whenever local boys Sevilla or Real Betis are playing, and live, gutsy flamenco shows every Friday night at 10pm.

🍷 Drinking & Entertainment

In summer dozens of *terrazas de verano* (summer terraces; temporary, open-air, late-night bars), many of them with live music and plenty of room to dance, spring up along both banks of the river. Classic spots include drinks on the banks of the Río Guadalquivir in Triana (the wall along Calle del Betis forms a fantastic makeshift bar), Plaza de la Alfalfa (cocktail and dive bars), the Barrio de Santa Cruz and the Alameda de Hércules. The latter is the hub for young *sevillanos* and the city's gay nightlife.

El Garlochi   BAR

(Calle Boteros 4; ☺ 10pm-6am) Dedicated entirely to the iconography, smells and sounds of Semana Santa, the ultracamp El Garlochi is a true marvel. Taste the rather revolting sounding cocktail, Sangre de Cristo (Blood of Christ), and the Agua de Sevilla, both heavily laced with vodka, whisky and grenadine, and pray they open more bars like this.

Bulebar Café BAR

(☑ 954 90 19 54; Alameda de Hércules 83; ⊙ 9am-2am) This place gets pretty *caliente* (hot) at night but is pleasantly chilled in the early evening, with friendly staff. Don't write off its spirit-reviving alfresco breakfasts that pitch early birds with up-all-nighters. It's in the uber-cool Alameda de Hércules.

★**Casa de la Memoria** FLAMENCO

(☑ 954 56 06 70; www.casadelamemoria.es; Calle Cuna 6; €18; ⊙ shows 7.30pm & 9pm) Neither a *tablao* (choreographed flamenco show) nor a private *peña* (club, usually of flamenco aficionados), this cultural centre offers what are, without doubt, the most intimate and authentic nightly flamenco shows in Seville. It's accommodated in the old stables of the Palacio de la Condesa de Lebrija.

It's perennially popular and space is limited to 100, so reserve tickets a day or so in advance by calling or visiting the venue.

ⓘ **Information**

Turismo Sevilla (www.turismosevilla.org; Plaza del Triunfo 1; ⊙ 10.30am-7pm Mon-Fri) Information on all of Sevilla province.

ⓘ **Getting There & Away**

Seville's **airport** (SVQ; ☑ 954 44 90 00; www.aena.es) has a fair range of international and domestic flights.

Estación de Autobuses Plaza de Armas is Seville's main bus station, with links including Málaga (€19, three hours, eight daily), Granada (€23, three hours, nine daily), Córdoba (€12, two hours, seven daily) and Madrid. Eurolines has international services to Germany Belgium, France and beyond.

Seville's Estación Santa Justa is 1.5km northeast of the centre. High-speed AVE trains go to/from Madrid (from €79, 2½ hours, 20 daily) and Córdoba (from €30, 40 minutes, 30 daily). Slower trains head to Granada (€30, three hours, four daily) and Málaga (€44, two hours, 11 daily).

ⓘ **Getting Around**

Seville offers a multitude of ways to get around, though walking still has to be the best option, especially in the centre. The Sevici bike-sharing scheme has made cycling easy and bike lanes

---

FLAMENCO

Seville is arguably Spain's flamenco capital and you're most likely to catch a spontaneous atmosphere (of unpredictable quality) in one of the bars staging regular nights of flamenco with no admission fee. The *soleá*, flamenco's truest *cante jondo* (deep song), was first concocted in Triana; head here to find some of the more authentic clubs.

---

are now almost as ubiquitous as pavements. The tram has recently been extended to the station of San Bernardo but its routes are still limited. Buses are more useful than the metro to link the main tourist sights.

Córdoba

POP 296,000

One building alone is enough to put Córdoba high on any traveller's itinerary: the mesmerising multiarched Mezquita. One of the world's greatest Islamic buildings, it's a symbol of the worldly and sophisticated Islamic culture that flourished here more than a millennium ago when Córdoba was the capital of Islamic Spain, and Western Europe's biggest and most cultured city. Once here, you'll find there's much more to this city: Córdoba is a great place for exploring on foot or by bicycle, staying and eating well in old buildings centred on verdant patios, diving into old wine bars, and feeling millennia of history at every turn.

◎ **Sights & Activities**

★**Mezquita** MOSQUE, CATHEDRAL

(Mosque; ☑ 957 47 05 12; www.catedraldecordoba.es; Calle Cardenal Herrero; adult/child €8/4, 8.30-9.30am Mon-Sat free; ⊙8.30-9.30am & 10am-7pm Mon-Sat, 8.30-11.30am & 3-7pm Sun Mar-Oct, to 6pm daily Nov-Feb) It's impossible to overemphasise the beauty of Córdoba's great mosque, with its remarkably serene (despite tourist crowds) and spacious interior. One of the world's greatest works of Islamic architecture, the Mezquita hints, with all its lustrous decoration, at a refined age when Muslims, Jews and Christians lived side by side and enriched their city with a heady interaction of diverse, vibrant cultures.

Córdoba

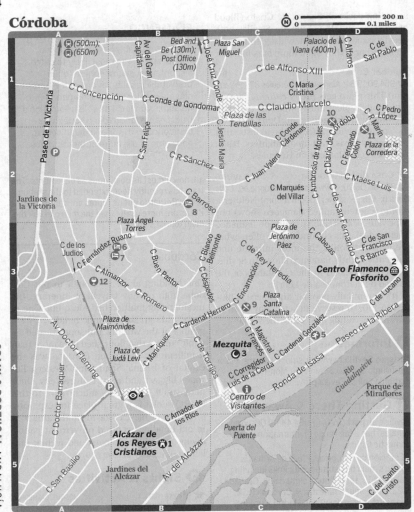

★ **Alcázar de los Reyes Cristianos** FORTRESS, GARDENS
(Fortress of the Christian Monarchs; www.alcazardelosreyescristianos.cordoba.es; Campo Santo de Los Mártires; admission 8.30am-2.30pm €4.50, other times incl water, light & sound show adult/child €7/free; ⊙ 8.30am-8.45pm Tue-Fri, to 4.30pm Sat, to 2.30pm Sun Sep-Jun, to 3pm Tue-Sun Jul-Aug; ⍟) Built under Castilian rule in the 13th and 14th centuries on the remains of a Moorish predecessor, this fort-cum-palace hosted both Fernando and Isabel, who made their first acquaintance with Columbus here in 1486. One hall displays some remarkable Roman mosaics, dug up from the Plaza de la Corredera in the 1950s. The Alcázar's terraced gardens – full of fish ponds, fountains, orange trees and flowers – are a delight to stroll around.

★ **Centro Flamenco Fosforito** MUSEUM
(☏ 957 47 68 29; www.centroflamencofosforito.cordoba.es; Plaza del Potro; €2; ⊙ 8.30am-7.30pm Tue-Fri, 8.30am-2.30pm Sat, 9.30am-2.30pm Sun) Possibly the best flamenco museum in Andalucía, the Fosforito centre has exhibits, film and information panels in English and Spanish telling you the history of the guitar

Córdoba

and all the flamenco greats. Touch-screen videos demonstrate the important techniques of flamenco song, guitar, dance and percussion – you can test your skill at beating out the *compás* (rhythm) of different *palos* (song forms). Regular live flamenco performances are held here too.

Palacio de Viana   MUSEUM
(www.palaciodeviana.com; Plaza de Don Gome 2; admission whole house/patios €8/5; ⊙10am-7pm Tue-Sat, to 3pm Sun Sep-Jun, 9am-3pm Tue-Sun Jul & Aug) A stunning Renaissance palace set around 12 beautiful patios, the Viana Palace is a particular delight to visit in spring. Occupied by the aristocratic Marqueses de Viana until 1980, the large building is packed with art and antiques. The whole-house charge covers a one-hour guided tour of the rooms and access to the patios and garden. It's an 800m walk northeast from Plaza de las Tendillas.

Hammam Baños Árabes   BATHHOUSE
(☑957 48 47 46; http://cordoba.hammamalandalus.com; Calle del Corregidor Luis de la Cerda 51; bath/bath & massage €24/36; ⊙2hr sessions 10am, noon, 2pm, 4pm, 6pm, 8pm & 10pm) Follow the lead of the medieval Cordobans and dip your toe in these beautifully renovated Arab baths, where you can enjoy an aromatherapy massage, with tea, hookah and Arabic sweets in the cafe afterwards.

🛏 Sleeping

⭐ Bed and Be   HOSTEL €
(☑661 42 07 33; www.bedandbe.com; Calle Cruz Conde 22; dm €17-20, d with shared bathroom €50-80; ❀🛜) 🅿 An exceptionally good hostel option a bit north of Plaza de las Tendillas. Staff are clued up about what's on and what's new in Córdoba, and they offer a social event every evening – anything from a bike tour to a sushi dinner. The assortment of double and dorm rooms are all super-clean and as gleaming white as a *pueblo blanco* (white town).

Hospedería Alma Andalusí   HOTEL €
(☑957 76 08 88; www.almaandalusi.com; Calle Fernández Ruano 5; r €50-60; ❀🛜) This guesthouse in a quiet section of the Judería (the old Jewish quarter) has been brilliantly converted from an ancient structure into a stylish, modern establishment, while rates have been kept down. There's an appealing floral theme throughout. Thoughtfully chosen furnishings, polished wood floors and blue-and-white colour schemes make for a comfortable base.

Hostal el Reposo de Bagdad   HOSTEL €
(☑957 20 28 54; http://hostalelreposodebagdad.com; Calle Fernández Ruano 11; s/d €40/60) Hidden away in a tiny street in the Judería, this place is excellent for anyone wanting a characterful place to stay at bargain prices. The house is over 200 years old, and the en suite rooms are simple with crisp, white linen. The (dark) ground-floor rooms have lovely Andalucian tiling.

🍴 Eating & Drinking

Córdoba's signature dish is *salmorejo*, a delicious, thick, chilled soup of blended tomatoes, garlic, bread, lemon, vinegar and olive oil, sprinkled with hard-boiled egg and strips of ham. Along with *rabo de toro* (bull's tail stew), it appears on every menu. Don't miss the strong white wines from nearby Montilla and Moriles.

Taberna Salinas   ANDALUCIAN €
(www.tabernasalinas.com; Calle Tundidores 3; raciones €7-8; ⊙12.30-4pm & 8-11.30pm Mon-Sat, closed Aug) A historic bar-restaurant (since 1879), with a patio and several rooms, Salinas is adorned in classic Córdoba fashion with tiles, wine barrels, art and photos of bullfighter Manolete. It's popular with tourists (and offers a five-language menu), but

SPAIN & PORTUGAL ANDALUCÍA

Alhambra

TIMELINE

900 The first reference to al-qala'at al-hamra (red castle) atop Granada's Sabika Hill.

1237 Founder of the Nasrid dynasty, Muhammad I, moves his court to Granada. Threatened by belligerent Christian armies he builds a new defensive fort, the **Alcazaba ❶**.

1302–09 Designed as a summer palace-cum-country estate for Granada's foppish rulers, the bucolic **Generalife ❷** is begun by Muhammad III.

1333–54 Yusuf I initiates the construction of the **Palacio Nazaríes ❸**, still considered the highpoint of Islamic culture in Europe.

1350–60 Up goes the **Palacio de Comares ❹**, taking Nasrid lavishness to a whole new level.

1362–91 The second coming of Muhammad V ushers in even greater architectural brilliance, exemplified by the construction of the **Patio de los Leones ❺**.

1527 The Christians add the **Palacio de Carlos V ❻**. Inspired Renaissance palace or incongruous crime against Moorish art? You decide.

1829 The languishing, half-forgotten Alhambra is 'rediscovered' by American writer Washington Irving during a protracted sleep-over.

1954 The Generalife gardens are extended southwards to accommodate an outdoor theatre.

For more information on the Alhambra and Granada's other sights, see p448-52.

TOP TIPS

» **Queue-dodger** Reserve tickets in advance online at www.alhambra-tickets.es

» **Money-saver** You can visit the general areas of the palace free of charge any time by entering through the Puerta de Justica.

» **Stay over** Two fine hotels are housed on the grounds: Parador de Granada (expensive) and Hotel América (more economical).

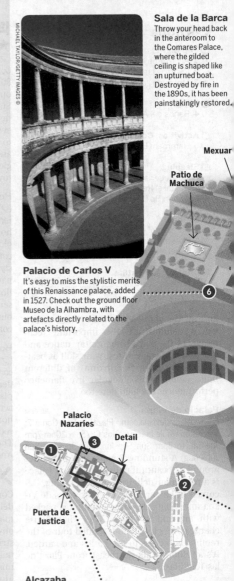

Sala de la Barca
Throw your head back in the anteroom to the Comares Palace, where the gilded ceiling is shaped like an upturned boat. Destroyed by fire in the 1890s, it has been painstakingly restored.

Mexuar

Patio de Machuca

Palacio de Carlos V
It's easy to miss the stylistic merits of this Renaissance palace, added in 1527. Check out the ground floor Museo de la Alhambra, with artefacts directly related to the palace's history.

Palacio Nazaríes

Detail

Puerta de Justica

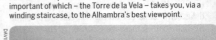

Alcazaba
Find time to explore the towers of the original citadel, the most important of which – the Torre de la Vela – takes you, via a winding staircase, to the Alhambra's best viewpoint.

Patio de los Arrayanes

If only you could linger longer beside the rows of *arrayanes* (myrtle bushes) that border this calming rectangular pool. Shaded porticos with seven harmonious arches invite further contemplation.

Palacio de Comares

The neck-ache continues in the largest room in the Comares Palace, renowned for its rich geometric ceiling. A negotiating room for the emirs, the Salón de los Embajadores is a masterpiece of Moorish design.

Sala de Dos Hermanas

Focus on the *dos hermanas* – two marble slabs either side of the fountain – before enjoying the intricate cupola embellished with 5000 tiny moulded stalactites. Poetic calligraphy decorates the walls.

Salón de los Embajadores

④

Patio de los Arrayanes

Baños Reales

Washington Irving Apartments

Patio de la Lindaraja

⑤

Sala de los Reyes

Sala de los Abencerrajes

Jardines del Partal

Palacio del Partal

Patio de los Leones

Count the 12 lions sculpted from marble, holding up a gurgling fountain. Then pan back and take in the delicate columns and arches built to signify an Islamic vision of paradise.

Generalife

...coda to most people's visits, the 'architect's garden' is no afterthought. While Nasrid in origin, the horticulture is relatively new: the pools and arcades were added in the early 20th century.

it retains a traditional atmosphere and the waiters are very helpful. Not least, the food is very good, from the orange-and-cod salad to the pork loin in hazelnut sauce.

Bar Santos TAPAS €
(Calle Magistral González Francés 3; tortilla €2; ⏱10am-midnight) Most restaurants close to the Mezquita are geared to an undiscriminating tourist market. But this legendary little bar serves the best *tortilla de patata* (potato omelette) in town – and don't the *cordobeses* know it. Thick wedges are deftly cut from giant wheels of the stuff and customarily served with plastic forks on paper plates to eat outside under the Mezquita's walls. Don't miss it.

★**El Astronauta** MEDITERRANEAN €€
(☑957 49 11 23; www.elastronauta.es; Calle Diario de Córdoba 18; media raciones €5.50-8.50, raciones €9-17; ⏱1.30-5pm & 8pm-late Mon-Thu, 1.30pm-late Fri & Sat; ☑) The Astronauta produces a galaxy of Mediterranean dishes with an emphasis on fresh, healthy ingredients: zesty salads, mezes, lamb moussaka, vegetarian burgers and much more. The decor is cosmic, the vibe alternative and the local clientele loyal.

★**Bodega Guzmán** WINE BAR
(Calle de los Judíos 7; ⏱noon-4pm & 8.15-11.45pm Fri-Wed) This atmospheric Judería drinking spot bedecked with bullfighting memorabilia is frequented by both locals and tourists. Montilla wine is dispensed from three giant barrels behind the bar: don't leave without trying some *amargoso* (bitter).

❶ Information

Centro de Visitantes (Visitors Centre; ☑957 35 51 79; www.andalucia.org; Plaza del Triunfo; ⏱9am-7.30pm Mon-Fri, 9.30am-3pm Sat & Sun) The main tourist information centre, with an exhibit on Córdoba's history, and some Roman and Visigothic remains downstairs.

❶ Getting There & Away

Córdoba's train station is 1.2km northwest of central Plaza de las Tendillas. Destinations include Granada (€38, 2¾ hours), Madrid (€38 to €71, 1¾ to two hours) and Seville (€14 to €30, 45 to 80 minutes).

Buses run from behind the train station to Granada (€15, 2¾ hours), Madrid (€17, five hours), Málaga (€12, three hours), Seville (€12, two hours) and more.

Granada
POP 258,000 / ELEV 738M

Granada's eight centuries as a Muslim capital are symbolised in its keynote emblem, the remarkable Alhambra, one of the most graceful architectural achievements in the Muslim world. Islam was never completely expunged here, and today it seems more present than ever in the shops, restaurants, tearooms and mosque of a growing North African community in and around the maze of the Albayzín. The tapas bars fill to bursting, while flamenco dives resound to the heart-wrenching tones of the south.

◉ Sights

Most major sights are an easy walk within the city centre, and there are buses for when the hills wear you out. Rectangular Plaza Nueva is Granada's main nexus. The Albayzín sits on a hill immediately to the north and is roughly demarcated by Gran Via de Colón and the Río Darro. The Alhambra lies on a separate hill on the opposite side of the Darro.

★**Alhambra** PALACE
(p446-7; ☑902 44 12 21; www.alhambra-tickets.es; adult/under 12yr €14/free, Generalife only €7; ⏱8.30am-8pm mid-Mar–mid-Oct, to 6pm mid-Oct–mid-Mar, night visits 10-11.30pm Tue-Sat mid-Mar–mid-Oct, 8-9.30pm Fri & Sat mid-Oct–mid-Mar) The Alhambra is Granada's – and Europe's – love letter to Moorish culture, a place where fountains trickle, leaves rustle, and ancient spirits seem to mysteriously linger. Part palace, part fort, part World Heritage site, part lesson in medieval architecture, the Alhambra has long enchanted a never-ending line of expectant visitors. As a historic monument, it is unlikely it will ever be surpassed – at least not in the lifetime of anyone reading this.

For most tourists, the Alhambra is an essential pilgrimage and, as a result, predictably crowded. It's worth booking in advance for the very earliest or latest time slots.

The central palace complex, **Palacios Nazaríes**, is the pinnacle of the Alhambra's design, a harmonious synthesis of space, light, shade, water and greenery that sought to conjure the gardens of paradise for the rulers who dwelt here.

The **Palacio de Carlos V** has a Renaissance-era circle-in-a-square ground plan. Inside, the Museo de la Alhambra has a collection of Alhambra artefacts.

Granada

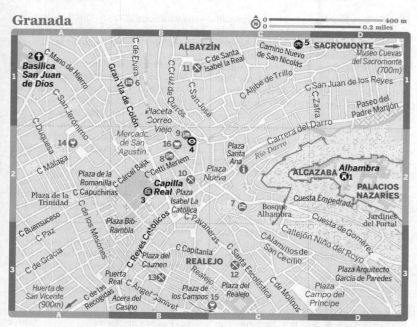

From the Arabic *jinan al-'arif* (the overseer's gardens), the **Generalife** is a soothing arrangement of pathways, patios, pools, fountains, tall trees and, in season, flowers of every imaginable hue.

It's highly recommended to **pre-book** (☎902 88 80 01, for international calls +34 958 92 60 31; www.alhambra-tickets.es) your entrance tickets as visitor numbers are limited to the Palacios Nazaríes and ticket queues are long.

See p446 for more information.

★**Capilla Real**　　　　HISTORIC BUILDING
(www.capillarealgranada.com; Calle Oficios; €4; ⊙10.15am-1.30pm & 3.30-6.30pm Mon-Sat, 11am-1.30pm & 2.30-5.30pm Sun) Here they lie, Spain's famed Catholic Monarchs, entombed in a chapel adjoining Granada's cathedral; far more peaceful in death than their tumultuous lives would have suggested. Isabel and Fernando commissioned the elaborate Isabelline-Gothic-style mausoleum that was to house them, but it was not completed until 1521, hence their temporary interment in the Alhambra's Convento de San Francisco.

Calle Calderería Nueva　　　　STREET
Linking the upper and lower parts of the Albayzín, Calle Calderería Nueva is a narrow street famous for its *teterías* (teahouses), but also a good place to shop for slippers, hookahs, jewellery and North African pottery from an eclectic cache of shops redolent of a Moroccan souq.

Granada

◎ Top Sights
1	Alhambra	D2
2	Basilica San Juan de Díos	A1
3	Capilla Real	B2

◎ Sights
4	Calle Calderería Nueva	B2
5	Mirador San Nicolás	C1

🛏 Sleeping
6	Hostal Arteaga	B1
7	Hostal Landázuri	C2
8	Hotel Posada del Toro	B2
9	Oasis Backpackers' Hostel	B2

🍴 Eating
10	Bodegas Castañeda	B2
11	El Ají	B1
12	Hicuri Art Restaurant	C3
	La Bella y La Bestia	(see 8)
13	Los Diamantes	B3

🍷 Drinking & Nightlife
14	El Bar de Eric	A2
15	Taberna La Tana	C3
16	Tetería As-Sirat	B2

Mirador San Nicolás   VIEWPOINT

(Callejón de San Cecilio) Callejón de San Cecilio leads to the Mirador San Nicolás, a lookout with unbeatable views of the Alhambra and Sierra Nevada. Come back here for sunset (you can't miss the trail then!). At any time of day take care: skilful, well-organised wallet-lifters and bag-snatchers operate here. Don't be put off – it is still a terrific atmosphere, with buskers and local students intermingling with camera-toting tourists.

★ Basilica San Juan de Díos   CHURCH

(Calle San Juan de Díos; €4; ⊙ 10am-1pm & 4-7pm) Bored of baroque churches? Seen every gilded altarpiece you want to see? Come to the Basilica of St John of God. If Seville cathedral is the world's most voluminous church, this basilica is surely one of the most opulently decorated. Barely a square inch of the interior lacks embellishment, most of it rich and glittering.

Huerta de San Vicente   MUSEUM

(☑ 958 25 84 66; Calle Virgen Blanca; admission only by guided tour in Spanish €3, Wed free; ⊙ 9.15am-1.30pm & 5-7.30pm Tue-Sun) This house where Federico García Lorca spent summers and wrote some of his best-known works is only 1.5km south of the city centre, but still retains the evocative aura of an early-20th-century country villa.

🛏 Sleeping

Hostal Landázuri   HOSTEL €

(☑ 958 22 14 06; www.hostallandazuri.com; Cuesta de Gomérez 24; s/d/t/q €36/45/60/70, s/d

EXPLORING THE ALBAYZÍN

On the hill facing the Alhambra across the Darro valley, Granada's old Muslim quarter (the Albayzín) is a place for aimless wandering; you'll get lost regularly whatever map you're using. The cobblestone streets are lined with signature only-in-Granada *cármenes* (large mansions with walled gardens, from the Arabic *karm* for garden). The Albayzín survived as the Muslim quarter for several decades after the Christian conquest in 1492.

Bus C1 runs circular routes from Plaza Nueva around the Albayzín about every seven to nine minutes, from 7.30am to 11pm.

without bathroom €24/34) This homely place boasts a terrace with Alhambra views, a cafe and a helpful mother–daughter team.

Oasis Backpackers' Hostel   HOSTEL €

(☑ 958 21 58 48; www.oasisgranada.com; Placeta Correo Viejo 3; dm from €13; ❄ @ 🛜 🚾) Facility-packed budget digs in a bohemian quarter, Oasis is seconds away from the *teterías* and bars on Calle Elvira. It has free internet access, a rooftop terrace and personal safes. As far as backpacker hostels go, it's a gem.

Hostal Arteaga   HOSTAL €

(☑ 958 20 88 41; www.hostalarteaga.es; Calle Arteaga 3; s/d €40/49; ❄ @ 🛜) A charming bargain option just off the Gran Vía de Colón, inching into the Albayzín. The rooms are spruced up with lavender walls, striped bedspreads and chequered blue bathroom tiles for a tidy, modern feel. Stay three nights and you get a free session, including the baths, sauna and jacuzzi, at the adjacent Baños de Elvira spa.

Hotel Posada del Toro   HOTEL €

(☑ 958 22 73 33; www.posadadeltoro.com; Calle de Elvira 25; d from €50; ❄ 🛜) A lovely small hotel with rooms set around a tranquil central patio. Walls are coloured like Italian gelato in pistachio, peach and cream flavours. The rooms are similarly tasteful with parquet floors, Alhambra-style stucco, rustic-style furniture and small but perfectly equipped bathrooms with double sinks and hydromassage showers. A bargain – especially considering its central location.

🍴 Eating

Granada is a bastion of the fantastic practice of free tapas with every drink. Place your drink order at the bar and, hey presto, a plate will magically appear with a generous portion of something delicious-looking on it. Order another drink and another plate will materialise. The process is repeated with every round you buy – and each time the tapa gets better. As Spanish bars serve only small glasses of beer (*cañas* measure just 250ml) it is perfectly easy to fill up on free tapas over an enjoyable evening without getting totally inebriated. Indeed, some people 'crawl' from bar to bar getting a drink and free tapa in each place. Packed shoulder-to-shoulder with tapas institutions, Calle de Elvira and Calle Navas are good places for bar crawls. If you're hungry you

WORTH A TRIP

SACROMONTE

Sacromonte, the primarily *gitano* (Roma) neighbourhood northeast of the Albayzín, is renowned for its flamenco traditions, drawing tourists to nightclubs and aficionados to music schools. But it still feels like the fringes of the city, literally and figuratively, as the homes dug out of the hillside alternate between flashy and highly extemporaneous, despite some of the caves having been established since the 14th century.

The area is good for a stroll – though solo women should avoid the uninhabited areas – yielding great views (especially from an ad hoc cafe on Vereda de Enmedio). For some insight into the area, the **Museo Cuevas del Sacromonte** (www.sacromontegranada.com; Barranco de los Negros; €5; ⊙10am-6pm) provides an excellent display of local folk art. This wide-ranging ethnographic and environmental museum and arts centre is set in large herb gardens and hosts art exhibitions, as well as flamenco and films (10pm on Wednesday and Friday from June to September).

can always order an extra plate or two to soak up the *cervezas*.

Bodegas Castañeda TAPAS €
(Calle Almireceros; tapas €2-3, raciones €6-8; ⊙11.30am-4.30pm & 7.30pm-1.30am) A much-loved relic among locals and tourists alike, the buzzing Castañeda is the Granada tapas bar to trump all others. Don't expect any fancy new stuff here, but do expect lightning-fast service, booze from big casks mounted on the walls, and eating as a physical contact sport.

Hicuri Art Restaurant VEGAN €
(Plaza de los Girones 3; mains €7-12; ⊙10am-10pm Mon-Sat; ☑) Granada's leading graffiti artist, El Niño de las Pinturas, has been let loose on the inner and outer walls of Hicuri, and the results are positively psychedelic. The food used to be vegetarian with a few dishes for diehard carnivores, but it recently went full-on vegan.

Tofu and seitan are liberally used in the food, and the almond tiramisu makes a persuasive dessert.

La Bella y La Bestia ANDALUCIAN, TAPAS €
(☑958 22 51 87; www.bodegaslabellaylabestia.com; Calle Carcel Baja 14; tapas €2-3; ⊙noor-midnight) Lots of beauty, but no real beast – this place wins the prize for Granada's most generous free tapas: a huge plate of bagels, chips and pasta arrives with your first drink. There are four branches, though this one is particularly well-placed, just off Calle de Elvira.

El Ají MODERN SPANISH €€
(☑958 29 29 30; Plaza San Miguel Bajo 9; mains €12-20; ⊙1-11pm; ☑) Up in the Albayzín, this chic but cosy neighbourhood restaurant is no bigger than a shoebox, but serves from breakfast right through to the evening. Chatty staff at the tiny marble bar can point out some of the highlights of the creative menu (such as prawns with tequila and honey). It's a good place to get out of the sun and rest up, especially if you are hiking up from Plaza Nueva.

Los Diamantes SEAFOOD €€
(www.barlosdiamantes.com; Calle Navas 26; raciones €8-10; ⊙noon-6pm & 8pm-2am Mon-Fri, 11am-1am Sat & Sun) Granada's great tapas institution has two central outlets. This old-school scruffy joint in tapa bar-lined Calle Navas, and a newer, hipper Ikea-esque version in Plaza Nueva. What doesn't change is the tapa specialty – fish, which you'll smell sizzling in the fryer as soon as you open the door.

 Drinking & Nightlife

The best street for drinking is the rather scruffy Calle de Elvira, but other chilled bars line Río Darro at the base of the Albayzín and Calle Navas. Just north of Plaza de Trinidad are a bunch of cool hipster-ish bars.

★Taberna La Tana BAR
(Calle Rosario; ⊙12.30-4pm & 8.30pm-midnight) Possibly the friendliest family-run bar in Granada, La Tana specialises in Spanish wines and backs it up with some beautifully paired tapas. You can't go wrong with the '*surtido*' plate of Spanish hams. Ask the bartender about the 'wines of the month' and state your preference – a *suave* (smooth) red, or a *fuerte* (strong).

El Bar de Eric BAR
(Calle Escuelas 8; ⊙8:30am-2am Sun-Thu, to 3am Fri & Sat) Imagine Keith Moon reincarnated as a punk rocker and put in charge of a

THE TEAHOUSES OF GRANADA

Granada's *teterías* (teahouses) have proliferated in recent years, but there's still something exotic and dandyish about their dark atmospheric interiors, stuffed with lace veils, stucco, low cushioned seats and an invariably bohemian clientele. Most offer a long list of aromatic teas along with sticky Arabic sweets. Some serve up music and more substantial snacks. Many still permit their customers to indulge in the *chachima* (shisha pipe). Narrow Calle Calderería Nueva is Granada's best 'tetería street'.

modern tapas restaurant. Eric's is the brainchild of Spanish rock-and-roll drummer Eric Jiménez, of Los Planetas – but in this new bastion of rock chic, things aren't as chaotic as you might think.

Tetería As-Sirat　　　　　　TEAHOUSE
(Calle Calderia Nueva 4) For a lung-filling hookah and tea experience try this little place next door to Kasbah. Among a head-spinning variety of teas popular with non-drinking Muslim youth you'll find Cocktail Cleopatra or a fruity mango infusion, which complements the honey-and-orange crepe nicely.

ℹ Information

Tourist Office (☎ 958 22 10 22; Calle Santa Ana 1; ⊙ 9am-7.30pm Mon-Sat, 9.30am-3pm Sun) Close to Plaza Nueva.

ℹ Getting There & Around

Granada's **bus station** (Carretera de Jaén) is 3km northwest of the city centre. Take city bus SN2 to Cruz del Sur and change onto the LAC bus for the Gran Via de Colón in the city centre. Destinations include Córdoba (€15, 2¾ hours), Málaga (€12, 1½ hours), Madrid (€25, six hours) and Seville (€23, three hours).

The **train station** (☎ 958 24 02 02; Avenida de Andaluces) is 1.5km northwest of the centre, off Avenida de la Constitución. For the centre, walk straight ahead to Avenida de la Constitución and turn right to pick up the LAC bus to Gran Vía de Colón. Destinations include Madrid (€69, four hours), Barcelona (€60, seven to 11 hours), Córdoba (€36 2½ hours) and Seville (€30, three hours).

Cádiz

POP 121,700

You could write several weighty tomes about Cádiz and still fall miles short of nailing its essence. Old age accounts for much of the complexity. Cádiz is generally considered to be the oldest continuously inhabited settlement in Europe, founded as Gadir by the Phoenicians in about 1100 BC. Now well into its fourth millennium, the ancient centre, surrounded almost entirely by water, is a romantic jumble of sinuous streets where Atlantic waves crash against eroded sea walls, salty beaches teem with sun-worshippers, and cheerful taverns echo with the sounds of cawing gulls and frying fish.

◉ Sights & Activities

★**Museo de Cádiz**　　　　　　MUSEUM
(www.museosdeandalucia.es; Plaza de Mina; €1.50, EU citizens free; ⊙ 9am-3.30pm Tue-Sun mid-Jun–mid-Sep, 9am-7.30pm Tue-Sat & 9am-3.30pm Sun mid-Sep–mid-Jun) The Museo de Cádiz is the province's top museum. Stars of the ground-floor archaeology section are two Phoenician marble sarcophagi carved in human likeness, along with lots of headless Roman statues and a giant marble Emperor Trajan (with head) from the Baelo Claudia ruins. Upstairs, the excellent fine arts collection displays 18 superb 17th-century canvases of saints, angels and monks by Francisco de Zurbarán.

★**Catedral de Cádiz**　　　　　　CATHEDRAL
(☎ 956 28 61 54; Plaza de la Catedral; adult/child €5/3; ⊙ 10am-6pm Mon-Sat, 1.30-6pm Sun) Cádiz' beautiful yellow-domed cathedral is an impressively proportioned baroque-neoclassical construction, best appreciated from seafront Campo del Sur in the evening sun. Though commissioned in 1716, the project wasn't finished until 1838, by which time neoclassical elements (the dome, towers and main facade) had diluted architect Vicente Acero's original baroque plan.

Playa de la Victoria　　　　　　BEACH
Often overshadowed by the city's historical riches, Cádiz' beaches are Copacabana-like in their size, vibe and beauty. This fine, wide strip of Atlantic sand starts 1km south of the Puerta de Tierra and stretches 4km back along the peninsula.

Take bus 1 (Plaza España-Cortadura; €1.10) from Plaza de España, or walk or jog along the promenade from the Barrio de Santa María.

Cádiz

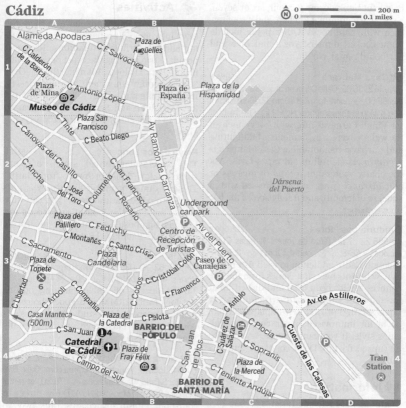

🎉 Festivals & Events

Carnaval CARNIVAL

(☉Feb) No other Spanish city celebrates Carnaval with as much spirit, dedication and humour as Cádiz. Here it becomes a 10-day singing, dancing and drinking fancy-dress street party spanning two February weekends. The fun, fuelled by huge amounts of alcohol, is irresistible. Check www.turismo.cadiz.es for updates on the next festival.

Costumed groups of up to 45 people, called *murgas,* tour the city on foot or on floats and tractors, dancing, drinking, singing satirical ditties or performing sketches. The biggest hits are the 12-person *chirigotas* with their scathing humour, irony and double meanings, often directed at politicians. Most of their famed verbal wit will be lost on all but fluent Spanish speakers.

Cádiz

🛏 Sleeping & Eating

★**Casa Caracol** HOSTEL €

(☎956 26 11 66; www.hostel-casacaracol.com; Calle Suárez de Salazar 4; hammock/dm/d incl breakfast €10/18/40; @🛜) 🖋 Casa Caracol is Cádiz' original old-town backpacker hostel. Friendly as only Cádiz can be, it has colourful bunk dorms for four, six or seven, a sociable communal kitchen, and a roof terrace with hammocks. Other perks include home-cooked dinners, yoga, and bike and surfboard rental. No lift.

★ **Casa Manteca**   TAPAS €
(☑ 956 21 36 03; Calle Corralón de los Carros 66; tapas €2.50; ⊙ noon-4pm & 8.30pm-12.30am, closed Sun & Mon evenings approx Nov-Mar) The hub of La Viña's Carnaval fun, with every inch of its walls covered in flamenco, bullfighting and Carnaval memorabilia, Casa Manteca is a *barrio* classic full of old tapas faves. Ask the chatty waiters for a *tapa* of mussels or *chicharrones* (pressed pork dressed with a squeeze of lemon), and it'll fly across the bar on wax paper.

Freiduría Las Flores   SEAFOOD €
(☑ 956 22 61 12; Plaza de Topete 4; tapas €1.50, raciones €6-8; ⊙ noon-4.30pm & 8.30pm-midnight) Cádiz' addiction to fried fish reaches new heights here. If it comes from the sea, chances are it's been fried and dished up at Las Flores as *tapa, media racion* (larger tapas serving) or *racion* (full-plate serving), or in an improvised paper cup, fish-and-chips style. If you can't choose, try a *surtido* (mixed fry-up). Don't count on getting a table.

🛈 **Information**

Centro de Recepción de Turistas (☑ 956 24 10 01; www.turismo.cadiz.es; Paseo de Canalejas; ⊙ 9am-6.30pm Mon-Fri, to 5pm Sat & Sun) Near the bus and train stations.

🛈 **Getting There & Away**

Buses run regularly to Seville (€13, 1¾ hours), Málaga (€28, 4½ hours), Tarifa (€10, 1¾ hours) and other destinations. From the nearby train station are services to Seville (€16 to €24, 1¾ hours, 15 daily) and Madrid (€74, 4½ hours, three to four daily) among others.

Tarifa

POP 13,500

Tarifa's tip-of-Spain location, where the Mediterranean and the Atlantic meet, gives it a different climate and character to the rest of Andalucía. Stiff Atlantic winds draw in surfers, windsurfers and kitesurfers who, in turn, lend this ancient yet deceptively small settlement a refreshingly laid-back international vibe.

 Activities

Tarifa's legendary winds have turned the town into one of Europe's premier windsurfing and kitesurfing destinations. The most popular strip is along the coast between Tarifa and Punta Paloma, 10km northwest. Over 30 places offer equipment hire and classes, from beginner to expert. The best months are May, June and September, but bear in mind that the choppy seas aren't always beginner's territory.

Playa de los Lances   BEACH
This spectacular, broad sweep of sand stretches for 7km northwest from Tarifa. The low dunes behind it are a *paraje natural* (protected natural area); you can hike across them on the 1.5km **Sendero de los Lances**, signposted towards the northwest end of Calle Batalla del Salado.

FIRMM   WHALE-WATCHING
(☑ 956 62 70 08; www.firmm.org; Calle Pedro Cortés 4; adult/child €30/20; ⊙ Apr-Oct) Of Tarifa's dozens of whale-watching outfits, not-for-profit FIRMM is a good choice. Its primary purpose is to study the whales, record data and encourage environmentally sensitive tours.

Hot Stick Kite School   KITESURFING, SURFING
(☑ 647 155516; www.hotsticktarifa.com; Calle Batalla del Salado 41; 1-day courses €70-80, kit rental per day €60; ⊙ Mar–mid-Nov) Daily three- to four-hour kitesurfing classes, plus two- to five-day courses (Spanish, English, French and German). Also two-hour surfing and paddle-boarding sessions (€50).

🍴 **Sleeping & Eating**

★ **Hostal África**   HOSTAL €
(☑ 956 68 02 20; www.hostalafrica.com; Calle María Antonia Toledo 12; s/d €50/65, with shared bathroom €35/50; ⊙ Mar-Nov; 🛜) This revamped 19th-century house just southwest of the Puerta de Jerez is one of the Costa de la Luz' best *hostales*. Full of pot plants and sky-blue-and-white arches, it's run by hospitable owners, and the 13 all-different rooms sparkle with bright colours. Enjoy the lovely, big roof terrace, with exotic cabana and views of Africa.

Melting Pot   HOSTEL €
(☑ 956 68 29 06; www.meltingpothostels.com; Calle Turriano Gracil 5; dm/d incl breakfast from €13/35; 🅿 @ 🛜) Small laid-back hostel in an equally laid-back town, equipped with four-

to eight-bed dorms along with some single and double rooms for privacy seekers.

★ **Café Azul**   BREAKFAST €

(www.facebook.com/cafeazultarifa; Calle Batalla del Salado 8; breakfasts €3.50-7.50; ⊙ 9am-3pm) This eccentric Italian-run place with eye-catching blue-and-white Moroccan-inspired decor whips up the best breakfasts in town, if not Andalucía. You'll want to eat everything. It does a wonderfully fresh fruit salad topped with muesli and yoghurt, plus good coffee, smoothies, juices, *bocadillos* (filled rolls) and cooked breakfasts. The fruit-and-yoghurt-stuffed crêpe is a work of art.

❶ Getting There & Away

Buses run regularly to Cádiz (€10, 1½ hours), Málaga (€17, 2¾ hours) and Seville (€20, three hours).

Málaga

POP 568,500

Málaga – a world apart from the adjoining Costa del Sol – is a historic and culturally rich provincial capital which has long lived in the shadow of the iconic Andalucian cities of Granada, Córdoba and Seville. Yet, it has rapidly emerged as the province's city of culture with its so-called 'mile of art' being compared to Madrid, and its dynamism and fine dining to Barcelona. The tastefully restored historic centre is a delight.

◉ Sights

★ **Museo Picasso Málaga**   MUSEUM

(❷902 44 33 77; www.museopicassomalaga.org; Calle San Agustín 8; €7, incl temporary exhibition €10; ⊙ 10am-8pm Tue-Thu & Sun, to 9pm Fri & Sat) The Museo Picasso has an enviable collection of 204 works, 155 donated and 49 loaned to the museum by Christine Ruiz-Picasso (wife of Paul, Picasso's eldest son) and Bernard Ruiz-Picasso (his grandson), and includes some wonderful paintings of the family, including the heartfelt *Paulo con gorro blanco* (Paulo with a white cap), a portrait of Picasso's eldest son painted in the 1920s.

★ **Centre Pompidou Málaga**   MUSEUM

(❷951 92 62 00; www.centrepompidou.es; Pasaje Doctor Carrillo Casaux, Muelle Uno; €7, incl temporary exhibition €9; ⊙ 9.30am-8pm Wed-Mon) Opened in 2015 in the port, this offshoot of the Paris Centre Pompidou is housed in a low-slung modern building crowned by a playful multicoloured cube. The permanent

TRIPPING TO MOROCCO

At once African and Arab, and looming large across the Straits of Gibraltar across from Tarifa, Morocco is an exciting detour from your Western European journey. The country's attractions are endless, from the fascinating souqs and medieval architecture of Marrakesh and Fès to the Atlantic charms of Asilah and Essaouira, from the High Atlas and Rif Mountains to the soulful sand dunes of the Sahara.

Several ferry services zip from southern Spain across to Morocco, including a fast **ferry** (❷956 68 18 30; www.frs. es; Avenida de Andalucía 16) from Tarifa that makes a day-trip an easy prospect. For further information, head to shop. lonelyplanet.com to purchase Lonely Planet's Morocco guide.

exhibition includes the extraordinary *Ghost* by Kader Attia depicting rows of Muslim women bowed in prayer created from domestic aluminum foil, plus works by such contemporary masters as Frida Kahlo, Francis Bacon and Antoni Tàpies. There are also audiovisual installations, talking 'heads' and temporary exhibitions.

Museo Carmen Thyssen   MUSEUM

(www.carmenthyssenmalaga.org; Calle Compañía 10; €4.50, incl temporary exhibition €9; ⊙ 10am-7.30pm Tue-Sun) Located in an aesthetically renovated 16th-century palace in the heart of the city's former Moorish quarter, the extensive collection concentrates on 19th-century Spanish and Andalucian art and includes paintings by some of the country's most exceptional painters, including Joaquín Sorolla and Ignacio Zuloaga. Temporary exhibitions similarly focus on 19th-century art.

★ **Alcazaba**   CASTLE

(Calle Alcazabilla; €2.20, incl Castillo de Gibralfaro €3.40; ⊙ 9.30am-8pm Tue-Sun) No time to visit Granada's Alhambra? Then Málaga's Alcazaba can provide a taster. The entrance is next to the **Roman amphitheatre**, from where a meandering path climbs amid lush greenery: crimson bougainvillea, lofty palms, fragrant jasmine bushes and rows of orange trees. Extensively restored, this palace fortress dates from the 11th-century Moorish

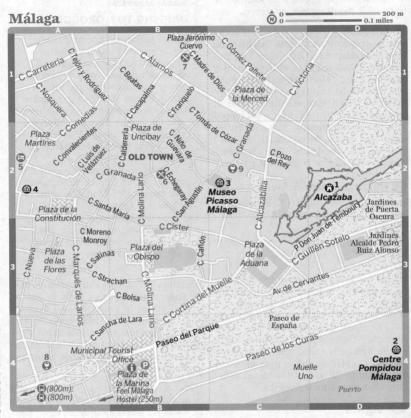

Málaga

period; the caliphal horseshoe arches, courtyards and bubbling fountains are evocative of this influential period in Málaga's history.

🎉 Festivals & Events

Feria de Málaga   FAIR
(⊙mid-Aug) Málaga's nine-day feria (fair), launched by a huge fireworks display, is the most ebullient of Andalucía's summer ferias. It resembles an exuberant Rio-style street party with plenty of flamenco and *fino* (sherry); the night-time action is at dedicated grounds and is a massive party.

🛏 Sleeping

★**Dulces Dreams**   HOSTEL €
(☎951 35 78 69; www.dulcesdreamshostel.com; Plaza de los Mártires 6; r incl breakfast €45-60; ❋ 🛜) Run by an enthusiastic young team, the rooms at Dulces (sweet) Dreams are ap-

propriately named after desserts; 'Cupcake' is a good choice with its terrace overlooking the imposing red-brick church across the way. This is an older building, so there's no lift and the rooms vary in size, but they are bright and whimsically decorated using recycled materials as far as possible.

Feel Málaga Hostel   HOSTEL €
(☑ 952 22 28 32; www.feelmalagahostel.com; Calle Vendeja 25; d €45, without bathroom €35, shared rooms per person from €16; @ 🛜) Located within a suitcase trundle of the city-centre train station, the accommodation here is clean and well equipped with a choice of doubles and shared rooms. The downstairs communal area has a colourful seaside look with stripey deckchairs and minifootball; bathrooms sport classy mosaic tiles; and the top-floor kitchen has all the essentials necessary to whip up a decent meal.

🍴 Eating & Drinking

El Piyayo   TAPAS €
(☑ 952 22 90 57; www.entreplatos.es; Calle Granada 36; raciones €6-10; ⏰ 12.30pm-midnight) A popular traditionally tiled bar and restaurant, famed for its *pescaitos fritos* (fried fish) and typical local tapas, including wedges of crumbly Manchego cheese the ideal accompaniment to a glass of hearty Rioja wine. The *berenjenas con miel de caña* (aubergine with molasses) are also good.

Tapeo de Cervantes   TAPAS €
(www.eltapeodecervantes.com; Calle Cárcer 8; tapas €4-6; ⏰ Tue-Sun) This place has caught on big time which, given its squeeze-in space, can mean a wait. Choose from traditional or more innovative tapas and *raciones* with delicious combinations and stylish presentation. Think polenta with oyster mushrooms, chorizo and melted cheese or the more conventional *tortilla de patatas* (potato omelette), spiked with a veg or two. Portions are generous.

Antigua Casa de Guardia   BAR
(www.antiguacasadeguardia.net; Alameda Principal 18; ⏰ 11am-midnight) This atmospheric old tavern dates to 1840 and is the oldest bar in Málaga. The peeling custard-coloured paintwork, black-and-white photographs of local boy Picasso and elderly bar staff look fittingly antique. Try the dark brown, sherry-like *seco* (dry) Málaga wine or the romantically named *lagrima trañañejo* (very old tear).

Bodegas El Pimpi   BAR
(www.bodegabarelpimpi.com; Calle Granada 62; ⏰ 11am-2am; 🛜) This rambling bar is an institution in this town. The interior encompasses a warren of rooms with a courtyard and open terrace overlooking the Roman amphitheatre. Walls are decorated with historic feria posters and photos of visitors, while the enormous barrels are signed by more well-known folk, including Tony Blair and Antonio Banderas. Tapas and meals are also available.

ℹ Information

Municipal Tourist Office (Plaza de la Marina; ⏰ 9am-8pm Mar-Sep, to 6pm Oct-Feb) Offers a range of city maps and booklets. It also operates information kiosks at the Alcazaba entrance (Calle Alcazabilla), at the main train station (Explanada de la Estación), on Plaza de la Merced and on the eastern beaches (El Palo and La Malagueta).

ℹ Getting There & Away

Málaga's airport is one of Spain's busiest, with budget connections from all over Europe. The airport is connected by train to central Málaga.

The bus station has links to all major cities in Spain, including Cádiz (€27, four hours), Córdoba (€12, three hours), Granada (€12, two hours), Madrid (€45, nine hours) and Seville (€19, 2¾ hours).

Train services include Córdoba (€26, 2½ hours, 18 daily), Seville (€24, 2¾ hours, 11 daily) and Madrid (€80, 2½ hours, 10 daily). Note that for Córdoba and Seville the daily schedule includes faster trains at roughly double the cost.

Ronda

POP 37,000

Perched on an inland plateau riven by the 100m fissure of El Tajo gorge, Ronda is Málaga province's most spectacular town. It has a superbly dramatic location, and owes its name ('surrounded' by mountains), to the encircling Serranía de Ronda.

◉ Sights

Puente Nuevo   BRIDGE
(€2; ⏰ 10am-6pm Mon-Fri, to 3pm Sat & Sun) Straddling the dramatic gorge and the Río Guadalevín (Deep River) is Ronda's most recognisable sight, the towering Puente Nuevo, best viewed from the Camino de los Molinos, which runs along the bottom of the gorge. The bridge separates the old and new towns.

ANDALUCÍA'S QUIETEST BEACHES

The coast east of Almería in eastern Andalucía is perhaps the last section of Spain's Mediterranean coast where you can have a beach to yourself. This is Spain's sunniest region – even in late March it can be warm enough to strip off and take in the rays. The best thing about the region is the wonderful coastline and semidesert scenery of the Cabo de Gata promontory. All along the 50km coast from El Cabo de Gata village to Agua Amarga, some of the most beautiful and empty beaches on the Mediterranean alternate with precipitous cliffs and scattered villages. The main village is laid-back San José, with excellent beaches nearby, such as Playa de los Genoveses and Playa de Mónsul.

Plaza de Toros BULLRING

(Calle Virgen de la Paz; €7, incl audioguide €8.50; ⊙10am-8pm) Ronda's Plaza de Toros is a mecca for bullfighting aficionados. In existence for more than 200 years, it is one of the oldest and most revered bullrings in Spain and has been the site of some of the most important events in bullfighting history.

The on-site **Museo Taurino** is crammed with memorabilia such as blood-spattered costumes worn by 1990s star Jesulín de Ubrique. It also includes artwork by Picasso and photos of famous fans such as Orson Welles and Ernest Hemingway.

Casa del Rey Moro GARDENS

(House of the Moorish King; Calle Santo Domingo 17; €4; ⊙10am-7pm) The terraces give access to La Mina, an Islamic stairway of more than 300 steps cut into the rock all the way down to the river at the bottom of the gorge. These steps enabled Ronda to maintain water supplies when it was under attack. It was also the point where Christian troops forced entry in 1485. The steps are not well lit and are steep and wet in places. Take care.

🛏 Sleeping & Eating

Hotel San Francisco HOSTAL €

(☎952 87 32 99; www.hotelsanfranciscoronda.com; Calle María Cabrera 18; s/d incl breakfast €38/60; ❄) This is possibly the best budget option in Ronda, offering a warm welcome. Once a *hostal*, it has been refurbished and

upgraded to hotel, with facilities to match – including wheelchair access.

★**Bodega San Francisco** TAPAS €

(www.bodegasanfrancisco.com; Calle Ruedo Alameda; raciones €6-10; ⊙1.30-5pm & 8pm-1am Wed-Mon) With three dining rooms and tables spilling out onto the narrow pedestrian street, this may well be Ronda's top tapas bar. The menu is vast – including nine-plus salad choices – and should suit the fussiest of families. Try the *revuelto de patatas* (scrambled eggs with potatoes and peppers). House wine is good.

ℹ Information

Tourist Office (www.turismoderonda.es; Paseo de Blas Infante; ⊙10am-7pm Mon-Fri, to 5pm Sat, to 2pm Sun) Helpful staff with a wealth of information on the town and region.

ℹ Getting There & Away

Slow buses reach Ronda from Málaga, Seville and Cádiz. Trains run to Málaga, Córdoba, Madrid and Granada, as well as Seville with a change in Bobadilla or Antequera.

Spain Survival Guide

ℹ Directory A–Z

ACCOMMODATION

At the budget end of the market, places listing accommodation use all sorts of overlapping names to describe themselves. *Pensiones, hospedajes* and *casas de huéspedes* all offer simple, cheap rooms, often with shared bathroom.

Hostales are a step up from *pensiones* and operate as simple, small hotels – you'll find them everywhere across the country

Spain has official youth hostels – *albergues juveniles* – as well as backpackers' hostels dotted around the country. These are often the cheapest places for lone travellers, but two people can usually get a better double room elsewhere for a similar price.

DISCOUNT CARDS

Many cities offer a card that includes entry to attractions, public transport, a city bus tour and restaurant discounts. Typically, you need to do lots of sightseeing to save money with it.

LGBT TRAVELLERS

Spain has become perhaps the most gay-friendly country in southern Europe.

Lesbians and gay men generally keep a fairly low profile, but are quite open in the cities. Ma drid, Barcelona, Sitges and Ibiza have particularly lively scenes. Sitges is a major destination on the international gay party circuit; gay participants take a leading role in the wild **Carnaval** (www.carnavaldesitges.com; ☺ Feb/Mar) there in February/March.

MONEY
ATMs are plentiful. Cards are widely accepted, but not as widely as in most of Europe – carry cash for cheaper restaurants and all bars.

Tipping is always optional in Spain. In restaurants, Spaniards leave small change, others up to 5%, which is considered generous. Tipping in bars is rare.

OPENING HOURS
Banks 8.30am to 2pm Monday to Friday; some also open 4pm to 7pm Thursday and 9am to 1pm Saturday

Central post offices 8.30am to 9.30pm Monday to Friday, 8.30am to 2pm Saturday (most other branches 8.30am to 8.30pm Monday to Friday, 9.30am to 1pm Saturday)

Nightclubs Midnight or 1am to 5am or 6am

Restaurants Lunch 1pm to 4pm, dinner 8.30pm to 11pm or midnight

Shops 10am to 2pm and 4.30pm to 7.30pm or 5pm to 8pm; big supermarkets and department stores generally open 10am to 10pm Monday to Saturday

PUBLIC HOLIDAYS
There are at least 14 official holidays a year – some observed nationwide, some locally. When a holiday falls close to a weekend, Spaniards like to make a *puente* (bridge), meaning they take the intervening day off too. Here are the national holidays:

Año Nuevo (New Year's Day) 1 January

Viernes Santo (Good Friday) March/April

Fiesta del Trabajo (Labour Day) 1 May

La Asunción (Feast of the Assumption) 15 August

Fiesta Nacional de España (National Day) 12 October

La Inmaculada Concepción (Feast of the Immaculate Conception) 8 December

Navidad (Christmas) 25 December

Regional governments set five holidays and local councils two more. Common dates include the following:

Epifanía (Epiphany) or **Día de los Reyes Magos** (Three Kings' Day) 6 January

Jueves Santo (Good Thursday) March/April; not observed in Catalonia and Valencia

Corpus Christi June. This is the Thursday after the eighth Sunday after Easter Sunday.

Día de Santiago Apóstol (Feast of St James the Apostle) 25 July

Día de Todos los Santos (All Saints Day) 1 November

Día de la Constitución (Constitution Day) 6 December

TELEPHONE
Local SIM cards with call and data packages are widely available. Spanish landline and mobile numbers have nine digits, with no separate area code.

International dialling code 00
Country code 34

ⓘ Getting There & Away
AIR
There are direct flights to Spain from most European countries, as well as North America, South America, Africa, the Middle East and Asia.

BUS
Apart from shorter cross-border services, Eurolines (www.eurolines.com) are the main operators of international bus services to Spain from most of Europe and Morocco. Other bus services connect Portugal and Spain, including three daily buses between Lisbon and Madrid.

FERRY
Regular car ferries and hydrofoils run to and from Morocco, and there are ferry links to the UK, Italy, the Canary Islands and Algeria. Check www.directferries.com for a run-down of routes.

TRAIN

The principal rail crossings into Spain pierce the Franco-Spanish frontier along the Mediterranean coast and via the Basque Country. From Portugal, the main line runs from Lisbon across Extremadura to Madrid. In addition to the rail services connecting Spain with France and Portugal, there are direct trains between Zurich and Barcelona (via Bern, Geneva, Perpignan and Girona), and between Milan and Barcelona (via Turin, Perpignan and Girona).

🛈 Getting Around

Spain has an extensive network of internal flights, many operated by budget airlines like Vueling and Ryanair.

The bus network is fast, cheap and comfortable. **Alsa** (www.alsa.es) is one of the main operators.

Renfe (www.renfe.com) is the main rail operator, and runs a wide network, which includes speedy but pricy AVE trains. Book ahead online for discounts.

Ferries and hydrofoils link Barcelona, Valencia and Dénia – with the Balearic Islands. There are also services to Spain's North African enclaves of Ceuta and Melilla.

PORTUGAL

Lisbon

POP 547,700 (2.7 MILLION IN URBAN AREA)

Spread across steep hillsides that overlook the Rio Tejo, Lisbon has captivated visitors for centuries. Windswept vistas reveal the city in all its beauty: Roman and Moorish ruins, white-domed cathedrals, grand plazas lined with sun-drenched cafes. The real delight of discovery though, is delving into the narrow cobblestone lanes.

As yellow trams clatter through tree-lined streets, *lisboêtas* stroll through lamplit old quarters, much as they've done for centuries. Gossip is exchanged over fresh bread and wine at tiny patio restaurants as fado singers perform in the background. In other parts of town, Lisbon reveals her youthful alter ego at bohemian bars and riverside clubs, late-night street parties and eye-catching boutiques selling all things classic and cutting-edge.

👁 Sights

At the riverfront is the grand Praça do Comércio. Behind it march the pedestrian-filled streets of Baixa (lower) district, up to Praça da Figueira and Praça Dom Pedro IV (aka Rossio). From Baixa it's a steep climb west, through swanky shopping district Chiado, into the narrow streets of nightlife-haven Bairro Alto. Eastwards from the Baixa it's another climb to Castelo de São Jorge and the Moorish, labyrinthine Alfama district around it. The World Heritage sites of Belém lie further west along the river – an easy tram ride from Praça do Comércio.

Castelo de São Jorge CASTLE
(www.castelodesaojorge.pt; adult/student/child €8.50/5/free; ⊙9am-9pm Mar-Oct, 9am-6pm Nov-Feb) Towering dramatically above Lisbon, the mid-11th-century hilltop fortifications of Castelo de São Jorge sneak into almost every snapshot. Roam its snaking ramparts and pine-shaded courtyards for superlative views over the city's red rooftops to the river. Guided tours daily (Portuguese, English and Spanish) at 1pm and 5pm are included in the admission price.

Alfama VILLAGE
Wander down (to save your legs) through Alfama's steep, narrow, cobblestoned streets and catch a glimpse of the more traditional side of Lisbon before it too is gentrified. Linger in a backstreet cafe along the way and experience some local bonhomie without the tourist gloss.

Museu do Fado MUSEUM
(www.museudofado.pt; Largo do Chafariz de Dentro; adult/child €5/3; ⊙10am-6pm Tue-Sun) Fado (traditional Portuguese melancholic song) was born in the Alfama. Immerse yourself in its bittersweet symphonies at Museu do Fado. This engaging museum traces fado's history from its working-class roots to international stardom.

★Núcleo Arqueológico da Rua dos Correeiros RUIN
(☏211 131 004; http://ind.millenniumbcp.pt; Rua Augusta 96; ⊙10am-noon & 2-5pm Mon-Sat) **FREE** Hidden under the Millennium BCP bank building are layers of ruins dating from the Iron Age discovered on a 1991 parking lot dig. Fascinating archaeologist-led tours, run by Fundacão Millennium (booking ahead year-round is highly advisable), descend into the depths in English (departing on the hour). The extremely well-done site is now rightfully a National Monument.

★**Mosteiro dos Jerónimos** MONASTERY
(www.mosteirojeronimos.pt; Praça do Império; adult/child €10/5, 1st Sun of month free; ⊙10am-6.30pm Tue-Sun, to 5.30pm Oct-May) Belém, 6km west of the centre on tram 15, has an undisputed heart-stealer in this Unesco-listed monastery. The *mosteiro* is the stuff of pure fantasy; a fusion of Diogo de Boitaca's creative vision and the spice and pepper dosh of Manuel I, who commissioned it to trumpet Vasco da Gama's discovery of a sea route to India in 1498.

Torre de Belém TOWER
(www.torrebelem.pt; adult/child €€/3, 1st Sun of month free; ⊙10am-6.30pm Tue-Sun, to 5.30pm Oct-Apr) Jutting out onto the Rio Tejo, this World Heritage-listed fortress epitomises the Age of Discoveries. Breathe in to climb a narrow spiral staircase to the tower, affording sublime views over Belém and the river.

Museu Nacional de Arte Antiga MUSEUM
(Ancient Art Museum; www.museudearteantiga.pt; Rua das Janelas Verdes; adult/child €€/3, 1st Sun of month free; ⊙10am-6pm Tue-Sun) Set in a lemon-fronted, 17th-century palace, the Museu Nacional de Arte Antiga is Lapa's biggest draw. It presents a star-studded collection of European and Asian paintings and decorative arts.

★**Museu Calouste Gulbenkian** MUSEUM
(www.museu.gulbenkian.pt; Avenida de Berna 45; adult/child €5/free, Sun free; ⊙10am-6pm Wed-Mon) Famous for its outstanding quality and breadth, the world-class Museu Calouste Gulbenkian showcases an epic collection of Western and Eastern art – from Egyptian treasures to Old Master and Impressionist paintings.

🛏 Sleeping

Lisbon Destination Hostel HOSTEL €
(📞213 466 457; www.destinationhostels.com; Rossio Train Station, 2nd floor; dm/s/d from €23/40/80; @🖤) Housed in Lisbon's loveliest train station, this world-class hostel has a glass ceiling lighting the spacious plant-filled common area. Rooms are crisp and well kept, and there are loads of activities (bar crawls, beach day trips etc), plus facilities including a shared kitchen, game consoles, movie room (with popcorn!) and a 24-hour self-service bar. Breakfast is top notch, with crêpes and fresh fruit.

Lisbon Calling HOSTEL €
(📞213 432 381; www.lisboncalling.net; Rua de São Paulo 126, 3rd fl; dm/d with shared bathroom €16/55, d €75; @🖤) This fashionable, unsigned backpacker favourite near Santa Catarina features original frescoes, *azulejos* (hand-painted tiles) and hardwood floors – all lovingly restored by friendly Portuguese owners. The bright, spacious dorms and a brick-vaulted kitchen are easy on the eyes, but the private rooms – specifically room 1812 – will floor you: boutique hotel-level dens of style and comfort that thunderously outpunch their price point.

Home Lisbon Hostel HOSTEL €
(📞218 885 312; www.homelisbonhostel.com; Rua São Nicolau 13; dm €26-30) In the heart of Baixa, this dorm-only hostel is one of the best maintained you'll come across. Facilities are above and beyond, from the professional-grade bar-reception to dark hardwood bunks spread across various floors with privacy curtains that might as well be luxury drapes. It's a family-run oasis, with the doting matriarch, known affectionately as Mamma, even cooking for guests.

Alfama Patio Hostel HOSTEL €
(📞218 883 127; www.alfama.destinationhostels.com; Rua das Escolas Gerais 3; dm €18-24, s/d without bathroom from €30/45, d €60; @🖤) In the heart of Alfama, this beautifully run hostel offers custom-made, Cappadocia-inspired particle-board dorms with privacy curtains and lockable drawers. From the upper-floor rooms, you can practically file your fingernails across the top of the tram as it rattles past. A bevy of activities (fado, street art and surfing tours) and barbecues on the garden-like patio mean it's notably social.

This is Lisbon HOSTEL €
(📞218 014 549; www.thisislisbonhostel.com; Rua da Costa do Castelo 63; dm €16-20, d with/without bathroom €64/60; @🖤) Great views and an easy-going vibe draw a good mix of travellers to this hilltop perch in Castelo. In addition to dorms, you'll trade a particularly spacious bathroom in the en suite double with a nice vanity in double with shared bathroom. The massive outdoor patio hosts BalconyTV's Lisbon concerts for their popular YouTube show.

O Bigode do Rato B&B €
(📞938 282 199; www.obigodedorato.com; Rua Dom João V 2A, 4th fl; r per person €25; 🖤) Independently minded travellers will find great

Central Lisbon

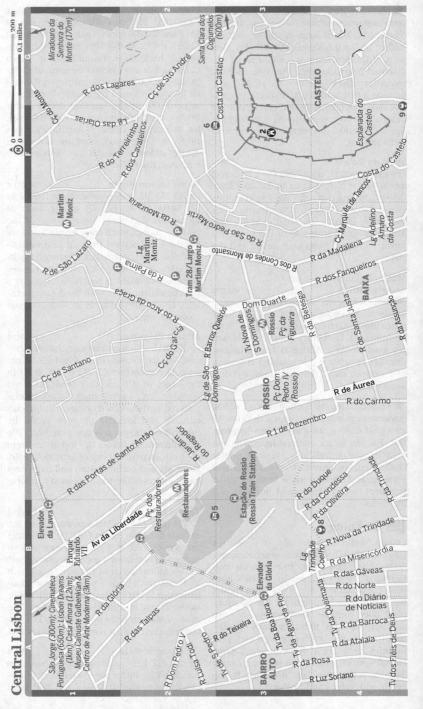

São Jorge (300m); Cinemateca Portuguesa (650m); Lisbon Dreams (1km); Casa Amora (1.2km); Museu Calouste Gulbenkian & Centro de Arte Moderna (3km)

Miradouro da Senhora do Monte (170m)

Santa Clara dos Cogumelos (600m)

CASTELO

Cç do Monte
R dos Lagares
Lg das Olarias
Cç de Sto André
Costa do Castelo
Esplanada do Castelo
Costa do Castelo

R do Terreirinho
R dos Cavaleiros

Martim Moniz
R da Mouraria
Lg Adelino Amaro da Costa

R de São Lázaro
Lg Martim Moniz
Tram 28/Largo Martim Moniz
R dos Condes de Monsanto
R do São Pedro Martir
R da Madalena

R da Palma
R do Arco da Graça
R dos Fanqueiros
BAIXA
R da Assunção

Cç de Santano
Cç do Garcia
R Barros Queirós
Dom Duarte
Tv Nova de S Domingos
Rossio Pç da Figueira
R da Betesga
R de Santa Justa

Lg de São Domingos
ROSSIO
Pç Dom Pedro IV (Rossio)
R de Áurea
R do Carmo

R das Portas de Santo Antão
R Jardim do Regedor
R 1 de Dezembro

Elevador da Lavra
Parque Eduardo VII
Pç dos Restauradores
Restauradores
Estação do Rossio (Rossio Train Station)
R do Duque
R da Trindade

Av da Liberdade
R da Condessa
R da Oliveira
R Nova da Trindade

Elevador da Glória
Lg Trindade Coelho
R da Misericórdia

R da Glória
R das Taipas
Tv da Boa Hora
Tv da Água da Flor
R das Gáveas
R do Norte

BAIRRO ALTO
R Dom Pedro V
R Luísa Todi
Tv de S Pedro
R do Teixeira
R da Queimada
R do Diário de Notícias
R da Barroca
R da Rosa
R da Atalaia
R Luz Soriano
Tv dos Fiéis de Deus

200 m
0.1 miles

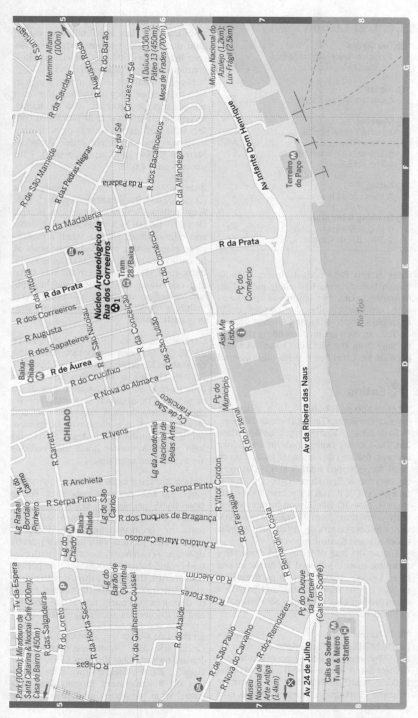

SPAIN & PORTUGAL LISBON

R de Santiago
Memmo Alfama (100m)
R da Saudade
R de São Mamede
R das Pedras Negras
R de São Mamede
R da Madalena
R da Vitória
R da Prata
R dos Correeiros
R Augusta
R dos Sapateiros
Baixa-Chiado
R de Áurea
CHIADO
R Garrett
R Anchieta
R Serpa Pinto
Lg de São Carlos
Baixa-Chiado
Lg do Chiado
Lg Rafael Bordalo Pinheiro
Tv do Carmo
R do Loreto
R da Horta Seca
Lg do Barão de Quintela
R Chiças
R das Salgadeiras
Park (100m); Miradouro de Santa Catarina & Noobai Café (200m); Casa do Bairro (450m)

R do Augusto Rosa
R do Barão
Lg da Sé
R Cruzes da Sé
R dos Bacalhoeiros
R da Padaria
R da Alfândega
R do Comércio
R da Conceição
R de São Nicolau
R de São Julião
R do Crucifixo
R Nova do Almaca
Cc de São Francisco
R Ivens
Lg da Academia Nacional de Belas Artes
R Serpa Pinto
R dos Duques de Bragança
R António Maria Cardoso
R das Flores
R do Alecrim
R de São Paulo
R do Ataíde
Tv de Guilherme Coussel
R Nova do Carvalho
Museu Nacional de Arte Antiga (1.4km)

A Duína (350m); Páteo 13 (450m); Mesa de Frades (700m)
Museu Nacional do Azulejo (1.2km); Lux-Frágil (2.5km)
Av Infante Dom Henrique
R da Prata
Pç do Comércio
Terreiro do Paço
Ask Me Lisboa
Rio Tejo
Pç do Município
Pç do Arsenal
R Vitor Cordon
R do Ferragial
R Bernardino Costa
Av da Ribeira das Naus
Pç do Duque da Terceira (Cais do Sodré)
Cais do Sodré Train & Metro Station
Av 24 de Julho

Tram 28/Baixa
Núcleo Arqueológico da Rua dos Correeiros

Central Lisbon

value at this Rato budget choice. Friendly Italian host Arianna has cutely gussied up a four-bedroom, two-bathroom apartment with eco-touches like lampshades made from old cassette tapes and vintage suitcases. You can even get an astounding view (especially from the Metallica room). Arianna pops in for breakfast but it's otherwise all yours.

✖ Eating

★ Mercado da Ribeira   MARKET €
(www.facebook.com/TimeOutMercadodaRibeira; Av 24 de Julho; ⊙ 10am-midnight Sun-Wed, 10am-2am Thu-Sat; 🛜) Doing trade in fresh fruit and veg, fish and flowers since 1892, this oriental food-topped market hall is the word on everyone's lips since Time Out transformed half of it into a gourmet food court in 2014. Now it's like Lisbon in microcosm, with everything from Garrafeira Nacional wines to Conserveira de Lisboa fish, Arcádia chocolate and Santini gelato.

Follow the lead of locals and come for a morning mooch followed by lunch at one of 35 kiosks – there's everything from Café de São Bento's famous steak and fries to a stand by top chef Henrique Sá Pessoa. Do not miss it.

★ Ti-Natércia   PORTUGUESE €
(📞 218 862 133; Rua Escola Gerais 54; mains €5-12; ⊙ 7pm-midnight Mon-Fri, noon-3pm & 7pm-midnight Sat) A decade in and a legend in the making, 'Aunt' Natércia and her downright delicious Portuguese home cooking is a

tough ticket: there are but a mere six tables and they fill up fast. She'll talk your ear off (and doesn't mince words!) while you devour her excellent take on the classics. Reservations essential (and cash only).

If you do manage to get a seat, you're in for a treat, especially with the *bacalhau com natas* (shredded codfish with bechamel, served au gratin) or *à Brás* (shredded codfish with eggs and potatoes) or, well, anything you else you might order. President Marcelo Rebelo de Sousa approved – his photo is on the wall.

Bota Feijão   PORTUGUESE €
(📞 218 532 489; Rua Conselheiro Lopo Vaz 5; half/whole portion €8.50/12; ⊙ noon-3pm Mon-Fri) Don't be fooled by the nondescript decor and railroad track views – when a tucked-away place is this crowded with locals at lunchtime midweek, it must be doing something right. They're all here for one thing and one thing only: *leitão*, suckling pig spit-roasted on an open fire until juicy and meltingly tender, doused in a beautiful peppery garlic sauce.

Cantinho Lusitano   PORTUGUESE €
(📞 218 065 185; www.cantinholusitano.com; Rua dos Prazeres 52; petiscos €4-8.50; ⊙ 7-11pm Tue-Sat; 🛜) Sharing is what this unassuming little place is all about. Its appealing menu of *petiscos* (tapas), such as Azeitão cheese, chorizo, garlic shrimps, *pica-pau* beef and fava bean salad, pairs nicely with Portuguese wines; and husband-wife team Silvia and João are consummate hosts. Reservations are a good idea at all times.

Antiga Confeitaria de Belém   PATISSERIE €
(📞 213 637 423; www.pasteisdebelem.pt; Rua de Belém 84-92; pastries from €1.05; ⊙ 8am-11pm Oct-Jun, to midnight Jul-Sep) Since 1837, this patisserie has been transporting locals to sugar-coated nirvana with heavenly *pastéis de belém* – crisp pastry nests filled with custard cream, baked at 200°C for that perfect golden crust, then lightly dusted with cinnamon. Admire *azulejos* in the vaulted rooms or devour a still-warm tart at the counter and try to guess the secret ingredient.

Enoteca de Belém   PORTUGUESE, WINE BAR €€
(📞 213 631 511; www.travessadaermida.com; Travessa do Marta Pinto 10; mains €16.50-18; ⊙ 1-11pm Tue-Sun; 🛜) Tucked down a quiet lane just off Belém's main thoroughfare, this casual wine bar serves modernised Portu-

guese classics (fantastic octopus, Iberian pork), matched by an excellent selection of full-bodied Douro reds and refreshing Alentejan whites. The experience – led by well-trained servers particularly adept at gravitating you towards a juice that marries with your tastes – is distinctively memorable.

Drinking & Entertainment

Alfama and Graça are perfect for a relaxed drink with a view while Bairro Alto is like a student at a house party: wasted on cheap booze, flirty and everybody's friend. At dusk, the nocturnal hedonist rears its head with bars trying to out-decibel each other, hash-peddlers lurking in the shadows and kamikaze taxi drivers forcing kerbside sippers to leap aside.

Portas do Sol BAR
(www.portasdosol.pt; Largo das Portas do Sol; cocktails €6; ⊙10am-1am, to 2am Fri-Sat; 🛜) Near one of Lisbon's iconic viewpoints, this spacious sun-drenched terrace has a mix of sofas and white patio furniture on which to sip cocktails while taking in magnificent river views. DJs bring animation to the darkly lit industrial interior on weekends.

★**Wine Bar do Castelo** WINE BAR
(☑218 879 093; www.winebardocastelo.blogspot.pt; Rua Bartolomeu de Gusmão 13; wines by the glass €4-30; ⊙1-10pm) Located near the entrance to the Castelo São Jorge, this laid-back wine bar serves more than 150 Portuguese wines by the glass, along with gourmet smoked meats, cheeses, olives and other tasty accompaniments (tapas from €10). Nuno, the multilingual owner, is a welcoming host and a fount of knowledge about all things wine-related.

Duque Brewpub BREWERY
(www.duquebrewpub.com; Duques da Calçada 49; pints €5.50-8.90; ⊙noon-1am; 🛜) Lisbon's first brewpub debuted in 2016 with 10 taps, five of which are brewed on-site (under the banner of Northern Portugal's Cerveja Aroeira) in true craft-beer style: no two batches are the same. Additional taps feature invited Portuguese craft beers like Passarola, Dois Coivos and Letra.

Take a load off with a hoppy IPA on the pleasant sidewalk seating or hang out in the cosy indoor space, where the tunes pop seamlessly between early '80s Depeche Mode to solo Morrissey to sexy modern fado from Gisela João.

Lux-Frágil CLUB
(www.luxfragil.com; Avenida Infante Dom Henrique, Armazém A - Cais de Pedra, Santo Apolónia; ⊙11pm-6am Thu-Sat) Lisbon's ice-cool, must-see club, Lux hosts big-name DJs spinning electro and house. It's run by ex-Frágil maestro Marcel Reis and part-owned by John Malkovich. Grab a spot on the terrace to see the sun rise over the Tejo; or chill like a king on the throne-like giant interior chairs.

A Baîuca FADO
(☑218 867 284; Rua de São Miguel 20; ⊙8pm-midnight Thu-Mon) On a good night, walking into A Baîuca is like gate-crashing a family party.

FADO

Infused by Moorish song and the ditties of homesick sailors, bluesy, bittersweet fado encapsulates the Lisbon psyche like nothing else. Ask 10 *lisboêtas* to explain it and each will give a different version. This is because fado is deeply personal and explanations hinge on the mood of the moment. Recurring themes are love, destiny, death and the omnipresent *saudade* or 'nostalgic longing'; a kind of musical soap opera.

Though a *fadista* (singer of fado) is traditionally accompanied by a classical and 12-string Portuguese guitar, many new-generation stars such as Mariza, Ana Moura and Joana Amendoeira are putting their own spin on the genre, giving it a twist of Cuban *son* or a dash of Argentine tango.

At Bairro Alto's touristy, folksy performances, you'll only be skating the surface. For authentic fado, go to where it was born – Alfama. While wandering the narrow lanes by night you'll be serenaded by mournful ballads.

There's usually a minimum cover of €15 to €25, and as food is often mediocre, it's worth asking if you can just order a bottle of wine. Book ahead at weekends. If you prefer a spontaneous approach, seek out *fado vadio* where anyone can – and does – have a warble.

It's a special place with *fado vadio*, where locals take a turn and spectators hiss if anyone dares to chat during the singing. There's a €25 minimum spend, which is as tough to swallow as the food, though the fado is spectacular. Reserve ahead.

❶ Information

Ask Me Lisboa (📞210 312 810; www.askme lisboa.com; Praça do Comércio; ⊙9am-8pm) Main branch of Turismo de Lisboa, providing free city maps, brochures, and hotel and tour booking services. Several other offices around town.

❶ Getting There & Away

AIR

Situated around 6km north of the centre, the ultramodern **Aeroporto de Lisboa** (Lisbon Airport; 📞218 413 700; www.ana.pt; Alameda das Comunidades Portuguesas) operates direct flights to major international hubs.

BUS

Lisbon's main long-distance bus terminal is **Sete Rios** (Praça General Humberto Delgado, Rua das Laranjeiras), adjacent to both Jardim Zoológico metro station and Sete Rios train station. The big carriers, Rede Expressos and Eva, run frequent services to almost every major town. **Intercentro** (📞707 200 512; www.intercentro. pt; Gare do Oriente) runs coaches to destinations all over Europe. The other major terminal is the **Gare do Oriente** (Oriente Station; Avenida Dom João II), concentrating on services to the north and Spain and beyond.

TRAIN

Lisbon has several major train stations. Santa Apolónia is the terminal for trains from northern and central Portugal. Gare do Oriente is Lisbon's biggest station. Trains to the Alentejo and the Algarve originate from here. Note that all of Santa Apolónia's services also stop here.

❶ Getting Around

Companhia Carris de Ferro de Lisboa (Carris; 📞213 500 115; www.carris.transporteslisboa. pt) operates all transport in Lisbon proper except the metro. Individual tickets on board cost €1.80 (bus) and €2.85 (tram).

The **metropoitano** (www.metro.trans porteslisboa.pt; single/day ticket €1.40/6; ⊙6.30am-1am) is useful for short hops and to reach the Gare do Oriente and nearby Parque das Nações.

Around Lisbon

Sintra

POP 26.000

With its rippling mountains, dewy forests thick with ferns and lichen, exotic gardens and glittering palaces, Sintra is like a page torn from a fairy tale. Its Unesco World Heritage–listed centre, Sintra-Vila, is dotted with pastel-hued manors folded into luxuriant hills that roll down to the blue Atlantic. It's the must-do day trip from Lisbon. Go early in the day midweek to escape the worst of the crowds.

◉ Sights

Castelo dos Mouros   CASTLE
(www.parquesdesintra.pt; adult/child €8/6.50; ⊙10am-6pm) Soaring 412m above sea level, this mist-enshrouded ruined castle looms high above the surrounding forest. When the clouds peel away, the vistas over Sintra's palace-dotted hill and dale to the glittering Atlantic are – like the climb – breathtaking.

★**Quinta da Regaleira**   NOTABLE BUILDING, GARDENS
(www.regaleira.pt; Rua Barbosa du Bocage; adult/child €6/3; ⊙10am-8pm high season, shorter hours in low season) This magical villa and gardens is a neo-Manueline extravaganza, dreamed up by Italian opera-set designer, Luigi Manini, under the orders of Brazilian coffee tycoon, António Carvalho Monteiro, aka Monteiro dos Milhões (Moneybags Monteiro). The villa is surprisingly homely inside, despite its ferociously carved fireplaces, frescoes and Venetian glass mosaics. Keep an eye out for mythological and Knights Templar symbols.

Palácio Nacional de Sintra   PALACE
(www.parquesdesintra.pt; Largo Rainha Dona Amélia; adult/child €10/8.50; ⊙9.30am-7pm, shorter hours in low season) The star of Sintra-Vila is this palace, with its iconic twin conical chimneys and lavish interior. The whimsical interior is a mix of Moorish and Manueline styles, with arabesque courtyards, barley-twist columns and 15th- and 16th-century geometric *azulejos* (hand-painted tiles) that figure among Portugal's oldest.

🛏 Sleeping & Eating

★ Moon Hill Hostel
HOSTEL €

(📞 219 243 755; www.moonhillhostel.com; Rua Guilherme Gomes Fernandes 19; dm €19, d with/without bathroom €89/59; ✳@🛜) 🐾 This design-forward, minimalist newcomer easily outshines the Sintra competition. Whether you book a boutique hotel-level private room, with colourful reclaimed wood headboards and wall-covering photos of enchanting Sintra forest scenes (go for 10 or 14 for Pena National Palace views, 12 or 13 for Moorish castle views) or a four-bed mixed dorm with lockers, you are sleeping in high style.

There's a modern shared kitchen, bar, courtyard, Portuguese fusion restaurant (mains €11 to €15) and, as if that all wasn't enough, it's perfectly situated in the middle of the Vila. Best in show!

Fábrica das Verdadeiras Queijadas da Sapa
PATISSERIE €

(www.facebook.com/queijadasdasapa; Alameda Volta do Duche 12; pastries from €0.85; ⊙9am-6pm Tue-Fri, 9.30am-6.30pm Sat & Sun) Fábrica das Verdadeiras Queijadas da Sapa has been rotting the teeth of royalty since 1756 with bite-sized *queijadas* – crisp pastry shells filled with a marzipan-like mix of fresh cheese, sugar, flour and cinnamon. Take a six-pack to go for €4.20.

Tulhas
PORTUGUESE €€

(Rua Gil Vicente 4; mains €10-18; ⊙noon-11pm, to 10pm winter; 🛜) This converted grain warehouse is dark, tiled and quaint, with wrought-iron chandeliers and a relaxed, cosy atmosphere. It's rightfully renowned for its *bacalhau com natas* (creamy bechamel with shredded cod, served au gratin) but the tasty *arroz de pato* (duck rice) is worth your consideration as well.

ℹ Information

Ask Me Sintra (Turismo; 📞 219 231 157; www.askmelisboa.com/sintra; Praça da Republica 23; ⊙9.30am-6pm) Near the centre of Sintra-Vila, Turismo de Lisboa's helpful multilingual office has expert insight into Sintra. There's also a small branch at the train station (📞 211 932 545; ⊙10am-noon & 2.30-6pm), often overrun by arriving visitors.

ℹ Getting There & Away

Trains (€2.15, 40 minutes) run every 15 minutes between Sintra and Lisbon's Rossio station. From Sintra station, it's a pleasant 1km walk (or short bus ride) into the village. Regular buses head from Sintra to Cascais (€4.10, one hour).

Cascais
POP 35,000

Cascais (kush-*kaish*) has rocketed from sleepy fishing village to much-loved summertime playground of wave-frolicking *lisboêtas* ever since King Luís I went for a dip in 1870. Its trio of golden bays attracts sun-worshipping holidaymakers, who come to splash in the ice-cold Atlantic. Don't expect to get much sand to yourself at the weekend, though.

👁 Sights & Activities

Cascais' three sandy bays – Praia da Conceição, Praia da Rainha and Praia da Ribeira – are fine for a sunbake or a tingly Atlantic dip, but there's not much towel space in summer.

The best beach is wild, windswept Praia do Guincho, 9km northwest, a mecca to surfers and windsurfers with massive crashing rollers, powder-soft sands, fresh seafood and magical sunsets.

You will find **Moana Surf School** (📞 964 449 436; www.moanasurfschool.com; Estrada do Abano, Praia do Guincho; private lessons per hour €40, group lesson €25, 4-lesson course €85) at Wave Center next door to Bar do Gunicho.

Boca do Inferno
VIEWPOINT

Atlantic waves pummel craggy Boca do Inferno (Mouth of Hell), 2km west of Cascais. It's about a 20-minute walk along the coast, or you can catch the BusCas (427) from Cascais Station (€1, every 10 to 15 minutes). Expect a mouthful of small splashes unless a storm is raging.

🛏 Sleeping & Eating

Perfect Spot Lisbon
HOSTEL €

(📞 924 058 643; www.perfectspot-lisbon.com; Avenida de Sintra 354; 3/4/7-day packages from €155/205/365; P🛜) New parents Jon and Rita run this lovely hostel – perfect for families in addition to surfers and climbers – in a large home just a smidgen outside the tourist zone. Spacious rooms and dorms are themed with unique art, but the real coup is the closed-in garden, a supreme hang space with day beds and a BBQ lounge.

Perhaps unfortunately, they work with all-inclusive three-day minimum-activity and cultural packages (check-ins on Monday

WALKING THE ALGARVE

If you like a good walk, by far the best way to appreciate the magnificent landscapes of inland Algarve is to hike part (or all) of the **Via Algarviana** (www.viaalgarviana.org). This 300km trail crosses the region from northeast to southwest. Some of the most beautiful sections are around Monchique, where splendid vistas open up as you climb through cork groves to the Algarve's highest hilltops.

and Friday only), so independent travellers are shut out (at time of writing, anyway).

★**Café Galeria
House of Wonders**   CAFE **€€**
(www.facebook.com/houseofwonders; Largo da Misericordia 53; buffet 1/2 people €14.95/24.50, light meals €2.50-9.75; ☉10am-midnight; 🛜🍴) 🍴 You'll find this fantastically whimsical, Dutch-owned cafe tucked away in the old quarter. It serves an astonishingly good Middle Eastern/Mediterranean vegetarian meze buffet downstairs amid a warm, welcoming ambience and an artwork-filled interior. Upstairs, you'll find set plates of similar food for €6.95 as well as delightful cakes, juices, cocktails and coffee, which can be taken on the rustic rooftop terrace.

★**Bar do Guincho**   PORTUGUESE **€€**
(www.bardoguincho.pt; Estrada do Abano, Praia do Guincho; mains €8.50-17.50; ☉noon-7pm Sun & Tue-Thu, noon-midnight Fri-Sat, to late Jul-Aug; 🛜) Sweeping the awards for most dramatic location in Cascais, this good-time bar/restaurant sits tucked behind a craggy ridge on the northern end of Guincho. From the sand, you would never know it's there, but it is – *and it is packed!* Revellers rake in the beach-friendly burgers, seafood and salads washed down with cold *cerveja*. Settle in for the afternoon.

❶ Information

Ask Me Cascais (Turismo; 📞912 034 214; www.visitcascais.com; Largo Cidade Vitória; ☉9am-8pm summer, to 6pm winter) The official Cascais tourist information booth has a handy map and an events guide *(What's In Cascais)*, and is helpful to an extent.

❶ Getting There & Away

Bus 417 goes about hourly from Cascais to Sintra (€4.10, 40 minutes).

Trains run from Lisbon's Cais do Sodré station to Cascais (€2.15, 40 minutes, every 20 to 30 minutes).

The Algarve

The Algarve is alluring. Coastal Algarve receives much exposure for its breathtaking cliffs, golden beaches, scalloped bays and sandy islands. But the letter 'S' (for sun, surf and sand) is only one letter in the Algarvian alphabet: activities, beach bars (and discos), castles (both sandy and real), diving, entertainment, fun...

Faro

POP 50,000

Algarve's capital has a more distinctly Portuguese feel than most resort towns. Many visitors only pass through this underrated city which is a pity as it makes for an enjoyable stopover. It has an attractive marina, well-maintained parks and plazas, and a historic old town full of pedestrian lanes and outdoor cafes. Its student population of 8000 ensures a happening nightlife.

❂ Sights & Activities

★**Sé**   CATHEDRAL
(www.paroquiasedefaro.org; Largo da Sé; adult/child €3.50/free; ☉10am-6.30pm Mon-Fri, 9.30am-1pm Sat Jun-Aug, slightly shorter hours Sep-May) The centrepiece of the Cidade Velha, the *sé* was

Faro

◉ **Top Sights**

➊ **Activities, Courses & Tours**

🛏 **Sleeping**

🍴 **Eating**

🍷 **Drinking & Nightlife**

completed in 1251, but heavily damaged in the 1755 earthquake. What you see now is a variety of Renaissance, Gothic and baroque features. Climb the tower for lovely views across the walled town and estuary islands. The cathedral also houses the **Museu Capitular**, with an assortment of chalices, priestly vestments and grisly relics (including both forearms of St Boniface) and a small 18th-century shrine built of bones.

★**Igreja de Nossa Senhora do Carmo & Capela dos Ossos** CHURCH
(Largo do Carmo; €3.50; ⊙10am-6.30pm Mon-Fri, 9.30am-1pm Sat, last admission 1hr before clos-

ing time, mass 7pm Mon-Fri, 6pm Sat, 10am Sun) This twin-towered baroque church was completed in 1719 under João V. The spectacular facade was completed after the 1755 earthquake. Brazilian gold paid for it, and the interior is gilded to the extreme. The numerous cherubs here seem comparatively serious and sober; they're no doubt contemplating the ghoulish attraction behind the church: the 19th-century Capela dos Ossos, built from the bones and skulls of over 1000 monks as a blackly reverent reminder of earthly impermanence. It's quite a sight.

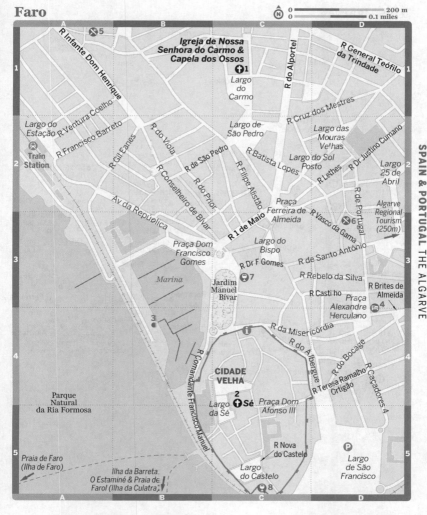

Faro

SPAIN & PORTUGAL THE ALGARVE

★ **Formosamar**   BOAT TOUR
(☑ 918 720 002; www.formosamar.com; Clube Naval, Faro Marina) 🖉 This recommended outfit genuinely embraces and promotes environmentally responsible tourism. Among the excellent tours it provides are two-hour birdwatching trips around the Parque Natural da Ria Formosa (€25), dolphin-watching (€45), and cycling tours (€37), and a two-hour small-boat trip that penetrates some of the narrower channels in the lagoon (€25). All trips have a minimum number of participants (usually two or three). It also runs kayaking trips and hires kayaks and bikes. It has departures from Olhão and Tavira, too, and various ticket offices around the Faro waterfront.

🛏 Sleeping

★ **Casa d'Alagoa**   HOSTEL €
(☑ 289 813 252; www.farohostel.com; Praça Alexandre Herculano 27; dm not incl breakfast €22-30, d €80; 🗟) Housed in a renovated mansion on a pretty square, this commendable budget option has all the elements of today's sophisticated hostel: it's funky, laid-back and cool (and clean!). Casa d'Alagoa boasts a range of spacious dorms, a great lounge and an upstairs terrace. There's a communal kitchen...

The Algarve

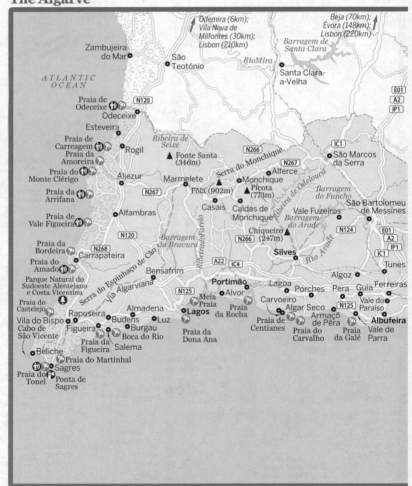

but hey, why do you need it when dinner is on offer? Bike rental also available.

A Doca
GUESTHOUSE €

(📞 289 820 716; www.residencialadoca.com; Rua 1 de Maio 21; s/d €40/50; 🕸🛜) This superbly run, spotless guesthouse does the basics well – the wi-fi signal is strong, the beds are comfortable and there are staff on hand 24 hours a day. Rooms are small with the double beds filling them out and the showers could run a little hotter in winter but the location near the waterfront is superb. Handy coffee machine at reception.

🍴 Eating & Drinking

Chefe Branco
PORTUGUESE €

(Rua de Loulé 9; mains €4.50-13.50; 🕒 noon-11pm) A fabulous local spot with appealing street-side seating and a slightly tacky but cosy interior. The delightful staff serve honest, homestyle fare including rabbit, goat and seafood dishes. The half portions are the biggest this side of the Rio Tejo. Finish off with an excellent Algarvian dessert.

Gengibre e Canela
VEGETARIAN €

(Travessa da Mota 10; buffet €7.50; 🕒 noon-3pm Mon-Sat, groups only evenings; 🛜📝) Give the

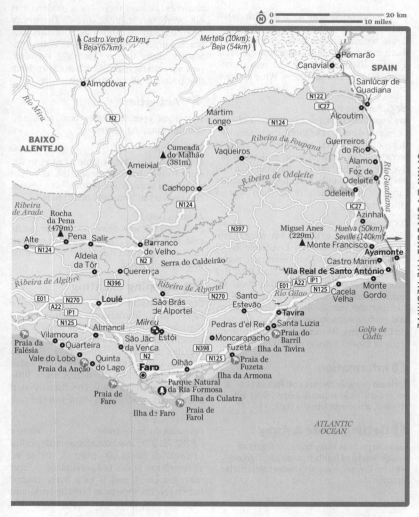

SPAIN & PORTUGAL THE ALGARVE

PARQUE NATURAL DA RIA FORMOSA

Ria Formosa Natural Park (www.icnf.pt) is mostly a lagoon system stretching for 60km along the Algarve coastline and encompassing 180 sq km, from west of Faro to Cacela Velha. It encloses a vast area of *sapal* (marsh), *salinas* (salt pans), creeks and dune islands, great for exploring by boat or kayak from Faro or other towns along the coast.

taste buds a break from meat and fish dishes and veg out (literally) at this Zen-like vegetarian restaurant. The buffet changes daily; there may be vegetable lasagne, vegetarian *feijoada* (bean casserole) and tofu dishes, but only the occasional curry. Wine and desserts are extra.

★**Columbus Bar** BAR
(www.barcolumbus.pt; Praça Dom Francisco Gomes 13; ⊘noon-4am; 🛜) Definitely the place to be, this popular central place has a streetside terrace in the heart of town and an attractive brick-vaulted interior. Bar staff do a fine job mixing cocktails, and there's a pleasing range of spirits. Gets lively from around 11pm onwards.

O Castelo BAR
(Rua do Castelo 11; ⊘10.30am-4am winter, 10am-4am summer Wed-Mon; 🛜) O Castelo is all things to all people: a bar, restaurant, nightclub and performance space. Start your day here with a coffee, grab a light meal for lunch or take in sunset over a cocktail. In summer the outside morphs into a party and performance space, and there are regular fado nights. Its location atop the historic walls of the old town is superb.

❶ Information

Turismo (www.visitalgarve.pt; Rua da Misericórdia 8; ⊘9am-1pm & 2-6pm) Busy but efficient office with friendly staff.

❶ Getting There & Away

Faro's airport has many domestic flights as well as dozens of flights from airports around Western Europe, many with budget and charter airlines.

Bus services run to Seville in Spain (€20, 3½ hours, four daily) and to Lisbon (€20, five hours, at least hourly).

There are three direct trains from Lisbon daily (€21.20 to €22.20, 3¾ hours) and connections to Porto. Locally, destinations include Lagos (€7.30, 1¾ hours, hourly).

Lagos
POP 22,000

As far as touristy towns go, Lagos *(lah-goosh)* has got the lot. It lies along the bank of the Rio Bensafrim, with 16th-century walls enclosing the old town's pretty, cobbled lanes and picturesque piazzas and churches. Beyond these lies a modern, but not overly unattractive, sprawl. The town's good restaurants and range of fabulous beaches nearby add to the allure. With every activity under the sun (literally) on offer, plus a pumping nightlife, it's not surprising that people of all ages are drawn here.

🏃 Activities

Numerous operators offer boat trips and dolphin-watching excursions.

Meia Praia BEACH
Meia Praia, the vast expanse of sand to the east of town, has outlets offering sailboard rental and waterskiing lessons, plus several laid-back restaurants and beach bars.

Algarve Dolphins BOAT TOUR
(📞282 788 513; www.algarve-dolphins.com; adult/child from €35/25) Offers dolphin-spotting trips in zippy rigid inflatables with marine biologists on board.

🛌 Sleeping & Eating

Old Town Hostel HOSTEL €
(📞282 087 221; Rua da Barroca 70; dm €23; @🛜) If you're in town to party, this highly rated hostel is the place to sleep it all off during the day. Located in atmospheric Rua da Barroca, it has a kitchen, terrace and small common room, but the dorms are a little cramped and often full. The friendly staff are more than willing to show you the best bars.

Pousada da Juventude HOSTEL €
(📞282 761 970; www.pousadasjuventude.pt; Rua Lançarote de Freitas 50; dm/d €17/45; @🛜) This well-run hostel is a good place to meet other travellers, and is in a lively, central bar street. It's sometime brutally basic and slightly worn, thanks to its popularity, but

Lagos

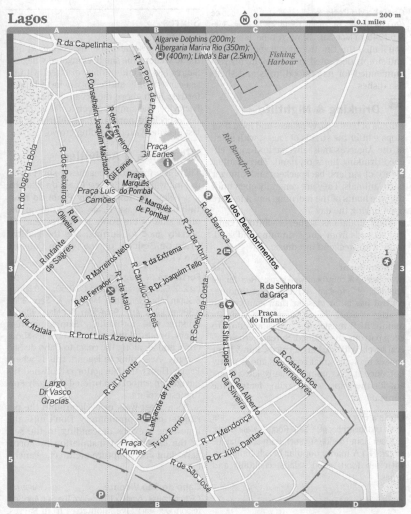

Algarve Dolphins (200m);
Albergaria Marina Rio (350m);
(400m); Linda's Bar (2.5km)

there's a kitchen and pleasantly sunny courtyard to chill in. Reception is very helpful and open 24 hours.

⭐ **A Forja** PORTUGUESE €€
(📞 282 768 588; Rua dos Ferreiros 17; mains €8-17.50; ⏱ noon-3pm & 6.30-10pm Sun-Fri) Like an Italian trattoria, this buzzing *adega tipica* pulls in the crowds – locals, tourists and expats – for its hearty, top-quality traditional food served in a bustling environment at great prices. Plates of the day are always reliable, as are the simply prepared fish dishes.

Lagos

Activities, Courses & Tours

1 Meia Praia	....	D3

Sleeping

2 Old Town Hostel	....	C3
3 Pousada da Juventude	....	B5

Eating

4 A Forja	....	B2
5 Casinha do Petisco	....	B3

Drinking & Nightlife

6 Bon Vivant	....	C3

Casinha do Petisco
SEAFOOD €€

(Rua da Oliveira 51; mains €8-14.50; ⊙10am-3pm & 6-10.45pm Mon-Sat) Blink (or be late) and you'll miss this tiny traditional gem. It's cosy and simply decorated and comes highly recommended for its seafood grills and shellfish dishes.

Drinking & Nightlife

Dozens of bars – party palaces and local beer stops – litter the streets of Lagos, with some of the Algarve's most diverse and most clichéd drinking holes on hand. These gather plenty of surfers, backpackers and younger party animals. They are generally open until the wee hours of the morning, and a few are open during the day.

Meia Praia has some beachfront gems just seconds from sun, swimming and sand, some with weekend live music.

★ Bon Vivant
BAR

(www.facebook.com/bonvivant.lagos; Rua 25 de Abril 105; ⊙2pm-4am; 🛜) This longstanding, central bar is far classier than some of the nearby options, takes some care over its mainly R&B music, and makes an effort to keep patrons entertained. Spread across several levels with various terraces, Bon Vivant shakes up some great cocktails and is pretty hot once it gets going (usually late). Look out for the impressive juggling feats of the bar staff.

Linda's Bar
BAR

(www.lindabeachbar.pt; São Roque, Meia Praia; ⊙10am-11pm Thu-Tue summer, 11am-6pm Thu-Tue winter; 🛜) A madly popular beach hang-out, with fab food, good salads, cocktails and tunes.

ⓘ Information

Turismo (✆282 763 031; www.visitalgarve.pt; Praça Gil Eanes; ⊙9am-7pm Jul & Aug, to 6pm Easter-Jun & Sep, to 5pm Oct-Easter) The very helpful staff offer excellent maps and leaflets.

ⓘ Getting There & Away

Buses services include Lisbon (€20, four hours, 10 expresses daily) and Sagres (€3.85, one hour, nearly hourly on weekdays, nine on Saturday and Sunday).

Lagos is at the western end of the Algarve train line, and has services to Faro (€7.30, 1¾ hours, nine daily) and, with a change, Lisbon (€22.70, four hours, five daily).

Sagres
POP 1940

Overlooking some of the Algarve's most dramatic scenery, the small, elongated village of Sagres has an end-of-the-world feel with its sea-carved cliffs and empty, wind-whipped fortress high above the ocean. It has a laid-back vibe, and simple, cheery cafes and bars. It's especially popular, particularly in the last decade, with the surfing crowd.

Sights & Activities

There are four good beaches a short drive or long walk from Sagres: **Praia da Mareta**, just below the town; lovely **Praia do Martinhal** to the east; **Praia do Tonel** on the other side of the Ponta de Sagres, and especially good for surfing; and the isolated **Praia de Beliche**, on the way to Cabo de São Vicente.

Fortaleza de Sagres
FORT

(✆282 620 140; adult/child €3/1.50; ⊙9.30am-6.30pm Apr, 9am-8pm May-Jun & Sep, 9am-8.30pm Jul & Aug, 9am-5pm Oct-Mar) Blank, hulking and forbidding, Sagres' fortress offers breathtaking views over the sheer cliffs, and all along the coast to Cabo de São Vicente. According to legend, this is where Prince Henry the Navigator established his navigation school and primed the early Portuguese explorers.

It's a great walk or cycle around the perimeter of the promontory. Don't miss the limestone crevices descending to the sea, or the labyrinth art installation by Portugal's famous sculpture-architect, Pancho Guedes.

Cabo de São Vicente
LANDMARK

(⊙lighthouse complex 10am-6pm Tue-Sun Apr-Sep, to 5pm Oct-Mar) Five kilometres from Sagres, Europe's southwesternmost point is a barren headland, the last piece of home that Portuguese sailors once saw as they launched into the unknown. It's a spectacular spot: at sunset you can almost hear the hissing as the sun hits the sea. The red **lighthouse** houses the small, but excellent, **Museu dos Faróis** (adult/child €1.50/1; ⊙10am-6pm Tue-Sun Apr-Sep, to 5pm Oct-Mar), showcasing Sagres' role in Portugal's maritime history.

Sagres Natura
SURFING

(✆282 624 072; www.sagresnatura.com; Rua São Vicente) This recommended surf school also rents out bodyboards (€15 per day), surfboards (€20) and wetsuits (€10). It also offers bikes for hire (€10) and the same company runs a surf equipment shop and hostel.

★ **Mar Ilimitado** · BOAT TOUR
(✆916 832 625; www.marilimitado.com; Porto da Baleeira) *✍* Mar Ilimitado, a team of marine biologists, offers a variety of highly recommended, ecologically sound boat trips, from dolphin-spotting (€35; 1½ hours) and seabird-watching (€45, 2½ hours) to excursions up to Cabo de São Vicente (€25, one hour).

🛏 Sleeping

Casa do Cabo de Santa Maria · GUESTHOUSE €€
(✆282 624 722; www.casadocabodesantamaria.com; Rua Patrão António Faustino; d €60-80, apt €80-120; ⓟ�☎) These squeaky-clean, welcoming rooms and apartments might not have sweeping views, but they are handsome and nicely furnished. Excellent value (breakfast not included).

🍴 Eating & Drinking

★ **A Casínha** · PORTUGUESE €€
(✆917 768 917; www.facebook.com/acasinha.restaurantesagres; Rua de São Vicente; mains €13-19; ⊙12.30-3pm & 7-10.30pm Tue-Sat, closed Jan & Feb) This cosy terracotta-and-white spot – built on the site of the owner's grandparents' house – serves up some fabulous Portuguese cuisine, including standout barbecued fish, a good variety of *cataplanas* (seafood stew) for two (€34) and *arroz de polvo* (octopus rice). High quality, with a pleasant atmosphere.

A Sagres · PORTUGUESE €€
(✆282 624 171; www.restaurenteasagres.com; Avenida Infante Dom Henrique; mains €8-15; ⊙lunch & dinner Thu-Tue) This popular local restaurant offers great fish (such as *massinha do mar* for two, €28) and grilled meat fare that won't break the bank. It's on the roundabout as you turn off to the fort.

Agua Salgada · BAR
(✆282 624 297; Rua Comandante Matoso; ⊙10am-late; ☎) Situated in a strip of cafebars, Agua Salgada has good crêpes and is one of the liveliest at night, with DJs and a party mood.

❶ Getting There & Away

Buses come from Lagos (€3.40, one hour, around 12 daily). On weekends there are fewer services.

OFF THE BEATEN TRACK

BEACHES OF THE WESTERN ALGARVE

Heading north along the Algarve's western coast you'll find some amazing beaches, backed by beautiful wild vegetation. Thanks to building restrictions imposed to protect the **Parque Natural do Sudoeste Alentejano e Costa Vicentina**, it's relatively unspoiled and well preserved. Although the seas can be dangerous, the area has a growing reputation for some of Europe's finest surf and attracts people from all over the world. If you like pristine sand and wild sea, these are some of Europe's most sublime beaches. Aljezur, Carrapateira and Odeceixe are the main bases: small, pretty towns with cheap lodging and eating options.

Évora
POP 41,000

One of Portugal's most beautifully preserved medieval towns, Évora is an enchanting place to delve into the past. Inside the 14th-century walls, Évora's narrow, winding lanes lead to striking architectural works: an elaborate medieval cathedral and cloisters; the cinematic columns of the Templo Romano (near the intriguing Roman baths); and a picturesque town square, once the site of some rather gruesome episodes courtesy of the Inquisition. Aside from its historic and aesthetic virtues, Évora is also a lively university town, and its many attractive restaurants serve up hearty Alentejan cuisine.

◉ Sights

Sé · CATHEDRAL
(Largo do Marquês de Marialva; €1.50, with cloister & towers €3.50, with museum €4.50; ⊙9am-noon & 2-4.30pm) Guarded by a pair of rose granite towers, Évora's fortress-like medieval cathedral has fabulous cloisters and a museum jam-packed with ecclesiastical treasures.

Templo Romano · RUIN
(Temple of Diana; Largo do Conde de Vila Flor) Once part of the Roman Forum, the remains of this temple dating from the 2nd or early 3rd century are a heady slice of drama right in town. It's among the best-preserved Roman monuments in Portugal, and probably on

the Iberian Peninsula. Though it's commonly referred to as the Temple of Diana, there's no consensus about the deity to which it was dedicated, and some archaeologists believe it may have been dedicated to Julius Caesar.

⟐ Sleeping & Eating

★ Hostel Namaste   HOSTEL €
(☎266 743 014; www.hostelnamasteevora.pt; Largo Doutor Manuel Alves Branco 12; dm/s/d €17/30/45; ☎) Maria and Carla Sofia are the kind souls that run these welcoming digs in the historic Arabic quarter. Rooms are bright, spotlessly clean and decorated with splashes of art and colour, and there's a lounge, library, kitchen and bike hire. Breakfast costs an extra €4.

Dom Joaquim   PORTUGUESE €€
(☎266 731 105; www.restaurantedomjoaquim.pai.pt; Rua dos Penedos 6; mains €14-17; ⊙noon-3pm & 7-10.45pm Tue-Sat, noon-3pm Sun) Amid stone walls and modern artwork, Dom Joaquim serves excellent traditional cuisine including meats (game and succulent, fall-off-the-bone lamb) and seafood dishes, such as caçao (dogfish).

❶ Information

Turismo (☎266 777 071; www.visitalentejo.pt; Praça do Giraldo 73; ⊙9am-7pm Apr-Sep, 9am-6pm Oct-Mar) This helpful, central tourist office dishes out a great town map.

❶ Getting There & Away

The bus station is west of town. Destinations include Coimbra (€19, 4½ hours), Faro (€18, four hours) and Lisbon (€12.40, 1½ to two hours).

The train station is outside the walls, 600m south of the jardim público (public garden). There are daily trains to/from Lisbon (€12.80, 1½ hours, four daily), Lagos (€31.60, 4½ to five hours, three daily) and Faro (€29.90, four to five hours, two daily).

Óbidos

POP 3100

Surrounded by a classic crenellated wall, Óbidos' gorgeous historic centre is a labyrinth of cobblestoned streets and flower-bedecked, whitewashed houses livened up with dashes of vivid yellow and blue paint. It's a delightful place to pass an afternoon, but there are plenty of reasons to stay overnight.

⊙ Sights

Igreja de Santa Maria   CHURCH
(Praça de Santa Maria; ⊙9.30am-12.30pm & 2.30-7pm summer, to 5pm winter) The town's elegant main church, near the northern end of Rua Direita, stands out for its interior, with a wonderful painted ceiling and walls done up in beautiful blue-and-white 17th-century azulejos. Paintings by the renowned 17th-century painter Josefa de Óbidos are to the right of the altar. There's a fine 16th-century Renaissance tomb on the left, probably carved by French sculptor Nicolas Chanterène.

⟐ Sleeping & Eating

Hostel Argonauta   HOSTEL €
(☎963 824 178, 262 958 088; Rua Adelaide Ribeirete 14; dm/d €25/50; ☎) In a pretty spot just outside the walls, this feels more like a friend's place than a hostel. Run with good cheer, it has an arty, colourful dorm with wood-stove heating and beds as well as bunks; there's also a cute double with a great view. The small capacity means it's a great personal, sociable experience. Breakfast is included.

Senhor da Pedra   PORTUGUESE €
(Largo do Santuário; mains €6-9; ⊙noon-3pm & 7-10pm Mon-Sat, noon-3pm Sun) Behind the striking church of Senhor da Pedra below town, this simple white-tiled eatery (the one on the right as you look at the row of restaurants) is a recommended place to try low-priced authentic Portuguese cuisine. It's a classic affair with Mum in the kitchen, and Dad and the boy on tables. The name isn't signed – it just says 'Snack Bar', but if these are snacks, we'd hate to see what is considered a full meal.

❶ Information

Turismo (☎262 959 231; www.obidos.pt; ⊙9.30am-7.30pm daily May-Sep, 9.30am-6pm Mon-Fri, 9.30am-12.30pm & 1.30-5.30pm Sat & Sun Oct-Apr) Just outside Porta da Vila, near the bus stop, with helpful multilingual staff offering town brochures and maps in four languages.

❶ Getting There & Away

There are at least six daily trains to Lisbon (€8.45 to €9.30, 2½ hours) mostly via connections at Mira Sintra-Meleças station on the suburban Lisbon line. It's a pretty but uphill walk to town.

Buses run hourly on weekdays to Lisbon (€8.15, one hour), plus five on Saturday and Sunday.

Nazaré

POP 10,500

With a warren of narrow, cobbled lanes running down to a wide, cliff-backed beach, Nazaré is a picturesque coastal resort. The sands are packed in summer; for a different perspective, take the funicular up to Promontório do Sítio, where picture-postcard coastal views unfold from the cliffs.

Nazaré has hit the headlines in recent years for the monster waves that roll in just north of town and the record-breaking feats of the gutsy surfers that ride them.

Sights & Activities

Promontório do Sítio   HISTORIC SITE

Until the 18th century the sea covered the present-day site of Nazaré; locals lived at this clifftop area 110m above the beach. Today this tourist-filled promontory is popular for its tremendous views and its religious associations. From Rua do Elevador, north of the *turismo*, an **ascensor** (Funicular; adult/child €1.20/0.90; ⊗7.30am-8.30pm winter, to 2am summer) climbs up the hill to Promontório do Sítio; it's nice to walk back down, escaping the crowds of trinket-sellers. There are plenty of places to stay and eat up on the clifftop too.

Festivals & Events

Carnaval   MARDI GRAS

One of Portugal's brashest Mardi Gras celebrations, with lots of costumed parades and general irreverence. Lots of people dress up and the nights go loud and long.

Sleeping & Eating

★**Vila Conde Fidalgo** GUESTHOUSE, APARTMENT €
(⊋262 552 361; www.facebook.com/VilaCondeFidalgo; Avenida da Independência Nacional 21a;

WORTH A TRIP

THE MONASTERY CIRCUIT

Three extraordinary monasteries are in fairly close proximity in central Portugal and make very rewarding visits from the coast or on the way between the south and north.

Mosteiro de Santa Maria de Alcobaça (⊋262 505 120; www.mosteiroalcobaca.pt; church free, monastery adult/child/family €6, with Tomar & Batalha €15; ⊗9am-5pm Apr-Sep, 9am-5.30pm Oct-Mar) One of Iberia's great monasteries, this utterly dominates the town of Alcobaça. Hiding behind the imposing baroque facade lies a high, austere, monkish church with a forest of unadorned 12th-century arches. But make sure you visit the rest too: the atmospheric refectory, vast dormitory and other spaces bring back the Cistercian life, which, according to sources, wasn't quite as austere here as it should have been.

Batalha (⊋244 765 497; www.mosteirobatalha.pt; church free, rest adult/child €6/free, with Alcobaça & Tomar €15; ⊗9am-6.30pm Apr-Sep, 9am-6pm Oct-Mar) This extraordinary abbey nearby was built to commemorate the 1385 Battle of Aljubarrota (fought just south of here). Most of the monument was completed by 1434 in Flamboyant Gothic, but Manueline exuberance steals the show, thanks to additions made in the 15th and 16th centuries.

Convento de Cristo (www.conventocristo.pt; Rua Castelo dos Templários; adult/child under 12 €6/free; ⊗9am-6.30pm Apr-Sep, 9am-5.30pm Oct-May) The larger town of Tomar is dominated from above by this monastery. Wrapped in splendour and mystery, the Knights Templar held enormous power in Portugal from the 12th to 16th centuries, and largely bankrolled the Age of Discoveries. Their headquarters sit on wooded slopes above the town and enclosed within 12th-century walls. The monastery is a stony expression of magnificence, founded in 1160 by Gualdim Pais, Grand Master of the Templars. It has chapels, cloisters and choirs in diverging styles, added over the centuries by successive kings and Grand Masters. The Charola, an extraordinary 16-sided Templar church, thought to be in imitation of the Church of the Holy Sepulchre in Jerusalem dominates the complex.

Batalha and Alcobaça are easily accessible by bus from each other and from Nazaré, while Tomar is reachable via a change from either.

d/apt €50/65; 🕿) Built around a series of flower-strewn courtyards and patios, this pretty family-run complex a few blocks up from the beach was a former fishermen's colony. Friendly manager Ana offers 10 clean, colourful and comfortable rooms with mini-fridges, plus a dozen apartments of varying sizes. Breakfast is €5 extra, served in your room or on the terrace outside.

⭐**A Tasquinha**   SEAFOOD €
(✆262 551 945; Rua Adrião Batalha 54; mains €7-11; ⊙noon-3pm & 7-10.30pm Tue-Sun) This exceptionally friendly family affair serves high-quality seafood in a pair of snug but pretty tiled dining rooms. Expect queues on summer nights.

However many people there are, the delightful owners always try and squeeze you in, even if it's at someone else's table! Top value.

❶ Information

Turismo (✆262 561 194; www.cm-nazare.pt; Avenida Vieira Giumarães, Edifício do Mercado Municipal; ⊙9.30am-1pm & 2.30-6pm Oct-Mar, 9.30am-12.30pm & 2.30-6.30pm Apr-Jun, 9am-9pm Jul & Aug) On the beachfront strip, in the cultural centre in the old fish market.

❶ Getting There & Away

Regular buses serve surrounding towns as well as Lisbon (€11.50, 1¾ hours).

Coimbra

POP 101,500

The medieval capital of Portugal for over a hundred years, and site of the country's greatest university, Coimbra's atmospheric, beautiful historic core cascades down a hillside in a lovely setting on the east bank of the Rio Mondego. If you visit during the academic year, you'll be sure to feel the university's influence. Students throng bars and cafes; posters advertise talks on everything from genetics to genocide; and graffiti scrawled outside *repúblicas* (communal student dwellings) address the political issues of the day.

◉ Sights

⭐**Museu Nacional de Machado de Castro**   MUSEUM
(✆239 853 070; www.museumachadocastro. pt; Largo Dr José Rodrigues; adult/child €6/free, cryptoportico only €3, with audioguide €7.50;

⊙2-6pm Tue, 10am-7pm Wed-Sun Apr-Sep, to 6pm Wed-Sun Oct-Mar) This great museum is a highlight of central Portugal. It's fitting that it has become a real centre of the local community, with people gathering to admire the views from its patio and cafe, for it's built over the Roman forum, the remains of which you can see. The artistic collection is wide-ranging and superb.

⭐**Universidade de Coimbra**   UNIVERSITY
(✆239 242 744; www.uc.pt/en/informacaopara/ visit/paco; adult/student €9/7, audio guide €3, tower €1; ⊙9am-7.30pm daily mid-Mar–Oct, 9.30am-1pm & 2-5.30pm Nov–mid-Mar) In every way the city's high point, the Old University consists of a series of remarkable 16th- to 18th-century buildings, all set around the vast **Patio des Escolas**, entered by way of the elegant 17th-century **Porta Férrea**, which occupies the same site as the main gate to Coimbra's Moorish stronghold. The highlight is the magnificent library.

Biblioteca Joanina   LIBRARY
(João V Library; ✆239 859 818; Universidade de Coimbra; ⊙9am-7.30pm daily mid-Mar–Oct, 9.30am-1pm & 2-5.30pm Nov–mid-Mar) The Old University's library, a gift from João V in the early 18th century, seems too extravagant and distracting for study with its rosewood, ebony and jacaranda tables, elaborately frescoed ceilings and gilt chinoiserie bookshelves. Its 300,000 ancient books deal with law, philosophy and theology. A lower floor has more tomes and the Prisão Acadêmica, a lock-up for misbehaving students.

⭐**Sé Velha**   CATHEDRAL
(Old Cathedral; ✆239 825 273; www.sevelha-coimbra.org; Largo da Sé Velha, Rua do Norte 4; €2.50; ⊙10am-6pm Mon-Sat, 1-6pm Sun) Coimbra's stunning 12th-century cathedral is one of Portugal's finest examples of Romanesque architecture. The main portal and facade are exceptionally striking. Its crenellated exterior and narrow, slit-like lower windows serve as reminders of the nation's embattled early days, when the Moors were still a threat. These buildings were designed to be useful as fortresses in times of trouble.

🛏 Sleeping

⭐**Serenata Hostel**   HOSTEL €
(✆239 853 130; www.serenatahostel.com; Largo da Sé Velha 21; dm/d without bathroom €15/38, d/ste/f €49/55/79; 🕿) In the pretty heart of the old town, this noble building with an in-

Central Coimbra

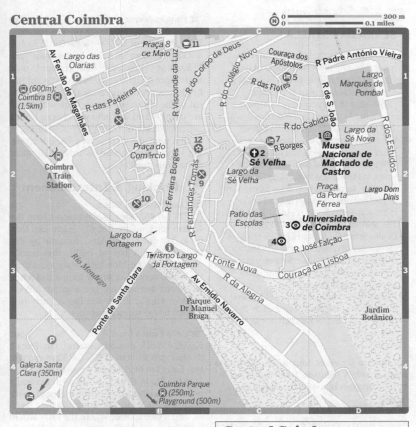

triguingly varied history is now a fabulous hostel, chock-full of modern comforts and facilities while maintaining a period feel in keeping with this historic zone. Great lounge areas, a cute secluded sun terrace, several computers, spacious dorms, friendly staff and a modern kitchen complete a very happy picture. Prices are often lower than listed here.

Riversuites   HOTEL €
(☑ 239 440 582; www.riversuites.pt; Av João das Regras 82; d €44-55, tr/q €69/79; ﹡🖥) Just across the bridge from the centre, this excellent hotel has slick, modern rooms (not suites) and comforts. A decent breakfast is included, and the showers are just great.

Casa Pombal   GUESTHOUSE €€
(☑ 239 835 175; www.casapombal.com; Rua das Flores 18; s with/without bathroom €55/40, d with/without bathroom €65/54; @🖥) In a lovely old-town location, this winning, Dutch-run

Central Coimbra

◎ Top Sights
1 Museu Nacional de Machado de Castro D2
2 Sé Velha C2
3 Universidade de Coimbra C3

◎ Sights
4 Biblioteca Joanina C3

🛏 Sleeping
5 Casa Pombal C1
6 Riversuites A4
7 Serenata Hostel C2

🍴 Eating
8 Adega Paço dos Condes B1
9 Fangas Mercearia Bar B2
10 Zé Manel dos Ossos B2

🍷 Drinking & Nightlife
11 Café Santa Cruz B1

🎭 Entertainment
12 Fado ao Centro B2

SPAIN & PORTUGAL COIMBRA

OFF THE BEATEN TRACK

SERRA DA ESTRELA

The forested Serra da Estrela has a raw natural beauty and offers some of the country's best hiking. This is Portugal's highest mainland mountain range (1993m), and the source of two great rivers: Rio Mondego and Rio Zêzere. The town of Manteigas makes a great base for hiking and exploring the area (plus skiing in winter). The main park office here provides details of popular walks in the Parque Natural da Serra da Estrela – some of which leave from town or just outside it. A solid budget option in town is **Pensão Estrela** (275 981 288; www.residencialestrela.web.pt; Rua Doutor Sobral 5; s/d from €25/35;). This recommended mother-and-son team in the heart of the village offers very clean, comfortable heated rooms with good bathrooms at a great price.

Two weekday buses connect Manteigas with Guarda, easily reached by bus from Porto, Coimbra and other major towns.

guesthouse squeezes tons of charm into a small space. A delicious breakfast is served in the gorgeous blue-tiled breakfast room.

✕ Eating

Adega Paço dos Condes PORTUGUESE €
(239 825 605; Rua do Paço do Conde 1; mains €5-10; 11.30am-3pm & 7-11pm Mon-Sat) Usually crowded with students and Coimbra locals, this straightforward family-run grill is one of the city's best budget eateries.

It's like something from a bygone era; prices are great and there's a long list of daily specials, which are usually your best way forward.

Zé Manel dos Ossos TASCA €€
(239 823 790; Beco do Forno 12; mains €7-15; noon-3pm & 7.30-10pm Mon-Fri, noon-3pm Sat) Tucked down a nondescript alleyway, this little gem, papered with scholarly doodles and scribbled poems, serves a terrific *feijoada á leitão* (a stew of beans and suckling pig).

Despite its hidden location, it's highly popular, so come early or be ready to wait. The charismatic service makes dining here a delight.

★**Fangas Mercearia Bar** PETISCOS €€
(934 093 636; www.fangas.pt; Rua Fernandes Tomás 45; petiscos €3-9; Fangas Bar 12.30-4pm & 7.30pm-12.30am Sat & Sun; Fangas 'Maior' 7pm-12.30am;) Top-quality deli produce is used to produce delightful *petiscos* (tapas) in this bright, cheery dining room, the best place to eat in the old town. Service is slow but staff are friendly and will help you choose from a delicious array of tasty platters – sausages, stuffed vegetables, conserves – and interesting wines. Book ahead as this small space always fills quickly.

🍷 Drinking & Entertainment

★**Galeria Santa Clara** BAR
(239 441 657; www.galeriasantaclara.com; Rua António Augusto Gonçalves 67; 1pm-2am Mon-Fri, to 3am Sat & Sun) Arty tearoom by day and chilled-out bar at night, this terrific place across the Mondego has good art on the walls, a series of sunny rooms and a fine riverfront terrace. It's got a great indoor-outdoor vibe and can feel like a party in a private house when things get going.

★**Café Santa Cruz** CAFE
(239 833 617; www.cafesantacruz.com; Praça 8 de Maio; snacks from €1.50; 7.30am-midnight Mon-Sat) One of Portugal's most atmospheric cafes, Santa Cruz is set in a dramatically beautiful high-vaulted former chapel, with stained-glass windows, graceful stone arches, and a Ché mosaic where the altar would have been, while the terrace grants lovely views of Praça 8 de Maio.

★**Fado ao Centro** FADO
(239 837 060; www.fadoaocentro.com; Rua Quebra Costas 7; show incl drink €10) At the bottom of the old town, this friendly fado centre makes a good place to introduce yourself to the genre. There's a performance every evening at 6pm. Shows include plenty of explanation in Portuguese and English about the history of Coimbra fado and the meaning of each song. It's tourist-oriented, but the performers enjoy it and do it well. You can chat with them afterwards over a glass of port (included).

❶ Information

Turismo Largo da Portagem (239 488 120; www.turismodecoimbra.pt; Largo da Portagem; 9am-8pm Mon-Fri, 9am-6pm Sat & Sun mid-Jun–mid-Sep, 9am-6pm Mon-Fri, 9am-1pm & 2-5.30pm Sat & Sun mid-Sep–mid-Jun) By the bridge, in the centre of things.

ⓘ Getting There & Away

From the rather grim **bus station** (Avenida Fernão de Magalhães) a 15-minute walk northwest of the centre, there are at least a dozen buses daily to Lisbon (€14.50, 2½ hours) and Porto (€12.50, 1½ hours), with almost as many to Braga (€14, 2¾ hours) and Faro (€27, six to nine hours).

Long-distance trains stop at Coimbra B station, north of the city. Cross the platform for quick, free connections to more-central Coimbra A (called just 'Coimbra' on timetables).

Coimbra is linked by regular Alfa Pendular (AP) and intercidade (IC) trains to Lisbon (AP/IC €22.80/19.20, 1¾/two hours) and Porto (€16.70/13.20, one/1¼ hours).

Porto

POP 1.5 MILLION (URBAN AREA)

From across the Rio Douro at sunset, romantic Porto looks like a pop-up town, a colourful tumbledown dream with medieval relics, soaring bell towers, extravagant baroque churches and stately beaux-arts buildings piled on top of one another, illuminated by streaming shafts of sun. If you squint you might be able to make out the open windows, the narrow lanes and the staircases zigzagging to nowhere. A lively walkable city with chatter in the air and a tangible sense of history, Porto's old-world riverfront district is a World Heritage Site. Across the water twinkle the neon signs of Vila Nova de Gaia, the headquarters of the major port manufacturers.

⊙ Sights

The Ribeira district – Porto's riverfront nucleus – is a remarkable window into Porto's history. Along the riverside promenade, *barcos rabelos* (the traditional boats used to ferry port wine down the Douro) bob beneath the shadow of the photogenic Ponte de Dom Luís I. From here you have a fine perspective of the port-wine lodges across the river in Vila Nova de Gaia. It's also packed with flocks of tourists.

Palácio da Bolsa   MONUMENT
(Stock Exchange; www.palaciodabolsa.com; Rua Ferreira Borges; tours adult/child €8/free; ⊙9am-6.30pm Apr-Oct, 9am-12.30pm & 2-5.30pm Nov-Mar) This splendid neoclassical monument (built from 1842 to 1910) honours Porto's past and present money merchants. Just past the entrance is the glass-domed **Pátio das Nações** (Hall of Nations), where the exchange once operated. But this pales in comparison with rooms deeper inside; to visit these, join one of the half-hour guided tours, which set off every 30 minutes.

Sé   CATHEDRAL
(Terreiro da Sé; cloisters adult/student €3/2; ⊙9am-12.30pm & 2.30-7pm Apr-Jun & Oct, 9am-7pm Jul-Sep, 9am-12.30pm & 2.30-6pm Nov-Mar) From Praça da Ribeira rises a tangle of medieval alleys and stairways that reach the hulking, hilltop fortress of the cathedral. Founded in the 12th century, it was largely rebuilt a century later and then extensively altered during the 18th century. However, you can still make out the church's Romanesque contours. Inside, a rose window and a 14th-century Gothic cloister remain from its early days.

Igreja de São Francisco   CHURCH
(Praça Infante Dom Henrique; adult/child €4/2; ⊙9am-8pm Jul-Sep, to 7pm Mar-Jun & Oct, to 5.30pm Nov-Feb) Igreja de São Francisco looks from the outside to be an austerely Gothic church, but inside it hides one of Portugal's most dazzling displays of baroque finery. Hardly an inch escapes unsmothered, as otherworldly cherubs and sober monks are drowned by nearly 100kg of gold leaf.

Jardim do Palácio de Cristal   GARDENS
(Rua Dom Manuel II; ⊙8am-9pm Apr-Sep, 8am-7pm Oct-Mar) Sitting atop a bluff, this gorgeous botanical garden is one of Porto's best-loved escapes, with lawns interwoven with sun-dappled paths and dotted with fountains, sculptures, giant magnolias, camellias, cypresses and olive trees. It's actually a mosaic of small gardens that open up little by little as you wander – as do the stunning views of the city and Rio Douro.

Museu de Arte Contemporânea   MUSEUM
(www.serralves.pt; Rua Dom João de Castro 210; adult/child museums & park €10/free, park €5/free; free 10am-1pm first Sun month; ⊙10am-7pm Tue-Fri, 10am-8pm Sat & Sun May-Sep, 10am-6pm Tue-Fri, 10am-7pm Sat & Sun Oct-Mar) This arrestingly minimalist, whitewashed space was designed by the eminent Porto-based architect Álvaro Siza Vieira. Cutting-edge exhibitions are showcased in the **Casa de Serralves**, a delightful pink art deco mansion, and there's a fine permanent collection featuring works from the late 1960s to the present. Both museums are accessible on a single ticket and sit within the marvellous 18-hectare **Parque de Serralves**.

Porto

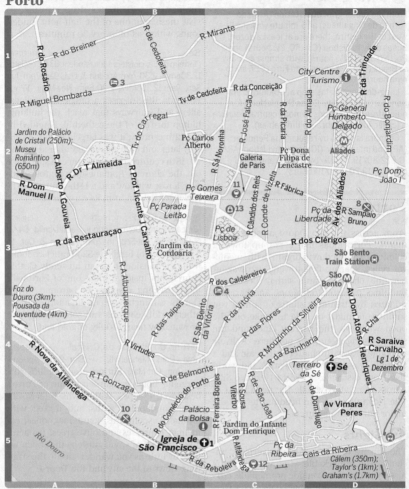

★ **Livraria Lello** HISTORIC BUILDING
(www.livrarialello.pt; Rua das Carmelitas 144; €3;
⏰10am-7.30pm Mon-Fri, 10am-7pm Sat, 11am-7pm
Sun) Even if you're not after books, don't
miss this exquisite 1906 neo-Gothic confection, with its lavishly carved plaster resembling wood and stained-glass skylight. Feels
magical? Its intricately wrought, curiously
twisting staircase was supposedly the inspiration for the one in Harry Potter, which JK
Rowling partly wrote in Porto while working here as an English teacher from 1991
to 1993.

🛏 Sleeping

Gallery Hostel HOSTEL €
(📞224 964 313; www.gallery-hostel.com; Rua
Miguel Bombarda 222; dm €22-25, d/ste €70/90;
🏵🛜) A true travellers' hub, this hostel-
gallery has clean and cosy dorms and doubles; a sunny, glass-enclosed back patio; a
grassy terrace; a cinema room; a shared
kitchen and a bar-music room. Throw in its
free walking tours, homemade dinners on
request, port wine tastings, concerts, and
you'll see why it's booked up so often – reserve ahead.

SPAIN & PORTUGAL PORTO

Tattva Design Hostel HOSTEL €

(📞 220 944 622; www.tattvadesignhostel.com; Rua do Cativo 26-28; dm €20-26, d €60-75, q €90-100; @ 🛜) Tattva knows precisely what makes backpackers tick – the facilities are superb and the attractive rooms have thoughtful touches – big lockers, good lighting, privacy curtains, and a bathroom and balcony in every room. The open-air rooftop lounge is a great place for a sundowner. Plus it offers free walking tours.

Poets Inn B&B €

(📞 223 324 209; www.thepoetsinn.com; Rua dos Caldeireiros 261; d €42-62, apt €72-92; 🛜) This laid-back B&B has a central but tucked-away location. Decorated by local artists, each of the doubles has a theme and some have fine city views. Most rooms share a bathroom. There's also a garden complete with hammock, a guest kitchen and a lounge with DVDs, plus a decent breakfast included in the price.

Residencial Santo André GUESTHOUSE €

(📞 222 000 115; www.residencialsantoandre.pt; Rua Santo Ildefonso 112; s/d/tr €22.50/30/40; 🛜) A charming four-floor walk-up with spiralled staircase and 10 oddly curvaceous rooms, some with bathrooms. They're all spick and span, but it's the smaller rooms that catch the most light. Set on a quiet street, it's a splendid cheapie.

🍴 Eating

⭐ **Mercado do Bolhão** MARKET €

(Rua Formosa; ⏰7am-5pm Mon-Fri, to 1pm Sat) The 19th-century, wrought-iron Mercado do Bolhão does a brisk trade in fresh produce, including cheeses, olives, smoked meats, sausages, breads and more. At its lively best on Friday and Saturday mornings, the market is also sprinkled with inexpensive stalls where you can eat fish so fresh it was probably swimming in the Atlantic that morning, or taste or sample local wines and cheeses.

Casa Guedes
TASCA €

(Praça dos Poveiros 130; mains €4-9; ⊙8am-midnight Mon-Sat) Come for tasty, filling and cheap meals, or for the famous pork sandwiches, served all day.

Space is tight and this no-frills *tasca* (tavern) is among Porto's favourites, so be prepared to wait for a table, inside or on the nice little terrace on the square.

Taberna do Barqueiro
PORTUGUESE €

(☎937 691 732; www.facebook.com/tabernadobarqueiro; Rua de Miragaia 123-124; mains €8-12; ⊙11am-10.30pm Mon & Wed-Sat, 11am-4pm Tue) Down by the river, the Taberna do Barqueiro is a rustic, homely bolthole, with a tiled mural of Porto on the wall and a terrace on the cobbles. Day specials like *bacalhau com natas* (baked salt cod with cream) and Portuguese-style tapas like sardines, cured ham, cheese and pork in red wine are served with a smile.

★Flor dos Congregados
PORTUGUESE €€

(☎222 002 822; www.flordoscongregados.pt; Travessa dos Congregados 11; mains €8-16; ⊙7-10pm Mon, 10am-10pm Tue-Sat) Tucked away down a narrow alley, this softly lit, family-run restaurant brims with stone-walled, wood-beamed, art-slung nooks. The frequently changing blackboard menu goes with the seasons.

Drinking & Nightlife

Nightlife rules in central Porto with some eclectic bar-gallery spaces leading the way.

It's worth exploring the narrow cobblestone streets just north of Rua das Carmelitas, which become an all-out street party (especially Rua Galeria de Paris, Cândido dos Reis and Conde de Vizela) on warm summer nights and on weekends throughout the year. Down by the water, the open-air bar scene on Praça da Ribeira is great for drinks with a view.

Wine Quay Bar
WINE BAR

(www.winequaybar.com; Cais da Estiva 111; ⊙4-11pm Mon-Sat) Sunset is prime-time viewing on the terrace of this terrific wine bar by the river. As you gaze across to the graceful arc of the Ponte Dom Luís I and over to the port cellars of Vila Nova de Gaia, you can sample some cracking Portuguese wines and appetisers (cured ham, cheese, olives and the like).

Casa do Livro
LOUNGE

(www.facebook.com/casadolivroporto; Rua Galeria de Paris 85; ⊙9.30pm-3am Sun-Thu, 9.30pm-4am Fri & Sat) Vintage wallpaper, gilded mirrors and walls of books give a discreet charm to this nicely lit beer and wine bar. On weekends, DJs spin funk, soul, jazz and retro sounds in the back room.

Information

City Centre Turismo (☎223 393 472; www.visitporto.travel; Rua Clube dos Fenianos 25; ⊙9am-7pm Nov-Apr, 9am-8pm May-Jul & Sep-Oct, 9am-9pm Aug) The main city *turismo* has a detailed city map, a transport map and the *Agenda do Porto* cultural calendar, among other printed materials.

VILA NOVA DA GAIA

While technically its own municipality, Vila Nova de Gaia ('Gaia') sits just across the Rio Douro from Porto and is woven into the city's fabric both by a series of stunning bridges and by its shared history of port-wine making. Since the mid-18th century, port-wine bottlers and exporters have been obliged to maintain their 'lodges' – basically dressed-up warehouses – here. Today some 30 of these lodges clamber up the steep riverbank.

From Porto's Ribeira district, a short walk across Ponte de Dom Luís I lands you on Gaia's inviting riverside promenade. Lined with beautiful *barcos rabelos* – flat-bottomed boats specially designed to carry wine down the Douro's once-dangerous rapids – the promenade offers grandstand views of Porto's historic centre.

Most people come here to taste the tipple, of course, and about 17 lodges oblige them. Tourist offices keep a list of lodges and opening times. **Taylor's** (☎223 772 956, 223 742 800; www.taylor.pt; Rua do Choupelo 250; tour €12; ⊙10am-6pm), **Cálem** (☎223 746 660; www.calem.pt; Avenida Diogo Leite 344 ; Visit to the cellars & tasting adult/reduced/under 12 €6/3/free; ⊙10am-7pm May-Oct, 10am-6pm Nov-Apr) and **Graham's** (☎223 776 484; www.grahams-port.com; Rua do Agro 141; tour incl tasting €10-100; ⊙9.30am-6pm Apr-Oct, 9.30am-5.30pm Nov-Mar) offer some of the best tours.

Getting There & Away

The airport, 19km northwest of the centre, is served from many European cities and is used by budget airlines.

There's no central bus terminal, but there are frequent services to nearly everywhere in the country, including Lisbon (€20, 3½ hours) and Braga (€6, 1¼ hours). Eurolines serves much of Europe from here.

Long-distance rail services start at Campanhã station, which is 3km east of the centre. Most urbano, regional and interregional (IR) trains depart from the stunning indoor-outdoor São Bento station, though all these lines also pass through Campanhã. Direct intercity trains head to Lisbon (€20, three hours hourly) via Coimbra. There are also trains north to Vigo in Spain.

Getting Around

An extensive bus network and newish metro system provide easy service around town. Porto's trams used to be one of its delights. Only three lines remain but they're very scenic.

For maximum convenience, Porto's transport system offers the rechargeable Andante Card (www.linhandante.com), allowing smooth movement between tram, metro, funicular and many bus lines.

Braga

POP 71,750

Portugal's third-largest city is an elegant town laced with ancient narrow lanes strewn with plazas and a splendid array of baroque churches. The constant chiming of bells is a reminder of Braga's age-old devotion to the spiritual world. But don't come expecting piety alone: Braga's upscale old centre is packed with lively cafes and trim boutiques, some excellent restaurants and low-key bars catering to students from the Universidade do Minho.

Sights

Sé CATHEDRAL

(www.se-braga.pt; Rua Dom Paio Mendes; ⏲9am-7pm high season, 9am-6.30pm low season) Braga's extraordinary cathedral, the oldest in Portugal, was begun when the archdiocese was restored in 1070 and completed in the following century. It's a rambling complex made up of differing styles, and architecture buffs could spend half a day happily distinguishing the Romanesque bones from Manueline musculature and baroque frippery.

OFF THE BEATEN TRACK

THE AZORES

Over a thousand kilometres west of mainland Portugal, the Azores consist of nine volcanic islands, the exposed tips of vast underwater mountains. Unesco designated three of them (Graciosa, Flores and Corvo) as biospheres, and the archipelago also contains Ramsar sites (important wetlands) and over 30 Blue Flag beaches. The government is committed to sustainability.

The Azores are best known for whale and dolphin watching; the archipelago is a pit stop or home for about a third of the world's species of cetacean. Diving, other watersports and hiking are other attractions.

Azores Airlines (SATA; www.azoresairlines.pt) flies direct from both Europe and North America. Budget carriers Ryanair and easyJet also fly here. Note that the time zone here is UTC/GMT minus one; one hour behind Portugal.

Escadaria do Bom Jesus RELIGIOUS SITE

(Monte do Bom Jesus) At Bom Jesus do Monte, a hilltop pilgrimage site 5km from Braga, is an extraordinary stairway, with allegorical fountains, chapels and a superb view. City bus 2 runs frequently from Braga to the site, where you can climb the steps (pilgrims sometimes do this on their knees) or ascend by funicular railway (one way/return €1.20/2).

Sleeping & Eating

Hotel dos Terceiros HOTEL €

(☎253 270 466; www.terceiros.com; Rua dos Capelistas 85; s/d €30/43; ❄📶) On a quiet pedestrian street near Praça da República, this simple hotel has recently updated rooms overlooking a small square, some with tiny balconies. Most rooms have one full and single bed each, and can sleep up to three people.

Anjo Verde VEGETARIAN €

(Largo da Praça Velha 21; mains €7.50-8.60; ⏲noon-3pm & 7.30-10.30pm Mon-Sat) Braga's vegetarian offering serves generous, elegantly presented plates in a lovely, airy dining room. Vegetarian lasagne, risotto and vegetable tarts are among the choices. The mains can be bland, but the spiced chocolate tart is a superstar.

ℹ Information

Turismo (☎253 262 550; www.cm-braga. pt; Avenida da Liberdade 1; ⏱9am-1pm & 2-6.30pm Mon-Fri, 9am-1pm & 2-6pm Sat & Sun) Braga's helpful tourist office is in an art-deco-style building facing the fountain.

ℹ Getting There & Away

There are bus services all over northern Portugal and to other major towns, including Lisbon (€19, 4½ hours) and Porto (€4.90, one hour).

Braga is within Porto's suburbano network, which means commuter trains travel every hour or so from Porto (€3.10, about one hour). Useful long-distance trains include Coimbra (€19, 2¼ hours, five to seven daily) and Lisbon (€31, four hours, two to four daily).

Parque Nacional da Peneda-Gerês

Spread across four impressive granite massifs, this vast park encompasses boulder-strewn peaks, precipitous valleys, gorse-clad moorlands and forests of oak and pine. It also shelters more than 100 granite villages that, in many ways, have changed little since Portugal's founding in the 12th century. For nature lovers, the stunning scenery here is unmatched in Portugal for camping, hiking and other outdoor adventures. The park's main centre is at Vila do Gerês, a sleepy, hot-springs village.

🏃 Activities

There are trails and footpaths through the park, some between villages with accommodation. Leaflets detailing these are available from the park offices. Day hikes around Vila do Gerês are popular. An adventurous op-

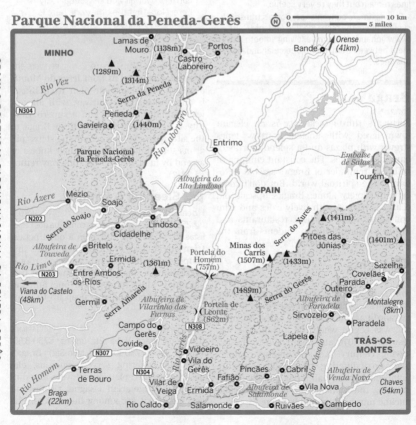

Parque Nacional da Peneda-Gerês

tion is the old Roman road from Mata do Albergaria (10km up-valley from Vila do Gerês), past the Vilarinho das Furnas reservoir to Campo do Gerês.

🛏 Sleeping & Eating

Gerês has plenty of *pensões* (guesthouses), though in summer you may find some are block-booked for spa patients and other visitors. Outside July and August, prices plummet.

Hotel Baltazar   HOTEL
(☑ 253 391 131; www.baltazarhotel.com; Rua Lagrifa Mendes 6; s/d €60/85; 🖥) In a fine old granite building, this friendly, family-run hotel just up from the hot springs has spacious rooms, many of which look onto a pleasant wooded park. The downstairs restaurant is excellent.

Lurdes Capela   PORTUGUESE €
(☑ 253 391 208; Rua Dr Manuel Gomes de Almeida 77; mains €6-13; ⊙ noon-3pm & 7-10pm) Family owned and operated, and almost always packed. Expect top-end service and even better food. We're talking massive fresh-fish platters with buttered potatoes and vegetables, fluffy, savoury omelettes and all the beef and cod dishes too.

ℹ Getting There & Away

Between three and seven buses daily run from Braga to Gerês (€4.50, 1½ hours).

Portugal Survival Guide

ℹ Directory A–Z

ACCOMMODATION

There's an excellent range of good-value accommodation in Portugal. Budget places provide some of Western Europe's cheapest rooms.

Guesthouses For a local experience, stay in a *pensão* or *residencial*. These are small, often family-run places, and some are set in historic buildings. Amenities range from simple to luxury.

Hostels Portugal has a growing network of hostels, with stylish, award-winning options in both Lisbon and Porto.

DISCOUNT CARDS

Lisbon and Porto offer a card that includes entry to attractions, public transport, a city bus tour and restaurant discounts. Typically, you need to do lots of sightseeing to save money with it.

> **ℹ PRICE RANGES**
>
> The following price ranges refer to a double room with bathroom in high season. Unless otherwise stated breakfast is included in the price.
>
> **€** less than €60
>
> **€€** €60 to €120
>
> **€€€** over €120
>
> Eating price ranges refer to the cost of an average main dish:
>
> **€** less than €8
>
> **€€** €8 to €14
>
> **€€€** over €14

LGBT TRAVELLERS

In 2010 Portugal legalised gay marriage, becoming the sixth European country to do so. Most Portuguese profess a laissez-faire attitude about same-sex couples, although how out you can be depends on where you are in Portugal. In Lisbon, Porto and the Algarve, acceptance has increased, whereas in most other areas, same-sex couples would be met with incomprehension.

Lisbon has the country's best gay and lesbian network and nightlife.

MONEY

Credit cards are accepted at smarter hotels and restaurants and in larger towns, but aren't much use to pay for things in the budget arena or in rural outposts.

Tipping

Restaurants Not necessary in cheaper places, where you can just round up, otherwise 5% to 10%.

Bars Not expected unless table service is provided.

OPENING HOURS

Restaurants noon to 3pm and 7pm to 10pm
Cafés 9am to 7pm
Shops 9.30am to noon & 2pm to 7pm Monday to Friday, 10am to 1pm Saturday
Bars 7pm to 2am
Nightclubs 11pm to 4am Thursday to Saturday
Malls 10am to 10pm
Banks 8.30am to 3pm Monday to Friday

PUBLIC HOLIDAYS

Some of these holidays have been cancelled in light of the economic crisis, but are scheduled to return.

New Year's Day 1 January

Carnaval Tuesday February/March; the day before Ash Wednesday

Good Friday March/April

Liberty Day 25 April; celebrating the 1974 revolution

Labour Day 1 May

Corpus Christi May/June; ninth Thursday after Easter

Portugal Day 10 June; also known as Camões and Communities Day

Feast of the Assumption 15 August

Republic Day 5 October; commemorating the 1910 declaration of the Portuguese Republic

All Saints' Day 1 November

Independence Day 1 December; commemorating the 1640 restoration of independence from Spain

Feast of the Immaculate Conception 8 December

Christmas Day 25 December

TELEPHONE

Local SIM cards with call and data packages are widely available.

Portuguese landline and mobile numbers have nine digits, with no separate area code.

International dialling code ☑ 00

Country code ☑ 351

❶ Getting There & Away

AIR

Most international flights arrive in Lisbon, though Porto and Faro also have some. For more information, including live arrival and departure schedules, see www.ana.pt.

BUS

The major long-distance carriers that serve European destinations are **Busabout** (www.busabout.com) and **Eurolines** (www.eurolines.com). From Spain, there's also daily service from Madrid to Lisbon and from Seville to Faro.

TRAIN

From Spain, the Sud-Expresso heads from the French border across to Portugal, continuing to Coimbra and Lisbon; change at Pampilhosa for Porto. From Madrid, the Talgo Lusitânia heads to Lisbon. A faster Madrid–Lisbon route is in the planning stages. There's also a train from Vigo in Spain's northwest to Porto.

❶ Getting Around

A host of small private bus operators, most amalgamated into regional companies, run a dense network of services across the country. Among the largest are **Rede Expressos** (☑ 707 223 344; www.rede-expressos.pt), **Rodonorte** (☑ 259 340 710; www.rodonorte.pt) and the Algarve line Eva Transportes (www.eva-bus.com). It's a reliable, cheap way to travel.

Portugal has an extensive railroad network, making for a scenic way of travelling between destinations; see www.cp.pt. Classes are:

Regional (R) Slow, stop everywhere;

Interregional (IR) Reasonably fast.

Intercidade (IC) Rápido or express trains.

Alfa Pendular Deluxe Marginally faster than express and much pricier.

Italy, Greece & Turkey

Best Places to Eat

➡ All'Arco (p504)

➡ Berberé (p511)

➡ Il Vesuvio (p542)

➡ Kalnterimi (p551)

➡ Antiochia (p586)

➡ Konak Konya Mutfağı (p593)

Best Places to Sleep

➡ Palazzo Guadagni Hotel (p511)

➡ Zorzis Hotel (p561)

➡ Angora House Hotel (p589)

➡ Kelebek Hotel & Cave Pension (p597)

Why Go?

Europe seems to ramp up the intensity as you head south-east – from the food to the sights to the scenery and the zest for life. This is where you dig into the freshest pasta, relish the tangiest local cheeses and savour the most aromatic pastries. Visit vineyards in Italy, drink ouzo with locals in Greek villages and experience Turkey's teahouses. You will witness history firsthand: sights like Pompeii, the Acropolis and Ephesus are merely the sprinkles on the gelato. The region is a cultural parade as well. See dervishes whirling; visit monasteries honed out of rock or built atop soaring pinnacles; get pampered in a Turkish bath; paddle down Venice's canals; lose yourself in Rhodes' walled, medieval city; and gaze up, spellbound by the Sistine Chapel. And as if this wasn't enough to lure you, it's all ringed by bewitching turquoise waters, silky soft sand and sunset-coloured cliffs. Prepare yourself: the southeast is boundless and magnetic.

Fast Facts

Capitals Rome (Italy), Athens (Greece), Ankara (Turkey)

Country code ☑ 39 (Italy), ☑ 30 (Greece), ☑ 90 (Turkey)

Currencies Euro € (Italy, Greece), Lira ₺ (Turkey)

Visas Not required for EU citizens or for stays of up to 90 days for many nationals (Italy, Greece). Required for many nationals and available online at www.evisa.gov.tr (Turkey).

Time zones GMT/UTC plus two hours (Italy), GMT/UTC plus three hours (Greece, Turkey)

Hello *Ciao* (Italian), *Yasas* (Greek), *Merhaba* (Turkish)

Italy, Greece & Turkey Highlights

1 **Venice** Take in gorgeous Venetian architecure from a gondola. (p498)

2 **Florence** Explore this exquisite Renaissance time capsule. (p505)

3 **Rome** Haunting sights, awe-inspiring art and must-see sights. (p516)

4 **Corfu** Beautiful architecure, a colourful history and fantastic cuisine. (p538)

5 **Athens** Ancient and contemporary come together, from the Acropolis to museums and atmospheric bars. (p544)

6 **Santorini** Be mesmerised by this island's dramatic

WORTH A TRIP: CAPPADOCIA

Explore this stunning landscape of underground cities. (p594)

ROMANIA

BUCHAREST ☆

BULGARIA

● SOFIA

Thessaloniki ●

● Çanakkale

● Bergama

TURKEY

İstanbul ●
⑩

ANKARA ☆

Cappadocia ●

Konya ●

● İzmir
Selçuk ●
Ephesus ⑨

Antalya
⑧

Delphi ●

⑤ **Athens**

ycenae ●
● Epidavros
Nafplio ●

3odrum ●
Marmaris ●
● Fethiye

● Sparta
⑥
● Gythio
Santorini

⑦
Rhodes
● Olymbos

CYPRUS

Hania ●
Iraklio ●
Crete

OFF THE BEATEN TRACK: KONYA

Visit the birthplace of the Whirling Dervishes and see some divine spinning. (p592)

400 km
200 miles

---

volcanic caldera and its world-famous sunsets. (p558)

⑦ **Rhodes** Lose yourself within the medieval walls of the city's Old Town and then head for sandy beaches. (p562)

⑧ **Antalya** Stroll lanes between Ottoman mansions in the shadow of the snowcapped Bey Mountains. (p571)

⑨ **Ephesus** Fulfil your toga-loaded daydreams in one of

the world's greatest surviving Graeco-Roman cities. (p578)

⑩ **İstanbul** Take in the minaret-studded skyline, along with the city's stately mosques and opulent palaces. (p578)

Italy's
TOP EXPERIENCES

A favourite destination since the days of the 18th-century grand tour, Italy (p498) may appear to hold few surprises. Its iconic monuments and masterpieces are known the world over, while cities such as Rome, Florence and Venice need no introduction. Yet Italy is far more than the sum of its sights. Its fiercely proud regions maintain customs and culinary traditions dating back centuries, resulting in passionate festivals and delectable food at every turn. And then there are those timeless landscapes, from Tuscany's gentle hillsides to icy Alpine peaks, vertiginous coastlines and spitting southern volcanoes. Drama is never far away in Italy and its theatrical streets and piazzas provide endless people-watching, ideally over a leisurely lunch or cool evening drink. This is, after all, the land of dolce far niente (sweet idleness), where simply hanging out is a pleasure and time seems to matter just that little bit less.

 Rome

Once *caput mundi* (capital of the world), Rome was legendarily spawned by a wolf-suckled boy, grew to be Western Europe's first superpower, became the spiritual centrepiece of the Christian world and is now the repository of over two millennia of European art and architecture. From the Pantheon and the Colosseum to Michelangelo's Sistine Chapel and countless works by Caravaggio, there's simply too much to see in one visit. So, do as countless others have done before you: toss a coin into the Trevi Fountain and promise to return. (p516)

 Venice

Step through the portals of Basilica di San Marco and try to imagine what it might have been like for a humble medieval labourer glimpsing those glittering gold mosaic domes for the first time. It's not such a stretch – seeing the millions of tiny gilt tesserae (hand-cut glazed tiles) fuse into a singular heavenly vision can make every leap of human imagination since the 12th century seem comparatively minor. Indeed, one visit is never enough; the basilica's sheer scale, exquisite detailing and ever-shifting light promises endless revelations. (p498)

Florence

Italy's most romanticised region, Tuscany was tailor-made for fastidious aesthetes. From Brunelleschi's Duomo to Masaccio's Cappella Brancacci frescoes, Florence, according to Unesco, contains 'the greatest concentration of universally renowned works of art in the world'. Beyond its blockbuster museums, jewel-box churches and flawless Renaissance streetscapes sprawls an undulating wonderland of regional masterpieces and the vine-laced hills of Italy's most famous wine region, Chianti. (p505)

GETTING AROUND

Air Italy offers an extensive network of internal flights. Alitalia is the main domestic carrier, with numerous low-cost airlines also operating across the country.

Bus Everything from meandering local routes to fast, reliable InterCity connections. Tickets are generally competitively priced with the train and often the only way to get to smaller towns.

Car Pre-booking via the internet often costs less than hiring a car in Italy. Online booking agency Rentalcars.com (www.rentalcars.com) compares the rates of numerous car-rental companies.

Train Trains in Italy are convenient and relatively cheap compared with other European countries.

★ Pompeii

Frozen in its death throes, the sprawling, time-warped ruins of Pompeii hurtle you 2000 years into the past. Wander through chariot-grooved Roman streets, lavishly frescoed villas and bathhouses, food stores and markets, theatres, even an ancient brothel. Then, in the eerie stillness, your eye on ominous Mt Vesuvius, ponder Pliny the Younger's terrifying account of the town's final hours: 'Darkness came on again, again ashes, thick and heavy. We got up repeatedly to shake these off; otherwise we would have been buried and crushed by the weight'. (p531)

★ Masterpieces

A browse through any art history textbook will no doubt highlight seminal movements in Western art, from classical, Renaissance and mannerist, to baroque, futurist and metaphysical. All were forged in Italy by a red carpet roll call of artists including Giotto, da Vinci, Michelangelo, Botticelli, Bernini, Caravaggio, Carracci, Boccioni, Balla and de Chirico. Find the best of them in Rome's Museo e Galleria Borghese and Vatican Museums, Florence's Uffizi and Venice's Gallerie dell'Accademia. (p508)

★ Cinque Terre

For the sinful inhabitants of the Cinque Terre's five sherbert-coloured villages – Monterosso, Vernazza, Corniglia, Manarola and Riomaggiore – penance involved a lengthy and arduous hike up the vertiginous cliffside to the local village sanctuary to appeal for forgiveness. Scale the same trails today, through terraced vineyards and hillsides smothered in macchia (shrubbery). As the heavenly views unfurl, it's hard to think of a more benign punishment. (p513)

★ Cuisine

It might look like a boot, but food-obsessed Italy feels more like a decadently stuffed Christmas stocking. From delicate tagliatelle al ragù to velvety cannoli, every bite feels like a revelation. The secret: superlative ingredients and strictly seasonal produce. And while Italy's culinary soul might be earthy and rustic, it's equally ingenious and sophisticated. Expect some of the world's top fine-dining destinations, from San Pellegrino 'World's Best 50' hotspots to Michelin-starred musts. So whether you're on a degustation odyssey, truffle hunting or swilling powerhouse reds, prepare to swoon.

if Italy were 100 people

93 would be Italian
4 would be Albanian and Eastern European
1 would be North African
2 would be other

belief systems
(% of population)

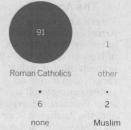

91
Roman Catholics

1
other

6
none

2
Muslim

population per sq km

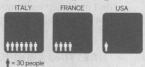

ITALY   FRANCE   USA

👤 ≈ 30 people

When to Go

Rome

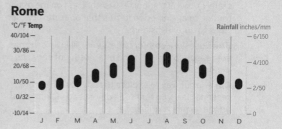

°C/°F **Temp**

Rainfall inches/mm

Greece's
TOP EXPERIENCES

The alluring combination of history and ravishing beauty that has made Greece (p538) one of the most popular destinations on the planet always seems to beckon. Within easy reach of magnificent archaeological sites such as the Acropolis and Delphi are breathtaking beaches and relaxed tavernas serving everything from ouzo to octopus. Hiking trails criss-cross islands like Corfu. Wanderers can island-hop to their heart's content (each island has its own character), while party types can enjoy pulsating nightlife in Greece's vibrant modern cities and on islands such as Santorini. Add welcoming locals with an enticing culture to the mix and it's easy to see why most visitors head home vowing to come back. Travellers to Greece inevitably end up with a favourite site they long to return to – get out there and find yours.

 The Acropolis

There's a reason the Acropolis remains the quintessential landmark of Western civilisation – it is spectacular. Whether experienced during an early-morning stroll or from a dinnertime terrace with the Parthenon lit up and glorious, the Acropolis embodies a power and beauty that speak to all generations. Look beyond the Parthenon and you will find more intimate spots like the exquisite Temple of Athena Nike, while the Acropolis Museum cleverly showcases the Acropolis' surviving treasures. (p544)

 Ancient Delphi

Arrive early to catch the magic of the sun's rays pouring over the Sanctuary of Athena Pronea at Delphi, the centre of the ancient Greek world. Only three columns remain of the magnificent sanctuary, but that's enough to let your imagination soar. Nearby, the Sacred Way meanders past the Temple of Apollo, where prophecies were uttered that sent armies to battle and made lovers swoon. (p556)

 Meteora

You're not likely to forget the first moment the magnificent Meteora comes into view – soaring pillars of rock that jut heavenward, and a handful of monasteries at the summit (some dating from the 14th century). The rope ladders that once enabled the monks to reach the top have long been replaced by steps carved into the rock. Today these spectacular stone towers beckon rock climbers from around the world. (p559)

 Athens

Life in Athens is a magnificent mash-up of the ancient and the contemporary. Beneath the majestic facades of venerable landmarks, the city teems with life and creativity. And Athenians love to get out and enjoy it

---

GETTING AROUND

Air It's sometimes cheaper to fly than take the ferry, especially if you book ahead online. Aegean Airlines (www.aegeanair.com) and Olympic Air (www.olympicair.com) are the two main carriers.

Boat Ferries come in all shapes and sizes, from state-of-the-art 'superferries' that run on the major routes, to ageing open ferries that operate local services to outlying islands.

Bus Buses are comfortable, generally run on time, are reasonably priced and offer frequent services on major routes.

Car A great way to explore the islands. Rates are reasonable if you rent for a day or two. Taking a car on the ferries is pricey.

FUN FOOD FACT

In Greece, a *vasilopita* (golden-glazed cake) is cut at midnight on New Year's Eve giving good fortune to whoever gets the lucky coin inside.

all. Galleries and clubs hold the exhibitions, performances and installations of the city's booming arts scene. Trendy restaurants and humble tavernas rustle up fine, fine fare. Ubiquitous cafes fill with stylin' locals and moods run from punk rock to haute couture. Discos and bars abound...and swing deep into the night. (p544)

★ Corfu

The story of Corfu is written across the handsome facades of its main town's buildings. This is a place that crams a remarkable mix of architecture in its small compass. Stroll past Byzantine fortresses, neoclassical British buildings of the 19th century, Parisian-style arcades, Orthodox church towers, and the narrow, sun-dappled streets of the Venetian Old Town. Beyond town, Corfu is lush green mountains, rolling countryside and dramatic coastlines. And if the architecture and scenery aren't enough, come for the Italian-influenced food. (p538)

★ Santorini

There's more to Santorini than sunsets, but this remarkable island, shaped by the fire of prehistoric eruptions, has made the celebratory sunset its own. On summer evenings the clifftop towns of Fira and Oia are packed with visitors awed by the vast blood-red canvas of the cliff face as the sun struts its stuff. You can catch the sunset without the crowds from almost anywhere along the cliff edge. And if you miss sundown, you can always face east at first light for some fairly stunning sunrises too... (p558)

★ Rhodes' Old Town

Getting lost in Rhodes' Old Town is a must. Away from the crowds, you will find yourself meandering down twisting, cobbled alleyways with archways above and squares opening up ahead. In these hidden corners your imagination will take off with flights of medieval fancy. Explore the ancient Knights' Quarter, the old Jewish neighbourhood or the Turkish Quarter. Hear traditional live music in tiny tavernas or dine on fresh seafood at atmospheric outdoor restaurants. Wander along the top of the city's walls, with the sea on one side and, on the other, a bird's-eye view into this living museum. (p564)

if Greece were 100 people

93 would be Greek
7 would be other

belief systems
(% of population)

98 Greek Orthodox
1 Muslim
1 Other

population per sq km

GREECE   USA   UK

♦ ≈ 30 people

When to Go

Athens

°C/°F Temp
40/104 —
30/86 —
20/68 —
10/50 —
0/32 —

Rainfall inches/mm
— 8/200
— 6/150
— 4/100
— 2/50
— 0

J F M A M J J A S O N D

Turkey's
TOP EXPERIENCES

Turkey (p571) walks the tightrope between Europe and Asia with ease. Its cities pack in towering minarets and spice-trading bazaars but also offer buzzing modern streetlife. Out in the countryside, this country's reputation as a bridge between continents is laid bare. Its expansive steppes and craggy mountain slopes are scattered with the remnants of once mighty empires. Lycian ruins peek from the undergrowth across the Mediterranean coast, the Roman era's pomp stretches out before you in Ephesus, while the swirling rock valleys of Cappadocia hide Byzantine monastery complexes whittled out by early Christian ascetics. Of course, if you just want to sloth on a prime piece of beach, Turkey has you covered. But when you've brushed off the sand, this land where East meets West, and the ancient merges seamlessly with the contemporary, is a fascinating mosaic of culture, history and visceral natural splendour.

⭐ İstanbul

In İstanbul, you can board a commuter ferry and flit between Europe and Asia in under an hour. Every day, a flotilla takes locals up the Bosphorus and over the Sea of Marmara, sounding sonorous horns as it goes. Morning services share the waterways with diminutive fishing boats and massive container ships, all accompanied by flocks of shrieking seagulls. At sunset, the tapering minarets and Byzantine domes of the Old City are thrown into relief against a dusky pink sky – it's the city's most magical sight. (p578)

⭐ Cappadocia

Cappadocia's hard-set honeycomb landscape looks sculpted by a swarm of genius bees. The truth – the effects of erosion on rock formed of ash from megalithic volcanic eruptions – is only slightly less cool. Humans have also left their mark here, in the Byzantine frescoes in rock-cut churches and in the bowels of complex underground cities. These days, Cappadocia is all about good times: fine wine, local dishes and five-star caves; horse riding, valley hikes and hot-air ballooning. There's enough to keep you buzzing for days. (p594)

⭐ Ephesus

Undoubtedly the most famous of Turkey's countless ancient sites, and considered the best-preserved ruins in the Mediterranean, Ephesus is a powerful tribute to Greek artistry and Roman architectural prowess. A stroll down the marble-coated Curetes Way provides myriad photo opportunities – not least the Library of Celsus with its two storeys of columns, and the Terraced Houses, their vivid frescoes and sophisticated mosaics giving insight into the daily lives of the city's elite. Much of the city is yet to be unearthed. (p578)

⭐ Hamams

At many hamams in Turkey, plenty of extras are on offer: bath treatments, facials, pedicures and so on. However, we recommend you stick with the tried and true hamam experience – a soak and a scrub followed by a good (and optional) pummelling. After this cleansing ritual and cultural experience, the world (and your body) will never

GETTING AROUND

Bus Turkey's intercity bus system is as good as any you'll find, with modern, comfortable coaches crossing the country at all hours and for very reasonable prices.

Car Driving takes nerves of steel, and not just because Turkey has the world's second-highest petrol prices. Avoid getting behind the wheel after dark.

Train The Turkish State Railways (www.tcdd.gov.tr) network covers the country, with the notable exception of the coastlines.

BAKLAVA, TURKISH-STYLE

As with many things Turkish, there's a ritual associated with eating baklava. Aficionados don't use a knife and fork. Instead, they turn their baklava upside down with the help of an index finger and thumb, and pop it into the mouth.

feel quite the same again; do leave time to relax with a çay afterwards. For a truly memorable hamam, seek out a soak in historic Sultanahmet, İstanbul.

⭐ Aya Sofya

Even in mighty İstanbul, nothing beats the Aya Sofya, or Church of the Divine Wisdom, which was for centuries the greatest church in Christendom. Emperor Justinian had it built in the 6th century, as part of his mission to restore the greatness of the Roman Empire; gazing up at the floating dome, it's hard to believe this fresco-covered marvel didn't single-handedly revive Rome's fortunes. Glittering mosaics depict biblical scenes and ancient Constantinople's figures of note such as Empress Zoe, one of only three standalone Byzantine empresses. (p579)

⭐ Whirling Dervishes

The *sema* (whirling dervish ceremony) crackles with spiritual energy as the robe-clad dervishes spin, a constellation of dancers performing this trancelike ritual. The ceremony begins and ends with chanted passages from the Koran and is rich with symbolism; the dervishes' conical felt hats represent their tombstones, as the dance signifies relinquishing earthly life to be reborn in mystical union

with God. You can see a *sema* in locations including İstanbul, Cappadocia, Bursa and Konya; the latter's Mevlâna Museum gives insight into the mystical Mevlevi, the original whirling dervishes. (p592)

⭐ Cuisine

The best thing about sampling Turkey's delicious specialties – ranging from meze on a Mediterranean harbour to a pension breakfast featuring products from the kitchen garden – is they take you to the heart of Turkish culture. For the sociable and family-orientated Turks, getting together and eating well is a time-honoured ritual. So get stuck into olive oil–lathered Aegean vegetables, spicy Anatolian kebaps and dishes from Turkey's many other corners – and as you drink a tulip-shaped glass of çay and contemplate some baklava for dessert, remember that eating is deepening your understanding of Turkey.

if Turkey were 100 people

70 would be Turkish
20 would be Kurdish
10 would be other

belief systems
(% of population)

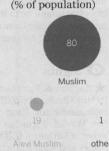

80
Muslim

19
Alevi Muslim

1
other

population per sq km

TURKEY · USA · UK

👤 ≈ 30 people

When to Go

İstanbul

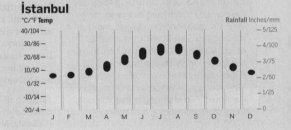

°C/°F Temp · Rainfall Inches/mm

ITALY

Venice

POP 264,500

Venice (Venezia) is a hauntingly beautiful city. At every turn you're assailed by unforgettable images: tiny bridges arching over limpid canals; chintzy gondolas sliding past working barges; towers and distant domes silhouetted against the watery horizon. Its celebrated sights are legion, and its labyrinthine alleyways exude a unique, almost eerie atmosphere, redolent of cloaked passions and dark secrets. Parts of the Cannaregio, Dorsoduro and Castello *sestieri* (districts) rarely see many tourists, and you can lose yourself for hours in the lanes between the Accademia and train station. Many of the city's treasures date to its time as a powerful medieval republic known as La Serenissima.

See p514-15 for our highlights of the Grand Canal.

⊙ Sights

★ Basilica di San Marco   BASILICA

(St Mark's Basilica; Map p502; ☑ 041 270 83 11; www.basilicasanmarco.it; Piazza San Marco; ⊙ 9.45am-5pm Mon-Sat, 2-5pm Sun summer, to 4pm Sun winter; ⛴ San Marco) FREE With its Byzantine domes and 8500 sq metres of luminous mosaics, Venice's basilica is an unforgettable sight. It dates to the 9th century when, according to legend, two merchants smuggled the corpse of St Mark out of Egypt in a barrel of pork fat. When the original burnt down in 932 Venice rebuilt the basilica in its own cosmopolitan image, with Byzantine domes, a

---

ⓘ FREE

Some of the most pivotal sites in Venetian history have free entry: **Rialto Market**, where an empire sprang up around fishmongers; **Basilica di Santa Maria della Salute** (p498), the domed church built as thanks for Venice's salvation from plague; and the **Basilica di San Marco**, the apotheosis of Venice's millennium of brilliant self-invention. While the Basilica di Santa Maria della Salute offers free afternoon organ vespers concerts, the Basilica di San Marco runs free guided tours of its astounding mosaics.

Greek cross layout and walls clad in marbles from Syria, Egypt and Palestine.

Piazza San Marco   PIAZZA

(Map p502; ⛴ San Marco) This grand showpiece square beautifully encapsulates the splendour of Venice's past and its tourist-fuelled present. Flanked by the arcaded **Procuratie Vecchie** and **Procuratie Nuove**, it's filled for much of the day with tourists, pigeons and tour guides. To get a bird's-eye view, head to the Basilica di San Marco's free-standing 99m *campanile*, which commands stunning 360-degree panoramas.

Ponte dei Sospiri   BRIDGE

(Map p502) One of Venice's most photographed sights, the Bridge of Sighs connects Palazzo Ducale to the 16th-century Priggione Nove (New Prisons). It's named after the sighs that condemned prisoners – including Giacomo Casanova – emitted as they were led down to the cells.

★ Gallerie dell'Accademia   GALLERY

(Map p502; ☑ 041 520 03 45; www.gallerieaccademia.org; Campo della Carità 1050; adult/reduced €11/8 plus supplement during special exhibitions, 1st Sun of the month free; ⊙ 8.15am-2pm Mon, to 7.15pm Tue-Sun; ⛴ Accademia) Venice's historic gallery traces the development of Venetian art from the 14th to 18th centuries, with works by Bellini, Titian, Tintoretto, Veronese and Canaletto among others. The former Santa Maria della Carità convent complex housing the collection maintained its serene composure for centuries until Napoleon installed his haul of Venetian art trophies here in 1807. Since then there's been nonstop visual drama inside its walls.

Peggy Guggenheim Collection   MUSEUM

(Map p502; ☑ 041 240 54 11; www.guggenheim-venice.it; Palazzo Venier dei Leoni 704; adult/reduced €15/9; ⊙ 10am-6pm Wed-Mon; ⛴ Accademia) After losing her father on the *Titanic*, heiress Peggy Guggenheim became one of the great collectors of the 20th century. Her palatial canalside home, Palazzo Venier dei Leoni, showcases her stockpile of surrealist, futurist and abstract expressionist art with works by up to 200 artists, including her ex-husband Max Ernst, Jackson Pollock (among her many rumoured lovers), Picasso and Salvador Dalí.

Basilica di Santa Maria
della Salute   BASILICA

(La Salute; Map p502; ☑ 041 241 10 18; www.seminariovenezia.it; Campo della Salute 1b; admission free, sacristy adult/reduced €3/1.50; ⊙9am-noon & 3-5.30pm; 🛥Salute) Guarding the entrance to the Grand Canal, this 17th-century domed church was commissioned by Venice's plague survivors as thanks for their salvation. Baldassare Longhena's uplifting design is an engineering feat that defies simple logic; in fact the church is said to have mystical curative properties. Titian eluded the plague until age 94, leaving 12 key paintings in the basilica's art-slung sacristy.

★**I Frari** CHURCH
(Basilica di Santa Maria Gloriosa dei Frari; Campo dei Frari, San Polo 3072; adult/reduced €3/1.50; ⊙9am-6pm Mon-Sat, 1-6pm Sun; ♿; 🛥San Tomà) A soaring Italian-brick Gothic church, I Frari's assets include marquetry choir stalls, Canova's pyramid mausoleum, Bellini's achingly sweet *Madonna with Child* triptych in the sacristy and Longhena's creepy Doge Pesaro funereal monument. Upstaging them

❶ NAVIGATING VENICE

Venice is not an easy place to navigate and even with a map you're bound to get lost. The main area of interest lies between Santa Lucia train station (signposted as the Ferrovia) and Piazza San Marco (St Mark's Sq) The path between the two – Venice's main drag – is a good 40- to 50-minute walk. It also helps to know that the city is divided into six *sestieri* (districts): Cannaregio, Castello, San Marco, Dorsoduro, San Polo and Santa Croce.

all, however, is the small altarpiece. This is Titian's lauded 1518 *Assunta* (Assumption), in which a radiant red-cloaked Madonna reaches heavenward, steps onto a cloud and escapes this mortal coil. Titian himself – lost

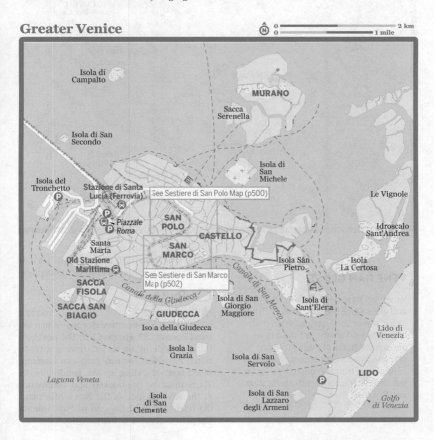

Sestiere di San Polo

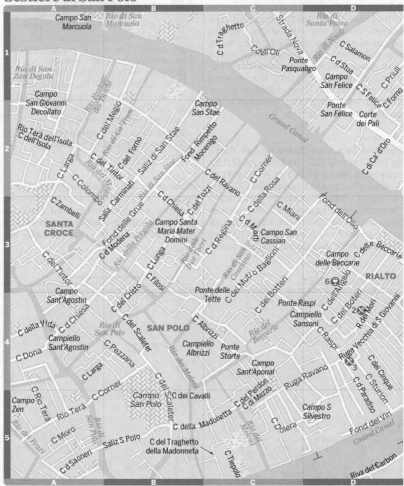

to the plague in 1576 at the age of 94 – is buried here near his celebrated masterpiece.

Tours

★ **Row Venice**   BOAT TOUR

(☑ 347 7250637; www.rowvenice.org; 90min lessons 1-2 people €80, 4 people €120) The next best thing to walking on water: rowing a traditional *batellina coda di gambero* (shrimp-tailed boat) standing up like gondoliers do. Tours must be pre-booked and commence at the wooden gate of the Sacca Misericordia boat marina at the end of Fondamenta Gasparo Contarini in Cannaregio.

VENETIAN GLASS

Venetians have been working in crystal and glass since the 10th century. Trade secrets were so closely guarded that any glass worker who left the city was considered guilty of treason. Today, along Murano's Fondamenta dei Vetrai, centuries of tradition are upheld by Davide Penso, Nason Moretti and Marina and Susanna Sent.

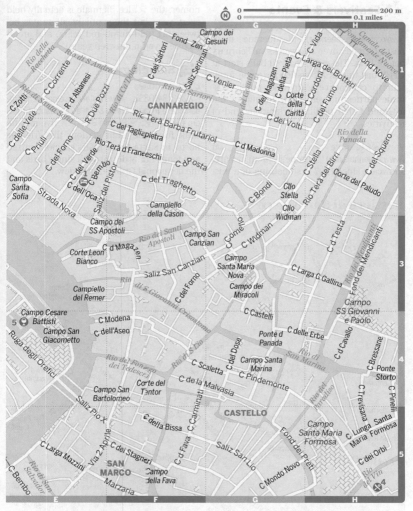

Walks Inside Venice   WALKING TOUR

(📞 041 524 17 06; www.walksinsidevenice.com; 2½hr group tours per person €60; 🚶) A spirited team runs both private tours (maximum six people) and public group tours (maximum eight people) exploring the city's major monuments and hidden backstreets. Group tours include explorations of the San Marco and San Polo, while private tour options include contemporary art and photography, and Venice's lagoon islands.

Sestiere di San Polo

🛏 Sleeping

🍴 Eating

🍷 Drinking & Nightlife

✿ Festivals & Events

Carnevale
CARNIVAL

(www.carnevale.venezia.it) Masquerade madness stretches over two weeks in February before Lent. Tickets to masked balls start at €140, but there's a free-flowing wine fountain to commence Carnevale, public costume parties in every *campo* (square) and a Grand Canal flotilla marking the end of festivities.

Venice Biennale
ART

(www.labiennale.org) Europe's premier arts showcase since 1907 is something of a misnomer: the Venice Biennale is actually held every year, but the spotlight alternates between art (odd-numbered years) and architecture (even-numbered years).

🛏 Sleeping

L'Imbarcadero
HOSTEL €

(☑ 392 3410861; www.hostelvenice.net; cnr Imbarcadero Riva de Biasio & Calle Zen, Santa Croce; dm €18-27; 🛜; 🚤 Riva de Biasio) A five-minute walk from the train station, this friendly hostel in Santa Croce offers spacious mixed and female-only dorms with single beds and the occasional Grand Canal view.

Sestiere di San Marco

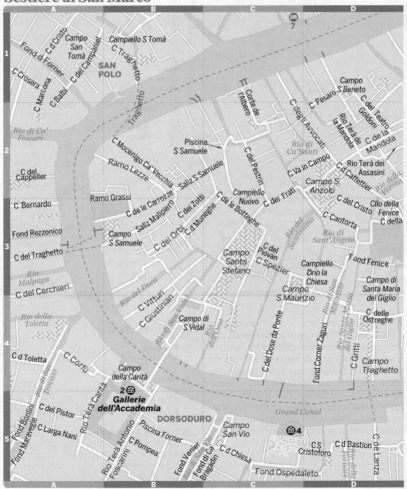

Hotel Bernardi   HOTEL **€**

(Map p500; ☎ 041 522 72 57; www.hotelbernardi.com; SS Apostoli Calle dell'Oca 4366, Cannaregio; s €48-110, d €57-90, f €75-140, without bathroom s €25-32, d €45-62; ❋ 🛜) Hospitable owners, a convenient location just off the main thoroughfare, and keen prices mean that the Bernardi is always heavily booked. Some of the best rooms – think timber-beamed ceilings, Murano chandeliers and gilt furniture – are in the annexe round the corner.

Ca' Angeli   BOUTIQUE HOTEL **€€**

(Map p502; ☎ 041 523 24 80; www.caangeli.it; Calle del Traghetto de la Madoneta 1434, San Polo;

BUILDING VENICE

Impossible though it seems, Venetians built their home on 117 small islands connected by some 400 bridges over 150 canals. But if floating marble palaces boggle the mind, consider what's underneath them: an entire forest's worth of wood pylons, rammed through silty barene (shoals) into the clay lagoon floor. Some 100,000 petrified pylons support the brick and Istrian stone base of Baldassare Longhena's 1631 Basilica di Santa Maria della Salute.

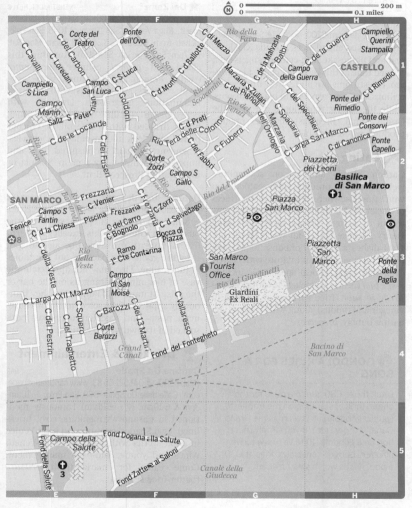

Sestiere di San Marco

Top Sights

1	Basilica di San Marco	H2
2	Gallerie dell'Accademia	B4

Sights

3	Basilica di Santa Maria della Salute	E5
4	Peggy Guggenheim Collection	C5
5	Piazza San Marco	G3
6	Ponte dei Sospiri	H3

Sleeping

7	Ca' Angeli	C1

Entertainment

8	Teatro La Fenice	E3

d €95-225, ste from €200; ; San Silvestro) Murano glass chandeliers, a Louis XIV loveseat and namesake 16th-century angels set a refined tone at this restored, canalside *palazzo.* Guestrooms are a picture with beamed ceilings, antique carpets and big bathrooms, while the dining room looks out onto the Grand Canal. Breakfast includes organic products where possible.

Eating

Garden islands and lagoon aquaculture yield speciality produce and seafood you won't find elsewhere, with tantalising traces of ancient spice routes. The city knows how to put on a royal spread, as France's King Henry III once found out when faced with 1200 dishes and 200 bonbons. Today such feasts are available in miniature with *cicheti* (Venetian tapas). Local specialities include *risi e bisi* (peasoup thickened with rice) and *sarde in saor* (fried sardines marinated in vinegar and onions), along with Veneto's signature bubbly, *prosecco.*

> **GONDOLA RIDES FOR A SONG**
>
> Ditch those €80 gondola rides for the cheap thrill of standing on the *traghetto* (public gondola) as you cross the Grand Canal (€2 per ride). If you simply must hop on a gondola, Tu.Ri.Ve (www.turive.it) offers budget-conscious rides at €30 a pop. That's worth singing about.

★ All'Arco — VENETIAN €

(Map p500; 041 520 56 66; Calle dell'Ochialer 436, San Polo; cicheti from €1.50; 8am-8pm Wed-Fri, to 3pm Mon, Tue & Sat ; Rialto-Mercato) Search out this authentic neighbourhood *osteria* (casual tavern) for some of the best *cicheti* (bar snacks) in town. Armed with ingredients from the nearby Rialto market, father-son team Francesco and Matteo serve miniature masterpieces such as *cannocchia* (mantis shrimp) with pumpkin and roe, and *otrega crudo* (raw butterfish) with mint-and-olive-oil marinade.

Even with copious *prosecco,* hardly any meal here tops €20 or falls short of five stars.

★ Dai Zemei — VENETIAN, CICHETI €

(Map p500; 041 520 85 46; www.ostariadaizemei.it; Ruga Vecchia San Giovanni 1045, San Polo; cicheti from €1.50; 8.30am-8.30pm Mon-Sat, to 7pm Sun; San Silvestro) Running this closet-sized *cicheti* counter are *zemei* (twins) Franco and Giovanni, who serve loyal regulars small meals with outsized imagination: gorgonzola lavished with *peperoncino* (chilli) marmalade, duck breast drizzled with truffle oil, or chicory paired with leek and marinated anchovies. A gourmet bargain for inspired bites and impeccable wines – try a crisp Nosiola or invigorating Prosecco Brut.

Osteria Ruga di Jaffa — OSTERIA €

(Map p500; Ruga Giuffa 4864; meals €20-25; 8am-11pm) Hiding in plain sight on the busy Ruga Giuffa is this excellent *osteria* (casual tavern). You should be able to spot it by the *gondolieri* packing out the tables at lunch time. They may not appreciate the vase of blooming hydrangeas on the bar or the artsy Murano wall lamps, but they thoroughly approve of the select menu of house-made pastas and succulent over-roast pork soaked in its own savoury juices.

Drinking & Entertainment

Cantina Do Spade — BAR

(Map p500; 041 521 05 83; www.cantinadospade.com; Calle delle Do Spade 860, San Polo; 10am-3pm & 6-10pm; ; Rialto) Famously mentioned in Casanova's memoirs, cosy, brick-lined 'Two Spades' continues to keep Venice in good spirits with its bargain Tri-Veneto wines and young, laid-back management. Come early for market-fresh *fritture* (batter-fried seafood).

★Al Mercà WINE BAR
(Map p500; Campo Cesare Battisti 213, San Polo; ⏱10am-2.30pm & 6-9pm Mon-Thu, to 9.30pm Fri & Sat; ⛴Rialto) Discerning drinkers throng to this cupboard-sized counter on a Rialto market square to sip on top-notch *prosecco* and DOC wines by the glass (from €2). Edibles usually include meatballs and mini *panini* (from €1), proudly made using super-fresh ingredients.

Teatro La Fenice OPERA
(Map p502; ☎041 78 65 11, theatre tours 041 78 66 75; www.teatrolafenice.it; Campo San Fantin 1965; theatre visits adult/reduced €9/6, concert/opera tickets from €15/45; ⏱tours 9.30am-6pm; ⛴Santa Maria dei Giglio) La Fenice, one of Italy's top opera houses, hosts a rich program of opera, ballet and classical music. With advance booking you can tour the theatre, but the best way to see it is with the *loggionisti* – opera buffs in the cheap top-tier seats. Get tickets at the theatre, online or through **HelloVenezia** (☎041 24 24; Piazzale Roma; ⏱transport tickets 7am-8pm events tickets 8.30am-6.30pm; ⛴Piazzale Roma).

Information

Airport Tourist Office (☎041 529 87 11; www.turismovenezia.it; Arrivals Hall, Marco Polo Airport; ⏱8.30am-7.30pm)

San Marco Tourist Office (Map p502; ☎041 529 87 11; www.turismovenezia.it; Piazza San Marco 71F; ⏱8.30am-7pm; ⛴San Marco)

Getting There & Away

Marco Polo Airport (VCE) Located on the mainland 12km from Venice, east of Mestre. Alilaguna operates a ferry service (€15) to Venice from the airport ferry dock (an eight-minute walk from the terminal); expect it to take 45 to 90 minutes to reach most destinations. Water taxis to Venice from airport docks cost from €110, or from €25 for shared taxis with up to 10 passengers. ATVO buses (€6) depart from the airport every 30 minutes from 7.50am to 12.20am, and reach Venice's Piazzale Roma within 20 to 30 minutes, traffic permitting.

Piazzale Roma This car park is the only point within central Venice accessible by car or bus. *Vaporetto* (water-bus) lines to destinations throughout the city depart from Piazzale Roma docks.

Stazione Santa Lucia Venice's train station. *Vaporetto* lines depart from Ferrovia (Station) docks to all parts of Venice. There is also a handy water-taxi stand just out front if you are heavily laden.

DISCOUNT PASSES

Access some of Venice's finest masterpieces in 16 churches with a Chorus Pass. It costs €12 (for a total saving of €35), and includes such spectacular sights as I Frari, Chiesa di Santa Maria dei Miracoli, Chiesa di San Sebastiano and Chiesa della Madonna dell'Orto.

The San Marco Museums Pack (€17) covers the Palazzo Ducale, Museo Correr, Museo Archeologico Nazionale and Biblioteca Nazionale Marciana. Or get even more history for your money: for €7 extra, buy the Civic Museum Pass, which grants access to an extra seven museums.

Stazione Venezia Mestre Mestre's mainland train station; transfer here to Stazione Santa Lucia.

Getting Around

Vaporetto Venice's main public transport. Single rides cost €7; for frequent use, get a timed pass for unlimited travel within a set period (one/two/three/seven-day passes cost €20/30/40/60). Tickets and passes are available dockside from ACTV ticket booths and ticket vending machines, or from tobacconists.

Gondola Daytime rates run to €80 for 30 minutes (six passengers maximum) or €100 for 35 minutes from 7pm to 8am, not including songs (negotiated separately) or tips.

Traghetto Locals use this daytime public gondola service (€2) to cross the Grand Canal between bridges.

Water taxi Sleek teak boats offer taxi services for €15 plus €2 per minute, plus €5 for pre-booked services and extra for night-time, luggage and large groups. Ensure the meter is working when boarding.

Florence

POP 377,200

Return time and again and you still won't see it all. Surprisingly small as it is, this riverside city looms large on the world's 'must-sees' list. Cradle of the Renaissance and of tourist masses that flock here to feast on world-class art, Florence (Firenze) is magnetic, romantic and busy. Its urban fabric has hardly changed since the Renaissance, its narrow streets evoke a thousand tales, and its food and wine are so wonderful the

Florence

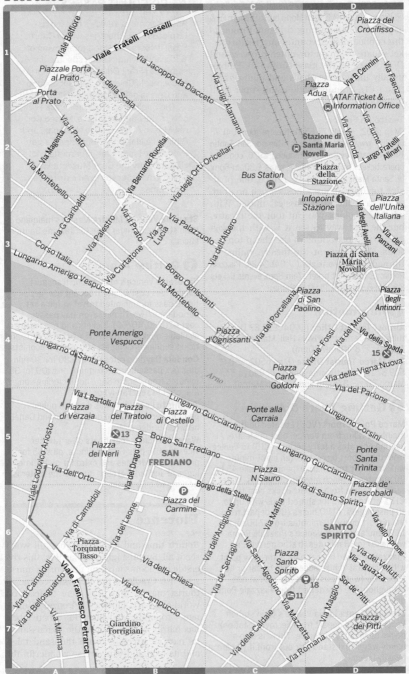

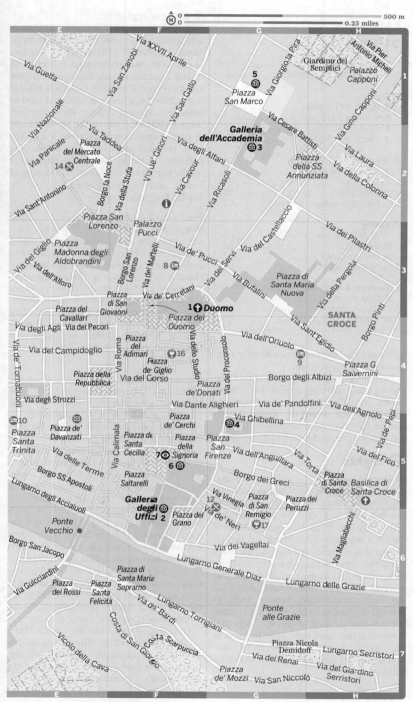

N
0 ———————————————— 500 m
0 ———————————————— 0.25 miles

Via Pier
Antonio Micheli

Via Guelfa

Via XXVII Aprile

Via Giorgio la Pira

Giardino dei
Semplici

Palazzo
Capponi

Via San Zanobi

5
Piazza
San Marco

Via Nazionale

Via San Gallo

Via Taddea

Piazza
del Mercato
Centrale

Via Panicale

14

Via degli Alfani

Galleria
dell'Accademia
3

Via Cesare Battisti

Piazza
della SS
Annunziata

Via Gino Capponi

Via Laura

Via della Colonna

Via Sant'Antonino

Borgo la Noce

Via de' Ginori

Via Cavour

Via Ricasoli

Via della Stufa

Piazza San
Lorenzo

Palazzo
Pucci

Via dei Pilastri

Via dei Martelli

Borgo San
Lorenzo

Piazza
Madonna degli
Aldobrandini

Via de' Pucci

Via de' Servi

Via Bufalini

Piazza di
Santa Maria
Nuova

Via della Pergola

Via del Giglio

Via dell'Alloro

8

Via de' Cerretani

Piazza
di San
Giovanni

1 Duomo

Piazza del
Duomo

Via dello Studio

Via del Castellaccio

SANTA
CROCE

Borgo Pinti

Piazza del
Cavallari

Via degli Agli   Via dei Pecori

Piazza
del
Adimari

Via dell'Oriuolo

Via Sant'Egidio

Piazza G
Salvemini

Via del Campidoglio

Piazza
de' Giglio
Via del Corso

16

Via del Proconsolo

9

Piazza della
Repubblica

Via degli Strozzi

Piazza
de'Donati

Via Dante Alighieri

Borgo degli Albizi

Via de' Pandolfini

Via dell'Agnolo

Via de' Tornabuoni

10

Piazza
Santa
Trinita

Piazza de'
Davanzati

Via delle Terme

Piazza di
Santa
Cecilia

Via Calimala

Piazza
de' Cerchi

Piazza
della
Signoria

Piazza
San
Firenze

4

Via Ghibellina

Via dell'Anguillara

Via Torta

Via de' Pepi

Via del Fico

Borgo SS Apostoli

7

6

Borgo dei Greci

Piazza
di Santa
Croce

Basilica di
Santa Croce

Lungarno degli Acciaiuoli

Piazza
Saltarelli

Galleria
degli
Uffizi 2

Piazza del
Grano

12

Via Vinegia

Via de' Neri

Piazza
di San
Remigio

17

Piazza dei
Peruzzi

Via Magliabechi

Ponte
Vecchio

Borgo San Jacopo

Lungarno Generale Diaz

Via dei Vagellai

Lungarno delle Grazie

Via Guicciardini

Piazza
dei Rossi

Piazza
Santa
Felicità

Piazza di
Santa Maria
Soprarno

Lungarno Torrigiani

Via de' Bardi

Ponte
alle Grazie

Vicolo della Cava

Costa di San Giorgio

Costa Scarpuccia

Piazza
de' Mozzi

Piazza Nicola
Demidoff

Via dei Renai

Via San Niccolò

Lungarno Serristori

Via del Giardino
Serristori

E   F   G   H

Florence

tag 'Fiorentina' has become an international label of quality assurance.

Fashion designers parade on Via de' Tornabuoni. Gucci was born here, as was Roberto Cavalli, who, like many a smart Florentine these days, hangs out in wine-rich hills around Florence. After a while in this absorbing city, you might want to do the same.

◉ Sights

★ Duomo   CATHEDRAL
(Cattedrale di Santa Maria del Fiore; www.operaduomo.firenze.it; Piazza del Duomo; ⊙10am-5pm Mon-Wed & Fri, to 4.30pm Thu, to 4.45pm Sat, 1.30-4.45pm Sun) FREE Florence's Duomo is the city's most iconic landmark. Capped by Filippo Brunelleschi's red-tiled cupola, it's a staggering construction whose breathtaking pink, white and green marble facade and graceful *campanile* (bell tower) dominate the medieval cityscape. Sienese architect Arnolfo di Cambio began work on it 1296, but construction took almost 150 years and it wasn't consecrated until 1436. In the echoing interior, look out for frescoes by Vasari and Zuccari and up to 44 stained-glass windows.

★ Galleria degli Uffizi   GALLERY
(Uffizi Gallery; www.uffizi.beniculturali.it; Piazzale degli Uffizi 6; adult/reduced €8/4, incl temporary exhibition €12.50/6.25; ⊙8.15am-6.50pm Tue-Sun) Home to the world's greatest collection of Italian Renaissance art, Florence's premier gallery occupies the vast U-shaped Palazzo degli Uffizi, built between 1560 and 1580 to house government offices. The collection, bequeathed to the city by the Medici family in 1743 on condition that it never leave Florence, contains some of Italy's best-known paintings including Piero della Francesco's profile potaits of the Duke and Duchess of Urbino, and a room full of masterpieces by Sandro Botticelli.

Piazza della Signoria   PIAZZA
(Piazza della Signoria) The hub of local life since the 13th century, Florentines flock here to meet friends and chat over early-evening *aperitivi* at historic cafes. Presiding over everything is **Palazzo Vecchio**, Florence's city hall, and the 14th-century **Loggia dei Lanzi**, an open-air gallery showcasing Renaissance sculptures, including Giambologna's *Rape of the Sabine Women* (c 1583), Benvenuto Cellini's bronze *Perseus* (1554) and Agnolo Gaddi's *Seven Virtues* (1384–89).

Palazzo Vecchio   MUSEUM
(🖅 055 276 82 24; www.musefirenze.it; Piazza della Signoria; museum adult/reduced €10/8, tower €10/8, museum & tower €14/12, guided tour €4; ⊙museum 9am-11pm Fri-Wed, to 2pm Thu summer, 9am-7pm Fri-Wed, to 2pm Thu winter; tower 9am-9pm Fri-Wed, to 2pm Thu summer, 10am-5pm Fri-Wed, to 2pm Thu winter) This fortress palace, with its crenellations and 94m-high tower, was designed by Arnolfo di Cambio between 1298 and 1314 for the *signoria* (city government). It remains the seat of the city's power, home to the mayor's office and the municipal council. From the top of the **Torre d'Arnolfo** (tower), you can revel in unforgettable rooftop views. Inside, Michelangelo's *Genio della Vittoria* (Genius of Victory) sculpture graces the Salone dei Cinquecento, a magnificent painted hall created for the city's 15th-century ruling Consiglio dei Cinquecento (Council of 500).

On rain-free days, take the 418-step hike up the palace's striking Torre d'Arnolfo. No more than 25 people are allowed at any one time and you have just 30 minutes to lap up the brilliant city panorama.

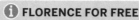

Ponte Vecchio
BRIDGE

Dating to 1345, Ponte Vecchio was the only Florentine bridge to survive destruction at the hands of retreating German forces in 1944. Above the jewellers' shops on the eastern side, the **Corridoio Vasariano** (Vasari corridor) is a 16th-century passageway between the Uffizi and Palazzo Pitti that runs around, rather than through, the medieval **Torre dei Mannelli** at the bridge's southern end. The first documentation of a stone bridge here, at the narrowest crossing point along the entire length of the Arno, dates from 972.

Museo del Bargello
MUSEUM

(www.polomuseale.firenze.it; Via de Proconsolo 4; adult/reduced €4/2; ⊙ 8.15am-4.50pm summer, to 1.50pm winter, closed 1st, 3rd & 5th Sun & 2nd & 4th Mon of month) It was behind the stark walls of Palazzo del Bargello, Florence's earliest public building, that the *podestà* meted out justice from the late 13th century until 1502. Today the building safeguards Italy's most comprehensive collection of Tuscan Renaissance sculpture with some of Michelangelo's best early works and a hall full of Donatello's. Michelangelo was just 21 when a cardinal commissioned him to create the drunken grape-adorned Bacchus (1496-97), displayed in Bargello's downstairs **Sala di Michelangelo**.

Basilica di Santa Croce
CHURCH, MUSEUM

(www.santacroceopera.it; Piazza di Santa Croce; adult/reduced €6/4; ⊙ 9.30am-5.30pm Mon-Sat,

---

❶ FLORENCE FOR FREE

To cut costs, visit on the first Sunday of the month, when admission to state museums, including the Uffizi and Galleria dell'Accademia, is free. EU passport holders aged under 18 and over 65 get into Florence's state museums for free, and EU citizens aged 18 to 25 pay half-price. Have your ID with you at all times.

DON'T MISS

PALAZZO VECCHIO TOURS

Join the 'Secret Passages' tour (adult/reduced €12/10, 1½ hours, twice daily), which leads small groups along the secret staircase built between the palace's super-thick walls in 1342 as an escape route for French Duke of Athens Walter de Brienne, who seized the palace and nominated himself Lord of Florence, only to be sent packing back to France by the Florentines a year later. It follows this staircase to the Tesoretto (Treasury) of Cosimo I – a tiny room no larger than a cupboard for his private collection – and the equally intimate, sumptuous Studiolo (Study) of his introverted, alchemy-mad son Francesco I. Cosimo commissioned Vasari and a team of Florentine mannerist artists to decorate the study; Francesco appears in one of the 34 emblematic paintings covering the walls not as a prince, but as a scientist experimenting with gunpowder. The lower paintings concealed 20 cabinets in which the young prince hid his shells, crystals and other treasures. The tour ends in the palace roof above the Salone dei Cinquecento, where you can see the huge wooden trusses supporting Vasari's ornate ceiling.

The 'Invitation to Court' tour (adult/child €12/2, 1¼ hours) is open to visitors aged eight years and upwards. Actors dressed in Renaissance costume rope young participants into the performance. A sumptuously attired Eleonora of Toledo, clearly shocked by the casual attire of today's children, has been known to give advice about proper grooming for young ladies, and Cosimo I is happy to lay down the law about the proper age for a Medici to take on duties as a cardinal (the answer is 14, the age of his son Ferdinando when he became a cardinal). Other engaging tours specifically designed with children in mind include 'At Court with Donna Isabelle' (adult/child €12/2, 1¼ hours) for kids from age 10, led by a gregarious Spanish Isabel de Reinoso; and 'Life at Court' (adult/child €12/2, 70 minutes) for four to seven year olds, which ends with a 16th-century dressing-up session. There are also story-telling sessions for children and hands-on fresco and panel painting workshops (adult/child €12/2, 1¼ hours) led by an actor dressed up as Giorgio Vasari.

Reserve tours and workshops in advance by telephone (☎ 055 276 82 24, ☎ 055 276 85 58) or email info@muse.comune.fi.it.

ⓘ LOOKING THE PART

Churches enforce a strict dress code for visitors: no shorts, sleeveless shirts or plunging necklines. Photography with no flash is allowed in museums, but leave the selfie stick at home.

2-5.30pm Sun) The austere interior of this Franciscan basilica is a shock after the magnificent neo-Gothic facade enlivened by varying shades of coloured marble. Most visitors come to see the tombs of Michelangelo, Galileo and Ghiberti inside this church, but frescoes by Giotto in the chapels right of the altar are the real highlights. The basilica was designed by Arnolfo di Cambio between 1294 and 1385 and owes its name to a splinter of the Holy Cross donated by King Louis of France in 1258.

★ Galleria dell'Accademia   GALLERY

(☑ 055 29 48 83; www.firenzemusei.it; Via Ricasoli 60; adult/reduced €8/4; ◷ 8.15am-6.50pm Tue-Sun) A queue marks the door to this gallery, built to house one of the Renaissance's most iconic masterpieces, Michelangelo's *David*. But the world's most famous statue is worth the wait. The subtle detail of the real thing – the veins in his sinewy arms, the leg muscles, the change in expression as you move around the statue – *is* impressive. Carved from a single block of marble, Michelangelo's most famous work was his most challenging – he didn't choose the marble himself and it was veined.

Museo di San Marco   MUSEUM

(☑ 055 238 86 08; Piazza San Marco 3; adult/reduced €4/2; ◷ 8.15am-1.50pm Mon-Fri, 8.15am-4.50pm Sat & Sun, closed 1st, 3rd & 5th Sun & 2nd & 4th Mon of month) At the heart of Florence's university area sits **Chiesa di San Marco** and adjoining 15th-century Dominican monastery where both gifted painter Fra' Angelico (c 1395–1455) and the sharp-tongued Savonarola piously served God. Today the monastery, aka one of Florence's most spiritually uplifting Museo museums, showcases the work of Fra' Angelico. After centuries of being known as 'Il Beato Angelico' (literally 'The Blessed Angelic One') or simply 'Il Beato' (The Blessed), the Renaissance's most blessed religious painter was made a saint by Pope John Paul II in 1984.

🛏 Sleeping

Hotel Dalí   HOTEL €

(☑ 055 234 07 06; www.hoteldali.com; Via dell'Oriuolo 17; d €90, s/d without bathroom €40/70, apt from €95; 🅿 🛜) A warm welcome from hosts Marco and Samanta awaits at this lovely small hotel. A stone's throw from the Duomo, it has 10 sunny rooms, some overlooking a leafy inner courtyard, decorated in a low-key modern way and equipped with kettles, coffee and tea. No breakfast, but – miraculous for downtown Florence – free parking in the rear courtyard.

The icing on the cake is a trio of gorgeous self-catering apartments – one with a Duomo view – sleeping two, four or six.

Academy Hostel   HOSTEL €

(☑ 055 239 86 65; www.academyhostel.eu; Via Ricasoli 9r; dm €32-36, s/d €42/100, d without bathroom €85; ✳ @ 🛜) This classy 10-room, 40-bed hostel sits on the 1st floor of Baron Ricasoli's 17th-century *palazzo*. The inviting lobby area was once a theatre and 'dorms' sport maximum four or six beds, high moulded ceilings and brightly coloured lock-

ⓘ SHORT ON TIME?

In July, August and other busy periods such as Easter, unbelievably long queues are a fact of life at Florence's key museums – if you haven't prebooked your ticket, you could well end up standing in line for four hours or so.

For a fee of €3 per ticket (€4 for the Uffizi and Galleria dell'Accademia), tickets to nine *musei statali* (state museums) can be reserved, including the Uffizi, Galleria dell'Accademia (where *David* lives), Palazzo Pitti, Museo del Bargello and the Medicean chapels (Cappelle Medicee). In reality, the only museums where prebooking is vital are the Uffizi and Accademia – to organise your ticket, go online or call **Firenze Musei** (p512), with ticketing desks (open 8.30am to 7pm Tuesday to Sunday) at the Uffizi and Palazzo Pitti. Many hotels in Florence also prebook museum tickets for guests.

You'll still have to queue to collect your ticket and with other pre-booked ticket holders to enter the gallery, but you'll save hours of time.

WHO'S THAT BLOKE?

Name *David*.

Occupation World's most famous sculpture.

Vital statistics Height: 516cm tall; weight: 19 tonnes of mediocre-quality pearly white marble from the Fantiscritti quarries in Carrara.

Commissioned In 1501 by the Opera del Duomo for the cathedral, but subsequently placed in front of the Palazzo Vecchio on Piazza della Signoria, where it stayed until 1873.

Outstanding features (a) His expression, which, from the left profile, appears serene, Zen and boy-like, and from the right, concentrated, manly and highly charged in anticipation of the gargantuan Goliath he is about to slay; (b) the sense of counterbalanced weight rippling through his body, from the tension in his right hip on which he leans to his taut left arm.

Why the small penis? In classical art a large or even normal-sized packet was not deemed elegant, hence the daintier size.

And the big head and hands? *David* was designed to stand up high on a cathedral buttress in the apse, from where his head and hands would have appeared in perfect proportion.

Beauty treatments Body scrub with hydrochloric acid (1843); clay and cellulose pulp 'mud pack', bath in distilled water (2004).

Occupational hazards Over the centuries he's been struck by lightning, attacked by rioters and had his toes bashed with a hammer. The two pale white lines visible on his lower left arm is where his arm got broken during the 1527 revolt when the Medici were kicked out of Florence.

ers. The terrace is a perfect spot to chill. No credit cards for payments under €100.

★ Palazzo Guadagni Hotel HOTEL €€
(☑ 055 265 83 76; www.palazzoguadagni.com; Piazza Santo Spirito 9; d €130-220; ❄ 🤶) This romantic hotel overlooking Florence's liveliest summertime square is legendary – Zefferelli shot scenes from *Tea with Mussolini* here. Housed in an artfully revamped Renaissance palace, it has 15 spacious if old-fashioned rooms and an impossibly romantic loggia terrace with wicker chairs and predictably dreamy views. Off season, double room rates drop to as low as €90.

Hotel Scoti PENSION €€
(☑ 055 29 21 28; www.hotelscoti.com; Via de' Tornabuoni 7; s/d €75/130; 🤶) Wedged between the designer stores on Florence's smartest shopping strip, this hidden *pensione* is a splendid mix of old-fashioned charm and value for money. Its 16 traditionally styled rooms are spread across the 2nd floor of a towering 16th-century *palazzo*, with some offering lovely rooftop views. The star of the show, though, is the frescoed lounge from 1780. Breakfast €5.

Eating

All'Antico Vinaio OSTERIA €
(☑ 055 238 27 23; www.allanticovinaio.com; Via dei Neri 65r; tasting platters €8-30, focaccia €5-7; ☺ 10am-4pm & 6-11pm Tue-Sat, noon-3.30pm Sun) The crowd spills out the door of this noisy Florentine thoroughbred. Push your way to the tables at the back and pray for a pew to taste cheese and salami in situ. Or join the queue at the deli counter for a well-stuffed focaccia (€5 to €7) wrapped in waxed paper to take away – quality is outstanding. Pour yourself a glass of wine (€2) while you wait.

★ Berberé PIZZA €
(☑ 055 238 29 46; www.berberepizza.it; Piazza dei Nerli 1; pizza €6.50-13; ☺ noon-2.30pm & 7pm-midnight Fri-Sun, 7pm-midnight Mon-Thu) Florence's stunning new kid on the block, this modern pizza space in San Frediano is an inspirational cocktail of perfect pizza, delicious craft beers brewed by small producers and striking contemporary interior design. Grab a stool at the white marble bar and pick from 14 pizza types – several are vegetarian – made with organic flour and live yeast. Reservations essential.

Trattoria Marione

TRATTORIA €

(☑055 21 47 56; Via della Spada 27; meals €25; ⊗noon-3pm & 7-11pm) For the quintessential 'Italian dining' experience, Marione is gold. It's busy, it's noisy, it's 99.9% local and the cuisine is right out Nonna's Tuscan kitchen. No one appears to speak English so go for Italian – the tasty excellent-value traditional fare is worth it. If you don't get a complimentary *limoncello* with the bill you clearly failed the language test.

Mercato Centrale

TUSCAN €

(☑055 239 97 98; www.mercatocentrale.it; Piazza del Mercato Centrale 4; dishes €7-15; ⊗10am-1am, food stalls noon-3pm & 7pm-midnight; 🛜) Meander the maze of stalls rammed with fresh produce at Florence's oldest and largest food market, on the ground of a 19th-century iron-and-glass structure. Then head up to the shiny new 1st floor – a vibrant food fair with dedicated bookshop, cookery school, bar and stalls cooking up steaks, grilled burgers, vegetarian dishes, pizza, gelato, pastries and pasta. Load up and find a free table.

🍷 Drinking & Nightlife

★ Coquinarius

WINE BAR

(www.coquinarius.com; Via delle Oche 11r; crostini & carpacci €4, meals €35; ⊗noon-10.30pm) With its old stone vaults, scrubbed wooden tables and refreshingly modern air, this *enoteca* run by the dynamic and charismatic Nicolas is spacious and stylish. The wine list features bags of Tuscan greats and unknowns, and outstanding *crostini* and *carpacci* (cold sliced meats) ensure you don't leave hungry.

Ditta Artigianale

BAR

(☑055 274 15 41; www.dittaartigianale.it; Via dei Neri 32r; ⊗8am-10pm Mon-Thu, 8am-midnight Fri, 9.30am-midnight Sat, 9.30am-10pm Sun; 🛜) With industrial decor and welcoming laid-back vibe, ingenious coffee roastery–cafe-bar Ditta Artigianale rocks. Behind the bar is well-travelled Florentine barista Francesco

Sanapo and gin queen Cecilia who together shake and mix what the city's most compelling hybrid is famed for – first-class coffee and outstanding gin cocktails.

Brunch is served from 10am to 4pm, and a gourmet *aperitivo* kicks in at 7pm, making it a perfect place to hang out whatever the time of day.

Volume

BAR

(www.volumefirenze.com; Piazza Santo Spirito 3r; ⊗9am-1.30am) Armchairs, recycled and up-cycled vintage furniture, books to read, a juke box, crepes and a tasty choice of nibbles with coffee or a light lunch give this hybrid cafe-bar-gallery real appeal – all in an old hat-making workshop with tools and wooden moulds strewn around. Watch for various music, art and DJ events and happenings.

ℹ Information

Central Tourist Office (☑055 29 08 32; www.firenzeturismo.it; Via Cavour 1r; ⊗9am-6pm Mon-Sat)

Firenze Musei (Florence Museums; ☑055 29 48 83; www.firenzemusei.it)

Infopoint Stazione (☑055 21 22 45; www.firenzeturismo.it; Piazza della Stazione 5; ⊗9am-7pm Mon-Sat, to 2pm Sun)

ℹ Getting There & Away

AIR

Tuscany's main international **airport** (Galileo Galilei Airport; ☑050 84 93 00; www.pisa-airport.com) is in Pisa and offers flights to most major European cities.

To get to/from Pisa airport, daily buses are operated by Terravision (www.terravision.eu; one way €4.99, 70 minutes) and Autostradale (www.airportbusexpress.it; one way €5, 80 minutes, hourly) between the airport and the bus stops outside Florence's Stazione di Santa Maria Novella on Via Luigi Alamanni (under the digital station clock). For either company, buy tickets online, on board and in Pisa at the Pisa Airport Information Desk in the arrrivals hall.

Regular trains link Florence's Stazione di Santa Maria Novella with the central train station in Pisa, Pisa Centrale (€8, 1½ hours, at least hourly from 4.30am to 10.25pm), from where the PisaMover shuttle bus (€1.30, eight minutes) continues to Pisa International Airport.

BUS

Services from the **SITA bus station** (Autostazione Busitalia-Sita Nord; ☑800 37 37 60; Via Santa Caterina da Siena 17r; ⊗5.30am-8.30pm Mon-Sat, 6am-8pm Sun), just west of Piazza della Stazione, are limited; the train is better.

CINQUE TERRE

Set amid some of the most dramatic coastal scenery on the planet, these five ingeniously constructed fishing villages can bolster the most jaded of spirits. A Unesco World Heritage Site since 1997, Cinque Terre isn't the undiscovered Eden it once was but, frankly, who cares? Sinuous paths traverse seemingly impregnable cliffsides, while a 19th-century railway line cut through a series of coastal tunnels ferries the footsore from village to village. Thankfully cars were banned over a decade ago.

Rooted in antiquity, Cinque Terre's five villages date from the early medieval period. Monterosso, the oldest, was founded in AD 643, followed by Riomaggiore, Vernazza, Corniglia and Manarola. Much of what remains in the villages today dates from the late High Middle Ages, including several castles and a quintet of illustrious parish churches.

Fetching vernacular architecture aside, Cinque Terre's unique historical feature is the steeply terraced cliffs bisected by a complicated system of fields and gardens that have been hacked, chiselled, shaped and layered over the course of nearly two millennia. So marked are these artificial contours that some scholars have compared the extensive *muretti* (low stone walls) to the Great Wall of China in their grandeur and scope.

In October 2011 flash floods along the Ligurian coast wreaked havoc in Vernazza and Monterosso, burying historic streets and houses under metres of mud and killing half-a-dozen people. The villages, in resiliant Ligurian style, recovered swiftly, but some of the walking trails remain fragile and closed to visitors.

However, Cinque Terre has a whole network of spectacular trails and you can still plan a decent village-to-village hike by choosing from any of 30 numbered paths. Check ahead for the most up-to-date trail information at www.parconazionale5terre.it/sentieri_parco.asp. Also see www.cinque terre.it and www.cinqueterre.com.

Sleeping & Eating

Hotel Pasquale (☑ 0187 81 74 77; www.hotelpasquale.it; Via Fegina 4; s €80-160, d €140-220, tr €170-300; ☺ Mar–mid-Nov ❀ ☎) Offering soothing views and 15 unusually stylish, modern guest rooms, this friendly seafront hotel is built into Monterosso's medieval sea walls. To find it, exit the train station and go left through the tunnel towards the *centro storico*.

Dau Cila (☑ 0187 76 00 32; www.ristorantedaucila.com; Via San Giacomo 65; meals €40; ☺ 8am-2am Mar-Oct) Perched within pebble-lobbing distance of Riomaggiore's wee harbour, Dau Cila is a smart, kitsch-free zone, and specialises in classic seafood and hyper-local wines. Pair the best Cinque Terre whites with cold plates such as smoked tuna with apples and lemon, or lemon-marinated anchovies.

Getting There & Around

Cinque Terre is sandwiched between Genoa (accessible by regular train services from Venice) and La Spezia (reached by regular train services from Florence). Between 6.30am and 10pm, one to three trains an hour trundle along the coast between Genoa and La Spezia, stopping at each of the Cinque Terre's villages. In summer the Golfo Paradiso SNC runs boats to the Cinque Terre from Genoa (one way/return €18/33).

Easily the best way to get around the Cinque Terre is with a **Cinque Terre card**, which includes unlimited use of walking paths and electric village buses, as well as cultural exhibitions. The basic one-/two-day card for those aged over four years costs €7.50/14.50. With unlimited train trips between the town, the card costs €12/23. A one-day family card for two adults and two children (under 12) costs €31.50/19.60 with/without train travel. An all-day train ticket between the villages is also good value at €4. Cards are sold at all Cinque Terre park information offices and each of Cinque Terre's train stations.

Venice's Grand Canal

The 3.5km route of vaporetto (passenger ferry) No 1, which passes some 50 palazzi (mansions), six churches and scene-stealing backdrops featured in four James Bond films, is public transport at its most glamorous.

The Grand Canal starts with controversy: **Ponte di Calatrava** ❶ a luminous glass-and-steel bridge that cost triple the original €4 million estimate. Ahead are castle-like **Fondaco dei Turchi** ❷, the historic Turkish trading-house; Renaissance **Palazzo Vendramin** ❸, housing the city's casino; and double-arcaded **Ca' Pesaro** ❹. Don't miss **Ca' d'Oro** ❺, a 1430 filigree Gothic marvel.

Points of Venetian pride include the **Pescaria** ❻, built in 1907 on the site where fishmongers have been slinging lagoon crab for 600 years, and neighbouring **Rialto Market** ❼ stalls, overflowing with island-grown produce. Cost overruns for 1592 **Ponte di Rialto** ❽ rival Calatrava's, but its marble splendour stands the test of time.

The next two canal bends could cause architectural whiplash, with Sanmicheli-designed Renaissance **Palazzo Grimani** ❾ and Mauro Codussi's **Palazzo Corner-Spinelli** ❿ followed by Giorgio Masari-designed **Palazzo Grassi** ⓫ and Baldassare Longhena's baroque jewel box, **Ca' Rezzonico** ⓬.

Wooden **Ponte dell'Accademia** ⓭ was built in 1930 as a temporary bridge, but the beloved landmark remains. Stone lions flank the **Peggy Guggenheim Collection** ⓮, where the American heiress collected ideas, lovers and art. You can't miss the dramatic dome of Longhena's **Chiesa di Santa Maria della Salute** ⓯ or **Punta della Dogana** ⓰, Venice's triangular customs warehouse reinvented as a contemporary art showcase. The Grand Canal's grand finale is pink Gothic **Palazzo Ducale** ⓱ and its adjoining **Ponte dei Sospiri** ⓲.

For more information on Venice and its sights, see p498-505.

Palazzo Grassi
French magnate François Pinault scandalised Paris when he relocated his contemporary art collection here, to be displayed in galleries designed by Gae Aulenti and Tadao Ando.

Ca' Rezzonico
See how Venice lived in baroque splendour at this 18th-century art museum with Tiepolo ceilings, silk-swagged boudoirs and even an in-house pharmacy.

Ponte dell'Accademia

Peggy Guggenheim Collection

Chiesa di Santa Maria delle Salute

Punta della Dogana
Minimalist architect Tadao Ando creatively repurposed abandoned warehouses as galleries, which now host contemporary art installations from François Pinault's collection.

LONELY PLANET/GETTY IMAGES ©

ALVARO LEIVA/GETTY IMAGES ©

Ponte di Calatrava
With its starkly streamlined fish-fin shape, the 2008 bridge was the first to be built over the Grand Canal in 75 years.

Fondaco dei Turchi
Recognisable by its double colonnade, watchtowers, and dugout canoe parked at the Museo di Storia Naturale's ground-floor loggia.

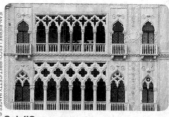

Ca' d'Oro
Behind the triple Gothic arcades are priceless masterpieces: Titians looted by Napoleon, a rare Mantegna and semiprecious stone mosaic floors.

② ③ **Palazzo Vendramin**

④ ⑤

⑥ **Pescaria**

⑦ **Rialto Market**

Palazzo Grimari ⑩
Palazzo Corner-Spinelli ⑨

⑧ **Ponte di Rialto**

Ponte dei Sospiri ⑱

Palazzo Ducale ⑰

Ponte di Rialto
Antonio da Ponte beat out Palladio for the commission of this bridge, but construction costs spiralled to 250,000 Venetian ducats – about €19 million today.

a' Pesaro
iginally designed by Baldassare Longhena, this lazzo was bequeathed to the city in 1898 to house e Galleria d'Arte Moderna and Museo d'Arte ientale.

TRAIN

Florence's central train station is **Stazione di Santa Maria Novella** (Piazza della Stazione). The **left-luggage counter** (Deposito Bagagliamano; Stazione di Santa Maria Novella; first 5hr €6, then per hr €0.90; ⊙ 6am-11pm) is located on platform 16. Tickets for all trains are sold in the main ticketing hall, but skip the permanently long queue by buying tickets from the touchscreen automatic ticket-vending machines; machines have an English option and accept cash and credit cards.

Florence is on the Rome–Milan line. Services include the following:

DESTINATION	COST (€)	DURATION
Milan	50-60	2¼-3½hr
Pisa	8	45min-1hr
Rome	43-52	1¾-4¼hr
Venice	45	2¾-4½hr

🛈 Getting Around

Florence is small and best navigated on foot, with most major sights within easy walking distance. There are bicycles for rent and an efficient network of buses and trams. Unless you're mad, forget a car.

Buses and electric minibuses run by public transport company ATAF serve the city. Most buses start/terminate at the ATAF bus stops opposite the southeastern exit of Stazione di Santa Maria Novella. Tickets valid for 90 minutes (no return journeys) cost €1.20 (€2 on board – drivers don't give change!) and are sold at kiosks, tobacconists and at the **ATAF ticket & information office** (⌨ 199 10 42 45, 800 42 45 00; www.ataf.net; Piazza della Stazione, Stazione di Santa Maria Novella; ⊙ 6.45am-8pm Mon-Sat) inside the main ticketing hall at Santa Maria Novella train station. A travel pass valid for one/three/seven days is €5/12/18. Upon boarding, time-stamp your ticket (punch on board) or risk an on-the-spot €50 fine. One tramline is up and running; more are meant to follow in 2017.

Rome

POP 2.86 MILLION

Even in this country of exquisite cities, Rome is special. Pulsating, seductive and utterly disarming, the Italian capital is an epic, monumental metropolis. They say a lifetime's not enough *(Roma, non basta una vita)*, but even on a short visit you'll be swept off your feet by its artistic and architectural masterpieces, its operatic piazzas, romantic corners and cobbled lanes. Yet while history reverberates all around, modern life is lived to the full – and it's this intoxicating mix of past and present, of style and urban grit that makes Rome such a compelling place.

◉ Sights

◉ Ancient Rome

★**Colosseum**　　　　　　　　　　RUIN
(Colosseo; Map p517; ⌨ 06 3996 7700; www.coopculture.it; Piazza del Colosseo; adult/reduced incl Roman Forum & Palatino €12/7.50; ⊙ 8.30am-1hr before sunset; Ⓜ Colosseo) Rome's great gladiatorial arena is the most thrilling of the city's ancient sights. Inaugurated in AD 80, the 50,000-seat Colosseum, originally known as the Flavian Amphitheatre, was clad in travertine and covered by a huge canvas awning held aloft by 240 masts. Inside, tiered seating encircled the arena, itself built over an underground complex (the hypogeum) where animals were caged and stage sets prepared. Games involved gladiators fighting wild animals or each other.

Palatino　　　　　　ARCHAEOLOGICAL SITE
(Palatine Hill; Map p517; ⌨ 06 3996 7700; www.coopculture.it; Via di San Gregorio 30 & Via Sacra; adult/reduced incl Colosseum & Roman Forum €12/7.50; ⊙ 8.30am-1hr before sunset; Ⓜ Colosseo) Sandwiched between the Roman Forum and the Circo Massimo, the Palatino (Palatine Hill) is an atmospheric area of towering pine trees, majestic ruins and memorable views. It was here that Romulus supposedly founded the city in 753 BC and Rome's emperors lived in unabashed luxury. Look out for the **stadio** (stadium), the ruins of the

Ancient Rome

Domus Flavia (imperial palace), and grandstand views over the Roman Forum from the **Orti Farnesiani**.

Roman Forum   ARCHAEOLOGICAL SITE
(Foro Romano; Map p517; ☑ 06 3996 7700; www.coopculture.it; Largo della Salara Vecchia & Via Sacra; adult/reduced incl Colosseum & Palatino €12/7.50; ⏰8.30am–1hr before sunset; ☐ Via dei Fori Imperiali) An impressive – if rather confusing – sprawl of ruins, the Roman Forum was ancient Rome's showpiece centre, a grandiose district of temples, basilicas and vibrant public spaces. The site, which was originally an Etruscan burial ground, was

first developed in the 7th century BC, growing over time to become the social, political and commercial hub of the Roman empire. Landmark sights include the **Arco di Settimio Severo** (Arch of Septimius Severus), the **Curia**, and the **Casa delle Vestali** (House of the Vestal Virgins).

⊙ The Vatican

★**St Peter's Basilica**   BASILICA
(Basilica di San Pietro; Map p520; www.vatican.va; St Peter's Sq; ⏰7am–7pm summer, to 6.30pm winter; Ⓜ Ottaviano-San Pietro) FREE In this city of outstanding churches, none can hold a

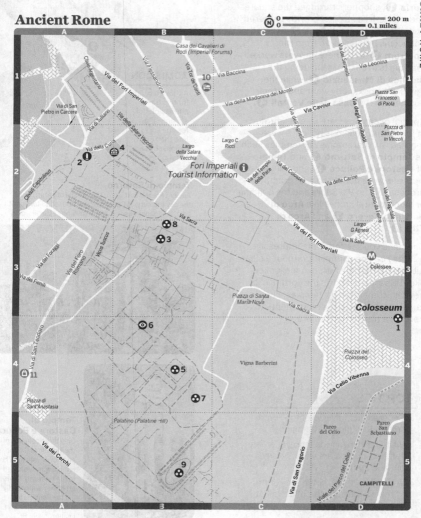

Ancient Rome

Roman Forum

In ancient times, a forum was a market place, civic centre and religious complex all rolled into one, and the greatest of all was the Roman Forum (Foro Romano). Situated between the Palatino (Palatine Hill), ancient Rome's most exclusive neighbourhood, and the Campidoglio (Capitoline Hill), it was the city's busy, bustling centre. On any given day it teemed with activity. Senators debated affairs of state in the **Curia ❶**, shoppers thronged the squares and traffic-free streets, crowds gathered under the **Colonna di Foca ❷** to listen to politicians holding forth from the **Rostrum ❷**. Elsewhere, lawyers worked the courts in basilicas including the **Basilica di Massenzio ❸**, while the Vestal Virgins quietly went about their business in the **Casa delle Vestali ❹**.

Special occasions were also celebrated in the Forum: religious holidays were marked with ceremonies at temples such as **Tempio di Saturno ❺** and **Tempio di Castore e Polluce ❻**, and military victories were honoured with dramatic processions up Via Sacra and the building of monumental arches like **Arco di Settimio Severo ❼** and **Arco di Tito ❽**.

The ruins you see today are impressive but they can be confusing without a clear picture of what the Forum once looked like. This spread shows the Forum in its heyday, complete with temples, civic buildings and towering monuments to heroes of the Roman Empire.

TOP TIPS

» Get grandstand views of the Forum from the Palatino and Campidoglio.

» Visit first thing in the morning or late afternoon; crowds are worst between 11am and 2pm.

» In summer it gets hot in the Forum and there's little shade, so take a hat and plenty of water.

Colonna di Foca & Rostrum

The free-standing, 13.5m-high Column of Phocus is the Forum's youngest monument, dating to AD 608. Behind it, the Rostrum provided a suitably grandiose platform for pontificating public speakers.

Campidoglio (Capitoline Hill)

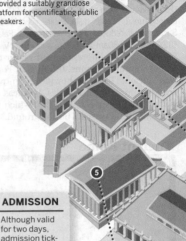

ADMISSION

Although valid for two days, admission tickets only allow for one entry into the Forum, Colosseum and Palatino.

Tempio di Saturno

Ancient Rome's Fort Knox, the Temple of Saturn was the city treasury. In Caesar's day it housed 13 tonnes of gold, 114 tonnes of silver and 30 million sestertii worth

JONATHAN SMITH/GETTY IMAGES ©

LONELY PLANET/GETTY IMAGES ©

Tempio di Castore e Polluce

Only three columns of the Temple of Castor and Pollux remain. The temple was dedicated to the Heavenly Twins after they supposedly led the Romans to victory over the Latin League in 496 BC.

Arco di Settimio Severo
One of the Forum's signature monuments, this imposing triumphal arch commemorates the military victories of Septimius Severus. Relief panels depict his campaigns against the Parthians.

Curia
This big barn-like building was the official seat of the Roman Senate. Most of what you see is a reconstruction, but the interior marble floor dates to the 3rd-century reign of Diocletian.

THE/JPEN/GETTY IMAGES ©

Basilica di Massenzio
Marvel at the scale of this vast 4th-century basilica. In its original form the central hall was divided into enormous naves; now only part of the northern nave survives.

JULIUS CAESAR
Julius Caesar was cremated on the site where the Tempio di Giulio Cesare now stands.

Via Sacra

Tempio di Giulio Cesare

Arco di Tito
Said to be the inspiration for the Arc de Triomphe in Paris, the well-preserved Arch of Titus was built by the emperor Domitian to honour his elder brother Titus.

Casa delle Vestali
White statues line the grassy atrium of what was once the luxurious 50-room home of the Vestal Virgins. The virgins played an important role in Roman religion, serving the goddess Vesta.

MANAKIN/GETTY IMAGES ©

Greater Rome

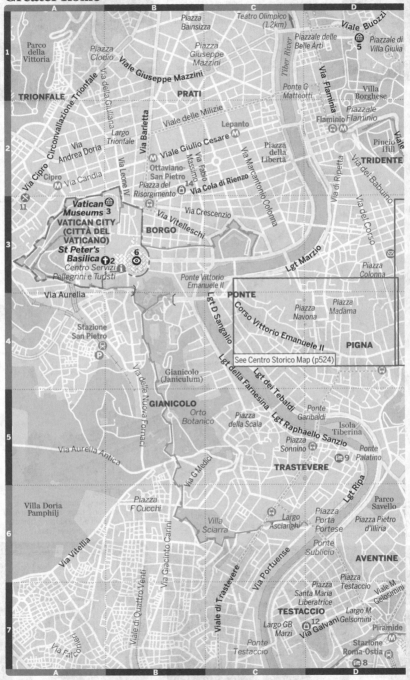

Parco della Vittoria

TRIONFALE

Piazza Clodio

Via Andrea Doria

Circonvallazione Trionfale

Via della Giuliana

Largo Trionfale

Via Cipro

Cipro

Via Candia

Via Leone IV

Piazza Bainsizza

Piazza Giuseppe Mazzini

Viale Giuseppe Mazzini

PRATI

Viale delle Milizie

Via Barletta

Lepanto

Viale Giulio Cesare

Via Fabio Massimo

Ottaviano San Pietro

Piazza del Risorgimento

Teatro Olimpico (1.2km)

Piazzale delle Belle Arti

5

Piazzale di Villa Giulia

Viale Buozzi

Tiber River

Ponte G Matteotti

Via Flaminia

Villa Borghese

Piazza della Libertà

Piazza della Liberta

Via Marcantonio Colonna

14

Via Cola di Rienzo

Via Crescenzio

Via di Ripetta

Flaminio

Piazzale Flaminio

Pincio Hill

TRIDENTE

Via del Babuino

Vatican Museums 3

VATICAN CITY (CITTÀ DEL VATICANO)

St Peter's Basilica 2

Centro Servizi Pellegrini e Turisti

6

Via Vitelleschi

BORGO

Ponte Vittorio Emanuele II

Via del Corso

Lgt Marzio

Piazza Colonna

Via Aurelia

Stazione San Pietro

Via delle Nuova Fornaci

GIANICOLO

Orto Botanico

Gianicolo (Janiculum)

Lgt D Sangallo

PONTE

Corso Vittorio Emanuele II

Piazza Navona

Piazza Madama

PIGNA

See Centro Storico Map (p524)

Lgt dei Tebaldi

Lgt della Farnesina

Piazza della Scala

Piazza Sonnino

Lgt Raphaello Sanzio

Ponte Garibaldi

Isola Tiberina

9

Ponte Palatino

TRASTEVERE

Via Aurelia Antica

Villa Doria Pamphilj

Via Vitellia

Piazza F Cucchi

Via G Medici

Via Giacinto Carini

Villa Sciarra

Largo Asciarghi

Piazza Porta Portese

Ponte Sublicio

Lgt Ripa

Parco Savello

Piazza Pietro d'Illiria

AVENTINE

Via di Trastevere

Via di Quattro Venti

Via Portuense

Piazza Santa Maria Liberatrice

TESTACCIO

Largo GB Marzi

12

Via Galvani

Ponte Testaccio

Piazza Testaccio

Viale M Gelsomini

Largo M Gelsomini

Piramide

Stazione Roma-Ostia

8

Via Falconieri

11

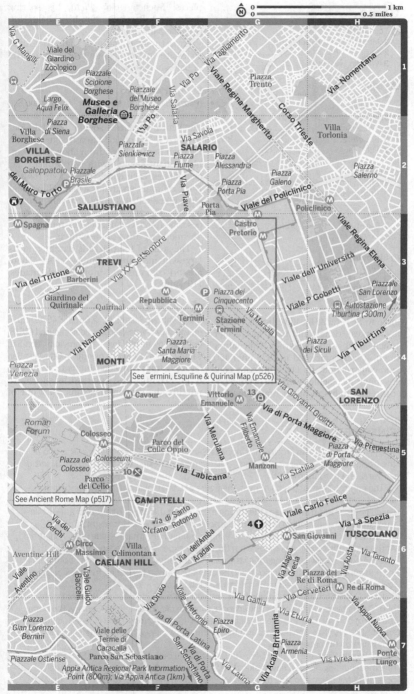

0 | 1 km
0 | 0.5 miles

E

Via G Mangili
Viale del Giardino Zoologico
Piazzale Scipione Borghese
Largo Aqua Felix
Piazza di Siena
Museo e Galleria Borghese 1
Piazzale del Museo Borghese
Villa Borghese
VILLA BORGHESE
Galoppatoio Piazzale Brasile
del Muro Torto
7
SALLUSTIANO

F

Via Tagliamento
Via Po
Via Salaria
Via Po
Piazzale Sienkiewicz
Via Savoia
SALARIO
Piazza Fiume
Via Piave
Piazza Porta Pia
Porta Pia

G

Viale Regina Margherita
Piazza Trento
Corso Trieste
Villa Torlonia
Piazza Alessandria
Piazza Galeno
Viale del Policlinico

H

Via Nomentana
Piazza Salerno
Policlinico
Viale Regina Elena

1

2

Spagna
TREVI
Via del Tritone
Barberini
Giardino del Quirinale
Quirinal
Via XX Settembre
Repubblica
Termini
Piazza dei Cinquecento
Stazione Termini
Via Marsala
Castro Pretorio
Viale dell'Università
Viale P Gobetti
Piazzale San Lorenzo
Autostazione Tiburtina (300m)

3

Piazza Venezia
Via Nazionale
MONTI
Piazza Santa Maria Maggiore
See Termini, Esquiline & Quirinal Map (p526)
Piazza dei Siculi
Via Tiburtina

4

Roman Forum
Colosseo
Colosseum
Piazza del Colosseo
Parco del Celio
10
See Ancient Rome Map (p517)
Cavour
Parco del Colle Oppio
Vittorio Emanuele 13
Via Merulana
Via di Porta Maggiore
Via Emanuele Filberto
Via Labicana
Manzoni
Via Statilia
Via Giovanni Giolitti
SAN LORENZO
Piazza di Porta Maggiore
Via Prenestina

5

Via dei Cerchi
Circo Massimo
Aventine Hill
Villa Celimontana
CAELIAN HILL
CAMPITELLI
Via di Santo Stefano Rotondo
4
Viale Carlo Felice
San Giovanni
Via La Spezia
TUSCOLANO
Via Taranto

6

Viale Aventino
Viale Guido Baccelli
Via dell'Amba Aradam
Via Druso
Viale Metronio
Piazza Epiro
Via Magna Grecia
Piazza dei Re di Roma
Via Cerveteri
Re di Roma
Via Aosta

Piazza Gian Lorenzo Bernini
Viale delle Terme di Caracalla
Parco San Sebastiano
Via di Porta Latina
Via di Porta San Sebastiano
Via Gallia
Via Eturia
Via Acaia Britannia
Piazza Armenia
Via Ivrea
Via Appia Nuova
Ponte Lungo

7

Piazzale Ostiense
Via Latina
Appia Antica Regional Park Information Point (800m); Via Appia Antica (1km)

E **F** **G** **H**

Rome

candle to St Peter's (Basilica di San Pietro), Italy's largest, richest and most spectacular basilica. Built atop an earlier 4th-century church, it was completed in 1626 after 120 years' construction. Its lavish interior contains many spectacular works of art, including three of Italy's most celebrated master-

pieces: Michelangelo's *Pietà,* his soaring dome, and Bernini's 29m-high baldachin over the papal altar.

Expect queues and note that strict dress codes are enforced, so no shorts, miniskirts or bare shoulders.

St Peter's Square   PIAZZA
(Piazza San Pietro; Map p520; Ⓜ Ottaviano-San Pietro) Overlooked by St Peter's Basilica, the Vatican's central square was laid out between 1656 and 1667 to a design by Gian Lorenzo Bernini. Seen from above, it resembles a giant keyhole with two semicircular colonnades, each consisting of four rows of Doric columns, encircling a giant ellipse that straightens out to funnel believers into the basilica. The effect was deliberate – Bernini described the colonnades as representing 'the motherly arms of the church'.

The scale of the piazza is dazzling: at its largest it measures 340m by 240m. There are 284 columns and, atop the colonnades, 140 saints.

⭐ **Vatican Museums**   MUSEUM
(Musei Vaticani; Map p520; ☎ 06 6988 4676; http://mv.vatican.va; Viale Vaticano; adult/reduced €16/8, last Sun of month free; ⊙ 9am-4pm Mon-Sat, 9am-12.30pm last Sun of month; Ⓜ Ottaviano-San Pietro) Founded by Pope Julius II in the early 16th century and enlarged by successive pontiffs, the Vatican Museums boast one of

---

FINER DETAILS

The jewel in the Vatican crown, the *Cappella Sistina* (Sistine Chapel) is home to two of the world's most famous works of art – Michelangelo's ceiling frescoes and his *Giudizio Universale* (Last Judgment).

The central focus of the painting is the figure of Christ, near the top. Around him, in a kind of vortex, the souls of the dead are torn from their graves to face his judgment. The saved get to stay up in heaven (the throng of bodies in the upper right quadrant), while the damned are sent down to face the demons in hell (in the bottom right).

An interesting point to note is the striking amount of ultramarine blue in this painting. At the time, this colour was made from the hugely expensive stone lapis lazuli. But as it was the pope who was paying for all the paint Michelangelo had no qualms about applying it in generous measure. In contrast, he didn't use any in his ceiling frescoes because he had to pay for all his own materials on that job.

Look in the bottom right-hand corner and you'll see a nude figure with a snake around him. This is Minos, judge of the underworld, with the face of Biagio de Cesena, the papal master of ceremonies and one of Michelangelo's loudest critics. Look closer and you'll see that he also has donkey ears and that the snake wrapped around him is actually biting him on his crown jewels.

Further up the painting, just beneath Christ, is the bald, beefy figure of St Bartholomew holding his own flayed skin. The face painted in the skin is said to be a self-portrait of Michelangelo, its anguished look reflecting the artist's tormented faith.

VATICAN MUSEUMS ITINERARY

Follow this three-hour itinerary for the museums' greatest hits.

At the top of the escalator after the entrance, head out to the **Cortile della Pigna**, a courtyard named after the Augustan-era bronze pine cone in the monumental niche. Cross the courtyard into the long corridor that is the **Museo Chiaramonti** and head left up to the **Museo Pio Clementino**, home of the Vatican's finest classical statuary. Follow through the **Cortile Ottagono** (Octagonal Courtyard) onto the **Sala Croce Greca** (Greek Cross Room) from where stairs lead up to the 1st floor.

Continue through the **Galleria dei Candelabri** (Gallery of the Candelabra), **Galleriadegli Arazzi** (Tapestry Gallery) and **Galleria delle Carte Geografiche** (Map Gallery) to the **Sala di Costantino**, the first of the four **Stanze di Raffaello** (Raphael Rooms) – the others are the **Stanza d' Eliodoro**, the **Stanza della Segnatura**, home to Raphael's superlative *La Scuola di Atene* (The School of Athens), and the **Stanza dell'Incendio di Borgo**. Anywhere else these frescoed chambers would be the star attraction, but here they're the warm-up act for the museums' grand finale, the **Sistine Chapel**.

Originally built in 1484 for Pope Sixtus IV, this towering chapel boasts two of the world's most famous works of art: Michelangelo's ceiling frescoes (1508–12) and his *Giudizio Universale* (Last Judgment; 1535–41).

the world's greatest art collections. Exhibits, which are displayed along about 7km of halls and corridors, range from Egyptian mummies and Etruscan bronzes to ancient busts, old masters and modern paintings. Highlights include the spectacular collection of classical statuary in the Museo Pio-Clementino, a suite of rooms frescoed by Raphael, and the Michelangelo-painted Sistine Chapel.

You'll never cover it all in one day, so it pays to be selective.

👁 Historic Centre

★Pantheon CHURCH
(Map p524; www.pantheonroma.com; Piazza della Rotonda; ⊙8.30am-7.30pm Mon-Sat, 9am-6pm Sun; 🚌Largo di Torre Argentina) FREE A striking 2000-year-old temple, now a church, the Pantheon is the best preserved of Rome's ancient monuments and one of the most influential buildings in the Western world. Built by Hadrian over Marcus Agrippa's earlier 27 BC temple, it has stood since around AD 125, and although its greying, pockmarked exterior looks its age, it's still a unique and exhilarating experience to pass through its vast bronze doors and gaze up at the largest unreinforced concrete dome ever built.

Piazza Navona PIAZZA
(Map p524; 🚌Corso del Rinascimento) With its ornate fountains, baroque *palazzi* (mansions) and colourful cast of street artists, hawkers and tourists, Piazza Navona is central Rome's elegant showcase square. Built over the 1st-century **Stadio di Domiziano** (Domitian's Stadium; ☎06 4568 6100; www.stadio domiziano.com; Via di Tor Sanguigna 3; adult/reduced €8/6; ⊙10am-7pm Sun-Fri, to 8pm Sat), it was paved over in the 15th century and for almost 300 years hosted the city's main market. Its grand centrepiece is Bernini's **Fontana dei Quattro Fiumi** (Fountain of the Four Rivers), an ornate, showy fountain featuring personifications of the rivers Nile, Ganges, Danube and Plate.

Piazza di Spagna & the Spanish Steps PIAZZA
(Map p526; Ⓜ Spagna) A magnet for visitors since the 18th century, the Spanish Steps (Scalinata della Trinità dei Monti) provide a perfect people-watching perch and you'll almost certainly find yourself taking stock here at some point.

★Trevi Fountain FOUNTAIN
(Fontana di Trevi; Map p526; Piazza di Trevi; Ⓜ Barberini) The Fontana di Trevi, scene of Anita Ekberg's dip in *La Dolce Vita,* is a flamboyant baroque ensemble of mythical figures and wild horses. It takes up the entire side of the 17th-century Palazzo Poli. A Fendi-sponsored restoration finished in 2015, and the fountain now gleams brighter than it has for years. The tradition is to toss a coin into the water, thus ensuring that you'll return to Rome.

Centro Storico

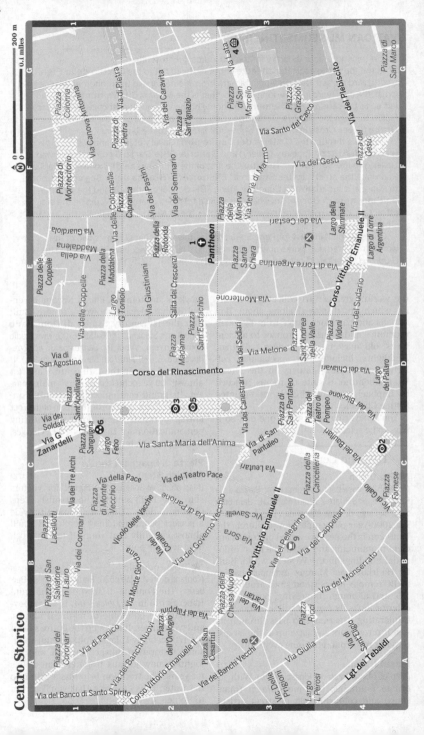

200 m
0.1 miles

Via di San Salvatore in Lauro

Piazza del Coronari

Piazza Lacellotti

Via dei Coronari

Via dei Tre Archi

Piazza di Monte Vecchio

Via della Pace

Via del Teatro Pace

Via di Panico

Via del Banchi Nuovi

Via Monte Giordano

Vicolo delle Vacche

Via del Corallo

Via di Parione

Via del Governo Vecchio

Corso Vittorio Emanuele II

Piazza dell'Orologio

Piazza San Cesarini

Via dei Filippini

Via dei Banco di Santo Spirito

Corso Vittorio Emanuele II

Via dei Banchi Vecchi

Vic Delle Prigioni

Largo L Perosi

Via Giulia

Piazza della Chiesa Nuova

Via dei Cartari

Via Sora

Via del Pellegrino

Piazza della Cancelleria

Via dei Cappellari

Via del Monserrato

Piazza Ricci

Via di Sant'Eligia

Lgt del Tebaldi

Via Santa Maria dell'Anima

Largo Febo

Piazza Tor Sanguigna

Via dei Soldati

Via G Zanardelli

Piazza Sant'Apollinare

Via di San Agostino

Via delle Coppelle

Piazza delle Coppelle

Corso del Rinascimento

Piazza Madama

Piazza Sant'Eustachio

Via dei Sediari

Via Melone

Via di Torre Argentina

Via di San Pantaleo

Piazza di San Pantaleo

Via Leutari

Piazza del Teatro di Pompeo

Via del Biscione

Largo del Pallaro

Via dei Chiavari

Via dei Baullari

Vic di Gallo

Piazza Fornese

Via Santo del Cacco

Via Canova

Piazza Colonna

Piazza di Montecitorio

Via di Pietra

Piazza di Pietra

Via del Caravita

Via delle Colonnelle

Via della Maddalena

Via Guardiola

Piazza della Maddalena

Via dei Pastini

Piazza Capranica

Via del Seminario

Piazza di Sant'Ignazio

Via di Pie' di Marmo

Via del Gesù

Piazza di San Marcello

Piazza Grazioli

Via Lata

Piazza di San Marco

Piazza del Plebiscito

Via del Plebiscito

Piazza del Gesù

Piazza della Minerva

Via dei Cestari

Largo della Stimmate

Corso Vittorio Emanuele II

Largo di Torre Argentina

Piazza Santa Chiara

Via Monterone

Piazza della Rotonda

Salita dei Crescenzi

Via Giustiniani

Largo G Toniolo

Sant'Andrea della Valle

Piazza Vidoni

Via del Sudario

1 Pantheon

2

3

5

6

7

8

9

4

Centro Storico

◉ **Top Sights**

◉ **Sights**

✖ **Eating**

◉ **Drinking & Nightlife**

Villa Medici PALACE

(Map p520; ☑ 06 6 76 11; www.villamedici.it; Viale Trinità dei Monti 1; gardens adult/reduced €12/6; ☺ tours Tue-Sun in Italian, French & English, check website for current times; cafe 11am-6pm Tue-Sun; Ⓜ Spagna) This sumptuous Renaissance palace was built for Cardinal Ricci da Montepulciano in 1540, but Ferdinando dei Medici bought it in 1576. It remained in Medici hands until 1801, when Napoleon acquired it for the French Academy. Take a tour to see the wonderful landscaped gardens, cardinal's painted apartments, and incredible views over Rome. Note the pieces of ancient Roman sculpture from the Ara Pacis embedded in the villa's walls.

Galleria Doria Pamphilj MUSEUM

(Map p524; ☑ 06 679 73 23; www.dopart.it; Via del Corso 305; adult/reduced €11/7.50; ☺ 9am-7pm, last admission 6pm; Ⓡ Via del Corso) Hidden behind the grimy grey exterior of Palazzo Doria Pamphilj, this wonderful gallery boasts one of Rome's richest private art collections, with works by Raphael, Tintoretto, Brueghel, Titian, Caravaggio, Bernini and Velázquez. Masterpieces abound, but the undisputed star is Velázquez' portrait of an implacable Pope Innocent X, who grumbled that the depiction was 'too real'. For a comparison, check out Gian Lorenzo Bernini's sculptural interpretation of the same subject.

Campo de' Fiori PIAZZA

(Map p524; Ⓡ Corso Vittorio Emanuele II) Noisy, colourful 'Il Campo' is a major focus of Roman life: by day it hosts one of Rome's best-known markets, while at night it morphs into a raucous open-air pub. For centuries the square was the site of public executions, and it was here that the philosopher Giordano Bruno was burned at the stake for heresy in 1600. The spot is marked by a sinister statue of the hooded monk, created by Ettore Ferrari and unveiled in 1889.

◉ Villa Borghese

Accessible from Piazzale Flaminio, Pincio Hill and the top of Via Vittorio Veneto, Villa Borghese is Rome's best-known park.

Museo Nazionale Etrusco di Villa Giulia MUSEUM

(Map p520; www.villagiulia.beniculturali.it; Piazzale di Villa Giulia; adult/reduced €8/4; ☺ 8.30am-7.30pm Tue-Sun; Ⓡ Via delle Belle Arti) Pope Julius III's 16th-century villa provides the charming setting for Italy's finest collection of Etruscan and pre-Roman treasures. Exhibits, many of which came from burial tombs in the surrounding Lazio region, range from bronze figurines and black *bucchero* tableware to temple decorations, terracotta vases and a dazzling display of sophisticated jewellery.

Must-sees include a polychrome terracotta statue of Apollo, the 6th-century-BC *Sarcofago degli Sposi* (Sarcophagus of the Betrothed), and the *Euphronios Krater,* a celebrated Greek vase.

★ **Museo e Galleria Borghese** MUSEUM

(Map p520; ☑ 06 3 28 10; www.galleriaborghese.it; Piazzale del Museo Borghese 5; adult/reduced €11/6.50; ☺ 9am-7pm Tue-Sun; Ⓡ Via Pinciana)

ⓘ **ROMA PASS**

The useful Roma Pass comes in two forms: the three-day classic pass (€36) provides free admission to two museums or sites, unlimited city transport, and discounted entry to other sites, exhibitions and events; and a 48-hour pass (€28), which gives free admission to one museum or site and then as per the classic pass. They're available online, from tourist information points or from participating museums.

Note that EU citizens aged between 18 and 25 generally qualify for a discount at most galleries and museums, while those under 18 and over 65 often get in free. In both cases you'll need proof of your age, ideally a passport or ID card.

Termini, Esquiline & Quirinal

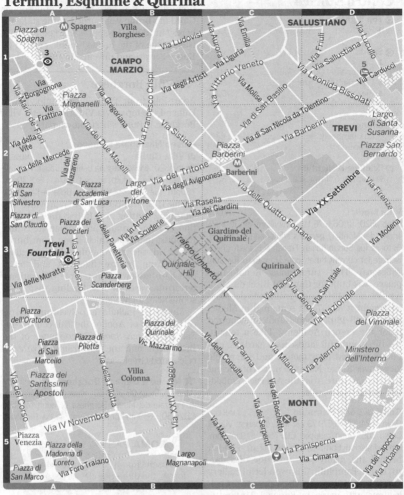

Termini, Esquiline & Quirinal

If you only have the time (or inclination) for one art gallery in Rome, make it this one. Housing what's often referred to as the 'queen of all private art collections', it boasts paintings by Caravaggio, Raphael and Titian, as well as some sensational sculptures

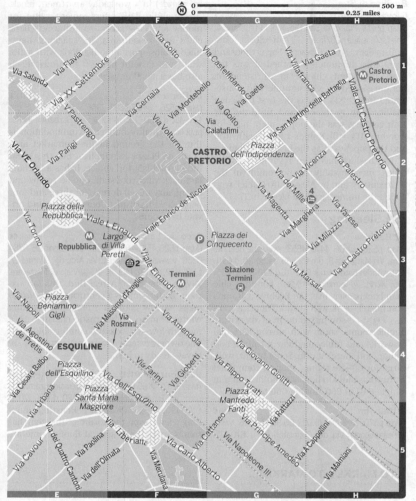

by Bernini. Highlights abound, but look out for Bernini's *Ratto di Proserpina* (Rape of Proserpina) and Canova's *Venere vincitrice* (Venus Victrix).

To limit numbers, visitors are admitted at two-hourly intervals, so you'll need to pre-book your ticket and get an entry time.

Esquiline & San Giovanni

Museo Nazionale Romano:
Palazzo Massimo alle Terme MUSEUM
(Map p526; ☎06 3996 7700; www.coopculture. it; Largo di Villa Peretti 1; adult/reduced €7/3.50;

⊙9am-7.45pm Tue-Sun; MTermini) One of Rome's great unheralded museums, this is a fabulous treasure trove of classical art. The ground and 1st floors are devoted to sculpture with some breathtaking pieces – check out the *Pugile* (Boxer), a 2nd-century-BC Greek bronze; the graceful 2nd-century-BC *Ermafrodite dormiente* (Sleeping Hermaphrodite); and the idealised *Il discobolo* (Discus Thrower). It's the magnificent and vibrantly coloured frescoes on the 2nd floor, however, that are the undisputed highlight of the museum.

Basilica di San Giovanni in Laterano
BASILICA

(Map p520; Piazza di San Giovanni in Laterano 4; cloister/basilica €5/free; ⏰ 7am-6.30pm, cloister 9am-6pm; Ⓜ San Giovanni) For a thousand years this monumental cathedral was the most important church in Christendom. Commissioned by Constantine and consecrated in AD 324, it was the first Christian basilica built in the city and, until the late 14th century, was the pope's main place of worship. It's still Rome's official cathedral and the pope's seat as the bishop of Rome.

The basilica has been revamped several times, most notably by Borromini in the 17th century, and by Alessandro Galilei, who added the immense white facade in 1735.

🛏 Sleeping

★ Beehive
HOSTEL €

(Map p526; ☎ 06 4470 4553; www.the-beehive.com; Via Marghera 8; dm €25-35, s €50-80, d €90-100, without bathroom s €60-70, d €70-80, tr €95-105; ❄ @ 🛜; Ⓜ Termini) 🌱 More boutique chic than backpacker dive, the Beehive is Rome's best hostel; book well ahead. There's a spotless, eight-person mixed dorm or six private double rooms, some with air-con. Original artworks and funky modular furniture add colour, and there's a cafe. Some bright, well-cared-for off-site rooms, sharing communal bathrooms and kitchen, are another bargain (single €40 to €50, double €60 to €80).

Althea Inn
B&B €

(Map p520; ☎ 339 4353717, 06 9893 2666; www.altheainn.com; Via dei Conciatori 9; d €70-125; Ⓜ Piramide) In a workaday apartment block, this friendly B&B offers superb value for money and easy access to Testaccio's bars, clubs and restaurants. Its spacious, light-filled rooms sport a modish look with white walls and tasteful modern furniture. Each also has a small terrace.

La Controra
HOSTEL €

(Map p526; ☎ 06 9893 7366; Via Umbria 7; dm €20-40, d €80-110; ❄ @ 🛜; Ⓜ Barberini, Ⓜ Repubblica) Quality budget accommodation is thin on the ground in the upmarket area north of Piazza Repubblica, but this great little hostel is a top choice. It has a friendly laid-back vibe, cool staff, double rooms and bright, airy mixed dorms (for three and four people), with parquet floors, air-con and private bathrooms.

Arco del Lauro
B&B €€

(Map p520; ☎ 346 2443212, 9am-2pm 06 9784 0350; www.arcodellauro.it; Via Arco de' Tolomei 27; s €72-132, d €132-145; ❄ 🛜; 🚊 Viale di Trastevere, 🚊 Viale di Trastevere) A real find, this fab six-room B&B occupies a centuries-old *palazzo* on a narrow cobbled street. Its gleaming white rooms combine rustic charm with a modern low-key look and comfortable beds. The owners extend a warm welcome and are always ready to help.

Residenza Maritti
GUESTHOUSE €€

(Map p517; ☎ 06 678 82 33; www.residenzamaritti.com; Via Tor de' Conti 17; s €50-120, d €80-170, tr €100-190; ❄ 🛜; Ⓜ Cavour) Boasting stunning views over the forums, this gem has rooms spread over several floors. Some are

---

TO MARKET, TO MARKET...

Rome's well-stocked delis and fresh-produce markets are a fabulous feature of the city's foodscape. Most neighbourhoods have a few local delis and their own daily food market, operating from around 7am to 1.30pm, Monday to Saturday.

Rome's most famous markets include the following:

Mercato di Circo Massimo (Map p517; www.mercatocircomassimo.it; Via di San Teodoro 74; ⏰ 9am-6pm Sat, to 4pm Sun, closed Sun Jul & all Aug; 🚊 Via dei Cerchi) Rome's best and most popular farmers market is a colourful showcase for seasonal, zero-kilometre produce.

Nuovo Mercato Esquilino (Map p520; Via Lamarmora; ⏰ 5am-3pm Mon-Sat; Ⓜ Vittorio Emanuele) Cheap and the best place to find exotic herbs and spices.

Piazza dell' Unità (Map p520; 🚊 Piazza del Risorgimento) Near the Vatican, perfect for stocking up for a picnic.

Nuovo Mercato di Testaccio (Map p520; entrances Via Galvani, Via Beniamino Franklin; ⏰ 6am-3pm Mon-Sat; 🚊 Via Marmorata) A purpose-built site crammed with enticing stalls and local shoppers.

bright and modern, others are more cosy in feel with antiques and family furniture. There's no breakfast but you can use a fully equipped kitchen.

Eating

★ Supplizio
FAST FOOD €

(Map p524; Via dei Banchi Vecchi 143; supplì €3-5; ⊘noon-4pm Mon-Sat plus 5.30-10pm Mon-Thu, to 11pm Fri & Sat; 🚊Corso Vittorio Emanuele II) Rome's favourite snack, the *supplì* (a fried croquette filled with rice, tomato sauce and mozzarella), gets a gourmet makeover at this elegant new streetfood joint. Sit back on the vintage leather sofa and dig into the classic article or throw the boat out and try something different, maybe a mildly spicy fish *supplì* stuffed with anchovies, tuna, parsley, and just a hint of orange.

Cafè Cafè
BISTRO €

(Map p520; 🕿06 700 87 43; www.cafecafebistrot. it; Via dei Santissimi Quattro Coronati 44; meals €15-20; ⊘9.30am-11pm; 🚊Via di San Giovanni in Laterano) Cosy, relaxed and welcoming, this cafe-bistro is a far cry from the usual impersonal eateries in the Colosseum area. With its rustic wooden tables, butternut walls and wine bottles, it's a charming spot to recharge your batteries over tea and homemade cake, a light lunch or laid-back dinner. There's also brunch on Sundays.

Pizzarium
PIZZA €

(Map p520; Via della Meloria 43; pizza slices from €3; ⊘11am-10pm; 🇲Cipro–Musei Vaticani) Pizzarium, or 'Bonci pizza rustica #pizzarium', as it has recently re-branded itself, serves some of Rome's best sliced pizza. Scissor-cut squares of meticulously crafted dough are topped with original combinations of seasonal ingredients and served on paper trays for immediate consumption. There's also a daily selection of freshly fried *supplì*.

★ L'Asino d'Oro
ITALIAN €€

(Map p526; 🕿06 4891 3832; Via del Boschetto 73; meals €45; ⊘12.30-2.30pm Sat, 7.30-11pm Tue-Sat; 🇲Cavour) This fabulous restaurant was transplanted from Orvieto and its Umbrian origins resonate in Lucio Sforza's delicious, exceptional cooking. It's unfussy yet innovative, with dishes featuring lots of flavourful contrasts, such as lamb meatballs with pear and blue cheese. Save room for the amazing desserts. For such excellent food, this intimate, informal yet classy place is one of

---

Rome's best deals. Hours are changeable so call ahead.

La Ciambella
ITALIAN €€

(Map p524; www.laciambellaroma.com; Via dell'Arco della Ciambella 20; fixed-price lunch menus €10-25, meals €30; ⊘7.30am-midnight; 🚊Largo di Torre Argentina) From breakfast pastries and lunchtime pastas to afternoon tea, Neapolitan pizzas and aperitif cocktails, this all-day eatery is a top find. Central but as yet undiscovered by the tourist hordes, it's a spacious, light-filled spot set over the ruins of the Terme di Agrippa, visible through transparent floor panels. The mostly traditional food is spot on, and the atmosphere laid back and friendly.

Drinking & Nightlife

Ai Tre Scalini
WINE BAR

(Map p526; Via Panisperna 251; ⊘12.30pm-1am; 🇲Cavour) The 'Three Steps' is always packed, with crowds spilling out into the street. Apart from a tasty choice of wines, it sells the damn fine Menabrea beer, brewed in northern Italy. You can also tuck into a heart-warming array of cheeses, salami and dishes such as *polpette al sugo* (meatballs with sauce; €7.50).

Co.So
BAR

(Via Braccio da Montone 80; cocktails €10; ⊘7pm-3am Mon-Sat; 🚊Via Prenestina) The chicest

ⓘ STOP, THIEF!

The greatest risk visitors face in Rome is from pickpockets and thieves. Pickpockets go where the tourists go, so watch out around the most touristed and crowded areas, such as the Colosseum, Piazza di Spagna, St Peter's Sq and Stazione Termini. Note that thieves prey on disoriented travellers at the bus stops around Termini, fresh in from airports. Crowded public transport is another hot spot – the 64 Vatican bus is notorious. If travelling on the metro, try to use the end carriages, which are usually less busy.

A money belt with your essentials (passport, cash, credit cards) is a good idea. However, to avoid delving into it in public, carry a wallet with a day's cash. Don't flaunt expensive goods. If you're carrying a bag or camera, wear the strap across your body and away from the road – moped thieves can swipe a bag and be gone in seconds. Be careful when you sit down at a streetside table – never drape your bag over an empty chair by the road or put it where you can't see it.

A common method is for one thief to distract you while their assistant makes away with your purse. Beware of gangs of kids or others demanding attention. If you notice that you've been targeted, either take evasive action or shout 'va via!' ('go away!') in a loud, angry voice. Remember also that some of the best pickpockets are well dressed.

In case of theft or loss, always report the incident to the police within 24 hours and ask for a statement.

---

bar in the Pigneto district, this tiny place, opened by Massimo D'Addezio, former master mixologist at Hotel de Russie, is buzzing and hipster to the hilt, with its Carbonara Sour cocktail (with vodka infused with pork fat), bubblewrap coasters, and popcorn and M&M bar snacks.

Barnum Cafe　　　　　　　　　　CAFE
(Map p524; www.barnumcafe.com; Via del Pellegrino 87; ⊙9am-10pm Mon, 8.30am-2am Tue-Sat; 🖥; 🚇 Corso Vittorio Emanuele II) A relaxed, friendly spot to check your email over a freshly squeezed orange juice or spend a pleasant hour reading a newspaper on one of the tatty old armchairs in the white bare-brick interior. Come evenings and the scene is cocktails, smooth tunes and coolly dressed-down locals.

Yeah! Pigneto　　　　　　　　　　BAR
(🖉 06 6480 1456; www.yeahpigneto.com; Via Giovanni de Agostini 41; small beer €3; aperitivo €7; ⊙7pm-2am Mon-Fri, 8pm-2am Sat & Sun) We say si! to Yeah! Pigneto. A relaxed boho-feeling bar with DJs playing jazz and the walls covered in collages and classic album covers, this is a good place for lingering over not-too-expensive beer. Regular live gigs.

ⓘ Information

Centro Servizi Pellegrini e Turisti (Map p520; 🖉 06 6988 1662; St Peter's Sq; ⊙8.30am-6pm Mon-Sat) The Vatican's official tourist office.

Fori Imperiali Tourist Information (Map p517; Via dei Fori Imperiali; ⊙9.30am-7pm)

National Bank of Greece (🖉 210 334 0500; cnr Karageorgi Servias & Stadiou, Syntagma; Ⓜ Syntagma) Has a 24-hour automated exchange machine.

ⓘ Getting There & Away

AIR

Rome's main international airport, **Leonardo da Vinci**, is 30km west of the city. The easiest way to get into town is by train, but there are also buses and private shuttle services.

Leonardo Express (one way €14) Runs to/from Stazione Termini. Departures from the airport every 30 minutes between 6.23am and 11.23pm; from Termini between 5.35am and 10.35pm. Journey time is 30 minutes.

FL1 (one way €8) Connects to Trastevere, Ostiense and Tiburtina stations, but not Termini. Departures from the airport every 15 minutes (half-hourly on Sundays and public holidays) between 5.57am and 10.42pm; from Tiburtina every 15 minutes between 5.46am and 7.31pm, then half-hourly to 10.02pm.

BUS

Long-distance national and international buses use **Autostazione Tiburtina** (Piazzale Tiburtina; Ⓜ Tiburtina).

From the bus station, cross under the overpass for the Tiburtina train station, where you can pick up metro line B and connect with Termini for onward buses, trains and metro line A.

TRAIN

Almost all trains arrive at and depart from **Stazione Termini** (Piazza dei Cinquecento; Ⓜ Termini), Rome's main train station and principal transport hub. There are regular connections to other European countries, all major Italian cities, and many smaller towns.

Train information is available from the Customer Service area on the main concourse to the left of the ticket desks. Alternatively, check www.trenitalia.com or phone ☑ 892021.

From Termini, you can connect with the metro or take a bus from Piazza dei Cinquecento out front. Taxis are outside the main entrance/exit.

❶ Getting Around

Rome's public transport system includes buses, trams, metro and a suburban train network. The main hub is Stazione Termini, the only point at which the city's two main metro lines cross. The metro is quicker than surface transport but the network is limited and the bus is often a better bet. Children under 10 travel free.

Metro The main lines are: A (orange; 5.30am to 9.30pm Thursday to Sunday, replacement bus MA1-MA2 to 11.30pm, to 1.30am Saturday) and B (blue; 5.30am to 11.30pm Monday to Thursday, to 1.30am Friday and Saturday). The new line C runs between Monte Compatri, about 12 miles southeast of the city, to Parco di Centocelle.

Buses Most routes pass through Stazione Termini. Buses run 5.30am until midnight, with limited services throughout the night.

WORTH A TRIP

POMPEII

The ghostly **Ruins of Pompeii** (☑ 081 857 53 47; www.pompeiisites.org; entrances at Porta Marina, Piazza Esedra & Piazza Anfiteatro; adult/reduced €12/6.50, incl Herculaneum €22/12; ⏱ 8.30am-7.30pm Apr-Oct, to 5pm Nov-Mar) – Pompeii in Italian – make for one of the world's most engrossing archaeological experiences. Much of the site's value lies in the fact that the town wasn't simply blown away by Vesuvius in AD 79 but buried under a layer of *lapilli* (burning fragments of pumice stone). The result is a remarkably well-preserved slice of ancient life, where visitors can walk down Roman streets and snoop around millennia-old houses temples, shops, cafes, amphitheatres, and even a brothel.

The origins of Pompeii are uncertain, but it seems likely that it was founded in the 7th century BC by the Campanian Oscans. Over the next seven centuries the city fell to the Greeks and the Samnites before becoming a Roman colony in 80 BC.

In AD 62, a mere 17 years before Vesuvius erupted, the city was struck by a major earthquake. Damage was widespread and much of the city's 20,000-strong population was evacuated. Fortunately, many had not returned by the time Vesuvius blew, but 2000 men, women and children perished nevertheless.

After its catastrophic demise, Pompeii receded from the public eye until 1594, when the architect Domenico Fontana stumbled across the ruins while digging a canal. Exploration proper, however, didn't begin until 1748. Of Pompeii's original 66 hectares, 44 have now been excavated. Of course that doesn't mean you'll have unhindered access to every inch of the Unesco-listed site – expect to come across areas cordoned off for no apparent reason, a noticeable lack of clear signs, and the odd stray dog. Audioguides are a sensible investment (€6.50 cash only).

Getting There & Away

There are regular train services between Rome and Naples with National rail company Trenitalia (2nd class €11.80 to €43, 70 minutes to 2¾ hours, up to 49 daily). High-speed private rail company Italo also runs daily services (2nd class €15 to €39, 70 minutes, up to 15 daily).

To reach the *scavi* (ruins) from Naples, hop the Circumvesuviana train (€3.20) or a regional trains (www.trenitalia.com).

From late May to October, tourist train Campania Express runs three times daily between Naples (Porta Nolana and Piazza Garibaldi Circumvesuviana stations) and Pompei-Scavi-Villa dei Misteri . One-day return tickets (€15, €10 for Artecard holders) can be purchased at the stations, online at www.eavsrl.it or www.campaniartecard/grandtour, or by phone on ☑ 800 60060 .

Tragedy in Pompeii

24 AUGUST AD 79

8am Buildings including the **Terme Suburbane ❶** and the **foro ❷** are still undergoing repair after an earthquake in AD 63 caused significant damage to the city. Despite violent earth tremors overnight, residents have little idea of the catastrophe that lies ahead.

Midday Peckish locals pour into the **Thermopolium di Vetutius Placidus ❸**. The lustful slip into the **Lupanare ❹**, and gladiators practise for the evening's planned games at the **anfiteatro ❺**. A massive boom heralds the eruption. Shocked onlookers witness a dark cloud of volcanic matter shoot some 14km above the crater.

3pm–5pm Lapilli (burning pumice stone) rains down on Pompeii. Terrified locals begin to flee; others take shelter. Within two hours, the plume is 25km high and the sky has darkened. Roofs collapse under the weight of the debris, burying those inside.

25 AUGUST AD 79

Midnight Mudflows bury the town of Herculaneum. Lapilli and ash continue to rain down on Pompeii, bursting through buildings and suffocating those taking refuge within.

4am–8am Ash and gas avalanches hit Herculaneum. Subsequent surges smother Pompeii, killing all remaining residents, including those in the **Orto dei Fuggiaschi ❻**. The volcanic 'blanket' will safeguard frescoed treasures like the **Casa del Menandro ❼** and **Villa dei Misteri ❽** for almost two millennia.

TOP TIPS

» Visit in the afternoon
» Allow three hours
» Wear comfortable shoes and a hat
» Bring drinking water
» Don't use flash photography

Terme Suburbane
The *laconicum* (sauna), *caldarium* (hot bath) and large, heated swimming pool weren't the only sources of heat here; scan the walls of this suburban bathhouse for some of the city's raunchiest frescoes.

Villa di Diomede

Casa del Poeta Tragico
Porta Ercolano
Casa d Faun

Tempio di Apollo
Basilica

Porta Marina

Terme del Foro

Macellum

Teatro Grande

Quadriportico dei Teatri
Porta di Stabia
Teatro Piccolo

Foro
An ancient Times Square of sorts, the forum sits at the intersection of Pompeii's main streets and was closed to traffic in the 1st century AD. The plinths on the southern edge featured statues of the imperial family.

Villa dei Misteri
Home to the world-famous *Dionysiac Frieze* fresco. Other highlights at this villa include *trompe l'oeil* wall decorations in the *cubiculum* (bedroom) and Egyptian-themed artwork in the *tablinum* (reception).

Lupanare
The prostitutes at this brothel were often slaves of Greek or Asian origin. Mattresses once covered the stone beds and the names engraved in the walls are possibly those of the workers and their clients.

Thermopolium di Vetutius Placidus
The counter at this ancient snack bar once held urns filled with hot food. The *lararium* (household shrine) on the back wall depicts Dionysus (the god of wine) and Mercury (the god of profit and commerce).

Casa dei Vettii

Porta del Vesuvio

Porta di Nola

EYEWITNESS ACCOUNT

Pliny the Younger (AD 61–c 112) gives a gripping, first-hand account of the catastrophe in his letters to Tacitus (AD 56–117).

Casa della Venere in Conchiglia

Porta di Sarno

Grande Palestra

Tempio di Iside

Casa del Menandro
This dwelling most likely belonged to the family of Poppaea Sabina, Nero's second wife. A room to the left of the atrium features Trojan War paintings and a polychrome mosaic of pygmies rowing down the Nile.

Orto dei Fuggiaschi
The Garden of the Fugitives showcases the plaster moulds of 13 locals seeking refuge during Vesuvius' eruption – the largest number of victims found in any one area. The huddled bodies make for a moving scene.

Anfiteatro
Magistrates, local senators and the games' sponsors and organisers enjoyed front-row seating at this veteran amphitheatre, home to gladiatorial battles and the odd riot. The parapet circling the stadium featured paintings of combat, victory celebrations and hunting scenes.

Italy Survival Guide

❶ Directory A–Z

BARGAINING

Gentle haggling is common in markets. Haggling in stores is generally unacceptable, though good-humoured bargaining at smaller artisan or craft shops in southern Italy is not unusual if making multiple purchases.

DISCOUNT CARDS

Some cities or regions offer discount passes, such as Roma Pass (three days €36), which offers free use of public transport and free or reduced admission to Rome's museums.

In many places around Italy, you can also save money by purchasing a *biglietto cumulativo*, a ticket that allows admission to a number of associated sights for less than the combined cost of separate admission fees.

ELECTRICITY

Electricity in Italy conforms to the European standard of 220V to 230V, with a frequency of 50Hz. Wall outlets typically accommodate plugs with two or three round pins (the latter grounded, the former not).

EMBASSIES & CONSUATES

For foreign embassies and consulates in Italy not listed here, look under 'Ambascíate' or 'Consolati' in the telephone directory.

Australian Embassy/Consulate Rome (☑ emergencies 800 877790, info 06 85 27 21; www.italy.embassy.gov.au; Via Antonio Bosio 5, Rome; ◷ 9am-5pm Mon-Fri)

Canadian Embassy/Consulate Rome (☑ 06 85 44 41; www.canadainternational.gc.ca/italy-italie; Via Zara 30, Rome); **Milan** (☑ 02 6269 4238; Piazza Cavour 3)

New Zealand Embassy/Consulate Rome (☑ 06 853 75 01; www.nzembassy.com/italy; Via Clitunno 44, Rome); **Milan** (☑ 02 7217 0001; www.nzembassy.com/italy; Via Terraggio 17, Milan; Ⓜ Cadorna)

UK Embassy/Consulate Rome (☑ 06 4220 0001; www.ukinitaly.fco.gov.uk; Via XX Settembre 80a, Rome); **Milan** (☑ 06 4220 2431;

Via San Paolo 7, Milan; Ⓜ San Babila); **Naples** (☑ 081 423 89 11; www.ukinitaly.fco.gov.uk; Via dei Mille 40, Naples)

US Embassy/Consulate Rome (☑ 06 4 67 41; www.italy.usembassy.gov; Via Vittorio Veneto 121, Rome); **Florence** (☑ 055 26 69 51; www.italy.usembassy.gov; Lungarno Vespucci 38, Florence); **Milan** (☑ 02 29 03 51; www.milan.usconsulate.gov; Via Principe Amedeo 2/10; Ⓜ Turati); **Naples** (☑ 081 583 81 11; www.italy.usembassy.gov; Piazza della Repubblica 2, Naples; Ⓜ Mergellina)

EMERGENCY & IMPORTANT NUMBERS

From outside Italy, dial your international access code, Italy's country code (39) then the number (including the '0').

Italy country code	☑ 39
International access code	☑ 00
Ambulance	☑ 118
Police	☑ 113
Fire	☑ 115

ETIQUETTE

Italy is a surprisingly formal society; the following tips will help avoid awkward moments.

Greetings Shake hands and say *buongiorno* (good day) or *buona sera* (good evening) to strangers; kiss both cheeks and say *come stai* (how are you) to friends. Use *lei* (you) in polite company; use *tu* (you) with friends and children. Only use first names if invited.

Asking for help Say *mi scusi* (excuse me) to attract attention; and use *permesso* (permission) when you want to pass someone in a crowded space.

Religion Dress modestly (cover shoulders, torsos and thighs) and show respect when visiting religious sites.

LEGAL MATTERS

Drugs & Alcohol

➡ If you're caught with what the police deem to be a dealable quantity of hard or soft drugs, you risk prison sentences of between six and 20 years.

➡ The legal limit for blood-alcohol when driving is 0.05% and random breath tests do occur.

Police

If you do run into trouble in Italy, you're likely to end up dealing with the *polizia statale* or the *carabinieri*. The former wear powder-blue trousers with a fuchsia stripe and a navy blue jacket, the latter wear black uniforms with a red stripe and drive dark-blue cars with a red stripe.

To contact the police in an emergency, dial ☑ 113.

---

❶ SLEEPING PRICE RANGES

The following price ranges refer to a double room with private bathroom (breakfast included) in high season.

€ under €110

€€ €110-200

€€€ over €200

LGBT TRAVELLERS

Homosexuality is legal (over the age of 16) and even widely accepted, but Italy is notably conservative in its attitudes, largely keeping in line with those of the Vatican. Overt displays of affection by homosexual couples can attract a negative response, especially in smaller towns. There are gay venues in Rome and a handful in Florence. Online resources include the following Italian-language websites:

Arcigay (www.arcigay.it) Bologna-based national organisation for the LGBTI community.

Circolo Mario Mieli (www.mariomieli.org) Rome-based cultural centre that organises debates, cultural events and social functions, including Gay Pride.

Coordinamento Lesbiche Italiano (CLR; www.clrbp.it) National organisation for lesbians, holding regular conferences and literary evenings.

Gay.it (www.gay.it) Website featuring LGBT news, feature articles and gossip

Pride (www.prideonline.it) National monthly magazine of art, music, politics and gay culture.

MONEY

Credit and debit cards can be used almost everywhere with the exception of some rural towns and villages.

Visa and MasterCard are widely recognised. American Express is only accepted by some major chains and big hotels, and few places take Diners Club.

ATMs are everywhere, but be aware of transaction fees. Some ATMs in Italy reject foreign cards. If this happens, try a few before assuming your card is the problem.

Tipping

Tipping is not generally expected nor demanded in Italy as it is in some other countries. This said, a discretionary tip for good service is appreciated in some circumstances. Use the following table as a guide.

PLACE	SUGGESTED TIP
Restaurant	10-15%, if service charge (*servizio*) not included
Bar	€0.10–0.20 if drinking at bar, 10% for table service
Taxi	Round up to the nearest euro

OPENING HOURS

Opening hours vary throughout the year. Hours will generally decrease in the shoulder and low seasons. 'Summer' times generally refer to the period from April to September or October, while 'winter' times generally run from October or November to March.

Banks 8.30am to 1.30pm and 2.45pm to 3.45 or 4.30pm Monday to Friday

Restaurants noon to 2.30pm & 7.30pm to 11pm or midnight

Cafes 7.30am to 8pm

Bars and clubs 10pm to 4am or 5am

Shops 9am to 1pm and 4pm to 8pm Monday to Saturday, some also open Sunday

PUBLIC HOLIDAYS

Most Italians take their annual holiday in August, with the busiest period occurring around 15 August, known locally as Ferragosto. As a result, many businesses and shops close for at least part of that month. Settimana Santa (Easter Holy Week) is another busy holiday period for Italians.

National public holidays include the following:

Capodanno (New Year's Day) 1 January

Epifania (Epiphany) 6 January

Pasquetta (Easter Monday) March/April

Giorno della Liberazione (Liberation Day) 25 April

Festa del Lavoro (Labour Day) 1 May

Festa della Repubblica (Republic Day) 2 June

Ferragosto (Feast of the Assumption) 15 August

Festa di Ognisanti (All Saints' Day) 1 November

Festa dell'Immacolata Concezione (Feast of the Immaculate Conception) 8 December

Natale (Christmas Day) 25 December

Festa di Santo Stefano (Boxing Day) 26 December

TELEPHONE

➡ Italian telephone area codes all begin with ☑ 0 and consist of up to four digits. The area code is followed by anything from four to eight digits. The area code is an integral part of the telephone number and must always be dialled, even when calling from next door.

➡ Mobile-phone numbers begin with a three-digit prefix such as ☑ 330.

➡ Toll-free (free-phone) numbers are known as *numeri verdi* and usually start with ☑ 800.

➡ To call Italy from abroad, call your international access number, then Italy's country code (☑ 39) and then the area code of the location you want, including the leading 0.

➡ To call abroad from Italy dial ☑ 00, then the country and area codes, followed by the telephone number.

➡ To make a reverse-charge (collect) international call from a public telephone, dial ☑ 170. All phone operators speak English.

Mobile Phones

➡ Italian mobile phones operate on the GSM 900/1800 network, which is compatible with the rest of Europe and Australia but not always with the North American GSM or CDMA systems – check with your service provider.

➡ If you have a GSM dual-, tri- or quad-band phone that you can unlock (check with your service provider), it can cost as little as €10 to activate a prepaid (*prepagato*) SIM card in Italy. TIM (Telecom Italia Mobile; www.tim.it), Wind (www.wind.it) and Vodafone (www.vodafone. it) all offer SIM cards and have retail outlets across town. All SIM cards must be registered in Italy, so make sure you have a passport or ID card with you when you buy one.

TIME

➡ Italy is one hour ahead of GMT. When it is noon in London, it is 1pm in Italy.

➡ Italy operates on a 24-hour clock.

TOURIST INFORMATION

Provincial and local offices deal directly with the public and most will respond to written and telephone requests for information. Staff can usually provide a city map, lists of hotels and information on the major sights. In larger towns and major tourist areas, English is generally spoken, along with other languages.

Main offices are generally open Monday to Friday; some also open on weekends, especially in urban areas or during peak summer season. Affiliated information booths (at train stations and airports, for example) may keep slightly different hours.

TRAVEL WITH CHILDREN

Italians love children but there are few special amenities for them. Always make a point of asking staff members at tourist offices if they know of any special family activities or have suggestions on hotels that cater for kids.

Book accommodation in advance whenever possible to avoid inconvenience. In hotels, some double rooms can't accommodate an extra bed for kids, so it's best to check ahead. If your child is small enough to share your bed, some hoteliers will let you do this for free. The website www.booking.com is good because it tells you the 'kid policy' for every hotel it lists and what extra charges you will incur.

On public transport, discounts are available for children (usually aged under 12 but sometimes based on the child's height), and admission to many sites is free for children under 18.

When travelling by train, reserve seats where possible to avoid finding yourselves standing. You can hire car seats for infants and children from most car-rental firms, but you should always book them in advance.

You can buy baby formula in powder or liquid form, as well as sterilising solutions such as Milton, at pharmacies. Disposable nappies (diapers) are available at supermarkets and pharmacies. Fresh cow's milk is sold in cartons in supermarkets and in bars with a 'Latteria' sign. UHT milk is popular and in many out-of-the-way areas the only kind available.

Kids are welcome in most restaurants, but do not count on the availability of high chairs. Children's menus are uncommon but you can generally ask for a *mezzo piatto* (half-portion) off the menu.

For more information and ideas, see the superb Italy-focused website www.italiakids.com.

VISAS

EU citizens do not need a visa to enter Italy. Nationals of some other countries, including Australia, Canada, Israel, Japan, New Zealand, Switzerland and the USA, do not need a tourist visa for stays of up to 90 days. To check the visa requirements for your country, go to www.schengenvisainfo.com/tourist-schengen -visa.

WIFI

➡ Numerous Italian cities and towns offer public wi-fi hotspots, including Rome and Venice. To use them, you will generally need to register online using a credit card or an Italian mobile number. An easier option (no need for a local mobile number) is to head to a cafe or bar offering free wi-fi.

➡ Most hotels, B&Bs, hostels and *agriturismi* offer free wi-fi to guests, though signals can vary in quality. There will usually be at least one fixed computer for guest use.

ⓘ Getting There & Away

AIR

Italy's main intercontinental gateways are Rome's **Leonardo da Vinci airport** (www.adr.it/fiumicino) and Milan's **Malpensa airport** (www.milanomalpensa-airport.com). Both are served by nonstop flights from around the world. Venice's **Marco Polo airport** (www.veniceairport.it) is also served by a handful of intercontinental flights.

Intra-European flights serve plenty of other Italian cities; the leading mainstream carriers include Alitalia, Air France, British Airways, Lufthansa and KLM.

Cut-rate airlines, led by Ryanair and easyJet, fly from a growing number of European cities to more than two dozen Italian destinations, typically landing in smaller airports such as Rome's **Ciampino** (www.adr.it/ciampino).

BUS

Buses are the cheapest overland option to Italy, but services are less frequent, less comfortable and significantly slower than the train.

Eurolines (www.eurolines.com) is a consortium of coach companies with offices throughout Europe. Italy-bound buses head to Milan, Rome, Florence, Venice and other Italian cities. It offers a bus pass valid for 15/30 days that costs €375/490 (reduced €315/405) in high season and €225/340 (reduced €195/265) in low season.

This pass allows unlimited travel between 53 European cities, including Milan, Venice, Florence and Rome.

TRAIN

Regular trains on two western lines connect Italy with France (one along the coast and the other from Turin into the French Alps). Trains from Milan head north into Switzerland and on towards the Benelux countries. Further east, two main lines head for the main cities in Central and Eastern Europe. Those crossing the Brenner Pass go to Innsbruck, Stuttgart and Munich. Those crossing at Tarvisio proceed to Vienna, Salzburg and Prague. The main international train line to Slovenia crosses near Trieste.

Depending on distances covered, rail can be highly competitive with air travel. Those travelling from neighbouring countries to northern Italy will find it is frequently more comfortable, less expensive and only marginally more time-consuming than flying.

Those travelling longer distances (say, from London, Spain, northern Germany or Eastern Europe) will doubtless find flying cheaper and quicker. Bear in mind, however, that the train is a much greener way to go – a trip by rail can

contribute up to 10 times fewer carbon dioxide emissions per person than the same trip by air.

SEA

Multiple ferry companies connect Italy with countries throughout the Mediterranean. Many routes only operate in summer, when ticket prices also rise. Prices for vehicles vary according to their size.

The helpful website www.directferries.co.uk allows you to search routes and compare prices between the numerous international ferry companies servicing Italy. Another useful resource for ferries from Italy to Greece is www.ferries.gr. You'll find services from Bari and Brindisi to Corfu.

ⓘ Getting Around

AIR

Italy offers an extensive network of internal flights. The privatised national airline, Alitalia, is the main domestic carrier, with numerous low-cost airlines also operating across the country. Useful search engines for comparing multiple carriers' fares (including those of cut-price airlines) are www.skyscanner.com, www.kayak.com and www.azfly.it. Airport taxes are factored into the price of your ticket.

BUS

Routes Everything from meandering local routes to fast, reliable InterCity connections provided by numerous bus companies.

Timetables and tickets Available on bus company websites and from local tourist offices. Tickets are generally competitively priced with the train and often the only way to get to smaller towns. In larger cities most of the InterCity bus companies have ticket offices or sell tickets through agencies. In villages and even some good-sized towns, tickets are sold in bars or on the bus.

Advance booking Generally not required, but advisable for overnight or long-haul trips in high season.

LOCAL TRANSPORT

Major cities all have good transport systems, including bus and underground-train networks. In Venice, the main public transport option is *vaporetti* (small passenger ferries).

Bus & Metro

➡ Cities and towns of any size have an efficient *urbano* (urban) and *extraurbano* (suburban) bus system. Services are generally limited on Sundays and holidays.

➡ Purchase bus and metro tickets before boarding and validate them once on board. Passengers with unvalidated tickets are subject to a fine (between €50 and €110). Buy tickets from a *tabaccaio* (tobacconist's shop), news-stands, ticket booths or dispensing machines at bus and metro stations. Tickets usually cost around €1.20 to €2. Many cities offer good-value 24-hour or daily tourist tickets.

Taxi

➜ You can catch a taxi at the ranks outside most train and bus stations, or simply telephone for a radio taxi. Radio taxi meters start running from when you've called rather than when you're picked up.

➜ Charges vary somewhat from one region to another. Most short city journeys cost between €10 and €15. Generally, no more than four people are allowed in one taxi.

TRAIN

Trains in Italy are convenient and relatively cheap compared with other European countries. The better train categories are fast and comfortable.

Trenitalia (☑ 892021; www.trenitalia.com) is the national train system that runs most services. Train tickets must be stamped in the green machines (usually found at the head of rail platforms) just before boarding. Failure to do so usually results in fines.

Italy operates several types of trains:

Regionale/interregionale Slow and cheap, stopping at all or most stations.

InterCity (IC) Faster services operating between major cities. Their international counterparts are called Eurocity (EC).

Alta Velocità (AV) State-of-the-art, high-velocity trains, including Frecciarossa, Frecciargento, Frecciabianca and Italo trains, with speeds of up to 300km/hr and connections to the major cities. More expensive than InterCity express trains, but journey times are cut by almost half.

GREECE

Corfu

POP 102,071

Ever since it was first settled by the Corcyrans in the 8th century, Corfu, or Kerkyra (*ker*-kih-rah) in Greek, has been an object of desire for both its untamed beauty and strategic position in the Mediterranean. It was a seat of European learning in the early days of modern Greece, with cultural institutions such as libraries and academic centres. To this day, Corfiots remain fiercely proud of their intellectual and artistic roots, a legacy visible from its fine museums and cultural life.

There are pockets of overdeveloped resorts, particularly north of Corfu Town and in the far north, but the island is sufficiently large enough to easily escape the crowds – venture up its woody mountains studded with spear-sharp cypress trees and explore vertiginous villages, coves fringed by cobalt-blue water, and the fertile interior ashimmer with olive groves.

🛈 Getting There & Away

AIR

Corfu's **airport** (CFU; ☑ 26610 89600; www.corfu-airport.com) is about 2km southwest of the town centre. There are three flights daily to Athen (€105, one hour) from where you can connect to the rest of Greece.

EasyJet (www.easyjet.com) has daily direct flights between the UK and Corfu (May to October) and high-season flights to Milan, Rome and Paris, while **British Airways** (BA; ☑ 210 890 6666; www.britishairways.com) now flies from the UK to Corfu. **Air Berlin** (AB; ☑ 210 353 5264; www.airberlin.com) serves Germany. From May to September, many charter flights come from northern Europe and the UK.

BOAT

Neo Limani (New Port), with all ferry departures, lies west of hulking Neo Frourio (New Fortress). As well as services to neighbouring islands, there are regular services to Bari (€85, eight hours) and Brindisi (€80, six hours) in Italy and to Saranda (€19, 25 minutes) in Albania.

BUS

KTEL (☑ 26610 28927, 26610 28898; www.ktelkerkyras.gr) services go to Athens (€45, 8½ hours, three daily) and Thessaloniki (€35, eight hours, twice daily). For both, budget another €10 for the ferry to the mainland. Purchase tickets from Corfu Town's **long-distance bus station** (☑ 26610 28927; www.ktelkerkyras.gr; Ioannou Theotoki, Corfu Town).

🛈 Getting Around

TO/FROM THE AIRPORT

Corfu local bus 15 goes between the airport and Plateia San Rocco in Corfu Town (€1.50, seven daily Monday to Friday, four or five Saturday and Sunday); buy tickets on board. The schedule is posted at the stop. If you miss bus 15, buses 6 and 10 stop on the main road 800m from the airport (en route to Benitses and Achillion).

Taxis between the airport and Corfu Town cost €10.

BUS

Local blue buses depart from the **local bus station** (📞 26610 31595; Plateia San Rocco) in Corfu Old Town.

Tickets are €1.10 or €1.50 depending on journey length; purchase them at the booth on Plateia San Rocco (although tickets for Achillion, Benitses and Kouramades are bought on the bus). All trips are under 30 minutes. Service is reduced on weekends.

CAR & MOTORCYCLE

Car- and motorbike-hire outlets (Alamo, Hertz, Europcar etc) abound at the airport, in Corfu Town and resort towns. Prices start at around €50 per day (less for longer-term hire). Most local companies have offices along the northern waterfront.

Budget (📞 26610 22062; www.budgetrentacar.gr; Eleftheriou Venizelou 50, Corfu Town)

Sunrise (📞 26610 26511, 26610 44325; www.corfusunrise.com; Ethnikis Antistaseos 6, Corfu Town)

Top Cars (📞 26610 35237; www.car-rental-corfu.com; Donzelot 25, Corfu Town)

Corfu Town

Elegant Corfu Town (also known as Kerkyra) leaves you spellbound from the moment you wander its tangle of cobbled streets lined

Corfu

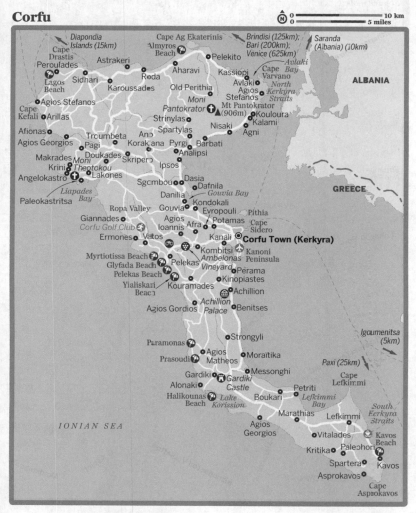

ITALY, GREECE & TURKEY CORFU

with stunning Venetian buildings. Corfu means 'twin peaks' – the town is bookended by two hills, on which two massive fortresses were built to repel the aggression of five successive Ottoman sieges. Besides some fascinating museums, there are some of the region's top restaurants to savour.

⊙ Sights

★ Palace of St Michael & St George
PALACE

Originally the residence of a succession of British high commissioners, this palace now houses the world-class **Museum of Asian**

Corfu Old Town

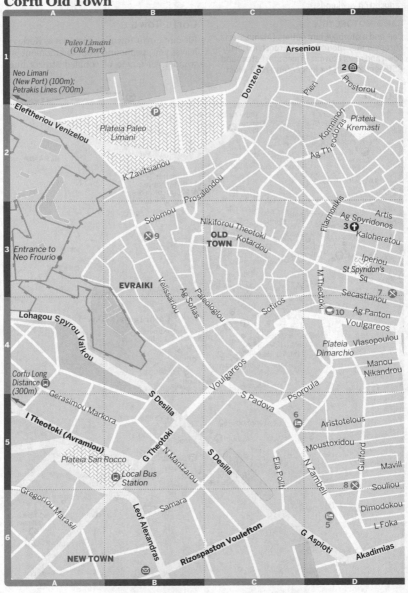

Art (☎26610 30443; www.matk.gr; adult/child incl audioguide €3/free, with Antivouniotissa Museum & Old Fortress €8; ◎8.30am-3.30pm Tue-Sun), founded in 1929. Expertly curated with extensive, informative English-language placards, the collection's approximately 10,000 artefacts, collected from all over Asia, include priceless prehistoric bronzes, ceramics, jade figurines, coins and works of art in onyx, ivory and enamel. Additionally, the palace's **throne room** and **rotunda** are impressively adorned in period furnishings and art.

Palaio Frourio FORTRESS

(Old Fortress; ☎26610 48310; adult/concession €4/2; ◎8am-8pm Apr-Oct, 8.30am-3pm Nov-Mar) Constructed by the Venetians in the 15th century on the remains of a Byzantine castle (and further altered by the British), this spectacular landmark offers respite from the crowds and superb views of the region. Climb to the summit of the inner outcrop, which is crowned by a lighthouse, for a 360-degree panorama. The gatehouse contains a Byzantine **museum**.

Church of Agios Spyridon CHURCH

(Agios Spyridonos; ◎7am-8pm) **FREE** The sacred relic of Corfu's beloved patron saint, St Spyridon, lies in an elaborate silver casket in the 16th-century basilica.

Antivouniotissa Museum MUSEUM

(☎26610 38313; www.antivcuniotissamuseum.gr; off Arseniou; adult/child €2/1; ◎9am-3.30pm Tue-Sun) The exquisite, timber-roofed, 15th-century **Church of Our Lady of Antivouniotissa** holds an outstanding collection of Byzantine and post-Byzantine icons and artefacts dating from the 13th to the 17th centuries.

Mon Repos Estate PARK

(Kanoni Peninsula; ◎8am-7pm May-Oct, to 5pm Nov-Apr) **FREE** On the Kanoni Peninsula on

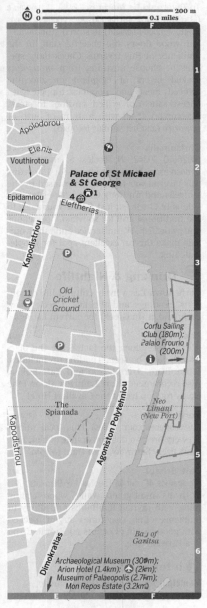

ITALY, GREECE & TURKEY CORFU

> ### ℹ CORFU TOWN SIGHTS PASS
>
> A joint sightseeing pass (adult/concession €8/4) is good for the Palaio Frourio (Old Fortress), Antivouniotissa Museum, the Archaeological Museum and the Museum of Asian Art. Get it at any of the included sights.

the southern outskirts of town, an extensive, wooded parkland estate surrounds an elegant neoclassical villa. It houses the **Museum of Palaeopolis** (ℹ 26610 41369; www.corfu. gr; adult/concession €3/2; ⊙ 8am-7pm Tue-Sun May-Oct), with entertaining archaeological displays and exhibits on the history of Corfu Town. Paths lead through lush grounds to the ruins of two Doric temples; the first is truly a ruin, but the southerly **Temple of Artemis** is serenely impressive.

Take a picnic and plenty of water, as there are no nearby shops. Bus 2a goes to Kanoni from the Spianada (€1.70, every 20 minutes).

🛏 Sleeping

★ Bella Venezia　　　　BOUTIQUE HOTEL **€€**
(ℹ 26610 46500; www.bellaveneziahotel.com; N Zambeli 4; s/d incl breakfast from €120/125; ❄✳🛜) From the instant you enter this neoclassical former girls' school – with its elegant lobby decked in candelabras, velvet chairs and grand piano – the place will charm you with its pure old-world charm. The Venezia has plush, high-ceilinged rooms with fine city views (some with balcony). Conscientious staff welcome you, and the gazebo breakfast room in the garden is delightful.

Siorra Vittoria　　　　BOUTIQUE HOTEL **€€**
(ℹ 26610 36300; www.siorravittoria.com; Stefanou Padova 36; s/d incl breakfast from €99/135, ste €193; Ⓟ✳🛜) Expect luxury and style at this quiet 19th-century mansion where painstakingly restored traditional architecture meets modern amenities; marble bathrooms, crisp linens and genteel service make for a relaxed stay. Breakfast in the peaceful garden beneath an ancient magnolia tree. The Vittoria suite encompasses the atelier and has views to the sea.

🍴 Eating

★ Il Vesuvio　　　　　GREEK **€**
(ℹ 26610 21284; Guilford; mains €10; ⊙ noon-late) The Neapolitan owner of this classy Italian restaurant, which has premises on both sides of the street, won the 'Best Italian Restaurant in Greece' award for his moreish homemade gnocchi, tortellini and ravioli. Eat on the street or inside but don't neglect a taste of the silky-smooth panna cotta – so fresh it will make your taste buds sing.

To Tavernaki tis Marinas　　　TAVERNA **€**
(ℹ 69816 56001; 4th Parados, Agias Sofias 1; mains €6-16; ⊙ noon-midnight) Restored stone walls, hardwood floors and cheerful staff lift the ambience of this taverna. Check daily specials or choose anything from *mousakas* (baked layers of eggplant or zucchini, minced meat and potatoes topped with cheese sauce) or grilled sardines to steak. Accompany it all with a dram of ouzo or *tsipouro* (a spirit similar to ouzo).

Chrisomalis　　　　　TAVERNA **€**
(ℹ 26610 30342; N Theotoki 6; mains €8-12; ⊙ noon-midnight) Going strong for 150 years, this taverna was formerly patronised by the Durrells and Anthony Quinn. The sign outside is in Greek, so just follow your nose to the traditional grill for souvlaki, pork chops and swordfish. Warm service and tables outside make this an excellent spot for people-watching.

🍷 Drinking & Nightlife

Corfu Town has a lively cultural life of concerts, readings and the like. Check www. corfuland.gr (in Greek) for current listings.

The Liston　　　　　　　BAR
All the bars along the Liston are the places to be and be seen. The line-up includes: Libro d'Oro, Arco, Liston and Kafe Koklia. Also recommended are Lounge Café and the classy rooftop bar at the Cavalieri Hotel.

Corfu Beer　　　　　　BREWERY
(www.corfubeer.com; Arillas) This local microbrewery brews a delicious range of ales. Free tours every Saturday from 11am to 1pm.

Café Bristol　　　　　　CAFE
(Voulgareos 40, cnr M Theotoki; ⊙ 9am-late; 🛜) With its mint-green walls, wood ceiling hung with myriad lightbulbs and dimly lit ambience, this easy-tunes haunt packed with good-looking Corfiots may remind you of a Parisian cafe.

ℹ Information

Municipal Tourist Kiosk (Palaio Frourio; ⊙ 9am-4pm Mon-Sat Jun-Sep) Offers helpful information for things to do around Corfu, accommodation and transport timetables.

Pachis Travel (☑ 26610 28298; Guilford 7; ⊘ 9am-2.30pm & 5.30pm-9pm, closed Sun) This helpful travel agency can assist with ferry and plane tickets, and hotels. It also organises charter boats and excursions to Paxi.

South of Corfu Town

The coast road south from Corfu Town leads to well-signposted Achillion Palace near the village of Gastouri.

Further south again are the popular beach resorts of **Moraïtika** and **Messonghi**, from where the winding coastal road follows at sea level through twisty sun-dappled woods to more appealing, and endlessly tranquil, **Boukari** with its little harbour. It's incredibly low-key.

Lefkimmi, in the southern part of the island, is one of Corfu's most down-to-earth towns, where the locals just get on with everyday life. Fascinating churches dot the older section; it's divided by a rather quaint (though sometimes odorous) canal.

◉ Sights

Achillion Palace HISTORIC BUILDING
(☑ 26610 56210; www.achillion-corfu.gr; Gastouri; adult/child €7/2, audioguide €3; ⊘ 8am-8pm Apr-Oct, 8.45am-4pm Nov-Mar) In the 1890s the Achillion Palace was the summer palace of Austria's Empress Elizabeth (King Otho of Greece was her uncle). Be sure to climb the stairs to the right of the villa to the marbled terrace for a view of the fresco depicting Achilles, to whom she dedicated the villa. The beautifully landscaped garden is guarded by elaborate statues of mythological heroes. Kaiser Wilhelm II bought the palace in 1907, and added a ferocious statue of Achilles Triumphant.

Arrive early to beat the crowds and journey through neoclassicism, fabulous furnishings and bold statuary (high style or low kitsch?).

⌂ Sleeping & Eating

Golden Sunset Hotel HOTEL €€
(☑ 26620 51853; www.goldensunsetcorfu.gr; Boukari; s/d incl breakfast €45/60; ❄) Offers stunning views from its simple 16 rooms. There's also a terraced **restaurant**.

★ Klimataria TAVERNA €€
(☑ 26610 71201; www.klimataria restaurant.gr; Benitses; mains €8-14; ⊘ 7pm-midnight Feb-Nov)

This tiny, humble taverna in Benitses is worth a pilgrimage in its own right – every item on the menu is absolutely delicious. From the olive oil and specially sourced feta to the tender octopus or range of mezedhes, the owners will not serve anything that they cannot find fresh. Call for reservations in summer.

West Coast

Some of Corfu's prettiest countryside, villages and beaches line the west coast. The scenic and popular resort area **Paleokastritsa**, 26km from Corfu Town, rambles for nearly 3km down a valley to a series of small, picturesque coves between tall cliffs. Craggy mountains swathed in cypresses and olive trees tower above. Venture to nearby grottoes or one of the dozen or so local beaches by small **boat** (per person €8.50; ⊘ 30min); water taxis take you to your beach of choice, or partake in a range of water sports.

Perched on the rocky promontory at the end of Paleokastritsa is the icon-filled **Moni Theotokou** (⊘ 9am-1pm & 3-8pm) FREE, a monastery founded in the 13th century (although the present building dates from the 18th century). Just off the monastery's lovely garden, a small **museum** (⊘ Apr-Oct) FREE and olive-mill exhibition have a shop selling oils and herbs.

From Paleokastritsa a path ascends 5km inland to the unspoilt village of **Lakones**, which is fantastic for coastal views.

⌂ Sleeping & Eating

Hotel Zefiros HOTEL €€
(☑ 26630 41244; www.hotel-zefiros.gr; Paleokastritsa; d/tr/q incl breakfast €64/80/130; ❄ ☎) Wine-coloured Zefiros, just 20m from the pretty beach, has a shabby-chic cafe with a tasty menu of mezedhes and snacks, plus beautiful rooms with modern flourishes and balconies. Room 107 has the best view.

Levant Hotel HOTEL €€
(☑ 26610 94230; www.levantcorfu.com; Pelekas Village; s/d incl breakfast €70/90; ⊘ May–mid-Oct; ⓟ❄☎❄) This grand hotel exudes romance with pastel-blue rooms, wood floors, belle époque–style lights and balcony. Rooms also have fridges and marble-accented bathrooms. Add to this a refined **restaurant** serving shrimp, risotto and *stifadho* on a terrace overlooking the island of Corfu. Tempted?

Athens

POP 3.1 MILLION

Ancient and modern, with equal measures of grunge and grace, bustling Athens is a heady mix of history and edginess. Iconic monuments mingle with first-rate museums, lively cafes and alfresco dining, and it's down right fun. With Greece's financial difficulties, Athens has revealed its more agitated side, but take the time to look beneath the surface and you'll discover a complex metropolis full of vibrant subcultures.

◉ Sights

★ **Acropolis**   HISTORIC SITE
(☑ 210 321 0219, disabled access 210 321 4172; http://odysseus.culture.gr; adult/child/concession €12/free/6; ☺ 8am-8pm Apr-Oct, to 5pm Nov-Mar, last entry 30min before closing; M Akropoli) The Acropolis is the most important ancient site in the Western world. Crowned by the Parthenon, it stands sentinel over Athens, visible from almost everywhere within the city. Its monuments and sanctuaries of Pentelic marble gleam white in the midday sun and gradually take on a honey hue as the sun sinks, while at night they stand brilliantly illuminated above the city. A glimpse of this magnificent sight cannot fail to exalt your spirit. Free admission first Sunday of the month from November to March.

★ **Acropolis Museum**   MUSEUM
(☑ 210 900 0901; www.theacropolismuseum.gr; Dionysiou Areopagitou 15, Makrygianni; adult/child €5/free; ☺ 8am-4pm Mon, to 8pm Tue-Sun, to 10pm Fri Apr-Oct, 9am-5pm Mon-Thu, to 10pm Fri, 9am-8pm Sat & Sun Nov-Mar; M Akropoli) This

> ### ⓘ ACROPOLIS PASS & ENTRY HOURS
> ....
> ➡ The Acropolis admission includes entry to Athens' main ancient sites: the Theatre of Dionysos, Ancient Agora, Roman Agora, Hadrian's Library, Keramikos and the Temple of Olympian Zeus. The ticket is valid for four days; otherwise individual site fees apply.
>
> ➡ Double-check hours as they fluctuate from year to year, with closing sometimes as early as 3pm.
>
> ➡ Box offices close 15 minutes to half an hour before the sites. Check www.culture.gr for free-admission holidays.

dazzling modernist museum at the foot of the Acropolis' southern slope showcases its surviving treasures still in Greek possession. While the collection covers the Archaic and Roman periods, the emphasis is on the Acropolis of the 5th century BC, considered the apotheosis of Greece's artistic achievement. The museum cleverly reveals layers of history, floating over ruins with the Acropolis visible above, showing the masterpieces in context. The surprisingly good-value **restaurant** has superb views; there's also a fine museum **shop**.

Ancient Agora   HISTORIC SITE
(☑ 210 321 0185; http://odysseus.culture.gr; Adrianou; adult/child €4/free, with Acropolis pass free; ☺ 8am-8pm daily, reduced hours in low season; M Monastiraki) The heart of ancient Athens was the Agora, the lively, crowded focal point of administrative, commercial, political and social activity. Socrates expounded his philosophy here, and in AD 49 St Paul came here to win converts to Christianity. The site today is a lush, refreshing respite, with beautiful monuments and temples and a fascinating **museum**.

Temple of Olympian Zeus   TEMPLE
(Olympieio; ☑ 210 922 6330; http://odysseus.culture.gr; cnr Leoforos Vasilissis Olgas & Leoforos Vasilissis Amalias, Syntagma; adult/child €2/free, with Acropolis pass free; ☺ 8am-8pm Apr-Oct, 8.30am-3pm Nov-Mar; M Akropoli, Syntagma) You can't miss this striking marvel smack in the centre of Athens. It is the largest temple in Greece; begun in the 6th century BC by Peisistratos, it was abandoned for lack of funds. Various other leaders had stabs at completing it, but it was left to Hadrian to complete the work in AD 131 – taking more than 700 years in total to build.

Hadrian's Arch   MONUMENT
(cnr Leoforos Vasilissis Olgas & Leoforos Vasilissis Amalias, Syntagma; M Akropoli, Syntagma) FREE The Roman emperor Hadrian had a great affection for Athens. Although he did his fair share of spiriting its classical artwork to Rome, he also embellished the city with many monuments influenced by classical architecture. His arch is a lofty monument of Pentelic marble that stands where busy Leoforos Vasilissis Olgas and Leoforos Vasilissis Amalias meet. Hadrian erected it in AD 132, probably to commemorate the consecration of the Temple of Olympian Zeus.

> **WORTH A TRIP**
>
> ## CAPE SOUNION
>
> The Ancient Greeks certainly knew how to choose a site for a temple. Nowhere is this more evident than at Cape Sounion, 70km south of Athens, where the **Temple of Poseidon** (☑22920 39363; http://odysseus.culture.gr; adult/child €4/free; ⊗8am-sunset, from 9.30am winter) stands on a craggy spur that plunges 65m down to the sea. Built in 444 BC – at the same time as the Parthenon – it is constructed of local marble from Agrilesa; its slender columns, of which 16 remain are Doric.
>
> It looks gleaming white when viewed from the sea, which gave great comfort to sailors in ancient times: they knew they were nearly home when they saw the first glimpse of white, far off in the distance. The views from the temple are equally impressive: on a clear day you can see Kea, Kythnos and Serifos to the southeast, and Aegina and the Peloponnese to the west. The site also contains scant remains of a **propylaeum**, a fortified **tower** and, to the northeast a 6th-century **temple to Athena**.
>
> Visit early in the morning before the tourist buses arrive, or head there for sunset to enact Byron's lines from *Don Juan*:
>
> 'Place me on Sunium's marbled steep / Where nothing save the waves and I / May hear our mutual murmurs sweep.'
>
> Byron was so impressed by Sounion that he carved his name on one of the columns (sadly, many other not-so-famous travellers followed suit).
>
> The temple can be reached by KTEL services from the Mavromateon terminal. There are a couple of tavernas just below the site – perfect for lunch and a swim.

Panathenaic Stadium HISTORIC SITE
(☑210 752 2984; www.panathenaicstadium.gr; Leoforos Vasileos Konstantinou, Pangrati; adult/child €5/2.50; ⊗8am-7pm Mar-Oct, to 5pm Nov-Feb; Ⓜ Akropoli) The grand Panathenaic Stadium lies between two pine-covered hills between the neighbourhoods of Mets and Pangrati. It was originally built in the 4th century BC as a venue for the Panathenaic athletic contests. It's said that at Hadrian's inauguration in AD 120, 1000 wild animals were sacrificed in the arena. Later, the seats were rebuilt in Pentelic marble by Herodes Atticus. There are seats for 70,000 spectators, a running track and a central area for field events.

★**National**
Archaeological Museum MUSEUM
(☑213 214 4800; www.namuseum.gr; 28 Oktovriou-Patision 44, Exarhia; adult/child €7/free; ⊗8am-8pm Apr-Oct, reduced hours Nov-Mar; Ⓜ Viktoria, 🚌 2, 4, 5, 9 or 11 to Polytechnio) One of the world's most important museums, the National Archaeological Museum houses the world's finest collection of Greek antiquities. Treasures offering a view of Greek art and history – dating from the Neolithic era to classical periods – include exquisite sculptures, pottery, jewellery, frescoes and artefacts found throughout Greece. The beautifully presented exhibits are displayed mainly thematically. Allow plenty of time to view the vast and spectacular collections (over 11,000 items) housed in this enormous (8000-sq-metre) 19th-century neoclassical building.

The museum is a 10-minute walk from Viktoria metro station, or catch trolleybus 2, 4, 5, 9 or 11 from outside St Denis Cathedral on Panepistimiou and get off at the Polytechnio stop.

Byzantine & Christian Museum MUSEUM
(☑213 213 9500; www.byzantinemuseum.gr; Leoforos Vasilissis Sofias 22, Kolonaki; adult/child €4/free; ⊗8am-8pm Apr-Oct, reduced hours Nov-Mar; Ⓜ Evangelismos) This outstanding museum – on the grounds of former Villa Ilissia, an urban oasis – presents a priceless collection of Christian art from the 3rd to 20th centuries. Thematic snapshots of the Byzantine and post-Byzantine world are exceptionally presented in expansive, well-lit, multilevel galleries, clearly arranged chronologically with English translations. The collection includes icons, frescoes, sculptures, textiles, manuscripts, vestments and mosaics.

The villa grounds, which sit next to **Aristotle's Lyceum** (cnr Rigillis & Leof Vasilissis Sofias; ⊗8am-8pm Mon-Fri; Ⓜ Evangelismos) FREE,

The Acropolis

Cast your imagination back in time, two and a half millennia ago, and envision the majesty of the Acropolis. Its famed and hallowed monument, the Parthenon, dedicated to the goddess Athena, stood proudly over a small city, dwarfing the population with its graceful grandeur. In the Acropolis' heyday in the 5th century BC, pilgrims and priests worshipped at the temples illustrated here (most of which still stand in varying states of restoration). Many were painted brilliant colours and were abundantly adorned with sculptural masterpieces crafted from ivory, gold and semiprecious stones.

As you enter the site today, elevated on the right, perches one of the Acropolis' best-restored buildings: the diminutive **Temple of Athena Nike ❶**. Follow the Panathenaic Way through the Propylaia and up the slope toward the Parthenon – icon of the Western world. Its **majestic columns ❷** sweep up to some of what were the finest carvings of their time: wraparound **pediments, metopes and a frieze ❸**. Stroll around the temple's exterior and take in the spectacular views over Athens and Piraeus below.

As you circle back to the centre of the site, you will encounter those renowned lovely ladies, the **Caryatids ❹** of the Erechtheion. On the Erechtheion's northern face, the oft-forgotten **Temple of Poseidon ❺** sits alongside ingenious **Themistocles' Wall ❻**. Wander to the Erechtheion's western side to find Athena's gift to the city: **the olive tree ❼**.

TOP TIP

» **The Acropolis** is a must-see for every visitor to Athens. Avoid the crowds by arriving first thing in the morning or late in the day.

Themistocles' Wall
Crafty general Themistocles (524–459 BC) hastened to build a protective wall around the Acropolis and in so doing incorporated elements from archaic temples on the site. Look for the column drums built into the wall.

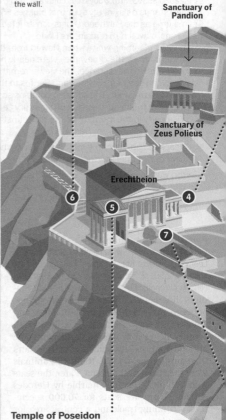

Sanctuary of Pandion

Sanctuary of Zeus Polieus

Erechtheion

❻ ❺ ❹
❼

Temple of Poseidon
Though he didn't win patronage of the city, Poseidon was worshipped on the northern side of the Erechtheion which still bears the mark of his trident-strike. Imagine the finely decorated coffered porch painted in rich colours, as it was before.

VWB PHOTOS / GETTY IMAGES ©

Porch of the Caryatids
Perhaps the most recognisable sculptural elements at the Acropolis are the majestic Caryatids (circa 415 BC). Modelled on women from Karyai (modern-day Karyes, in Lakonia) the maidens are thought to have held a libation bowl in one hand, and to be drawing up their dresses with the other.

Parthenon Pediments, Metopes & Frieze
The Parthenon's pediments (the triangular elements topping the east and west facades) were filled with elaborately carved three-dimensional sculptures. The west side depicted Athena and Poseidon in their contest for the city's patronage, the east Athena's birth from Zeus' head. The metopes are square carved panels set between channelled triglyphs. They depicted battle scenes, including the sacking of Troy and the clash between the Lapiths and the Centaurs. The cella was topped by the Ionic frieze, a continuous sculptured band depicting the Panathenaic Procession.

Parthenon

Chalkotheke

Sanctuary of Artemis Brauronia

Panathenaic Way

Statue of Athena Promachos

Arrephorion

Propylaia

Pinakothiki

Entrance

Spring of Klepsydra

Parthenon Columns
The Parthenon's fluted Doric columns achieve perfect form. Their lines were ingeniously curved to create an optical illusion: the foundations (like all the 'horizontal' surfaces of the temple) are slightly concave and the columns are slightly convex making both appear straight.

Temple of Athena Nike
Recently restored, this precious tiny Pentelic marble temple was designed by Kallicrates and built around 425 BC. The cella housed a wooden statue of Athena as Victory (Nike) and the exterior friezes illustrated Athenian battle triumphs.

Athena's Olive Tree
The flourishing olive tree next to the Erechtheion is meant to be the sacred tree that Athena produced to seize victory in the contest for Athens.

SILKFACTORY / GETTY IMAGES ©

WESTEND61 / GETTY IMAGES ©

ANTON_IVANOV / SHUTTERSTOCK ©

Central Athens

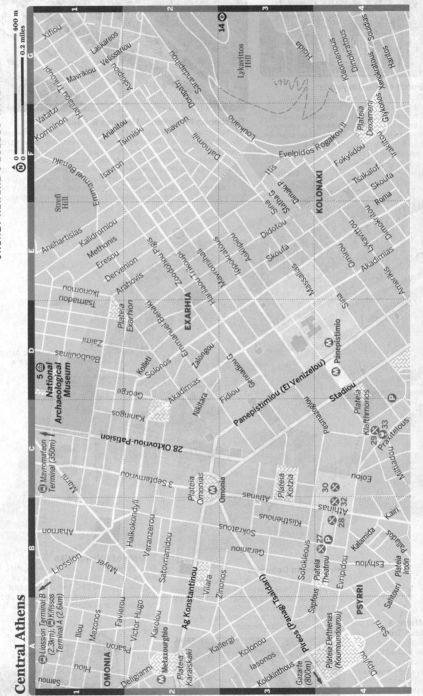

OMONIA

METAXOURGHIO

PSYRRI

EXARHIA

KOLONAKI

National Archaeological Museum

Lykavittos Hill

Panepistimiou (El Venizelou)

Panepistimio

Stadiou

Omonia

Plateia Omonias

Plateia Kotzia

Plateia Karaiskaki

Plateia Theatrou

Plateia Eleftherias (Koumoundourou)

Plateia Exarhion

Piraeos (Panagi Tsaldari)

28 Oktovriou-Patision

Ag Konstantinou

Liossion Terminal B (2.3km); Kifissos Terminal A (2.6km)

Mavromateon Terminal (350m)

Gazarte (800m)

400 m
0.2 miles

N

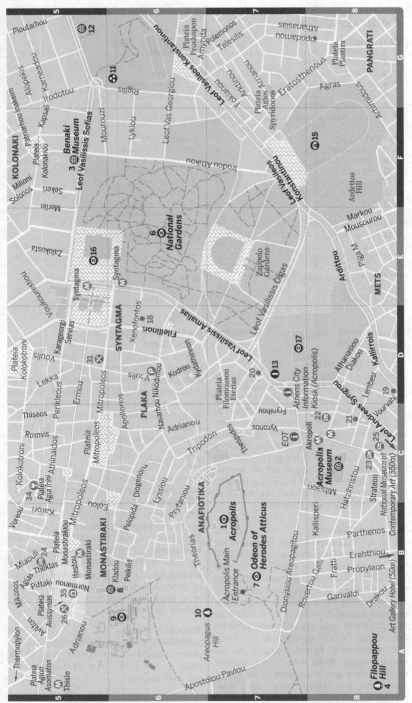

Central Athens

include ancient ruins such as the Peisistratos aqueduct.

National Museum of Contemporary Art
MUSEUM
(☏210 924 2111; www.emst.gr; Kallirrois & Frantzi, Koukaki-Syngrou; adult/child €3/free; ⊙11am-7pm Tue, Wed & Fri-Sun, to 10pm Thu; ⓜSyngrou-Fix) In 2015 this museum inaugurated spectacularly renovated quarters at the former Fix Brewery on Leoforos Syngrou. It shows top-notch rotating exhibitions of Greek and international contemporary art. Its permanent exhibitions include paintings, installations, photography, video and new media, as well as experimental architecture.

★ Benaki Museum
MUSEUM
(☏210 367 1000; www.benaki.gr; Koumbari 1, cnr Leoforos Vasilissis Sofias, Kolonaki; adult/child €7/ free, Thu free; ⊙9am-5pm Wed & Fri, to midnight Thu & Sat, to 3pm Sun; ⓜSyntagma, Evangelismos) Greece's finest private museum contains the vast collection of Antonis Benakis, accumulated during 35 years of avid collecting in Europe and Asia. The collection includes Bronze Age finds from Mycenae and Thessaly; works by El Greco; ecclesiastical furniture brought from Asia Minor; pottery, copper, silver and woodwork from Egypt, Asia Minor and Mesopotamia; and a stunning collection of Greek regional costumes.

Parliament & Changing of the Guard
BUILDING
(Plateia Syntagmatos; ⓜSyntagma) FREE In front of the parliament building on Plateia Syntagmatos, the traditionally costumed *evzones* (guards) of the Tomb of the Unknown Soldier change every hour on the hour. On Sunday at 11am, a whole platoon marches down Vasilissis Sofias to the tomb, accompanied by a band.

☞ Tours

Three main companies – CHAT (☏210 323 0827; www.chatours.gr; Xenofontos 9, Syntagma; ⓜSyntagma), GO Tours (☏210 921 9555; www.gotours.com.gr; Kallirrois 12, Makrygianni; ⓜAkropoli) and Hop In Sightseeing (☏210 428 5500; www.hopin.com; Leoforos Vasilissis Amalias 44, Makrygianni; ⊙6.30am-10pm; ⓜAkropoli) – run almost identical air-conditioned city coach tours, as well as excursions to nearby sights. Hotels act as booking agents and often offer discounts. More unusual tours include the following:

Alternative Athens
TOUR
(☏6948405242; www.alternativeathens.com) Experience-based tours and workshops to get off the beaten path – from food to street art and bar-hopping.

Solebike   BICYCLE RENTAL
(☑ 210 921 5620; www.solebike.eu; Lembesi 11, Makrygianni; 10hr from €20; ⊙9am-3pm Mon-Sat, also 6-8.30pm Tue, Thu & Fri; M̄Akropoli) Solebike hires out electric bikes, and offers tours (from €36).

This Is My Athens   TOUR
(http://myathens.thisisathens.org) Volunteer program that pairs you with a local to show you around for two hours. You must book online 72 hours ahead.

✪ Festivals

★Hellenic Festival   PERFORMING ARTS
(Athens & Epidavros Festival; www.greekfestival.gr; ⊙Jun-Aug) The ancient theatre at Epidavros and Athens' Odeon of Herodes Atticus are the headline venues of Greece's annual cultural festival featuring a top line-up of local and international music, dance and theatre.

Major shows in its **Athens Festival** take place at the superb **Odeon of Herodes Atticus** (☑ 210 324 1807; M̄Akropoli), one of the world's prime historic venues, with the floodlit Acropolis as a backdrop. Events are also held in modern venues around town.

🛏 Sleeping

★Athens Backpackers   HOSTEL €
(☑ 210 922 4044; www.backpackers.gr; Makri 12, Makrygianni; dm incl breakfast €24-29, 2-/4-/6-person apt from €100/130/160; 🕸@🔊; M̄Akropoli) The popular rooftop bar with cheap drinks and Acropolis views is a major drawcard for this modern and friendly Australian-run backpacker favourite. There's a barbecue in the courtyard, a well-stocked kitchen and a busy social scene. Spotless dorms with private bathrooms and lockers have bedding, but towel use costs €2.

Art Gallery Hotel   PENSION €
(☑ 210 923 8376; www.artgalleryhotel.gr; Erehthiou 5, Koukaki; s/d/tr/q from €50/60/70/80; 🕸🔊; M̄Syngrou-Fix) Staying in this quaint, family-run place feels like staying in a home. Original furniture from the 1960s decorates the communal areas. Some rooms are a little small, but the upstairs balcony has a bit of an Acropolis view. A few cheaper rooms have shared bathrooms.

AthenStyle   HOSTEL €
(☑ 210 322 5010; www.athenstyle.com; Agias Theklas 10, Psyrri; dm €18-26, s/d €50/75, apt from €84; 🕸@🔊; M̄Monastiraki) This bright, arty place has friendly staff, well-equipped studio apartments and hostel beds within walking distance of the Monastiraki metro, major sights and nightlife. Each dorm has lockers; some balconies have Acropolis views. Murals bedeck reception; the cool basement lounge, with pool table, home cinema and internet corner, holds art exhibitions. The small Acropolis-view rooftop bar hosts evening happy hours.

★Hera Hotel   BOUTIQUE HOTEL €€
(☑ 210 923 6682; www.herahotel.gr; Falirou 9, Makrygianni; d incl breakfast €130-145, ste €250; 🕸@🔊; M̄Akropoli) This elegant boutique hotel, a short walk from the Acropolis and Plaka, was totally rebuilt – but the formal interior design is in keeping with the lovely neoclassical facade. There's lots of brass and timber, and stylish classic furnishings. The rooftop garden, restaurant and bar have spectacular views.

Athens Studios   APARTMENT €€
(☑ 210 923 5811; www.athensstudios.gr; Veïkou 3a, Makrygianni; apt incl breakfast €80-120; @🔊; M̄Akropoli) Run by the folk from Athens Backpackers, these relaxed apartments are spacious, with kitchenettes, colourful bathrooms, and a lounge area with shared balcony (top-floor balconies are largest). The bedroom has either two beds or four bunks, making it a well-priced alternative to dormitory living.

🍴 Eating

★Kalnterimi   TAVERNA €
(☑ 210 331 0049; www.kalnterimi.gr; Plateia Agion Theodoron, cnr Skouleniou, Monastiraki; mains €5-8; ⊙noon-11pm Mon-Sat; 🔊; M̄Panepistimio) Find your way behind the Church of Agii Theodori to this hidden, open-air taverna offering Greek food at its most authentic. Everything is fresh-cooked and delicious: you can't go wrong. Hand-painted tables spill onto the footpath along a pedestrian

---

STREET FOOD

From vendors selling *koulouria* (fresh pretzel-style bread) and grilled corn or chestnuts to the raft of fast-food offerings, there's no shortage of snacks on the run in Athens. You can't go wrong with *tiropites* (cheese pies) or Greece's favourite savoury snack, souvlaki, which packs more punch for €2.50 than anything else.

street and give a feeling of peace in one of the busiest parts of the city.

★ Diporto Agoras   TAVERNA €

(☑210 321 1463; cnr Theatrou & Sokratous; plates €5-6; ⊙7am-7pm Mon-Sat, closed 1-20 Aug; Ⓜ Omonia, Monastiraki) This quirky old taverna is one of the dining gems of Athens. There's no signage, only two doors leading to a rustic cellar where there's no menu, just a few dishes that haven't changed in years. The house speciality is *revythia* (chickpeas), usually followed by grilled fish and washed down with wine from one of the giant barrels lining the wall. The often erratic service is part of the appeal.

Café Avyssinia   MEZEDHES €€

(☑210 321 7047; Kynetou 7, Monastiraki; mains €10-16; ⊙11am-1am Tue-Sat, to 7pm Sun; Ⓜ Monastiraki) Hidden away on colourful Plateia Avyssinias, in the middle of the flea market, this bohemian *mezedhopoleio* (restaurant specialising in mezedhes) gets top marks for atmosphere, food and friendly service. It specialises in regional Greek cuisine, from warm fava to eggplant baked with tomato and cheese, and has a great selection of ouzo, *raki* (Cretan firewater) and *tsipouro* (a distilled spirit similar to ouzo but usually stronger).

There is acoustic live Greek music on weekends. Snag fantastic Acropolis views upstairs.

Tzitzikas & Mermingas   MEZEDHES €

(☑210 324 7607; www.tzitzikasmermigas.gr; Mitropoleos 12-14, Syntagma; mezedhes €6-12; ⊙noon-11pm; Ⓜ Syntagma) Greek merchandise lines the walls of this cheery, modern *mezedhopoleio* that sits smack in the middle of central Athens. It serves a tasty range of delicious and creative mezedhes (like the honey-drizzled, bacon-wrapped Naxos cheese) to a bustling crowd of locals.

REMBETIKA

Athens has some of the best *rembetika* (Greek blues) in intimate, evocative venues. Performances usually include both *rembetika* and *laïka* (urban popular music), start at around 11.30pm and do not have a cover charge, though drinks can be expensive. Most close May to September, so in summer try live-music tavernas around Plaka and Psyrri.

Varvakios Agora   MARKET €

(Athens Central Market; Athinas, btwn Sofokleous & Evripidou, Omonia; ⊙7am-3pm Mon-Sat; Ⓜ Monastiraki, Panepistimio, Omonia) The streets around the colourful and bustling Varvakios Agora are a sensory delight. The meat and fish market fills the historic building on the eastern side, and the fruit and vegetable market is across the road. The meat market might sound like a strange place to go for a meal, but its tavernas are an Athenian institution. Clients range from hungry market workers to elegant couples emerging from nightclubs in search of a bowl of hangover-busting *patsas* (tripe soup).

🍷 Drinking & Entertainment

The city's hottest scene masses around Kolokotroni St north of Syntagma Sq, and around Plateia Agia Irini in Monastiraki. A cafe-thick area in Monastiraki is Adrianou, along the Ancient Agora, where people fill shady tables.

Get off the metro at Keramikos and you'll be smack in the middle of the thriving Gazi scene. In Thisio, cafes along the pedestrian promenade Apostolou Pavlou have great Acropolis views; those along pedestrianised Iraklidon pack 'em in at night.

In summer much of the city's serious nightlife moves to glamorous, enormous seafront clubs radiating out from Glyfada. Many sit on the tram route, which runs to 2.30am on Friday and Saturday. If you book for dinner you don't pay cover; otherwise admission ranges from €10 to €20 and includes one drink. Glam up to get in.

★ Tailor Made   BAR

(☑213 004 9645; www.tailormade.gr; Plateia Agia Irini 2, Monastiraki; ⊙8am-2am; Ⓜ Monastiraki) This popular new micro-roastery offers its array of coffee blends as well as hand-pressed teas. Cheerful Athenians spill from the mod-art-festooned interior to the tables alongside the flower market. At night it turns into a happening cocktail and wine bar.

Clumsies   BAR

(☑210 323 2682; www.theclumsies.gr; Praxitelous 30, Syntagma; ⊙9am-late; Ⓜ Syntagma) Warm welcoming decor with a design-retro feel and a packed, babbling crowd of happy sippers (from coffee to creative cocktail) makes this new all-day bar a go-to hangout for locals and visitors alike.

Gazarte
BAR

(📞 210 346 0347; www.gazarte.gr; Voutadon 32-34, Gazi; Ⓜ Keramikos) Upstairs you'll find a cinema-sized screen playing videos, amazing city views taking in the Acropolis, mainstream music and a trendy 30-something crowd. There's occasional live music and a restaurant to boot.

🛍 Shopping

Plaka and Monastiraki are happy hunting grounds for souvenirs, folk art and leather.

Monastiraki Flea Market
MARKET

(btwn Adrianou, Ifestou & Ermou, Monastiraki; ⊙ daily; Ⓜ Monastiraki) This traditional market has a festive atmosphere, combined with an onslaught of more modern souvenir stalls. Permanent antique and collectables shops are open all week, while the streets around the station and Adrianou fill with vendors selling jewellery, handicrafts and bric-a-brac.

❶ Information

DANGERS & ANNOYANCES

➜ Streets surrounding Omonia have become markedly seedier, with an increase in prostitutes and junkies; avoid the area, especially at night.

➜ Watch for pickpockets on the metro and at the markets.

➜ When taking taxis, ask the driver to use the meter or negotiate a price in advance. Ignore stories that the hotel you've chosen is closed or full: they're angling for a commission from another hotel.

➜ Bar scams are commonplace, particularly in Plaka and Syntagma. Beware the over-friendly!

➜ With the recent financial reforms in Greece have come strikes in Athens (check http://livingingreece.gr/strikes). Picketers tend to march in Plateia Syntagmatos.

EMERGENCY

SOS Doctors (📞 1016, 210 821 1838; ⊙ 24hr) Pay service with English-speaking doctors.

Visitor Emergency Assistance (📞 112) Toll-free 24-hour service in English.

TOURIST INFORMATION

Athens Airport Information Desk (⊙ 24hr) This 24-hour desk has Athens info booklets and the Athens Spotlighted discount card for goods and services.

Athens City Information Kiosk (Acropolis) (📞 210 321 7116; Dionysiou Areopagitou &

Leoforos Syngrou; ⊙ 9am-9pm May-Sep; Ⓜ Akropoli)

EOT (Greek National Tourist Organisation; 📞 210 331 0716, 210 331 0347; www.visitgreece.gr; Dionysiou Areopagitou 18-20, Makrygianni; ⊙ 8am-8pm Mon-Fri, 10am-4pm Sat & Sun May-Sep, 9am-7pm Mon-Fri Oct-Apr; Ⓜ Akropoli) Free Athens map, transport information and *Athens & Attica* booklet. There's also a desk at **Athens Airport** (⊙ 9am-5pm Mon-Fri & 10am-4pm Sat).

❶ Getting There & Away

AIR

Modern **Eleftherios Venizelos International Airport** (ATH; 📞 210 353 0000; www.aia.gr), at Spata, is east of Athens.

BOAT

Most ferry, hydrofoil and high-speed catamaran services to the islands leave from Athens' massive port at Piraeus.

Purchase tickets at booths on the quay next to each ferry, over the phone or online; travel agencies selling tickets also surround each port.

BUS

Athens has two main intercity (IC) **KTEL** (📞 14505; www.ktel.org) bus stations, 5km and 7km to the north of Omonia. Pick up timetables at the tourist office, or look online.

Kifissos Terminal A (📞 210 512 4910; Leoforos Kifisou 100, Peristeri; Ⓜ Agios Antonios) Buses to Thessaloniki, the Peloponnese, Ionian Islands and destinations in western Greece. Local bus 051 goes to central Athens (junction of Zinonos and Menandrou, near Omonia) every 15 minutes from 5am to midnight. Local bus X93 goes to/from the airport. Local bus 420 goes to/from Piraeus (junction of Akti Kondili and Thermopilon). Taxis to Syntagma cost about €9.

Liossion Terminal B (📞 210 831 7153; Liossion 260, Thymarakia; Ⓜ Agios Nikolaos, Attiki) Buses to central and northern Greece, such as Trikala (for Meteora) and Delphi. To get here take bus 024 from the main gate of the National Gardens on Amalias and ask to get off at Praktoria KTEL. Taxis to Syntagma cost about €9. Local bus X93 connects Kiffisos Bus Terminal A, Liossion Terminal B, and the Athens Airport.

Mavromateon Terminal (📞 210 880 8080, 210 822 5148, 210 880 8000; www.ktelattikis.gr; cnr Leoforos Alexandras & 28 Oktovriou-Patision, Pedion Areos; Ⓜ Viktoria) Buses for destinations in southern Attica leave from this station, about 250m north of the National Archaeological Museum.

MICHAL KRAKOWIAK / GETTY IMAGES ©

. Seville, Spain
eville's cathedral (p439) is one of the largest
hristian churches in the world.

. Cinque Terre, Italy
xplore the colourful old fishing harbour at
omaggiore (p513).

. Ephesus, Turkey
hese ruins, which are some of the best preserved
the Mediterranean, include the stunning Library
Celsus (p578).

. Porto, Portugal
ome of the best views of Porto (p481) can be
ken in from the other side of the Rio Douro.

CHRISTIAN KOBER / ROBERTHARDING / GETTY IMAGES ©

ℹ PUBLIC TRANSPORT TICKETS

Tickets good for 70 minutes (€1.20) and a 24-hour/five-day travel pass (€4/10) are valid for all forms of public transport except for airport services; the three-day tourist ticket (€20) includes one round-trip airport ride. Bus/trolleybus-only tickets (€1.20) cannot be used on the metro. Children under six travel free; people under 18 and over 65 pay half-fare.

Buy tickets in metro stations or transport kiosks or most *periptera* (kiosks). Validate the ticket in the machine as you board your transport of choice.

TRAIN

Intercity (IC) trains to central and northern Greece depart from the central **Larisis train station** (Stathmos Larisis; ☑ 210 529 8837, 14511; www.trainose.gr; Ⓜ Larisis), about 1km northwest of Plateia Omonias. For the Peloponnese, take the **suburban rail** (☑ 1110; www.trainose.gr) to Kiato and change for a bus there.

ℹ Getting Around

TO/FROM THE AIRPORT
Bus

Express buses operate 24 hours between the airport and the city centre, Piraeus and KTEL bus terminals. At the airport, buy tickets (€5; not valid for other forms of public transport) at the booth near the stops.

Plateia Syntagmatos Bus X95, one to 1½ hours, every 30 minutes, 24 hours. The Syntagma stop is on Othonos St.

Kifissos Terminal A bus station Bus X93, one hour, every 30 minutes (60 minutes at night), 24 hours.

Piraeus Bus X96, 1½ hours, every 20 minutes, 24 hours. To Plateia Karaïskaki.

Metro

Metro line 3 goes to the airport. Some trains terminate early at Doukissis Plakentias; disembark and wait for the airport train (displayed on the train and platform screen). Trains run every 30 minutes, leaving Monastiraki between 5.50am and midnight, and the airport between 5.30am and 11.30pm.

Airport tickets costs €8 per adult or €14 return (return valid 48 hours). The fare for two or more passengers is €7 each, so purchase tickets together (same with suburban rail). Tickets are valid for all forms of public transport for 90 minutes (revalidate your ticket on final mode of transport).

Taxi

Fixed fares are posted. Expect day/night (midnight to 5am) €35/50 to the city centre, and €47/72 to Piraeus. Both trips often take at least an hour, longer with heavy traffic. Check www.athensairporttaxi.com for more info.

PUBLIC TRANSPORT
Bus & Trolleybus

Local express buses, regular buses and electric trolleybuses operate every 15 minutes from 5am to midnight. The free OASA map shows most routes.

Metro

The metro works well and posted maps are self-explanatory (with icons and English translations). Trains operate from 5am to midnight (every four minutes during peak periods and every 10 minutes off peak); on Friday and Saturday, lines 2 and 3 run till 2am. Get information at www.stasy.gr and www.ametro.gr. All stations have wheelchair access.

TAXIS

Despite the many yellow taxis, it can be tricky getting one, especially during rush hour. Make sure the meter is on. The smartphone app Uber (www.uber.com) is usable in Athens.

If a taxi picks you up while already carrying passengers, the fare is not shared: each person pays the fare on the meter minus any diversions to drop others (note what it's at when you get in). Short trips around central Athens cost about €5; there are surcharges for pickups at the airport and transport hubs, as well as holiday and night tariffs. Taxi services include **Athina 1** (☑ 210 921 7942), **Enotita** (☑ 210 645 9000, 18388; www.athensradiotaxienotita.gr), **Taxibeat** (www.taxibeat.gr) and **Parthenon** (☑ 210 581 4711).

Delphi

POP 854

If the ancient Greeks hadn't chosen Delphi (from *delphis,* womb) as their navel of the Earth and built the Sanctuary of Apollo here, someone else would have thought of a good reason to make this eagle's-nest town a tourist attraction. Its cliff-side location is spectacular and, despite its overt commercialism and the constant passage of tour buses through the modern village, it still has a special feel. Ancient Delphi (and the adjoining village of Delphi) is 178km northwest of Athens.

THE DELPHI ORACLE

The Delphic oracle was considered one of the most important religious (and political) sanctuaries in Greece. Worshippers flocked here from far and wide to consult the god Apollo on serious decisions. Apollo's instrument of communication was the Pythia, or priestess, usually an older woman, who sat on a tripod in the Temple of Apollo.

During visitations and consultations, the priestess chewed laurel leaves and entered a trance after inhaling vapours from a chasm below. Archaeologists believe this could have been ethylene wafting through a crack from a fault line (carried by water running underground). Her vapour-inspired, if somewhat vague, answers were spoken in tongue then 'translated' by the priests of Apollo. In fact, the oracle's reputation for infallibility may have rested on the often ambiguous or cryptic answers. Wars were fought, marriages sealed, leaders chosen and journeys begun on the strength of the oracle's visions. After all, the prophecies were the will of a god, so the oracle's reputation remained throughout antiquity.

Legend holds that one priestess suffered for her vagueness. When Alexander the Great visited, hoping to hear a prophecy that he would soon conquer the ancient world, the priestess refused direct comment, instead asking that he return later. Enraged, he dragged her by the hair out of the chamber until she screamed, 'Let go of me; you're unbeatable'. He quickly dropped her, saying, 'I have my answer'.

⊙ Sights

★ Ancient Delphi
ARCHAEOLOGICAL SITE
(☑ 22650 82312; www.culture.gr; site or museum adult/child €6/free, combined €9 ⊙ 8am-3pm, longer hours summer) Of all the archaeological sites in Greece, Ancient Delphi is the one with the most potent spirit of place. Built on the slopes of Mt Parnassos, overlooking the Gulf of Corinth and extending into a valley of cypress and olive trees, this World Heritage Site's allure lies both in its stunning setting and its inspiring ruins.

The ancient Greeks regarded Delphi as the centre of the world – according to mythology, Zeus released two eagles at opposite ends of the world and they met here.

Check ahead for opening hours as these are subject to change. In summer, visit the site early to avoid the crowds and the heat. Don't head into the site just before closing time; staff are already rounding visitors up by then and you won't be permitted a thorough visit.

Delphi Museum
MUSEUM
(☑ 22650 82312; www.culture.gr; site or museum adult €6, adult/student combined €9/5; ⊙ 8am-8pm summer, to 2.45pm winter) From around the 8th century BC, Ancient Delphi managed to amass a considerable treasure trove, much of it reflected in its magnificent museum. It's worth visiting here before your site visit. It helps construct an image of what the site must have looked like with its wealthy buildings, statues (remember, these were then painted in colour) and other valuable offerings.

🏃 Activities

Two popular day hikes, both part of the E4 European long-distance path, start and end at Delphi.

The wonderful **Korykeon Cave walk** connects two ancient sites, the Temple of Apollo and Korykeon Cave, a sacred mountain cave-shrine for Pan. The cavern comprises a natural amphitheatre filled with stalactites and stalagmites. You can walk as far as 80m inside (caution: it can be slippery). Many hikers hire a taxi in Arahova as far as Kalyvia (around €25), hike to the cave (500m) and return to Delphi along a well-marked path (four hours). Along the way, there are awesome views of Delphi, the Amfissa plain and Galaxidi.

The **Delphi to Ancient Kirra hike** meanders through shady olive groves – the largest continuous olive grove in Greece – and takes three to four hours. After lunch and a swim, return by bus (around €2) to Delphi. The E4 trailhead is marked 100m east of the Hotel Acropole.

🛏 Sleeping & Eating

Rooms Pitho
PENSION €
(☑ 22650 82850; www.pithohotel.gr; Vasileon Pavlou & Friderikis 40a; s/d/tr incl breakfast from €45/55/70; ❄ 🛜) Pitho's eight spotless, modern rooms (some on the small side), excellent service, extremely friendly owners and location – about halfway along the street above a gift shop – make it a good choice.

Delphi Town

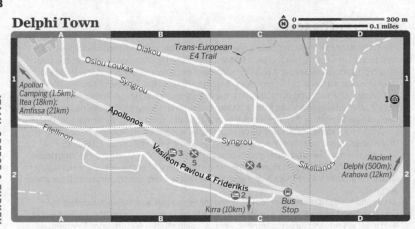

Delphi Town

⊙ Sights
1 Delphi Museum D1

🛏 Sleeping
2 Hotel Sibylla..C2
3 Rooms Pitho B2

⊗ Eating
4 Souvlaki Pita Gyros..............................C2
5 Taverna Vakhos B2

Because it's incorporated into a home-style lodging, it's quieter than some hotels.

Hotel Sibylla HOTEL €
(☎ 22650 82335; www.sibylla-hotel.gr; Vasileon Pavlou & Friderikis 9; s/d/tr €26/30/40; ▣ 🛜) A top budget choice, cosy Sibylla has delightful owners and seven light and tidy rooms, all with fans and several with views across to the gulf.

Souvlaki Pita Gyros KEBAB €
(Apollonos; mains €2-6; ⊙ 8am-3pm) Run by a family who conscientiously and efficiently whip up tasty budget options, including souvlaki and great Greek salads. Eat in or takeaway. Opposite Hotel Leto.

Taverna Vakhos TAVERNA €€
(☎ 22650 83186; www.vakhos.com; Apollonos 31; mains €8-14.50; ⊙ noon-midnight; 🛜) Take the steps above the National Bank to this excellent family taverna featuring traditional local fare. Ask for what's fresh that day – it gets local produce if possible and staff gather the herbs themselves. If nothing appeals,

make a meal of appetisers alone, eg *formae-la*, the local cheese (€6).

ⓘ Information

Almost everything you'll need in Delphi is on Vasileon Pavlou & Friderikis. Delphi's other through roads are Apollonos, which runs north of and parallel to Vasileon Pavlou & Friderikis, and Filellinon, which runs south and parallel to the main drag. Four steep stairways connect all three roads.

Incredibly, there is no tourist office. Several ATMs are on Friderikis.

ⓘ Getting There & Away

Buses (☎ 22650 82317; www.ktel-fokidas.gr; Vasileon Pavlou & Friderikis) depart from the eastern end of Friderikis, opposite the old Hotel Vouza. Tickets must be purchased from the Delphi restaurant between 9am and 8pm (the bus system's closing time). If you're taking an early bus, you will need to plan ahead; buy tickets one day earlier. The same applies in high season when buses fill up quickly. Travellers to Kalambaka/Meteora should find better connections via Lamia and Trikala, rather than Larissa.

Santorini

POP 15,550

Santorini may well have conquered a corner of your imagination before you've even set eyes on it. With multicoloured cliffs soaring over 300m from a sea-drowned caldera, it rests in the middle of the indigo Aegean, looking like a giant slab of layered cake. The island spoons the vast crater left by one of the biggest volcanic eruptions in history. Smaller islands curl around the fragmented western edge of the caldera, but it is the main island of Thira that will take your breath away with its snow-drift of white Cycladic houses lining the cliff tops and, in places, spilling like icy cornices down the terraced rock. When the sun sets, the reflection on the buildings and the glow of the orange and red in the cliffs can be truly spectacular.

Sights

Museum of Prehistoric Thera MUSEUM
(☑22860 22217; Mitropoleos; adult/child €3/free; ☺8am-3pm Tue-Sun) Opposite the bus station, this well-presented museum houses extraordinary finds excavated from Akrotiri and is all the more impressive when you realise just how old they are. Most remarkable is the

---

WORTH A TRIP

METEORA

Meteora (meh-teh-o-rah) should be a certified Wonder of the World with its magnificent late-14th-century monasteries perched dramatically atop enormous rocky pinnacles. Try not to miss it.

From the 11th century, hermit monks lived here in scattered caverns. By the 14th century, Turkish incursions into Greece were on the rise, so monks began to seek safe havens away from the bloodshed. The inaccessibility of the rocks of Meteora made them an ideal retreat. While there were once monasteries on all 24 pinnacles, six remain active religious sites.

Keen walkers should definitely explore the area on foot on the old and once-secret *monopatia* (monk paths).

Sights

Entry to each monastery is €3 and dress codes apply: no bare shoulders are allowed, men must wear trousers and women must wear skirts below the knee (wraparound skirts are generally provided at the entrances). Before planning your route, double-check days and opening hours. The six accessible monasteries are: **Moni Agias Triados** (Holy Trinity; ☺9am-5pm Fri-Wed Apr-Oct, 9am-3pm Sat-Wed Nov-Mar), **Moni Agias Varvaras Rousanou** (☺9am-6pm Thu-Tue Apr-Oct, to 2pm Nov-Mar), **Moni Agiou Nikolaou** (Monastery of St Nikolaou Anapafsa; ☺9am-3.30pm Sat-Thu Nov-Mar, to 2pm Apr-Oct), **Moni Agiou Stefanou** (☺9am-1.30pm & 3.30-5.30pm Tue-Sun Apr-Oct, 9.30am-1pm & 3-5pm Tue-Sun Nov-Mar), **Moni Megalou Meteorou** (Grand Meteoron; a☺9am-5pm Wed-Mon Apr-Oct, to 4pm Thu-Mon Nov-Mar) and **Moni Varlaam** (☺9am-4pm Sat-Thu Apr-Oct, 9am-3pm Sat-Wed Nov-Mar).

Sleeping & Eating

Doupiani House (☑24320 75326; www.doupianihouse.com; s/d/tr incl breakfast from €50/60/75; P ❄ @ 🛜) The delightful Doupiani House has the lot: spotless, tastefully decorated rooms, with balconies or garden access. Its location – just outside the village – provides a window to Meteora, boasting one of the region's best panoramic views. There's breakfast on the terrace, birdsong and attentive hosts, Toula and Thanasis.

Taverna Paradisos (mains €6.50-9; ☺noon-4pm & 6pm-late; P) The traditional meals at roomy Paradisos will have you exclaiming *'nostimo!'* (delicious!) all the way through your dishes, thanks to local and high-quality ingredients and owner-chef Koula's magic touch. Excellent fried zucchini.

Getting There & Around

From Athens, buses head north to Trikala (€29, five hours, six daily), where you can hop a bus to Kalambaka (€2.30, 30 minutes), Meteora's nearest village. Trains run between Athens and Kalambaka (regular/IC €18/29, 5½/4½ hours, both twice daily).

The main sealed road surrounding the entire Meteora complex of rocks and monasteries is about 15km in length. A bus (€1.20, 20 minutes) departs from Kalambaka and Kastraki at 9am and returns at 1pm (12.40pm on weekends). That's enough time to explore three monasteries – Moni Megalou Meteorou, Moni Varlaam and Moni Agias Varvaras Rousanou.

glowing gold ibex figurine, dating from the 17th century BC and in amazingly mint condition. Also look for fossilised olive tree leaves from within the caldera from 60,000 BC.

★ **Ancient Akrotiri** ARCHAEOLOGICAL SITE
(☑ 22860 81366; adult/child €5/free; ☺ 8am-8pm) In 1967 excavations began at the site of Akrotiri. What they uncovered was phenomenal: an ancient Minoan city buried deep beneath volcanic ash from the catastrophic eruption of 1613 BC. Today, the site retains a strong sense of place. Housed within a cool, protective structure, wooden walkways allow you to pass through various parts of the city.

Art Space GALLERY
(☑ 22860 32774; www.artspace-santorini.com; Exo Gonia; ☺ 11am-sunset) **FREE** This unmissable, atmospheric gallery is just outside Kamari, in Argyros Canava, one of the oldest wineries on the island. The atmospheric old wine caverns are hung with superb artworks, while sculptures transform lost corners and niches. The collection features some of Greece's finest modern artists.

Winemaking is still in the owner's blood, and part of the complex is given over to producing some stellar vintages. Tastings (€5) enhance the experience.

Santorini (Thira)

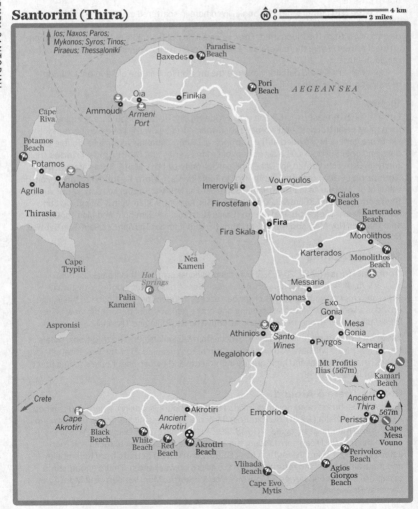

⚡ Activities

Walking

Walks in and around the capital, Fira, are spectacular, particularly heading north to Firostefani and Imerovigli along the caldera-edge pathway. This is about a 30-minute walk, one way.

If you want to keep walking, you can eventually reach **Oia**, but be aware that this is no small undertaking, and the trail beyond Imerovigli can be rough. It's about 9km in all, and a good three to four hours' walk one way. It's best not to undertake it in the heat of the day.

Beaches

The best beaches are on the east and south coasts. Sunbeds, beach bars and watersports operators are here to serve.

One of the main beaches is the long stretch at **Perissa**. **Perivolos** and **Agios Georgios**, further south, are long stretches of black sand, pebbles and pumice stones. While they're backed by bars, tavernas, hotels and shops, they remain fairly relaxed.

Red (Kokkini) Beach, near Ancient Akrotiri, has impressive red cliffs. It's a bit of a trek over uneven rock to reach it, or caïques from Akrotiri Beach can take you there for about €5 return.

Vlihada, also on the south coast, has a beach backed by weirdly eroded cliffs, tavernas plus a photogenic fishing harbour.

Kamari is 10km from Fira and is Santorini's best-developed resort. It has a long beach of black sand, with the rugged limestone cliffs of Cape Mesa Vouno framing its southern end and the site of Ancient Thira on its summit. The beachfront road is dense with restaurants and bars. Boats connect it with Perissa in summer.

Note: at times, Santorini's black-sand beaches become so hot that a sun lounge or mat is essential.

🛏 Sleeping

★ Karterados Caveland Hostel   HOSTEL €€

(☎ 22860 22122; www.cave-land.com; Karterados; incl breakfast dm €17-25, d with/without bathroom €70/50, apt €100; P ❄ 🛜 🏊) This fabulous, chilled-out hostel is based in an old winery complex in Karterados about 2km from central Fira (see website for directions). Accommodation is in the big old wine caves, all of them with creative, colourful decor and good facilities. The surrounding garden is relaxing, with weekly barbecues held, and there are yoga classes on offer too.

OIA

Perched on the northern tip of the island, the village of Oia (ee-ah) reflects the renaissance of Santorini after the devastating earthquake of 1956. Restoration work has whipped up beauty and you will struggle to find a more stunning Cyclades village. Built on a steep slope of the caldera, many of its dwellings nestle in niches hewn into the volcanic rock.

Not surprisingly, Oia draws enormous crowds. Try to visit in the morning or spend the night here. At sunset the town feels like a magnet for every traveller on the island.

Villa Roussa   HOTEL €€

(☎ 22860 23220; www.villaroussa.gr; Dekigala; s/d/tr from €60/85/100; P ❄ 🛜 🏊) This place is all about location. Minutes from the caldera (without the prices to match) and seconds from Fira's bus station (but thankfully out of earshot), it has fresh, immaculate rooms and helpful staff.

★ Zorzis Hotel   BOUTIQUE HOTEL €€

(☎ 22860 81104; www.santorinizorzis.com; Perissa; d incl breakfast €95; ❄ 🛜 🏊) Behind a huge bloom of geraniums on Perissa's main street, Hirohiko and Spiros (a Japanese-Greek couple) run an immaculate 10-room hotel. It's a pastel-coloured sea of calm (no kids), with delightful garden, pool and mountain backdrop.

🍴 Eating

Galini Cafe   CAFE €

(☎ 22860 22095; www.galinicafesantorini.com; mains €6-14; ⊘ 8am-midnight) Just as you reach Firostefani, this breezy cafe welcomes you with brightly coloured flowerpots and a handcrafted school of fish swimming overhead. Chilled and friendly, with unparalleled caldera views, it's a great place for breakfast or a light meal and a cocktail at sunset.

Ouzeri   TAVERNA €

(☎ 22860 21566; Fabrika Shopping Centre; mains €7-15; ⊘ lunch & dinner) Central and cheerfully dressed in red gingham, this terrace Fira restaurant has surprisingly reasonable prices. It's a longstanding favourite with locals and tourists alike, with top traditional dishes like mussels *saganaki,* baked feta and stuffed calamari.

Lolita's Gelato ICE CREAM €
(☑ 22860 71279; cones €3-6) Near Oia's bus station, Lolita's sells scoopfuls of heaven, including classics like blueberry or pistachio, plus original flavours like rosewater and red pepper.

ⓘ Information

Dakoutros Travel (☑ 22860 22958; www.dakoutrostravel.gr; Fira; ⊙ 8.30am-10pm) Travel agency on the main street, just before Plateia Theotokopoulou. Ferry and air tickets sold; assistance with excursions, accommodation and transfers.

Information Kiosk (⊙ 9am-8pm Mon-Fri May-Sep)

National Bank of Greece (Dekigala) South of Plateia Theotokopoulou, on the caldera side of the road. Has an ATM.

ⓘ Getting There & Around

AIR
Santorini Airport (☑ 22860 28400; www.santoriniairport.com) has flights year-round to/from Athens (from €64, 45 minutes) with Olympic Air (www.olympicair.com) and Aegean Airlines (www.aegeanair.com). Seasonal European connections are plentiful, including easyJet from London, Rome and Milan.

BOAT
There are plenty of ferries each day to and from Piraeus and many Cyclades islands.

Thira's main port is Athinios. Buses (and taxis) meet all ferries and then cart passengers up the towering cliffs through an ever-rising series of S-bends to Fira. Accommodation providers can usually arrange transfers (to Fira per person is around €10).

BUS
There are frequent bus connections between Fira's bus station and the airport, located southwest of Monolithos Beach. The first leaves Fira around 7am and the last 9pm (€1.60, 20 minutes). Most accommodation providers will arrange (paid) transfers.

KTEL Santorini Buses (☑ 22860 25404; http://ktel-santorini.gr) has a good website with schedules and prices. Tickets are purchased on the bus.

In summer buses leave Fira twice-hourly for Oia, with more services pre-sunset (€1.60). There are also numerous daily departures for Akrotiri (€1.80), Kamari (€1.60), Perissa and Perivolos Beach (€2.20), and a few to Monolithos (€1.60).

Buses leave Fira, Perissa and Kamari for the port of Athinios (€2.20, 30 minutes) a half-dozen times per day, but it's wise to check times in advance. Buses for Fira meet all ferries, even late at night.

CAR
A car is the best way to explore the island during high season, when buses are intolerably overcrowded. Be very patient and cautious when driving – the narrow roads and heavy traffic, especially in and around Fira, can be a nightmare. Note that Oia has no petrol station, the nearest being just outside Fira.

There are representatives of all the major international car-hire outfits, plus dozens of local operators in all tourist areas. A good local hire outfit is **Damigos Rent a Car** (☑ 22860 22048; www.santorini-carhire.com). You'll pay from around €50 per day for a car.

Rhodes
POP 115,000

By far the largest and always the most powerful of the Dodecanese Islands, Rhodes (*rodos*) abounds in beaches, wooded valleys and ancient history. Whether you arrive in search of buzzing nightlife, languid sun worshipping or diving in crystal-clear waters, or embark on a culture-vulture journey through past civilisations, it's all here. The atmospheric Old Town of Rhodes is a maze of cobbled streets that will spirit you back to the days of the Byzantine Empire and beyond. Further south is the picture-perfect town of Lindos, a magical vision of sugar-cube houses spilling down to a turquoise bay.

ⓘ Getting There & Away

AIR
Olympic Air (☑ 22410 24571; www.olympicair.com; Ierou Lohou 9) connects Rhodes' Diagoras airport with Athens and destinations throughout Greece, including several Dodecanese islands. Taxis charge a set fare of €22 to Rhodes Town, while buses connect the airport with Rhodes Town's Eastern Bus Terminal (€2.40, 25 minutes) between 6.30am and 11.15pm daily.

Minoan Air (www.minoanair.com) flies once weekly to Santorini (€79, 50 minutes).

BOAT
Rhodes is the main port in the Dodecanese. Two inter-island ferry operators operate from the Commercial Harbour, immediately outside the walls of Rhodes Old Town. **Dodekanisos Seaways** (☑ 22410 70590; www.12ne.gr; Afstralias 3, Rhodes Town) runs daily high-speed catamarans north up the chain. **Blue Star Ferries** (☑ 21089 19800; www.bluestarferries.com) provides slower and less frequent services. Tickets are available at the dock and from travel agents in Rhodes Town.

Getting To/From Turkey

Catamarans connect Rhodes' Commercial Harbour with Marmaris, Turkey (50 minutes), with two daily services in summer and two weekly in winter. Tickets cost €27 each way, plus €13 Turkish port tax. Same-day returns cost €45, including tax, and longer-stay returns, €63. For schedules and bookings, visit www.rhodes.marmarisinfo.com.

ⓘ Getting Around

BOAT

The quay at Mandraki Harbour is lined with excursion boats offering day trips to east-coast towns and beaches including Lindos.

Several islands can also be visited as day trips on Dodekanisos Seaways catamarans, departing from the Commercial Harbour. These include Symi and Kos (both daily), Halki and Tilos (both twice weekly), and Kastellorizo (once weekly).

BUS

Two bus terminals, a block apart in Rhodes Town, serve half the island each. There is regular transport across the island all week, with fewer services on Saturday and only a few on Sunday. Pick up schedules from the kiosks at either terminal, or from the EOT (Greek National Tourist Organisation) office.

The **Eastern Bus Terminal** (☑ 22410 27706; www.ktelrodou.gr) has frequent services to the

Rhodes

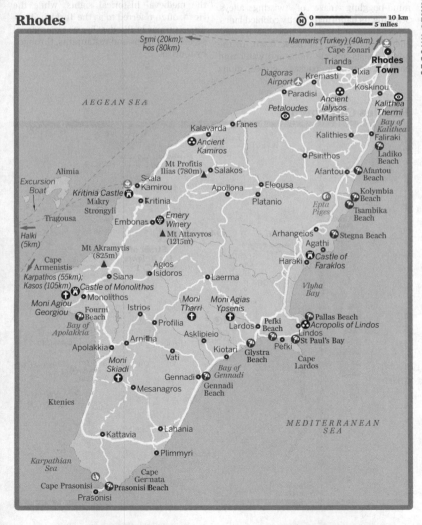

airport (€2.40) and Kalithea Thermi (€2.20). From the **Western Bus Terminal** (☎ 22410 26300) there are services to East Coast beaches (€2.20 to €4) and Lindos (€5).

Rhodes Town

Rhodes Town is really two distinct and very different towns. The **Old Town** lies within but utterly apart from the New Town, sealed like a medieval time capsule behind a double ring of high walls and a deep moat. Nowhere else in the Dodecanese can boast so many layers of architectural history, with ruins and relics of the classical, medieval, Ottoman and Italian eras entangled in a mind-boggling maze of twisting alleys. Strolling its hauntingly pretty cobbled lanes, especially at night, is an experience no traveller should miss. The **New Town**, to the north, boasts upscale shops and waterfront bars servicing the package crowd, along with the city's best beach, while bistros and bars lurk in the backstreets behind.

◉ Sights

A wander around Rhodes' Unesco World Heritage–listed Old Town is a must. It is reputedly the world's finest surviving example of medieval fortification, with 12m-thick walls. A mesh of Byzantine, Turkish and Latin architecture, the Old Town is divided into the Kollakio (the Knights' Quarter, where the Knights of St John lived during medieval times), the Hora and the Jewish Quarter. The **Knights' Quarter** is in the northern end of the Old Town and contains most of the medieval historical sights, while the **Hora**, often referred to as the Turkish Quarter, is primarily Rhodes Town's commercial sector with shops and restaurants, thronged by tourists.

Rhodes Old Town

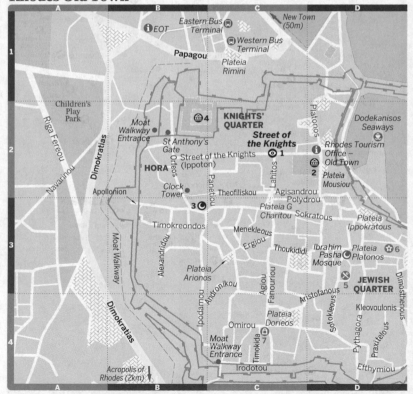

Archaeological Museum MUSEUM
(☎22410 65256; Plateia Mousiou; admission
€6; ☺8am-8pm) By far the best museum
in the Dodecanese, spreading through the
15th-century Knights' Hospital and out into
its beautiful and surprisingly wild gardens.
Room after room holds magnificently preserved ancient treasures, excavated from all
over the island and ranging over 7000 years.
Highlights include an exquisite marble statue of Aphrodite from the 2nd century BC,
a pavilion displaying wall-mounted mosaics,
and a reconstructed burial site from 1700 BC
that held not only a helmeted warrior but
also his horse.

Palace of the Grand Master HISTORIC BUILDING
(☎22410 65270; admission €6; ☺8.30am-8pm)
From the outside, the magnificent Palace of
the Grand Master looks much as it did when
erected by the Knights Hospitaller during the
14th century. During the 19th century, however, it was devastated by an explosion, so

the interior as you see it today is an Italian
reconstruction, completed in the '18th year of
the Fascist Era' (1940). The dreary magisterial chambers upstairs hold haphazard looted
artworks, so the most interesting section is
the exhibit on ancient Rhodes downstairs.

Mosque of Süleyman MOSQUE
(Sokratous) The Hora bears many legacies
of its Ottoman past. During Turkish times
churches were converted to mosques, and
many more Muslim houses of worship were
built from scratch, although most are now
dilapidated. The most important is the pink-
domed Mosque of Süleyman. Built in 1522 to
commemorate the Ottoman victory against
the knights, it was renovated in 1808.

★ Street of the Knights HISTORIC SITE
(Ippoton) Austere and uncommercialised, the
cobbled Street of the Knights (Ippoton, in
Greek) is lined with magnificent medieval
buildings. It was home from the 14th century to the Knights Hospitaller who ruled
Rhodes. They were divided by birthplace
into seven 'tongues', or languages – England,
France, Germany, Italy, Aragon, Auvergne
and Provence – each responsible for a specific section of the fortifications.

🛏 Sleeping

New Village Inn PENSION €
(☎22410 34937, 6976475917; www.newvillageinn.
gr; Konstantopedos 10; d €50; ❄) Hidden on a
back alleyway, a few steps from the bustle
of the New Town, this well-kept little pension centres on an attractive, leafy courtyard ornamented with icons. Two of its four

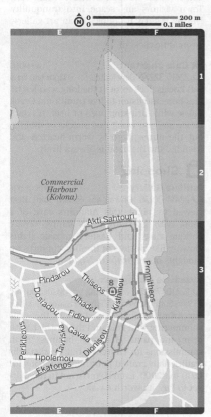

Rhodes Old Town

whitewashed en-suite rooms have their own private balconies.

★ Hotel Anastasia
PENSION €€

(☑ 22410 28007; www.anastasia-hotel.com; 28 Cktovriou 46; s/tw/d/tr €47/55/65/75; ✳@☎) The New Town's friendliest and most peaceful accommodation option, this handsome white-painted villa is set well back from the road and offers charming ochre-coloured en-suite rooms with wooden shutters, tiled floors and traditional furnishings. Some have private balconies and there's an inviting breakfast bar in the lush garden.

✗ Eating

★ Koykos
GREEK €

(☑ 22410 73022; Mandilana 20-26; mains €3-8; ☺ breakfast, lunch & dinner; ✳☎) This inviting complex, off a pedestrian shopping street, consists of several antique-filled rooms – a couple hold vintage jukeboxes – along with two bougainvillea-draped courtyards and a floral roof terrace. Best known for fabulous homemade pies, it also serves all the classic mezedhes, plus meat and fish dishes, or you can drop in for a coffee or sandwich.

Niohori
TAVERNA €

(☑ 22410 35116; I Kazouli 29; mains €6-10; ☺ noon-midnight) This simple, great-value taverna – the open courtyard is basically a garage – delivers with a meat-accented menu. The owner is a butcher, with a shop across the street, so he selects the best cuts. Tuck into veal liver with oil and oregano, *stifadho* (meat with onions in a tomato puree), steak and meatballs, seasoned with organ music from the nearby church.

★ Nireas
SEAFOOD €€

(☑ 22410 21703; Sofokleous 45-47; mains €8-16; ✳) Nireas' status as Rhodes' favourite seafood restaurant owes much to the sheer enthusiasm and verve of genial owner Theo, from Symi – that and the beautifully prepared food, served beneath a vine-shaded canopy outside, or in the candlelit, lemon-walled interior. Be sure to sample the Symi shrimp, salted mackerel and, if you're in the mood, the 'Viagra' salad of small shellfish.

🍷 Drinking & Entertainment

Christos Garden
BAR

(☑ 22410 32144; Griva 102; ☺ 10pm-late) With its grotto-like bar and pebble-mosaic courtyard abloom with flowers, Christos offers New Town visitors an escape into tranquillity. During the day it doubles as an art gallery; after dark the fairy lights twinkle. Perfect for a romantic cocktail.

★ Cafe Chantant
LIVE MUSIC

(☑ 22410 32277; Dimokratou 3; ☺ 11pm-late Fri & Sat) Locals flock to sit at the long wooden tables here and listen to live traditional Greek music while drinking ouzo or beer. It's dark inside and you won't find snacks or nibbles, but the atmosphere is warm-hearted and friendly, and the band is always lively.

🛍 Shopping

Antique Gallery
ARTS, CRAFTS

(☑ 22414 00126; Omirou 45; ☺ 9am-9pm) Best viewed by night, this Aladdin's cave of a shop, with its shiny brass lamps, ornate antique rings and Eastern mosaic lights glowing like clusters of fireflies, conjures up thoughts of the *Arabian Nights*.

Byzantine Iconography
ARTS, CRAFTS

(☑ 22410 74127; www.sirimis.gr; Kisthiniou 42; ☺ 9am-5pm Mon-Fri) Visit artisan Basilios Per Sirimis in his cramped studio, the walls shimmering with gold and the air thick with resin and paint. His main business is in commissions for churches, but he also sells traditionally crafted paintings and icons for €210 to €2000. Even if you're not in the market to buy, it's worth a visit.

DON'T MISS

KALITHEA THERMI

Italian architect Pietro Lombardi constructed this opulent art-deco spa Kalithea Thermi (☑ 22410 65691; www.kalitheasprings.gr; Kalithea; admission €3; ☺ site 8am-8pm Apr-Oct, to 5pm Nov-Mar, cafe stays open later), on the site of ancient thermal springs, in 1929. Its dazzling white-domed pavilions, pebble-mosaic courtyards and sweeping sea-view colonnades appeared in movies such as *Zorba the Greek* and *Guns of Navarone*, and have now been restored after years of neglect. In peak season, though, its small sandy bathing beach and cafe get impossibly crowded.

Located just 9km south of Rhodes Town, with frequent buses from the Eastern Bus Terminal (€2.20).

ℹ Information

EOT (Greek Tourist Information Office; ☏ 22410 44335; www.ando.gr/eot; cnr Makariou & Papagou; ☻8am-2.45pm Mon-Fri) National tourism information, including brochures, maps and transport details.

Rhodes Guide (www.rhodesguide.com) What's on, where to stay and where to hang out in Rhodes.

Rhodes Tourism Office – Old Town (☏ 22410 35945; www.rhodes.gr; cnr Platonos & Ippoton; ☻7am-3pm Mon-Fri) In an ancient building at the foot of the Street of the Knights, this helpful office supplies excellent street maps, leaflets and brochures.

Lindos

Your first glimpse of the ancient and unbelievably pretty town of Lindos is guaranteed to steal your breath away: the towering Acropolis radiant on the cypress-silvered hill, and the sugar-cube houses of the whitewashed town tumbling below it towards the aquamarine bay. Entering the town itself, you'll find yourself in a magical warren of hidden alleys, packed with the ornate houses of long-vanished sea captains that now hold appetising tavernas, effervescent bars and cool cafes. Pick your way past donkeys as you coax your calves up to the Acropolis and one of the finest views in Greece.

◉ Sights

Two magnificent beaches line the crescent harbour that curves directly below the village. The larger, logically known as **Main Beach**, is a perfect swimming spot – sandy with shallow water – for kids. Follow a path north to the western tip of the bay to reach the smaller, taverna-fringed **Pallas Beach**. Don't swim near the jetty here, which is home to sea urchins.

Ten minutes' walk from town on the other, western, side of the Acropolis, sheltered **St Paul's Bay** is similarly caressed by turquoise waters.

★**Acropolis of Lindos**   ARCHAEOLOGICAL SITE
(☏ 22440 31258; entry €6; ☻8am-8pm Apr-Oct, 8.30am-3pm Nov-Mar) A steep footpath climbs the 116m-high rock above Lindos to reach the beautifully preserved Acropolis. First walled in the 6th century BC, the clifftop is now enclosed by battlements constructed by the Knights of St John. Once within, you're confronted by stunning ancient remains that include a **Temple to Athena Lindia**

and a 20-columned **Hellenistic stoa**. Silhouetted against the deep blue sky, the stark white columns are dazzling, while the long-range coastal views are out of this world.

Be sure to pack a hat and some water, as there's no shade at the top, and take care to protect young kids from the many dangerous drop-offs.

🛏 Sleeping & Eating

Electra Studios   PENSION €
(☏ 22440 31266; www.electra-studios.gr; s/d/tr €40/50/60; ☻Apr-Oct; ❉) Simple family-run pension, where the plain, but very pleasant, whitewashed rooms have varnished wooden twin beds, fridges and air-con. Some have balconies and there's also a lovely communal roof terrace overlooking a lemon grove and the sea.

Mare Mare   CAFE €
(☏ 22440 31651; Pallas Beach; mains €9; ☻breakfast, lunch & dinner; 🤚✎) This chic beach bar, near the jetty on the smaller of the two beaches below Lindos, makes a wonderful place to relax at any time of day, with a menu that ranges from breakfasts and souvlakia to succulent steaks and calamari. To miss the crowds, come early, or in the late afternoon.

★**Kalypso**   TAVERNA €€
(☏ 22440 32135; www.kalypsolindos.gr; mains €8-15; ☻lunch & dinner; ❉🤚) Dine in the high-ceilinged main room of this 17th-century sea captain's house, or simply admire the facade from the roof terrace. The menu ranges through seafood, meat and vegetarian delights, plus tasty Lyndian dishes, including 'Kalypso bread' with feta and tomato. Take the second right off the main drag.

ℹ Information

Lindos Tourist Office (Plateia Eleftherias; ☻9am-3pm Mon-Sat, 10am-1pm Sun) Small information kiosk at the entrance to central Lindos.

Greece Survival Guide

ℹ Directory A–Z

BARGAINING

Bargaining is acceptable in flea markets and markets, but elsewhere you are expected to pay the stated price.

CUSTOMS REGULATIONS

Import regulations for medicines are strict; if you are taking medication, make sure you get a statement from your doctor before you leave home. It is illegal, for instance, to take codeine into Greece without an accompanying doctor's certificate.

It is strictly forbidden to export antiquities (anything more than 100 years old) without an export permit. This crime is second only to drug smuggling in the penalties imposed. It is an offence to remove even the smallest article from an archaeological site.

DANGERS & ANNOYANCES

Adulterated & Spiked Drinks

Adulterated drinks (known as *bombes*) are served in some bars and clubs in Athens and at resorts known for partying. These drinks are diluted with cheap illegal imports that leave you feeling worse for wear the next day.

At many of the party resorts catering to large budget-tour groups, spiked drinks are not uncommon; keep your hand over the top of your glass. More often than not, the perpetrators are foreign tourists rather than locals.

Tourist Police

The *touristikí astynomía* (tourist police) work in cooperation with the regular Greek police and are found in cities and popular tourist destinations. Each tourist police office has at least one member of staff who speaks English. If you need to report a theft or loss of passport, go to the tourist police first, and they will act as interpreters between you and the regular police.

EMBASSIES & CONSULATES

All foreign embassies in Greece are in Athens and its suburbs.

Australian Embassy (☑ 210 870 4000; www. greece.embassy.gov.au; Ambelokipi, 6th fl, Thon Building, cnr Leoforos Alexandras & Leoforos Kifisias, Athens)

Canadian Embassy (☑ 210 727 3400; www. greece.gc.ca; Ethnikis Antistaseos 48, Chalandri, Athens)

French Embassy (☑ 210 361 1663; www. ambafrance-gr.org; Leoforos Vasilissis Sofias 7, Athens)

German Embassy (☑ 210 728 5111; www. athen.diplo.de; Dimitriou 3, cnr Karaoli, Kolonaki, Athens)

Irish Embassy (☑ 210 723 2771; www.embassy ofireland.gr; Leoforos Vasileos Konstantinou 5-7, Athens)

Italian Embassy (☑ 210 361 7260; www. ambatene.esteri.it; Sekeri 2, Athens)

Netherlands Embassy (☑ 210 725 4900; www. dutchembassy.gr; Leoforos Vasileos Konstantinou 5-7, Athens)

New Zealand Embassy (☑ (+39) 06 853 7501; www.nzembassy.com/italy; Via Clitunno 44, Rome) Travellers from New Zealand should contact the embassy in Rome.

Turkish Embassy (☑ 210 726 3000; embassy. athens@mfa.gov.tr; Vassileos Gheorgiou B'8, Athens) Has an additional branch in **Athens** (☑ 210 724 5915; turkbaskon@kom.forthnet.gr; Leoforos Vasileos Georgiou 8, Athens).

UK Embassy (☑ 210 727 2600; www.ukin greece.fco.gov.uk; 1 Ploutarchou, Athens)

US Embassy (☑ 210 721 2951; http://athens. usembassy.gov; 91 Vasilisis Sophias, Athens)

EMERGENCY & IMPORTANT NUMBERS

In Greece, the area code must be dialled, meaning you always dial the full 10-digit telephone number.

Country code	☑ 30
International access code	☑ 00
Ambulance	☑ 166
Highway rescue (ELPA)	☑ 104
Police	☑ 100
Tourist police	☑ 171

ETIQUETTE

Eating & dining Always accept an offer of a drink as it's a show of goodwill. Don't insist on paying if invited out; it insults your hosts. In restaurants, the pace of service might feel slow; dining is a drawn-out experience in Greece and it's impolite to rush waitstaff.

Photography In churches, avoid using a flash or photographing the main altar, which is considered taboo. At archaeological sites, you'll be stopped from using a tripod as this marks you as a professional and thereby requires special permissions.

Places of worship If you plan to visit churches, carry a shawl or long sleeves and a long skirt or trousers to cover up in a show of respect. Some

---

ⓘ SLEEPING PRICE RANGES

We have divided accommodation into budgets based on the rate for a double room in high season (May to August). Unless otherwise stated, all rooms have private bathroom facilities.

€ less than €60 (less than €80 in Athens)

€€ €60–150 (€80–150 in Athens)

€€€ more than €150

places will deny admission if you're showing too much skin.

Body language If you feel you're not getting a straight answer, you might need literacy in Greek body language. 'Yes' is a swing of the head and 'no' is a curt raising of the head or eyebrows, often accompanied by a 'ts' click-of-the-tongue sound.

INTERNET ACCESS

Free wi-fi is available in most cafes, restaurants and hotels. Some cities have free wi-fi zones in shopping and eating areas.

LGBT TRAVELLERS

In a country where the church still plays a prominent role in shaping society's views on issues such as sexuality, it comes as no surprise that homosexuality is generally frowned upon by many locals – especially outside major cities. While there is no legislation against homosexual activity, it pays to be discreet.

MONEY
ATMS

ATMs are found in every town large enough to support a bank and in almost all the tourist areas. Be aware that many ATMs on the islands can lose their connection for a day or two at a time, making it impossible for anyone (locals included) to withdraw money. It's useful to have a backup source of money.

Tipping

In restaurants a service charge is normally included in the bill, and while a tip is not expected (as it is in North America), it is always appreciated and should be left if the service has been good. Taxi drivers normally expect you to round up the fare.

OPENING HOURS

Always try to double-check opening hours before visiting. In summer, many shops in major tourist destinations are also open on Sunday.

Banks 8am to 2.30pm Monday to Thursday, 8am to 2pm Friday

Bars 8pm to late

Cafes 10am to midnight

Clubs 10pm to 4am

Post offices 7.30am to 8pm Monday to Friday, 7.30am to 2pm Saturday (urban offices)

Restaurants 11am to 3pm and 7pm to 1am

Shops 8am to 3pm Monday, Wednesday and Saturday, 8am to 2.30pm and 5pm to 8.30pm Tuesday, Thursday and Friday

PUBLIC HOLIDAYS

All banks and shops and most museums and ancient sites close on public holidays. National public holidays:

 FOOD PRICE RANGES

The following price ranges refer to the average cost of a main course (not including service charges):

€ less than €10

€€ €10–20

€€€ more than €20

New Year's Day 1 January

Epiphany 6 January

First Sunday in Lent February

Greek Independence Day 25 March

Good Friday March/April

Orthodox Easter Sunday 1 May 2016, 16 April 2017, 8 April 2018, 28 April 2019

May Day (Protomagia) 1 May

Whit Monday (Agiou Pnevmatos) 50 days after Easter Sunday

Feast of the Assumption 15 August

Ohi Day 28 October

Christmas Day 25 December

St Stephen's Day 26 December

TELEPHONE

The Greek telephone service is maintained by the public corporation known as OTE (pronounced o-*teh*). There are public telephones just about everywhere. The phones are easy to operate and can be used for local, long-distance and international calls. The 'i' at the top left of the push-button dialling panel brings up the operating instructions in English. Note that in Greece the area code must always be dialled when making a call (ie all Greek phone numbers are 10-digit).

All public phones use OTE phonecards, known as *telekarta*, not coins. These cards are widely available at *periptera* (street kiosks), corner shops and tourist shops. A local call costs around €0.30 for three minutes. There are also discount-card schemes with instructions in Greek and English; the talk time is enormous compared to the standard phonecard rates.

Mobile Phones

There are several mobile service providers in Greece. Panafon, Cosmote, Vodofone and Wind are the best known. Cosmote tends to have the best coverage in remote areas. All offer 2G connectivity and pay-as-you-talk services for which you can buy a rechargeable SIM card and have your own Greek mobile number. If you're buying a package, be sure to triple-check the fine print. There are restrictions on deals such as 'free-minutes' only being available to phones using the same provider.

TRAVEL WITH CHILDREN

While Greece doesn't cater to kids in the way that some countries do – you won't find endless theme parks and children's menus here – children will be welcomed and included wherever you go. Greeks will generally make a fuss over your kids, who may find themselves receiving many small gifts and treats. Teach them a few Greek words and they will be made to feel even more appreciated.

VISAS

EU citizens do not need a visa to enter Greece. Nationals of some other countries, including Australia, Canada, Israel, Japan, New Zealand, Switzerland and the USA, do not need a tourist visa for stays of up to 90 days. To check the visa requirements for your country, see www.schengenvisainfo.com/tourist-schengen-visa.

ℹ️ Getting There & Away

AIR

Greece has four main international airports that take chartered and scheduled flights.

Eleftherios Venizelos International Airport (ATH; ☎ 210 353 0000; www.aia.gr) Athens' Eleftherios Venizelos International Airport lies near Spata, 27km east of Athens. It has all the modern conveniences, including 24-hour luggage storage in the arrivals hall and a children's playroom – even a small archaeological museum above the check-in hall for passing time.

Nikos Kazantzakis International Airport (HER; ☎ general 28103 97800, info 28103 97136; www.heraklion-airport.info) About 5km east of Iraklio (Crete). Has a bank, an ATM, a duty-free shop and a cafe-bar.

Diagoras Airport (RHO; ☎ 22410 88700; www.rhodes-airport.org) On the island of Rhodes.

Makedonia International Airport (SKG; ☎ 2310 985 000; www.thessalonikiairport.com) About 17km southeast of Thessaloniki. Served by local bus 78 (half-hourly); a taxi costs around €15 to €20.

LAND & SEA

You can now travel from London to Athens by train and ferry in less than two days. By choosing to travel on the ground instead of the air, you'll also be reducing your carbon footprint.

Train

The Greek railways organisation **OSE** (Organismos Sidirodromon Ellados; www.trainose.gr) runs daily trains from Thessaloniki to Sofia and to Belgrade (via Skopje), with a weekly onward train to and from Budapest.

Ferry

Ferries can get very crowded in summer. If you want to take a vehicle across it's wise to make a reservation beforehand. Please note that tickets for all ferries to Turkey must be bought a day in advance – and you will almost certainly be asked to turn in your passport the night before the trip. It will be returned the next day before you board the boat. Port tax for departures to Turkey is around €15.

ℹ️ Getting Around

Greece is an easy place to travel around thanks to a comprehensive public transport system. Buses are the mainstay of land transport, with a network that reaches out to the smallest villages. Trains are a good alternative, where available. If you're in a hurry, Greece also has an extensive domestic air network. To most visitors, though, travelling in Greece means island-hopping via the multitude of ferries that criss-cross the Adriatic and the Aegean.

AIR

The vast majority of domestic mainland flights are handled by the country's national carrier **Aegean Airlines** (A3; ☎ 801 112 0000; www.aegeanair.com) and its subsidiary, **Olympic Air** (☎ 801 801 0101; www.olympicair.com). You'll find offices wherever there are flights, as well as in other major towns.

The prices listed in this guide are for full-fare economy, and include domestic taxes and charges. There are discounts for return tickets for travel between Monday and Thursday, and bigger discounts for trips that include a Saturday night away. Find full details and timetables on airline websites.

The baggage allowance on domestic flights is 15kg, or 20kg if the domestic flight is part of an international journey.

BOAT

Greece has an extensive network of ferries – the only means of reaching many of the islands. Schedules are often subject to delays due to poor weather and industrial action, and prices fluctuate regularly. In summer, ferries run regular service between all but the most out-of-the-way destinations; however, services seriously slow down in winter (and in some cases stop completely).

BUS

The bus network is comprehensive. All long-distance buses, on the mainland and the islands, are operated by regional collectives known as **KTEL** (Koino Tamio Eispraxeon Leoforion; www.ktel.org). Details of inter-urban buses throughout Greece are available by dialling ☎ 14505. Bus fares are fixed by the government and bus travel is very reasonably priced. A journey costs approximately €5 per 100km.

CAR & MOTORCYCLE

No one who has travelled on Greece's roads will be surprised to hear that the country's road fatality rate is one of the highest in Europe. More than a thousand people die on the roads every year, with 10 times that number of people injured. Overtaking is listed as the greatest cause of accidents.

Heart-stopping moments aside, your own car is a great way to explore off the beaten track. The road network has improved enormously in recent years; many roads marked as dirt tracks on older maps have now been asphalted and many of the islands have very little traffic. There are regular (if costly) car-ferry services to almost all islands.

TURKEY

Antalya

POP 1 MILLION

Once seen simply as the gateway to the Turkish Riviera, Antalya today is very much a destination in its own right. Situated smack on the Gulf of Antalya (Antalya Körfezi), the largest Turkish city on the western Mediterranean coast is both classically beautiful and stylishly modern. At its core is the wonderfully preserved old city district of Kaleiçi – literally 'within the castle'. The old city wraps around a splendid Roman-era harbour with cliff-top views of hazy-blue silhouettes of the Beydağları (Bey Mountains). Just outside of the central city is one of Turkey's finest museums.

◎ Sights

★ **Antalya Museum** MUSEUM
(☑236 5688; www.antalyamuzesi.gov.tr/en; Konyaaltı Caddesi 1; admission ₺20; ⊙9am-7.30pm Apr-Oct, 8.30am-5pm Nov-Mar, closed Mon) On no account should you miss this comprehensive museum with exhibitions covering everything from the Stone and Bronze Ages to Byzantium. The Hall of Regional Excavations exhibits finds from ancient cities in Lycia (such as Patara and Xanthos) and Pamphylia, while the Hall of Gods displays beautiful and evocative statues of some 15 Olympian gods, many of them in near-perfect condition. Most of the statues, including the sublime *Three Graces,* were found at Perge.

The museum is about 2km west of the Kaleiçi district, accessible on the old-fashioned *tramvay* (tram) from Kale Kapısı tramstop.

Hadrian's Gate GATE
(Hadriyanüs Kapısı; Atatürk Caddesi) Commonly known as Üçkapılar (the 'Three Gates') in Antalya, the monumental Hadrian's Gate was erected for the Roman emperor's visit to Antalya in 130 AD.

**Suna & İnan Kıraç
Kaleiçi Museum** MUSEUM
(☑243 4274; www.kaleicimuzesi.org; Kocatepe Sokak 25; adult/child ₺3/2; ⊙9am-noon & 1-5pm Thu-Tue) This small ethnography museum is housed in a lovingly restored Antalya mansion. The 2nd floor contains a series of life-size dioramas depicting some of the most important rituals and customs of Ottoman Antalya. Much more impressive is the collection of Çanakkale and Kütahya ceramics housed in the former Greek Orthodox church of Aya Yorgi (St George), just behind the main house, which has been fully restored and is worth a look in itself.

Yivli Minare HISTORIC SITE
(Fluted Minaret; Cumhuriyet Caddesi) Antalya's symbol is the Yivli Minare, a handsome and distinctive 'fluted' minaret erected by the Seljuk Sultan Aladdin Keykubad I in the early 13th century. The adjacent mosque (1373) is still in use. Within the Yivli Minare complex is the heavily restored **Mevlevi Tekke** (Whirling Dervish Monastery), which probably dates from the 13th century.

🏃 Activities

Boat Excursions BOAT TOUR
(Roman Harbour) Excursion yachts tie up in the Roman harbour in Kaleiçi. Some trips go as far as Kemer, Phaselis, Olympos, Demre and even Kaş. You can take one-/two-hour trips (₺30/45) or a six-hour voyage (₺95 with lunch) which visits Kemer and Phaselis, the Gulf of Antalya islands and some beaches for a swim.

🛏 Sleeping

The most atmospheric – and central – place to stay in Antalya is the old town of Kaleiçi, a virtually vehicle-free district that has everything you need. Kaleiçi's winding streets can be confusing to navigate, although signs pointing the way to most pensions are posted on street corners. Most midrange and budget pensions offer decent discounts from October through to April.

★ Sabah Pansiyon
PENSION €

(☑ 247 5345, 0555 365 8376; www.sabahpansiyon.com; Hesapçı Sokak 60; dm ₺42, s/d/tr ₺110/130/200, 2-bedroom self-catering apt €90; ❄ 🏠 ❄) Our favourite budget digs in Antalya is still going strong. The Sabah has long been the first port of call for travellers watching their kuruş, thanks to the Sabah brothers who run the place with aplomb. Rooms vary in size but all are sweet, simple and super-clean. The shaded courtyard is prime territory for meeting other travellers.

If you're looking for self-catering facilities, check out their complex of five modern, spacious apartments nearby which can accommodate up to six people. Great for families.

Abad Pansiyon
PENSION €

(☑ 0537 691 4164, 248 9723; www.antalyahostel.com; Hesapçı Sokak 65; dm ₺30, s/d/tr ₺60/95/145; ❄ 🏠) Right on the main thoroughfare through the Kaleiçi district, this lovely old Ottoman house has simple, bright, if rather bland, rooms that are a solid choice for budget travellers.

Kaleiçi District

★ **White Garden Pansiyon** PENSION €€
(☑241 9115; www.whitegardenpansion.com; Hesapçı Geçidi 9; s/d ₺100/130, self-catering apt ₺350; ❄🕸🐾) A positively delightful place to stay – full of quirky Ottoman character – the White Garden combines tidiness and class beyond its price level, with impeccable service from Metin and his staff. The building itself is a fine restoration and the courtyard is particularly charming. The breakfast here is one of the best you'll see in Turkey.

There are also four self-catering apartments with good-sized rooms that would be an excellent choice for families.

🍴 Eating

A nearly endless assortment of cafes and restaurants are tucked in and around the Kaleiçi area. For cheap eating, walk east to the Dönerciler Çarşısı or north to the rooftop kebap places across the street from **Kale Kapısı** (Fortress Gate).

₺ KEBAP €
(☑243 2548; Arık Caddesi 4/A; pide & dürüm ₺8; ⊙7am-midnight Mon-Sat) Looking for something very cheap and cheerful? Fantastically prepared *çorba* (soup), pide and Adana *dürüm* (beef kebap rolled in pitta) are here at bargain prices, as are *mantı* (Turkish ravioli). It's opposite the landmark Antalya 2000 building and its Plaza Cinema.

Dönerciler Çarşısı MARKET €
(Market of Döner Makers; Atatürk Caddesi) Budget-eating central in Antalya; this entire alleyway is devoted to kebap shops churning out grilled meat dishes.

Yemenli TURKISH €€
(☑247 5346; Zeytin Sokak 16; mains ₺15-30; 🍴) Tried-and-true Turkish favourites are served up at this lovely restaurant with dining either in the leafy garden courtyard or inside the charmingly renovated stone house. It's run by the same team behind the Sabah Pansiyon, so service is friendly and on-the-ball. There's a couple of excellent vegetarian options here too.

🍷 Drinking & Nightlife

Castle Café CAFE
(☑248 6594; Hıdırlık Sokak 48/1; ⊙8am-11pm) Our favourite place along the cliff's edge is this lively cafe and bar which attracts a good crowd of young Turks with its affordable drinks. Service can be slow but the jaw-dropping views from the terrace more than make up for it.

Access is either from the path just opposite the Hıdırlık Kalesi or through the back, down the stairs, off Hıdırlık Sokak.

Pupa Cafe CAFE
(Paşa Camii Sokak) We really like this casual garden-cafe with tables next to a slab of Byzantine wall. It's a relaxed and friendly place scattered with pot plants and hanging lamps. A good choice for a quiet evening of chatting and drinking. The good-value menu of seafood and Turkish staples (₺10 to ₺18) makes this place worthy of a visit too.

ℹ Information

Tourist Office (☑241 1747; Cumhuriyet Meydanı; ⊙8am-6pm) Tiny information office just west of the Yivli Minare. Has city maps and a few brochures.

ℹ Getting There & Away

The otogar (bus station) is 4km north of the centre. A tram (₺1.50) runs from here to the city centre (İsmetpaşatram stop). From the otogar, buses whizz to destinations across the country including services to Denizli (₺40, four hours), Göreme (₺50, nine hours) and Istanbul (₺80, 11½ hours).

Aya Sofya

TIMELINE

537 Emperor Justinian, depicted in one of the church's famous **mosaics ❶**, presides over the consecration of Byzantium's new basilica, Hagia Sophia (Church of the Holy Wisdom).

557 The huge **dome ❷**, damaged during an earthquake, collapses and is rebuilt.

843 The second Byzantine Iconoclastic period ends and figurative **mosaics ❸** begin to be added to the interior. These include a depiction of the Empress Zoe and her third husband, Emperor Constantine IX Monomachos.

1204 Soldiers of the Fourth Crusade led by the Doge of Venice, Enrico Dandolo, conquer and ransack Constantinople. Dandolo's **tomb ❹** is eventually erected in the church whose desecration he presided over.

1453 The city falls to the Ottomans; Mehmet II orders that Hagia Sophia be converted to a mosque and renamed Aya Sofya.

1577 Sultan Selim II is buried in a specially designed tomb, which sits alongside the **tombs ❺** of four other Ottoman Sultans in Aya Sofya's grounds.

1847–49 Sultan Abdül Mecit I orders that the building be restored and redecorated; the huge **Ottoman Medallions ❻** in the nave are added.

1935 The mosque is converted into a museum by order of Mustafa Kemal Atatürk, president of the new Turkish Republic.

2009 The face of one of the four **seraphs ❼** is uncovered during major restoration works in the nave.

2012 Restoration of the exterior walls and western upper gallery commences.

For more information on the Aya Sofya and İstanbul's other sights, see p578-88.

TOP TIPS

Bring binoculars if you want to properly view the mosaic portraits in the apse and under the dome.

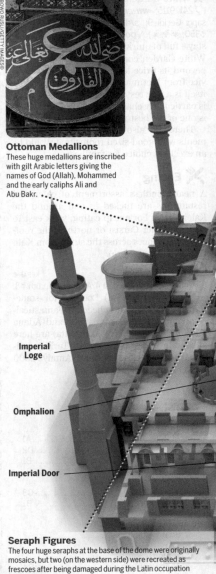

Ottoman Medallions
These huge medallions are inscribed with gilt Arabic letters giving the names of God (Allah), Mohammed and the early caliphs Ali and Abu Bakr.

Imperial Loge

Omphalion

Imperial Door

Seraph Figures
The four huge seraphs at the base of the dome were originally mosaics, but two (on the western side) were recreated as frescoes after being damaged during the Latin occupation (1204–61).

Dome

Soaring 56m from ground level, the dome was originally covered in gold mosaics but was decorated with calligraphy during the 1847–49 restoration works overseen by Swiss-born architects Gaspard and Giuseppe Fossati.

Christ Enthroned with Empress Zoe and Constantine IX Monomachos

This mosaic portrait in the upper gallery depicts Zoe, one of only three Byzantine women to rule as empress in their own right.

Ottoman Tombs

The tombs of five Ottoman sultans and their families are located in Aya Sofya's southern corner and can be accessed via Kabasakal Caddesi. One of these occupies the church's original Baptistry.

Aya Sofya Tombs

Former Baptistry

Astronomer's House & Workshop

Ablutions Fountain

Exit

Primary School

Main Entrance

Grave of Enrico Dandolo

Venetian doge in 1205, only year after he and Crusaders had med the city. A -century marker e upper gallery cates the probable tion of his grave.

Constantine the Great, the Virgin Mary and the Emperor Justinian

This 11th-century mosaic shows Constantine (right) offering the Virgin Mary the city of Constantinople. Justinian (left) is offering her Hagia Sophia.

OLYMPOS & ÇIRALI

The tiny beach hamlets of Olympos and Çıralı are where you head if you're looking for days of sandy-sloth action. Olympos is an old hippy hang-out with an all-night party reputation in summer and the vine-covered ancient **Olympos ruins** (admission incl Olympos Beach ₺5, long-stay ticket allowing 10 entries over 10 days ₺7.50; ⏱9am-7.30pm) lining the dirt track to the beach. A couple of kilometres down the beach is more sedate Çıralı, where a clutch of simple pensions sit back from the sand and life is simplified to a choice between swinging in a hammock or sunning yourself on the beach. In the evening, trips to the famed **Chimaera** (admission ₺5), a cluster of natural flames on the slopes of Mt Olympos, is the major activity. At night the 20-odd flames are visible at sea.

Sleeping

Şaban Pansion (☎0507 007 6600, 892 1265; www.sabanpansion.com; dm ₺40, tree house ₺65, bungalow with bathroom & air-con ₺80; ❄🛜) Our personal favourite in Olympos, this is the place to come if you want to snooze in a hammock or on cushions in the shade of orange trees. In the words of the charming manager Meral: 'It's not a party place'. Instead it sells itself on tranquillity, space and great home cooking, plus room 7 really is a tree house.

Hotel Canada (☎825 7233, 0532 431 3414; www.canadahotel.net; s/d ₺110/145, 4-person bungalow ₺250; ❄🛜🏊) This is a beautiful place offering the quintessential Çıralı experience: warmth, friendliness and house-made honey. The main house rooms are comfortable and the garden is filled with hammocks, citrus trees and 11 bungalows. Canadian Carrie and foodie husband Şaban also offer excellent set meals (€10). It's 750m from the beach; grab a free bike and pedal on down.

Getting There & Away

Buses and dolmuşes plying the Fethiye–Antalya coast road will stop near the Olympos and Çıralıjunction. From there, dolmuşes (₺5) serve Olympos (9km) hourly from 8am to 8pm between May and October; and Çıralı (7km) hourly between June and September. Outside of these months, ring your guesthouse beforehand to check dolmuş times.

Selçuk

POP 28,213

Were it not for nearby Ephesus, Selçuk might be just another Turkish farming town, with its lively weekly markets and ploughs rusting away on side streets. That said, the gateway to Ephesus does have plenty of its own attractions – many topped with a picture-perfect stork's nest: Roman/Byzantine aqueduct arches, a lone pillar remaining from one of the Seven Wonders of the Ancient World, and the hilltop Byzantine ruins of the Basilica of St John and Ayasuluk Fortress.

👁 Sights

Ayasuluk Fortress   CASTLE
(2013 Sokak; admission incl Basilica of St John ₺10; ⏱8am-6.30pm Apr-Oct, to 4.30pm Nov-Mar) Selçuk's crowning achievement is accessed on the same ticket as the neighbouring Basilica of St John. Excavation is ongoing and, at the time of writing, entry was by intermittent guided tours; hopefully regular access will soon be established. The digs here, begun in 1990, have proven that there were castles on Ayasuluk Hill going back beyond the original Ephesian settlement to the Neolithic age. The partially restored fortress' remains today date from Byzantine, Seljuk and Ottoman times.

Basilica of St John   RUIN, HISTORIC SITE
(St Jean Caddesi; admission incl Ayasuluk Fortress ₺10; ⏱8am-6.30pm Apr-Oct, to 4.30pm Nov-Mar) Despite a century of restoration, the once-great basilica built by Byzantine Emperor Justinian (r 527–65) is still but a skeleton of its former self. Nonetheless, it is an atmospheric site with excellent hilltop views, and the best place in the area for a sunset photo. The information panels and scale model highlight the building's original grandeur, as do the marble steps and monumental gate.

Ephesus Museum   MUSEUM
(Uğur Mumcu Sevgi Yolu Caddesi; admission ₺10; ⏱8.30am-6.30pm Apr-Oct, to 4.30pm Nov-Mar)

Selçuk

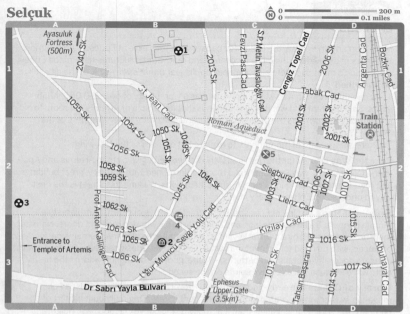

Selçuk

This museum holds artefacts from Ephesus' Terraced Houses, including scales, jewellery and cosmetic boxes, plus coins, funerary goods and ancient statuary. The famous effigy of Phallic god Priapus, visible by pressing a button, draws giggles, and a whole room is dedicated to Eros in sculpted form. The punters also get a rise out of the multi-breasted marble Artemis statue, a very fine work indeed.

Temple of Artemis RUIN
(Artemis Tapınağı; off Dr Sabrı Yayla Bulvarı; ⊙ 8am-7pm Apr-Oct, 8.30am-6pm Nov-Mar) FREE In an empty field on Selçuk's western extremities, this solitary reconstructed pillar is all that remains of the massive Temple of Artemis, one of the Seven Wonders of the Ancient World. At its zenith, the structure had 127 columns; today, the only way to get any sense of this grandeur is to see Didyma's better-preserved Temple of Apollo (which had 122 columns).

🛏 Sleeping & Eating

★ **Atilla's Getaway** HOSTEL, RESORT €
(☏ 0232-892 3847; www.atillasgetaway.com; Acarlar Köyü; dm/s/d/tr €16/26/42/63, camping €8; ❋@🛜≋) This 'backpacker resort', named after its friendly Turkish-Australian

owner, is all about relaxation, with a classically themed chill-out area gazing at the hills and a bar with pool table and nightly fires. Twice-weekly barbecues and six kinds of breakfast are offered and the volleyball court and table tennis add to the fun.

The roadside complex is about 3km south of Selçuk, linked by free shuttles, and a 50-minute walk through the hills from Ephesus' Upper Gate.

★ **Boomerang** GUESTHOUSE €€
(☏ 0232-892 4879; www.boomerangguesthouse.com; 1047 Sokak 10; dm/s/d/tr/f from €10/30/40/60/70; ❋🛜) 🌿 People do indeed keep coming back to this Turkish-Chinese operation, to spend chilled-out evenings among the trees in the stone courtyard,

EPHESUS

More than anywhere else, the Greco-Roman world comes alive at Ephesus. After almost 150 years of excavation, the city's recovered and renovated structures have made Ephesus Europe's most complete classical metropolis – and that's with 82% of the city still to be unearthed.

As capital of Roman Asia Minor, Ephesus was a vibrant city of over 250,000 inhabitants. So important and wealthy was Ephesus that its Temple of Artemis (en route to present-day Selçuk) was the biggest on earth, and one of the Seven Wonders of the Ancient World.

There are a wealth of monuments to explore but don't miss the following:

Curetes Way Named for the demigods who helped Lena give birth to Artemis and Apollo, the Curetes Way was Ephesus' main thoroughfare, lined with statuary, great buildings, and rows of shops selling incense, silk and other goods. Walking this street is the best way to understand Ephesian daily life.

Temple of Hadrian One of Ephesus' star attractions, this ornate, Corinthian-style temple honours Trajan's successor, and originally had a wooden roof and doors. Note its main arch; supported by a central keystone, this architectural marvel remains perfectly balanced, with no need for cement or mortar. The temple's designers also covered it with intricate decorative details and patterns – Tyche, goddess of chance, adorns the first arch, while Medusa wards off evil spirits on the second.

Library of Celsus The early-2nd-century-AD governor of Asia Minor, Celsus Polemaeanus, was commemorated in this magnificent library. Originally built as part of a complex, the library looks bigger than it actually is: the convex facade base heightens the central elements, while the central columns and capitals are larger than those at the ends. Facade niches hold replica statues of the Greek Virtues: Arete (Goodness), Ennoia (Thought), Episteme (Knowledge) and Sophia (Wisdom).

Great Theatre Originally built under Hellenistic King Lysimachus, the Great Theatre was reconstructed by the Romans between AD 41 and AD 117. However, they incorporated original design elements, including the ingenious shape of the *cavea* (seating area). Seating rows are pitched slightly steeper as they ascend, meaning that upper-row spectators still enjoyed good views and acoustics – useful, considering that the theatre could hold 25,000 people.

A taxi from Selçuk costs about ₺15, but it's also a pleasant 2.5km walk from town.

where the recommended bar-restaurant (mains ₺12 to ₺20) serves dishes including kebaps, Chinese food and cheesy *köfte*. Some rooms have balconies, while budget options are also available (single/double/triple €20/30/45) along with extras such as a travel desk and bike hire.

Sişçi Yaşar'ın Yeri   KÖFTE, KEBAP €
(✆8923487; Atatürk Caddesi; mains from ₺8; ⏲lunch & dinner) Under overhanging leaves next to a 14th-century mosque, Yaşar's place is good for a simple lunch of *köfte* (meatballs), *çöp şiş* (*şiş* kebap served rolled in a thin pita with onions and parsley) and *ayran* (yoghurt drink).

🛈 Getting There & Away

At least two buses head to İstanbul (₺80, 10 hours) daily. For Antalya and other destinations along the Mediterranean coast, you usually have to change buses at Denizli (₺30, three hours).

İstanbul

POP 14 MILLION

Former capital of both the Byzantine and Ottoman empires, İstanbul manages to doff its cap to its grand past while stridantly forging a vibrant, modern path. Stately mosques, opulent palaces and elaborately decorated domed churches cram into the Old City quarter, while the hilly streets of Beyoğlu host state-of-the-art museums and art galleries, chic boutiques and funky cafes. Hop on a commuter ferry to cross between Europe and Asia. Haggle your heart out in the Grand Bazaar. Join the gregarious crowds bar-hopping in the alleys off İstiklal Caddesi This marvellous metropolis is a showcase of Turkey at its most energetic, innovative and cosmopolitan. The Bosphorus strait, between the Black Sea and the Sea of Marmara, divides Europe from Asia. On its western shore, European İstanbul is further divided by the Golden Horn (Haliç) into the Old City in the southwest and Beyoğlu in the northeast.

⊙ Sights

★ Aya Sofya   MUSEUM
(p574-5; Hagia Sophia; Map p584 ☑ 0212-522 0989, 0212-522 1750; www.ayasofyamuzesi.gov.tr; Aya Sofya Meydanı 1; adult/child under 12yr ₺40/ free; ⊙ 9am-7pm Tue-Sun mid-Apr-mid-Oct, to 5pm mid-Oct–mid-Apr; ⊠ Sultanahmet) There are many important monuments in İstanbul,

🛈 MUSEUM PASS

The Museum Pass İstanbul (www. muze.gov.tr/museum_pass; ₺85) offers savings on entry to the Old City's major sights, and allows holders to skip admission queues.

but this venerable structure – commissioned by the great Byzantine emperor Justinian, consecrated as a church in 537, converted to a mosque by Mehmet the Conqueror in 1453 and declared a museum by Atatürk in 1935 – surpasses the rest due to its innovative architectural form, rich history, religious importance and extraordinary beauty. (See p574-5 for more information.)

Museum of Turkish & Islamic Arts MUSEUM
(Türk ve Islam Eserleri Müzesi; Map p584; Atmeydanı Caddesi 46, Hippodrome; adult/child under

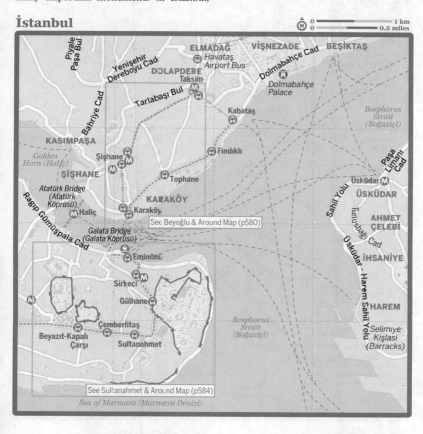

İstanbul

12yr ₺20/free; 9am-5pm; Sultanahmet) This Ottoman palace on the western edge of the Hippodrome was built in 1524 for İbrahim Paşa, childhood friend, brother-in-law and grand vizier of Süleyman the Magnificent. Undergoing a major renovation at the time of research, it has a magnificent collection

of artefacts, including exquisite examples of calligraphy and one of the world's most impressive collections of antique carpets.

★ **Topkapı Palace**   PALACE
(Topkapı Sarayı; Map p584; 0212-512 0480; www. topkapisarayi.gov.tr; Babıhümayun Caddesi; palace

Beyoğlu & Around

adult/child under 12yr ₺40/free, Harem adult/child under 6yr ₺25/free; ⊙9am-6.45pm Wed-Mon mid-Apr–Oct, to 4.45pm Nov–mid-Apr; 🚇Sultanahmet) Topkapı is the subject of more colourful stories than most of the world's museums put together. Libidinous sultans, ambitious courtiers, beautiful concubines and scheming eunuchs lived and worked here between the 15th and 19th centuries when it was the court of the Ottoman empire. Visiting the palace's opulent pavilions, jewel-filled Treasury and sprawling Harem gives a fascinating glimpse into their lives.

İstanbul Archaeology Museums   MUSEUM
(İstanbul Arkeoloji Müzeleri; Map p584; ☑0212-520 7740; www.istanbularkeoloji.gov.tr; Osman Hamdi Bey Yokuşu Sokak, Gülhane; adult/child under 12yr ₺20/free; ⊙9am-7pm, last admission 6pm; 🚇Gülhane) This superb museum showcases archaeological and artistic treasures from the Topkapı collections. Housed in three buildings, its exhibits include ancient artefacts, classical statuary and an exhibition tracing İstanbul's history. There are many highlights, but the sarcophagi from the Royal Necropolis of Sidon are particularly striking.

★**Süleymaniye Mosque**   MOSQUE
(Map p584; Professor Sıddık Sami Onar Caddesi; 🚇Laleli-Üniversite) The Süleymaniye crowns one of İstanbul's seven hills and dominates the Golden Horn, providing a landmark for the entire city. Though it's not the largest of the Ottoman mosques, it is certainly one of the grandest and most beautiful. It's also unusual in that many of its original *külliye* (mosque complex) buildings have been retained and sympathetically adapted for reuse.

Beyoğlu & Around

BOSPHORUS BOAT EXCURSION

İstanbul's soul is the Bosphorus. Don't miss seeing the city's iconic skyline and riverside views from the city's real highway aboard a Bosphorus excursion boat. Plenty of boats depart from Eminönü and stop at various points before turning around at Anadolu Kavağ (one way/return ₺15/25). Along the way you soak up sights such as the ornate **Dolmabahçe Palace** (Dolmabahçe Sarayı; ☑212-327 2626; www.millisaraylar.gov.tr; Dolmabahçe Caddesi, Beşiktaş; adult Selâmlık ₺30, Harem ₺20, joint ticket ₺40; ⊙9am-4pm Tue, Wed & Fri-Sun; 🚇Kabataş then walk) and majestically modern Bosphorus Bridge, along with plenty of lavish *yalıs* (seafront mansions).

★**Grand Bazaar**   MARKET
(Kapalı Çarşı, Covered Market; Map p584; ⊙8.30am-7pm Mon-Sat, final entry 6pm; 🚻; Ⓜ Veznecilar, 🚇Beyazıt-Kapalı Çarşı) The colourful and chaotic Grand Bazaar is the heart of İstanbul's Old City and has been so for centuries. Starting as a small vaulted *bedesten* (warehouse) built by order of Mehmet the Conqueror in 1461, it grew to cover a vast area as laneways between the *bedesten*, neighbouring shops and *hans* (caravanserais) were roofed and the market assumed the sprawling, labyrinthine form that it retains today.

★**İstanbul Modern**   GALLERY
(İstanbul Modern Sanat Müzesi; Map p580; ☑212-334 7300; www.istanbulmodern.org; Meclis-i Mebusan Caddesi, Tophane; adult/student/under 12yr ₺25/14/free; ⊙10am-6pm Tue, Wed & Fri-Sun, to 8pm Thu; 🚇Tophane) The big daddy of a slew of newish, privately funded art galleries in the city, this impressive institution has a stunning location on the shores of the Bosphorus, an extensive collection of Turkish 20th-century paintings on the ground floor, and a constantly changing and uniformly excellent program of mixed-media exhibitions by local and international artists in the basement galleries. There's also a well-stocked gift shop, a cinema that shows art-house films and a stylish cafe-restaurant with superb views of the Bosphorus.

ℹ FOR FREE

Topping the seven hills of the Old City and adorning many of its streets, İstanbul's Ottoman mosques are the jewels in the city's crown. Entry to these architectural wonders is open to everyone regardless of their religion. The *türbes* (tombs) attached to these mosques are often sumptuously decorated with İznik tiles and can also be visited; head to the **Aya Sofya Tombs** (Aya Sofya Müzesi Padişah Türbeleri; Map p584; ☏0212-522 1750; ayasofyamuzesi.gov.tr/en; Babıhümayun Caddesi; ⊙9am-5pm; ⊟Sultanahmet) `FREE` to see some great examples.

Remember to dress modestly if you plan to visit mosques; women should have a shawl or scarf to cover their heads.

Museum of Innocence   MUSEUM
(Masumiyet Müzesi; Map p580; ☏212-252 9738; www.masumiyetmuzesi.org; Çukurcuma Caddesi, Dalgıç Çıkmazı, 2; adult/student ₺25/10; ⊙10am-6pm Tue-Sun, to 9pm Thu; ⊟Tophane) The painstaking attention to detail in this fascinating museum/piece of conceptual art will certainly provide every amateur psychologist with a theory or two about its creator, Nobel Prize–winning novelist Orhan Pamuk. Vitrines display a quirky collection of objects that evoke the minutiae of İstanbullu life in the mid-to-late 20th century, when Pamuk's novel of the same name is set.

İstiklal Caddesi   STREET
(Independence Ave; Map p580) Once called the Grand Rue de Pera but renamed İstiklal (Independence) in the early years of the Republic, Beyoğlu's premier boulevard is a perfect metaphor for 21st-century Turkey, being an exciting mix of modernity and tradition. Contemporary boutiques and cutting-edge cultural centres are housed in its grand 19th-century buildings, and an antique tram traverses its length alongside crowds of pedestrians making their way to the bustling cafes, bistros and bars that Beyoğlu is known for.

Kariye Museum (Chora Church)   MUSEUM
(Kariye Müzesi; ☏212-631 9241; www.choramuseum.com; Kariye Camii Sokak, Edirnekapı; admission ₺15; ⊙9am-7pm mid-Apr–Sep, to 5pm Oct–mid-Apr; ⊟31E, 32, 36K & 38E from Eminönü, 87 from Taksim, ⊞Ayvansaray) İstanbul has more than its fair share of Byzantine monuments, but few are as drop-dead gorgeous as this mosaic- and fresco-laden church. Nestled in the shadow of Theodosius II's monumental land walls and now a museum overseen by the Aya Sofya curators, it receives a fraction of the visitor numbers that its big sister attracts but offers an equally fascinating insight into Byzantine art. Parts of the museum were closed for renovation as of 2015; check the website for more information.

☞ Tours

★ **İstanbul Eats**   WALKING TOUR
(www.culinarybackstreets.com/culinary-walks/istanbul/; tours per person ₺215-355) Culinary walks around the Old City, Bazaar District, Beyoğlu, Kadıköy or the Bosphorus suburbs, with themes like the Kebab Krawl or Shop-Cook-Feast. All are conducted by the dedicated foodies who produce the excellent blog of the same name. Tours involve lots of eating, all of which is included in the price.

İstanbul Walks   WALKING TOUR
(Map p584; ☏0554 335 6622, 0212-516 6300; www.istanbulwalks.com; 1st fl, Şifa Hamamı Sokak 1; tours €35-75, child under 2/7yr free/30% discount; ⊟Sultanahmet) Specialising in cultural tourism, this company is run by history buffs and offers a large range of guided walking tours conducted by knowledgeable English-speaking guides. Tours concentrate on İstanbul's various neighbourhoods, but there are also tours of major monuments, a Turkish Coffee Trail, Whirling Dervishes and a tour of the Bosphorus and Golden Horn by private boat. Student discounts are available.

✸ Festivals

★ **İstanbul Music Festival**   MUSIC
(http://muzik.iksv.org/en; ⊙Jun) The city's premier arts festival includes performances of opera, dance, orchestral concerts and chamber recitals. Acts are often internationally renowned and the action takes place in atmosphere-laden venues including Aya İrini in Sultanahmet.

İstanbul Tulip Festival   CULTURAL
(⊙Mar-Apr) The tulip (*lale* in Turkish) is one of İstanbul's traditional symbols, and the local government celebrates this fact by plant-

ing over three million of them annually. These bloom in late March and early April, endowing almost every street and park with vivid spring colours and wonderful photo opportunities.

🛏 Sleeping

⭐ Marmara Guesthouse   PENSION €
(Map p584; ☑0212-638 3638; www.marmaraguesthouse.com; Terbıyık Sokak 15, Cankurtaran; s €60-80, d & tw €65-85, tr €80-100, f €95-115; ❄❈☏; ☐Sultanahmet) There are plenty of family-run pensions in Sultanahmet, but few can claim the Marmara's levels of cleanliness and comfort. Manager Elif Aytekin and her family go out of their way to make guests feel welcome, offering plenty of advice and serving a delicious breakfast on the vine-covered, sea-facing roof terrace. Rooms have comfortable beds, good bathrooms and double-glazed windows.

Hotel Alp Guesthouse   HOTEL €
(Map p584; ☑0212-517 7067; www.alpguesthouse.com; Adliye Sokak 4, Cankurtaran; s/d €55/80; ❄❈☏; ☐Sultanahmet) The Alp lives up to its location in Sultanahmet's premier small-hotel enclave, offering a range of attractive, well-priced rooms. Bathrooms are small but very clean, and there are plenty of amenities. The roof terrace is one of the best in this area, with great sea views, comfortable indoor and outdoor seating, and free tea and coffee.

Cheers Hostel   HOSTEL €
(Map p584; ☑0212-526 0200; www.cheershostel.com; Zeynep Sultan Camii Sokak 21, Sultanahmet; dm €15-24, s €60, d & tw €60-70, tr €90-105, q €88-120, f €135; ℙ❄❈@☏; ☐Gülhane) The dorms here are worlds away from the impersonal barracks-like spaces in bigger hostels. Bright and airy, they feature wooden floorboards, rugs, lockers and comfortable beds; most have air-con. Bathrooms are clean and plentiful. It's a great choice in winter because the cosy rooftop bar has an open fire and a great view. Private rooms aren't as nice.

⭐ Hotel Empress Zoe   BOUTIQUE HOTEL €€
(Map p584; ☑0212-518 2504; www.emzoe.com; Akbıyık Caddesi 10, Cankurtaran; s €60-90, d €140-160, tr €150, ste €180-300; ❄❈☏; ☐Sultanahmet) Named after the feisty Byzantine Empress, this is one of the most impressive boutique hotels in the city. There's a range of room types but the garden suites are particularly enticing as they overlook a gorgeous flower-filled courtyard where breakfast is served in warm weather. You can enjoy an early-evening drink there, or while admiring the sea view from the terrace bar.

ITALY, GREECE & TURKEY İSTANBUL

DON'T MISS

HAMAMS

Succumbing to a soapy scrub in a steamy hamam is one of the city's quintessential experiences.

The concept of the steam bath was passed from the Romans to the Byzantines and then on to the Turks. Until recent decades, many homes in İstanbul didn't have bathroom facilities, and due to Islam's emphasis on personal cleanliness, the community relied on the hundreds of hamams throughout the city, often as part of the *külliye* (mosque complex). Today, many carry on due to their roles as local meeting places.

The cheapest bath is the one you do yourself, having brought your own soap, shampoo and towel. But the real Turkish bath experience is to have an attendant wash, scrub and massage you. Our top three picks for sudsy relaxation after a long day of sightseeing:

Ayasofya Hürrem Sultan Hamamı (Map p584; ☑0212-517 3535; www.ayasofyahamami.com; Aya Sofya Meydanı 2; bath treatments €85-170, massages €40-75; ⊗8am-10pm; ☐Sultanahmet) Built by order of Süleyman the Magnificent, and meticulously restored.

Cağaloğlu Hamamı (Map p584; ☑0212-522 2424; www.cagalogluhamami.com.tr; Prof Kazım İsmail Gürkan Caddesi 24 ; bath, scrub & massage packages €40-120, self-service €30; ⊗8am-10pm; ☐Sultanahmet) The most beautiful of the city's Ottoman hamams.

Çemberlitaş Hamamı (Map p534; ☑212-522 7974; www.cemberlitashamami.com; Vezir Han Caddesi 8; self-service ₺60, bath, scrub & soap massage ₺90; ⊗6am-midnight; ☐Çemberlitaş) An architecturally splendid Ottoman hamam.

Sultanahmet & Around

HOCA GIYASETTIN

Şemsettin Sk
Sarı Beyazıt Cad
Namahrem Sk
Vefa Cad
Oluk Sk
Sıfahane Cad

Hayriye Hanım Sk

Kıble Çeşme Cad

Ragıp Gümüşpala Cad

SARIDEMİR

Turyol
Bosphorus
Ferry

Reşadiye Cad

13 ⊗ Hasırcılar Cad

YENİ CAMİ
MEYDANI

Tahmis Sk
Yenicami Meydanı Sk

Fetva Yokuşu
Mimar Sinan Cad

15

Prof Cemil Birsel Cad

RÜSTEM
PAŞA

Tahtakale Cad

Çiçek Pazarı Sk

EMİNÖNÜ

Süleymaniye
Mosque ☉

Dökmeciler
Hamamı Sk

Silyavuşpaşa Sk

Sabuncu Hanı Sk

TAHTAKALE

Büyük
Postane Cad

Prof Sıddık Sami
Onar Cad

Vasıf Çınar Cad

Aşir Efendi Cad

MOLLA
HÜSREV

Kazlı Mescit Sk

Süleymaniye Cad

MERCAN

Havancı Sk

Yenicami Cad

Nargileci Sk

Cemal
Nadir Sk

SÜLEYMANİYE

Bozdoğan
Kemeri Cad

Besim Ömer Paşa Cad

Semaver Sk

Çakmakçılar Yokuşu

SURURİ

Hanımeli Sk
Hoca Hanı Sk

Türkocağı
Cad

Mercan Cad

Tarakçılar Cad

Örücüler
Hamamı Sk

Sultan Mektep Sk

Bezciler Sk

Mengene Sk

Tasvir Sk

Vezneciler Cad

Bakırcılar Cad

FABRIC

2 ⊙ Grand
Bazaar

CARPETS

Fesçiler Cad

Kalpakçılar Cad

GOLD

Şeref Efendi Sk

Nuruosmaniye Cad

NURUOSMANİYE

Divan Yolu (Ordu) Cad

Beyazıt
Meydanı

BEYAZIT

Beyazıt-
Kapalı Çarşı

Kürkçüler
Çarşısı

Tavuk Pazarı Sk

Türbedar Sk

Bab-ı Ali Cad

14 ⊡ Divan Yolu (Ordu) Cad ⊙ 7

ÇEMBERLİTAŞ

Çemberlitaş

Derin Kuyu Sk

Soğanağa Camii Sk

Abuhayat Sk

Asma Kandil Sk

Direkli
Camii Sk

Yahya Paşa Sk

Divan-ı Ali Sk

Doğramacı Sk

EMİN
SİNAN

Gedikpaşa Camii Sk

Klodfarer Cad

Mabeyinci Yokuşu

Molla Bey Sk

Tatlı Kuyu Sk

Emin Sinan Hamamı Sk

Peykhane Cad

Saraç İshak Sk

Asmalı Han Sk

GEDİK
PAŞA

Tuğcu Sk

Piyer Loti Cad

Dizdariye Çeşmesi Sk

Dağhan Sk

Katip Sinan Camii Sk

TürkeliCad

KUMKAPI

Kumkapı Hanı Sk

Arayıcı Sk

Ustad Sk

KADIRGA

Çifte Gelinler Cad

Sarayiçi Sk

Neviye Sk

Katip
Sinan Sk

Özbekler Sk

Mollataşı Cad

Samsa Sk

Telli Odalar Sk

Çaparız Sk

Paye Sk

Kadırga Limanı Cad

Sarapnel Sk

Tavası Çeşme Sk

Babayiğit Sk

Arapzade Sk

Işık Sk

ŞEHSUVARBEY

KÜÇÜK
AYASOFYA

Kaleci Sk

Alişan Sk

Cinci Meydanı Sk

Kennedy Cad (Sahil Yolu)

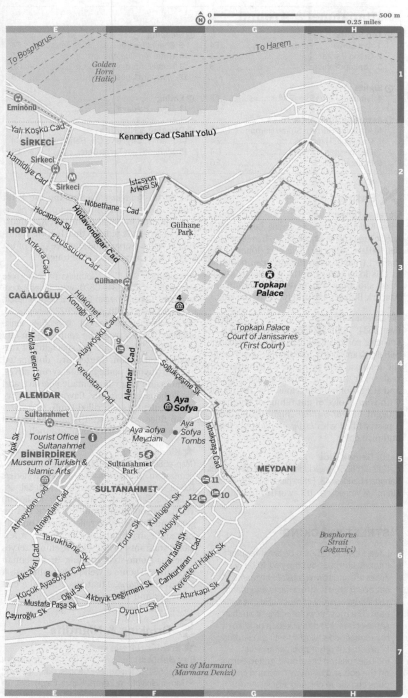

N 0 ————————— 500 m
0 ————————— 0.25 miles

To Bosphorus
To Harem

Golden Horn (Haliç)

Eminönü

Yalı Köşkü Cad

Kennedy Cad (Sahil Yolu)

SİRKECİ

Hamidiye Cad

Sirkeci

Sirkeci

İstasyon Arkası Sk

Nöbethane Cad

Hocapaşa Sk

Hüdavendigar Cad

HOBYAR

Ebussuud Cad

Ankara Cad

Gülhane Park

Gülhane

3
Topkapı Palace

4

CAĞALOĞLU

Hükümet Konağı Sk

6

Alayköşkü Cad

9

Yerebatan Cad

Alemdar Cad

Soğukçeşme Sk

Molla Fenari Sk

ALEMDAR

Topkapı Palace Court of Janissaries (First Court)

Sultanahmet

1 Aya Sofya

Tourist Office – Sultanahmet

Işık Sk

BİNBİRDİREK

Museum of Turkish & Islamic Arts

Aya Sofya Meydanı

Aya Sofya Tombs

İshakpaşa Cad

5

Sultanahmet Park

MEYDANI

SULTANAHMET

Atmeydanı Cad

11

Atmeydanı Cad

12

10

Torun Sk

Kutlugün Sk

Akbıyık Cad

Tavukhane Sk

Amiral Tafdil Sk

Cankurtaran Cad

Bosphorus Strait (Boğaziçi)

Aksakal Cad

8

Küçük Ayasofya Cad

Oğul Sk

Akbıyık Değirmeni Sk

Keresteci Hakkı Sk

Ahırkapı Sk

Mustafa Paşa Sk

Çayıroğlu Sk

Oyuncu Sk

Sea of Marmara (Marmara Denizi)

Sultanahmet & Around

✗ Eating

Bereket Döner
KEBAP €

(Hacı Kadın Caddesi, cnr Tavanlı Çeşme Sokak, Küçük Pazar; döner ekmek ₺5; ⊙ 11am-8pm Mon-Sat; Ⓜ Halıc, Vezneciler) The best döner in the district (maybe even the city) can be found at this local eatery in the run-down Küçük Pazar shopping strip between Eminönü and Atatürk Bulvarı. Definitely worth the trek.

★ Develi Baklava
SWEETS €

(Map p584; 🖉 212-512 1261; Hasırcılar Caddesi 89, Eminönü; portions ₺8-9; ⊙ 6.30am-7pm Mon-Sat; Ⓜ Haliç, 🚋 Eminönü) Close to the Spice Bazaar, the baklava here is made with butter and real sugar (inferior products use glucose) and it's absolutely delicious. Try the classic with your choice of nut filling, or try the indulgent *bülbül yuvası* (nightingale's nest), a pastry filled with *kaymak* (clotted cream) and pistachio.

Fatih Damak Pide
PIDE €

(🖉 212-521 5057; www.fatihdamakpide.com; Büyük Karaman Caddesi 48, Fatih; pides ₺17-25; ⊙ 7am-11pm; Ⓜ Vezneciler) It's worth making the trek to this *pidecisi* overlooking the Fatih İtfaiye Park near the Aqueduct of Valens, as its reputation for making the best Karadeniz (Black Sea)–style pide on the Historic Peninsula is well deserved and the free pots of tea served with meals are a nice touch.

Antiochia
SOUTHEASTERN ANATOLIA €€

(Map p580; 🖉 0212-244 0820; www.antiochiaconcept.com; General Yazgan Sokak 3, Asmalımescit; mezes & salads ₺13-18, pides ₺21-22, kebaps ₺24-52; ⊙ noon-midnight Mon-Sat; ✷🛜🖉🚻; funicularTünel) Dishes from the southeastern city of Antakya (Hatay) are the speciality at this foodie destination. Mezes are dominated by wild thyme, pomegranate syrup, olives, walnuts and tangy homemade yoghurt, and the kebaps are equally flavoursome – try the succulent *şiş et* (grilled lamb) or *dürüm* (wrap filled with minced meat, onions and tomatoes). There's a discount at lunch.

★ Klemuri
ANATOLIAN €€

(Map p580; 🖉 212-292 3272212-292 3272; www.klemuri.com; Büyükparmakkapı Sokak 2; starters TL8-12, mains ₺12-24; ⊙ noon-11pm Mon-Sat; 🖉; Ⓜ Taksim, 🚋 Kabataş, then funicular to Taksim) The Laz people hail from the Black Sea region, and their cuisine relies heavily on fish, kale and dairy products. One of only a few Laz restaurants in the city, Klemuri serves delicious home-style cooking in bohemian surrounds. There's a well-priced wine list, a dessert *(Laz böreği)* that has attained a cult following and interesting choices for vegetarians and vegans.

🍷 Drinking & Nightlife

★ Erenler Nargile ve Çay Bahçesi
TEA GARDEN

(Map p584; Yeniçeriler Caddesi 35, Beyazıt; ⊙ 7am-midnight; 🚋 Beyazıt-Kapalı Çarşı) Set in

---

STREET SNACKING

Locals love to eat, and do so at regular intervals throughout the day. In busy areas around town (*iskeles*, bazaars, shopping strips) street carts and stands sell a huge variety of quick and cheap eats. The most popular of these are fish sandwiches and döner kebap or *kokoreç* (seasoned grilled intestines) stuffed in bread, but other popular snacks include roasted chestnuts, grilled corn on the cob and *pis pilav* (rice and chickpeas cooked in chicken stock).

the vine-covered courtyard of the Çorlulu Ali Paşa Medrese, this nargile cafe near the Grand Bazaar is the most atmospheric in the Old City.

Mimar Sinan Teras Cafe   NARGILE CAFE
(Map p584; ☎ 212-514 4414; Mimar Sinan Han, Fetva Yokuşu 34-35, Süleymaniye; ⏲ 8am-1am; Ⓜ Vezneciler, Haliç, 🚋 Laleli-Üniversite) A magnificent panorama of the city can be enjoyed from the spacious outdoor terrace of this popular student cafe in a ramshackle building located in the shadow of the Süleymaniye Mosque. Head here during the day or in the evening to admire the view over a coffee, unwind with a nargile or enjoy a glass of çay and game of backgammon.

360   BAR
(Map p580; www.360istanbul.com; 8th fl, İstiklal Caddesi 163; ⏲ noon-2am Sun-Thu, to 4am Fri & Sat; Ⓜ Şişhane, 🚋 Karaköy, then funicular to Tünel) İstanbul's most famous bar, and deservedly so. If you can score one of the bar stools on the terrace you'll be happy indeed – the view is truly extraordinary. It morphs into a club after midnight on Friday and Saturday, when a cover charge of around TL40 applies.

★Unter   BAR
(Map p580; ☎ 212 244-5151; www.unter.com.tr; Kara Ali Kaptan Sokak 4, Karaköy; ⏲ 9am-midnight Tue-Thu & Sun, to 2am Fri & Sat; 🚋 Tophane) This scenester-free zone epitomises the new Karaköy style: it's glam without trying too hard, and has a vaguely arty vibe. The ground-floor windows open to the street in fine weather, allowing the action to spill outside during busy periods. Good cocktails and a wine list strong in boutique Thracian drops are major draws, as is the varied food menu.

❶ Information

Tourist Office – Sultanahmet (Map p584; ☎ 212-518 8754; Hippodrome, Sultanahmet; ⏲ 9.30am-6pm mid-Apr–Sep, 9am-5.30pm Oct–mid-Apr; 🚋 Sultanahmet)

❶ Getting There & Away

AIR

İstanbul's **Atatürk International Airport** (IST, Atatürk Havalimanı; ☎ 212-463 3000; www.ataturkairport.com) is 23km west of Sultanahmet. Close by, the domestic terminal (İç Hatlar) is smaller but no less efficient.

WHIRLING DERVISHES

These sultans of spiritual spin known as the 'whirling dervishes' have been twirling their way to a higher plane ever since the 13th century and show no sign of slowing down.

There are a number of opportunities to see dervishes whirling in İstanbul. The best known of these is the weekly ceremony in the *semahane* (whirling dervish hall) in the **Galata Mevlevi Museum** (Galata Mevlevihanesi Müzesi; Map p580; www.galatamevlevihanesimuzesi.gov.tr; Galipdede Caddesi 15, Tünel; TL50; ⏲ performances 5pm Sun; 🚋 Karaköy, then funicular to Tünel) in Tünel. This one-hour ceremony is held on Sundays at 5pm and costs ₺50 per person. Come early (preferably days ahead) to buy your ticket.

Sabiha Gökçen International Airport (SAW, Sabiha Gökçen Havalimanı; ☎ 216-588 8888; www.sgairport.com) is 50km east, on the Asian side of the city.

BUS

The **Büyük İstanbul Otogarı** (Big İstanbul Bus Station; ☎ 212-658 0505; www.otogaristanbul.com) is the city's main bus station for both intercity and international routes. Often called simply 'the otogar' (bus station), it's located at Esenler in the municipality of Bayrampaşa, about 10km west of Sultanahmet. The metro service from Aksaray stops here (₺4; Otogar stop) on its way to the airport.

TRAIN

At the time of research, only one international service – the daily Bosfor Ekspresi between İstanbul and Bucharest via Sofia – was operating in and out of İstanbul, departing at 10pm daily (€39 to €59 plus couchette surcharge). Check Turkish State Railways (TCDD; www.tcdd.gov.tr) for updates.

❶ Getting Around

Rechargable İstanbulkarts (travelcards) can be used on public transport city-wide. Purchase (₺10, including ₺4 credit) and recharge them at kiosks and machines at metro and tram stops, bus terminals and ferry docks. It reduces single fares from ₺4 to ₺2.30. If you're only using public transport for a few city journeys, *jetons* (single trip travel token; ₺4) can be purchased from machines at tram, metro and ferry docks.

ℹ GETTING INTO İSTANBUL FROM THE AIRPORTS

Havataş Airport Bus (☎212-444 2656; http://havatas.com) travels between the airports and Cumhuriyet Caddesi, just off Taksim Meydanı. Buses leave Atatürk (₺10, one hour) every 30 minutes between 4am and 1am. Its service between Sabiha Gökçen (₺13, 1½ hours) and Taksim leaves every 30 minutes between 3.30am and 1am – easily the cheapest way to get to the city from Sabiha Gökçen.

Metro From Atatürk to Zeytinburnu, where you can connect with the tram to Sultanahmet (total ₺8, one hour).

Shuttle Most hotels can book airport shuttles to/from both Atatürk (€5) and Sabiha Gökçen (€12). Check shuttle schedules at reception.

Taxi From Atatürk/Sabiha Gökçen to Sultanahmet costs around ₺45/130.

BOAT

İstanbul's commuter ferries ply the Bosphorous between the city's European and Asian sides. Ferries for Üsküdar and the Bosphorus leave from Eminönü dock; ferries depart from Kabataş (Adalar İskelesi dock) for the Princes' Islands. From Karaköy, ferries depart for Kadıköy on the Asian shore.

BUS

İstanbul's efficient bus system runs between 6.30am and 11.30pm. You must have an İstanbulkart to use the buses. The major bus terminals are at Taksim Meydanı and at Beşiktaş, Kabataş, Eminönü, Kadıköy and Üsküdar.

METRO

The most useful metro service is the M1A Line connecting Aksaray with Atatürk Airport, stopping at 15 stations including the otogar (main bus station) along the way. Services leave every two to 10 minutes between 6am and midnight.

TAXI

İstanbul is full of yellow taxis, all of them with meters – insist that drivers use them. From Sultanahmet to Taksim Meydanı costs around ₺15.

TRAM & FUNICULAR

A tramvay (tramway) service runs from Zeytinburnu (where it connects with the M1A Metro) to Kabataş (connecting with the funicular to Taksim) via Sultanahmet, Eminönü and Karaköy (connecting with the funicular to Tünel). Trams run every five minutes from 6am to midnight. An antique tram rattles up and down İstiklal Caddesi between Tünel funicular station and Taksim Meydanı. The one-stop Tünel funicular between Karaköy and İstiklal Caddesi runs between 7am and 10.45pm. Another funicular runs from Kabataş (where it connects with the tram) up to the metro station at Taksim.

Ankara

POP 4.7 MILLION

İstanbullus may quip that the best view in Ankara is the train home, but the Turkish capital has more substance than its reputation as a staid administrative centre suggests. The capital established by Atatürk boasts two of the country's most important sights; the hilltop *hisar* (citadel) district is full of old-fashioned charm, and the cafe-crammed Kızılay neighbourhood is one of Turkey's hippest urban quarters.

◉ Sights

Museum of Anatolian Civilisations MUSEUM
(Anadolu Medeniyetleri Müzesi; ☎0312-324 3160; http://www.anadolumedeniyetlerimuzesi.gov.tr/; Gözcü Sokak 2; admission ₺15; ⊗8.30am-5pm; ⓂUlus) The superb Museum of Anatolian Civilisations is the perfect introduction to the complex weave of Turkey's ancient past, housing artefacts cherry-picked from just about every significant archaeological site in Anatolia.

The museum is housed in a 15th-century *bedesten* (covered market). The central room houses reliefs and statues, while the surrounding hall displays exhibits from Palaeolithic, Neolithic, Chalcolithic, Bronze Age, Assyrian, Hittite, Phrygian, Urartian and Lydian periods. Downstairs are classical Greek and Roman artefacts and a display on Ankara's history.

Anıt Kabir MONUMENT
(Atatürk Mausoleum & Museum; www.anitkabir. org; Gençlik Caddesi; audioguide ₺10; ⊗9am-5pm May-Oct, to 4pm Nov-Apr; ⓂTandoğan) FREE The monumental mausoleum of Mustafa Kemal Atatürk (1881–1938), the founder of modern Turkey, sits high above the city with its abundance of marble and air of veneration. The tomb itself actually makes up only a small part of this fascinating complex, which consists of museums and a ceremonial courtyard. For many Turks a visit is virtually a pilgrimage, and it's not unusual to

see people visibly moved. Allow at least two hours in order to visit the whole site.

Citadel
AREA

(Ankara Kalesi; M Ulus) The imposing *hisar* is the most interesting part of Ankara to poke about in. This well-preserved quarter of thick walls and intriguing winding streets took its present shape in the 9th century AD, when the Byzantine emperor Michael II constructed the outer ramparts. The inner walls date from the 7th century.

After you've entered **Parmak Kapısı** (Finger Gate), the main gate, and passed through a gate to your left, you'll see **Alaettin Camii** (Alitaş Sokak) on the left. The citadel mosque dates from the 12th century, but has been extensively rebuilt. To your right a steep road leads to a flight of stairs that leads to the **Şark Kulesi** (Eastern Tower), with panoramic city views. Although it's much harder to find, a tower to the north, **Ak Kale** (White Fort), also offers fine views.

🛌 Sleeping

Book ahead, as many rooms are snapped up by business people. There are a number of budget and midrange hotels around Ulus Meydanı. However, given that most of the restaurants and nightlife are in Kızılay and Kavaklıdere, if you want to go out for the evening the added cost of a taxi back to Ulus may mean that a room in Kızılay costs the same overall.

★ Deeps Hostel
HOSTEL €

(☑ 0312-213 6338; www.deepshostelankara.com; Ataç Sokak 46; dm ₺35-50, s/d without breakfast ₺65-100; 🕾; M Kızılay) At Ankara's best budget choice, friendly Şeyda, the owner of Deeps, has created a colourful, light-filled hostel with spacious dorms and rooms, and squeaky-clean, modern shared bathrooms. It's all topped off by masses of advice and information, a fully equipped kitchen and a cute communal area downstairs where you can swap your Turkish travel tales.

Otel Mithat
HOTEL €

(☑ 0312-311 5410; www.otelmithat.com.tr; Tavus Sokak 2; s/d/tr ₺95/140/175; ❄🕾; M Ulus) With groovy carpeting and sleek neutral bed linen, the Mithat's rooms are fresh and modern. The teensy bathrooms do let the side down somewhat, but this is a minor complaint about what is, overall, an excellent budget choice. Nonsmokers will be pleased that unlike most Ankara hotels in this price range, the Mithat takes its no-smoking policy seriously.

Angora House Hotel
HISTORIC HOTEL €€

(☑ 0312-309 8380; www.angorahouse.com.tr; Kale Kapısı Sokak 16; s/d/tr ₺140/190/240; 🕾; M Ulus) Be utterly charmed by this restored Ottoman house, which oozes subtle elegance at every

---

ESSENTIAL TURKISH CUISINE

Kebaps and *köfte* (meatballs) in all their variations are the mainstay of restaurant meals. Look out particularly for the following:

Adana kebap Spicy *köfte* grilled on a skewer and served with onions, sumac, parsley, tomatoes and pide bread.

İskender kebap Döner kebap (spit-roasted lamb slices) on fresh pide and topped with savoury tomato sauce and browned butter.

Tokat kebap Lamb cubes grilled with potato, tomato, aubergine and garlic.

Meze is where Turkish cuisine really comes into its own. *Acılı ezme* (spicy tomato and onion paste), *fasulye pilaki* (white beans cooked with tomato paste and garlic), and *yapraksarma* (vine leaves stuffed with rice, herbs and pine nuts) are just a few of the myriad meze dishes on offer.

For quick cheap eats, try pide (Turkish pizza), *lahmacun* (Arabic-style pizza), *gözleme* (stuffed savoury crepe) and *börek* (filled pastries).

Popular non-kebap mains include *mantı* (Turkish ravioli), *saç kavurma* (stir-fried cubed meat dishes) and *güveç* (meat and vegetable stews cooked in a terracotta pot).

The national hot drink is *çay*, served black in tulip-shaped glasses. The Turkish liquor of choice is *rakı*, a fiery aniseed drink similar to Greek ouzo; do as the Turks do and cut it by half with water. *Ayran* is a refreshing yoghurt drink made by whipping up yoghurt with water and salt and is the perfect accompaniment to a kebap.

Ankara

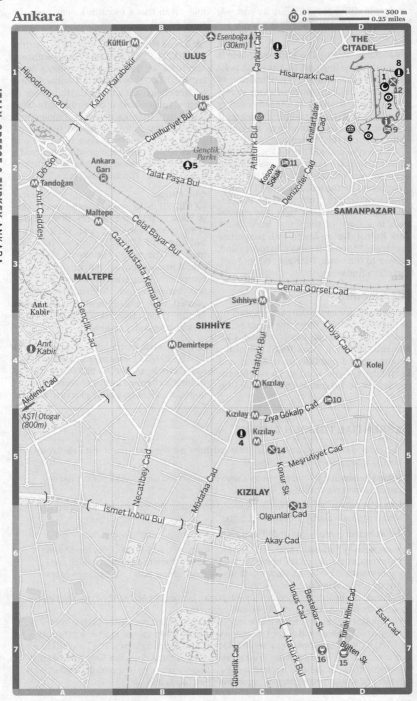

Ankara

0 — 500 m
0 — 0.25 miles

THE CITADEL

Esenboğa (30km)

ULUS

Kültür

Hisarparkı Cad

8

1
12
2

Çankırı Cad

Ulus

6
7
9

Cumhuriyet Bul

3

Atatürk Bul

Anatatalar Cad

Hipodrom Cad

Kâzım Karabekir

Gençlik Parkı

Ankara Garı

5

Tandoğan

Talat Paşa Bul

Kosova Sokak

11

Denizciler Cad

SAMANPAZARI

Anıt Caddesi

Dö Göl

Maltepe

Celal Bayar Bul

MALTEPE

Gazi Mustafa Kemal Bul

Gençlik Cad

Anıt Kabir

Cemal Gürsel Cad

Anıt Kabir

Sıhhiye

Libya Cad

SIHHİYE

Demirtepe

Kolej

Akdeniz Cad

Atatürk Bul

AŞTİ Otogar (800m)

Kızılay

Necatibey Cad

Müdafaa Cad

Kızılay

Ziya Gökalp Cad

10

Kızılay

4

Kızılay

14

Meşrutiyet Cad

KIZILAY

Konur Sk

13

Olgunlar Cad

İsmet İnönü Bul

Akay Cad

Güvenlik Cad

Tunus Cad

Bestekar Sk

Atatürk Bul

Tunalı Hilmi Cad

Esat Cad

16

Bülten Sk

15

turn. The six spacious rooms are infused with loads of old-world atmosphere, featuring dark wood accents, creamy 19th-century design textiles and colourfu Turkish carpets, while the walled courtyard garden is the perfect retreat from the citadel streets. Delightfully helpful staff add to the appeal.

✗ Eating

It's all about street stalls, hip bistros and cafe culture in Kızılay, where terraces line virtually every inch of space south of Ziya Gökalp Caddesi. Kızılay's tall, thin buildings also pack in up to five floors of nightspots.

Çomlek Ev Yemekleri TURKISH €
(Konur Sokak; set menu ₺7; ☺noon-9pm Mon-Sat; Ⓜ Kızılay) This unpretentious place is crammed with students who slurp down simple but filling daily lunch specials. Choose the *güveç* (meat and vegetable stews cooked in a terracotta pot) for a tasty, wholesome meal.

Leman Kültür INTERNATIONAL €
(☎0312-310 8617; www.lmk.com.tr Konur Sokak 8; mains ₺10-20; Ⓜ Kızılay) Named after a cult Turkish comic strip – and decorated accordingly – this is still the pre-party pick for a substantial feed and for spotting beautiful young educated things. The food is generally of the meatballs, burgers and grilled

GOAT OR RABBIT?

Can you tell the difference between a goat and a rabbit? It's not as easy as you think – or at least not if all you have to go on is the wool. One of the most popular misconceptions about Ankara's famous angora wool is that it comes from angora goats, a hardy breed believed to be descended from wild Himalayan goats. Not so: the soft, fluffy wool produced from these goats is correctly known as mohair. Angora wool in the strictest sense comes from angora rabbits, also local but much cuter and whose fur, weight for weight, was once worth as much as gold.

meats variety. Drinks are reasonably priced and the speakers crank everything from indie-electro to Türk pop.

And Evi Cafe MODERN TURKISH €€
(☎0312-312 7978; İçkale Kapısı; mains ₺12-24; Ⓜ Ulus) Even if the food was so-so this cafe, set into the citadel walls, would be a winner for the cosy Ottoman-style interior and incredible panoramic views of the city from the terrace. Luckily, the food is great. Tuck into a lunchtime crepe (₺11), sample a slice of the divine carrot cake (₺6) with a latte for afternoon tea, or choose one of the pasta dishes for dinner. It's all good.

🍷 Drinking & Nightlife

Café des Cafés CAFE
(☎0312-428 0176; Tunalı Hilmi Caddesi 83; ☺8.30am-11pm) Quirky vintage styling and comfy sofas make Café des Cafés a popular Kavaklıdere haunt. Pull up a chair on the tiny streetside terrace and sharpen up your people-watching skills. The orange and cinnamon hot chocolate is bliss in a glass.

Hayyami WINE BAR
(☎0312-466 1052; Bestekar Sokak 82B; ☺noon-late) Named after the renowned Sufi philosopher, this thriving wine house–restaurant attracts a hobnobbing crowd to its lowered courtyard. It boasts a long and diverse wine selection, which you can savour with a tapas-like array of dishes including *salçalı sosis* (barbecued sausage) and devilishly large cheese platters (mains ₺12 to ₺25).

ⓘ Information

Tourist Office (📞 0312-310 3044; Kale Kapısı Sokak ; ⊙10am-5pm; Ⓜ Ulus) Ankara's main tourist office is inside the Citadel. There are also (usually unmanned) branches at the AŞTİ otogar and at the train station.

ⓘ Getting There & Away

BUS

From Ankara's huge **AŞTİ otogar** (Ankara Şehirlerarası Terminali İşletmesi; Mevlâna Bulvarı), buses depart to all corners of Turkey day and night. Services to İstanbul (₺40 to ₺80, six hours) leave half-hourly. The AŞTİ is at the western end of Ankara's Ankaray Metro line (fare ₺1.75), by far the easiest way to travel between the otogar and the centre.

TRAIN

Ankara Train Station (Ankara Garı; Talat PaşaBulvarı) has high-speed trains to Konya (economy/business class ₺27.50/35, two hours, eight daily); and to Pendik, a suburb 25km east of İstanbul (₺70, 3½ hours).

ⓘ Getting Around

BUS

Ankara has a good bus, dolmuş and minibus network. Signs on the front and side of the vehicles are better guides than route numbers. Buses marked 'Ulus' and 'Çankaya' run the length of Atatürk Bulvarı. Those marked 'Gar' go to the train station, those marked 'AŞTİ' to the otogar.

Standard ₺3.50 transport cards (valid for two journeys) are available at subway stations and major bus stops or anywhere displaying an EGO Bilet sign. They work on most buses as well as the subway. These tickets are not valid on express buses, which are the longer buses with ticket counters halfway down the vehicle.

METRO

Ankara's underground train network is the easiest way to get between Ulus and Kızılay and the transport terminals. Tickets are available at all stations.

TAXI

Taxis are everywhere and they all have meters (normally built into the mirror), with a ₺2.70 base rate. It costs about ₺10 to cross the centre; charges rise at night and the same trip will cost well over ₺15.

Konya

The home of the whirling dervish orders is a bastion of Seljuk culture. The centre is dotted with imposing historic monuments all topped off by the city's turquoise-domed Mevlâna Museum, one of Turkey's finest sights and most important centres of pilgrimage. It's worthwhile planning your Konya trip to be here on a Thursday evening when the *sema* ceremony is performed at the Mevlâna Culture Centre.

⊙ Sights

★ Mevlâna Museum   MUSEUM

(📞 0332-351 1215; admission ₺5, audioguide ₺10; ⊙10am-5pm Mon, 9am-5pm Tue-Sun) For Muslims and non-Muslims alike, the main reason to come to Konya is to visit the Mevlâna Museum, the former lodge of the whirling dervishes. It's Celaleddin Rumi (later known as Mevlâna) that we have to thank for giving the world the whirling dervishes and, indirectly, the Mevlâna Museum. Calling it a mere museum, however, makes it sound dead and stale, but the truth couldn't be more different. As one of the biggest pilgrimage centres in Turkey, the museum constantly buzzes with energy.

Mevlâna Culture Centre   CULTURAL CENTRE

(Whirling Dervish Performance; http://www.emav.org/; Aslanlı Kışla Caddesi; ⊙7.30-11pm Thu) 𝗙𝗥𝗘𝗘 The Mevlevi worship ceremony, or *sema*, is a ritual dance representing union with God; it's what gives the dervishes their famous whirl, and appears on Unesco's third Proclamation of Masterpieces of the Oral and Intangible Heritage of Humanity. Watching a *sema* can be an evocative, romantic, unforgettable experience. There are many dervish orders worldwide that perform similar rituals, but the original Turkish version is the smoothest and purest, more of an elegant, trancelike dance than the raw energy seen elsewhere.

The dervishes dress in long white robes with full skirts that represent their shrouds. Their voluminous black cloaks symbolise their worldly tombs, their conical felt hats their tombstones.

By holding their right arms up, they receive the blessings of heaven, which are communicated to earth by holding their left arms turned down. As they whirl, they form a 'constellation' of revolving bodies, which itself slowly rotates.

Tile Museum   MUSEUM

(Karatay Medresesi Çini Müzesi; 📞 0332-351 1914; Alaaddin Meydanı; admission ₺5; ⊙9am-6.40pm) Gorgeously restored, the interior central dome and walls of this former Seljuk theo-

Konya

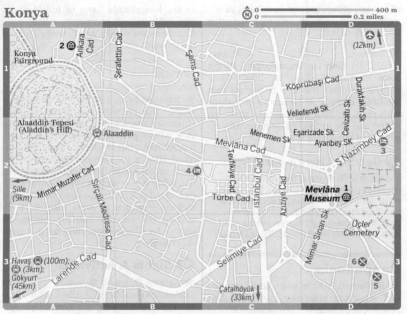

logical school (1251) showcase some finely preserved blue-and-white Seljuk tilework. There is also an outstanding collection of ceramics on display including exhibits of the octagonal Seljuk tiles unearthered during excavations at Kubad Abad Palace on Lake Beyşehir. Emir Celaleddin Karatay, a Seljuk general, vizier and statesman who built the *medrese,* is buried in one of the corner rooms.

🛏 Sleeping

Ulusan Otel HOTEL €
(☑ 0332-351 5004; Çarşı PTT Arkasi 4; s/d without bathroom ₺40/75; 🛜) This is the pick of the Konya cheapies. The rooms may be totally basic, but they're bright and spotlessly clean. Shared bathrooms are immaculately kept (some rooms have private bathrooms) and the communal area is full of homely knick-knacks.

Derviş Otel BOUTIQUE HOTEL €€
(☑ 0332-350 0842; www.dervishotel.com; Güngör Sokak 7; s/d/tr ₺160/190/260; ✳🛜) This airy, light-filled 200-year-old house has been converted into a rather wonderful boutique hotel. All of the seven spacious rooms have lovely soft colour schemes with local carpets covering the wooden floors, comfortable

Konya
◎ **Top Sights**
1 Mevlâna Museum D2

◎ **Sights**
2 Tile Museum A1

🛏 **Sleeping**
3 Derviş Otel..D2
4 Ulusan Otel...B2

🍴 **Eating**
5 Konak Konya Mutfağı D3
6 Somatçi D3

beds and modern bathrooms to boot. With enthusiastic management providing truly personal service this is a top-notch alternative to Konya's more anonymous hotels.

🍴 Eating

★**Konak Konya Mutfağı** ANATOLIAN €€
(☑ 0332-352 8547; Piriesat Caddesi 5; mains ₺10-20; ⊙11am-10pm) This excellent traditional restaurant is run by well-known food writer Nevin Halıcı, who puts her personal twist on Turkish classics. Grab an outside table and dine beside vine-draped pillars and a fragrant rose garden. Aubergine aficionados shouldn't miss the *sebzeli közleme* (a grill

of smoked aubergine and lamb) and sweet-tooths should definitely save room to try the unusual desserts.

★ Somatçi ANATOLIAN **€€**

(📞 0332-351 6696; www.somatci.com; Mengüc Sokak 36; mains ₺12-20; ⊙ 9am-11pm) Rekindling old recipes, this new restaurant uses the finest ingredients and cooks everything with panache. Staff are happy to advise on dishes and the setting inside a carefully restored old building is spot on.

ℹ Getting There & Away

The otogar is 7km north of the centre and connected by tram. There are frequent buses to all major destinations, including Ankara (₺30, 3½ hours), İstanbul (₺70, 11½ hours) and Göreme (₺30, three hours). Eight express trains run to/from Ankara daily (adult/child ₺30/15, 1¾ hours).

Cappadocia

As if plucked from a whimsical fairy tale and set down upon the stark Anatolian plains, Cappadocia is a geological oddity of honeycombed hills and towering boulders of otherworldly beauty. The fantastical topography is matched by the human history here. People have long utilised the region's soft stone, seeking shelter underground. Rock-hewn churches covered in Byzantine frescoes are secreted into cliffs, the villages are honeycombed out of hillsides and vast subterranean complexes, where early Christians once hid, are tunnelled under the ground.

Göreme

POP 2101

Surrounded by epic sweeps of moonscape valley, this remarkable honey-coloured village hollowed out of the hills may have long since grown beyond its farming-hamlet roots, but its charm has not diminished. Nearby, the Göreme Open-Air Museum is an all-in-one testament to Byzantine life, while if you wander out of town you'll find storybook landscapes and little-visited rock-cut churches at every turn. With its easygoing allure and stunning setting, it's no wonder Göreme continues to send travellers giddy.

◎ Sights & Activities

★ Göreme Open-Air Museum MUSEUM

(Göreme Açık Hava Müzesi; 📞 0384-271 2167; Müze Caddesi; admission ₺30; ⊙ 8.30am-6.45pm Apr-Nov, 8.30am-4.45pm Dec-Mar) One of Turkey's Unesco World Heritage sites, the Göreme Open-Air Museum is an essential stop on any Cappadocian itinerary and deserves a two-hour visit. First an important Byzantine monastic settlement that housed some 20 monks, then a pilgrimage site from the 17th

---

GOING UNDERGROUND

Thought to have been carved out by the Hittites, the vast network of Cappadocia's underground cities was first mentioned by the ancient Greek historian Xenophon in his *Anabasis* (written in the 4th century BC).

During the 6th and 7th centuries, Byzantine Christians extended and enlarged the cities and used them as a means by which to escape persecution. If Persian or Arab armies were approaching, a series of beacons would be lit in warning – the message could travel from Jerusalem to Constantinople in hours. When it reached Cappadocia, the Christians would gather their belongings and relocate to the underground cities, hiding in the subterranean vaults for months at a time.

Some of the cities are remarkable in scale – it is thought that Derinkuyu and Kaymaklı housed about 10,000 and 3000 people respectively.

Around 37 underground cities have already been opened. There are at least 100 more, though the full extent of these subterranean refuges may never be known.

Touring the cities is like tackling an assault course for history buffs. Narrow walkways lead you into the depths of the earth, through stables with handles used to tether animals, churches with altars and baptism pools, walls with air-circulation holes, granaries with grindstones, and blackened kitchens with ovens. While it's a fascinating experience, be prepared for unpleasantly crowded and sometimes claustrophobic passages. Avoid visiting on weekends, when busloads of domestic tourists descend. Even if you don't normally like having a guide, it's worth having one: they can conjure up the details of life below the ground better than you can on your own.

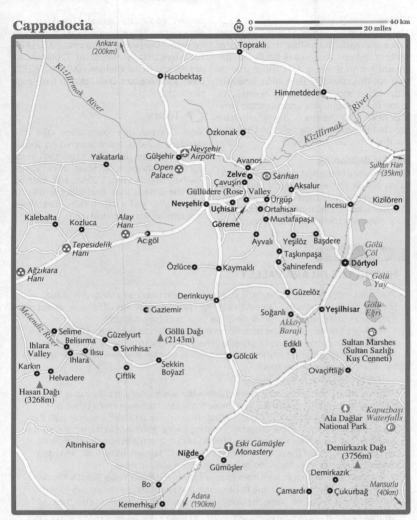

century, this splendid cluster of monastic Byzantine artistry with its rock-cut churches, chapels and monasteries is 1km uphill from Göreme's centre.

The stunning, fresco-filled **Karanlık Kilise** (Dark Church; admission ₺10) is the most famous of the Open-Air Museum's churches. It takes its name from the fact that it originally had very few windows. Luckily, this lack of light preserved the vivid colour of the frescoes, which show, among other things, Christ as Pantocrator, Christ on the cross and the Betrayal by Judas. The church was restored at great expense and the entrance fee is intended to limit visitor numbers to further preserve the frescoes.

When you exit the Open-Air Museum, don't forget to cross the road to visit the **Tokalı Kilise** (Buckle Church), 50m down the hill towards Göreme and covered by the same ticket. This is one of Göreme's biggest and finest churches, with an underground chapel and fabulous, recently restored frescoes. The holes in the floor once contained tombs, taken by departing Greek Christians during Turkey's population exchange.

Hiking

The trails that loop around Güllüdere (Rose) Valley are easily accessible to all levels of walkers and provide some of the finest fairy chimney–strewn vistas in Cappadocia. As well as this, though, they hide fabulous, little-visited rock-cut churches boasting vibrant fresco fragments and intricate carvings hewn into the stone. If you only have time to hike through one valley in Cappadocia, this is the one to choose.

Hot Air Ballooning

Göreme is one of the best places in the world to go hot-air ballooning. Flight conditions are especially favourable here and seeing this remarkable landscape from above is a truly magical experience. Flights start from around ₺560 and include breakfast and champagne. The Göreme-based ballooning agencies **Butterfly Balloons** (☏0384-271 3010; www.butterflyballoons.com; Uzundere Caddesi 29) and **Royal Balloon** (☏0384-271 3300; www.royalballoon.com; Dutlu Sokak 9) have good credentials:

Tours

Most Göreme tour companies offer two standard full-day tours referred to locally as the Red Tour (including visits to Göreme Open-Air Museum, Uçhisar rock castle, Paşabağı and Devrent Valleys, and Avanos), and the Green Tour (including a hike in Ihlara Valley and a trip to either Derinkuyu or Kaymaklı underground city).

WORTH A TRIP

HIKING THE IHLARA VALLEY

The Ihlara Valley scythes through the stubbly fields and today is home to one of the prettiest strolls in the world. Once called Peristrema, the valley was a favourite retreat of Byzantine monks, who cut churches into the base of its towering cliffs.

Following the Melendiz River, hemmed in by jagged cliffs as it snakes between painted churches, piles of boulders and a sea of greenery ringing with birdsong and croaking frogs, is an unforgettable experience. Good times to visit are midweek in May or September, when fewer people are about.

There is an ATM in Ihlara village.

Ihlara Valley (Ihlara Vadısı; admission incl Selime Monastery, Güzelyurt's Monastery Valley & Aksaray Museum ₺20; ⊙8am-6.30pm) Hiking the full trail between Ihlara village and Selime is a wonderfully bucolic day out. Most visitors come on a tour and only walk the short stretch with most of the churches, entering via the 360 steps of the **Ihlara Vadısı Turistik Tesisleri** (Ihlara Valley Tourist Facility) ticket booth and exiting at Belisırma. This means the rest of the path is blissfully serene, with farmers tilling their fields and shepherds grazing their flocks the only people you're likely to meet.

It takes about an hour to walk from Ihlara village to the Ihlara Vadısı Turistik Tesisleri stairs, 1½ hours to walk from there to Belisırma, and about another two hours to walk from Belisırma to Selime. Along the valley floor, signs mark the different churches.

Selime Monastery (Selime village ; admission incl Ihlara Valley, Güzelyurt's Monastery Valley & Aksaray Museum ₺20; ⊙8am-6pm) The monastery at Selime is an astonishing rock-cut structure incorporating a vast kitchen with a soaring chimney, a church with a gallery around it, stables with rock-carved feed troughs and other evidence of the troglodyte lifestyle.

Akar Pansion & Restaurant (☏0382-453 7018; www.ihlara-akarmotel.com; Ihlara Village; s/d/tr ₺50/90/120; ☂) Akar's basic rooms have cheerful linen and are kept spotlessly clean. Grab one of the rooms in the new building with private balconies. Helpful English-speaking staff can fill you in on any Ihlara queries, the restaurant serves tasty local dishes (₺10 to ₺20) and the attached shop sells picnic ingredients.

Star Restaurant & Pension (☏0382-453 7020; Ihlara Village; mains ₺15-20; ☂☑) Right beside the river, the wonderful shady terrace at this friendly, family-run place is just the spot for dinner and chilling out with a beer after a day's hike. Local trout is the speciality, but there are also meaty casseroles and vegetarian options. It also has 10 bright, simple rooms upstairs (singles/doubles ₺40/80) and a small, grassy camping area (sites ₺30).

Heritage Travel TOUR

(☑0384-271 2687; www.turkishheritagetravel.com; Uzundere Caddesi; day-tours per person cash-payment/credit card €45/55) This highly recommended local agency specialises in tailor-made Turkey packages but also runs three popular guided day tours (€60 per person), including an excellent 'Undiscovered Cappadocia' trip to Soğanlı. A range of more offbeat activities, from photography safaris (₺400 per person) to cooking classes (₺160 per person) and day trips to Hacıbektaş are also offered.

Yama Tours TOUR

(☑0384-271 2508; www.yamatours.com; Müze Caddesi 2; group day-tours ₺110-120) This popular backpacker-friendly travel agency runs daily Red (regional highlights; ₺110) and Green (Ihlara Valley; ₺120) tours and can book a bag full of other Cappadocia adventures and activities for you.

Ihlara Valley

Map of Ihlara Valley showing: Aksaray (45km), Çatlak Hotel, Selime, Selime Monastery, Güzelyurt (9km), Piri Pension, Çatlak Restaurant, Ticket Office, Yaprakhisar, Melendiz River, Anatolia Valley Restaurant & Camping; Tandırcı Restaurant & Camping; Belisırma Restaurant, Belisırma, Ticket Office, Bahattin'in Samanlığı Kilise, Direkli Kilise, Kırk Dam Altı Kilise, Yılanlı Kilise, Sümbüllü Kilise, Ihlara Vadısı Turistik Tesisleri, Ağaçaltı Kilise, Pürenli Sek Kelises, Kokar Kilise, Ticket Office, Star Restaurant & Pension, Ihlara Village, Akar Pansion & Restaurant, Ilısu (2km), Güzelyurt (13km)

🛏 Sleeping

★ Shoestring Cave Pension HOSTEL €

(☑0384-271 2450; www.shoestringcave.com; Kazım Eren Sokak; dm ₺40, d/ste ₺130/210; ⊜🌐🏊) The double rooms at this old-school backpacker paradise have been jazzed up significantly in recent years, while the funky cave dorm means those counting their kuruş still have a dependable place to crash. The courtyard picnic tables and cool terrace swimming-pool area provide a proper communal feel, so pull up a pew and swap a couple of Turkish travel tales.

Köse Pension PENSION €

(☑0384-271 2294; www.kosepension.com; Ragıp Üner Caddesi; dm ₺20, rooftop hut per person ₺35, d/tr ₺120/135, ; ⊜🌐🏊) It may have no cave character, but traveller favourite Köse is still the pick of Göreme's budget digs. Ably managed by Sabina, this friendly place provides a range of spotless rooms featuring brilliant bathrooms, bright linens and comfortable beds, more basic rooms, and a spacious rooftop dorm. The swimming pool is a bonus after a long, hot hike.

Breakfasts here (not included; ₺5 to ₺8) include a swag of options.

★ Kelebek Hotel BOUTIQUE HOTEL €€

(☑0384-271 2531; www.kelebekhotel.com; Yavuz Sokak 31; fairy-chimney r from ₺175-420; 🅿⊜❄🌐🏊) It's reassuring to know the oldie is still the goodie. Local guru Ali Yavuz leads a charming team at one of Göreme's original boutique hotels that has seen a travel industry virtually spring from beneath its stunning terrace. Exuding Anatolian inspiration at every turn, the rooms are spread over two gorgeous stone houses, each with a fairy chimney protruding skyward.

Kemal's Guest House GUESTHOUSE €€

(☑0384-271 2234; www.kemalsguesthouse.com; Ayzazefedi Sokak 4 ; s/d/tr ₺130/160/225; ⊜❄🌐) It may not have the razzmatazz of Göreme's newer offerings, but this pension delivers old-fashioned hospitality in spades. Kemal is a terrific cook (dinner feasts €15) and his Dutch wife, Barbara, knows her way around Cappadocia's hiking trails like no other hotelier. Pull up a comfy seat in the sun-dappled garden.

🍴 Eating

Fırın Express PIDE €

(☑0384-271 2266; Camı Sokak; pide ₺7-13; 🌐☑) Simply the best pide (Turkish-style pizza) in town is found in this local haunt. The cavernous wood oven fires up meat and vegetarian options and anything doused with egg. We suggest adding an *ayran* (yogurt drink) and a *çoban salatası* (shepherd's salad) for a delicious bargain feed.

Nazar Börek   TURKISH €

(📞0384-271 2441; Müze Caddesi; gözleme & börek ₺7-9; 🛜📷) Head here for supremely tasty traditional Turkish staples served up by friendly Rafik and his team. Nazar remains our longstanding favourite for its hearty plates of *gözleme* and *sosyete böregi* (stuffed spiral pastries served with yogurt and tomato sauce). The convivial atmosphere encourages diners to linger long after their meal has finished.

Göreme Market   MARKET €

(🕐9am-4pm Wed) Pick up fresh produce, locally made cheese and all sorts of other foodie delights at Göreme's Wednesday market.

Köy Evi   ANATOLIAN €€

(📞0384-271 2008; Aydınkıragı Sokak 40; meze ₺7-10, mains ₺12-18, kebap plates ₺20-40; 📷) The simple, wholesome flavours of village food are the main act at this brilliant rustic-style restaurant where charming staff serve up a taste-bud tour of Göreme while the female chefs shovel out more steaming-hot bread from the *tandır* (oven). The warren of cave rooms has been kept authentically basic, which adds to the homespun appeal.

Bring your appetite and prepare to feast on the soul food that fuelled Cappadocian farmers for centuries.

❶ Getting There & Away

AIR

Two airports serve central Cappadocia: **Kayseri Airport** (Kayseri Erkilet Havalimanı ; 📞0352-337 5494; www.kayseri.dhmi.gov.tr; Kayseri Caddesi) and **Nevşehir Airport** (Nevşehir Kapadokya Havalimanı ; 📞0384-421 4451; www.kapadokya.dhmi.gov.tr; Nevşehir Kapadokya Havaalanı Yolu, Gülşehir). Both have several flights daily to/from İstanbul.

Airport shuttle buses to Göreme from either airport must be pre-booked. All hotels can do this for you or book directly through **Helios Transfer** (www.heliostransfer.com; Adnan Menderes Caddesi 24/A,Göreme; per passenger to/from either airport ₺32).

BUS

Most long-distance buses from western Turkey terminate in Nevşehir, from where the bus company runs a free *servis* that takes you on to Göreme. Make sure your ticket states your final destination, not Nevşehir. Beware of touts at Nevşehir otogar and only usethe bus company's official *servis* shuttle.The major bus companies all have offices in Göreme otogar and service destinations nationwide.

Turkey Survival Guide

❶ Directory A–Z

BARGAINING

Haggling is common in bazaars, as well as for out-of-season accommodation and long taxi journeys. In other instances, you're expected to pay the stated price.

DANGERS & ANNOYANCES

Although Turkey is by no means a dangerous country to visit, it's always wise to be a little cautious, especially if you're travelling alone.

Assaults

Sexual assaults have occurred against travellers of both sexes in hotels in central and eastern Anatolia. Make enquiries, check forums and do a little research in advance if you are travelling alone or heading off the beaten track.

Flies & Mosquitoes

In high summer, mosquitoes are troublesome even in İstanbul; they can make a stay along the coast a nightmare. Some hotel rooms come equipped with nets and/or plug-in bugbusters, but it's a good idea to bring some insect repellent and mosquito coils.

Lese-Majesty

The laws against insulting, defaming or making light of Atatürk, the Turkish Republic, the Turkish flag, the Turkish government, the Turkish people and so on are taken very seriously. Making derogatory remarks, even in the heat of a quarrel, can be enough to get a foreigner carted off to jail.

Scams & Druggings

Various scams operate in İstanbul. In the most notorious, single men (the usual target) are

---

❶ SLEEPING PRICE RANGES

Ranges are based on the cost of a double room. Unless otherwise mentioned, rates include tax (KDV), an en suite bathroom and breakfast.

€ less than €90

€€ €90 to €200

€€€ more than €200

befriended, invited to a bar and, after a few drinks, presented with an astromical bill. The proprietors can produce a menu showing the same prices. If you don't have enough cash, you'll be frogmarched to the nearest ATM. If this happens to you, report it to the tourist police; some travellers have taken the police back to the bar and received a refund.

A less common variation on this trick involves the traveller having their drink spiked and waking up in an unexpected place with their belongings, right down to their shoes, missing – or worse.

The spiking scam has also been reported on overnight trains, with passengers getting robbed. Turks are often genuinely sociable and generous travelling companions, but be cautious about accepting food and drinks from people you are not 100% sure about.

Traffic

As a pedestrian, note that some Turks are aggressive, dangerous drivers; 'right of way' doesn't compute with many motorists, despite the little green man on traffic lights. Give way to vehicles in all situations, even if you have to jump out of the way.

ELECTRICITY

➡ Electrical current is 230V AC, 50Hz.

➡ You can buy plug adaptors at most electrical shops.

EMBASSIES & CONSULATES

Australian Embassy (📞 0312-459 9500; www.turkey.embassy.gov.au; 7th fl, MNG Building, Uğur Mumcu Caddesi 88, Gaziosmanpaşa)

Canadian Embassy (📞 0312-409 2700; turkey.gc.ca; Cinnah Caddesi 58, Çankaya)

New Zealand Embassy (📞 0312-446 3333; www.nzembassy.com/turkey; Kizkulesi Sokak 11, Gaziosmanpaşa)

UK Embassy (📞 0312-455 3344; ukinturkey.fco.gov.uk; Şehit Ersan Caddesi 46a, Çankaya)

US Embassy (📞 0312-455 5555; turkey.usembassy.gov; Atatürk Bulvarı 110, Kavaklıdere)

EMERGENCY & IMPORTANT NUMBERS

Turkey country code	📞90
International access code from Turkey	📞00
Ambulance	📞112
Fire	📞110
Police	📞155

ETIQUETTE

Religion Dress modestly and be quiet and respectful around mosques.

Restaurants Generally, whoever extended the invitation to eat together picks up the bill.

🛈 FOOD PRICE RANGES

This section uses the following price ranges, based on the cost of a main course.

İstanbul & Bodrum Peninsula

€ less than ₺20

€€ ₺20 to ₺30

€€€ more than ₺30

Rest of Turkey

€ less than ₺9

€€ ₺9 to ₺18

€€€ more than ₺18

Alcohol Bars are common, but public drinking and inebriation are less acceptable away from tourist towns.

Greetings Turks value respect; greet or acknowledge people.

Language Learn a few Turkish phrases; immeasurably helpful and appreciated by Turks.

Relationships Do not be overly tactile with your partner in public; beware miscommunications with locals.

Politics Be tactful; criticising Turkish nationalism can land you in prison.

Shopping Visiting the bazaar, be prepared to haggle and drink tea with shopkeepers.

Queues Turks can be pushy in public situations; be assertive.

LGBT TRAVELLERS

Homosexuality is not a criminal offence in Turkey, but prejudice remains strong and there are sporadic reports of violence towards gay people – the message is discretion.

BHN Mavi Tours (www.turkey-gay-travel.com) Gay-friendly İstanbul travel agent, with useful links on its website.

Kaos GL (www.kaosgl.com) Based in Ankara, the LGBT rights organisation publishes a gay-and-lesbian magazine and its website has news and information in English.

Lambdaistanbul (www.lambdaistanbul.org) The Turkish branch of the International Lesbian, Gay, Bisexual, Trans and Intersexual Association.

MONEY

➡ Turkey's currency is the Türk Lirası (Turkish lira; ₺). The lira comes in notes of five, 10, 20, 50, 100 and 200, and coins of one, five, 10, 25 and 50 kuruş and one lira.

➡ ATMs are widely available.

→ Visa and MasterCard are widely accepted by hotels, shops and restaurants, although often not by pensions and local restaurants outside the main tourist areas. You can also get cash advances on these cards. Amex is less commonly accepted outside top-end establishments.

Moneychangers

The Turkish lira is weak against Western currencies, and you will probably get a better exchange rate in Turkey than elsewhere. The lira is virtually worthless outside Turkey, so make sure you spend it all before leaving.

US dollars and euros are the easiest currencies to change. You'll get better rates at exchange offices, which often don't charge commission, than at banks. Turkey has no black market.

Tipping

Turkey is fairly European in its approach to tipping and you won't be pestered for baksheesh. Tipping is customary in restaurants, hotels and taxis; optional elsewhere.

Restaurants A few coins in budget eateries; 10% to 15% of the bill in midrange and top-end establishments.

Taxis Round up metered fares to the nearest 50 kuruş.

OPENING HOURS

Standard hours.

Information 8.30am to noon and 1.30pm to 5pm Monday to Friday

Eating breakfast 7.30am to 10am, lunch noon to 2.30pm, dinner 6.30pm to 10pm

Drinking 4pm to late

Nightclubs 11pm to late

Shopping 9am to 6pm Monday to Friday (longer in tourist areas and big cities – including weekend opening)

Government departments, offices and banks 8.30am to noon and 1.30pm to 5pm Monday to Friday

PUBLIC HOLIDAYS

New Year's Day (Yılbaşı) 1 January

National Sovereignty & Children's Day (Ulusal Egemenlik ve Çocuk Günü) 23 April

International Workers' Day (May Day) 1 May

Youth & Sports Day (Gençlik ve Spor Günü) 19 May

Şeker Bayramı (Ramazan Bayramı) Varies; June 2017 and 2018

Victory Day (Zafer Bayramı) 30 August

Kurban Bayramı (Festival of the Sacrifice) Varies; September 2017, August 2018. The most important holiday of the year, transport and accommodation fill up fast.

Republic Day (Cumhuriyet Bayramı) 28 to 29 October

TELEPHONE

→ Payphones require cards that can be bought at telephone centres or, for a small mark-up, at some shops.

→ If you set up a roaming facility with your home phone provider, you should be able to connect your mobile to a network.

→ If you buy a local SIM card and use it in your home mobile, the network detects and bars foreign phones within a month.

→ To avoid barring, register your phone when you buy your Turkish SIM. At a certified cell phone shop, show your passport and fill in a short form declaring your phone is in Turkey.

TRAVEL WITH CHILDREN

Your *Çocuklar* (children) will be welcomed wherever they go. Your journey will be peppered with exclamations of *Maşallah* (glory be to God) and your children will be clutched into the adoring arms of strangers.

→ Cots are increasingly common; many hotels will organise one with advance notice.

→ Children's menus are uncommon outside tourist areas, but restaurants will often prepare special dishes for children.

→ High chairs are by no means common, but increasingly widespread in tourist areas (apart from İstanbul).

→ Public baby-changing facilities are rare.

→ Breastfeeding in public is uncommon; best to do so in a private or discreet place.

→ Free travel on public transport within cities, and discounts on longer journeys, are common for children.

→ Dangerous drivers and uneven surfaces make using strollers an extreme sport.

→ Pasteurised UHT milk is sold in cartons everywhere, but fresh milk is harder to find.

→ Migros supermarkets have the best range of baby food.

→ Most supermarkets stock formula (although it is very expensive) and vitamin-fortified rice cereal.

→ Disposable *bebek bezi* (nappies or diapers) are readily available.

VISAS

→ Nationals of countries including Denmark, Finland, France, Germany, Israel, Italy, Japan, New Zealand, Sweden and Switzerland don't need a visa to visit Turkey for up to 90 days.

→ Nationals of countries including Australia, Austria, Belgium, Canada, Ireland, the Netherlands, Norway, Portugal, Spain, the UK and USA need a visa, which must be purchased online at www.evisa.gov.tr before travelling.

→ Most nationalities, including the above, are given a 90-day multiple-entry visa.

➡ In most cases, the 90-day visa stipulates 'per period 180 days'. This means you can spend three months in Turkey within a six-month period; when you leave after three months, you can't re-enter for three months.

➡ At the time of writing, the e-visa cost US$20 for most nationalities, with a few exceptions including Australians and Canadians, who pay US$60, and South Africans, who receive it free.

➡ Your passport must be valid for at least six months from the date you enter the country.

WOMEN TRAVELLERS

Travelling in Turkey is straightforward for women, provided you follow some simple guidelines.

➡ Outside tourist areas, the cheapest hotels are generally not suitable for lone women. Stick with family-oriented midrange hotels.

➡ If there is a knock on your hotel door late at night, don't open it; in the morning, complain to the manager.

➡ Look at what local women are wearing. Cleavage and short skirts without leggings are a no-no everywhere except nightclubs in İstanbul and heavily touristed destinations along the coast.

➡ When travelling by taxi and dolmuş, avoid getting into the seat beside the driver, as this can be misinterpeted as a come-on.

ⓘ Getting There & Away

AIR
Airports

Atatürk International Airport (p537) İstanbul's main airport is in Yeşilköy, 23km west of Sultanahmet. The international terminal (Dış Hatlar) is polished and organised.

Sabiha Gökçen International Airport (p587) This airport on İstanbul's Asian side is popular with low-cost European airlines, but is not as conveniently located as Atatürk.

Antalya International Airport (Antalya Havalimanı; ☎ 444 7423; www.aytport.com) Receives flights from across Turkey and Europe.

Adnan Menderes Airport (☎ 455 0000; www.adnanmenderesairport.com) There are many flights to İzmir's Adnan Menderes Airport from European destinations.

Bodrum International Airport (www.bodrum-airport.com) Receives flights from all over Europe, mostly with charters and budget airlines in summer, and from İstanbul and Ankara with the Turkish airlines. Also known as Milas-Bodrum Airport.

Airlines

Turkish Airlines (☎ 0850-333 0849 www.thy.com), the national carrier, has extensive international and domestic networks including budget subsidiaries **Sun Express** (☎ 444 0797; www.sunexpress.com) and **Anadolu**

Jet (☎ 444 2538; www.anadolujet.com). It is generally considered a safe airline, and its operational safety is certified by the International Air Transport Association (IATA).

LAND

There are direct bus services to İstanbul from Austria, Albania, Bulgaria, Germany, Greece, Hungary, Kosovo, Macedonia, Romania and Slovenia.The major bus companies that operate these routes are **Metro Turizm** (☎ 0850 222 3455; www.metroturizm.com.tr), **Ulusoy** (☎ 0850 811 1888; www.ulusoy.com.tr) and **Varan** (☎ 0850 811 1999; www.varan.com.tr). Currently the only train route operating between Europe and İstanbul is the daily Bosfor/Balkan Ekspresi to Bucharest (Romania) andSofia (Bulgaria). See **Turkish State Railways** (☎ 444 8233; www.tcdd.gov.tr) for details.

SEA

Departure times and routes change between seasons, with fewer ferries generally running in the winter. Ferry lines (www.ferrylines.com) is a good starting point for information. The following is a list of ferry routes from Turkey:

Ayvalık–Lesvos, Greece Jale Tour (www.jaletour.com)

Bodrum–Kos, Greece Bodrum Ferryboat Association (www.bodrumferryboat.com); Bodrum-Express Lines (www.bodrumexpresslines.com)

Bodrum–Rhodes, Greece Bodrum Ferryboat Association

Datça–Rhodes, Greece Knidos Yachting (www.knidosyachting.com)

Datça–Simi, Greece Knidos Yachting

Marmaris–Rhodes, Greece Yeşil Marmaris-Travel & Yachting (www.yesilmarmaris.com)

Trabzon–Sochi, Russia Olympia Line (www.olympia-line.ru), Öz Star Denizcilik (Princess-Victoria), Sarı Denizcilik (www.saridenizcilik.com/en); see also www.seaport-sochi.ru andwww.al-port.com

Turgutreis–Kos, Greece Bodrum Ferryboat Association

ⓘ Getting Around

BUS

➡ Turkey's intercity bus system is as good as any you'll find, with modern, comfortable coaches crossing the country at all hours and for very reasonable prices.

➡ Major companies with extensive networks include **Kamil Koç** (☎ 444 0562; www.kamilkoc.com.tr), Metro Turizm and Ulusoy.

➡ A town's otogar is often on the outskirts, but most bus companies provide a *servis* (free shuttle bus) to/from the centre.

➡ Local routes are usually operated by dolmuşes (minibuses), which might run to a timetable or set off when full.

CAR & MOTORCYCLE

» Turkey has the world's second-highest petrol prices. Petrol/diesel costs about ₺5 per litre.

» An international driving permit (IDP) is not obligatory, but handy if your driving licence is from a country likely to seem obscure to a Turkish police officer.

» You must be at least 21 years old to hire a car. Rental charges are similar to those in Europe.

» You must have third-party insurance if you are bringing your own car into the country. Buying it at the border is a straightforward process (one month €80).

» Road accidents claim about 10,000 lives in Turkey each year.

TRAIN

The Turkish State Railways network covers the country fairly well, with the notable exception of the coastlines. Most train journey times are notoriously long with roundabout routes, but the entire system is currently being overhauled. Check out the website The Man In Seat Sixty-One (www.seat61.com/turkey2) for details on Turkish train travel.

InterRail, Balkan Flexipass and Eurodomino passes are valid on the Turkish railway network, but Eurail passes are not.

Balkans

Best Places to Eat

➡ To Je To (p663)

➡ Kaj Pero (p656)

➡ Manastirska Magernitsa (p671)

➡ Villa Spiza (p622)

➡ Stariya Chinar (p682)

Best Places to Sleep

➡ Goli + Bosi (p622)

➡ Green Studio Hostel (p663)

➡ Old Town Hostel (p642)

➡ Trip N Hostel (p649)

➡ Hotel-Mehana Gurko (p680)

Why Go?

The Balkans are fascinating and fast-changing slices of Europe, where the influence of the Ottoman Empire is never far away and the ancient and modern often coexist. Fabulous Croatia, famed for its islands and dramatic coastline, as well as the walled city of Dubrovnik, is the most visited of the pack. But don't discount exciting Serbia with its fortress cities and famous music festival, Muslim-influenced Bosnia's dramatic countryside and two gorgeous Old Towns, the magnificent scenery of Macedonia and Montenegro, or the sublime beaches of Albania. Travel here is a little rough around the edges compared with destinations further north and west, but few people visit the Balkans without leaving in awe, with their preconceptions smashed.

Fast Facts

Capitals Zagreb (Croatia), Sofia (Bulgaria), Sarajevo (Bosnia & Hercegovina), Belgrade (Serbia), Podgorica (Montenegro), Skopje (Macedonia), Pristina (Kosovo), Tirana (Albania)

Currencies Euro € (Montenegro, Kosovo), Kuna KN (Croatia), Lev lv (Bulgaria), Convertible Mark KM (Bosnia & Hercegovina), Dinar DIN (Serbia), Denar MKD (Macedonia), lekë (Albania)

Languages Albanian, Bosnian, Bulgarian, Croatian, Montenegrin, Macedonian, Serbian

Visas Not needed for EU, US, Canadian, Australian or New Zealand citizens

Time zones Central European Time; GMT/UTC plus one hour

WORTH A TRIP: HVAR ISLAND

Admire the Venetian architecture and vibrant nightlife of Hvar Town. (p623)

WORTH A TRIP: MOSTAR

Take a day trip to Hercegovina's most charming town. (p634)

Balkans Highlights

1 Zagreb Croatia's capital beckons, with superb museums and sophisticated cafe culture. (p614)

2 Split Dalmatia's great Adriatic port boasts the fabulous Diocletian's Palace and a stunning setting. (p619)

3 Dubrovnik See the unforgettable city walls and marble streets in Croatia's most famous city. (p625)

4 Kotor Montenegro's most beautiful town sits at the end of an enormous bay, with impressive scenery. (p640)

5 Albanian Riviera Fabulous scenery and long stretches

OFF THE BEATEN TRACK:
PRISTINA

Explore Kosovo's plucky and
fast-changing capital.
(p661)

of magnificent beach make
Albania's coast a must. (p652)

6 Berat Albania's 'town of a
thousand windows'. (p651)

7 Ohrid take a dip in this
ancient lake. (p656)

8 Belgrade Serbia's
hedonistic capital is a
fascinating and fast-changing
place. (p662)

9 Veliko Târnovo Bulgaria's
most beautiful town sits

towering above the fast-
flowing Yantra River. (p678)

10 Black Sea Bulgaria's
gorgeous sandy coast has
great beaches to relax on.
(p680)

Croatia & Serbia's
TOP EXPERIENCES

Precariously poised between the Balkans and Central Europe, this land has been passed between competing kingdoms, empires and republics for millennia, and they left a rich cultural legacy. Venetian palazzos snuggle up to Napoleonic forts, Roman columns protrude from early Slavic churches, and Viennese mansions face off with Socialist Realist sculpture. Museums showcase treasures from most key stages of Europe's history, telling a story that is in equal parts fascinating and horrifying.

While political correctness is about as commonplace as a nonsmoking bar, Serbia (p662) is a cultural crucible: the art nouveau town of Subotica revels in its proximity to Hungary, bohemian Niš echoes to the clip-clop of Roma horse carts, and minaret-studded Novi Pazar nudges some of the most sacred sites in Serbian Orthodoxy. And in the mountains, ancient traditions coexist with après-ski bling.

★ Dubrovnik

Croatia's most popular attraction, Dubrovnik is a Unesco World Heritage Site for good reason. This historic walled city was relentlessly shelled during Croatia's 1990s' Homeland War. Now, its mighty walls, monasteries, medieval churches, graceful squares and fascinating residential quarters all look magnificent again. For an unrivalled perspective of this Adriatic pearl, first take the cable car up to Mt Srđ, then get up close to the city by walking Dubrovnik's walls, as history unfolds from the battlements. (p625)

★ Hvar Island

Come high summer, there's no better place to get your groove on than Hvar Town. Gorgeous tanned people descend from their yachts in droves for round-the-clock fun on this glam isle. With après-beach parties as the sun drops below the horizon far out in the Adriatic, designer cocktails sipped seaside to fresh house tunes spun by DJs, and full-moon beach parties, Hvar caters to a well-dressed, party-happy crowd. Plus there's Hvar beyond the party scene, with its gorgeous interior largely uncharted by tourist crowds. (p623)

★ Split

Experience life as it's been lived for thousands of years in Diocletian's Palace, one of the world's most imposing Roman ruins. The mazelike streets of this buzzing quarter, the living heart and soul of Split, are chock-full of bars, shops and restaurants. Getting lost in the labyrinth of narrow streets, passageways and courtyards is one of Croatia's most enchanting experiences – and it's small enough that you'll always find your way out easily. Escape the palace walls for a drink on the marble-paved, palm-fringed Riva along the water's edge. (p619)

GETTING AROUND

➡ Both Croatia and Serbia are easy countries to travel in, with good bus and train networks connecting all major cities and towns.

➡ There are multiple international airports in both countries, the busiest of which are Zagreb, Belgrade, Dubrovnik and Split.

➡ Croatia has many ferries connecting the mainland to its many islands, as well as to more distant ports in Italy.

➡ Car hire is easy and straightforward in both countries.

➡ No city in either country currently has a subway system: buses and trams are the best way to get around urban areas.

➡ Taxis are affordable and a reliable way to get around cities after dark.

★ Zagreb

Elevated to the status of ritual, having coffee in one of Zagreb's outdoor cafes is a must, involving hours of people-watching, gossiping and soul-searching, unhurried by waiters. To experience the truly European and vibrant cafe culture, grab a table along the pedestrian cobbled Tkalčićeva, or one of the pavement tables on Trg Petra Preradovića or Bogovićeva. Don't miss the Saturday morning *špica*, the coffee-drinking and people-watching ritual in the city centre that forms the peak of Zagreb's weekly social calendar. (p614)

★ Plitvice Lakes National Park

A turquoise ribbon of crystal water and gushing waterfalls in the forested heart of continental Croatia, Plitvice Lakes National Park is an awesome sight. There are dozens of lakes, all in an incredible hue that's a product of the karst terrain. Travertine expanses covered with mossy plants divide the lakes, while boardwalks allow you to step right over this exquisite water world. (p618)

★ Belgrade

Outspoken, adventurous, proud and audacious: Belgrade is by no means a 'pretty' capital, but its gritty exuberance makes it one of the most happening cities in Europe. Marvel at its mighty Kalemegdan Citadel and its creative headquarters in the riverside Savamala quarter, walk in the footsteps of Tesla and Tito, and party the night away on a *splav* (river barge nightclub). Whatever you do in Belgrade, you won't be bored for a moment. (p662)

★ EXIT Festival

The now world-famous EXIT Festival (p667) takes place each July in Novi Sad's atmospheric Petrovaradin Citadel (p666). The first event in 2000 lasted 100 days and galvanised a generation of young Serbs against the Milošević regime. Today it's Eastern Europe's most famous music festival and attracts around 200,000 revelers from around the world, and the likes of Patti Smith, Kraftwerk and the Pet Shop Boys.

★ Croatia's Coastline

Croatia's extraordinary island-speckled coastline is indisputably its main attraction. Part of the appeal lies in its diversity. You'll find glitz and glamour in places like Hvar, where fancy yachts and fancier threads are de rigueur. In other locales Croatian families get busy with buckets and spades. For those wanting peace and quiet, there are plenty of secluded coves and Robinson Crusoe–style islets to discover.

if Croatia were 100 people

90 would be Croat
6 would be Other
4 would be Serb

religious groups
(% of population)

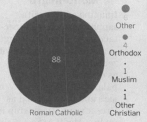

88
Roman Catholic

Other

4
Orthodox

1
Muslim

1
Other Christian

population per sq km

SERBIA   HEGARY   BOSNIA & HERCEGOVINA

= 15 people

When to Go

Zagreb

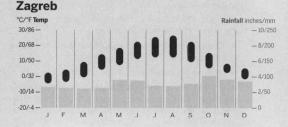

Bosnia & Hercegovina & Montenegro's
TOP EXPERIENCES

This craggily beautiful land retains some lingering scars from the heartbreaking civil war in the 1990s. But today visitors will more likely remember Bosnia and Hercegovina (BiH; p630) for its deep, unassuming human warmth and for the intriguing East-meets-West atmosphere born of fascinatingly blended Ottoman and Austro-Hungarian histories. Major drawcards are the reincarnated antique centres of Sarajevo and Mostar, where rebuilt historical buildings counterpoint fashionable bars and wi-fi–equipped cafes. Elsewhere Socialist-era architectural monstrosities are surprisingly rare blots on predominantly rural landscapes. Many Bosnian towns are lovably small, wrapped around medieval castles and surrounded by mountain ridges or cascading river canyons. Few places in Europe offer better rafting or such accessible, inexpensive skiing.

Montenegro

Imagine a place with sapphire beaches as spectacular as Croatia's, rugged peaks as dramatic as Switzerland's, canyons nearly as deep as Colorado's, palazzos as elegant as Venice's and towns as old as Greece's, and then wrap it up in a Mediterranean climate and squish it into an area two-thirds of the size of Wales, and you start to get a picture of Montenegro. You could easily drive clear across the country in a day – or spend a month and be left wanting more. Ironically, this tiny place is populated by giants – arguably the tallest people in the world. (p638)

Mostar

Mostar's world-famous 16th-century stone bridge is the centrepiece of its alluring, extensively restored Old Town, and as you explore the narrow cobbled streets you'll discover ever-new angles from which to photograph young men throwing themselves off this famous structure into the deep river below: an unforgettable sight. Further from the centre a scattering of shattered building shells remain as moving testament to the terrible 1990s conflict that divided the city. Contradictory and charismatic, Mostar never fails to beguile. (p634)

Sarajevo

Despite its name being synonymous with the 1990s conflict that tore the region around, Sarajevo today boasts an impressively restored historic centre full of welcoming cafes and good-value lodgings. The bullet holes have been largely plastered over on the city's curious architectural mixture of Ottoman and Austro Hungarian buildings. The antique stone-flagged alleys of Baščaršija may give the Old Town core a certain Turkish feel, but the spirit of the Bosnian capital is progressive and looking determinedly towards the future. (p630)

GETTING AROUND

➡ Bosnia & Hercegovina and Montenegro are both fairly easy to get around.

➡ Montenegro in particular has a good train network.

➡ In both countries bus is the most common way to get around.

➡ In the cities, buses, trolleybuses and trams are the only forms of public transport.

➡ Taxis are generally affordable for short hops and in urban areas.

➡ Neither country has domestic flights.

➡ Driving is possible and fairly hassle-free in both countries, with car-hire agencies present in all cities and a decent and well-maintained road network.

⭐ Kotor

Time-travel back to a Europe of moated walled towns with shadowy lanes and stone churches on every square. It may not be as impressive as Dubrovnik's or as shiny as Budva's, but Kotor's Old Town feels much more lived in and ever so dramatic. The way it seems to grow out of the surrounding sheer grey mountains adds a thrill of foreboding to the experience – it's as if they could at any point choose to squeeze the little town in a rocky embrace. (p640)

⭐ Perast

An oversized village comprised almost entirely of elegant baroque palaces and churches, romantic Perast forms a worthy centrepiece to the entire Bay of Kotor. The positioning is perfect, sitting at the apex of the inner bay, looking straight down the narrow channel leading to the outer section. Catch a boat to Gospa od Škrpjela (Our-Lady-of-the-Rocks), one of two tiny islands sitting just offshore, where a sky-blue dome covers a church filled with votive offerings left by grateful sailors. (p642)

⭐ Durmitor National Park

Reflecting the beauty of the imposing grey peaks of the Durmitor range are 18 glacial lakes, known locally as *gorske oči* (mountain eyes). The largest and most beautiful of them is the Black Lake, its inky appearance caused by the black pines that surround it and the peak known as

The Bear (Meded) rearing above it. The Black Lake is a breeze to get to and a delight to walk around, but other, more remote lakes await discovery further up, along the park's hiking trails. (p645)

⭐ Montenegro's Coast

It's barely 100km from tip to toe, but Montenegro's coast is quite extraordinary. Mountains jut sharply from crystal-clear waters in such a way that the word 'looming' is unavoidable. As if that wasn't picturesque enough, ancient walled towns cling to the rocks and dip their feet in the water like they're the ones on holiday. In summer the whole scene is bathed in the scent of wild herbs, conifers and Mediterranean blossoms. The word 'magical' is similarly impossible to avoid.

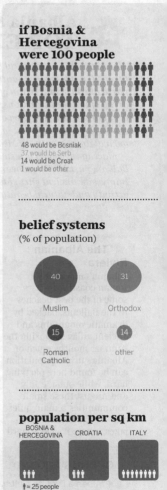

if Bosnia & Hercegovina were 100 people

48 would be Bosniak
37 would be Serb
14 would be Croat
1 would be other

belief systems
(% of population)

40 Muslim
31 Orthodox
15 Roman Catholic
14 other

population per sq km

BOSNIA & HERCEGOVINA | CROATIA | ITALY

† ≈ 25 people

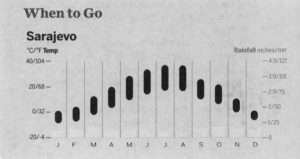

When to Go

Sarajevo

°C/°F Temp

40/104 —
20/68 —
0/32 —
-20/-4 —

Rainfall inches/mm

— 4.9/125
— 3.9/100
— 2.9/75
— 2/50
— 1/25
— 0

J F M A M J J A S O N D

Albania & Macedonia's
TOP EXPERIENCES

Albania (p647) has natural beauty in such abundance that you might wonder why it's taken 20 years for the country to take off as a tourist destination, since the end of a particularly brutal strain of communism in 1991. Today Albania offers a remarkable array of unique attractions, not least due to its former isolation: ancient mountain behaviour codes, forgotten archaeological sites and villages where time seems to have stood still. With stunning mountain scenery, a thriving capital in Tirana and beaches to rival anywhere in the Mediterranean, it has become the sleeper hit of the Balkans.

Macedonia (p654) is a small nation with a complex and fascinating history. Part Balkan, part Mediterranean and rich in Greek, Roman and Ottoman history, it offers impressive ancient sites side by side with buzzing modernity, packing in much more activity and natural beauty than would seem possible for a country its size.

The Albanian Riviera

Albania's magnificent Ionian coastline boasts some of the best beaches in the Balkans, backed by dramatic mountains and ancient villages. During the summer months much of Albania's urban population can be found here partying hard, while outside July and August these small communities remain quiet and laid-back fishing villages, where it's never hard to escape the crowds and find your own idyll among the olive groves. Beaches to look out for include Drymades, Dhërmi, Jal, Bunec and Borsh. (p652)

Berat

Explore the Unesco World Heritage–listed museum town of Berat, the so-called 'city of a thousand windows', one of Albania's most charming and popular destinations. Clamber around the ancient hilltop Kalaja (Fortress) and witness a residential neighbourhood where locals go about their daily lives surrounded by crumbling churches and haunting ruins. Meanwhile, down in the valley from the quiet Gorica quarter, the view of the white-painted Ottoman mansions overlooking the river from the other side is quite simply unforgettable. (p651)

Tirana

The plucky Albanian capital is something of a comeback kid. Once a byword for backwardness and isolation, the city has in the past two decades transformed itself into a vibrant, young and exciting place, the mad whirl around which modern Albania now spins. Sip cocktails in the trendy Blloku neighbourhood, join locals on their *xhiro* (evening stroll) along the city's Italianate boulevards, and marvel at Albania's complex and brutal history at the excellent National Museum. Tirana bores nobody. (p647)

GETTING AROUND

➡ Albania is quite a bit harder to get around than many of its neighbours.

➡ Albania's train network is ancient and not worth bothering with unless you're a train enthusiast.

➡ Buses and furgons (minibuses) are the main means of transport, though they are often slow, irregular and crowded.

➡ Macedonia is easier to get around, with a more modern train network and better roads.

➡ Driving is possible in both countries: hiring cars is easy, though be prepared for some pretty crazy drivers.

➡ Neither country operates internal flights.

➡ In towns, buses and taxis are the only public transport options.

⭐ The Accursed Mountains

Albania's natural landscape is its greatest drawcard, and it is best experienced in the country's north, where the Accursed Mountains offer superb hiking, traditional villages that still look like they're living in the 19th century, and ferry rides across stunning Lake Koman. The most popular hike is the gorgeous and only moderately challenging day trek between Valbona and Theth, which shouldn't be missed. For keen hikers there are dozens more opportunities to walk in Albania's northern wilderness. (p650)

⭐ Lake Ohrid

Wonderful Lake Ohrid's rich azure waters enchant visitors wherever they encounter them along the long shoreline shared between Macedonia and Albania. But the Macedonian town of Ohrid wins the most affection and is definitely the best place to experience the lake. Here the placid waters are backed by an ancient town filled with churches and overseen by a huge fortress. Beaches and rocky promontories can be easily accessed, boat trips taken, and delicious fresh fish enjoyed in the town's restaurants. (p656)

⭐ Skopje

The Macedonian capital is a quirky and charming place, and one that presents many faces to visitors. Its soul is arguably to be found in the wonderful Čaršija (old Turkish bazaar) though, a tangle of cobbled streets and ancient houses where you can get lost for hours. Here you'll find the famous Sveti Spas Church, with its ornate, hand-carved iconostasis, several beautiful mosques, some excellent museums and Tvrdina Kale Fortress, Skopje's guardian since the 5th century. Constant urban renewal has made the city a bizarre jigsaw puzzle the older sites, communist-era centre and contemporary building spree combine to create a multifaceted city that never fails to surprise. (p654)

⭐ Regional Macedonia

Hiking, mountain biking, wine tasting and climbing beckon in Macedonia, while the remote mountains conceal fascinating medieval monasteries, superb alpine trails and traditional Balkan villages. Ohrid, noted for its beaches, summer festival, sublime Byzantine churches and 34km-long lake, is the centre of the country's tourism industry, while in the winter months skiing at resorts such as Mavrovo become the main draw.

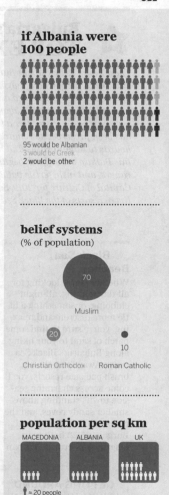

if Albania were 100 people

95 would be Albanian
3 would be Greek
2 would be other

belief systems
(% of population)

70
Muslim

20
Christian Orthodox

10
Roman Catholic

population per sq km

MACEDONIA ALBANIA UK

♦ = 20 people

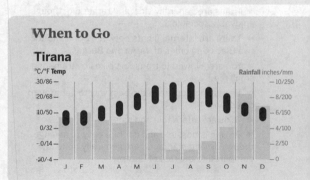

When to Go

Tirana

°C/°F Temp

-30/86-
-20/68-
-10/50-
-0/32-
--0/14-
--20/4-

Rainfall inches/mm

-10/250
-8/200
-6/150
-4/100
-2/50
-0

J F M A M J J A S O N D

Bulgaria's
TOP EXPERIENCES

There's a lot to love about Bulgaria (p670): just ask the Greeks, Romans, Byzantines and Turks, all of whom fought to claim it as their own. Billed as the oldest nation on the continent – it preceded ancient Greece by at least 1500 years – Bulgaria is rich with ancient treasure: stories abound of locals planting gardens only to have them ripped up by archaeologists after a turn of the spade unearthed priceless antiquities. The past has been preserved to remarkable effect; everything from Thracian tombs and Hellenic hoards to Roman ruins and medieval fortresses are easily accessible. Centuries later, this Balkan beauty still beguiles, with a come-hither coastline, voluptuous mountain ranges, and lush, fertile valleys laden with vines and roses. Plovdiv is the European Capital of Culture for 2019, Sofia has cool cred to rival any major metropolis, and the lively resorts of the Black Sea coast teem with modern-day pleasure pilgrims.

 Black Sea Beaches

Whether you're looking for all-day tanning, all-night clubbing, or something a little more discrete and relaxing, you're sure to find some patch of sand to your liking along Bulgaria's Black Sea coast. Away from the big, brash package resorts, you'll come across charming seaside towns standing above smaller sandy coves, and the cities of Varna (p680) and Burgas (p682) both have lengthy, less-crowded urban beaches. If it's solitude you seek, head for the more remote beaches to the far north and south.

 Rila Monastery

Set peacefully in a forested valley south of Sofia, Rila Monastery is Bulgaria's biggest and most storied spiritual treasure; a former centre of learning and culture that kept national spirits up during the Ottoman occupation. A Unesco World Heritage Site since 1983, the monastery grew from a 10th-century hermit's hut, and has been rebuilt many times since. Its elaborate arches and precious frescoes and icons create a sublime and sumptuous atmosphere. Today's architectural incarnation of the monastery is considered a 19th-century Bulgarian Renaissance masterpiece. (p676)

Veliko Târnovo

The unquestioned highlight of Bulgaria's central heartland – the grand old city of the tsars, Bulgaria's capital in medieval times – offers a mix of antiquity, boutique bliss and nightlife. This university town, set high above the ribboning Yantra River, is popular with visitors both local and foreign, who marvel at the oddly endearing 'Sound and Light Show' held nightly at the impressive Tsarevets Fortress, a still-robust medieval citadel. It's also a great base for local hikes. (p678)

Plovdiv

Arty, fun-loving Plovdiv makes a great alternative

GETTING AROUND

➡ Bulgaria's bus and train network is extensive and affordable.

➡ Trains are generally slow and rather old, though enjoyably sociable.

➡ There are internal flights between Sofia and the two Black Sea cities of Varna and Burgas.

➡ You are allowed to transport bikes by train for a small fee.

➡ Trams and buses are the best way to get around cities.

➡ Taxis are affordable and safe.

➡ Driving is possible and car hire easy to arrange, though driving standards are generally quite low compared to the rest of Europe.

if Bulgaria were 100 people

77 would be Bulgarian
8 would be Turk
4 would be Roma
11 would be other

to Sofia. It's an eminently walkable and safe student city, loaded with great restaurants, bars, and galleries, and boasting a dynamic cultural scene. The evocative Old Town features National Revival–era homes clinging to cobblestoned lanes, museums and galleries, and a magnificent Roman amphitheatre; while the hip Kapana district is home to unpretentious indie cafes and bars. Plovdiv also makes a great base for forays into the Rodopi Mountains, famous for hiking and caving. (p674)

★ Sofia's Alexander Nevski Memorial Church

Rising majestically over the rooftops of the Bulgarian capital, this beautiful Orthodox church, dedicated to the memory of the 200,000 Russian soldiers who died fighting for Bulgaria's independence in the Russo-Turkish War (1877–78), took 30 years to construct, and was completed in 1912. The shimmering golden domes and half-domes are visible several streets away, while the vast, candlelit interior, heavy with incense, is decorated with Italian marble, alabaster and fading murals. Daily services, led by robed, white-bearded

priests, and accompanied by chanting choirs, can be moving experiences. (p670)

★ Wine Tasting

Bulgaria's winemaking tradition dates to ancient Thracian times. Fine wine has been enjoyed here by everyone from Roman writers and French crusaders to former British Prime Minister Winston Churchill, who used to order barrels of the local red from Melnik (p677) – a village in the southwest of the country that remains a great place for sampling wines. Distinct wine-growing regions exist from the Danube to the Black Sea to the Thracian Plain, and numerous wineries offer tastings that are usually complemented by meats, cheeses and memorable rustic views.

belief systems
(% of population)

60 — Eastern Orthodox
7 — Muslim (Sunni)
1 — Muslim (Shia)
28 — other
4 — none

population per sq km

BULGARIA   GREECE   ROMANIA

⸙ ≈ 15 people

When to Go

Sofia

°C/°F Temp · Rainfall inches/mm
30/86 — — 10/250
20/68 — — 8/200
10/50 — — 6/150
0/32 — — 4/100
-10/14 — — 2/50
-20/-4 — — 0

J F M A M J J A S O N D

CROATIA

Zagreb

📋 01 / POP 792,875

Zagreb has culture, arts, music, architecture, gastronomy and all the other things that make a quality capital city – it's no surprise that the number of visitors has risen sharply in the last couple of years. Croatia's coastal attractions aside, Zagreb has finally been discovered as a popular city-break destination in its own right.

◉ Sights

Museum of Broken Relationships MUSEUM
(www.brokenships.com; Ćirilometodska 2; adult/concession 30/20KN; ⊙9am-10.30pm) Explore mementos that remain after a relationship ends at Zagreb's quirkiest museum. The innovative exhibit toured the world until it settled here in its permanent home. On display are donations from around the globe, in a string of all-white rooms with vaulted ceilings and epoxy-resin floors.

Dolac Market MARKET
(⊙6.30am-3pm Mon-Fri, to 2pm Sat, to 1pm Sun) Zagreb's colourful fruit and vegetable market is just north of Trg Bana Jelačića. Traders from all over Croatia come to sell their products at this buzzing centre of activity. Dolac has been heaving since the 1930s, when the city authorities set up a market space on the 'border' between the Upper and Lower Towns.

**Cathedral of the Assumption
of the Blessed Virgin Mary** CHURCH
(Katedrala Marijina Uznešenja; Kaptol 31; ⊙10am-5pm Mon-Sat, 1-5pm Sun) Kaptol Square is dominated by this cathedral, formerly known as St Stephen's. Its twin spires – seemingly permanently under repair – soar over the city. Although the cathedral's original Gothic structure has been transformed many times over, the sacristy still contains a cycle of **frescoes** dating from the 13th century. An earthquake in 1880 badly damaged the cathedral; reconstruction in a neo-Gothic style began around the turn of the 20th century.

Lotrščak Tower HISTORIC BUILDING
(Kula Lotrščak; Strossmayerovo Šetalište 9; adult/concession 20/10KN; ⊙9am-9pm) The tower was built in the middle of the 13th century in order to protect the southern city gate. Climb it for a sweeping 360-degree view of the city.

Near the tower is a **funicular railway** (www.zet.hr/english/funicular.aspx; ticket 4KN; ⊙6.30am-10pm), constructed in 1888, which connects the Lower and Upper Towns.

Trg Bana Jelačića SQUARE
Zagreb's main orientation point and its geographic heart is Trg Bana Jelačića – it's where most people arrange to meet up. If you enjoy people-watching, sit in one of the cafes and watch the tramloads of people getting out, greeting each other and dispersing among the newspaper and flower sellers.

St Mark's Church CHURCH
(Crkva Svetog Marka; Trg Svetog Marka 5; ⊙Mass 7.30am & 6pm Mon-Fri, 7.30am Sat, 10am, 11am & 6pm Sun) This 13th-century church is one of Zagreb's most emblematic buildings. Its colourful tiled roof, constructed in 1880, has the medieval coat of arms of Croatia, Dalmatia and Slavonia on the left side, and the emblem of Zagreb on the right. The Gothic portal, composed of 15 figures in shallow niches, was sculpted in the 14th century. The interior contains sculptures by Ivan Meštrović. You can enter the anteroom only during opening hours; the church itself is open only at Mass times. From late April to October there's a guard-changing ceremony outside the church every Saturday and Sunday at noon.

City Museum MUSEUM
(Muzej Grada Zagreba; 📞01-48 51 926; www.mgz.hr; Opatička 20; adult/concession/family 30/20/50KN; ⊙10am-6pm Tue-Fri, 11am-7pm Sat, 10am-2pm Sun; 🖶) Since 1907, the 17th-century Convent of St Claire has housed this historical museum, which presents the history of Zagreb through documents, artwork and crafts, as well as interactive exhibits that fascinate kids. Look for the scale model of old Gradec. Summaries of the exhibits are posted in English.

Museum of Contemporary Art MUSEUM
(Muzej Suvremene Umjetnosti; 📞01-60 52 700; www.msu.hr; Avenija Dubrovnik 17; adult/concession 30/15KN; ⊙11am-6pm Tue-Fri & Sun, to 8pm Sat) Housed in a stunning city icon designed by local star architect Igor Franić, this swanky museum displays both solo and thematic group shows by Croatian and international artists in its 17,000 sq metres. The permanent display, called *Collection in Motion*, showcases 620 edgy works by 240 artists, roughly half of whom are Croatian. There's a packed schedule of film, theatre, concerts and performance art year-round.

☞ Tours

Blue Bike Tours   BICYCLE TOUR
(☑ 098 18 83 344; www.zagrebbybike.com) To experience Zagreb on a bike, book one of the tours – choose between Lower Town, Upper Town or Novi Zagreb – departing daily at 10am and 2pm from Trg Bana Jelačića 15. Tours last around two hours and cost 175KN.

Funky Zagreb   TOUR
(www.funky-zagreb.com) Personalised tours that range in theme from wine tasting (340KN for 2½ to three hours) to hiking in Zagreb's surroundings (from 720KN per person for a day trip).

🛏 Sleeping

Zagreb's accommodation scene has been undergoing a noticeable change with the arrival of some of Europe's budget airlines. The budget end of the market has picked up greatly and hostels have mushroomed in the last couple of years – as of writing, there are over thirty in Zagreb, from cheap backpacker digs to more stylish hideaways. Several of them have organised a pub crawl three nights per week, with free entrance to clubs and shots to boot (enquire at your hostel).

The city's business and high-end hotels are in full flow, thanks to Zagreb's role as an international conference hot spot.

Prices usually stay the same in all seasons, but be prepared for a 20% surcharge if you arrive during a festival or major event (in particular the autumn fair).

Chillout Hostel Zagreb Downtown   HOSTEL €
(☑ 01-48 49 605; www.chillout-hostel-zagreb.com; Tomićeva 5a; dm 105-125KN, s/d 300/350KN; P✳
@🤶) Located in the tiny pedestrian street with the funicular, this cheerful spot has no less than 170 beds just steps away from Trg Bana Jelačića. The trimmings are plentiful and the vibe friendly. Breakfast is available.

Hobo Bear Hostel   HOSTEL €
(☑ 01-48 46 636; www.hobobearhostel.com; Medulićeva 4; dm from 153KN, d from 436KN; ✳@🤶) Inside a duplex apartment, this sparkling five-dorm hostel has exposed brick walls, hardwood floors, free lockers, a kitchen with free tea and coffee, a common room and book exchange. The three doubles are across the street. Take tram 1, 6 or 11 from Trg Bana Jelačića.

Funk Lounge Hostel   HOSTEL €
(☑ 01-55 52 707; www.funkhostel.hr; Rendićeva 28b; dm 135-180KN, s/d 450/450KN; ✳@🤶)

Located steps from Maksimir Park, this outpost of the original Funk Hostel (southwest of the centre) has friendly staff, neat rooms and a range of freebies, including breakfast, a shot of *rakija* (grappa), toiletries and lockers. On site is a restaurant and bar, and a full kitchen.

Swanky Mint Hostel   HOSTEL €€
(☑ 01-40 04 248; www.swanky-hostel.com/mint/; Ilica 50; dm 125-160KN, s/d 320/520KN, apt 620-760KN; @🤶) Inside a restored textile-dye factory from the 19th century, this new hostel at the heart of town combines industrial chic with creature comforts. Freebies include wi-fi, lockers, towels and a welcome shot of *rakija*. The garden bar serves breakfast and drinks.

✗ Eating

Karijola   PIZZA €
(Vlaška 63; pizzas from 42KN; ⏱11am-midnight Mon-Sat, to 11pm Sun) Locals swear by the crispy, thin-crust pizza churned out of a clay oven at this newer location of Zagreb's best pizza joint. Pizzas come with high-quality ingredients, such as smoked ham, olive oil, rich mozzarella, cherry tomatoes, rocket and shiitake mushrooms.

Tip Top   SEAFOOD €
(Gundulićeva 18; mains from 40KN; ⏱7am-11pm Mon-Sat) We love Tip Top and its wait staff, who still sport old socialist uniforms and scowling faces that eventually turn to smiles. But we mostly love the excellent Dalmatian food. Every day has a different set menu.

★ Mundoaka Street Food   INTERNATIONAL €€
(☑ 01-78 88 777; Petrinjska 2; mains from 45KN; ⏱8am-midnight Mon-Thu, to 1am Fri, 9am-1am Sat) This adorable eatery clad in light wood, with tables outside, serves up American classics – think chicken wings and pork ribs – and a global spectrum of dishes, from Spanish tortillas to *shakshuka* eggs. Great breakfasts, muffins and cakes, all prepared by one of Zagreb's best-known chefs. Reserve ahead.

★ Vinodol   CROATIAN €€
(www.vinodol-zg.hr; Teslina 10; mains from 56KN; ⏱noon-11pm) The well-prepared Central European fare here is much-loved by local and overseas patrons. On warm days, eat on the covered patio (entered through an ivy-clad passageway off Teslina); the cold-weather alternative is the dining hall with vaulted stone ceilings. Highlights include the succulent lamb or veal and potatoes cooked under

Zagreb

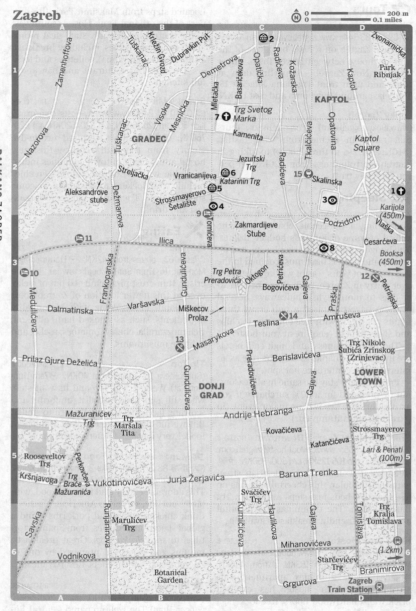

peka (a domed baking lid), as well as *buk-ovače* (local mushrooms).

Lari & Penati MODERN CROATIAN **€€**
(Petrinjska 42a; mains from 60KN; ⊙noon-11pm
Mon-Fri, to 5pm Sat) Small, stylish bistro that

serves up innovative lunch and dinner specials – they change daily according to what's market-fresh. The food is fab, the music cool and the few sidewalk tables lovely in warm weather. Closes for two weeks in August.

Zagreb

🍷 Drinking

In the Upper Town, the chic Tkalčićeva is throbbing with bars and cafes. In the Lower Town, there's bar-lined Bogovićeva and Trg Petra Preradovića (known locally as Cvjetnitrg), the most popular spot in the Lower Town for street performers and occasional bands. One of the nicest ways to see Zagreb is to join in on the špica – Saturday-morning prelunch coffee drinking on the terraces along Bogovićeva, Preradovićeva and Tkalčićeva.

★**Cica**   BAR
(Tkalčićeva 18; ⊘10am-2am) This tiny storefront bar is as underground as it gets on Tkalčićeva. The funky interior has cutting-edge work by local artists and cool flea-market finds. Sample one or – if you dare – all of the 25 kinds of *rakija* that the place is famous for. Herbal, nutty, fruity: if you can think it, they've got it.

Booksa   CAFE
(www.booksa.hr; Martićeva 14d; ⊘11am-8pm Tue-Sun; 🛜) Bookworms and poets, writers and performers, oddballs and artists...basically anyone creative in Zagreb comes here to chat and drink coffee, browse the library, surf with free wi-fi and hear readings at this lovely, book-themed cafe. There are English-language readings here, too; check the website. Closes for three weeks from late July.

Basement Wine Bar   WINE BAR
(Tomićeva 5; ⊘9am-2am Mon-Sat, 4pm-midnight Sun) A city-centre hotspot for sampling Croatian wines by the glass, this basement bar (with a few sidewalk tables) sits right by the funicular. Pair the tipple with meat and cheese platters.

❶ Getting There & Away

BUS

Zagreb's **bus station** (📞060 313 333; www.akz.hr; Avenija M Držića 4) is 1km east of the train station. If you need to store bags, there's a **left-luggage office** (per hour 5KN; ⊘24hr). Trams 2 and 6 run from the bus station to the train station. Tram 6 goes to Trg Bana Jelačića.

Domestic destinations include: Dubrovnik (205KN to 250KN, 9½ to 11 hours, nine to 12 daily), Rovinj (150KN to 195KN, four to six hours, nine to 11 daily) and Split (115KN to 205KN, five to 8½ hours, 32 to 34 daily).

International destinations include Belgrade (220KN, six hours, five daily), Sarajevo (160KN to 210KN, seven to eight hours, four to five daily) and Vienna (225KN to 247KN, five to six hours, three daily).

TRAIN

The **train station** (📞060 333 444; www.hznet.hr; Trg Kralja Tomislava 12) is in the southern part of the city centre. As you come out, you'll see a series of parks and pavilions, directly in front of you, which lead into the town centre.

Domestic trains head to Split (197KN to 208KN, five to seven hours, four daily). There are international departures to Belgrade (188KN, 6½ hours, daily), Ljubljana (127KN, 2½ hours, four daily), Sarajevo (238KN, eight to 9½ hours, daily) and Vienna (520KN, six to seven hours, two daily).

Rovinj

📞052 / POP 14,365

Rovinj (Rovigno in Italian) is coastal Istria's star attraction. While it can get overrun with tourists in summer, and residents have developed a sharp eye for maximising profits by upgrading hotels and restaurants to four-star status, it remains one of the last true Mediterranean fishing ports. Fishers haul their catch into the harbour in the early morning, followed by a horde of squawking gulls, and mend their nets before lunch. Prayers for a good catch are sent forth at the massive Church of St Euphemia, the

WORTH A TRIP

PLITVICE LAKES NATIONAL PARK

The absolute highlight of Croatia's Adriatic hinterland, this glorious expanse of forested hills and turquoise lakes is exquisitely scenic – so much so that in 1979 Unesco proclaimed the **park** (053-751 015; www.np-plitvicka-jezera.hr; adult/child Jul & Aug 180/80KN, Apr-Jun, Sep & Oct 110/55KN, Nov-Mar 55/35KN; 7am-8pm) a World Heritage Site.

Sixteen crystalline lakes tumble into each other via a series of waterfalls and cascades, while clouds of butterflies drift about. It takes upwards of six hours to explore the 18km of wooden footbridges and pathways that snake around the edges of the rumbling water on foot, but you can slice two hours off by taking advantage of the park's free boats and buses (departing every 30 minutes from April to October).

While the park is beautiful year-round, spring and autumn are the best times to visit. In spring and early summer the falls are flush with water, while in autumn the changing leaves put on a colourful display. Winter is also spectacular, although snow can limit access and free park transport doesn't operate. If possible, avoid the peak months of July and August, when the falls reduce to a trickle, parking is problematic, and the sheer volume of visitors can turn the walking tracks into a conga line.

60m-high tower of which punctuates the peninsula. Wooded hills and low-rise hotels surround the Old Town, which is webbed with steep cobbled streets and piazzas. The 14 green islands of the Rovinj archipelago make for a pleasant afternoon away; the most popular are Sveta Katarina and Crveni Otok (Red Island), also known as Sveti Andrija.

The Old Town is contained within an egg-shaped peninsula. About 1.5km south is the Punta Corrente Forest Park and the wooded cape of Zlatni Rt (Golden Cape), with its age-old oak and pine trees, and several large hotels. There are two harbours: the northern open harbour and the small, protected harbour to the south.

◉ Sights

★ **Church of St Euphemia** CHURCH
(Sveta Eufemija; Petra Stankovića; 10am-6pm Jun-Sep, to 4pm May, to 2pm Apr) The town's showcase, this imposing church dominates the old town from its hilltop location in the middle of the peninsula. Built in 1736, it's the largest baroque building in Istria, reflecting the period during the 18th century when Rovinj was its most populous town. Inside, look for the marble **tomb of St Euphemia** behind the right-hand altar.

Batana House MUSEUM
(Pina Budicina 2; adult/concession 10/5KN, with guide 15KN; 10am-2pm & 7-11pm) On the harbour, Batana House is a museum dedicated to the *batana,* a flat-bottomed fishing boat that stands as a symbol of Rovinj's seafaring and fishing traditions. The multimedia

exhibits inside the 17th-century town house have interactive displays, excellent captions and audio with bitinada, which are typical fishers' songs. Check out the spacio, the ground-floor cellar where wine was kept, tasted and sold amid much socialising (open on Tuesday and Thursday).

Grisia STREET
Lined with galleries where local artists sell their work, this cobbled street leads uphill from behind the Balbi Arch to St Euphemia. The winding narrow backstreets that spread around Grisia are an attraction in themselves. Windows, balconies, portals and squares are a pleasant confusion of styles – Gothic, Renaissance, baroque and neoclassical. Notice the unique *fumaioli* (exterior chimneys), built during the population boom, when entire families lived in a single room with a fireplace.

Punta Corrente Forest Park PARK
(Zlatni Rt) Follow the waterfront on foot or by bike past Hotel Park to this verdant area, locally known as Zlatni Rt, about 1.5km south. Covered in oak and pine groves and boasting 10 species of cypress, the park was established in 1890 by Baron Hütterott, an Austrian admiral who kept a villa on Crveni Otok. You can swim off the rocks or just sit and admire the offshore islands.

🛏 Sleeping

Porton Biondi CAMPGROUND €
(052-813 557; www.portonbiondi.hr; Aleja Porton Biondi 1; campsites per person/tent 55/44KN; mid-Mar–Oct) This beachside camping

ground, which sleeps 1200, s about 700m north of the Old Town.

Polari Camping　　　CAMPGROUND **€**
(☑052-801 501; www.campingrovinjvrsar.com; Polari bb; campsites per person/tent 81/92KN; ☺Apr-Sep; @🛜🐕) On the beach about 3km southeast of town, Polari features swimming pools, restaurants and playgrounds.

Villa Baron Gautsch　　　GUESTHOUSE **€€**
(☑052-840 538; www.baron-gautsch.com; IM Ronjgova 7; s/d incl breakfast 293/586KN; ❄🛜) This German-owned *pansion* (guesthouse), up the leafy street leading up from Hotel Park, has 17 spick-and-span rooms, some with terraces and lovely views of the sea and the Old Town. Breakfast is served on the small terrace out the back. It's cash (kuna) only.

✖ Eating

Male Madlene　　　TAPAS **€**
(☑052-815 905; Svetog Križa 2E; snacks from 30KN; ☺11am-2pm & 7-11pm May-Sep) Adorable spot in the owner's tiny living room hanging over the sea, where she serves up creative finger food, with market-fresh ingredients, based on old Italian recipes. Think tuna-filled zucchini, goat-cheese-stuffed peppers and bite-size savoury pies and cakes. A 12-snack plate for two is 100KN. Great Istrian wines by the glass. Reserve ahead, especially for evenings.

Maestral　　　MEDITERRANEAN **€**
(Vladimira Nazora bb; mains from 45KN; ☺11am-midnight) Grab an alfresco table at this tavern on the sea edge for great views of the Old Town and well-prepared simple food that's priced just right. Its *ribarska pogača* (pizza-like pie with salted fish and veggies) is delicious. Located in an old stone house away from the tourist buzz.

Veli Jože　　　SEAFOOD **€**
(Svetog Križa 3; mains from 50KN; ☺11am-11pm) Graze on good Istrian standards, either in the eclectic interior crammed with knick-knacks or at the clutch of outdoor tables with water views.

❶ Getting There & Away

The bus station is just to the southeast of the Old Town. There are daily services to Zagreb (145KN to 180KN, four to five hours), Split (444KN, 11 hours) and Dubrovnik (628KN,15 to 16 hours).

Split

☑021 / POP 178,190

The second-largest city in Croatia, Split (Spalato in Italian) is a great place to see Dalmatian life as it's really lived. Always buzzing, this exuberant city has just the right balance of tradition and modernity. Step inside Diocletian's Palace (a Unesco World Heritage Site and one of the world's most impressive Roman monuments) and you'll see dozens of bars, restaurants and shops thriving amid the atmospheric old walls where Split life has been going on for thousands of years. To top it off, Split has a unique setting: its dramatic coastal mountains act as the perfect backdrop to the turquoise waters of the Adriatic. You'll get a chance to appreciate this gorgeous cityscape when making a ferry journey to or from the city.

◉ Sights

★**Diocletian's Palace**　　　HISTORICAL CENTRE
Facing the harbour, Diocletian's Palace is one of the most imposing Roman ruins in existence and where you'll spend most of your time while in Split. Don't expect a palace though, nor a museum – this is the city's living heart, its labyrinthine streets packed with people, bars, shops and restaurants. A military fortress, imperial residence and fortified town, the palace measures 215m from east to west and is 181m wide at the southernmost point, altogether covering 31,000 sq metres.

Although the original structure was modified in the Middle Ages, the alterations have only served to increase the allure of this fascinating site. The palace was built from lustrous white stone from the island of Brač, and construction lasted 10 years. Diocletian spared no expense, importing marble from Italy and Greece, and columns and sphinxes from Egypt.

Each wall has a gate named after a metal: at the northern end is the Golden Gate, while the southern end has the Bronze Gate. To the east is the Silver Gate and to the west is the Iron Gate. Between the eastern and western gates there's a straight road (Krešimirova, also known as Decumanus), which separates the imperial residence on the southern side, with its state rooms and temples, from the northern side, once used by soldiers and servants. The Bronze Gate, in the southern wall, led from the living quarters to the sea. Just beyond the palace walls are two city landmarks made by sculptor Ivan Meštrović;

BALKANS SPLIT

Central Split

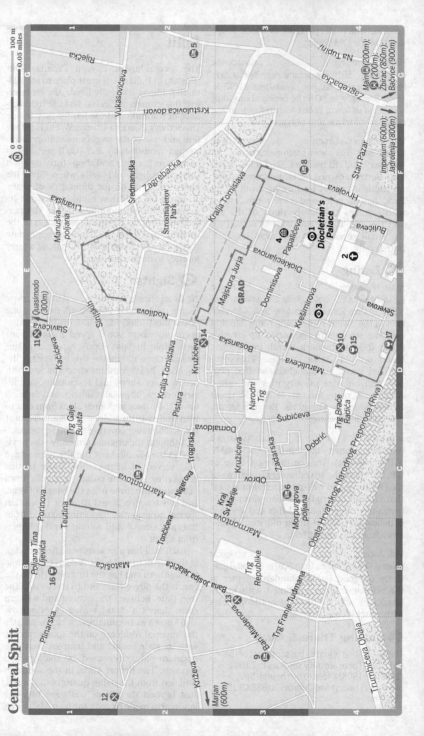

Diocletian's Palace

GRAD

Marjan (600m);

Quasimodo (300m);

Main (200m); Zbirac (850m); Bačvice (900m)

Imperium (600m); Jadrolinija (800m)

Stari Pazar

Narodni Trg

Trg Gaje Bulata

Trg Republike

Poljana Tina Ujevića

Štrosmajerov Park

Trg Braće Radica

Central Split

◎ Top Sights

◎ Sights

🛏 Sleeping

⊗ Eating

◎ Drinking & Nightlife

the medieval bishop Grgur Ninski guards the Golden Gate and the literary scholar Marko Marulić watches over Trg Braće Radić (Voćni Trg) just off Riva.

There are 220 buildings with n the palace boundaries, home to about 3000 people. The narrow streets hide passageways and courtyards, some deserted and eerie, others thumping with music from bars and cafes; local residents hang out their washing overhead, kids play football amid the ancient walls, and grannies sit in their windows watching the action below. Each street has small signs at its beginning and end, marking what you'll find upon it: bars, cafes, restaurants, shops, museums. It makes moving around much easier, though one of the best things you can do is get lost in the palace – it's small enough that you'll always find your way out easily.

Town Museum MUSEUM
(Muzej Grada Splita; www.mgst.net; Papalićeva 1; adult/concession 20/10KN; ⊘9am-9pm Tue-Fri, to 4pm Sat-Mon) Built by Juraj Dalmatinac for one of the many noblemen who lived within the palace in the Middle Ages, Papalić Palace is considered a fine example of late Gothic style, with an elaborately carved entrance gate that proclaimed the importance of its original inhabitants. The interior has been thoroughly restored to house this museum.

Captions are in Croatian, but wall panels in a variety of languages provide a historical framework for the exhibits. The museum has three floors, with drawings, heraldic coats of arms, 17th-century weaponry, fine furniture, coins and documents from as far back as the 14th century.

Cathedral of St Domnius CHURCH
(Katedrala Svetog Duje; Duje 5; cathedral/treasury/belfry 15/15/10KN; ⊘8am-7pm Mon-Sat, 12.30-6.30pm Sun) FREE Split's octagonal-shaped cathedral was originally built as Diocletian's mausoleum, encircled by 24 columns, almost completely preserved to this day. Its round domed interior has two rows of Corinthian columns and a frieze showing Emperor Diocletian and his wife. Note that admission also gets you free access to the Temple of Jupiter and its crypt. For 35KN, you can get a ticket that includes access to all these highlights.

Temple of Jupiter TEMPLE
(temple/temple & cathedral 10/35KN; ⊘8am-7pm Mon-Sat, 12.30-6.30pm Sun) The headless sphinx in black granite guarding the entrance to the temple was imported from Egypt at the time of the temple's construction in the 5th century. Of the columns that supported a porch the temple once had, only one remains. Take a look at the barrel-vaulted ceiling and a decorative frieze on the walls. You can also pop into the crypt, which was used as a church back in the day.

🏃 Activities

Bačvice SWIMMING
A flourishing beach life gives Split its aura of insouciance in summer. The pebbly **Bačvice** is the most popular beach, awarded with a Blue Flag eco label. You'll find good **swimming**, lively ambience and *picigin* games galore. There are showers and changing rooms at both ends of the beach. Bačvice is also a popular summer bar and club area for visitors and Split's younger crowd.

Marjan FISHING
For an afternoon away from the city buzz, Marjan hill (178m) is the perfect destination. Considered the lungs of the city, this hilly nature reserve offers trails through fragrant pine forests, scenic lookouts and ancient chapels. There are different ways of reaching Marjan. One is to head up Plinarska street just behind the National Theatre, cross Nazorova street and continue west down Mandalinski Put until you get to the Northern Gate

BALKANS SPLIT

(Spinutska Vrata). Otherwise, you can start the walk closer to the centre, from the stairway (Marjanske Skale) in Varoš, right behind the Church of Sveti Frane. It's a mild incline along old stone stairs and a scenic 10-minute trek to get to Vidilica cafe at the top. From here, right by the old Jewish cemetery, you can follow the marked trail, stopping en route to see the chapels, all the way to Kašjuni cove, a quieter beach option than buzzing Bačvice.

🛏 Sleeping

CroParadise Split Hostels
HOSTEL €

(📞091 444 4194; www.croparadise.com; Čulića Dvori 29; dm 200KN, s/d 250/500KN, apt from 500KN; ❄️@📶) A great collection of three hostels – Blue, Green and Pink – inside converted apartments in the neighbourhood of Manuš. The shared bar Underground (open June to September) is a starting point for pub crawls (Monday to Saturday nights). Other facilities include laundry, bike and scooter rental. Five apartments are also available.

Silver Central Hostel
HOSTEL €

(📞021-490 805; www.silvercentralhostel.com; Kralja Tomislava 1; dm 180KN; ❄️@📶) In an upstairs apartment, this light-yellow-coloured boutique hostel has four dorm rooms and a pleasant lounge. It has a two-person apartment nearby (250KN to 520KN) and another hostel, Silver Gate (📞021-322 857; www.silvergatehostel.com; Hrvojeva 6; dm 180KN, d with kitchen 525KN), near the food market.

★ Goli + Bosi
HOSTEL €€

(📞021-510 999; www.gollybossy.com; Morpurgova Poljana 2; dm/s/d 240/700/800KN) Split's design hostel is the premier destination for flashpackers, with its sleek futuristic decor, hip vibe and a cool lobby cafe-bar-restaurant. For 1130KN you get the superior double (called Mala Floramy), with breakfast included and gorgeous views.

Villa Varoš
GUESTHOUSE €€

(📞021-483 469; www.villavaros.hr; Miljenka Smoje 1; d/ste 586/887KN; P❄️📶) Midrangers are getting a better deal in Split nowadays, with places such as Villa Varoš around. Owned by a New Yorker Croat, Villa Varoš is central, the rooms are simple, bright and airy, and the apartment has a Jacuzzi and a small terrace.

🍴 Eating

★ Villa Spiza
DALMATIAN €

(Kružićeva 3; mains from 50KN; ⏱9am-midnight Mon-Sat) Locals' favourite within the palace walls, this low-key joint offers great-quality Dalmatian mainstays that change daily – think calamari, risotto and stuffed peppers – at low prices. Fresh home cooking is served at the bar inside, or at a couple of benches outside. Service is slow but the food is prepared with care.

Figa
INTERNATIONAL €

(📞021-274 491; Buvinina 1; mains from 50KN; ⏱8.30am-1am) A cool little restaurant and bar, with a funky interior and tables on the stairs outside, Figa serves nice breakfasts, seafood dishes and a wide range of salads. There's live music some nights and the kitchen stays open late. Service can be slow but comes with smiles and jokes.

Gušt
PIZZA €

(📞021-486 333; Slavićeva 1; pizzas from 32KN; ⏱9am-11pm Mon-Sat, 6-11pm Sun, closed Sun Jul-Sep) Split's die-hard pizza fans swear by this joint – it's cheap and very local.

Makrovega
VEGETARIAN €

(📞021-394 440; Leština 2; buffets from 60KN; ⏱9am-8pm Mon-Fri, to 5pm Sat) This meat-free haven has a stylish, spacious interior and delicious buffets. À la carte food includes macrobiotic and vegetarian offerings. Lots of seitan, tofu and tempeh, and excellent cakes.

Paradigma
MEDITERRANEAN €€

(📞021-645 103; Bana Josipa Jelačića 3; mains from 95KN; ⏱8am-midnight) Bringing culinary innovation to Split, this new restaurant sports modern interiors with hand-painted murals, and a rooftop terrace featuring Riva views in an old building resembling a ship's bow. It's slightly hidden from the tourist scene. Highlights are its top-notch wine list and Mediterranean-inspired dishes, like olive oil *sorbetto,* sous vide steaks and *pršut* (prosciutto) powder.

🍷 Drinking & Nightlife

Split is great for nightlife, especially in spring and summer. The palace walls are generally throbbing with loud music on Friday and Saturday nights, and you can spend the night wandering the mazelike streets, discovering new places.

After all the bars in the palace go quiet at 1am (as people live within the palace walls), the entertainment complex of Bačvice has a multitude of open-air bars and clubs that stay open till the wee hours.

Paradox WINE BAR

(Poljana Tina Ujevića 2; ☺9am-1am Mon-Sat, 4pm-1am Sun) Stylish wine bar with cool wine-glass chandeliers inside, alfresco tables and a great selection of well-priced Croatian wines and local cheeses to go with them.

Tri Volta BAR

(Dosud 9; ☺7am-midnight) A mixed crowd of misfits, fishers and bohos gathers at this legendary hang-out under three ancient vaults, with low-priced drinks and *sir i pršut* (cheese and prosciutto).

Ghetto Club BAR

(Dosud 10; ☺6pm-midnight Mon-Thu, to 2am Fri-Sat) Head for Split's most bohemian and gay-friendly bar, in an intimate courtyard amid flower beds, a trickling fountain, great music and a friendly atmosphere.

Imperium CLUB

(Gat Sv Duje bb; ☺8am-11pm Sun-Thu, to 4am Fri-Sat) Split's only megaclub overlooks the harbour from the 1st floor of the ferry terminal, with two large dance floors and an outdoor terrace with a bar. It's quiet on weekdays but fills up with a mixed crowd for concerts and DJ events on weekends.

Quasimodo CLUB

(Gundulićeva 26; ☺7pm-2am Mon-Thu & Sun, 9pm-4am Fri-Sat Oct-May) Splićani have been partying at this 1st-floor miniclub for decades. There's live and DJ-spun alternative music: rock, indie rock, jazz, blues… It shuts down in summer months from June to September.

Žbirac CAFE

(Šetalište Petra Preradovića 1b; ☺7am-1am Sun-Thu, to 2am Fri-Sat) This beachfront cafe is like the locals' open-air living room, a cult hang-out with great sea views, swimming day and night, *picigin* games and occasional concerts.

❶ Getting There & Away

BOAT

Jadrolinija (☎021-338 333; www.jadrolinija.hr; Gat Sv Duje bb) Handles most of the coastal ferry lines and catamarans that operate between Split and the islands. There is also a twice-weekly ferry service between Rijeka and Split (147KN, 7.30pm Thursday and Sunday, arriving at 6am).

BlueLine (www.blueline-ferries.com) Car ferries to Ancona (Italy), on some days via Hvar Town and Vis (per person/car from 480KN/540KN, 10 to 12 hours).

Krilo (www.krilo.hr) A fast passenger boat that goes to Hvar Town (70KN, one hour, twice daily) and to Vis (55KN, 2¾ hours, daily); the Vis catamaran stops in Hvar on Tuesdays. There's also a new connection to Dubrovnik from mid-May through mid-October (170KN, 4½ hour, twice weekly).

SNAV (☎021-322 252; www.snav.it) Ferries to Ancona (660KN, five hours, daily) from June through mid-September. In the ferry terminal.

BUS

Advance bus tickets with seat reservations are recommended. Most buses leave from the main **bus station** (☎060 327 777; www.ak-split.hr) beside the harbour, which has a **garderoba** (left-luggage office; 1st hour 5KN, then per hour 1.50KN; ☺6am-10pm), to the following destinations: Dubrovnik (115KN to 137KN, 4½ hours, 15 daily), Pula (308KN to 423KN, 10 to 11 hours, three daily) and Zagreb (144KN to 175KN, seven hours, 40 daily). Note that Split–Dubrovnik buses pass briefly through Bosnian territory, so keep your passport handy for border-crossing points.

TRAIN

Trains run between Split **train station** (☎021-338 525; www.hznet.hr; Kneza Domagoja 9) and Zagreb (189KN, six to eight hours, five daily), two of which are overnight. There are trains between Šibenik and Split (45KN, two hours, three daily), with a change in Perković, and from Split to Zadar (107KN, five hours, two daily) via Knin.

Hvar Island

☎021 / POP 11,080

Hvar is the number-one holder of Croatia's superlatives: it's the most luxurious island, the sunniest place in the country (2724 sunny hours each year) and, along with Dubrovnik, the most popular tourist destination. Hvar Town, the island's capital, is all about swanky hotels, elegant restaurants, trendy bars and clubs, posh yachties, and a general sense that if you care about seeing and being seen, this is the place to be. The coastal towns of Stari Grad and Jelsa, the cultural and historical centres of the island, are the more serene and discerning spots.

Hvar is also famed for the lilac lavender fields that dot its interior, as well as other aromatic plants such as rosemary and heather. You'll find that some of the deluxe hotels use skincare products made out of these gorgeous-smelling herbs.

The interior of the island hides abandoned ancient hamlets, towering peaks and verdant, largely uncharted landscapes. It's worth exploring on a day trip, as is the southern end of the island, which has some of Hvar's most beautiful and isolated coves.

◉ Sights

St Stephen's Square
SQUARE

(Trg Svetog Stjepana) The centre of town is this rectangular square, which was formed by filling in an inlet that once stretched out from the bay. At 4500 sq metres, it's one of the largest old squares in Dalmatia. The town first developed in the 13th century to the north of the square and later spread south in the 15th century. Notice the **well** at the square's northern end, which was built in 1520 and has a wrought-iron grill dating from 1780.

Franciscan Monastery & Museum
MONASTERY

(admission 25KN; ⊙9am-1pm & 5-7pm Mon-Sat) This 15th-century monastery overlooks a shady cove. The elegant **bell tower** was built in the 16th century by a well-known family of stonemasons from Korčula. The **Renaissance cloister** leads to a refectory containing lace, coins, nautical charts and valuable documents, such as an edition of Ptolemy's *Atlas*, printed in 1524.

Fortica
FORTRESS

(admission 25KN; ⊙9am-9pm) Through the network of tiny streets northwest of St Stephen's Square, climb up through a park to the citadel built on the site of a medieval castle to defend the town from the Turks. The Venetians strengthened it in 1557, and the Austrians renovated it in the 19th century by adding barracks. Inside is a tiny collection of ancient amphorae recovered from the seabed. The view over the harbour is magnificent, and there's a lovely cafe at the top.

🛏 Sleeping

Helvetia Hostel
HOSTEL €

(📞091 34 55 556; hajduk.hvar@gmail.com; Grge Novaka 6; dm/d 230/500KN; ❄🤖) Run by a friendly islander, this hostel inside his family's old stone house just behind Riva has three dorms and two doubles. The highlight is the giant rooftop terrace, where guests hang out and enjoy undisturbed views of Hvar bay and the Pakleni Islands.

Hostel Marinero
HOSTEL €

(📞091 174 1601; Put Sv Marka 7; dm 240-320KN; ❄🤖) Location is the highlight at this six-dorm hostel right off the seafront. Dorms are basic but clean. There is no shared kitchen, but the restaurant downstairs is a good place to mingle. The hostel wristband gets you discounts and perks at spots around town. Be ready for some noise, as the Kiva Bar is right next door.

Luka's Lodge
HOSTEL €

(📞021-742 118; www.lukalodgehvar.hostel.com; Šime Buzolića Tome 75; dm 150-190KN; d 350-400KN; ❄@🤖) Friendly owner Luka really takes care of his guests at this homey hostel, a five-minute walk from town. All rooms come with fridges, some with balconies. There's a living room, two terraces and a kitchen and laundry service. Upon request, Luka does pick-ups from the ferry dock.

🍴 Eating

Konoba Menego
DALMATIAN €

(📞021-742 036; www.menego.hr; Kroz Grodu 26; mains from 60KN; ⊙11.30am-2pm & 5.30pm-midnight) This rustic old house on the stairway towards Fortica is kept as simple and authentic as possible. As they say: no grill, no pizza, no Coca-Cola. The place is decked out in Hvar antiques, the staff wear traditional outfits, the service is informative, and the marinated meats, cheeses and vegetables are prepared the old-fashioned Dalmatian way.

Konoba Luviji
DALMATIAN €

(📞091 519 8444; Jurja Novaka 6; mains from 50KN; ⊙7pm-1am) Food brought out of the wood oven at this tavern is simple, unfussy and tasty, although portions are modestly sized. Downstairs is the *konoba* (tavern) where Dalmatian-style tapas are served, while the restaurant is upstairs on a small terrace, with Old Town and harbour views.

Divino
MEDITERRANEAN €€€

(📞021-717 541; www.divino.com.hr; Put Križa 1; mains from 130KN; ⊙10am-1am) The fabulous location and the island's best wine list are reason enough to splurge at this swank restaurant. Add innovative food (think rack of lamb with crusted pistachio) and dazzling views of the Pakleni Islands, and you've got a winning formula for a special night out. Or have some sunset snacks and wine on the gorgeous terrace. Book ahead.

🍷 Drinking

★Falko
BEACH BAR

(⊙8am-9pm mid-May–mid-Sep) A 3km walk from the town centre brings you to this adorable hideaway in a pine forest just above the beach. A great unpretentious alternative to the flashy spots closer to town, it serves yummy sandwiches and salads from a hut, as well as its own limoncello and *rakija*. Think low-key artsy vibe, hammocks and a local crowd.

Hula-Hula
BEACH BAR

(www.hulahulahvar.com; ⊙9am-1pm) *The* spot to catch the sunset to the sound of techno and house music, Hula-Hula is known for its après-beach party (4pm to 9pm), where all of young trendy Hvar seems to descend for sundowner cocktails.

Kiva Bar
BAR

(www.kivabarhvar.com; Fabrika bb; ⊙9pm-2am) A happening place in an alleyway just off the Riva. It's packed to the rafters most nights, with a DJ spinning old dance, pop and rock classics that really get the crowd going.

❶ Getting There & Away

The local **Jadrolinija car ferry** from Split calls at Stari Grad (47KN, two hours, six daily) in summer. Jadrolinija also has catamarans to Hvar Town (55KN to 70KN, one hour, three to five daily) and Jelsa (40KN, 1½ hours, two daily). **Krilo** (www.krilo.hr), the fast passenger boat, travels between Split and Hvar Town (70KN, one hour, two daily) in summer. You can buy tickets at **Pelegrini Tours** (🖉021-742 743; www.pelegrini-hvar.hr; Riva bb) in Hvar.

Connections to Italy are available in the summer season: two Jadrolinija ferries a week (on Saturday and Sunday night) go from Stari Grad to Ancona; Blue Line also runs boats to Ancona from Hvar Town in August and September. Pelegrini Tours sells these tickets.

Dubrovnik

🖉020 / POP 28,500

Regardless of whether you are visiting Dubrovnik for the first time or the hundredth, the sense of awe never fails to descend when you set eyes on the beauty of the Old Town. Indeed it's hard to imagine anyone becoming jaded by the city's marble streets and baroque buildings, or failing to be inspired by a walk along the ancient city walls that have protected a civilised, sophisticated republic for centuries.

◉ Sights

★City Walls & Forts
FORT

(Gradske Zidine; adult/child 100/30KN; ⊙9am-6.30pm Apr-Oct, 10am-3pm Nov-Mar) No visit to Dubrovnik would be complete without a walk around the spectacular city walls, the finest in the world and the city's main claim to fame. From the top, the view over the Old Town and the shimmering Adriatic is sublime. You can get a good handle on the extent of the shelling damage in the 1990s by gazing over the rooftops: those sporting bright new terracotta suffered damage and had to be replaced.

The first set of walls to enclose the city was built in the 9th century. In the middle of the 14th century the 1.5m-thick defences were fortified with 15 square forts. The threat of attacks from the Turks in the 15th century prompted the city to strengthen the existing forts and add new ones, so that the entire Old Town was contained within a stone barrier 2km long and up to 25m high. The walls are thicker on the land side – up to 6m – and range from 1.5m to 3m on the sea side.

The round **Minčeta Tower** protects the northern edge of the city from land invasion, while the western end is protected from land and sea invasion by the detached **Lovrjenac Fort**. Pile Gate is protected by the **Bokar Tower**, and the **Revelin Fort** guards the eastern entrance.

There are entrances to the walls from near the Pile Gate, the Ploče Gate and the Maritime Museum. The Pile Gate entrance tends to be the busiest; entering from the Ploče Gate has the added advantage of getting the steepest climbs out of the way first (you're required to walk in an anticlockwise direction). Don't underestimate how strenuous the wall walk can be, especially on a hot day. There's very little shelter and the water sold by the few vendors on the route tends to be overpriced.

★War Photo Limited
GALLERY

(🖉020-322 166; www.warphotoltd.com; Antuninska 6; adult/child 40/30KN; ⊙10am-10pm daily Jun-Sep, 10am-4pm Tue-Sun May & Oct) An immensely powerful experience, this gallery features compelling exhibitions curated by New Zealand photojournalist Wade Goddard, who worked in the Balkans in the 1990s. Its declared intention is to 'expose the myth of war...to let people see war as it is, raw, venal, frightening, by focusing on how war inflicts injustices on innocents and combatants alike'. There's a permanent exhibition on the upper floor devoted to the wars in Yugoslavia, but the changing exhibitions cover a multitude of conflicts.

Franciscan Monastery & Museum
MONASTERY

(Muzej Franjevačkog Samostana; Placa 2; adult/child 30/15KN; ⊙9am-6pm) Within this

Dubrovnik

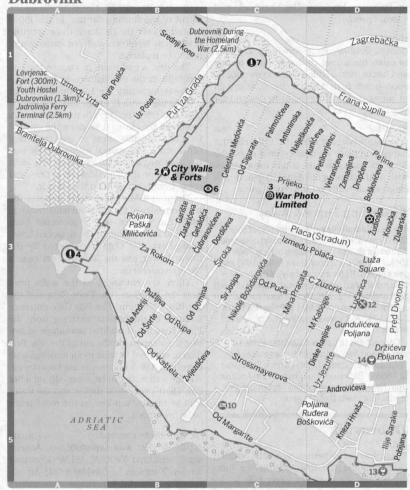

monastery's solid stone walls is a gorgeous mid-14th-century **cloister**, a historic **pharmacy**, and a small **museum** with a collection of relics and liturgical objects, including chalices, paintings, gold jewellery and pharmacy items such as laboratory gear and medical books. Artillery remains that pierced the monastery walls during the 1990s war have been saved, too.

Dominican Monastery & Museum
MONASTERY

(Muzej Dominikanskog Samostana; off Sv Dominika 4; admission 30KN; ⊙9am-5pm) This imposing structure is an architectural highlight, built in a transitional Gothic-Renaissance style, and containing an impressive art collection. Constructed around the same time as the city wall fortifications in the 14th century, the stark exterior resembles a fortress more than a religious complex. The interior contains a graceful 15th-century **cloister** constructed by local artisans after the designs of the Florentine architect Maso di Bartolomeo.

The large, single-naved church features some bright, modern, stained glass and a painting by Vlaho Bukovac above one of the side altars. Other priceless pieces of art are hung in rooms off the cloister, including

N
0 — 100 m
0 — 0.05 miles

Petra Frešimira IV

Dubrovnik

Adriatic and distant Elafiti Islands filling the horizon.

Synagogue　SYNAGOGUE
(Sinagoga; Žudioska 5; admission 35KN; ⊙10am-8pm May-Oct, to 3pm Nov-Apr) Dating to the 15th century, this is the second-oldest synagogue (the oldest Sephardic one) in the Balkans. Inside is a museum that exhibits religious relics and documentation on the local Jewish population, including records relating to their persecution during WWII.

🛏 Sleeping

Solitudo　CAMPGROUND €
(☎020-448 686; www.camping-adriatic.com; Vatroslava Lisinskog 17; per adult/child/site from €12/6/16, units from €69; ⊙Apr-Nov; P🚭🐕🏊) Solitudo is a strange name for a giant camping ground that's filled to the gills in summer, but to its credit it has bright, modern shower blocks, is close to Copacabana Beach, and allows guests access to a pool at a nearby hotel. Tenters will find the ground hard and rocky – or muddy and rocky when it rains.

Youth Hostel Dubrovnik　HOSTEL €
(☎020-423 241; www.hfhs.hr; Vinka Sagrestana 3; dm 157KN; @🛜) Thankfully there are now better, cosier hostels in the Old Town, but this Hostelling International establishment is considerably cheaper. The location is pretty good, in a quiet area 1.4km west of the Pile Gate. Dorms are spacious if plain, and can get hot. Rates include breakfast.

15th- and 16th-century works by Lovro Dobričević, Nikola Božidarević and Titian.

★ Cable Car　CABLE CAR
(www.dubrovnikcablecar.com; Petra Krešimira IV bb; adult/child return 120/50KN; ⊙9am-5pm Nov-Mar, to 8pm Apr, May & Oct, to midnight Jun-Aug, to 10pm Sep) Dubrovnik's cable car whisks you from just north of the city walls to Mt Srđ in under four minutes. Operations cease if there are high winds or a thunderstorm brewing. At the end of the line there's a stupendous perspective of the city from a lofty 405m, taking in the terracotta-tiled rooftops of the old town and the island of Lokrum, with the

WORTH A TRIP

OTHER PLACES WORTH A VISIT

Istria Don't miss the peninsula's main city, Pula, with its wealth of Roman architecture. The star of the show is the remarkably well-preserved amphitheatre dating back to the1st century. About 10km south along the indented shoreline, the Premantura Peninsula hides a spectacular nature park, the protected cape of Kamenjak with its lovely rolling hills, wild flowers, low Mediterranean shrubs, fruit trees and medicinal herbs, and around 30km of virgin beaches and coves.

South Dalmatia The island of Korčula, rich in vineyards and olive trees, is the largest island in an archipelago of 48, with plenty of opportunities for scenic drives, many quiet coves and secluded beaches, as well as Korčula Town, a striking walled town of round defensive towers, narrow stone streets and red-roofed houses that resembles a miniature Dubrovnik.

Around Dubrovnik A great excursion from Dubrovnik is the seductive island of Mljet, its northwestern half showcasing Mljet National Park, where the lush vegetation, pine forests and spectacular saltwater lakes are exceptionally scenic. It's an unspoiled oasis of tranquillity that, according to legend, captivated Odysseus for seven years.

City Walls Hostel HOSTEL €€
(📱091 79 92 086; www.citywallshostel.com; Sv Šimuna 15; dm/r from €36/76; ❄ @ 🛜) Tucked away by the city walls, this classic backpackers is warm and welcoming with a lively atmosphere. Downstairs there's space for socialising. Upstairs you'll find clean and simple dorms and a cosy double with a sea view. The same welcoming crew also runs a B&B near the cathedral.

✕ Eating

Oliva Pizzeria PIZZA €
(📱020-324 594; www.pizza-oliva.com; Lučarica 5; mains 40-89KN; ◷noon-10pm) There are a few token pasta dishes on the menu, but this attractive little place is really all about pizza. And the pizza is worthy of the attention. Grab a seat on the street and tuck in.

★ Atlantic Kitchen MEDITERRANEAN €€
(📱020-435 726; www.facebook.com/atlantic kitchen; Kardinala Stepinca 42; mains 89-139KN; ◷9am-11pm Apr-Nov) With its checked tablecloths and handwritten blackboard menus, there's a distinctly French feel to this breezy bistro – although the food meanders from France to Spain, Italy and Croatia. It's all excellent, and the service is great too.

Konoba Ribar DALMATIAN €€
(📱020-323 194; Kneza Damjana Jude bb; mains 60-120KN; ◷10am-midnight) Serving local food the way locals like it, at more or less local prices, this little family-run eatery is a blissfully untouristy choice. They don't attempt anything fancy or clever, just big serves of traditional favourites such as risotto and stuffed squid. It's set in a little lane pressed hard up against the city walls.

🍷 Drinking

Cave Bar More BAR
(www.hotel-more.hr; below Hotel More, Kardinala Stepinca 33; ◷10am-midnight) This little beach bar serves coffee, snacks and cocktails to bathers by the dazzlingly clear waters in Lapad. But that's not the half of it: the main bar is set in an actual cave. Cool off beneath the stalactites in the side chamber, where a glass floor exposes a water-filled cavern.

Buža BAR
(off Ilije Sarake; ◷8am-late) Finding this ramshackle bar-on-a-cliff feels like a real discovery as you duck and dive around the city walls and finally see the entrance tunnel. Emerging by the sea, it's quite a scene, with tasteful music (soul, funk) and a mellow crowd soaking up the vibes and views. Grab a cool drink in a plastic cup, perch on a concrete platform, and enjoy.

Jazz Caffe Troubadour BAR
(Bunićeva Poljana 2; ◷9am-1am) Tucked into a corner behind the cathedral, Troubadour looks pretty nondescript during the day. That all changes on summer nights, when jazz musicians set up outside and quickly draw crowds.

ℹ Getting There & Away

BOAT

The ferry terminal and the bus station are next to each other at Gruž, 3km northwest of the Old

Town. A twice-weekly Jadrolinija coastal ferry (Obala Papelvana Pavla II 1) heads north to Hvar and Split.

BUS

Buses out of **Dubrovnik Bus Station** (060 305 070; Obala Pape Ivana Pavla I 44a) can be crowded, so book tickets in advance in summer.

Split–Dubrovnik buses pass briefly through Bosnian territory, so keep your passport handy for border-crossing points.

All bus schedules are detailed at www.libertas dubrovnik.hr.

Croatia Survival Guide

ℹ Directory A–Z

ACCOMMODATION

Private accommodation is often great value in Croatia, plus it gets you a glimpse of Croatia's own brand of hospitality. Many of the owners treat their guests like long-lost friends. Some offer the option of eating with them which is a great way to get to know the culture.

Note that many establishments add a 30% charge for stays of less than three nights, and sometimes 50% or even 100% more for a one-night stay. Some will even insist on a seven-night minimum stay in the high seasons. The surcharge may be waived in low season.

Whether you rent from an agency or from the owners privately, don't hesitate to bargain, especially for longer stays.

Prices include 'residence tax', which is around 7KN per person per day. Prices quoted in this chapter do not include the residence tax.

BUSINESS HOURS

Banks 9am to 8pm Monday to Friday, 7am to 1pm or 8am to 2pm Saturday

Bars and cafes 8am to midnight

Offices 8am to 4pm or 8.30am to 4.30pm Monday to Friday

Restaurants Noon to 11pm or midnight, closed Sunday out of peak season

Shops 8am to 8pm Monday to Friday, to 2pm or 3pm Saturday

ELECTRICITY

Electrical supply is 220V, 50Hz AC. Croatia uses the standard European (round-pronged) plugs.

INTERNET RESOURCES

Adriatica.net (www.goadriatica.net)

Croatian National Tourist Board (www. croatia.hr)

Taste of Croatia (www.tasteofcroatia.org)

MONEY

The kuna has a fixed exchange rate tied to the euro and the rate varies little from year to year. However, to amass hard currency, the government makes the kuna more expensive in summer when tourists visit. You'll get the best exchange rate from mid-September to mid-June. ATMs are widely available. Credit cards are accepted in most hotels and restaurants. Smaller restaurants, shops and private accommodation owners only take cash.

TELEPHONE

➡ To call Croatia from abroad, dial your international access code, then ☑ 385 (the country code for Croatia), then the area code (without the initial 0) and the local number.

➡ To call from region to region within Croatia, start with the area code (with the initial zero); drop it when dialling within the same region.

➡ Phone numbers with the prefix ☑ 060 can be either free or charged at a premium rate, so watch out for the fine print.

➡ Phone numbers that begin with ☑ 09 are mobile phone numbers, calls to which are billed at a much higher rate than regular numbers.

➡ Users with unlocked phones can buy a local SIM card, which are easy to find. Otherwise, you'll be roaming.

VISAS

Citizens of the EU, the USA, Canada, Australia, New Zealand, Israel, Ireland, Singapore and the UK do not need a visa for stays of up to 90 days. South Africans must apply for a 90-day visa in Pretoria. Contact any Croatian embassy, consulate or travel agency abroad for information.

ℹ Getting There & Away

Getting to Croatia is becoming ever easier, especially if you're arriving in summer. Low-cost carriers have established routes to Croatia – you can now fly to Dubrovnik, Split, Zadar, Rijeka, Pula and Zagreb on budget airlines. A plethora of bus and ferry routes also shepherd holidaymakers to the coast.

AIR

There are direct flights to Croatia from a variety of European cities, but no nonstop flights from North America.

LAND

Croatia has border crossings with Hungary, Slovenia, Bosnia and Hercegovina, Serbia and Montenegro.

SEA

Regular ferries connect Croatia with Italy.

Blue Line (www.blueline-ferries.com)

Jadrolinija (www.jadrolinija.hr)

SNAV (www.snav.com)

Ustica Lines (www.usticalines.it)

Venezia Lines (www.venezialines.com)

❶ Getting Around

Transport in Croatia is reasonably priced, quick and generally efficient.

Car Useful for travelling at your own pace, or for visiting regions with minimal public transport. Cars can be hired in every city or larger town. Drive on the right.

Bus Reasonably priced, with extensive coverage of the country and frequent departures.

Boat Extensive network of car ferries and catamarans all along the coast and the islands.

Train Less frequent and much slower than buses, with limited network.

BOSNIA & HERCEGOVINA

Sarajevo

✔ 033 / POP 419,000

In the 1990s Sarajevo was besieged and on the edge of annihilation. Today, its restored historic centre is full of welcoming cafes and good-value lodgings, the bullet holes largely plastered over on the city's curious architectural mixture of Ottoman and Austro-Hungarian buildings.

The antique stone-flagged alleys of Baščaršija give the delightful Old Town core a certain Turkish feel. Directly north and south, steep valley sides are fuzzed with red-roofed Bosnian houses and prickled

with uncounted minarets, climbing towards green-topped mountain ridges. Westward, Sarajevo sprawls for over 10km through Novo Sarajevo and dreary Dobrijna, past dismal ranks of scarred apartment blocks. At the westernmost end of the tramway spine, affluent Ilidža gives the city a final parkland flourish. In winter, Bjelašnica and Jahorina offer some of Europe's best-value skiing, barely 30km away.

◉ Sights

The best way to really 'feel' the city is to stroll Old Sarajevo's pedestrian lanes and grand avenues, and climb the gently picturesque slopes of Bjelave and Vratnik for sweeping views. Seeking out key museums is likely to take you into modern, business-like Novo Sarajevo, and on to park-filled Ilidža.

Franz Ferdinand's Assassination Spot HISTORIC SITE

(cnr Obala Kulina Bana & Zelenih Beretki) On 28 June 1914, Archduke Franz Ferdinand, heir to the Habsburg throne of Austro-Hungary, was shot by 18-year-old Gavrilo Princip. This assassination, which would ultimately be the fuse that detonated WWI, happened by an odd series of coincidences on a street corner outside what is now the Sarajevo 1878–1918 museum.

Bezistan ARCHITECTURE

(http://vakuf-gazi.ba/english/index.php/objects/ottoman-era/bezistan-tasli-han; ⊙ 8am-8pm Mon-Fri, 9am-2pm Sat) The 16th-century stone-vaulted covered bazaar is little more than 100m long, but squint and you could be in Istanbul. Most of the 50-plus shops sell inexpensive souvenirs, scarves, cheap handbags and knock-off sunglasses. The structure is one of Ottoman governor Gazi-Husrevbey's great bequests.

★ Svrzo House MUSEUM

(Svrzina Kuća; ✔ 033-535264; http://muzejsarajeva.ba; Glođina 8; admission 3KM; ⊙ 10am-6pm Mon-Fri mid-Apr–mid-Oct, to 4pm mid-Oct–mid-Apr, 10am-3pm Sat year-round) An oasis of white-washed walls, cobbled courtyards and partly vine-draped dark timbers, this 18th-century house-museum is brilliantly restored and appropriately furnished, helping visitors imagine Sarajevo life in eras past.

Notice the *čekme dolaf* (food hatch), designed to prevent inter-sex fraternisation.

History Museum
MUSEUM

(☑ 033-226 098; www.muzej.ba; Zmaja od Bosne 5; admission 5KM; ⊙ 9am-7pm Mon-Fri, 10am-2pm Sat & Sun) Around half of the small but engrossing History Museum 'non-ideologically' charts the course of the 1990s conflict. Affecting personal exhibits include examples of food aid, stacks of Monopoly-style 1990s dinars and a makeshift siege-time 'home'. The exhibition's maudlin effect is emphasised by the museum building's miserable and still partly war-damaged 1970s architecture. Opening hours are shorter in winter.

★ Tunnel Museum
MUSEUM

(Tunel Spasa; http://tunelspasa.ba; Tuneli bb 1; adult/student 10/5KM; ⊙ 9am-5pm, last entry 4.30pm Apr-Oct, 3.30pm Nov-Mar) The most visceral of Sarajevo's many 1990s warexperience 'attractions', this unmissable museum's centrepiece and raison d'être is a section of the 1m-wide, 1.6m-high hand-dug tunnel under the airport runway, which acted as the city's lifeline to the outside world during the 1992–95 siege, when Sarajevo was virtually surrounded by Serb forces.

Equipped with rails, the tunnel proved just enough to keep Sarajevo supplied with food and arms for nearly four years.

Most of the tunnel has since collapsed, but this museum lets you walk through the short section that survives. Photos and maps are displayed around the shell-pounded house that hid the tunnel entrance, there's a new museum section of tools and documents, and the garden houses a demonstration minefield as well as two projection rooms showing wordless videos: five minutes' footage of the city bombardment and around 12 minutes depicting the wartime tunnel experience.

Getting here by public transport is a bit of a fiddle. Take tram 3 to Ilidža (the far terminus, 35 minutes, 11km from Baščaršija), then switch to Kotorac-bound bus 32 (10 minutes). Get off at the last stop, walk across the Tilava bridge, then turn immediately left down Tuneli for 500m. The bus runs around twice hourly weekdays, but only every 90 minutes on Sundays, so it's often faster to walk from Ilidža (around 30 minutes). Many city tours include a visit here – if you're alone, joining such a tour can prove cheaper than coming by taxi. And your guide can add a lot of useful insight.

🛏 Sleeping

Hostels are multiplying at an incredible rate. There are now several right on Ferhadija, and several great options on the narrow 'party street', Muvekita. Prices often rise during city festivals and at New Year.

BOSNIA & HERCEGOVINA & THE 1990S CONFLICT

Today's Bosnia & Hercegovina (BiH) remains deeply scarred by the 1990s civil war that began when post-Tito-era Yugoslavia imploded.

Seen very simply, the core conflict was a territorial battle between the Bosnians, Serbs and Croats. The war that ensued is often portrayed as 'ethnic', but in fact all sides were Slavs, differing only in their (generally secularised) religious backgrounds. Indeed, many Bosniaks (Muslims), Serbs (Orthodox Christians) and Croats (Catholics) had intermarried or were friends. Yet for nearly four years a brutal and extraordinarily complex civil war raged, with atrocities committed by all sides. Best known is the campaign of 'ethnic' cleansing in northern and eastern BiH, which aimed at creating a Serb republic.

Meanwhile in Mostar, Bosnian Croats and Bosniaks traded fire across a 'front line', with Croat bombardment eventually destroying the city's world-famous Old Bridge. Sarajevo endured a long siege and, in July 1995, Dutch peacekeepers monitoring the supposedly 'safe' area of Srebrenica proved unable to prevent a Bosnian Serb force from killing an estimated 8000 Muslim men in Europe's worst mass killings since WWII. By this stage, Croats had renewed their own offensive, expelling Serbs from western BiH and the Krajina region of Croatia

Finally, two weeks of NATO air strikes in September 1995 added force to an ultimatum to end the Serbs' siege of Sarajevo and a peace conference was held in Dayton, Ohio, in the US. The resultant accords maintained BiH's pre-war external boundaries, but divided the country into a complex jigsaw of semi-autonomous 'entities' and cantons to balance 'ethnic' sensibilities.This succeeded in maintaining the fragile peace, but the complex political structure resulting from the war has led to bureaucratic tangles and economic stagnation.

Central Sarajevo

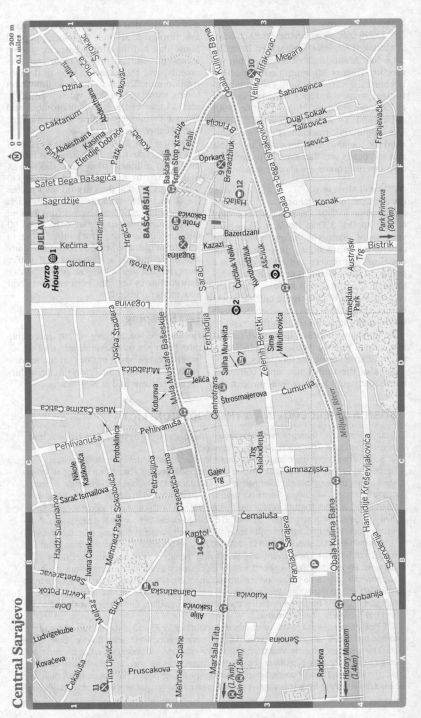

200 m
0.1 miles

BJELAVE

Svrzo House 🏛1

BAŠČARŠIJA

Tram Stop Kračule

 Očaktanum
Džina
Mlini
Ploča
Srijokac
Abdesthana
Kasima Efendije Dobrače
Kovači
Pirluša
Jekovac

Safet Bega Bašagiča
Sagrdžije
Kečima
Glođina
Cemerlina
Hrgiča
Na Varoši
Logavina

Baščaršija
Telali
Oprkanj ✗9
Bravadžiluk
Halači
💲12
Prote Bakovica 🍴9
Bazerdzani
Kazazi
Dugalina 💲8
Čurčiluk Veliki
Kundurdžiluk
Aščiluk 💲3
Ašiluk

Obala Kulina Bana
B Fincija
Velika Alifakovca ✗10
Megara
Šahinaginca
Dugi Sokak
Talirovića
Isevića
Franjevačka
Obala Isa-bega Ishakovića
Konak
Park Prinčeva (800m)
Austrijski Trg
Bistrik

Saraći
Ferhadija
Salina Muvekita
Zelenih Beretki
Sime Milutinovića
Strosmajerova
Ćumurija
Ćurčiluk Veliki
Atmejdan Park

💲2
Jelića 🍴4
Centrotrans
Trg Oslobođenja
Miljacka River

Josipa Štadlera
Mula Mustafe Bašeskije
Mladbdica
Koturova
Pehlivanuša
Muse Čazime Čatica
Pehlivanuša
Protoklinica
Petrakijna
Gajev Trg
Gimnazijska
Hamdije Kreševljakovića

Nikole Kašikovića
Hadži Sulemanov
Sarač Ismailova
Ivana Cankara
Mehmed Paše Sokolovića
Dženetića čikma
Čemaluša
13 🍴
Branilaca Sarajeva
Obala Kulina Bana
Skenderija

Špetarevac
Kevrin Potok
Buka
Dalmatinska 💲5
Kaptol 14 🍴
Kulovica
🅿
Čobanija

Dola
Meitaš
Alije Isakovića
Šenoina
Radiceva
History Museum (1.4km)

Ludvigekube
Kovačeva
Čekaluša
Tina Ujevića ✗11
Pruscakova
Mehmeda Spahe
Maršala Tita
(1.7km); Main 🚌(1.8km)

Central Sarajevo

Hostel For Me   HOSTEL €
(☑033-840135, 062 328658; www.hostelforme.com; 4th fl, Prote Bakovica 2; dm €0; ❄🛜) One of Sarajevo's best-appointed new hostels sits right within the Old Town, albeit hidden away up four flights of stairs. It's worth the climb for good-headroom bunks, huge lockers, and a decent lounge area and a two-table kitchen with fine views across the Old Town roofs to the Gazi Husrevbegov Mosque. Breakfast is €3.

Franz Ferdinand Hostel   HOSTEL €
(☑033-834625; http://franzferdinandhostel.com/; Jelića 4; dm 19-27KM, d 62-82KM; ❄@🛜) Giant sepia photos and a floor timeline recall characters and scenes related to Sarajevo WWI history. Bunks have private powerpoints and ample headroom, and the comfortably stylish kitchen-lounge is well designed to encourage conversation between travellers. Reception is open 24 hours.

Hostel Story   HOSTEL €
(☑033-551555; www.hostel-story.com; Muvekita 4; dm €12-16, d without bathroom from €34) Of several hostels right on Sarajevo's 'party street', Story wins for the quality of its dorms, the super-sized lockers and the lift access saving all those sweaty climbs upstairs in summer. There's a loungey cafe and shisha bar downstairs, but the hostel itself lacks a lounge area, so tends to be less sociable than many of its competitors.

Hostel Balkan Han   HOSTEL €
(☑Unkas 061 538331; www.balkanhan.com; Dalmatinska 6; dm/apt €12/64; 🛜) Lively, charming owner Unkas welcomes guests with a shot of herb *rakija* in this two-dorm hostel's small, characterful private bar area. Beds are close packed but with storage spaces.

✖ Eating

Barhana   PIZZA, BOSNIAN €
(Đugalina 8; pizza 5-12KM; ⊘10am-midnight, kitchen till 11.30pm) Barhana's remarkably reasonable prices pair unbeatably with its charming part-wooden cottage interior, the centrepiece of which is the large brick pizza oven and open kitchen, partly masked by collections of bottles and candles.

Tables spill out onto a shared courtyard. Myriad varieties of chilled *rakija* are served in teardrop-shaped phials.

Buregdžinica Bosna   PIES €
(Bravadžuluk; 250g portions 2-3.50KM; ⊘7am-11pm) The classic Old City spot for *burek* (heavy pastry stuffed with meat or cheese) and other fresh-cooked pies, sold by weight.

The interior is decorated with Sarajevo 1984 ski scenes. Eat on the street terrace.

★ Mala Kuhinja   FUSION €€
(☑061 144741; www.malakuhinja.ba; Tina Ujevića 13; mains 12-25KM; ⊘10am-11pm Mon-Sat; ❄🛜🐾) Run by former TV celebrity chefs, the novel concept here is to forget menus and simply ask you what you do/don't like. Spicy? Vegan? Gluten free? No problem. Armed with this knowledge the team sets about making culinary magic in the show-kitchen. Superb.

Food is locally sourced; reservations are wise for peak meal times. Before 11am there's a 6KM breakfast.

Inat Kuća   BOSNIAN €€
(Spite House; ☑033-447867; www.inatkuca.ba; Velika Alifakovac 1; mains 8-15KM, steak 25KM; ⊘10am-10pm; ❄🛜) This Sarajevo institution occupies a classic Ottoman-era house that's a veritable museum piece, with a central stone water-trough, a case of antique guns, and fine metal-filigree lanterns. A range of Bosnian specialities are served using pewter crockery at glass-topped display tables containing traditional local jewellery.

Instead of the usual insipid 1980s pop played in many restaurants, the soundtrack here is Bosnian *sevdah* (traditional music). The menu tells the story of the restaurant's odd name, which might be better phrased 'house of strong will'. The riverside terrace offers a fine view of the restored City Hall.

Drinking & Nightlife

★ Zlatna Ribica   BAR
(Kaptol 5; beer/wine from 4/5KM; ⊙9am-1am) Sedate and outwardly grand, this tiny bar is inspiringly eccentric, adding understated humour to a cosy treasure trove of antiques and kitsch, all mixed together and reflected in big art-nouveau mirrors.

Kuća Sevdaha   CAFE
(www.artkucasevdaha.ba/en/; Halači 5; tea/coffee/sherbet from 2/2/3KM; ⊙10am-11pm) Sip Bosnian coffee, juniper sherbet, rose water or herb-tea infusions while nibbling local sweets and listening to the lilting wails of *sevdah*. The ancient building that surrounds the cafe's fountain courtyard is now used as a museum, celebrating great 20th-century *sevdah* performers (admission 3KM, open 10am to 6pm Tuesday to Sunday).

Pink Houdini   BAR
(www.facebook.com/JazzBluesClubPinkHoudini; Branilaca Sarajeva 31; beer 3KM; ⊙24hr) One of Sarajevo's relatively rare 24-hour drinking spots, this quirky basement jazz bar has live gigs at 10pm on Fridays and Sundays.

The ceiling is an abstract sculpture in gilded scrap metal and mic stands. The rough whitewashed walls are dotted with lit niches, art books and luminous green hand-prints.

Getting There & Away

BUS
Sarajevo's **main bus station** (⊉033-213100; www.centrotrans.com; Put Života 8; ⊙6am-10pm) primarily serves locations in the Federation, Croatia and Western Europe. Many services to the Republik Srpska (RS) and Serbia leave from **East Sarajevo (Lukovica) Bus Station** (Autobuska Stanica Istočno Sarajevo; ⊉057-317377; www.balkanexpress-is.com; Nikole Tesle bb; ⊙6am-11.15pm). The latter lies way out in the suburb of Dobrijna, 400m beyond the western terminus stop of trolleybus 103 and bus 31E. To some destinations, buses leave from both stations. For Jajce (23.50KM to 27KM, 3½hr) take Banja Luka buses.

TRAIN
The only international rail service is to Zagreb, departing at 10.46am (61KM, nine hours via Banja Luka). Domestically there are Mostar trains at 6.51am and 6.57pm (11KM, 2¾ hours) and nine local chuggers to Zenica, Doboj, Konjic or Kakanj.

Mostar
⊉036 / POP 113,200

Mostar's world-famous 16th-century stone bridge is the centrepiece of its alluring, extensively restored old town where, at dusk, the lights of numerous millhouse restaurants twinkle across streamlets. Further from the centre a scattering of shattered building shells remain as moving testament to the terrible 1990s conflict that divided the city. The surrounding sun-drenched Hercegovinian countryside produces excellent wines and offers a series of tempting day-trip attractions.

Sights

Stari Most   BRIDGE
The world-famous Stari Most (Old Bridge) is Mostar's indisputable visual focus. Its pale stone arch magnificently throws back the golden glow of sunset or the tasteful nighttime floodlighting. The bridge's swooping stone arch was originally built between 1557 and 1566 on the orders of Suleyman the Magnificent.

The 16th-century stone version replaced a previous suspension bridge whose wobbling had previously terrified tradesmen as they gingerly crossed the fast-flowing Neretva River. An engineering marvel of its age, that new bridge had long become the 'old' bridge when, after 427 years, it was pounded into the river during a deliberate Croat artillery atack in 1993. Footage of this sad moment is shown on many a video in Mostar. But the structure was laboriously reconstructed using original techniques and reopened in 2004. It's now a Unesco World Heritage Site.

Numerous well-positioned cafes and restaurants tempt you to sit and savour the splendidly restored scene.

Bridge Diving   SPECTACLE
In summer, young men leap over 20m from Stari Most's parapet. These aren't suicide attempts but a professional sport – donations are expected from spectators. Daredevil tourists can try jumping for themselves, but only after paying 50KM and doing a brief training course. Enquire at the Bridge-Divers' Clubhouse and listen very carefully to advice: diving incorrectly can prove fatal.

Crooked Bridge   BRIDGE
(Kriva Ćuprija) Resembling Stari Most but in miniature, the pint-sized Crooked Bridge crosses the tiny Rabobolja creek amid a

layered series of picturesque millhouse restaurants. The original bridge, weakened by wartime assaults, was washed away by 2000 floods, but rebuilt a year later.

Kajtaz House MUSEUM
(Gaše Ilića 21; admission 4KM; ⊕9am-7pm Apr-Oct) Hidden behind tall walls, Mostar's most historic old house was once the harem section of a larger homestead built for a 16th-century Turkish judge. Full of original artefacts, it still belongs to descendents of the original family.

Spanski Trg HISTORIC SITE
Over 20 years ago Croat and Bosniak forces bombarded each other into the rubble across a 'front line' which ran along the Bulevar and Alese Šantića St. Even now, several shell-pocked skeletal buildings remain in ruins around Spanski Trg, notably the triangular nine-storey tower that was once **Ljubljanska Banka** (Kralja Zvonimira bb).

War Photo Exhibition GALLERY
(Helebija Kula, Stari Most; admission 6KM; ⊕9am-8.30pm Apr-Nov) Collection of around 50 wartime photos of Mostar.

🛏 Sleeping

Backpackers HOSTEL €
(☑036-552408, 063 199019; www.backpackers-mostar.com; Braće Felića 67; dm/d/tr €10/30/45; ⊖❄🛜) With its graffiti-chic approach and music-till-late sitting area, this is Mostar's party hostel. It's above a main-street shop and currently quite small, but owner Ermin has big plans for expansion.

Ask about private inter-hostel shared taxi transfers, notably to Kotor and Dubrovnik via Stolac and Trebinje.

Hostel Nina HOSTEL €
(☑061 382743; www.hostelnina.ba; Čelebica 18; dm/d without bathroom €10/20; ❄@) This popular homestay-hostel is run by an obliging English-speaking lady whose husband, a war survivor and former bridge jumper, runs regional tours. There's a little patch of garden, a shared kitchen and one or two possibilities for parking.

Hostel Majdas HOSTEL €
(☑061 382940; www.facebook.com/HostelMajdasMostar; Pere Lažetića 9; dm 20-23KM; ❄@🛜) Mostar's cult traveller getaway, Majdas now has a garden where breakfast is served, and a loveable cat. It still offers the classic multisite around-Mostar day tours, which manager-guide Bata pioneered.

ESSENTIAL FOOD & DRINK

Bosanski Lonac Slow-cooked meat-and-veg hotpot.

Burek Cylindrical or spiral lengths of filo-pastry filled with minced meat. *Sirnica* is filled instead with cheese, *krompiruša* with potato and *zeljanica* with spinach. Collectively these pies are called pitta.

Ćevapi (Ćevapčići) Minced meat formed into cylindrical pellets and served in freshbread with melting *kajmak*.

Kajmak Thick, semi-soured cream.

Klepe Small, ravioli-like triangles served in a butter-pepper drizzle with grated raw garlic.

Kljukuša Potato-dough-milk dish cooked like a pie then cut into slices.

Pljeskavica Patty-shaped ćevapi.

Ražnjići Barbequed meat skewers.

Sač Traditional cooking technique using a metal hood loaded with hot charcoals.

Sarma Steamed *dolma;* parcels of rice and minced meat wrapped in cabbage or other green leaves.

Sogan Dolma Slow-roasted onions filled with minced meat.

Tufahija Whole stewed apple with walnut filling.

Uštipci Bready, fried dough-balls.

🍴 Eating

Eko-Eli BOSNIAN €
(Maršala Tita 115; mains 2.50-3.50KM; ⊕7am-9.30pm) Escape the tourists and watch typical Bosnian *pitta* snacks (including *krompirača, sirnica, burek* and *zeljanica*) being baked over hot coals beneath traditional sač iron hoods.

Takeaway, eat at the communal table, or dine in the almost comically uninspired bar next door.

Balkan 1 BOSNIAN €
(Aščinica Balkan; Braće Fejića 61; mains 3-7KM; ⊕6am-9.45pm) In business since the mid 1960s, Balkan 1 serves precooked home-cooking specialities, including various forms of dolma (meat-stuffed vegetables) in a dining room decked with

Mostar

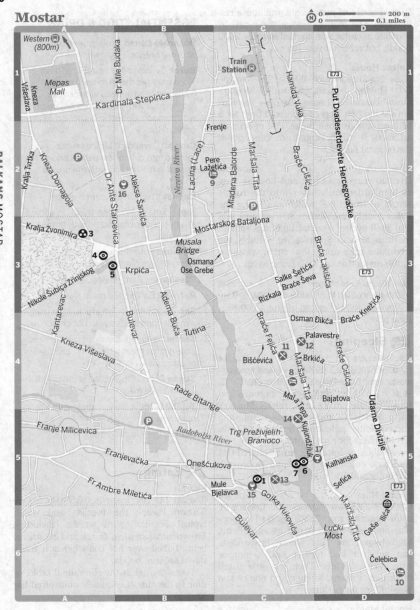

enough local metalwork and such a jumble of framed pictures that you might not notice the darkly mirrored high ceiling and dustily kitsch plastic flowers. Street terrace available too.

Hindin Han

BALKAN €€

(☎ 036-581054; Jusovina bb; mains 7-20KM; ⏱ 11am-11pm; 🛜) Hindin Han is a rebuilt historic building with several layers of summer terrace perched pleasantly above a side stream. Locals rate its food as better than

Mostar

◎ Sights
	Bridge Diving	(see 7)
1	Crooked Bridge	C5
2	Kajtaz House	D5
3	Ljubljanska Banka Tower Ruin	A3
4	Spanski Trg	A3
5	Stara Gimnazija	A3
6	Stari Most	C5
7	War Photo Exhibition	C5

🛏 Sleeping
8	Backpackers	C4
9	Hostel Majdas	B2
10	Hostel Nina	D6

🍴 Eating
11	Balkan 1	C4
12	Eko-Eli	C4
13	Hindin Han	C5
14	Urban Grill	C5

🍷 Drinking & Nightlife
15	Black Dog Pub	C5
16	OKC Abrašević	B2
17	Wine & More	D5

most other equivalent tourist restaurants. The stuffed squid we tried (13KM) was perfectly cooked and generously garnished.

Urban Grill   BOSNIAN €€
(Mala Tepa 26; mains 8-27KM; ⊙8am-11pm Mon-Sat, 9am-11pm Sun; ▒) From the street level Urban Grill seems to be a slightly up-market Bosnian fast-food place. But the menu spans a great range and the big attraction is the seven-table lower terrace with unexpectedly perfect framed views of the Old Bridge.

🍺 Drinking & Nightlife

Black Dog Pub   PUB
(Crooked Bridge; beer/wine from 2/4KM; ⊙10am-late) Old Mostar's best hostelry features four specially brewed draft beers, happy hours and live acoustic music on Monday nights.

The decor of flags, posters and old car numberplates add further character to the ancient millhouse building; the stream-side terrace has great Crooked Bridge views.

OKC Abrašević   BAR
(☑036-561107; www.okcabrasevic.org; Alekse Šantića 25; coffee/beer 1/2KM; ⊙8am-midnight) This understatedly intellectual smoky box of a bar offers Mostar's most vibrantly alternative scene, and has an attached venue for offbeat gigs. It's hidden away in an unsigned courtyard on the former front line.

Wine & More   WINE BAR
(Mala Tepa; ⊙9am-11pm; 🤟) Sedately sample Trebinje's celebrated Tvrdoš Monastery wines in this cosy, thick-walled shop or at its four tables set on the Old Town's time-polished stone stairways.

ℹ Getting There & Away

BUS
The main **bus station** (☑036-552025; Ivana Krndelja Trg) beside the train station handles half a dozen daily services to Sarajevo, Split and Zagreb plus morning departures to Belgrade, Herceg Novi, Kotor and Vienna. For Dubrovnik there are direct buses (38KM, 4½ hours) at 7am and 10am, or you could take a bus to attractive Trebinje (21KM, four hours, three daily), from where there's a 10am bus to Dubrovnik (not on Sundays). Three extra Split-bound buses use the **Western Bus Station** (AutobusniKolodvor; ☑036-348680; Vukovarska bb), 800m beyond Mepas Mall.

TRAIN
Trains to Sarajevo (11KM, 2¼ hours) depart at 7.05am and 7.10pm daily. The morning train continues to Zagreb (74.60KM, 13¼ hours).

Bosnia & Hercegovina Survival Guide

ℹ Directory A–Z

DANGERS & ANNOYANCES
Landmines and unexploded ordnance still affect 2.4% of BiH's area. BHMAC (www.bhmac.org) clears more every year, but total removal of the land-mine threat isn't envisaged before 2019, while earth movements caused by the 2014 floods are likely to add to the complexity of locating the last mines. For your safety, stick to asphalt/concrete surfaces or well-worn paths in affected areas, and avoid war-damaged buildings.

MONEY
➤ Bosnia's convertible mark (KM or BAM) is pronounced *kai-em* or *maraka*. It is divided into

---

ℹ **SLEEPING PRICE RANGES**

Room prices are for high season (June to September) and assume a private bathroom and breakfast, except in hostels or where otherwise indicated.

€ less than 80KM

€€ 80KM to 190KM

EATING PRICE RANGES

The following are average costs for restaurant main courses:

€ less than 10KM

€€ 10KM to 25KM

---

100 fenig. It's tied to the euro at approximately €1 = 1.96KM.

➡ Though no longer officially sanctioned, many businesses still unblinkingly accept euros, for minor purchases using a slightly customer-favourable 1:2 rate. Exchanging euros is markedly better than other currencies as there's usually no rate-split.

➡ Exchanging travellers cheques can prove awkward and usually requires the original purchase receipt.

➡ ATMs accepting Visa and MasterCard are ubiquitous.

VISAS

Stays of under 90 days require no visa for citizens of the EU, Australia, Canada, Israel, Japan, New Zealand and the USA. Other nationals should see www.mfa.ba for visa details and where to apply.

Getting There & Away

BUS

Buses to Zagreb and/or Split (Croatia) run at least daily from most towns in the Federation. Some services to Herceg Novi (Montenegro) and Dubrovnik (Croatia) run summertime only. Buses to several destinations in Serbia and/or Montenegro from many Republik Srpska (RS) towns. Buses to Vienna and Germany run several times weekly from bigger BiH cities.

TRAIN

The only international rail service links Sarajevo to Zagreb, daily, via Banja Luka.

Getting Around

Bus stations pre-sell tickets. Between towns it's normally easy enough to wave down any bus en route. Advance reservations are sometimes necessary for overnight routes or at peak holiday times. The biggest company, **Centrotrans** (www.centrotrans.com; Ferhadija 16, Sarajevo), has online timetables (click 'Red Vožnje').

Trains are slower and less frequent than buses, but generally slightly cheaper. **RS Railways** (www.zrs-rs.com/red_voznje.php) has timetables for services in the RS.

MONTENEGRO

Budva

♫ 033 / POP 13,400

The poster child of Montenegrin tourism, Budva – with its atmospheric Stari Grad (Old Town) and numerous beaches – certainly has a lot to offer. Yet the child has moved into a difficult adolescence, fuelled by rampant development that has leeched much of the charm from the place. In high season the sands are blanketed with package holidaymakers from Russia and Ukraine, while the nouveau riche park their multimillion-dollar yachts in the town's guarded marina. By night you'll run a gauntlet of scantily clad women attempting to cajole you into the beachside bars. But it's the buzziest place on the coast so if you're in the mood to party, this is the place to be.

⊙ Sights

Budva's best feature and star attraction is its Old Town – a mini-Dubrovnik, with marbled streets and Venetian walls rising from the clear waters below. You can still see the remains of Venice's emblem, the winged lion of St Mark, over the main gate. Much of the Old Town was ruined in two earthquakes in 1979, but it has since been completely rebuilt and now houses more shops, bars and restaurants than residences.

Citadela   FORTRESS
(admission €2.50; ⊙ 9am-midnight May-Oct, to 5pm Nov-Apr) At the Stari Grad's seaward end, the old citadel offers striking views, a small museum and a library full of rare tomes and maps. It's thought to be built on the site of the Greek acropolis, but the present incarnation dates to the 19th-century Austrian occupation. Its large terrace serves as the main stage of the annual Theatre City festival.

Town Walls   FORTRESS
(admission €1.50) A walkway about a metre wide leads around the landward walls of the Stari Grad, offering views across the rooftops and down on some beautiful hidden gardens. Admission only seems to be charged in the height of summer; at other times it's either free or locked. The entrance is near the Citadela.

Ploče Beach   BEACH
(www.plazaploce.com) If the sands are getting too crowded in Budva itself, head out

Budva

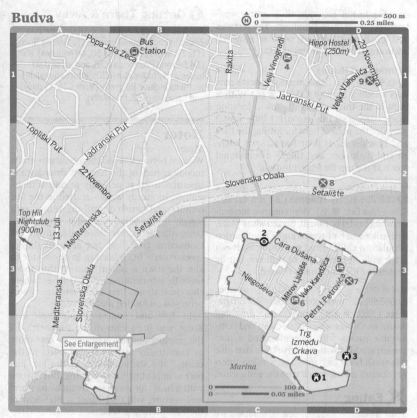

Budva

◎ Sights
1 Citadela	D4
2 Main Gate	C3
3 Town Walls	D4

🛏 Sleeping
4 Hotel Oliva	C1
5 Montenegro Freedom Hostel	D3
6 Montenegro Hostel	C3

🍽 Eating
7 Pizza 10 Maradona	D3
8 Restoran Lim	D2
9 Stari Ribar	D1

to this little pebbly beach at the end of a scrub-covered peninsula, 10km west of town (take the road to Kotor, turn off towards Jaz Beach and keep going). The water is crystal-clear, but if you prefer fresh water there are little pools set into the sunbathing terraces.

Jaz Beach   BEACH

FREE The blue waters and broad sands of Jaz Beach look spectacular when viewed from high up on the Tivat road. While it's not built up like Budva and Bečići, the beach is still lined with loungers, sun umbrellas and noisy beach bars. Head down the Budva end of the beach for a little more seclusion.

Parking will set you back €2.50 and camping is possible (per adult/child/tent/car/caravan €3/1/2.50/1/3), but the facilities are extremely basic and the field can get muddy.

🛏 Sleeping

Montenegro Freedom Hostel   HOSTEL €
(☑ 067 523 496; montenegrofreedom@gmail.com; Cara Dušana 21; dm/tw/d €14/30/36; ❄ 🛜) In a quieter section of the Old Town, this

sociable hostel has tidy little rooms scattered between three buildings. The terraces and small courtyard are popular spots for impromptu guitar-led singalongs.

Montenegro Hostel
HOSTEL €

(☑069 039 751; www.montenegrohostel.com; Vuka Karadžića 12; dm/r €15/53; ❋🛜) With a right-in-the-thick-of-it Old Town location (pack earplugs), this colourful little hostel provides the perfect base for hitting the bars and beaches. Each floor has its own kitchen and bathroom, and there's a communal space at the top for fraternisation.

Hippo Hostel
HOSTEL €

(☑069 256 117; IV Proleterska 37; dm €11-12, r €28; ☉Apr-Oct; @🛜) Montenegro's longest-standing hostel is a small, tucked-away place, with colourful bathrooms and a front garden popular for chilling and socialising in. It can get frantic in the height of summer, but by September it's much more relaxed.

Hotel Oliva
HOTEL €€

(☑069 551 769; www.hotel-oliva.com; Velji Vinogradi bb; r €50; P❋🛜) Don't expect anything flashy, just a warm welcome, clean and comfortable rooms with balconies, and a nice garden studded with the olive trees that give this small hotel its name. The wireless internet doesn't extend much past the restaurant.

✖ Eating

Stari Ribar
SEAFOOD, MONTENEGRIN €

(☑033-459 543; 29 Novembra 19; mains €3-12; ☉7am-11pm) You'll be relieved to learn that the name means Old Fisherman, not Old Fish. This humble eatery in the residential part of town serves grilled fish (fresh, naturally) and meat dishes at local prices. The squid here is definitely worth trying.

Pizza 10 Maradona
PIZZA €

(Petra I Petrovića 10; pizza slice €2) A reader alerted us to this late-night hole-in-the-wall eatery selling pizza by the slice. We can confirm that after a hard night's 'researching' the city's nightspots, Maradona's crispy based pizza does indeed seem to come straight from the hand of God.

Restoran Lim
EUROPEAN €€

(Slovenska Obala; mains €6-19; ☉8am-1am) Settle into one of the throne-like carved wooden chairs and feast on the likes of grilled meat and fish, homemade sausages, pizza, beef Stroganoff, veal Parisienne or Weiner schnitzel. The octopus salad is excellent.

❶ Getting There & Away

The **bus station** (☑033-456 000; Popa Jola Zeca bb) has frequent services to Herceg Novi (€6, 1¾ hours), Kotor (€3.50, 40 minutes), Bar (€4.50) and Podgorica (€6), and around six buses a day to Kolašin (€10). International destinations include Belgrade (from €26, 15 daily) and Sarajevo (€22, four daily).

Kotor

☑032 / POP 4800

Wedged between brooding mountains and a moody corner of the bay, this dramatically beautiful town is perfectly at one with its setting. Its sturdy walls – started in the 9th century and tweaked until the 18th – arch steeply up the slopes behind it. From a distance they're barely discernible from the mountain's grey hide, but at night they're spectacularly lit, reflecting in the water to give the town a golden halo. Within those walls lie labyrinthine marbled lanes, where churches, shops, bars and restaurants surprise you on hidden piazzas.

In July and August people pour into Kotor, and the yachts of the super-rich fill the marina, but this town never gets quite as Euro-trashy as some other parts of the coast – the sheltered arm of the bay just isn't as appealing for swimming. But anyone with a heart for romance, living history and architecture, will find Kotor a highlight of their Montenegrin travels.

◉ Sights

The best thing to do in Kotor is to let yourself get lost and found again in the maze of streets. You'll soon know every corner, since the town is quite small, but there are plenty of old churches to pop into and many coffees to be drunk in the shady squares.

Town Walls
FORTRESS

(admission €3; ☉24hr, fees apply 8am-8pm May-Sep) Kotor's fortifications started to head up St John's Hill in the 9th century, and by the 14th century a protective loop was completed, which was added to right up until the 19th century. The energetic can make a 1200m ascent up the fortifications via 1350 steps to a height of 260m above sea level.

There are entry points near the North Gate and behind Trg od Salate. Avoid the heat of the day and bring lots of water.

St Nicholas' Church
CHURCH

(Crkva Sv Nikole; Trg Sv Luke) Breathe in the smell of incense and beeswax in this relatively unadorned Orthodox church (1909). The silence, the iconostasis with its silver bas-relief panels, the dark wood against bare grey walls, the filtered light through the dome, and the simple stained glass conspire to create a mystical atmosphere.

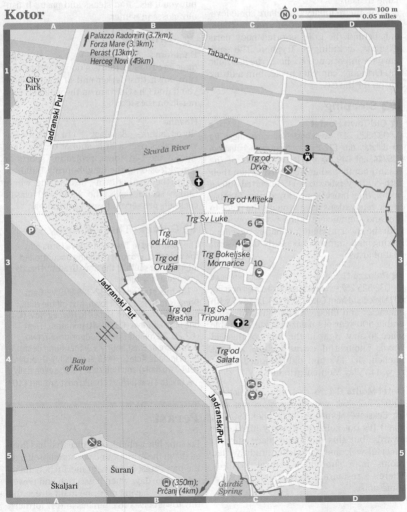

Kotor

St Tryphon's Cathedral   CHURCH

(Katedrala Sv Tripuna; Trg Sv Tripuna; admission €2.50; ☉8am-7pm) Kotor's most impressive building, this Catholic cathedral was consecrated in the 12th century but reconstructed after several earthquakes. When the entire frontage was destroyed in 1667, the baroque bell towers were added; the left one remains unfinished. The cathedral's gently hued interior is a masterpiece of Romanesque architecture, with slender Corinthian columns alternating with pillars of pink stone, thrusting upwards to support a series of vaulted roofs. Its gilded silver bas-relief altar screen is considered Kotor's most valuable treasure.

Up in the reliquary chapel are some lovely icons, a spooky wooden crucifix (1288) and, behind the grill, assorted body parts of saints, including St Tryphon. The early martyr's importance to both the Catholic and Orthodox churches makes him a fitting patron for the city.

🛏 Sleeping

★ Old Town Hostel   HOSTEL €

(☏032-325 317; www.hostel-kotor.me; near Trg od Salata; dm €12-15, r without/with bathroom €39/44, apt €49; ❀🗲) If the ghosts of the Bisanti family had any concerns when their 13th-century palazzo was converted into a hostel, they must be overjoyed now. Sympathetic renovations have brought the place to life, and the ancient stone walls now echo with the cheerful chatter of happy travellers, mixing and mingling beneath the Bisanti coat of arms.

★ Palazzo Drusko   GUESTHOUSE €€

(☏032-325 257; www.palazzodrusko.me; near Trg od Mlijeka; s/d from €49/75; ❀🗲) Loaded with character and filled with antiques, this venerable 600-year-old palazzo is a memorable place to stay, right in the heart of the Old Town. Thoughtful extras include a guest kitchen, 3D TVs and old-fashioned radios rigged to play Montenegrin music.

Hotel Monte Cristo   HOTEL €€

(☏032-322 458; www.montecristo.co.me; near Trg Bokeljske Mornarice; r/apt from €90/125; ❀🗲) It's not going to win any hip design awards, but this old stone place offers a cheerful welcome and clean, brightly tiled rooms in a supremely central location. There's a restaurant downstairs, so expect some noise.

✗ Eating

Bastion   MONTENEGRIN, SEAFOOD €€

(www.bastion123.com; Trg od Drva; mains €8-18; ☉10am-midnight) At a slight remove from the frenetic heart of the Old Town, Bastion offers a mixture of fresh seafood and traditional meaty grills. If the weather's well behaved, grab a table outside.

★ Galion   SEAFOOD €€€

(☏032-325 054; Šuranj bb; meals €12-23; ☉noon-midnight) With an achingly romantic setting, extremely upmarket Galion gazes directly at the Old Town across the millionaire yachts in the marina. Fresh fish is the focus, but you'll also find steaks and pasta. It usually closes in winter.

🍷 Drinking

Bandiera   BAR

(near Trg od Salata) Tourists don't tend to venture down this darker end of town, where you'll find Che Guevara on the wall and rock music on the stereo.

Havana   BAR

(Trg od Zatvora; ☉8am-1am; 🗲) In summer Havana takes over a little square on the dark side of the Old Town, projecting sports or pop videos onto the neighbouring building. When the weather turns, head inside, where Cuban scenes cover the walls and classic cocktails are served from a central bar.

❶ Getting There & Away

The main road to Tivat and Budva turns off the waterfront road at a baffling uncontrolled intersection south of the Stari Grad and heads through a long tunnel.

The **bus station** (☏032-325 809; ☉6am-9pm) is to the south of town, just off the road leading to the tunnel. Buses to Herceg Novi (€4, one hour), Budva (€3.50, 40 minutes), Tivat (€2.20, 20 minutes) and Podgorica (€7, two hours) are at least hourly. Further flung destinations include Kolašin (€12, four daily), Dubrovnik (€14, two daily) and Belgrade (€32, seven daily).

A taxi to Tivat airport should cost around €10.

Perast

☏032 / POP 270

Looking like a chunk of Venice that has floated down the Adriatic and anchored itself onto the bay, Perast hums with melancholy memories of the days when it was rich and powerful. Despite having only one main street, this tiny town boasts 16 churches and 17 formerly grand palazzos. While some are just enigmatic ruins sprouting bougainvillea and wild fig, others are caught up in the whirlwind of renovation that has hit the town. Michael Douglas and Catherine Zeta-Jones are said to have paid €2 million for a house here.

The town slopes down from the highway to a narrow waterfront road (Obala Marka Martinovića) that runs along its length. At its heart is St Nicholas' Church, set on a small square lined with date palms and the bronze busts of famous citizens.

Sights

Sveti Đorđe & Gospa od Škrpjela ISLAND
(St George's Island & Our Lady of the Rocks Island) Just offshore from Perast are two peculiarly picturesque islands. The smaller, Sveti Đorđe (St George), rises from a natural reef and houses a Benedictine monastery shaded by cypresses. Boats (€5 return) ferry people to its big sister, Gospa od Škrpjela (Our Lady of the Rocks), which was artificially created in the 15th century around a rock where an image of the Madonna was found. Every year on 22 July the locals row over with stones to continue the task.

St Nicholas' Church CHURCH
(Crkva Sv Nikole; treasury €1; ⏲10am-6pm) This large church has never been completed, and given that it was commenced in the 17th century and the bay's Catholic community has declined markedly since then, one suspects it never will be. Its treasury contains beautifully embroidered vestments and the remains of various saints. Climb the imposing 55m bell tower for views over the bay.

Perast Museum MUSEUM
(Muzej grada Perasta; adult/child €2.50/1.50; ⏲9am-7pm) The Bujović Palace, dating from 1694, has been lovingly preserved and converted into a museum showcasing the town's proud seafaring history. It's worth visiting for the building alone and for the wondrous photo opportunities afforded by its balcony.

Sleeping

Boka Bay B&B APARTMENT €€
(www.bokabay.com; apt €50-75; ❄) There are only two cosy sloped-ceiling apartments here – a studio and a one-bedroom – but they both have water views, en suites and kitchenettes. Bookings must be made by email.

Hotel Conte APARTMENT €€€
(☎032-373 687; www.hotel-conte.com; apt €80-160; ❄📶) Conte is not so much a hotel as a series of deluxe studio to two-bedroom apartments in historic buildings scattered around St Nicholas' Church. The sense of age resonating from the stone walls is palpable, even with the distinctly nontraditional addition of a spa bath and sauna in the flashest apartment. It's worth paying €20 extra for a sea view.

Eating

Konoba Otok Bronza MONTENEGRIN, SEAFOOD €€
(☎032-373 607; mains €7-13) Dating from the 12th century (yes, you read that right), this memorable place has a cavelike interior with a spring spouting mountain water from its rock walls. Settle in for a reasonably priced traditional meal or just soak up the mood over a glass of local vino under the canopy of grapevines.

Restaurant Conte SEAFOOD €€€
(☎032-373 687; mains €9-20; ⏲8am-midnight; 📶) Meals come with lashings of romance on the flower-bedecked waterside terrace of the Hotel Conte. You'll be presented with platters of whole fish to select from; the chosen one will return, cooked and silver-served, to your table.

Getting There & Away

Paid parking is available on either approach to town; car access into the town itself is restricted.

There's no bus station but buses stop at least hourly on the main road at the top of town. Expect to pay less than €3 for any journey within the bay between Kotor (25 minutes) and Herceg Novi (40 minutes).

Boat tours of the bay invariably stop here.

Lovćen National Park

Directly behind Kotor is **Mt Lovćen** (1749m, pronounced '*lov*·chen'), the black mountain that gave Crna Gora (Montenegro) its name (*crna/negro* means 'black', *gora/monte* means 'mountain' in Montenegrin and Italian respectively). This locale occupies a special place in the hearts of all Montenegrins. For most of its history it represented the entire nation – a rocky island of Slavic resistance in an Ottoman sea. The old capital of Cetinje nestles in its foothills and many of its residents head up here for picnics during summer.

Two-thirds of the national park's 6220 hectares are covered in woods, particularly the black beech that gives it its moody complexion. Even the rockier tracts sprout wild herbs such as St John's wort, mint and sage. The park is home to various types of reptile, 85 species of butterfly and large mammals such as brown bears and wolves. The 200 avian species found here include regal birds of prey such as the peregrine falcon, golden eagle and imperial eagle (but you'll be looking for a long time for the two-headed variety featured on the Montenegrin flag). Several species migrate between here and Lake Skadar.

The mountains are criss-crossed with hiking paths and mountain-biking trails, which can be accessed from Kotor, Budva or Cetinje, and the Coastal Mountain Traversal runs straight through. If you're planning on hiking, come prepared, as the temperature is on average 10°C cooler than on the coast, and Lovćen's prone to sudden changes in summer. Despite the high average rainfall, water supplies are limited, as the moisture quickly leaches into the karstic limestone.

The park's main hub is **Ivanova Korita**, near its centre, where there are a few eateries and accommodation providers and, in winter, a beginners' ski slope. Here you'll also find the **National Park Visitor Centre** (www.nparkovi.me; ⊙9am-5pm), which rents bikes (per hour €2) and offers accommodation in four-bed bungalows (€40). Informal camping is possible within the park (small/large tent €3/5, campervan €10), with additional charges for using established camping grounds (€10) or lighting fires in designated places (€5, including wood).

ℹ Getting There & Away

If you're driving, the park can be approached from either Kotor or Cetinje (entry fee €2). Tour buses are the only buses that head into the park.

Cetinje

⌨ 041 / POP 14,000

Rising from a green vale surrounded by rough grey mountains, Cetinje is an odd mix of former capital and overgrown village, where single-storey cottages and stately mansions share the same street. Several of those mansions - dating from times when European ambassadors rubbed shoulders with Montenegrin princesses - have become museums or schools for art and music.

Cetinje seems to expect its visitors to flit in and out on tour buses - as indeed most

of them do. Accommodation is limited and there are only a few proper restaurants. Come the weekend, competing sound systems blast the cobwebs from the main street. If war broke out on a Saturday night you probably wouldn't hear it.

◉ Sights

A collection of four Cetinje museums and two galleries are collectively known as the **National Museum of Montenegro**. A joint ticket will get you into all of them (adult/child €10/5), or you can buy individual tickets.

History Museum   MUSEUM
(Istorijski muzej; ☎041-230 310; www.mnmuseum. org; Novice Cerovića 7; adult/child €3/1.50; ⊙9am-5pm) Housed in Cetinje's most imposing building, the former parliament (1910), this fascinating museum is well laid out, following a timeline from the Stone Age to 1955. There are few English signs, but the enthusiastic staff will walk you around and give you an overview before leaving you to your own devices.

Montenegrin Art Gallery   GALLERY
(Crnogorska galerija umjetnosti; www.mnmuseum. org; Novice Cerovića 7; adult/child €4/2; ⊙9am-5pm) The national collection is split between the former parliament and a striking modern building on Cetinje's main street (mainly used for temporary exhibitions). All of Montenegro's great artists are represented, with the most famous (Milunović, Lubarda, Đurić, etc) having their own separate spaces.

King Nikola Museum   PALACE
(Muzej kralja Nikole; www.mnmuseum.org; Dvorski Trg; adult/child €5/2.50; ⊙9am-5pm) Entry to this 1871 palace, home to the last sovereign of Montenegro, is by guided tour (you may need to wait for a group to form). Although looted during WWII, enough plush furnishings, stern portraits and taxidermied animals remain to capture the spirit of the court.

Njegoš Museum   PALACE
(Njegošev muzej; www.mnmuseum.org; Dvorski Trg; adult/child €3/1.50; ⊙9am-5pm) This castle-like palace was the residence of Montenegro's favourite son, prince-bishop and poet Petar II Petrović Njegoš. It was built and financed by the Russians in 1838 and housed the nation's first billiard table, hence the museum's alternative name, Biljarda.

DURMITOR NATIONAL PARK

Magnificent scenery ratchets up to stupendous in this national park, where ice and water have carved a dramatic landscape from the limestone. Forty-eight peaks soar to over 2000m in altitude, with the highest, **Bobotov Kuk**, reaching 2523m. From December to March Durmitor is a major ski resort, while in summer it's a popular place for hiking, rafting and other active pursuits.

The park is home to enough critters to cast a Disney movie, including 163 species of bird, about 50 types of mammals, and purportedly the greatest variety of butterflies in Europe. It covers the Durmitor mountain range and a narrow branch heading east along the Tara River towards Mojkovac. **Žabljak**, at the eastern edge of the range, is the park's principal gateway and the only town within its boundaries. It's not very big and neither is it attractive, but it has a supermarket, a post office, a bank, hotels and restaurants, all gathered around the car park masquerading as the main square.

All of the approaches to Durmitor are spectacular. The bus station is at the southern edge of Žabljak, on the Šavnik road. Buses head to Nikšić (€9, six daily), Podgorica (€9.50, three daily) and Pljevlja (€4.50, three daily).

BALKANS MONTENEGRO SURVIVAL GUIDE

Cetinje Monastery
MONASTERY

(Cetinjski Manastir; ☉8am-6pm) It's a case of four times lucky for the Cetinje Monastery, having been repeatedly destroyed during Ottoman attacks and rebuilt. This sturdy incarnation dates from 1786, with its only exterior ornamentation being the capitals of columns recycled from the original building, founded in 1484.

🛏 Sleeping

Pansion 22
GUESTHOUSE €

(☎069 055 473; www.pansion22.com; Ivana Crnojevića 22; s/d €22/40; ☎) They may not be great at speaking English or answering emails, but the family who run this central guesthouse offer a warm welcome nonetheless. The rooms are simply decorated, clean and comfortable, with views of the mountains from the top floor.

Hotel Grand
HOTEL €€

(☎041-231 651; www.hotelgrand.me; Njegoševa 1; s/d from €45/65; ⓟ☎☒) Step back into an era of brass trim, dark wood, parquet floors and keys dangling behind disinterested reception staff. While it may have passed for grand in its Yugoslav heyday, the Hotel Grand could hardly be accused of that now. That said, it's not a terrible place to stay and the beds are comfortable.

🍴 Eating

Vinoteka
ITALIAN, MONTENEGRIN €

(Njegoševa 103; mains €4-12) The wood-beamed porch and astroturfed terrace facing the garden is such a pleasant place to sit that the reasonably priced pizza, pasta and Montene-

grin cuisine feels like a bonus – the decent wine list even more so. The breakfasts are good too.

Kole
MONTENEGRIN, EUROPEAN €€

(☎041-231 620; www.restaurantkole.me; Bul Crnogorskih Junaka 12; mains €3-12; ☉7am-11pm) They serve omelettes and pasta at this snazzy modern eatery, but it's the local specialities that shine. Try the Njeguški ražanj, smoky spit-roasted meat stuffed with *pršut* (smoke-dried ham) and cheese.

❶ Getting There & Away

Cetinje is on the main Budva–Podgorica highway and can also be reached by a glorious back road from Kotor via Lovćen National Park. The **bus station** (Trg Golootočkih Žrtava) is basically derelict but buses still stop outside, including regular services from Herceg Novi (€7, 2½ hours), Budva (€4, 40 minutes) and Podgorica (€4, 30 minutes).

Montenegro Survival Guide

❶ Directory A–Z

ACCOMMODATION

Private accommodation (rooms and apartments for rent) and hotels form the bulk of the sleeping options, although there are some hostels in the more touristy areas. Camping grounds operate in summer, and some of the mountainous areas have cabin accommodation in 'eco villages' or mountain huts. In the peak summer season, some places require minimum stays (three days to a week). Many establishments on the coast

ℹ PRICE RANGES

The following price indicators apply for accommodation in a double room in the shoulder season (roughly June and September):

€ less than €40

€€ €40 to €100

Tipping isn't expected at restaurants, although it's common to round up to the nearest euro. The following price categories refer to a standard main course in restaurants/eateries:

€ less than €7

€€ €7 to €12

€€€ more than €12

close during winter. An additional tourist tax (usually less than €1 per night) is added to the rate for all accommodation types.

DANGERS & ANNOYANCES

➡ The roads can be treacherous. The main hazard is from other motorists, who have no qualms about overtaking on blind corners while talking on their mobile phones or stopping in the middle of the road without warning.

➡ Chances are you'll see some snakes if you're poking around ruins during summer. Montenegro has two types of venomous vipers but they'll try their best to keep out of your way. If bitten, you will have time to head to a medical centre for the antivenom, but you should go immediately. Water snakes are harmless.

➡ Check with the police before photographing any official building they're guarding.

➡ Since Montenegro is in an active seismic zone, earthquakes strike from time to time. The last major one that caused a loss of life was in 1979.

EMERGENCY & IMPORTANT NUMBERS

International access code	☏ 00
Country code	☏ 382
Police	☏ 122
Ambulance	☏ 124
Roadside Assistance	☏ 9807

INTERNET ACCESS

Most accommodation providers (excluding private accommodation) now offer free wireless connections, although they often don't penetrate to every part of the building and may be limited to

the reception area. Many bars and cafes also offer wireless. Most towns also have an internet cafe; hourly rates start from around 50c.

OPENING HOURS

Montenegrins have a flexible approach to opening times. Even if hours are posted on the door of an establishment, don't be surprised if they're not heeded. Many tourist-orientated businesses close between November and March.

Banks 8am-5pm Monday to Friday, 8am-noon Saturday

Post offices 7am-8pm Monday to Friday, sometimes Saturday. In smaller towns they may close midafternoon, or close at noon and reopen at 5pm.

Restaurants, Cafes & Bars 8am-midnight. Cafe-bars may stay open until 2am or 3am.

Shops 9am-8pm. Sometimes they'll close for a few hours in the late afternoon.

PUBLIC HOLIDAYS

New Year's Day 1 and 2 January

Orthodox Christmas 6, 7 and 8 January

Orthodox Good Friday & Easter Monday date varies, usually April/May

Labour Day 1 May

Independence Day 21 May

Statehood Day 13 July

TELEPHONE

➡ The international access prefix is ☏ 00 or + from a mobile phone.

➡ Press the *i* button on public phones for dialling commands in English.

➡ Mobile numbers start with 06.

Local SIM cards are a good idea if you're planning a longer stay. The main providers (T-Mobile, M:tel and Telenor) have storefronts in most towns. Many shopping centres have terminals where you can top-up your prepay account. Mobile calls are expensive in Montenegro, but the main providers offer heavily discounted rates to calls within their networks, so it's not uncommon for businesses to advertise three different mobile numbers on different networks.

TOURIST INFORMATION

Official tourist offices (usually labelled *turistič-ka organizacija*) are hit and miss. Some have wonderfully helpful English-speaking staff, regular opening hours and a good supply of free material, while others have none of the above. Thankfully the **National Tourist Office** (www.montenegro.travel) is more switched on and its website is a great resource for travellers. It doesn't have a public office but you can dial 1300 at any time to receive tourist information from multilingual staff.

VISAS

Visas are not required for citizens of most European countries, Turkey, Israel, Singapore, South Korea, Israel, Australia, New Zealand, Canada and the USA. In most cases this allows a stay of up to 90 days. If your country s not covered by a visa waiver, you will need a valid passport, verified letter of invitation, return ticket, proof of sufficient funds and proof of medical cover in order to obtain a visa.

❶ Getting There & Away

Montenegro may be a wee slip of a thing, but it borders five other states: Croatia, Bosnia and Hercegovina (BiH), Serbia, Kosovo and Albania. You can easily enter Montenegro by land from any of its neighbours.

BUS

There's a well-developed bus network linking Montenegro with the major cities of the former Yugoslavia and onwards to Western Europe and Turkey. At the border, guards will often enter the bus and collect passports, checking the photos as they go. Once they're happy with them they return them to the bus conductor, who will return them to you as the driver speeds off. Make sure you get yours back and that it's been stamped.

TRAIN

Montenegro's main train line starts at Bar and heads north through the middle of Montenegro and into Serbia. At least two trains go between Bar and Belgrade daily (€21, 11 hours), with one continuing on to Novi Sad and Subotica. You'll find timetables on the website of **Montenegro Railways** (www.zpcg.me).

From Belgrade it's possible to connect to destinations throughout Europe; see the website of **Serbian Railways** (www.serbianrailways. com) for timetables.

❶ Getting Around

Bus Buses link all major towns and are affordable, reliable and reasonably comfortable.

Car While you can get most places by bus, hiring a car will give you freedom to explore some of Montenegro's scenic back roads. Some of these are extremely narrow and cling to the sides of canyons, so it may not suit the inexperienced or faint-hearted.

Train Trains are cheap, but the network is limited and the carriages are old and can get hot. The main line links Bar, Virpazar, Podgorica, Kolašin, Mojkovac and Bijelo Polje, and there's a second line from Podgorica to Danilovgrad and Nikšić.

ALBANIA

Tirana

📞 04 / POP 802,000

Lively, colourful Tirana is the beating heart of Albania, where this tiny nation's hopes and dreams coalesce into a vibrant whirl of traffic, brash consumerism and unfettered fun. Trendy Blloku buzzes, with the well-heeled and flush hanging out in bars or zipping between boutiques, while the city's grand boulevards are lined with fascinating relics of its Ottoman, Italian and communist past – from delicate minarets to loud socialist murals. Loud and crazy, Tirana is never dull.

◉ Sights

The centre of Tirana is Skanderbeg Sq, a large traffic island. Running through the square is Tirana's main avenue, Blvd Zogu I, which becomes Blvd Dëshmorët e Kombit (Martyrs of the Nation Blvd) south of the square. Most of the city's sights are within walking distance, though Tirana itself is now one huge urban sprawl.

Sheshi Skënderbej   SQUARE
(Skanderbeg Sq) Skanderbeg Sq is the best place to start witnessing Tirana's daily goings-on. Until it was pulled down by an angry mob in 1991, a 10m-high bronze statue of Enver Hoxha stood here, watching over a mainly car-free square. Now only the **equestrian statue of Skanderbeg**, the Albanian national hero, remains.

★**National History Museum**   MUSEUM
(Muzeu Historik Kombëtar; www.mhk.gov.al; Sheshi Skënderbej; adult/student 200/60 lekë; ⊙10am-5pm Tue-Sat, 9am-2pm Sun) The largest museum in Albania holds many of the country's archaeological treasures and a replica of Skanderbeg's massive sword (how he held it, rode his horse and fought at the same time is a mystery). The excellent collection is almost entirely signed in English and takes you chronologically from ancient Illyria to the postcommunist era. One highlight of the museum is a terrific exhibition of icons by Onufri, a renowned 16th-century Albanian master of colour.

★**National Art Gallery**   GALLERY
(Galeria Kombëtare e Arteve; Blvd Dëshmorët e Kombit; adult/student 200/100 lekë; ⊙10am-6pm Wed-Sun) Tracing the relatively brief history of Albanian painting from the early 19th

Tirana

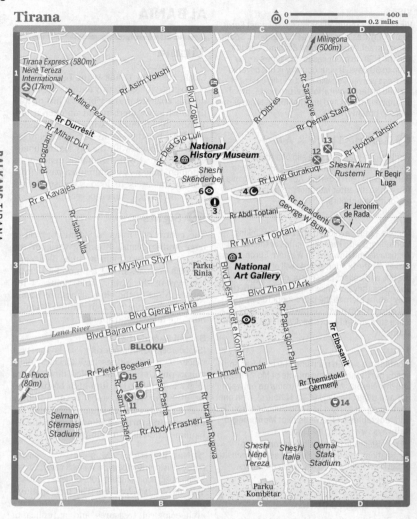

Tirana

◎ Top Sights
1 National Art Gallery		C3
2 National History Museum		B2

◎ Sights
3 Equestrian Statue of Skanderbeg		C2
4 Et'hem Bey Mosque		C2
5 Pyramid		C4
6 Sheshi Skënderbej		B2

🛏 Sleeping
7 Brilant Antik Hotel		D3
8 Freddy's B&B		C1
9 Tirana Backpacker Hostel		A2
10 Trip N Hostel		D1

✕ Eating
11 Era		B4
12 Oda		D2
13 Stephen Centre		D2

🍷 Drinking & Nightlife
14 Kaon Beer Garden		D4
15 Nouvelle Vague		B4
16 Radio		B4

century to the present day, this beautiful space also has temporary exhibits that are worth a look. Downstairs there's a small but interesting collection of 19th-century paintings depicting scenes from daily Albanian life, while upstairs the art takes on a political dimension with some truly fabulous examples of Albanian socialist realism.

Et'hem Bey Mosque
MOSQUE

(Sheshi Skënderbej; ⊘ 8am-11am) To one side of Skanderbeg Sq, the 1789-1823 Et'hem Bey Mosque was spared destruction during the atheism campaign of the late 1960s because of its status as a cultural monument. Small and elegant, it's one of the oldest buildings left in the city. Take your shoes off to look inside at the beautifully painted dome.

Pyramid
NOTABLE BUILDING

(Blvd Dëshmorët e Kombit) Designed by Enver Hoxha's daughter and son-in-law and completed in 1988, this monstrously unattractive building was formerly the Enver Hoxha Museum, and more recently a convention centre and nightclub. Today, covered in graffiti and surrounded by the encampments of Tirana's homeless, its once white marble walls are now crumbling; no decision on whether to demolish or restore it appears to have yet been reached. It's sometimes open for temporary exhibits, for which it's a surprisingly great venue.

🛏 Sleeping

★ Tirana Backpacker Hostel
HOSTEL €

(☑ 068 4682 353, 068 3133 451; www.tiranahostel.com; Rr e Bogdaneve 3; dm €10-11, s/d €28/35, cabin per person €14 ; ❄ @ ⊚) Albania's first ever hostel has now moved to an ever better location, and remains one of the best value and most enthusiastically run places to stay in the country. It's housed in a charmingly decorated house with a garden in which there are several cute cabins for those wanting something more than a dorm room, though there are also great private rooms available.

★ Trip N Hostel
HOSTEL €

(☑ 068 2055 540, 068 3048 905 www.tripnhostel.com; Rr Musa Maci 1; dm/d €10/30) Tirana's coolest hostel is this recently opened place, housed in a large design-conscious house in a residential neighbourhood, with a garden out the back and a cool bar-hangout area. Dorms have handmade fixtures, curtains between beds for privacy and private lockable drawers, while there's also a roof terrace

strewn with hammocks. There's a great vibe and a cool crowd as well.

Milingona
HOSTEL €

(☑ 069 2049 836, 069 2070 076; www.milingona-hostel.com; Rr Risa Cerova 197/2, off Rr e Dibres; dm €8-10, d €30; @ ⊚) This friendly, female-run, community-conscious hostel takes up a large house in a residential district and is cared for by multilingual sisters. There are large dorms (sleeping six and eight people), each of which shares facilities with another dorm on the same floor. There's a large shared kitchen, a living room, a roof terrace and a garden.

To get here from the centre, walk up Rr e Dibres, and when it splits, bear right after the Medresa – Rr Risa Cerova is the first street on the right.

★ Brilant Antik Hotel
HOTEL €€

(☑ 04-2251 166; www.hotelbrilant.com; Rr Jeronim de Rada 79; s/d €60/90; ❄ ⊚) This charming house-cum-hotel has plenty of character, a central location and welcoming English-speaking staff to ease you into Tirana life. Rooms are spacious, decently furnished with the odd antique, and breakfast downstairs is a veritable feast.

Freddy's B&B
HOTEL €€

(☑ 04 2266 077, 068 2035 261; www.freddyshostel.com; Rr Bardhok Biba 75; s/d/tr/qu €33/38/50/59; ❄ @ ⊚) Having transitioned from a hostel to a small hotel (though its website is yet to catch up), Freddy's is run by a local family with years of experience. Following a renovation in 2014, all rooms are now comfortable, ensuite and even have their own PC desktops. It's also got an excellent location right in the city centre.

🍴 Eating

Era
ALBANIAN, ITALIAN €€

(☑ 04-224 3845; www.era.al; Rr Ismail Qemali; mains 400-800 lekë; ⊘ 11am-midnight; 🖉) This local institution serves traditional Albanian and Italian fare in the heart of Blloku. The inventive menu includes oven-baked veal and eggs, stuffed eggplant, pizza, and pilau with chicken and pine nuts. Be warned: it's sometimes quite hard to get a seat as it's fearsomely popular, so you may have to wait. Delivery and takeaway are both available.

Stephen Centre
CAFE €€

(www.stephencenter.com; Rr Hoxha Tahsim 1; mains 400-700 lekë; ⊘ 7am-11pm Mon-Sat; ⊚) Looking better than ever after a 2014 refit, this

Tirana classic is where to come for a great burger, fantastic Tex-Mex and voluminous, great-value breakfasts. Run by Christian missionaries to Albania who do wonderful work with local orphans, Roma and the disabled, the Centre has no booze on the menu, but is a super friendly and relaxed hang out.

Oda
ALBANIAN €€

(Rr Luigj Gurakuqi; mains 350-650 lekë; ⊙noon-11pm; 🖉) This tourist favourite is stuffed full of traditional Albanian arts and crafts, and while its popularity with travellers means you won't feel like you've discovered a truly authentic slice of the country, the delicious menu and pleasant atmosphere make it well worth a visit. You can choose from two brightly lit dining rooms or an atmospheric terrace.

🍷 Drinking & Nightlife

Radio
BAR

(Rr Ismail Qemali 29/1; ⊙9am-1am; 🛜) This place remains one of the city's coolest bars, and attracts a young and alternative crowd. Set back from the street, you have to know it's here, but once inside this understated and friendly place be sure to check out the owner's collection of antique Albania-made radios.

Nouvelle Vague
BAR

(Rr Pjetër Bogdani; ⊙9am-midnight; 🛜) A Blloku hotspot favoured by a cool crowd, Nouvelle Vague is one of the places to head any night of the week for a great atmosphere, full cocktail list and interesting music.

Kaon Beer Garden
BEER HALL

(www.kaonbeer.com; Rr Asim Zeneli; ⊙noon-1am) For those who hate the hassle of ordering beer after beer, here's Kaon. Its popular 'keg-on-the-table' approach means it can be hard to get a table in the evening (queuing is normal), but once you get in, it's a pleasant outdoor bar and restaurant in the fancy villa-filled part of town. You won't go hungry; Albanian meals start from 200 lekë. Locally brewed beer comes in standard glasses, or tabletop 2- and 3-litre 'roxys'.

ℹ Getting There & Away

Unless you fly to Tirana, you'll almost certainly arrive by bus. There is no official bus station in Tirana, instead there are a large number of geographically dispersed bus stops around the city centre, from which buses to specific destinations leave. Do check locally for the latest departure points: hostels usually have up-to-date information.

Most international services depart from various parts of Blvd Zogu I, with multiple services to Skopje, Macedonia (€20, eight hours) and Pristina, Kosovo (€20, five hours), leaving from near the Tirana International Hotel, and services to Ulcinj, Montenegro (€20, four hours) leaving from in front of the Tourist Information Centre.

Departures to the south leave from Rr Myhedin Llegami near the corner with Blvd Gjergj Fishta.

WORTH A TRIP

THE ACCURSED MOUNTAINS & THE KOMAN FERRY

The 'Accursed Mountains' offer some of Albania's most impressive scenery, and have exploded in recent years as a popular backpacker destination. You'll see a totally different side of the country here: that of blood feuds, deep tradition, extraordinary landscapes and fierce local pride. It's absolutely a highlight of any trip to Albania, and quite extraordinary to be so easily removed from modern life in the middle of 21st-century Europe. The two main villages with tourist infrastructure are Theth and Valbona, and a superb dayhike links the two.

Another reason to head to this remote part of Albania is for the excellent three-hour ferry ride across Lake Koman, connecting the towns of Koman and Fierzë. The best way to experience the region is to make a loop beginning and ending in Shkodra, and taking in Koman, Fierzë, Valbona and Theth. To do this, arrange to have the morning 6.30am *furgon* (shared minibus) from Shkodra to Koman (500 lekë, two hours) pick you up at your hotel, which will get you to the departure point for the boats by 8.30am. There are two ferries daily in the summer months – both leave from Koman at 9am and arrive in Fierzë around 1pm. On arrival in Fierzë the boats are met by buses that will take you to Valbona (400 lekë). Stay in Valbona for a night or two before doing the stunning day hike to Theth. After the hike you can stay for another night or two in Theth, before taking a *furgon* back to Shkodra.

These include services to Berat (400 lekë, three hours, every 30 minutes until 6pm), and to towns on the Albanian Riviera, including Himara (1000 lekë, five hours, 1pm and 6pm) and Saranda (1300 lekë, 6½ hours, roughly hourly 5am to noon).

There are no international train connections to Albania, and the aged domestic train network is extremely limited, slow and only of interest as a curiosity.

Berat

📍 032 / POP 71,000

Berat weaves its own very special magic, and is easily a highlight of visiting Albania. Its most striking feature is the collection of white Ottoman houses climbing up the hill to its castle, earning it the title of 'town of a thousand windows' and helping it join Gjirokastra on the list of Unesco World Heritage sites in 2008. Its rugged mountain setting is particularly evocative when the clouds swirl around the tops of the minarets, or break up to show the icy top of Mt Tomorri.

◎ Sights

★ Kalaja   CASTLE

(admission 100 lekë; ◎24hr) The area inside the castle's walls still lives and breathes; if you walk around this busy, ancient neighbourhood for long enough you'll invariably stumble into someone's courtyard thinking it's a church or ruin (no one seems to mind). In spring and summer the fragrance of camomile is in the air (and underfoot), and wildflowers burst from every gap between the stones.

The highest point is occupied by the Inner Fortress, where ruined stairs lead to a Tolkienesque water reservoir. Views are spectacular in all directions and guided tours are available from the entry gate for €10. It's a steep ten-minute walk up the hill from the centre of town.

★ Onufri Museum   GALLERY

(admission 200 lekë; ◎9am-1pm & 4-7pm Tue-Sat, to 2pm Sun May-Sep, to 4pm Tue-Sun Oct-Apr) Kala was traditionally a Christian neighbourhood, but fewer than a dozen of the 20 churches remain. The quarter's biggest church, **Church of the Dormition of St Mary** (Kisha Fjetja e Shën Mërisë), is the site of the Onufri Museum. The church itself dates from 1797 and was built on the foundations of a 10th-century church. Onu-

fri's spectacular 16th-century artworks are displayed on the ground level along with a beautifully gilded iconostasis.

Mangalem Quarter   NEIGHBOURHOOD

Down in the traditionally Muslim Mangalem quarter, there are three grand mosques. The 16th-century **Sultan's Mosque** (Xhamia e Mbretit) is one of the oldest in Albania. The **Helveti teqe** behind the mosque has a beautiful carved ceiling and was specially designed with acoustic holes to improve the quality of sound during meetings. The Helveti, like the Bektashi, are a dervish order, or brotherhood, of Muslim mystics.

Ethnographic Museum   MUSEUM

(admission 200 lekë; ◎9am-1pm & 4-7pm Tue-Sat, to 2pm Sun May-Sep, to 4pm Tue-Sun Oct-Apr) Down from the castle, this museum is in an 18th-century Ottoman house that's as interesting as the exhibits. The ground floor has displays of traditional clothes and the tools used by silversmiths and weavers, while the upper storey has kitchens, bedrooms and guest rooms decked out in traditional style.

🛏 Sleeping

Berat Backpackers   HOSTEL €

(📞069 7854 219; www.beratbackpackers.com; Gorica; tent/dm/r €6/12/30; ◎mid-Mar–Nov; @🛜) This transformed traditional house in the Gorica quarter (across the river from Mangalem) houses one of Albania's friendliest and best-run hostels. The vine-clad establishment contains a basement bar, alfresco drinking area and a cheery, relaxed atmosphere that money can't buy. There are two airy dorms with original ceilings, and one excellent-value double room that shares the bathroom facilities with the dorms.

There's also a shaded camping area on the terrace and cheap laundry available.

**Lorenc Guesthouse
& Hostel**   GUESTHOUSE €

(📞069 6337 254, 032 231 215; lorencpushi@ hotmail.com; Gorica; dm/d €12/26; 🛜) This 400-year-old Gorica house once beloged to King Zog's Minister of Finance, and the quirkiness doesn't stop there; loquacious owner Lorenc is a former opera singer who is happy to put his talents on display with a little urging. The rooms all share bathrooms, but some have truly gorgeous original ceilings, while the shaded garden is a little slice of heaven.

✖ Eating

White House ITALIAN €€
(Rr Antipatrea; mains 300-600 lekë; ⊙8am-11pm)
On the main road that runs north of the river, this place has a superb roof terrace with sweeping views over Berat, and serves up a mean pizza to boot. There's also a classier dining room downstairs, with air-conditioning – perfect for a blowout meal.

Wildor ALBANIAN €€
(Rr Antipatrea; mains 450-700 lekë; ⊙9am-10pm; ☏) On the river front main road, this renovated old stone mansion has rather unconvincing decor that hints at tradition without really being anything of the kind. But that's unimportant as the traditional Berati food is hearty and fresh.

ℹ Getting There & Away

Buses and *furgons* run between Tirana and Berat (400 lekë, three hours, half-hourly until 3pm). Services arrive in and depart from Sheshi Teodor Muzaka, next to the Lead Mosque in the centre of town. There are also buses to Vlora (300 lekë, two hours, hourly until 2pm), Durrës (300 lekë, two hours, six daily), Saranda (1200 lekë, six hours, two daily at 8am and 2pm) and Gjirokastra (800 lekë, four hours, daily at 8am).

The Albanian Riviera

The Albanian Riviera was a revelation a decade or so ago, when travellers began to discover the last virgin stretch of the Mediterranean coast in Europe. Since then, things have become significantly less pristine, with overdevelopment blighting many of the once charming coastal villages. But worry not, while Dhërmi and Himara may be well and truly swarming, there are still spots to kick back and enjoy the empty beaches the region was once so famous for.

🛏 Sleeping

★ Sea Turtle CAMPGROUND €
(☑069 4016 057; Drymades; per person incl half-board from 1000 lekë; ⊙Jun-Sep; ☏) This great little set-up is run by two brothers. Each summer they turn the family orange orchard into a vibrant tent city, and the price includes the tent (with mattresses, sheets and pillows), breakfast and a family-cooked dinner (served up in true camp style). Hot showers are under the shade of old fig trees, or it's a short walk to the beach.

★ Shkolla Hostel HOSTEL €
(☑069 2119 596; www.tiranahostel.com; Vuno; tent/dm €4/8; ⊙late Jun-Sep) A unique summer-only hostel housed in the village school at Juno, this is a wonderful place to get off the beaten track and enjoy the tranquil isolation of this mountain village.

Kamping Himare CAMPGROUND €
(☑068 5298 940; www.himaracamping.com; Potami Beach; tent per person 800 lekë; ⊙May-Sep) On the second beach in Himara if you're coming from Tirana, this chilled out camping ground across the main road from the beach is housed in an olive and orange grove. Nice touches include midnight movies in an open-air cinema and sublime pancakes for breakfast. Rates includes mattresses, sheets and pillows, while breakfast is 200 lekë extra.

✖ Eating

★ Pastarella MEDITERRANEAN €€
(☑068 2044 481; www.pastarellarestaurant.com; Dhërmi; mains 300-8000 lekë; ⊙11am-11pm Jun-Sep) At the southern far end of Dhërmi beach, this offshoot of a popular Tirana restaurant is a hugely popular place come the summer months, where its dining room, which opens onto the beach and has gorgeous views, functions as an all-day restaurant and bar. The enticing menu is all about seafood, fresh fish and pasta.

Gërthëla SEAFOOD €€
(Rr Jonianët; mains 300-1000 lekë; ⊙11am-midnight; ☏) One of Saranda's original restaurants, 'the crab' is a long-standing taverna that only has fish and seafood on the menu, and locals will tell you with certainty that it offers the best-prepared versions of either available in town. The charming glass-fronted dining room is full of traditional knickknacks and there's a big wine selection to boot.

ℹ Getting There & Away

The towns of the Albanian Riviera, which include Dhërmi, Hirmara, Borsh and Bunec, are connected by one main coastal road between Vlora and Saranda. Buses run down the road in both directions several times a day. Sample prices from Tirana include Himara (800 lekë, four hours) and Saranda (1300 lekë, eight hours).

Albania Survival Guide

ⓘ Directory A–Z

EMERGENCY & IMPORTANT NUMBERS
Ambulance ☏127
Fire ☏128
Police ☏129

MONEY
The lekë is the official currency, though the euro is widely accepted; you'll get a better deal for things in general if you use lekë.

Accommodation is generally quoted in euros but can be paid in either currency.

ATMs can be found in all but the most rural of Albania's towns, and often dispense cash in either currency.

Credit cards are accepted only in the larger hotels, shops and travel agencies, and few of these are outside Tirana.

PUBLIC HOLIDAYS
New Year's Day 1 January
Summer Day 16 March
Nevruz 23 March
Catholic Easter March or April
Orthodox Easter March or April
May Day 1 May
Mother Teresa Day 19 October
Independence Day 28 November
Liberation Day 29 November
Christmas Day 25 December

TELEPHONE
Albania's country phone code is ☏355.

Mobile coverage is excellent, though it's limited in very remote areas (most places have some form of connection including Theth).

Prepaid SIM cards cost around 500 lekë and include credit. Mobile numbers begin with ☏06.

To call an Albanian mobile number from abroad, dial ☏355 then either 67, 68 or 69 (drop the 0).

VISAS
Visas are not required for citizens of EU countries or nationals of Australia, Canada, New Zealand, Japan, South Korea, Norway, South Africa or the USA. Travellers from other countries should check www.mfa.gov.al.

ⓘ Getting There & Away

Albania has good connections in all directions: daily buses go to Kosovo, Montenegro, Macedonia and Greece.

The southern seaport of Saranda is a short boat trip from Greece's Corfu, while in summer

The following price categories for the cost of a double room in high season are used in the accommodation listings in this chapter.

€ less than €30

€€ €30 to €80

The following price categories for the cost of a main course are used in the listings for restaurants/eateries in this chapter.

€ less than 200 lekë

€€ 200 lekë to 500 lekë

ferries also connect Himara and Vlora to Corfu. Durrës has regular ferries to Italy.

Travellers heading south from Croatia can pass through Montenegro to Shkodra (via Ulcinj), and loop through Albania before heading into Macedonia via Pogradec or Kosovo via the Lake Koman Ferry, or the new super-fast Albania–Kosovo highway. There are no international passenger trains into Albania.

BORDER CROSSINGS
Your border-crossing options are buses, taxis or walking across a border and picking up transport on the other side.

Montenegro The main crossings link Shkodra to Ulcinj (Muriqan) and to Podgorica (Hani i Hotit).

Kosovo The closest border crossing to the Koman Ferry terminal is Morina, and further south is Qafë Prush. Near Kukës, use Morinë for the highway to Tirana.

Macedonia Use Blato to get to Debar, Qafë e Thanës or Sveti Naum, each to one side of Pogradec, for accessing Ohrid.

Greece The main border crossing to and from Greece is Kakavija, on the road from Athens to Tirana. It's about half an hour from Gjirokastra and 250km west of Tirana, and can take up to three hours to pass through during summer. Kapshtica (near Korça) also gets long lines in summer. Konispoli is near Butrint in Albania's south.

ⓘ Getting Around

Bus and *furgon* are the main form of public transport in Albania. Fares are low, and you either pay the conductor on board or when you hop off, which can be anywhere along the route.

Municipal buses operate in Tirana, Durrës, Shkodra and Vlora, and trips cost 30 lekë.

Trains are dirt cheap and travelling on them is an adventure. Daily passenger trains leave suburban Tirana (the main train station in the city has been demolished and a new one is currently under construction) for Durrës, Shkodra, Fier, Vlora, Elbasan and a few kilometres shy of Pogradec. Check timetables at the station in person, and buy your ticket 10 minutes before departure.

MACEDONIA

Skopje

📞 02 / POP 670,000

Skopje is among Europe's most entertaining and eclectic small capital cities. While an expensive and rather kitschy government construction spree has sparked controversy in recent years, Skopje's new abundance of statuary, fountains, bridges, museums and other structures built to encourage a national identity has visitors' cameras snapping like never before and has defined the ever-changing city for the 21st century.

But plenty survives from earlier times – Skopje's Ottoman- and Byzantine-era wonders include the 15th-century Kameni Most (Stone Bridge), the wonderful Čaršija (old Turkish bazaar), where you can get lost for hours, Sveti Spas Church, with its ornate, hand-carved iconostasis, and Tvrdina Kale Fortress, Skopje's guardian since the 5th century.

⊙ Sights

The Čaršija houses Skopje's main historic sights. Other museums are on the Vardar's southern bank, where cafes line pedestrianised ul Makedonija. Buzzing Ploštad Makedonija (Macedonia Sq) stands smack by the Ottoman stone bridge (Kameni Most), which accesses Čaršija. The residen-

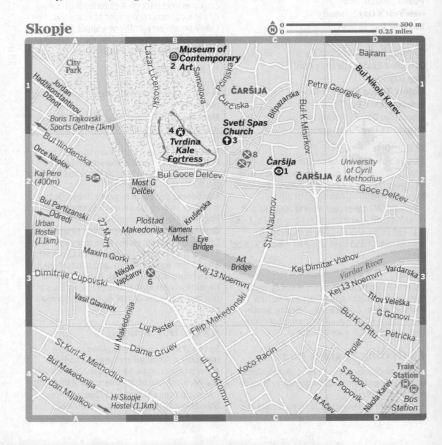

Skopje

0 500 m / 0 0.25 miles

tial district of Debar Maalo, to the west of the city centre, is a very popular area for locals to eat, and has retained its local character more than the deeply altered city centre.

★ Čaršija NEIGHBOURHOOD

Čaršija is the hillside Turkish old town of Skopje and evokes the city's Ottoman past with its winding lanes filled with teahouses, mosques, craftsmen's stores, and even good nightlife. It also boasts Skopje's best historic structures and museums, and is the first place any visitor should head. Čaršija runs from the Stone Bridge to the Bit Pazar, a big, busy vegetable market purveying bric-a-brac, household goods and anything random. Expect to get pleasantly lost in its maze of narrow streets.

★ Sveti Spas Church CHURCH

(Church of the Holy Saviour; Makarije Frčkoski 8; adult/student 120/50MKD; ⊙ 9am-5pm Tue-Fri, to 3pm Sat & Sun) Partially underground (the Turks banned churches from being taller than mosques), this church dates from the 14th century and is the most historically important in the city. Its dark interior boasts a stunning wood-carved iconostasis 10m wide and 6m high, built by early-19th-century master craftsmen Makarije Frčkovski and brothers Petar and Marko Filipovski. It's rather tricky to find as its sunken design means it doesn't really look like a church from the outside.

★ Tvrdina Kale Fortress FORTRESS

(⊙ daylight hours) **FREE** Dominating the skyline of Skopje, this *Game of Thrones*-worthy 6th-century AD Byzantine (and later, Ottoman) fortress is an easy walk up from the Čaršija, and its ramparts offer great views over city and river. Inside are various archaeological finds from neolithic to Ottoman times.

★ Museum of Contemporary Art MUSEUM

(NIMoCA; www.msuskopje.org.mk; Samoilova bb; admission 50MKD; ⊙ 10am-5pm Tue-Sat, 9am-1pm Sun) Definitely a highlight of Skopje, this excellent museum is housed in an impressive building at the top of a hill, with wonderful city views and an extraordinarily good collection for a city of Skopje's size. The museum was formed in the aftermath of the devastating 1963 earthquake, with artists and collections around the world donating works to form a collection that now includes works by Picasso, Léger, Hockney, Alexander Calder, Jasper Johns, Meret Oppenheim, Christo and Bridget Riley.

🛏 Sleeping

★ Hi Skopje Hostel HOSTEL €

(☑ 6091 242; www.hiskopjehostel.com; Crniche 15; dm/s/d from 540/1200/2100MKD) In the cool shade of Mt Vodno, this cheerful new hostel offers dorms and two rooms (with a shared bathroom). There's a communal kitchen, and the relaxing back garden adds to the out-of-city vibe. The friendly young owners offer tons of info on city sights and events. It's located on a hilly street 2.5km from the bus/train stations (take a taxi for 150MKD).

★ Urban Hostel HOSTEL €

(☑ 02-6142 785; www.urbanhostel.com.mk; Adolf Ciborovski 22; dm/s/d €13/24/35, apt from €46; ❄ 🛜) A short walk from the centre in the leafy Debar Maalo neighbourhood, this excellent hostel takes great care of its guests, with super-clean rooms, comfy beds, and some quirky extras including a fireplace and a piano. The friendly, helpful staff members are another highlight. It's about a 15-minute walk from the city centre.

Unity Hostel HOSTEL €

(☑ 078 277 557; www.unityhostel.mk; Bul Ilidenska 1; dm €10-12, s/d €30/35; ❄ 🛜) It may be housed in a fairly unappealing-looking communist era building, but the new Unity Hostel's location is great, just across the river from the Kale Fortress. Inside it's bright and cheerfully run by a friendly team. There are two dorms and one double room, complimented by a balcony, full kitchen and living room.

SKOPJE 2014: A GARISH VISION?

The central district of Skopje has undergone monumental change in recent years, as the Macedonian government under Prime Minister Nikola Gruevski has implemented the controversial Skopje 2014 project. The project, begun in 2010, has seen the construction of 20 new buildings and 40 new monuments in the area around the river. It's an attempt to give the city a more uniform appearance while helping to bolster Macedonian national pride by linking the modern state to its forerunners, many of whose Macedonian credentials are in fact debatable.

Detractors bemoan the tens – if not hundreds – of millions of euros spent on the project to date, while others point to the inherent kitschiness of the plan, with its stylised buildings, and blatantly nationalist leanings (the inclusions of Alexander the Great and Philip II of Macedon, for example, being interpreted by many as broad snubs to the Greek government, which objects to Macedonia's interpretation of its ancient history).

But Skopje 2014 has at least given visitors lots of fountains, statues and other facades to . Some prominent highlights include the Art Bridge and Eye Bridge over the Vadar River, and the new National Theatre, a replica of the original building that once stood here on the riverside but was destroyed by the 1963 earthquake. Look out also for the new Museum of Archeology and the Porta Macedonia, a triumphal arch just off Skopje's main plaza.

✖ Eating

★ Kebapčilnica Destan   KEBAB €
(ul 104 6; set meal 180MKD; ⊙7am-11pm) Skopje's best beef kebabs, accompanied by seasoned grilled bread, are found at this classic Čaršija place. There's no menu and everyone gets the same thing, served gruffly by the non-English speaking staff. But that's the charm, and the terrace is usually full – that's how good they are. There's a second, more sanitised branch on **Ploštad Makedonija** (Ploštad Makedonija; kebabs 180MKD; ⊙10am-11pm).

Pivnica An   MACEDONIAN €€
(Kapan An; mains 300-600MKD; ⊙11am-11pm) Housed in a *caravansarai* (inn) that is famously tricky to find (it's through an archway off the busy little square in the heart of the Čaršija, where the kebab restaurants are concentrated), this place is all about Ottoman tradition in its sumptuous courtyard. The food is very good, and far superior to that served immediately outside its front door.

★ Kaj Pero   MACEDONIAN €€
(Orce Nikolov 109; mains 200-600MKD; ⊙8am-midnight) This neighbourhood favourite has outside tables that are low lit by the street lights, giving it a great atmosphere for al fresco dining in the summer months. Inside it's a cosy, traditional feel, perfect for winter meals. The menu is focused on *skara*, but also has an excellent local wine selection and a range of inventive non-grill dishes.

ℹ Getting There & Away

BUS
Skopje's **bus station** (☎ 02-2466 313; www.sas. com.mk; bul Nikola Karev), with an ATM, exchange office and English-language info, adjoins the train station. Bus schedules are online.

Buses to Ohrid go via Kičevo (three hours, 167km) or Bitola (four to five hours, 261km) – book ahead in summer. Most intercity buses are air-conditioned and are generally faster than trains, though more expensive.

TRAIN
The **train station** (Železnička Stanica; bul Jane Sandanski) serves local and international destinations. Disagreements with the Greek government have led to periodically suspended train routes to Greece, but the Skopje–Thessaloniki connection (760MKD, 4½ hours, daily at 5.06am) was running at the time of research. A train serves Belgrade (1430MKD, eight hours, daily at 8.20am and 8.10pm), and another reaches Pristina (330MKD, three hours, daily at 4.10pm) in Kosovo.

Ohrid
☎ 046 / POP 55,000

Sublime Ohrid has an atmospheric Old Town with beautiful churches along a graceful hill, topped by a medieval castle overlooking serene, 34km-long Lake Ohrid. It's undoubtedly Macedonia's most alluring attraction, especially when you factor in nearby Galičica National Park and the secluded beaches that dot the lake's eastern shore.

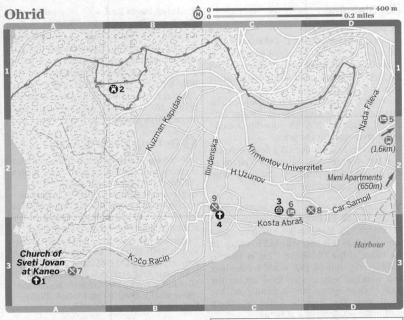

Ohrid

Sights

★**Church of Sveti Jovan at Kaneo**   CHURCH
(admission 100MKD; ⊗9am-6pm) This stunning
13th-century church is set on a cliff over the
lake, and is possibly Macedonia's most photographed structure. Peer down into the
azure waters and you'll see why medieval
monks found spiritual inspiration here. The
small church has original frescoes behind
the altar.

Sveta Sofija Cathedral   CHURCH
(Car Samoil bb; adult/student 100/30MKD;
⊗10am-7pm) Ohrid's grandest church,
11th-century Sveta Sofia is supported by columns and decorated with elaborate, if very
faded Byzantine frescoes, though they are
well preserved and very vivid in the apse.
Its superb acoustics mean it's often used for
concerts (300MKD). The exposed beams reveal the very real achievment that construct-
ing a church this size would have been in the
11th century.

Car Samoil's Castle   CASTLE
(admission 30MKD; ⊗9am-7pm) The massive,
turreted walls of this 10th-century castle indicate the power of the medieval Bulgarian
state. Ascend the stairways to the ramparts
for fantastic views over the town and lake.

Ohrid

◎ Top Sights
  1 Church of Sveti Jovan at Kaneo..........A3

◎ Sights
  2 Car Samoil's Castle B1
  3 Robev Family House National
       Museum C2
  4 Sveta Sofija Cathedral C2

⊟ Sleeping
  5 Sunny Lake Hostel...............................D2
  6 Villa Jovan C2

⊗ Eating
  7 Letna Bavča Kaneo...............................A3
  8 Restaurant Antiko................................D2
  9 Restoran Sveta Sofija..........................C2

**Robev Family House
National Museum**   MUSEUM
(Car Samoil 62; adult/student 100/50MKD; ⊗9am-
2pm & 7-10pm Tue-Sun) In the heart of the Old
Town, this 1827 museum is housed over several floors of the remarkably well-preserved
Robev Residence. On display is everything
from Greek archaeological finds, prehistoric
implements and metal work to pottery, jewellery and some wonderful interiors. Across
the road the Urania Residence, a further part
of the museum, has an ethnographic display.

🛏 Sleeping

★ Sunny Lake Hostel
HOSTEL €
(www.sunnylakehostel.mk/; 11 Oktombri 15; dm €10, d €20-24; 🛜) This excellent new hostel is a bustling hub for backpackers stopping off in Ohrid. There are good facilities, including a great terrace with lake views, lockers under each bed, and a kitchen to cook in. The bathrooms aren't great, and hot water isn't always available, but it's superbly located and a great deal for the price.

Bikes can be hired for €3 a day. There are also laundry facilities, hammocks, plenty of ball games, and a pleasant garden for summer-evening beer drinking.

★ Villa Jovan
HISTORIC HOTEL €
(☑ 076 377 644; vila.jovan@gmail.com; Car Samoli 44; s/d/ste €25/35/49; 🕸🛜) There are nine rooms within this 200-year-old mansion in the heart of the Old Town. They're charmingly rustic, full of old world-furnishings and wooden beams, with local art on the walls. While rooms are definitely on the small side, the friendly English-speaking staff make you feel right at home.

The suite has panoramic views and a super balcony.

Mimi Apartments
APARTMENT €
(☑ 250 103; mimioh@mail.com.mk; Strašo Pinđur 2; r incl breakfast 800MKD) Spacious, centrally located private rooms with fridge.

🍴 Eating

★ Letna Bavča Kaneo
SEAFOOD €
(Kočo Racin 43; fish 100-200MKD; ⊙10am-midnight; 🛜) This simple 'summer terrace' on Kaneo beach is inexpensive and great. A fry-up of diminutive *plasnica* (a small fish commonly eaten fried in the Balkans), plus salad, feeds two, or try other specialties such as eel or carp. Swim in Lake Ohrid directly from the restaurant's dock, then soak up the sun while drinking a local beer – it doesn't get much better than this.

★ Restaurant Antiko
MACEDONIAN €€
(Car Samoil 30; mains 300-650MKD) In an old Ohrid mansion in the middle of the Old Town, the famous Antiko has great traditional ambience and pricey, but good, traditional dishes. Don't miss the excellent *tavče gravče*, a traditional Macedonian dish of beans cooked in spices and peppers, the Antiko version of which is widely held to be a classic of the genre.

Restoran Sveta Sofija
MACEDONIAN €€
(Car Samoil 88; mains 300-500MKD; ⊙10am-midnight; 🛜) This upscale restaurant opposite the Sveta Sofija Cathedral couldn't have a better location, and in the warmer months you can dine al fresco across the road on a little terrace. This is a great spot to try traditional fare, and oenophiles will delight in being able to choose from more than 100 Macedonian wines.

ℹ Getting There & Away

From the **bus station** (7 Noemvri bb), 1.5km east of centre, buses serve Skopje, either via Kičevo (500MKD, three hours, eight daily) or (the longer route) via Bitola (560MKD). In summer, reserve ahead for Skopje buses, or be prepared to wait. Some *kombi* (minibuses) and taxis wait at the end of Bul Makedonski Prosveiteli.

International buses serve Belgrade (via Kičevo; 1800MKD, 15 hours, one daily at 5.45am). A 7pm bus serves Sofia (1450MKD, eight hours). For Albania, take a bus to Sveti Naum (110MKD, 50 minutes, eight daily). Cross the border and take a cab (€5, 6km) to Pogradeci. An Ohrid–Sveti Naum taxi costs 1000MKD.

Bitola

📋 047 / POP 95,400

With elegant buildings and beautiful people, elevated Bitola (660m) has a sophistication inherited from its Ottoman days as the 'City of Consuls'. Its 18th- and 19th-century colourful townhouses, Turkish mosques and cafe culture make it Macedonia's most intriguing and liveable major town. An essential experience is sipping a coffee and people-watching along the pedestrianised Širok Sokak ('Wide Street' – still officially called ul Maršal Tito), the main promenade and heart of the city.

◉ Sights

Širok Sokak
STREET
(ul Maršal Tito) Bitola's Širok Sokak is the city's most representative and stylish street, with its multicoloured facades and European honorary consulates attesting to the city's Ottoman-era sophistication. Enjoying the cafe life here as the beautiful people promenade past is an essential Bitola experience.

Church of Sveti Dimitrija
CHURCH
(11 Oktomvri bb; ⊙7am-6pm) This Orthodox church (1830) has rich frescoes, ornate lamps and a huge iconostasis.

Heraclea Lyncestis
ARCHAEOLOGICAL SITE

(admission 100MKD, photos 500MKD; ⊙9am-3pm winter, to 5pm summer) Located 1km south of Bitola (70MKD by taxi), Heraclea Lyncestis is among Macedonia's best archaeological sites. Founded by Philip II of Macedon, Heraclea became commercially significant before Romans conquered (168 BC) and its position on the Via Egnatia kept it prosperous. In the 4th century Heraclea became an episcopal seat, but it was sacked by Goths and then Slavs.

See the Roman baths, portico and amphitheatre, and the striking Early Christian basilica and episcopal palace ruins, with beautiful, well-preserved floor mosaics. They're unique in depicting endemic trees and animals. Excavations continue, so you may see newer discoveries.

🛏 Sleeping

⭐ Chola Guest House
GUESTHOUSE €

(☑047-224 919; www.chola.mk; Stiv Naumov 80; s/d €12/20; ❄🐾) Overall an excellent value place to stay, with a quiet location in an atmospheric old mansion that has clean, well-kept rooms and colourful modern bathrooms. It's a short walk from the main drag: there is a useful map on the website, well worth consulting as it's hard to find otherwise.

Hotel De Niro
HOTEL €

(☑047-229 656; hotel-deniro@t-home.mk; Kiril i Metodij 5; s/d/ste from €17/34/67; ❄🐾) Central yet discreet with lovely old Bitola style rooms can be found here, including a spacious apartment that sleeps four people upstairs. The owner owns an art gallery, as you'll quickly see from the paintings that cover almost every inch of wall space. There's a good pizza-and-pasta restaurant (mains 200MKD to 450MKD) downstairs. Breakfast is €2 extra.

🍴 Eating

El Greko
PIZZA €

(☑071 279 848; cnr Maršal Tito & Elipda Karamandi; mains 150-350MKD; ⊙10am-1am) This Sokak taverna and pizzeria has a great beer-hall ambience and is popular with locals. It's one of many decent places along the main street, all of which heave with locals from mid-afternoon until late in the evening.

WORTH A TRIP

VILLA DIHOVO

One of Macedonia's most remarkable guesthouses, **Villa Dihovo** (☑047 293 040, 070 544 744; www.villadihovo.com; 🐾) comprises three traditionally decorated rooms in the 80-year-old home of former professional footballer Petar Cvetkovski and family. Its big flowering lawn is great for kids, and the only fixed prices are for the homemade wine, beer and *rakija* (firewater); all else, room price included, is your choice. Petar himself is a mine of information, deeply involved in the Slow Food movement, and can arrange everything from hikes to Pelisterski Oči to mountain-bike rides and an evening of wine tasting in his cellar. There's also a superb shared kitchen on the premises, where guests can cook with the hosts, as well as a living room with an open fireplace – perfect for colder nights. Booking in advance is essential.

🍷 Drinking

⭐ Porta Jazz
BAR

(Kiril i Metodij; ⊙8am-1am; 🐾) There's a notably Bohemian vibe at this rightly popular, funky place that's packed when live jazz and blues bands play. It's located near the Centar na Kultura, one block back from the Širok Sokak. During the day it's a very pleasant cafe where you can sip espresso on the terrace.

ℹ Getting There & Away

The **bus** and **train stations** (Nikola Tesla) are adjacent, 1km south of the centre. Buses serve Skopje (480MKD, 3½ hours, 12 daily) via Prilep (140MKD, one hour), Kavadarci (280MKD, two hours, five daily), Strumica (460MKD, four hours, two daily) and Ohrid (210MKD, 1¼ hours, 10 daily). Four daily trains serve Skopje (315MKD) via Prilep (85MKD) and Veles (170MKD).

Pelister National Park

Macedonia's oldest national park covers 125 sq km on its third-highest mountain range, the quartz-filled Baba massif. Eight peaks top 2000m, crowned by Mt Pelister (2601m). Two glacial lakes, Pelisterski Oči (Pelister's Eyes), provide chilly refreshment.

Pelister's 88 tree species include the rare five-leafed Molika pine. It also hosts endemic Pelagonia trout, deer, wolves, chamois, wild boars, bears and eagles.

◉ Sights

Only 5km from Bitola, the 830m-high mountainside hamlet of **Dihovo** is a charming and increasingly popular base for Pelister hikes, with appealing stone houses and the icon-rich **Church of Sveti Dimitrije** (1830). The setting is gorgeous, surrounded by thick pine forests and rushing mountain streams. Indeed, Dihovo's **outdoor swimming pool** is basically a very large basin containing ice-cold mountain-spring waters, rushing from the boulder-filled Sapungica River. Locals have shown impressive initiative in developing this traditional village into an eco-tourism destination.

❶ Getting There & Away

The village of Dihovo is the best base for exploring the park and is just a short distance outside the town of Bitola, which can easily be reached by bus from Skopje (480MKD, 3½ hours, 12 daily) or Ohrid (210MKD, 1½ hours, 10 daily). Take a taxi from Bitola's bus station to Dihovo.

Macedonia Survival Guide

❶ Directory A–Z

DANGERS & ANNOYANCES
The all-pervasive fear of a draft (*promaja*), which causes otherwise sane Macedonians to compulsively shut bus windows on sweltering hot days, is undoubtedly the most incomprehensible and aggravating thing foreigners complain about – fight for your rights, or suffer in silence.

EMERGENCY & IMPORTANT NUMBERS
Ambulance 🗷194
Fire 🗷193
Police 🗷192

MONEY
Macedonian denars (MKD) come in 10-, 50-, 100-, 500-, 1000- and 5000-denar notes, and one-, two-, five-, 10- and 50- denar coins. Taxi drivers hate it when you pay with a 1000-denar note, and may make you go into a shop to get change. Euros are generally accepted – some hotels quote euro rates, but it's always possible (and usually beneficial) to pay in denar.

Macedonian exchange offices (*menuvačnici*) work commission-free. ATMs are widespread.

Credit cards can often be used in larger cities, but you can't really rely on then outside Skopje. Avoid travellers cheques altogether.

TELEPHONE
Macedonia's country code is 🗷389. Drop the initial zero in city codes and mobile prefixes (🗷07) when calling from abroad. Buying a local SIM card is good for longer stays.

VISAS
Citizens of former Yugoslav republics, Australia, Canada, the EU, Iceland, Israel, New Zealand, Norway, Switzerland, Turkey and the USA can stay for three months, visa-free. Otherwise, visa fees average from US$30 for a single-entry visa and US$60 for a multiple-entry visa. Check the Ministry of Foreign Affairs website (www.mfa.gov.mk) if unsure of your status.

❶ Getting There & Away

Skopje's buses serve Sofia, Belgrade, Budapest, Pristina, Tirana, İstanbul, Thessaloniki and more. Trains connect Skopje to Pristina, Belgrade and Thessaloniki. The long-awaited arrival of budget airlines has improved Skopje's modest number of air connections, and it's now connected pretty well to major European cities.

BORDER CROSSINGS
Macedonia and Albania have four border crossings. The busiest are Kafasan–Qafa e Thanës, 12km southwest of Struga, and Sveti Naum–Tushëmishti, 29km south of Ohrid. Blato, 5km northwest of Debar, and Stenje, on Lake Prespa's southwestern shore, are the least used.

For Bulgaria, Deve Bair (90km from Skopje, after Kriva Palanka) accesses Sofia. The Delcevo crossing (110km from Skopje) leads to Blagoevgrad, while the southeastern Novo Selo crossing, 160km from Skopje beyond Strumica, reaches Petrich.

KOSOVO

Kosovo is Europe's newest country and a fascinating land at the heart of the Balkans. Welcoming smiles, charming mountain towns, superb hiking opportunities and 13th-century domed Serbian monasteries are all on the menu – and that's just for starters. It's safe to travel here now, and it's well worth doing so, as this is one of the last corners of Europe that remains off the beaten track.

Kosovo declared independence from Serbia in 2008, and while it has been diplomatically recognised by 110 countries, there are still many nations that do not accept Kosovan independence, including Serbia. Do note that it's currently not possible to cross into Serbia from Kosovo, unless you entered Kosovo from Serbia first.

The bustling capital, **Pristina**, is no oil painting, but it's a fun and fascinating place, with its Turkish-style bazaar, imposing minarets and an international population that manages to give the city the feel of somewhere far bigger. Elsewhere in the small country you'll find no shortage of things to do: charming **Prizren** is home to the famous Dokufest film festival each August, and houses an impressive fortress and some gorgeous mosques. The town of **Peja** is a good base for exploring Kosovo's beautiful Rugova Mountains, which are becoming a popular destination for hikers and climbers, while in the winter months, the ski slopes of Brezovica are tipped as the next big thing for skiers in the Balkans.

Kosovo

Blace, 20 minutes north of Skopje, reaches Pristina in Kosovo, while Tetovo's Jazince crossing is closer to Prizren.

Tabanovce is the major road/rail crossing for Belgrade, Serbia.

ⓘ Getting Around

Skopje serves most domestic destinations. Larger buses are new and air-conditioned; *kombi* are usually not. During summer, pre-book for Ohrid.

SERBIA

Belgrade

📞 011 / POP 1.6 MILLION

Outspoken, adventurous, proud and audacious: Belgrade is by no means a 'pretty' capital, but its gritty exuberance makes it one of the most happening cities in Europe. While it hurtles towards a brighter future, its chaotic past unfolds before your eyes: socialist blocks are squeezed between art nouveau masterpieces, and remnants of the Habsburg legacy contrast with Ottoman relics. It is here where the Sava River meets the Danube (Dunav), contemplative parkland nudges hectic urban sprawl, and old-world culture gives way to new-world nightlife.

◎ Sights

★**Kalemegdan Citadel**   FORTRESS
(Kalemegdanska tvrđava) **FREE** Some 115 battles have been fought over imposing, impressive Kalemegdan; the citadel was destroyed more than 40 times throughout the centuries. Fortifications began in Celtic times, and the Romans extended it onto the flood plains during the settlement of 'Singidunum', Belgrade's Roman name. The fort's bloody history, discernible despite today's plethora of jolly cafes and funfairs, only makes Kalemegdan all the more fascinating.

Military Museum   MUSEUM
(www.muzej.mod.gov.rs; Kalemegdan Citadel; adult/child 150/70DIN; ⊙10am-5pm Tue-Sun) Tucked away in Belgrade's sprawling Kalemegdan Citadel, this museum presents the complete military history of the former Yugoslavia. Gripping displays include captured Kosovo Liberation Army weapons, bombs and missiles (courtesy of NATO), rare guns, and bits of the American stealth fighter that

was shot down in 1999. You'll find the museum through the Stambol Gate, built by the Turks in the mid-1700s and used for public executions.

National Museum   MUSEUM
(Narodni Muzej; www.narodnimuzej.rs; Trg Republike 1a; adult/child 200/100DIN; ⊙10am-5pm Tue-Wed & Fri, noon-8pm Thur & Sat, 10am-2pm Sun) Trg Republike (Republic Sq), a meeting point and outdoor exhibition space, is home to the National Museum. Lack of funding for renovations has kept it mostly shuttered for the last decade, though some exhibitions are again open to the public.

Nikola Tesla Museum   MUSEUM
(www.tesla-museum.org; Krunska 51; admission incl guided tour in English 500DIN; ⊙10am-6pm Tue-Sun) Meet the man on the 100DIN note at one of Belgrade's best museums. Release your inner nerd with some wondrously sci-fi-ish interactive elements. Tesla's ashes are kept here in a glowing, golden orb: at the time of research, debate was raging between the museum and its supporters and the church as to whether they should be moved to hallowed ground.

Maršal Tito's Grave   MONUMENT
(House of Flowers; www.mij.rs; Botićeva 6; incl entry to Museum of Yugoslav History 200DIN; ⊙10am-8pm Tue-Sun May-Oct, to 6pm Nov-April) A visit to Tito's mausoleum is obligatory. Also on display are thousands of elaborate relay batons presented to him by young 'Pioneers', plus gifts from political leaders and the voguish set of the era. It's attached to the fascinating **Museum of Yugoslav History**. Take trolleybus 40 or 41 at the south end of Parliament on Kneza Miloša. It's the second stop after turning into Bul Mira: ask the driver to let you out at Kuća Cveća.

Sveti Sava   CHURCH
(www.hramsvetogsave.com; Svetog Save) Sveti Sava is the world's biggest Orthodox church, a fact made entirely obvious when looking at the city skyline from a distance or standing under the dome. The church is built on the site where the Turks apparently burnt relics of St Sava. Work on the church interior (frequently interrupted by wars) continues today.

Ada Ciganlija   BEACH
(www.adaciganlija.rs) In summertime, join the hordes of sea-starved locals (up to 250,000 a day) for sun and fun at this artificial is-

land on the Sava. Cool down with a swim, kayak or windsurf after a leap from the 55m bungee tower. Take bus 52 or 53 from Zeleni Venac.

Aviation Museum
MUSEUM
(www.muzejvazduhoplovstva.org.rs; Nikola Tesla airport; admission 500DIN; ⊘9am–6.30pm Tue-Sun Apr-Oct, to 4pm Nov-Mar) This airport-based museum contains rare planes, a WWII collection and bits of the infamous American stealth fighter shot down in 1999.

🛌 Sleeping

★ Green Studio Hostel
HOSTEL €
(📞011-218 5943; www.greenstudiohostel.com; Karađorđeva 61, 6th floor, Savamala; dm from €9, r €9-40, apt €40; ✳🤖) Clean, airy and staffed by your new best friends, this sunny spot has a handy location near the bus and train stations, as well as Belgrade's main attractions. Nightly happy hours, daily activities, tons of local advice, and free *rakija*!

Bed 'n' Beer Hostel
HOSTEL €
(📞011-406 6788; www.bednbeerhostel.com; ul Zetska 5; dm from €10; ✳🤖) This new hostel offers what it proffers, plus a great location smack bang in the boho quarter of Skadarlija, spacious, sunny dorms and fun, informed English-speaking staff. Unsurprisingly, there's a beer bar on-site.

Arka Barka
HOSTEL €
(📞064 925 3507; www.arkabarka.net; Bul Nikole Tesle bb; dm €15; ✳🤖) Bobbing off Ušće Park, a mere stagger from the Danube barges, this 'floating house' offers sparkling rooms in 'wake-up!' colours, party nights and fresh river breezes. It's a moderate walk, or a short ride on bus 15 or 84 from Zeleni Venac. Cash only.

YOLOstel
HOSTEL €
(📞064 141 9339; www.yolostel.rs; ul Uzun Mirkova 6, Apt 6, 3rd floor; dm/d from €11/35; ✳🤖) This new designer hostel enjoys an awesome location just a short stumble from Savamala. With custom-made furniture, quirky, gorgeous decor and a hip, refined air, this is not your usual backpacker flophouse.

Soul House Apartments
APARTMENT €€
(📞064 135 2255; www.soul-house.net; ul Makedonska 15; one person/two people stays from €25/35; ✳🤖) These three themed apartments are located within the same building, a quick amble from Trg Republike. The 'hippie suite' (€25/35) is yellow and bright, the 'modern-

istic studio' (€30/40) has trippy, fun furnishings, and the 'retro apartment' (€40/50) is done up Tito-era style. All have good kitchens. There's a minimum two-night stay on weekends.

✘ Eating

★ To Je To
BALKAN €
(bul Despota Stefana 21; 220-750DIN; ⊘8am-midnight) 'To je to' means 'that's it', and in this case, they're talking about meat. Piles of the stuff, grilled in all its juicy glory, make up the menu here in the forms of Sarajevo-style *ćevapi* (spicy skinless sausages), turkey kebab, sweetbreads and more. It serves homemade *sarma* (stuffed cabbage rolls) on the weekends. Cheap, scrumptious and highly recommended by locals.

Institut za Burger Praše i Gulaš
INTERNATIONAL €
(Institute of Burger, Pig and Goulash; www.institut bpg.rs; ul Maršala Birjuzova 22; mains 300-600DIN; ⊘24hr) Decadent, delicious and strictly for carnivores, the Institut serves up the best American-style burgers in the Balkans; they're pricier than *pljeskavica* (spicy hamburger), but worth every juicy mouthful. As the name suggests, they also do wicked things with pork (dismiss the succulent *drapano praše* at your peril) and goulash. Huge portions, Western-style breakfasts (8am-noon) and fun 50s-diner decor make this a winner.

Radost Fina Kuhinjica
VEGETARIAN €€
(📞060 603 0023; Pariska 3; mains 450-1300DIN; ⊘2pm-midnight Tue-Sat, 1pm-9pm Sun ; 🍴) Barbecue-obsessed Serbia isn't the easiest place for vegetarians, but thanks to this cheery eatery, you'll never have to settle for eating garnish and chips again. Its ever-changing menu features curries, veggie burgers, innovative pastas and meat substitutes galore, some of which are vegan. The healthy cupcakes are a delight.

?
SERBIAN €€
(Znak Pitanja; www.varoskapija.rs; Kralja Petra 6; 550-1100DIN; ⊘9am-1am) Belgrade's oldest *kafana* (cafe) has been attracting the bohemian set since 1823 with dishes such as stuffed chicken and 'lamb under the iron pan'. Its quizzical name follows a dispute with the adjacent church, which objected to the boozy tavern – originally called 'By the Cathedral' – referring to a house of god.

🍷 Drinking & Nightlife

Belgrade has a reputation as one of the world's top party cities, with a wild club scene limited only by imagination and hours in the day. Many clubs move to river barges in summertime, known collectively as *splavovi*. The Sava boasts a 1.5km strip of *splavovi* on its west bank: these are the true wild-and-crazy party boats. Walk over Brankov Most or catch tram 7, 9 or 11 from the city.

Central Belgrade

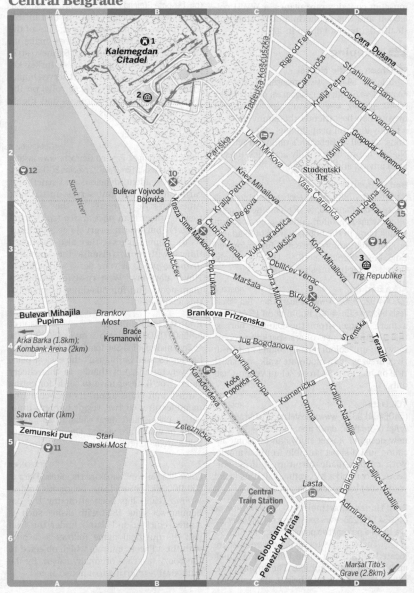

★**Kafana Pavle Korčagin** TAVERNA
(☎011-240 1980; Ćirila i Metodija 2a; ⊘8pm-1am)
Raise a glass to Tito at this frantic, festive
kafana. Lined with communist memorabilia
and packed to the rafters with revellers and
grinning accordionists, this table-thumping
throwback fills up nightly; reserve a table in
advance.

Rakia Bar BAR
(www.rakiabar.com; Dobračina 5, Dorćol;
⊘9am-midnight Sun-Thu, to 1am Fri & Sat) An
ideal spot for *rakija* rookies to get their first
taste of the spirit of Serbia. English-speaking
staff will gently guide you through the extensive drinks menu, but beware: this stuff
is strong.

Radionica Bar BAR
(Dobračina 59, Dorćol; ⊘8pm-3am, 9pm-4am Fri-
Sat) 'Radionica' means 'workshop', and that's
exactly what this place once was. Traces
of its blue-collar past remain in its indus-
trial-cool decor, but there's nothing rough
about its hipster clientele or swish cocktail
menu.

Hot Mess RIVER BARGE
(Ušće bb, Sava River; ⊘9am-3am) Hot Mess epitomises the sybaritic *splav*, with selfie-snap-
pers posing by the on-board pool, blinding
neon lights and a young, uninhibited crowd
going wild to disco, house and RnB. They
also do great hangover breakfasts.

Blaywatch RIVER BARGE
(www.blaywatch.com; Brodarska bb, Sava River;
⊘midnight-late) This throbbing place gets
crowded and dress codes may be enforced
(scruffy bad on boys, skimpy good on girls).

BALKANS BELGRADE

Central Belgrade

The crowd is a mix of local 'beautiful people' and foreigners, all occupied with each other and the turbo tunes.

Plastic
NIGHTCLUB

(cnr Dalmatinska & Takovska; ⊙ Wed-Sat 10pm-6am Oct-May) A perennial favourite among electro-heads and booty shakers, this slick venue is frequented by top local and international DJs. The more intimate Mint Club is within Plastic. Between May and October, head to Plastic Light, the floating version of the club on the Sava River.

Tube
NIGHTCLUB

(www.thetube.rs; Simina 21; ⊙ 11pm-6am Thu-Sat) Lovers of all music electronic will have a blast in this beautifully designed former nuclear bunker. It's a big club, but does get packed: get in early to stake yourself some space.

❶ Getting There & Away

BUS

Belgrade has two adjacent bus stations, near the eastern banks of the Sava River: BAS (☑ 011-263 6299; www.bas.rs; Železnička 4) and Lasta (☑ 011-334 8555; www.lasta.rs; Železnička 2). Buses run from both to international and Serbian destinations. Sample daily routes include Belgrade to Sarajevo (2340DIN, eight hours), Ljubljana (4000DIN, 7½ hours) and Vienna (4400DIN, 9½ hours); frequent domestic services include Subotica (800DIN, three hours), Novi Sad (520DIN, one hour), Niš (1380DIN, three hours) and Novi Pazar (1400DIN, three hours).

TRAIN

The central train station (Savski Trg 2) has an information office on Platform 1, tourist information office, exchange bureau (⊙ 6am-10pm) and sales counter (Savski Trg 2; ⊙ 24hrs).

Frequent trains go to Novi Sad (288DIN, 1½ hours), Subotica (560DIN, three hours) and Niš (784DIN, four hours). See www.serbianrailways.com for timetables and fares.

Novi Sad

☑ 021 / POP 366,860

As convivial as a *rakija* toast – and at times just as carousing – Novi Sad is a chipper town with all the spoils and none of the stress of the big smoke. Locals sprawl in pretty parks and outdoor cafes, and laneway bars pack out nightly. The looming Petrovaradin Citadel keeps a stern eye on proceedings, loosening its tie each July to host Serbia's largest music festival. You can walk to all of Novi Sad's attractions from the happening pedestrian thoroughfare, Zmaj Jovina, which stretches from the town square (Trg Slobode) to Dunavska street.

⊙ Sights

The formidable Petrovaradin Citadel notwithstanding, Novi Sad is less about 'sights' than soaking up the city's vibrant spirit. Simply strolling by the Danube along Sunčani Kej (Sunny Quay), peoplewatching in Zmaj Jovina or splashing on the Štrand is enough to have you racing to your accommodation desk and begging to extend your stay.

★ Petrovaradin Citadel
FORTRESS

(museum 200DIN; ⊙ museum 9am-5pm Tue-Sun) Towering over the river on a 40m-high volcanic slab, this mighty citadel (*tvrđava*) is aptly nicknamed 'Gibraltar on the Danube'. Constructed with slave labour between 1692 and 1780, its dungeons have held notable prisoners including Karađorđe (leader of the first uprising against the Turks and founder of a dynasty) and Tito. Have a good gawk at the iconic clock tower: the size of the minute and hour hands are reversed so far-flung fishermen can tell the time.

Within the citadel walls, a museum offers insight (sans English explanations) into the site's history. The museum can also arrange tours (300DIN) of Petrovaradin's creepy – but cool – underground passageways.

Museum of Vojvodina
MUSEUM

(Muzej Vojvodine; www.muzejvojvodine.org.rs; Dunavska 35-7; admission 200DIN, free on Sundays; ⊙ 9am-7pm Tue-Fri, 10am-6pm Sat & Sun) This museum houses historical, archaeological and ethnological exhibits. Building 35 covers Vojvodinian history from Palaeolithic times to the late 19th century. Building 37 takes the story to 1945, with harrowing emphasis on WWI and WWII.

Štrand
BEACH

One of Europe's best by-the-Danube beaches, this 700m-long stretch of sand morphs into a city of its own come summertime, with bars, stalls and all manner of recreational diversions attracting thousands of sun'n'fun seekers from across the globe. It's also the ultimate Novi Sad party venue, hosting everything from local punk gigs to EXIT raves.

DON'T MISS

NOVI PAZAR & STUDENICA MONASTERY

Novi Pazar is the cultural centre of the Raška/Sandžak region, with a large Muslim population. Turkish coffee, cuisine and customs abound, but some idyllic Orthodox sights are in the vicinity: this was the heartland of the Serbian medieval state. One of the most sacred sites in Serbia, Unesco-listed Studenica was established in the 1190s by founder of the Serbian empire (and future saint) Stefan Nemanja, and developed by his sons Vukan, Stefan and Rastko (St Sava). Active monastic life was cultivated by Sava and continues today, though this thriving little community doesn't mind visitors. Two well-preserved churches lie within impressive white-marble walls. Bogorodičina Crkva (Church of Our Lady), a royal funeral church, contains Stefan's tomb. Smaller Kraljeva Crkva (King's Church) houses the acclaimed *Birth of the Virgin* fresco and other masterpieces. From Novi Pazar, catch a Kraljevo-bound bus to the village of Ušće (about one hour) and hop on a local bus from there, or negotiate a return taxi journey.

✪ Festivals & Events

EXIT Festival　　　　　　　　　　　MUSIC
(www.exitfest.org) The Petrovaradin Citadel is stormed by thousands of revellers each July during this epic festival. The first event in 2000 lasted 100 days and galvanised a generation of young Serbs against the Milošević regime. The festival has been attended by the likes of Chemical Brothers, Gogol Bordello and Patti Smith, and an annual tally of about 200,000 merrymakers from around the world.

🛏 Sleeping

★ Hostel Sova　　　　　　　　　　HOSTEL €
(☑ 021-527 556; www.hostelsova.com; Ilije Ognjanovića 26; dm from €10, d €15 pp; P ⓢ) This cute spot is akin to a mini Novi Sad: super-friendly, attractive and given to laid-back socialising (not to mention the odd *rakija* or two). It's perched above a deceptively quiet street that's just around the corner from buzzy Zmaj Jovina and a couple of minutes' stagger from the best bars in town.

Downtown　　　　　　　　　　　　HOSTEL €
(☑ 021-524 818; www.hostelnovisad.com; Njegoševa 2; dm from €12, s/d €21/30; @) Super-friendly staff and an 'in the thick of it' location off Trg Slobode make this rambunctious, slightly ramshackle hostel a classic Novi Sad experience in itself.

🍴 Eating

★ Fish i Zeleniš　　　　MEDITERRANEAN €€
(Fish and Greens; ☑ 021-452 000; www.fishizelenis.com; Skerlićeva 2; mains from €80DIN; ⊙ noon-midnight ; ✐) This bright, snug little nook serves up the finest vegetarian/pescatarian

meals in northern Serbia. Organic, locally sourced ingredients? Ambient? Ineffably delicious? Tick, tick, tick. A three-minute walk from Zmaj Jovina.

Piknik　　　　　　　　　　　　SERBIAN €€
(☑ 069 174 5645; Ribarac bb, Ribarsko Ostrvo; mains 500-1400DIN; ⊙ 10am-11pm Mon-Sat; ✈) This utterly charming restaurant by the Danube ladles out hearty Vojvodinian cuisine to an appreciative crowd of city slickers, jolly fishermen and local families (who visit as much for the wonderful on-site playground and petting zoo as for the grub). The amusing menu alone makes this happy place worth the trip.

ℹ Getting There & Away

The **bus station** (Bul Jaše Tomića; ⊙ information counter 6am-11pm) has regular departures to Belgrade (520DIN, one hour, every 10 minutes) and Subotica (600DIN, 1½ hours), plus services to Užice (1120DIN, five hours) and Zlatibor (1300DIN, six hours). From here, four stops on bus 4 will take you to the town centre: nip down the underpass and you'll see Trg Slobode on emerging.

Frequent trains leave the **train station** (Bul Jaše Tomića 4), next door to the bus station, for Belgrade (288DIN, 1½ hours) and Subotica (384DIN, 1½ hours).

Subotica

☑ 024 / POP 148,000

Sugar-spun art nouveau marvels, a laid-back populace and a delicious sprinkling of Serbian and Hungarian flavours make this quaint town a worthy day trip or stopover.

MADNESS, MADE IN SERBIA

On the surface, the Dragačevo Trumpet Assembly (an annual gathering of brass musicians) sounds harmless; nerdily endearing, even. But band camp this ain't: it's the most boisterous music festival in all of Europe, if not the world. Known simply as 'Guča', after the western Serbian village that has hosted it each August since 1961, the four-day debauch is hedonism at its most rambunctious. Tens of thousands of beer-and-brass-addled visitors dance wild *kola* (fast-paced circle dances) through the streets, gorging on spit-meat and slapping dinar on the sweaty foreheads of the (mostly Roma) *trubači* performers.

The music itself is relentless and frenzy-fast; even Miles Davis confessed, 'I didn't know you could play trumpet that way.' Sleep is a dubious proposition, but bring a tent or book ahead anyway: www.guca.rs has information on accommodation and transport.

◉ Sights

Town Hall   HISTORIC BUILDING
(Trg Slobode) Built in 1910, this behemoth is a curious mix of art nouveau and something Gaudí may have had a playful dab at. The council chambers – with exquisite stained-glass windows and elaborate decor – are not to be missed.

Modern Art Gallery   HISTORIC BUILDING
(www.likovnisusret.rs; Park Ferenca Rajhla 5; dult/student 100/50DIN; ⊙8am-7pm Mon-Fri, 9am-1pm Sat) This mansion was built in 1904 as an architect's design studio, and it shows. One of the most sumptuous buildings in Serbia, it's a vibrant flourish of mosaics, ceramic tiles, floral patterns and stained glass.

⌂ Sleeping & Eating

Hostel Incognito   HOSTEL €
(☎062 666 674; www.hostel-subotica.com; Hugo Badalića 3; s/d/tr/apt 1000/1800/2400/7000DIN; P 🕙) This basic but clean, friendly hostel is a couple of minutes' walk from all the Subotica sights. Reception is in the restaurant downstairs: call before lobbing up.

Hostel Bosa Milićević   HOSTEL €
(☎548 290; Segedinski put 9-11; dm 1019DIN) Stay with the students at this cheapie, tucked well away behind the Ekonomski Fakultet.

Ravel   CAFE €
(Nušićeva 2; cakes 60-200DIN; ⊙9am-10pm Mon-Sat, 11am-10pm Sun) Dainty nibbles at *gateaux* and twee tea-taking is the name of the game at this adorable art nouveau classic.

Boss Caffe   INTERNATIONAL €€
(www.bosscaffe.com; Matije Korvina 7-8; 450-1000DIN; ⊙7am-midnight Mon-Thu, to 1am Fri & Sat, 9am-midnight Sun) The best restaurant in town has a huge menu spanning Chinese, Italian, Mexican and Serbian cuisines; somehow it pulls it off with aplomb. It's directly behind the Modern Art Gallery.

❶ Getting There & Away

From the **bus station** (www.sutrans.rs; Senćanski put 3) there are hourly services to Novi Sad (600DIN, two hours) and Belgrade (800DIN, 3½ hours). See the website for other destinations. Subotica's **train station** (Bose Milećević bb) has two trains to Szeged, Hungary (320DIN, 1¾ hours), and trains to Belgrade (560DIN, 3½ hours), which stop at Novi Sad (384DIN, 1½ hours).

Niš

☑018 / POP 183,000

Niš is a lively city of curious contrasts, where Roma in horse-drawn carriages trot alongside new cars, and posh cocktails are sipped in antiquated alleyways.

◉ Sights

Niš Fortress   FORTRESS
(Niška tvrđava; Jadranska; ⊙24hr) While its current incarnation was built by the Turks in the 18th century, there have been forts on this site since ancient Roman times. Today it's a sprawling recreational area with restaurants, cafes, market stalls and ample space for moseying. It hosts the **Nišville International Jazz Festival** (www.nisville.com) each August and **Nišomnia** (www.facebook.com/festivalnisomnia), featuring rock and electro acts, in September. The city's main pedestrian boulevard, Obrenovićeva, stretches before the citadel.

Tower of Skulls   MONUMENT
(Ćele Kula; Bul Zoran Đinđić; adult/child 150/130DIN; ⊙9am-7pm Tue-Fri, to 3pm Sat &

Sun) With Serbian defeat in minent at the 1809 Battle of Čegar, the Duke of Resava kamikazeed towards the Turkish defences, firing at their gunpowder stores, killing himself, 4000 of his men, and 10,000 Turks. The Turks triumphed regardless, and to deter future acts of rebellion, they beheaded, scalped and embedded the skulls of the dead Serbs in this tower. Only 58 of the initial 952 skulls remain. Contrary to Turkish intention, the tower serves as a proud monument of Serbian resistance.

Get there on any bus marked 'Niška Banja' from the stop opposite the Ambassador Hotel: ask to be let out at Ćele Kula.

Red Cross Concentration Camp MUSEUM
(Crveni Krst; Bul 12 Februar; adult/child 150/130DIN; ⊙9am-4pm Tue-Fri, 10am-3pm Sat & Sun) One of the best-preserved Nazi camps in Europe, the deceptively named Red Cross held about 30,000 Serbs, Roma, Jews and Partisans during the German occupation of Serbia (1941–45). Harrowing displays tell their stories, and those of the prisoners who attempted to flee in the biggest ever breakout from a concentration camp. A short walk north of the Niš bus station.

🛏 Sleeping

Day 'n' Night Hostel HOSTEL €
(☑064 481 5869; www.daynnighthostel.com; Božidarčeva 9; dm/s/d from €9/15/20; P☀🛜) This spanking new hostel is clean and bright, and has a kitchen and common room on each of its two floors. Friendly English-speaking staff do their utmost to ensure you have a good stay, and can organise excursions. It's a ten-minute walk to downtown Niš.

Hostel Niš HOSTEL €
(☑513 703; www.hostelnis.rs; Dobrička 3a; dm/d per person 1260/1780DIN; @) Perfectly central with outgoing, helpful staff, good-sized rooms and lockable storage? Winner. It's a five-minute walk (towards the river) from the bus station.

★Hotel Sole HOTEL €€
(☑018-292 432; www.hotelsole.rs; Kralja Stefana Prvovenčanog 11; s/d from €50/60 incl breakfast; P☀🛜) Sitting pretty right in the heart of Niš, this totally refurbished hotel has modern, super-spacious rooms and one of the best free breakfasts you'll find anywhere. Staff is top-notch.

🍴 Eating

Restoran Sindjelić SERBIAN €
(Nikole Pasića 36; meals from 400DIN; ⊙8am-1am Sun-Fri, to 2am Sat) Hearty traditional fare.

Stara Srbija SERBIAN €€
(Old Serbia; ☑018-521 902; Trg Republike 12; mains 220-1500DIN; ⊙8am-midnight) Right at home in a restored 1876 house in the centre of Niš, this atmospheric spot serves up filling, fantastic traditional southern Serbian cuisine, including baked beans with smoked meat and the divine chicken stuffed with prosciutto and *kaymak* (clotted cream).

ℹ Getting There & Away

The **bus station** (Bul 12 Februar) behind the fortress has frequent services to Belgrade (1380DIN, three hours) and Brus (710DIN, 1½ hours) for Kopaonik, and three daily to Novi Pazar (1120DIN, four hours).

From the **train station** (Dimitrija Tucovića), there are seven trains to Belgrade (784DIN, 4½ hours) and two to Sofia (730DIN, five hours).

Serbia Survival Guide

ℹ Directory A–Z

DANGERS & ANNOYANCES
Travelling around Serbia is generally safe for travellers who exercise the usual caution. The exceptions can be border areas, particularly the southeast Kosovo border, where Serb–Albanian tensions remain. Check the situation before attempting to cross overland, and think thrice about driving there in Serbian-plated cars.

As evidenced by the neverending furore over Belgrade's Pride Parades (chronicled in the brilliant 2011 film *Parada*), life is not all rainbows for homosexuals in this conservative country. Discretion is highly advised.

EMERGENCY & IMPORTANT NUMBERS
Ambulance ☑94
Fire ☑93
Police ☑92

> ### ℹ SLEEPING PRICE RANGES
> The following price categories for the cost of a high-season double room are used in the listings in this chapter. Although accommodation prices are often quoted in euro, you must pay in dinar.
>
> **€** less than €30 (3000DIN)
>
> **€€** €30 to €75 (3000DIN to 7000DIN)

EATING PRICE RANGES

The following price categories for the cost of a main course are used in the listings in this chapter

€ less than €6 (600DIN)

€€ €6 to €10 (600DIN to 1000DIN)

MONEY

Serbia retains the dinar (DIN).

ATMs are widespread and cards are accepted by established businesses. Exchange offices (*menjačnica*) are on every street corner.

Exchange machines accept euros, US dollars and British pounds.

TELEPHONE

The country code is ☑ 381. Press the *i* button on public phones for dialling commands in English. Long-distance calls can also be made from booths in post offices.

Local and international phonecards can be bought in post offices and tobacco kiosks.

Mobile-phone SIM cards (around 200DIN) and recharge cards can be purchased at supermarkets and kiosks.

All mobile numbers in Serbia start with 06.

VISAS

Tourist visas for stays of less than 90 days aren't required by citizens of EU countries, most other European countries, Australia, New Zealand, Canada and the USA. The **Ministry of Foreign Affairs** (www.mfa.gov.rs/en) has full details.

Officially, all visitors must register with the police. Hotels and hostels will do this for you, but if you're camping or staying in a private home, you are expected to register within 24 hours of arrival. Unofficially? This is rarely enforced, but being unable to produce registration documents upon leaving Serbia could result in a fine.

ⓘ Getting There & Away

BORDER CROSSINGS

Serbia is landlocked by accessible neighbours. Subotica is 10km from the Hungarian border, Vršac is the same distance from Romania, and Bulgaria is 45 minutes from Pirot. When things are calm on the Kosovo border, €5 and three hours get you from Novi Pazar to Priština.

Because Serbia does not acknowledge crossing points into Kosovo as international border crossings, it may not be possible to enter Serbia from Kosovo unless you first entered Kosovo from Serbia. Check with your embassy.

BUS

Bus services to both Western Europe and Turkey are well developed, with regular services to destinations including Vienna, Sarajevo and Podgorica.

TRAIN

All of Europe is accessible from Belgrade: Bucharest, Budapest, Ljubljana, Moscow, Sofia and Zagreb are a train ride away. Heading north and west, most trains call in at Novi Sad and Subotica. Heading east, they go via Niš.

Several trips from Serbia offer a nice slice of scenery, such as the route to Bar on the Montenegrin coast. For more information, visit **Serbian Railways** (www.serbianrailways.com).

ⓘ Getting Around

Bus services are extensive, though outside major hubs connections can be sporadic. Reservations are only worthwhile during festivals.

Trains usually aren't as regular and reliable as buses, and can be murderously slow.

BULGARIA

Sofia

☑ 02 / POP 1.2 MILLION

Bulgaria's pleasingly laid-back capital, Sofia, is often overlooked by tourists heading straight to the coast or the ski resorts, but they're missing something special. It's no grand metropolis, true, but it combines a largely modern, youthful city with an old East-meets-West atmosphere – a scattering of onion-domed churches, Ottoman mosques and stubborn Red Army monuments shares the skyline with vast shopping malls and glassy five-star hotels. Sofia's grey, blocky civic architecture lends a lingering Soviet feel to the place, but it's also a surprisingly green city. Vast parks and manicured gardens offer welcome respite from the busy city streets, and the ski slopes and hiking trails of mighty Mt Vitosha are just a short bus ride from the centre. Home to many of Bulgaria's finest museums, galleries, restaurants and entertainment venues, Sofia may persuade you to stick around and explore further.

◉ Sights

★ **Aleksander Nevski Church**　　　CHURCH
(pl Aleksander Nevski; ⊙ 7am-7pm) One of *the* symbols not just of Sofia but of Bulgar-

ia itself, this massive, awe-inspiring church was built between 1882 and 1912 in memory of the 200,000 Russian soldiers who died fighting for Bulgaria's independence during the Russo-Turkish War (1877–78).

Aleksander Nevski Crypt
GALLERY

(Museum of Icons; pl Aleksander Nevski; adult/student 6/3 lv; ⊙10am-5.30pm Tue-Sun; 🚇1) Originally built as a final resting place for Bulgarian kings, this crypt now houses Bulgaria's biggest and best collection of icons, stretching back to the 5th century. Enter to the left of the eponymous church's main entrance.

★ Sveta Sofia Church
CHURCH

(ul Parizh; museum adult/student 6/2 lv; ⊙7am-7pm Apr-Oct, to 6pm Nov-Mar, museum 9am-5pm Tue-Sun; 🚇9) Sveta Sofia Church is the capital's oldest, and gave the city its name. A newly opened subterranean museum houses an ancient necropolis, with 56 tombs and the remains of four other churches. Outside are the Tomb of the Unknown Soldier and an eternal flame, and the grave of Ivan Vazov, Bulgaria's most revered writer.

Archaeological Museum
MUSEUM

(www.naim.bg; pl Nezavisimost; adult/student 10/2 lv; tours in English 20 lv; ⊙10am-6pm May-Oct, to 5pm Tue-Sun Nov-Apr; 🚇10) Housed in a former mosque built in 1496, this museum displays a wealth of Thracian, Roman and medieval artefacts. Highlights include a mosaic floor from the Church of Sveta Sofia, a 4th-century BC Thracian gold burial mask, and a magnificent bronze head, thought to represent a Thracian king.

Museum of Socialist Art
MUSEUM

(ul Lachezar Stanchev 7, Iztok; admission 6 lv; ⊙10am-5.30pm Tue-Sun; Ⓜ GM Dimitrov) If you wondered where all those unwanted statues of Lenin ended up, you'll find some here, along with the red star from atop Sofia's **Party House** (pl Nezavisimost; 🚇20). There's a gallery of paintings, rejoicing in such catchy titles as 'Youth Meeting at Kilifarevo Village to Send Worker-Peasant Delegation to the USSR', and stirring old propaganda films are shown.

The museum isn't the easiest to find. Catch the metro to the GM Dimitrov station, in the Iztok suburb, walk north up bul Tsankov and then turn right onto ul Lachezar Stanchev. The museum is housed in a gated Ministry of Culture building next to the Sopharma Business Towers. There is

no sign anywhere, but you can see the big red star in the garden.

🛏 Sleeping

Art Hostel
HOSTEL €

(🕿02-987 0545; www.art-hostel.com; ul Angel Kânchev 21a; dm/s/d from 20/47/66 lv; 🛜; 🚇12) This bohemian hostel stands out from the crowd with its summertime art exhibitions, live music, dance performances and more. Dorms are appropriately arty and bright; private rooms are airy and very welcoming. There's a great basement bar and peaceful little garden at the back.

Canapé Connection
HOSTEL €

(🕿02-441 6373; www.canapeconnection.com; ul William Gladstone 12a; dm/s/d from 18/52/62 lv; @🛜; 🚇1) Run by three young travellers, Canapé is a homely place with eight- and four-bed dorms featuring wide bunks and wooden floors, as well as private rooms. Homemade *banitsa* (cheese pastry), pancakes and croissants are on the breakfast menu.

Red B&B
B&B €€

(🕿088 922 6822; www.redbandb.com; ul Lyuben Karavelov 15; s/d from 40/70 lv; @; Ⓜ Vasil Levski, 🚇10) Attached to the Red House cultural centre in a wonderful '20s building, once home to Bulgaria's most famous sculptor, this six-room hotel offers digs with a difference. All rooms are individually decorated, and the general air is one of boho bonhomie. Shared bathrooms.

🍴 Eating

K.E.V.A
BULGARIAN €€

(🕿087 731 3233; School for Performing Arts, ul Rakovski 112; 5-15 lv; ⊙11am-midnight; Ⓜ Sofia Universitet) All is not as it seems at K.E.V.A, a simple-looking place with a cheap menu: this restaurant offers five-star cuisine at cafeteria prices. A favourite hangout of Sofia's arty elite and students from the attached School for Performing Arts, it also hosts regular mealtime theatrical performances.

★ Manastirska Magernitsa
BULGARIAN €€

(🕿02-980 3883; www.magernitsa.com; ul Han Asparuh 67; mains 6-10 lv; ⊙11am-2am; Ⓜ NDK) This traditional *mehana* (tavern) is among the best places in Sofia to sample authentic Bulgarian cuisine. The enormous menu features recipes collected from monasteries across the country, with dishes such as 'drunken rabbit' stewed in wine, as well as salads, fish, pork and game options. Portions are generous and service attentive.

The Little Things INTERNATIONAL €€
(📞 088 249 0030; ul Tsar Ivan Shishman 37; mains 7-18 lv; ⏰ noon-midnight; 🚎 1) It's the little things – knickknacks, toys, books, flowers –

that give this charming spot its name, but it's the large portions of delightful, home-style food that keep locals coming back. Mains includes handmade meatballs, sinful pastas and creamy fish dishes; whatever you do, try the fig cheesecake.

Sofia

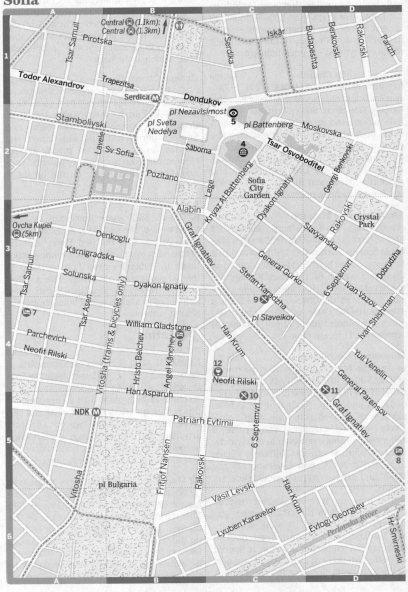

BALKANS SOFIA

🍷 Drinking & Nightlife

One More Bar   BAR

(📱 088 253 9592; ul Shishman 12; ⏱ 8am-2am;
Ⓜ Sofia Universitet) Inside a gorgeous old
house, this shabby-chic hotspot wouldn't
be out of place in Melbourne or Manhattan:
an extensive cocktail list, delightful summer
garden and jazzy background music add to
its cosmopolitan appeal.

Bar Up   BAR

(📱 087 654 1641; ul Neofit Rilski 55; ⏱ 9am-mid-
night Mon-Thu, 9am-2am Fri & Sat, 11am-1am Sun;
Ⓜ NPK) As you'd expect from a place that
serves cocktails in jars and has furniture
made from shipping pallets, this is a laid-
back and arty place, with a regular roster of
changing exhibitions to seal the deal.

ℹ Getting There & Away

BUS

Sofia's central **bus station** (Tsentralna Avtoga-
ra; www.centralnaavtogara.bg; bul Maria Luisa
100; ⏱ 24hr) is 100m south of the train station.
There are dozens of counters for individual
private companies, an information desk and an
OK-Supertrans (www.oktaxi.net; ⏱ 6am-10pm)
taxi desk. Frequent buses depart Sofia for Plovdiv (14 lv, 2½ hours), VelikoTârnovo (22 lv, four
hours), Varna (33 lv, seven hours) and more; the
easy-to-navigate website www.bgrazpisanie.
com has full local and international timetables
and fare listings. Departures are less frequent
between November and April.

TRAIN

The central train station is a massive, rather
cheerless concrete hive, built in the brutalist
style in the '70s.

Destinations for all domestic and international
services are listed on timetables in Cyrillic, but
departures (for the following two hours) and

arrivals (for the previous two hours) are listed in English on a large computer screen on the ground floor. Directions and signs around the station are sometimes translated into French. Other facilities include a post office, left luggage office, cafes, a supermarket and accommodation agencies. The rates at the foreign exchange offices are very poor, so best wait until you get into town.

Same-day tickets are sold at counters on the ground floor, while advance tickets are sold in the gloomy basement, accessed via an unsigned flight of stairs obscured by another set of stairs that heads up to some snack bars. Counters are open 24 hours, but normally only a few are staffed and queues are long, so don't turn up at the last moment to purchase your ticket, and allow some extra time to work out the confusing system of platforms (indicated with Roman numerals) and tracks.

Sample fast train routes include Sofia to Plovdiv (12 lv, 2½ hours) and Varna (31 lv, seven hours). See www.bgrazpisanie.com or www.bdz.bg for all domestic and international routes.

Plovdiv

☎ 032 / POP 338,184

With its art galleries, winding cobbled streets and bohemian cafes, Plovdiv equals Sofia in things cultural and is a determined

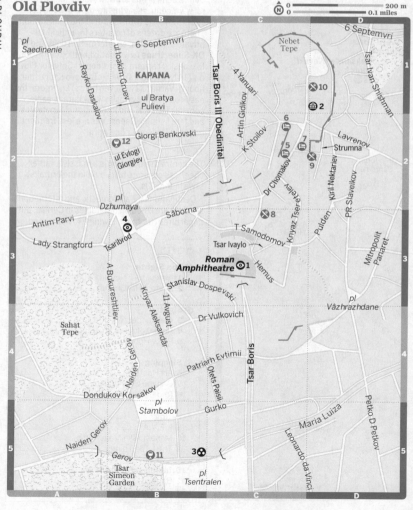

Old Plovdiv

rival in nightlife as well – it has a lively, exuberant spirit befitting its status as a major university town. Being a smaller and less stressful city than Sofia, Plovdiv is also great for walking.

Always one of Bulgaria's wealthiest and most cosmopolitan cities, Plovdiv is also Bulgaria's second-largest road and railway hub and economic centre. Although travellers often regard it as a mere stopover point between Bulgaria and Greece or Turkey, Plovdiv repays a longer visit and will certainly draw you in if you let it.

⊙ Sights

★ Roman Amphitheatre   HISTORIC SITE
(ul Hemus; adult/student 5/2 lv; ⊙9am-6pm) Plovdiv's magnificent 2nd-century-AD amphitheatre, built during the reign of Emperor Trajan, was only uncovered during a freak landslide in 1972. It once held about 6000 spectators. Now largely restored, it's one of Bulgaria's most magical venues, once again hosting large-scale special events and concerts. Visitors can admire the amphitheatre for free from several lookouts along ul Hemus, or pay admission for a scarper around.

Roman Stadium   HISTORIC SITE
(www.ancient-stadium-plovdiv.eu; ⊙9am-6pm) While the once-huge 2nd-century Roman Stadium is mostly hidden under the pedestrian mall, there are stairways from different sides allowing for at-your-leisure explora-

tion. A new onsite 3D movie (adult/student 6/3 lv, 10 showings daily) offers an immersive insight into the stadium's glory days as a venue for gladiator matches.

Roman Odeon   RUIN
Constructed between the 2nd and 5th centuries AD, the Odeon was once the seat of the city council. It now hosts occasional performances in its tiny reconstructed amphitheatre: check out the original columns. It's adjacent to the tourist information centre.

Ethnographical Museum   MUSEUM
(☑032-626 328; www.ethnograph.info; ul Dr Chomakov 2; adult/student 5/2 lv; ⊙9am-6pm Tue-Sun May-Oct, to 5pm Nov-Apr) This intriguing museum houses 40,000 exhibits, including folk costumes, musical instruments, jewellery and traditional craftworks such as winemaking and beekeeping. Built in 1847, it's Plovdiv's most renowned National Revival-period home; the gorgeous garden and exquisite exterior are reasons enough to visit.

🛏 Sleeping

Hikers Hostel   HOSTEL €
(☑089 676 4854; www.hikers-hostel.org; ul Sâborna 53; dm/tw from 14/50 lv; @🛜) With a mellow, central location in the Old Town, Hikers has standard dorms and facilities, but bonuses such as a garden lounge, hammocks and mega-friendly staff make it a worthy option. They also have off-site private rooms available; ask when booking.

Plovdiv Guest House   HOSTEL €
(☑622 432; www.plovdivguest.com; ul Sâborna 20; dm/s/d/q €9/25/30/45; ❄@🛜) Another backpacker option on Sâborna, this place offers clean and bright dorms with 10, eight or four beds, and there's one spacious attic double. Dorms feature their own self-contained and modern bathroom or shower. There's an outdoor cafe out the back, above the ancient Roman wall.

★ Hostel Old Plovdiv   HOSTEL €€
(☑032-260 925; www.hosteloldplovdiv.com; ul Chetvarti Yanuari 3; dm/s/tw/tr/q €12/25/35/39/45; P🛜) This marvellous old building (1868) is more akin to a boutique historical hotel than a run-of-the-mill hostel. Remarkably restored by charismatic owner Hristo Giulev and his wife, this genial place – smack bang in the middle of the Old Town – is all about warm welcomes and old-world charm.

Every room features hand-picked local antiques (from the decor to the beds themselves), and the courtyard is desperately romantic, with a history all its own (Hristo will fill you in over a glass of their special iced tea).

✕ Eating

King's Stables
BULGARIAN €

(☑ 088 981 4255; ul Sâborna 40; mains 4-7 lv; ☺ 9am-2am) The sprawling, summer-only King's Stables occupies a rolling hill ending in Roman walls. Offerings range from breakfast crepes to hearty meat dishes: be prepared to be shaken down for whatever you're eating by the trillion (clean) kittens roaming the joint. It's a lively spot, with local bands playing most nights.

Rahat Tepe
GRILL €

(☑ 087 845 0259; ul Dr Chomakov 20; mains 4-8 lv; ☺ 10am-midnight) Way up in the Old Town, the al fresco Rahat Tepe serves simple meals such as salads, beef kebabs and fried fish. Suitably rustic with great city views, it's an ideal spot for a nosh after clambering around Nebet Tepe (Nebet Hill).

★ Grazhdanski Klub
BULGARIAN €€

(Citizens Club; ul Stoyan Chalukov 1; mains 5-12 lv; ☺ 8am-1am Mon-Fri, 10am-1am Sat & Sun; ☎) A locals' favourite, this fabulous, friendly nook is just a totter down the hill from the Roman Amphitheatre. Its cool, green courtyard is a haven in hotter months; inside is cosy. The food – mostly Bulgarian staples and sinful salads – is moreish: thankfully, portions are huge! It's attached to the endearing, free-to-enter **Vazrazdane Gallery** (☺ 10am-6.30pm Mon-Sat, 11am-5pm Sun).

🍷 Drinking & Nightlife

★ Art Club Nylon
BAR

(☑ 088 949 6750; ul Giorgi Benkovski 8, Kapana; ☺ noon-4am Mon-Sat; ☎) A bastion of bohemia, this damp, bare-bones, but somehow wonderful place often hosts rock and indie bands playing to Plovdiv's cool kids.

Apartment 101
BAR

(ul William Gladston 8; ☺ 10am-1am Sun-Thu, to 2am Fri & Sat) A hip – but not painfully so – spot in a wonderfully ramshackle building with chill-out music and occasional live acts. The interior is op-shop chic; you'll have to be crowbarred out of the eminently hangoutable courtyard.

ℹ Getting There & Away

BUS

Plovdiv's main station is **Yug bus station** (☑ 032-626 937; bul Hristo Botev 47). Yug is diagonally opposite the train station and a 15-minute walk from the centre. Taxis cost 5 to 7 lv; local buses 7, 20 and 26 stop across the street.

WORTH A TRIP

RILA MONASTERY

Bulgaria's largest and most renowned monastery emerges abruptly out of a forested valley in the Rila Mountains. It's a major attraction for both Bulgarian pilgrims and foreign tourists. On summer weekends the site is especially busy, though at other times it provides more solitude. Stay at a nearby hotel or camping ground, or even at the monastery itself, to experience Rila's photogenic early mornings and late evenings. You can also hike the surrounding mountains.

Drivers usually park near the western **Dupnitsa gate**; the eastern entrance is called the **Samokov gate**. At both you'll find multilingual placards with historical details.

The nearby 23m-high stone **Hreliova Tower** (1335), named after a significant benefactor, is the only 14th-century structure remaining here. The monastery's kitchen (1816) is in the northern wing's courtyard. The 22m-high chimney, caked with centuries' worth of soot, cuts through all storeys, with 10 arched rows crowned by a small dome. Thousands of pilgrims formerly dined here simultaneously, with food prepared in giant cauldrons – a single cauldron could fit an entire cow. The upper balcony offers outstanding views over Rila Mountains.

Monastery day trips from Sofia by bus require leaving before 8am to travel to Dupnitsa (1½ hours) from the central bus station, or Ovcha Kupel bus station. Then grab the next bus to Rila village or monastery. To return, catch a bus back to Dupnitsa, which also has train connections to Sofia.

Frequent routes include Plovdiv to Sofia (12 lv, 2½ hours), Burgas (20 lv, five hours) and Varna (26 lv, seven hours). Check out www.bgraz-pisanie.com for full destination and fare info. The **Sever bus station** (ul Dimitar Stambolov 2), in the northern suburbs, serves destinations to the north of Plovdiv, including Veliko Târnovo (18 lv, four hours).

TRAIN

Daily direct services from the **train station** (bul Hristo Botev) include trains to Sofia (9 lv, three hours) and Burgas (14.60 lv, five hours); see www.bgrazpisanie.com or www.bdz.bg for all fares and timetables.

Koprivshtitsa

📞 07184 / POP 2900

Quiet Koprivshtitsa is a well-preserved 'museum village' filled with gorgeous National Revival–period mansions. This was the place where revolutionary Todor Kableshkov declared an uprising against the Turks on 20 April 1876, from Kalachev Bridge (also called Kableshkov Bridge).

Koprivshtitsa once had 12,000 residents, rivalling Sofia, but after 1878 and independence, many of its merchants, shepherds and intellectuals left for the cities; the village remained essentially unchanged, and the post-WWII communist government declared it variously a 'town-museum' and a 'historical reserve'.

⊙ Sights

Koprivshtitsa boasts six house-museums. Some are closed either on Monday or Tuesday (all operate Wednesday through Sunday). To buy a combined ticket for all (adults/students 5/3 lv) visit the **souvenir shop Kupchinitsa** (near the tourist information centre). The best museums include the following.

Oslekov House   HISTORIC BUILDING
(ul Gereniloto 4; ⊙ 9.30am-5.30pm Apr-Oct, 9am-5pm Nov-Mar, closed Mon) The Oslekov House (built 1853–56) was built by a rich merchant killed in the line of duty during the 1876 April Uprising against the Turks. It's arguably the best example of Bulgarian National Revival–period architecture in Koprivshtitsa, with a triple-arched entrance, spacious interior, stylish furniture and brightly coloured walls.

Kableshkov House   HISTORIC BUILDING
(ul Todor Kableshkov 8; ⊙ 9.30am-5.30pm Apr-Oct, 9am-5pm Nov-Mar, closed Mon) Todor Kableshkov is revered as having (probably) been the person who fired the first shot in the 1876 uprising. This, his glorious former home (1845) has exhibits about the uprising.

🛏 Sleeping

Hotel Kozlekov   HOTEL €
(📞 87989-1077; www.hotelkozlekov.com; ul Georgi Benkovski 8; d/studio from 50/60 lv; 🅿 @) Rustic as it gets but with amazingly modern service, this hilltop hotel is attached to a superb restaurant serving up hearty Bulgarian classics. Staff speak English; some rooms have balconies.

Hotel Astra   HOTEL €
(📞 07184-2033; www.hotelastra.org; bul Hadzhi Nencho Palaveev 11; d/apt 45/66 lv; 🅿) Set beautifully in a garden, the hospitable Astra is a popular place with large, well-kept rooms.

✗ Eating

Dyado Liben   BULGARIAN €€
(📞 07184-2109; bul Hadzhi Nencho Palaveev 47; mains 4-9 lv; ⊙ 11am-midnight; 🛜) Traditional fare is served at this atmospheric 1852 mansion with tables set in a warren of halls, graced with ornate painted walls and heavy, worn wood floors. Find it just across the bridge leading from the main square inside the facing courtyard.

ⓘ Getting There & Away

Getting to Koprivshtitsa is a bit of a challenge. Being 9km north of the village, the train station requires a shuttle bus (2 lv, 15 minutes), which isn't always dependably timed for meeting incoming and outgoing trains. Trains do come from Sofia (11 lv, 2½ hours, four daily) and connections can be made for Plovdiv and other points like Burgas, which gets a daily train (18 lv, five hours).

Alternatively, Koprivshtitsa's bus stop is central and has more frequent connections including buses to Sofia (13 llv, two hours, five daily), and Plovdiv (12 lv, two hours, one daily).

Melnik

📞 07437 / POP 385

Tiny Melnik is one of Bulgaria's most unique villages, due to its traditional architecture, local wine, and location (about 20km north of Greece). Tucked beneath imposing sandstone cliffs, the village has historically been a wine-production centre, and you'll find plenty to sample at restaurants and National Revival–era house museums where vintners once lived.

◉ Sights

The major sights here, unsurprisingly, are wineries. Melnik's wines, celebrated for more than 600 years, include the signature dark red, Shiroka Melnishka Loza; it was a favourite tipple of Winston Churchill. Shops and stands dot Melnik's cobblestone paths, with reds and whites for 3 lv to 4 lv and up.

Museum of Wine   MUSEUM
(www.muzei-na-vinoto.com; ul Melnik 91; admission 5 lv; ☺10am-7pm) Learn the history of wine-making in Melnik, ogle the 400-plus bottles on display (the dirt vault is especially cool), and work your way through a tasting menu at this fun museum attached to the Hotel Bulgari. Once you find one (or four) wines that you like, fill a bottle and they'll personalise a label for you.

Mitko Manolev Winery   WINERY
(Shestaka; ☎88754-5795, 07437-2215; www.shestaka.com; admission incl tasting 2 lv; ☺9am-dusk) For the most atmospheric adventures in *degustatsia* (wine tasting), clamber up the cobblestones to this winery, also known as Shestaka ('six-fingered'); it's named after the founder, who had an extra digit (as does his modern-day descendant Mitko). This place is basically a cellar dug into the rocks, plus a hut with tables and chairs outside. It's along the hillside trail between the Bolyaskata Kâshta ruins and the Kordopulov House. Accommodation is also available (double rooms are 35 lv).

Kordopulov House   MUSEUM
(☎07437-2265; www.kordopulova-house.com; admission 3 lv; ☺8am-8pm) Built in 1754, this four-storey former home of a prestigious wine merchant is an impressive structure. The sitting rooms have been carefully restored, and boast 19th-century murals, stained-glass windows and exquisitely carved wooden ceilings. An enormous wine cellar (tasting available) includes 180m of illuminated labyrinthine passageways; look out for the wall full of glittering coins. The house is on the cliff face at the street's end, south of the creek: you can't miss it.

🛏 Sleeping

Lumparova Kâshta   PENSION €
(☎088 880 4512; r per person 25 lv; 🅿) The Lumparova has cosy rooms with balconies that enjoy fantastic cliff views, and attractive decor and beds. There's traditional food and wine tasting, too. It's up a steep path starting behind the village.

Chavkova Kâshta   PENSION €
(☎089 350 5090; www.themelnikhouse.com; ul Melnik 12; s/d 30/40 lv; 🛜) This friendly pension, a two-minute walk straight in from the bus on the left, under the square's giant plane tree, has airy and clean rooms (the only drawback being that the shower shoots onto the floor). There's a tasty *mehana* (tavern) attached for dinner or drinks.

✕ Eating

★Mehana Chavkova House   BULGARIAN €€
(☎089 350 5090; ul Melnik 112; 5-10 lv) Sit beneath the 500-year-old trees and watch Melnik meander past at this superb spot. Like many places in town, grilled meats and Bulgarian dishes are specialties (try the 'sach', a sizzling flat pan of meat and vegetables); the atmosphere and super-friendly service gives it that extra nudge above the rest.

Mehana Mencheva Kâshta   BULGARIAN €€
(☎07437-2339; mains 6-11 lv; ☺10am-11.30pm) This tiny tavern has a lovely upper porch overlooking the main street down towards the end of the village. It's popular with locals and does the full run of Bulgarian dishes.

ℹ Getting There & Away

One daily direct bus connects Melnik with Sofia (17 lv, four hours); times vary.

Veliko Târnovo

☑ 062 / POP 68,735

The evocative capital of the medieval Bulgarian tsars, sublime Veliko Târnovo is dramatically set amidst an amphitheatre of forested hills, divided by the ribboning Yantra River. Commanding pride of place is the magisterial, well-restored Tsarevets Fortress, citadel of the Second Bulgarian Empire. It's complemented by scores of churches and other ruins, many still being unearthed.

As the site of Bulgaria's most prestigious university, Veliko Târnovo also boasts a revved-up nightlife of which many larger

Veliko Târnovo

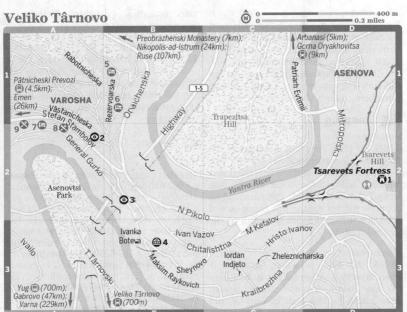

0 ——————— 400 m
0 ——————— 0.2 miles

towns would be jealous. There's great food and drink, too, in restaurants offering commanding views of the river and castle, or the old-world ambience of the Varosha quarter, with its terracotta rooftops and lounging cats.

◉ Sights

★ Tsarevets Fortress
FORTRESS

(adult/student 6/2 lv, scenic elevator 2 lv; ⊙8am-7pm Apr-Oct, 9am-5pm Nov-Mar) The inescapable symbol of Veliko Târnovo, this reconstructed fortress dominates the skyline, and is one of Bulgaria's most beloved monuments. The former seat of the medieval tsars, it boasts the remains of more than 400 houses, 18 churches, the royal palace, an execution rock and more. Watch your step: there are lots of potholes, broken steps and unfenced drops. The fortress morphs into a psychedelic spectacle with a magnificent nighttime sound-and-light show, held on public holidays.

Veliko Târnovo
Archaeological Museum
MUSEUM

(ul Ivanka Boteva 2; adult/student 6/2 lv; ⊙9am-6pm Tue-Sun) Housed in a grand old building with a courtyard full of Roman sculptures, this museum contains Roman artefacts and

Veliko Târnovo

medieval Bulgarian exhibits, including a huge mural of the tsars, plus some ancient gold from nearby neolithic settlements.

Samovodska Charshiya
HISTORIC AREA

This atmospheric, cobblestoned historical quarter was Veliko Târnovo's biggest market square in the 1880s, and remains the place to come to shop, stroll and admire the town's many National Revival–era houses.

Ulitsa Gurko
HISTORIC SITE

The oldest street in Veliko Tãrnovo, ul Gurko is a must-stroll. Overlooking the Yantra River, its charmingly crumbling period houses – which appear to be haphazardly piled on one another – provide a million photo-ops and conversations that start with 'Imagine living here...' Sturdy shoes a must.

🛏 Sleeping

Hotel Comfort
HOTEL €

(🖉 088 777 7265; www.hotelcomfortbg.com; ul P Tipografov 5; d/apt from 40/100 lv; 🅿❄🛜) With jaw-dropping views of the fortress and surrounding hills, plus a stellar location just around the corner from the Samovodska Charshia market square, this family-owned hotel is a winner. English is spoken by the amiable staff.

Hikers Hostel
HOSTEL €

(🖉 088 969 1661; www.hikers-hostel.org; ul Rezervoarska 91; dm/d from 14/52 lv; @🛜) Tãrnovo's most laid-back hostel, Hikers has an unassuming location high in Varosha's old quarter (a 10-minute walk from downtown). Owner Toshe Hristov does free bus/train station pick-ups and runs trips. Dorms are spartan but clean.

★ Hotel-Mehana Gurko
HISTORIC HOTEL €€

(🖉 062-627 838; www.hotel-gurko.com; ul General Gurko 33; s/d/apt from 50/90/100 lv; ❄@🛜) You can't miss this gorgeous place, with riotous blooms and ye olde curios bedecking its restored 19th-century facade. Sitting pretty on Veliko Tãrnovo's oldest street, the Gurko is one of the best places to sleep (and eat) in town; rooms are spacious and soothing, each individually decorated and offering great views.

🍴 Eating

Shtastlivetsa
BULGARIAN €€

(🖉 062-600 656; www.shtastliveca.com; ul Stefan Stambolov 79; mains 7-17 lv; ⏱11am-1am; 🛜) A local institution, the 'Lucky Man' (as the impossible-to-pronounce name means in Bulgarian) has an ideal location overlooking the river's bend and a long menu of inventive meat dishes, baked-pot specials, superb pizzas and lunchtime soups. Every visitor to Veliko Tãrnovo comes here at least once.

Hotel-Mehana Gurko
BULGARIAN €€

(🖉 627 838; ul General Gurko 33; mains 5-11 lv; 🛜) This traditional-style *mehana* of the Hotel Gurko is a cosy place with great views and tasty Bulgarian specialities. Portions are hearty and service is prompt and friendly.

Ego Pizza & Grill
PIZZA €€

(🖉 601 804; ul Nezavisimost 17; mains 5-12 lv; ⏱9am-midnight; 🛜) Probably Tãrnovo's best pizza place, Ego has a new location overlooking the river's bend. It's a spacious restaurant, with outdoor and indoor seating and excellent views. Service can be hit-or-miss.

❶ Getting There & Away

BUS

Three bus stations serve Veliko Tãrnovo. **Zapad** (🖉 062-640 908; ul Nikola Gabrovski 74), about 4km southwest from the centre, is the main station. From here, buses serve Plovdiv (24 lv, four hours, at least two daily), Burgas (23 lv, four hours, three daily), Kazanlâk (10 lv, two hours, three daily) and elsewhere. The more central **Yug bus station** (🖉 062-620014; ul Hristo Botev 74) has many daily buses to Sofia (22 lv, three hours), Varna (17 lv, four hours) and Burgas (23 lv, four hours). **Etap Adress** (🖉 062-630 564; Hotel Etâr, ul Ivailo 2), right by the tourist information centre, also runs hourly buses to Sofia and Varna.

TRAIN

Gorna Oryakhovitsa station (🖉 062-826 118), 8.5km from town, and the smaller **Veliko Târnovo train station** (🖉 062-620 065), 1.5km west of the centre, both run frequent trains to Plovdiv (23 lv, five hours), Burgas (19 lv, five hours), Varna (14 lv, five hours) and Sofia (21 lv, five hours). The latter station may be closer, but many trains require a change at Gorna Oryakhovitsa anyway. Get there on bus 10.

Varna

🖉 052 / POP 335,000

Bulgaria's third city and maritime capital, Varna is by far the most interesting and cosmopolitan town on the Black Sea coast. A combination of port city, naval base and seaside resort, it's an appealing place to while away a few days, packed with history yet thoroughly modern, with an enormous park to amble round and a lengthy beach to lounge on. In the city centre you'll find Bulgaria's largest Roman baths complex and its finest archaeological museum, as well as a lively cultural and restaurant scene.

◉ Sights

Archaeological Museum
MUSEUM

(www.archaeo.museumvarna.com; ul Maria Luisa 41; adult/student 10/2 lv; ⏱10am-5pm Tue-Sun Apr-

Varna

Sep, Tue-Sat Oct-Mar; 🚍 3 9, 109) Exhibits at this vast museum, the best of its kind in Bulgaria, include 6500-year-old bangles, necklaces and earrings said to be the oldest worked gold found in the world. You'll also find Roman surgical implements, Hellenistic tombstones and touching oddments including a marble plaque listing, in Greek, the names of the city's school graduates for AD 221.

Roman Thermae RUIN
(cnr ul Han Krum & ul San Stefano; adult/student 4/2 lv; ⊙10am-5pm Tue-Sun May-Oct, Tue-Sat Nov-Apr) The well-preserved ruins of Varna's 2nd-century-AD Roman Thermae are the largest in Bulgaria, although only a small part of the original complex still stands.

🛏 Sleeping

Flag Hostel HOSTEL €
(📞089 740 8115; www.varnahostel.com; ul Bratya Shkorpil 13a; dm incl breakfast 22 lv; 🅿☕📶; 🚍3, 9) The Flag is a long-established, sociable

spot with a party atmosphere. The three dorms are basic, with comfortable single beds (no bunks). Free pick ups from the bus and train stations.

Yo Ho Hostel HOSTEL €
(📞088 472 9144; www.yohohostel.com; ul Ruse 23; dm/s/d/tw incl breakfast from 14/30/40/40 lv;

@ 🖥; 🖥109) Shiver your timbers at this pirate-themed place, with four- and 11-bed dorm rooms and private options. Staff offer free pick-ups, and can organise camping and rafting trips.

Hotel Astra   HOTEL €€

(📞052-630 524; www.hotelastravarna.com; ul Opalchenska 9; s/d 60/70 lv; ✳🖥; 🖥9) A real bargain by Varna standards, this central, cheerful family-run hotel has 10 spacious rooms, all with terraces and basic but good-sized bathrooms.

🍴 Eating

★ Stariya Chinar   BULGARIAN €€

(📞052-949 400; www.stariachinar.com; ul Preslav 11; mains 7-19 lv; ⊙8am-midnight) This is upmarket Balkan soul food at its best. Try the baked lamb, made to an old Bulgarian recipe, or the divine barbecue pork ribs; they also create some rather ornate salads. Outdoors is lovely in summer; park yourself in a traditional interior when the cooler weather strikes.

Balkanska Skara Nashentsi   BULGARIAN €€

(📞052-630 186; ul Tsar Simeon 1 27; mains 5-10lv; ⊙11am-1am Mon-Sat, 6pm-1am Sun) This big, riotous restaurant is popular with locals for its prodigious portions of grilled meats, live music and fun atmosphere. Set menus are available.

Bistro Dragoman   SEAFOOD €€

(📞052-621 688; www.bistro-dragoman.net; ul Dragoman 43; mains 4-16 lv; ⊙10am-11.30pm) This welcoming little place specialises in delicious takes on seafood and locally caught fish. This being the Balkans, grilled meats are also on the menu.

❶ Getting There & Away

BUS

Varna's **central bus station** (bul Vladislav Varenchik158) is about 2km northwest of the city centre. There are regular buses to Sofia (33 lv, seven hours), Burgas (14 lv, two hours) and all the major destinations in Bulgaria: see www.bgrazpisanie.com for fares and schedules.

TRAIN

Facilities at Varna's **train station** (📞052-662 3343; pl Slaveikov) include a left-luggage office and cafe. Destinations include the following:

Ruse (12.20 lv, four hours, two daily)

Sofia (23.60 lv, seven to eight hours, seven daily)

Plovdiv (24.20 lv, seven hours, three daily)

Shumen (6.50 lv, 1½ hours, 10 daily)

The **Rila Bureau** (📞632 348; ul Preslav 13; ⊙8.30am-5.30pm Mon-Fri, 8am-3.30pm Sat) sells tickets for international services and advance tickets for domestic trains.

Burgas

📞 056 / POP 212,000

For most visitors, the port city of Burgas (sometimes written as 'Bourgas') is no more than a transit point for the more obviously appealing resorts and historic towns further up and down the coast. If you do decide to stop

---

WORTH A TRIP

NESEBÂR

On a small rocky outcrop 37km northeast of Burgas, connected to the mainland by a narrow, artificial isthmus, pretty-as-a-postcard Nesebâr is famous for its surprisingly numerous, albeit mostly ruined, medieval churches. It has, inevitably, become heavily commercialised, and transforms into one huge, open-air souvenir market during the high season; outside summer, it's a ghost town. Designated by Unesco as a World Heritage Site, Nesebâr has its charms, but in summer these can be overpowered by the crowds and the relentless parade of tacky shops. With **Sunny Beach** (Slânchev Bryag) just across the bay, you have every conceivable water sport on hand. The 'new town' on the other side of the isthmus has the newest and biggest hotels and the main beach, but the sights are all in the Old Town. Nesebâr was once home to about 80 churches, but most are now in ruins, giving the town a particularly haunting air. Characteristic of the Nesebâr style are horizontal strips of white stone and red brick, and facades decorated with green ceramic discs.

Nesebâr is well connected to coastal destinations by public transport, and the town's bus station is on the small square just outside the city walls. From here there are buses to nearby Sunny Beach (1 lv, 10 minutes, every 15 minutes), Burgas (6 lv, 40 minutes, every 30 minutes), Varna (15 lv, two hours, seven daily) and Sofia (30 lv, seven hours, several daily).

over, you'll find a lively, well-kept city with a neat, pedestrianised centre, a long, uncrowded beach and some interesting museums. A clutch of reasonably priced hotels, as well as some decent restaurants, makes it a practical base for exploring the southern coast, too.

◉ Sights

Burgas Beach — BEACH
Burgas' 2km-long beach isn't the best the Black Sea has to offer, but the northern end is clean and patrolled by lifeguards in summer. It's lined with many beach bars and fish restaurants, and umbrellas and loungers can be hired. Running along the beach is the leafy, flower-filled **Maritime Park**, which has a predictably graffiti-covered communist monument, as well as lots of statues, fountains and a couple of bars.

🛏 Sleeping

★ Old House Hostel — HOSTEL €
(087 984 1559; www.burgashostel.com; ul Sofroniy 2; dm/d 17/33 lv; ❄ 🤖) This charming hostel makes itself right at home in a lovely 1895 house. Dorms are airy and bright (and bunk-free!), while doubles have access to a sweet little courtyard. Located downtown and only 400m to the beach, this place is a winner.

🍴 Eating

★ Ethno — SEAFOOD €€
(088 787 7966; ul Aleksandrovska 49; 7-20 lv; 11am-11.30pm) This downtown restaurant does splendid things with seafood: the Black Sea mussels alone are worth a trip to Burgas. With ambient blue-and-white surrounds that recall the city's Greek heritage, superb (English-speaking) service and a summery vibe, Ethno is classy without being uptight.

ℹ Getting There & Away

BUS

Yug bus station (pl Tsaritsa Yoanna), outside the train station at the southern end of ul Aleksandrovska, is where most travellers arrive or leave. There are regular buses to coastal destinations, including Nesebâr (6 lv, 40 minutes), Varna (14lv, 2½ hours) and Sozopol (4.50 lv, 40 minutes). Buses also go to and from Sofia (30 lv, five to six hours) and Plovdiv (17 lv, four hours). Departures are less frequent outside summer.

TRAIN

The **train station** (ul Ivan Vazov) has ticket windows (8am to 6pm) on the right, where you can buy advance tickets for domestic and international services; same-day tickets can be bought at the windows (24 hours) on the left. Trains run to Varna (19 lv, five to six hours, five to seven daily) and Sofia (23.60 lv, seven to eight hours, six daily).

Sozopol
📞 0550 / POP 5000
Ancient Sozopol, with its charming Old Town of meandering cobbled streets and pretty wooden houses, huddled together on a narrow peninsula, is one of the coast's real highlights. With two superb beaches, a genial atmosphere, plentiful accommodation and good transport links, it has long been a popular seaside resort and makes an excellent base for exploring the area. Although not

Sozopol map

Sozopol

◉ **Sights**
1 Archaeological Museum A2
2 Southern Fortress Wall & Tower Museum A2

🛏 **Sleeping**
3 Hotel Radik A3
4 Sasha Khristov's Private Rooms B1

🍴 **Eating**
5 Panorama B1

683 · BALKANS SOZOPOL

quite as crowded as Nesebâr, it is becoming ever more popular with international visitors. There's a lively cultural scene, too, with plenty of free concerts and other events in summer.

◉ Sights

The town's two beaches are attractive, though waves can be quite high. The 1km-long **Harmanite Beach** is wide and clean, and offers a water slide, paddle boats, volleyball nets and beach bars. At the southern end, incongruously, archaeological excavations have uncovered stone sarcophagi on the site of the ancient **Apollonia necropolis**. The **Town Beach** (or Northern Beach) is another pleasant curve of sand, but it's smaller, gets *very* crowded, and doesn't offer the same number of beachside cafes, restaurants and bars.

Archaeological Museum   MUSEUM
(ul Han Krum 2; adult/child 8/3 lv; ⊗ 9am-6pm, closed Sat & Sun Oct-Apr) Housed in a drab concrete box near the port, this museum has a small but fascinating collection of local finds from its Apollonian glory days and beyond. In addition to a wealth of Hellenic treasures, the museum occasionally exhibits the skeleton of a local 'vampire', found with a stake driven through its chest.

Southern Fortress Wall
& Tower Museum   RUIN, MUSEUM
(ul Milet 40; museum admission 3 lv; ⊗ 9.30am-8pm Jul-Aug, to 5pm May, Jun, Sep & Oct) The reconstructed walls and walkways along the rocky coastline, and a 4th-century-BC well that was once part of a temple to Aphrodite here, are free to explore; the views are ridiculously glorious. The attached museum is a bit of an anticlimax.

⌕ Sleeping

Sozopol has countless private homes offering rooms. Look for signs along Republikanska in the new town, and pretty much anywhere in the Old Town.

Sasha Khristov's
Private Rooms   PENSION €
(☑ 23 434; ul Venets 17; s/d 20/30 lv) This lovely family home in the Old Town faces the art gallery at the end of the Sozopol peninsula. It comprises good-sized rooms and a large apartment. Book ahead in summer.

★ Hotel Radik   HOTEL €€
(☑ 055-023 706; ul Republikanska 4; d/studio/apt from 68/75/95 lv; P☀🛜🏊) Run by a

lovely English ex-pat/Bulgarian couple, the Radik is cheap, cheerful and perfectly located 100m from the Old Town and a quick stagger to the beach. Rooms have sea views and balconies; studios and apartments have good kitchenettes.

✗ Eating

★ Panorama   SEAFOOD €€
(ul Morski Skali 21; mains 8-20 lv; ⊗ 10am-1am) This lively place has an open terrace with a fantastic view towards Sveti Ivan Island. Fresh, locally caught fish is a mainstay of the menu. It's one of the best of many seafood spots on the street.

❶ Getting There & Away

The small public **bus station** (ul Han Krum) is just south of the Old Town walls. Buses leave for Burgas (4.50 lv, 40 minutes) about every 30 minutes between 6am and 9pm in summer, and about once an hour in the low season.

Buses also arrive and depart from spots around the new town's main square. Three or four buses go to Sofia daily and one or two depart for Plovdiv.

Fast Ferry (www.fastferry.bg), operating from a kiosk at the harbour, runs ferries at least four days a week to Nesebâr (single/return from 27/54 lv, 30 minutes) between June and September.

Bulgaria Survival Guide

❶ Directory A–Z

ACCOMMODATION
Sofia, Plovdiv, Veliko Târnovo, Varna and Burgas all have hostels; for cheap accommodation elsewhere, look out for signs reading 'стаи под наем' (rooms for rent). Many hotels offer discounts for longer stays or on weekends; prices may rise during summer.

EMERGENCY & IMPORTANT NUMBERS
Bulgarian area codes have between two and five numerals. When dialing a local number, drop the initial '0'.

Country Code ☑ 359
Ambulance ☑ 150
Fire ☑ 160
Police ☑ 166
24-hour Pharmacy Information ☑ 178

MONEY
The local currency is the lev (plural: leva), comprised of 100 stotinki. It is almost always

abbreviated to lv. The lev is a stable currency. For major purchases such as organised tours, airfares, car rental and midrange and top-end hotels, prices are almost always quoted by staff in euros, although payment is possible in leva too. Bulgaria has no immediate plans to adopt the euro as its national currency.

ATMs that accept major credit cards (Visa, MasterCard and American Express) are common, and can be found in all sizeable towns and cities. The total amount you can withdraw depends on how much your bank will allow; the maximum allowed per day by most Bulgarian banks is usually 200 lv.

PUBLIC HOLIDAYS

During official public holidays all government offices, banks, post offices and major businesses will be closed. All hotels, restaurants, bars, national parks/reserves and museums stay open (unless the holiday coincides with a normal day off), as do most shops and petrol stations; border crossings and public transport continue to operate normally.

New Year's Day 1 January
Liberation Day 3 March
Easter March/April
May Day 1 May
St George's Day/Bulgarian Army Day 6 May
Cyrillic Alphabet Day 24 May
Unification Day 6 September
Bulgarian Independence Day 22 September
National Revival Day 1 November
Christmas 25 and 26 December

TELEPHONE

To call Bulgaria from abroad, dial the international access code (which varies from country to country), add 359 (the country code for Bulgaria), the area code (minus the first zero) and then the number.

To make an international call from Bulgaria, dial 00 followed by the code of the country you are calling, then the local area code, minus the first zero.

VISAS

Bulgaria is a member of the EU. Visas are not required for EU citizens. Citizens of Australia, Canada, New Zealand and the USA can visit visa-free for up to 90 days.

ⓘ Getting There & Away

BORDER CROSSINGS

You can expect delays at each of Bulgaria's border crossings, especially if you are using public transport. Delays at the Turkish border tend to be longest.

Greece to Bulgaria
➡ Promahonas–Kulata

ⓘ PRICE RANGES

Price ranges in accommodation listings are based on the cost of a double room with a bathroom.

€ less than 60 lv

€€ 60 lv to 120 lv (to 200 lv in Sofia)

The following price ranges used in listings of restaurants/eateries refer to a typical main course.

€ less than 5 lv

€€ 5 lv to 15 lv

➡ Ormenio–Svilengrad
➡ Xanthi–Zlatograd
Macedonia to Bulgaria
➡ Deve Bair–Gyushevo
➡ Delčevo–Zlatarevo
➡ Novo Selo–Stanke Lisichkovo
Romania to Bulgaria
➡ Giurgiu–Ruse; toll-bridge
➡ Calafat–Vidin; ferry
➡ Calarasi–Silistra; ferry
➡ Kardam–Negru Vodă
➡ Durankulak–Vama Veche (accessible from Varna)
Serbia to Bulgaria
➡ Dimitrovgrad–Kalotina
➡ Zajc–Vrâshka Chuka (near Vidin)
➡ Klisura–Strezimirovtsi (near Pernik)
Turkey to Bulgaria
➡ Derekoy–Malko Târnovo
➡ Edirne–Kapitan Andreevo

BUS

Buses travel to Bulgarian cities from destinations all over Europe, with most arriving in Sofia. You will have to get off the bus at the border and walk through customs to present your passport. Long delays can be expected. When travelling out of Bulgaria by bus, the cost of entry visas for the countries concerned are not included in bus ticket prices.

TRAIN

There are a number of international trains from Bulgaria, including services to Serbia. Romania, Greece and Turkey. Sofia is the main hub, although trains stop at other towns.

Bulgarian international train services are operated by **Bulgarian State Railway** (BDZ; www.bdz.bg). Other resources to check include **Romanian State Railway** (CFR; www.cfr.ro) and **Serbian Railways** (www.serbianrailways.com).

ⓘ Getting Around

BUS

Buses provide the most comfortable and quickest mode of public transport in Bulgaria. They link all cities and major towns and connect villages with the nearest transport hub. There are several private companies operating frequent modern, comfortable buses between the larger towns, while older, often cramped minibuses also run on routes between smaller towns.

Union-Ivkoni (www.union-ivkoni.com) Links most major towns and many smaller ones, including Sofia, Burgas, Varna, Plovdiv, Pleven, Ruse, Sliven and Shumen.

Biomet (www.biomet.bg) Runs between Sofia and Veliko Târnovo, Varna, Burgas and Stara Zagora.

Etap-Grup (www.etapgroup.com) Another extensive intercity network, with buses between

Sofia, Burgas, Varna, Ruse and Veliko Târnovo as well as routes between Sofia and Sozopol, Primorsko, Tsarevo and Pomorie.

TRAIN

Bulgarian State Railways (БДЖ; www.bdz.bg) boasts an impressive 4278km of tracks across the country, linking most sizeable towns and cities, although some are on a spur track and only connected to a major railway line by infrequent services.

Most trains tend to be antiquated, shabby and not especially comfortable, and journey times are slower than buses. On the plus side, you'll have more room in a train compartment, and the scenery is likely to be more rewarding.

Trains are classified as *ekspresen* (express), *bârz* (fast) or *pâtnicheski* (slow passenger). Unless you absolutely thrive on train travel or you want to visit a more remote town, use a fast or express train.

Central & Eastern Europe

Best Places to Eat

➡ Restauracja Pod Norenami (p723)

➡ Klassz (p743)

➡ Prince of Orange (p729)

➡ Bistro de l'Arte (p757)

➡ Kanapa (p765)

Best Places to Sleep

➡ Mosaic House (p705)

➡ Mundo Hostel (p723)

➡ Hostel Tresor (p729)

➡ Kapital Inn (p741)

➡ Little Bucharest Old Town Hostel (p751)

Why Go?

Though the countries of Central and Eastern Europe emerged from communism a quarter-century ago, they still retain a feeling of the 'other' Europe – wilder, less-refined, and more remote than their cousins in the west. Medieval capitals like Prague, Kraków and Budapest number among the continent's most beautiful cities and belong on any first-timer's list. More exotic destinations such as Slovakia, Slovenia and Romania boast rustic charm and extreme natural beauty. All are members of the European Union.

The situation changes as you move further east. The former Soviet countries of Belarus, Ukraine, Moldova and Georgia lie well off the beaten track for most travellers and will appeal mainly to adventurers. Eastern Ukraine remains embroiled in conflict, though the western parts of the country, particularly the majestic cities of Kyiv and Lviv, are peaceful. Mountainous Georgia is one of the most beautiful countries anywhere.

Fast Facts

Capitals Prague (Czech Republic), Warsaw (Poland), Bratislava (Slovakia), Budapest (Hungary), Ljubljana (Slovenia), Bucharest (Romania), Chișinău (Moldova), Kyiv (Ukraine), Minsk (Belarus), Tbilisi (Georgia)

Currency Euro € (Slovakia, Slovenia), crown Kč (Czech Republic), złoty zł (Poland), forint ft (Hungary), lei (Romania), Moldovan lei (Moldova), hryvnia UAH (Ukraine), Belarusian rouble BR (Belarus), lari GEL (Georgia)

Languages Czech (Czech Republic), Polish (Poland), Slovak (Slovakia), Hungarian (Hungary), Slovenian (Slovenia), Romanian (Romania), Moldovan and Russian (Moldova) Ukrainian, Russian (Ukraine); Belarusian, Russian (Belarus); Georgian (Georgia)

Visas Required for Belarus for most visitors; other countries visa-free for most visitors for stays up to 90 days

**OFF THE BEATEN TRACK:
MINSK**

Isolated capital with surprisingly
attractive Soviet style.
(p775)

**OFF THE BEATEN TRACK:
HIGH TATRAS**

Alpine adventure in the heart of
Central Europe. (p714)

**WORTH A TRIP:
LVIV**

The old-world charm of Prague or
Krakow without the tourists.
(p769)

Central & Eastern Europe Highlights

1 Prague Ramble around an intact 14th-century town core and cross the continent's most beautiful bridge. (p700)

2 Kraków Admire the biggest medieval public square in

Europe at the heart of Poland's historic capital. (p719)

3 Auschwitz-Birkenau Bow your head in remembrance of the more than a million murdered here in WWII. (p725)

4 Slovenia Climb, raft and cave in this prettiest of possible places in a tiny package. (p727)

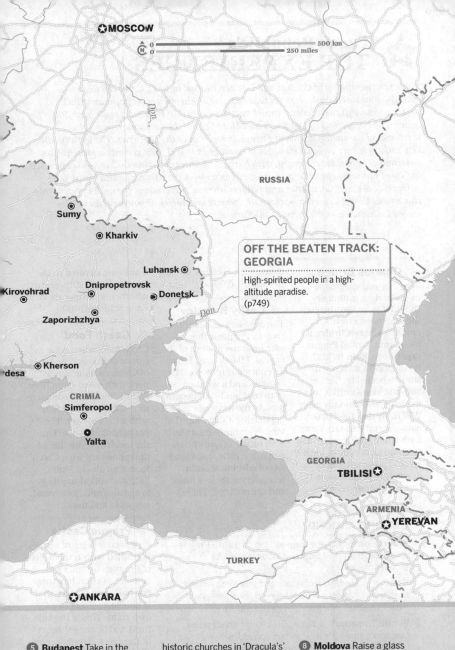

MOSCOW

N
0   500 km
0   250 miles

RUSSIA

Sumy

Kharkiv

Luhansk

Dnipropetrovsk

Kirovohrad   Donetsk

Zaporizhzhya

Don

desa   Kherson

CRIMIA

Simferopol

Yalta

Don

OFF THE BEATEN TRACK: GEORGIA

High-spirited people in a high-altitude paradise. (p749)

GEORGIA

TBILISI

ARMENIA

YEREVAN

TURKEY

ANKARA

⑤ **Budapest** Take in the Danubian metropolis with a bowl of goulash and a soak in a thermal bath. (p738)

⑥ **Transylvania** Enjoy resplendent nature and

historic churches in 'Dracula's' old stomping ground. (p755)

⑦ **Bucharest** Gawk at one of the world's biggest buildings and absorb Romania's energetic capital. (p749)

⑧ **Moldova** Raise a glass of wine and plant your flag of personal conquest in this little-visited land. (p762)

Czech Republic's
TOP EXPERIENCES

Since the opening up of Central and Eastern Europe in 1989, the Czech Republic (p700) – and its capital – has evolved into one of Europe's most popular travel destinations. Prague offers an intact medieval core that transports you back 500 years. The backstreets of Old Town and Malá Strana, in particular, are living textbooks of the steady march of European styles over the centuries. Thankfully, the city's historic core escaped significant damage in WWII, so it records a millennium of continuous urban development, with baroque facades encasing Gothic houses perched on top of Romanesque cellars – all following a street plan from the 11th century.

Outside the capital, castles and palaces abound – including the audacious hilltop chateau at Český Krumlov – which illuminate the stories of powerful dynasties whose influence was felt throughout Europe.

⭐ Charles Bridge

Whether you visit alone in the early morning or shoulder your way through the afternoon crowds, crossing Charles Bridge is the quintessential Prague experience. Built in 1357, its 16 elegant arches withstood wheeled traffic for 500-odd years until it was made pedestrian-only after WWII. By day, the famous baroque statues stare down with stony indifference on a fascinating parade of buskers and postcard sellers; at dawn, they regain something of the mystery and magic their creators sought to capture. (p704)

⭐ Český Krumlov

The only serious beauty rival to Prague is this former royal town south of the capital. Like Prague, it has an enormous hilltop castle complex and a winding river to confound your geography. As the town has gained popularity, it's developed a kind of summer-resort feel, with plenty of quirky bars and cafes, little shops, and lots of adventure outfitters offering cycling tours and rafting trips. There's a museum devoted to the works of early 20th-century painter and former resident Egon Schiele. (p709)

⭐ Czech Food

Czech food, when done well, can be delicious. The heart of Czech cooking is roast pork with bread dumplings, and the meal isn't complete unless it's washed down with a mug of beer. The pork should fall apart at the touch of a fork. Bread dumplings are what Czech food is all about. Fluffy, light and soft, dumplings are made from flour, yeast, egg yolks and milk.

⭐ Prague Castle

A thousand years of history is cradled within the walls of Prague's hilltop castle, a complex of churches, towers, halls and palaces that is almost a village in its own right. This is the cultural and historical heart of the Czech Republic, comprising not only collections of physical treasures, such as the golden reliquaries of St Vitus Treasury and the Bohemian crown jewels, but also the sites of great

GETTING AROUND

Train Good for moving between big cities like Prague and Brno, but often slow and inconvenient for smaller places.

Bus Buses are faster, cheaper and more convenient than trains. Modern Student Agency coaches run from Prague to cities around the country.

Public Transport All large cities have decent public transport, mainly buses and (in some cases) trolleybuses. Prague is the only city with a metro.

Car The easiest way to move between destinations, but highways are often two-laned and clogged. The country's main four-lane motorway, the D1, links Prague and Brno.

historic events such as the murder of St Wenceslas and the Second Defenestration of Prague. (p700)

⭐ Classical Music

The country that nurtured Smetana, Dvořák and Janáček, and saw performances by Wolfgang Amadeus Mozart, has a place in musical history alongside that of Austria and Germany. The Prague Spring Music Festival (www.festival.cz) is the main event on the cultural calendar, though locales around the country hold their own festivals. Every major town will have a classical music hall, and more often than not, leading theaters give themselves over to opera and dance.

⭐ Old Town Square, Prague

Despite swarms of tourists, crowded pavement cafes and over-the-top commercialism, it's impossible not to enjoy the spectacle of Prague's premier public space: tour leaders, umbrellas aloft like battle standards, thrusting through the crowds gathered to watch the town hall's amazing Astronomical Clock; students dressed as frogs and chickens handing out flyers for a drama production; middle-aged couples in matching rain jackets, frowning at pink-haired, leather-clad punks with too many piercings. Verily, all of human life is here. (p700)

⭐ St Vitus Cathedral

Occupying the site of a 10th-century Romanesque rotunda built by the Good King Wenceslas of Christmas carol fame, St Vitus is the heart of Czech Catholicism, its spires and bell tower the focus of the city skyline. Its soaring Gothic nave is lit by gorgeous stained glass, and is home to the cultural jewels of St Wenceslas Chapel and the magnificent silver tomb of St John of Nepomuk. (p700)

⭐ Czech Beer

No matter how many times you tell yourself, 'today is an alcohol-free day', Czech beer *(pivo)* will be your undoing. Light, clear, refreshing and cheaper than water, Czech beer is recognised as one of the world's best – the Czechs claim it's so pure it's impossible to get a hangover from drinking it. Brewing traditions go back 1000 years, and the beer has only gotten better since then.

⭐ The Bone Church

When the Schwarzenbergs purchased Sedlec monastery in 1870 they allowed a local woodcarver to get creative with the bones piled in the crypt (the remains of around 40,000 people), resulting in the remarkable 'bone church' of Sedlec Ossuary. Garlands of skulls hang from the vaulted ceiling, around a chandelier containing at least one of each bone in the human body. (p708)

if the Czech Republic were 100 people

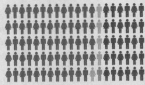

64 would be Czech
5 would be Moravian
1 would be Slovak
30 would be other

belief systems
(% of population)

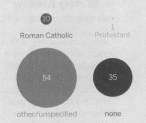

10 Roman Catholic
1 Protestant
54 other/unspecified
35 none

population per sq km

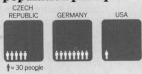

CZECH REPUBLIC GERMANY USA

⬤ = 30 people

When to Go

Prague

°C/°F Temp
30/86 —
20/68 —
10/50 —
0/32 —
-10/14 —
-20/-4 —

Rainfall inches/mm
— 10/250
— 8/200
— 6/150
— 4/100
— 2/50
— 0

J F M A M J J A S O N D

Poland's
TOP EXPERIENCES

Poland (p714) has spent centuries at the pointy end of history, grappling with war and invasion. Nothing, however, has succeeded in suppressing Poles' strong sense of nationhood and cultural identity. As a result, centres such as Warsaw and Kraków exude a sophisticated energy that's a heady mix of old and new.

Away from the cities, Poland is a diverse land, from its northern shore on the Baltic to a row of majestic mountains along the southern border. Here the architecture is decidedly folksy – log cabins and timbered houses. If the word 'skansen', referring to an open-air museum of folk architecture, isn't a regular part of your vocabulary yet, it will be after your trip to Poland. These great gardens make for a wonderful ramble and are testament to centuries of peasant life in Poland. You'll find these open-air folk museums all around the country.

⭐ Stately Kraków

A unique atmosphere drifts through the attractive streets and squares of this former royal capital, with its heady blend of history and harmonious architecture. From the vast Rynek Główny, Europe's largest medieval market square, to the magnificent Wawel Royal Castle on a hill above the Old Town, every part of the city is fascinating. Add to that the former Jewish district of Kazimierz and its scintillating nightlife, and it's easy to see why Kraków is an unmissable destination. (p719)

⭐ Warsaw's Museums & Palaces

Poland's capital (p714) has an extravagantly dramatic history, and its best museums reflect that complex past. The city's darkest hour in the revolt against German Nazi rule is powerfully retold at the Warsaw Rising Museum; while Poland's long Jewish presence is related with energy at the Museum of the History of Polish Jews. Beautiful music can be heard at the Chopin Museum. For stately charm, head to Wilanów Palace.

⭐ Malbork Castle

Medieval monster mother ship of the Teutonic order, Gothic blockbuster Malbork Castle is a mountain of bricks held together by a lake of mortar. It was home to the all-powerful order's grand master and later to visiting Polish monarchs. They have all now left the stage of history, but not even the shells of WWII could dismantle this baby. (p718)

⭐ Auschwitz-Birkenau

The Auschwitz-Birkenau Memorial & Museum, established by the German military occupiers in 1941, is a grim reminder of a part of history's greatest genocide, the killing of more than a million people here in the pursuit of Nazi ideology. Now it's a highly moving museum and memorial to the victims. (p725)

GETTING AROUND

Air The national carrier LOT operates a comprehensive network of domestic routes.

Train The rail network is extensive, easy to use and reasonably priced. It's likely to be your main means of transport for covering long distances.

Bus The bus network covers nearly every town and village accessible by road. Buses are often more convenient than trains over short distances.

Public Transport Every large and medium-sized city will have a comprehensive bus network, while some cities will also have tram and trolleybus systems. Warsaw is the only city with a metro.

Car Driving for long distances in Poland is no fun. Roads are crowded, and road-building and repair has led to many detours and delays.

★ Nightlife in Kazimierz

Once a lively blend of both Jewish and Christian cultures, the western half of Kraków's Kazimierz has in recent years become one of the city's nightlife hubs. Hidden among its narrow streets and distressed facades are numerous small bars, ranging from grungy to glamorous. The centre of all this activity is Plac Nowy, a small, atmospheric square dominated by a circular central building that was once the quarter's meat market.

★ Sampling Vodka

For most Poles, the day-to-day tipple of choice is beer. But when it comes time to celebrate, someone's bound to break out the vodka. And once it's on the table, no one leaves until the bottle is finished. Poles make some of the world's best and are not afraid to experiment. Proof: *Żubrówka* ('bison vodka') is flavoured with grass from the Białowieża Forest on which bison feed.

★ Eating Pierogi

Pierogi (or 'Polish raviolis') are square- or crescent-shaped dumplings made from dough and stuffed with anything from cottage cheese, potato and onion to minced meat, sauerkraut and fruit. They are usually boiled and served doused in melted butter. *Pierogi* are highly versatile and can be eaten as a snack or as a main course for lunch or dinner. They can also be a vegetarian's best friend. The ubiquitous *pierogi ruskie* (Russian-style) are meatless, stuffed with cottage cheese, potato and onion.

★ Warsaw's Old Town

Though it's a relatively recent reconstruction, having been built from war rubble after WWII, Warsaw's Old Town *(Stare Miasto)* looks as though it's been there for centuries. It's the first (and sometimes only) part of the city tourists hit, and with good reason: this small quarter holds numerous historic attractions, including the Royal Castle. It's also fun just to hang around here; the attractive Old Town Square is always buzzing. (p714)

★ Wieliczka Salt Mine

The Unesco-heritage Wieliczka Salt Mine, near Kraków, is an inspiring, easy day trip and the most amazing salt mine you'll ever see. The cavernous interior is filled with lovingly crafted salt-hewn formations, including enormous chapels, with altarpieces and figures – and there are even underground lakes. The showpiece is the ornamented Chapel of St Kinga, which is actually a fair-sized church. Every single element here, from chandeliers to altarpieces, is made of salt. (p722)

if Poland were 100 people

15 would be aged 0-14
12 would be aged 15-24
44 would be aged 25-54
15 would be aged 55-64
14 would be aged 65+

belief systems
(% of population)

90 Roman Catholic
1 Eastern Orthodox
1 Protestant
8 other

population per sq km

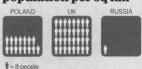

POLAND   UK   RUSSIA

♦ ≈ 8 people

When to Go

Warsaw

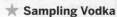

°C/°F Temp
30/86
20/68
10/50
0/32
-10/14
-20/-4

Rainfall inches/mm
10/250
8/200
6/150
4/100
2/50
0

J F M A M J J A S O N D

Slovenia's
TOP EXPERIENCES

It's a pint-sized place with just over 2 million people. But 'good things come in small packages' and never was that old chestnut more appropriate than in describing Slovenia (p727). The capital, Ljubljana, is a culturally rich city that values quality of life and sustainability over unfettered growth. This sensibility extends to rural and less-developed parts of the country, and to treasures like Lake Bled in the north and the coastal resort of Piran to the south.

Climbing Mt Triglav

They say you're not really a Slovene until you climb Mt Triglav and get 'spanked' at the summit. And it's all but stamped in locals' passports once they've made the trek up the country's tallest mountain. The good news for the rest of us is that Triglav is a challenging but accessible peak that just about anyone in decent shape can 'conquer' with an experienced guide. There are several popular approaches, but whichever path you choose, the reward is the same: sheer exhilaration. (p733)

Ljubljana

Slovenia's capital city strikes that perfect yet elusive balance between size and quality of life. It's big enough to offer discoveries yet small enough to walk – or better yet, cycle – around at a leisurely pace. And no place in Slovenia waltzes through architecture so adroitly as the capital named 'beloved', from its ancient hilltop castle and splendid art nouveau banks to local urban planner Jože Plečnik's wondrously decorative pillars, obelisks and orbs found everywhere. (p727)

Piran

Venice in Slovenia? That busy merchant empire left its mark up and down the Adriatic coast, and Slovenia was lucky to end up with one of the best-preserved medieval Venetian ports anywhere. Piran attracts tourist numbers on a massive scale in season, but the beautiful setting means it's never less than a constant delight. Enjoy fresh fish on the harbour, then wander the narrow streets and end up for drinks and people-watching in a glorious central square. (p735)

River Adventures

Rarely does a river beckon to be rafted as convincingly as the Soča. Maybe it's that piercing sky-blue-bordering-on-green – or is it turquoise? – colour of the water, or the river's refreshing froth and foam as it tumbles down the mountains. Even if you're not the rafting type, you'll soon find yourself strapping on a wetsuit for that exhilarating ride of the summer. Outfitters in Bled specialise in guided rafting trips.

Slovenian Food

Slovenia is in the midst of a slow-food, organic-food, local-food revolution that prizes original recipes and

---

GETTING AROUND

Train Clean, modern and quick, trains are ideal for travelling across the country and between cities and large towns.

Bus Less comfortable than trains, buses are useful for reaching places along the Adriatic coast that are not connected by rail.

Public Transport All cities and towns of any size have decent, affordable public transportation. The capital Ljubljana is small enough to walk, but buses are handy if saving time is important.

Car Four-lane highways link major cities and the country is small enough that you can cross the country in a few hours.

Bike Ljubljana is mostly flat and cycling is a popular and scenic way of getting around. There's a city bike-share system or ask the Ljubljana Tourist Information Centre about rentals.

fresh, quality ingredients. If Slovenian cooking has a signature side, it would have to be stick-to-your-ribs barley or buckwheat groats. Another must-try is *žlikrofi*, pasta stuffed with potatoes, chives and a local form of bacon. Pumpkin-seed oil is Slovenia's most unique condiment. It can be green or red nut, roasted or cold-pressed, but always nutty.

⭐ Lake Bled

With its sky-blue lake, picture-postcard church on a tiny island, medieval castle clinging to a rocky cliff and some of the country's highest peaks as backdrops, Bled seems to have been designed by the very god of tourism. But Slovenia's biggest draw is more than just a pretty face. There's a raucous adventure scene too, with diving, cycling, rafting and canyoning, among other active pursuits, as well as excellent camping grounds, hostels and hotels. (p732)

⭐ Postojna Cave

Postojna Cave is Slovenia's biggest subterranean attraction. The entrance might not look like much, but when you get whisked 4km underground on a train and only then start exploring, you start to get a sense of the scale. The caverns are a seemingly endless parade of crystal fancies – from frilly chandeliers and dripping spaghetti-like stalactites, to paper-thin sheets and stupendous stalagmites, all laid down over the centuries by the simple dripping of mineral-rich water. (p736)

⭐ Rustic-Glam Accommodation

Slovenia is well known as an outdoor destination and is at the forefront of new ways to stay in and experience nature close-up. One trend we're embracing is 'glamping' – classic camping in a tent or cabin but with an emphasis on glamour (think safari tents with private hot-tubs). An inventive and fun way to escape the everyday. The best place is Camping Bled (p733), on the shores of Lake Bled.

⭐ Folklore Festivals

Expect booze, colourful costumes and accordion music as Slovenes let their hair down at centuries-old festivals. Kurentovanje is a rite-of-spring party celebrated in the days leading up to Shrove Tuesday and the start of Lent. Jurjevanje in the town of Črnomelj in June celebrates an ancient Slavic deity called Green George and is Slovenia's oldest international folklore festival. The zany Cows' Ball not far from Bled in September sees bovines trip the light fantastic.

if Slovenia were 100 people

83 would be Slovenes
2 would be Serbs
2 would be Croats
1 would be Bosniaks
12 would be other

belief systems

(% of population)

58 Catholic
3 Muslim
2 Orthodox Christian
1 Protestant
36 other/none

population per sq km

SLOVENIA   ITALY   UK

🚶 ≈ 50 people

When to Go

Ljubljana

°C/°F Temp

40/104 —

20/68 —

0/32 —

-20/-4 —

J F M A M J J A S O N D

Rainfall inches/mm
— 4.9/125
— 3.9/100
— 2.9/75
— 2/50
— 1/25
— 0

Hungary's
TOP EXPERIENCES

Hungary (p738) has always marched to a different drummer – speaking a language, preparing dishes and drinking wines like no others.

The allure of Budapest, once an imperial city, is obvious at first sight and it also boasts the hottest nightlife in the region. Other cities, such as Eger, the wine capital of the north, have much to offer travellers. Lake Balaton can be an attractive hot-weather respite in a landlocked country.

★ Budapest's Royal Palace

Bombed and rebuilt at least half a dozen times since King Béla IV established a royal residence here in the mid-13th century, the Royal Palace has been home to kings and queens, occupiers like the Turks in the 16th and 17th centuries, and non-domiciled rulers like the Habsburg royalty. Today the Royal Palace contains two important museums, the national library and an abundance of statues and monuments. It is the focal point of Buda's Castle Hill and the city's most visited sight. (p738)

★ Budapest's Parliament

Budapest's historic Parliament is the centrepiece along the Danube on the Pest side. Stretching for some 268m along the river and counting a superlative number of rooms (690), courtyards (10) and gates (27), it is Hungary's largest building. Parliament is the seat of the unicameral National Assembly, but parts of it, including the awesome Domed Hall, which contains the iconic Crown of St Stephen, can be visited by guided tour. (p740)

★ The Great Synagogue, Budapest

The largest Jewish temple in Europe, the Moorish-style Great Synagogue, is one of Budapest's most eye-catching buildings. Built in 1859 for 3000 conservative faithful, the copper-domed structure is next to the Hungarian Jewish Museum and the haunting Holocaust Memorial Room. In the courtyard stands the Holocaust Memorial, a 'tree of life' designed by sculptor Imre Varga whose leaves bear the family names of many of the victims. (p739)

★ Thermal Baths

With more than 300 thermal hot springs in public use across Hungary, it's not hard to find a place to take the waters. Some of the most atmospheric thermal baths, like the Király (p739) in Budapest, date back to the 16th century. The popular Széchenyi Baths (p739) in the capital are a nice compromise between historic atmosphere and modern sanitation.

GETTING AROUND

Train The Hungarian National Railway, MÁV, operates clean, punctual and comfortable train services. Budapest is the main rail hub.

Bus Better than trains for travelling in rural areas and between towns and villages. Hungary's Volánbusz network covers the country.

Public Transport All cities have efficient bus (and, in some cases, trolleybus) services. Budapest is the only city with a metro.

Car Roads in Hungary are generally good – in some cases excellent. High-speed motorways cross the country in all directions.

Ferry During the warm months, Budapest-based Mahart PassNave runs excursion boats on the Danube from Budapest to towns north of the capital. There's also high-speed water transport to Vienna and Bratislava.

Lake Balaton

Hungary's 'sea' (and Continental Europe's largest lake) is where the populace comes to sun and swim in summertime. The quieter northern side of Lake Balaton mixes sizzling beaches and oodles of fun on the water with historic waterside towns like Keszthely and Balatonfüred. Tihany, a 30m-high peninsula jutting 4km into the lake, is home to a stunning abbey church. (p745)

★ **Eger**

Everyone loves Eger, and it's immediately apparent why. Beautifully preserved baroque architecture gives the town a relaxed, almost Mediterranean feel; it is flanked by two of the Northern Uplands' most beautiful ranges of hills (Bükk and Mátra), and it is the home of some of Hungary's best wines, including the celebrated Bull's Blood. Sample this at cellars in the evocatively named Valley of the Beautiful Women, within walking distance of the city. (p745)

★ **The Folkloric Northeast**

Preserved through generations, Hungary's folk-art traditions are particularly prominent in the northeast of the country, not far from Eger. You'll find exquisitely detailed embroidery, pottery, hand-painted or carved wood, dyed Easter eggs and graphic woven cloth across the region. Differences in colours and styles easily identify the art's originating area. The culture of the tiny villages of this region, including

those brightly dyed Easter eggs, has much in common with Hungary's neighbours to the east.

★ **Great Food**

Hungary can arguably boast having Central and Eastern Europe's finest cuisine. It's very meaty, that's true, but it's also big on flavour. Try one of the staples like paprika-laced *pörkölt* (a stew not unlike what we call goulash) or *gulyá* (or *gulyásleves*), a thick beef soup cooked with onions and potatoes. And don't overlook specialties such as *libamaj* (goose liver prepared in an infinite number of ways) and *halászlé*, a rich fish soup.

★ **Varied Scenery**

Hungary cannot claim any point higher than 1000m, and it's nowhere near the sea, yet the country has an amazingly varied topography. There's the low-lying salty grasslands of the Great Plain, a half-dozen ranges of hills to the north and northeast, and two major (and very scenic) rivers: the Danube and the Tisza. Hungary also has well over 1000 lakes, of which the largest and most famous is Lake Balaton.

if Hungary were 100 people

92 would be Hungarian
2 would be Roma
6 would be other

belief systems
(% of population)

52 — Roman Catholic
16 — Calvinist
3 — Lutheran
3 — Greek Catholic
12 — other
14 — unaffiliated

population per sq km

HUNGARY   GERMANY   USA

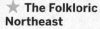 ≈ 11 people

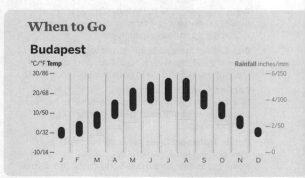

When to Go

Budapest

°C/°F **Temp**

30/86 —
20/68 —
10/50 —
0/32 —
-10/14 —

Rainfall inches/mm

— 6/150
— 4/100
— 2/50
— 0

J F M A M J J A S O N D

Romania's
TOP EXPERIENCES

Beautiful and beguiling, the rural landscape of Romania (p749) remains relatively untouched by the country's urban evolution. It's a land of aesthetically stirring hand-ploughed fields, sheep-instigated traffic jams and lots of homemade plum brandy.

The vibrant capital, Bucharest, is all energy, while Transylvania's Saxon towns, animated by plenty of 'Dracula' tat, feel untouched by time. Unesco-listed painted monasteries dot the country's northeastern region.

⭐ Bucharest's Palace of Parliament

Depending on your point of view, this modern colossus is either a mind-blowing testament to the waste and folly of dictatorship or an awe-inspiring showcase of Romanian materials and craftsmanship, albeit applied to sinister ends. Whatever emotions the Palace of Parliament – or 'House of the People', as it's often called – happens to elicit, the sheer scale of Romania's entry into the 'World's Largest Buildings' competition must be seen to be believed. (p749)

⭐ The Perils of Plum Brandy

Big meals traditionally begin with a shot of Romanian moonshine, *țuică*, but treat this innocent-looking liquid with a measure of respect. Home-brewed batches can weigh in at as much as 60% alcohol, and the wallop can be fast and furious. Classic *țuică* is usually distilled from plums – purists say only plums – but we've seen other fruits, like apricots and pears, employed to this nefarious end. In smaller villages, you'll likely be offered some of grandpa's best. *Noroc!*

⭐ Monasteries

In the Carpathian foothills, the Unesco-listed painted monasteries in northeastern Moldavian province proudly show off Romania's unique, Latin-flavoured Orthodox tradition. The churches are at one with their natural surroundings, and the dizzying kaleidoscope of colours and intricate details in the frescoes bring to life everything from biblical stories to the 15th-century siege of Constantinople. The monasteries are the genius of Moldavian Prince Stefan the Great (Ștefan cel Mare), who was later canonised for his work. (p760)

⭐ Cuisine

Romania's de facto, delicious national dish of stuffed cabbage (or sometimes grape) leaves, *sarmale cu mămăligă*, is traditionally served at weddings, Christmas dinners and big celebrations. It's also a staple on restaurant menus around the country. The leaves are typically filled with spiced pork, but occasionally veal or lamb is mixed in. *Mămăligă*, a thick porridge made from yellow corn (maize) flour, is a welcome sidekick to soak up the savoury juices. Our favourite bit is the dollop of

---

GETTING AROUND

Air Flying between cities is a feasible option if time is a concern. The Romanian national carrier Tarom operates a comprehensive network of domestic routes.

Train Trains are slow but reliable. The extensive network covers much of the country, including main tourist sights and key destinations.

Bus A mix of buses and minibuses form the backbone of the Romanian national transport system, but the system is confusing to navigate.

Car Roads are generally crowded and in poor condition. There are only a few short stretches of four-lane motorway, meaning most travel is along clogged two-lane roads.

Public Transport Cities generally have good public transport systems, comprised of buses, trams and trolleybuses. Bucharest is the only city with a metro.

sour cream usually dropped on top. *Pofta buna!*

⭐ Trekking in the Carpathians

Romania is looped by the Carpathian mountains that slice through the middle of the country around Braşov. There are dense primeval forests that leap from the pages of a Brothers Grimm story, with bears, wolves, lynx and boar, rugged mountain plateaus, well-marked trails and a network of cabins en route to keep you warm. Trekking is the best way to absorb this vibrant landscape of forests and rolling pastureland.

⭐ Medieval Towns

Transylvania is filled with medieval towns that run the gamut from the historic cores of large cities like Braşov to more-isolated, tiny hamlets. One of our favourites is timeless Sighişoara (p758), where you can climb the cobblestones to the town's ancient citadel and marvel at how little has changed in more than five centuries. Nestled in buttery-soft hills, nearby Viscri is as rustic as it gets; powder-blue shuttered houses with old ladies knitting socks on doorsteps while livestock wanders the streets.

⭐ Folk Traditions

Folk traditions are alive and kicking, especially in Romania's rural areas. There's tremendous variety across regions. The open-air folk museums are a treat, and every town or city has some type of ethnographic exhibition. Bucharest has two great museums dedicated to folk arts: the National Village Museum (p750) and the Museum of the Romanian Peasant (p750).

⭐ Bucharest Nightlife

Romanians love to party. University towns get manic on weekends and in summer the party moves to the coast – but the undisputed centre of the action is the capital, Bucharest. The tiny lanes of the city's scruffy Old Town have been converted into an unbroken string of bars, pubs and clubs. The latter can be dressy affairs, so pack some suitable clubbing garb. (p751)

⭐ Bran Castle

Perched on a bluff in Transylvania, Bran Castle overlooks a desolate mountain pass swirling with mist and dense forest. Its spectral exterior is like a composite of every horror film you've ever seen, but don't expect to be scared. Inside, Bran is anything but spooky, with its white walls and geranium-filled courtyard. Legend has it Vlad the Impaler (the inspiration for Count Dracula) was briefly imprisoned here, and you can follow his footsteps through an 'Escheresque' maze of hidden passages. (p758)

if Romania were 100 people

83 would be Romanian
6 would be Hungarian
3 would be Roma
8 would be other

belief systems
(% of population)

86 Eastern Orthodox

8 Protestant

5 Roman Catholic

1 other

population per sq km

ROMANIA   BULGARIA   UKRAINE

👤 ≈ 15 people

When to Go

Bucharest

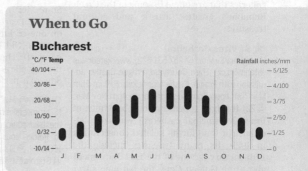

°C/°F Temp
40/104 —
30/86 —
20/68 —
10/50 —
0/32 —
-10/14 —

Rainfall inches/mm
— 5/125
— 4/100
— 3/75
— 2/50
— 1/25
— 0

J F M A M J J A S O N D

CZECH REPUBLIC

Prague

POP 1.22 MILLION

The Velvet Revolution that freed the Czechs from communism bequeathed to Europe a gem of a city to stand beside stalwarts such as Rome, Amsterdam and London. Not surprisingly, visitors from around the world have come in droves, and on a hot summer's day it can feel like you're sharing Charles Bridge with half of humanity. But even the crowds can't take away from the spectacle of a 14th-century stone bridge, a hilltop castle and a lovely, lazy river.

◉ Sights

◉ Prague Castle & Hradčany

Mighty Prague Castle is perched on a hilltop high above the Vltava River, with the attractive and peaceful residential area of Hradčany stretching westward to the Loreta and Strahov Monastery.

★ Prague Castle — CASTLE

(Pražský hrad; ☑ 224 372 423; www.hrad.cz; Hradčanské náměstí 1; grounds free, sights adult/concession long tour 350/175Kc, short tour 250/125Kc; ☉ grounds 5am-midnight Apr-Oct, 6am-11pm Nov-Mar, gardens 10am-6pm Apr & Oct, to 7pm May & Sep, to 9pm Jun-Aug, closed Nov-Mar, historic buildings 9am-5pm Apr-Oct, to 4pm Nov-Mar; Ⓜ Malostranská, 🚊 22) Prague Castle – Pražský hrad, or just *hrad* to Czechs – is Prague's most popular attraction. Looming above the Vltava's left bank, its serried ranks of spires, towers and palaces dominate the city centre like a fairy-tale fortress. Within its walls lies a varied and fascinating collection of historic buildings, museums and galleries that are home to some of the Czech Republic's greatest artistic and cultural treasures.

★ St Vitus Cathedral — CHURCH

(Katedrála Sv Víta; ☑ 257 531 622; www.katedralasvatehovita.cz; Third Courtyard, Prague Castle; admission with Prague Castle tour ticket; ☉ 9am-5pm Mon-Sat, noon-5pm Sun Apr-Oct, to 4pm Nov-Mar; 🚊 22) It might appear ancient, but much of Prague's principal cathedral was completed just in time for its belated consecration in 1929. Its many treasures include the 14th-century mosaic of the Last Judgement above the Golden Gate, the baroque silver tomb of St John of Nepomuck, the ornate Chapel of St Wenceslas, and art nouveau stained glass by Alfons Mucha.

Old Royal Palace — PALACE

(Starý královský palác; admission with Prague Castle tour ticket; ☉ 9am-5pm Apr-Oct, to 4pm Nov-Mar; 🚊 22) The Old Royal Palace is one of the oldest parts of Prague Castle, dating from 1135. It was originally used only by Czech princesses, but from the 13th to the 16th centuries it was the king's own palace. At its heart is the grand Vladislav Hall and the Bohemian Chancellery, scene of the famous Defenestration of Prague in 1618.

Lobkowicz Palace — MUSEUM

(Lobkovický palác; ☑ 233 312 925; www.lobkowicz.cz; Jiřská 3; adult/concession/family 275/200/690Kč; ☉ 10am-6pm; 🚊 22) This 16th-century palace houses a private museum which includes priceless paintings, furniture and musical memorabilia. You tour with an audio guide dictated by owner William Lobkowicz and his family – this personal connection really brings the displays to life, and makes the palace one of the castle's most interesting attractions.

Strahov Library — HISTORIC BUILDING

(Strahovská knihovna; ☑ 233 107 718; www.strahovskyklaster.cz; Strahovské nádvoří 1; adult/concession 100/50Kč; ☉ 9am-noon & 1-5pm; 🚊 22) Strahov Library is the largest monastic library in the country, with two magnificent baroque halls dating from the 17th and 18th centuries. You can peek through the doors but, sadly, you can't go into the halls themselves – it was found that fluctuations in humidity caused by visitors' breath was endangering the frescoes.

◉ Staré Město

Staré Město – meaning 'Old Town' – is the historic heart of medieval Prague, centred on one of Europe's most spectacular town squares (Old Town Square, or Staroměstské náměstí). The maze of cobbled streets and narrow alleys leading away from Old Town Square is perfect for exploring.

Old Town Hall — HISTORIC BUILDING

(Staroměstská radnice; ☑ 236 002 629; www.staromestskaradnicepraha.cz; Staroměstské náměstí 1; guided tour adult/child 100/50Kč, incl tower 160Kč; ☉ 11am-6pm Mon, 9am-6pm Tue-Sun; Ⓜ Staroměstská) Prague's Old Town Hall,

Prague Castle

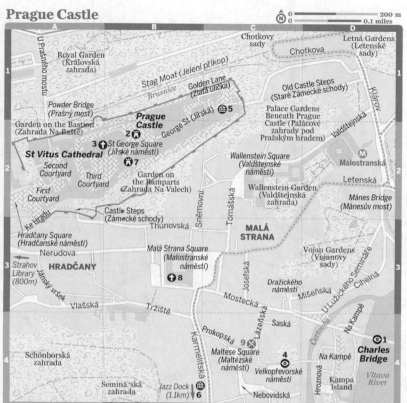

founded in 1338, is a hotchpotch of medieval buildings acquired piecemeal over the centuries, presided over by a tall Gothic tower with a splendid Astronomical Clock. As well as housing the Old Town's main tourist information office, the town hall has several historic attractions, and hosts art exhibitions on the ground floor and the 2nd floor.

★ **Astronomical Clock**   HISTORIC SITE
(Staroměstské náměstí; ⊙chimes on the hour 9am-9pm; Ⓜ Staroměstská) Every hour, on the hour, crowds gather beneath the Old Town Hall Tower to watch the Astronomical Clock in action. Despite a slightly underwhelming performance that takes only 45 seconds, the clock is one of Europe's best-known tourist attractions, and a must for visitors to Prague. After all, it's historic, photogenic and – if you take time to study it – rich in intriguing symbolism.

Prague Castle

Church of Our Lady Before Týn   CHURCH
(Kostel Panny Marie před Týnem; ☏ 222 318 186; www.tyn.cz; Staroměstské náměstí; suggested donation 25Kč; ⊙10am-1pm & 3-5pm Tue-Sat, 10.30am-noon Sun Mar-Oct, shorter hours Nov-Feb; Ⓜ Staroměstská) Its distinctive twin Gothic

Central Prague

CENTRAL & EASTERN EUROPE PRAGUE

Mánes Bridge
(Mánesův
most)

JOSEFOV

U starého
hřbitova
6

Červená

Vězeňská

Kozí

9

V Kolkovně

Masná

Jan Palach Square
(Náměstí
Jana Palacha)

Široká

Maiselova

Pařížská

Krásnohorské

Dušní

Týnská ulička

Týnská

Veleslavínova

M Staroměstská

Žatecká

Valentinská

Kaprova

U radnice

Dlouhá

Astronomical
Clock

Týn Courtyard
(Týnský dvůr)

2 ⊕

Štupartská

Celetná

Platnéřská

Mariánské
náměstí

Linhartská

Prague City
Tourism – Old ⓘ
Town Hall

5 ⊜ ◎1

STARÉ MĚSTO

Křižovnické
náměstí

Karlova

Little Square
(Malé náměstí)

Železná

Former Fruit
Market
(Ovocný trh)

Vltava River

Alšovo nábřeží

17.listopadu

Křižovnická

Karel Zeman
Museum (350m);
Lokál Inn (450m);
St Nicholas
Church (650m);
U Modré Kachničky
(800m)

Anenská

Lilíová

Řetězová

Husova

Jilská

Melantrichova

Michalská

Havelská

Open-Air
Market

Rytířská

Havlíška

Provaznická

13 ☕

Zlatá

V Kotcích

Můstek M

Anenské
náměstí

Náprstkova

Bethlehem Square
(Betlémské
náměstí)

Uhelný
trh

28. října

Jungmannovo
náměstí

Skořepka

Perlová

Betlémská

Karolíny Světlé

Divadelní

Konviktská

Na Perštýně

Martinská

V Kotcích

M Můstek

Smetanovo nábřeží

Bartolomějská

Národní
Třída

Franciscan Garden
(Františkánská
zahrada)

Národní třída

11 🏛

M Třída

Legion
Bridge
(Legií
most)

P
15

Voršilská

Mikulandská

Purkyňova

Jungmannova

Palackého

Ostrovní

Vladislavova

Masarykovo nábřeží

Nastruze

Pštrossova

Křemencova

V Jirchářích

Spálená

Vodičkova

Slav Island
(Slovanský
ostrov)

8 ☕

Vyšehrad
Citadel (2.1km)

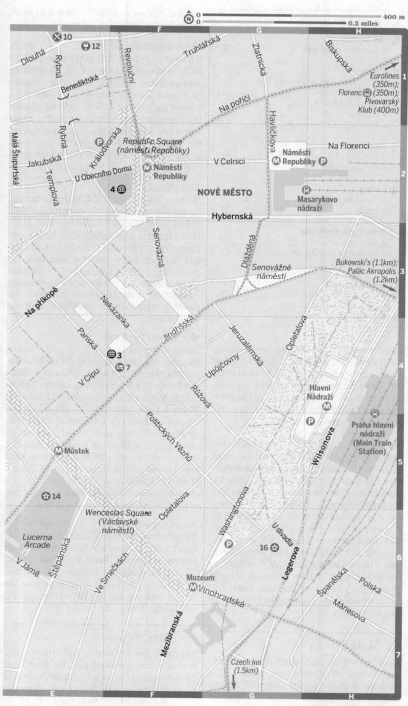

Ⓝ 0 _____ 400 m
0 _____ 0.2 miles

Dlouhá
Rybná
❌ 10
🍴 12
Benediktská
Revoluční
Truhlářská
Zlatnická
Biskupská
Eurolines (350m);
Florenc 🚇 (350m);
Pivovarský Klub (400m)
Na poříčí
Havlíčkova
Malá Štupartská
Rybná
Jakubská
Templová
🅿
Kralodvorská
Republic Square
(náměstí Republiky)
V Celnici
Na Florenci
Náměstí Republiky
🚇
🅿
U Obecního Domu
Ⓝ Náměstí Republiky
4 🏛
NOVÉ MĚSTO
Masarykovo nádraží 🚉
Hybernská
Senovážná
Dlážděná
Senovážné náměstí
Bukowski's (1.1km);
Palác Akropolis (1.2km)
Na příkopě
Nekázanka
Panská
Jindřišská
Jeruzalémská
Opletalova
🏛 3
💺 7
V Cípu
Upujčovny
Růžová
Hlavní Nádraží
🚇
🅿
Praha hlavní nádraží (Main Train Station) 🚉
Ⓜ Můstek
Politických Vězňů
Wilsonova
⭐ 14
Opletalova
Wenceslas Square
(Václavské náměstí)
Washingtonova
U divadla
Lucerna Arcade
V Jámě
Štěpánská
🅿
16 ⭐
Legerova
Ve Smečkách
Muzeum
Ⓜ Vinohradská
Španělská
Polská
Mánesova
Mezibranská
Czech Inn (1.5km)

Central Prague

spires make Týn Church an unmistakable Old Town landmark. Like something out of a 15th-century fairy tale, they loom over the Old Town Square, decorated with a golden image of the Virgin Mary made in the 1620s from the melted down Hussite chalice that previously adorned the church.

Municipal House HISTORIC BUILDING
(Obecní dům; ☏ 222 002 101; www.obecnidum. cz; náměstí Republiky 5; guided tour adult/concession/child under 10yr 290/240Kč/free; ◷ public areas 7.30am-11pm, information centre 10am-8pm; Ⓜ Náměstí Republiky) Prague's most exuberant and sensual art nouveau building was a labour of love, every detail of its design and decoration carefully considered, every painting and sculpture loaded with symbolism. The restaurant and cafe flanking the entrance are like walk-in museums of early-20th-century design; upstairs are half a dozen sumptuously decorated halls that you can visit by guided tour.

◎ Malá Strana

Malá Strana (the 'Little Quarter') is a charming district of Renaissance palaces and gardens, with an idyllic riverside setting. Prague's scenic centrepiece, the 650-year-old Charles Bridge, links Malá Strana to Staré Město on the far side of the river.

★ Charles Bridge BRIDGE
(Karlův most; ◷ 24hr; 🚋 17, 18 to Karlovy lázně, 12, 20, 22 to Malostranské náměstí) FREE Strolling across Charles Bridge is everybody's favourite Prague activity. However, by 9am it's a 500m-long fairground, with an army of tourists squeezing through a gauntlet of hawkers and buskers beneath the impassive gaze of the baroque statues that line the parapets. If you want to experience the bridge at its most atmospheric try to visit at dawn.

St Nicholas Church CHURCH
(Kostel sv Mikuláše; ☏ 257 534 215; www.stnicholas. cz; Malostranské náměstí 38; adult/child 70/50Kč; ◷ 9am-5pm Mar-Oct, to 4pm Nov-Feb; 🚋 12, 20, 22) Malá Strana is dominated by the huge green cupola of St Nicholas Church, one of Central Europe's finest baroque buildings. On the ceiling, Johann Kracker's 1770 *Apotheosis of St Nicholas* is Europe's largest fresco (clever trompe l'oeil technique has made the painting merge almost seamlessly with the architecture).

Museum of the Infant Jesus of Prague MUSEUM
(Muzeum Pražského Jezulátka; ☏ 257 533 646; www. pragjesu.info; Karmelitská 9; ◷ church 8.30am-7pm Mon-Sat & 8.30am-8pm Sun, museum 9.30am-5.30pm Mon-Sat & 1-6pm Sun, closed 1 Jan, 25 & 26 Dec & Easter Mon; 🚋 12, 20, 22) FREE The Church of Our Lady Victorious (kostel Panny Marie Vítězné), built in 1613, has on its central altar a 47cm-tall waxwork figure of the baby Jesus, brought from Spain in 1628 and known as the Infant Jesus of Prague (Pražské Jezulátko). At the back of the church is a museum, displaying a selection of the frocks used to dress the Infant.

John Lennon Wall HISTORIC SITE
(Velkopřevorské náměstí; 🚋 12, 20, 22) After his murder on 8 December 1980 John Lennon became a pacifist hero for many young Czechs. An image of Lennon was painted on a wall in a secluded square opposite the French Embassy, along with political graffiti and Beatles lyrics.

◎ Nové Město

The 'New Town' – new in the 14th century, that is – wraps around the Old Town, and finds a focus in the broad, historic boulevard of Wenceslas Square. Its sprawl of mostly

DON'T MISS

PRAGUE'S JEWISH MUSEUM

The slice of Staré Město bounced by Kaprova, Dlouhá and Kozí streets is home to the remains of the once-thriving mini-town of Josefov, Prague's former Jewish ghetto. The **Prague Jewish Museum** (Židovské muzeum Praha; ☎222 317 191; www.jewishmuseum.cz; Reservation Centre, Maiselova 38/15; ordinary ticket adult/child 300/200Kč, combined ticket incl entry to Old-New Synagogue 480/320Kč; ⏲9am-6pm Sun-Fri Apr-Oct, to 4.30pm Nov-Mar; Ⓜ Staroměstská) encompasses half a dozen ancient synagogues, a ceremonial hall and former mortuary, and the powerful melancholy of the Old Jewish Cemetery. These exhibits tell the often tragic and moving story of Prague's Jewish community, from the 16th-century creator of the Golem, Rabbi Loew, to the horrors of Nazi persecution.

An ordinary ticket gives admission to all six main monuments; a combined ticket includes the Old-New Synagogue as well. Completed around 1270, the Old-New Synagogue is Europe's oldest working synagogue and one of Prague's earliest Gothic buildings.

19th- and early 20th-century buildings encompasses important museums and galleries, impressive architecture and the city centre's main shopping streets.

Mucha Museum GALLERY
(Muchovo muzeum; ☎221 451 333; www.mucha.cz; Panská 7; adult/child 240/140Kč; ⏲10am-6pm; Ⓜ Můstek) This fascinating (and busy) museum features the sensuous art nouveau posters, paintings and decorative panels of Alfons Mucha (1860–1939), as well as many sketches, photographs and other memorabilia. The exhibits include countless artworks showing Mucha's trademark Slavic maidens with flowing hair and piercing blue eyes, bearing symbolic garlands and linden boughs.

Vyšehrad Citadel FORTRESS
(☎261 225 304; www.praha-vysehrad.cz; information centre at V pevnosti 159/5b; admission to grounds free; ⏲grounds 24hr; Ⓜ Vyšehrad) FREE The Vyšehrad Citadel, about 2km south of the centre, refers to the complex of buildings and structures atop Vyšehrad Hill that have played a role in Czech history for over 1000 years. While most structures date from the 18th century, the citadel is still viewed as the city's spiritual home. The sights are spread out over a wide area, with commanding views.

Sleeping

★**Fusion Hotel** HOSTEL, BOUTIQUE HOTEL €
(☎226 222 800; www.fusionhotels.com; Panská 9; dm from 500Kč, d/tr from 2100/2700Kč; @ 📶; 🚊3, 9, 14, 24) Billing itself as an 'affordable design hotel', Fusion certainly has style in abundance. From the revolving bar and spaceship-like UV corridor lighting, to the individually decorated rooms that resemble miniature modern-art galleries, the place exudes 'cool'. You can choose from the world's most stylish backpacker dorm, private doubles, triples and family rooms.

★**Czech Inn** HOSTEL, HOTEL €
(☎267 267 600; www.czech-inn.com; Francouzská 76, Vršovice; dm 260-450Kč, s/d 1320/1540Kč, apt from 3100Kč; P ⊖ @ 📶; 🚊4, 22) The Czech Inn calls itself a hostel, but the boutique label wouldn't be out of place. Everything seems sculpted by an industrial designer, from the iron beds to the brushed-steel flooring and minimalist square sinks. It offers a variety of accommodation, from standard hostel dorm rooms to good-value private doubles (with or without private bathroom) and apartments.

★**Mosaic House** HOTEL, HOSTEL €€
(☎221 595 350; www.mosaichouse.com; Odborů 4; dm/tw from 370/2400Kč; ⊖ ❄ @ 📶; Ⓜ Karlovo Náměstí) 🌿 A blend of four-star hotel and boutique hostel, Mosaic House is a cornucopia of designer detail, from the original 1930s mosaic in the entrance hall to the silver spray-painted tree branches used as clothes racks. The backpackers dorms are kept separate from the private rooms, but have the same high-quality decor and design, as does the in-house music bar and lounge.

Eating

Traditional Czech cuisine can be heavy, built around meat (usually pork) and accompanied by high-calorie dumplings, all washed down with copious quantities of beer. Most pubs also serve food.

KARLŠTEJN CASTLE

Rising above the village of Karlštejn, 30km southwest of Prague and easily reachable by train, **Karlštejn Castle** (Hrad Karlštejn; ☑ tour booking 311 681 617; www.hradkarlstejn.cz; adult/child Tour 1 270/180Kč, Tour 2 300/200Kč, Tour 3 150/100Kč; ⊙ 9am-6.30pm Jul & Aug, 9.30am-5.30pm Tue-Sun May, Jun & Sep, to 5pm Apr, to 4.30pm Oct, to 4pm Mar, reduced hours Sat & Sun only Dec-Feb) is rightly one of the top attractions in the Czech Republic. This fairytale medieval fortress is in such good shape that it wouldn't look out of place on Disney World's Main Street. Unfortunately, the crowds that throng its courtyards come in theme-park proportions too – in summer it's mobbed with visitors, ice-cream vendors and souvenir stalls.

Thankfully, the peaceful surrounding countryside offers views of Karlštejn's stunning exterior that rival anything you'll see on the inside. If at all possible, visit midweek or out of season, and avoid the queues at the castle ticket office by purchasing your tickets in advance via the link on the castle's website.

Karlštejn is easily reachable by frequent train service that leaves from Praha hlavní nádraží (Prague's main train station).

Lokál
CZECH €

(☑ 222 316 265; http://lokal-dlouha.ambi.cz; Dlouhá 33; mains 110-270Kč; ⊙ 11am-1am Mon-Fri, noon-1am Sat, noon-10pm Sun; ⊜ 5, 8, 24) Who'd have thought it possible? A classic Czech beer hall (albeit with slick modern styling); excellent *tankové pivo* (tanked Pilsner Urquell); a daily-changing menu of traditional Bohemian dishes; smiling, efficient, friendly service; and a nonsmoking area. Top restaurant chain Ambiente has turned its hand to Czech cuisine, and the result has been so successful that the place is always busy, mostly with locals.

Bakeshop Praha
BAKERY €

(☑ 222 316 823; www.bakeshop.cz; Kozí 1; sandwiches 75-200Kč; ⊙ 7am-9pm; Ⓜ Staroměstská) This fantastic bakery sells some of the best bread in the city, along with pastries, cakes and takeaway sandwiches, wraps, salads and quiche. Very busy at lunchtime.

Cukrkávalimonáda
EUROPEAN €

(☑ 257 225 396; www.cukrkavalimonada.com; Lázeňská 7; mains 100-200Kč; ⊙ 9am-7pm; ⊜ 12, 20, 22) A cute little cafe-cum-restaurant that combines minimalist modern styling with Renaissance-era painted timber roof-beams, CKL offers fresh, homemade pastas, frittatas, ciabattas, salads and pancakes (sweet and savoury) by day and a slightly more sophisticated bistro menu in the early evening. There's also a good breakfast menu offering ham and eggs, croissants, and yoghurt, and the hot chocolate is to die for.

🍷 Drinking & Nightlife

Cafe Louvre
CAFE

(☑ 224 930 949; www.cafelouvre.cz; Národní třída 22, 1st fl; ⊜ 6, 9, 18, 22) Others are more famous, but the French-style Louvre is arguably Prague's most amenable grand cafe. The atmosphere is wonderfully olde worlde, but there's a proper nonsmoking section among its warren of rooms and it serves good coffee, as well as food. Pop in for breakfast, play a little billiards and check out the associated art gallery downstairs when leaving.

Bukowski's
COCKTAIL BAR

(☑ 222 212 676; Bořivojova 86, Žižkov; ⊙ 7pm-3am; ⊜ 5, 9, 26) Like many of the drinking dens that are popular among expats, Bukowski's is more a cocktail dive than a cocktail bar. Named after hard-drinking American writer Charles Bukowski, it cultivates a dark and slightly debauched atmosphere – the decor is self-consciously 'interesting' (when you can see it through the smoke-befogged candlelight) – but it has friendly bartenders and cool tunes.

Pivovarský Klub
PUB

(☑ 222 315 777; www.pivovarskyklub.com; Křižíkova 17, Karlín; ⊙ 11.30am-11.30pm; Ⓜ Florenc) This bar is to beer what the Bodleian Library is to books – wall-to-wall shelves lined with myriad varieties of bottled beer from all over the world, and six guest beers on tap. Perch on a bar stool or head downstairs to the snug cellar and order some of the pub's excellent grub (such as authentic *guláš* – goulash – with bacon dumplings) to soak up the beer.

U Tří růží
BREWERY

(☑ 601 588 281; www.u3r.cz; Husova 10; ⊙ 11am-11pm Sun-Thu, to midnight Fri & Sat; ⊜ 17, 18) In the 19th century there were more than 20 breweries in Prague's Old Town, but by 1989 there was only one left (U Medvídku). The

Three Roses brewpub, on the site of one of those early breweries, helps revive the tradition, offering six beers on tap, including a tasty *světlý ležák* (pale lager), good food, and convivial surroundings.

Prague Beer Museum PUB
(📞732 330 912; www.praguebeermuseum.com; Dlouhá 46; ☺noon-3am; 🖥; 🚋5, 8, 14) Although the name seems aimed at the tourist market, this lively and always-heaving pub is very popular with Praguers. There are no fewer than 30 Czech-produced beers on tap (plus a beer menu with tasting notes to guide you). Try a sample board – a wooden platter with five 0.15L glasses containing five beers of your choice.

⭐**Cross Club** CLUB
(📞736 535 010; www.crossclub.cz; Plynární 23; admission free-150Kč; ☺cafe noon-2am, club 6pm-4am; 🖥; Ⓜ Nádraží Holešovice) An industrial club in every sense of the word: the setting in an industrial zone; the thumping music (both DJs and live acts); and the interior, an absolute must-see jumble of gadgets, shafts, cranks and pipes, many of which move and pulsate with light to the music. The program includes occasional live music, theatre performances and art happenings.

☆ **Entertainment**

Lucerna Music Bar LIVE MUSIC
(📞224 217 108; www.musicbar.cz; Palác Lucerna, Vodičkova 36; cover 100-500Kč; ☺8pm-4am; Ⓜ Můstek) Nostalgia reigns supreme at this atmospheric old theatre, now looking a little dog-eared, which hosts a hugely popular 1980s and '90s video party every Friday and Saturday night. There's an impressively eclectic program of live bands on midweek nights, with everything from Slovakian ska and Belgian pop-rock to Dutch electro-funk and US heavy metal.

Jazz Dock JAZZ
(📞774 058 838; www.jazzdock.cz; Janáčkovo nábřeží 2, Smíchov; admission 150Kč; ☺4pm-3am; Ⓜ Anděl, 🚋7, 9, 12, 14) Most of Prague's jazz clubs are smoky cellar affairs – this riverside club is a definite step up, with clean, modern decor and a decidedly romantic view out over the Vltava. It draws some of the best local talent and occasional international acts. Go early or book to get a good table. Shows normally begin at 7pm and 10pm.

Palác Akropolis LIVE MUSIC
(📞296 330 911; www.palacakropolis.cz; Kubelíkova 27, Žižkov; admission free-200Kč; ☺club 7pm-5am; 🖥; 🚋5, 9, 26 to Lipanska) The Akropolis is a Prague institution, a smoky, labyrinthine, sticky-floored shrine to alternative music and drama. Its various performance spaces host a smorgasbord of musical and cultural events, from DJs to string quartets to Macedonian Roma bands to local rock gods to visiting talent.

Prague State Opera OPERA, BALLET
(Státní opera Praha; 📞224 901 448; www.narodni-divadlo.cz; Wilsonova 4; tickets 180-1190Kč; ☺box office 10am-6pm; Ⓜ Muzeum) The impressive neo-rococo home of the Prague State Opera provides a glorious setting for performances of opera and ballet. An annual Verdi festival takes place here in August and September, and less conventional shows, such as Leoncavallo's rarely staged version of *La Bohème*, are also performed here.

National Theatre OPERA, BALLET
(Národní divadlo; 📞224 901 448; www.narodni-divadlo.cz; Národní třída 2; tickets 50-1100Kč; ☺box offices 10am-6pm; 🚋6, 9, 18, 22) The much-loved National Theatre provides a stage for traditional opera, drama and ballet by the likes of Smetana, Shakespeare and Tchaikovsky, sharing the program alongside more modern works by composers and playwrights such as Philip Glass and John Osborne.

ℹ️ **Information**

Prague City Tourism – Old Town Hall (Prague Welcome; 📞221 714 444; www.prague.eu; Old Town Hall, Staroměstské náměstí 5; ☺9am-7pm; Ⓜ Staroměstská) The busiest of the Prague City Tourism branches occupies the ground floor of the Old Town Hall (enter to the left of the Astronomical Clock).

ℹ️ **Getting There & Away**

See p713 for details on the main overland and air routes to Prague and the Czech Republic.

ℹ️ **Getting Around**

TO/FROM THE AIRPORT

From the airport, buy a full-price public transport ticket (32Kč) from the **Prague Public Transport Authority** (DPP; 📞296 191 817; www.dpp.cz; ☺7am-9pm) desk and take bus 119 (20 minutes; every 10 minutes from 4am to midnight) to the end station at metro line A, then continue by metro into the city centre (another 10 to 15 minutes; no new ticket needed).

There's also an **Airport Express** bus (AE, 60Kč, 35 minutes, every 30 minutes from 5am to 10pm) which runs to **Praha hlavní nádraží** (Prague's main train station), where you can connect to metro line C (buy ticket from driver, luggage goes free).

AAA Radio Taxi (☑ 14014, 222 333 222; www.aaataxi.cz) operates a 24-hour taxi service, charging around 500Kč to 650Kč to get to the centre of Prague.

PUBLIC TRANSPORT

Prague has an integrated metro, tram and bus network – tickets are valid on all types of transport, and for transfers between them. A basic ticket (32Kč) is good for 90 minutes – validate tickets once in yellow machines on trams and buses, and at the entrance to metro stations. Convenient one- and three-day passes are also available.

Bohemia

Kutná Hora

Enriched by the silver ore that veined the surrounding hills, the medieval city of Kutná Hora became the seat of Wenceslas II's royal mint in 1308, producing silver *groschen* that were then the hard currency of Central Europe. Boom-time Kutná Hora rivalled Prague in importance, but by the 16th century the mines began to run dry, and its demise was hastened by the Thirty Years' War and a devastating fire in 1770. The town became a Unesco World Heritage Site in 1996, luring visitors with a smorgasbord of historic sights, including an eerie monastery crafted entirely from human bones. Most visitors come here as a day trip from Prague.

⊙ Sights

Sedlec Ossuary   CHURCH
(Kostnice; ☑ information centre 326 551 049; www.ossuary.eu; Zámecká 127; adult/concession 90/60Kč; ⊙ 8am-6pm Mon-Sat, 9am-6pm Sun Apr-Sep, 9am-5pm Mar & Oct, 9am-4pm Nov-Feb) When the Schwarzenbergs purchased Sedlec monastery in 1870 they allowed a local woodcarver to get creative with the bones piled in the crypt (the remains of around 40,000 people), resulting in the remarkable 'bone church' of Sedlec Ossuary. Garlands of skulls hang from the vaulted ceiling, around a chandelier containing at least one of each bone in the human body.

Barborská   STREET
Barborská street runs along the front of the 17th-century former Jesuit College, and is decorated with a row of 13 baroque **statues** of saints, an arrangement inspired by the statues on Prague's Charles Bridge. All are related to the Jesuits and/or the town; the second statue – the woman holding a chalice, with a stone tower at her side – is St Barbara, the patron saint of miners and therefore of Kutná Hora.

Czech Silver Museum   MUSEUM
(České muzeum stříbra; ☑ 327 512 159; www.cms-kh.cz; Barborská 28; adult/concession Tour 1 70/40Kč, Tour 2 120/80Kč, combined 140/90Kč; ⊙ 10am-6pm Jul & Aug, 9am-6pm May, Jun & Sep, 9am-5pm Apr & Oct, 10am-4pm Nov, closed Mon year-round) Originally part of the town's fortifications, the **Hrádek** (Little Castle) was rebuilt in the 15th century as the residence of Jan Smíšek, administrator of the royal mines, who grew rich from silver mined illegally right under the building. It now houses the Czech Silver Museum. Visiting is by guided tour, which includes the chance to visit an ancient silver mine.

✖ Eating

Pivnice Dačický   BEER HALL €
(☑ 327 512 248; www.dacicky.com; Rakova 8; mains 140-360Kč; ⊙ 11am-11pm; ☎ 👪) Get some froth on your moustache at this old-fashioned, wood-panelled Bohemian beer hall, where you can dine on dumplings and choose from five draught beers including Pilsner Urquell, Primátor yeast beer and local Kutná Hora lager.

ℹ Information

Kutná Hora Tourist Office (Informační centrum; ☑ 327 512 378; www.guide.kh.cz; Palackého náměstí 377; ⊙ 9am-6pm Apr-Sep, 9am-5pm Mon-Fri & 10am-4pm Sat & Sun Oct-Mar) Books accommodation, rents bicycles (per day 220Kč) and offers internet access (per minute 1Kč, minimum 15Kč).

ℹ Getting There & Away

Direct trains from Prague's main train station to Kutná Hora station every two hours (201Kč return, 55 minutes). It's a 10-minute walk from here to Sedlec Ossuary, and a further 2.5km to the Old Town.

There are hourly buses on weekdays (three or four on Saturdays) from Háje bus station on the southern edge of Prague to Kutná Hora (136Kc return, 1¾ hours). The train is a better bet.

Český Krumlov

POP 14,050

Crowned by a spectacular castle, and centred on an elegant old town square, Český Krumlov is a pocket-sized Prague. Renaissance and baroque buildings enclose the meandering arc of the Vltava river. Following architectural neglect during the communist era, the undeniable fairy-tale beauty of Český Krumlov is radiant again, with thoughtful restoration transforming the heritage buildings lining the narrow lanes into cosy restaurants and classy boutique hotels.

⊙ Sights

★**Český Krumlov State Castle**   CASTLE
(☎380 704 711; www.zamek-ceskykrumlov.eu; Zámek 59; adult/concession Tour 1 250/160Kč, Tour 2 240/140Kč, Theatre Tour 300/200Kč; ⊙9am-6pm Tue-Sun Jun-Aug, to 5pm Apr May, Sep & Oct) Český Krumlov's striking Renaissance castle, occupying a promontory high above the town, began life in the 13th century. It acquired its present appearance in the 16th to 18th centuries under the stewardship of the noble Rožmberk and Schwarzenberg families. The interiors are accessible by guided tour only, though you can stroll the grounds on your own.

Castle Museum & Tower   MUSEUM, TOWER
(☎380 704 711; www.zamek-ceskykrumlov.eu; Zámek 59; combined entry adult/concession 130/60Kč, museum only 100/50Kč, tower only 50/30Kč; ⊙9am-6pm Jun-Aug, to 5pm Apr & May, to 5pm Tue-Sun Sep & Oct, to 4pm Tue-Sun Jan-Mar) Located within the castle complex, this small museum and adjoining tower is an ideal option if you don't have the time or energy for a full castle tour. Through a series of rooms, the museum traces the castle's history from its origins through to the present day.

Egon Schiele Art Centrum   MUSEUM
(☎380 704 011; www.schieleartcentrum.cz; Široká 71; adult/concession 160/90Kč; ⊙10am-6pm Tue-Sun) This excellent private gallery houses a small retrospective of the controversial Viennese painter Egon Schiele (1890–1918), who lived in Krumlov in 1911 and raised the ire of townsfolk by hiring young girls as nude models. For this and other sins he was eventually driven out.

🛏 Sleeping

★**Krumlov House**   HOSTEL €
(☎380 711 935; www.krumlovhostel.com; Rooseveltova 68; dm/d/tr 300/1000/1350Kč; ⊛@🗟) 🖉 Perched above the river, Krumlov House is friendly and comfortable, and has plenty of books, DVDs and local information to feed your inner wanderer. Accommodation is in six-bed en suite dorms as well as private double and triple rooms or private, self-catered apartments. The owners are English-speaking and traveller-friendly.

Hostel Skippy   HOSTEL €
(☎380 728 380; www.hostelskippy.webs.com; Plešivecká 123; dm/d 350/880Kč; ⊛🗟) Located in the near suburb of Plešivec on the Vltava, about 15 minutes walk south of the historic centre. The owners are a musician and an artist and the hostel has a relaxed, indie vibe. Unlike some hostels with racks of bunks, Skippy is more like hanging out at a friend's place. It's small, so you'll need to book ahead.

U Malého Vítka   HOTEL €€
(☎380 711 925; www.vitekhotel.cz; Radnični 27; s/d 1200/1500Kč; P⊛🗟) We like this small hotel in the heart of the Old Town. The simple room furnishings are of high-quality, hand-crafted wood, and each room is named after a traditional Czech fairy-tale character. The downstairs restaurant and cafe are very good too.

🍴 Eating

Laibon   VEGETARIAN €
(☎728 676 654; www.laibon.cz; Parkán 105; mains 90-180Kč; ⊙11am-11pm; 🗟🖉) This rustic vegetarian restaurant, with several riverside picnic tables with castle views, is extremely popular on user-generated sites. Menu items such as guacamole and hummus can start the mouth watering after too many days of pork or chicken. Book in advance in summer and request an outside table.

★**Krčma v Šatlavské**   CZECH €€
(☎380 713 344; www.satlava.cz; Horní 157; mains 180-280Kč; ⊙11am-midnight) This medieval barbecue cellar is hugely popular with visitors and your tablemates are much more likely to be from Austria or Asia than from the town itself, but the grilled meats served up with gusto in a funky labyrinth illuminated by candles are excellent and perfectly in character with Český Krumlov. Advance booking is essential.

Český Krumlov

CENTRAL & EASTERN EUROPE MORAVIA

Český Krumlov

⊙ **Top Sights**
1 Český Krumlov State Castle B1

⊙ **Sights**
2 Castle Museum & Tower B1
3 Egon Schiele Art Centrum A3

🛏 **Sleeping**
4 Krumlov House D4
5 U Malého Vítka B2

🍴 **Eating**
6 Krčma v Šatlavské B3
7 Laibon B2

ℹ Information

Infocentrum (📞 380 704 622; www.ckrumlov.info; náměstí Svornosti 2; ⊙ 9am-7pm Jun-Aug, to 6pm Apr, May, Sep & Oct, to 5pm Nov-Mar) One of the country's best tourist offices. Good source for transport and accommodation info, maps, internet access (per five minutes 5Kč) and audio guides (per hour 100Kč).

ℹ Getting There & Away

TRAIN

From Prague (260Kč, 3½ hours), the train requires a change in České Budějovice. There's regular train service between České Budějovice and Český Krumlov (40Kč, 45 minutes). Český Krumlov train station is a long 30-minute walk north of the historic centre.

BUS

Student Agency coaches (195Kč, three hours) leave regularly from Prague's Na Knížecí bus station at Anděl metro station (Line B). Book in advance for weekends or in July and August.

Moravia

The Czech Republic's easternmost province, Moravia is yin to Bohemia's yang. If Bohemians love beer, Moravians love wine. If

Bohemia is towns and cities, Moravia is rolling hills and pretty landscapes. Once you've seen the best of Bohemia, head east for a different side of the Czech Republic.

Brno

POP 387,200

Among Czechs, Moravia's capital (and the country's second-biggest city) has a dull rep; a likeable enough place where not much actually happens. The reality, though, is very different. Tens of thousands of students ensure lively cafe and club scenes that easily rival Prague's.

◎ Sights

★**Vila Tugendhat**   ARCHITECTURE
(Villa Tugendhat; ☑ tour booking 515 511 015; www.tugendhat.eu; Černopolni 45; adult/concession basic tour 300/180Kč, extended tour 350/210Kč; ⊗ 10am-6pm Tue-Sun; ⛟ 3, 5, 11 to Černopclní) Brno had a reputation in the 1920s as a centre for modern architecture in the functionalist and Bauhaus styles. Arguably the finest example is this family villa, designed by modern master Mies van der Rohe in 1930. Entry is by guided tour booked in advance by phone or email. Two tours are available: a 60-minute basic tour and a 90-minute extended visit.

Capuchin Monastery   CEMETERY
(Kapucínský klášter; www.kapucini.cz; Kapucínské náměstí; adult/concession 70/35Kč; ⊗ 9am-noon & 1-4.30pm Mon-Sat, 11am-11.45am & 1-4.30pm Sun May-Sep, closed Mon mid-Feb–Apr & Oct–mid-Dec, weekends only mid-Dec–mid-Feb) One of the city's leading attractions is this ghoulish cellar crypt that holds the mummified remains of several city noblemen from the 18th century. Apparently the dry, well-ventilated crypt has the natural ability to turn dead bodies into mummies. Up to 150 cadavers were deposited here prior to 1784, the desiccated corpses including monks, abbots and local notables.

Špilberk Castle   CASTLE
(Hrad Špilberk; ☑ 542 123 611; www.spilberk.cz; Špilberk 210/1; combined entry adult/concession 400/240Kč, casements only 90/50Kč, tower only 50/30Kč; ⊗ 9am-5pm daily May & Jun, 10am-6pm daily Jul-Sep, 9am-5pm Tue-Sun Oct-Apr) Brno's spooky hilltop castle is considered the city's most important landmark. Its history stretches back to the 13th century, when it was home to Moravian margraves and later a fortress. Under the Habsburgs in the 18th

and 19th centuries, it served as a prison. Today it's home to the **Brno City Museum**, with several temporary and permanent exhibitions.

Labyrinth under the Cabbage Market   TUNNELS
(Brněnské podzemí; ☑ 542 427 150; www.ticbrno.cz; Zelný trh 21; adult/concession 160/80Kč; ⊗ 9am-6pm Tue-Sun) In recent years the city has opened several sections of extensive underground tunnels to the general public. This tour takes around 40 minutes to explore several cellars situated 6m to 8m below the Cabbage Market, which has served as a food market for centuries. The cellars were built for two purposes: to store goods and to hide in during wars.

🛌 Sleeping

★**Hostel Mitte**   HOSTEL €
(☑ 734 622 340; www.hostelmitte.com; Panská 22; incl breakfast dm 500Kč, s/d 1000/1300Kč; ⊛@🛜) Set in the heart of the Old Town, this clean and stylish hostel smells and looks brand new. The rooms are named after famous Moravians (eg Milan Kundera) or famous events (Austerlitz) and decorated accordingly. There are dorms in six-bed rooms and private singles and doubles.

Hotel Europa   HOTEL €€
(☑ 515 143 100; www.hotel-europa-brno.cz; třída kpt Jaroše 27; s/d 1400/1800Kč; 🅿⊛🛜) Set in a quiet neighbourhood a 10-minute walk from the city centre, this self-proclaimed 'art' hotel (presumably for the wacky futuristic lobby furniture) offers clean and tastefully furnished modern rooms in a historic 19th-century building. The lobby has free wi-fi, while the rooms have cable (ethernet) connections. There is free parking out the front and in the courtyard.

🍴 Eating

Annapurna   INDIAN €
(☑ 774 995 122; www.indicka-restaurace-brno.cz; Josefská 14; mains 140-220Kč; ⊗ 10.30am-10.30pm Mon-Fri, noon-10.30pm Sat & Sun; 🍽) The weekday lunch specials (110Kč for soup, main, rice and salad) are absolutely mobbed at this cramped space not far from the train station. People come for the very good Indian food and prompt service. Outside of lunch, it's less crowded but still worth a trip for curries and lots of varied vegetarian dishes.

Spolek CZECH €

(☑774 814 230; www.spolek.net; Orli 22; mains 80-180Kč; ☺9am-10pm Mon-Fri, 10am-10pm Sat & Sun; ☎🚲🎨) You'll get friendly, unpretentious service at this coolly 'bohemian' (yes, we're in Moravia) haven with interesting salads and soups, and a concise but diverse wine list. It has excellent coffee too.

🍷 Drinking & Nightlife

★**Cafe Podnebi** CAFE

(☑542 211 372; www.podnebi.cz; Údolní 5; ☺8am-midnight Mon-Fri, from 9am Sat & Sun; ☎🎨) This homey, student-oriented cafe is famous citywide for its excellent hot chocolate, but it also serves very good espresso drinks. In summer the garden terrace is a hidden oasis and there's a small play area for kids.

U Richarda PUB

(☑775 027 918; www.uricharda.eu; Údolní 7; ☺11am-11pm Mon-Sat) This microbrewery is highly popular with students, who come for the great house-brewed, unpasteurised yeast beers (including a rare cherry-flavoured lager) and the good traditional Czech cooking (mains 109Kč to 149Kč). Book in advance.

ℹ️ Information

Tourist Information Centre (TIC Brno ; ☑542 211 090; www.ticbrno.cz; Old Town Hall, Radnická 8; ☺8am-6pm Mon-Fri, 9am-6pm Sat & Sun) Lots of great information on hand in English, including free maps. There's a free computer to check email.

ℹ️ Getting There & Away

TRAIN

Express trains to Brno depart Prague's main station, Praha hlavní nádraží every couple of hours during the day (220Kč, three hours). Brno is a handy junction for onward train travel to Vienna (220Kč, two hours) and Bratislava (210Kč, 1½ hours).

BUS

Buses depart Prague's Florenc bus station hourly for Brno (210Kč, 2½ hours). Brno has two bus stations. Yellow Student Agency buses use the small bus stop in front of the main train station, while most other buses use the Zvonařka bus station, behind the train station.

Czech Republic Survival Guide

ℹ️ Directory A–Z

ACCOMMODATION

The Czech Republic offers a wide range of accommodation options, from budget hostels and pensions to international chains and sharply styled boutique hotels.

➜ Prague, Brno and Český Krumlov all have backpacker-oriented hostels. Dorm bed prices vary according to the season, with the highest rates over holidays and in summer.

➜ The **Czech Youth Hostel Association** (www. czechhostels.com) is a handy website for scouting hostels and booking rooms.

➜ Campsites are normally open from May to September and charge from 60Kč to 120Kč per person. Camping on public land is prohibited.

MONEY

➜ Banks are the best places to exchange cash. They normally charge around a 2% commission with a 50Kč minimum.

➜ The easiest and cheapest way to carry money is in the form of a credit or debit card from your bank, which you can use to withdraw cash either from an ATM or over the counter in a bank.

➜ Avoid private exchange booths (směnárna) in the main tourist areas. They lure you in with attractive-looking exchange rates that quickly get eaten up in hidden fees.

OPENING HOURS

Banks 9am to 4pm Monday to Friday, limited hours 9am to 1pm Saturday

Bars & Clubs 11am to 1am Tuesday to Saturday, shorter hours Sunday and Monday

Restaurants 11am to 11pm, many kitchens close by 10pm

Shops 9am to 6pm Monday to Friday, 9am to 1pm Saturday

PUBLIC HOLIDAYS

New Year's Day 1 January

Good Friday & Easter Monday March/April

Labour Day 1 May

ℹ️ ACCOMMODATION PRICE RANGES

In this section we've used the following general price indicators (double room in high season):

€ less than 1600Kč

€€ 1600Kč to 3700Kč

€€€ more than 3700Kč

ℹ️ EATING PRICE RANGES

In this section we've used the following price indicators (for a main meal):

€ less than 200Kč

€€ 200Kč to 500Kč

€€€ more than 500Kč

Liberation Day 8 May

Sts Cyril & Methodius Day 5 July

Jan Hus Day 6 July

Czech Statehood Day 28 September

Republic Day 28 October

Struggle for Freedom & Democracy Day 17 November

Christmas Eve 24 December

Christmas Day 25 December

St Stephen's Day 26 December

TELEPHONES

→ All Czech telephone numbers, both landline and mobile (cell), have nine digits. There are no city or area codes, so to call any Czech number, simply dial the nine-digit number.

→ To call abroad from the Czech Republic, dial the international access code (📞 00), then the country code, then the area code (minus any initial zero) and the number. To dial the Czech Republic from abroad, dial your country's international access code, then 📞 420 (the Czech Republic country code) and the unique nine-digit local number.

→ Mobile phones use the GSM 900/1800 system. Czech SIM cards can be used in European and Australian mobile phones. Standard North American GSM1900 phones will not work, though dual-band GSM 1900/900 phones will.

WI-FI

Nearly every hostel and hotel will have free wi-fi available. In addition, cafes, restaurants and bars will usually offer free wi-fi for customers.

ℹ️ Getting There & Away

Prague sits at the heart of Europe and is well served by air, road and rail.

AIR

Václav Havel Airport Prague (Prague Ruzyně International Airport; 📞 220 111 888; www.prg.aero; K letišti 6, Ruzyně; 📶; 🚌 100, 119), 17km west of the city centre, is the main international gateway to the Czech Republic and the hub for the national carrier **Czech Airlines** (www.csa.com), which operates direct flights to Prague from many European cities.

The airport has two terminals: Terminal 1 for flights to/from non–Schengen Zone countries (including the UK, Ireland and countries outside Europe); Terminal 2 for flights to/from Schengen Zone countries (most EU nations plus Switzerland, Iceland and Norway).

LAND

The Czech Republic has border crossings with Germany, Poland, Slovakia and Austria. These are all EU-member states within the EU's Schengen Zone, meaning there are no passport or customs checks, though international travellers are always expected to carry their passports.

Bus

Several bus companies offer coach service connecting Prague to cities around Europe. Nearly all international buses (and most domestic services) use the renovated and user-friendly **Florenc bus station** (ÚAN Praha Florenc; 📞 900 144 444; www.florenc.cz; Křižíkova 2110/2b, Karlín; ⏱️ 4am-midnight, information counter 6am-10pm; 📶; Ⓜ Florenc).

International bus operators include the excellent **Student Agency** (📞 bus information 841 101 101, nonstop info line 800 100 300; www.studentagency.cz; ÚAN Praha Florenc, Křižíkova 2110/2b) and **Eurolines** (📞 245 005 245; www.elines.cz; ÚAN Praha Florenc, Křižíkova 2110/2b; ⏱️ 6.30am-10.30pm Mon-Fri, 6.30am-9pm Sat; 📶; Ⓜ Florenc); both have offices at Florenc bus station, or you can buy tickets online.

Train

The Czech Republic is well integrated into European rail networks. **České dráhy** (📞 840 112 113; www.cd.cz), the Czech state rail operator, sells tickets for international destinations.

For Prague, nearly all domestic and international trains arrive at **Praha hlavní nádraží** (Prague main train station; 📞 840 112 113; www.cd.cz; Wilsonova 8, Nové Město; Ⓜ Hlavní nádraží), which is located on metro line C (red). Major international rail connections linking Prague to Bratislava, Vienna and Budapest also pass through Brno.

For outbound travel from Prague, buy tickets at ticket counters on the lower level of the main station.

ℹ️ Getting Around

The Czech Republic is well served by train and bus.

In Prague, most trains arrive at and depart from the main station, Praha hlavní nádraží. In other cities, train stations are generally located near the centre and within walking distance of sights and attractions.

Buses generally use the main Florenc bus station. Student Agency is a reliable domestic bus operator and runs regularly from Prague to Český Krumlov and Brno, among many other destinations.

SLOVAKIA

Going strong over two decades as an independent state after the break-up of Czecho-slovakia, Slovakia – Europe's most castellated country – is a bastion of untrammelled wildernesses, where some of the continent's densest forest coverage gives way to dramatic fortresses and craggy mountains harbouring outstanding hiking. It savours wine over beer and, in its tradition-steeped hinterland, cradles an entrancing folk culture most European nations have lost. Slovakia's small size is possibly its biggest attraction. You can traipse woodsy waterfall-filled gorges one day and yodel from 2500m-plus peaks the next.

Travellers normally begin their exploration with the country's tiny capital, Bratislava, which sits astride the Danube River. The city's charming Old Town (Starý Mesto) is filled with narrow pedestrian streets of pastel-coloured 18th-century buildings and myriad sidewalk cafes, all under the watchful gaze of the city's solemn castle.

From here, head north and east to the High Tatras, where you'll find true Alpine peaks, seemingly in the middle of nowhere. As you look upon the snow-strewn jagged mountains rising like an apparition east of Liptovský Mikuláš, you may think you're imagining things. But there they are indeed. The High Tatras are undoubtedly where the adventure junkies head, along with those who can afford the luxury mountain resorts, mostly located here. Tucked into the eastern end of the peaks is the Belá Tatras: the loveliest and least discovered region.

Bratislava is well served by international rail, with frequent connections to Vienna (one hour, hourly), Prague (4¼ hours, six daily) and Budapest (2¾ hours, seven daily). Rail is also the main way to get around Slovakia.

POLAND

Warsaw

POP 1.7 MILLION

Once you've travelled around Poland, you realise this: Warsaw is different. Rather than being centred on an old market square, the capital is spread across a broad area with diverse architecture: restored Gothic, communist concrete, modern glass and steel. Warsaw has suffered the worst history could throw at it, including virtual destruction at the end of World War II – and survived. As a result, it's a fascinating collection of neighbourhoods and landmarks.

☉ Sights

Though it's a relatively recent reconstruction, Warsaw's Old Town (Stare Miasto) looks as though it's been there for centuries. Running south from Castle Sq to busy al Jerozolimskie is the stamping ground of Warsaw's students, shoppers and socialites.

◉ Old Town

Plac Zamkowy SQUARE
(Castle Square) A natural spot from which to start exploring the Old Town is triangular Castle Square. Attracting snap-happy tourists by the hundreds each day is the square's centrepiece, the Sigismund III Vasa Column (Kolumna Zygmunta III Wazy).

★ **Royal Castle** CASTLE
(Zamek Królewski; www.zamek-krolewski.pl; Plac Zamkowy 4; adult/concession 23/15zł; ⊙10am-6pm Mon-Sat, 11am-6pm Sun) This massive brick edifice, a copy of the original blown up by the Germans in WWII, began life as a wooden stronghold of the dukes of Mazovia in the 14th century. Its heyday came in the mid-17th century, when it became one of Europe's most splendid royal residences. It then served the Russian tsars and, in 1918, after Poland regained independence, became the residence of the president. Today it is filled with period furniture and works of art.

Barbican FORTRESS
(Barbakan; ul Nowomiejska) Heading north out of the Old Town along ul Nowomiejska you'll soon see the redbrick Barbican, a semicircular defensive tower topped with a decorative Renaissance parapet. It was partially dismantled in the 19th century, but reconstructed after WWII, and is now a popular spot for buskers and art sellers.

◉ Royal Way

St Anne's Church CHURCH
(Kościół Św Anny; ul Krakowskie Przedmieście 68) Marking the start of the Royal Way, this is arguably the most ornate church in the city. It escaped major damage during WWII, which explains why it sports an original trompe l'oeil ceiling, a Rococo high altar and a gorgeous organ. The facade is also Baroque in style, although there are neoclassical touches here and there.

★ Chopin Museum MUSEUM
(📞 22 441 6251; www.chopin.museum; ul Okólnik 1; adult/concession 22/13zł, Sun free; ⊘11am-8pm Tue-Sun) High-tech, multimedia museum within the Baroque Ostrogski Palace, showcasing the work of the country's most famous composer. You're encouraged to take your time through four floors of displays, including stopping by the listening booths in the basement where you can browse Chopin's oeuvre to your heart's content. Limited visitation is allowed each hour; your best bet is to book your visit in advance by phone or email.

★ Łazienki Park GARDENS
(Park Łazienkowski; www.lazienki-krolewskie.pl; ul Agrykola 1; ⊘dawn-dusk) Pronounced wah-*zhen*-kee, this park is a beautiful place of manicured greens and wild patches. Its popularity extends to families, peacocks and fans of classical music, who come for the al fresco Chopin concerts on Sunday afternoons at noon and 4pm from mid-May through September. Once a hunting ground attached to Ujazdów Castle, Łazienki was acquired by King Stanisław August Poniatowski in 1764 and transformed into a splendid park complete with palace, amphitheatre, and various follies and other buildings.

◉ City Centre & Around

★ Palace of Culture & Science HISTORIC BUILDING
(Pałac Kultury i Nauki; www.pkin.pl; Plac Defilad 1; observation terrace adult/concession 20/14zł; ⊘9am-8.30pm) Love it or hate it, every visitor to Warsaw should visit the iconic, socialist realist PKiN (as its full Polish name is abbreviated). This 'gift of friendship' from the Soviet Union was built in the early 1950s, and at 231m high remains the tallest building in Poland. It's home to a huge congress hall, theatres, a multiscreen cinema and museums. Take the high-speed lift to the 30th-floor (115m) observation terrace to take it all in.

★ Warsaw Rising Museum MUSEUM
(Muzeum Powstania Warszawskiego; www.1944.pl; ul Grzybowska 79; adult/concession 18/14zł, Sun free; ⊘8am-6pm Mon, Wed & Fri, to 8pm Thu, 10am-6pm Sat & Sun; Ⓜ Rondo Daszyńskiego, 🚊9, 22 or 24 along al Jerozolimskie) One of Warsaw's best, this museum traces the history of the city's heroic but doomed uprising against the German occupation in 1944 via three levels of interactive displays, photographs, film archives and personal accounts. The volume of material is overwhelming, but the museum does an excellent job of instilling in visitors a sense of the desperation residents felt in deciding to oppose the occupation by force, and of illustrating the dark consequences, including the Nazis' destruction of the city in the aftermath.

★ Wilanów Palace PALACE
(Pałac w Wilanowie; 📞 22 544 2850; www.wilanow-palac.pl; ul Potockiego 10/16; adult/concession 20/15zł; ⊘10am-7pm Tue-Sun; 🚊116 or 180) Warsaw's top palace is Wilanów (vee-*lah*-noof), 6km south of Łazienki. It dates to 1677, when King Jan III Sobieski bought the land and turned an existing manor house into an Italian Baroque villa fit for a royal summer residence (calling it in Italian 'villa nuova', from which the Polish name is derived). Wilanów changed hands several times over the centuries, and with every new owner it acquired a bit of Baroque here and a touch of neoclassical there.

◉ Former Jewish District

★ Museum of the History of Polish Jews MUSEUM
(Polin; www.polin.pl; ul Anielewicza 6; adult/concession 25/15zł, incl temporary exhibits 30/20zł; ⊘10am-6pm Mon, Wed-Fri & Sun, to 8pm Sat; 🚊4, 15, 18 or 35 along ul Marszałkowska) This exceptional museum's permanent exhibition opened in late 2014. Impressive multimedia exhibits document 1000 years of Jewish history in Poland, from accounts of the earliest Jewish traders in the region through waves of mass migration, progress and pogroms, all the way to WWII and the destruction of Europe's largest Jewish community. It's worth booking online first, and you can hire an audio guide (10zł) to get the most out of the many rooms of displays, interactive maps, photos and videos.

Central Warsaw

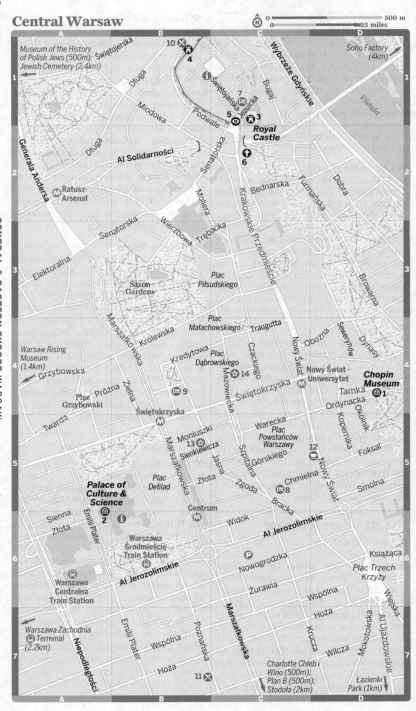

N
0   500 m
0   0.25 miles

Museum of the History
of Polish Jews (500m);
Jewish Cemetery (2.4km)

Świętojerska

Długa

Miodowa

10

4

Świętojańska

Jezuicka

5

3

Bulaj

Wybrzeże Gdyńskie

Soho Factory
(4km)

Vistula

Podwale

Royal
Castle

6

Al Solidarności

Senatorska

Długa

Generala Andersa

Ratusz-
Arsenał

Bednarska

Furmańska

Dobra

Elektoralna

Senatorska

Wierzbowa

Trębacka

Moliera

Krakowskie Przedmieście

Saxon
Gardens

Plac
Piłsudskiego

Browarna

Marszałkowska

Królewska

Plac
Małachowskiego

Traugutta

Nowy Świat

Obozna

Sewerynów

Dynasy

Warsaw Rising
Museum
(1.4km)

Grzybowska

Plac
Próżna

Zielna

Plac
Grzybowski

Kredytowa

Plac
Dąbrowskiego

Mazowiecka

Czackiego

14

Świętokrzyska

9

Nowy Świat -
Uniwersytet

Chopin
Museum

1

Tamka

Ordynacka

Okólnik

Kopernika

Foksal

Twarda

Świętokrzyska

Marszałkowska

Moniuszki

13

Sienkiewicza

Jasna

Szpitalna

Górskiego

Plac
Powstańców
Warszawy

Warecka

12

Nowy Świat

Chmielna

Smolna

Palace of
Culture &
Science

2

Plac
Defilad

Złota

Zgoda

Bracka

8

Sienna

Złota

Emilii Plater

Centrum

Widok

Al Jerozolimskie

Warszawa
Śródmieście
Train Station

Nowogrodzka

Książąca

Plac Trzech
Krzyży

Warszawa
Centralna
Train Station

Al Jerozolimskie

Żurawia

Wspólna

Hoża

Mokotowska

Al Ujazdowskie

Wiejska

Warszawa Zachodnia
Terminal
(2.2km)

Emilii Plater

Wspólna

Poznańska

Marszałkowska

Krucza

Wilcza

Hoża

Niepodległości

11

Charlotte Chleb i
Wino (500m);
Plan B (500m);
Stodoła (2km)

Łazienki
Park (1km)

Jewish Cemetery CEMETERY
(Cmentarz Żydowski; ul Okopowa 49/51; adult/concession 10/5zł; ⊙10am-5pm Mon-Thu, 9am-1pm Fri, 11am-4pm Sun) Founded in 1806, Warsaw's main Jewish Cemetery incredibly suffered little during WWII and contains more than 150,000 tombstones, the largest collection of its kind in Europe. A notice near the entrance lists the graves of many eminent Polish Jews, including Ludwik Zamenhof, creator of the international artificial language Esperanto.

🛏 Sleeping

⭐**Oki Doki Hostel** HOSTEL €
(🖉22 828 0122; www.okidoki.pl; Plac Dąbrowskiego 3; dm 29-90zł, r 128-260zł; 🛜) Arguably Warsaw's most popular hostel, and certainly one of the best. Each of its bright, large rooms is individually named and decorated. Accommodation is in three- to eight-bed dorms, with a special three-bed dorm for women only. The owners are well travelled and know the needs of backpackers, providing a kitchen and a laundry service. Breakfast available (15zł).

⭐**Castle Inn** HOTEL €€
(🖉22 425 0100; www.castleinn.pl; ul Świętojańska 2; s/d from 280/300zł; ❄🛜) Nicely decorated 'art hotel', housed in a 17th-century town house. All rooms overlook either Castle Sq

---

Central Warsaw

---

or St John's Cathedral, and come in a range of playful styles. Our favourite would be No 121, 'Viktor', named for a reclusive street artist, complete with tasteful graffiti and a gorgeous castle view. Breakfast costs an extra 35zł.

Chmielna Guest House GUESTHOUSE €€
(🖉22 828 1282; www.chmielnabb.pl; ul Chmielna 13; r 190-210zł; 🛜) Handily situated in the middle of a bustling shopping and restaurant zone, this sister property of New World Hostel offers a small number of comfortable budget rooms, some of which have shared bathrooms. Rooms are decked out in colourful contemporary decor, and there's a basic kitchen for guest use. Note that the rooms are on the 3rd floor.

✗ Eating

⭐**Charlotte Chleb i Wino** FRENCH €
(al Wyzwolenia 18; mains 9-25zł; ⊙7am-midnight Mon-Fri, 9am-1am Sat, 9am-10pm Sun; 🛜) Dazzling French bakery and bistro facing Plac Zbawiciela. It dishes up tantalising croissants and pastries at the break of dawn, then transitions to big salads and crusty sandwiches through the lunch and dinner hours, and finally to wine on the terrace in the evening. Great value for money.

Bar Mleczny Pod Barbakanem CAFETERIA €
(ul Mostowa 27; mains 7-10zł; ⊙8am-4pm Mon-Fri, 9am-4pm Sat; 🖉) In the Old Town, just outside the Barbican, look for Bar Mleczny Pod Barbakanem, a staple that's been around for decades. Don't be put off by the faded exterior; this remains a popular place for lunch.

Tel Aviv VEGETARIAN €
(ul Poznańska 11; mains 10-34zł; ⊙9am-midnight; 🛜🖉) Warm, welcoming Tel Aviv offers vegetarian, vegan and gluten-free mains, including lots of salads and vegan burgers. Where this place especially excels is in its comfortable interior, where you can relax with a book or laptop.

🍷 Drinking & Nightlife

⭐**Kofi** CAFE
(ul Mińska 25; ⊙9am-5pm; 🛜) If you're weary of the weak filtered coffee of Central Europe, you'll shed a happy tear when you enter this cool cafe within the sprawling Soho Factory compound in Praga. Excellent coffee is served in an atmospheric industrial interior, enhanced by the aroma of coffee beans being roasted on the premises.

Cafe Blikle
CAFE

(ul Nowy Świat 35; ⊘9am-8pm Mon-Sat, 10am-8pm Sun; 🛜) The mere fact that Blikle has survived two world wars and the challenges of communism makes it a household name locally. But what makes this legendary cafe truly famous is its doughnuts, for which people have been queuing up for generations. Enter its cake shop via the separate entrance to the right, and find out why.

Plan B
BAR

(al Wyzwolenia 18; ⊘11am-late) Phenomenally popular, this upstairs bar on Plac Zbawiciela draws a mix of students and young office workers. Find some couch space and relax to smooth beats from regular DJs. On warm summer evenings the action spills out onto the street, giving the square the feel of a summer block party.

☆ Entertainment

Live Music

Tygmont
LIVE MUSIC

(✆22 828 3409; www.tygmont.com.pl; ul Mazowiecka 6/8; ⊘7pm-late) Hosting both local and international acts, the live music here (occasionally including jazz) is both varied and plentiful. Concerts start around 9pm; it fills up early, so either reserve a table or turn up at opening time. Dinner is also available.

Stodoła
LIVE MUSIC

(✆22 825 6031; www.stodola.pl; ul Batorego 10; ⊘9am-9pm Mon-Fri, to 2am Sat) Originally the canteen for builders of the Palace of Culture & Science, Stodoła is one of Warsaw's biggest and longest-running live music venues. A great place to catch touring bands.

WORTH A TRIP

MALBORK CASTLE

Northeast of Warsaw, along the main train line to Gdańsk, stands a show-stoppingly massive castle that merits a visit for sheer outrageousness. The Marienburg (Fortress of Mary) was built by the then-dominant Teutonic Knights and was the headquarters of their order for almost 150 years. Its vast bulk is an apt embodiment of its weighty history.

The immense castle took shape in stages. First was the so-called High Castle, the formidable central bastion that was begun around 1276. When Malbork became the capital of the order in 1309, the fortress was expanded considerably. The Middle Castle was built to the side of the high one, followed by the Lower Castle still further along. The whole complex was encircled by three rings of defensive walls and strengthened with dungeons and towers. The castle eventually spread over 21 hectares, making it the largest fortress built anywhere in the Middle Ages.

The castle was seized by the Polish army in 1457, during the Thirteen Years' War, when the military power of the knights had started to erode. Malbork then became the residence of Polish kings visiting Pomerania, but from the Swedish invasions onwards it gradually went into decline. After the First Partition in 1772, the Prussians turned it into barracks, destroying much of the decoration and dismantling sections of no military use.

Despite sustaining damage during WWII, almost the entire complex has been preserved, and the castle today looks much as it did six centuries ago, dominating the town and the surrounding countryside. The best view is from the opposite side of the river (you can get there via the footbridge), especially in the late afternoon when the brick turns an intense red-brown in the setting sun.

The entrance to the complex is from the northern side. The audio commentary takes you round 38 stops – accept the fact that you will get lost at some point. From the main gate, you walk over the drawbridge, then go through five iron-barred doors to the vast courtyard of the Middle Castle (Zamek Średni).

On the western side (to your right) is the Grand Masters' Palace (Pałac Wielkich Mistrzów), which has some splendid interiors. Alongside is the Knights' Hall (Sala Rycerska), which is the largest chamber in the castle at 450 sq metres. The remarkable ceiling has its original palm vaulting preserved. The tour proceeds to the High Castle (Zamek Wysoki), over another drawbridge and through a gate (note the ornamented 1280 doorway) to a spectacular arcaded courtyard.

Because of Malbork's position on the busy Gdańsk–Warsaw railway route, trains leave hourly through the day. The journey costs from 55 to 110zł and takes around three hours.

Performing Arts

Filharmonia Narodowa　　CLASSICAL MUSIC
(National Philharmonic; ☑ 22 551 7128; www.fil
harmonia.pl; ul Jasna 5; ⊙ box office 10am-2pm &
3-7pm Mon-Sat) Home of the world-famous
National Philharmonic Orchestra and Choir
of Poland, founded in 1901, this venue has
a concert hall (enter from ul Sienkiewicza
10) and a chamber-music hall (enter from
ul Moniuszki 5), both of which stage regular concerts. The box office entrance is on ul
Sienkiewicza.

❶ Information

Lux Med (☑ 22 332 2888; www.luxmed.pl;
Marriott Hotel Bldg, al Jerozolimskie 65/79;
⊙ 7am-8pm Mon-Fri, 8am-4pm Sat) Private
clinic with English-speaking specialist doctors
and its own ambulance service; carries out
laboratory tests and arranges house calls.
Warsaw Tourist Office (www.warsawtour.
pl; Plac Defilad 1, enter from ul Emilii Plater;
⊙ 8am-8pm May-Sep, to 6pm Oct-Apr; ☎) The
Palace of Culture & Science branch of Warsaw's
official tourist information organisation is a
central resource for maps and advice. The staff
can also help with accommodation. There's no
phone number, so visit in person or contact
via email. Also note the other helpful branches
at the airport (Terminal A; ⊙ 8am-8pm May-
Sep, to 6pm Oct-Apr) and the Old Town (Rynek
Starego Miasta 19/21; ⊙ 9am-8pm May-Sep, to
6pm Oct-Apr; ☎).

❶ Getting There & Away

AIR

The main airport, **Warsaw Frédéric Chopin
Airport** (Lotnisko Chopina Warszawa; ☑ 22
650 4220; www.lotnisko-chopina.pl; ul Żwirki
i Wigury 1), lies in the suburb of Okęcie, 10km
south of the city centre; it handles most
domestic and international flights. **Warsaw
Modlin Airport** (☑ 801 80 1880; www.modlin
airport.pl; ul Generała Wiktora Thommée 1a),
35km north of Warsaw handles some budget
carriers, including Ryanair flights to and from
the UK.

BUS

West of the city centre, **Warszawa Zachodnia bus terminal** (☑ 708 208 888; www.
dworzeconline.pl; al Jerozolimskie 144; ⊙
information & tickets 6am-9pm) handles the
majority of international and domestic routes
in and out of the city, run by various bus
operators. Bus tickets are sold at the terminal.
The private bus company **Polski Bus** (www.
polskibus.com) operates buses to cities across
Poland and beyond from the **Młociny bus**
station (Dworzec Autobusowy Młociny; ul
Kasprowicza 145) north of the city centre, and
the **Wilanowska bus station** (Dworzec Autobusowy Wilanowska; ul Puławska 145), south of
the centre.

TRAIN

Warsaw has several train stations, but the one
most travellers use is **Warszawa Centralna**
(Warsaw Central; ☑ 22 391 9757; www.pkp.pl;
al Jerozolimskie 54; ⊙ 24hr). You can travel by
rail from Warsaw to every major Polish city and
many other places in between; check the useful
online timetable in English at www.rozklad-pkp.
pl for details of times and fares.

❶ Getting Around

TO/FROM THE AIRPORT

Train Regular services run between Warsaw
Frédéric Chopin Airport and Warszawa Centralna stations every 30 minutes between
about 5am and 10.30pm (4.40zł, 20 minutes).

Bus Bus 175 (4.40zł, every 15 minutes, 5am
to 11pm) runs from the airport, passing along
ul Jerozolimskie and ul Nowy Świat before
terminating at Plac Piłsudskiego, within walking
distance of the Old Town.

From Modlin Airport the Modlin bus travels regularly between the airport and major landmarks,
such as the Palace of Culture, along three different routes (33zł, 40 minutes, twice an hour).

PUBLIC TRANSPORT

Warsaw's integrated public-transport system
is operated by **Zarząd Transportu Miejskiego**
(Urban Transport Authority; ☑ 19 115; www.ztm.
waw.pl) and consists of tram, bus and metro
lines, all using the same ticketing system. Trams
are especially handy for moving around the
city's sprawling centre.

Kraków

POP 758,000

If you believe the legends, Kraków was
founded on the defeat of a dragon, and it's
true a mythical atmosphere permeates its
attractive streets and squares. Wawel Castle is a major drawcard, while the Old Town
contains soaring churches, impressive museums and the vast Rynek Główny, Europe's
largest market square. However, there's
more to the former royal capital than history and nightlife. As you walk through the
Old Town, you'll sometimes find yourself
overwhelmed by the harmony of a quiet
back street, the 'just so' nature of the architecture and light.

CENTRAL & EASTERN EUROPE KRAKÓW

Kraków – Old Town & Wawel

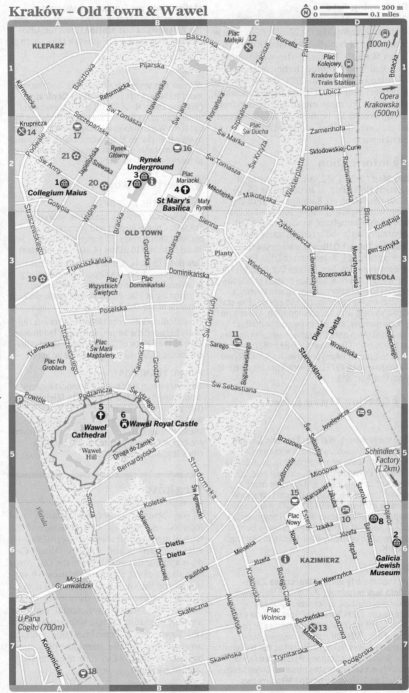

Kraków – Old Town & Wawel

◉ Sights

Wawel Hill

South of Old Town, this hilltop location is enveloped in the heady atmosphere of Polish history perhaps more than any other site in the country. Its great castle was the seat of the kings for over 500 years from the early days of the Polish state.

★ Wawel Royal Castle CASTLE
(Zamek Królewski na Wawelu; Wawel Visitor Centre 12 422 5155; www.wawel.krakow.pl; Wawel Hill; grounds admission free, attractions priced separately; grounds 6am-dusk; 6, 8, 10, 13, 18) As the political and cultural heart of Poland through the 16th century, Wawel Castle is a potent symbol of national identity. It's now a museum containing five separate sections: the Crown Treasury & Armoury; the State Rooms; the Royal Private Apartments; Lost Wawel; and the Exhibition of Oriental Art. Each requires a separate ticket. Of the five, the State Rooms and the Royal Private Apartments are most impressive.

Leonardo da Vinci's masterpiece, The Lady with an Ermine (adult/concession 10/8zł; 9.30am-5pm Tue-Fri, 10am-5pm Sat & Sun), is on display at Wawel Castle for the foreseeable future as the painting's permanent home, the Czartoryski Museum is undergoing a multiyear renovation. Along with the Mona Lisa, the 'Lady' is one of a handful of da Vinci portraits of women. The painting has had a remarkable history. It was stolen from Kraków by the Germans in WWII and was returned by the Americans after the war in 1946.

★ Wawel Cathedral CHURCH
(12 429 9515; www.katedra-wawelska.pl; Wawel 3, Wawel Hill; cathedral free, combined entry for crypts, bell tower & museum adult/concession 12/7zł; 9am-5pm Mon-Sat, from 12.30pm Sun; 6, 8, 10, 13, 18) The Royal Cathedral has witnessed many coronations, funerals and burials of Poland's monarchs and strongmen over the centuries. This is the third church on this site, consecrated in 1364. The original was founded in the 11th century by King Bolesław I Chrobry and replaced with a Romanesque construction around 1140. When that burned down in 1305, only the Crypt of St Leonard survived. Highlights include the Holy Cross Chapel, Sigismund Chapel, Sigismund Bell, and the Crypt of St Leonard and Royal Crypts.

Old Town

Kraków's atmospheric Old Town is packed with historical buildings and monuments, including several museums and many churches. It's been included on Unesco's World Heritage List since 1978, and is largely car-free.

★ St Mary's Basilica CHURCH
(Basilica of the Assumption of Our Lady; 12 422 0737; www.mariacki.com; Plac Mariacki 5, Rynek Główny; adult/concession church 10/5zł, tower 15/10zł; 11.30am-5.30pm Mon-Sat, 2-5.30pm Sun; 1, 6, 8, 13, 18) Overlooking Rynek Główny, this striking brick church, best known simply as St Mary's, is dominated by two towers of different heights. The first church here was built in the 1220s and following its destruction during a Tatar raid, construction of the basilica began. Tour

the exquisite interior, with its remarkable carved wooden altarpiece, and in summer climb the tower for excellent views. Don't miss the hourly *hejnał* (bugle call) from the taller tower.

★**Rynek Underground** MUSEUM
(☑12 426 5060; www.podziemiarynku.com; Rynek Główny 1; adult/concession 19/16zł, Tue free; ⏱10am-8pm Mon, to 4pm Tue, to 10pm Wed-Sun; ☺1, 6, 8, 13, 18) This fascinating attraction beneath the market square consists of an underground route through medieval market stalls and other long-forgotten chambers. The 'Middle Ages meets 21st century' experience is enhanced by holograms and audiovisual wizardry. Buy tickets at an office on the western side of the Cloth Hall (Sukiennice 21), where an electronic board shows tour times and tickets available.

Cloth Hall HISTORIC BUILDING
(Sukiennice; www.museum.krakow.pl; Rynek Główny 1/3; adult ☺1, 6, 8, 13, 18) FREE Dominating the middle of Rynek Główny, this building was once the centre of Kraków's medieval clothing trade. Created in the early 14th century when a roof was put over two rows of stalls, it was extended into a 108m-long Gothic structure, then rebuilt in Renaissance style after a 1555 fire; the arcades were a late-19th-century addition.

★**Collegium Maius** HISTORIC BUILDING
(☑12 663 1521; www.maius.uj.edu.pl; ul Jagiellońska 15; adult/concession 16/12zł; ⏱10am-2.20pm Mon-Fri, to 1.20pm Sat; ☺2, 13, 18, 20) The Collegium Maius, built as part of the Kraków Academy (now the Jagiellonian University), is the oldest surviving university building in Poland, and one of the best examples of 15th-century Gothic architecture in the city. It has a magnificent arcaded **courtyard** (7am to dusk) and a fascinating university collection. Visit is by guided-tour only.

⊙ **Kazimierz & Podgórze**

For much of its early history, the former mixed Jewish and Christian quarter of Kazimierz was an independent town with its own municipal charter and laws. Though the ethnic make-up of Kazimierz is now wholly different, the architecture gives hints of the past, with clearly distinguishable elements of what were Christian and Jewish areas.

Podgórze, across the river from Kazimierz, would pique few travellers' curiosities if it wasn't for the notorious role it played during WWII. It was here that the Germans herded some 16,000 Jews into a ghetto, centred around today's Plac Bohaterów Getta. Both ghetto and camp were chillingly recreated in the movie *Schindler's List*.

★**Schindler's Factory** MUSEUM
(Fabryka Schindlera; ☑12 257 0096; www.mhk. pl; ul Lipowa 4; adult/concession 21/16zł, free Mon; ⏱10am-4pm Mon, 9am-8pm Tue-Sun; ☺3, 9, 19, 24, 50) This impressive interactive museum covers the Nazi occupation of Kraków in WWII. It's housed in the former enamel factory of Oskar Schindler, the German industrialist who famously saved the lives of members of his Jewish labour force during the Holocaust. Well-organised, innovative exhibits tell the moving story of the city from 1939 to 1945.

★**Galicia Jewish Museum** MUSEUM
(☑12 421 6842; www.galiciajewishmuseum.org; ul Dajwór 18; adult/concession 15/10zł; ⏱10am-6pm; ☺3, 9, 19, 24, 50) This museum both commemorates Jewish victims of the Holocaust and celebrates the Jewish culture and history of the former Austro-Hungarian region of Galicia. It features an impressive photographic exhibition depicting modern-day remnants of southeastern Poland's once-thriving Jewish community, called 'Traces of Memory', along with video testimony of survivors and regular temporary exhibits.

Jewish Museum MUSEUM
(Old Synagogue; ☑12 422 0962; www.mhk.pl; ul Szeroka 24; adult/concession 9/7zł, free Mon; ⏱10am-2pm Mon, 9am-5pm Tue-Sun; ☺3, 9, 19, 24, 50) This museum is housed in the Old Synagogue, which dates to the 15th century. The prayer hall, complete with a reconstructed *bimah* (raised platform at the centre where the Torah is read) and the original *aron kodesh* (the niche in the eastern wall where Torah scrolls are kept), houses an exhibition of liturgical objects.

⊙ **Outside the Centre**

★**Wieliczka Salt Mine** MUSEUM
(☑12 278 7302; www.kopalnia.pl; ul Daniłowicza 10; adult/concession 79/64zł; ⏱7.30am-7.30pm Apr-Oct, 8am-5pm Nov-Mar) Some 14km southeast of Kraków, Wieliczka (vyeh-leech-kah) is famous for its deep salt mine. It's an eerie world of pits and chambers, and everything within its depths has been carved by hand from salt blocks. The mine has a labyrinth of tunnels, about 300km distributed over nine

levels, the deepest being 327m underground. A section of the mine, some 22 chambers connected by galleries, from 64m to 135m below ground, is open to the public by guided tour, and it's a fascinating trip.

★ **Kościuszko Mound**　　　MONUMENT
(Kopiec Kościuszki; ☑ 12 425 1116; www.kopiecko sciuszki.pl; Al Waszyngtona 1; adult/concession 12/10zł; ⊙ 9am-dusk; ☒ 1, 2, 6) The mound, dedicated to Polish (and American) military hero Tadeusz Kościuszko, was erected between 1820 and 1823, soon after the great man's death. The mound stands 34m high, and soil from the Polish and American battlefields where Kościuszko fought was placed here. The views over the city are spectacular. The memorial is located in the suburb of Zwierzyniec, just under 3km west of the Old Town.

🛏 Sleeping

★ **Mundo Hostel**　　　HOSTEL €
(☑ 12 422 6113; www.mundohostel.eu; ul Sarego 10; dm 60-65zł, d 170-190zł; @ 🛜; ☒ 6, 8, 10, 13, 18) Attractive, well-maintained hostel in a quiet courtyard location neatly placed between the Old Town and Kazimierz. Each room is decorated for a different country; for example, the Tibet room is decked out with colourful prayer flags. Barbecues take place in summer. There's a bright, fully equipped kitchen for do-it-yourself meals.

Good Bye Lenin Hostel　　　HOSTEL €
(☑ 12 421 2030; www.goodbyelerin.pl; ul Joselewicza 23; dm 40-55zł, d 140zł; ℙ 🛜; ☒ 3, 9, 19, 24, 50) This cheerful place has a cheeky communist theme with absurd paintings and statues mocking the imagery of the era. Most dorm rooms have four to six beds and a small garden out front is popular for lounging and barbecues. The hostel can be tricky to find. It's located in an alley to the right as you approach from ul Starowiślna.

Hotel Eden　　　HOTEL €€
(☑ 12 430 6565; www.hoteleden.pl; ul Ciemna 15; s/d 240/320zł; 🛜; ☒ 3, 9, 19, 24, 50) Located within three meticulously restored 15th-century townhouses, the Eden has comfortable rooms and comes complete with a sauna and the only *mikvah* (traditional Jewish bath) in Kraków. Kosher meals are available on request.

U Pana Cogito　　　HOTEL €€
(☑ 12 269 7200; www.pcogito.pl; ul Bałuckiego 6; s/d/q 240/290/390zł; ℙ ❄ @ 🛜; ☒ 11, 18, 22, 52) White and cream seem to be the colours of choice at this friendly 14-room hotel in a lovely mansion across the river and southwest of the centre. All rooms have big bathrooms and refrigerators, and for extra privacy, the one apartment has a separate entrance.

🍴 Eating

★ **Glonojad**　　　VEGETARIAN €
(☑ 12 346 1677; www.glonojad.com; Plac Matejki 2; mains 16-20zł; ⊙ 8am-10pm; 🛜 🗺; ☒ 2, 4, 14, 19, 20, 24) Attractive modern vegetarian restaurant with a great view onto Plac Matejki, just north of the Barbican. The diverse menu has a variety of tasty dishes including samosas, curries, potato pancakes, burritos, gnocchi and soups.

★ **Restauracja Pod Norenami**　　　ASIAN €€
(☑ 661 219 289; www.podnorenami.pl; ul Krupnicza 6; mains 18-30zł; ⊙ 10am-10pm; 🛜 🗺; ☒ 2, 4, 8, 13, 14, 18, 20, 24) This warm and inviting Asian-fusion restaurant is ideal for vegans and vegetarians. The menu pivots from Japanese to Thai and Vietnamese, with lots of spicy noodle and rice dishes, vegetarian sushi and many other choices. Breakfast (served from 10am to noon) has Middle Eastern overtones, with hummus and pita and spicy scrambled eggs. Book in advance.

★ **Marchewka z Groszkiem**　　　POLISH €€
(☑ 12 430 0795; www.marchewkazgroszkiem.pl; ul Mostowa 2; mains 20-30zł; ⊙ 9am-10pm; 🛜; ☒ 6, 8, 10, 13) Traditional Polish cooking, with hints of influence from neighbouring countries like Ukraine (beer), Hungary (wine) and Lithuania. Excellent potato pancakes and a delicious boiled beef with horseradish sauce highlight the menu.

🍷 Drinking & Nightlife

★ **Café Bunkier**　　　CAFE
(☑ 12 431 0585; http://en.bunkiercafe.pl; Plac Szczepański 3a; ⊙ 9am-late; 🛜; ☒ 2, 4, 14, 18, 20, 24) The 'Bunker' is a wonderful cafe with a positively enormous glassed-in terrace tacked onto the Bunkier Sztuki (Art Bunker), a cutting-edge gallery northwest of the Rynek. The garden space is heated in winter and seems to always have a buzz. Enter from the Planty.

★ **Café Camelot**　　　CAFE
(☑ 12 421 0123; www.camelot.pl; ul Św Tomasza 17; ⊙ 9am-midnight; ☒ 2, 4, 14, 19, 20, 24) For coffee and cake, try this genteel haven

hidden around an obscure street corner in the Old Town. Its cosy rooms are cluttered with lace-covered candle-lit tables, and a quirky collection of wooden figurines featuring spiritual or folkloric scenes.

★ **Forum Przestrzenie**   BAR
(☑514 342 939; www.forumprzestrzenie.com; ul Konopnickiej 28; ☉10am-2am; 🛜; 🚊11,18,22,52) In a highly creative re-use of a communist-era eyesore, the Hotel Forum has been repurposed as a trendy, retro coffee and cocktail bar – and occasional venue for DJs, live music and happenings.

Alchemia   CAFE
(☑12 421 2200; www.alchemia.com.pl; ul Estery 5; ☉9am-late; 🚊3, 9, 19, 24, 50) This Kazimierz venue exudes a shabby-is-the-new-cool look with rough-hewn wooden benches, candlelit tables and a companionable gloom. It hosts occasional live-music gigs and theatrical events through the week.

☆ Entertainment

★ **Harris Piano Jazz Bar**   JAZZ
(☑12 421 5741; www.harris.krakow.pl; Rynek Główny 28; ☉1pm-late; 🚊1, 6, 8, 13, 18) This active jazz haunt is housed in an atmospheric, intimate cellar space. Harris hosts jazz and blues bands most nights of the week from around 9.30pm, but try to arrive an hour earlier to get a seat (or book in advance by phone). Wednesday nights see weekly (free) jam sessions.

Piec' Art   JAZZ
(☑12 429 1602; www.piecart.pl; ul Szewska 12; performances 15-20zł; ☉noon-late; 🛜; 🚊2, 13, 18, 20) Dark and inviting, this intimate basement bar is a seductive place for a drink even when it's quiet. Several times a week, there's live acoustic jazz, which makes it all the more appealing.

Filharmonia Krakowska   CLASSICAL MUSIC
(Filharmonia im. Karola Szymanowskiego w Krakowie; ☑reservations 12 619 8722, tickets 12 619 8733; www.filharmonia.krakow.pl; ul Zwierzyniecka 1; ☉box office 10am-2pm & 3-7pm Tue-Fri; 🚊1, 2, 6) Home to one of the best orchestras in the country.

Opera Krakowska   OPERA
(☑12 296 6260; www.opera.krakow.pl; ul Lubicz 48; tickets 20-200zł; ☉10am-7pm Mon-Fri, or two hours before performances at box office; 🚊4, 10, 14, 20, 52) The Kraków Opera performs in the

strikingly modern red building at the Mogilskie roundabout.

ⓘ Information

InfoKraków – Cloth Hall (☑12 433 7310; www.infokrakow.pl; Cloth Hall, Rynek Główny 1/3; ☉9am-7pm May-Sep, to 5pm Oct-Apr; 🛜; 🚊1, 6, 8, 13, 18)
InfoKraków – Kazimierz (☑12 422 0471; www.infokrakow.pl; ul Józefa 7; ☉9am-5pm; 🚊6, 8, 10, 13)

ⓘ Getting There & Away

AIR

Kraków's **John Paul II International Airport** (KRK ; ☑information 12 295 5800; www.krakowairport.pl; Kapitana Mieczysława Medweckiego 1, Balice ; 🛜) is located in the town of Balice, about 15km west of the centre. The airport terminal hosts several car-hire desks, bank ATMs, and a branch of the InfoKraków tourist information office.

BUS

Kraków's bus station is conveniently located next to the main train station on the fringe of the Old Town. Modern **Polski Bus** (www.polskibus.com) coaches depart from here to Warsaw (five hours, several daily); check fares and book tickets online.

TRAIN

Newly remodeled and gleaming **Kraków Główny Train Station** (Dworzec Główny; ☑information 22 391 9757; www.pkp.pl; Plac Dworcowy; 🚊2, 3, 4, 10, 14, 19, 24, 52), on the northeastern outskirts of the Old Town, handles all international trains and most domestic rail services. Hourly trains make the three-hour run to Warsaw (60zł). Popular international connections include Bratislava (seven hours, one daily), Budapest (10½ hours, one daily), Lviv (7½ to 9½ hours, two daily) and Prague (10 hours, one daily).

ⓘ Getting Around

TO/FROM THE AIRPORT

Bus Public buses 292 and 208 both run from the airport to Kraków's main bus station (and back) and require a 4zł ticket.
Train Trains depart once or twice an hour between 4am and 11.30pm between the airport and Kraków Główny station. On exiting the airport terminal, take a free shuttle bus to a nearby train station for the onward journey. Buy tickets on board the train from a vending machine or the conductor (10zł). The trip takes about 20 minutes.

AUSCHWITZ-BIRKENAU MEMORIAL & MUSEUM

Auschwitz-Birkenau (Auschwitz-Birkenau Miejsce Pamięci i Muzeum; ☑ guides 33 844 8100; www.auschwitz.org; ul Więźniów Oświęcimia 20; tours adult/concession 40/30zł; ⊘ 8am-7pm Jun-Aug, to 6pm Apr-May, to 5pm Mar & Sep, to 4pm Feb & Oct, to 3pm Jan & Nov, to 2pm Dec) FREE is synonymous with genocide and the Holocaust. More than a million Jews, and many Poles and Roma, were murdered here by the German occupiers during WWII. Both sections of the camp, base camp Auschwitz I and a much larger outlying camp at Birkenau (Auschwitz II), have been preserved and are open for visitors. It's essential to visit both to appreciate the extent and horror of the place.

From April to October it's compulsory to join a tour if you arrive between 10am and 3pm; book well ahead either via www.visit.auschwitz.org, or by phoning. English-language tours leave at numerous times throughout the day, generally most frequently between 11.30am and 1.30pm, when they operate half-hourly.

The Auschwitz extermination camp was established in April 1940 by the Germans in prewar Polish army barracks on the outskirts of Oświęcim. Auschwitz was originally intended for Polish political prisoners, but the camp was then adapted for the wholesale extermination of the Jews of Europe in fulfilment of Nazi ideology. For this purpose, the much larger camp at Birkenau (Brzezinka) was built 2km west of the original site in 1941 and 1942.

The museum's visitor centre is at the entrance to the Auschwitz site. Photography and filming are permitted throughout the camp without the use of a flash or stands.

Auschwitz

Auschwitz was only partially destroyed by the fleeing Germans, and many of the original brick buildings stand to this day as a bleak testament to the camp's history. Some 13 of the 30 surviving prison blocks now house museum exhibitions – either general, or dedicated to victims from particular countries or ethnic groups that lost people at Auschwitz.

From the visitor centre in the entrance building, you enter the barbed-wire encampment through the infamous gate, displaying the grimly cynical message in German: 'Arbeit Macht Frei' (Work Brings Freedom). The sign is in fact a replica, which replaced the original when it was stolen in late 2009. Though it was recovered within a few days, it had been cut into pieces by the thieves and took 17 months to restore.

Birkenau (Auschwitz II)

It was actually at Birkenau, not Auschwitz, that most of the killing took place. Massive (175 hectares) and purpose-built for efficiency, the camp had more than 300 prison barracks – they were actually stables built for horses, but housed 300 people each. Birkenau had four huge gas chambers, complete with crematoria. Each could asphyxiate 2000 people at one time and there were electric lifts to raise the bodies to the ovens.

Though much of Birkenau was destroyed by the retreating Germans, the size of the place, fenced off with long lines of barbed wire and watchtowers stretching almost as far as your eye can see, will give you some idea of the scale of the crime; climb the tower at the entrance gate to get the full effect.

Getting There

For most tourists, the jump-off point for Oświęcim is Kraków. **Buses** (12zł, 1½ hours, hourly) can be a more convenient option than trains, as they generally drop you off in the parking lot opposite the entrance to Auschwitz. The alternative is catching a **train** from Kraków (14zł, 1½ hours, hourly) to Oświęcim train station, then walking 1.5km to the museum entrance.

PUBLIC TRANSPORT

Kraków has an efficient network of buses and trams that run between 5am and 11pm. Trams are especially handy for moving between the Old Town and Kazimierz.

Two types of individual tickets are available: short-term tickets are valid for 20 minutes and are fine for short journeys, as well as normal 40-minute tickets. Both can be used interchangeably on buses and trams. You can also buy one-/two-/three-day passes for longer stays. Buy tickets from machines located on-board vehicles (have coins ready) or from news kiosks at important stops.

Poland Survival Guide

ℹ Directory A–Z

ACCOMMODATION

Poland has a wide choice of accommodation options to suit most budgets, including hotels, pensions and guesthouses, hostels, apartment rentals and camping grounds.

➔ Warsaw is the most expensive place to stay, followed by other large cities. The further away from the big cities you go, the cheaper accommodation gets.

➔ Prices are quoted in złoty, though some larger hotels geared to foreign clients may also quote rates in euros for guests' convenience. All hotels accept złoty as payment.

➔ The most popular lodging website for Polish hotels is Booking.com. Nearly all of the more popular hotels, as well as pensions and even hostels, will have a listing on the site.

➔ Hostel accommodation is abundant in Kraków. Expect amenities like shared kitchens, laundry facilities and sometimes a lounge and bar, and free wi-fi. **Hostels.com** (www.hostels.com) maintains an updated inventory of Polish hostels.

➔ Poland has over 500 camping and bivouac sites registered at the **Polish Federation of Camping & Caravanning** (☎ 22 810 6050; www.pfcc.eu).

ℹ ACCOMMODATION PRICE RANGES

In this section we've used the following general price indicators (double room in high season):

€ less than 150zł

€€ 150zł to 400zł

€€€ more than 400zł

ℹ EATING PRICE RANGES

In this section we've used the following price indicators (for a main meal):

€ less than 20zł

€€ 20zł to 40zł

€€€ more than 40zł

MONEY

➔ The Polish currency is the złoty, abbreviated to zł and pronounced zwo-ti. It is divided into 100 groszy, which are abbreviated to gr.

➔ ATMs are ubiquitous in cities and towns, and even the smallest hamlet is likely to have at least one.

➔ Change money at banks or *kantors* (private currency-exchange offices). Find these in town centres as well as travel agencies, train stations, post offices and department stores. Rates vary, so it's best to shop around.

➔ In restaurants, tip 10% of the bill to reward good service. Leave the tip in the pouch the bill is delivered in or hand the money directly to the server.

OPENING HOURS

Most places adhere to the following hours. Museums are usually closed on Mondays, and have shorter hours outside of the high season.

Banks 9am to 4pm Monday to Friday, 9am to 1pm Saturday

Offices 9am to 5pm Monday to Friday, 9am to 1pm Saturday

Post Offices 8am to 7pm Monday to Friday, 8am to 1pm Saturday

Restaurants 11am to 10pm

Shops 8am to 6pm Monday to Friday, 10am to 2pm Saturday

PUBLIC HOLIDAYS

New Year's Day 1 January
Epiphany 6 January
Easter Sunday March or April
Easter Monday March or April
State Holiday 1 May
Constitution Day 3 May
Pentecost Sunday Seventh Sunday after Easter
Corpus Christi Ninth Thursday after Easter
Assumption Day 15 August
All Saints' Day 1 November
Independence Day 11 November
Christmas 25 and 26 December

TELEPHONE

➔ All Polish telephone numbers, landline and mobile (cell), have nine digits. Landlines are written ☑12 345 6789, with the first two numbers corresponding to the former city code. Mobile phone numbers are written ☑123 456 789.

➡ To call abroad from Poland, dial the international access code (☑00), then the country code, then the area code (minus any initial zero) and the number.

➡ To dial Poland from abroad, dial your country's international access code, then ☑48 (Poland's country code) and then the unique nine-digit local number.

➡ Poland uses the GSM 900/1800 network, which is compatible with the rest of Europe and Australia but not always with the North American GSM systems – check with your service provider.

➡ Prepaid SIM cards are readily available from telephone provider shop (GSM, Orange etc). No ID is required, and top-ups can be bought at phone shops, newspaper kiosks and even some ATMs.

WI-FI

Poland is well wired, and the majority of hotels, above a basic pension, offer some form of internet access (normally wi-fi) for you to log on with your own laptop, smartphone or tablet.

ⓘ Getting There & Away

AIR

Most international flights to Poland arrive at Warsaw's **Frédéric Chopin Airport**. Warsaw has a second, smaller airport, **Warsaw Modlin Airport**, 35km north of the city, which handles budget flights. Other important international air gateways include:

Gdańsk Lech Wałęsa Airport (☑801 066 808, 52 567 3531; www.airport.gdansk.pl; ul Słowackiego 210)

Katowice Airport (Port Lotniczy Katowice; ☑32 392 7000; www.katowice-airport.com; ul Wolności 90, Pyrzowice; 🕿)

Kraków John Paul II International Airport (p724)

LAND

EU-member Poland has open borders (and plenty of rail and road crossings) on its western and southern frontiers with Germany, the Czech Republic and Slovakia. Crossings with EU-member Lithuania, on the northeastern end of the country, are also open.

It's a different story moving east and north into Ukraine, Belarus and Russia's Kaliningrad enclave, which form part of the EU's external border and may require visas and advance planning.

ⓘ Getting Around

BUS

Poland is easily accessible by bus. Most of Poland's bus transport is operated by the former state bus company, **Państwowa Komunikacja Samochodowa** (PKS), although deregulation of the bus system has made room for dozens of private operators. One of the best private companies is **Polski Bus** (www.polskibus.com), which runs a modern fleet to big cities around the country.

TRAIN

Poland's train network is extensive and reasonably priced. Prices of Polish trains can vary greatly, even along the same lines. The **Express InterCity** trains (marked EIC) tend to be the most expensive, while trains marked **TLK** can be nearly as fast and much cheaper. Ask at ticket windows for the cheapest tickets available.

SLOVENIA

Ljubljana

POP 280,600

Slovenia's capital and largest city also happens to be one of Europe's greenest and most liveable capitals. Indeed, the European Commission awarded Ljubljana with the coveted Green Capital of Europe title for 2016. Car traffic is restricted in the centre, leaving the leafy banks of the emerald-green Ljubljanica River, which flows through the city's heart, free for pedestrians and cyclists.

◉ Sights

The easiest way to see Ljubljana is on foot. The oldest part of town, with the most important historical buildings and sights (including Ljubljana Castle) lies on the right (east) bank of the Ljubljanica River. The centre, which has the lion's share of the city's museums and galleries, is on the left (west) side of the river.

★**Ljubljana Castle** CASTLE
(Ljubljanski Grad; ☑01-306 42 93; www.ljubljanski grad.si; Grajska Planota 1; adult/child incl funicular & castle attractions €8/5, castle attractions only €6/3; ⊙castle 9am-11pm Jun-Sep, 9am-9pm Apr, May & Oct, 10am-8pm Jan-Mar & Nov, 10am-10pm Dec, castle attractions 9am-9pm Jun-Sep, to 8pm Jan-May & Oct-Nov, 10am-6pm Dec) Crowning a 375-m-high hill east of the Old Town, the castle is an architectural mishmash, but most of it dates to the early 16th century when it was largely rebuilt after a devastating earthquake. It's free to ramble around the castle grounds, but you'll have to pay to enter the Watchtower and the Chapel of St

Slovenia

George, to see the worthwhile Exhibition on Slovenian History, to visit the new Puppet Theatre and to take the Time Machine tour.

★National
& University Library ARCHITECTURE
(Narodna in Univerzitetna Knjižnica (NUK); ☎01-200 11 10; www.nuk.uni-lj.si; Turjaška ulica 1; ⊙8am-8pm Mon-Fri, 9am-2pm Sat) This library is designer Jože Plečnik's masterpiece, completed in 1941. To appreciate this great man's minimalist design philosophy, enter through the main door (note the horse-head doorknobs) on Turjaška ulica – you'll find yourself in near darkness, entombed in black marble. As you ascend the steps, you'll emerge into a colonnade suffused with light – the light of knowledge, according to the architect's plans.

Triple Bridge BRIDGE
(Tromostovje) Running south from the square to the Old Town is the much celebrated Triple Bridge. Originally called Špital (Hospital) Bridge when it built as a single span in 1842, it was nothing spectacular, but between 1929 and 1932 superstar architect Jože Plečnik added the two pedestrian side bridges, furnished all three with stone balustrades and lamps and forced a name change. Stairways on each of the side bridges lead down to the poplar-lined terraces along the Ljubljanica River.

Museum of Contemporary
History of Slovenia MUSEUM
(Muzej Novejše Zgodovine Slovenije; ☎01-300 96 10; www.muzej-nz.si; Celovška cesta 23; adult/student €3.50/2.50, 1st Sun of month free; ⊙10am-6pm Tue-Sat) This museum, housed in the 18th-century Cekin Mansion (Grad Cekinov), traces the history of Slovenia in the

20th century through multimedia and artefacts. Note the contrast between the sober earnestness of the communist-era rooms and the exuberant, logo-mad commercialism of the industrial exhibits. The sections focusing on Ljubljana under occupation during WWII are very effective.

🛏 Sleeping

Accommodation prices in Ljubljana are the highest in the country, so expect to shell out a bit more here than elsewhere. For tighter budgets, there is a growing number of high-quality modern hostels, some with private singles and doubles. The website of the Tourist Information Centre (www.visit ljubljana.com) maintains a comprehensive list of hotels and sleeping options

⭐ Hostel Vrba   HOSTEL €
(☑ 064 133 555; www.hostelvrba.si Gradaška ulica 10; dm €15-18, d €40; @🛜) Probably our favourite new budget accommodation in Ljubljana, this nine-room hostel on the Gradiščica Canal is just opposite the bars and restaurants of delightful Trnovo. There are three doubles, dorms with four to eight beds, hardwood floors and always a warm welcome. Free bikes, too, in summer.

⭐ Hostel Tresor   HOSTEL €€
(☑ 01-200 90 60; www.hostel-tresor.si; Čopova ulica 38; dm €15-24, s/d €40/70; ❄@🛜) This new 28-room hostel in the heart of Center is housed in a Secessionist-style former bank, and the money theme continues right into rooms named after currencies and financial aphorisms on the walls. Dorms have between four and 12 beds but are spacious. The communal areas (we love the atrium) are stunning; breakfast is in the vaults.

⭐ Adora Hotel   HOTEL €€
(☑ 082 057 240; www.adorahotel.si/en; Rožna ulica 7; s €68-109, d €78-119, apt €110-150; ⓟ❄@🛜) This small hotel below Gornji trg is a welcome addition to accommodation in the Old Town. The 10 rooms are small but fully equipped, with lovely hardwood floors and tasteful furnishings. The breakfast room looks out onto a small garden, bikes are free for guest use and the staff are overwhelmingly friendly and helpful.

🍴 Eating

⭐ Prince of Orange   ITALIAN €
(☑ 083 802 447; Komenskega ulica 30; dishes €4.50-9, set lunch from €7; ⏱ 7.30am-9.30pm Mon-Thu, 9.30am-midnight Fri, 10am-2pm Sat) This true find – a bright and airy cafe just above Trubarjeva cesta – serves outstanding shopmade soups and bruschetta. Ask for some of the farmer's goat cheese and about the link between the cafe and England's King William III (the pub sign on the wall is a clue).

⭐ Druga Violina   SLOVENIAN €
(☑ 082 052 506; Stari trg 21; mains €5-9, set lunch from €6; ⏱ 8am-midnight) Just opposite the Academy of Music, the 'Second Fiddle' is an extremely pleasant and affordable place for a meal in the Old Town. There are lots of very Slovenian dishes like *ajdova kaša z jurčki* (buckwheat groats with ceps) and *obara* (a thick stew of chicken and vegetables) on the menu. It's a social enterprise designed to help those with disabilities.

Ajdovo Zrno   VEGAN €
(☑ 041 832 446; www.ajdovo-zrno.si; Trubarjeva cesta 7; mains €4-6, set lunch €7.50; ⏱ 10am-7pm Mon-Fri; 🍽) 'Buckwheat Grain' serves soups, lots of different salads and baked vegetarian dishes. It also has terrific, freshly squeezed juices. Enter from Mali trg.

Julija   INTERNATIONAL €€
(☑ 01-425 64 63; http://julijarestaurant.com; Stari trg 9; mains €9-19; ⏱ noon-10pm) This is arguably the best of a trio of restaurants standing side by side on touristy Stari trg. We love the baroque decor and the three-course set lunches (€9) served on the sidewalk terrace. The cuisine here revolves around risottos and pastas, though the duck confit with polenta and sour cherries was one of the best meals this visit.

🍷 Drinking & Nightlife

Le Petit Café   CAFE
(☑ 01-251 25 75; www.lepetit.si; Trg Francoske Revolucije 4; ⏱ 7.30am-midnight; 🛜) Just opposite the Križanke, this pleasant, boho place offers great coffee and a wide range of breakfast goodies, lunches and light meals, plus an excellent restaurant on the 1st floor with a provincial-style decor and menu.

⭐ Klub Daktari   BAR
(☑ 059 055 538; www.daktari.si; Krekov trg 7; ⏱ 8am-1am Mon-Sat, 9am-midnight Sun) This rabbit-warren of a watering hole at the foot of the funicular to Ljubljana Castle is so chilled out there's practically frost on the windows. The décor is

retro-distressed, with shelves full of old books and a player piano in the corner. More of a cultural centre than a club, Daktari hosts live-music sets and an eclectic mix of other cultural events.

★**Postaja Centralna**　　COCKTAIL BAR
(Central Station; ☎059 190 400; www.central napostaja.com; Trubarjeva cesta 23; ⊗8am-1am Mon-Wed, to 3am Thu & Fri, 9am-3am Sat) This classy place tries — and largely succeeds – at being just about everything to everyone. It's

Ljubljana

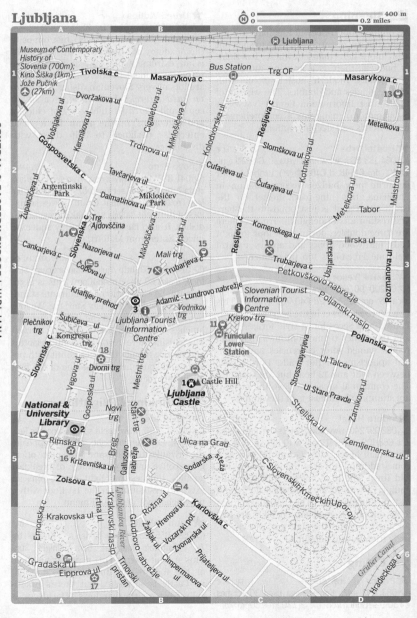

a slightly louche cocktail bar, with street-art tags on the walls and lots of dazzling neon, a club with DJs at the weekend, a cafe with its own homemade fruit teas and a restaurant with burgers.

★ **Nebotičnik** CLUB
(☐040 233 078, 040 601 787; www.neboticnik. si; 11th fl, Štefanova ulica 1; ☺10pm-3am Thu-Sat) An elegant old cafe with its breathtaking terrace atop Ljubljana's famed art-deco Skyscraper (1933), its spectacular 360-degree views attract punters throughout the day. Ljubljana's beau monde returns at night to party in the flashy club and lounge on the floor below — No 11.

Metelkova Mesto CLUB
(Metelkova Town; www.metelkovamesto.org; Masarykova cesta 24) This ex-army garrison taken over by squatters in the 1990s and converted into a free-living commune comes to life with concerts and performances generally after midnight daily in summer and on Friday and Saturday the rest of the year. While it's certainly not for the genteel, and the quality of the acts varies, there's usually a little of something for everyone.

Ljubljana

◎ **Top Sights**

☆ Entertainment

★ **Sax Pub** JAZZ
(☐040 168 804; www.saxhostelljubljana.com/sax-pub.html; Eipprova ulica 7; ☺8am-1am) More than a quarter-century in Trnovo and decorated with colourful murals and graffiti outside, the tiny and convivial Sax has live jazz as well as blues, folk and hip-hop at 8pm on Thursday year-round. Canned stuff rules at other times.

Slovenia Philharmonic Hall CLASSICAL MUSIC
(Slovenska Filharmonija; ☐01-241 08 00; www.filharmonija.si; Kongresni trg 10; ☺box office 11am-1pm & 3-6pm Mon-Fri) Home to the Slovenian Philharmonic founded in 1701, this small but very atmospheric venue in the southeast corner of Kongresni trg also stages concerts and hosts performances of the Slovenian Chamber Choir (Slovenski Komorni Zbor) founded in 1991. Haydn, Beethoven and Brahms were honorary Philharmonic members, and Gustav Mahler was resident conductor for a season (1881–82).

Križanke PERFORMING ARTS
(☐01-241 60 00, box office 01-241 60 26; www.ljubljanafestival.si; Trg Francoske Revolucije 1-2; ☺box office 10am-8pm Mon-Fri, 10am-1pm Sat Apr-Sep, noon-5pm Mon-Fri Oct-Mar, 1hr before performance) The open-air theatre seating more than 1200 spectators at this sprawling 18th-century monastery, remodelled by Plečnik in the 1950s, hosts the events of the summer Ljubljana Festival. The smaller Knights Hall (Viteška Dvorana) is the venue for chamber concerts.

ⓘ Information

Ljubljana Tourist Information Centre (TIC; ☐01-306 12 15; www.visitljubljana.com; Adamič-Lundrovo nabrežje 2; ☺8am-9pm Jun-Sep, to 7pm Oct-May) Knowledgeable and enthusiastic staff dispense information, maps and useful literature and help with accommodation. Maintains an excellent website.

Slovenian Tourist Information Centre (STIC; ☐01-306 45 76; www.slovenia.info; Krekov trg 10; ☺8am-9pm Jun-Sep, 8am-7pm Mon-Fri, 9am-5pm Sat & Sun Oct-May) Good source of information for the rest of Slovenia, with internet and bicycle rental also available.

ⓘ Getting There & Away

Ljubljana is Slovenia's main travel hub. See p737 for international arrival and departure details.

BUS

Buses to destinations both within Slovenia and abroad leave from the **bus station** (Avtobusna Postaja Ljubljana; ☎01-234 46 00; www.ap-ljubljana.si; Trg Osvobodilne Fronte 4; ⏰5am-10.30pm Mon-Sat, 5.30am-10.30pm Sun) just next to the train station. Next to the ticket windows are multilingual information phones and a touch-screen computer. There's another touch-screen computer outside too.

TRAIN

Domestic and international trains arrive at and depart from central Ljubljana's **train station** (Železniška Postaja; ☎01-291 33 32; www.slo-zeleznice.si; Trg Osvobodilne Fronte 6; ⏰5am-10pm), where you'll find a separate information centre on the way to the platforms. Buy domestic tickets from windows No 1 to 8 and international ones from either window No 9 or the information centre.

ℹ Getting Around

TO/FROM THE AIRPORT

The cheapest way to Ljubljana's **Jože Pučnik Airport**, 27km away, is by public bus (€4.10, 45 minutes) from stop No 28 at the bus station. These run at 5.20am and hourly from 6.10am to 8.10pm Monday to Friday; at the weekend there's a bus at 6.10am and then one every two hours from 9.10am to 7.10pm. Buy tickets from the driver.

Two airport-shuttle services that get consistently good reviews are **GoOpti** (☎01-320 45 30; www.goopti.com) and **Markun Shuttle** (☎041 041 792 865, 051 321 414; www.prevozi-markun.com), which will transfer you from Brnik to central Ljubljana for €9 in half an hour. Book by phone or online.

PUBLIC TRANSPORT

Ljubljana's city buses operate every five to 15 minutes from 5am (6am on Sunday) to around 10.30pm. There are also a half-dozen night buses. A flat fare of €1.20 (good for 90 minutes of unlimited travel, including transfers) is paid with a stored-value magnetic Urbana card, which can be purchased at newsstands and tourist offices.

Lake Bled & the Julian Alps

Bled

POP 10,900

Yes, it's every bit as lovely in real life. With its emerald-green lake, picture-postcard church on an islet, a medieval castle clinging to a rocky cliff and some of the highest peaks of the Julian Alps and the Karavanke as backdrops, Bled is Slovenia's most popular resort, drawing everyone from honeymooners lured by the over-the-top romantic setting to backpackers, who come for the hiking, biking, watersports and canyoning.

◉ Sights & Activities

★ Lake Bled   LAKE

(Blejsko jezero) Bled's greatest attraction is its exquisite blue-green lake, measuring just 2km by 1.4km. The lake is lovely to behold from almost any vantage point, and makes a beautiful backdrop for the 6km walk along the shore. Mild thermal springs warm the water to a swimmable 26°C (79°F) from June through August.

★ Bled Castle   CASTLE

(Blejski Grad; ☎04-572 97 82; www.blejski-grad.si; Grajska cesta 25; adult/child €9/4.50; ⏰8am-9pm mid-Jun–mid-Sep, to 8pm Apr–mid-Jun & mid-Sep–Oct, to 6pm Nov-Mar) Perched atop a steep cliff more than 100m above the lake, Bled Castle is how most people imagine a medieval fortress to be, with towers, ramparts, moats and a terrace offering magnificent views. The castle houses a **museum collection** that traces the lake's history from earliest times to the development of Bled as a resort in the 19th century.

★ Bled Island   ISLAND

(Blejski Otok; www.blejskiotok.si) Tiny, tear-shaped Bled Island beckons from the shore. There's the **Church of the Assumption** and a small **museum**, but the real thrill is the ride out by *pletna* (gondola). The *pletna* will set you down on the south side at the monumental **South Staircase** (Južno Stopnišče), built in 1655. The staircase comprises 99 steps – a local tradition is for the husband to carry his new bride up them.

★ 3glav Adventures   ADVENTURE SPORTS

(☎041 683 184; www.3glav.com; Ljubljanska cesta 1; ⏰9am-noon & 4-7pm mid-Apr–Sep) The number-one adventure-sport specialists in Bled for warm-weather activities. Its most popular trip is the Emerald River Adventure, an 11-hour hiking and swimming foray into Triglav National Park and along the Soča River that covers a huge loop from Bled over the Vršič Pass and down the Soča Valley, with optional rafting trip (see boxed text, below).

🛏 Sleeping

Camping Bled
CAMPGROUND €

(☑04-575 20 00; www.camping bled.com; Kidričeva cesta 10c; site per adult/child €13.40/9.38, glamping huts from €61; 🅿@🛜) Bled's hugely popular, amenity-laden campground is in a rural valley at the western end of the lake, about 4km from the bus station. You don't need a tent: the campground is also home to glamping possibilities: four family-sized 'mobile homes' and a dozen cute wooden A-frame huts.

★ Old Parish House
GUESTHOUSE €€

(☑070 865 738; www.blejskiotok.si/hotel; Slovenski trg 3; s/d from €50/68; 🅿🛜) In a privileged position, the Old Parish House (Stari Farovž), belonging to the Parish Church of St Martin, has been newly transformed into a simple, welcoming guesthouse, with timber beams, hardwood floors and neutral, minimalist style. Pros include car parking, lake views and waking to church bells.

Traveller's Haven
HOSTEL €

(☑041 396 545; www.travellers-haven.si; Riklijeva cesta 1; dm/d from €21/48; 🅿🛜) This is arguably the nicest of several hostels clustered on a hillside on the eastern shore of the lake, about 500m north of the centre. The setting is a renovated villa, with six rooms (including one double), a great kitchen, a low-cost laundry and bike hire.

🍴 Eating

Slaščičarna Šmon
CAFE €

(☑04-574 16 16; www.smon.si; Grajska cesta 3; kremna rezina €2.70; ⏱7.30am-10pm) Bled's culinary speciality is the delicious *kremna rezina*, also known as the *kremšnita*: it's a layer of vanilla custard topped with whipped cream and sandwiched between two layers of flaky pastry. While Šmon patisserie may not be its place of birth, it remains the best place in which to try it – retro decor and all.

Gostilna Murka
SLOVENIAN €€

(☑04-574 33 40; www.gostilna-murka.com; Riklijeva cesta 9; mains €9-19; ⏱10am-10pm Mon-Fri, noon-11pm Sat & Sun) This traditional eatery set within a large, leafy garden may at first appear a bit theme-park-ish – but the food is super-authentic (lots of old-school national dishes) and the welcome warm. Offers good-value lunch specials for around €5.

Grajska Plaža
SLOVENIAN €€

(☑031 813 886; www.grajska-plaza.com; Veslaška promenada 11; mains €8-20; ⏱9am-11pm May–mid-Oct) Even the locals say that dining at this place feels like a summer holiday. It's built on a terrace over the Castle Lido and has a relaxed vibe, helpful service and an easy all-day menu that stretches from morning coffee to end-of-day cocktails. Meal options like grilled trout or octopus salad are generous and tasty.

CLIMBING & RAFTING IN THE GREAT OUTDOORS

Bled is a popular jumping-off spot for exploring the nearby Triglav National Park and taking part in boundless adventure opportunities like climbing, canyoning and rafting.

Climbers will no doubt be tempted to scale the country's tallest peak: the 2864m-high Mt Triglav. It's a rite of passage for Slovenians and accessible to anyone who is reasonably fit and confident.

We strongly recommend hiring a guide for the ascent, even if you have some mountain-climbing experience under your belt. A local guide will know the trails and conditions.

Rafting and kayaking on the beautiful Soča River, northwest of Bled, provides all the adrenaline of a mountain climb, but has the added advantage of a cooling swim on a hot summer day. The rafting season lasts from April to October.

Rafting trips on the Soča over a distance of around 8km (1½ hours) usually cost from €35 to €40; longer trips may be possible when water levels are high. Prices include guiding, transport to/from the river, a neoprene suit, boots, life jacket, helmet and paddle. Wear a swimsuit and bring a towel.

The town of **Bovec** in the middle of the Soča Valley is the epicentre for rafting in these parts, but several agencies in Bled organise day-out-and-back excursions.

Outfitter 3glav Adventures (above) offers both climbing and rafting trips, among other outdoor pursuits. For climbing, another useful contact is the **Alpine Association of Slovenia** (PZS; ☑01-434 56 80; www.pzs.si; Dvoržakova ulica 9, Ljubljana; ⏱9am-3pm Mon & Thu, 9am-5pm Wed, 8am-1pm Fri).

Bled

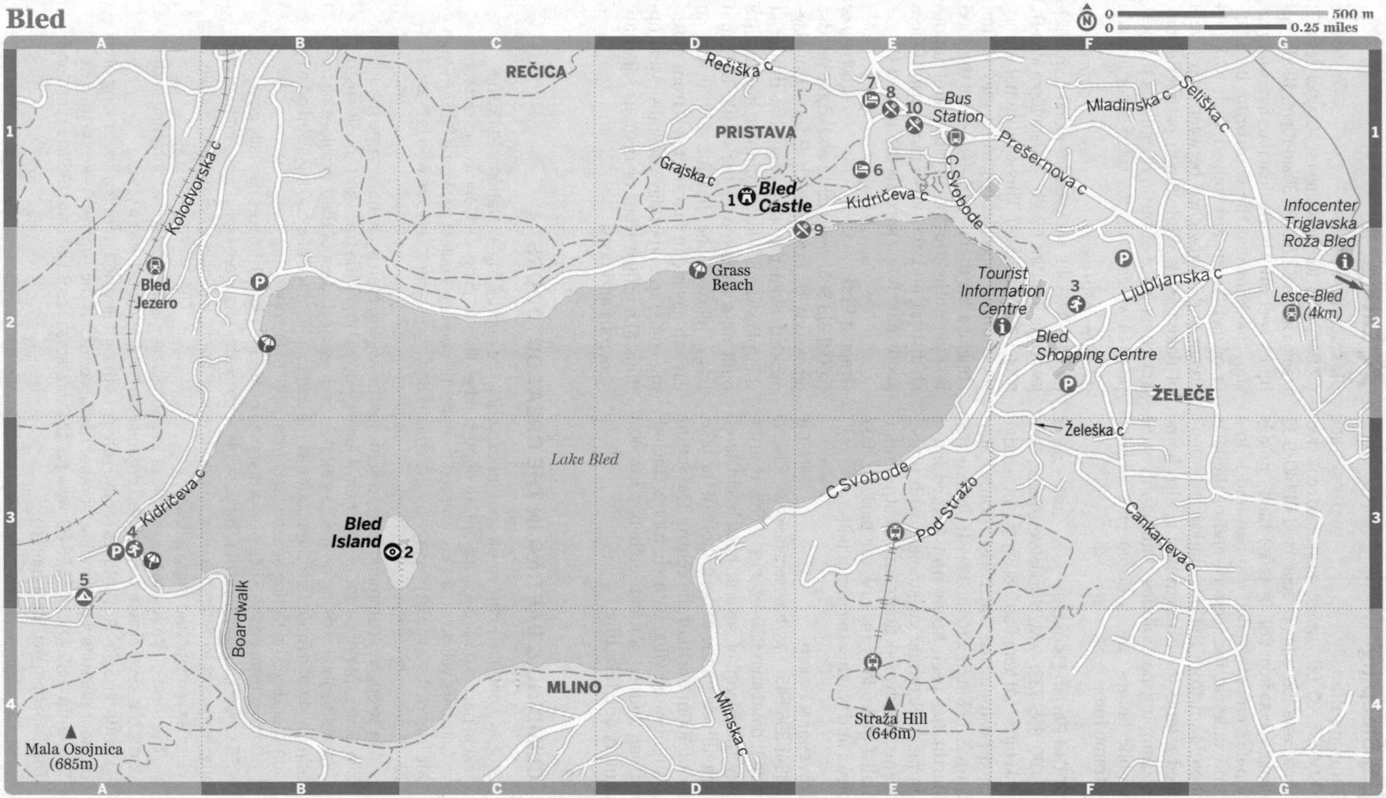

Bled Island

Lake Bled

Bled Castle

Mala Osojnica (685m)

Straža Hill (646m)

ŽELEČE

MLINO

REČICA

PRISTAVA

Infocenter Triglavska Roža Bled

Lesce-Bled (4km)

Seliška c

Mladinska c

Prešernova c

Ljubljanska c

Želeška c

Cankarjeva c

Bled Shopping Centre

Tourist Information Centre

Bus Station

C Svobode

Kidričeva c

Grajska c

Rečiška c

C Svobode

Pod Stražo

Mlinska c

Grass Beach

Kidričeva c

Kolodvorska c

Bled Jezero

Boardwalk

Mala Osojnica (685m)

Bled

◉ **Top Sights**

◆ **Activities, Courses & Tours**

◉ **Sleeping**

◉ **Eating**

ⓘ Information

Infocenter Triglavska Roža Bled (☏ 04-578 02 05; www.tnp.si; Ljubljanska cesta 27; ⊘ 8am-6pm mid-Apr–mid-Oct, to 4pm mid-Oct–mid-Apr) An excellent info centre for Bled and the entire region, with maps, guides and displays on Triglav National Park.

Tourist Information Centre (☏ 04-574 11 22; www.bled.si; Cesta Svobode 10; ⊘ 8am-9pm Mon-Sat, 9am-5pm Sun Jul & Aug, reduced hr Sep-Jun) Occupies a small office behind the Casino at Cesta Svobode 10; sells maps and souvenirs, rents bikes and has internet access.

ⓘ Getting There & Away

BUS

Bled is well connected by bus; the **bus station** (Cesta svobode 4) is a hub of activity at the lake's northeast. More than a dozen buses daily make the run to and from Ljubljana (€6.30, 80 to 90 minutes, 57km).

TRAIN

Bled has two train stations, though neither is close to the centre. The Lesce-Bled station, 4km east of Bled township on the road to Radovljica, is on the rail line to Ljubljana (€5.08 to €6.88, 40 minutes to one hour, 51km, up to 20 daily). Buses connect the station with Bled.

The Karst Region & Coast

Slovenia's astonishing diversity comes to the fore in its western coastal region. Separated by short distances, you can traipse through remarkable Unesco-recognised caves that yawn open to reveal karstic treasures, or admire the Venetian history and architectural legacy of photogenic seaside towns like Piran.

Piran

POP 4470

Picturesque Piran (Pirano in Italian), sitting pretty at the tip of a narrow peninsula, is everyone's favourite town on the Slovenian coast. Its Old Town – one of the best-preserved historical towns anywhere on the Adriatic – is a gem of Venetian Gothic architecture, but it can be a mob scene at the height of summer. In quieter times, it's hard not to fall instantly in love with the atmospheric winding alleyways, the sunsets and the seafood restaurants.

◉ Sights

★ **Tartinijev Trg**   SQUARE

The much-photographed, pastel-toned Tartinijev trg is a marble-paved square (oval-shaped, really) that was the inner harbour until it was filled in 1894. The statue of the nattily dressed gentleman in the centre is of native son, composer and violinist Giuseppe Tartini (1692–1770). To the east is the 1818 Church of St Peter. Across from the church is Tartini House, the composer's birthplace.

★ **Venetian House**   HISTORIC BUILDING

(Benečanka; Tartinijev trg 4) One of Piran's most eye-catching structures is the red mid-15th-century Gothic Venetian House, with its tracery windows and balcony, in the northeast of Tartinijev trg.

★ **Cathedral of St George**   CATHEDRAL

(Župnijska Cerkev Sv Jurija; www.zupnija-piran.si; Adamičeva ulica 2) A cobbled street leads from behind the Venetian House to Piran's hilltop cathedral, baptistery and bell tower. The cathedral was built in baroque style in the early 17th century, on the site of an earlier church from 1344. The cathedral's doors are usually open and a metal grille allows you to see some of the richly ornate and newly restored interior.

🛏 Sleeping

Prices are higher in Piran than elsewhere on the coast, and it's not a good idea to arrive without a booking in summer.

Val Hostel   HOSTEL €

(☏ 05-673 25 55; www.hostel-val.com; Gregorčičeva ulica 38a; per person €22-25; @ 🛜) Location is the winner here – this central hostel has 22 rooms (including a few singles) with shared bathrooms, and access to a kitchenette and a laundry.

WORTH A TRIP

POSTOJNA CAVE

The karst cave at **Postojna** (Postojnska Jama; ☑ 05-700 01 00; www.postojnska-jama.eu; Jamska cesta 30; adult/child €22.90/13.70; ⊙ tours hourly 9am-5pm or 6pm May-Sep, 3-4 daily 10am-3pm or 4pm Oct-Apr), one of the largest in the world, is among Slovenia's most popular attractions, and its stalagmite and stalactite formations are unequalled anywhere. It's a busy destination – the amazing thing is how the large crowds at the entrance seem to get swallowed whole by the size of the cave, and the tourist activity doesn't detract from the wonder.

The cave has been known – and visited – by residents of the area for centuries (you need only look at Passage of New Signatures inside the Vivarium Proteus). But people in the Middle Ages knew only the entrances; the inner parts were not explored until April 1818, just days before Habsburg Emperor Franz I (r 1792–1835) came to visit.

Since then more than 36 million people have visited it (with some 6000 a day in August; rainy summer days bring the biggest crowds).

Postojna is accessible by bus from Ljubljana (€6, one hour, hourly) or Piran (€8.30, 1¾ hours, four daily). It's also on a main rail line from Ljubljana (€5.80, one hour). In July and August there is a free shuttle bus from the train station to the cave entrance.

★**PachaMama** GUESTHOUSE, APARTMENT €€
(☑ 059 183 495; www.pachamama.si; Trubarjeva 8; per person €30-35; ❋ 🔊) Built by travellers for travellers, this excellent new guesthouse ('PachaMama Pleasant Stay') sits just off Tartinijev trg and offers 12 simple, fresh rooms, decorated with timber and lots of travel photography. Cool private bathrooms and a 'secret garden' add appeal.

★**Max Piran** B&B €€
(☑ 041 692 928, 05-673 34 36; www.maxpiran.com; Ul IX Korpusa 26; d €65-70; ❋ 🔊) Piran's most romantic accommodation is in a delightful, coral-coloured, 18th-century townhouse. It has just six handsome, compact rooms, each bearing a woman's name rather than a number. It's just down from the Cathedral of St George, and excellent value.

✕ Eating

One of Piran's attractions is its plethora of fish restaurants, especially along Prešernovo nabrežje.

★**Cantina Klet** SEAFOOD €
(Trg 1 Maja 10; mains €5-9; ⊙ 10am-11pm) This small wine bar sits pretty under a grapevine canopy on Trg 1 Maja. You order drinks from the bar (cheap local wine from the barrel or well-priced beers), but we especially love the self-service window (labelled 'Fritolin pri Cantini') where you order from a small blackboard menu of fishy dishes, like fish fillet with polenta, fried calamari, or fish tortilla.

Restaurant Neptune SEAFOOD €
(☑ 05-673 41 11, 041 715 890; Župančičeva ul 7; mains €8-20; ⊙ noon-4pm, 6-10pm) It's no bad thing to be more popular with locals than tourists, and this family-run place hits all the buttons – a friendly welcome, big seafood platters (as well as meat dishes and salads), and a good-value daily two-course set lunch (you might want to wrap up with mama's dessert though).

ℹ Information

Tourist Information Centre (TIC; ☑ 05-673 44 40; www.portoroz.si; Tartinijev trg 2; ⊙ 9am-10pm Jul & Aug, to 5pm Sep-Jun)

ℹ Getting There & Away

The **bus station** (Dantejeva ulica) is south of the centre. Around three buses daily make the journey to Ljubljana (€12, three hours, 140km), via Postojna.

Slovenia Survival Guide

ℹ Directory A–Z

ACCOMMODATION

Accommodation in Slovenia runs the gamut from riverside camping grounds, hostels, mountain huts, cosy *gostišča* (inns) and farmhouses, to elegant castle hotels and five-star places in Ljubljana.

➡ Accommodations tends to book up quickly in summer in Bled and along the coast, so try to reserve at least a few weeks in advance.

- Hotel rates vary seasonally, with July and August the peak season and September/October and May/June the shoulders.

- Slovenia has a growing stable of excellent hostels, especially in popular spots like Ljubljana and Bled.

- There's a *kamp* (camping ground) in virtually every corner of the country; seek out the Slovenian Tourist Board's *Camping in Slovenia* brochure. Some rent inexpensive bungalows. Camping 'rough' is illegal.

MONEY

- Slovenia uses the euro. One euro is divided into 100 cents. There are seven euro notes in denominations of €5, €10, €20, €50, €100, €200 and €500.

- Exchange cash at banks, post offices, tourist offices, travel agencies and private exchange offices.

- ATMs are ubiquitous throughout Slovenia.

- Credit cards, especially Visa, MasterCard and American Express, are widely accepted.

- When a gratuity is not included in your bill, which may or may not be the case, paying an extra 10% is customary.

OPENING HOURS

Stores 8am to 7pm Monday to Friday, to 1pm Saturday

Restaurants 11am to 10pm

Banks 9am to 5pm Monday to Friday (lunch break 12.30pm to 2pm)

Museums 10am to 6pm Tuesday to Sunday, shorter hours in winter

PUBLIC HOLIDAYS

New Year 1 and 2 January

Prešeren Day (Slovenian Culture Day) 8 February

Easter & Easter Monday March/April

Insurrection Day 27 April

Labour Day holidays 1 and 2 May

National Day 25 June

Assumption Day 15 August

Reformation Day 31 October

ℹ️ EATING PRICE RANGES

The following price ranges refer to a two-course, sit-down meal, including a drink, for one person. Many restaurants also offer an excellent-value set menu of two or even three courses at lunch.

€ less than €15

€€ €16 to 30

€€€ more than €30

ℹ️ ACCOMMODATION PRICE RANGES

The following price ranges refer to a double room with en suite toilet and bath or shower, and include tax and breakfast.

€ less than €50

€€ €51 to 100

€€€ more than €100

All Saints' Day 1 November

Christmas Day 25 December

Independence Day 26 December

TELEPHONES

- There are six area codes in Slovenia (☎ 01 to ☎ 05 and ☎ 07).

- Public telephones require a *telefonska kartica* or *telekartica* (telephone card) available at post offices and some newsstands.

- To call Slovenia from abroad, dial the international access code, ☎ 386 (the country code for Slovenia), the area code (minus the initial zero) and the number.

- To call abroad from Slovenia, dial ☎ 00 followed by the country and area codes and then the number. Numbers beginning with ☎ 80 are toll-free.

- Slovenia uses GSM 900, which is compatible with the rest of Europe and Australia but not with the North American GSM 1900 or the Japanese system.

- Local SIM cards are available from providers SiMobil, Telekom Slovenija and Telemach.

WI-FI

Virtually every hotel and hostel in the land offers wi-fi for guests' use, usually for free.

ℹ️ Getting There & Away

AIR

Slovenia's main international airport receiving regular scheduled flights is Ljubljana's **Jože Pučnik Airport** (Aerodrom Ljubljana; ☎ 04-206 19 81; www.lju-airport.si/eng; Zgornji Brnik 130a, Brnik), 27km north of Ljubljana. In the arrivals hall there's a Slovenia Tourist Information Centre desk, several travel agencies and ATMs.

From its base at Brnik, the Slovenian flag-carrier, **Adria Airways** (☎ 01-369 10 10, 04-259 45 82; www.adria-airways.com), serves more than 20 European destinations on regularly scheduled flights.

LAND

Slovenia is well connected by road and rail with its four neighbours: Italy, Austria, Hungary and

Croatia. Bus and train timetables sometimes use Slovenian names for foreign cities.

Bus Most international buses arrive and depart from Ljubljana's bus station.

Train The **Slovenian Railways** (Slovenske Železnice, SŽ; ☑ 01-291 33 32; www.slo-zeleznice.si) network links up with the European railway network via Austria, Germany, Czech Republic, Croatia, Hungary (Budapest), Switzerland (Zürich) and Serbia (Belgrade).

❶ Getting Around

Bus Generally efficient and good value but can be very crowded on Friday afternoons. Buy your ticket at the *avtobusna postaja* (bus station) or simply pay the driver as you board.

Train Cheaper but usually slower than buses (with the exception of intercity high-speed services). Getting from A to B often requires returning to Ljubljana.

HUNGARY

Budapest

POP 1.75 MILLION

Straddling the Danube River, with the Buda Hills to the west and sprawling Pest to the east, Budapest is a dazzling city. Its beauty is not all God given; humankind has played a role in shaping this pretty face too. Architecturally, the city is a treasure trove, with enough baroque, neoclassical, Eclectic and Art Nouveau (or Secessionist) buildings to satisfy everyone.

◉ Sights

◉ Buda Hills

The hilly terrain lining the Danube's western bank is home to Castle Hill (Várhegy). This is the nerve centre of Budapest's history and the area is packed with many of the capital's most important museums and other attractions.

Royal Palace   PALACE
(Királyi Palota; I Szent György tér; ☐ 16, 16A, 116) The former Royal Palace has been razed and rebuilt at least half a dozen times over the past seven centuries. Béla IV established a royal residence here in the mid-13th century, and subsequent kings added to the structure. The palace was levelled in the battle to rout the Turks in 1686; the Habsburgs rebuilt it but spent very little time here. To-

day the Royal Palace contains two important museums as well as the National Széchenyi Library.

Hungarian National Gallery   GALLERY
(Nemzeti Galéria; ☑ 1-201 9082; www.mng.hu; I Szent György tér 2, Bldgs A-D; adult/concession 1800/900Ft, audio guide 1000Ft; ◉ 10am-6pm Tue-Sun; ☐ 16, 16A, 116) The Hungarian National Gallery is an overwhelming collection spread across four floors that traces Hungarian art from the 11th century to the present. The largest collections include medieval and Renaissance stonework, Gothic wooden sculptures and panel paintings, late Gothic winged altars, and late Renaissance and baroque art.

Matthias Church   CHURCH
(Mátyás templom; ☑ 1-355 5657; www.matyas-templom.hu; I Szentháromság tér 2; adult/concession 1500/1000Ft; ◉ 9am-5pm Mon-Sat, 1-5pm Sun; ☐ 16, 16A, 116) Parts of Matthias Church date back 500 years, notably the carvings above the southern entrance. But basically Matthias Church (so named because King Matthias Corvinus married Beatrix here in 1474) is a neo-Gothic confection designed by the architect Frigyes Schulek in 1896.

Fishermen's Bastion   MONUMENT
(Halászbástya; I Szentháromság tér; adult/concession 700/500Ft; ◉ 9am-11pm mid-Mar–mid-Oct; ☐ 16, 16A, 116) The bastion is a neo-Gothic masquerade that looks medieval and offers among the best views in Budapest. Built as a viewing platform in 1905 by Frigyes Schulek, the architect behind Matthias Church, the bastion's name was taken from the medieval guild of fishermen responsible for defending this stretch of the castle wall. The seven gleaming white turrets represent the Magyar tribes that entered the Carpathian Basin in the late 9th century.

★ Memento Park   HISTORIC SITE
(☑ 1-424 7500; www.mementopark.hu; XXII Balatoni út 16; adult/student 1500/1000Ft; ◉ 10am-dusk; ☐ 150) Home to more than 40 statues, busts and plaques of Lenin, Marx, Béla Kun and others whose likenesses have ended up on trash heaps elsewhere in the former-socialist world, Memento Park, 10km southwest of the city centre, is truly a mind-blowing place to visit. Ogle the socialist realism and try to imagine that at least four of these relics were erected as recently as the late 1980s; a few of them, including a memorial of Béla Kun in a crowd by

fence-sitting sculptor Imre Varga were still in place when one of us moved to Budapest in early 1992.

Citadella
FORT

(🖵27) FREE The Citadella is a fortress that never saw a battle. Built by the Habsburgs after the 1848–49 War of Independence to defend the city from further insurrection, the structure was obsolete by the time it was ready in 1851 because the political climate had changed.

⊙ Pest

The flat eastern bank of the Danube is where you begin to appreciate Budapest's size and urban character. You'll probably spend the bulk of your time here, which takes in the former Jewish quarter as well as high-heeled Andrássy út, the long, dramatic and très chic boulevard that slices through the area.

★ Great Synagogue
SYNAGOGUE

(Nagy zsinagóga; www.greatsynagogue.hu; VII Dohány utca 2; adult/student & child incl museum 3000/2000Ft; ☺10am-5.30pm Sun-Thu, to 4.30pm Fri Apr-Oct, reduced hours Nov-Mar; Ⓜ M2 Astoria) Budapest's stunning Great Synagogue is the largest Jewish house of worship in the world outside New York City. Built in 1859, the synagogue has both Romantic and Moorish architectural elements. Inside, the Hungarian Jewish Museum contains objects relating to religious and everyday life, as well as the Holocaust Memorial Room, which relates the events of 1944–45. On the synagogue's north side, the Holocaust Memorial presides over the mass graves of those murdered by the Nazis.

Hungarian State Opera House
NOTABLE BUILDING

(Magyar Állami Operaház; www.operavisit.hu; VI Andrássy út 22; tours adult/concession 2900/1900Ft; ☺tours 3pm & 4pm; 🔹; Ⓜ M1 Opera) The neo-Renaissance Hungarian State Opera House was designed by Miklós Ybl in 1884 and is among the city's most beautiful buildings. Its facade is decorated with statues of muses and opera greats such as Puccini and Mozart, while its interior dazzles with marble columns, gilded vaulted ceilings and chandeliers, and superb acoustics. If you cannot attend a performance, join one of the tours. Tickets are available from the souvenir shop inside to the left.

House of Terror
MUSEUM

(Terror Háza; www.terrorhaza.hu; VI Andrássy út 60; adult/concession 2000/1000Ft; ☺10am-6pm Tue-Sun; Ⓜ M1 Oktogon) The headquarters of the dreaded secret police have been turned into the striking House of Terror, an engrossing and evocative museum focusing on the crimes and atrocities of Hungary's fas-

CENTRAL & EASTERN EUROPE BUDAPEST

DON'T MISS

IN HOT WATER

Hungarians have been 'taking the waters' supplied by an estimated 300 thermal springs since togas were all the rage, and the practice really got a boost during the centuries-long Ottoman occupation (some baths retain their original Turkish appearance).

Gellért Baths (Gellért gyógyfürdő; ☎1-466 6166; www.gellertbath.hu; XI Kelenhegyi út 4, Danubius Hotel Gellért; weekdays/weekends incl locker 5100/5300Ft, cabin 5500/5700Ft; ☺6am-8pm; 🚋7, 86, Ⓜ M4 Szent Gellért tér, 🚋18, 19, 47, 49) Soaking in the Art Nouveau Gellért Baths, open to both men and women in mixed sections, has been likened to taking a bath in a cathedral.

Széchenyi Baths (Széchenyi Gyógyfürdő; ☎1-363 3210; www.szechenyibath.hu; XIV Állatkerti körút 9-11; ticket incl locker/cabin Mon-Fri 4700/4900Ft, Sat & Sun 4900/5400Ft; ☺6am-10pm; Ⓜ M1 Széchenyi fürdő) At the northern end of City Park, the Széchenyi Baths is unusual for three reasons: its immense size (with 15 indoor pools and three outdoor); its bright, clean atmosphere; and its water temperatures (up to 38°C), which really are what the wall plaques say they are.

Király Baths (Király Gyógyfürdő; ☎1-202 3688; www.spasbudapest.com; II Fő utca 84; daily ticket incl cabin 2700Ft; ☺9am-9pm; 🚋86, 🚋4, 6) The four pools here, with water temperatures of between 26°C and 40°C, are genuine Turkish baths erected in 1570 and have a wonderful skylit central dome. The Király is open to both men and women every day of opening, so pack a swimsuit.

Buda

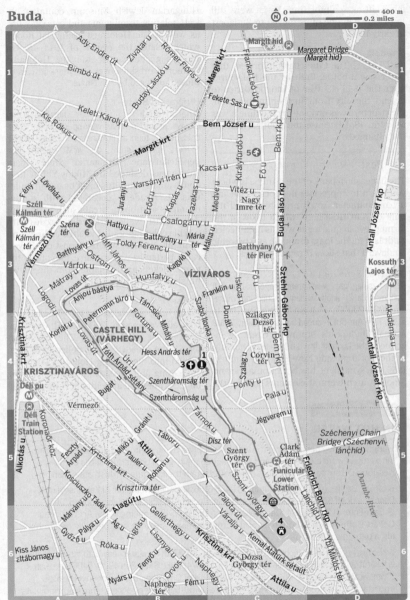

cist and Stalinist regimes. The years leading up to the 1956 Uprising get the lion's share of the exhibition space. The reconstructed prison cells in the basement and the Perpetrators' Gallery, featuring photographs of the turncoats, spies and torturers, are chilling.

Parliament   HISTORIC BUILDING

(Országház; ☎1-441 4904; www.parlament.hu; V Kossuth Lajos tér 1-3; adult/student EU citizen 2200/1200Ft; non-EU citizen 5400/2800Ft; ☉8am-6pm Mon-Fri, to 4pm Sat & Sun Apr-Oct, 8am-4pm daily Nov-Mar; Ⓜ M2 Kossuth Lajos tér)

Buda

The Eclectic-style Parliament, designed by Imre Steindl and completed in 1902, has 691 sumptuously decorated rooms, but you'll only get to see several on a guided tour of the North Wing: the main staircase and landing; the Domed Hall, where the **Crown of St Stephen**, the nation's most important national icon, is on display; the Loge Hall; and the Congress Hall, where the House of Lords of the one-time bicameral assembly sat until 1944.

Basilica of St Stephen   CHURCH
(Szent István Bazilika; ☑ 06 30 703 6599; www.basilica.hu; V Szent István tér; requested donation 200Ft; ☺ 9am-5pm Apr-Sep, 10am-4pm Oct-Mar; Ⓜ M2 Arany János utca) Budapest's neoclassical cathedral was built over half a century and completed in 1905. Much of the interruption had to do with a fiasco in 1868 when the dome collapsed during a storm, and the structure had to be demolished and then rebuilt from the ground up. The basilica is rather dark and gloomy inside, but take a trip to the top of the dome for incredible views.

Heroes' Square   SQUARE
(Hősök tere; ☐ 105. Ⓜ M1 Hősök tere) This public space holds a sprawling monument constructed to honour the millennial anniversary (in 1896) of the Magyar conquest of the Carpathian Basin.

🛏 Sleeping

Accommodation in Budapest runs the gamut from hostels in converted flats and private rooms in far-flung housing estates to luxury guesthouses in the Buda Hills and five-star properties. The booking site **Hostelworld** (www.hostelworld.com) maintains a good list of Budapest hostels.

Wombat's   HOSTEL €
(☑ 1-883 5005; www.wombats-hostels.com; Király utca 20; dm €16-20, d €29; ☏; Ⓜ M1/2/3 Deák Ferenc tér) Well located for Erzsébetváros nightlife – it's directly opposite buzzing Gozsdu udvar – this slick and well-equipped hostel can accommodate a whopping 465 guests in its 120 rooms. Choose from four- to eight-bed dorms or doubles, all of which are en suite. There's a clean, cool design throughout and a large common area set in a colourful glass-roofed atrium.

Carpe Noctem   HOSTEL €
(☑ 06 70 670 0384; www.budapestpartyhostels.com; VI Szobi utca 5; dm 5400Ft; @☏; Ⓜ M3 Nyugati pályaudvar, ☐ 4, 6) Part of the Budapest Party Hostels chain, this relaxed place offers a smaller, more laidback option than its sister establishments. With just three rooms of six- to eight-bed dorms, it has an intimate, easygoing atmosphere. It's right at the top of an apartment block – so expect quite a hike with your bags.

Central Backpack King Hostel   HOSTEL €
(☑ 06 30 667 9669; www.centralbackpackking.hostel.com; V Október 6 utca 15; dm €12-18, d €45-52; @☏; ☐ 15, 115, Ⓜ M3 Arany János utca) This upbeat place in the heart of the Inner Town has dorm rooms with seven or eight beds on one floor and doubles, triples and quads on another. There's a small but scrupulously clean kitchen, a large, bright common room, and views across Október 6 utca.

★ **Kapital Inn**   B&B €€
(☑ 06 30 915 2029; www.kapitalinn.com; VI Aradi utca 30, 4th fl; r €89-125, ste €199; ☕✳@☏☒; Ⓜ M1 Vörösmaty utca) Stylishly decorated and well-run B&B with just four luxurious rooms and a two-bed suite on the fourth floor of a beautiful 1893 building. The sleek, recently revamped breakfast room has a fridge stocked with goodies that can be raided at any time, and the 56-sq-metre terrace is a great place to take breakfast or just relax in the sun.

✖ Eating

The dining scene in Budapest has undergone a sea change in recent years. Hungarian food has 'lightened up', offering the same wonderfully earthy and spicy tastes but in less calorific dishes.

Nagyi Palacsintázója   HUNGARIAN €
(Granny's Crepe Place; www.nagyipali.hu; I Hattyú utca 16; pancakes 190-680Ft, set menus

Central Pest

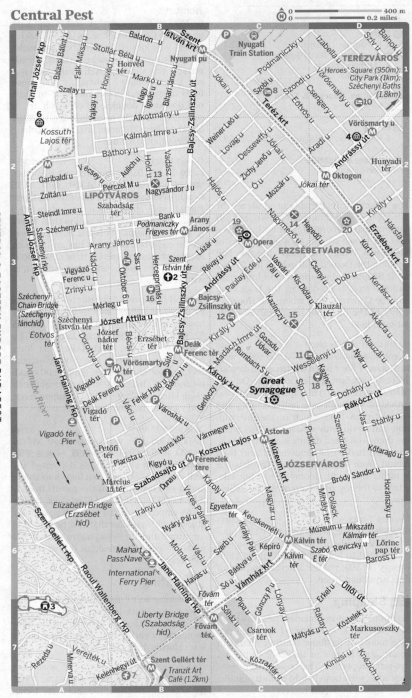

0   400 m
0   0.2 miles

TERÉZVÁROS

Nyugati
Train Station

Heroes' Square (950m);
City Park (1km);
Széchenyi Baths
(1.8km)

ERZSÉBETVÁROS

Opera

Oktogon

Andrássy út

LIPÓTVÁROS

Kossuth
Lajos tér

Szent
István tér

Deák
Ferenc tér

JÓZSEFVÁROS

Great
Synagogue

Astoria

Vörösmarty
tér

Ferenciek
tere

Kossuth Lajos u

Kálvin tér

Danube River

Széchenyi
Chain Bridge
(Széchenyi
lánchíd)

Elizabeth Bridge
(Erzsébet
híd)

Mahart
PassNave
International
Ferry Pier

Liberty Bridge
(Szabadság
híd)

Vigadó tér
Pier

Szent Gellért tér
Tranzit Art
Café (1.2km)

1090-1190Ft; ⊘24hr; ☑; Ⓜ M2 Széll Kálmán tér) This small eatery serves Hungarian pancakes – both savoury and sweet – round the clock and is always packed.

★**Klassz** INTERNATIONAL €€
(www.klasszetterem.hu; VI Andrássy út 41; mains 1890-5490Ft; ⊘11.30am-11pm; Ⓜ M1 Oktogon) Owned by the local wine society, Klassz is mostly about wine – Hungarian, to be precise – and here you can order by the 10cL measure from an ever-changing list of up to four dozen wines to sip and compare.

★**Kispiac** HUNGARIAN €€
(☑1-269 4231; www.kispiac.eu; V Hold utca 13; mains 1950-3500Ft; ⊘noon-10pm Mon-Sat; Ⓜ M3 Arany János utca) This hole-in-the-wall retro-style restaurant next to the Hold utca market serves *seriously* Hungarian things like stuffed *csülök* (pig's trotter – and way better than it sounds), roast *malac* (piglet) and an infinite variety of *savanyúság* (sour pickled vegetables).

Central Pest

◎ Top Sights

★**Macesz Bistro** JEWISH, HUNGARIAN €€
(☑1-787 6164; http://maceszbistro.hu; VII Dob utca 26; mains 1990-5190Ft; ⊘noon-4pm, 6-11pm Sun-Thurs, till midnight Fri-Sat) A wonderful marriage of modern and traditional, the Macesz Huszár serves up Hungarian Jewish dishes in a swish bistro-style dining room, handsomely dressed up with lace tablecloths, flock wallpaper and rocking horses. The Jewish-style eggs and matzo-ball soup are standout starters.

🍷 Drinking & Nightlife

In recent years Budapest has gained a reputation as one of Europe's top nightlife destinations. Alongside its age-old cafe culture, it offers a magical blend of unique drinking holes, fantastic wine, homegrown fire waters and emerging craft beers.

★**Bambi Presszó** CAFE
(☑1-213 3171; www.facebook.com/bambiesz presszo; II Frankel Leó út 2-4; ⊘7am-10pm Mon-Fri, 9am-10pm Sat & Sun; ☐86) The words 'Bambi' and 'modern' do not make comfortable bedfellows; nothing about this place (named after a communist-era local soft drink) has changed since the 1960s. And that's just the way the crowd here likes it. Friendly, though set-it-down-with-a-crash service completes the picture.

Tranzit Art Café CAFE
(☑1-209 3070; www.tranzitcafe.com; XI Bukarest utca & Ulászló utca; ⊘9am-11pm Mon-Fri, 10am-10pm Sat; ☐7, ☐19, 49) As chilled a place to drink and nosh as you'll find in south Buda, the Tranzit made its home in a small disused bus station, put art on the walls and filled the leafy courtyard with hammocks and comfy sofas. Breakfast and sandwiches are available, and two-course lunches (including a veggie one) can be had for 1200Ft during the week.

Gerbeaud CAFE
(☑1-429 9001; www.gerbeaud.hu; V Vörösmarty tér 7; ⊘9am-9pm; Ⓜ M1 Vörösmarty tér) Founded on the northern side of Pest's busiest square in 1858, Gerbeaud has been the most fashionable meeting place for the city's elite since 1870. Along with exquisitely prepared cakes and pastries, it serves continental/full breakfast and sandwiches. A visit here is mandatory.

LOCAL KNOWLEDGE

EAT, DRINK & BE MAGYAR

There is a lot more to Hungarian food than goulash and it remains one of the most sophisticated styles of cooking in Europe. Magyars even go so far as to say there are three essential world cuisines: French, Chinese and their own.

That may be a bit of an exaggeration but Hungary's reputation as a food centre dates largely from the late 19th century and the first half of the 20th and, despite a fallow period during the chilly days of communism, is once again commanding attention. So too are the nation's world-renowned wines.

★ **DiVino Borbár**   WINE BAR
(☑ 06 70 935 3980; www.divinoborbar.hu; V Szent István tér 3; ☺ 4pm-midnight Sun-Wed, to 2am Thu-Sat; Ⓜ M1 Bajcsy-Zsilinszky út) Central and always heaving, DiVino is Budapest's most popular wine bar and the crowds spilling out into the square in front of the basilica will immediately tell you that. Choose from 120 types of wine produced by some 30 winemakers under the age of 35 at the bar, but be careful: those 0.1L glasses go down quickly.

Szimpla Kert   RUIN PUB
(www.szimpla.hu; VII Kazinczy utca 14; ☺ noon-3am; Ⓜ M2 Astoria) Budapest's first *romkocsma* (ruin pub), Szimpla Kert is firmly on the drinking-tourists' trail (you can even buy a T-shirt) but remains a landmark place for a drink. It's a huge building with nooks filled with bric-a-brac, grafitti, art and all manner of unexpected items. Sit in an old Trabant, watch open-air cinema, down shots or join in an acoustic jam session.

☆ Entertainment

Hungarian State Opera House   OPERA
(Magyar Állami Operaház; ☑ box office 1-353 0170; www.opera.hu; VI Andrássy út 22; ☺ box office 11am-5pm, from 4pm Sun; Ⓜ M1 Opera) The gorgeous neo-Renaissance opera house is worth a visit as much to admire the incredibly rich decoration inside as to view a performance and hear the perfect acoustics.

Liszt Academy   CLASSICAL MUSIC
(Liszt Zeneakadémia; ☑ 1-321 0690; www.zeneakademia.hu; VI Liszt Ferenc tér 8; ☺ ticket office 11am-6pm; Ⓜ M1 Oktogon) Budapest's most

important concert hall has emerged from extensive renovations and is looking more fantastic than ever. Performances are usually booked up at least a week in advance, but (expensive) last-minute tickets can sometimes be available – it's always worth checking.

ⓘ Information

Budapest Info (www.budapestinfo.hu; V Sütő utca 2; ☺ 8am-8pm; Ⓜ M1/M2/M3 Deák Ferenc tér) Centrally located tourist office, but often hopelessly crowded in summer. There are also tourist desks in the arrivals sections of Ferenc Liszt International Airport, terminals 2A and 2B.

ⓘ Getting There & Away

Most people arrive in Budapest by air, but you can also get here from dozens of European cities by bus and train. See p747 for international arrival and departure details.

AIR

Budapest's **Ferenc Liszt International Airport** (☑ 1-296 7000; www.bud.hu) has two modern terminals side by side, 2A and 2B, 24km southeast of the city centre.

BUS

Volánbusz (☑ 1-382 0888; www.volanbusz.hu), the national bus line, has an extensive list of destinations from Budapest. All international buses and domestic ones to/from western Hungary arrive at and depart from Népliget bus station in Pest.

TRAIN

Magyar Államvasutak (MÁV, Hungarian State Railways; ☑ 06-40 49 49 49, from abroad +36-1 444 4499; www.mav.hu) links up with the European rail network in all directions. Most international trains (and domestic traffic to/from the north and northeast) arrive at the train station **Keleti pályaudvar**.

ⓘ Getting Around

TO/FROM THE AIRPORT

MiniBUD (☑ 1-550 0000; www.minibud.hu; one way from 1900Ft) is the airports official bus shuttle service and runs regularly from the airport to the center and back. Order tickets by telephone or from the service website. There are MiniBUD information counters in the arrivals terminals.

The cheapest way to get into the city centre from the airport is to take bus 200E – look for the stop on the footpath between terminals 2A and 2B – which terminates at the Kőbánya-

Kispest metro station. From there take the M3 metro into the city centre.

PUBLIC TRANSPORT

Public transport is run by **BKK** (Budapesti Közlekedési Központ, Centre for Budapest Transport; ☑1-258 4636; www.bkk.hu). Travel passes valid for one day to one month are valid on all trams, buses, trolleybuses, HÉV (within city limits) and metro lines. Public transport runs generally from 4.30am to about 11.30pm.

The basic fare for all forms of transport is 350Ft (3000Ft for a block of 10), allowing you to travel as far as you like on the same metro, bus, trolleybus or tram line without changing/transferring. A 'transfer ticket' allowing unlimited stations with one change within one hour costs 530Ft.

Northeastern Hungary

Hungary is mainly flat, though here in the northeastern part of the country, the foothills of the Carpathians begin. The region is known for its forested hiking trails, traditional folk culture and hilltop castle ruins. It's also know for its superb wine. The region capital of Eger makes for an excellent base to explore and taste the grape.

Eger

POP 56,500

Blessed with beautifully preserved baroque architecture, Eger is a jewellery box of a town with loads to see and do. Explore the bloody history of Turkish occupation and defeat at the hilltop castle, climb an original Ottoman minaret, and then spend time traipsing from cellar to cellar in the Valley of Beautiful Women, tasting the celebrated Eger Bull's Blood (Egri Bikavér) and other local wines.

⊙ Sights & Activities

★ Eger Castle   FORTRESS

(Egri Vár; ☑36-312 744; www.egrivar.hu; Vár köz 1; castle grounds adult/child 800/400Ft, incl museum 1400/700Ft; ⊙ exhibits 10am-5pm Tue-Sun May-Oct, 10am-4pm Tue-Sun Nov-Apr, castle grounds 8am-8pm May-Aug, to 7pm Apr & Sep, to 6pm Mar & Oct, to 5pm Nov-Feb) Climb up cobbled Vár köz from Dózsa György tér to reach Eger Castle, erected in the 13th century after the Mongol invasion. Models and drawings in the **István Dobó Museum**, housed in the former Bishop's Palace (1470), painlessly explain the history of the castle. The **Eger Art Gallery**

LAKE BALATON

Extending roughly 80km like a skinny, lopsided paprika, at first glance Lake Balaton, to the southwest of Budapest, seems to simply be a happy, sunny expanse of tourmaline-coloured water to play in. But step beyond the beaches of Europe's biggest and shallowest body of water and you'll encounter the vine-filled forested hills, a national park and a wild peninsula jutting out 4km, nearly cutting the lake in half.

High season in Lake Balaton is July and August; crowds descend and prices skyrocket. If you're keen to enjoy the water activities but don't want the crowds, try to visit in June or September – the water is still warm (versus a bathtub-like 28 to 29 degrees in the heat of summer), everything is still open and it feels summery.

Regular trains to Lake Balaton (four hours, six daily) usually leave from Déli or Kelenföld train stations in Budapest, and buses (three hours, seven daily) from Népliget bus station.

on the northwestern side of the courtyard has works by Canaletto and Ceruti. Beneath the castle are **casemates** hewn from solid rock, which can be visited.

Minaret   ISLAMIC

(☑06 70 202 4353; www.minareteger.hu; Knézich Károly utca; admission 300Ft; ⊙10am-6pm daily Apr-Sep, 10am-5pm daily Oct, 10am-3pm Sat & Sun Nov-Mar) This 40m-high minaret, topped incongruously with a cross, is one of the few reminders of the Ottoman occupation of Eger. Nonclaustrophobes can brave the 97 narrow spiral steps to the top for the awesome views.

★ Valley of the
Beautiful Women   WINE TASTING

(Szépasszony-völgy) Wine tasting is popular in the wine cellars of this evocatively named valley. Try ruby-red Bull's Blood or any of the whites: Leányka, Olaszrizling and Hárslevelű from nearby Debrő. The choice of wine cellars can be a bit daunting so walk around and have a look yourself. The valley is a little over 1km southwest across Rte 25 and off Király utca.

🛏 Sleeping

Agria Retur Vendégház GUESTHOUSE €
(☏36-416 650; www.returvendeghaz.hu; Knézich Károly utca 18; s/d/tr 3800/6400/9300Ft; 📶)
You couldn't find sweeter hosts than the daughter and mother who own this guesthouse near the minaret. Walking up three flights of stairs, you enter a cheery communal kitchen/eating area central to four mansard rooms with fridge. Out the back is a huge garden with tables and a barbecue at your disposal.

Dobó Vendégház GUESTHOUSE €€
(☏36-421 407; www.dobovendeghaz.hu; Dobó István utca 19; s 9000-10,500Ft, d 13,500-15,900Ft; 📶) Tucked away along one of the old town's pedestrian streets, just below Eger Castle, this lovely little hotel has seven spic-and-span rooms, some with balconies. Check out the museum-quality Zsolnay porcelain collection in the breakfast room.

🍴 Eating

Palacsintavár CREPERIE €
(Pancake Castle; ☏36-413 980; www.palacsintavar.hu; Dobó István utca 9; mains 1850-2250Ft; ⊙noon-11pm Tue-Sat, to 10pm Sun) Pop art and a fascinating collection of antique cigarettes still in their packets line the walls in this eclectic eatery. Savoury *palacsinták* – pancakes, for a better word – are served with an abundance of fresh vegetables and range in flavour from Asian to Mexican. There's a large choice of sweet ones (from 1690Ft) too. Enter from Fazola Henrik utca.

★ Fő Tér HUNGARIAN €€
(Main Square; ☏36-817 482; http://fotercafe.hu; Gerl Matyas utca 2; mains 1300-3400Ft; ⊙10am-10pm) This restaurant adds a bit of colour to Eger's dining scene, with its chartreuse-and-plum pop-art decor and a glassed-in terrace with a tented roof. The food is Hungarian with a contemporary taste; we loved the grilled smoked-ewe cheese with orange salad (1950Ft) and pork knuckle braised in dark beer (2000Ft).

❶ Getting There & Away

Up to seven direct trains a day connect to/from Budapest's Keleti train station (two hours, 120km).

Hungary Survival Guide

❶ Directory A–Z

ACCOMMODATION

➡ Except during the peak summer season (ie July and most of August), you should have no problem finding accommodation to fit your budget in Hungary.

➡ Hotels run the gamut from luxurious five-star palaces to the run-down old socialist-era hovels that still survive in some towns.

➡ The youth hostel (*ifjúsági szállók*) scene in Budapest has exploded in the last couple of years. However, in the rest of Hungary quality hostels are a rare breed. Useful websites for online booking include www.hostelworld.com and www.hihostels.hu.

➡ Campsites are plentiful. One of the best resources for finding a campsite in a particular part of the country is en.camping.info; another good website is www.camping.hu.

MONEY

➡ The Hungarian currency is the forint (Ft).

➡ Credit and debit cards can be used almost everywhere and there is usually no minimum-purchase requirement.

➡ Bank ATMs are everywhere and are usually the easiest way to exchange money.

➡ Exchange cash at banks rather than moneychangers.

➡ Tip waiters and bartenders 10% to reward good service.

OPENING HOURS

Banks 8am to 5pm Monday to Thursday, to 4pm Friday

Bars 11am to midnight Sunday to Thursday, to 1am or 2am Friday and Saturday

Clubs 4pm to 2am Sunday to Thursday, to 4am Friday and Saturday

Grocery stores 7am to 7pm Monday to Friday, to 3pm Saturday

---

❶ ACCOMMODATION PRICE RANGES

In this section, the price breakdown for a double room in high season is as follows:

€ less than 15,000Ft

€€ 15,000Ft to 33,500Ft

€€€ more than 33,500Ft

Restaurants 11am to 11pm
Shops 9am to 6pm Monday to Friday, to 1pm Saturday

PUBLIC HOLIDAYS

New Year's Day 1 January
1848 Revolution/National Day 15 March
Easter Monday March/April
International Labour Day 1 May
Whit Monday May/June
St Stephen's/Constitution Day 20 August
1956 Remembrance Day/Republic Day 23 October
All Saints' Day 1 November
Christmas holidays 25 & 26 December

TELEPHONES

➡ All localities in Hungary have a two-digit telephone area code, except for Budapest, which has just a '1'.

➡ To make an intercity landline call within Hungary and whenever ringing a mobile telephone, dial the prefix ⬚06, then dial the area code and phone number.

➡ To make an international call from Hungary, dial ⬚00 then the country code, the area code and the number.

➡ The country code for Hungary is ⬚36.

➡ Most North American mobile (cell) phones won't work here. Consider buying a recharge-able SIM chip at mobile-phone shops and newsagents, which cuts the cost of making local calls.

WI-FI

Almost all hostels and hotels offer internet and/or wi-fi, mostly free but sometimes for a small surcharge. Free wi-fi is also available at major airports, and many restaurants and cafes.

❶ Getting There & Away

Hungary is well connected with all seven of its neighbours by air, road and rail, though most transport begins or ends its journey in Budapest.

AIR

Budapest is the main air gateway to Hungary. International flights land at Terminals 2A and 2B of **Ferenc Liszt International Airport** on the outskirts of Budapest. Budget carriers use Terminal 2B. **Hévíz-Balaton Airport** (SOB; ⬚83-200 304; www.hevizairport.com; Repülőtér 1, Sármellék), in season, serves some German destinations, and is located 15km southwest of Keszthely near Lake Balaton.

Malév Hungarian Airlines, the national carrier, was liquidated due to bankruptcy in 2012.

LAND

Bus

Crossing the continent by bus is cheapest. Most international buses are run by **Eurolines** (www.eurolines.hu) and link with its Hungarian associate, **Volánbusz** (p744).

Train

Hungarian State Railways, **Magyar Állam-vasutak** or MÁV, links up with the European rail network in all directions. Its trains run as far as London (via Munich and Paris), Stockholm (via Hamburg and Copenhagen), Moscow, Rome and Istanbul (via Belgrade). Almost all international trains bound for Hungary arrive and depart from Budapest's Keleti station; Deli handles trains to Croatia, Slovenia, Bosnia and Herzegovina and Serbia.

WATER

Hydrofoils to Bratislava and Vienna run by **Mahart PassNave** (⬚1-484 4025; www.mahart passnave.hu; V Belgrád rakpart; ⏱8am-6pm Mon-Fri; ⬚2) from May to late September arrive at and depart from the **International Ferry Pier** (Nemzetközi hajóállomás; ⬚1-318 1223; V Belgrád rakpart; ⬚2).

❶ Getting Around

Hungary's domestic transport system is efficient, comprehensive and inexpensive. Towns are covered by a system of frequent buses, trams and trolleybuses. The majority of Hungary's towns and cities are easily negotiated on foot.

Hungary's **Volánbusz** (p744) network covers the whole country.

The national rail operator **MÁV** offers clean, punctual and relatively comfortable (if not ultra-modern) train services. Budapest is the hub of all the main railway lines, though many secondary lines link provincial cities and towns.

Georgia

100 km
60 miles

RUSSIA

AZERBAIJAN

ARMENIA

TURKEY

BLACK SEA

Sochi
Gantiadi
Psou
Gagra
Gudauta
Novy Afon
ABKHAZIA
Lake Ritsa
Sukhumi
Ochamchyra
Chkhalta
Kodori Gorge
Gali
Jvari Reservoir
Mt Elbrus (5642m)
Becho
Enguri River
Jvari
Mestia (5193m)
Mt Shkhara (5193m)
SVANETI
Ushguli
RACHA
Onj
Ambrolauri
Oni
Sachkhere
Chiatura
Tqibuli
Gelati
Sataplia Nature Reserve
Martvili
Prometheus Cave
Okatse Canyon
IMERETI
Rioni River
Kutaisi
Molsameta
Zestaponi
Vani
Khashuri
Likhi Range
Kvirila
Kareli
Gori
Uplistsikhe
Tskhinvali
SOUTH OSSETIA
Liakhvi
Dzau
Gudauri
Georgian Military Highway
Aragvi
Mtiuletis
Ananuri
Mtskheta
TBILISI
Tbilisi Airport
Rustavi
Marneuli
Gardabani
Böyük K-sik
Tsiteli Khidi (Krasny Most)
Bagratashen
Sadakhlo
Guguti
Bolnisi
Bavra
KVEMO KARTLI
Tsalka
Lake Paravani
Akhalkalaki
Ninotsminda
Çıldır
Kartsakhi Lake
Vardzia
Aspindza
Akhaltsikhe
Sapara Monastery
Vale
Abastumani
Khulo
ADJARA
Mtirala National Park
Akhtsiskali River
Batumi
Batumi Botanical Garden
Sarpi
Hopa
Rize
Posof
Ardahan
SAMTSKHE-JAVAKHETI
SAMTSKHE
Borjomi-Kharagauli National Park
Borjomi
Bakuriani
Atsuri River
Ateni Sioni
GURIA
Ozurgeti
Supsa River
Ureki
Lanchkhuti
Kobuleti
Poti
Lake Paliastomi
Kolkheti National Park
Samtredia
Senaki
Khobi
SAMEGRELO
Zugdidi
Tsalenjikha
Mestia
KHEVSURETI
Shatili
Barisakho
Mt Diklos (4285m)
Tusheti
Dartlo
Omalo
Shenaqo
Mt Kazbek (5047m)
Roki Tunnel
Mamisoni Pass
Kazbegi
Larsi
Jvari Pass
KHEVI
PSHAVI
Akhmeta
Ikalto
Alaverdi Cathedral
Telavi
Tsinandali
Gremi
Nekresi Monastery
Lagodekhi
Lagodekhi Protected Areas
Shenaqo
Pshavis Aragvi River
Iori River
Sagarejo
Gurjaani
Sighnaghi
KAKHETI
Tsnori
Bodbe Convent
Dedoplistskaro
Vashlovani Protected Area
Balak-n
Gardabani Davit Gareja
Sagarejo
Nazran
Grozny
Nalchik
Vladikavkaz
Alazani River
(Border closed)

1
2
3
4
5
6
7
8
9
11

Illyichevsk (Ukraine); Burgas (Bulgaria); Varna (Bulgaria)

GEORGIA

From its green valleys spread with vineyards to its old churches and watchtowers perched in fantastic mountain scenery, Georgia (Saqartvelo) is one of the most beautiful countries on earth and a marvellous canvas for walkers, horse riders, cyclists, skiers, rafters and travellers of every kind. Equally special are its proud, high-spirited, cultured people: Georgia claims to be the birthplace of wine, and this is a place where guests are considered blessings and hospitality is the very stuff of life.

Tbilisi, the capital and usual first port of call for visitors, is redolent of an age-old Eurasian crossroads, with its winding lanes, balconied houses, leafy squares and handsome churches, all overlooked by the 17-centuries old Narikala Fortress. Neighbourhoods not far from the centre retain a village feel with narrow streets, small shops and community atmosphere. But this is also a country moving forward in the 21st century, with spectacular contemporary buildings, a minimal crime rate and ever-improving facilities for the visitors who are a growing part of its future.

The **Georgian National Tourism Administration** (www.georgia.travel) maintains an excellent website in English on tourist attractions and guidelines for visitors.

There are many small or medium-sized, midrange hotels with character in cities and towns around the country, and a handful of super-luxury top-end places, mainly located in big cities like Tbilisi. There are perhaps 50 travellers' hostels around Georgia (the majority in Tbilisi). They provide dormitory beds or bunks, sometimes a few private doubles, and shared bathrooms and kitchens.

Most travellers arrive by air to **Tbilisi's international airport** (www.tbilisiairport. com), located 15km east of the city centre. Direct flights head to/from more than 40 international destinations spread from Paris to China. There are also a few international bus connections, including daily service to/from Athens, Istanbul and Moscow.

Once in Georgia, *marshrutky* (minibuses) are the main transport option for moving around the country. Trains are mostly slower and less frequent than road transport.

ROMANIA

Bucharest

POP 2.1 MILLION

Romania's capital gets a bad rap, but in fact it's dynamic, energetic and quite fun. It's where still-unreconstructed communism meets unbridled capitalism; where the soporific forces of the EU meet the passions of the Balkans. While much of the centre is modern and garish, you will find some splendid 17th- and 18th-century Orthodox churches tucked away in quiet corners and graceful art nouveau villas. Communism changed the face of the city for good, and nowhere is this more evident than at the gargantuan Palace of Parliament.

⊙ Sights

Bucharest teems with museums and attractions; all are relatively cheap and many are among the nation's best. The historic thoroughfare Calea Victoriei makes a nice walk, as it connects the two main squares of the city: Piaţa Victoriei in the north, and Piaţa Revoluţiei in the centre.

Palace of Parliament   HISTORIC BUILDING
(Palatul Parlamentului/Casa Poporului; ☑ tour bookings 021-311 3611; http://cic.cdep.ro/en/visiting/visiting-routes; B-dul Naţiunile Unite; complete tour adults/students 45/23 lei, standard adult/students 25/13 lei; ⊙10am-4pm; Ⓜ Izvor) The Palace of Parliament is the world's second-largest building (after the Pentagon) and former dictator Nicolae Ceauşescu's most infamous creation. Built in 1984 (and still unfinished), the building has more than 3000 rooms and covers 330,000 sq metres. Entry is by guided tour only (book in advance). Bring your passport since they check IDs. Today it houses the parliament.

Stavropoleos Church   CHURCH
(☑ 021-313 4747; www.stavropoleos.ro; Str Stavropoleos 4; ⊙7am-8pm) The tiny and lovely Stavropoleos Church, which dates from 1724, perches a bit oddly a block over from some of Bucharest's craziest Old Town carousing. It's one church, though, that will make a lasting impression, with its courtyard filled with tombstones and an ornate wooden interior and carved wooden doors.

Romania

Old Princely Court
RUIN

(Palatul Voievodal, Curtea Veche; Str Franceză 21-23; admission 3 lei; ⏰10am-6pm) The Old Princely Court dates to the 15th century, when Bucharest was the capital of the Wallachian principality. The ruins are being slowly excavated but for now you can wander around some of the rooms of the former court. The Vlad Țepeș statue out the front makes a good photo.

Rebirth Memorial
MONUMENT

(Memorialul Renaşterii; Calea Victoriei) This striking memorial, respected and reviled in equal measure, marks the dramatic events of 1989, when many people died in this area for their opposition to the Ceauşescu regime. The white obelisk piercing a basket-like crown stands on an island in Calea Victoriei. Local wags have dubbed it the 'potato of the revolution'.

Museum of the Romanian Peasant
MUSEUM

(Muzeul Țăranului Român; ☎021-317 9661; www.muzeultaranuluiroman.ro; Şos Kiseleff 3; adult/child 8/2 lei; ⏰10am-6pm Tue-Sun) The collection of peasant bric-a-brac, costumes, icons and partially restored houses make this one of the most popular museums in the city. There's not much English signage, but little cards in English posted in each room give a flavour of what's on offer. An 18th-century church stands in the back lot, as does a great gift shop and restaurant.

National Village Museum
MUSEUM

(Muzeul Naţional al Satului; ☎021-317 9103; www.muzeul-satului.ro; Şos Kiseleff 28-30; adult/child 10/5 lei; ⏰9am-7pm Tue-Sun, to 5pm Mon; 👶) On the shores of Herăstrău Lake, this museum is a terrific open-air collection of several dozen homesteads, churches, mills and windmills relocated from rural Romania.

Built in 1936 by royal decree, it is one of Europe's oldest open-air museums and a good choice for kids to boot.

🛏 Sleeping

Hotels are typically aimed at businesspeople, and prices are higher here than in the rest of the country. Tips for getting discounts include booking in advance or using the hotel's website.

★ Little Bucharest
Old Town Hostel   HOSTEL €
(☏ 0786-055 287; www.littlebucharest.ro; Str Smârdan 15; dm 45-60 lei, r 225 ei; ❄@🖙) Bucharest's most central hostel is super clean, white walled and well run. Accommodation is over two floors, with dorms ranging from six to 12 beds. Private doubles are also available. The staff is travel-friendly and youth-oriented and can advise on sightseeing and fun. The location is in the middle of Bucharest's lively Old Town.

Midland Youth Hostel   HOSTEL €
(☏ 021-314 5323; www.themidlandhostel.com; Str Biserica Amzei 22; dm 40-60 le ; ❄✱@🖙) A happening hostel, with an excellent central location not far from Piaţa Romană. Accommodation is in four-, eight- or 12-bed dorms. There's a common kitchen too.

Rembrandt Hotel   HOTEL €€
(☏ 021-313 9315; www.rembrandt.ro; Str Smârdan 11; tourist s/d 180/230 lei, standard 260/300 lei, business 350/380 lei; ❄✱@🖙) It's hard to say enough good things about this place. Stylish beyond its three-star rating, this 16-room, Dutch-run hotel faces the landmark National Bank in the historic centre. Rooms come in three categories, tourist, standard and business, with the chief difference size. All rooms have polished wooden floors, timber headboards, and DVD players. Book well in advance.

🍴 Eating

Many restaurants are concentrated in the Old Town, with the rest spread out all around the city. Self-caterers will want to head to the daily market on Piaţa Amzei, with a good selection of fresh fruit and veg.

★ Caru' cu Bere   ROMANIAN €€
(☏ 021-313 7560; www.carucubere.ro; Str Stavropoleos 3-5; mains 20-45 le ; ⏰ 8am-midnight Sun-Thu, 8am-2am Fri & Sat; 🖙) Despite a decidedly tourist-leaning atmosphere, with peasant-girl hostesses and sporadic traditional song-and-dance numbers, Bucharest's oldest beer house continues to draw in a strong local crowd. The colourful belle-epoque interior and stained-glass windows dazzle, as does the classic Romanian food. Dinner reservations recommended.

Sindbad   MIDDLE EASTERN €€
(☏ 021-317 7788; www.restaurantsindbad.ro; Str Lipscani 19 ; mains 20-30 lei ; 🖙) This small Lebanese restaurant may lack a little something in presentation, but it makes up for this with great food, belly-dancing and water pipes. In a word: authentic.

Lente & Cafea   INTERNATIONAL €€
(☏ 021-310 7424; www.lente.ro; Str Gen Praporgescu 31; mains 25-40 lei; ⏰ 11.30am-1am; 🖙) The *tomatina*, tomato soup served with croutons and yellow cheese, is a classic, but all the entrees are creative, filling and good value. We especially like the 'Anthos' main, which are strips of beef tenderloin flavoured with celery soy sauce and served with basmati rice. The garden terrace is a respite on a hot day.

🍷 Drinking & Nightlife

★ Grădina Verona   CAFE
(☏ 0732-003 060; Str Pictor Verona 13-15; ⏰ 9am-1am; 🖙) A garden oasis hidden behind the Cărtureşti bookshop, serving standard-issue but excellent espresso drinks and some of the wackiest iced-tea infusions ever concocted in Romania, such as peony flower, mango and lime (it's not bad).

Control   CLUB
(☏ 0733-927 861; www.control-club.ro; Str Constantin Mille 4; ⏰ 6pm-4am; 🖙) This is a favorite among club-goers who like alternative, indie and garage sounds. Hosts both live acts and DJs, depending on the night.

La Muse   CLUB
(☏ 0734-000 236; www.lamuse.ro; Str Lipscani 53; ⏰ 9am-3am Sun-Wed, to 6am Thu-Sat; 🖙) Just about anything goes at this popular Old Town dance club. Try to arrive early, around 11pm, since it can get crowded later. La Muse draws everyone from university students to young professionals in their 20s and 30s. Everyone looks great.

Central Bucharest

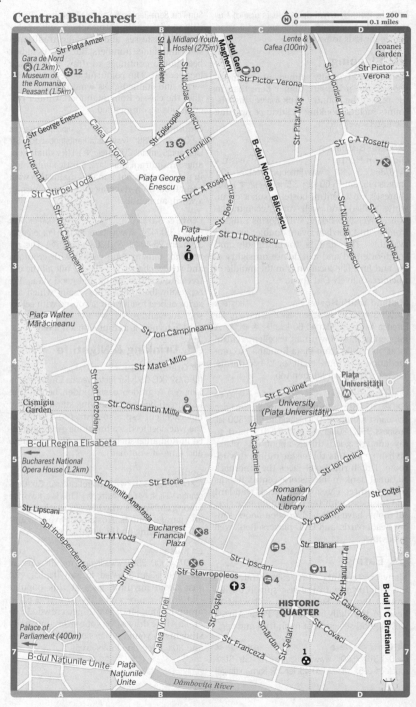

0   200 m
0   0.1 miles

A · **B** · **C** · **D**

Str Piaţa Amzei
Gara de Nord
(1.2km);
Museum of
the Romanian
Peasant (1.5km)
⊕ 12

Str Mendeleev
Midland Youth
Hostel (275m)
B-dul Gen
Magheru
Lente &
Cafea (100m)
Icoanei
Garden
Str Pictor
Verona

Str George Enescu
Calea Victoriei
Str Nicolae Golescu
Str Episcopiei
☉ 10
Str Pictor Verona
Str Dionisie Lupu

Str Luterană
Str Ştirbei Vodă
☉ 13
Str Franklin
Piaţa George
Enescu
Str C A Rosetti
Str Boteanu
B-dul Nicolae Bălcescu
Str Pitar-Moş
Str C A Rosetti
7 ✕
Str Nicolae Filipescu
Str Tudor Arghezi

Str Ion Câmpineanu
Piaţa
Revoluţiei
2 ❶
Str D I Dobrescu

Piaţa Walter
Mărăcineanu
Str Ion Câmpineanu

Str Ion Brezoianu
Str Matei Millo

Cişmigiu
Garden
Str Constantin Mille
9 ⬛
Str E Quinet
University
(Piaţa Universităţii)
Piaţa
Universităţii
Ⓜ

B-dul Regina Elisabeta
Str Academiei
Str Ion Ghica

Bucharest National
Opera House (1.2km)
Str Domnita Anastasia
Str Eforie
Str Colţei

Str Lipscani
Spl Independenţei
Str M Vodă
Bucharest
Financial
Plaza
✕ 8
Romanian
National
Library
Str Doamnei
5 ⬛
Str Blănari

Str Ilfov
Str Stavropoleos
✕ 6
Str Lipscani
✝ 3
4 ⬛
11 ⬛
Str Hanul cu Tei

Calea Victoriei
Str Poştei
Str Şelari
Str Smârdan
HISTORIC
QUARTER
Str Gabroveni
B-dul I C Brătianu

Palace of
Parliament (400m)
B-dul Naţiunile Unite
Piaţa
Naţiunile
Unite
Str Franceză
Str Covaci
1 ☢

Dâmboviţa River

Central Bucharest

☆ Entertainment

Green Hours 22 Jazz Club   JAZZ
(🖉 concerts 0788-452 485; www.greenhours.ro; Calea Victoriei 120; ⊙ 6pm-2am) This old-school basement jazz club runs a lively program of jazz nights through the week and hosts an international jazz fest in May/June. Check the website for the schedule during your trip and try to book in advance.

**Bucharest National
Opera House**   OPERA
(Opera Națională București; 🖉 box office 021-310 2661; www.operanb.ro; B-dul Mihail Kogălniceanu 70-72; tickets 10-70 lei; ⊙ box office 9am-1pm & 3-7pm) The city's premier venue for classical opera and ballet. Buy tickets online or at the venue box office.

Romanian Athenaeum   CLASSICAL MUSIC
(Ateneul Roman; 🖉 box office 021-315 6875; www. fge.org.ro; Str Franklin 1-3; tickets 15-65 lei; ⊙ box office noon-7pm Tue-Fri, 4-7pm Sat, 10-11am Sun) The historic Athenaeum is home to the respected George Enescu Philharmonic and offers a wide array of classical-music concerts from September to May as well as a number of one-off musical shows and spectacles throughout the year. Buy tickets at the venue box office.

🛈 Getting There & Away

Bucharest is Romania's main travel gateway. See p763 for international arrival and departure details.

AIR

All international and domestic flights use **Henri Coandă International Airport** (often referred to in conversation by its previous name 'Otopeni'). Henri Coandă is 17km north of Bucharest on the road to Brașov.

BUS

It's possible to get just about anywhere in the country by bus from Bucharest, but figuring out where your bus or maxitaxi departs from can be tricky. Bucharest has several bus stations and they don't seem to follow any discernible logic. The website **Autogari.ro** (www. autogari.ro) has an online timetable.

TRAIN

The central station for most national and all international trains, **Gara de Nord** (🖉 phone reservations 021-9522; www.cfrcalatori.ro; Piața Gara de Nord 1; Ⓜ Gara de Nord) is accessible by metro from the centre of the city. Check the latest train schedules on either www. cfr.ro or the reliable German site www.bahn.de.

🛈 Getting Around

TO/FROM THE AIRPORT

Bus Express bus No 783 leaves every 15 minutes between 6am and 11pm (every half-hour at weekends) from Piața Unirii and Piața Victoriei and points in between. Buy a ticket, valid for one round trip or two people one way, at any RATB bus-ticket booth near a bus stop. The airport is 45 to 60 minutes from the centre, depending on traffic.

Train There's a regular shuttle train service (35 minutes) from the main station, Gara de Nord, to Henri Coandă International Airport. The trains leave hourly at 10 minutes past the hour, starting at 8.10am and continuing until 7.10pm.

Taxi A reputable taxi should cover the distance from the centre to Henri Coandă International Airport for no more than 50 lei. Order a taxi from machines standing in the arrivals hall. You'll receive an order ticket stamped with the number of the taxi.

PUBLIC TRANSPORT

Bucharest's public transport system of metros, buses, trams and trolleybuses is operated by the transport authority **RATB** (Regia Autonomă de Transport București; 🖉 info 021-9391; www. ratb.ro). The system runs daily from about 5am to approximately 11.30pm. For buses, trams and trolleybuses, buy tickets at any RATB street kiosk, marked 'casa de bilete', located at major stops and public squares.

CENTRAL & EASTERN EUROPE BUCHAREST

Transylvania

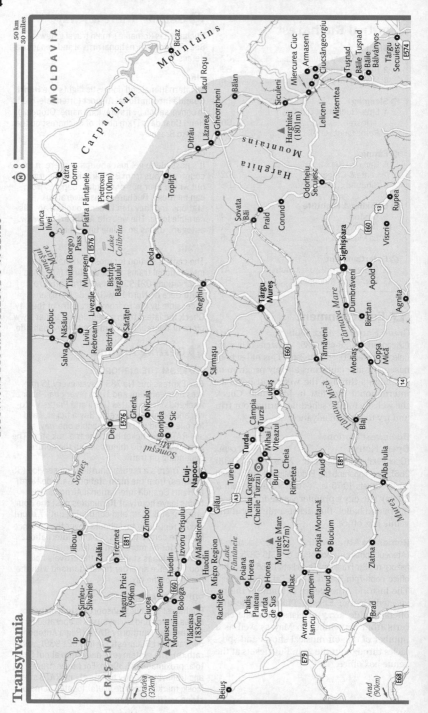

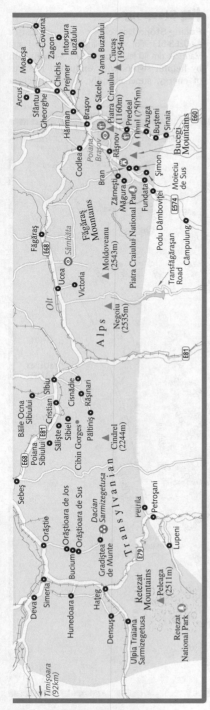

Transylvania

The northwestern Romanian province of Transylvania conjures a vivid landscape of mountains, castles, fortified churches and a wicked, sharp-fanged nobleman of a certain ilk (see boxed text, p757). A melange of architecture and chic sidewalk cafes punctuate the towns of Braşov and Sighişoara, while many of Transylvania's Saxon villages are dotted with fortified churches that date back half a millennium.

Braşov

POP 274,400

Legend has it the Pied Piper reemerged from Hamelin in Braşov, and indeed there's something whimsically enchanting about the city, with its fairy-tale turrets and cobbled streets. Dramatically overlooked by Mt Tâmpa, with trees sporting a russet-gold coat (and cocky Hollywood-style sign), this is a remarkably relaxed city.

◉ Sights

Piaţa Sfatului   SQUARE

This wide square, chock with cafes, was once the heart of medieval Braşov. In the centre stands the 1420 **Council House** (Casa Sfatului), topped by the **Trumpeter's Tower**, in which town councillors, known as centurions, would meet. These days at midday, traditionally costumed musicians appear from the top of the tower like figures in a Swiss clock.

Black Church   CHURCH

(Biserica Neagră; ☑ 0268-511 824; www.honterusgemeinde.ro; Curtea Johannes Honterus 2; adult/child 9/6 lei; ⊙ 10am-7pm Tue-Sat, noon-7pm Sun) Braşov's main landmark, the Black Church is the largest Gothic church between Vienna and Istanbul, and is still used by German Lutherans today. Built between 1383 and 1480, it was named for its appearance after a fire in 1689. The original statues from the exterior of the apse are now inside.

Mt Tâmpa   MOUNTAIN

(Telecabina Tampa; ☑ 0268-478 657; Aleea Tiberiu Brediceanu; cable car one way/return 10/16 lei; ⊙ Tue-Sun 9.30am-5pm) Towering over the city from the east, 940m Mt Tâmpa – with its Hollywood-style sign – was Braşov's original defensive wall. You can hike up (about an hour) or take a cable car to reach a small viewing platform offering stunning views over the city and the possibility of a light bite or drink at a communist-era dining room.

Sleeping

Rolling Stone Hostel   HOSTEL €

(☎0268-513 965; www.rollingstone.ro; Str Piatra Mare 2a; dm 40 lei, r from 120 lei; ☻@☎) Run by helpful sisters with unlimited reserves of energy, super-friendly Stone attracts a

Braşov

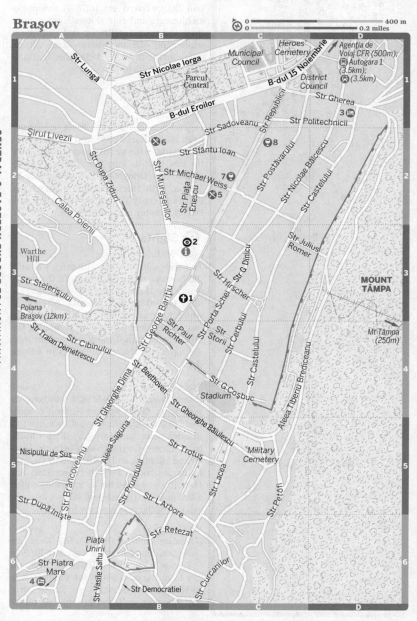

0 _____ 400 m
0 _____ 0.2 miles

THE SKINNY ON DRACULA

Transylvania is best known as the alleged stomping ground of one bloodthirsty count named Dracula.

But there are two things worth pointing out, that might come as a surprise. The first is that Dracula is real (well, sort of). The second is that he did not actually spend much time in Transylvania.

Bram Stoker's 1897 vampire novel was inspired by centuries-old superstition and the real-life exploits of Vlad Dracula. Known by his murderous moniker, Vlad Țepeș (the Impaler), the 15th-century nobleman was said to have skewered up to 80,000 enemies on long spikes.

Though he was reputedly born in the Transylvanian town of Sighişoara, the real Dracula's exploits took place further to the south, across the Carpathians, in the Romanian region of Wallachia.

Despite Dracula's wicked ways, particularly for fending off the invading Ottoman Turks, he is considered a hero in Transylvania and throughout Romania – so not everyone is thrilled with the count's bloodsucking reputation.

cosmo stew of travellers. Dorms are a little crowded, but for the smaller one downstairs. The private double room (without bathroom) has couches and armoire. You'll be given a map and bags of info on arrival. Personal lockers, organised tours and basic breakfast.

★ **Casa Reims** BOUTIQUE HOTEL €€
(☑0368-467 325; www.casareims.ro; Str Castelului 85; s/d 200/250 lei ; P❂❄☎) High-end mom-and-pop boutique with glamour touches like quality linens, flower-print spreads and hardwood floors. You'll get an enthusiastic welcome at the reception desk and a hearty home-cooked breakfast. There's a big enclosed parking lot for drivers and the pedestrian centre is five minutes away on foot. Recommended.

Braşov

⊙ **Sights**
1 Black Church......................................B3
2 Piaţa Sfatului...................................B3

🛏 **Sleeping**
3 Casa Reims.......................................D1
4 Rolling Stone Hostel.......................A6

🍴 **Eating**
5 Bistro de l'Arte...............................C2
6 Sergiana...B2

🍸 **Drinking & Nightlife**
7 Deane's Irish Pub & Grill...............C2
8 Festival 39.......................................C2

🍴 Eating

★ **Bistro de l'Arte** BISTRO €€
(☑0720-535 566; www.bistrodelarte.ro; Str Piaţa Enescu 11; mains 15-35 lei; ☻9am-1am Mon-Sat, noon-1am Sun; ☎) Tucked down a cobbled street straight out of a folk tale, this joint has decidedly boho genes with walls dotted with local artists' work. Gazpacho soup, shrimps and tomato gratin, snails… or just a croque monsieur. Perfect for nursing a cappuccino and working on your laptop.

Sergiana ROMANIAN €€
(☑0268-419 775; http://sergianagrup.ro; Str Mureşenilor 28; mains 25-40 lei; ☻11am-11pm) Authentically Saxon, this subterranean carnivore's heaven has two sections: the white room for 'pure' nonsmokers, and the exposed brick vaults for *fumeurs*. Choose from a menu of venison, stag, boar, pork ribs, sirloin steak, and Transylvanian sour soup with smoked gammon and tarragon (11.50 lei). A hunter's dream.

🍸 Drinking & Nightlife

Festival 39 BAR
(☑0268-478 664; www.festival39.com; Str Republicii 62; ☻7am-midnight) This watering hole is a romantic art-deco dream of stained-glass ceilings, wrought-iron finery, candelabra and leather banquettes, and has a bar long enough to keep an army of barflies content.

Deane's Irish Pub & Grill PUB
(☑0268-474 542; Str Republicii 19; ☻10am-1am Mon-Thu, 10am-3am Fri & Sat, noon-1am Sun) As if transplanted from Donegal, this subterranean Irish pub with its early-20th-century

WORTH A TRIP

FORTIFIED SAXON CHURCHES

The rolling hills stretching to the north and west of Braşov are filled with fortified churches and villages that can easily feel lost in centuries past; especially when you see a horse and cart rattle past laden with milk churns, or a shepherd ushering his flock across your path. Bus service is practically nonexistent; visitors come by hire car, taxi, bike or tour bus.

A couple of highlights get nearly all the visits, notably the fortified church at **Biertan** and the atmospheric Saxon village of **Viscri**. Much of the restoration in the area has been carried out by the Mihai Eminescu Trust, of which Britain's Prince Charles is a major driving force, along with author William Blacker (*Along The Enchanted Way*).

cloudy mirrored bar, shadowy booths and old-world soundtracks, is a haven for the Guinness-thirsty.

ℹ Information

Tourist Information Centre (☑ 0268-419 078; www.brasovcity.ro; Piaţa Sfatului 30; ⊙10am-6pm Mon-Fri) Easily spotted in the gold city council building in the centre of the square, the English-speaking staff offer free maps and brochures and track down hotel vacancies and train and bus times.

ℹ Getting There & Away

BUS

Maxitaxis and minibuses are the best way to reach places near Braşov, including Bran. Braşov has two main bus stations: **Autogara 1** (Bus Station 1; ☑ 0268-427 267; www.autogari. ro; B-dul Gării 1), located next to the train station, is the main departure point for bus service to Bucharest (2½ hours); **Autogara 2** (Bus Station 2; ☑ 0268-426 332; www.autogari.ro; Str Avram Iancu 114), 1km northwest of the train station, sends half-hourly buses marked 'Moieciu-Bran' to Bran (40 minutes) from roughly 6am to 11pm.

TRAIN

The train station is 2km northeast of the centre. There are convenient rail connections to both Bucharest (2½ hours) and Sighişoara (2½ hours). International train services include daily trains to Budapest (14 hours) and Vienna (18 hours).

Bran

Just to the southwest of Braşov, the tiny town of Bran once occupied a crucial border post along the Carpathians that separated Transylvania to the north from the lands south of the peaks. Not surprising, then, that such a gargantuan castle would arise here. More surprising is that the castle would develop such a strong association with Vlad Ţepeş (aka Dracula), who by all accounts didn't spend much time here.

◉ Sights

Bran Castle   CASTLE
(☑0268-237 700; www.bran-castle.com; Str General Traian Moşoiu 24; adult/student 35/20 lei; ⊙9am-6pm Tue-Sun & noon-6pm Mon May-Sep, 9am-4pm Tue-Sun & noon-4pm Mon Oct-Apr) The 60m-tall Bran Castle, sometimes mistakenly called 'Dracula's Castle', is spectacular and one of the country's leading attractions. It was built by Saxons from Braşov in 1382 to defend Bran pass against the Turks. It may have housed Vlad Ţepeş (aka Dracula) for a few nights on his flight from the Turks in 1462. Castle ticket includes entry to the open-air village museum, with a dozen traditional buildings at the foot of the castle.

🛏 Sleeping

The Guest House   PENSION €
(☑0744-306 062; www.guesthouse.ro; Str General Traian Moşoiu 7; r from 120-140 lei; tr 150 lei; P❉❀🛜) With terrific views of Bran Castle, this guesthouse is clean and family-friendly with a kids' adventure playground and communal lounge and dining room.

ℹ Getting There & Away

Bran is an easy DIY day trip from Braşov. Buses marked 'Bran-Moieciu' (one hour) depart every half-hour from Braşov's Autogara 2. Return buses to Braşov leave Bran every half-hour from roughly 7am to 6pm in winter, and 7am to 10pm in summer.

Sighişoara

POP 26,400

From the moment you enter its fortified walls, wending your way along cobblestones to its centrepiece square, Sighişoara burns itself into your memory. It's like stepping into a kid's fairy tale, the narrow streets aglow with lustrously coloured 16th-century houses, their gingerbread roofs tumbling

Sighişoara

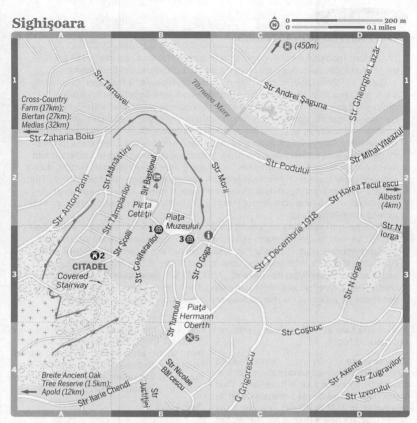

N 0 _____ 200 m
0 _____ 0.1 miles

Sighişoara

◉ **Sights**
1 Casa Dracula B3
2 Citadel A3
3 Clock Tower B3

🛏 **Sleeping**
4 Burg Hostel B2
Pensiune Cristina & Pave ....(see 2)

🍴 **Eating**
Casa Dracula .... (see 1)
5 Central Park B4

down to pretty cafes. Horror fans won't be disappointed either, for this Unesco-protected citadel, the best preserved of its kind in Europe, was the purported birthplace of one of history's great 'monsters' – Vlad Ţepeş (The Impaler).

◉ Sights

Citadel FORTRESS

Most of Sighişoara's sights are clustered in the compact Old Town – the delightful medieval Citadel – perched on a hillock and fortified with a 14th-century wall, to which 14 towers and five artillery bastions were later added. Today the citadel, which is on the Unesco World Heritage list, retains nine of its original towers (named for the guilds in charge of their upkeep) and two bastions.

Clock Tower MUSEUM

(Turnul cu Ceas; ✆ 0265-771 108; Piaţa Muzeului 1; adult/child 12/3 lei; ⊙ 9am-6.30pm Tue-Fri, 10am-

5.30pm Sat & Sun) The symbol of the town is this magnificent medieval clock tower, built in the 14th century and expanded 200 years later. It originally housed the town council, but these days it's purely decorative. The clock and figurines were added in the 17th century. The figurines represent different medieval characters, including Peace,

WORTH A TRIP

THE PAINTED MONASTERIES

The historic monasteries of Romania's northeastern Moldavia province – dating from the 15th and 16th centuries – are among the most distinctive in all Christendom.

Unusually, some have frescoes both outside and inside. While the region's prevailing winds and rains mean that north-facing exterior walls have largely lost their five-century-old paintings, frescoes facing other directions have survived – almost a miracle, considering that the plaster is only 5mm thick on some of the most impressive paintings.

While wall paintings and icons are common in Orthodox churches, external frescoes are more rare. Different explanations have been given for this too. Since these fortified monasteries were created when the Turks threatened, large numbers of soldiers would have been garrisoned within; they, like the villagers, were largely illiterate. Further, during services, these small churches could hold few parishioners (generally, the nobility). The edifying outdoor paintings thus helped explain biblical stories and ethical concepts to the masses – useful too, considering that liturgies in Old Church Slavonic were unintelligible to most Romanians.

While several monastery complexes are scattered throughout the province, the most impressive – and easiest to reach – churches are those at **Humor** (Mănăstirea Humorului; Gura Humorului; adult/student 5/2 lei; ⊘8am-7pm summer, to 5pm winter), **Moldoviţa** (Mânăstirea Moldoviţa; Vatra Moldoviţei; adult/student 5/2 lei; ⊘8am-7pm summer, to 5pm winter) and **Voroneţ** (Mănăstirea Voroneţ; ✆0741-612 529; Voroneţ, Gura Humorului; adult/child 5/2 lei; ⊘8am-7pm summer, to 4pm winter). The region's biggest city, **Suceava**, is a good base for exploring the monasteries and is reachable from Bucharest by train.

Justice and Law, as well as those representing Day and Night.

Casa Dracula HISTORIC BUILDING
(✆0265-771 596; www.casavladdracul.ro; Str Cositorarilor 5 ; admission 5 lei; ⊘10am-10pm) Vlad Ţepeş (aka Dracula) was reputedly born in this house in 1431 and lived here until the age of four. It's now a decent restaurant, but for a small admission, the staff will show you Vlad's old room (and give you a little scare). Bubble-burster: the building is indeed centuries old, but has been completely rebuilt since Vlad's days.

🛏 Sleeping

Burg Hostel HOSTEL €
(✆0265-778 489; www.burghostel.ro; Str Bastionului 4-6; dm 40 lei, s/d without bathroom 70/90 lei, with bathroom 80/95 lei; ⊛🔊) Basic Burg is ubiquitously wood-walled with a number of cosy rooms – the triples have the most space. Single rooms are adequate. There's a bar downstairs, plus a pleasant courtyard to read in.

Pensiune Cristina & Pavel PENSION €
(✆0744-159 667, 0744-119 211; www.pensiuneafaur.ro; Str Cojocarilor 1; dm/s/d 50/95/140 lei; 🅿⊛) The floors are so clean at this four-room,

one-dorm guesthouse, you could eat your lunch off them. En suite rooms are spearmint white, plus there's an idyllic garden bursting with flowers. The dining/self-catering area is welcoming and, should you need it, there's a laundry service.

🍴 Eating

★ Central Park INTERNATIONAL €€
(✆0365-730 006; www.hotelcentralpark.ro; Piaţa Hermann Oberth 25; mains 25-40 lei ; ⊘11am-11pm; 🔊) Even if you're not staying at the Central Park hotel, plan a meal here. Sighişoara is short on good restaurants and this is the best around. The food is a mix of Romanian and international dishes, and the carefully selected wine list offers the best domestic labels.

Casa Dracula ROMANIAN €€
(✆0265-771 596; www.casavladdracul.ro; Str Cositorarilor 5; mains 30 lei; ⊘11am-11pm ; 🔊👶) Despite the ghoulish Dracula bust mounted to the wall, the house where Vlad was born could have been dealt a worse blow than this atmospheric, wood-panelled restaurant. The menu scuttles from tomato soup to salmon fillet – all with Dracula related references. With a little embellishing from you, your kids will love it.

ℹ Information

Tourist Information (☑ 0265-770 415; www.
infosighisoara.ro; Str O Goga 8; ☺10am-6pm
Tue-Sat) Private accommodation service masquerading as a tourist information office. Can
help find rooms but don't expect anything else.

ℹ Getting There & Away

BUS

The bus station is located next to the train
station, about 15 minutes walk north of the
citadel. Buses to Braşov (2½ hours) stop at the
bus station a couple of times per day.

TRAIN

About a dozen trains connect Sighişoara with
Braşov (two hours), nine of which (none of
the slow ones) go on to Bucharest (4½ hours).
Five daily trains go to Cluj-Napoca (59 lei, 3½
hours). A few daily trains pass through town on
their way to Budapest (nine hours). Buy tickets
at the train station.

Romania Survival Guide

ℹ Directory A–Z

ACCOMMODATION

Romania has a wide choice of accommodation
options to suit most budgets, including hotels,
pensions and private rooms, hostels and camping grounds. Prices across these categories
have risen in recent years, but are still generally
lower than comparable facilities in Western
Europe.

➜ Bucharest is the most expensive place to
stay, followed by other large cities. The further away from the cities you go the cheaper
accommodation gets.

➜ Hostels in Romania are not as well developed
as in other European countries. Large cities,
like Bucharest and Braşov, do have several,
good-quality private hostels.

➜ Camping grounds (popas turistic) run the
gamut between a handful of nicely maintained

**ℹ ACCOMMODATION PRICE
RANGES**

The following price ranges refer to a
double room with a bathroom, including
breakfast:

€ Under 150 lei

€€ 150 to 300 lei

€€€ Over 300 lei

ℹ EATING PRICE RANGES

We've broken down the eating price
ranges into three categories – budget,
midrange and top end – depending on
the price of an average main-course
item.

€ Under 15 lei

€€ 15 to 30 lei

€€€ Over 30 lei

---

properties in scenic areas to grungy affairs,
with wooden huts packed unattractively side-
by-side like sardines. Rough camping is generally not permitted but in remote areas, the laws
are rarely enforced.

MONEY

➜ The Romanian currency is the leu (plural: lei),
noted in this guide as 'lei' but listed in some
banks and currency exchange offices as RON.
One leu is divided into 100 bani.

➜ ATMs are everywhere and give 24-hour with-
drawals in lei on a variety of international bank
cards, including Visa and MasterCard.

➜ The best place to exchange money is at a
bank. You'll pay a small commission, but get a
decent rate. You can also change money at a
private exchange booth (casa de schimb) but
be wary of commission charges and always ask
how many lei you will receive before handing
over your bills.

➜ In restaurants, tip 10% of the bill to reward
good service. Leave the tip in the pouch that
the bill is delivered in or hand the money
directly to the waiter.

OPENING HOURS

Banks 9am to 5pm Monday to Friday, 9am to
1pm Saturday

Museums 10am to 5pm Tuesday to Friday,
10am to 4pm Saturday and Sunday

Offices 8am to 5pm Monday to Friday, 9am to
1pm Saturday

Restaurants 9am to 11pm Monday to Friday,
10am to 11pm Saturday and Sunday

Shops 9am to 6pm Monday to Friday, 8am to
2pm Saturday

PUBLIC HOLIDAYS

New Year 1 and 2 January

Orthodox Easter Monday April/May

Labour Day 1 May

Pentecost May/June, 50 days after Easter
Sunday

Assumption of Mary 15 August

Feast of St Andrew 30 November

Romanian National Day 1 December
Christmas 25 and 26 December

TELEPHONE

➤ All Romanian landline numbers have 10 digits, consisting of a zero, plus a city code and the number.

➤ To reach a Romanian landline from abroad, dial your country's international access code, then ☎ 40 (Romanian country code), then the city code (minus the zero) and the six- (or seven-) digit local number.

➤ Mobile phone numbers can be identified by a three-digit prefix starting with ☎ 7. All mobile numbers have 10 digits: ☎ 0 + three-digit prefix (7xx) + six-digit number.

➤ Romanian mobile (cell) phones use the GSM 900/1800 network, which is the standard throughout much of Europe as well as in Australia and New Zealand, but is not compatible with most mobile phones in North America or Japan.

➤ Local SIM cards can be used in European, Australian and some American phones. Other phones must be set to roaming.

WORTH A TRIP

MOLDOVA
....

Sandwiched between Romania and Ukraine, Moldova is as 'off the beaten track' as you can get in Europe. Attracting just a fraction of the number of visitors of neighbouring countries (12,000 to 20,000 annually in recent years), it's a natural destination for travellers who like to plant the flag and visit lands few others have gone to.

But Moldova's charms run deeper than being merely remote. The country's wines are some of the best in Europe and a fledgling wine-tourism industry, where you can tour wineries and taste the grape, has taken root. The countryside is delightfully unspoiled and the hospitality of the villagers is authentic.

The capital Chişinău is by far Moldova's largest and liveliest city and its main transport hub. While the city's origins date back six centuries to 1420, much of Chişinău was levelled in WWII and a tragic earthquake that struck in 1940. The city was rebuilt in Soviet style from the 1950s onwards, and both the centre and outskirts are dominated by utilitarian (and frankly not very attractive) high-rise buildings. That said, the centre is surprisingly green and peaceful. The capital also has a lively restaurant and cafe scene.

Wine lovers will want to explore one of the country's two amazing wine cellars – both located within easy day-trip distance from Chişinău. The cave cellars at **Cricova** (☎ tours 069 077 734; www.cricova.md; Str Ungureanu 1, Cricova; guided tours per person from 295 lei ; ☉ 10am-5pm Mon-Fri) and **Mileştii Mici** (☎ tours 022 382 333; www.milestii-mici.md; Mileştii Mici , Ialoveni; guided 40-min tour per person 250 lei; tasting & lunch per person 600-1000 lei; ☉ tours at 10am, 1pm, 3.30pm Mon-Fri) are both tens of kilometers long and house literally millions of bottles of wine.

For something completely different, across the Dniestr River lies the separatist, Russian-speaking region of **Transdniestr**. Although it's formally still part of Moldova, it's a time-warp kind of place, where the Soviet Union reigns supreme and busts of Lenin line the main boulevards. The region's capital, Tiraspol, is accessible from Chişinău by train.

The hotel situation in Chişinău is improving, but most new properties aim for the high end, leaving budget and midrange travellers with less to choose from. This may be one town where a splurge is in order as the difference in quality from top to bottom is very noticeable. Our top choice remains the **Jazz Hotel** (☎ 212 626; www.jazz-hotel.md; Str Vlaicu Pârcălab 72; s/d 1250/1800 lei ; P ☻ ✳ @ ☎), with bright, clean rooms and an excellent location in the heart of the city.

The easiest way to get to Moldova is by plane. Modern **Chişinău International Airport** (KIV; ☎ 525 111; www.airport.md; Str Aeroportului 80/3), 16km southeast of the city centre, has flights to and from several major European cities.

There is also regular train service to Chişinău from the Romanian capital Bucharest (14 hours, daily) and Moscow (28 to 32 hours, four to five daily) among a handful of other cities.

Once in Moldova, getting around can be tricky. Most locals navigate the country via a dense network of minibuses, as train travel tends to be slow and the rail network not very comprehensive.

WI-FI

Romania is well-wired, and the majority of hotels, above a basic pension or guestroom, usually offer some form of internet access, normally wi-fi. Many bars, cafes and restaurants offer free wi-fi for customers.

ⓘ Getting There & Away

Romania shares a border with five countries: Bulgaria, Hungary, Moldova, Serbia and Ukraine. Romania is not a member of the EU's common customs and border area, the Schengen area, so even if you're entering from an EU member state (Bulgaria or Hungary), you'll still have to show a passport or valid EU identity card.

AIR

➜ Romania has good air connections to Europe and the Middle East.

➜ The majority of international flights to Romania arrive at Bucharest's **Henri Coandă International Airport** (OTP/Otopeni; ☏ 021-204 1000; www.bucharestairports.ro; Şos Bucureşti-Ploieşti). The airport is home base for Romania's national carrier **Tarom** (☏ call centre 021-204 6464, office 021-316 0220; www.tarom.ro; Spl Independenţei 17, City Centre; ⊗ 8.30am-7.30pm Mon-Fri, 9am-1.30pm Sat), which has an extensive network of flights around Europe and to the Middle East.

➜ Several other cities have international airports that service mostly domestic flights and those to and from European cities. International airports that serve Transylvania include: Cluj's **Avram Iancu International Airport** (CLJ; ☏ 0264-307 500, 0264-416 702; www.airportcluj.ro; Str Traian Vuia 149-151) and **Sibiu International Airport** (SBZ; ☏ 0269-253 135; www.sibiuairport.ro; Sos Alba Iulia 73).

Land

Bus Long-haul bus services remain a popular way of travelling from Romania to Western Europe as well as to parts of southeastern Europe and Turkey. **Eurolines** (www.eurolines.ro) and **Atlassib** (☏ 0748-111 111, call centre 080-10 100 100; www.atlassib.ro; Soseaua Alexandriei 164) both maintain vast networks from cities throughout Europe to destinations all around Romania.

CENTRAL & EASTERN EUROPE ROMANIA SURVIVAL GUIDE

Moldova

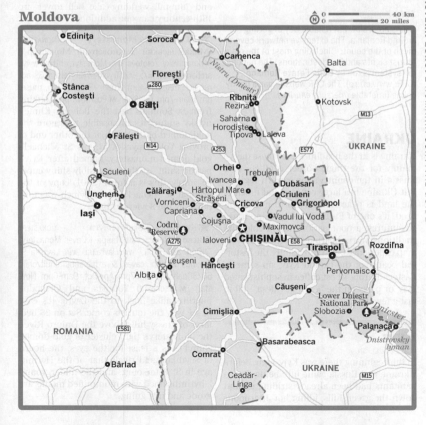

Train Romania is integrated into the European rail grid, and there are decent connections to Western Europe and neighbouring countries. Nearly all of these arrive at and depart from Bucharest's main station, Gara de Nord.

ℹ Getting Around

AIR

Given the distances and poor state of the roads, flying between cities is a feasible option if time is a concern. **Tarom** operates a comprehensive network of domestic routes.

BUS

A mix of buses and minibuses form the backbone of the national transport system. If you understand how the system works, you can move across the country easily and cheaply. Unfortunately, there's little logic behind how the system is organised. Buses and minibus routes change frequently and changes are communicated by word of mouth. Your best bet is to rely on tourist offices and your hotel to sort out transport options.

TRAIN

Trains are a slow but reliable way of getting around Romania. The extensive network covers much of the country, including most of the main tourist sights and key destinations. The national rail system is run by **Căile Ferate Române** (CFR; www.cfr.ro). The CFR website has a handy online timetable (mersul trenurilor).

UKRAINE

Ukraine is in the headlines a lot these days – mainly for the tragic border conflicts with Russia in the country's far eastern regions. But Ukraine is a large country and much of the land is peaceful and worth a visit. Indeed, it's one of Europe's last genuine travel adventures: a poor nation rich in colourful traditions, warm-hearted people and off-the-map experiences. You can admire the historical beauty of the capital Kyiv, sip some of Eastern Europe's best coffee in sophisticated Lviv, or party on the beach in Odesa – all in just a few days.

Kyiv

POP 2.8 MILLION

In the beginning there was Kyiv. Long before Ukraine and Russia came into being, its inhabitants had been already striding up and down the green hills, idling hot afternoons away on the Dnipro River and promenading along Kreshchatyk – then a stream, now the main avenue. These days, the city has a fair few must-sees, mostly related to the glorious Kyivan Rus past, as well as both charming and disturbingly eclectic architecture. But its main asset is the residents – a merry, tongue-in-cheek lot, who act as one when their freedoms are threatened.

◉ Sights

★ **St Sophia's Cathedral**   CHURCH
(pl Sofiyska; admission grounds/cathedral/bell tower 17/60/40uah; ⊘grounds 9am-7pm, cathedral 10am-6pm Thu-Tue, to 5pm Wed; Ⓜ Maydan Nezalezhnosti) The interior is the most astounding aspect of Kyiv's oldest standing church, St Sophia's Cathedral. Many of the mosaics and frescoes are original, dating back to 1017–31, when the cathedral was built to celebrate Prince Yaroslav's victory in protecting Kyiv from the Pechenegs (Tribal Raiders). While they're equally attractive, the building's gold domes and 76m-tall wedding-cake bell tower are 18th-century baroque additions.

★ **St Michael's Monastery**   MONASTERY
(Михайлівський Золотоверхий Монастир | Mykhaylivsky Zolotoverkhy Monastyr; http://www.archangel.kiev.ua/; vul Tryokhsvyatytelska 6; admission free, museum 17uah; ⊘8am-8pm, museum 10am-7pm Tue-Sun; Ⓜ Poshtova pl) Looking from St Sophia's past the Bohdan Khmelnytsky statue, it's impossible to ignore the gold-domed blue church at the other end of proyizd Volodymyrsky. This is St Michael's gold-domed monastery, named after Kyiv's patron saint. As the impossibly shiny cupolas imply, this is a fresh (2001) copy of the original St Michael's (1108), which was torn down by the Soviets in 1937.

★ **Kyevo-Pecherska Lavra**   MONASTERY
(Києво - Печерська Лавра | Caves Monastery; ☑044 280 3071; www.lavra.ua; vul Lavrska 9; grounds 20uah, caves & exhibitions adult/child 60/30uah; ⊘8am-7pm Apr-Oct, 9am-6pm Nov-Mar; Ⓜ Arsenalna) Tourists and Orthodox pilgrims alike flock to the Lavra. It's easy to see why the tourists come. Set on 28 hectares of grassy hills above the Dnipro River, the monastery's tight cluster of gold-domed churches is a feast for the eyes, the hoard of Scythian gold rivals that of the Hermitage in St Petersburg, and the underground labyrinths lined with mummified monks are exotic and intriguing.

★ Holodomor Memorial
MEMORIAL

(vul Ivana Mazepy 15A; Ⓜ Arsenalna) **FREE** At the far end of Vichnoy Slavy Park, centred around a Soviet-era war memorial, you will find a monument from an entirely different epoch. President Viktor Yushchenko's pet project, it is dedicated to almost four million victims of the famine, artificially induced by Stalin's policy of collectivisation in 1932–33.

Andriyivsky Uzviz
STREET

(Ⓜ Kontraktova Pl) According to legend a man walked up the hill, erected a cross and prophesied: 'A great city will stand on this spot'. That man was the Apostle Andrew, hence the name of Kyiv's quaintest thoroughfare, a steep cobbled street that winds its way up from Kontraktova Pl to vul Volodymyrska. Its vague Monparnasse feel has attracted Ukraine's lowbrow rich, but despite gentrification it still retains an atmosphere unique for Kyiv.

🛏 Sleeping

Lodging in the capital can be expensive outside of staying in a hostel. There are plenty of these as well as luxury hotels, but not much in the middle.

Dream House Hostel
HOSTEL €

(📞 044 580 2169; www.dream-family.com; Andriyivsky uzviz 2D; dm/d from 150/500uah; ✳@🛜; Ⓜ Kontraktova pl) Kyiv's most happening hostel is this gleaming 100-bed affair superbly located at the bottom of Andriyivsky uzviz. An attached cafe-bar, a basement kitchen, a laundry room, key cards, bike hire and daily events and tours make this a comfortable and engaging base from which to explore the capital.

★ Bohdan Khmelnitsky Boatel
CRUISE BOAT €

(📞 229 1919; vul Naberezhno-Khreshchatytska, moorage 5; r from 450uah; ⏱ Oct-Apr; Ⓜ Kontraktova pl) The grand dame of the Dnipro River fleet, this paddle boat built in Budapest in 1954 is now permanently moored in Podil. The dark-wood panelling in its corridors and smallish cabins looks immaculate, but it may be stuffy in the summer heat.

Ibis
HOTEL €€

(📞 591 2222; www.ibis.com; bul Tarasa Shevchenka 25; r from 1100uah; Ⓜ Universytet) Yes, it is a predictable chain hotel, but it still feels sparklingly new and is about the best value you can get for US$100 a night – and the most

comfortable bed, too. Otherwise, it is Ibis – with minimalistically designed, slightly cramped rooms and no minibar.

🍴 Eating

★ Musafir
CRIMEAN TATAR €

(Мусафір; 📞 050 930 4164; www.musafir.com.ua; vul Saksahanskoho 57; mains 60-90uah; ⏱ 10am-10pm; 🛜) The informal, traditional Musafir opened here in 2015 and specialises in Eastern-influenced Tatar cuisine, with an emphasis on grilled meats, stews, *yantyk* (pie-like pastry) and Turkish coffee. The latter is served with lumps of sugar that you are expected to put straight in your mouth, rather than in your cup. Gets crowded so best to book in advance.

★ Kanapa
UKRAINIAN €€

(Канапа; 📞 425 4548; www.kanapa-restaurant. kiev.ua/; Andriyivsky uzviz 19; mains 160uah; ⏱ 9am-11pm; 🛜) Sneak away from the busy street and you find yourself in what seems like a treehouse – a wooden terrace perched above the dense canopy of trees underneath. A unique place, Kanapa serves gentrified, 21st-century Ukrainian food, largely made from locally sourced farm produce.

★ Spotykach
UKRAINIAN €€

(Спотикач; 📞 044 586 4095; vul Volodymyrska 16; mains 100-180uah; ⏱ 11am-midnight; 🛜; Ⓜ Zoloti Vorota) A tribute to the 1960s, this discreetly stylish retro-Soviet cellar will make even a hardened dissident shed a nostalgic tear.

THE UKRAINIAN TABLE

Ukrainians admit theirs is a cuisine of comfort – full of hearty dishes designed for fierce winters rather than for gastronomic zing. And yet, while it's suffered from negative stereotypes of Soviet-style cabbage slop and pernicious pickles, Ukrainian cooking isn't bad. Look especially for **borshch** (борщ), the national soup made with beetroot, pork fat and herbs. **Cabbage rolls** (*holubtsy* голубці) are stuffed with seasoned rice and meat and stewed in a tomato and soured cream sauce. **Varenyky** (вареники), similar to Polish *pierogi*, are small, half-moon-shaped dumplings that have more than 50 different traditional vegetarian and meat fillings.

Central Kyiv

500 m
0.25 miles

Dnipro River

Mezhyhirya (30km)

vul Naberezhno-Khreshchatytska

Naberezhne shose

pl Poshtova

Volodymyrsky uzviz

Poshtova pl

PODIL

vul Voloska

vul Spaska

Kontraktova pl

vul Hryhoriya Skovorody

vul Illinska

vul Bratska

vul Sahaydachnoho

Z hyvopysna aleya

vul Desyatynna

St Michael's Monastery

vul Mykhaylivska

Maydan Nezalezhnosti

vul Mala Zhytomyrska

prov Tarasa Shevchenka

vul Sofiyska

vul Volodymyrska

St Sophia's Cathedral

vul Striletska

Kontraktova pl

vul Pokrovska

vul Khoryva

Provulok Khoreviv

vul Prytytsko-Mykilska

vul Borychiv Tik

vul Kostyantynivska

vul Verkhniy Val

vul Frunze

Andriyivsky Uzviz

vul Vozdvyzhenska

vul Kozhumyatska

VERKHNIY GOROD

Peyzazhna aleya

vul Velyka Zhytomyrska

vul Reytarska

vul Yaroslaviv Val

vul Hlybochytska

vul Petrivska

vul Kudryavska

vul Voznesensky uzviz

vul Observatorna

vul Yuriya Kotsyubynskoho

vul Olesya Honchara

prov Chekhovsky

vul Vorovskoho

Lukyanivska

vul Lukyanivska

vul Hlybochytska

vul Mykoly Rymonenka

vul Artyoma

vul Vyacheslava Chornovola

vul Poltavska

vul Pavlivska

vul Gogolivska

vul Turgenivska

vul Dmytrivska

vul Zolotoustivska

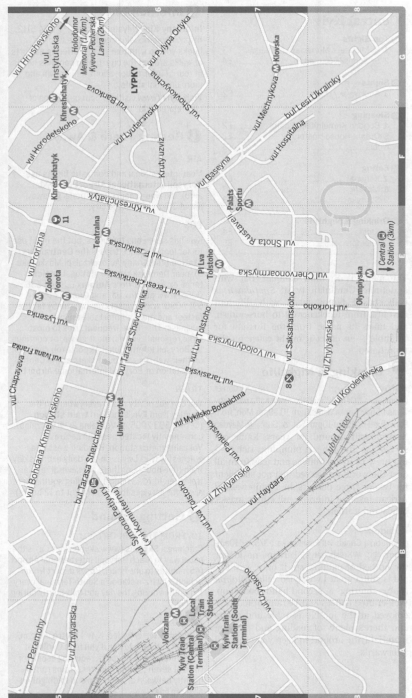

LYPKY

vul Hrushevskoho

vul Instytutska

Holodomor
Memorial (1.7km);
Kyevo-Pecherska
Lavra (2km)

vul Bankova

vul Pylypa Orlyka

vul Shovkovychna

Khreshchatyk

vul Horodetskoho

vul Lyuteranska

vul Mechnykova

Klovska

bul Lesi Ukrainky

Kruty uzviz

vul Hospitalna

Khreshchatyk

vul. Khreshchatyk

vul Baseyna

Palats
Sportu

vul Shota Rustaveli

Teatralna

11

vul Proprizna

vul Pushkinska

Pl Lva
Tolstoho

vul Chervonoarmiyska

Olympiyska

Central
Station (3km)

Zoloti
Vorota

vul Lysenka

vul Tereshchenkivska

bul Tarasa Shevchenka

vul Lva Tolstoho

vul Horkoho

vul Saksahanskoho

vul Zhylyanska

vul Ivana Franka

vul Chapayeva

vul Tarasivska

vul Volodymyrska

8

vul Korolenkivska

vul Bohdana Khmelnytskoho

bul Tarasa Shevchenka

Universytet

vul Mykilsko-Botanichna

vul Pankivska

vul Zhylyanska

vul Haydara

Lybid River

vul Symona Petlyury
(vul Kominternu)

9

vul Lva Tolstoho

vul Peremohy

vul Zhylyanska

vul Urytskoho

Vokzalna

Local
Train Station

Kyiv Train
Station (Central
Terminal)

Kyiv Train
Station (South
Terminal)

Central Kyiv

The menu is Kremlin banquet, but with a definite Ukrainian twist. *Spotykach* is vodka-based liquor made with different flavours, from blackcurrant to horseradish, and takes its name from the Russian for 'stumble' – an effect it might cause on the uninitiated.

🍷 Drinking & Nightlife

Kaffa   COFFEE

(Каффа; ☎044 425 3845; www.kaffa.ua; prov Tarasa Shevchenka 3; ☺11am-10.30pm Mon, from 9am Tue-Fri, 10am-10pm Sat & Sun; Ⓜ Maydan Nezalezhnosti) Around for years, Kaffa still serves the most heart-pumping, rich-tasting brew in town. Coffees and teas from all over the world are served in a pot sufficient for two or three punters, in a whitewashed African-inspired interior – all ethnic masks, beads and leather.

Kupidon   PUB

(Купідон | Cupid; vul Pushkinska 1-3/5; ☺10am-10pm; 🛜; Ⓜ Kreshchatyk) Perhaps no longer the hotbed of nationalism it once was, Cupid is still a great Lviv-styled cellar *knaypa* (pub) abutting a second-hand bookshop. Well-crafted coffees and Ukrainian food are enjoyed at the jumble of table and chairs and there's plenty of reading and drawing material lying around to keep you occupied afterwards.

ℹ Information

Interesny Kiev (Mysterious Kiev; ☎364 5112; http://mysteriouskiev.com/) The website hooks you up with tour guides offering all sorts of walks around the city. It also contains heaps of tourist information about well-known and more unusual sights.

Visit Kyiv (www.visitkyiv.com.ua) Heaps of city-related info.

ℹ Getting There & Away

AIR

Most international and domestic flights use **Boryspil International Airport** (www.kbp. aero), Ukraine's main international gateway, about 30km east of the city.

BUS

Kyiv has seven bus terminals, but the most useful for long-distance trips is the **Central Bus Station** (Tsentralny Avtovokzal; pl Moskovska 3), near Demiivska metro station. Long-distance express carriers **Autolux** (☎044 536 0055; www.autolux.ua) and **Gunsel** (☎044 591 9090; www.gunsel.com.ua) run by far the fastest and most comfortable buses in the business. They have frequent trips to most large regional centres; most go via, or continue to, Boryspil International Airport. You can book on their websites, or buy tickets at the Central Bus Station or Boryspil International Airport.

TRAIN

You can get pretty much everywhere in the country from Kyiv's modern **train station** (☎044 503 7005; pl Vokzalna 2; Ⓢ Vokzalna), conveniently located near the centre at Vokzalna metro station. Heading west, the quickest way to Lviv is on the daily express day train (five hours), or there are several regular trains (eight to 13 hours). Heading south, there are night services to Odesa (eight to 12 hours).

ℹ Getting Around

TO/FROM THE AIRPORT

Catching a **Sky Bus** (www.skybus.kiev.ua) is the usual way to reach Boryspil International Airport (45 minutes to one hour). Buses depart from behind Kyiv train station's South Terminal every 15 minutes during the day and half-hourly during the night.

METRO

Although often crowded, Kyiv's **metro** is clean, efficient and easy to use if you read Cyrillic. It is also the world's deepest, requiring escalator rides of seven to eight minutes. Trains run frequently between around 6am and midnight on all three lines.

Lviv

POP 756,000

If you've spent time in any other region of Ukraine, Lviv will come as a shock. Mysterious and architecturally lovely, this Unesco World Heritage Site is the country's least 'Soviet' and exudes much of the same authentic Central European charm as Prague or Kraków. Its quaint cobbles, bean-perfumed coffeehouses and rattling trams are half a continent away from the post-Soviet badlands to the east. It's also a place where the candle of Ukrainian national identity burns brightest and where Russian is definitely a minority language.

Sights

Ploshcha Rynok SQUARE

`FREE` Lviv was declared a Unesco World Heritage Site in 1998, and this old market square lies at its heart. The square was progressively rebuilt after a major fire in the early 16th century destroyed the original. The 19th-century **Ratusha** (Town Hall) stands in the middle of the plaza, with fountains featuring Greek gods at each of its

---

`WORTH A TRIP`

THE BLACK SEA PORT OF ODESA

The Black Sea coastal city of Odesa is a city straight from literature – an energetic, decadent boomtown. Its famous Potemkin Steps sweep down to the Black Sea and Ukraine's biggest commercial port. Behind them, a cosmopolitan cast of characters makes merry among pastel neoclassical buildings lining a geometrical grid of leafy streets.

Immigrants from all over Europe were invited to make their fortune here when Odesa was founded in the late 18th century by Russia's Catherine the Great. These new inhabitants gave Russia's southern window on the world a singular, subversive nature.

As well as becoming a duty-free port, Odesa also attracted ordinary holidaymakers with its sunny climate and sandy beaches. True, the city's appearance grows tattier as you head south past half-empty sanatoriums towards its beachside nightclubs. However, this east–west crossroads makes up for that with sheer panache, and Odesans are known across the old USSR for being stylish, funny, savvy and not easily impressed.

Sooner or later everyone gravitates to the tree-lined pedestrian zone of **Bul Prymorsky**, with its replica 19th-century gas lamps and park benches. At the boulevard's eastern end, you'll spot the pink-and-white colonnaded **City Hall**, originally the stock exchange and later the Regional Soviet Headquarters. The cannon here is a war trophy captured from the British during the Crimean War. In the square in front of City Hall is Odesa's most photographed monument, the **Pushkin Statue** (Пам'ятник Пушкіну). The plaque reads 'To Pushkin – from the Citizens of Odesa'.

Continuing along the boulevard, at the top of the Potemkin Steps you'll reach the **statue of Duc de Richelieu** (Пам'ятник герцогу де Рішельє), Odesa's first governor, looking like a Roman in a toga.

At the western end of bul Prymorsky stands the semi-derelict **Vorontsov Palace** (Воронцовський палац). This was the residence of the city's third governor, built in 1826 in a classical style with interior Arabic detailing. The Greek-style colonnade behind the palace offers brilliant views over Odesa's bustling port.

Lots of people swim at Odesa's crowded beaches in summer, but that's not really the aim of going to the beach here. Rather, it's about strolling disheveled promenades and observing local beach life, Ukrainian style. Be aware that drinking is now banned on and around Odesa's beaches, so don't give the ever-present police an excuse to extract money from you by carrying a cool one.

Odesa is well connected by train to major Ukrainian, Russian and Central European cities. Despite the addition of 'summer trains' on the most popular routes (eg Kyiv and Lviv), seats to/from Odesa fill up fast from June to August, so book ahead.

Frequent **Gunsel** (www.gunsel.com.ua) buses are the most comfortable and quickest way to travel to Kyiv (six to seven hours, five daily). Its nonstop VIP service has airline-style seats and a stewardess serving free refreshments.

KELLY CHENG TRAVEL PHOTOGRAPHY / GETTY IMAGES ©

1. Moscow, Russia
Be awed by the playful jumble of patterns and colours adorning St Basil's Cathedral (p784).

2. Plitvice Lakes National Park, Croatia
This national park (p618) is the highlight of any visit to Croatia's Adriatic hinterland.

3. Prague, Czech Republic
Grab yourself a drink and watch the world go by in Prague's Old Town Square (p700).

4. Budvar, Montenegro
Lose yourself in Budvar's atmospheric Stari Grad (Old Town; p638).

DANITA DELIMONT / GETTY IMAGES ©

corners. Vista junkies can climb the building's 65m-high neo-Renaissance **tower**.

Lviv History Museum
MUSEUM

(Львівський історичний музей; www.lhm.lviv. ua; admission 10uah to each branch; ⊙ all branches 10am-5.30pm Thu-Tue) Lviv's main museum is split into three collections dotted around pl Rynok. The best branch is at **No 6**. Here you can enjoy an Italian-Renaissance inner courtyard and slide around the exquisitely decorated interior in cloth slippers on the woodcut parquetry floor made from 14 kinds of hardwood. It was here on 22 December 1686 that Poland and Russia signed the treaty that partitioned Ukraine. **No 2**, the Palazzo Bandinelli, covers 19th- and 20th-century history. **No 24** expounds on the city's early days.

★ Lychakiv Cemetery
CEMETERY

(Личаківський цвинтар; ☑ 032 275 5415; www. lviv-lychakiv.ukrain.travel; vul Pekarska; admission 25uah; ⊙ 9am-6pm) Don't leave town until you've seen this amazing cemetery only a short ride on tram 7 from the centre. This is the Père Lachaise of Eastern Europe, with the same sort of overgrown grounds and Gothic aura as the famous Parisian necropolis (but containing less well-known people). Pride of place goes to the grave of revered nationalist poet Ivan Franko.

🛏 Sleeping

Lviv has a shortage of budget accommodation. Expect to pay around twice as much in Lviv as you would elsewhere in western Ukraine. The hostel situation also seems to be in constant flux, with expats setting them up and selling them off with alarming speed.

★ Old City Hostel
HOSTEL €

(☑ 032 294 9644; www.oldcityhostel.lviv.ua; vul Beryndy 3; dm/d from 160/450uah; @ 🛜) Occupying two floors of an elegantly fading tenement just steps from pl Rynok this expertly run hostel with period features and views of the Shevchenko statue from the wrap-around balcony long since established itself as the city's best. Fluff-free dorms hold four to 16 beds, shower queues are unheard of, sturdy lockers keep your stuff safe and there's a well-endowed kitchen.

Central Square Hostel
HOSTEL €

(☑ 095 225 6654; www.cshostel.com; pl Rynok 5; dm/d from 120/400; 🛜) This hostel may be small, but its location on pl Rynok puts you in the heart of the Lviv action. Free tea and coffee, a pint-sized kitchen and thief-proof lockers, but just one shower.

Hotel George
HOTEL €€

(☑ 032 232 6236; www.georgehotel.com.ua; pl Mitskevycha 1; s 480-900uah; d 600-1250uah; 🛜) The George is a historic hotel that offers decent value. The rooms have been given a modern makeover and have lost some of their antique, old-world charm, though the communal spaces remain elegant and untouched. The English-speaking staff are great and the buffet breakfast is still served in the amazing Oriental-style restaurant.

🍴 Eating

Lviv is more famous for cafes than restaurants, but the food scene has seen dramatic developments in recent years with some weird and wonderful theme restaurants popping up across the city centre.

Puzata Khata
CAFE €

(Пузата хата; ☑ 044 391 4699; www.puzatahata.com.ua; vul Sichovykh Striltsiv 12; mains 20-40uah; ⊙ 8am-11pm) This super-sized version of Ukraine's number-one restaurant chain stands out for its classy, Hutsul-themed interior and pure Ukrainian-rock soundtrack.

Dim Lehend
UKRAINIAN €€

(Дім легенд; vul Staroyevreyska 48; mains 30-70uah; ⊙ 11am-2am) Dedicated to the city of Lviv, there's nothing dim about the 'House of Legends'. The five floors contain a library stuffed with Lviv-themed volumes, a room showing live webcam footage of Lviv's underground river, rooms dedicated to lions and cobblestones, and another featuring the city in sounds. The menu is limited to Ukrainian staples but the coffee and desserts are excellent.

🍸 Drinking & Nightlife

★ Kabinet Cafe
CAFE

(Кафе Кабінет; vul Vynnychenka 12; ⊙ 10am-11pm) The jumble of moth-eaten antique chairs and sofas, book-lined walls and dusty parquet floors are no product of a restaurateur's imagination – this place is real. Evoking pre-war (and pre-tourism) Lviv, it would be a shame to sit outside on busy vul Vynnychenka in summer, and in winter this is the perfect spot to curl up with a book, order a warming cup of aromatic Lviv coffee and pretend it's 19-something.

Dzyga
CAFE

(Дзига; www.dzyga.com.ua; vul Virmenska 35; ⊙10am-midnight; ☎) This café-cum-art gallery in the shadow of the Dominican Cathedral has a relaxed vibe. It's particularly popular with bohemian, alternative types, but seems to attract pretty much everyone, really. The summertime outdoor seating is gathered around the city's Monument to the Smile.

ℹ Information

Tourist Information Centre (☑ 032 254 6079; www.touristinfo.lviv.ua; pl Rynok 1, Ratusha; ⊙10am-8pm Mon-Fri, to 7pm Sat, to 6pm Sun May-Sep, shorter hours Oct-Apr) Ukraine's best tourist information centre. Branches at the airport and the train station.

ℹ Getting There & Away

AIR

The city's **Danylo Halytskyi International Airport** (☑ 032 229 8112; www. wo.aero; vul Lyubinska 168) stands 7km west of the city centre. The main domestic carrier **Ukraine International Airlines** (www.flyuia.com) offers regulars flights to and from the capital, Kyiv. Internationally, Lviv is attracting an ever-increasing number of flights to European destinations, and flights service cities like Warsaw, Vienna and Munich among others.

BUS

The city's **Main Bus Station** (Holovny Avtovokzal; vul Stryska) is inconveniently located 7km south of the centre, though trolleybus No 5 can bring you back and forth. This is the main on/off spot for significant domestic and nearly all international coach services. Several buses daily ply the roads to Kyiv (nine hours). There are numerous external connections from here to the Czech Republic, Italy, Spain and Germany.

TRAIN

Lviv's Main Train Station is 2km west of the centre. The quickest way to Kyiv is on the daily Intercity+ express (travel time five hours), though this leaves at a bleary-eyed 5.55am. There are also several regular trains per day, but travel times vary from eight to 13 hours. International trains serve Moscow (25 hours, daily), Bratislava (18 hours, daily) and Minsk (12 hours, daily). There's a handy timetable at www.uz.gov.ua.

Ukraine Survival Guide

ℹ Directory A–Z

ACCOMMODATION

Accommodation will be your single biggest expense in Ukraine. Rooms are slightly more affordable than they once were due to favourable exchange rates. Big cities like Kyiv and Lviv are the most expensive.

➡ Hotel rates are listed in hryvnya, but you may still come across places where US dollars or euros are quoted.

➡ Hostelling is a well-established sector in Ukraine's accommodation market, especially in tourist hotspots like Kyiv and Lviv. These websites are useful for finding a hostel: **Hostelling Ukraine International** (www.hihostels.com.ua) and **Hostelworld** (www.hostelworld.com).

➡ Most so-called campsites are really former Soviet holiday camps, and slightly more formalised than most Western campers prefer. Facilities are usually poor. Wild camping is tolerated in most areas of the country, but not recommended. Lighting fires in national parks is forbidden.

MONEY

➡ The Ukrainian currency, the hryvnya, is divided into 100 kopecks. Kopecks have become worthless and prices are often rounded up or down.

➡ As this edition was being researched, price inflation was running at about 30% per year, meaning prices may be out of date.

➡ ATMs are widespread, even in small towns. Credit cards accepted at most hotels and upmarket restaurants. The best way to manage your money is to withdraw with your card.

➡ Exchange money at banks or exchange kiosks (обмін валюти) scattered along main streets and dotting markets. Some upmarket shops have their own exchange offices, as do

---

ℹ ACCOMMODATION PRICE RANGES

In this section we've used the following price indicators (double room in high season). Note: As this edition was being researched, price inflation was running at about 30% per year, meaning price information may be out of date.

€ less than 400uah

€€ 400–800uah

€€€ more than 800uah

> ### ⓘ EATING PRICE RANGES
>
> Price categories used per main course:
>
> **€** less than 70uah
>
> **€€** 70–180uah
>
> **€€€** more than 180uah

department stores and train stations. Rates are usually the same.

➡ Tipping is not common in Ukraine.

OPENING HOURS

Opening hours are consistent throughout the year with very few seasonal variations. Lunch breaks (usually 1pm to 2pm) are a throwback to Soviet days. Sunday closing is rare.

Banks 9am to 5pm Monday to Friday
Cafes 9am to 10pm
Restaurants 11am to 11pm
Bars and Clubs 10pm to 3am

Shops 9am to 9pm Monday to Saturday
Sights 9am to 5pm or 6pm, closed at least one day a week

PUBLIC HOLIDAYS

The main public holidays in Ukraine are the following:

New Year's Day 1 January
Orthodox Christmas 7 January
International Women's Day 8 March
Orthodox Easter (Paskha) April/May
Labour Day 1–2 May
Victory Day (1945) 9 May
Constitution Day 28 June
Independence Day (1991) 24 August

TELEPHONES

➡ Ukraine simplified the way numbers are dialled a few years ago, banishing the confusing system of Soviet-era prefixes and dialling tones. All numbers now start with 📞0.

➡ Ukraine's country code is 📞38.

Belarus

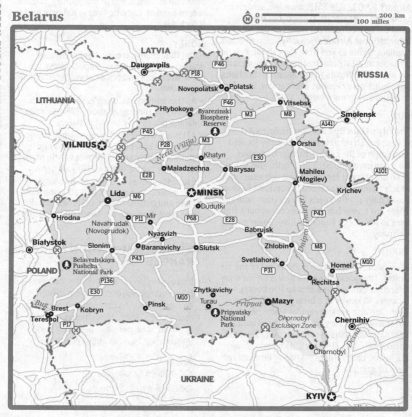

→ To call Kyiv from abroad, for example, dial the international access code plus ☏ 38, Ukraine's country code, plus ☏ 44, Kyiv's city code (dropping the first zero), and the subscriber number. There's no need to dial the city code if dialling within that city, unless you're calling from a mobile

→ To call internationally, dial ☏ 0, wait for a second tone, then dial ☏ 0 again, followed by the country code, city code and number.

→ European GSM phones usually work in Ukraine; double-check with your provider before leaving. However, if you're going to be making a few calls, it's more economical to get a prepaid SIM card. Top up credit using vouchers available from mobile-phone shops and news kiosks.

WI-FI
Internet service in Ukraine has improved immensely in recent years, and most hotels as well as upmarket cafes and restaurants offer free wi-fi.

❶ Getting There & Away

The majority of visitors fly to Ukraine – generally to Kyiv. However, low-cost flights to neighbouring

---

WORTH A TRIP

BELARUS

Eastern Europe's outcast, Belarus (Беларусь), lies at the edge of the region and seems determined to avoid integration with the rest of the continent at all costs. Taking its lead from the former Soviet Union, rather than the European Union, this little-visited dictatorship may seem like a strange choice for travellers, but its isolation lies at the heart of its appeal.

While the rest of Central and Eastern Europe has charged headlong into capitalism, Belarus allows the chance to visit a Europe with minimal advertising and no litter or graffiti.

Visitors typically begin in the capital **Minsk** (Мінск), which suffered tremendous damage in WWII and was built anew in the late 1940s and '50s as a flagship Stalinist city. The result is a remarkably uniform conurbation that is actually strangely attractive in the centre, the 1950s' Stalinist style being far grander and more colourful than the later, drabber Soviet architecture of the 1960s and '70s. The **Minsk Tourist Information Centre** (Інфармацыйны цэнтр Мінск Турыст; www.minsktourism.by) maintains a helpful website on attractions in the city, with information in English.

Another popular destination is the southwestern city of **Brest** (Брэст), a relatively prosperous and cosmopolitan border town that looks far more to the neighbouring EU than it does to Minsk. It has plenty of charm and has performed a massive DIY job on itself over the past few years in preparation for its millennial celebrations in 2019.

The city's main sight is the **Brest Fortress** (Брэсцкая крэпасць; Brestskaya krepost; pr Masherava) `FREE`, a moving WWII memorial where Soviet troops held out far longer than expected against the Nazi onslaught in the summer and autumn of 1941. But there are also several good museums here, and the impressive **Belavezhskaya Pushcha National Park** (☏ 01631 56 370; www.belarus.by/en/travel/belarus-life/belovezhskaya-pushcha) is nearby.

Outside the large cities, Belarus offers a simple yet pleasing landscape of cornflower fields, thick forests and picturesque villages. The country also is home to Europe's largest mammal, the *zoobr* (European bison). While travellers will always be a subject of curiosity, they'll also be on the receiving end of warm hospitality and a genuine welcome. The official **Belarus website** (www.belarus.by) is an excellent source of general information.

Most visitors arrive in Belarus by air. The national airline **Belavia** (☏ 017 220 2555; www.belavia.by; vul Nyamiha 14, Minsk) runs regular flights to and from several major European cities, including London, Paris, Frankfurt and Vienna.

Belarus is also accessible by bus, though long queues at border crossings are not uncommon. The most frequently used bus links are the four-hour trip between Vilnius (Lithuania) and Minsk, and the seven-hour trip between Minsk and Białystok (Poland). Services also run to/from Białystok and Brest. There are slower train connections to Belarus from Russia, Lithuania and Poland.

countries mean some travellers enter the country overland.

AIR

Kyiv's **Boryspil International Airport** (☑ 044 393 4371; www.kbp.aero), 30km southeast of the city centre, is the country's main international air gateway. The airport is home to Ukraine's major international air carrier: **Ukraine International Airlines** (www.flyuia.com).

LAND

Ukraine shares borders with Russia, Belarus, Poland, Slovakia, Hungary, Romania and Moldova. Both Kyiv and Lviv are well connected by bus and train to destinations around Europe. The easiest points of access are via Poland, Slovakia, Hungary and Moldova.

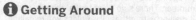 Getting Around

Ukraine International Airlines (www.flyuia.com) operates regular flights between Kyiv and Lviv and Odesa as well connecting other large cities around the country.

For overland travel, consult the Kyiv and Lviv sections for details. All trains are operated by **Ukrainian Railways** (www.uz.gov.ua). **Bus.com.ua** (www.bus.com.ua) has bus timetables but is hard to navigate.

Russia & the Baltic Coast

Best Places to Eat

➡ Varenichnaya No 1 (p790)

➡ V (p812)

➡ Miit (p826)

➡ Senamiesčio Krautuvė (p838)

Best Places to Sleep

➡ Soul Kitchen Hostel (p799)

➡ Tabinoya (p811)

➡ Naughty Squirrel (p825)

➡ Hostelgate B&B (p838)

Why Go?

When it comes to cultural mileage, the central and north-eastern reaches of the Baltic is as fuel-efficient a destination as you could ever hope for. First comes Russia, the big bear that lorded it over the region during the Soviet era and still casts a mighty shadow. This epic-scale nation packs a double whammy with Moscow and St Petersburg, among Europe's most impressive and dynamic cities, graced with imperial palaces, magnificent museums and stunning streetscapes.

In comparison, Estonia, Latvia and Lithuania are tiny. Yet in this wonderfully compact space there are three completely distinct cultures to discover – with different languages, different traditions and markedly different temperaments. By way of example, you need only look at the three unique yet equally compelling capitals: flamboyantly baroque Vilnius, chic art-nouveau Rīga and majestically medieval Tallinn.

Fast Facts

Capitals Moscow (Russia), Tallinn (Estonia), Rīga (Latvia), Vilnius (Lithuania)

Emergency ☑ 112 (Estonia)

Currency Rouble (R; Russia), Euro (€; Baltic States)

Languages Russian, Estonian, Latvian, Lithuanian

Visas Russia: required by all – apply at least a month in advance of your trip; Baltic States: not required for citizens of the EU, USA, Canada, Japan, New Zealand and Australia

Time zones Russia GMT plus three hours (GMT plus four hours in summer), Baltic States GMT plus two hours (GMT plus three hours in summer)

OFF THE BEATEN TRACK: LAHEMAA NATIONAL PARK

Discover the open-air museum of stones and picturesque fishing village of Alja. (p813)

OFF THE BEATEN TRACK: ŽEMAITIJA NATIONAL PARK

Visit the Cold War Museum in an ex-Soviet nuclear missile base. (p846)

WORTH A TRIP: KALININGRAD

Explore this tiny slice of Russia and its lovely Baltic coast. (p802)

OFF THE BEATEN TRACK: DAUGAVPILS

Check out the new Mark Rothko Art Centre. (p832)

SWEDEN
STOCKHOLM
HELSINKI
Fårö
Gotland
BALTIC SEA
Hiiumaa
Saaremaa
Tallinn 3
Lahemaa National Park
Narva
Gulf of Finland
ESTONIA
Pärnu
Lake Võrtsjärv
Tartu 4
Narva
Lake Pihkva
Ventspils
Gulf of Riga
Valmiera
Cēsis
Smiltene
Pskov
Pechory
Kuldiga
Jūrmala Riga 6
5 Gauja National Park
Sigulda
Liepāja
Jelgava
LATVIA
Lake Lubāns
Klaipēda
Žemaitija National Park
Šiauliai
Rēzekne
Kurshskaya Kosa National Park
Lake Lūkstas
Panevėžys
Daugavpils
Curonian Spit 7
Neman (Nemunas)
LITHUANIA
Svetlogorsk
Yantarny
Zelenogradsk
Sovetsk
Baltiysk
Kaliningrad
Cernyakhovsk
Kaunas
Vilnius 8
Trakai
Olsztyn
Druskininkai
Velikaya
Dnipro (Dnieper)
BELARUS
MINSK
WARSAW

Russia & the Baltic Coast Highlights

① **Moscow** Russia's mega-capital offers historical showstoppers, such as the Kremlin and Red Square, as well as cool creativity. (p784)

② **St Petersburg** Home to the amazing Hermitage and gilded palaces, the old imperial capital is a stunner. (p793)

③ **Tallinn** Explore the Estonian capital's Old Town

of polished medieval abodes. (p806)

④ **Tartu** Further your education among the museums and student bars of this electric university town. (p814)

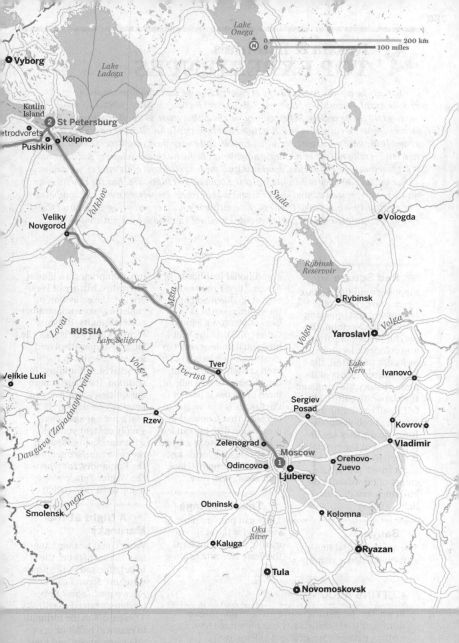

Russia & Estonia's
TOP EXPERIENCES

Could there be a more iconic image of eastern Europe than the awe-inspiring architectural ensemble of Moscow's Red Square? Russia's capital (p784) is a must on any trip to the region. St Petersburg, on the Baltic coast, is another stunner. The former imperial capital is still Russia's most beautiful and alluring city, with its grand Italianate mansions, wending canals and enormous Neva River. Emulating the tourist-friendly nature of its Baltic neighbours is the Russian exclave of Kaliningrad: it's a fascinating destination, combining all the best elements of its enormous mother.

For the last 300 years Estonia's history been linked to Russia, but the two have as much in common as a barn swallow and a bear (their respective national symbols). The capital Tallinn (p806) is one of the continent's most captivating cities, and the sparsely populated countryside provide spiritual sustenance for nature-lovers.

⭐ Red Square

Stepping onto Red Square never ceases to inspire: the tall towers and imposing walls of the Kremlin, the playful jumble of patterns and colours adorning St Basil's Cathedral, the majestic red bricks of the State History Museum and the elaborate edifice of GUM, all encircling a vast stretch of cobblestones. Individually they are impressive, but the ensemble is electrifying. Come at night to see the square empty of crowds and the buildings awash with lights. (p784)

⭐ Banya

The quintessential Russian experience is visiting a traditional bathhouse, or *banya*. Forget your modesty, strip down and brave the steam room at the likes of Moscow's Sanduny Baths (p791). As the heat hits, you'll understand why locals wear felt hats to protect their hair. A light thrashing with a bundle of birch branches is part of the fun, as is the invigorating blast that follows the post-steam dive into an icy pool or the douse in a frigid shower – as the locals say, '*S lyogkim parom!*' (Hope your steam was easy!).

⭐ The Hermitage

Little can prepare most visitors for the scale and quality of the exhibits at the State Hermitage Museum. Comprising an almost unrivalled history of Western art, the collection includes a staggering number of Rembrandts, Rubens, Picassos and Matisses – the latter two now displayed in new galleries in the General Staff Building. In addition, there are superb antiquities, sculpture and jewellery on display. If that's not enough, then simply content yourself with wandering through the private apartments of the Romanovs, for whom the Winter Palace was home until 1917. (p793)

⭐ A Night at the Mariinsky

What could be more Russian than a night at the ballet, dressed to the nines, watching *Swan Lake* or *Romeo and Juliet*? St Petersburg's famed Mariinsky Theatre offers the ultimate in classical ballet or operatic experiences, and now with a contemporary twist as the Mariinsky's long-awaited second stage has finally opened. Also worth a visit is Moscow's Bolshoi Theatre, looking better

---

GETTING AROUND

Train Best for getting between the major cities in both countries; particularly recommended for connecting between Moscow and St Petersburg.

Bus Bus routes are extensive in both Russia and Estonia and cover places where trains don't reach.

Urban Transport Moscow and St Petersburg both have excellent and cheap metro systems. Tallin's network of buses, trams and trolleybuses is also good.

than ever after a long renovation. Tickets are no longer cheap, but the experience will stay with you forever. (p800)

 Tallinn's Old Town

There was a time when sturdy walls and turreted towers enclosed most of Europe's cities, but wartime bombing and the advent of the car put paid to most of them. Tallinn's Old Town is a magical window into that bygone world, inducing visions of knights and ladies, merchants and peasants – not least due to the locals' proclivity for period dress. Rambling lanes lined with medieval dwellings open onto squares once covered in the filth of everyday commerce – now lined with cafes and altogether less gory markets selling souvenirs and handicrafts. (p807)

Tartu

Tartu is to Estonia what Oxford and Cambridge are to England. Like those towns, it's the presence of an esteemed ancient university and its attendant student population (with associated high japes and insobriety) that gives it its special character. There's a museum on nearly every corner of Tartu's elegant streets and, it seems, a grungy bar in every other cellar. When the sun shines, the hill in the centre of town is the best place to observe those eternal clichés of undergraduate life: earnest prattling, hopeless romancing and enthusiastic drinking. (p814)

Pärnu

Chances are you're not visiting the Baltic with images of endless sandy beaches hovering before your eyes, but Pärnu offers exactly that. When the quirky notion of sea-bathing became fashionable at the dawn of the 20th century, Pärnu became Estonia's most popular seaside resort – and it's hardly less so today. Architectural gems of that period combine with relics of the Hanseatic past to create very pleasant streets to explore, with interesting eateries and bars lurking within them. (p817)

Lahemaa National Park

Providing a one-stop shop of all of Estonia's major habitats – coast, forests, plains, peat bogs, lakes and rivers – within a very convenient 80km of the capital, Lahemaa is the slice of rural Estonia that travellers on a tight schedule really shouldn't miss. On top of the natural attractions, there are graceful baroque manors to peruse, pocket-sized villages to visit and country taverns to take refuge in whenever the weather turns and the stomach growls. (p813)

if Russia were 100 people

80 would be Russian
4 would be Tatar
2 would be Ukrainian
1 would be Bashkir
1 would be Chuvash
12 would be other

belief systems
(% of population)

Orthodox Christian 75 Muslim 5 Buddhist 1
Catholic 1 other 18

population per sq km

ESTONIA FINLAND RUSSIA

= 3 people

When to Go

Moscow

Latvia & Lithuania's
TOP EXPERIENCES

A tapestry of sea, lakes and woods, Latvia (p821) is is a vast pristine parkland with just one real city – its cosmopolitan capital, Rīga. The country might be small, but the amount of personal space it provides is enormous. You can always secure a chunk of pristine nature all for yourself, be it for trekking, cycling or dreaming away on a white-sand beach amid pine-covered dunes. People here fancy themselves the least pragmatic and the most artistic of the Baltic lot. They prove the point with myriad festivals and a merry, devil-may-care attitude – well, a subdued Nordic version of it.

A land of wood and water, proud, independent Lithuania (Lietuva; p834) is fast being recognised as one of Europe's gems. Southernmost of the Baltic states, it's a pocket-sized republic that's a nature-lover's delight, yet lacks nothing in urban excitement. The capital, Vilnius, is a beguiling artists' enclave, its timeworn courtyards, cobbled streets and baroque churches animated by the vibrant, optimistic culture of today. However, the county's foremost attraction is its stunning Baltic coastline, especially the unique sliver of white sand known as Curonian Spit. Lonely coastal wetlands lure migrating birds by the tens of thousands while inland, lush forests watch over burnished lakes.

⭐ Rīga's Art Nouveau Architecture

If you ask any Rīgan where to find the city's world-famous art nouveau architecture, you will always get the same answer: 'Look up!' Over 750 buildings in Latvia's capital – more than any other city in Europe – boast this flamboyant and haunting style of decor. Spend a breezy afternoon snapping your camera at the imaginative facades in the city's Quiet Centre district to find an ethereal (and almost eerie) melange of screaming demons, enraptured deities, overgrown flora and bizarre geometrical patterns. (p821)

⭐ Jūrmala

Jūrmala was once the most fashionable spa centre and beach resort in all of the former Russian Empire. And while the sanatorium craze has come and gone, it's still an uberpopular place to pamper oneself silly, with unending menus of bizarre services (chocolate massages?). Even if you're not particularly keen to swim at the shallow beach, it's well worth the day trip from the Latvian capital to check out the wonderful old wooden mansions and witness the ostentatious presentations of the nouveau riche. (p827)

⭐ Gauja National Park

Dotted with sweet little towns, such as Sigulda, and dramatic fortifications, Latvia's Gauja National Park entrances all who visit. The tower of Turaida Castle rises majestically over the huddling pines, a glorious reminder of the fairy-tale kingdoms that once ruled the land. And after you've had your history lesson, it's time to spice things up with a bevy of adrenalin-inducing sports, such as bungee jumping from a cable car or careering down a frozen bobsled track. (p828)

GETTING AROUND

Train Services are limited in Latvia compared to Lithuania. Generally the best way for getting between the major cities.

Bus In Latvia, buses are more frequent than trains and serve more of the country. In Lithuania the bus network is extensive, efficient and relatively cheap.

Urban Transport Rīga and Vilnius are easily explored on foot or by bicycle, but both cities also have excellent public transport.

FORAGED FOOD

The Baltic locavore movement isn't just up-and-coming: it has arrived with much ado, and its mascot is the mushroom. The damp climate makes places like Lithuania's Dzūkija National Park a wonderful spot for finding all sorts of scrumptious fungi. But if you want to indulge in some foraging of your own, it's safer to wait until berry season.

⭐ Vilnius's Baroque Old Town

Tempting hideaways, inviting courtyards, baroque churches and terrace bars serving beer – the Lithuanian capital's Old Town is one of the best places to get lost in throughout the Baltics. Old and new seem to coexist seamlessly here: whether you're looking for that thrift-shop boutique, an organic bakery, a cosy little bookshop or just a quiet spot to have a coffee, they're all likely to be standing side-by-side down some as-yet-unexplored cobblestone alleyway. (p835)

⭐ Curonian Spit

There's something elemental – even slightly old-fashioned – about Lithuania's loveliest seaside retreat: a long, thin strip of rare and majestic sand dunes that lines the southeastern corner of the Baltic Sea. Maybe it's the pine scent or the sea breezes, or the relative isolation that so vividly recalls German writer Thomas Mann's sojourns here in the early 1930s. Come to Curonian Spit to recharge your batteries and renew your faith in the redemptive powers of wind, water, earth and sky. (p846)

⭐ Hill of Crosses

Your first thought as you traverse the flat Lithuanian landscape in search of this landmark is likely to be something along the lines of, 'Where did they ever find a hill?' And then you glimpse it in the distance – more a mound than a mountain – covered in crosses by the tens of thousands. The hill takes on even more significance when you realise that the crosses planted here represent not just religious faith but an affirmation of the country's very identity. (p844)

⭐ Midsummer's Eve

Although church affiliations are widespread, ancient pagan rituals are still deeply woven into the fabric of all three countries. Storks are revered, even-numbered bouquets of flowers are superstitiously rebuffed and the summer solstice is held in the highest regard. While every town and village has a celebration, one great place to see in the solstice is Lithuania's Lake Plateliai (p846).

if Latvia were 100 people

61 would be Latvian
26 would be Russian
4 would be Belarusian
2 would be Ukrainian
2 would be Polish
5 would be other

belief systems
(% of population)

23 — Roman Catholic
20 — Lutheran
17 — Orthodox Christian
40 — other or none

population per sq km

LITHUANIA   LATVIA   RUSSIA

⬤ ≈ 9 people

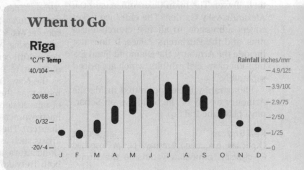

When to Go

Rīga

°C/°F **Temp**
40/104 —
20/68 —
0/32 —
-20/-4 —

Rainfall inches/mm
— 4.9/125
— 3.9/100
— 2.9/75
— 2/50
— 1/25
— 0

J F M A M J J A S O N D

RUSSIA

Moscow

📋 495 OR 499 / POP 12 MILLION

Intimidating in scale, but also exciting and unforgettable, Moscow is a place that inspires extreme passion or loathing. History, power and wild capitalism hang in the air, alongside an explosion of creative energy throwing up edgy art galleries and a dynamic restaurant, bar and nightlife scene.

The sturdy stone walls of the Kremlin occupy the city's founding site on the northern bank of the Moscow River. Remains of the Soviet state, such as Lenin's Tomb, are nearby in Red Square and elsewhere in the city which radiates from the Kremlin in a series of ring roads.

👁 Sights

👁 The Kremlin & Red Square

Kremlin MUSEUM
(Кремль; 📋495-695 4146; www.kreml.ru; R500; ⏱10am-5pm Fri-Wed, ticket office 9.30am-4.30pm Fri-Wed; Ⓜ Aleksandrovsky Sad) The apex of Russian political power and once the centre of the Orthodox Church, the Kremlin is not only the kernel of Moscow but of the whole country. It's from here autocratic tsars, communist dictators and modern-day presidents have done their best – and worst – for Russia.

Covering Borovitsky Hill on the north bank of the Moscow River, the Kremlin is enclosed by high walls 2.25km long, with Red Sq outside the east wall. The best views of the complex are from Sofiyskaya nab across the river.

Before entering the Kremlin, deposit bags at the **left-luggage office** (per bag R60; ⏱9am-6.30pm Fri-Wed), beneath the Kutafya Tower. The main ticket office is in the Alexandrovsky Garden. The entrance ticket covers admission to all five church-museums, and the Patriarch's Palace. It does not include the Armoury, the Diamond Fund Exhibition or special exhibits, which are priced separately.

Photography is not permitted inside the Armoury or any of the buildings on Sobornaya pl (Cathedral Sq).

Red Square HISTORIC SITE
(Красная площадь; Krasnaya pl; Ⓜ Ploshchad Revolyutsii) Immediately outside the Krem-

lin's northeastern wall is the celebrated Red Square, the 400m by 150m area of cobblestones that is at the very heart of Moscow. Commanding the square from the southern end is **St Basil's Cathedral** (Покровский собор, Храм Василия Блаженного; www.saint-basil.ru; adult/student R250/50, audio guide R200; ⏱11am-5pm; Ⓜ Ploshchad Revolyutsii). This panorama never fails to send the heart aflutter, especially at night.

Lenin's Mausoleum MEMORIAL
(Мавзолей Ленина; www.lenin.ru; ⏱10am-1pm Tue-Thu & Sat; Ⓜ Ploshchad Revolyutsii) FREE Although Vladimir Ilych requested that he be buried beside his mum in St Petersburg, he still lies in state at the foot of the Kremlin wall, receiving visitors who come to pay their respects. Line up at the western corner of the square (near the entrance to Alexander Garden) to see the embalmed leader, who has been here since 1924. Note that photography is not allowed; and stern guards ensure that all visitors remain respectful and silent.

👁 South of the Moscow River

**State Tretyakov Gallery
Main Branch** GALLERY
(Главный отдел Государственной Третьяковской галереи; www.tretyakovgallery.ru/en; Lavrushinsky per 10; R400; ⏱10am-6pm Tue, Wed, Sat & Sun, to 9pm Fri & Sun, last tickets 1hr before closing; Ⓜ Tretyakovskaya) The exotic boyar (high-ranking noble) castle on a little lane in Zamoskvorechie contains the main branch of the State Tretyakov Gallery, housing the world's best collection of Russian icons and an outstanding collection of other prerevolutionary Russian art. Show up early to beat the queues.

New Tretyakov Gallery GALLERY
(Новая Третьяковская галерея; www.tretyakovgallery.ru/en/; ul Krymsky val 10; R400; ⏱10am-6pm Tue, Wed & Sun, to 9pm Thu-Sat , last tickets 1hr before closing; Ⓜ Park Kultury) The premier venue for 20th-century Russian art is this branch of the State Tretyakov Gallery, better known as the New Tretyakov. This place has much more than the typical socialist realist images of muscle-bound men wielding scythes, and busty women milking cows (although there's that too). The exhibits showcase avant-garde artists such as Malevich, Kandinsky, Chagall, Goncharova and Popova. A joint ticket for both Tretyakov galleries (R700) saves R100.

Art Muzeon & Krymskaya Naberezhnaya
SCULPTURE PARK

(ul Krymsky val 10; M Park Kultury) FREE Now fully revamped and merged with the wonderfully reconstructed Krymskaya Naberezhnaya embankment is this motley collection of (mostly kitschy) sculpture and monuments to Soviet idols (Stalin, Sverdlov, a selection of Lenins and Brezhnevs) that were ripped from their pedestals in the post-1991 wave of anti-Soviet feeling. All of these stand in a lovely gardens with boardwalks and many inviting benches.

★ Gorky Park
PARK

(Парк Горького; ⊙24hr; 🚼; M Oktyabrskaya) FREE Moscow's main escape from the city within the city is not your conventional expanse of nature preserved deep inside an urban jungle. It is not a fun fair either, though it used to be one. Its official name says it all – Maxim Gorky's Central Park of Culture & Leisure. That's exactly what it provides: culture and leisure in all shapes and forms. Designed by avant-garde architect Konstantin Melnikov as a piece of communist utopia in the 1920s, these days it showcases the enlightened transformation Moscow has undergone in the recent past.

◎ West of the Kremlin

Pushkin Museum of Fine Arts
MUSEUM

(Музей изобразительных искусств им Пушкина; ☎495-697 9578; www.arts-museum.ru; ul Volkhonka 12; single gallery/combined galleries R300/550, from 5pm Fri R500/800; ⊙11am-7pm Tue, Wed, Sat & Sun, to 8pm Thu & Fri; M Kropotkinskaya) This is Moscow's premier foreign-art museum, split over three branches and showing off a broad selection of European works, including masterpieces from ancient civilisations, the Italian Renaissance and the Dutch Golden Age. To see the incredible collection of Impressionist and post-Impressionist paintings, visit the Gallery of European & American Art.

Novodevichy Convent
CONVENT

(Новодевичий монастырь; adult/student R300/100, photos R100; ⊙grounds 8am-8pm, museums 9am-5pm Wed-Mon; M Sportivnaya) The Novodevichy Convent was founded in 1524 to celebrate the taking of Smolensk from Lithuania, an important step in Moscow's conquest of the old Kyivan Rus lands. The oldest and most dominant building in the grounds is the white Smolensk Cathe-

DON'T MISS

JEWISH MUSEUM & CENTRE OF TOLERANCE

Occupying a heritage garage, purpose-built to house a fleet of Leyland double-deckers that plied Moscow streets in the 1920s, this vast **museum** (Еврейский музей и Центр терпимости; ☎495-645 0550; www.jewish-museum.ru; ul Obraztsova 11 str 1A; adults/students R400/200; ⊙noon-10pm Sun-Thu; M Novoslobodskaya), filled with cutting-edge multimedia technology, tackles the uneasy subject of relations between Jews and the Russian state over the centuries. The exhibition tells the stories of pogroms, Jewish revolutionaries, the Holocaust and Soviet anti-Semitism in a calm and balanced manner. The somewhat limited collection of material exhibits is compensated for by the abundance of interactive video displays.

dral, with a sumptuous interior covered in 16th-century frescoes. Novodevichy is a functioning monastery. Women are advised to cover their heads and shoulders when entering the churches, while men should wear long pants.

Cathedral of Christ the Saviour
CHURCH

(Храм Христа Спасителя; www.xxc.ru; ul Volkhonka 15; ⊙1-5pm Mon, 10am-5pm Tue-Sun; M Kropotkinskaya) FREE This gargantuan cathedral was completed in 1997 – just in time to celebrate Moscow's 850th birthday. It is amazingly opulent, garishly grandiose and truly historic. The cathedral's sheer size and splendour guarantee its role as a love-it-or-hate-it landmark. Considering Stalin's plan for this site (a Palace of Soviets topped with a 100m statue of Lenin), Muscovites should at least be grateful they can admire the shiny domes of a church instead of the shiny dome of Ilyich's head.

☞ Tours

Moscow Free Tour
WALKING TOUR

(☎495-222 3466; http://moscowfreetour.com; Nikolskaya ul 4/5; paid tours R950-1550) Every day these enthusiastic ladies offer an informative, inspired two-hour guided walk around Red Square and Kitay Gorod – and it's completely free. It's so good you'll likely sign up for one of their excellent paid tours, covering the Kremlin, the Arbat and the

The Kremlin

A DAY AT THE KREMLIN

Only at the Kremlin can you see 800 years of Russian history and artistry in one day. Enter the ancient fortress through the Trinity Gate Tower and walk past the impressive Arsenal, ringed with cannons. Past the Patriarch's Palace, you'll find yourself surrounded by white-washed walls and golden domes. Your first stop is **Assumption Cathedral** ❶ with the solemn fresco over the doorway. As the most important church in prerevolutionary Russia, this 15th-century beauty was the burial site of the patriarchs. The **Ivan the Great Bell Tower** ❷ now contains a nifty multimedia exhibit on the architectural history of the Kremlin. The view from the top is worth the price of admission. The tower is flanked by the massive **Tsar Cannon & Bell** ❸.

In the southeast corner, **Archangel Cathedral** ❹ has an elaborate interior, where three centuries of tsars and tsarinas are laid to rest. Your final stop on Sobornaya pl is **Annunciation Cathedral** ❺, rich with frescoes and iconography.

Walk along the Great Kremlin Palace and enter the **Armoury** ❻ at the time designated on your ticket. After gawking at the goods, exit the Kremlin through Borovitsky Gate and stroll through the Alexander Garden to the **Tomb of the Unknown Soldier** ❼.

TOP TIPS

» **Lunch** There are no eating options. Plan to eat before you arrive or stash a snack.

» **Lookout** After ogling the sights around Sobornaya pl, take a break in the park across the street, which offers wonderful views of the Moscow River and points south.

WALTER BIBIKOW / GETTY IMAGES ©

Assumption Cathedral

Once your eyes adjust to the colourful frescoes, the gilded fixtures and the iconography, try to locate *Saviour with the Angry Eye*, a 14th-century icon that is one of the oldest in the Kremlin.

Arsenal

BOROVITSKY TOWER

Use the entrance at Borovitsky Tower if you intend to skip the churches and visit only the Armoury or Diamond Fund.

Borovitsky Tower

Trinity Gate Tower

Alexander Garden

❻

Great Kremlin Palace

LONELY PLANET / GETTY IMAGES ©

Armoury

Take advantage of the free audio guide to direct you to the most intriguing treasures of the Armoury, which is chock-full of precious metalworks and jewellery, armour and weapons, gowns and crowns, carriages and sledges.

Tomb of the Unknown Soldier

Visit the Tomb of the Unknown Soldier honouring the heroes of the Great Patriotic War. Come at the top of the hour to see the solemn synchronicity of the changing of the guard.

AVOID CONFUSION

Regular admission to the Kremlin does not include Ivan the Great Bell Tower. But admission to the bell tower does include the churches on the Kremlin grounds.

Ivan the Great Bell Tower

Check out the artistic electronic renderings of the Kremlin's history, then climb 137 steps to the belfry's upper gallery, where you will be rewarded with super, sweeping vistas of Sobornaya pl and beyond.

Patriarch's Palace

⑦ ① ② ③ ⑤ ④

Moscow River

Sobornaya pl

Tsar Cannon & Bell

Peer down the barrel of the monstrous Tsar Cannon and pose for a picture beside the oversized Tsar Bell, both of which are too big to serve their intended purpose.

Annunciation Cathedral

Admire the artistic mastery of Russia's greatest icon painters – Theophanes the Greek and Andrei Rublyov – who are responsible for many of the icons in the deesis and festival rows of the iconostasis.

Archangel Cathedral

See the final resting place of princes and emperors who ruled Russia for more than 300 years, including the visionary Ivan the Great, the tortured Ivan the Terrible and the tragic Tsarevitch Dmitry.

Central Moscow

1 km
0.5 miles

MAYAKOVSKAYA

Jewish Museum & Centre of Tolerance (2km)

ul Fadeeva
Dolgorukovskaya ul
ul Vasnetskaya
1-ya Tverskaya-Yamskaya ul
1-ya Brestskaya ul
Triumfalnaya pl
Mayakovskaya
Bolshaya Sadovaya (Garden Ring)
Oruzheyny per
Sadovaya-Karetnaya ul
Kosoy per
Delegatskaya ul
Vasilevskaya ul

Sadovaya-Karetnaya ul
Maly Karetny per
ul Karetny Ryad
Hermitage Gardens
Uspensky per
ul Malaya Dmitrovka

(Garden Ring)
ul Shchepkina
Samotechnaya
Troitskaya ul
Tsvetnoy Bulvar
Tsvetnoy Bulvar
Tsvetnoy bul
Trubnaya ul
Trubnaya pl
Trubnaya
Petrovsky
per Daev
Posledny per
Pushkarev per
Pushkarev per

Leningradsky Vokzal
Yaroslavsky Vokzal
Kazansky Vokzal
Komsomolskaya
Komsomolskaya pl
Izmaylovsky Market (7.7km)
Komsomolskaya
Kalanchevskaya
Ryazansky per
Kalanchevskaya ul
Park im Bauman
ul Zemlyanoy val
Kurskaya
Maly Kazenny per
Lyapin per

ul Mashi Poryvaevoy
Dokuchaev per
Skornyazhny per
1-y Koptelsky per
Sadovaya-Spasskaya ul
Sadovaya-Sukharevskaya ul

pr Akademika Sakharova
Olkhov per
Krasnye Vorota
Pl Krasnye Vorota
Krasnye Vorota
(Garden Ring)
ul Mashkova
ul Pokrovka
ul Chaplygina
ul Zhukovskogo
Bolshoy Kharitonyevsky per
Furmanny per
Furmanny per
Chistoprudny bul
Chistye Prudy
Chistye Prudy
pl Pokrovskie Vorota
Pokrovsky bul
Kolpachny per

pr Mira
Sukharevskaya
Sukharevskaya pl
ul Gilyarovskogo

Myasnitskaya ul
Turgenevskaya
Turgenevskaya pl
Turgenevskaya
Sretensky Bulvar
Sretensky Bulvar
Myasnitskaya ul
ul Malaya Lubyanka
ul Bolshaya Lubyanka
Milyutinsky per
Krivokolenny per
Armyansky per
Potapovsky per
Potapovsky per

(Boulevard Ring)
Rozhdestvensky bul
Lukov per
Ulansky per

Lubyanskaya pl
Lubyanka
Lubyanka
Kitay-Gorod
Lubyansky proezd
Novaya pl
Kitay-Gorod
Kitay-Gorod

Rozhdestvensky bul
per Kolokolnikov
per Pechatnikov
Bolshoy Kiselny per
Varsonofevsky per
Kuznetsky Most
Pushechnaya ul
Kuznetsky Most

Zvonarsky per
Bolshoy Kiselny per
⊕ 11
ul Neglinnaya

ul Neglinnaya
ul Kuznetsky most
★ 24
★ 23
Teatralny proezd
Teatralnaya pl
Teatralnaya
Ploshchad Revolyutsii
Teatralny proezd
● 10

Petrovsky bul
🏨 13
ul Petrovka
ul Petrovka
per Petrovsky
ul Bolshaya Dmitrovka
21
Stoleshnikov per
Kamergersky per
Georgievsky per
12
Okhotny Ryad
Okhotny Ryad
Manezhnaya pl

Strastnoy bul
Putinkovsky per
🏛 14
Chekhovskaya
Pushkinskaya
Tverskaya
Tverskaya ul
Bryusov per
Gazetny per
ul Bolshaya Nikitskaya
Bolshaya Nikitskaya ul

20
Bolshoy Kozikhinsky per
Malaya Bronnaya ul
Bolshaya Bronnaya ul
Tverskoy bul (Boulevard Ring)
Leontievsky per
Voznesensky per
Maly Gnezdnikovsky
Bryusov per
Bolshaya Nikitskaya ul
Kalashny per
Nikitsky bul

Tverskaya ul
22 🏨
Pushkinskaya pl
Pushkinskaya
Bolshaya Bronnaya ul
15 🏨
Bolshoy Kozikhinsky per
pl Nikitskie Vorota
Merzlyakovsky
16

Patriarch's Pond
Malaya Bronnaya ul
Bolshoy Patriarshy per
Granatny per
Spiridonovka
Malaya Nikitskaya ul
Bolshaya Nikitskaya ul
★ 25

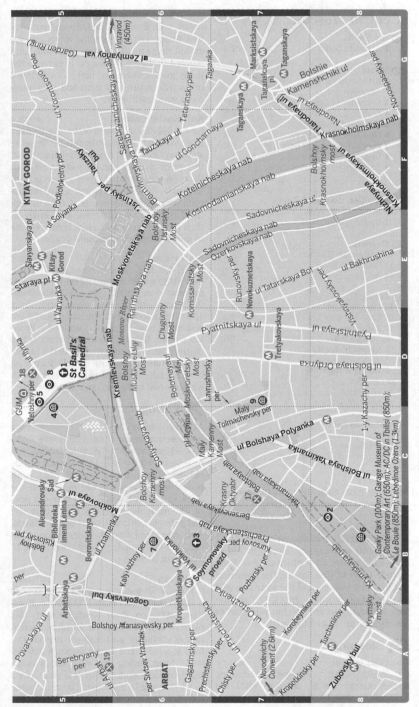

KITAY GOROD

ul Vorontsovo Pole

ul Zemlyanoy val (Garden Ring)

Vinzavod (450m)

Marksistskaya

Taganskaya pl

Bolshie Kamenshchiki ul

Taganskaya

Novoradishchevskaya per

Narodnaya ul

Nizhnyaya Krasnokholmskaya

Krasnokholmskaya nab

Bolshoy Krasnokholmsky most

Teterinsky per

Taganka

ul Goncharnaya

Tauzskaya ul

Serebryanicheskaya nab

Serebryanicheskaya nab

Ustinsky per Yauzsky

Podkolokolny per

ul Solyanka

Kotelnicheskaya nab

Kosmodamianskaya nab

Sadovnicheskaya ul

Bernikovskaya nab

Ustinsky most

Bolshoy Ustinsky Most

Moskvoretskaya nab

Moskva River

Raushskaya nab

Sadovnicheskaya nab

Ozerkovskaya nab

ul Bakhrushina

Vishnyakovskiy per

Chugunny Most

Komissariatsky Most

Runovsky per

Novokuznetskaya

ul Tatarskaya Bol

Pyatnitskaya ul

Tretyakovskaya

Pyatnitskaya ul

Slavyanskaya pl

Kitay-Gorod

Staraya pl

ul Varvarka

ul Ilinka

St Basil's Cathedral

1

8

18

GUM

5

Vetoshny per

4

Kremlevskaya nab

Bolshoy Moskvoretsky Most

Sofiyskaya nab

Bolotnaya ul

Bolotnaya ul

Moskvoretsky Most

Lavrushinsky per

Maly Tolmachevsky per

9

ul Bolshaya Ordynka

1-y Kazachy per

ul Bolshaya Polyanka

Garage Museum of Contemporary Art (650m); AC/DC in Tbilisi (850m); Le Boule (850m); Lebedinoe Ozero (1.3km)

Gorky Park (100m);

Alexandrovsky Sad

Biblioteka imeni Lenina

Borovitskaya

ul Znamenka

Mokhovaya ul

Bolshoy Kamenny most

pl Repina

Maly Kamenny Most

Bolotnaya nab

Bersenevskaya nab

Krasny Oktyabr

17

ul Bolshaya Yakimanka

Yakimanskaya nab

Vodootvodny

2

6

Krymskaya nab

Kadashevskaya nab

Bolshoy Kislovsky per

Arbatskaya

per

Povarskaya ul

Serebryany per

ul Arbat

ARBAT

19

per Sivtsev Vrazhek

Bolshoy Afanasyevsky per

Gagarinsky per

ul Volkhonka

Koly Jazhny per

Gogolevsky bul

Kropotkinskaya

Soymonovsky proezd

1

3

7

ul Prechistenka

Prechistensky per

ul Ostozhenka

Chisty per

Pozharsky per

Kursovoy per

Prechistenskaya nab

Soymonovsky proezd

Novodevichy Convent (2.6km)

Kropotkinsky per

Koroteynikov per

Turchaninov per

Krymsky most

Zubovsky bul

Metro, or more thematic tours like communist Moscow or mystical Moscow.

Moscow 360 WALKING TOUR
(☑ 985-447 8688; www.moscow360.org) FREE This ambitious company offers four different walking tours, all of which are free. They include tours of Red Square, the Cathedral of Christ the Saviour and the Metro, as well as – the most unusual – an AK-47 Tour (the tour and transport are free, but you'll pay to shoot). Tips are gratefully accepted.

🛏 Sleeping

Godzillas Hostel HOSTEL €
(☑ 495-699 4223; www.godzillashostel.com; Bolshoy Karetny per 6; dm from R820, s/d R2730/3070; ✳ @ 🛜; Ⓜ Tsvetnoy Bulvar) Tried and true, Godzillas is Moscow's best-known hostel, with dozens of beds spread out over four floors. The rooms come in various sizes, but they are all spacious, light-filled and painted in different colours. To cater to the many guests, there are bathroom facilities on each floor, three kitchens and a big living room with satellite TV.

Anti-Hostel Cosmic HOSTEL €
(☑ 499-390 8132; http://anti-hostel.ru; ul Bolshaya Dmitrovka 7/5 str 3; capsules from R1350; 🛜; Ⓜ Teatralnaya) Occupying a converted apartment, this place marries the idea of hostel with that of a capsule hotel. The location is hard to beat – Red Square is just a five-minute walk away. Capsules create a tiny, though comfortable, universe for guests to enjoy on their own. There is also a nice common area to mingle with fellow capsule-dwellers.

iVAN Hostel HOSTEL €
(☑ 916-407 1178; www.ivanhostel.com; per Petrovsky 1/30 apt 23; dm from R1000, d with shared bathroom from R3000; 🛜; Ⓜ Chekhovskaya) iVAN consists of two clean and quiet apartments located in the same tsarist-era residential building, a short walk from Pushkin square. Being a hostel, it naturally has dorms – and very nice ones at that – but its main virtues are several simply furnished but tastefully designed private rooms with whitewashed walls and large windows.

✕ Eating

★ Varenichnaya No 1 RUSSIAN €
(www.varenichnaya.ru; ul Arbat 29; mains R200-400; ⊙ 10am-midnight; ☑ 🛗; Ⓜ Arbatskaya) Retro Soviet is all the rage in Moscow, but this old-style Varenichnaya does it right, with books lining the walls, old movies on the black-and-white TV, and Cold War–era prices. The menu features tasty, filling *vareniki* and *pelmeni* (different kinds of dumplings), with sweet and savoury fillings. Bonus: an excellent housemade pickled veggie plate to make you pucker.

Stolovaya 57 CAFETERIA €
(Столовая 57; www.gum.ru/en/projects/s57; 3rd fl, GUM, Krasnaya pl 3; mains R200-300; ⊙ 10am-10pm; Ⓜ Okhotny Ryad) Newly minted, this old-style cafeteria offers a nostalgic recreation of dining in post-Stalinist Russia. The food is good – and cheap for such a fancy store. Meat cutlets and cold salads come highly recommended. This is a great place to try 'herring in a fur coat' (herring, beets, carrots and potatoes).

Cafe Receptor
FUSION €

(Кафе Рецептор; ☑ 499-216 7483; www.cafere
ceptor.ru; Bolshaya Nikitskaya ul 22/2; mains R250-
500; ⊙noon-midnight; 🛜🖉📶; Ⓜ Okhotny Ryad)
Colourful graffiti, amateur artwork and old
photographs adorn the walls of this quirky
basement cafe. It creates an arty setting for
healthy, veg-heavy meals, fresh juices and
fancy teas. There's also free-flowing wine,
house cocktails and occasional live music.
There is another outlet near **Patriarch's
Ponds** (☑ 499-216 9224; Bolshoy Kozikhinsky per
10; Ⓜ Tverskaya).

★ Mizandari
GEORGIAN €

(☑ 903-263 9990; www.mizandari.ru; nab Bolotnaya 5, str 1; mains R300-500; ⊙ 11am-11pm
Sun-Thu, to midnight Fri & Sat; Ⓜ Kropotkinskaya)
Georgian restaurants in Moscow tend to
be either expensive or tacky. This small,
family-run place is neither. Come with
friends and order a selection of appetizers,
such as *pkhali* (vegetable puree) and *lobio*
(spicy beans; both made of walnut paste),
khachapuri (cheese pastry) and *kharcho*
(lamb soup). Bless you if you can still accommodate a main course after all that!

🍷 Drinking & Nightlife

★ 32.05
CAFE

(☑ 905-703 3205; www.veranda3205.ru; ul Karetny
Ryad 3; ⊙ 11am-3am; Ⓜ Pushkinskaya) The biggest drinking/eating establishment in Hermitage Gardens, this verandah positioned at
the back of the main building looks a bit like
a greenhouse. In summer, tables (and patrons) spill out into the park, making it one
of the city's best places for outdoor drinking.
With its long bar and joyful atmosphere, the
place also heaves in winter.

Enthusiast
BAR

(Энтузиаст; per Stoleshnikov str 5; ⊙ noon-11pm
Sun-Thu, to 2am Fri & Sat; Ⓜ Teatralnaya) Scooter
enthusiast, that is. But you don't have to be
one in order to enjoy this superbly laid-back
bar, hidden at the far end of a fancifully
shaped courtyard and disguised as a spare-
parts shop. On a warm day, grab a beer or
cider, settle into a beach chair and let harmony descend on you.

Noor / Electro
BAR

(☑ 903-136 7686; www.noorbar.com; ul Tverskaya
23/12; ⊙ 8pm-3am Mon-Wed, 8pm-6am Thu-Sun;
Ⓜ Pushkinskaya) There is little to say about
this misleadingly unassuming bar, apart
from the fact that everything in it is close to

SANDUNY BATHS

Although entry is pricey, the **Sanduny
Baths** (Map p788; www.sanduny.ru;
Neglinnaya ul 14; per person R1600-2500;
⊙ 8am-10pm Wed-Mon, Second Male Top
Class 10am-midnight Tue-Fri, 8am-10pm Sat
& Sun). Moscow's most luxurious *banya* (hot bath), is an experience worth
sampling. The Gothic Room is a work of
art, with its rich woodcarvings, while the
main shower room has an aristocratic
Roman feel to it. There are several classes, as on trains, though regulars say
that, here, second male class is actually
better than the premium class. You can
cut the cost by bringing your own towel
or sheet to wrap yourself into, a felt hat
to avoid burning your hair, and flip flops
(thongs) to protect your feet.

---

perfection. It has it all – prime location, convivial atmosphere, eclectic DJ music, friendly bartenders and superb drinks. Though
declared 'the best' by various magazines on
several occasions, it doesn't feel like they
care about the accolades.

☆ Entertainment

★ Bolshoi Theatre
BALLET, OPERA

(Большой театр; ☑ 495-455 5555; www.bolshoi.
ru; Teatralnaya pl 1; tickets R100-12,000; ⊙ closed
Jul-Aug; Ⓜ Teatralnaya) An evening at the
Bolshoi is still one of Moscow's most romantic and entertaining options for a night on
the town. The glittering six-tier auditorium
has an electric atmosphere, evoking over
200 years of premier music and dance. Both
the ballet and opera companies perform a
range of Russian and foreign works here.
After the collapse of the Soviet Union, the
Bolshoi was marred by politics, scandal and
frequent turnover. But the show must go on –
and it does.

Tchaikovsky Concert Hall
CLASSICAL MUSIC

(Концертный зал имени Чайковского; ☑ 495-
232 0400; www.meloman.ru; Triumfalnaya pl 4/31;
tickets R300-3000; ⊙ closed Jul-Aug; Ⓜ Mayakovskaya) Home to the famous Moscow State
Philharmonic (Moskovskaya Filharmonia),
the capital's oldest symphony orchestra,
Tchaikovsky Concert Hall was established in
1921. It's a huge auditorium, with seating for
1600 people. This is where you can expect to
hear the Russian classics, such as Stravinsky,

METRO TOUR

For just R49 you can spend 90 minutes touring around Moscow's magnificent metro stations. Many of these are marble-faced, frescoed, gilded works of art. Among our favourites are **Komsomolskaya**, a huge stuccoed hall, its ceiling covered with mosaics depicting military heroes; **Novokuznetskaya**, featuring military bas-reliefs done in sober khaki, and colourful ceiling mosaics depicting pictures of the happy life; and **Mayakovskaya**, Grand Prize winner at the 1939 World's Fair in New York.

Rachmaninov and Shostakovich, as well as other European favourites. Look out for special children's concerts.

Masterskaya LIVE MUSIC
(Мастерская; ☎ 495-621 9043; www.mstrsk.ru; Teatralny proezd 3 str 3; ☺ noon-6am; ☎; Ⓜ Lubyanka) All the best places in Moscow are tucked into far corners of courtyards, and they often have unmarked doors. Such is the case with this super-funky music venue. The eclectic, arty interior makes a cool place to chill out during the day. Evening hours give way to a diverse array of live-music acts or the occasional dance or theatre performance.

 ## Shopping

Ul Arbat has always been a tourist attraction and is littered with souvenir shops and stalls.

GUM MALL
(ГУМ; www.gum.ru; Krasnaya pl 3; ☺ 10am-10pm; Ⓜ Ploshchad Revolyutsii) With an elaborate 240m facade on the northeastern side of Red Square, GUM is a bright, bustling shopping mall with hundreds of fancy stores and restaurants. With a skylight roof and three-level arcades, the spectacular interior was a revolutionary design when it was built in the 1890s, replacing the Upper Trading Rows previously occupying this site.

Izmaylovsky Market MARKET
(www.kremlin-izmailovo.com; Izmaylovskoye shosse 73; ☺ 10am-8pm; Ⓜ Partizanskaya) This sprawling area, also known as Vernisazh market, is packed with art, handmade crafts, antiques, Soviet paraphernalia and just about anything you might want for a souvenir. You'll

find Moscow's biggest original range of *matryoshki* (nesting dolls), *palekh* (painted laquer work) and *khokhloma* (laquer bowls) ware, as well as less traditional woodworking crafts. There are also rugs from the Caucasus and Central Asia, pottery, linens, jewellery, fur hats, chess sets, toys, Soviet posters and much more.

ℹ Information

International Clinic MEDSI (☎ 495-933 7700; http://medsi.ru/eng/icm; Grokholsky per 1; ☺ 24hr; Ⓜ Pr Mira) Emergency service, consultations and a full range of medical specialists. On-site pharmacy with English-speaking staff.

Maria Travel Agency (☎ 495-775 8226; www.maria-travel.com; ul Maroseyka 13; Ⓜ Kitay-Gorod) Visa support, apartment rental and some local tours, including the Golden Ring.

Moscow Times (www.themoscowtimes.com) Locally published English-language newspaper, free of charge.

Unifest Travel (☎ 495-234 6555; http://unifest.ru/en.html; Komsomolsky prospekt 16/2) On-the-ball travel company offers rail and air tickets, visa support and more.

ℹ Getting There & Away

International flights land and take off from Moscow's three airports – **Domodedovo** (Домодедово; ☎ 495-933 6666; www.domodedovo.ru), **Sheremetyevo** (Шереметьево, SVO; ☎ 495-578 6565; www.svo.aero) and **Vnukovo** (Внуково; ☎ 495-937 5555; www.vnukovo.ru).

ℹ Getting Around

TO/FROM THE AIRPORT

All three airports are accessible by the convenient **Aeroexpress Train** (☎ 8-800-700 3377; www.aeroexpress.ru; R420; ☺ 6am-midnight) from the city centre; a reduced rate is available for online purchase.

Alternatively, order an official airport taxi from the dispatcher's desk in the terminal (R2000 to R2200 to the city centre). You can save some cash by booking in advance to take advantage of the fixed rates offered by most companies (usually from R1500 to R1800 to/from any airport). Driving times vary wildly depending on traffic.

Bicycle

Cycling on the streets is dangerous, but it's a pleasant way to get around if you stick to the cycling routes along the river and in the city parks. Bikes are available from **VeloBike** (http://velobike.ru) and various rental stations around town.

PUBLIC TRANSPORT

The **Moscow Metro** (www.mosmetro.ru) is by far the easiest, quickest and cheapest way of getting around the city. Magnetic tickets (single ride R32, '90 minutes' fare R49) are sold at ticket booths. Save time by buying a Troika card, which can be topped up with any amount up to R3000 and used on all forms of public transport.

Buses, trolleybuses and trams are useful along a few radial or cross-town routes that the metro misses, and are necessary for reaching sights away from the city centre. Tickets (R31) are sold on the vehicle by a conductor.

TAXI

Unofficial taxis are still common in Moscow. Expect to pay R200 to R400 for a ride around the city centre, depending on your haggling skills.

St Petersburg

📞 812 / POP 4.9 MILLION

Affectionately known as Piter to locals, St Petersburg is a visual delight. The Neva River and surrounding canals reflect unbroken facades of handsome 18th- and 19th-century buildings that house a spellbinding collection of cultural storehouses, culminating in the incomparable Hermitage. Home to many of Russia's greatest creative talents (Pushkin, Dostoevsky, Tchaikovsky), Piter still inspires a contemporary generation of Russians, making it a liberal, hedonistic and exciting place to visit as well as a giant warehouse of culture.

The city covers many islands, some real, some created through the construction of canals. The central street is Nevsky pr, which extends some 4km from the Alexander Nevsky Monastery to the Hermitage.

👁 Sights

👁 Historic Centre

⭐ **State Hermitage Museum**   MUSEUM
(Государственный Эрмитаж; www.hermitage museum.org; Dvortsovaya pl 2; adult/student R400/free, 1st Thu of month free; ⏱ 10.30am-6pm Tue, Thu, Sat & Sun, to 9pm Wed & Fri; Ⓜ Admiralteyskaya) Mainly set in the magnificent Winter Palace and adjoining buildings, the Hermitage fully lives up to its sterling reputation. You can be absorbed by its treasures for days and still come out wanting more.

The enormous collection (over three million items, only a fraction of which are on display in around 360 rooms) almost amounts to a comprehensive history of Western European art. Viewing it demands a little planning, so choose the areas you'd like to concentrate on before you arrive.

General Staff Building   MUSEUM
(Здание Главного штаба; www.hermitagemu seum.org; Dvortsovaya pl 6-8; admission including main State Hermitage R400 ; ⏱ 10.30am-6pm Tue, Thu, Sat & Sun, to 9pm Wed & Fri; Ⓜ Admiralteyskaya) The east wing of this magnificent building, wrapping around the south of Dvortsovaya pl and designed by Carlo Rossi in the 1820s, marries restored interiors with contemporary architecture to create a series of galleries displaying the Hermitage's amazing collection of Impressionist and post-Impressionist works. Contemporary art is here, too, often in temporary exhibitions by major artists.

Russian Museum   MUSEUM
(Русский музей; 📞 812-595 4248; www.rusmuse um.ru; Inzhenernaya ul 4; adult/student R450/200, 4-palace ticket adult/child R600/300; ⏱ 10am-6pm Mon, Wed & Fri-Sun, 1pm-9pm Thu; Ⓜ Nevsky Prospekt) The handsome Mikhailovsky Palace is home to the country's biggest collection of Russian art. After the Hermitage you may feel you have had your fill of art, but try your utmost to make some time for this gem. There's also a lovely garden behind the palace.

⭐ **Church on the Spilled Blood**   CHURCH
(Церковь Спаса на Крови; http://cathedral. ru; Konyushennaya pl; adult/student R250/150; ⏱ 10.30am-6pm Thu-Tue; Ⓜ Nevsky Prospekt) This five-domed dazzler is St Petersburg's most elaborate church with a classic Russian Orthodox exterior and interior decorated with some 7000 sq m of mosaics. Officially called the Church of the Resurrection of Christ, its far more striking colloquial name references the assassination attempt on Tsar Alexander II here in 1881.

St Isaac's Cathedral   MUSEUM
(Isaakievsky Sobor; www.cathedral.ru; Isaaki-evskaya pl; cathedral adult/student R250/150, colonnade R150; ⏱ cathedral 10.30am-6pm Thu-Tue, colonnade 10.30am-10.30pm May-Oct, to 6pm Nov-Apr, 3rd Wed of month closed; Ⓜ Admiralteyskaya) The golden dome of St Isaac's Cathedral dominates the St Petersburg skyline. Its obscenely lavish interior is open as a museum, although services are held in the cathedral on major religious holidays. Most people bypass the museum to climb the 262 steps

The Hermitage

A HALF-DAY TOUR

Successfully navigating the State Hermitage Museum, with its four vast interconnecting buildings and around 360 rooms, is an art form in itself. Our half-day tour of the highlights can be done in four hours, or easily extended to a full day.

Once past ticket control start by ascending the grand **Jordan Staircase** ❶ to Neva Enfilade and Great Enfilade for the impressive staterooms, including the former throne room St George's Hall and the 1812 War Gallery (Room 197), and the Romanovs' private apartments. Admire the newly restored **Great Church** ❷ then make your way back to the Neva side of the building via the Western Gallery (Room 262) to find the splendid **Pavilion Hall** ❸ with its view onto the Hanging Garden and the gilded Peacock Clock, always a crowd pleaser.

Make your way along the series of smaller galleries in the Large Hermitage hung with Italian Renaissance art, including masterpieces by **Da Vinci** ❹ and **Caravaggio** ❺. The Loggia of Raphael (Room 227) is also impressive. Linger a while in the galleries containing Spanish art before taking in the Dutch collection, the highlight of which is the hoard of **Rembrandt** ❻ canvases in Room 254.

Descend the Council Staircase (Room 206), noting the giant malachite vase, to the ground floor where the fantastic Egyptian collection awaits in Room 100 as well as the galleries of Greek and Roman Antiquities. If you have extra time, it's well worth booking tours to see the two special exhibitions in the **Gold Rooms** ❼ of the Treasure Gallery.

TOP TIPS

» **Queues** Reserve tickets online to skip the long lines.

» **Dining** Bring a sandwich and a bottle of water with you: the cafe is dire.

» **Footwear** Wear comfortable shoes.

» **Cloakroom** Bear in mind the only one is before ticket control, so you can't go back and pick up a sweater.

KEVEN OSBORNE / FOX FOTOS / GETTY IMAGES ©

Jordan Staircase
Originally designed by Rastrelli, in the 18th century this incredible white marble construction was known as the Ambassadorial Staircase because it was the way into the palace for official receptions.

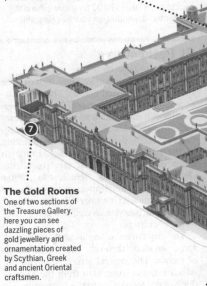

The Gold Rooms
One of two sections of the Treasure Gallery, here you can see dazzling pieces of gold jewellery and ornamentation created by Scythian, Greek and ancient Oriental craftsmen.

IMAGE SOURCE / GETTY IMAGES ©

Great Church
This stunningly ornate church was the Romanovs' private place of worship and the venue for the marriage of the last tsar, Nicholas II, to Alexandra Feodorovna in 189

Rembrandt
A moving portrait of contrition and forgiveness, *Return of the Prodigal Son* (Room 254) depicts the biblical scene of a wayward son returning to his father.

Da Vinci
Along with the *Benois Madonna*, also here, *Madonna and Child (Madonna Litta;* Room 214) is one of just a handful of paintings known to be the work of Leonardo da Vinci.

St George's Hall

Hermitage Theatre

Pavilion Hall
Apart from the Peacock Clock, the Pavilion Hall also contains beautifully detailed mosaic tables made by Italian and Russian craftsmen in the mid-19th century.

Caravaggio
The Lute Player (Room 237) is the Hermitage's only Caravaggio, and a work that the master of light and shade described as the best piece he'd ever painted.

Central St Petersburg

Maly pr
Bolshoy pr
Sportivnaya
Zverinskaya ul
ul Blokhina
ul Yablochkova
Kronverksky pr
Kronverksky
Kronverkskaya nab
Kronverksky Alexandrovsky
Island Park
Troitskaya
pl
Petrovskaya nab
pr Dobrolyubova
Sportivnaya
Zayachy Island
Kronversky
Proliv
Tuchkov
most
Petrogradsky
Island
Troitsky
most
Malaya Neva
nab Makarova
Birzhevoy
most
Suvorovskaya pl
Birzhevaya pl
9
Summer
Garden
VASILYEVSKY
ISLAND
Birzhevoy
proezd
4
Dvortsovy
most
State
Hermitage
Museum
2
Bolshoy
Konyushenny
most
2-y Sadovy
most
Church on the
Spilled Blood
1
l-ya liniya i Kadetskaya liniya
ul Repina
Pevchesky
most
14
26
Bol Konyushennaya
Inzhenernaya ul
7
28
Pl Iskusstv
Vasileostrovsky
Gardens
3
Dvortsovaya
pl
ADMIRALTEYSKY
Nevsky pr
Zelyony
most
23
24
Nevsky
Prospekt
Bolshaya Neva
Dekabristov
pl
Alexander
Garden
Admiralteyskaya
Kazanskaya pl
15
Gostiny
Dvor
Blagoveshchensky
most
Angliyskaya nab
Galernaya ul
Isaakievskaya pl
8
Malaya Morskaya ul
Bol Morskaya ul
nab reki Moyki
Krasny
most
25
18
Bankovsky
per
ul Lomonosova
16
Sadovaya ul
SPASSKY
Pl Truda
Konnogvardeysky bul
Pochtamtskaya ul
Bol Morskaya ul
Siny
most
22
Griuvtsova pr
Kazanskaya ul
nab kanala Griboyedova
Gorokhovaya ul
Apraksin per
ul Truda
Kryukov Canal
Potseluev
most
Fonarny
most
KAZANSKY
Kazanskaya ul
Demidov
most
Sennaya pl
Sennaya
Ploshchad
Semyonovsky
most
per Matveeva
ul Dekabristov
Lviny
most
27
Teatralnaya Pl
ul Glinki
Voznesensky pr
Stolyarny per
Sadovaya
Moskovsky pr
SENNAYA
nab reki Fontanki
Zvenigorodskaya
ul Soyuza Pechatnikov
Pr Rimskogo-Korsakova
Nikolsky per
Yusupov
Gardens
Obukhovsky
most
Pushkinskaya
Vitebskaya pl
Griboyedov Canal
Nikolsky
Gardens
Fontanka
Vitebsk Station
(Vitebsky vokzal)
Kanonerskaya ul
Sadovaya ul
POKROVSKY
ul Labutina
nab reki Fontanki
Egypetsky
most
Izmailovsky pr
Polsky
Gardens
pr Moskvinoy
Tékhnologichesky
Institut
Pulkovo
(12km)

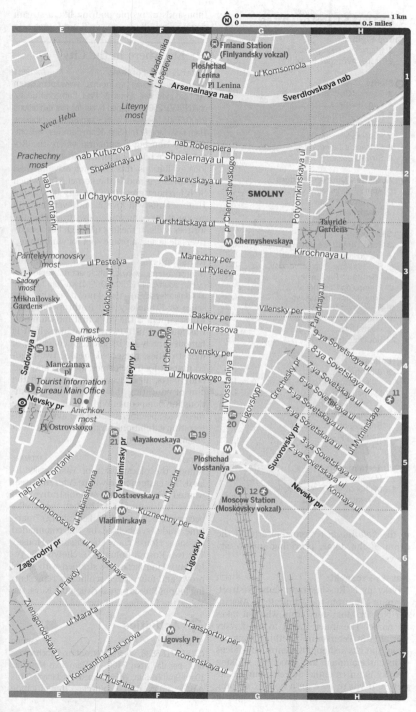

Central St Petersburg

to the *kolonnada* (colonnade) around the drum of the dome, providing superb city views.

Nevsky Prospekt   STREET
Nevsky pr is Russia's most famous street, running 4km from the Admiralty to Alexander Nevsky Monastery, from which it takes its name. The inner 2.5km to Moskovsky vokzal is St Petersburg's seething main avenue, the city's shopping centre, and focus of its entertainment and street life. Walking Nevsky is an essential St Petersburg experience. If you're here on a holiday evening (such as 27 May – City Day), the sight of thousands of people pouring like a stream down its middle is one you'll not forget.

⊙ Elsewhere in the City

Peter & Paul Fortress   FORTRESS
(Петропавловская крепость; www.spbmuseum.ru; grounds free, Peter & Paul Cathedral adult/child R450/250, combined ticket for five exhibitions R600/350; ⊗grounds 8.30am-8pm, exhibitions 11am-6pm Mon & Thu-Sun, 10am-5pm Tue; MGorkovskaya) Housing a cathedral where the Romanovs are buried, a former prison and various exhibitions, this large defensive fortress on Zayachy Island is the kernel from which St Petersburg grew into the city it is today. History buffs will love it and everyone will swoon at the panoramic views from atop the fortress walls, at the foot of which lies a sandy riverside beach, a prime spot for sunbathing.

Kunstkamera   MUSEUM
(Кунсткамера; www.kunstkamera.ru; Tamozhenny per; adult/child R250/50; ⊗11am-7pm Tue-Sun; MAdmiralteyskaya) Also known as the Museum of Ethnology and Anthropology, the Kunstkamera is the city's first museum and was founded in 1714 by Peter himself. It is famous largely for its ghoulish collection of monstrosities, preserved 'freaks', two-headed mutant foeti, deformed animals and odd body parts, all collected by Peter with the aim of educating the notoriously superstitious Russian people. While most rush to see these sad specimens, there are also very interesting exhibitions on native peoples from around the world.

Strelka   LANDMARK
Among the oldest parts of Vasilyevsky Island, this eastern tip is where Peter the Great wanted his new city's administrative and intellectual centre to be. In fact, the Strelka became the focus of St Petersburg's maritime trade, symbolised by the colonnaded Customs House (now the Pushkin House). The two Rostral Columns, archetypal St Petersburg landmarks, are studded with ships' prows and four seated sculptures representing four of Russia's great rivers: the Neva, the Volga, the Dnieper and the Volkhov.

🏃 Activities

Skatprokat   CYCLING
(☏812-717 6838; www.skatprokat.ru; Goncharnaya ul 7; per day from R400; ⊗11am-8pm Mon-Thu, 10am-9pm Fri-Sun; MPloshchad Vosstaniya) This outfit offers rental bicycles that include

brand-new mountain bikes by the Russian company Stark. You'll need to leave either R2000 and your passport, or R7000, as a deposit per bike. If you are in town for a while, this place also sells secondhand bikes and does repairs. They also offer excellent Saturday- and Sunday-morning bike tours of the city.

Mytninskiye Bani BANYA
(Мытнинские бани; www.mybanya.spb.ru; Mytninskaya ul 17-19; per hr R200-300; ⊘8am-10pm Fri-Tue; ⓂPloshchad Vosstaniya) Unique in the city, Mytninskiye Bani is heated by a wood furnace, just like the log-cabin bathhouses that are still found in the Russian countryside. It's actually the oldest communal *banya* in the city, and in addition to a *parilka* (steam room) and plunge pool, the private 'lux' *banya* includes a swanky lounge area with leather furniture and a pool table.

☞ Tours

Peter's Walking Tours WALKING TOUR
(☎812-943 1229; www.peterswalk.com; Original tour/other tours R1500/from R2200 per person) Established in 1996, Peter Kozyrev's innovative and passionately led tours are highly recommended as a way to see the city with knowledgable locals. The daily Original Peterswalk is one of the favourites, and leaves daily from **Hostel Life** (☎812-318 1808; www.hostel-life.ru; Nevsky pr 47, Vosstaniya; dm from R950, tw/tr R3325/3515; ⊘🛜; ⓂMayakovskaya) at 10.30am from late March to late October.

Anglo Tourismo BOATING
(☎921-989 4722; www.anglotourismo.com; 27 nab reki Fontanki; 1hr tour adult/student R1000/850; ⓂGostiny Dvor) There's a huge number of companies offering cruises all over the Historic Heart, all with similar prices and itineraries. But Anglo Tourismo is the only operator to run tours with commentary in English. Between May and September the schedule runs every 1½ hours between 11am and 6.30pm. From 1 June to 31 August there are also additional night cruises.

The company also runs free daily walking tours starting at 10.30am and lasting three hours.

Sputnik Tours WALKING TOUR
(☎499-394 1600; www.sputnik8.com) This online tour agency is one with a difference: they act as a market place for locals wanting to give their own unique tours of the city. Browse, select a tour, register and pay a de-

WORTH A TRIP

STREET ART MUSEUM

Covering 11 hectares and with 150,000–200,000 sq m of walls, a large disused section of the laminated plastics factory SLOPAST is the location of the amazing **Street Art Museum** (☎812-448 1593; http://streetartmuseum.ru; shosse Revolutsii 84, Okhta; adult/student R350/250; ⓂPloshchad Lenina, then bus 137 or 530). The complex, in the industrial zone of Okhta, a 20-minute bus ride east of Ploshchad Lenina, has some 70 works of varying formats, including epic pieces by the likes of top Russian streets artists Timothy Radya, Kirill Kto and Nikita Nomerz, as well as the Spanish artist Escif. You need to register for a tour on the website. Concerts and events are also held here.

posit and you'll be given the contact number of the guide. A superb way to meet locals.

🛏 Sleeping

Soul Kitchen Hostel HOSTEL €
(☎965-816 3470; www.soulkitchenhostel.com; nab reki Moyki 62/2, apt 9, Sennaya; dm/d from R790/3380; ⊘@🛜; ⓂAdmiralteyskaya) Soul Kitchen blends boho hipness and boutique-hotel comfort, scoring perfect 10s in many key categories: private rooms (chic), dorm beds (double-wide with privacy-protecting curtains), common areas (vast), kitchen (vast *and* beautiful) and bathrooms (downright inviting). There is also bike hire, table football, free Macs to use, free international phone calls and stunning Moyka views from a communal balcony.

Friends Hostel on Griboedov HOSTEL €
(☎812-331 7799; www.friendsplace.ru; nab kanala Griboyedova 20; dm/d from R500/1800; @🛜; ⓂNevsky Prospekt) In a quiet courtyard near Kazan Cathedral, this is our favourite out of the many branches of this truly friendly, very colourful hostel chain. The dorms and rooms are spotless, have lockers and share good bathrooms and a kitchen. Perks include free international calls, English-speaking staff and organised daily events such as pub crawls and historical walks.

Baby Lemonade Hostel HOSTEL €
(☎812-570 7943; www.facebook.com/babylemonadehostel; Inzhernernaya ul 7; dm/d with shared

bathroom from R790/2590, d from R3250; @ 🛜; Ⓜ Gostiny Dvor) The owner of Baby Lemonade is crazy about the 1960s and it shows in the pop-art, psychedelic design of this friendly, fun hostel with two pleasant, large dorms and a great kitchen and living room. It's worth splashing out for the boutique-hotel-worthy private rooms that are in a separate flat with great rooftop views.

✕ Eating

Marketplace   RUSSIAN, INTERNATIONAL €
(http://market-place.me; Nevsky pr 24; mains R200-300; ⊙ 8am-5.30am; 🛜 ✍; Ⓜ Nevsky Prospekt) The most central branch of this mini-chain that brings a high-class polish to the self-serve canteen concept, with many dishes cooked freshly on the spot . The hip design of the multi-level space is very appealing, making this a great place to linger, especially if you indulge in one of the desserts or cocktails served on the 1st floor.

Jack & Chan   INTERNATIONAL €
(✒812-982 0535; http://jack-and-chan.com; Inzhenernaya ul 7; mains R350; ⊙ 10am-midnight; 🛜; Ⓜ Gostiny Dvor) The restaurant name, a punning reference to Jackie Chan in Russian, neatly sums up the burger-meets-Asian menu at this fine and stylish casual diner. Try the sweet-and-sour fish and the prawn-and-avocado salad with glass noodles.

Biblioteka   INTERNATIONAL €
(✒812-244 1594; www.ilovenevsky.ru; Nevsky pr 20; mains R250-450; ⊙ cafe/restaurant 8am-11pm Sun-Thu, to midnight Fri & Sat, bar 5pm-2am; 🛜; Ⓜ Nevsky Prospekt) You could spend the better part of a day here. Ground floor is a waiter-service cafe where it's difficult to avoid being tempted by the cake and dessert display by the door; next up is a more formal restaurant; and on the top floor there's a multi-roomed lounge bar with live music and DJs late into the night.

🍷 Drinking & Nightlife

★ Ziferberg   ANTI-CAFE
(✒981-180 7022; http://ziferburg.ziferblat.net; Bolshaya Konyushennaya 9; R2-480; ⊙ 11am-midnight Sun-Thu, 11am-7am Fri & Sat; 🛜; Ⓜ Nevsky Prospekt) Occupying much of the 3rd-floor gallery of Passage is this anti-cafe with a range of quirky, boho-hipster decorated spaces, some intimate, others very social.

There's an excellent range of activities to enjoy with your coffee or tea, from boardgames and movies to concerts by classical music students, particularly on the weekends.

Borodabar   COCKTAIL BAR
(Kazanskaya ul 11; ⊙ 5pm-2am Sun-Thu, to 4am Fri & Sat; 🛜; Ⓜ Nevsky Prospekt) Boroda means beard in Russian, and sure enough you'll see plenty of facial hair and tattoos in this hipster cocktail hangout. The mixologists really know their stuff – we can particularly recommend their smoked old fashioned, which is infused with tobacco smoke, and their colourful (and potent) range of shots.

Radiobaby   BAR, CLUB
(Kazanskaya ul 7; ⊙ 6pm-6am; Ⓜ Nevsky Prospekt) Go through the arch at Kazanskaya 5 (not 7 – that's just the street address), turn left through a second arch and you'll find this super-cool barnlike bar on your right. It's divided into several different rooms, there's a 'no techno, no house' music policy, table football, a relaxed crowd and an atmosphere of eternal hedonism. After 10pm the place becomes more a club than a bar.

☆ Entertainment

Mariinsky Theatre   OPERA, BALLET
(Мариинский театр; ✒812-326 4141; www.mariinsky.ru; Teatralnaya pl 1; tickets R1000-6000; Ⓜ Sadovaya) Petersburg's most spectacular venue for ballet and opera, the Mariinsky Theatre is an attraction in its own right. Tickets can be bought online or in person, but they should be bought in advance during the summer months. The magnificent interior is the epitome of imperial grandeur, and any evening here will be an impressive experience.

**Mikhailovsky Opera &
Ballet Theatre**   OPERA, BALLET
(✒812-595 4305; www.mikhailovsky.ru; pl Iskusstv 1; tickets R300-4000; Ⓜ Nevsky Prospekt) While not quite as grand as the Mariinsky, this illustrious stage still delivers the Russian ballet or operatic experience, complete with multi-tiered theatre, frescoed ceiling and elaborate concerts. Pl Iskusstv (Arts Square) is a lovely setting for this respected venue, which is home to the State Academic Opera & Ballet Company.

It's generally easier and cheaper to get tickets to the performances staged here than those at the Mariinsky.

ℹ Information

American Medical Clinic (☑ 812-740 2090; www.amclinic.ru; nab reki Moyki 78; ⊙ 24hr; Ⓜ Admiralteyskaya) One of the city's largest private clinics.

Apteka Petrofarm (Nevsky pr 22; ⊙ 24hr) All-night pharmacy.

Ost-West Kontaktservice (☑ 812-327 3416; www.ostwest.com; Ligovsky pr 10; ⊙ 9am-6pm Mon-Sat; Ⓜ Ploshchad Vosstanya) Can find you an apartment to rent and organise tours and tickets.

Tourist Information Bureau (☑ 812-310 2822; http://eng.ispb.info; Sadovaya ul 14/52; ⊙ 10am-7pm Mon-Fri, noon-6pm Sat; Ⓜ Gostiny Dvor) There are also branches outside the Hermitage, St Isaac's Cathedral and at Pulkovo Airport.

ℹ Getting There & Away

International and domesitc flights touch down at **Pulkovo International Airport** (LED; ☑ 812-337 3822; www.pulkovoairport.ru).

ℹ Getting Around

TO/FROM THE AIRPORT

From Pulkovo International Airport, an official taxi to the centre should cost around R900, or you can take the bus to Moskovskaya metro station for R30, then take the metro from Moskovskaya (Line 2) all over the city for R35 – a journey of about 50 minutes as I told.

PUBLIC TRANSPORT

The metro is usually the quickest way around the city. *Zhetony* (tokens) and credit-loaded cards can be bought from booths in the stations (R35).

If you are staying more than a day or two, it's worth buying one of the multiple journey passes, starting with the 10 journey pass (R330) valid for seven days.

The **St Petersburg Card** (https://petersburg card.com; from R2500 for two days) a sightseeing smart card, can also be used to travel on public transport and also includes entrance to over 50 city museums, free or discounted tours, and a rechargeable transport card.

Buses, trolleybuses and *marshrutky* (minibuses; fares R35) often get you closer to the sights and are especially handy to cover long distances along main avenues like Nevsky pr.

TAXI

Unofficial taxis are common. Official taxis (fourdoor Volga sedans with a chequerboard strip down the side and a green light in the front window) have meters that drivers sometimes use, though you most often pay a negotiated price.

MOSCOW TO ST PETERSBURG

The fastest trains between Moscow and St Petersburg are the Sapsan services (from R2600, three to four hours, six daily). There are also around 10 overnight services, which can take anywhere from seven to 11 hours (*platskart/kupe* from R1000/2200). Tickets often sell out in the high months, but keep your plans flexible and you should be able to find something, even at the last minute. Many flights (from R2300) also connect the two cities and they rarely sell out.

Peterhof

The 'Russian Versailles', Peterhof (Петергоф, also known as Petrodvorets), 29km west of the city, was built for Peter the Great. A major casuality of WWII, the palace and grounds are largely a reconstruction best visited for its **Grand Cascade** (ul Razvodnaya 2; ⊙ 10am-6pm Mon-Fri, to 8.30pm Sat, to 7pm Sun, May-early Oct) and Water Avenue, a symphony of over 140 fountains and canals located in the **Lower Park** (Нижний парк; http://eng.peterhofmuseum.ru; adult/student R500/250, free Nov-Apr; ⊙ 9am-8pm). There are several additional palaces, villas and parks here, each of which charges its own hefty admission price.

Buses and *marshrutky* to Petrodvorets (R55, 30 minutes) run frequently from outside metro stations Avtovo and Leninsky Prospekt. From May to September, the **Peterhof Express** (http://www.peterhof-express. com/; adult single/return R700/1200, student single/return R500/900; ⊙ 10am-6pm) hydrofoil leaves from jetties behind the Hermitage and behind the Admiralty.

Tsarskoe Selo

Tsarskoe Selo (Царское Село), 25km south of the city in the town of Pushkin, is home to the baroque **Catherine Palace** (Екатерининский дворец; http://eng.tzar.ru; Sadovaya ul 7; adult/student R400/200, audioguide R150; ⊙ 10am-4.45pm Wed-Sun), expertly restored following its near destruction in WWII. From May to September individual visits to Catherine's Palace are limited to noon to 2pm and 4pm to 4.45pm, other times being reserved for tour groups.

From late April to October there is also an entry charge to the beautiful surrounding **Catherine Park** (adult/child R120/60), otherwise this is free.

The easiest way to get to Tsarskoe Selo is by *marshrutka* (R35) from Moskovskaya metro station.

Kaliningrad Region

Sandwiched between Poland and Lithuania, the Kaliningrad Region is a Russian exclave that's both intimately attached to the Motherland also a world apart. This 'Little Russia' – only 15,100 sq km with a population of 941,873 – offers an intriguing capital, beautiful countryside, charming old Prussian seaside resorts and splendid beaches.

Kaliningrad

☑ 4012 / POP 431,900

The region's capital, Kaliningrad (Калининград, formely Königsberg), was once a Middle European architectural gem equal to Prague or Kraków. Precious little of this built heritage remains, but there are attractive residential suburbs and remnants of the city's old fortifications that evoke the Prussian past.

◉ Sights

The once densely populated Kant Island is now a parkland dotted with sculptures and dominated by the Cathedral. A few nearby buildings – the former Stock Exchange from the 1870s and the neo-traditional row of shops, restaurants and hotels known as **Fish Village** – hint at what this area looked like pre-WWII. Get a bird's-eye view from the 31m-high **lighthouse viewing tower** (R50; ⊙10am-10pm).

Kaliningrad Cathedral   CHURCH
(Кафедральный собор Кёнигсберга; ☑4012-631 705; www.sobor-kaliningrad.ru; Kant Island; adult/student R150/130, photos R50, concerts R250-300; ⊙10am-5pm) Photos displayed inside this Unesco World Heritage Site attest to how dilapidated the cathedral was until the early 1990s – the original dates back to 1333. The lofty interior is dominated by an ornate organ used for regular **concerts**. Upstairs, the carved-wood **Wallenrodt Library** has interesting displays of old Königsberg. The top floor is devoted to Immanuel Kant; the exhibition includes his death mask. Kant's **tomb** (могила Канта) is on the building's outer north side.

Kaliningrad Region

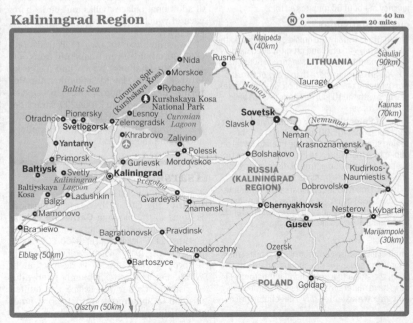

★ Museum of the World Ocean   MUSEUM

(Музей Мирового Океана; www.world-ocean.ru/en; nab Petra Velikogo 1; adult/student R300/150, individual vessels adult/student R150/100; ⊙ 10am-6pm Wed-Mon) Strung along the banks of the Pregolya River are the several ships, a sub, maritime machinery and exhibition halls that make up this excellent museum. The highlight is the handsome former scientific expedition vessel *Vityaz*, moored alongside the *Viktor Patsaev*, with its exhibits relating to space research; visits are by guided tour (included in admission price) every 45 minutes. The pre-atomic B-413 submarine gives a taste of what life was like for its former 300 inhabitants.

🛌 Sleeping

Akteon Lindros Hostel   HOSTEL €

(Хостел Актеон Линдрос; ⌨ 900-568 3333; www.akteon-hostel.ru; ul Svobodnaya 23; dm/d from R400/1200; 🖃) Quiet and clean, this new hostel offers standard-issue bunks, a good kitchen and happy-to-help staff. It's well serviced by public transport: buses 5, 9, 12, 14 and 35 will get you there from the city centre.

ℹ️ Information

Citizens of Japan and many European countries can visit Kaliningrad on a 72-hour visa, but this needs to be arranged in advance with local travel agents.

Regional Tourism Information Centre
(✉ 4012-555 200; www.visit-kaliningrad.ru; pr Mira 4; ⊙ 9am-8pm Mon-Fri & 11am-6pm Sat May-Sep, 9am-7pm Mon-Fri & 11am-4pm Sat Oct-Apr) Helpful, English-speaking staff and lots of information on the region.

ℹ️ Getting There & Away

AIR

Khrabrovo airport (✉ 4012-610 620; www.kgd.aero) is 24km north of the city.

BUS

Mainly local buses depart from the **Yuzhny bus station** (ul Zheleznodorozhnaya 7), as well as international bus services run by **Ecolines** (✉ 4012-758 733; www.ecolines.net) to Warsaw and several German cities. **König Avto** (✉ 4012-999 199; www.kenigauto.com) international services leave from the **international bus station** (Moskovsky pr 184); there's a König Avto booking office at Yuzhny vokzal.

WORTH A TRIP

SVETLOGORSK & KURSHSKAYA KOSA NATIONAL PARK

It's easy to access the region's other key sights on day trips from Kaliningrad, but if you did want to spend time away from the city, base yourself in the charming seaside resort of **Svetlogorsk** (Светлогорск) which is only a few hours' drive down the Baltic coast from the pine forests and Sahara-style dunes of the **Kurshskaya Kosa National Park** (Национальный парк Куршская коса; www.park-kosa.ru; admission per person/car R40/300), a Unesco World Heritage Site.

TRAIN

All long-distance and most local trains go from **Yuzhny vokzal** (Южный вокзал, South Station; pl Kalinina), some passing through, but not always stopping, at **Severny vokzal** (Северный вокзал, North Station; pl Pobedy).

Local train services (ie those between Kaliningrad and Svetlogorsk) run on local time, but those beyond the region to Moscow, St Petersburg and abroad have their arrival and departure times listed in Moscow time; if a Moscow-bound train is scheduled to depart at 10am it will leave at 9am Kaliningrad time.

ℹ️ Getting Around

Trams, trolleybuses (both R10), buses (R12) and minibuses (R12 to R17) will get you most places. For the airport, take bus 144 from the Yuzhny bus station (R30, 30 minutes). A taxi to/from the airport is R450 with **Taxi Kaliningrad** (✉ 4012-585 858; www.taxi-kaliningrad.ru).

Russia Survival Guide

ℹ️ Directory A–Z

ACCOMMODATION

There has been a boom in hostels in both Moscow and St Petersburg, and if you're on a budget you'll want to consider these. Prices run at R600 to R1000 for a dorm bed, and under R3000 for a private room with a shared bathroom. Elsewhere hotel rooms with a bathroom start at about R3000.

BUSINESS HOURS

Note that most museums close their ticket offices one hour (in some cases 30 minutes) before the official closing time.

> ### ⓘ EATING PRICE RANGES
>
> The following price categories are for the cost of a main course:
>
> € less than R500
>
> €€ R500 to R1000

Banks 9am to 6pm Monday to Friday, some open 9am to 5pm Saturday

Bars & Restaurants noon to midnight

Shops 10am to 9pm Monday to Friday, to 7pm Saturday and Sunday

INTERNET RESOURCES

Redtape.ru (www.redtape.ru)

Visit Russia (www.visitrussia.org.uk)

Way to Russia (http://waytorussia.net)

LGBT TRAVELLERS

➡ Russia is a conservative country and being gay is generally frowned upon. LGBT people face stigma, harassment, and violence in their everyday lives.

➡ Homosexuality isn't illegal, but promoting it (and other LGBT lifestyles) is. What constitutes promotion is at the discretion of the authorities.

➡ There are active and relatively open gay and lesbian scenes in both Moscow and St Petersburg. Elsewhere, the gay scene tends to be underground.

➡ For a good overview, visit http://english.gay.ru.

MONEY

The Russian currency is the rouble, written as'рубль' and abbreviated as 'руб' or 'р'. Coins come in amounts of R1, R2, R5 and R10 roubles, with banknotes in values of R10, R50, R100, R500, R1000 and R5000.

ATMs that accept all major credit and debit cards are everywhere, and most restaurants, shops and hotels in major cities take plastic. You can exchange dollars and euros (and some other currencies) at most banks; when they're closed, try the exchange counters at top-end hotels. You may need your passport. Note that crumpled or old banknotes are often refused. Many banks cash travellers cheques for a small commission.

PUBLIC HOLIDAYS

Many businesses are closed from 1 to 7 January. Russia's main public holidays are as follows:

New Year's Day 1 January

Russian Orthodox Christmas Day 7 January

Defender of the Fatherland Day 23 February

International Women's Day 8 March

Easter Monday April

International Labour Day/Spring Festival 1 May

Victory Day 9 May

Russian Independence Day 12 June

Unity Day 4 November

SAFE TRAVEL

Petty theft and pickpockets are prevalent in both Moscow and St Petersburg, so be vigilant with your belongings.

Some police officers can be bothersome, especially to dark-skinned or foreign-looking people. Other members of the police force target tourists, though reports of tourists being hassled about their documents and registration have declined. Still, you should always carry a photocopy of your passport, visa and registration stamp. If you are stopped for any reason – legitimate or illegitimate – you will surely be hassled if you don't have these.

Sadly, racism is a problem in Russia. Be vigilant on the streets around Hitler's birthday (20 April), when bands of right-wing thugs have been known to roam around spoiling for a fight with anyone who doesn't look Russian.

TELEPHONE

The international code for Russia is 🖉 7. The international access code from landline phones in Russia is 🖉 8, followed by 🖉 10 after the second tone, followed by the country code.

The three main mobile-phone companies, all with prepaid and 4G internet options, are **Beeline** (www.beeline.ru), **Megafon** (www.megafon.ru) and **MTS** (www.mts.ru). Company offices are everywhere. It costs almost nothing to purchase a SIM card, but bring your passport.

Local telecom rules mean mobile calls or texts from your 'home' city or region to another city or region are more expensive – essentially long-distance calls/texts. So active callers should consider purchasing a Moscow SIM while in Moscow, and a St Petersburg SIM while in St Petersburg.

Mobile phone numbers start interchangeably with either the country code (🖉 7) or the internal mobile code (🖉 8), plus three digits that change according to the service provider, followed by a seven-digit number. Nearly all Russians will give you their mobile number with an initial 8, but if you're dialing from a non-Russian number (ie your own on roaming), replace this 8 with a 7.

To call a mobile phone from a landline, the line must be enabled to make paid calls (all local numbers are free from a landline anywhere in Russia). To find out if this is the case, dial 8, and then if you hear a second tone you can dial the mobile number in full. If you hear nothing, hang up – you can't call anywhere but local landlines from here.

VISAS

Practically everyone needs a visa to visit Russia. For most travellers a tourist visa (single- or double-entry, valid for a maximum of 30 days) will be sufficient. If you plan to stay longer than a month, you can apply for a business visa or – if you are a US citizen – a three-year multi-entry visa.

To obtain a visa, everyone needs an invitation, also known as 'visa support'. Hotels and hostels will usually issue anyone staying with them an invitation voucher free or for a small fee (typically around €20 to €30). If you are not staying in a hotel or hostel, you will need to buy an invitation – this can be done through travel agents or specialist visa agencies, also for around €20.

Invitation voucher in hand, you can then apply for a visa. Start by entering details in the online form of the Consular Department of the Russian Ministry of Foreign Affairs (https://visa.kdmid. ru/PetitionChoice.aspx).

Take care in answering the questions accurately on this form, including listing all the countries you have visited in the last 10 years and the dates of the visits – stamps in your passport will be checked against this information and if there are anomalies you will likely have to restart the process. Keep a note of the unique identity number provided for your submitted form – if you have to make changes later, you will need this to access it without having to fill in the form again from scratch.

Some Russian embassies (eg those in the UK and US) have contracted separate agencies to process the submission of visa applications; these companies use online interfaces that direct the relevant information into the standard visa application form.

Consular offices apply different fees and slightly different application rules country by country. Avoid potential hassles by checking well in advance what these rules might be.

The charge for the visa will depend on the type of visa applied for and how quickly you need it. We highly recommend applying for your visa in your home country rather than on the road.

Registration

Every visitor to Russia must have their visa registered within seven days of arrival, excluding weekends and public holidays. Registration is handled by your accommodating party. If staying in a homestay or rental apartment, you'll need to make arrangements with either the landlord or a friend to register you through the post office. See http://waytorussia.net/RussianVisa/Registration.html for how this can be done.

Once registered, you'll receive a registration slip. Keep this safe – that's the document that any police who stop you will ask to see. You do not need to register more than once unless you stay in additional cities for more than seven days, in which case you'll need additional registration slips.

Immigration Form

Immigration forms are produced electronically by passport control at airports. If you are arriving by land, ask for the form at the border if it is not provided by the immigration officials.

Take good care of your half of the completed form as you'll need it for registration and could face problems while travelling in Russia – and certainly will on leaving – if you can't produce it.

❶ Getting There & Away

AIR

There are international flights into and out of Moscow and St Petersburg.

LAND

Russia has excellent train and bus connections with the rest of Europe. However, many routes connecting St Petersburg and Moscow with points east – including Kaliningrad – go through Belarus, for which you'll need a transit visa. Buses are the best way to get from St Petersburg to Tallinn. St Petersburg to Helsinki can be done by bus or train, as well as by boat.

From Eastern Europe you are most likely to enter Russia from Estonia at Narva; from Latvia at Rēzekne; from Belarus at Krasnoye or Ezjaryshcha; and from Ukraine at Chernihiv. You can enter Kaliningrad from Lithuania and Poland at any of seven border posts.

SEA

Between early April and late September, international passenger ferries connect Stockholm, Helsinki and Tallinn with St Petersburg's **Morskoy Vokzal** (Морской вокзал; pl Morskoy Slavy 1).

❶ Getting Around

AIR

Booking flights within Russia online is easier than ever, and domestic flights are relatively cheap. Tickets can also be purchased at ubiquitous *avia kassa* (ticket offices). Online agencies specialising in Russian air tickets with English interfaces include **Anywayanyday** (☐ 8-800-775 7753; www.anywayanyday.com) and **Pososhok. ru** (☐ 8-800-333 8118; www.pososhok.ru).

BUS

Buses and *marshrutky* (fixed-route vans or minibuses) are often more frequent, more convenient and faster than trains, especially on short-distance routes. There's almost no need to reserve a seat – just arrive a good 30 minutes before the scheduled departure and buy a ticket. Prices are comparable to 3rd-class train fares. *Marshrutky* fares tend to be double those of buses and they usually leave when full, rather than according to a schedule. Where roads are good, *marshrutky* can be twice as fast as buses.

TAXI

Russian cities have plenty of official taxis, but few people think twice about flagging down any car to request a ride. A fare is negotiated for the journey – simply state your destination and ask '*skolko?*' (how much?), and off you go. Proceed with caution if you are alone and/or it's late at night, especially if you are a woman. While exceedingly rare, violent attacks on passengers have occurred.

TRAIN

Russia's extensive train network is efficiently run by **Russian Railways** (RZD; http://rzd.ru). *Prigorodny* (suburban) or short-distance trains – also known as *elektrichki* – do not require advance booking: you can buy your ticket at the *prigorodny poezd kassa* (suburban train ticket offices) at train stations.

Tickets can be bought online from RZD. Bookings open 45 days before the date of departure. You'd be wise to buy well in advance over the busy summer months and holiday periods such as New Year and early May, when securing berths at short notice on certain trains can be difficult. On long-distance trains the cheapest fares are 3rd class (*platskartny*) followed by 2nd-class sleeper (*kupe*) and 1st-class (*SV*).

At stations, you'll need your passport (or a photocopy) to buy tickets. You can buy tickets for others if you bring their passports or photocopies. Be prepared for long, slow queues. At train ticket offices ('*Zh/D kassa*' ,short for '*zheleznodorozhnaya kassa*'), which are all over most cities, you can pay a surcharge of around R200 and avoid the queues. Alternatively, most travel agencies will organise the reservation and delivery of train tickets for a substantial mark-up.

ESTONIA

Tallinn

POP 414,000

Estonia's capital city has charm by the bucketload, fusing the modern and medieval to come up with a vibrant vibe all of its own. It's an intoxicating mix of ancient church spires, glass skyscrapers, baroque palaces, appealing eateries, brooding battlements, shiny shopping malls, rundown wooden houses and cafes set on sunny squares – with a few Soviet throwbacks in the mix, for added spice.

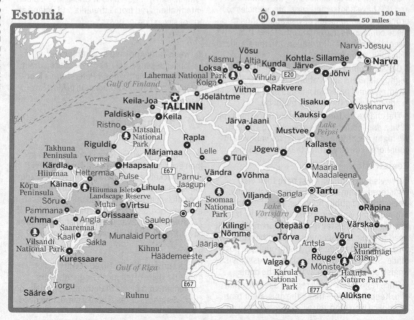

Estonia

◉ Sights

Most of Tallinn's sights are conveniently located within the medieval Old Town (vana-linn), made up of the lower town, surrounded by by much of its 2.5km defensive wall, and the Toompea (upper town). However, given Tallinn's relatively compact size, it's worth venturing out to the further-flung attractions – Kadriorg, in particular, should not be missed.

◉ Lower Town

★ Town Hall Square   SQUARE
(Raekoja plats) Raekoja plats has been the pulsing heart of Tallinn since markets began here in the 11th century. One side is taken is taken up by the Gothic town hall, while the rest is ringed by pretty pastel-coloured buildings dating from the 15th to 17th centuries. Whether bathed in sunlight or sprinkled with snow, it's always a photogenic spot.

Tallinn Town Hall   HISTORIC BUILDING
(Tallinna raekoda; ☎ 645 7900; www.raekoda.tal-linn.ee; Raekoja plats; adult/student €5/2; ⊙10am-4pm Mon-Sat Jul-Aug, by appointment Sep-Jun) Completed in 1404, this is the only surviving Gothic town hall in northern Europe. Inside, you can visit the Trade Hall (housing a visitor book dripping in royal signatures), the Council Chamber (featuring Estonia's oldest woodcarvings, dating from 1374), the vaulted Citizens' Hall, a yellow-and-black-tiled councillor's office, and a small kitchen. The steeply sloped attic has displays on the building and its restoration.

Town Hall Tower   VIEWPOINT
(adult/child €3/1; ⊙11am-6pm Jun-Aug) Old Thomas (Vana Toomas), Tallinn's symbol and guardian, has been keeping watch from his perch on the town hall's weathervane since 1530 (although his previous incarnation now resides in the City Museum). You can enjoy much the same views as Thomas by climbing the 115 steps to the top of the tower. According to legend, this elegant 64m minaret-like structure was modelled on a sketch made by an explorer following his visit to the Orient.

Holy Spirit Lutheran Church   CHURCH
(Pühavaimu kirik; www.eelk.ee/tallinna.puhav aimu/; Pühavaimu 2; adult/child €1/0.50; ⊙noon-2pm Mon-Fri & 10am-4pm Sat Jan–mid-Mar, 10am-3pm Mon-Sat mid-Mar–Apr & Oct-Dec, 10am-5pm Mon-Sat May-Sep) The blue-and-gold clock on the facade of this striking 13th-century Gothic church is the oldest in Tallinn, dating from 1684. Inside there are exquisite wood-carvings and painted panels, including an altarpiece dating to 1483 and a 17th-century baroque pulpit.

Great Guild Hall   MUSEUM
(Suurgildi hoone; www.ajaloomuuseum.ee; Pikk 17; adult/child €5/3; ⊙10am-6pm, closed Wed Oct-Apr) The Estonian History Museum has filled the striking 1410 Great Guild building with a series of ruminations on the Estonian psyche, presented through interactive and unusual displays. Coin collectors shouldn't miss the display in the old excise chamber, while military nuts should head downstairs. The basement also covers the history of the Great Guild itself.

Lower Town Wall   FORTRESS
(Linnamüür; Väike-Kloostri 3; adult/child €1.50/0.75; ⊙11am-7pm Jun-Aug, to 5pm Fri-Wed Apr, May, Sep & Oct, to 4pm Fri-Tue Nov-Mar) The most photogenic stretch of Tallinn's remaining walls connects nine towers lining the western edge of the Old Town. Visitors can explore the barren nooks and crannies of three of them, with cameras at the ready for the red-rooftop views.

St Olaf's Church   CHURCH
(Oleviste kirik; www.oleviste.ee; Lai 50; tower adult/child €2/1; ⊙10am-6pm Sep-Jun, to 8pm Jul & Aug) From 1549 to 1625, when its 159m steeple was struck by lightning and burnt down, this (now Baptist) church was one of the tallest buildings in the world. The current spire reaches a still respectable 124m, and you can take a tight 258-step staircase up the tower for wonderful views of Toompea over the Lower Town's rooftops.

City Museum   MUSEUM
(Linnamuuseum; www.linnamuuseum.ee; Vene 17; adult/child €4/3; ⊙10.30am-5.30pm Tue-Sun) Tallinn's City Museum is actually split over 10 different sites. This, its main branch, is set in a 14th-century merchant's house and traces the city's development from its earliest days. The displays are engrossing and very well laid out, with plenty of information in English, making the hire of the audio-guide quite unnecessary.

RUSSIA & THE BALTIC COAST TALLINN

Toompea

★ Alexander Nevsky Orthodox Cathedral
CHURCH

(Lossi plats; ☉8am-7pm) The positioning of this magnificent, onion-domed Russian Orthodox cathedral (completed in 1900) at the heart of the country's main administrative hub was no accident: the church was one of many built in the last part of the 19th century as part of a general wave of Russification in the empire's Baltic provinces. Orthodox believers come here in droves, alongside tourists ogling the interior's striking icons

Tallinn

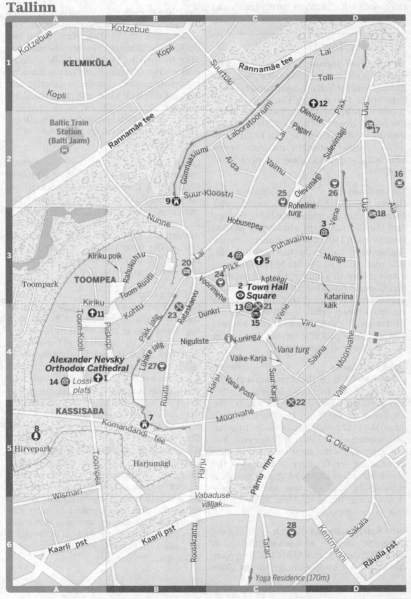

Yoga Residence (170m)

and frescoes. Quiet, respectful, demurely dressed visitors are welcome but cameras aren't.

St Mary's Lutheran Cathedral CHURCH
(Tallinna Püha Neitsi Maarja Piiskoplik toomkirik; www.toomkirik.ee; Toom-Kooli 6 church/tower

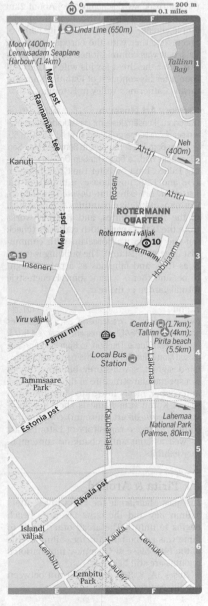

€2/5; ◷9am-5pm daily May-Sep, 10am-4pm Tue-Sun Oct-Apr) Tallinn's cathedral (now Lutheran, originally Catholic) was founded by at least 1233, although the exterior dates mainly from the 15th century, with the tower completed in 1779. This impressive building was a burial ground for the rich and titled, and the whitewashed walls are decorated with the elaborate coats-of-arms of Estonia's noble families. Fit viewseekers can climb the tower.

Toompea Castle HISTORIC BUILDING
(Lossi plats) Three towers have survived from the Knights of the Sword's hilltop castle, the finest of which is 14th-century Pikk Hermann (best viewed from the rear). In the

RUSSIA & THE BALTIC COAST TALLINN

18th century the fortress underwent an extreme makeover at the hands of Russian empress Catherine the Great, converting it into the pretty-in-pink baroque palace that now houses Estonia's parliament (Riigikogu).

Linda Hill   PARK
(Lindamägi; Falgi tee) Shaded by 250-year-old linden trees, this small mound near the top of Toompea is named after Linda, wife of Kalev, the heroic first leader of the Estonians. Accorded to legend, Toompea is the burial mound she built for him. During the Soviet years the statue of the grieving Linda became the unofficial memorial to victims of Stalin's deportations and executions.

Kiek in de Kök   CASTLE, MUSEUM
(🗹 644 6686; www.linnamuuseum.ee; Komandandi tee 2; adult/child €5/3; ⏱ 10.30am-5.30pm Tue-Sun) Built around 1475, this tall, stout fortress is one of Tallinn's most formidable cannon towers. Its name (amusing as it sounds in English) is Low German for 'Peep into the Kitchen'; from the upper floors medieval voyeurs could peer into the houses below. Today it houses a branch of the City Museum, focusing mainly on the development of the town's elaborate defences.

Bastion Passages   FORTRESS
(Bastionikäigud; 🗹 644 6686; www.linnamuuseum.ee; Komandandi tee 2; adult/child €6/3.50) Guided tours depart from Kiek in de Kök exploring the 17th-century Swedish-built tunnels connecting the towers. Bookings are required, and warm clothes and sensible shoes are recommended. Combined tour and tower tickets are available (€9).

◉ City Centre

Hotel Viru & the KGB   MUSEUM
(🗹 680 9300; www.viru.ee; Viru väljak 4; tour €10; ⏱ daily May-Oct, Tue-Sun Nov-Apr) When the Hotel Viru was built in 1972, it was not only Estonia's first skyscraper, it was the only place for tourists to stay in Tallinn – and we mean that literally. Having all the foreigners in one place made it much easier to keep tabs on them and the locals they had contact with, which is exactly what the KGB did from their 23rd-floor spy base. The hotel offers fascinating tours of the facility in various languages; bookings essential.

Rotermann Quarter   AREA
(Rotermanni kvartal; www.rotermann.eu) With impressive contemporary architecture wedged between 19th-century brick warehouses, this development has transformed a former factory complex into the city's swankiest shopping and dining precinct.

◉ Kadriorg Park

Kadriorg Park   PARK
(Kadrioru park; www.kadriorupark.ee) About 2km east of the Old Town, this beautiful park's ample acreage is Tallinn's favourite patch of green. Together with the baroque Kadriorg Palace, it was commissioned by the Russian tsar Peter the Great for his wife Catherine I soon after his conquest of Estonia (Kadriorg means Catherine's Valley in Estonian).

Kadriorg Art Museum   PALACE, GALLERY
(Kadrioru kunstimuuseum; www.kadriorumuuseum.ee; A Weizenbergi 37; adult/child €5.50/3.50; ⏱ 10am-6pm Tue & Thu-Sun, to 8pm Wed May-Sep, 10am-8pm Wed, to 5pm Thu-Sun Oct-Apr) Kadriorg Palace, built by Peter the Great between 1718 and 1736, now houses a branch of the Estonian Art Museum devoted to Dutch, German and Italian paintings from the 16th to the 18th centuries, and Russian works from the 18th to early 20th centuries (check out the decorative porcelain with communist imagery upstairs). The building is exactly as frilly and fabulous as a palace ought to be, and there's a handsome French-style formal garden at the rear.

Kumu   GALLERY
(www.kumu.ee; A Weizenbergi 34; all galleries adult/student €6/4, permanent only €4.50/3; ⏱ 11am-6pm Tue & Thu-Sun, to 8pm Wed Apr-Sep, closed Mon & Tue Oct-Apr) This futuristic, Finnish-designed, seven-storey building (2006) is a spectacular structure of limestone, glass and copper, nicely integrated into the landscape. Kumu (the name is short for *kunstimuuseum* or art museum) contains the country's largest repository of Estonian art as well as constantly changing contemporary exhibits.

◉ Pirita & Around

Just past Maarjamäe the Pirita River enters Tallinn Bay and the city's favourite beach begins to unfurl. The area's other claim to fame was as the base for the sailing events of the 1980 Moscow Olympics; international regattas are still held here.

Buses 1A, 8, 34A and 38 all run between the city centre and Pirita.

Tallinn TV Tower   VIEWPOINT

(Tallinna teletorn; www.teletorn.ee; Kloostrimetsa tee 58a; adult/child €8/5; ⊙10am-7pm) Opened in time for the 1980 Olympics, this futuristic 314m tower offers brilliant views from its 22nd floor (175m). Press a button and frosted glass disks set in the floor suddenly clear, giving a view straight down. Once you're done gawping, check out the interactive displays in the space-age pods. Daredevils can try the open-air 'edge walk' (€20).

Maarjamäe Palace   MUSEUM

(Maarjamäe loss; www.ajaloomuuseum.ee; Pirita tee 56; adult/child €4/2; ⊙10am-5pm Wed-Sun) A kilometre north of Kadriorg Park, Maarjamäe is a neo-Gothic limestone manor house built in 1874 for a Russian count. It's now home to the **Estonian Film Museum** and a less-visited branch of the **Estonian History Museum**, detailing the twists and turns of the 20th century. Don't miss the Soviet sculpture graveyard at the rear of the building.

⊙ Other Neighbourhoods

Estonian Open-Air Museum   MUSEUM

(Eesti vabaõhumuuseum; www.evm.ee; Vabaõhu-muuseumi tee 12, Rocca Al Mare; adult/child May-Sep €7/3.50, Oct-Apr €5/3; ⊙10am-8pm May-Sep, to 5pm Oct-Apr) If tourists won't go to the countryside, bring the countryside to them. That's the modus operandi of this excellent, sprawling complex, where historic buildings have been plucked and transplanted among the tall trees. In summer the time-warping effect is highlighted by staff in period costume performing traditional activities among the wooden farmhouses and windmills.

Lennusadam Seaplane Harbour   MUSEUM

(www.lennusadam.eu; Vesilennuki 6; adult/child €14/7, incl Fat Margaret €16/10; ⊙10am-7pm daily May-Sep, Tue-Sun Oct-Apr; ℗) When this triple-domed hangar was completed in 1917, its reinforced-concrete shell frame construction was unique in the world. Resembling a classic Bond-villain lair, the vast space was completely restored and opened to the public in 2012 as a fascinating maritime museum, filled with interactive displays. Highlights include exploring the cramped corridors of a 1930s naval submarine, and the icebreaker and minehunter ships moored outside.

🏃 Activities

Kalev Spa Waterpark   SWIMMING

(www.kalevspa.ee; Aia 18 2½hr visit adult/child €13/10; ⊙6.45am-9.30pm Mon-Fri, 8am-9.30pm Sat & Sun) For serious swimmers there's an indoor pool of Olympic proportions, but there are plenty of other ways to wrinkle your skin here, including waterslides, spa pools, saunas and a kids' pool. There's also a gym, a day spa and three private saunas, with the largest holding up to 15 of your closest hot-and-sweaty mates.

☞ Tours

Tallinn Traveller Tours   TOUR

(☑5837 4800; www.traveller.ee) Entertaining, good-value tours – including a two-hour Old Town walking tour that departs at midday from outside the tourist information centre (it's nominally free but tips are encouraged). There are also ghost tours (€15), pub crawls (€20), bike tours (from €19) and day trips to as far afield as Rīga (€55).

Euro Audio Guide   WALKING TOUR

(www.euroaudioguide.com; iPod rental €13) Pre-loaded iPods are available from the tourist office offering commentary on various Old Town sights. If you've got your own iPod, iPhone or iPad you can download the tour and an e-book for €15.

🛏 Sleeping

⭐Tabinoya   HOSTEL €

(☑632 0062; www.tabincya.com; Nunne 1; dm/s/d from €15/30/40; @🛜) The Baltic's first Japanese-run hostel occupies the two top floors of a charming old building, with dorms and a communal lounge at the top, and spacious private rooms, a kitchen and a sauna below. Bathroom facilities are shared. The vibe's a bit more comfortable and quiet than most of Tallinn's hostels. Book ahead.

Red Emperor   HOSTEL €

(☑615 0035; www.redemperorhostel.com; Aia 10; dm/s/d from €12/21/32; @🛜) Situated above a wonderfully grungy live-music bar, Red Emperor is Tallinn's premier party hostel for those of a beardy, indie persuasion. Facilities are good, with brightly painted rooms, wooden bunks and plenty of showers, and there are organised activities every day (karaoke, shared dinners etc). Pack heavy-duty earplugs if you're a light sleeper.

Old House Hostel & Guesthouse
HOSTEL €

(☑641 1281; www.oldhouse.ee; Uus 22 & Uus 26; dm/s/d from €14/29/48; P@?) Although one is called a hostel and one a guesthouse, these twin establishments both combine a cosy guesthouse feel with hostel facilities (bunkless dorm rooms, shared bathrooms, guest kitchens and lounges). The homey, old-world decor (antiques, wacky wallpaper, plants, lamps) and the relatively quiet Old Town location will appeal to budget travellers who like things to be nice and comfortable.

Old Town Backpackers
HOSTEL €

(☑5351 7266; www.tallinnoldtownbackpackers. com; Uus 14; dm/s €15/35; @?) Enter this baroque house and the whole hostel is laid out before you: a large room with half a dozen beds that also serves as the kitchen and living room. Given the tightness, late-night partying isn't encouraged, but you'll certainly get to know your fellow guests. Especially as there's a sauna and spa.

✗ Eating

★V
VEGAN €

(☑626 9087; Rataskaevu 12; mains €6-9; ⊙noon-11pm; ☑) Visiting vegans are spoiled for choice in this wonderful restaurant. In summer everyone wants one of the four tables on the street, but the atmospheric interior is just as great. The food is excellent; expect the likes of sweet potato peanut curry, spicy tofu with quinoa, and stuffed zucchini.

III Draakon
CAFE €

(Raekoja plats; mains €1-3; ⊙9am-midnight) There's bucketloads of atmosphere at this Lilliputian tavern below the Town Hall, and super-cheap elk soup, sausages and oven-hot pies baked fresh on site. The historic setting is amped up – expect costumed wenches with a good line in tourist banter, and beer served in ceramic steins.

Must Puudel
CAFE €

(Müürivahe 20; mains €6.50-11; ⊙9am-11pm Sun-Wed, to 2am Thu-Sat; ?) Mismatched 1970s furniture, an eclectic soundtrack, courtyard seating, excellent coffee, cooked breakfasts (less than €5), tasty light meals, long opening hours and a name that translates as 'Black Poodle' – yep, this is the Old Town's hippest cafe.

🍷 Drinking & Nightlife

Tallinn's hipsters tend to leave the pricey bars of the Old Town to the tourists and head to Kalamaja instead. **Telliskivi Creative City** (Telliskivi Loomelinnak; www.telliskivi. eu; Telliskivi 60a; ⊙shops 8.30am-9pm Mon-Sat, 9am-7pm Sun) is the liveliest nook – especially **F-hoone** (www.fhoone.ee; Telliskivi 60a; mains €5.50-8.70; ⊙9am-11pm Mon-Sat, 10am-9pm Sun; ?☑) – but there are cosy local pubs scattered throughout the neighbourhood.

DM Baar
BAR

(www.depechemode.ee; Voorimehe 4; ⊙noon-4am) If you just can't get enough of Depeche Mode, this is the bar for you. The walls are covered with all manner of memorabilia, including pictures of the actual band partying here. And the soundtrack? Do you really need to ask? If you're not a fan, leave in silence.

Kultuuriklubi Kelm
BAR

(Vene 33; ⊙5pm-2am Mon-Thu, to 6am Fri, 7pm-6am Sat, 7pm-2am Sun) It may be a 'culture club', but you're unlikely to hear *Karma Chameleon* blasting out in this artsy rock bar. Expect lots of live music, art exhibitions, ping-pong competitions and movies on Wednesday nights.

Hell Hunt
PUB

(www.hellhunt.ee; Pikk 39; ⊙noon-2am; ?) Billing itself as 'the first Estonian pub', this trusty old trooper boasts an amiable air and a huge beer selection – local and imported. Don't let the menacing-sounding name put you off – it actually means 'gentle wolf'. In summer, it spills onto the little square across the road.

Põrgu
PUB

(www.porgu.ee; Rüütli 4; ⊙noon-midnight Mon-Thu, to 2am Fri & Sat) While the name may mean 'hell', the descent to this particular underworld is nothing short of heavenly for craft beer fans. There's a good mix of local and imported drops, including 13 beers and two ciders on tap and dozens more by the bottle. The food's good too.

X-Baar
GAY & LESBIAN

(www.xbaar.ee; Tatari 1; ⊙4pm-1am Sun-Thu, to 3am Fri & Sat) This long-standing bar is the mainstay of the gay and lesbian scene, attracting a mixed crowd of mainly local men and women. It's a relaxed kind of place, with a snug bar and a large dancefloor.

LAHEMAA NATIONAL PARK

A microcosm of Estonia's natural charms, this park takes in a stretch of deeply indented coast with several peninsulas and bays, plus 475 sq km of pine-fresh hinterland encompassing forest, lakes, rivers and peatbogs, and areas of historical and cultural interest.

Fully restored **Palmse Manor** (www.palmse.ee; adult/child €7/5; ⊙10am-7pm) is the park's showpiece, housing the **visitor centre** (⊘329 5555; www.loodusegakoos.ee; ⊙9am-5pm daily May-Oct, Mon-Fri Oct-Apr) in its former stables. The pretty manor house (1720, rebuilt in the 1780s) is now a museum containing period furniture and clothing. Other estate buildings have also been restored and put to new use: the distillery is a hotel, the steward's residence is a guesthouse, the lakeside bathhouse is a summertime restaurant, and the farm labourers' quarters became a tavern.

First mentioned in 1465, the fishing village of **Alja** has many restored or reconstructed traditional buildings, including a wonderfully ancient-looking tavern that was actually built in 1976. Altja's Swing Hill (Kiitemägi), complete with a traditional Estonian wooden swing, has long been the focus of Midsummer's Eve festivities in Lahemaa. The 3km circular **Altja Nature & Culture Trail** starts at Swing Hill and takes in net sheds, fishing cottages and the stone field known as the 'open-air museum of stones'.

Lahemaa is best explored by car or bicycle. The main bus routes through the park include Tallinn to Altja (€6.30, 1¾ hours, daily)

☆ Entertainment

Events are posted on walls, advertised on flyers found in shops and cafes, and listed in newspapers. Tallinn's best English-language listings guide is *Tallinn In Your Pocket* (www.inyourpocket.com), published every two months; buy it at bookshops or the tourist office (€2.50), or download it for free from the website. Despite the name, *Tallinn This Week* is also bimonthly; it's available from the tourist office and venues around town. For performing arts listings, see www.culture.ee, www.concert.ee and www.teater.ee.

Buy tickets for concerts and big events at Piletilevi (www.piletilevi.ee), either online or inside the Viru Keskus shopping centre in Viru väljak.

ℹ Information

Tallinn Tourist Information Centre (⊘645 7777; www.visittallinn.ee; Niguliste 2; ⊙9am-7pm Mon-Fri, to 5pm Sat & Sun May-Aug, 9am-6pm Mon-Fri, to 3pm Sat & Sun Sep-Apr) Brochures, maps, event schedules and other info.

ℹ Getting There & Away

AIR

Tallinn Airport (Tallinna Lennujaam; ⊘605 8888; www.tallinn-airport.ee; Tartu mnt 101) is 4km southeast of the Old Town. Numerous airlines fly to Tallinn from within the Baltic region and from further afield.

BOAT

Ferries head to Tallinn from Helsinki and other Baltic ports.

BUS

Regional and international buses depart from the **Central Bus Station** (Tallinna bussijaam; ⊘12550; www.bussijaam.ee; Lastekodu 46; ⊙5am-1am), about 2km southeast of the Old Town; tram 2 or 4 will get you there. Services depart from here for Latvia and other European destinations. Main domestic routes include Tartu (€7 to €12, 2½ hours, at least every half-hour) and Pärnu (€6.50 to €11, two hours, at least hourly)

TRAIN

The **Baltic Train Station** (Balti Jaam; Toompuiestee 35) is on the northwestern edge of the Old Town. Despite the name, there are no direct services to the other Baltic states. Destinations includeTartu (€11, two to 2½ hours, eight daily) and Pärnu (€7.60, 2¼ hours, three daily)

ℹ Getting Around

TO/FROM THE AIRPORT

➡ Bus 2 runs roughly every 20 minutes (6.30am to around midnight) from the A Laikmaa stop, opposite the Tallink Hotel, next to Viru Keskus. From the airport, bus 2 will take you via six bus stops to the centre and on to the passenger port. Buy tickets from the driver (€1.60); journey time depends on traffic but rarely exceeds 20 minutes.

➡ A taxi between the airport and the city centre should cost less than €10.

TO/FROM THE FERRY TERMINALS

Most ferries and cruise ships dock at the Old City Harbour (Vanasadama). Eckerö Line, Viking Line and St Peter Line use **Terminals A & B** (Sadama) while Tallink uses **Terminal D** (Lootsi), just across the marina. Linda Line ferries dock a little further west at the hulking **Linnahall** (Kalasadama).

All terminals are a short (less than 1km) walk from the Old Town, but there are also buses and tram connections. A taxi between the city centre and any of the terminals should only cost about €5.

PUBLIC TRANSPORT

Tallinn has an excellent network of buses, trams and trolleybuses that run from around 6am to midnight. The major local bus station is on the basement level of the Viru Keskus shopping centre in Viru väljak, although some buses terminate their routes on the surrounding streets. All local public transport timetables are online at www.tallinn.ee.

Public transport is free for Tallinn residents. Visitors still need to pay, either from the driver with cash (€1.60 for a single journey) or by using the e-ticketing system. Buy a plastic smartcard (€2 deposit) and top up with credit, then validate the card at the start of each journey using the orange card-readers. Fares using the e-ticketing system cost €1.10/3/6 for an hour/day/five days.

The Tallinn Card includes free public transport. Travelling without a valid ticket runs the risk of a €40 fine.

TAXI

Taxis are plentiful in Tallinn but each company sets its own fare; prices should be posted prominently. However, if you hail a taxi on the street, there's a chance you'll be overcharged. To save yourself the trouble, order a taxi by phone (operators speak English):

Krooni Takso (☑1212; www.kroonitakso.ee; base fare €2.50, per km 6am-11pm €0.50, 11pm-6am €0.55)

Reval Takso (☑1207; www.reval-takso.ee; base fare €2.29, per km €0.49)

Tartu

POP 98,000

Tartu lays claim to being Estonia's spiritual capital, with locals talking about a special Tartu *vaim* (spirit), created by the time-stands-still feel of its wooden houses and stately buildings, and by the beauty of its parks and riverfront. It's also Estonia's premier university town, with students making up nearly a seventh of the population – guaranteeing a vibrant nightlife for a city of its size.

◉ Sights

◉ Old Town

★ Town Hall Square   SQUARE

(Raekoja plats) Tartu's main square is lined with grand buildings and echoes with the chink of glasses and plates in summer. The centrepiece is the Town Hall itself, fronted by a statue of students kissing under a spouting umbrella. On the south side of the square, look out for the communist hammer-and-sickle relief that still remains on the facade of number 5.

Tartu Art Museum   GALLERY

(Tartu kunstimuuseum; www.tartmus.ee; Raekoja plats 18; adult/student €4/3; ⊙11am-6pm Wed & Fri-Sun, to 9pm Thu) If you're leaving one of the plaza's pubs and you're not sure whether you're seeing straight, don't use this building as your guide. Foundations laid partially over an old town wall have given a pronounced lean to this, the former home of Colonel Barclay de Tolly (1761–1818) – an exiled Scot who distinguished himself in the Russian army. It now contains an engrossing gallery spread over three levels, the bottom of which is given over to temporary exhibitions.

Tartu University   UNIVERSITY

(Tartu Ülikool; www.ut.ee; Ülikooli 18) Fronted by six Doric columns, the impressive main building of Tartu University was built between 1803 and 1809. The university itself was founded in 1632 by the Swedish king Gustaf II Adolf (Gustavus Adolphus) to train Lutheran clergy and government officials. It was modelled on Uppsala University in Sweden.

Tartu University Art Museum   MUSEUM

(Tartu Ülikooli kunstimuuseum; www.kunstimuuseum.ut.ee; Ülikooli 18; adult/child €3/2; ⊙10am-6pm Mon-Sat May-Sep, 11am-5pm Mon-Fri Oct-Apr) Within the main university building, this collection comprises mainly plaster casts of ancient Greek sculptures made in the 1860s and 1870s, along with an Egyptian mummy. The rest of the collection was evacuated to Russia in 1915 and has never returned. Admission includes entry to the graffiti-covered attic lock-up, where students were held in solitary confinement for various infractions.

St John's Lutheran Church   CHURCH

(Jaani kirik; www.jaanikirik.ee; Jaani 5; steeple adult/child €2/1.50; ⊙10am-7pm Mon-Sat Jun-Aug, to 6pm Tue-Sat Sep-May) Dating to at least 1323, this imposing red-brick church is unique for the rare terracotta sculptures placed in niches around its exterior and interior (look up). It lay in ruins and was left derelict following a Soviet bombing raid in 1944 and wasn't fully restored until 2005. Climb the 135 steps of the 30m steeple for a bird's-eye view of Tartu.

⊙ Toomemägi

Rising to the west of the town hall, Toomemägi (Cathedral Hill) is the original reason for Tartu's existence functioning on and off as a stronghold from around the 5th or 6th century. It's now a tranquil park, with walking paths meandering through the trees and a pretty-as-a-picture rotunda which serves as a summertime cafe.

Tartu University Museum   MUSEUM

(Tartu Ülikool muuseum; www.muuseum.ut.ee; Lossi 25; adult/child €4/3; ⊙10am-6pm Tue-Sun May-Sep, 11am-5pm Wed-Sun Oct-Apr) Atop Toomemägi are the ruins of a Gothic cathedral, originally built by German knights in the 13th century. It was substantially rebuilt in the 15th century, despoiled during the Reformation in 1525, used as a barn, and partly rebuilt between 1804 and 1809 to house the university library, which is now a museum. Inside there are a range of interesting exhibits chronicling student life.

⊙ Other Neighbourhoods

Estonian National Museum   MUSEUM

(Eesti rahva muuseum; www.erm.ee; Narva mnt 177) When we last visited, the immense, low-slung, architectural showcase built to house the Estonian National Museum had yet to open its doors. Built on a Soviet airstrip on the grounds of Raadi Manor (the museum's original pre-war home), the new building has a floor space of nearly 34,000 sq metres and will contain a cafe, restaurant and displays on august themes such as 'Estonian Dialogues' and 'Echo of the Urals'. Check the website for details.

Science Centre AHHAA   MUSEUM

(Teaduskeskus AHHAA; www.ahhaa.ee; Sadama 1; adult/child €12/9, planetarium €4, flight simulator €1, 4D theatre €2; ⊙10am-7pm) Head under the dome for a whizz-bang series of interactive exhibits that are liable to bring out the mad scientist in kids and adults alike. Allow at least a couple of hours for button pushing, water squirting and knob twiddling. And you just haven't lived until you've set a tray of magnetised iron filings 'dancing' to Bronski Beat's *Smalltown Boy*. Upstairs there's a nightmarish collection of pickled organs and deformed fetuses courtesy of the university's medical faculty.

KGB Cells Museum   MUSEUM

(KGB kongide muuseum; http://linnamuuseum.tartu.ee; Riia mnt 15b, enter from Pepleri; adult/child €4/2; ⊙11am-4pm Tue-Sat) What do you do when a formerly nationalised building is returned to you with cells in the basement and a fearsome reputation? In this particular case, the family donated the basement to the Tartu City Museum, which created this sombre and highly worthwhile exhibition. Chilling in parts, the displays give a fascinating rundown on deportations, life in the gulags, the Estonian resistance movement and what went on in these former KGB headquarters, known as the 'Grey House'.

🛏 Sleeping

Terviseks   HOSTEL €

(☑565 5382; www.terviseksbbb.com; top fl, Raekoja plats 10; dm €15-17, s/d €22/44; @ 🤶) Occupying a historic building in a perfect main-square location, this excellent 'backpacker's bed and breakfast' offers dorms (maximum four beds, no bunks), private rooms, a full kitchen and lots of switched-on info about the happening places in town. It's like staying in your rich mate's cool European pad. Cheers (*terviseks!*) to that.

Looming   HOSTEL €

(☑5699 4398; www.loominghostel.ee; Kastani 38; dm €15-17, s/d €32/39; @ 🤶) 🍃 Run by urban greenies with a commitment to recycled materials and sustainable practices, Looming ('creation' in Estonian) offers smart, bunk-free dorms and private rooms in a converted art-nouveau factory building. There's an appealing roof terrace and bikes for rent (per day €10).

Academus Hostel   HOSTEL €

(☑5306 6620; www.academus.ee; Pepleri 14; s/tw/f €30/40/50; P 🤶) The university runs three hostels, but only this one is open to nonstudents year-round. Rooms are clean, bright and reasonably large, and have

Tartu

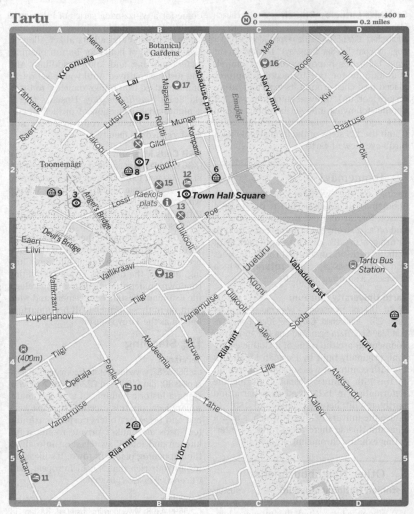

private kitchenettes and bathrooms. Despite being a tad institutional, they're excellent value for money. Advance reservations are a must.

✖ Eating

Werner   CAFE €
(www.werner.ee; Ülikooli 11; baked items €2-3; ⏰7.30am-11pm Mon-Thu, 8am-1am Fri & Sat, 9am-9pm Sun) Upstairs there's a proper restaurant serving pasta and meaty mains, but we prefer the buzzy cafe downstairs. The counter positively groans under a hefty array of quiches and tempting cakes, plus there's a sweet little courtyard at the back.

Noir   EUROPEAN €
(🕿744 0055; www.cafenoir.ee; Ülikooli 7; mains €7-8; ⏰11am-11pm Mon-Sat, to 6pm Sun; ⊞) Definitely a place to impress a date, this sexy, black-walled restaurant-cum-*vinoteque* is a fine place for wining, dining and reclining. It's tucked away in a courtyard off Ülikooli, with outdoor tables and a well-priced menu of salads and pasta.

Tartu

University Cafe CAFE €€
(Ülikooli Kohvik; ☑737 5405; www.kohvik.ut.ee; Ülikooli 20; mains €7-16; ⊙11.30am-9pm Mon-Wed, to midnight Thu-Sat) This venerable institution inhabits a labyrinth of elegantly decorated rooms. It's simultaneously grand and cosy, with serves to sate the most ravenous of scholars. In the evening the Tartu Jazz Club takes over the bottom floor.

 Drinking & Nightlife

Genialistide Klubi BAR, CLUB
(www.genklubi.ee; Magasini 5 ⊙noon-3am Mon-Sat) The Genialists' Club is an all-purpose, grungy 'subcultural establishment' that's simultaneously a bar, a cafe, an alternative nightclub, a live-music venue, a cinema, a specialist Estonian CD store and, just quietly, the hippest place in Tartu.

Naiiv BAR
(www.naiiv.ee; Vallikraavi 6; ⊙6pm-1am Tue-Thu, to 3am Fri & Sat) An imperious white cat holds court at this very cool craft beer and cocktail bar. The selection is extensive, so ask the clued-up staff for suggestions on good local brews, then find a comfy sofa to sink into, or head out to the small rear courtyard.

Club Tallinn CLUB
(www.facebook.com/ClubTallinn; Narva mnt 27; admission €5-7; ⊙11pm-3am Wed-Sat) Tartu's best dance club is a multifloored extravaganza with many nooks and crannies. Some top-notch DJs spin here, drawing a fashionable, up-for-it crowd.

❶ Information

Tartu Tourist Information Centre (☑744 2111; www.visittartu.com; Town Hall, Raekoja plats; ⊙9am-6pm mid-May–mid-Sep, 9am-5pm Mon-Fri, 10am-2pm Sat & Sun mid-Sep–mid-May) Stocks local maps and brochures, books accommodation and tour guides, and has free internet access.

❶ Getting There & Away

AIR
Tartu Airport (TAY; ☑605 8888; www.tartu-airport.ee; Lennu tn 44, Reola küla), 9km south of the city centre, offers daily Finnair services to and from Helsinki.

BUS
Regional and international (p820) buses depart from **Tartu Bus Station** (Tartu Autobussijaam; ☑12550; Turu 2 (enter from Soola); ⊙6am-9pm), which is attached to the Tasku shopping centre.

Major domestic routes include Tallinn (€7 to €12, 2½ hours, at least every half hour) and Pärnu (€9.60 to €12, 2¾ hours, 12 daily)

TRAIN
Tartu's beautifully restored wooden **train station** (☑673 7400; www.elron.ee; Vaksali 6), is 1.5km southwest of the Old Town at the end of Kuperjanovi street. Four express (2½-hour) and four regular (two-hour) services head to Tallinn daily (both €11).

Pärnu

POP 39,800

Local families, hormone-sozzled youths and German, Swedish and Finnish holidaymakers join together in a collective prayer for sunny weather while strolling the beaches, sprawling parks and picturesque historic centre of Pärnu (*pair*-nu), Estonia's premier seaside resort.

◎ Sights

Pärnu straddles both sides of the Pärnu River at the point where it empties into Pärnu Bay. The south bank contains the major attractions, including the Old Town and the beach. The main thoroughfare of the historic centre is Rüütli, lined with splendid buildings dating back to the 17th century.

Pärnu Beach
BEACH

Pärnu's long, wide, sandy beach – sprinkled with volleyball courts, cafes and changing cubicles – is easily the city's main drawcard. A curving path stretches along the sand, lined with fountains, park benches and an excellent playground. Early-20th-century buildings are strung along Ranna pst, the avenue that runs parallel to the beach. Across the road, the formal gardens of **Rannapark** are ideal for a summertime picnic.

Museum of New Art
GALLERY

(Uue kunstimuuseum; ☎ 443 0772; www.mona.ee; Esplanaadi 10; adult/child €3/1.50; ☺ 9am-9pm) Pärnu's former Communist Party headquarters now houses one of Estonia's edgiest galleries. As part of its commitment to pushing the cultural envelope, it stages an international nude art exhibition every summer. Founded by filmmaker Mark Soosaar, the gallery also hosts the annual Pärnu Film Festival.

Tallinn Gate
GATE

(Tallinna Värav) The typical star shape of the 17th-century Swedish ramparts that once

Pärnu

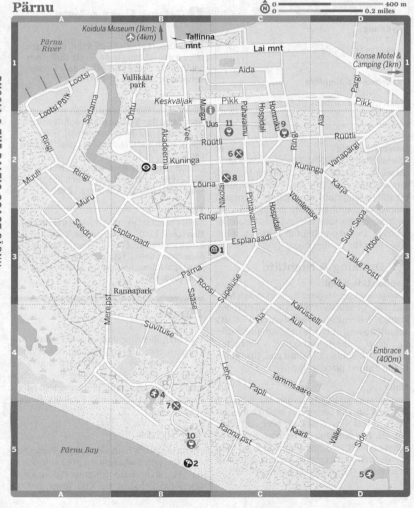

surrounded the Old Town can easily be spotted on a colour map, as most of the pointy bits are now parks. The only intact section, complete with its moat, lies to the west of the centre. Where the rampart meets the western end of Kuninga, it's pierced by this tunnel-like gate, which once defended the main road that headed to the river-ferry crossing and on to Tallinn.

🏃 Activities

Tervise Paradiis Veekeskus — WATER PARK
(www.terviseparadiis.ee; Side 14; adult/child 3hr €13/9, day €20/15; ⊙10am-10pm) At the far end of the beach, Estonia's largest water park beckons with pools, slides, tubes and other slippery fun. It's a big family-focused draw, especially when bad weather ruins beach plans. The large resort also offers spa treatments, fitness classes and ten-pin bowling.

Hedon Spa — SPA
(☑449 9011; www.hedonspa.com; Ranna pst 1; treatments from €25; ⊙9am-7pm Mon-Sat, to 5pm Sun) Built in 1927 to house Pärnu's famous mud baths, this handsome neoclassical building has recently been fully restored and opened as a day spa. All manner of pampering treatments are offered, only some of which involve mud.

🛏 Sleeping & Eating

Konse Motel & Camping — CAMPGROUND €
(☑5343 5092; www.konse.ee; Suur-Jõe 44a; sites €9-15, r with/without bathroom from €52/40; P@🤶) Crammed beside the river about 1km from the centre, Konse offers camp-

ing and a variety of rooms, all with kitchen access. It's not an especially charming spot but there is a sauna (per hour €15), and bike (per day €10) and rowboat (per hour €10) rental.

Steffani — PIZZA €
(www.steffani.ee; Nikolai 24; mains €6.10-8.30; ⊙11am-midnight Sun-Thu, to 2am Fri & Sat; 🐕) The queue out front should alert you – this is a top choice for thin-crust and pan pizzas, particularly in summer when you can dine alfresco on the big, flower-filled terrace. The menu also stretches to pasta and, oddly, burritos. During summer it also operates out of a **beach branch** (Ranna pst 1; mains €7.10-9.90).

Piccadilly — CAFE, VEGETARIAN €
(www.wine.kohvila.com; Pühavaimu 15; mains €4.50-7.50; ⊙9am-11pm Mon-Sat, 10am-8pm Sun; 🐕) Piccadilly offers a down-tempo haven for wine-lovers and vegetarians and an extensive range of hot beverages. Savoury options include delicious salads, sandwiches and omelettes, but really it's all about the sweeties, including moreish cheesecake and handmade chocolates.

🍷 Drinking & Nightlife

Veerev Õlu — PUB
(Uus 3a; ⊙11am-1am Mon-Sat, 1pm-1am Sun) Named after the Rolling Stones, the 'Rolling Beer' wins the award for the friendliest and cosiest pub by a long shot. It's a tiny rustic space with good vibes, cheap beer and the occasional live folk-rock band (with compulsory dancing on tables, it would seem).

Puhvet APTEK — BAR, CLUB
(www.aptek.ee; Rüütli 40; ⊙10pm-2am Wed & Thu, to 4am Fri & Sat) Drop by the old 1930s pharmacy to admire the clever restoration that has turned it into a smooth late-night haunt. Fabulous decor (including original cabinets, vials and bottles) competes for your attention with cocktails and DJs.

Sunset — CLUB
(www.sunset.ee; Ranna pst 3; ⊙11pm-6am Fri & Sat Jun-Aug) Pärnu's biggest and most famous summertime nightclub has an outdoor beach terrace and a sleek multifloor interior with plenty of nooks for when the dance floor gets crowded. Imported DJs and bands keep things cranked until the early hours.

ⓘ Information

Pärnu Tourist Information Centre (☑ 447 3000; www.visitparnu.com; Uus 4; ⊙ 9am-6pm mid-May–mid-Sep, 9am-5pm Mon-Fri & 10am-2pm Sat & Sun mid-Sep–mid-May) A very helpful centre stocking maps and brochures, booking accommodation and rental cars (for a small fee), and providing a left-luggage service (per day €2). There's a small gallery attached as well as a toilet and showers.

ⓘ Getting There & Away

Buses stop at the corner of Pikk and Ringi, but the main **bus station ticket office** (Ringi 3; ⊙ 6.30am-7.30pm) is about 100m away (look for the red 'bussijaam' sign). International coaches head from here to as far afield as St Petersburg and Vilnius. Domestic destinations includeTallinn (€6.50 to €11, two hours, at least hourly) and Tartu (€9.60 to €12, 2¾ hours,12 daily).

Three daily trains run between Tallinn and Pärnu (€7.60, 2¼ hours), but this isn't a great option given that **Pärnu station** (Liivi tee) is an inconvenient 5km east of the town centre in a difficult to find and to access spot on a major road.

Estonia Survival Guide

ⓘ Directory A–Z

ACCOMMODATION

If you like flying by the seat of your pants when you're travelling, you'll find July and August in Estonia very problematic. The best accommodation books up quickly and in Tallinn, especially on weekends, you might find yourself scraping for anywhere at all to lay your head. In fact, Tallinn gets busy most weekends, so try to book about a month ahead anytime from May through to September (midweek isn't anywhere near as bad).

Budget catagory accommodation (€) has double rooms and/or dorm beds for less than €35.

PUBLIC HOLIDAYS

New Year's Day (Uusaasta) 1 January

Independence Day (Iseseisvuspäev) Anniversary of 1918 declaration on 24 February

Good Friday (Suur reede) March/April

Easter Sunday (Lihavõtted) March/April

Spring Day (Kevadpüha) 1 May

Pentecost (Nelipühade) Seventh Sunday after Easter (May/June)

Victory Day (Võidupüha) Commemorating the anniversary of the Battle of Võnnu (1919) on 23 June.

St John's Day (Jaanipäev, Midsummer's Day). Taken together, Victory Day and St John's Day

on 24 June are the excuse for a week-long midsummer break for many people.

Day of Restoration of Independence (Taasiseseisvumispäev) On 20 August, marking the country's return to Independence in 1991.

Christmas Eve (Jõululaupäev) 24 December

Christmas Day (Jõulupüha) 25 December

Boxing Day (Teine jõulupüha) 26 December

TELEPHONE

There are no area codes in Estonia; if you're calling anywhere within the country, just dial the number as it's listed. All landline phone numbers have seven digits; mobile (cell) numbers have seven or eight digits and begin with 5. Estonia's country code is ☑ 372.

TOURIST INFORMATION

In addition to the info-laden, multilingual website of the **Estonian Tourist Board** (www.visitestonia.com), there are tourist offices in most cities and many towns and national parks throughout the country. At nearly every one you'll find English-speaking staff and lots of free material.

ⓘ Getting There & Away

AIR

Eleven European airlines have scheduled services to Tallinn year-round, with additional routes and airlines added in summer. There are also daily flights between Helsinki and Tartu.

LAND

Bus

The following bus companies have services between Estonia and the other Baltic states:

Ecolines (☑ 606 2217; www.ecolines.net)

Lux Express & Simple Express (☑ 680 0909; www.luxexpress.eu)

UAB Toks (www2.toks.lt)

Train

Valga is the terminus for both the Estonian and Latvian rail systems, but the train services don't connect up. From Valga, Estonian trains operated by **Elron** (www.elron.ee) head to Tartu, while Latvian trains operated by **Pasažieru vilciens** (www.pv.lv) head to Valmiera, Cēsis, Sigulda and Rīga. There are also direct trains to Tallinn from St Petersburg and Moscow.

SEA

Tallinn has ferry connections to Helsinki and other Baltic ports.

ⓘ Getting Around

BUS

➡ The national bus network is extensive, linking all the major cities to each other and the smaller towns to their regional hubs.

- All services are summarised on the extremely handy **T pilet** (www.tpilet.ee) site.
- Don't presume that drivers will speak English.
- Concessions are available for children and seniors.

TRAIN

Train services have been steadily improving in recent years. Domestic routes are run by **Elron** (www.elron.ee) but it's also possible to travel between Tallinn and Narva on the Russian-bound services run by **GoRail** (www.gorail.ee).

LATVIA

Rīga

The Gothic spires that dominate Rīga's cityscape might suggest austerity, but it is the flamboyant art nouveau that forms the flesh and the spirit of this vibrant cosmopolitan city, the largest of all three Baltic capitals. Like all northerners, it is quiet and reserved on the outside, but there is some powerful chemistry going on inside its hip bars, modern art centres, and in the kitchens of its cool experimental restaurants. Standing next to a gulf named after itself, Rīga is a short drive from jet-setting sea resort Jūrmala, which comes with a stunning whitesand beach. But if you are craving solitude and a pristine environment, gorgeous sand dunes and blueberry-filled forests, begin right outside the city boundaries.

◉ Sights

◉ Old Rīga (Vecrīga)

★**Rīga Cathedral** CHURCH
(Rīgas Doms; ☑6721 3213; www.doms.lv; Doma laukums 1; admission €3; ◉9am-5pm) Founded in 1211 as the seat of the Rīga diocese, this enormous (once Catholic, now Evangelical Lutheran) cathedral is the largest medieval church in the Baltic. The architecture is an amalgam of styles from the 13th to the 18th centuries: the eastern end, the oldest portion, has Romanesque features; the tower is 18th-century baroque; and much of the rest dates from a 15th-century Gothic rebuilding.

★**Art Museum Rīga Bourse** MUSEUM
(Mākslas muzejs Rīgas Birža; www.lnmm.lv; Doma laukums 6; adult/child €6.40/2.85; ◉10am-6pm

ART NOUVEAU RĪGA

Just when you thought that Old Rīga was the most beautiful neighbourhood in town, the city's audacious art nouveau district (focused around Alberta iela, Strēlnieku iela and Elizabetes iela) swoops in to vie for the prize. Rīga boasts over 750 Jugendstil (art nouveau) buildings, making it the city with the most art nouveau architecture in the world.

Alberta iela is like a huge painting that you can spend hours staring at, as your eye detects more and more intriguing details. But this must-see Rīga sight is a rather functional street with residential houses, restaurants and shops. The master responsible for most of these is Mikhail Eisenstein (father of filmmaker Sergei Eisenstein). Named after the founder of Rīga, Bishop Albert von Buxthoeven, the street was the architect's gift to Rīga on its 700th anniversary.

Tue-Thu, Sat & Sun, to 8pm Fri) Rīga's lavishly restored stock exchange building is a worthy showcase for the city's art treasures. The elaborate facade features a coterie of deities that dance between the windows, while inside, gilt chandeliers sparkle from ornately moulded ceilings. The Oriental section features beautiful Chinese and Japanese ceramics and an Egyptian mummy, but the main halls are devoted to Western art, including a Monet painting and a scaled-down cast of Rodin's *The Kiss*.

★**Arsenāls Exhibition Hall** GALLERY
(Izstāžu zāle Arsenāls; www.lnmm.lv; Torņa iela 1; adult/child €3.56/2.13; ◉noon-5pm Tue, Wed & Fri-Sun, to 8pm Thu) Behind a row of spooky granite heads depicting Latvia's most prominent artists, the imperial arsenal, constructed in 1832 to store weapons for the Russian tzar's army, is now a prime spot for international and local art exhibitions, which makes it worth a visit. Also check out the massive wooden stairs at the back of the building – their simple yet funky geometry predates modern architecture.

Blackheads House HISTORIC BUILDING
(Melngalvju nams; www.melngalvjunams.lv; Rātslaukums 7) Built in 1344 as a veritable fraternity house for the Blackheads guild of

Latvia

unmarried German merchants, the original house was decimated in 1941 and flattened by the Soviets seven years later. Somehow the original blueprints survived and an exact replica of this fantastically ornate structure was completed in 2001 for Rīga's 800th birthday.

Rīga History & Navigation Museum
MUSEUM

(Rīgas vēstures un kuģniecības muzejs; www.rigamuz.lv; Palasta iela 4; adult/child €4.27/0.71; ⊙10am-5pm May-Sep, 11am-5pm Wed-Sun Oct-Apr) Founded in 1773, this is the oldest museum in the Baltic, situated in the old cathedral monastery. The permanent collection features artefacts from the Bronze Age all the way to WWII, ranging from lovely pre-Christian jewellery to preserved hands removed from Medieval forgers. A highlight is the beautiful neo-classical Column Hall, built when Latvia was part of the Russian empire and filled with relics from that time.

Cat House
HISTORIC BUILDING

(Kaķu māja; Miestaru iela 10/12) The spooked black cats mounted on the turrets of this 1909 art nouveau–influenced building have become a symbol of Rīga. According to local legend, the building's owner was rejected from the Great Guild across the street and

exacted revenge by pointing the cats' butts towards the hall. The members of the guild were outraged, and after a lengthy court battle the merchant was admitted into the club on the condition that the cats be turned in the opposite direction.

Museum of Decorative Arts & Design
MUSEUM

(Dekoratīvi lietišķās mākslas muzejs; ☑6722 7833; www.lnmm.lv; Skārņu iela 10/20; adult/child €4.27/2.13; ⊙11am-5pm Tue & Thu to Sun, till 7pm Wed) The former St George's Church houses a museum devoted to applied art from the art nouveau period to the present, including an impressive collection of furniture, woodcuts, tapestries and ceramics. The building's foundations date back to 1207, when the Livonian Brothers of the Sword erected their castle here. Since the rest of the original knights' castle was leveled by rioting citizens at the end of the same century, it is the only building that remains intact since the birth of Rīga.

◉ Central Rīga (Centrs)

Pilsētas Kanāls (City Canal)
PARK

Pilsētas kanāls, the city's old moat, once protected the medieval interior from invaders. Today, the snaking ravine has been incorpo-

rated into a thin belt of stunning parkland splitting Old and Central Rīga. Stately Raiņa bulvāris follows the rivulet on the north side, and used to be known as 'Embassy Row' during Latvia's independence between the world wars.

Freedom Monument
MONUMENT

(Brīvības bulvāris) Affectionately known as 'Milda', Rīga's Freedom Monument towers above the city between Old and Central Rīga. Paid for by public donations, the monument was designed by Kārlis Zāle and erected in 1935 where a statue of Russian ruler Peter the Great once stood.

Rīga Art Nouveau Museum
MUSEUM

(Rīgas jūgendstila muzejs; www.jugendstils.riga.lv; Alberta iela 12; adult/child May-Sep €6/4, Oct-Apr €3.50/2.50; ⊙10am-6pm Wed-Sun) If you're curious about what lurks behind Rīga's imaginative art nouveau facades, then it's definitely worth stopping by here. Once the home of Konstantīns Pēkšēns (a local architect responsible for over 250 of the city's buildings), the interiors have been completely restored to resemble a middle-class apartment from the 1920s. Enter from Strēlnieku iela; push No 12 on the doorbell.

Nativity of Christ Cathedral
CHURCH

(Kristus Piedzimšanas katedrāle; pravoslavie.lv; Brīvības bulvāris 23; ⊙7am-7pm) With gilded cupolas peeking through the trees, this Byzantine-styled Orthodox cathedral (1883) adds a dazzling dash of Russian bling to the skyline. During the Soviet period the church was converted into a planetarium, but it's since been restored to its former use. Mind the dress code – definitely no shorts; women are asked to cover their heads.

◉ Maskavas Forštate

Separated from the Old Town by the Central Railway Station, Rīga's 'Moscow Suburb' is in fact one of its oldest central districts, though unlike the rest of the centre it looks like it has never got over the economic hardships of the 1990s. The place also feels haunted because of its dark history – it was the site of the Jewish ghetto during the Nazi occupation of Latvia.

★ Rīga Central Market
MARKET

(Rīgas Centrāltirgus; www.centraltirgus.lv; Nēģu iela 7; ⊙8am-5pm) Haggle for your huckleberries at this vast market, housed in a series of WWI Zeppelin hangars and spilling outdoors. It's an essential Rīga experience, providing bountiful opportunities both for people-watching and to stock up for a picnic lunch. Although the number of traders is dwindling, the dairy and fish departments, each occupying a separate hangar, present a colourful picture of abundance that activates ancient foraging instincts in visitors.

Spīķeri
AREA

(www.spikeri.lv) The shipping yard behind the Central Market is the latest district to benefit from a generous dose of gentrification. These crumbling brick warehouses were once filled with swinging slabs of hanger meat; these days you'll find hip cafes and start-up companies. Stop by during the day to check out **Kim?** (⊘6722 3321; www.kim.lv; Maskavas iela 12/1; €3; ⊙noon-8pm Tue, to 6pm Wed-Sun) – an experimental art zone that dabbles with contemporary media – or come in the evening to peruse the surplus of farm produce at the night market.

Latvian Academy of Science
HISTORIC BUILDING

(Latvijas Zinātņu Akadēmija; www.panoramariga. lv; Akadēmijas laukums 1; panorama €4; ⊙8am-10pm) Rising above the Moscow suburb, this Stalinesque tower is in fact a not-so-welcome

Rīga

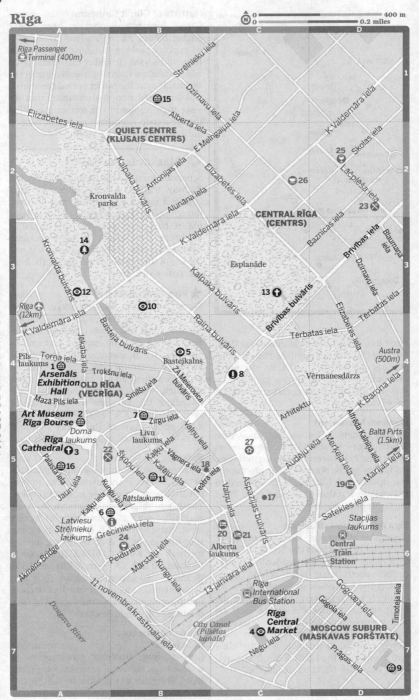

RUSSIA & THE BALTIC COAST RĪGA

0 ————— 400 m
0 ————— 0.2 miles

Riga Passenger
Terminal (400m)

Strēlnieku iela

Dzirnavu iela

15

Elizabetes iela

**QUIET CENTRE
(KLUSAIS CENTRS)**

Alberta iela

E Melngaiļa iela

K Valdemāra iela

Skolas iela

Kalpaka bulvāris

Antonijas iela

Elizabetes iela

25

26

Lāčplēša iela

Kronvalda
parks

Alunāna iela

K Valdemāra iela

**CENTRAL RĪGA
(CENTRS)**

23

Baznīcas iela

Brīvības iela

Blaumaņa iela

14

Esplanāde

Kalpaka bulvāris

13

Brīvības bulvāris

Dzirnavu iela

Kronvalda bulvāris

12

10

Raina bulvāris

Tērbatas iela

Elizabetes iela

Rīga
(12km)

K Valdemāra iela

Basteja bulvāris

Tērbatas iela

Austra
(500m)

Jēkaba iela

5

Bastejkalns

ZA Meierovica bulvāris

8

Vērmanesdārzs

K Barona iela

Alfrēda Kalniņa iela

Baltā Pirts
(1.5km)

Pils
laukums

Torņa iela

1

**Arsenāls
Exhibition
Hall**

Trokšņu iela

Smilšu iela

**OLD RĪGA
(VECRĪGA)**

Mazā Pils iela

Art Museum 2
Rīga Bourse

7

Zirgu iela

Arhitektu

Mērķeļa iela

Audēju iela

27

**Rīga
Cathedral**

3

Doma
laukums

Līvu
laukums

Kaļķu iela

Vāgnera iela

Vaļņu iela

19

Pasta iela

16

Šķūņu iela

22

11

18

Teātra iela

Vaļņu iela

Aspazijas bulvāris

Satekles iela

Stacijas
laukums

Jauņu iela

Kaļķu iela

Kungu iela

6

Rātslaukums

17

**Central
Train
Station**

**Latviešu
Strēlnieku
laukums**

Grēcinieku iela

24

Peldu iela

20

21

Alberta
laukums

Akmens Bridge

Marstaļu iela

Kungu iela

13 janvāra iela

Rīga
International
Bus Station

Gogoļa iela

Gogoļa iela

**MOSCOW SUBURB
(MASKAVAS FORŠTATE)**

Timoteja iela

11 novembra krastmala iela

Dungava River

City Canal
(Pilsētas
kanāls)

4

**Rīga
Central
Market**

Negu iela

Prāgas iela

9

Rīga

present from the Russian capital, which has seven towers like it, only bigger. Construction of what is often dubbed 'Stalin's birthday cake' commenced in 1951 but wasn't completed until 1961, by which time Stalin had run out of birthdays. Those with an eagle eye will spot hammers and sickles hidden in the convoluted facade. The wonderful viewing terrace at floor 17 is Rīga's best vantage point.

☞ Tours

E.A.T. Rīga WALKING, CYCLING
(☑ 22469888; www.eatriga.lv; tours from €12) Foodies may be initially disappointed to dis-

cover that the name stands for 'Experience Alternative Tours' and the focus is on off-the-beaten-track themed walking tours (Old Rīga, Art Nouveau, Alternative Rīga, Retro Rīga). But don't fret – Rīga Food Tasting is an option. It also offers a cycling tour of Jūrmala.

Rīga Bike Tours BICYCLE TOUR
(☑ 28225773; rigabikerent.com; Riharda Vagnera iela 14; ◷10am-6pm) These folks run daily bicycle tours of Rīga that last for three hours and cost €15 (€10 with your own bike). Longer cycling tours of Latvia are also on offer. Their useful office operates under the Rīga Explorers Club brand.

Riga Culture Free Tour CULTURAL TOUR
(☑ 20338877; www.rigaculturefreetour.lv) FREE A daily English-language walk conducted by local cultural experts. It lasts for two hours and begins at noon from Rainis monument on Esplanāde.

Retro Tram CULTURAL TOUR
(☑ 6710 4817; rigassatiksme. v/en/services/retro-tram/; €2) Two routes, aboard a restored tram, meander through the art nouveau district and on to Mežaparks. Free guided walking tours of the art nouveau district are available on weekends and public holidays, departing five time a day from the Ausekļa tram stop.

⮥ Sleeping

★**Naughty Squirrel** HOSTEL €
(☑ 6722 0073; www.thenaughtysquirrel.com; Kalēju iela 50; dm from €18; ❄@☎) Slashes of bright paint and cartoon graffiti brighten up the city's capital of backpackerdom, which buzzes with travellers rattling the foosball table and chilling out in the TV room. Sign up for regular pub crawls, adrenaline-charged day trips to the countryside and summer BBQs.

★**Cinnamon Sally** HOSTEL €
(☑ 22042280; www.cinnamonsally.com; Merķeļa iela 1; dm from €12, tr/q from €45/50; @☎) Convenient for the train/bus stations, Cinnamon Sally comes with perfectly clean rooms, very helpful staff and a common area cluttered with sociable characters. It might feel odd to be asked to take off your shoes at reception, but it's all part of its relentless effort to create a homey atmosphere.

Rīga Old Town Hostel HOSTEL €
(☑ 6722 3406; www.rigaoldtownhostel.lv; Vaļņu iela 43; dm from €17; ❄☎) The Aussie pub

on the ground floor doubles as the hostel's hang-out space. If you can manage to lug your suitcase past the faux bookshelf door and up the twisting staircase, you'll find spacious dorms with chandeliers and plenty of sunlight.

✖ Eating

★ Miit
CAFE €

(www.miit.lv; Lāčplēša iela 10; mains €5; ⊘ 7am-9pm Mon, to 11pm Tue & Wed, to 1am Thu, to 3am Fri, 9am-1am Sat, 10am-6pm Sun) Rīga's hipster students head here to sip espresso and blog about Nietzsche amid comfy couches and discarded bicycle parts. The two-course lunch is a fantastic deal for penny-pinchers – expect a soup and a main course for under €5 (dishes change daily).

Austra
INTERNATIONAL €

(www.facebook.com/cafe.austra; Krišjāna Barona iela 41/43; mains €5-8; ⊘ noon-9pm Mon & Tue, to 10pm Wed, to 11pm Thu, to midnight Fri, 1-11pm Sat) The inventive fusion food served in this small, unpretentious place achieves the quality of a fashionable upmarket restaurant, but goes for the price of a cafeteria. The €5 two-course lunch is one of the best deals in town.

LIDO Alus Sēta
LATVIAN €

(www.lido.lv; Tirgoņu iela 6; mains around €5; ☎) The pick of the LIDO litter (Rīga's ubiquitous smorgasbord chain), Alus Sēta feels like an old Latvian brew house. It's popular with locals as well as tourists – everyone flocks here for cheap, tasty traditional fare and homemade beer. Seating spills onto the cobbled street during the warmer months.

🍷 Drinking & Nightlife

★ Folksklub Ala Pagrabs
BEER HALL

(www.folkklubs.lv; Peldu iela 19; ⊘ 12pm-1am Sun-Tue, to 3am Wed, to 4am Thu, to 6am Fri & Sat) A huge cavern filled with the bubbling magma of relentless beer-infused joy, folk-punk music, dancing and Latvian nationalism, this is an essential Rīga drinking venue, no matter what high-browed locals say about it. The bar strives to reflect the full geography and diversity of Latvian beer production, but there is also plenty of local cider, fruit wine and *šmakouka* moonshine.

Kaņepes Kultūras Centrs
BAR

(Skolas iela 15; ⊘ 2pm-1am) The crumbling building of a former musical school, which half of Rīgans over 40 seems to have attended, is now a bar with a large outdoor area filed with an artsy studenty crowd. Wild dancing regularly erupts in the large room, where parents of the patrons once suffered through their violin drills.

Piens
BAR, CLUB

(Milk; www.klubspiens.lv; Aristida Briāna iela 9; noon-midnight Sun-Tue, to 4pm Wed-Sat) Located up in the Miera iela area, this bar-club hybrid occupies a large chunk of industrial land. There's an appealing mix of eclectic decor, old sofas and sunny terraces.

Trusis Kafe
CAFE

(☎ 26582462; www.trusiskafe.lv; Dzirnavu iela 43; ⊘ 10am-10pm Mon-Fri, to 8pm Sat) This sweet unassuming hipster den (its name translates as Rabbit) has an impressive array of Latvian-produced drinks – from Malduguns craft beer and cider to Sabile wines and rhubarb 'champagne'. The right place to drink and chat with friends without needing to shout over music to be heard, but also good for a quick coffee meditation during the day.

☆ Entertainment

Rīga in Your Pocket and *Rīga This Week* have the most up-to-date listings for opera, ballet, guest DJs, live music and other events around town. The tourist office in the Blackheads House (p821) can help travellers book tickets at any concert venue around town. Several trip operators offer bar and club tours if you'd rather have someone else arrange your big night out. Backpackers staying at sociable digs might find hostel-organised pub crawls and parties.

ℹ Information

ARS (☎ 6720 1006; www.ars-med.lv; Skolas iela 5) English-speaking doctors; 24-hour consultation available.

Tourist Information Centre (☎ 6730 7900; www.liveriga.com; Rātslaukums 6; ⊘ 10am-6pm) Dispenses tourist maps and walking-tour brochures, helps with accommodation, books and day trips, and sells concert tickets. It also stocks the Rīga Card, which offers discounts on sights and restaurants, and free rides on public transport. Satellite offices can be found in Livu laukums (May to September only) and at the bus station.

ℹ️ Getting There & Away

AIR

Rīga airport (Starptautiskā Lidosta Rīga; ☎ 1817; www.riga-airport.com; Mārupe District; 🚌 22) is 13km southwest of the city centre.

BUS

Buses depart from Rīga's **international bus station** (Rīgas starptautiskā autoosta; www.autoosta.lv; Prāgas iela 1), located behind the railway embankment just beyond the south-eastern edge of Old Rīga. Latvian destinations include Cēsis (€4.15, two hours, every 30 minutes), Kuldīga (€6.40, 2½ to 3¼ hours, hourly), Sigulda (€2.15, one hour, every 45 minutes) and Ventspils (€7.55, three to four hours, hourly).

TRAIN

Rīga's **central train station** (Centrālā stacija; ☎ 6723 2135; www.pv.lv; Stacijas laukums 2) is convenient to Old and Central Rīga. Visit www.ldz.lv to view the timetables and prices for long-haul international and domestic trains. Local destinations include Cēsis (€3.50, two hours, four daily) and Jūrmala (Majori; €1.40, 30 minutes, two to three per hour).

ℹ️ Getting Around

TO/FROM THE AIRPORT

The cheapest way to get from Rīga airport to the centre is bus 22 (€2, 25 minutes), which runs at least every 30 minutes and stops at several points around town, including the Stockmanns complex and on the river side of the Old Town. A taxi ride between the airport and the centre typically costs €12.

BICYCLE

Zip around town with **Sixt Bicycle Rental** (Sixt velo noma; ☎ 6767 6780; www.sixtbicycle.lv; per 30min/day €0.90/9). A handful of stands are conveniently positioned around Rīga and Jūrmala; simply choose your bike, call the rental service and receive the code to unlock your wheels.

PUBLIC TRANSPORT

The centre of Rīga is too compact for most visitors even to consider public transport, but trams, buses or trolleybuses may come in handy if you are venturing further out. For routes and schedules, consult www.rigassatiksme.lv. Tickets cost €1.15 (€0.30 for ISIC-holding students). Unlimited tickets are available for 24 hours (€5), three days (€10) and five days (€15). Tickets are available from Narvessen newspaper kiosks, as well as vending machines on board new trams, and in the underground pass by the train station.

TAXI

Taxis charge €0.60 to €0.80 per kilometre. Insist on having the meter on before you set off. Meters usually start running at around €1.50. It shouldn't cost more than €5 for a short journey (like crossing the Daugava for dinner in Ķīpsala). There are taxi ranks outside the bus and train stations, at the airport and in front of a few major hotels in Central Rīga, such as Radisson Blu Hotel Latvija.

Jurmala

POP 56,000

The Baltic's version of the French Riviera, Jūrmala (pronounced *yoor*-muh-lah) is a 32km strip of 14 townships with Prussian-style villas, each unique in shape and decor. Even during the height of communism, Jūrmala was always a place to '*sea*' and be seen. On summer weekends, vehicles clog the roads when jetsetters and day-tripping Rīgans flock to the resort town for some serious fun in the sun.

If you don't have a car or bicycle, you'll want to head straight to the heart of the action – the townships of Majori and Dzintari.

👁 Sights & Activities

Besides its 'Blue Flag' beach, Jūrmala's main attraction is its colourful art nouveau **wooden houses**, distinguishable by frilly awnings, detailed facades and elaborate towers. There are over 4000 wooden structures found throughout Jūrmala (most are lavish summer cottages), but you can get your fill of wood by taking a leisurely stroll along **Jūras iela**, a 1km-long pedestrian street connecting Majori and Dzintari.

Ķemeri National Park   NATIONAL PARK
(Ķemeru nacionālais parks; ☎ 6673 0078; www.kemerunacionalaisparks.lv) Beyond Jūrmala's stretch of celebrity summer homes lies a verdant hinterland of drowsy fishing villages, quaking bogs and thick forests. At the end of the 19th century Ķemeri was known for its curative mud and spring water, attracting visitors from as far away as Moscow.

Baltic Beach Spa   SPA
(☎ 6777 1446; www.balticbeach.lv; Jūras iela 23/25; treatments from €15; ⏰ 8am-10pm) Attached to a beachfront resort, this is the largest treatment centre in the Baltic, with three rambling storeys full of massage rooms, saunas, yoga studios, swimming pools and spa pools.

ℹ Information

Tourist Office (🖊6714 7900; Lienes iela 5; ⊗9am-7pm Mon-Fri, 10am-5pm Sat, 10am-3pm Sun) Located across from Majori train station, this helpful office has scores of brochures outlining walks, bike routes and attractions. Staff can assist with accommodation bookings and bike rental. A giant map outside helps orient visitors when the centre is closed.

ℹ Getting There & Around

BICYCLE

Six Rent a Bicycle (sixtbicycle.lv) has several locations in Jūrmala. The most useful one is across the square from Majori station. You can also drop its bikes here if you rode them from Rīga.

MINIBUSES

From Rīga take minibuses (30 minutes) in the direction of Sloka, Jaunķemeri or Dubulti and ask the driver to let you off at Majori. These vans depart every five to 15 minutes between 6am and midnight and leave opposite Rīga's central train station. Catch the bus at Majori train station for a lift back. From 9am to midnight, minibuses also connect Jūrmala to Rīga International Airport.

SLOW BOAT

Slow Boat (🖊2923 7123; www.pie-kapteina.lv; adult/child €15/10) departs from Rīga Riflemen Sq and docks in Majori near the train station. The journey takes one hour, and only runs on weekends.

TRAIN

Two to three trains per hour link Jūrmala to Central Rīga. Take a suburban train bound for Sloka, Tukums or Dubulti and disembark at Majori station (€1.50, 30 to 35 minutes).

Sigulda

POP 17,800

With a name that sounds like a mythical ogress, it comes as no surprise that the gateway to the **Gauja National Park** (www.gnp.gov.lv) is an enchanting spot with delightful surprises tucked behind every dappled tree. Locals proudly call their town the 'Switzerland of Latvia', but if you're expecting the majesty of a mountainous snow-capped realm, you'll be rather disappointed. Instead, Sigulda mixes its own brew of scenic trails, extreme sports and 800-year-old castles steeped in legends.

⊙ Sights

Sigulda sprawls between its three castles, with most of the action occurring on the east side of the Gauja River near New Sigulda Castle. Take your own walking tour for an abridged version of Sigulda's greatest hits, and don't forget to take a ride on the **cable car** (🖊29212731; Poruka iela 14; one way adult/child €5/4; ⊗10am-6.30pm Jun-Aug, to 4pm Sep-May) across the valley for an awesome aerial perspective.

★**Turaida Museum Reserve**   CASTLE
(Turaidas muzejrezervāts; 🖊6797 1402; www.turaida-muzejs.lv; Turaidas iela 10; adult/child €5/1.14; ⊗9am-8pm May-Sep, to 7pm Oct, 10am-5pm Nov-Apr) Turaida means 'God's Garden' in ancient Livonian, and this green knoll capped with a fairy-tale castle is certainly a heavenly place. The red-brick castle with its tall cylindrical tower was built in 1214 on the site of a Liv stronghold. A museum inside the castle's 15th-century granary offers an interesting account of the Livonian state from 1319 to 1561, and additional exhibitions can be viewed in the 42m-high Donjon Tower, and the castle's western and southern towers.

Sigulda Medieval Castle   CASTLE
(Pils iela 18; adult/child €1.50/0.80; ⊗9am-8pm May-Sep, 9am-5pm Mon-Fri, to 8pm Sat & Sun Oct, 9am-5pm Nov-Apr) Constructed between 1207 and 1209 by the Livonian Brothers of the Sword, this castle lies mainly in picturesque ruins after being severely damaged during the Great Northern War. Some sections have been restored and you can now walk along the front ramparts and ascend a tower at the

Sigulda

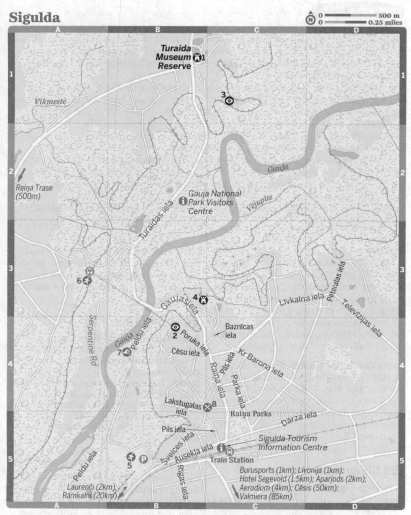

rear, where there are wonderful views over the forested Gauja Valley. See if you can spy Krimulda Manor and Turaida Castle poking through the trees.

🏃 Activities

Sigulda is prime hiking territory, so bring your walking shoes. Many outfitters around Sigulda offer bicycle and mountain-bike rentals costing around €15 per day. Brochures detailing hiking, cycling and hiking routes are available at the tourist office.

Bobsled Track   ADVENTURE SPORTS
(Bob trase; ☎ 6797 3813; www.bobtrase.lv; Šveices iela 13; ⊘ noon-5pm Sat & Sun) Sigulda's 1200m bobsled track was built for the Soviet team. In winter you can fly down the 16-bend track at 80km/h in a five-person Vučko **soft bob** (per person €10, from October to mid-March), or book in for the real Olympian experience on the hair-raising **taxi bob** (per person €15, from November to mid-March). Summer speed fiends can ride a wheeled **summer bob** (per person €15, from May to September).

KULDĪGA

Famed locally for its cute toy Niagara, lovely old Kuldīga is a place where your immersion into the epoche of chivalry won't be spoiled by day-tripping camera-clickers – the place is simply too far from Rīga.

In its heyday, Kuldīga served as the capital of the Duchy of Courland (1596–1616), but it was badly damaged during the Great Northern War and never quite able to regain its former lustre. Today, this blast from the past is a favourite spot to shoot Latvian period-piece films.

There's not a lot to do here except to stroll the streets and the park in the grounds of the old castle (of which nothing much remains), admiring the sculpture garden and gazing down on pretty **Ventas Rumba**. Said to be Europe's widest waterfall, it stretches for 249m, but is only a couple of metres high. During spawning season salmon would have little difficulty launching themselves up and over it, giving Kuldīga the curious epithet 'city where salmon fly'.

Buses run to/from Rīga (€6.40, 2½ to 3½ hours, every two hours) and Ventspils (€3, 1¼ hours, seven daily).

Aerodium ADVENTURE SPORTS
(☑ 28384400; www.aerodium.lv; 2min weekday/weekend €33/37) The one-of-a-kind aerodium is a giant wind tunnel that propels participants up into the sky as though they were flying. Instructors can get about 15m high, while first-timers usually rock out at about 3m. To find the site, look for the sign along the A2 highway, 4km west of Sigulda.

Cable Car Bungee Jump ADVENTURE SPORTS
(☑ 28383333; www.bungee.lv; Poruka iela 14; bungee jump from €40; ⏲ 6.30pm, 8pm & 9.30pm Wed-Sun Apr-Oct) Take your daredevil shenanigans to the next level with a 43m bungee jump from the bright-orange cable car that glides over the Gauja River. For an added thrill, jump naked.

🛏 Sleeping & Eating

Kempings Siguldas Pludmale CAMPGROUND €
(☑ 29244948; www.makars.lv; Peldu iela 2; per person/tent/car/caravan €5/3/3/6; ⏲ mid-May–mid-Sep) Pitch your tent in the grassy camping area beside the sandy beach along the Gauja. The location is perfect but there's only one men's and one women's bathroom for the scores of campers. Two-person tents can be hired for €4.50 per day. There's a second camping area up the river in Līgatne that's owned and operated by Makars as well. Ask at this location for directions.

Kaķu Māja LATVIAN €
(www.cathouse.lv; Pils iela 8; mains around €3; ⏲ 8am-11pm) A top spot for a cheap bite, the 'Cat's House' has pick-and-point bain-marie

meals and an attached bakery with pastries, pies and cakes. On Friday and Saturday nights, the restaurant in the back busts out the disco ball and morphs into a nightclub until 2am.

ⓘ Information

Gauja National Park Visitors Centre
(☑ 26657661; www.gnp.lv; Turaida iela 2a; ⏲ 9am-7pm) Sells maps to the park, town and cycle routes nearby.

Sigulda Tourism Information Centre (☑ 6797 1335; www.tourism.sigulda.lv; Ausekļa iela 6; ⏲ 9am-6pm; 🛜) Located within the train station, this extremely helpful centre has stacks of information about activities and accommodation.

ⓘ Getting There & Around

Buses trundle the 50-odd kilometers between Sigulda's bus station and Rīga (€2.15, one hour, every 30 minutes between 8am and 10.30pm).

One train per hour (between 6am and 9pm) travels the Rīga–Sigulda–Cēsis–Valmiera Line. Destinations from Sigulda include Rīga (€2.35, one or 1¼ hours) and Cēsis (€2, 40 minutes).

Sigulda's attractions are quite spread out, and after a long day of walking, bus 12 will become your new best friend. It plies the route to/from New Sigulda Castle, Turaida Castle and Krimulda Manor hourly during business hours (more on weekends).

Cēsis

POP 19,500

Not only is sweet little Cēsis (tsay-sis) one of Latvia's prettiest towns, it's also one of its oldest. Nestled within the forested con-

Cēsis

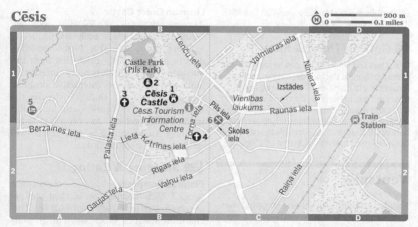

fines of Gauja National Park its cobbled lanes wend around a sturdy castle, a soaring church spire and a lazy lakeside park.

◉ Sights

★ Cēsis Castle   CASTLE
(Cēsu pils; www.cesupils.lv; both castles adult/student €5/2.50, excursions from €33; ☺10am-6pm daily May-Sep, 10am-5pm Tue-Sun Oct-Apr) This is actually two castles in one. The first is the old Wenden castle, with its sorrowful dark-stone towers. Founded by Livonian knights in 1214, it was sacked by Russian tsar Ivan the Terrible in 1577, but only after its 300 defenders blew themselves up with gunpowder. The other is the more cheerful castle-like 18th-century manor house once inhabited by the dynasty of German counts von Sievers. It houses a museum that features original fin de siècle interiors.

St John's Church   CHURCH
(Svētā Jāņa baznīca; http://cesujana.lelb.lv; admission free; ☺11am-5pm) Switch on your imagination in this 13th-century church where armour-clad Livonian knights prayed and buried their dead in what then was a lonely island of Christianity surrounded by the lands of pagans. Currently the home of the town's Lutheran community, the church contains tombs of the order's grand masters and top bishops.

🛏 Sleeping & Eating

Glūdas Grava   MOTEL €
(☎27036862; www.gludasgrava.lv; Glūdas iela 6a; r €40) An unusual one. A garage has been transformed into five studios with glassy

Cēsis

◉ Top Sights
  1 Cēsis Castle B1

◉ Sights
  2 Castle Park (Pils Park) B1
  3 Russian Orthodox Church of
     Transfiguration B1
  4 St John's Church B2

🛏 Sleeping
  5 Glūdas Grava A1

✖ Eating
  6 Mākslas telpa Mala C1

front walls and individual entrances. Each studio is equipped with a kitchen and sleeps up to four people. There is no reception – book your stay on its website or on www.booking.com and you'll be given instructions about the keys.

Mākslas Telpa Mala   CAFE €
(www.facebook.com/telpamala; Lielā Skolas iela 4; mains €3-4; ☺noon-9pm) A truly heart-warming place inside an old wooden house, featuring an antiquated tiled wood stove. Cheapish lunch food is on offer, along with craft beer, Latvian cider and fruit wine. We also liked the Latvian rock classics (not something you would hear in your average cafe) on the soundtrack. A small souvenir and cloth shop is attached.

❶ Information

Cēsis Tourism Information Centre (☎6412 1815; www.tourism.cesis.lv; Pils laukums 9;

⏰10am-5pm daily May-Sep, Tue-Sun Oct-Apr) Within the Cēsis Castle.

ℹ️ Getting There & Away

Cēsis' bus and train station can be found in the same location: at the roundabout connecting Raunas iela to Raiņa iela. There are up to five trains per day between 6.35am and 9pm linking Cēsis and Rīga (€3.50, two hours). Bikes are allowed on board. Two or three buses per hour between 6.15am and 10.20pm ply the route from Cēsis to Rīga, stopping in Līgatne and Sigulda.

Ventspils

POP 42,500

Fabulous amounts of oil and shipping money have turned Ventspils into one of Latvia's most beautiful and dynamic cities. Although locals coddle their Užavas beer and claim that there's not much to do, tourists will find a weekend's worth of fun in the form of brilliant beaches, interactive museums and winding Old Town streets dotted with the odd boutique and cafe.

◎ Sights

Ventspils Beach
BEACH

For Liepāja, the wide stretch of dazzlingly white sand south of the Venta River is what the Louvre is for Paris – its main treasure. During the warmer months, beach bums of every ilk – from nudist to kiteboarder – line the sands to absorb the sun's rays. Backed by a belt of dunes and a lush manicured park, the Blue Flag beach feels as pristine and well cared for as an urban beach can get.

Livonian Order Castle
CASTLE

(Livonijas ordeņa pils; ☑6362 2031; www.ventspilsmuzejs.lv; Jāņa iela 17; adult/child €2.10/1.10; ⏰10am-6pm Tue-Sun) This blocky building doesn't look obviously castle-like from the outside, but the 13th-century interior is home to a cutting-edge interactive local history and art museum. During Soviet rule the castle was used as a prison and an exhibit in the stables recounts its horrors (in Latvian only). An adjacent Zen rock garden will soothe your soul afterwards.

🛏️ Sleeping & Eating

Piejūras Kempings
CAMPGROUND €

(☑6362 7925; Vasarnīcu iela 56; tent sites per person €5, 4-person cottage from €40; @) This charming campus of grassy tent grounds and pine cottages is a full-service operation with an on-site laundrette, bicycle rental, and tennis, volleyball and basketball courts.

Krogs Zītari
EASTERN EUROPEAN €€

(☑25708337; www.facebook.com/KrogsZitari/info?tab=overview; Tirgus iela 11; mains €7-12; ⏰11am-midnight) Tucked in the courtyard of a pretty timber-framed German house, this beer garden serves large portions of traditional (or not so traditional) Latvian fare. But whether it is herring rollmops with cottage cheese and boiled potatoes or – more exotically – oven-baked vegetables with Georgian suluguni cheese, all food is designed to make a perfect match for excellent Latvian beer.

ℹ️ Information

Tourist Information Centre (☑6362 2263; www.visitventspils.com; Dārzu iela 6; ⏰8am-6pm Mon-Sat, 10am-4pm Sun) In the ferry terminal.

OFF THE BEATEN TRACK

DAUGAVPILS

Latvia's second-largest city has an undeserved reputation as a grim Soviet Gotham City – mostly among Latvians who have never been to it. In reality, it has a fairly well-preserved historical centre and a mighty fortress, reminding of the times when it was a provincial Russian imperial town with a thriving Jewish community. Native son Mark Rothko, became one of America's most notable 20th-century artists: his name is attached to the new **contemporary art centre,** (www.rothkocenter.com; Mihaila iela 3; adult/student €8/4, half-price for people born on 24 Apr & 25 Sep; ⏰11am-7pm Wed-Sat, to 5pm Tue & Sun) one of the country's best.

Four trains a day depart Daugavpils' **train station** (☑6548 7261; Stacijas iela) for Rīga (€7, three to four hours). Other service include St Petersburg in Russia (€49, 10 hours, daily) and Minsk in Belarus (€43, nine hours, three weekly).

From the **bus station** (☑6542 3000; www.buspark.lv; Viestura iela 10) buses run to/from Rīga (€9, 3¾ hours, hourly) as well as Vilnius in Lithuania (€12, 3½ hours, two daily).

ⓘ Getting There & Away

Ventspils' **bus terminal** (☎ 6362 4262; Kuldīgas iela 5) is served by buses to/from Rīga (€7.50, 2¾ to four hours, hourly) and Kuldīga (€3, 1¼ hours, five daily).

Scandlines (www.scandlines.com) runs ferries to Nynäshamn, Sweden (€21, 12 hours, five weekly) and to Travemünde, Germany (€21, 25 hours, twice weekly).

Latvia Survival Guide

ⓘ Directory A–Z

ACCOMMODATION

We highly advise booking ahead during the high season (summer). Rates drop significantly in the colder months. Budget range accommodation (€) cost less than €40.

Check out www.camping.lv for details on pitching a tent.

INTERNET RESOURCES

Latvian Tourism Development Agency (www.latvia.travel)

Latvian Institute (www.latinst.lv)

1188 search engine (www.1188.lv)

PUBLIC HOLIDAYS

New Year's Day 1 January

Easter March/April

Labour Day 1 May

Restoration of Independence of the Republic of Latvia 4 May

Mothers' Day Second Sunday in May

Whitsunday A Sunday in May or June

Līgo Eve (Midsummer festival) 23 June

Jāņi (St John's Day and Summer Solstice) 24 June

National Day Anniversary of proclamation of Latvian Republic, in 1918, on 18 November

Christmas (Ziemsvētki) 25 December

Second Holiday 26 December

New Year's Eve 31 December

TELEPHONE

Latvian telephone numbers have eight digits; landlines start with ☎ 6 and mobile numbers start with ☎ 2. To make any call within Latvia, simply dial the eight-digit number. To call a Latvian telephone number from abroad, dial the international access code, then the country code for Latvia (☎ 371) followed by the subscriber's eight-digit number.

ⓘ Getting There & Away

AIR

There are direct flights to over 50 destinations within Europe from **Rīga International Airport** (Starptautiskā Lidosta Rīga; ☎1817; www.riga-airport.com; Mārupe District; ⊟22).

LAND

There are no border controls between Latvia and both Estonia and Lithuania. However, we advise carrying your travel documents with you at all times, as random border checks do occur.

International trains head from Rīga to Moscow (€142, 16 hours, daily), St Petersburg (€107, 15 hours, daily) and Minsk (€66, 12 hours, daily).

SEA

Ferry services from Rīga and Ventspils connect Latvia to Swedish and German ports.

ⓘ Getting Around

BUS

Buses are much more convenient than trains if you're travelling beyond the capital's clutch of suburban rail lines. Updated timetables are available at www.autoosta.lv and www.1188.lv.

CAR & MOTORCYCLE

➡ Driving is on the right-hand side.

➡ Headlights must be on at all times.

➡ Local car-hire companies usually allow you to drive in all three Baltic countries, but not beyond.

TRAIN

Rīga's network of commuter rails makes it easy for tourists to reach day-tripping destinations. Latvia's further attractions are best explored by bus. Train schedule queries can be answered at www.pv.lv as well as at www.1188.lv.

RUSSIA & THE BALTIC COAST LATVIA SURVIVAL GUIDE

LITHUANIA

Vilnius

📷 5 / POP 546,700

Europe's largest baroque Old Town is at Vilnius' heart. Viewed from a hot air balloon, the skyline – pierced by countless Orthodox and Catholic church steeples – looks like a giant bed of nails. Adding to this heady mix is a combination of cobbled alleys, crumbling corners, majestic hilltop views, breakaway states and traditional artists' workshops – all in a city so small you'd sometimes think it was a village.

It has not always been so happy here, though. There are reminders of loss and pain too, from the horror of the KGB's torture cells to the ghettos where the Jewish community was concentrated before being murdered by the Nazis. Yet the spirit of freedom and resistance has prevailed, and the city is forging a new identity, combining the past with a present and future that involves world cuisine, a burgeoning nightlife and shiny new skyscrapers.

👁 Sights

👁 Cathedral Square & Gediminis Hill

At the base of Gediminas Hill sprawls Cathedral Square (Katedros aikštė), dominated by Vilnius Cathedral and its 57m-tall **belfry** (📷 8-6001 2080; www.bpmuziejus.lt; Katedros aikštė; adult/student €4.50/2.50; ⏰ 10am-7pm Tue-Sat May-Sep, to 6pm Oct-Apr). The square buzzes with local life, especially during Sunday morning Mass.

★ Palace of the Grand Dukes of Lithuania   MUSEUM

(Valdovų rumai; 📷 5-212 7476; www.valdovurumai.lt; Katedros aikštė 4; adult/student €2.90/1.45, guided

Lithuania

Ⓝ 0 ___ 100 km
0 ___ 50 miles

Gulf of Riga

BALTIC SEA

✪RĪGA

Jaunspils   **Jelgava**

Liepāja

LATVIA

Biržai

Mazeikiai   Joniškis   E67

Skuodas   Pasvalys   Rokiškis   **Daugavpils**

Salantai   Kuršenai   **Šiauliai**   Pampenai

Telšiai   **Panevėžys**   Aukštaitija National Park

Palanga   Plungė   E77   Utena

Kretinga   Kelme   Anykščiai   Ⓘ

Klaipėda   E67   E262   Ignalina

Smiltynė   Kėdainiai   Ukmergė   Molėtai

Juodkrantė   Sveksna   E271

Curonian Spit   Skautvile   Jonava   E272

Šilutė   Tauragė   Kernavė   **VILNIUS**   ✪

Preila

Nida   Jurbakas   **Kaunas**   E271   Neris (Vilnia)

Neman (Nemunas)   Vievis   E28

RUSSIA   Paneriai

Marijampolė   Juozapinė (294m) ▲

Nevskoye   Kalvarija   Alytus   Šalčininkai   Dieveniskes

Merkine

Lazdijai   Grūtas Park Ⓐ

Druskininkai

POLAND

BELARUS

JEWISH VILNIUS

Over the centuries Vilnius developed into one of Europe's leading centres of Jewish life and scholarship, until the community was wiped out by the occupying Nazis and their Lithuanian sympathisers during WWII. The former Jewish quarter lay in the streets west of Didžiojigatvė, including present-day Žydų gatvė (Jews St) and Gaono gatvė, named after Vilnius' most famous Jewish resident, Gaon Elijahu ben Shlomo Zalman (1720–97). The **Tolerance Centre** (☑ 5-262 9666; www.jmuseum.lt; Naugarduko gatvė 10/2; adult/concession €3/1.10; ⊙10am-6pm Mon-Thu, to 4pm Fri & Sun), a beautifully restored former Jewish theatre, houses thought-provoking displays on the history and culture of Jews in Lithuania before the Shoah (Holocaust) and occasional exhibitions. The **Holocaust Museum** (Holokausto Muziejus; ☑ 5-262 0730; www.jmuseum.lt; Pamėnkalnio gatvė 12; adult/child €2.40/1.20; ⊙9am-5pm Mon-Thu, 9am-4pm Fri, 10am-4pm Sun), in the so-called Green House, is an unvarnished account detailing the suffering of Lithuanian Jews in an un-edited display of horrific images and letters by local survivors. Vilnius' only remaining synagogue, the **Choral Synagogue** (Choralinė Sinagoga; ☑ 5-261 2523; Pylimo gatvė 39; donations welcome; ⊙10am-2pm Sun-Fri) FREE, was built in a Moorish style in 1903 and survived because it was used as a medical store.

tour €20.27; ⊙museum 10am-6pm Tue-Thu & Sat, to 8pm Fri, to 4pm Sun) On a site that has been settled since at least the 4th century AD stands the latest in a procession of fortified palaces, repeatedly remodelled, extended, destroyed, and rebuilt over the centuries. What visitors now see is a painstaking restoration of its final grand manifestation, the baroque palace built for the Grand Dukes in the 17th century. While the gleamingly white complex is evidently new, it contains fascinating historical remains, and is a potent symbol of revitalised, independent Lithuania.

Gediminas Castle & Museum
MUSEUM

(Gedimino Pilis ir Muziejus; ☑ 5-261 7453; www.lnm.lt; Gediminas Hill, Arsenalo gatvė 5; adult/child €2/1; ⊙10am-7pm daily Apr-Sep, 10am-5pm Tue-Sun Oct-Mar) With its prime hilltop location above the junction of the Neris and Vilnia rivers, Gediminas Castle is the last of a series of settlements and fortified buildings occupying this site since Neolithic times. This brick version, built by Grand Duke Vytautas in the early 15th century, offers commanding 360-degree views of Vilnius, and an exhibition tracing the history of the castle across the centuries, complete with scale models.

Funicular to Gediminas Hill
CABLE CAR

(☑ 5-261 7453; www.lnm.lt; Arsenalo gatvė 5; adult/student €1.50/1; ⊙10am-7pm May-Sep, to 5pm Oct-Apr) This is the quickest and easiest way to the top of Gediminas Hill, with great views en route. The entrance is behind the northeastern side of the Cathedral, inside a small courtyard at the rear of the Museum of Applied Art.

Vilnius Cathedral
CHURCH

(Vilniaus Arkikatedra; ☑ 5-261 0731; www.katedra.lt; Katedros aikštė 1; crypts adult/child €4.50/2.50; ⊙7am-7pm, crypts 10am-4pm Mon-Sat) Known in full as the Cathedral of St Stanislav and St Vladislav, this national symbol occupies a spot originally used for the worship of Perkūnas, the Lithuanian thunder god. Seventeenth-century St Casimir's Chapel, with its a baroque cupola, coloured marble and frescoes of the saint's life, is the showpiece, while the crypts are the final resting places of many prominent Lithuanians, including Vytautas the Great (1350–1430). The website has details of Mass.

National Museum of Lithuania
MUSEUM

(Lietuvos Nacionalinis Muziejus; ☑ 5-262 7774; www.lnm.lt; Arsenalo gatvė 1; adult/child €2/1; ⊙10am-6pm Tue-Sun) FREE Building on the collections complied by the Museum of Antiquities since 1855, this splendid museum shows artefacts from Lithuanian life from Neolithic times to the 20th century. It has special collections devoted to the country's different folk traditions, to numismatics (including some of the very first Lithuanian coins) and to burial goods. A statue of Mindaugas, Lithuania's sole king, stands guard over the entrance.

👁 Old Town

Eastern Europe's largest Old Town deserves its Unesco status. The area, stretching 1.5km south from Katedros aikštė, was built up in the 15th and 16th centuries, and its narrow

RUSSIA & THE BALTIC COAST VILNIUS

winding streets, hidden courtyards and lavish old churches retain the feel of bygone centuries. One of the purest pleasures the city has to offer is aimlessly wandering Old Town backstreets.

★**Vilnius University** HISTORIC BUILDING
(Vilniaus Universitetas; ☑5-268 7298; www.vu.lt; Universiteto gatvė 3; admission to architectural ensemble adult/child €1.50/0.50; ☺9am-6pm Mon-Fri Mar-Oct, 9.30am-5.30pm Mon-Sat Nov-Apr) Founded in 1579 during the Counter-Reformation, Vilnius University was run by Jesuits for two centuries and became one of the greatest centres of Polish learning. It

produced many notable scholars, but was closed by the Russians in 1832 and didn't reopen until 1919. Today it has 23,000 students and Lithuania's oldest library, shelving five million books (including one of two originals of *The Catechism* by Martynas Mažvydas, the first book ever published in Lithuanian).

St Anne's Church CHURCH
(Šv Onos Bažnyčia; ☑8-6981 7731; www.onosba-znycia.lt; Maironio gatvė 8-1; ☺11am-7pm Jun-Aug, from 5pm Sep-May; Mass 6pm Mon-Sat, 9am & 11am Sun) This gorgeous, late-15th-century Gothic church is a tiny confection of red

Vilnius

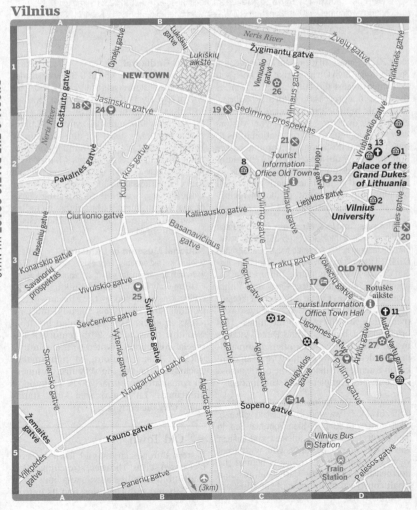

brick, glass and arches, dwarfed by the Bernadine Church outside which it stands. The building marries 33 different kinds of brick into a whole that many regard as the most beautiful in Vilnius. It's reputed that Napoleon was so charmed by St Anne's that he wanted to relocate it to Paris.

St Casimir's Church
CHURCH
(Šv Kazimiero Bažnyčia; ☑ 5-212 1715; www.kazimiero.lt; Didžioji gatvė 34; ⊙ 9am-6.30pm Mon-Fri, 8am-1.30pm Sun) This striking church is the city's oldest baroque place of worship. St Casimir's dome and cross-shaped ground plan defined a new style for 17th-century

churches when the Jesuits built it between 1604 and 1615. It was destroyed and rebuilt several times over the centuries and has recently emerged from another bout of renovation.

Gates of Dawn
HISTORIC BUILDING
(Aušros Vartai; ☑ 5-212 3513; www.ausrosvartai.lt; Aušros Vartų gatvė 12; ⊙ 6am-7pm) **FREE** The southern border of Old Town is marked by the last-standing of five portals that were once built into the city walls. A suitably grand way to enter one of the best-preserved sections of the Old Town, it's also the site of the Gate of Dawn Chapel of Mary the Mother of Mercy and the 'Vilnius Madonna', a 17th-century painting of Our Lady said to work miracles.

RUSSIA & THE BALTIC COAST VILNIUS

☞ Tours

Two-hour walking tours of the Old Town in English (€10), starting at 11am on Monday, Wednesday, Friday and Sunday from mid-May to mid-September, are organised by any tourist information centre. They also supply audio guides (€10) for self-guided tours, and hand out free copies of thematic walking tours, including Jewish Vilnius, Musical Vilnius, and Castles & Palaces of Vilnius.

🛏 Sleeping

Filaretai Hostel
HOSTEL €

(☎5-215 4627; www.filaretaihostel.com; Filaretų gatvė 17; dm/s/d/tr per person without bathroom €10/21/15/12; P@🛜) Affiliated with the Lithuanian Hostels Association, Filaretai occupies a quaint old villa 15 minutes' walk (uphill) from Old Town. Dorms are five- to eight-bedded; bed linen is provided, towels are extra, and there's a communal kitchen and washing machine. Reception is open 24 hours. To get here take bus 34 from the bus and train stations to the seventh stop.

Hostelgate B&B
B&B €

(☎8-689 60292; www.hostelgate.lt; Šv Mikalojaus gatvė 3; d/f €38/58; @🛜) With a great location (just off Vokiečių gatvė), wi-fi, cheery decor, friendly staff, a well-stocked kitchen and some rooms with en suite or balconies, Hostelgate makes a great base for exploring the Old Town. The same operation also runs a hostel on **Aušros Vartų gatvė** (☎6383 2818; http://www.hostelgate.lt; Aušros Vartų gatvė 7-1; d/tr €11/39), with 24-hour reception.

Come to Vilnius
HOSTEL €

(☎8-6202 9390; www.cometovilnius.eu; Šv Stepano gatvė 15; dm/d/tr €16/35/44; @🛜) Bright colours, timber furnishings, proximity to transport, and free drinks, hot drinks, towels and wi-fi are the draws at this decent indie hostel. Prices fall slightly in the low season.

✗ Eating

★Senamiesčio Krautuvė
LITHUANIAN €

(☎5-231 2836; www.senamiesciokrautuve.lt; Literatų gatvė 5; ⊙10am-10pm Mon-Sat, 11am-5pm Sun) Look no further than this wonderful, quiet hobbit-hole for the very best Lithuanian comestibles, many unique to the country. Cured meats, fresh sausages, cheeses, fresh fruit and vegetables, honey and preserves, breads and pastries: all are arranged in irresistible profusion around the walls of this snug trove on Literatu gatvė.

Radharanė
VEGETARIAN €

(☎5-240 4720; www.radharane.lt; Gedimino prospektas 32; mains €4; ⊙11am-9pm; ✔) In a town where light, tasty vegetarian fare isn't thick on the ground, Radharanė's Indian-with-a-Lithuanian-twist fare is a godsend. Try the kofta, paneer with eggplant or channa dahl, all served with rice and salad. It's all good.

Senoji Kibininė
LITHUANIAN €

(www.kibinas.lt; Vilniaus gatvė; mains €3.50; ⊙9am-9pm Mon-Fri, 10am-9pm Sat, 10am-8pm Sun) You can fill up on *cepelinai* or potato pancakes here, but its real thing is *kibinai:* pasties traditional to the country's Turkic Karaite minority that deserve to share the fame of their Cornish rivals. Whether it's mutton, chicken'n'mushroom, or spinach and curd you fancy, these toothsome shortcrust pockets are ideal after a few drinks in the Old Town.

Pietausim
LITHUANIAN €

(☎8-6151 8454; www.pietausim.lt; J Jasinskio gatvė 16; mains €4; ⊙11am-2.30pm) Like a Soviet-era canteen, but with sleek decor and a bustling, youthful clientele, Pietausim bangs out great-value Lithuanian food to the lunchtime *cognoscenti*. Baked fish, *šaltibarščiai* (cold beetroot soup), salads and more: all gets hoovered up by the early afternoon, so get in quickly.

🍷 Drinking & Nightlife

Bukowski
BAR

(☎8-6405 8855; Visų Šventų gatvė 7; ⊙11am-2am Mon-Wed, to 5am Thu-Sun) The eponymous Barfly is the spiritual patron of this charismatic boho bar in a less-trodden pocket of the Old Town. It has a back terrace for finer weather, great beers on tap, a full program of poetry, music and other events, and a welcoming, unpretentious atmosphere. One of Vilnius's best.

Soho
GAY & LESBIAN

(☎8-6993 9567; www.sohoclub.lt; Švitrigailos gatvė 7/16; 11pm-1am €3,1-4am €6, other times free; ⊙10pm-7am Fri & Sat) Proud, friendly and party-obsessed, Soho proudly bills itself as Lithuania's 'most popular' LGBTQ club. On a regular night, DJs play house and pop; on special nights, live perfomers take over.

Būsi Trečias   MICROBREWERY

(☑ 5-231 2698; www.busitrecias.lt; Totorių gatvė 18; ⊙ 11am-11pm Sun-Fri, to 3am Sat) Locals know this microbrewery-pub is a great place to get a cheap, sustaining Lithuanian lunch. It also offers charismatic wooden decor, 12 varieties of beer (including lime, raspberry and caramel) and courtyard tables for the warmer months.

Exit   CLUB

(☑ 8-6985 9116; J Jasinskio gatvė 16a; admission from €3; ⊙ 11pm-4am Fri & Sat) Probably Lithuania's biggest club, Exit has the sound system, atmosphere and hedonistic crowd to attract big-name internationals to play alongside local DJs.

☆ Entertainment

The tourist office publishes events listings, as does the *Baltic Times*.

**Lithuanian National Opera
& Ballet Theatre**   OPERA

(Lietuvos Nacionalinis Operos ir Baleto Teatras; ☑ 8-615 51000; www.opera.lt; Vienuolio gatvė 1; ⊙ box office 10am-7pm Mon-Fri, to 6.30pm Sat, to 3pm Sun) This stunning (or gaudy, depending on your taste) Soviet-era building, with its huge, cascading chandeliers and grandiose dimensions, is home to Lithuania's national ballet and opera companies. You can see world-class performers for as little as €4 (or as much as €200...).

**Lithuanian National
Philharmonic**   CLASSICAL MUSIC

(Lietuvos Nacionalinė Filharmonija; ☑ 5-266 5233; www.filharmonija.lt; Aušros Varių gatvė 5; ⊙ box office 10am-7pm Tue-Sat, to noon Sun) Lithuania's premier venue for orchestral, chamber and sacral music. But it's not all classical: prominent international jazz acts often ply their trade here.

ⓘ Information

Baltic-American Medical & Surgical Clinic
(☑ 5-234 2020; www.bak.lt; Nemenčinės gatvė 54a; ⊙ 24hr) English-speaking health care inside Vilnius University Antakalnis hospital.

Tourist Information Office Old Town (☑ 5-262 9660; www.vilnius-tourism.lt; Vilniaus gatvė 22, LT-01119; ⊙ 9am-6pm) The head office of Vilnius' tourist information service is great for brochures, advice and accommodation bookings.

Tourist Information Office Town Hall (☑ 5-262 6470; www.vilnius-tourism.lt; Didžioji gatvė 31; ⊙ 9am-12.30pm & 1.15-6pm) Good for maps, brochures, bike rentals, accommodation booking, advice and more.

ⓘ Getting There & Away

AIR

There are no domestic flights within Lithuania, unless you detour via another regional capital.

BUS

Vilnius' **bus station** (Autobusų Stotis; ☑ information 1661; www.autobusustotis.lt; Sodų gatvė 22) is just south of the Old Town. Timetables are displayed on a board here and on the handy website www.autobusubilietai.lt. Several bus lines run from here to international destinations.

Buses to destinations within Lithuania include Druskininkai (€10, two hours, 15 daily), Kaunas (€6, 1¾ hours, regularly from 5.45am to 11pm), Klaipėda (€18, four to 5½ hours, 17 daily) and Šiauliai (€13, three to 4½ hours, 15 daily).

TRAIN

The **train station** (Geležinkelio Stotis; ☑ information 233 0088; www.litrail.lt; Geležinkelio gatvė 16) is opposite the bus station. There is no direct or convenient rail link between Vilnius and Rīga or Tallinn. Direct daily services within Lithuania to/from Vilnius include Kaunas (€6, 1½ hours, 14 daily), Klaipėda (€16, four hours, three daily) and Trakai (€1.70, 40 minutes, up to 10 daily).

ⓘ Getting Around

TO/FROM THE AIRPORT

Vilnius International Airport (Tarptautinis Vilniaus Oro Uostas; ☑ 6124 4442; www.vno.lt; Rodūnios kelias 10a; 🚕; 🚌 1, 2) lies 5km south of the centre. The airport is accessible by bus, train or taxi. Bus 1 runs between the airport and the train station; bus 2 runs between the airport and the northwestern suburb of Šeškinė via the Žaliasis bridge across the Neris and on to Lukiškių aikštė. Have small change handy for a ticket (€1 from the driver)

Trains run to the central station every 30 minutes between 6am and 11.30pm. On-board tickets cost €0.72 and the trip is only 10 minutes.

Taxi rates vary depending on whether you hail one from out the front of the arrivals hall (about €15), or call a reputable firm in advance (around €10).

BICYCLE

Bikes can be easily hired and returned at the 37 orange **Cyclocity** (☑ 8-800 22008; www.cyclocity.lt; ⊙ 24hr Apr-Oct) stations across Vilnius. Either credit cards or Cyclocity Cards (available by advance subscription) can be used to hire a bike. A three-day ticket is €2.90.

Velo-City (☑ 8-674 12123; www.velovilnius.lt; Palangos gatvė 1; per hr/24hr €4/12; ⊙ 10am-

9pm Apr-Sep, by appointment Oct to Mar) is a well-established bike-hire operation on the edge of the Old Town with decent, well-maintained bikes.

PUBLIC TRANSPORT

The city is efficiently served by buses and trolleybuses from 5.30am or 6am to midnight; Sunday services are less frequent. Single-trip tickets cost €1 from the driver, €0.64 if you have a Vilniečio Kortelė (an electronic ticket sold at kiosks; see www.vilniusticket.lt for details) or nothing if you have a Vilnius City Card with public transport included (sold in tourist information centres). Fare evaders risk a small fine.

Quicker minibuses shadow most routes. They pick up/drop off passengers anywhere en route (not just at official bus stops) and can be flagged down on the street. Tickets costs €1 from the driver.

For destinations within the Old Town, you'll normally have to hoof it.

For route details see www.vilniustransport.lt or pick up a transport map from tourist offices.

TAXI

Taxi rates in Vilnius can vary; they are generally cheaper if ordered in advance by telephone than if hailed directly off the street or picked up at a taxi stand. Ask the hotel reception desk or restaurant to call one for you. Reliable companies include **Ekipažas** (📞1446; www.ekipazastaksi.lt) and **Mersera** (📞278 8888).

Trakai

📞 528 / POP 5400

With its red-brick, fairy-tale castle, Karaites culture, quaint wooden houses and pretty lakeside location, Trakai is a must-see just 28km from the capital.

Most of the town stands on a 2km-long, north-pointing tongue of land between Lake Luka (east) and Lake Totoriškių (west). Lake Galvė opens out from the northern end of the peninsula and boasts 21 islands.

Gediminas probably made Trakai his capital in the 1320s and Kęstutis certainly based his 14th-century court here. Protected by the 82-sq-km **Trakai Historical National Park** (📞528-55 776; www.seniejitrakai.lt), Trakai today is a quiet town, outside summer weekends.

⊙ Sights

★ **Trakai Castle**   CASTLE
(Trakų Pilis; www.trakaimuziejus.lt; adult/senior/student & child €6/4/3; ⊙10am-7pm May-Sep, to 6pm Mar, Apr & Oct, to 5pm Nov-Feb; 🚗) The

centrepiece of Trakai is its picture-postcard Island Castle, atop an island on Lake Galvė. The painstakingly restored red-brick Gothic castle probably dates from around 1400, when Gran Duke Vytautas needed stronger defences than the peninsula castle afforded. The castle closes on Mondays between October and March, and charges €1.16 for photography in its grounds.

**Church of the Visitation
of the Blessed Mary**   CHURCH
(Birutės gatvė 5) Founded around the same time as Trakai Castle, and also by Grand Duke Vytautas, this grand 15th-century parish church has a large collection of ecclesiastical art, including the Trakai Mother of God, a revered image thought to have been donated by Vytautas himself.

Karaite Ethnographic Museum   MUSEUM
(Karaimų etnografinė paroda; 📞 528-55 286; www.trakaimuziejus.lt; Karaimų gatvė 22; adult/child €1.16/0.58; ⊙10am-6pm Wed-Sun) The Karaite Ethnographic Museum traces the ancestry of the Karaites, a Judaic sect and Turkic minority originating in Baghdad, which adheres to the Law of Moses. Their descendants – some 380 families – were brought to Trakai from the Crimea around 1400 to serve as bodyguards. Only 12 families (60 individuals) still live in Trakai and their numbers – 280 throughout Lithuania – are dwindling rapidly.

ℹ Information

Tourist Information Centre (📞 528-51 934; www.trakai-visit.lt; Karaimų gatvė 41; ⊙9am-6pm) Lavishly stocked with brochures, staffed by English speakers who can organise everything from boat trips to accommodation, and with an adjoining handicrafts shop, this little office by the lake has everything you need. Closed on weekends between October and April.

ℹ Getting There & Away

Up to 10 daily trains (€1.48, 30 minutes) travel between Trakai's **train station** (📞 51 055; Vilniaus gatvė 5) and Vilnius.

Druskininkai

📞 313 / POP 16,450

Nineteenth-century Druskininkai (drus-ki-nin-key) on the Nemunas River is Lithuania's oldest and most chic spa town. Today it attracts plenty of investment and young, hip and wealthy Lithuanians seeking a quick detox from city life.

◎ Sights & Activities

Bikes and two- or four-seater buggies are the best way to get around. The tourist office gives away maps covering three local cycling trails: the southbound riverside **Sun Path** (Saulės takas; 24km) goes to the windmill museum, **Stars Orbit** (Žvaigzdžių orbita; 24km) snakes south into the Raigardas Valley, and the forested eastbound **Žilnas Path** (Žilvino takas; 20km) links Druskininkai with Grūtas Park (8km east) The river and lake are also foci of fun.

★ **Grūtas Park**   PARK
(Grūto Parkas; ☑ 313-55 511; www.grutoparkas.lt; Grūtas; adult/child €6/3; ☺ 9am-10pm summer, to 5pm rest of year; ⓘ) Both entertaining and educational, the black-humoured Grūtas Park (aka 'Stalin World') has been an enormous hit since it opened in 2001. The sprawling grounds, built to resemble a concentration camp (complete with loudspeakers bellowing Soviet anthems), feature socialist realist statues of Lenin, Stalin and Lithuanian luminaries, and exhibits on Soviet history (with a focus on the oppression of Lithuania). To get there, take bus no 2 from Druskininkai, via Viečiūnai, or drive 8km east to Grūtas village.

Bike Rental   BICYCLE RENTAL
(☑ 8-686 8 7022; Laisvės alėja 10; bikes per hr/day €2/9, buggies per 30/60min €5/8; ☺ 8am-9pm) Between May and October bikes and buggies can be hired from Vilniaus alėja 10, the corner of Vilniaus and Laisvės alėjas, or opposite the tourist office at MK Čiurlionio gatvė 52.

Aqua Park   WATER PARK
(☑ 313-52 338; www.akvapark.lt; Vilniaus gatvė 13-2; 2hr water entertainment adult/child €9/4.5; ☺ noon-10pm Mon-Thu, noon-11pm Fri, 10am-11pm Sat, 10am-9pm Sun) Families need look no further than this humid wonderland, which brings together six waterslides (the longest over 200m), spas, saunas, a wavepool, kids' play area and more. Prices rise during summer and on weekends and public holidays.

ⓘ Information

Tourist Information Centre (☑ 313-51 777; www.info.druskininkai.lt; MK Čiurlionio gatvė

65; ☺ 10am-1pm & 1.45-6.45pm Mon-Sat, 10am-5pm Sun) Brochures, bike rental, accommodation and bookings advice.

ⓘ Getting There & Away

From the **bus station** (☑ 313 51 333; Gardino gatvė 1; ☺ 5.15am-6.50pm) there are up to 15 daily buses (€10, two hours) to/from Vilnius, hourly buses to/from Kaunas (€10, two to three hours), six to/from Panevėžys (€17, 4¼ hours) and seven to/from Šiauliai (€19, 5¼ hours).

Kaunas
☑ 37 / POP 353,000

Kaunas (kow-nas), a sprawling city 100km west of Vilnius at the confluence of the Nemunas and Neris Rivers, has a compact Old Town, an abundance of artistic and educational museums, and a fascinating history. A sizeable student population provides plenty of energy, and some rough edges give it that extra bit of spice.

◎ Sights

◉ Old Town

Rotušės Aikštė, a large, open square at the heart of the Old Town is lined with pretty 15th- and 16th-century German merchants' houses and is centred on the 17th-century former **town hall** (Kauno rotušė; ☑ 37-203 572; www.kaunas.lt; Rotušės aikštė 15). The first two floors also serve as a wedding hall (Saturdays usually see a procession of brides and grooms in their finery) and there's a small ceramics museum in the cellar.

**St Francis Xavier
Church & Monastery**   CHURCH
(☑ 8-6405 2621; www.jesuit.lt; Rotušės aikštė 7-9; tower €1.50; ☺ 4-6pm daily, plus 9am-1pm Sun) The southern side of Rotušės aikštė is dominated by the twin-towered St Francis Xavier Church, college and Jesuit monastery complex, built between 1666 and 1720. Take a peek inside and then climb the tower for the best aerial views of Kaunas.

Sts Peter & Paul Cathedral   CHURCH
(Šventų Apaštalų Petro ir Povilo Arkekatedra Bazilika; ☑ 37-324 093; www.kaunoarkikatedra.lt; Vilniaus gatvė 1; ☺ 7am-6.30pm) With its single tower, this church owes much to baroque reconstruction, especially inside, but the original 15th-century Gothic shape of its windows remains. The largest Gothic build-

Kaunas

RUSSIA & THE BALTIC COAST KAUNAS

500 m
0.25 miles

Kaunas International (10km)

Žemaičių gatvė

Vytautas Park

NEW TOWN

Nepriklausomybes aikštė

Vytauto prospektas

Putvinskio gatvė

Ramybės Park

Sugihara House (700m)

Long-distance (50m); (200m)

Gedimino gatvė

Miško gatvė

Kęstučio gatvė

Mickevičiaus gatvė

Donelaičio gatvė

Putvinskio gatvė

GREEN HILL (ŽALIAKALNIS)

MK Čiurlionis National Museum of Art

Vienybės aikštė

Laisvės alėja

Daukanto gatvė

Savanorių prospektas

Ožeškienės gatvė

Maironio gatvė

City Garden

Kanto gatvė

Šv Gertrūdos gatvė

Gruodžio gatvė

Nemuno gatvė

Kurpių gatvė

Karaliaus Mindaugo prospektas

Jablonskio gatvė

Birštono gatvė

Jonavos gatvė

Jurbarko gatvė

Jonavos gatvė

Neris River

Nemunas River

Minkovskiu gatvė

OLD TOWN

Sladkevičiaus gatvė

Valančiaus gatvė

Mapu gatvė

Vilniaus gatvė

Daukšos gatvė

Zamenhofo gatvė

Muitinės gatvė

Aleksoto gatvė

Aleksoto tiltas

Veiverių gatvė

Veiverių gatvė

Kaunas Botanical Gardens (1km); Birštonas (40km)

Papilio gatvė

Rotušės aikštė

Muziejaus gatvė

Daubrido gatvė

Jakšto gatvė

Ninth Fort (7km)

Kaunas

ing in Lithuania, it was probably founded by Vytautas around 1410 and now has nine altars. The **tomb of Maironis** stands outside the south wall.

👁 New Town

Kaunas expanded east from the Old Town in the 19th century, giving birth to the modern centre and its striking 1.7km pedestrian street, **Laisvės alėja** (Freedom Ave).

⭐ MK Čiurlionis National Museum of Art
GALLERY
(MK Čiurlionio Valstybinis Dailės Muziejus; ☎37-229 475; www.ciurlionis.lt; Putvinskio gatvė 55; adult/child €2/1; ⏱11am-5pm Tue, Wed & Fri-Sun, to 7pm Thu) In this, Kaunas' leading gallery, you'll find extensive collections of the romantic paintings of Mikalojus Konstantinas Čiurlionis (1875–1911), one of Lithuania's greatest artists and composers, as well as Lithuanian folk art and 16th- to 20th-century European applied art.

Museum of Devils
MUSEUM
(Velnių Muziejus; ☎37-221 587; www.ciurlionis.lt; Putvinskio gatvė 64; adult/child €1.74/0.87; ⏱11am-5pm Tue, Wed & Fri-Sun, to 7pm Thu; 🚼) Diabolical is the best word to describe the collection of 3000-odd devil statuettes in this museum, collected over the years by landscape artist Antanas Žmuidzinavičius (1876–1966). While the commentary aims for a pseudo-intellectual veneer, linking the devils to Lithuanian folklore, the fun of this museum is all about the spooky masks and stories. Great for kids.

👁 Outside the Centre

Museum of the Ninth Fort
MUSEUM
(IX Forto Muziejus; ☎37-377 750; www.9fortomuziejus.lt; Žemaičių plentas 73; adult/child €2.30/1.40, catacombs with guide €6; ⏱10am-6pm Wed-Mon Apr-Oct, to 4pm Nov-Mar) A poignant memorial to the tens of thousands of people, mainly Jews, who were murdered by the Nazis, the excellent Museum of the Ninth Fort, 7km north of Kaunas, comprises an old WWI-era fort and the bunker-like church of the damned. Displays cover deportations of Lithuanians by the Soviets and graphic photo exhibitions track the demise of Kaunas' Jewish community. Take bus 23 from Jonavos gatvė to the 9-ojo Forto Muziejus stop, then cross under the motorway.

🛏 Sleeping

Kauno Arkivyskupijos Svečių Namai
GUESTHOUSE €
(☎37-322 597; www.kaunas.lcn.lt/sveciunamai; Rotušės aikštė 21; s/d/tr from €15/25/32; 🅿❄@) 🌿 This Catholic archdiocesan guesthouse couldn't have a better location, snuggled between venerable churches and overlooking the Old Town square. Rooms are spartan but spacious; breakfast is not included. Book well in advance, since it fills up fast.

Apple Economy Hotel
HOTEL €
(☎37-321 404; www.applehotel.lt; Valančiaus gatvė 19; s/d from €36/45; 🅿➿@📶) This simple hotel in a quiet courtyard on the edge of the Old Town is a recommended no-frills option. The rooms are tiny, but bright and cheerful, and the beds are very comfy.

Metropolis
HOTEL €
(☎37-205 992; www.metropolishotel.lt; S Daukanto gatvė 21; d/tr €42/56; 📶) Still redolent of former glories, the Metropolis ('Lietuva' in Soviet times) is a good-value option on a quiet, tree-lined street just off Laisvės alėja. Rooms are well fitted out, and time-worn features (such as the sculpted-stone balconies and hefty wooden turnstile leading into the moulded-ceilinged lobby, enhance its charm.

THE HILL OF CROSSES

One of Lithuania's most awe-inspiring sights is the legendary **Hill of Crosses** (Kryžių kalnas; ☑ 41-370 860; Jurgaičiai). The sound of the thousands of crosses – which appear to grow on the hillock – tinkling in the breeze is wonderfully eerie.

Planted here since at least the 19th century and probably much older, the crosses were bulldozed by the Soviets, but each night people crept past soldiers and barbed wire to plant more, risking their lives or freedom to express their national and spiritual fervour. Some of the crosses are devotional, others are memorials (many for people deported to Siberia), and some are finely carved folk-art masterpieces.

The hill is 10km north of Šiauliai, 2km east off the road to Joniškis and Rīga, in the village of Jurgaičiai. To get here, take one of up to eight daily buses from Šiauliai bus station to Joniškis and get off at the Domantai stop, from where the hill is a 2km walk. The return taxi fare from Šiauliai is €18 to €22; ask Šiauliai tourist office to order one for you by telephone to avoid paying more than you should.

Šiauliai is reachable by bus from Vilnius, Kaunas and Klaipėda. For accommodation, consult the **Tourist Information Centre** (☑ 41-523 110; www.siauliai.lt/tic; Vilniaus gatvė 213; ⊙ 9am-1pm & 2-6pm Mon-Fri, 10am-4pm Sat, to 3pm Sun).

✕ Eating

Raw Inn VEGETARIAN €
(☑ 8-652 00360; www.rawinn.lt; Vilniaus gatvė 30-1; mains €4-6; ⊙ 10am-9pm Mon to Fri, 11am-9pm Sat, 1-8pm Sun; ☑) Bursting with cheery wholesomeness, Raw Inn serves only two types of food: raw and vegan. If you've had your fill of *cepelinai,* and can't face anything too challenging, its salads, falafel, soup and other virtuous treats are well worth seeking out.

Žalias Ratas LITHUANIAN €
(☑ 37-200 050; Laisvės alėja 36b; mains €6; ⊙ 11am-midnight) Tucked away behind the tourist office, the 'Green Circle' is one of those pseudo-rustic inns where staff don traditional garb and bring out the piping-hot Lithuanian fare to eager customers. It's better than it sounds and a great choice in summer, when the terrace is buzzing with diners.

Motiejaus Kepyklėlė BAKERY €
(☑ 8-616 15599; Vilniaus gatvė 7; ⊙ 8am-10pm Mon-Sat, 9am-6pm Sun) Perhaps the best bakery in Kaunas, Motiejaus has settled into grand new redbrick digs in the heart of Vilniaus gatvė. Alongside Lithuanian cookies and pastries you'll find excellent international dainties such as canelles, cupcakes, macaroons and croissants. The coffee can also be counted on.

♟ Drinking & Nightlife

W1640 BAR
(☑ 37-203 984; www.viskiobaras.lt; Kurpių gatvė 29; ⊙ 5pm-1am Tue-Thu, to 5am Fri & Sat; ☺) Tucked away down a shabby side street,

this bar is a real find. Not only does it have a mind-boggling collection of whiskeys (150 types, to be precise) – mostly Scotch, but also some rarer Japanese ones – the bar staff are the friendliest in town. If whiskey isn't your poison, then one of its ales just might be.

Skliautas BAR
(☑ 37-206 843; www.skliautas.com; Rotušės aikštė 26; ⊙ 11am-midnight Mon-Thu, to 2am Fri & Sat, to 11pm Sun) Great for cheap Lithuanian food and a boisterous atmosphere, Skliautas bursts with energy most times of the day and night, and in summer its crowd basically takes over the adjoining alley. Also good for coffee and cake.

ⓘ Information

Tourist Office (☑ 37-323 436; www.visit.kaunas.lt; Laisvės alėja 36; ⊙ 9am-7pm Mon-Fri, 10am-3pm Sat & Sun) Books accommodation, sells maps and guides, and arranges bicycle rental and guided tours of the Old Town.

ⓘ Getting There & Away

AIR
Kaunas International Airport (☑ 8-612 44442; www.kaunas-airport.lt; Vilniaus gatvė, Karmėlava; ⊙ 9am-midnight; ☑ 29, 29E) is situated 10km north of the city centre. Bus 29 or minibus 120 run to the centre of town; a taxi should cost around €18.

BUS
The **long-distance bus station** (Autobusų Stotis; ☑ 37-409 060; www.autobusubilietai. lt; Vytauto prospektas 24; ⊙ ticket office 5.45am-9.30pm) handles intercity buses within

Lithuania and further afield. Daily services within Lithuania include Klaipėda (€14, 2¾ to four hours, 20 daily) and Vilnius (€6, 1¾ hours, at least every 30 minutes).

TRAIN

From the **train station** (Geležinkelio Stotis; ☑ 7005 5111; www.litrail.lt; MK Č urlionio gatvė 16; ☺ ticket office 4.10am-9.20pm) there are 14 trains daily to/from Vilnius (€5, 1¼ to 1¾ hours).

🛈 Getting Around

Buses and trolleybuses run from 5am to 11pm, and tickets cost €0.70 from the driver. Alternatively, you can buy a *Kauno Miesto Kortelė* (Kaunas City Card) from a Kauno Spauda or Naversen kiosk for €1.74, top it up, and pay only €0.58. While the City Card is cheaper, it's only really worth it if you'll be in Kaunas for an extended stay.

Minibuses shadow routes and run later than regular buses; drivers sell tickets for €0.87, and will stop wherever you wish. For information on public transport, including routes and timetables, see the website **Kaunas Public Transport** (www.kvt.lt).

Klaipėda

☑ 46 / POP 161,300

Lithuania's third-largest city is a mix of old and new. This former Prussian capital

(when it was named Memel) has retained a distinct German flavour in the architecture of its heavily cobbled Old Town and one remaining tower of its red-brick castle. It's also Lithuania's only port of call for *Titanic*-sized cruise ships, and a vital sea link for cargo and passenger ferries between Lithuania, Scandinavia and beyond.

Most people will only catch a glimpse of Klaipėda (klai-pey-da) as they rush headlong for the ferry to Curonian Spit, but spend a few hours – or even better, a day – and you'll be justly rewarded.

⊙ Sights

Klaipėda Castle Museum   MUSEUM
(Klaipėda Pilies Muziejus; ☑ 410 527; www.mlimuziejus.lt; Pilies gatvė 4; adult/child €1.74/0.87; ☺ 10am-6pm Tue-Sat) This small museum is based inside the remains of Klaipėda's old moat-protected castle, which dates back to the 13th century. It tells the castle's story through the ages until the 19th century, when most of the structure was pulled down. You'll find fascinating photos from WWII and the immediate postwar years, when the city was rebuilt by Soviet planners.

History Museum of Lithuania Minor   MUSEUM
(Mažosios Lietuvos Istorijos Muziejus; ☑ 46-410 524; www.mlimuziejus.lt; Didžioji Vandens gatvė 6; adult/child €1.45/0.72; ☺ 10am-6pm Tue-Sat) This small museum traces the origins of 'Lithuania Minor' (Kleinlitauen) – as this coastal region was known during several centuries as part of East Prussia. It exhibits Prussian maps, coins, artefacts of the Teutonic order, traditional weaving machines and traditional folk art.

Švyturys   BREWERY
(☑ 46-484 000; www.svyturys.lt; Kūlių Vartų gatvė 7) Klaipėda is home to the country's oldest operating brewery, where its most popular beer, Švyturys, has been brewed since 1784.

Klaipėda

Klaipėda
⊙ 0 ————— 200 m
0 ————— 0.1 miles

RUSSIA & THE BALTIC COAST KLAIPĖDA

ŽEMAITIJA NATIONAL PARK

The 200-sq-km Žemaitija National Park, a magical landscape of lake and forest, is as mysterious as it is beautiful. It's easy to see why it spawns fables of devils, ghosts and buried treasure.

The draw here is two-fold. You can swim, boat and bike around at your leisure, as well as pay a visit to one of the country's newest and most bizarre attractions: the **Cold War Museum** (Šaltojo Karo Muziejus; ☑ 8-677 86574; www.zemaitijosnp.lt; Plokštinė; adult/child €5/2.50; ⊙ 9am-6pm Tue-Fri, 10am-5pm Sat & Sun), housed in what was once a Soviet nuclear missile base.

The best access point is the small town of **Plateliai**, on the western shore of the lake of the same name, and home to the helpful **Žemaitija National Park Visitor Centre** (☑ 448-49 231; www.zemaitijosnp.lt; Didžioji gatvė 8; ⊙ 8am-5pm Mon-Thu, to 3.45pm Fri, 10am-5pm Sat Jun-Aug).

About 20km northeast of the park is **Samogitian Calvary** (Žemaičių Kalvarija), built on the site of 9th- to 13th-century burial grounds. Pilgrims come here during the first two weeks of July to climb the seven hills, where 20 chapels form a 7km 'Stations of the Cross' route in commemoration of Christ's life, death and resurrection.

Plungė, the nearest city, is best reached by train from Klaipėda (€4, one hour, four daily) and from Vilnius (€13, four hours, two daily). There are several buses daily from Kaunas (€13, four hours). From Plungė, there are limited buses onward to Plateliai.

Organised by the tourist office, tours of the brewery are 1½ to two hours, cost €10 per person (including tastings), and leave any time between 10am and 4pm Monday to Friday.

🛏 Sleeping & Eating

Klaipėda Hostel HOSTEL €
(☑ 46-211 879; www.klaipedahostel.com; Butkų Juzės gatvė 7/4; dm/d €12/32; 🅿@🛜) This friendly hostel close to the bus station looks terrible from the outside, but is very homey and pleasant inside. Two small dorms sleep 12 people and there's one double, as well as a kitchen, and free tea and coffee. Book in advance; no credit cards accepted.

Katpėdėlė LITHUANIAN €
(☑ 8-618 28343; www.katpedele.lt; Žvejų gatvė 12; mains €4-6; ⊙ 10am-1am Sun-Wed, to 2am Thu, to 3am Fri & Sat; 🛜) It may be a franchise, but Katpėdėlė does the Lithuanian standards really well, and makes the most of a brick merchant's building in a prime spot by the Danė. Try the grilled pork neck with thyme and whiskey sauce, or the salmon with peanuts.

🍷 Drinking & Nightlife

Žvejų Baras BAR
(☑ 46-412 060; www.zvejubaras.lt; Kurpių gatvė 8; ⊙ 5pm-midnight Sun-Wed, to 2am Thu-Sat) The beautiful, lead-lit, timbered interior of this portside pub (the name means 'Fisherman's Bar') is one of Klaipėda's nicest places to catch live music, or chat over a few interesting beers.

ℹ Information

Tourist Office (☑ 46-412 186; www.klaipedainfo.lt; Turgaus gatvė 7; ⊙ 9am-7pm Mon-Fri, 10am-4pm Sat & Sun) Exceptionally efficient tourist office selling maps and locally published guidebooks, and arranging accommodation, tours and more. Operates reduced hours outside high season, closing on Sundays.

ℹ Getting There & Away

The train and bus stations are situated near each other in the modern part of town, about 2km north of Old Town. Three daily trains run to Vilnius (€18, 4 hours). There's regular bus service to Vilnius (€18, four to 5½ hours, 17 daily) and Kaunas (€14, 2¾ to four hours, 20 daily).

Curonian Spit National Park

This magical sliver of land, covered by pine forest, hosts some of Europe's most precious sand dunes and a menagerie of elk, deer and avian wildlife. Recognised by Unesco as a World Heritage Site, the fragile spit is divided evenly between Lithuania and Russia's Kaliningrad region, with Lithuania's half protected as **Curonian Spit National Park** (☑46-402 256; www.neria.lt; Smiltynės gatvė 11, Smiltynė; ☺9am-5pm Sun-Thu, to 6pm Fri & Sat).

Smiltynė, where the ferries from Klaipėda dock, draws weekend crowds with the fascinating **Lithuania Sea Museum** (Lietuvos Jūrų Muziejus; ☑46-490 740; www.juru. muziejus.lt; Smiltynės gatvė 3; adult/student €9/6; ☺10.30am-6.30pm Tue-Sun Jun-Aug; ♿) inside a 19th-century fort. Further south, the village of **Juodkrantė** is awaft with the tempting smells of smoked fish (*žuvis*) and home to a 6500-strong colony of grey herons and cormorants, while picture-perfect **Nida** is close by the unmissable 52m-high **Parnidis Dune**, with its panoramic views of the 'Lithuanian Sahara' – coastline, forest and sand extending towards Kaliningrad.

The tourist office (p846) in Klaipėda can help arrange transport and accommodation.

Curonian Spit is accessible only via boat or ferry (there are no bridges linking the spit to the mainland). From Klaipėda, two ferries run regularly: a passenger ferry, known as the 'Old Ferry', goes to Smiltynė; and a vehicle ferry, the 'New Ferry', connects to a point on the spit around 2km south of Smiltynė, and departs from a port 2km south of Klaipėda's Old Town.

Regular buses run to villages on the spit, including Nida (€3.40) and Juodkrantė (€1.40), but these depart from **Smiltynė** (Smiltynės gatvė), meaning you'll first have to use the passenger ferry to get to the bus.

Ift the weather is fine cycling is a great way to explore the spit. There is a well-marked trail that runs the entire length of the spit from Smiltynė to Nida via Juodkrantė (about 50km). Hire bikes in Klaipėda and take them across the lagoon via the passenger ferry for free.

Lithuania Survival Guide

ⓘ Directory A–Z

ACCOMMODATION

Book ahead in the high season for Vilnius and the Curonian Spit. High-season prices are around 30% higher than low-season prices. Prices are higher in Vilnius.

Budget accommodation in Lithuania (**€**) is less than €50.

INTERNET RESOUCES

In Your Pocket (www.inyourpocket.com)
Lithuania Travel (www.lithuania.travel)

LGBT TRAVELLERS

The scene is low-key and underground. For general information, chat rooms and guides, contact Vilnius-based **Lithuanian Gay League** (☑5-233 3031; www.gay.lt), which publishes a solid online entertainment guide in English.

PUBLIC HOLIDAYS

New Year's Day 1 January
Independence Day (Nepriklausomybės diena) 16 February; anniversary of 1918 independence declaration
Lithuanian Independence Restoration Day 11 March
Easter Sunday March/April
Easter Monday March/April
International Labour Day 1 May
Mothers' Day First Sunday in May
Fathers' Day First Sunday in June
Feast of St John (Midsummer) 24 June
Statehood Day 6 July; commemoration of coronation of Grand Duke Mindaugas in the 13th century
Assumption of Blessed Virgin 15 August
All Saints' Day 1 November
Christmas (Kalėdos) 25 and 26 December

TELEPHONE

➡ To call a landline within Lithuania, dial ☑8 followed by the city code and phone number.

➡ To call a mobile phone within Lithuania, dial ☑8 followed by the eight-digit number.

➡ To make an international call dial ☑00 before the country code.

➡ Mobile companies Bitė (www.bite.lt), Omnitel (www.omnitel.lt) and Tele 2 (www.tele2.lt) sell prepaid SIM cards. Tele2 offers free roaming with its prepaid cards, making it the best choice for those travelling in Estonia, Latvia and Poland, too. It also offers the cheapest rates.

ⓘ Getting There & Away

AIR

Between them, airBaltic and Estonian Air connect Vilnius with Tallinn up to five times daily, and Rīga up to seven times daily.

Ryanair handles the bulk of Kaunas airport's traffic, operating flights to/from 11 European destinations.

BOAT

From Klaipėda's **International Ferry Port** (☑46-395 051; www.dfdsseaways.lt; Perkėlos gatvé 10), **DFDS Seaways** (☑ 46-395 000; www.dfdsseaways.lt; Šaulių gatvė 19) runs big passenger and car ferries regularly to Kiel and Sassnitz (in Germany), and to Karlshamn (in Sweden).

BUS

The main international bus companies operating in Lithuania are **Lux Express** (☑ 680 0909; www.luxexpress.eu) and **Ecolines** (☑ in Rīga 67214512, in Tallinn 6062217, in Vilnius 52133300; www.ecolines.net).

TRAIN

➡ Many international train routes, including to Warsaw and Moscow, pass through Belarus and require a transit visa.

➡ See **Lithuanian Rail** (p848) for further information.

ℹ Getting Around

BIKE, CAR & MOTORCYCLE

Lithuanian roads are generally very good and driving is easy, though winter poses particular problems for those not used to driving in ice and snow. Four-lane highways link the main cities of Vilnius, Kaunas and Klaipėda and the drive from Vilnius all the way to the Baltic coast (330km) generally takes three to four hours. Car hire is offered in all the major cities.

Touring cyclists will find Lithuania mercifully flat. Some roads are unsealed, but they're usually kept in good condition. Bike hire is offered in all the major cities.

BUS

Most services are summarised on the handy website **Bus Tickets** (www.autobusubilietai.lt).

PUBLIC TRANSPORT

Lithuanian cities generally have good public transport, with buses, trolleybuses and minibuses. A ride usually costs around €1.

TRAIN

The country's efficient train network, **Lithuanian Rail** (☑ information 7005 5111; www.litrail.lt), links Vilnius to Kaunas, Klaipėda and Trakai. For some journeys, including Kaunas to Klaipėda, buses are faster.

Survival Guide

Directory A–Z

Accommodation

Europe offers the fullest possible range of accommodation for all budgets. In this guide we've listed reviews by budget, then by author preference within the budget sections.

Price Ranges

Rates are for high season and often drop outside high season by as much as 50%. High season in ski resorts is usually between Christmas and New Year and around the February to March winter holidays.

Reservations

During peak holiday periods, particularly Easter, summer and Christmas – and any time of year in popular destinations such as London, Paris and Rome – it's wise to book ahead. Most places can be reserved online. Always try to book directly with the establishment; this means you're paying just for your room, with no surcharge going to a hostel- or hotel-booking website.

B&Bs & Guesthouses

Guesthouses (pension, gasthaus, *chambre d'hôte*, etc) and B&Bs (bed and breakfasts) offer greater comfort than hostels for a marginally higher price. Most are simple affairs, normally with shared bathrooms.

In some destinations, particularly in Eastern Europe, locals wait in train stations touting rented rooms. Just be sure such accommodation isn't in a far-flung suburb that requires an expensive taxi ride to and from town. Confirm the price before agreeing to rent a room and remember that it's unwise to leave valuables in your room when you go out.

B&Bs in the UK and Ireland often aren't really budget accommodation – even the lowliest tend to have midrange prices and there is a new generation of 'designer' B&Bs which are positively top end.

Camping

Most camping grounds are some distance from city centres; we list easily accessible camping grounds only, or include sites where it's common for travellers to bed down en masse under the stars (for example, on some Greek islands).

National tourist offices provide lists of camping grounds and camping organisations. Also see www.coolcamping.co.uk for details on prime campsites across Europe.

There will usually be a charge per tent or site, per person and per vehicle. In busy areas and in busy seasons, it's sometimes necessary to book.

Camping other than at designated grounds is difficult in Western Europe, because it's hard to find a suitably private spot.

Camping is also illegal without the permission of the local authorities (the police or local council office) or the landowner. Don't be shy about asking; you might be pleasantly surprised.

In some countries, such as Austria, the UK, France and Germany, free camping is illegal on all but private land, and in Greece it's illegal altogether but not enforced. This doesn't prevent hikers from occasionally pitching their tent, and you'll usually get away with it if you have a small tent, are discreet, stay just one or two nights, decamp during the day and don't light a fire or leave rubbish. At worst, you'll be

BOOK YOUR STAY ONLINE

For more accommodation reviews by Lonely Planet authors, check out http://lonelyplanet.com/hotels/. You'll find independent reviews, as well as recommendations on the best places to stay. Best of all, you can book online.

woken by the police and asked to move on.

In Eastern Europe, free camping is more widespread.

Homestays & Farmstays

You needn't volunteer on a farm to sleep on it. In Switzerland and Germany, there's the opportunity to sleep in barns or 'hay hotels'. Farmers provide cotton undersheets (to avoid straw pricks) and woolly blankets for extra warmth, but guests need their own sleeping bag and torch. For further details, visit Agrotourismus Schweiz (www.schlaf-im-stroh.ch) and Hay Hotels (www.heu-hotel.de).

Hostels

There's a vast variation in hostel standards across Europe.

HI Hostels (those affiliated to Hostelling International, www.hihostels.com), usually offer the cheapest (secure) roof over your head in Europe and you don't have to be particularly young to use them. Only southern German hostels enforce a strict age limit of 26 years. That said, if you're over 26 you'll frequently pay a small surcharge (usually about €3) to stay in an official hostel.

You need to be a YHA or HI member to use HI-affiliated hostels, but nonmembers can stay by paying a few extra euros, which will be set against future membership. After sufficient nights (usually six), you automatically become a member. To join, ask at any hostel or contact your national hostelling office, which you'll find on the HI website – where you can also make online bookings.

Europe has many private hostelling organisations and hundreds of unaffiliated backpacker hostels. These have fewer rules, more self-catering kitchens and fewer large, noisy school groups. Dorms in many private hostels can be mixed

sex. If you aren't happy to share mixed dorms, be sure to ask when you book.

Hotels

Hotels are usually the most expensive accommodation option, though at their lower end there is little to differentiate them from guesthouses or even hostels.

Cheap hotels around bus and train stations can be convenient for late-night or early-morning arrivals and departures, but some are also unofficial brothels or just downright sleazy. Check the room beforehand and make sure you're clear on price and what it covers.

Discounts for longer stays are usually possible and hotel owners in Southern Europe *might* be open to a little bargaining if times are slack. In many countries it's common for business hotels (usually more than two stars) to slash their rates by up to 40% on Friday and Saturday nights.

University Accommodation

Some university towns rent out their student accommodation during the holiday periods. This is a popular practice in France, the UK and many Eastern European countries. University accommodation will sometimes be in single rooms (although it's more commonly in doubles or triples) and might have cooking facilities. For details ask at individual colleges or universities, at student information offices or local tourist offices.

Customs Regulations

The European Union (EU) has a two-tier customs system: one for goods bought duty-free to import to or export from the EU, and one for goods bought in another EU country where taxes and duties have already been paid.

➡ Entering or leaving the EU, you are allowed to carry duty-free: 200 cigarettes, 50 cigars or 250g of tobacco; 2L of still wine plus 1L of spirits over 22% alcohol or another 2L of wine (sparkling or otherwise); 50g of perfume, 250cc of eau de toilette.

➡ Travelling from one EU country to another, the duty-paid limits are 800 cigarettes, 200 cigars, 1kg of tobacco, 10L of spirits, 20L of fortified wine, 90L of wine (of which not more than 60L is sparkling) and 110L of beer.

➡ Non-EU countries often have different regulations and many countries forbid the export of antiquities and cultural treasures.

Electricity

Europe generally runs on 220V, 50Hz AC, but there are exceptions. The UK runs on 230/240V AC, and some old buildings in Italy and Spain have 125V (or even 110V in Spain). The continent is moving towards a 230V standard. If your home country has a vastly different voltage you will need a transformer for delicate and important appliances.

The UK and Ireland use three-pin square plugs. Most of Europe uses the 'europlug' with two round pins. Greece, Italy and Switzerland use a third round pin in a way that the two-pin plug usually – but not always in Italy and Switzerland – fits. Buy an adapter before leaving home; those on sale in Europe generally go the other way, but ones for visitors to Europe are also available – airports are always a good place to buy them.

Embassies & Consulates

Generally speaking, your embassy won't be much help in emergencies if the trouble you're in is remotely your own fault. Remember, you're bound by the laws of the country you're in.

In genuine emergencies you might get some assistance, but only if other channels have been exhausted. For example, if you need to get home urgently, a free ticket is exceedingly unlikely – the embassy would expect you to have insurance. If you have all your money and documents stolen, it might assist with getting a new passport, but a loan for onward travel is out of the question.

Health

Good health care is readily available in Western Europe and, for minor illnesses, pharmacists can give valuable advice and sell over-the-counter medication. They can also advise if you need specialised help and point you in the right direction. The standard of dental care is usually good.

While the situation in Eastern Europe is improving since the EU accession of many countries, quality medical care is not always readily available outside major cities, but embassies, consulates and five-star hotels can usually recommend doctors or clinics.

No jabs are necessary for Europe. However, the World Health Organization (WHO) recommends that all travellers be covered for diphtheria, tetanus, measles, mumps, rubella and polio, regardless of their destination. Since most vaccines don't produce immunity until at least two weeks after they're given, visit a physician at least six weeks before departure.

Tap water is generally safe to drink in Western Europe. However, bottled water is recommended in most of Eastern Europe, and is a must in some countries, including Russia and Ukraine, where giardia can be a problem. Do not drink water from rivers or lakes as it may contain bacteria or viruses.

Condoms are widely available in Europe, however emergency contraception may not be, so take the necessary precautions.

Insurance

It's foolhardy to travel without insurance to cover theft, loss and medical problems. There are a wide variety of policies, so check the small print.

Some policies specifically exclude 'dangerous activities', which can include scuba diving, motorcycling, winter sports, adventure sports or even hiking.

Check that the policy covers ambulances or an emergency flight home.

Worldwide travel insurance is available online at www.lonelyplanet.com/travel-insurance. You can buy, extend and claim online anytime – even if you're already on the road.

Internet Access

Internet access varies enormously across Europe. In most places, you'll be able to find wireless (wi-fi, also called WLAN in some countries), although whether it's free varies greatly.

Where the wi-fi icon (🛜) appears in this book, it means that the establishment offers free wi-fi that you can access immediately, or by asking for the access code from staff.

Access is generally straightforward, although a few tips are in order. If you can't find the @ symbol on a keyboard, try Alt Gr + 2, or Alt Gr + Q. Watch out for German and some Balkans keyboards, which reverse the Z and the Y positions. Using a French keyboard is an art unto itself.

Where necessary in relevant countries, click on the language prompt in the bottom right-hand corner of the screen or hit Ctrl + Shift to switch between the Cyrillic and Latin alphabets.

Legal Matters

Alcohol & Smoking

You can generally purchase alcohol (beer and wine) from between 16 and 18 (usually 18 for spirits), but if in doubt, ask. Although you can drive at 17 or 18, you might not be able to hire a car until you're 25.

Cigarette-smoking bans in bars and restaurants and other public places are increasingly common across Europe so ask before lighting up.

HEALTH RESOURCES

The **World Health Organization** publishes the annually revised, free online book *International Travel and Health* (www.who.int/ith/en). **MD Travel Health** (www.mdtravelhealth.com) provides up-to-date travel-health recommendations for every country.

It's usually a good idea to consult your government's website before departure, if one is available:

Australia (http://smartraveller.gov.au)

Canada (www.phac-aspc.gc.ca)

UK (www.gov.uk/foreign-travel-advice)

USA (www.wnc.cdc.gov/travel)

Drugs

Drugs are often quite openly available in Europe, but that doesn't mean they're legal. The Netherlands is most famed for its liberal attitudes, with coffeeshops openly selling cannabis even though the drug is not technically legal. However, a blind eye is generally turned to the trade as the possession and purchase of small amounts (5g) of 'soft drugs' (ie marijuana and hashish) is allowed and users won't be prosecuted for smoking or carrying this amount. Don't take this relaxed attitude as an invitation to buy harder drugs; if you get caught, you'll be punished. Since 2008 magic mushrooms have been banned in the Netherlands.

In Belgium, the possession of up to 5g of cannabis is legal, but selling the drug isn't, so if you get caught at the point of sale, you could be in trouble. Switzerland has also decriminalised possession of up to 10g of marijuana.

In Portugal, the possession of all drugs has been decriminalised. Once again, however, selling is illegal.

Getting caught with drugs in other parts of Europe, particularly countries such as Turkey and Russia, can lead to imprisonment.

For more details see the website of the European Monitoring Centre for Drugs and Drug Addiction (http://www.emcdda.europa.eu). If in any doubt, err on the side of caution, and don't even think about taking drugs across international borders.

LGBT Travellers

Across Western Europe you'll find very liberal attitudes towards homosexuality. London, Paris, Berlin, Munich, Amsterdam, Madrid and Lisbon have thriving gay communities and pride events. The Greek islands of Mykonos and Lesvos are popular gay beach destinations. Gran Canaria and Ibiza in Spain are big centres for both gay clubbing and beach holidays.

Eastern Europe, and in particular Russia, tends to be far less progressive. Outside the big cities, attitudes become more conservative and discretion is advised, particularly in Turkey and most parts of Eastern Europe.

Maps

Tourist offices usually provide free but fairly basic maps.

Road atlases are essential if you're driving or cycling. Leading brands are Freytag & Berndt, Hallwag, Kümmerly + Frey, and Michelin.

Maps published by European automobile associations, such as Britain's AA (www.theaa.co.uk) and Germany's ADAC (www.adac.de), are usually excellent and sometimes free if membership of your local association gives you reciprocal rights.

Money

The euro, used in 19 EU states as well as several other non-EU states, is made up of 100 cents. Notes come in denominations of €5, €10, €20, €50, €100, €200 and €500 euros, though any notes above €50 are rarely used on a daily basis. Coins come in 1c, 2c, 5c, 10c, 20c, 50c, €1 and €2.

Denmark, the UK and Sweden have held out against adopting the euro for political reasons, while non-EU nations, such as Albania, Belarus, Norway, Russia, Switzerland, Turkey and Ukraine, also have their own currencies.

ATMs

Across major European towns and cities international ATMs are common, but you should always have a back-up option, as there can be glitches. In some remote areas, ATMs might be scarce, too.

Much of Western Europe now uses a chip-and-pin system for added security. You will have problems if you don't have a four-digit PIN number and might have difficulties if your card doesn't have a metallic chip. Check with your bank.

Always cover the keypad when entering your PIN and make sure there are no unusual devices attached to the machine, which can copy your card's details or cause it to stick in the machine. If your card disappears and the screen goes blank before you've even entered your PIN, don't enter it – especially if a 'helpful' bystander tells you to do so. If you can't retrieve your card, call your bank's emergency number, if you can, before leaving the ATM.

Cash

It's a good idea to bring some local currency in cash, if only to cover yourself until you get to an exchange facility or find an ATM. The equivalent of €150 should usually be enough. Some extra cash in an easily exchanged currency is also a good idea, especially in Eastern Europe.

Credit Cards

Visa and MasterCard/Eurocard are more widely accepted in Europe than Amex and Diners Club; Visa (sometimes called Carte Bleue) is particularly strong in France and Spain.

There are, however, regional differences in the general acceptability of credit cards; in Germany for example, it's rare for restaurants to take credit cards. Cards are not widely accepted off the beaten track.

To reduce the risk of fraud, always keep your card in view when making transactions; for example, in restaurants that do accept cards, pay as you leave, following your card to the till. Keep transaction records and either check your statements when you return home, or check your account online while still on the road.

Letting your credit-card company know roughly where you're going lessens the chance of fraud – or of your bank cutting off the card when it sees (your) unusual spending.

Debit Cards

It's always worthwhile having a Maestro-compatible debit card, which differs from a credit card in deducting money straight from your bank account. Check with your bank or MasterCard (Maestro's parent) for compatibility.

Exchanging Money

Euros, US dollars and UK pounds are the easiest currencies to exchange. You may have trouble exchanging some lesser-known ones at small banks.

Importing or exporting some currencies is restricted or banned, so try to get rid of any local currency before you leave. Get rid of Scottish pounds before leaving the UK; nobody outside Britain will touch them.

Most airports, central train stations, big hotels and many border posts have banking facilities outside regular business hours, at times on a 24-hour basis. Post offices in Europe often perform banking tasks, tend to open longer hours and outnumber banks in remote places. While they always exchange cash, they might baulk at handling travellers cheques not in the local currency.

The best exchange rates are usually at banks. *Bureaux de change* usually – but not always – offer worse rates or charge higher commissions. Hotels and airports are almost always the worst places to change money.

International Transfers

International bank transfers are good for secure one-off movements of large amounts of money, but they might take three to five days and there will be a fee (about £25 in the UK, for example). Be sure to specify the name of the bank, plus the sort code and address of the branch where you'd like to pick up your money.

In an emergency it's quicker but more costly to have money wired via an Amex office (www.americanexpress.com), Western Union (www.westernunion.com) or MoneyGram (www.moneygram.com).

Taxes & Refunds

When non-EU residents spend more than a certain amount (around €75) they can usually reclaim any sales tax when leaving the country.

Making a tax-back claim is straightforward. First, make sure the shop offers duty-free sales (often a sign will be displayed reading 'Tax-Free Shopping'). When making your purchase, ask the shop attendant for a tax-refund voucher, filled in with the correct amount and the date. This can be used to claim a refund directly at international airports, or stamped at ferry ports or border crossings and mailed back for a refund.

Travellers Cheques

It's become more difficult to find places that cash travellers cheques. In parts of Eastern Europe only a few banks handle them, and the process can be quite bureaucratic and costly.

That said, having a few cheques is a good back-up. If they're stolen you can claim a refund, provided you have a separate record of cheque numbers.

Amex and Thomas Cook are reliable brands of travellers cheques, while cheques in US dollars, euros or British pounds are the easiest to cash. When changing them ask about fees and commissions as well as the exchange rate.

Post

From major European centres, airmail typically takes about five days to North America and about a week to Australasian destinations, although mail from such countries as Albania or Russia is much slower.

Courier services such as DHL are best for essential deliveries.

Safe Travel

Travelling in Europe is usually very safe. The following outlines a range of general guidelines.

Discrimination

In some parts of Europe travellers of African, Arab or Asian descent might encounter unpleasant attitudes that are unrelated to them personally. In rural areas travellers whose skin colour marks them out as foreigners might experience unwanted attention.

Attitudes vary from country to country. People tend to be more accepting in cities than in the country. Race is also less of an issue in Western Europe than in parts of the former Eastern Bloc. For example, there has been a spate of racially motivated attacks in St Petersburg and other parts of Russia in recent years.

Druggings

Although rare, some drugging of travellers does occur in Europe. Travellers are especially vulnerable on trains and buses where a new 'friend' may offer you food or a drink that will knock you out, giving them time to steal your belongings.

Gassings have also been reported on a handful of overnight international trains. The best protection is to lock the door of your compartment (use your own lock if there isn't one) and to lock your bags to luggage racks, preferably with a sturdy combination cable.

If you can help it, never sleep alone in a train compartment.

Pickpockets & Thieves

Theft is definitely a problem in parts of Europe and you have to be aware of unscrupulous fellow travellers. The key is to be sensible with your possessions.

➡ Don't store valuables in train-station lockers or luggage-storage counters and be careful about people who offer to help you operate a locker. Also be vigilant if someone offers to carry your luggage: they might carry t away altogether.

➡ Don't leave valuables in your car, on train seats or in your room. When going out, don't flaunt cameras, laptops and other expensive electronic goods.

➡ Carry a small day pack, as shoulder bags are an open invitation for snatch-thieves. Consider using small zipper locks on your packs.

➡ Pickpockets are most active in dense crowds, especially in busy train stations and on public transport during peak hours. Be careful in these situations.

➡ Spread valuables, cash and cards around your body or in different bags.

➡ A money belt with your essentials (passport, cash, credit cards, airline tickets) is usually a good idea. However, so you needn't delve into it in public, carry a wallet with a day's worth of cash.

➡ Having your passport stolen is less of a disaster if you've recorded the number and issue date or, even better, photocopied the relevant data pages. You can also scan them and email them to yourself. If you lose your passport, notify the police immediately to get a statement and contact your nearest consulate.

➡ Record the serial numbers of travellers cheques and carry photocopies of your credit cards, airline tickets and other travel documents.

Scams

Most scams involve distracting you – either by kids running up to you, someone asking for directions or spilling something on you – while another person steals your wallet. Be alert in such situations.

In some countries, especially in Eastern Europe, you may encounter people claiming to be from the tourist police, the special police, the super-secret police, whatever. Unless they're wearing a uniform and have good reason for accosting you, treat their claims with suspicion.

Needless to say, never show your passport or cash to anyone on the street. Simply walk away. If someone flashes a badge, offer to accompany them to the nearest police station.

Unrest & Terrorism

Civil unrest and terrorist bombings are rare in Europe, but they do occur. Attacks by ETA (the Basque separatist group in Spain and France) and attacks by Muslim extremists in the UK, Belgium, France, Denmark, Spain and Russia have all occurred in recent years. Keep an eye on the news and avoid areas where any flare-up seems likely.

Telephone

If your mobile phone is European, it's often perfectly feasible to use it on roaming throughout the continent.

If you're coming from outside Europe, it's usually worth buying a prepaid local SIM in one European country. Even if you're not staying there long, calls across Europe will still be cheaper if they're not routed via your home country and the prepaid card will enable you to keep a limit on your spending. In several countries you need your passport to buy a SIM card.

In order to use other SIM cards in your phone, you'll need to have your handset unlocked by your home provider. Even if your phone is locked, you can use apps such as 'whatsapp' to send free text messages internationally wherever you have wi-fi access, or Skype to make free international calls whenever you're online.

Europe uses the GSM 900 network, which also covers Australia and New Zealand, but is not compatible with the North American GSM 1900 or the totally different system in Japan and South Korea. If you have a GSM phone, check with your service provider about using it in Europe. You'll need international roaming, but this is usually free to enable.

You can call abroad from almost any phone box in Europe. Public telephones accepting phonecards (available from post offices, telephone centres, news stands or retail outlets) are virtually the norm now; coin-operated phones are rare if not impossible to find.

Without a phonecard, you can ring from a telephone booth inside a post office or telephone centre and settle your bill at the counter. Reverse-charge (collect) calls are often possible. From many countries the Country Direct system lets you phone home by billing the long-distance carrier you use at home. These numbers can often be dialled from public phones without even inserting a phonecard.

Time

Europe is divided into four time zones. From west to east these are

UTC (Britain, Ireland, Portugal) GMT (GMT+1 in summer)

CET (the majority of European countries) GMT+1 (GMT+2 in summer)

EET (Greece, Turkey, Bulgaria, Romania, Moldova, Ukraine, Belarus, Lithuania, Latvia, Estonia, Kaliningrad, Finland) GMT+2 (GMT+3 in summer)

MSK (Russia) GMT+3 (GMT+4 in summer)

At 9am in Britain it's 1am (GMT/UTC minus eight hours) on the US west coast, 4am (GMT/UTC minus five hours) on the US east coast, 10am in Paris and Prague, 11am in Athens, midday in Moscow and 7pm (GMT/UTC plus 10 hours) in Sydney.

In most European countries, clocks are put forward one hour for daylight-saving time on the last Sunday in March, and turned back again on the last Sunday in October.

Toilets

Many public toilets require a small fee either deposited in a box or given to the attendant. Sit-down toilets are the rule in the vast majority of places. Squat toilets can still be found in rural areas,

although they are definitely a dying breed.

Public-toilet provision remains changeable from city to city. If you can't find one, simply drop into a hotel or restaurant and ask to use theirs.

Tourist Information

Unless otherwise indicated, tourist offices are common and widespread, although their usefulness varies enormously.

Travellers with Disabilities

Cobbled medieval streets, 'classic' hotels, congested inner cities and underground subway systems make Europe a tricky destination for people with mobility impair-

THE SCHENGEN AREA

Twenty-six European countries are signatories to the Schengen Agreement, which has effectively dismantled internal border controls between them. They are Austria, Belgium, Czech Republic, Denmark, Estonia, Finland, France, Germany, Greece, Iceland, Italy, Hungary, Latvia, Liechtenstein, Lithuania, Luxembourg, Malta, the Netherlands, Norway, Poland, Portugal, Slovenia, Slovakia, Spain, Sweden and Switzerland.

Citizens of the US, Australia, New Zealand, Canada and the UK only need a valid passport to enter these countries. However, other nationals, including South Africans, can apply for a single visa – a Schengen visa (www.schengenvisainfo.com) – when travelling throughout this region.

Non-EU visitors (with or without a Schengen visa) should expect to be questioned, however perfunctorily, when first entering the region. However, later travel within the zone is much like a domestic trip, with no border controls.

If you need a Schengen visa, you must apply at the consulate or embassy of the country that's your main destination, or your point of entry. You may then stay up to a maximum of 90 days in the entire Schengen area within a six-month period. Once your visa has expired, you must leave the zone and may only re-enter after three months abroad. Shop around when choosing your point of entry, as visa prices may differ from country to country.

If you're a citizen of the US, Australia, New Zealand or Canada, you may stay visa-free a total of 90 days, during six months, within the entire Schengen region.

If you're planning a longer trip, you need to inquire personally as to whether you need a visa or visas. Your country might have bilateral agreements with individual Schengen countries allowing you to stay there longer than 90 days without a visa. However, you will need to talk directly to the relevant embassies or consulates.

While the UK and Ireland are not part of the Schengen area, their citizens can stay indefinitely in other EU countries, only needing paperwork if they want to work long term or take up residency.

ments. However, the train facilities are good and some destinations boast new tram services or lifts to platforms. The following websites can help with specific details.

Accessible Europe (www. accessibleurope.com) Specialist European tours with van transport.

DisabledGo.com (www.disa bledgo.com) Detailed access information to thousands of venues across the UK and Ireland.

Lonely Planet (www.lonely planet.com/thorntree) Share experiences on the Travellers With Disabilities branch of the Thorn Tree message board.

Mobility International Schweiz (www.mis-ch.ch) Good site (only partly in English) listing 'barrier-free' destinations in Switzerland and abroad, plus wheelchair-accessible hotels in Switzerland.

Mobility International USA (www.miusa.org) Publishes guides and advises travellers with disabilities on mobility issues.

Society for Accessible Travel & Hospitality (SATH; http://sath. org) Reams of information for travellers with disabilities.

Visas

➡ Citizens of the USA, Canada, Australia, New Zealand and the UK need only a valid passport to enter nearly all countries in Europe, including the entire EU.

➡ Belarus and Russia require a prearranged visa before arrival and even an 'invitation' from (or booking with) a tour operator or hotel. It's simpler and safer to obtain these visas before leaving home.

➡ Australians and New Zealanders need a visa for both Ukraine and Moldova.

➡ Transit visas are usually cheaper than tourist or business visas but they allow only a very short stay (one to

---

ONLINE RESOURCES FOR FINDING WORK

EuroJobs (www.eurojobs.com) Links to hundreds of organisations looking to employ both non-Europeans (with the correct work permits) and Europeans.

Natives (www.natives.co.uk) Summer and winter resort jobs, and various tips.

Picking Jobs (www.pickingjobs.com) Includes some tourism jobs.

Season Workers (www.seasonworkers.com) Best for ski-resort work and summer jobs, although it also has some childcare jobs.

Ski-jobs.co.uk (www.ski-jobs.co.uk) Mainly service jobs such as chalet hosts, bar staff and porters. Some linguistic skills required.

---

five days) and can be difficult to extend.

➡ All visas have a 'use-by' date and you'll be refused entry afterwards. In some cases it's easier to get visas as you go along, rather than arranging them all beforehand. Carry spare passport photos (you may need from one to four every time you apply for a visa).

➡ Visas to neighbouring countries are usually issued immediately by consulates in Eastern Europe, although some may levy a hefty surcharge for 'express service'.

➡ Consulates are generally open weekday mornings (if there's both an embassy and a consulate, you want the consulate).

➡ Because regulations can change, double-check with the relevant embassy or consulate before travelling.

Volunteering

A short-term volunteer project might seem a good idea. However, most voluntary organisations levy high charges for airfares, food, lodging and recruitment (from about €250 to €800 per week), making such work impractical for most shoestringers.

One exception is WWOOF (www.wwoof.net) which helps link volunteers with organic farms across at least 25 European nations. A small membership fee is required to join the national chapter but in exchange for your labour you'll receive free lodging and food.

For more information, Lonely Planet publishes *Volunteer: A Traveller's Guide to Making a Difference Around the World.*

Women Travellers

➡ Women might attract unwanted attention in Turkey, rural Spain and Southern Italy, especially Sicily, where many men view whistling and catcalling as flattery. Conservative dress can help to deter lascivious gazes and wolf whistles; dark sunglasses help avoid unwanted eye contact.

➡ Marriage is highly respected in southern Europe, and a wedding ring can help, along with talk about 'my husband'. Hitchhiking alone is not recommended anywhere.

➡ Female readers have reported assaults at Turkish hotels with shared bathrooms, so women travelling to Turkey might want to consider a more expensive room with private bathroom.

➡ Useful websites include Journeywoman (www.journeywoman.com) which has a newsletter about solo female travels all over the world, and Women Travel the World (www.womentravel.info) promoting women's travel businesses.

Work

EU citizens are allowed to work in any other EU country, but there can still be tire-some paperwork involved. Other nationalities require special work permits that can be almost impossible to arrange, especially for temporary work. However, that doesn't prevent enterprising travellers from topping up their funds by working in the hotel or restaurant trades at beach or ski resorts, or teaching a little English – and they don't always have to do this illegally.

The UK, for example, issues special 'working holiday' visas to Common-wealth citizens who are aged between 17 and 30, valid for 12 months' work during two years (see www.gov.uk/browse/visas-immigration/work-visas). Your national student-exchange organisa-tion might be able to arrange temporary work permits to several countries.

If you have a grandparent or parent who was born in an EU country, you may have certain rights of residency or citizenship. Ask that coun-try's embassy about dual citizenship and work permits. With citizenship, also ask about any obligations, such as military service and res-idency. Be aware that your home country may not rec-ognise dual citizenship.

Transport

GETTING THERE & AWAY

Flights, tours and rail tickets can be booked online at lonelyplanet.com/bookings.index.do.

Entering Europe

All countries require travellers to have a valid passport, preferably with at least six months between the time of departure and the passport's expiry date.

EU travellers from countries that issue national identity cards are increasingly using these to travel within the EU, although it's impossible to use these as the sole travel documents outside the EU.

Some countries require certain nationalities to buy a visa allowing entry between certain dates. Specifically, Belarus and Russia require all nationalities to obtain visas, while Australian and New Zealand travellers also need visas to enter Moldova and Ukraine. Turkey requires Australian, Canadian, South African, UK and US passport holders to buy a visa on arrival. Other nationalities may have additional requirements.

Air

To save money, it's best to travel off-season. This means, if possible, avoid mid-June to early September, Easter, Christmas and school holidays.

Regardless of your ultimate destination, it's sometimes better to pick a recognised transport 'hub' as your initial port of entry, where high traffic volumes help keep prices down. The busiest, and therefore most obvious, airports are London, Frankfurt, Paris and Rome. Sometimes tickets to Amsterdam, Athens, Barcelona, Berlin, İstanbul, Madrid and Vienna are worth checking out.

Long-haul airfares to Eastern Europe are rarely a bargain; you're usually better flying to a Western European hub and taking an onward budget-airline flight or train. The main hubs in Eastern Europe are Budapest, Moscow, Prague and Warsaw.

Most of the aforementioned gateway cities are also well serviced by low-cost carriers that fly to other parts of Europe.

Land

It's possible to reach Europe by various different train routes from Asia. Most common is the Trans-Siberian Railway, connecting Moscow to Siberia, the Russian Far East, Mongolia and China.

It is also possible to reach Moscow from several Central Asian states and İstanbul from Iran and Jordan. See www.seat61.com for more information about these adventurous routes.

CLIMATE CHANGE & TRAVEL

Every form of transport that relies on carbon-based fuel generates CO_2, the main cause of human-induced climate change. Modern travel is dependent on aeroplanes, which might use less fuel per kilometre per person than most cars but travel much greater distances. The altitude at which aircraft emit gases (including CO_2) and particles also contributes to their climate change impact. Many websites offer 'carbon calculators' that allow people to estimate the carbon emissions generated by their journey and, for those who wish to do so, to offset the impact of the greenhouse gases emitted with contributions to portfolios of climate-friendly initiatives throughout the world. Lonely Planet offsets the carbon footprint of all staff and author travel.

Sea

There are numerous ferry routes between Europe and Africa, including links from Spain to Morocco, Italy and Malta to Tunisia, France to Morocco and France to Tunisia. Check out www.traghettiweb.it for comprehensive information on all Mediterranean ferries. Ferries are often filled to capacity in summer, so book well in advance if you're taking a vehicle across.

Passenger freighters (typically carrying up to 12 passengers) aren't nearly as competitively priced as airlines. Journeys also take a long time. However, if you have your heart set on a transatlantic journey, TravLtips Cruise and Freighter (www.travltips.com) has information on freighter cruises.

GETTING AROUND

In most European countries, the train is the best option for internal transport. Check the websites of national rail systems as they often offer fare specials and national passes that are significantly cheaper than point-to-point tickets.

Air
Airlines

In recent years low-cost carriers have revolutionised European transport. Most budget airlines have a similar pricing system – namely that ticket prices rise with the number of seats sold on each flight, so book as early as possible to get a decent fare.

Some low-cost carriers – Ryanair being the prime example – fly to smaller, less convenient airports on the outskirts of their destination city, or even to the airports of nearby cities, so check the exact location of the de-

parture and arrival airports before you book.

Departure and other taxes (including booking fees, checked-baggage fees and other surcharges) soon add up and are included in the final price by the end of the online booking process – usually a lot more than you were hoping to pay – but with careful choosing and advance booking you can get excellent deals.

Air Passes

Various travel agencies and airlines offer air passes, such as SAS's Visit Scandinavia/ Nordic Air Pass (www.flysas.com). Check with your travel agent for current promotions.

Bicycle
Rental & Purchase

It is easy to hire bikes throughout most of Europe. Many Western European train stations have bike-rental counters. It is sometimes possible to return the bike at a different outlet so you don't have to retrace your route. Hostels are another good place to find cheap bike hire.

There are plenty of places to buy bikes in Europe, but you'll need a specialist bicycle shop for a bike capable of withstanding a European trip. Cycling is very popular in the Netherlands and Germany, and those countries are good places to pick up a well-equipped touring bicycle.

European prices are quite high (certainly higher than in North America), however non-European residents should be able to claim back value-added tax (VAT) on the purchase.

Boat

Several different ferry companies compete on the main ferry routes, resulting in a comprehensive but complicated service. The same ferry company can have a host of

different prices for the same route, depending on the time of day or year, validity of the ticket and length of your vehicle. Vehicle tickets usually include the driver and often up to five passengers free of charge.

It's worth booking ahead where possible as there may be special reductions on off-peak crossings and advance-purchase tickets. On English Channel routes, apart from one-day or short-term excursion returns, there is little price advantage in buying a return ticket versus two singles.

Rail-pass holders are entitled to discounts or free travel on some lines. Food on ferries is often expensive (and lousy), so it is worth bringing your own. Also be aware that if you take your vehicle on board, you are usually denied access to it during the voyage.

Lake and river ferry services operate in many countries, Austria and Switzerland being just two. Some of these are very scenic.

Bus
International Buses

Often cheaper than trains, sometimes substantially so, long-distance buses also tend to be slower and less comfortable. However in Portugal, Greece and Turkey, buses are often a better option than trains.

Europe's biggest organisation of international buses operates under the name Eurolines (www.eurolines.com), comprised of various national companies.

National Buses

Domestic buses provide a viable alternative to trains in most countries. Again, they are usually slightly cheaper and somewhat slower. Buses are generally best for short hops, such as getting around cities and reaching remote villages, and they are often the only option in mountainous regions.

Reservations are rarely necessary. On many city buses you usually buy your ticket in advance from a kiosk or machine and validate it on entering the bus.

Car & Motorcycle

Travelling with your own vehicle gives flexibility and is the best way to reach remote places. However, the independence does sometimes isolate you from local life. Also, cars can be a target for theft and are often impractical in city centres, where traffic jams, parking problems and getting thoroughly lost can make it well worth ditching your vehicle and using public transport.

Fuel

➡ Fuel prices can vary enormously (though fuel is always more expensive than in North America or Australia).

➡ Only unleaded petrol is availablein Europe. Diesel is usually cheaper, though the difference is marginal in Britain, Ireland and Switzerland.

➡ Ireland's Automobile Association maintains a webpage of European fuel prices at www.theaa.ie/AA/Motoring-Advice/Petrol-Prices.aspx.

Motorcycle Touring

Europe is made for motorcycle touring, with quality winding roads, stunning scenery and an active motorcycling scene. Just make sure your wet-weather motorcycling gear is up to scratch.

➡ Rider and passenger crash helmets are compulsory everywhere in Europe.

➡ Austria, Belgium, France, Germany, Luxembourg, Portugal and Spain require that motorcyclists use headlights during the day; in other countries it is recommended.

➡ On ferries, motorcyclists rarely have to book ahead as they can generally be squeezed on board.

➡ Take note of the local custom about parking motorcycles on pavements (sidewalks). Though this is illegal in some countries, the police often turn a blind eye provided the vehicle doesn't obstruct pedestrians.

Preparation

Always carry proof of ownership of your vehicle (Vehicle Registration Document for British-registered cars). An EU driving licence is acceptable for those driving through Europe. If you have any other type of licence, you should obtain an International Driving Permit (IDP) from your motoring organisation. Check what type of licence is required in your destination prior to departure.

Third-party motor insurance is compulsory. Most UK policies automatically provide this for EU countries. Get your insurer to issue a Green Card (which may cost extra), an internationally recognised proof of insurance, and check that it lists every country you intend to visit. You'll need this in the event of an accident outside the country where the vehicle is insured.

Also ask your insurer for a European Accident Statement form, which can simplify things if worst comes to worst. Never sign statements that you can't read or understand – insist on a translation and sign that only if it's acceptable.

For non-EU countries, check the requirements with your insurer. Travellers from the UK can obtain additional advice and information from the Association of British Insurers (www.abi.org.uk).

Take out a European motoring assistance policy. Non-Europeans might find it cheaper to arrange international coverage with

their national motoring organisation before leaving home. Ask your motoring organisation for details about the free services offered by affiliated organisations around Europe.

Every vehicle that travels across an international border should display a sticker indicating its country of registration. A warning triangle, to be used in the event of breakdown, is compulsory almost everywhere.

Some recommended accessories include a first-aid kit (compulsory in Austria, Slovenia, Croatia, Serbia, Montenegro and Greece), a spare bulb kit (compulsory in Spain), a reflective jacket for every person in the car (compulsory in France, Italy and Spain) and a fire extinguisher (compulsory in Greece and Turkey).

Residents of the UK should contact the RAC (www.rac.co.uk) or the AA (www.theaa.co.uk) for more information. Residents of the US, contact AAA (www.aaa.com).

Purchase

Buying a car and then selling it at the end of your European travels may work out to be a better deal than renting one, although this isn't guaranteed and you'll need to do your sums carefully.

The purchase of vehicles in some European countries is illegal for non-nationals or non-EU residents. Britain is probably the best place to buy as second-hand prices are good there. Bear in mind that British cars have steering wheels on the right-hand side. If you wish to have left-hand drive and can afford to buy a new car, prices are generally reasonable in Greece, France, Germany, Belgium, Luxembourg and the Netherlands.

Paperwork can be tricky wherever you buy, and many countries have compulsory roadworthiness checks on older vehicles.

Rental

➡ Renting a car is ideal for people who will need cars for 16 days or less. Anything longer, it's better to lease.

➡ Big international rental firms will give you reliable service and good vehicles. National or local firms can often undercut the big companies by up to 40%.

➡ Usually you will have the option of returning the car to a different outlet at the end of the rental period, but there's normally a charge for this and it can be very steep if it's a long way from your point of origin.

➡ Book early for the lowest rates and make sure you compare rates in different cities. Taxes range from 15% to 20% and surcharges apply if rented from an airport.

➡ If you rent a car in the EU you might not be able to take it outside the EU, and if you rent the car outside the EU, you will only be able to drive within the EU for eight days. Ask at the rental agencies for other such regulations.

➡ Make sure you understand what is included in the price (unlimited or paid kilometres, tax, injury insurance, collision damage waiver etc) and what your liabilities are. We recommend taking the collision damage waiver, though you can probably skip the injury insurance if you and your passengers have decent travel insurance.

➡ The minimum rental age is usually 21 years and sometimes 25. You'll need a credit card and to have held your licence for at least a year.

➡ Motorcycle and moped rental is common in some countries, such as Italy, Spain, Greece and southern France.

Road Conditions & Road Rules

➡ Conditions and types of roads vary across Europe. The fastest routes are generally four- or six-lane highways known locally as motorways, autoroutes, autostrade, autobahnen, etc. These tend to skirt cities and plough through the countryside in straight lines, often avoiding the most scenic bits.

➡ Some highways incur tolls, which are often quite hefty (especially in Italy, France and Spain), but there will always be an alternative route. Motorways and other primary routes are generally in good condition.

➡ Road surfaces on minor routes are unreliable in some countries (eg Greece, Albania, Romania, Ireland, Russia and Ukraine), although normally they will be more than adequate.

➡ Except in Britain and Ireland, you should drive on the right. Vehicles brought to the continent from any of these locales should have their headlights adjusted to avoid blinding oncoming traffic (a simple solution on older headlight lenses is to cover up a triangular section of the lens with tape). Priority is often given to traffic approaching from the right in countries that drive on the right-hand side.

➡ Speed limits vary from country to country. You may be surprised at the apparent disregard for traffic regulations in some places (particularly in Italy and Greece), but as a visitor it is always best to be cautious. Many driving infringements are subject to an on-the-spot fine. Always ask for a receipt.

➡ European drink-driving laws are particularly strict. The blood-alcohol concentration (BAC) limit when driving is usually between 0.05% and 0.08%, but in certain areas (such as Gibraltar, Bulgaria and Belarus) it can be zero.

Hitching

Hitching is never entirely safe and we cannot recommend it. Travellers who decide to hitch should understand that they are taking a small but potentially serious risk. It will be safer if they travel in pairs and let someone know where they plan to go.

➡ A man and woman travelling together is probably the best combination. A woman hitching on her own is taking a larger than normal risk.

➡ Don't try to hitch from city centres; take public transport to the suburban exit routes.

➡ Hitching is usually illegal on highways – stand on the slip roads or approach drivers at petrol stations and truck stops.

➡ Look presentable and cheerful, and make a cardboard sign indicating your intended destination in the local language.

➡ Never hitch where drivers can't stop in good time or without causing an obstruction.

➡ In parts of Eastern Europe including Russia, Ukraine and Turkey, traditional hitchhiking is rarely practised. Instead, anyone with a car can be a taxi and it's quite usual to see locals stick their hands out (palm down) on the street, looking to hitch a lift. The difference with hitching here, however, is that you pay for the privilege. You will need to speak the local language (or at least know the numbers) to discuss your destination and negotiate a price.

Local Transport

European towns and cities have excellent local trans-port systems, often encompassing trams as well as buses and metro/subway/ underground-rail networks.

Most travellers will find areas of interest in European cities can be easily traversed by foot or bicycle. In Greece and Italy, travellers sometimes rent mopeds and motorcycles for scooting around a city or island.

Taxi

Taxis in Europe are metered and rates are usually high. There might also be supplements for things such as luggage, time of day, location of pick-up and extra passengers.

Good bus, rail and underground-railway networks often render taxis unnecessary, but if you need one in a hurry they can be found idling near train stations or outside big hotels. Lower fares make taxis more viable in some countries such as Spain, Greece, Portugal and Turkey.

Train

Express Trains

Eurostar (www.eurostar.com) links London's St Pancras International station, via the Channel Tunnel, with Paris' Gare du Nord (2¼ hours, up to 25 a day) and Brussels' international terminal (one hour 50 minutes, up to 12 a day). Some trains also stop at Lille and Calais in France. From early 2017, direct Eurostar trains will also link Amsterdam Centraal Station with London St Pancras, with stops at Schiphol airport and Rotterdam Centraal Station

(and Antwerp and Brussels in Belgium); the Amsterdam–London journey time will be around four hours.

The train stations at St Pancras International, Paris, Brussels and Amsterdam are much more central than the cities' airports. So, overall, the journey takes as little time as the equivalent flight, with less hassle.

Eurostar in London also sells tickets onwards to some Continental destinations. Holders of Eurail and InterRail passes are offered discounts on some Eurostar services; check when booking.

Within Europe, express trains are identified by the symbols 'EC' (EuroCity) or 'IC' (InterCity). The French TGV, Spanish AVE and German ICE trains are even faster, reaching up to 300km/h. Supplementary fares can apply on fast trains (which you often have to pay when travelling on a rail pass), and it is a good idea (sometimes obligatory) to reserve seats at peak times and on certain lines. The same applies for branded express trains, such as the Thalys (between Paris and Brussels, Bruges, Amsterdam and Cologne), and the Eurostar Italia (between Rome and Naples, Florence, Milan and Venice).

If you don't have a seat reservation, you can still obtain a seat that doesn't have a reservation ticket attached to it. Check which destination a seat is reserved for – you might be able to sit in it until the person boards the train.

Overnight Trains

There are usually two types of sleeping accommodation: dozing off upright in your seat or stretching out in a sleeper. Again, reservations are advisable, as sleeping options are allocated on a first-come, first-served basis. Couchette bunks are comfortable enough, if lacking in privacy. There are four per compartment in 1st class, six in 2nd class.

Sleepers are the most comfortable option, offering beds for one or two passengers in 1st class, or two or three passengers in 2nd class. Charges vary depending upon the journey, but they are significantly more costly than couchettes.

In the former Soviet Union, the most common options are either 2nd-class *kupey-ny* compartments (usually referred to as *kupe*) – which have four bunks – or the cheaper *platskartny*, which are open-plan compartments with reserved bunks.

The cheapest option – not usually available on overnight trains – are the very basic bench seats in *obshchiy* (*za-halney* in Ukrainian) class.

Security

Sensible security measures include always keeping your bags in sight (especially at stations), chaining them to the luggage rack, locking compartment doors overnight and sleeping in compartments with other people. However, horror stories are very rare.

Language

ALBANIAN

Note that uh is pronounced as the 'a' in 'ago'. Also, ll and rr in Albanian are pronounced stronger than when they are written as single letters. Albanian is also understood in Kosovo.

Hello.	Tungjatjeta.	toon·dya·tye·ta
Goodbye.	Mirupafshim.	mee·roo·paf·sheem
Please.	Ju lutem.	yoo loo·tem
Thank you.	Faleminderit.	fa·le·meen·de·reet
Excuse me.	Më falni.	muh fal·nee
Sorry.	Më vjen keq.	muh vyen kech
Yes./No.	Po./Jo.	po/yo
Help!	Ndihmë!	ndeeh·muh
Cheers!	Gëzuar!	guh·zoo·ar

I don't understand.
Unë nuk kuptoj.   oo·nuh nook koop·toy

Do you speak English?
A flisni anglisht?   a flees·nee ang·leesht

How much is it?
Sa kushton?   sa koosh·ton

Where's ...?
Ku është ...?   koo uhsh·tuh ...

Where are the toilets?
Ku janë banjat?   koo ya·nuh ba·nyat

WANT MORE?

For in-depth language information and handy phrases, check out Lonely Planet's *Europe Phrasebook*. You'll find it at **shop.lonelyplanet.com**, or you can buy Lonely Planet's iPhone phrasebooks at the Apple App Store.

BULGARIAN

Note that uh is pronounced as the 'a' in 'ago' and zh as the 's' in 'pleasure'.

Hello.	Здравейте.	zdra·vey·te
Goodbye.	Довиждане.	do·veezh·da·ne
Please.	Моля.	mol·ya
Thank you.	Благодаря.	bla·go·dar·ya
Excuse me.	Извинете.	iz·vee·ne·te
Sorry.	Съжалявам.	suh·zhal·ya·vam
Yes./No.	Да./Не.	da/ne
Help!	Помощ!	po·mosht
Cheers!	Наздраве!	na·zdra·ve

I don't understand.
Не разбирам.   ne raz·bee·ram

Do you speak English?
Говорите ли английски?   go·vo·ree·te lee ang·lees·kee

How much is it?
Колко струва?   kol·ko stroo·va

Where's ...?
Къде се намира ...?   kuh·de se na·mee·ra ...

Where are the toilets?
Къде има тоалетни?   kuh·de ee·ma to·a·let·nee

CROATIAN & SERBIAN

Croatian and Serbian are very similar and mutually intelligible (and using them you'll also be understood in Bosnia and Hercegovina, Montenegro and parts of Kosovo). In this section the significant differences between Croatian and Serbian are indicated with (C) and (S) respectively. Note that r is rolled and zh is pronounced as the 's' in 'pleasure'.

Hello.	Dobar dan.	daw·ber dan
Goodbye.	Zbogom.	zbo·gom
Please.	Molim.	mo·lim
Thank you.	Hvala.	hva·la

Excuse me.	Oprostite.	o·pro·sti·te
Sorry.	Žao mi je.	zha o mi ye
Yes./No.	Da./Ne.	da/ne
Help!	Upomoć!	u·po·moch
Cheers!	Živjeli!	zhi·vye·li

I don't understand.
Ja ne razumijem.   ya ne ra·zu·mi·yem

Do you speak English?
Govorite/Govoriš li   go·vo·ri·te/go·vo·rish
engleski? (pol/inf)   li en·gle·ski

How much is it?
Koliko stoji/   ko·li·ko sto·yi/
košta? (C/S)   kosh·ta

Where's ...?
Gdje je ...?   gdye ye ...

Where are the toilets?
Gdje se nalaze   gdye se na·la·ze
zahodi/toaleti? (C/S)   za·ho·di/to·a·le·ti

CZECH

An accent mark over a vowel in written Czech indicates it's pronounced as a long sound. Note that oh is pronounced as the 'o' in 'note', uh as the 'a' in 'ago', and kh as the 'ch' in the Scottish *loch*. Also, r is rolled in Czech and the apostrophe (') indicates a slight y sound.

Hello.	Ahoj.	uh·hoy
Goodbye.	Na shledanou.	nuh·skhle·duh·noh
Please.	Prosím.	pro·seem
Thank you.	Děkuji.	dye·ku·yi
Excuse me.	Promiňte.	pro·min'·te
Sorry.	Promiňte.	pro·min'·te
Yes./No.	Ano./Ne.	uh·no/ne
Help!	Pomoc!	po·mots
Cheers!	Na zdraví!	nuh zdruh·vee

I don't understand.
Nerozumím.   ne·ro·zu·meem

Do you speak English?
Mluvíte anglicky?   mlu·vee·te uhn·glits·ki

How much is it?
Kolik to stojí?   ko·lik to sto·yee

Where's ...?
Kde je ...?   gde ye ...

Where are the toilets?
Kde jsou toalety?   gde ysoh to·uh·le·ti

DANISH

All vowels in Danish can be long or short. Note that aw is pronounced as in 'saw', and ew as the 'ee' in 'see' with rounded lips.

Hello.	Goddag.	go·da
Goodbye.	Farvel.	faar·vel
Please.	Vær så venlig.	ver saw ven·lee
Thank you.	Tak.	taak
Excuse me.	Undskyld mig.	awn·skewl mai
Sorry.	Undskyld.	awn·skewl
Yes./No.	Ja./Nej.	ya/nai
Help!	Hjælp!	yelp
Cheers!	Skål!	skawl

I don't understand.
Jeg forstår ikke.   yai for·stawr i·ke

Do you speak English?
Taler De/du   ta·la dee/doo
engelsk? (pol/inf)   eng·elsk

How much is it?
Hvor meget koster det?   vor maa·yet kos·ta dey

Where's ...?
Hvor er ...?   vor ir ...

Where's the toilet?
Hvor er toilettet?   vor ir toy·le·tet

DUTCH

It's important to distinguish between the long and short versions of each vowel sound. Note that ew is pronounced as the 'ee' in 'see' with rounded lips, oh as the 'o' in 'note', uh as the 'a' in 'ago', and kh as the 'ch' in the Scottish *loch* (harsh and throaty).

Hello.	Dag.	dakh
Goodbye.	Dag.	dakh
Please.	Alstublieft.	al·stew·bleeft
Thank you.	Dank u.	dangk ew
Excuse me.	Pardon.	par·don
Sorry.	Sorry.	so·ree
Yes./No.	Ja./Nee.	yaa/ney
Help!	Help!	help
Cheers!	Proost!	prohst

I don't understand.
Ik begrijp het niet.   ik buh·khreyp huht neet

Do you speak English?
Spreekt u Engels?   spreykt ew eng·uhls

How much is it?
Hoeveel kost het?   hoo·veyl kost huht

Where's ...?
Waar is ...?   waar is ...

Where are the toilets?
Waar zijn de toiletten?   waar zeyn duh twa·le·tuhn

ESTONIAN

Double vowels in written Estonian indicate they are pronounced as long sounds. Note that air is pronounced as in 'hair'.

Hello.	*Tere.*	*te·re*
Goodbye.	*Nägemist.*	*nair·ge·mist*
Please.	*Palun.*	*pa·lun*
Thank you.	*Tänan.*	*tair·nan*
Excuse me.	*Vabandage.* (pol)	*va·ban·da·ge*
	Vabanda. (inf)	*va·ban·da*
Sorry.	*Vabandust.*	*va·ban·dust*
Yes./No.	*Jaa./Ei.*	*yaa/ay*
Help!	*Appi!*	*ap·pi*
Cheers!	*Terviseks!*	*tair·vi·seks*

I don't understand.
Ma ei saa aru. ma ay saa a·ru

Do you speak English?
Kas te räägite kas te rair·git·te
inglise keelt? ing·kli·se keylt

How much is it?
Kui palju see maksab? ku·i pal·yu sey mak·sab

Where's ...?
Kus on ...? kus on ...

Where are the toilets?
Kus on WC? kus on ve·se

FINNISH

In Finnish, double consonants are held longer than their single equivalents. Note that ew is pronounced as the 'ee' in 'see' with rounded lips, and uh as the 'u' in 'run'.

Hello.	*Hei.*	*hay*
Goodbye.	*Näkemiin.*	*na·ke·meen*
Please.	*Ole hyvä.*	*o·le hew·va*
Thank you.	*Kiitos.*	*kee·tos*
Excuse me.	*Anteeksi.*	*uhn·tayk·si*
Sorry.	*Anteeksi.*	*uhn·tayk·si*
Yes./No.	*Kyllä./Ei.*	*kewl·la/ay*
Help!	*Apua!*	*uh·pu·uh*
Cheers!	*Kippis!*	*kip·pis*

I don't understand.
En ymmärrä. en ewm·mar·ra

Do you speak English?
Puhutko englantia? pu·hut·ko en·gluhn·ti·uh

How much is it?
Mitä se maksaa? mi·ta se muhk·saa

Where's ...?
Missä on ...? mis·sa on ...

Where are the toilets?
Missä on vessa? mis·sa on ves·suh

FRENCH

The French r sound is throaty. French also has nasal vowels (pronounced as if you're trying to force the sound through the nose), indicated here with o or u followed by an almost inaudible nasal consonant sound m, n or ng. Syllables in French words are, for the most part, equally stressed.

Hello.	*Bonjour.*	*bon·zhoor*
Goodbye.	*Au revoir.*	*o·rer·vwa*
Please.	*S'il vous plaît.*	*seel voo play*
Thank you.	*Merci.*	*mair·see*
Excuse me.	*Excusez-moi.*	*ek·skew·zay·mwa*
Sorry.	*Pardon.*	*par·don*
Yes./No.	*Oui./Non.*	*wee/non*
Help!	*Au secours!*	*o skoor*
Cheers!	*Santé!*	*son·tay*

I don't understand.
Je ne comprends pas. zher ner kom·pron pa

Do you speak English?
Parlez-vous anglais? par·lay·voo ong·glay

How much is it?
C'est combien? say kom·byun

Where's ...?
Où est ...? oo ay ...

Where are the toilets?
Où sont les toilettes? oo son ley twa·let

GERMAN

Note that aw is pronounced as in 'saw', ew as the 'ee' in 'see' with rounded lips, while kh and r are both throaty sounds in German.

Hello.		
(in general)	*Guten Tag.*	*goo·ten taak*
(Austria)	*Servus.*	*zer·vus*
(Switzerland)	*Grüezi.*	*grew·e·tsi*
Goodbye.	*Auf Wiedersehen.*	*owf vee·der·zey·en*
Please.	*Bitte.*	*bi·te*
Thank you.	*Danke.*	*dang·ke*
Excuse me.	*Entschuldigung.*	*ent·shul·di·gung*
Sorry.	*Entschuldigung.*	*ent·shul·di·gung*
Yes./No.	*Ja./Nein.*	*yaa/nain*
Help!	*Hilfe!*	*hil·fe*
Cheers!	*Prost!*	*prawst*

I don't understand.
Ich verstehe nicht. ikh fer·shtey·e nikht

Do you speak English?
Sprechen Sie Englisch?   *shpre·khen zee eng·lish*

How much is it?
Wie viel kostet das?   *vee feel kos·tet das*

Where's ...?
Wo ist ...?   *vaw ist ...*

Where are the toilets?
Wo ist die Toilette?   *vo ist dee to·a·le·te*

GREEK

Note that dh is pronounced as the 'th' in 'that', and that gh and kh are both throaty sounds, similar to the 'ch' in the Scottish *loch*.

Hello.   Γεια σου.   *yia su*

Goodbye.   Αντίο.   *a·di·o*

Please.   Παρακαλώ.   *pa·ra·ka·lo*

Thank you.   Ευχαριστώ.   *ef·kha·ri·sto*

Excuse me.   Με συγχωρείτε.   *me sing·kho·ri·te*

Sorry.   Συγνώμη.   *si·ghno·mi*

Yes./No.   Ναι./Όχι.   *ne/o·hi*

Help!   Βοήθεια!   *vo·i·thia*

Cheers!   Στην υγειά μας!   *stin i·yia mas*

I don't understand.
Δεν καταλαβαίνω.   *dhen ka·ta·la·ve·no*

Do you speak English?
Μιλάς Αγγλικά;   *mi·las ang·gli·ka*

How much is it?
Πόσο κάνει;   *po·so ka·ni*

Where's ...?
Που είναι ...;   *pu i·ne ...*

Where are the toilets?
Που είναι η τουαλέτα;   *pu i·ne i tu·a·le·ta*

HUNGARIAN

A symbol over a vowel in written Hungarian indicates it's pronounced as a long sound. Double consonants should be drawn out a little longer than in English. Note that aw is pronounced as in 'law', eu as the 'u' in 'nurse', and ew as 'ee' with rounded lips. Also, r is rolled in Hungarian and the apostrophe (') indicates a slight y sound.

Hello. (to one person)
Szervusz.   *ser·vus*
Hello. (to more than one person)
Szervusztok.   *ser·vus·tawk*

Goodbye.   *Viszlát.*   *vis·lat*

Please.   *Kérem.* (pol)   *key·rem*
                      Kérlek. (inf)   *keyr·lek*

Thank you.   *Köszönöm.*   *keu·seu·neum*

Excuse me.   *Elnézést*   *el·ney·zeysht*
                       kérek.   *key·rek*

Sorry.   *Sajnálom.*   *shoy·na·lawm*

Yes.   *Igen.*   *i·gen*

No.   *Nem.*   *nem*

Help!   *Segítség!*   *she·geet·sheyg*

Cheers! (to one person)
Egészségedre!   *e·geys·shey·ged·re*
Cheers! (to more than one person)
Egészségetekre!   *e·geys·shey·ge·tek·re*

I don't understand.
Nem értem.   *nem eyr·tem*

Do you speak English?
Beszél/Beszélsz   *be·seyl/be·seyls*
angolul? (pol/inf)   *on·gaw·lul*

How much is it?
Mennyibe kerül?   *men'·nyi·be ke·rewl*

Where's ...?
Hol van a ...?   *hawl von o ...*

Where are the toilets?
Hol a vécé?   *hawl o vey·tsey*

ITALIAN

The r sound in Italian is rolled and stronger than in English. Most other consonants can have a more emphatic pronunciation too (in which case they're written as double letters).

Hello.   *Buongiorno.*   *bwon·jor·no*

Goodbye.   *Arrivederci.*   *a·ree·ve·der·chee*

Please.   *Per favore.*   *per fa·vo·re*

Thank you.   *Grazie.*   *gra·tsye*

Excuse me.   *Mi scusi.* (pol)   *mee skoo·zee*
                       Scusami. (inf)   *skoo·za·mee*

Sorry.   *Mi dispiace.*   *mee dees·pya·che*

Yes.   *Sì.*   *see*

No.   *No.*   *no*

Help!   *Aiuto!*   *ai·yoo·to*

Cheers!   *Salute!*   *sa·loo·te*

I don't understand.
Non capisco.   *non ka·pee·sko*

Do you speak English?
Parla inglese?   *par·la een·gle·ze*

How much is it?
Quant'è?   *kwan·te*

Where's ... ?
Dov'è ... ?   *do·ve ...*

Where are the toilets?
Dove sono i   *do·ve so·no ee*
gabinetti?   *ga·bee·ne·tee*

LATVIAN

A line over a vowel in written Latvian indicates it's pronounced as a long sound. Note that air is pronounced as in 'hair', ea as in 'ear', wa as in 'water', and dz as the 'ds' in 'adds'.

Hello.	Sveiks.	svayks
Goodbye.	Atā.	a·taa
Please.	Lūdzu.	loo·dzu
Thank you.	Paldies.	pal·deas
Excuse me.	Atvainojiet.	at·vai·nwa·yeat
Sorry.	Piedodiet.	pea·dwa·deat
Yes./No.	Jā./Nē.	yaa/nair
Help!	Palīgā!	pa·lee·gaa
Cheers!	Priekā!	prea·kaa

I don't understand.
Es nesaprotu.   es ne·sa·prwa·tu

Do you speak English?
Vai Jūs runājat   vai yoos ru·naa·yat
angliski?   ang·li·ski

How much is it?
Cik maksā?   tsik mak·saa

Where's ...?
Kur ir ...?   kur ir ...

Where are the toilets?
Kur ir tualetes?   kur ir tu·a·le·tes

LITHUANIAN

Symbols on vowels in written Lithuanian indicate that they're pronounced as long sounds. Note that ow is pronounced as in 'how'.

Hello.	Sveiki.	svay·ki
Goodbye.	Viso gero.	vi·so ge·ro
Please.	Prašau.	pra·show
Thank you.	Ačiū.	aa·choo
Excuse me.	Atleiskite.	at·lays·ki·te
Sorry.	Atsiprašau.	at·si·pra·show
Yes./No.	Taip./Ne.	taip/ne
Help!	Padėkit!	pa·dey·kit
Cheers!	Į sveikatą!	ee svay·kaa·taa

I don't understand.
Aš nesuprantu.   ash ne·su·pran·tu

Do you speak English?
Ar kalbate angliškai?   ar kal·ba·te aang·lish·kai

How much is it?
Kiek kainuoja?   keak kain·wo·ya

Where's ...?
Kur yra ...?   kur ee·ra ...

Where are the toilets?
Kur yra tualetai?   kur ee·ra tu·a·le·tai

MACEDONIAN

Note that r is pronounced as a rolled sound in Macedonian.

Hello.	Здраво.	zdra·vo
Goodbye.	До гледање.	do gle·da·nye
Please.	Молам.	mo·lam
Thank you.	Благодарам.	bla·go·da·ram
Excuse me.	Извинете.	iz·vi·ne·te
Sorry.	Простете.	pros·te·te
Yes./No.	Да./Не.	da/ne
Help!	Помош!	po·mosh
Cheers!	На здравје!	na zdrav·ye

I don't understand.
Јас не разбирам.   yas ne raz·bi·ram

Do you speak English?
Зборувате ли англиски?   zbo·ru·va·te li an·glis·ki

How much is it?
Колку чини тоа?   kol·ku chi·ni to·a

Where's ...?
Каде е ...?   ka·de e ...

Where are the toilets?
Каде се тоалетите?   ka·de se to·a·le·ti·te

NORWEGIAN

In Norwegian, each vowel can be either long or short. Generally, they're long when followed by one consonant and short when followed by two or more consonants. Note that aw is pronounced as in 'law', ew as 'ee' with pursed lips, and ow as in 'how'.

Hello.	God dag.	go·daag
Goodbye.	Ha det.	haa·de
Please.	Vær så snill.	veyr saw snil
Thank you.	Takk.	tak
Excuse me.	Unnskyld.	ewn·shewl
Sorry.	Beklager.	bey·klaa·geyr
Yes./No.	Ja./Nei.	yaa/ney
Help!	Hjelp!	yelp
Cheers!	Skål!	skawl

I don't understand.
Jeg forstår ikke.   yai fawr·stawr i·key

Do you speak English?
Snakker du engelsk?   sna·ker doo eyng·elsk

How much is it?
Hvor mye koster det?   vor mew·e kaws·ter de

Where's ...?
Hvor er ...?   vor ayr ...

Where are the toilets?
Hvor er toalettene?   vor eyr to·aa·le·te·ne

POLISH

Polish vowels are generally pronounced short. Nasal vowels are pronounced as though you're trying to force the air through your nose, and are indicated with n or m following the vowel. Note also that r is rolled in Polish.

Hello.	Cześć.	cheshch
Goodbye.	Do widzenia.	do vee·dze·nya
Please.	Proszę.	pro·she
Thank you.	Dziękuję.	jyen·koo·ye
Excuse me.	Przepraszam.	pshe·pra·sham
Sorry.	Przepraszam.	pshe·pra·sham
Yes./No.	Tak./Nie.	tak/nye
Help!	Na pomoc!	na po·mots
Cheers!	Na zdrowie!	na zdro·vye

I don't understand.
Nie rozumiem.   nye ro·zoo·myem

Do you speak English?
Czy pan/pani mówi   chi pan/pa·nee moo·vee
po angielsku? (m/f)   po an·gyel·skoo

How much is it?
Ile to kosztuje?   ee·le to kosh·too·ye

Where's ...?
Gdzie jest ...?   gjye yest ...

Where are the toilets?
Gdzie są toalety?   gjye som to·a·le·ti

PORTUGUESE

Most vowel sounds in Portuguese have a nasal version (ie pronounced as if you're trying to force the sound through your nose), which is indicated in our pronunciation guides with ng after the vowel.

Hello.	Olá.	o·laa
Goodbye.	Adeus.	a·de·oosh
Please.	Por favor.	poor fa·vor
Thank you.	Obrigado. (m)	o·bree·gaa·doo
	Obrigada. (f)	o·bree·gaa·da
Excuse me.	Faz favor.	faash fa·vor
Sorry.	Desculpe.	desh·kool·pe
Yes./No.	Sim./Não.	seeng/nowng
Help!	Socorro!	soo·ko·rroo
Cheers!	Saúde!	sa·oo·de

I don't understand.
Não entendo.   nowng eng·teng·doo

Do you speak English?
Fala inglês?   faa·la eeng·glesh

How much is it?
Quanto custa?   kwang·too koosh·ta

Where's ...?
Onde é ...?   ong·de e ...

Where are the toilets?
Onde é a casa de   ong·de e a kaa·za de
banho?   ba·nyoo

ROMANIAN

Note that ew is pronounced as the 'ee' in 'see' with rounded lips, uh as the 'a' in 'ago', and zh as the 's' in 'pleasure'. The apostrophe (') indicates a very short, unstressed (almost silent) i. Moldovan is the official name of the variety of Romanian spoken in Moldova.

Hello.	Bună ziua.	boo·nuh zee·wa
Goodbye.	La revedere.	la re·ve·de·re
Please.	Vă rog.	vuh rog
Thank you.	Mulțumesc.	mool·tsoo·mesk
Excuse me.	Scuzați-mă.	skoo·za·tsee·muh
Sorry.	Îmi pare rău.	ewm' pa·re ruh·oo
Yes./No.	Da./Nu.	da/noo
Help!	Ajutor!	a·zhoo·tor
Cheers!	Noroc!	no·rok

I don't understand.
Eu nu înțeleg.   ye·oo noo ewn·tse·leg

Do you speak English?
Vorbiți engleza?   vor·beets' en·gle·za

How much is it?
Cât costă?   kewt kos·tuh

Where's ...?
Unde este ...?   oon·de yes·te ...

Where are the toilets?
Unde este o toaletă?   oon·de yes·te o to·a·le·tuh

RUSSIAN

Note that zh is pronounced as the 's' in 'pleasure'. Also, r is rolled in Russian and the apostrophe (') indicates a slight y sound.

Hello.	Здравствуйте.	zdrast·vuyt·ye
Goodbye.	До свидания.	da svee·dan·ya
Please.	Пожалуйста.	pa·zhal·sta
Thank you.	Спасибо	spa·see·ba
Excuse me./ Sorry.	Извините, пожалуйста.	eez·vee·neet·ye pa·zhal·sta
Yes./No.	Да./Нет.	da/nyet
Help!	Помогите!	pa·ma·gee·tye
Cheers!	Пей до дна!	pyey da dna

I don't understand.
Я не понимаю.   ya nye pa·nee·ma·yu

Do you speak English?

Вы говорите	vi ga·va·*reet*·ye
по-английски?	pa·an·*glee*·skee

How much is it?

Сколько стоит?	*skol'*·ka sto·eet

Where's ...?

Где (здесь) ...?	gdye (zdyes') ...

Where are the toilets?

Где здесь туалет?	gdye zdyes' tu·al·*yet*

SLOVAK

An accent mark over a vowel in written Slovak indicates it's pronounced as a long sound. Note also that uh is pronounced as the 'a' in 'ago', and kh as the 'ch' in the Scottish *loch*. The apostrophe (') indicates a slight y sound.

Hello.	Dobrý deň.	do·bree dyen'
Goodbye.	Do videnia.	do *vi*·dye·ni·yuh
Please.	Prosím.	pro·seem
Thank you.	Ďakujem	dyuh·ku·yem
Excuse me.	Prepáčte.	pre·pach·tye
Sorry.	Prepáčte.	pre·pach·tye
Yes./No.	Áno./Nie.	a·no/ni·ye
Help!	Pomoc!	po·mots
Cheers!	Nazdravie!	nuhz·druh·vi·ye

I don't understand.

Nerozumiem.	nye·ro·zu·myem

Do you speak English?

Hovoríte po	ho·vo·*ree*·tye po
anglicky?	*uhng*·lits·ki

How much is it?

Koľko to stojí?	kol'·ko to sto·yee

Where's ...?

Kde je ...?	kdye ye ...

Where are the toilets?

Kde sú tu záchody?	kdye soo tu za·kho·di

SLOVENE

Note that r is pronounced as a rolled sound in Slovene.

Hello.	Zdravo.	zdra·vo
Goodbye.	Na svidenje.	na svee·den·ye
Please.	Prosim.	pro·seem
Thank you.	Hvala.	hva·la
Excuse me.	Dovolite.	do·vo·lee·te
Sorry.	Oprostite.	op·ros·tee·te
Yes./No.	Da./Ne.	da/ne
Help!	Na pomoč!	na po·moch
Cheers!	Na zdravje!	na zdrav·ye

I don't understand.

Ne razumem.	ne ra·*zoo*·mem

Do you speak English?

Ali govorite	a·lee go·vo·*ree*·te
angleško?	ang·*lesh*·ko

How much is it?

Koliko stane?	ko·lee·ko sta·ne

Where's ...?

Kje je ...?	kye ye ...

Where are the toilets?

Kje je stranišče?	kye ye stra·*neesh*·che

SPANISH

Note that the Spanish r is strong and rolled, th is pronounced 'with a lisp', and v is soft, pronounced almost like a 'b'.

Hello.	Hola.	o·la
Goodbye.	Adiós.	a·dyos
Please.	Por favor.	por fa·*vor*
Thank you.	Gracias.	gra·thyas
Excuse me.	Perdón.	per·*don*
Sorry.	Lo siento.	lo syen·to
Yes./No.	Sí./No.	see/no
Help!	¡Socorro!	so·*ko*·ro
Cheers!	¡Salud!	sa·*loo*

I don't understand.

Yo no entiendo.	yo no en·*tyen*·do

Do you speak English?

¿Habla/Hablas	a·bla/a·blas
inglés? (pol/inf)	een·*gles*

How much is it?

¿Cuánto cuesta?	kwan·to kwes·ta

Where's ...?

¿Dónde está ...?	don·de es·ta ...

Where are the toilets?

¿Dónde están los	don·de es·*tan* los
servicios?	ser·*vee*·thyos

SWEDISH

Swedish vowels can be short or long – generally the stressed vowels are long, except when followed by double consonants. Note that aw is pronounced as in 'saw', air as in 'hair', eu as the 'u' in 'nurse', ew as the 'ee' in 'see' with rounded lips, and oh as the 'o' in 'note'.

Hello.	Hej.	hey
Goodbye.	Hej då.	hey daw
Please.	Tack.	tak
Thank you.	Tack.	tak

Excuse me.	Ursäkta mig.	oor-shek-ta mey
Sorry.	Förlåt.	feur-lawt
Yes./No.	Ja./Nej.	yaa/ney
Help!	Hjälp!	yelp
Cheers!	Skål!	skawl

I don't understand.
Jag förstår inte.   yaa feur-shtawr in-te

Do you speak English?
Talar du engelska?   taa-lar doc eng-el-ska

How much is it?
Hur mycket kostar det?   hoor mew-ke kos-tar de

Where's ...?
Var finns det ...?   var finns ce ...

Where are the toilets?
Var är toaletten?   var air tol-aa-le-ten

TURKISH

Double vowels are pronounced twice in Turkish. Note also that eu is pronounced as the 'u' in 'nurse', ew as the 'ee' in 'see' with rounded lips, uh as the 'a' in 'ago', r is rolled and v is a little softer than in English.

Hello.	Merhaba.	mer-ha-ba
Goodbye.	Hoşçakal. (when leaving)	hosh-cha-kal
	Güle güle. (when staying)	gew-le gew-le
Please.	Lütfen.	lewt-fen
Thank you.	Teşekkür ederim.	te-shek-kewr e-de-reem
Excuse me.	Bakar mısınız.	ba-kar muh-suh-nuhz
Sorry.	Özür dilerim.	eu-zewr dee-le-reem
Yes./No.	Evet./Hayır.	e-vet/ha-yuhr
Help!	İmdat!	eem-dat
Cheers!	Şerefe!	she-re-fe

I don't understand.
Anlamıyorum.   an-la-nuh-yo-room

Do you speak English?
İngilizce konuşuyor musunuz?   een-gee-leez-je ko-noo-shoo-yor moo-soo-nooz

How much is it?
Ne kadar?   ne ka-dar

Where's ...?
... nerede?   ... ne-re-de

Where are the toilets?
Tuvaletler nerede?   too-va-let-ler ne-re-de

UKRAINIAN

Ukrainian vowels in unstressed syllables are generally pronounced shorter and weaker than they are in stressed syllables. Note that ow is pronounced as in 'how' and zh as the 's' in 'pleasure'. The apostrophe (') indicates a slight y sound.

Hello.	Добрий день.	do-bry den'
Goodbye.	До побачення.	do po-ba-chen-nya
Please.	Прошу.	pro-shu
Thank you.	Дякую.	dya-ku-yu
Excuse me.	Вибачте.	vy-bach-te
Sorry.	Перепрошую.	pe-re-pro-shu-yu
Yes./No.	Так./Ні.	tak/ni
Help!	Допоможіть!	do-po-mo-zhit'
Cheers!	Будьмо!	bud'-mo

I don't understand.
Я не розумію.   ya ne ro-zu-mi-yu

Do you speak English?
Ви розмовляєте англійською мовою?   vy roz-mow-lya-ye-te an-hliys'-ko-yu mo-vo-yu

How much is it?
Скільки це він/вона коштує? (m/f)   skil'-ki tse vin/vo-na ko-shtu-ye

Where's ...?
Де ...?   de ...

Where are the toilets?
Де туалети?   de tu-a-le-ti

LANGUAGE TURKISH

Behind the Scenes

SEND US YOUR FEEDBACK

We love to hear from travellers – your comments keep us on our toes and help make our books better. Our well-travelled team reads every word on what you loved or loathed about this book. Although we cannot reply individually to your submissions, we always guarantee that your feedback goes straight to the appropriate authors, in time for the next edition. Each person who sends us information is thanked in the next edition – the most useful submissions are rewarded with a selection of digital PDF chapters.

Visit **lonelyplanet.com/contact** to submit your updates and suggestions or to ask for help. Our award-winning website also features inspirational travel stories, news and discussions.

Note: We may edit, reproduce and incorporate your comments in Lonely Planet products such as guidebooks, websites and digital products, so let us know if you don't want your comments reproduced or your name acknowledged. For a copy of our privacy policy visit lonelyplanet.com/privacy.

OUR READERS

Many thanks to the travellers who used the last edition and wrote to us with helpful hints, useful advice and interesting anecdotes: Sain Alizada, Matthieu Brusseau, Tine Declerck, Stewart Gray, Balawyn Jones, Andy Leerock, Boyan Lin, Charlie Merry, Felicity Milanovic, Maria Skinnemoen, Jukka Sutinen, Connor Yocum, Zhu Zhengqing

Illustrations p66–7 by Javier Zarracina & Michael Weldon, p90–1, p92–3, p310–11, p318–19, p418–19, p446–7, p514–15, p518–19, p532–3, p546–7, p574–5, p786–7 and p794–5 by Javier Zarracina

Cover photograph: Detail of timber-framed buildings, Copenhagen, Denmark, The Picture Store / Alamy ©

ACKNOWLEDGEMENTS

Climate map data adapted from Peel MC, Finlayson BL & McMahon TA (2007) 'Updated World Map of the Köppen-Geiger Climate Classification', Hydrology and Earth System Sciences, 11, 163–344.

THIS BOOK

The 9th edition of Lonely Planet's *Europe on a Shoestring* guidebook was curated by Mark Baker, Tom Masters, Korina Miller, Simon Richmond, Andy Symington and Nicola Williams. This guidebook was produced by the following:

Associate Product Director Kirsten Rawlings

Destination Editors Helen Elfer, Gemma Graham, James Smart, Anna Tyler, Brana Vladisavljevic, Clifton Wilkinson

Product Editors Elizabeth Jones, Kate James

Senior Cartographer Valentina Kremenchutskaya

Book Designers Cam Ashley, Kerrianne Jenkins, Katherine Marsh, Jessica Rose, Wibowo Rusli

Assisting Editors Andrea Dobbin, Katie Connolly, Bella Li, Katie O'Connell, Gabrielle Stefanos, Saralinda Turner, Fionnuala Twomey

Cover Designer Campbell McKenzie

Thanks to James Hardy, Liz Heynes, Indra Kilfoyle, Claire Murphy, Darren O'Connell, Diana Saengkham, Eleanor Simpson, Angela Tinson, Tony Wheeler, Tracy Whitmey

Index

NOTES

Map Legend

Sights

- Beach
- Bird Sanctuary
- Buddhist
- Castle/Palace
- Christian
- Confucian
- Hindu
- Islamic
- Jain
- Jewish
- Monument
- Museum/Gallery/Historic Building
- Ruin
- Shinto
- Sikh
- Taoist
- Winery/Vineyard
- Zoo/Wildlife Sanctuary
- Other Sight

Activities, Courses & Tours

- Bodysurfing
- Diving
- Canoeing/Kayaking
- Course/Tour
- Sento Hot Baths/Onsen
- Skiing
- Snorkelling
- Surfing
- Swimming/Pool
- Walking
- Windsurfing
- Other Activity

Sleeping

- Sleeping
- Camping

Eating

- Eating

Drinking & Nightlife

- Drinking & Nightlife
- Cafe

Entertainment

- Entertainment

Shopping

- Shopping

Information

- Bank
- Embassy/Consulate
- Hospital/Medical
- Internet
- Police
- Post Office
- Telephone
- Toilet
- Tourist Information
- Other Information

Geographic

- Beach
- Gate
- Hut/Shelter
- Lighthouse
- Lookout
- Mountain/Volcano
- Oasis
- Park
- Pass
- Picnic Area
- Waterfall

Population

- Capital (National)
- Capital (State/Province)
- City/Large Town
- Town/Village

Transport

- Airport
- Border crossing
- Bus
- Cable car/Funicular
- Cycling
- Ferry
- Metro station
- Monorail
- Parking
- Petrol station
- S-Bahn/Subway station
- Taxi
- T-bane/Tunnelbana station
- Train station/Railway
- Tram
- Tube station
- U-Bahn/Underground station
- Other Transport

Routes

- Tollway
- Freeway
- Primary
- Secondary
- Tertiary
- Lane
- Unsealed road
- Road under construction
- Plaza/Mall
- Steps
- Tunnel
- Pedestrian overpass
- Walking Tour
- Walking Tour detour
- Path/Walking Trail

Boundaries

- International
- State/Province
- Disputed
- Regional/Suburb
- Marine Park
- Cliff
- Wall

Hydrography

- River, Creek
- Intermittent River
- Canal
- Water
- Dry/Salt/Intermittent Lake
- Reef

Areas

- Airport/Runway
- Beach/Desert
- Cemetery (Christian)
- Cemetery (Other)
- Glacier
- Mudflat
- Park/Forest
- Sight (Building)
- Sportsground
- Swamp/Mangrove

Note: Not all symbols displayed above appear on the maps in this book

Andy Symington

Scandinavia, Germany & Benelux, Spain & Portugal Andy hails from Australia but has been living in Spain for 15 years, where, to shatter a couple of stereotypes of the country, he can frequently be found huddled in sub-zero temperatures watching the tragically poor local football team. He has authored and co-authored many LP guidebooks and other publications on Spain and elsewhere; in his spare time he walks in the mountains, embarks on epic tapas trails, and co-bosses a rock bar.

Nicola Williams

France, Switzerland & Austria British writer and editorial consultant Nicola Williams has lived in France and written about it for more than a decade. From her hillside house on the southern shore of Lake Geneva, it's an easy hop to Paris where she has spent endless years revelling in its extraordinary art, urban architecture, boutique shopping and cuisine. Nicola has worked on numerous titles for Lonely Planet, including *France* and *Discover France*. Find Nicola on Twitter at @Tripalong.

OUR STORY

A beat-up old car, a few dollars in the pocket and a sense of
adventure. In 1972 that's all Tony and Maureen Wheeler needed
_____ overland to
_____ – broke but
_____ and stapling
_____ the Cheap.
_____ et was born.

Melbourne, Oa_____ klin, London,
that 'a great gu_____ Tony's belief

OUR W

_____ ter based in
_____ ng as a writer
_____ Radio Liberty,
_____ of several
_____ nia, Latvia &
_____ markbaker

_____ '90s when,
_____ ed 'Eastern
_____ novel. Having
_____ in the former
_____ gh it constantly
_____ ommasters.net.

_____ as been explor-
_____ 36 countries
_____ es and an MA in
_____ Lonely Planet

_____ urvival Guide
chapters UK-born writer and photographer Simon's first taste of continental
Europe was on a family holiday to Mallorca in the 1970s. Many subsequent
Euro trips have followed including work assignments to, among other places,
the Baltic States, Belgium and Portugal. Simon is co-author of Lonely Planet's
Russia and _Trans-Siberian Railway_ guides. Read more about Simon's travels at
www.simonrichmond.com and on Twitter and Instagram @simonrichmond.

OVER MORE
PAGE WRITERS

Published by Lonely Planet Global Limited
CRN 554153
9th edition – October 2016
ISBN 978 1 78657 113 7
© Lonely Planet 2016   Photographs © as indicated 2016
10 9 8 7 6 5 4 3 2 1
Printed in China

Although the authors and Lonely Planet have taken all reasonable care in preparing this book, we make no warranty about the
accuracy or completeness of its content and, to the maximum
extent permitted, disclaim all liability arising from its use.